THE MICHELIN GUIDE

2019

GREAT BRITAIN | IRELAND

MICHELIN

CONTENTS

Introduction

Michelin *(Restaurant Brat)*

DEAR READER

We are delighted to present the 2019 edition of the Michelin guide to Great Britain and Ireland – a guide to the best places to eat and stay in England, Wales, Scotland, Northern Ireland and the Republic of Ireland.

- ***The guide caters for every type of visitor, from business traveller to families on holiday, and lists the best establishments across all categories of comfort and price – from cosy bistros and intimate townhouses to celebrated restaurants and luxurious hotels. So, whether you're visiting for work or pleasure, you'll find something that's right for you.***

- ***All of the establishments in the guide have been selected by our team of famous Michelin inspectors, who are the eyes and ears of our readers. They always pay their own bills and their anonymity is key to ensuring that they receive the same treatment as any other guest. Each year, they search for new establishments to add to the guide – and only the best make it through. Once the annual selection has been made, the 'best of the best' are then recognised with awards: our famous One ✿, Two ✿✿ and Three ✿✿✿ Stars and our value-for-money Bib Gourmands ☺.***

- ***Restaurants – our readers' favourite part – appear at the front of each locality, with the hotels following afterwards. Restaurants are ordered according to the quality of their food, with Michelin Stars placed at the top, followed by Bib Gourmands and then Michelin Plates ℩O. Being chosen by the Michelin Inspectors for inclusion in the guide is a guarantee of quality in itself and the Plate symbol points out restaurants where you will have a good meal.***

Mews

2019 brings with it plenty of highlights

- *Three restaurants have been newly awarded Two Stars:* ***Kitchen Table at Bubbledogs*** *in Bloomsbury from chef James Knappett,* ***CORE by Clare Smyth*** *in North Kensington and* ***Moor Hall*** *in Aughton from Mark Birchall.*

- *The biggest winner is definitely the Republic of Ireland, specifically County Cork, which plays host to three new One Stars:* ***Chestnut, Mews*** *and* ***Ichigo Ichie.*** *Ireland also has three new Bib Gourmands.*

- *Three pubs in England that have entered the guide with a Star:* ***Blackbird*** *in Newbury,* ***White Swan,*** *Fence and* ***Fordwich Arms,*** *Fordwich.*

- *Simon Rogan follows the success of L'Enclume with a Star for his* ***Rogan & Co*** *restaurant in the same village of Cartmel, and also for his London outpost,* ***Roganic.***

- *When it comes to restaurants offering value for money, look no further than Bristol. Three restaurants have been awarded a Bib Gourmand:* ***Bell's Diner & Bar Rooms, Root*** *and* ***Tare.***

• *London's vitality and diversity is represented by its new One-Stars, which are all so different in their looks, their style and their cuisine.* ***Brat****, in a room above a converted pub in Shoreditch, is all about cooking over fire, while the highly original* ***Ikoyi*** *in St. James's introduces diners to the flavours of West Africa.* ***Hide****, opposite Green Park, was perhaps the most eagerly awaited unveiling of 2018 and marked the return of chef Ollie Dabbous. This bustling, three-storey all-day restaurant bucked the trend for small, intimate places. Many diners were equally thrilled when the team behind Ellory opened their new place,* ***Leroy****, also in Shoreditch. Meanwhile,* ***Sabor*** *proved that if you want wonderful tapas you need not travel to Spain.*

• *Our mission always remains the same: to help you find the best restaurants and hotels on your travels. Please don't hesitate to contact us, as we are keen to hear your opinions on the establishments listed within these pages, as well as those you feel could be of interest for future editions.*

• *We trust you will enjoy travelling with the 2019 edition of our Great Britain & Ireland guide.*

Hide

2019...NEW AWARDS IN THIS YEAR'S GUIDE

STARS...

✿✿

London	Camden/Bloomsbury	**Kitchen Table at Bubbledogs**
	Kensington & Chelsea/Chelsea	**CORE by Clare Smyth**
England	Aughton	**Moor Hall**

✿

London	Hackney/Shoreditch	**Brat**
	Hackney/Shoreditch	**Leroy**
	Westminster/Mayfair	**Hide**
	Westminster/Mayfair	**Sabor**
	Westminster/Regent's Park and Marylebone	**Roganic**
	Westminster/St James's	**Ikoyi**
England	Bath	**Olive Tree**
	Bristol	**Bulrush**
	Canterbury/Fordwich	**Fordwich Arms**
	Cartmel	**Rogan & Co**
	Dorking	**Sorrel**
	Fence	**White Swan**
	Little Dunmow	**Tim Allen's Flitch of Bacon**
	Newbury	**Blackbird**
	Oxford	**Oxford Kitchen**
	Stratford-upon-Avon	**Salt**
	Winteringham	**Winteringham Fields**
Republic of Ireland	Ballydehob	**Chestnut**
	Baltimore	**Mews**
	Cork	**Ichigo Ichie**

A complete list of Stars and Bib Gourmands 2019 are at the beginning of each region.

... AND BIB GOURMANDS

London

Hackney/Hoxton	**Petit Pois**
Islington/Highbury	**Farang**
Lambeth/Clapham	**Sorella**
Southwark/Peckham	**Kudu**

England

Aughton	**The Barn**
Brighton & Hove	**Cin Cin**
Bristol	**Bells Diner & Bar Rooms**
Bristol	**Root**
Bristol	**Tare**
Chelmsford	**The Windmill Chatham Green**
Crundale	**Compasses Inn**
Ilfracombe	**Antidote**
Langford	**Bell Inn**
Ludlow	**Charlton Arms**
Newcastle upon Tyne	**Route**
Sherborne	**The Green**
Skelton	**Dog and Gun**
Stanton	**Leaping Hare**
Upton	**Crown Inn**

Scotland

Glasgow	**Monadh Kitchen**
Helensburgh	**Sugar Boat**

Wales

Colwyn Bay	**Bryn Williams at Porth Eirias**

Northern Ireland

Aghalee	**Clenaghans**

Republic of Ireland

Dublin	**Clanbrassil House**
Galway	**Tartare**
Timoleague	**Dillon's**
Tuam	**Brownes**

Starred establishments 2019

London This location has at least one 3 star restaurant ***

Dublin This location has at least one 2 star restaurant **

Edinburgh This location has at least one 1 star restaurant *

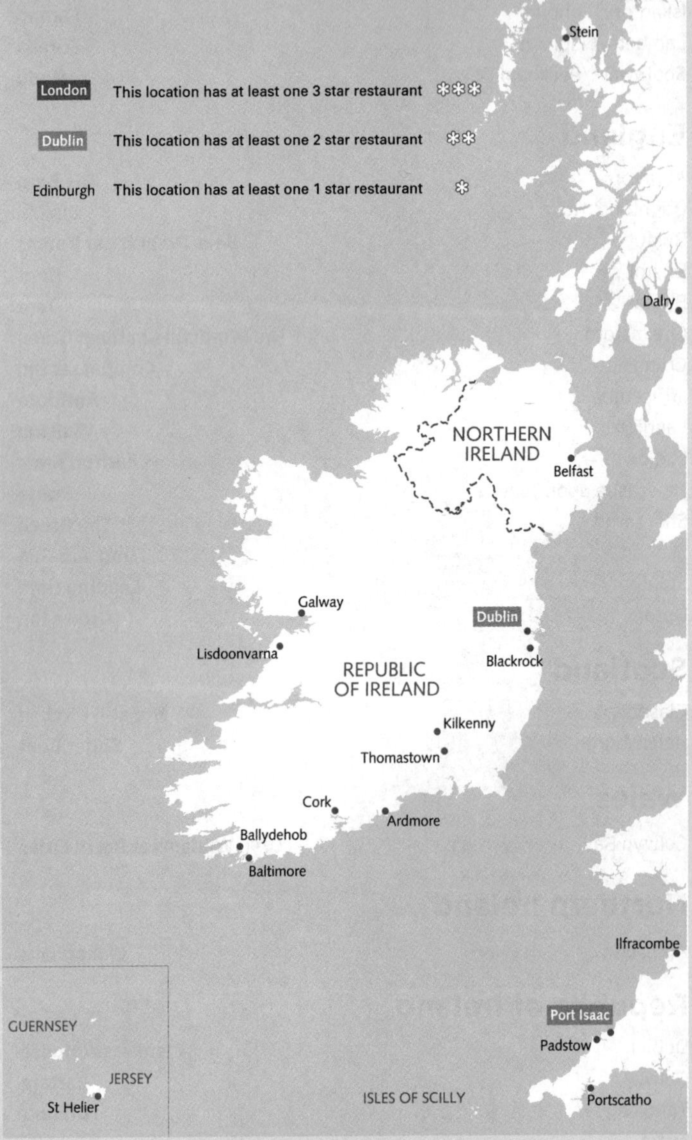

SCOTLAND
Auchterarder
Peat Inn
Anstruther
Edinburgh
Leith
Newcastle-upon-Tyne
Grasmere
Summerhouse
Bowness-on-Windermere
Cartmel
Pateley Bridge
Harome
Oldstead
Langho
Leeds
South Dalton
Aughton
Birkenhead
Fence
ENGLAND
Winteringham
Menai Bridge
Chester
Baslow
Llandrillo
Nottingham
Morston
Hunstanton
Machynlleth
Mountsorrel
Birmingham
Hambleton
Montgomery
Hampton in Arden
Kenilworth
Stratford-upon-Avon
WALES
Cambridge
Llanddewi Skirrid
Cheltenham
Murcott
Great Milton
Little Dunmow
Oxford
Burchett's Green
Whitebrook
Malmesbury
Castle Combe
Shinfield
Marlow
London
Penarth
Bristol
Newbury
Chew Magna
Colerne
Bath
Egham
Ascot
Seasalter
East Chisenbury
Bray
Dorking
Fordwich
Ripley
Knowstone
Winchester
Bagshot
Biddenden
East Grinstead
Horsham
Chagford
Lympstone
Torquay

Bib Gourmands 2019

• This location has at least one Bib Gourmand establishment

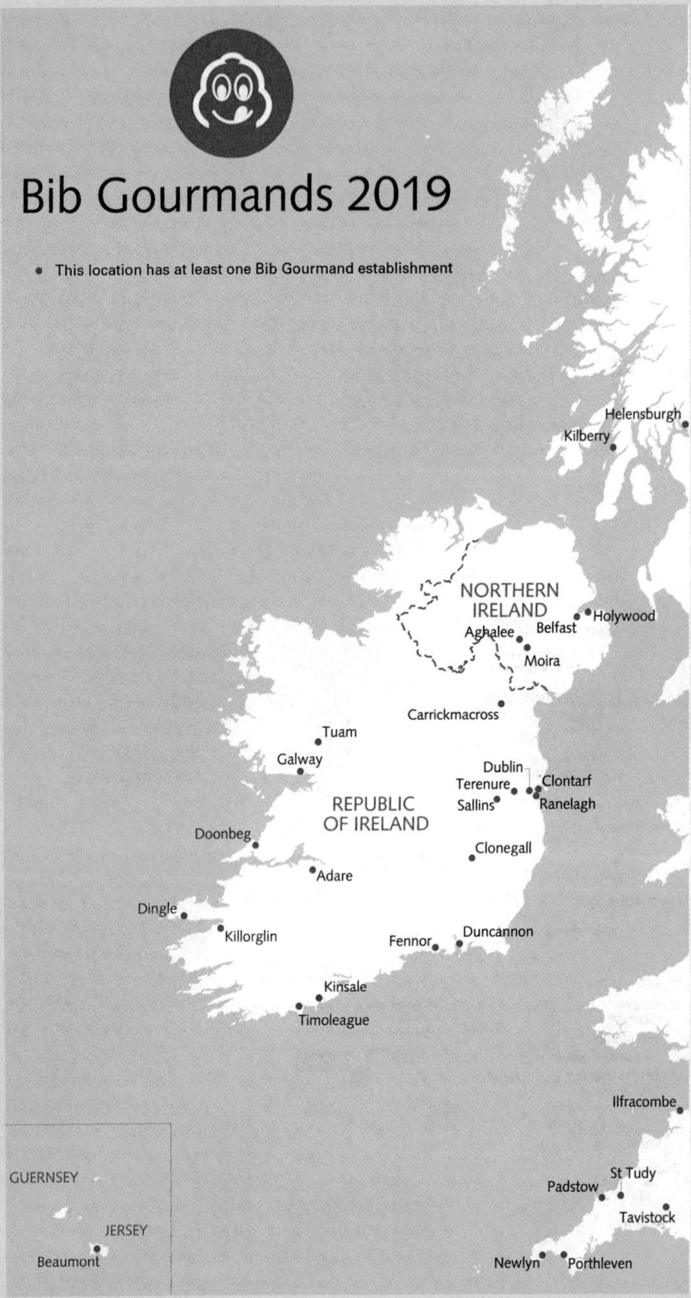

SCOTLAND
Glasgow
Edinburgh
Peebles
Ponteland
North Shields
Newcastle-upon-Tyne
Skelton
Maltby
Thornton
York
Drighlington
Aughton
Manchester
South Ferriby
Stockport
Sheffield
Colwyn Bay
Chester
Nottingham
Thorpe Market
Wymondham
WALES
ENGLAND
Stanton
Ludlow
Bury St. Edmunds
Welland
Aldeburgh
Brecon
Hunsdon
Cirencester
Oxford
Ashendon
Howe Street
Upper South Wraxall
Butlers Cross
Chelmsford
Langford
Ripley
Aberthin
Cookham
London
Bristol
Gerrards Cross
Ewell
Upton
Crundale
Sherborne
Old Alresford
West Hoathly
Tenterden
Donhead-St-Andrew
Brighton and Hove
Seaview

THE MICHELIN GUIDE'S COMMITMENTS

EXPERIENCED IN QUALITY!

Whether they are in Japan, the USA, China or Europe, our inspectors apply the same criteria to judge the quality of each and every hotel and restaurant that they visit. The Michelin guide commands a worldwide reputation thanks to the commitments we make to our readers – and we reiterate these below:

Anonymous inspections

Our inspectors make regular and anonymous visits to hotels and restaurants to gauge the quality of products and services offered to an ordinary customer. They settle their own bill and may then introduce themselves and ask for more information about the establishment. Our readers' comments are also a valuable source of information, which we can follow up with a visit of our own.

Independence

To remain totally objective for our readers, the selection is made with complete independence. Entry into the guide is free. All decisions are discussed with the Editor and our highest awards are considered at a European level.

Our famous One ✪, Two ✪✪ and Three ✪✪✪ stars identify establishments serving the highest quality cuisine – taking into account the quality of ingredients, the mastery of techniques and flavours, the levels of creativity and, of course, consistency.

Selection and choice

The guide offers a selection of the best hotels and restaurants in every category of comfort and price. This is only possible because all the inspectors rigorously apply the same methods.

THREE MICHELIN STARS

Exceptional cuisine, worth a special journey!

Our highest award is given for the superlative cooking of chefs at the peak of their profession. The ingredients are exemplary, the cooking is elevated to an art form and their dishes are often destined to become classics.

TWO MICHELIN STARS

Excellent cooking, worth a detour!

The personality and talent of the chef and their team is evident in the expertly crafted dishes, which are refined, inspired and sometimes original.

ONE MICHELIN STAR

High quality cooking, worth a stop!

Using top quality ingredients, dishes with distinct flavours are carefully prepared to a consistently high standard.

BIB GOURMAND

Good quality, good value cooking.

'Bibs' are awarded for simple yet skilful cooking for under £28 or €40.

THE MICHELIN PLATE

Good cooking

Fresh ingredients, carefully prepared: simply a good meal.

Annual updates

All the practical information, classifications and awards are revised and updated every year to give the most reliable information possible.

Consistency

The criteria for the classifications are the same in every country covered by the MICHELIN guide.

The sole intention of Michelin is to make your travels safe and enjoyable.

Follow our anonymous inspectors: @MichelinGuideUK

SEEK AND SELECT...

HOW TO USE THIS GUIDE

RESTAURANTS

Restaurants are listed by award.

Within each award category, they are ordered by comfort, from XXXXX to X.

Within each comfort category, they are then ordered alphabetically.

Awards:

- ✿✿✿ **Three Stars:** Exceptional cuisine, worth a special journey!
- ✿✿ **Two Stars:** Excellent cooking, worth a detour!
- ✿ **One Star:** High quality cooking, worth a stop!
- **Bib Gourmand:** Good quality, good value cooking.
- **The Michelin Plate:** Good cooking.

Comfort:

Level of comfort, from XXXXX to X, followed by for pubs.

Red: our most delightful places.

ENGLAND

BEAULIEU

Hampshire – ✉ Brockenhurst – Pop. 72

✿ **Scott's**

FRENCH • CLASSIC XXX This ele
18C inn; head to the terrace fo
and efficient, and only top quali
dishes. Cooking has a classical
→Spiced scallops with caulifl
Roast duck breast, smoked bac
soufflé with Sichuan spiced cho
Menu £30/50 (dinner only)
Town plan: D1-a – *Palace Ln* ✉
www.Scotts.com – Closed Dece

Sea Grill Ⓝ

MEATS AND GRILLS • BISTRO
lage, this laid-back bar-restaura
classic. The eggs are from their
nearby farms.
Menu £28 (weekday dinner
Town plan: D1-c – *12 Robert St*
www.seagrill.co.uk – Closed Dec

Manor of Roses

ROMANTIC • STYLISH With its
this charming 18C inn has a time
marry antique furniture with mo
lised. The wicker-furnished cons
18 rooms – ♦£62/ £120♦♦£6
Town plan: D1-a – *Palace Ln* ✉
✿ **Scott's** –See restaurant listin

Wentworth

FRIENDLY • COSY Ivy-clad Vic
the bedrooms; some are tradi
bright and modern. 19C restaur
28 rooms – ♦ £61/106♦♦£6
Town plan: D1-c – *35 Charles St*
www.wentworth.com – Closed

HOTELS

Hotels are listed by comfort, from to , followed by for guesthouses.

Within each comfort category, they are then ordered alphabetically.

Red: our most delightful places.

Locating the establishment

Location and coordinates on the town plan, with main sights.

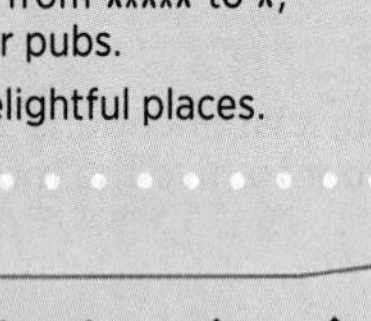

Key words

Each entry comes with two keywords, making it quick and easy to identify the type of establishment and/or the food that it serves.

Other Special Features

- Particularly interesting wine list
- Notable cocktail list
- Great view
- Peaceful establishment

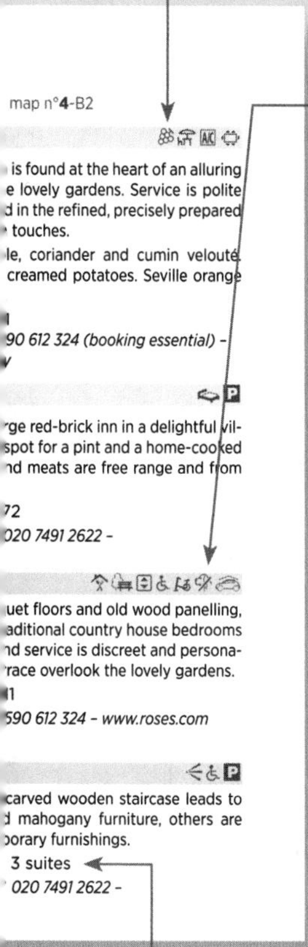
map n°4-B2
is found at the heart of an alluring
e lovely gardens. Service is polite
d in the refined, precisely prepared
touches.
le, coriander and cumin velouté
creamed potatoes. Seville orange
90 612 324 (booking essential) –
rge red-brick inn in a delightful vil-
spot for a pint and a home-cooked
nd meats are free range and from
72
020 7491 2622 –
uet floors and old wood panelling,
aditional country house bedrooms
nd service is discreet and persona-
race overlook the lovely gardens.
1
590 612 324 – www.roses.com
carved wooden staircase leads to
d mahogany furniture, others are
porary furnishings.
3 suites
020 7491 2622 –

Facilities & services

- Restaurant or pub with bedrooms
- Hotel with a restaurant
- Lift (elevator) • Wheelchair access
- Air conditioning (in all or part of the establishment)
- Outside dining available
- Open for breakfast • Small plates
- Restaurant offering vegetarian menus
- Restaurant offering lower priced theatre menus
- No dogs allowed
- Wellness centre
- Sauna • Exercise room
- Swimming pool: outdoor or indoor
- Garden or park • Tennis court
- Golf course
- Conference room
- Private dining room
- Car park • Garage
- Credit cards not accepted
- Nearest Underground station (London)
- N New establishment in the guide

Prices

- Prices are given in £ sterling, and in € euros for the Republic of Ireland.
- All accommodation prices include both service and V.A.T. Restaurant prices include V.A.T. and service is also included when an **s** appears after the prices.

Restaurants		**Hotels**	
Menu £13/28	Fixed price menu. Lowest/highest price.	£50/90 £100/120	Lowest/highest price for single and double room.
Carte £20/35	À la carte menu. Lowest/highest price.	£100/120	Bed & breakfast rate.
s	Service included.	£5	Breakfast price where not included in rate.

Great Britain & Ireland

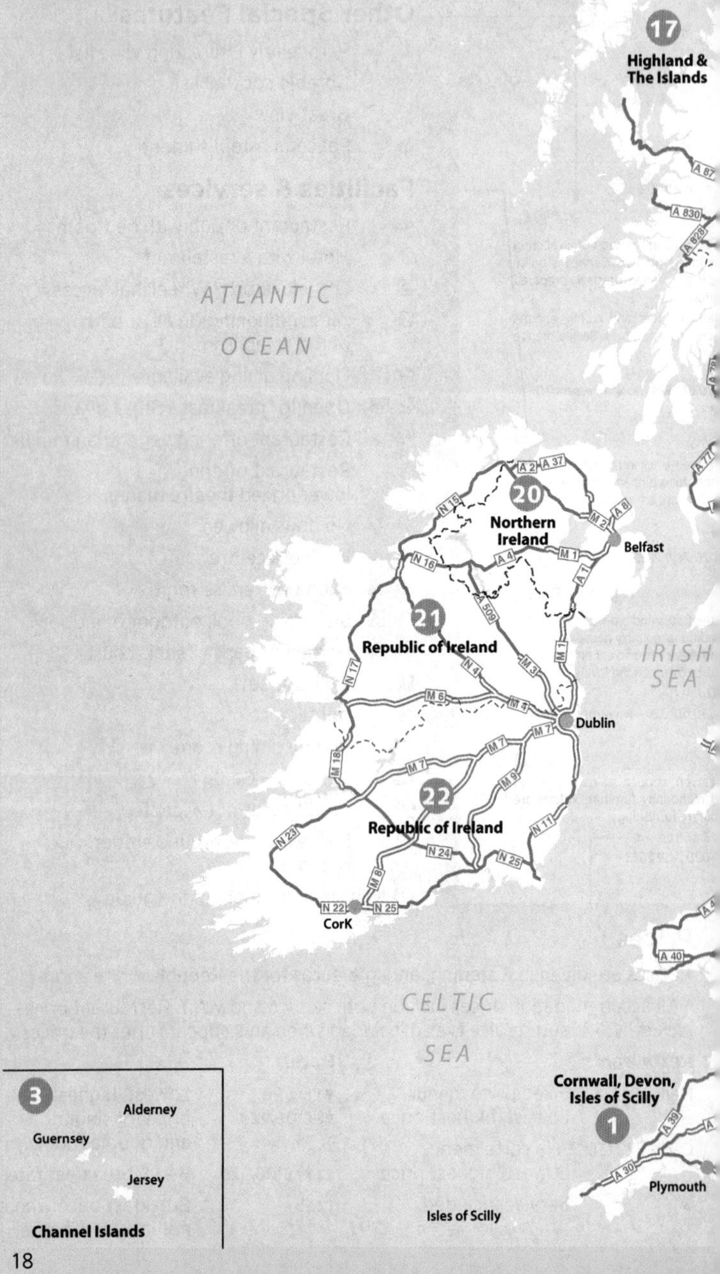

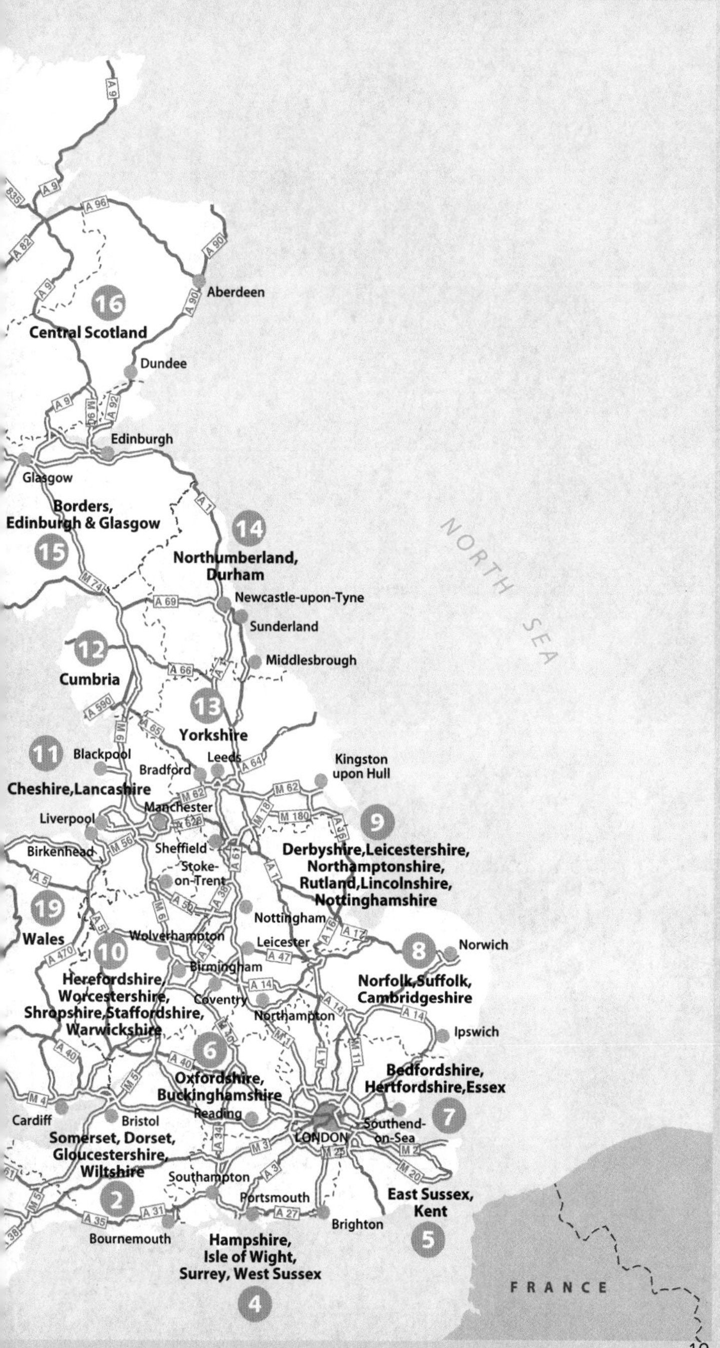
A 9
835
A 96
A 82
A 90
Aberdeen
16
Central Scotland
Dundee
A 92
M 90
Edinburgh
Glasgow
A 1
Borders,
Edinburgh & Glasgow
15
14
Northumberland,
Durham
NORTH SEA
M 74
A 69
Newcastle-upon-Tyne
Sunderland
12
Middlesbrough
A 66
Cumbria
13
A 590
M 6
A 65
Yorkshire
11
Blackpool
Leeds
A 64
Kingston
upon Hull
Bradford
Cheshire,Lancashire
M 62
Manchester
M 18
M 180
9
Liverpool
A 628
Birkenhead
M 56
Sheffield
A 61
Derbyshire,Leicestershire,
Northamptonshire,
Rutland,Lincolnshire,
Nottinghamshire
Stoke-
on-Trent
A 5
19
A 50
A 38
Nottingham
Wales
A 16
A 17
Wolverhampton
8
Norwich
A 470
10
Leicester
A 47
Birmingham
Herefordshire,
Worcestershire,
Shropshire,Staffordshire,
Warwickshire
Coventry
A 14
Norfolk,Suffolk,
Cambridgeshire
Northampton
Ipswich
M 1
M 11
A 40
6
M 5
Bedfordshire,
Hertfordshire,Essex
Oxfordshire,
Buckinghamshire
M 4
Cardiff
Bristol
Reading
7
Southend-
on-Sea
Somerset, Dorset,
Gloucestershire,
Wiltshire
A 34
LONDON
M 3
M 25
M 2
M 20
Southampton
A 3
2
Portsmouth
East Sussex,
Kent
A 35
A 31
A 27
Brighton
5
Bournemouth
Hampshire,
Isle of Wight,
Surrey, West Sussex
4
FRANCE

Alasdair James / iStock

GREAT BRITAIN

LONDON

London is one of the most cosmopolitan, dynamic, fashionable and cultured cities on earth, home not only to such iconic images as Big Ben, Tower Bridge and bear-skinned guards, but also Bengali markets, speedboat rides through the Docklands and stunning views of the city from the top of the very best of 21C architecture. From Roman settlement to banking centre to capital of a 19C empire, the city's pulse has never missed a beat; it's no surprise that a dazzling array of theatres, restaurants, museums, markets and art galleries populate its streets.

The city is one of the food capitals of the world, where you can eat everything from Turkish to Thai and Polish to Peruvian; diners here are an eclectic, well-travelled bunch who gladly welcome all-comers and every style of cuisine. Visit one of the many food markets like Borough or Brixton to witness the capital's wonderfully varied produce, or pop into a pop-up to get a taste of the latest trends. If it's traditional British you're after, try one of the many pubs in the capital; this was, after all, where the gastropub movement began.

- Michelin Road map n° 504
- Michelin Green Guide: London

B. Stevens/Cultura Creative/Photononstop

NOT TO BE MISSED

STARRED RESTAURANTS

✿✿✿

Exceptional cuisine, worth a special journey!

✿✿

Excellent cooking, worth a detour!

✿

High quality cooking, worth a stop!

Five Fields

BIB GOURMAND RESTAURANTS ☺
Good food, good value cooking

RESTAURANTS FROM A TO Z

Simon Harvey Photography / Pied a Terre

G

H

I

J

Michelin

Gymkhana

RESTAURANTS BY CUISINE TYPE

Yauatcha

Creative British

Creative French

Creole

Fish and chips

French

Fusion

Greek

Indian

Italian

Japanese

Meats and grills

Mediterranean cuisine

Mexican

Middle Eastern

Modern British

Modern French

Modern cuisine

Vegetarian

Vietnamese

World cuisine

Barrafina

OUR TOP PICKS

RESTAURANTS WITH OUTSIDE DINING

R

S

T

V-Y-Z

Trishna

THE BEST PUBS

Jan Macuch/istock

OUR SELECTION OF HOTELS

HOTELS FROM A TO Z

N-O

P

R

S-T

W

Z

loveguli/iStock

OUR MOST DELIGHTFUL HOTELS

Boroughs and areas

Greater London is divided, for administrative purposes, into 32 boroughs plus **the City:** these sub-divide naturally into minor areas, usually grouped around former villages or quarters, which often maintain a distinctive character.

BRENT

Church End

Shayona

INDIAN • **FAMILY** Opposite the striking Swaminarayan Temple is this simple, sattvic restaurant: it's vegetarian and 'pure' so avoids onion or garlic. Expect curries from the north, dosas from the south and Mumbai street food. No alcohol so try a lassi.

Menu £10 (weekday lunch) - Carte £12/19

Town plan: 2C3-a - *54-62 Meadow Garth ✉ NW10 8HD - ⊖ Stonebridge Park - ✆ 020 8965 3365 - www.shayonarestaurants.com - Closed 27-28 October and 25 December*

Kensal Green

Parlour

MODERN BRITISH • **PUB** A fun, warmly run and slightly quirky neighbourhood hangout. The menu is a wonderfully unabashed mix of tradition, originality and reinvention, and dishes are beautifully fresh, full of flavour and such great value. Don't miss the cow pie which even Dan, however Desperate, would struggle to finish.

Menu £18 - Carte £18/42

Town plan: 16L4-r - *5 Regent St ✉ NW10 5LG - ⊖ Kensal Green - ✆ 020 8969 2184 - www.parlourkensal.com - Closed 1 week late August, 1 week Christmas-New Year and Monday*

Queen's Park

Ostuni

ITALIAN • **NEIGHBOURHOOD** The cuisine of Puglia, the red hot heel in Italy's boot, is celebrated at this rustic local restaurant. Don't miss the olives, creamy burrata, fava bean purée, the sausages and bombette, or the orecchiette - the ear-shaped pasta.

Carte £24/45

Town plan: 10M3-b - *43-45 Lonsdale Rd ✉ NW6 6RA - ⊖ Queen's Park - ✆ 020 7624 8035 - www.ostuniristorante.co.uk - Closed 24-25 December*

BROMLEY

Farnborough

Chapter One

MODERN CUISINE • **FRIENDLY** Long-standing restaurant with many regulars, its stylish bar leading into an elegant, modern dining room. Wide-ranging menus offer keenly priced, carefully prepared modern European dishes; cooking is light and delicate, mixing classic and modern flavours. Assured service.

Menu £23/40

Town plan: 8G6-c - *Farnborough Common, Locksbottom ✉ BR6 8NF - ✆ 01689 854848 - www.chapteronerestaurant.co.uk - Closed 2-4 January*

Petts Wood

Indian Essence

INDIAN • **NEIGHBOURHOOD** At this smart, contemporary Indian restaurant everything is made in-house, from the masala paste to the kulfi; dishes are vibrant and flavoursome and the prices are good.

Menu £19 (weekday lunch)/25 - Carte £25/36

Town plan: 8G5-e - *176-178 Petts Wood Rd ✉ BR5 1LG - ✆ 01689 838700 - www.indianessence.co.uk*

Céleste

CAMDEN

Belsize Park

Tandis

WORLD CUISINE • NEIGHBOURHOOD X Persian and Middle Eastern food whose appeal stretches way beyond the Iranian diaspora. The specialities are the substantial and invigorating khoresh stew and the succulent kababs; end with Persian sorbet with rosewater.

Carte £ 21/32

Town plan: 11P2-x - *73 Haverstock Hill ✉ NW3 4SL*
- ⊖ Chalk Farm - ✆ 020 7586 8079 - www.tandisrestaurant.com
- Closed 25 December

Bloomsbury

Kitchen Table at Bubbledogs (James Knappett)

MODERN CUISINE • FASHIONABLE XX Ignore the throngs enjoying the curious combination of hotdogs with champagne and head for the curtain – behind it you'll find a horseshoe-shaped counter and a look of expectation on the faces of your fellow diners. Chef-owner James Knappett and his team prepare a no-choice menu of around 12 dishes; each one is described on the blackboard in a single noun so you have to place your trust in them. The produce is some of the best you can find and the small dishes come with a clever creative edge, without being overly complicated. The cooking has developed considerably over the years and now displays admirable poise.

With seating for just 19, the atmosphere is very convivial, especially if you're a fully paid-up member of the foodie community. The chefs interact with their customers over the counter and offer comprehensive explanations of each dish; they are helped out by James' wife Sandia, who is charm personified.

→ Orkney scallops with warm charcoal cream and Exmouth caviar. Duck with black garlic, blood orange purée, turnip and shiso. Milk ice cream with rhubarb and charred black pepper meringue.

Menu £ 125 – tasting menu only

Town plan: 31AN1-g - *70 Charlotte St ✉ W1T 4QG*
- ⊖ Goodge Street - ✆ 020 7637 7770 (booking essential)
- www.kitchentablelondon.co.uk - dinner only - Closed first 2 weeks January, 2 weeks September, 23-27 December and Sunday-Tuesday

An important business lunch or dinner with friends?
The symbol ⊕ indicates restaurants with private rooms.

Pied à Terre

CREATIVE • ELEGANT XXX One of the reasons for the impressive longevity of David Moore's restaurant has been its subtle reinventions: nothing ever too grandiose – just a little freshening up with some new art or clever lighting to keep the place looking relevant and vibrant. The cooking is still based on classical French techniques but dishes now display a more muscular edge.

→ Smoked quail spelt risotto with coral mushrooms and watercress. Poached turbot with langoustine and spinach. Pink and red pavlova with raspberries, kaffir lime and a lavender custard.

Menu £ 38/80

Town plan: 31AN1-a – *34 Charlotte St ✉ W1T 2NH – ⊖ Goodge Street – ✆ 020 7636 1178 (booking essential) – www.pied-a-terre.co.uk – Closed 23 December-9 January, Saturday lunch, Sunday and bank holidays*

Hakkasan Hanway Place

CHINESE • TRENDY XX There are now Hakkasans all over the world but this was the original. It has the sensual looks, air of exclusivity and glamorous atmosphere synonymous with the 'brand'. The exquisite Cantonese dishes are prepared with care and consistency by the large kitchen team; lunch dim sum is a highlight.

→ Dim sum platter. Grilled Chilean sea bass in honey. Chocolate and olive oil ganache.

Carte £ 35/135

Town plan: 31AP2-y – *8 Hanway Pl. ✉ W1T 1HD – ⊖ Tottenham Court Road – ✆ 020 7927 7000 – www.hakkasan.com – Closed 24-25 December*

The Ninth (Jun Tanaka)

MEDITERRANEAN CUISINE • BRASSERIE X Jun Tanaka's first restaurant – the ninth in which he has worked – is this neighbourhood spot with a lively downstairs and more intimate first floor. Cooking uses classical French techniques with a spotlight on the Med; dishes look appealing but the focus is firmly on flavour. Vegetables are a highlight.

→ Salted beef cheek, oxtail consommé and sauce ravigote. Chargrilled sea bream, lemon confit and miso. Pain perdu with vanilla ice cream.

Menu £ 27 (lunch) – Carte £ 39/66

Town plan: 31AN1-j – *22 Charlotte St ✉ W1T 2NB – ⊖ Goodge Street – ✆ 020 3019 0880 – www.theninthlondon.com – Closed Christmas-New Year, Sunday and bank holidays*

Barbary

WORLD CUISINE • TAPAS BAR X A sultry, atmospheric restaurant from the team behind Palomar: a tiny place with 24 non-bookable seats squeezed around a horseshoe-shaped, zinc-topped counter. The menu of small sharing plates lists dishes from the former Barbary Coast. Service is keen, as are the prices.

Carte £ 16/36

Town plan: 31AQ2-k – *16 Neal's Yard ✉ WC2H 9DP – ⊖ Covent Garden (bookings not accepted) – www.thebarbary.co.uk – Closed dinner 24-26 December*

Barrica

SPANISH • TAPAS BAR X All the staff at this lively little tapas bar are Spanish, so perhaps it's national pride that makes them run it with a passion lacking in many of their competitors. When it comes to the food, authenticity is high on the agenda. Dishes pack a punch and are fairly priced.

Carte £ 22/38

Town plan: 31AN1-x – *62 Goodge St ✉ W1T 4NE – ⊖ Goodge Street – ✆ 020 7436 9448 (booking essential) – www.barrica.co.uk – Closed 25-31 December, 1 January, Easter, Sunday and bank holidays*

Salt Yard

MEDITERRANEAN CUISINE • TAPAS BAR A ground floor bar and buzzy basement restaurant specialising in good value plates of tasty Italian and Spanish dishes, ideal for sharing. Ingredients are top-notch; charcuterie is a speciality. Super wine list and sincere, enthusiastic staff.

Carte £ 20/28

Town plan: 31AN1-d – *54 Goodge St. ✉ W1T 4NA – ⊖ Goodge Street – ✆ 020 7637 0657 – www.saltyard.co.uk – Closed 31 December-1 January and dinner 24-25 December*

Mere

MODERN CUISINE • FASHIONABLE Monica Galetti's first collaboration with her husband, David, is an understatedly elegant basement restaurant flooded with natural light. Global, ingredient-led cooking features French influences with a nod to the South Pacific.

Menu £ 35 (weekday lunch) – Carte £ 46/64

Town plan: 31AN1-r – *74 Charlotte St ✉ W1T 4QH – ⊖ Goodge Street – ✆ 020 7268 6565 – www.mere-restaurant.com – Closed Sunday and bank holidays*

Noizé (N)

MODERN FRENCH • NEIGHBOURHOOD A softly spoken Frenchman, an alumnus of Pied à Terre, took over the former Dabbous site and created a delightfully relaxed, modern bistro. The unfussy French food is served at fair prices; sauces are a great strength. The wine list, with plenty of depth and fair mark-ups, is another highlight.

Carte £ 34/56

Town plan: 31AN1-t – *39 Whitfield St ✉ W1T 2SF – ⊖ Goodge Street – ✆ 020 7323 1310 – www.noize-restaurant.co.uk – Closed 2 weeks August, 23 December-3 January, Easter, Saturday lunch, Sunday and Monday*

Roka

JAPANESE • FASHIONABLE The original Roka, where people come for the lively atmosphere as much as the cooking. The kitchen takes the flavours of Japanese food and adds its own contemporary touches; try specialities from the on-view Robata grill.

Carte £ 42/75

Town plan: 31AN1-k – *37 Charlotte St ✉ W1T 1RR – ⊖ Goodge Street – ✆ 020 7636 5228 – www.rokarestaurant.com – Closed 25 December*

Cigala

SPANISH • NEIGHBOURHOOD Longstanding Spanish restaurant, with a lively and convivial atmosphere, friendly and helpful service and an appealing and extensive menu of classics. The dried hams are a must and it's well worth waiting the 30 minutes for a paella.

Menu £ 24 (weekday lunch) – Carte £ 34/46

Town plan: 32AR1-a – *54 Lamb's Conduit St. ✉ WC1N 3LW – ⊖ Russell Square – ✆ 020 7405 1717 (booking essential) – www.cigala.co.uk – Closed 24-26 December and 1 January*

Honey & Co

WORLD CUISINE • SIMPLE The husband and wife team at this sweet little café were both Ottolenghi head chefs so expect cooking full of freshness and colour. Influences stretch beyond Israel to the wider Middle East. Open from 8am; packed at night.

Menu £ 35

Town plan: 18Q4-c – *25a Warren St ✉ W1T 5LZ – ⊖ Warren Street – ✆ 020 7388 6175 (booking essential) – www.honeyandco.co.uk – Closed 24-26, 31 December, 1-3 January and Sunday*

Noble Rot

TRADITIONAL BRITISH • RUSTIC A wine bar and restaurant from the people behind the wine magazine of the same name. Unfussy cooking comes with bold, gutsy flavours; expect fish from the Kent coast as well as classics like terrines, rillettes and home-cured meats.

Menu £ 16 (weekday lunch) - Carte £ 33/49

Town plan: 18R4-r - *51 Lamb's Conduit St ✉ WC1N 3NB - ⊖ Russell Square - ✆ 020 7242 8963 - www.noblerot.co.uk - Closed 25-26 December and Sunday*

Covent Garden

LUXURY • DESIGN Popular with those of a theatrical bent. Boldly designed, stylish bedrooms, with technology discreetly concealed. Boasts a very comfortable first floor oak-panelled drawing room with its own honesty bar. Easy-going menu in Brasserie Max.

58 rooms - £ 360/385 £ 360/475

Town plan: 31AP2-x - *10 Monmouth St ✉ WC2H 9HB - ⊖ Covent Garden - ✆ 020 7806 1000 - www.firmdalehotels.com*

Camden Town

York & Albany

MODERN CUISINE • INN This handsome 1820s John Nash coaching inn was rescued by Gordon Ramsay a few years ago after lying almost derelict. It's a moot point whether it's still an inn or more a restaurant; the food is sophisticated and the service is bright.

Menu £ 25 (weekday lunch) - Carte £ 32/49

9 rooms - £ 145/175 £ 175/305

Town plan: 12Q3-s - *127-129 Parkway ✉ NW1 7PS - ⊖ Camden Town - ✆ 020 7592 1227 - www.gordonramsayrestaurants.com/york-and-albany*

Dartmouth Park

Bull & Last

TRADITIONAL BRITISH • NEIGHBOURHOOD A busy Victorian pub with plenty of charm and character; the upstairs is a little quieter. Cooking is muscular, satisfying and reflects the time of year; charcuterie is a speciality.

Carte £ 34/47

Town plan: 12Q1-a - *168 Highgate Rd ✉ NW5 1QS - ⊖ Tufnell Park. - ✆ 020 7267 3641 (booking essential) - www.thebullandlast.co.uk - Closed 23-25 December*

Hatton Garden

Anglo

CREATIVE BRITISH • RUSTIC As its name suggests, British produce is the mainstay of the menu at this pared-down, personally run restaurant, with 'home-grown' ingredients often served in creative ways. Cooking is well-executed with assured flavours.

Menu £ 42/60 - Carte lunch £ 34/53

Town plan: 32AS1-o - *30 St Cross St ✉ EC1N 8UH - ⊖ Farringdon - ✆ 020 7430 1503 - www.anglorestaurant.com - Closed 22 December-4 January, Sunday and lunch Monday*

Holborn

Margot

ITALIAN • ELEGANT Bucking the trend of casual eateries is this glamourous, elegant Italian, where a doorman greets you, staff sport tuxedos and the surroundings are sleek and stylish. The seasonal, regional Italian cooking has bags of flavour and a rustic edge.

Menu £ 25 (lunch and early dinner) - Carte £ 30/61

Town plan: 31AQ2-m - *45 Great Queen St ✉ WC2 5AA - ⊖ Holborn - ✆ 020 3409 4777 - www.margotrestaurant.com - Closed 25 December*

Great Queen Street

MODERN BRITISH • RUSTIC X The menu is a model of British understatement and is dictated by the seasons; the cooking, confident and satisfying and served in generous portions. Lively atmosphere and enthusiastic service. Highlights include the shared dishes like the suet-crusted steak and ale pie for two.

Menu £ 18 (weekday lunch) - Carte £ 22/42

Town plan: 31AQ2-c - *32 Great Queen St ✉ WC2B 5AA - ⊖ Holborn - ✆ 020 7242 0622 (booking essential) - www.greatqueenstreetrestaurant.co.uk - Closed Christmas-New Year, Sunday dinner and bank holidays*

Rosewood London

HISTORIC • ELEGANT A beautiful Edwardian building that was once the HQ of Pearl Assurance. The styling is very British and the bedrooms are uncluttered and smart. Cartoonist Gerald Scarfe's work adorns the walls of his eponymous bar. A classic brasserie with a menu of British favourites occupies the former banking hall.

306 rooms - †£ 390/900 ††£ 390/900 - ☕ £ 25 - 44 suites

Town plan: 32AR1-x - *252 High Holborn ✉ WC1V 7EN - ⊖ Holborn - ✆ 020 7781 8888 - www.rosewoodhotels.com/london*

L'oscar (N)

HISTORIC BUILDING • ELEGANT No expense was spared in converting this Arts & Craft building and former HQ of the Baptist church. Silk, leather and marble have been used to create a seductive interior, with a peacock motif running through it. Baptist Grill is in the former chapel and serves a modern British menu.

39 rooms - †£ 310/965 ††£ 310/965 - ☕ £ 35

Town plan: 32AR1-e - *2-6 Southampton Row ✉ WC1B 4AA - ⊖ Holborn - ✆ 020 7405 5555 - www.loscar.com*

The Hoxton

TOWNHOUSE • CONTEMPORARY When the room categories are Shoebox, Snug, Cosy and Roomy, you know you're in a hip hotel. A great location and competitive rates plus a retro-style diner, a buzzy lobby and a 'Chicken Shop' in the basement.

174 rooms ☕ - †£ 99/269 ††£ 99/269

Town plan: 31AQ1-h - *199 - 206 High Holborn ✉ WC1V 7BD - ⊖ Holborn - ✆ 020 7661 3000 - www.thehoxton.com*

Primrose Hill

Michael Nadra Primrose Hill

MODERN CUISINE • NEIGHBOURHOOD XX The menu resembles Michael Nadra's Chiswick operation, which means flavours from the Med but also the occasional Asian note. The bar offers over 20 martinis. The unusual vaulted room adds to the intimacy and service is very friendly.

Menu £ 23/39

Town plan: 12Q3-m - *42 Gloucester Ave ✉ NW1 8JD - ⊖ Camden Town - ✆ 020 7722 2800 - www.restaurant-michaelnadra.co.uk/primrose - Closed 24-28 December and 1 January*

Odette's

MODERN CUISINE • NEIGHBOURHOOD XX A long-standing local favourite. Warm and inviting interior, with chatty yet organised service. Robust and quite elaborate cooking, with owner passionate about his Welsh roots. Good value lunch menu.

Menu £ 23 (lunch and early dinner) - Carte £ 34/53

Town plan: 11P3-b - *130 Regent's Park Rd. ✉ NW1 8XL - ⊖ Chalk Farm - ✆ 020 7586 8569 - www.odettesprimrosehill.com - Closed Christmas-New Year, Sunday dinner and Monday*

Swiss Cottage

Bradley's

MODERN CUISINE • NEIGHBOURHOOD XX A stalwart of the local dining scene and ideal for visitors to the nearby Hampstead Theatre. The thoughtfully compiled and competitively priced set menus of mostly classical cooking draw in plenty of regulars.

Menu £ 24/30 – Carte £ 36/47

Town plan: 11N2-e – *25 Winchester Rd. ✉ NW3 3NR – ⊖ Swiss Cottage – ✆ 020 7722 3457 – www.bradleysnw3.co.uk – Closed Sunday dinner and bank holidays*

Tufnell Park

Regional map n° **7**-B3

Ceremony

VEGETARIAN • NEIGHBOURHOOD X Zinc-topped tables, a raised bar and a contemporary look – vegetarian restaurants never used to look like this. The small menu is full of interesting dishes, with influences from the Med and Asia; some even use produce from the garden at the back. The booths are the prized seats.

Carte £ 27/33

Town plan: 12Q1-c – *131 Fortess Rd ✉ NW5 2HR – ⊖ Tufnell Park – ✆ 020 3302 4242 (booking essential) – www.ceremonyrestaurant.london – dinner only and Sunday lunch – Closed Christmas and Monday*

West Hampstead

Regional map n° **7**-B3

Hām

MODERN CUISINE • NEIGHBOURHOOD X A bright, modern space that perfectly complements the style of cooking, which is light, seasonal and unfussy. The restaurant has a warm neighbourhood feel – its name means 'home' – and its brunches are also popular.

Carte £ 35/46

Town plan: 10M2-h – *238 West End Ln ✉ NW6 1LG – ⊖ West Hampstead – ✆ 020 7813 0168 – www.hamwesthampstead.com – Closed Sunday dinner, Monday and Tuesday*

Michelin

CITY OF LONDON

Restaurants

✿ City Social

MODERN CUISINE • ELEGANT XXX Jason Atherton's dark and moody restaurant with an art deco twist, set on the 24th floor of Tower 42; the City views are impressive, especially from tables 10 and 15. The flexible menu is largely European and the cooking manages to be both refined and robust at the same time.

→ Brixham crab with pickled kohlrabi, nashi pear and pink grapefruit. Isle of Gigha halibut with Wye Valley asparagus and tomato consommé. Hazelnut plaisir sucré, chocolate syrup, biscuit and milk ice cream.

Carte £ 47/90

Town plan: 33AW2-s - *Tower 42 (24th floor), 25 Old Broad St ✉ EC2N 1HQ - ⊖ Liverpool Street - ✆ 020 7877 7703 - www.citysociallondon.com - Closed Sunday and bank holidays*

✿ La Dame de Pic

MODERN FRENCH • DESIGN XX A high-ceilinged, columned room in the impressive Beaux-Arts style Four Seasons Hotel at Ten Trinity Square; a charming brasserie deluxe with a spacious, stylish feel. Anne-Sophie Pic's cuisine is refined, colourful and original; it's rooted in classic French techniques yet delivered in a modern manner, relying on exciting flavour combinations of top quality ingredients.

→ Berlingots with smoked Brillat-Savarin, asparagus, bergamot and mint. Challans chicken with tonka bean tea, pumpkin parcels, chestnut and yuzu. The white millefeuille.

Menu £ 39 (lunch) - Carte £ 69/91

Town plan: 34AY3-d - *Four Seasons Hotel London at Ten Trinity Square, 10 Trinity Sq ✉ EC3N 4AJ - ⊖ Tower Hill - ✆ 020 3297 3799 - www.ladamedepiclondon.co.uk - Closed Sunday*

✿ Club Gascon (Pascal Aussignac)

FRENCH • ELEGANT XX Chef-owner Pascal Aussignac celebrates the gastronomy of Gascony and France's southwest in his restaurant noted for its vintage marble walls and beautiful floral display. Go for the tasting menu to sample the kitchen's full repertoire of robustly flavoured yet refined dishes.

→ Venison carpaccio with sea urchin jus, cauliflower and sansho pepper. Veal sweetbreads with lobster and cuttlefish tagliatelle. Pineapple and ginger soufflé with lemongrass sorbet.

Menu £ 40/84 - Carte £ 46/76

Town plan: 33AU1-z - *57 West Smithfield ✉ EC1A 9DS - ⊖ Barbican - ✆ 020 7600 6144 (booking essential) - www.clubgascon.com - Closed 22 December-7 January, Saturday lunch, Monday lunch, Sunday and bank holidays*

Bread Street Kitchen

MODERN CUISINE • TRENDY XX Gordon Ramsay's take on NY loft-style dining comes with a large bar, thumping music, an open kitchen and enough zinc ducting to kit out a small industrial estate. For the food, think modern bistro dishes with an element of refinement.

Carte £ 32/62

Town plan: 33AV2-e - *10 Bread St ✉ EC4M 9AJ - ⊖ St Paul's - ✆ 020 3030 4050 - www.gordonramsayrestaurants.com/bread-street-kitchen*

Brigadiers

INDIAN • EXOTIC DÉCOR XX The army mess clubs of India provide the theme for this large restaurant on the ground floor of the Bloomberg building. BBQ and street food from around India is the focus; with 'Feast' menus for larger parties. Beer and whisky are also a feature. The atmosphere is predictably loud and lively.

Menu £ 25 (lunch)
- Carte £ 27/45

Town plan: 33AV2-a - *1-5 Bloomberg Arcade ✉ EC4N 8AR - ⊖ Bank - ✆ 020 3319 8140 (booking essential) - www.brigadierslondon.com - Closed Christmas*

Cigalon

FRENCH • ELEGANT XX Hidden away among the lawyers offices on Chancery Lane, this bright, high-ceilinged restaurant pays homage to the food and wine of Provence. Expect flavoursome French classics like salade niçoise and bouillabaisse.

Menu £ 23/37 - Carte lunch £ 31/46

Town plan: 32AS2-x - *115 Chancery Ln ✉ WC2A 1PP - ⊖ Chancery Lane - ✆ 020 7242 8373 - www.cigalon.co.uk - Closed Christmas, New Year, Saturday, Sunday and bank holidays*

Fenchurch

MODERN CUISINE • DESIGN XX Arrive at the 'Walkie Talkie' early so you can first wander round the Sky Garden and take in the views. The smartly dressed restaurant is housed in a glass box within the atrium. Dishes are largely British and the accomplished cooking uses modern techniques.

Menu £ 35 (weekday lunch)
- Carte £ 53/68

Town plan: 34AX3-a - *Level 37, Sky Garden, 20 Fenchurch St ✉ EC3M 3BY - ⊖ Monument - ✆ 0333 772 0020 - www.skygarden.london - Closed 25-27 December*

Vanilla Black

VEGETARIAN • INTIMATE XX A vegetarian restaurant where real thought has gone into the creation of dishes, which deliver an array of interesting texture and flavour contrasts. Modern techniques are subtly incorporated and while there are some original combinations, they are well-judged.

Menu £ 22 (weekday lunch)/55

Town plan: 32AS2-e - *17-18 Tooks Ct. ✉ EC4A 1LB - ⊖ Chancery Lane - ✆ 020 7242 2622 (booking essential) - www.vanillablack.co.uk - Closed 2 weeks Christmas and bank holidays*

On a budget? Take advantage of lunchtime prices.

Yauatcha City

CHINESE • FASHIONABLE XX A more corporate version of the stylish Soho original, with a couple of bars and a terrace at both ends. All the dim sum greatest hits are on the menu but the chefs have some work to match the high standard found in Broadwick Street.

Menu £ 35/48
- Carte £ 32/77

Town plan: 34AX1-w - *Broadgate Circle ✉ EC2M 2QS - ⊖ Liverpool Street - ✆ 020 3817 9880 - www.yauatcha.com - Closed 24 December-3 January and bank holidays*

Cabotte

FRENCH • WINE BAR X A bistro de luxe with a stunning wine list - owned by two master sommeliers who share a passion for the wines of Burgundy. Cooking comes with the same regional bias and the accomplished classics are simple in style and rich in flavour.

Carte £ 35/51

Town plan: 33AV2-c - *48 Gresham St ✉ EC2V 7AY - ⊖ Bank - ✆ 020 7600 1616 (booking essential) - www.cabotte.co.uk - Closed Saturday, Sunday and bank holidays*

James Cochran EC3

MODERN CUISINE • SIMPLE X A spacious, simply furnished restaurant where the eponymous chef offers original combinations of interesting ingredients in an array of gutsy, good value small plates. The 6 course evening tasting menu is available with matching wines.

Carte £ 40/45

Town plan: 34AX2-v - *19 Bevis Marks ✉ EC3A 7JA - ⊖ Liverpool Street - ✆ 020 3302 0310 (booking essential at lunch) - www.jcochran.restaurant - Closed Christmas, Saturday lunch, Sunday and bank holidays*

José Pizarro

SPANISH • TAPAS BAR X The eponymous chef's third operation is a good fit here: it's well run, flexible and fairly priced - and that includes the wine list. The Spanish menu is nicely balanced, with the seafood dishes being the standouts.

Carte £ 17/56

Town plan: 34AX1-p - *36 Broadgate Circle ✉ EC2M 1QS - ⊖ Liverpool Street - ✆ 020 7256 5333 - www.josepizarro.com - Closed Sunday*

Paternoster Chop House

TRADITIONAL BRITISH • BRASSERIE X Appropriately British menu in a restaurant lying in the shadow of St Paul's Cathedral. Large, open room with full-length windows; busy bar attached. Kitchen uses thoughtfully sourced produce.

Menu £ 24 (lunch and early dinner) - Carte £ 29/58

Town plan: 33AU2-x - *Warwick Ct., Paternoster Sq. ✉ EC4M 7DX - ⊖ St Paul's - ✆ 020 7029 9400 - www.paternosterchophouse.co.uk - Closed 26-30 December, 1 January and dinner Sunday*

Temple and Sons

TRADITIONAL BRITISH • BISTRO X In a glass cube next to Tower 42 is this relaxed restaurant styled on a Victorian grocer's shop, with a bar serving home-canned cocktails, and a menu of traditional British dishes like sausage and mash and sticky toffee pudding.

Carte £ 22/52

Town plan: 33AW2-s - *22 Old Broad St ✉ EC2N 1HQ - ⊖ Liverpool Street - ✆ 020 7877 7710 - www.templeandsons.co.uk - Closed Sunday*

Jugged Hare

TRADITIONAL BRITISH • PUB Vegetarians may feel ill at ease – and not just because of the taxidermy. The atmospheric dining room, with its open kitchen down one side, specialises in stout British dishes, with meats from the rotisserie a highlight.

Menu £ 25 (early dinner) – Carte £ 27/58

Town plan: 33AV1-x – *42 Chiswell St ✉ EC1Y 4SA – ⊖ Barbican.*
– ✆ 020 7614 0134 (booking essential) – www.thejuggedhare.com
– Closed 25-26 December

Hotels

Four Seasons H. London at Ten Trinity Square

HISTORIC BUILDING • ELEGANT This extraordinary building, built in 1922, is the former headquarters of The Port of London Authority and boasts many original features including the impressive rotunda lounge with its domed ceiling and plaster reliefs. Classically furnished bedrooms; choose an Executive for more space and a contemporary look. Accomplished French cooking in La Dame de Pic. Asian dishes in Mei Ume.

100 rooms – †£ 390/525 ††£ 390/525 – ☕£ 28 – 7 suites

Town plan: 34AY3-d – *10 Trinity Sq ✉ EC3N 4AJ – ⊖ Tower Hill*
– ✆ 020 3297 9200
– www.fourseasons.com/tentrinity

❀ **La Dame de Pic** – See restaurant listing

Andaz Liverpool Street

BUSINESS • DESIGN A contemporary and stylish interior hides behind the classic Victorian façade. Bright and spacious bedrooms boast state-of-the-art facilities. Various dining options include a brasserie specialising in grilled meats, a compact Japanese restaurant and a traditional pub.

267 rooms – †£ 169/499 ††£ 169/499 – ☕£ 28 – 14 suites

Town plan: 34AX2-t – *40 Liverpool St ✉ EC2M 7QN – ⊖ Liverpool Street*
– ✆ 020 7961 1234
– www.andazliverpoolstreet.com

The Ned

HISTORIC BUILDING • CONTEMPORARY The former Midland bank headquarters, designed and built by Sir Edward Lutyens in 1926; now a hotel and members club offering relaxed luxury and considerable style. Edwardian-style bedrooms feature rug-covered wooden floors and beautiful furniture. There are numerous restaurants housed in the vast hall; pay a visit to the former bank vaults – now a quirky bar.

252 rooms – †£ 320/400 ††£ 320/550 – ☕£ 15

Town plan: 33AW2-n – *27 Poultry ✉ EC2R 8AJ – ⊖ Bank*
– ✆ 020 3828 2000 – www.thened.com

Montcalm London City at The Brewery

BUSINESS • CONTEMPORARY The majority of the stylish, modern bedrooms are in the original part of the Whitbread Brewery, built in 1714; ask for a quieter one overlooking the courtyard, or one of the 25 found in the 4 restored Georgian townhouses across the road. Enjoy a meal in the Chiswell Street Dining Rooms or The Jugged Hare.

236 rooms ☕ – †£ 253/496 ††£ 253/496 – 7 suites

Town plan: 33AV1-r – *52 Chiswell St ✉ EC1Y 4SA – ⊖ Barbican*
– ✆ 020 7614 0100
– www.themontcalmlondoncity.co.uk

Threadneedles

HISTORIC BUILDING • CONTEMPORARY A converted bank, dating from 1856, with a smart, boutique feel and a stunning stained-glass cupola in the lounge. Individually styled bedrooms feature Egyptian cotton sheets, iPod docks and thoughtful extras. Spacious Wheeler's with its marble, pillars and panelling specialises in grills and seafood.

74 rooms – †£ 149/599 ††£ 149/599 – ☕£ 15

Town plan: 33AW2-y – *5 Threadneedle St.* ✉ *EC2R 8AY* – ⊖ *Bank* – ✆ *020 7657 8080* – *www.hotelthreadneedles.co.uk*

EALING

Acton Green

Le Vacherin

FRENCH • BRASSERIE XX Authentic feel to this comfortable brasserie, with its brown leather banquette seating, mirrors and belle époque prints. French classics from snails to duck confit; beef is a speciality.

Menu £ 25 (weekdays) – Carte £ 25/53

Town plan: 6C4-f – *76-77 South Par* ✉ *W4 5LF* – ⊖ *Chiswick Park* – ✆ *020 8742 2121* – *www.levacherin.com* – *Closed Monday lunch*

Duke of Sussex

MEDITERRANEAN CUISINE • PUB Bustling Victorian pub, whose striking dining room was once a variety theatre complete with proscenium arch. Stick to the Spanish dishes; stews and cured meats are the specialities. BYO on Mondays.

Carte £ 19/54

Town plan: 6C4-f – *75 South Par* ✉ *W4 5LF* – ⊖ *Chiswick Park.* – ✆ *020 8742 8801* – *www.thedukeofsussex.co.uk*

Ealing

Charlotte's W5

MODERN CUISINE • NEIGHBOURHOOD X It's all about flexibility at this converted stable block – you can come for a drink, a snack or a full meal. Every dish is available in a choice of three sizes and every bottle of wine is offered by the glass or carafe. The charming service team add to the buzz.

Menu £ 18/30 – Carte £ 28/49

Town plan: 1B3-c – *Dickens Yard, Longfield Ave* ✉ *W5 2UQ* – ⊖ *Ealing Broadway* – ✆ *020 3771 8722* – *www.charlottes.co.uk*

Kiraku

JAPANESE • FRIENDLY X The name of this cute little Japanese restaurant means 'relax and enjoy' - easy with such charming service. Extensive menu includes zensai, skewers, noodles, rice dishes and assorted sushi; ask if you want them in a particular order.

Carte £ 14/35

Town plan: 2C3-v – *8 Station Par, Uxbridge Rd.* ✉ *W5 3LD* – ⊖ *Ealing Common* – ✆ *020 8992 2848* – *www.kiraku.co.uk* – *Closed Christmas-New Year*

South Ealing

Ealing Park Tavern

MODERN BRITISH • TRENDY An impressive Arts and Crafts property, dating from 1886 and brought up to date thanks to a splendid refurbishment from the Martin Brothers. Cooking is robust yet with a refined edge. The pub also boasts its own brewery at the back.

Carte £ 22/30

Town plan: 6C4-e – *222 South Ealing Rd* ✉ *W5 4RL* – ⊖ *South Ealing* – ✆ *020 8758 1879* – *www.ealingparktavern.com* – *Closed 25 December*

GREENWICH

Peninsula

MODERN CUISINE • ELEGANT Don't be put off by its being in a somewhat corporate hotel – the floor-to-ceiling windows ensure great views across the river. The menu is also creative and ambitious, with the occasional Nordic touch; the dishes are skilfully executed and attractively presented.

Menu £ 35 (early dinner) – Carte £ 39/58

Town plan: 7F4-p – *InterContinental London - The O2 Hotel (2nd floor), 1 Waterview Dr, Greenwich Peninsula ✉ SE10 0TW – ⊖ North Greenwich – ☎ 020 8463 6913 – www.iclondon-theo2.com – dinner only – Closed 1-14 January, 1 week summer and Sunday*

Craft London

MODERN BRITISH • DESIGN Chef Stevie Parle has created a striking space beside the O2 that includes a coffee shop, a cocktail bar, and a restaurant championing seasonal British produce. They do their own curing and smoking, and roast their own coffee.

Menu £ 32 – Carte £ 27/43

Town plan: 7F4-f – *Peninsula Sq ✉ SE10 0SQ – ⊖ North Greenwich – ☎ 020 8465 5910 – www.craft-london.co.uk – dinner only and Saturday lunch – Closed Christmas-New Year, Sunday and Monday*

Michelin

HACKNEY

Dalston

Jidori

JAPANESE • BISTRO A sweet, unadorned yakitori-style restaurant serving succulent skewers of chicken, cooked on a charcoal-fired Kama-Asa Shoten grill imported from Japan. Charming staff and a good selection of cocktails, sake and craft beers.

Carte £ 17/28

Town plan: 14U2-y – *89 Kingsland High St ✉ E2 8BP – ⊖ Dalston Kingsland – ✆ 020 7686 5634 (bookings not accepted) – www.jidori.co.uk – dinner only and lunch Wednesday-Friday – Closed 25-26 December, 1 January, bank holiday Mondays and Sunday*

Rotorino

ITALIAN • SIMPLE A stylish yet down to earth Italian serving Southern Italian specialities like caponata, gnudi and Sasso chicken. Staff are welcoming and knowledgeable; ask for one of the booths at the back.

Menu £ 19 (early dinner) – Carte £ 22/34

Town plan: 14U3-w – *434 Kingsland Rd ✉ E8 4AA – ⊖ Dalston Junction – ✆ 020 7249 9081 – www.rotorino.com – dinner only and Sunday lunch – Closed Christmas-New Year*

Hackney

Legs

MODERN BRITISH • NEIGHBOURHOOD An urban, no-frills bistro with a lively atmosphere, charming staff and food bursting with freshness and flavour. Dinner is a daily selection of small plates for sharing – and they also serve brunch on Saturdays. The wine list focuses on organic wines from small producers.

Carte £ 15/31

Town plan: 14V2-s – *120 Morning Ln ✉ E9 6LH – ⊖ Hackney Central – ✆ 020 3441 8765 – www.legsrestaurant.com – dinner only and lunch Saturday-Sunday – Closed Sunday dinner, Monday and Tuesday*

Laughing Heart

MODERN CUISINE • WINE BAR A wine bar for our age and as joyful as the name suggests. It comes with a great vibe, lovely service and a flexible menu of cleverly paired seasonal ingredients with occasional Asian flavours. Natural wines are the focus of the wine list and the small wine shop downstairs.

Carte £ 20/38

Town plan: 14U3-s – *277 Hackney Rd ✉ E2 8NA – ⊖ Hoxton – ✆ 020 7686 9535 – www.thelaughingheartlondon.com – dinner only – Closed 12-26 August, 1-6 January and Sunday*

Hackney Wick

Cornerstone

SEAFOOD • NEIGHBOURHOOD Fish dishes – which change according to seasons and catches – are the highlight here, which is hardly surprising as the owner-chef was Nathan Outlaw's chef at The Capital. Save room for the Cornish burnt cream. The pared-back back room is dominated by a large open kitchen.

Carte £ 26/46

Town plan: 3F3-c – *3 Prince Edward Rd ✉ E9 5LX – ⊖ Hackney Wick (Rail) – ✆ 020 8986 3922 (booking essential) – www.cornerstonehackney.com – Closed 23 December-2 January, 23-30 July, Sunday and Monday*

Gotto Trattoria

ITALIAN • BRASSERIE The sister to Soho's Mele e Pere is a modern trattoria in a canal-side setting. The imported Italian ingredients are treated with respect and some of the recipes – such as for the every-present lasagne – are family secrets. Many of the cocktails use their homemade vermouth.

Carte £ 18/26

Town plan: 3F3-t – *27 East Bay Ln ✉ E15 2GW – ⊖ Hackney Wick (Rail) – ✆ 020 3424 5035 – www.gotto.co.uk*

Hoxton

The Frog Hoxton

MODERN CUISINE In 2018 Adam Handling moved his Frog from Spitalfields to bigger premises here in Hoxton Square. The three operations under one roof all have their own identity: a coffee shop and deli, a large bar and a casual restaurant specialising in well-priced, creative sharing plates.

Carte £ 17/31

Town plan: 20U4-x – *45-47 Hoxton Sq ✉ N1 9PD – ⊖ Old Street – ✆ 020 3813 9832 – www.thefroghoxton.com*

Petit Pois

MODERN BRITISH • NEIGHBOURHOOD Some restaurants just have a certain honesty about them. The small, even cramped, dining room is full of life and the service team take it in their stride. The flavoursome cooking is all about allowing the main ingredient to shine. The chocolate mousse is scooped at the table.

Menu £ 14 (weekday lunch) – Carte £ 28/36

Town plan: 20U4-a – *9 Hoxton Sq ✉ N1 6NU – ⊖ Old Street – ✆ 020 7613 3689 – www.petitpoisbistro.com – Closed 24-26 December*

Sardine

FRENCH • FASHIONABLE A trendy, compact restaurant with a communal table at the heart of proceedings. The food comes from Southern France, and dishes are rustic, unfussy and very tasty; try the lamb à la ficelle, cooked over an open fire.

Menu £ 16 (lunch and early dinner) – Carte £ 27/40

Town plan: 19T4-r – *Parasol Art Gallery, 15 Micawber St ✉ N1 7TB – ⊖ Old Street – ✆ 020 7490 0144 (booking essential) – www.sardine.london – Closed Christmas-New Year and Monday lunch*

M by Montcalm

BUSINESS • DESIGN Contemporary hotel with a designer style, set within a striking modern building. Appropriately for a hotel in Tech City, you can control the bedroom lighting, music, etc. from the bedside iPad. Relaxed ground floor restaurant with a mezzanine cocktail bar; modern British brasserie with city views.

269 rooms – †£ 255/330 ††£ 255/400

Town plan: 19T4-m – *151-157 City Rd ✉ EC1V 1JH – ⊖ Old Street – ✆ 020 3837 3000 – www.mbymontcalm.co.uk*

London Fields

Hill & Szrok

MEATS AND GRILLS • NEIGHBOURHOOD Butcher's shop by day; restaurant by night, with a central marble-topped table, counters around the edge and a friendly, lively feel. Daily blackboard menu of top quality meats, including steaks aged for a minimum of 60 days. No bookings.

Carte £ 17/34

Town plan: 14V3-z - *60 Broadway Market ✉ E8 4QJ - ⊖ Bethnal Green - ✆ 020 7254 8805 (bookings not accepted) - www.hillandszrok.co.uk - dinner only and Sunday lunch - Closed 23 December-2 January*

Pidgin

MODERN BRITISH • NEIGHBOURHOOD A cosy, single room restaurant with understated décor and a lively atmosphere, tucked away on a residential Hackney street. The no-choice four course menu of modern British dishes changes weekly, as does the interesting wine list.

Menu £ 49 - tasting menu only

Town plan: 14V2-d - *52 Wilton Way ✉ E8 1BG - ⊖ Hackney Central - ✆ 020 7254 8311 (booking essential) - www.pidginlondon.com - dinner only and lunch Friday -Sunday - Closed Christmas-New Year and Monday*

Shoreditch

Brat (Tomos Parry)

TRADITIONAL BRITISH • NEIGHBOURHOOD In this room on the first floor of a pub, it's all about cooking over fire - the stove, grill and oven were all hand-built to chef-owner Tomos Parry's own specification. Whole turbot, grilled in a handmade basket over lump wood charcoal, is a speciality but there are plenty of other dishes to enjoy, some inspired by his Welsh heritage.

→ Soused red mullet. Herdwick lamb. Burnt cheesecake with rhubarb.

Carte £ 23/40

Town plan: 20U4-r - *4 Redchurch St (1st Floor) ✉ E1 6JL - ⊖ Shoreditch High Street (booking essential) - www.bratrestaurant.com - Closed 24-26 December, Easter, Sunday dinner and Monday*

The Clove Club (Isaac McHale)

MODERN CUISINE • TRENDY The smart, blue-tiled open kitchen takes centre stage in this sparse room at Shoreditch Town Hall. Menus showcase expertly sourced produce in dishes that are full of originality, verve and flair - but where flavours are expertly judged and complementary; seafood is a highlight.

→ Hot-smoked wild Irish trout with almond milk sauce and Oscietra caviar. Aylesbury duck with red cabbage, blackcurrant purée and beetroot. Loquat sorbet, loquat kernel mousse, amaranth and popcorn.

Menu £ 75/110

Town plan: 20U4-c - *380 Old St ✉ EC1V 9LT - ⊖ Old Street - ✆ 020 7729 6496 (booking essential) - www.thecloveclub.com - Closed 2 weeks Christmas-New Year, August bank holiday, Monday lunch and Sunday*

Leroy (Sam Kamienko)

MODERN BRITISH • NEIGHBOURHOOD How can you not fall for a place where the first thing you see is a couple of shelves of vinyl? Putting all their experience to bear, the owners have created a restaurant with a relaxed, easy vibe and great food. The core ingredient shines through in every unshowy dish; there's little division between starters and main courses - just order a few dishes to share.

→ Peas, lardo, mint and slow-cooked egg yolk. Brill, beurre blanc, borage and sorrel. Sauternes crème caramel.

Menu £ 20 (weekday lunch) - Carte £ 29/48

Town plan: 20U4-d - *18 Phipp St ✉ EC2A 4NU - ⊖ Old Street - ✆ 020 7739 4443 - www.leroyshoreditch.com - Closed 24-30 December, Monday lunch and Sunday*

Lyle's (James Lowe)

MODERN BRITISH • SIMPLE The young chef-owner is an acolyte of Fergus Henderson and delivers similarly unadulterated flavours from seasonal British produce, albeit from a set menu at dinner. This pared-down approach extends to a room that's high on functionality, but considerable warmth comes from the keen young service team.

→ Peas with Ticklemore cheese. Dexter rib, broccoli leaf and anchovy. Caramel ice cream with espresso meringue.

Menu £ 59 (dinner) - Carte lunch £ 34/48

Town plan: 20U4-g - *Tea Building, 56 Shoreditch High St ✉ E1 6JJ - ⊖ Shoreditch High Street - ✆ 020 3011 5911 - www.lyleslondon.com - Closed Sunday and bank holidays*

Popolo

MEDITERRANEAN CUISINE • TRENDY Skimmed concrete floors and exposed brick walls give this restaurant a utilitarian feel; sit at the counter and chat to the chefs as they work. Italian, Spanish and North African influences feature on the menu of small plates. Pasta is a highlight and classic, simply cooked dishes allow the ingredients to shine.

Carte £ 19/39

Town plan: 19T4-c - *26 Rivington St ✉ EC2A 3DU - ⊖ Old Street - ✆ 020 7729 4299 (bookings not accepted) - www.popoloshoreditch.com - dinner only - Closed Sunday*

Merchants Tavern

TRADITIONAL BRITISH • BRASSERIE The 'pub' part - a Victorian warehouse - gives way to a large restaurant with the booths being the prized seats. The cooking is founded on the sublime pleasures of seasonal British cooking, in reassuringly familiar combinations.

Carte £ 30/60

Town plan: 20U4-t - *36 Charlotte Rd ✉ EC2A 3PG - ⊖ Old Street - ✆ 020 7060 5335 - www.merchantstavern.co.uk - Closed 12-26 August, 24-27 December and 1 January*

Andina

PERUVIAN • SIMPLE Andina may be smaller and slightly more chaotic that its sister Ceviche, but this friendly picantería with live music is equally popular. The Peruvian specialities include great salads and skewers, and ceviche that packs a punch.

Carte £ 15/31

Town plan: 20U4-w - *1 Redchurch St ✉ E2 7DJ - ⊖ Shoreditch High Street - ✆ 020 7920 6499 (booking essential) - www.andinarestaurants.com - Closed 24-26 December and 1 January*

Red Rooster N

AMERICAN • FASHIONABLE An outpost of Marcus Samuelsson's famed Harlem restaurant. His Southern soul food classics include "Sammy's chicken 'n' waffles" and "Ol' man shrimp 'n' grits"; the "Bird Royale Feast" is proving popular. There's live music at night and a gospel choir to accompany Sunday brunch.

Carte £ 31/45

Town plan: 20U4-e - *The Curtain Hotel, 45 Curtain Rd ✉ EC2A 3PT - ⊖ Old Street - ✆ 020 3146 4545 - www.redroosterldn.com - dinner only and Sunday lunch - Closed Sunday dinner*

The sun's out? Enjoy eating outside on the terrace.

Princess of Shoreditch

TRADITIONAL BRITISH • PUB There has been a pub on this corner site since 1742 but it is doubtful many of the previous incarnations were as busy or as pleasant as the Princess is today. The best dishes are those with a rustic edge, such as goose rillettes or chicken pie.

Carte £ 26/40

Town plan: 19T4-a - *76-78 Paul St ✉ EC2A 4NE - ⊖ Old Street - ✆ 020 7729 9270 (booking essential) - www.theprincessofshoreditch.com - Closed 24-26 December*

Ace Hotel

BUSINESS • MINIMALIST What better location for this achingly trendy hotel than hipster-central itself – Shoreditch. Locals are welcomed in, the lobby has a DJ, urban-chic rooms have day-beds if you want friends over and the minibars offer everything from Curly Wurlys to champagne. British favourites in the stylish brasserie.

258 rooms - †£ 169/429 ††£ 169/429 - ☕ £ 14 - 3 suites

Town plan: 20U4-p - *100 Shoreditch High St ✉ E1 6JQ - ⊖ Shoreditch High Street - ✆ 020 7613 9800 - www.acehotel.com*

Courthouse H. Shoreditch

HISTORIC BUILDING • CONTEMPORARY Former magistrates' court and police station; a quirky mix of original features and modern amenities including a cinema, bowling alley and roof terrace. Contemporary bedrooms boast high levels of facilities. The Kray twins were once incarcerated in what is now the bar – and tried in the panelled dining room.

128 rooms ☕ - †£ 200/600 ††£ 200/600 - 42 suites

Town plan: 20U4-v - *335-337 Old St ✉ EC1V 9LL - ⊖ Old Street - ✆ 020 3310 5555 - www.shoreditch.courthouse-hotel.com*

The Curtain

BUSINESS • TRENDY A trendy, fun hotel which used to be a warehouse used for raves. The stylish, comfortable bedrooms feature original art and steam showers. Enjoy a taco and tequila in Tienda Roosteria, soul food in Red Rooster or brasserie dishes in rooftop Lido. Live music in members club, LP.

120 rooms ☕ - †£ 250/400 ††£ 275/450 - 5 suites

Town plan: 20U4-e - *45 Curtain Rd ✉ EC2A 3PT - ⊖ Old Street - ✆ 020 3146 4545 - www.thecurtain.com*

Red Rooster – See restaurant listing

Nobu H. Shoreditch

BUSINESS • DESIGN The UK's first Nobu hotel is an impressive modern building with a super-stylish interior, hidden away in the streets of Shoreditch. Comfortable bedrooms have a subtle industrial feel and offer state-of-the-art TVs. The 35th branch of the renowned Nobu restaurant serves its modern Japanese cuisine in the basement.

150 rooms ☕ - †£ 217/355 ††£ 217/355 - 4 suites

Town plan: 19T4-h - *10-50 Willow St ✉ EC2A 4BH - ⊖ Old Street - ✆ 020 7683 1200 - www.nobuhotelshoreditch.com*

Boundary

LUXURY • DESIGN A converted warehouse boasting individually styled bedrooms, studios and duplex loft suites which are cool, stylish and bursting with personality. Basement Tratra for rustic French-inspired cooking; Rooftop has a relaxed Mediterranean flavour; Albion is an all-day café with something for everyone.

17 rooms - †£ 145/650 ††£ 145/650 - ☕ £ 20 - 5 suites

Town plan: 20U4 - *2-4 Boundary St ✉ E2 7DD - ⊖ Shoreditch High Street - ✆ 020 7729 1051 - www.boundary.london*

The Hoxton

BUSINESS • QUIRKY Industrial-style urban lodge with a rakish, relaxed air, youthful clientele and even younger staff. Bedrooms are compact but have some nice touches; choose a 'concept' room for something different. Open-plan restaurant with American menu and great cocktails.

210 rooms – †£ 99/299 ††£ 99/349

Town plan: 19T4-x – *81 Great Eastern St.* ✉ *EC2A 3HU* – ⊖ *Old Street*
– ✆ *020 7550 1000* – *www.thehoxton.com*

South Hackney

Empress

TRADITIONAL BRITISH • PUB An 1850s neighbourhood pub with a short, simple and pleasingly seasonal menu of traditional British dishes with the occasional Mediterranean influence. Service is friendly and you can bring your own bottle on Tuesday nights.

Carte £ 21/42

Town plan: 3F3-d – *130 Lauriston Rd, Victoria Park* ✉ *E9 7LH* – ⊖ *Homerton.*
– ✆ *020 8533 5123* – *www.empresse9.co.uk* – *Closed 25-27 December and Monday lunch except bank holidays*

Michelin

HAMMERSMITH and FULHAM

Fulham

✿ Harwood Arms

MODERN BRITISH • PUB Its reputation may have spread like wildfire but this remains a proper, down-to-earth pub that just happens to serve really good food. The cooking is very seasonal, proudly British, full of flavour and doesn't seem out of place in this environment. Service is suitably relaxed and friendly.

→ Wood pigeon and prune faggots with onion cream and thyme. Roast fallow deer with baked crapaudine beetroot, smoked bone marrow and walnut. Rhubarb and sherry trifle.

Menu £ 33 (weekday lunch)/50

Town plan: 22M7-a - *Walham Grove ✉ SW6 1QP - ⊖ Fulham Broadway. - ✆ 020 7386 1847 (booking essential) - www.harwoodarms.com - Closed 24-26 December, lunch 27 December and 1 January and Monday lunch except bank holidays*

RIGO' Ⓝ

CREATIVE • DESIGN XX The Italian chef-owner uses his international experience to create menus that are made up of quite delicate compositions. While there's plenty of pasta and Italian produce like Fassona beef, you are also just as likely to see, say, some Japanese influences. Service is quite formal.

Menu £ 46

Town plan: 22M8-r - *277 New King's Rd ✉ SW6 4RD - ⊖ Parsons Green - ✆ 020 7751 3293 - www.rigolondon.com - dinner only and lunch Friday-Saturday - Closed 23 December-3 January, 11-25 August and Sunday*

Claude's Kitchen

MODERN CUISINE • BISTRO X Two operations in one converted pub: 'Amuse Bouche' is a well-priced champagne bar; upstairs is an intimate dining room with a weekly changing menu. The cooking is colourful and fresh, with the odd challenging flavour combination.

Menu £ 23 - Carte £ 31/36

Town plan: 22M8-a - *51 Parsons Green Ln ✉ SW6 4JA - ⊖ Parsons Green. - ✆ 020 3813 3223 (booking essential) - www.amusebouchelondon.com - dinner only - Closed 24-26 December, Sunday and Monday*

Koji

JAPANESE • WINE BAR X A fun, contemporary wine bar serving Japanese food. The menu mixes the modern and the classic, with tempura and dishes from the robata grill particularly popular; food is full of flavour and the kitchen clearly know their craft.

Carte £ 45/78

Town plan: 22NZH-e - *58 New King's Rd ✉ SW6 4LS - ⊖ Parsons Green - ✆ 020 7731 2520 - www.koji.restaurant - Closed 25-26 December and Monday*

Manuka Kitchen

MODERN CUISINE • RUSTIC The two young owners run their simple little restaurant with great enthusiasm and their prices are keen. Like the magical Manuka honey, the chef is from New Zealand; his menu is varied and his food is wholesome and full of flavour.

Menu £ 15 (weekday lunch) – Carte £ 24/33

Town plan: 22M8-k – *510 Fulham Rd ✉ SW6 5NJ – ⊖ Fulham Broadway – ✆ 020 7736 7588 – www.manukakitchen.com – Closed 25-26 December, Sunday dinner and Monday lunch*

Tendido Cuatro

SPANISH • NEIGHBOURHOOD Along with tapas, the speciality is paella. Designed for a hungry two, they vary from seafood to quail and chorizo; vegetarian to cuttlefish ink. Vivid colours used with abandon deck out the busy room.

Carte £ 26/47

Town plan: 22M8-x – *108-110 New Kings Rd ✉ SW6 4LY – ⊖ Parsons Green – ✆ 020 7371 5147 – www.cambiodetercio.co.uk – Closed 2 weeks Christmas*

Tommy Tucker

TRADITIONAL BRITISH • PUB The old Pelican pub was revamped by the owners of nearby Claude's Kitchen. It's bright and open plan, with an unstructured menu divided under headings of 'meat', 'fish' and 'fruit and veg'. The cooking is rustic and satisfying.

Carte £ 21/42

Town plan: 22M8-s – *22 Waterford Rd ✉ SW6 2DR – ⊖ Fulham Broadway. – ✆ 020 7736 1023 – www.thetommytucker.com*

Hammersmith

River Café (Ruth Rogers)

ITALIAN • FASHIONABLE It's more than 30 years since this iconic restaurant opened, and superlative ingredients are still at the centre of everything they do. Dishes come in hearty portions and are bursting with authentic Italian flavours. The on-view kitchen with its wood-fired oven dominates the stylish and buzzing riverside room.

→ Asparagus with anchovy butter and parmesan. Anjou pigeon with Allegrini Valpolicella and green beans 'in umido'. Nespole and almond tart.

Carte £ 64/70

Town plan: 21K7-c – *Thames Wharf, Rainville Rd ✉ W6 9HA – ⊖ Barons Court – ✆ 020 7386 4200 (booking essential) – www.rivercafe.co.uk – Closed Christmas-New Year and Sunday dinner*

L'Amorosa

ITALIAN • NEIGHBOURHOOD Former Zafferano head chef Andy Needham has created a warm and sunny Italian restaurant – one that we'd all like to have in our high street. The quality of the produce shines through and homemade pasta dishes are a highlight.

Carte £ 25/39

Town plan: 21K7-s – *278 King St ✉ W6 0SP – ⊖ Ravenscourt Park – ✆ 020 8563 0300 – www.lamorosa.co.uk – Closed 1 week August, 1 week Christmas, Sunday dinner, Monday and bank holidays*

Indian Zing

INDIAN • NEIGHBOURHOOD Chef-owner Manoj Vasaikar seeks inspiration from across India. His cooking balances the traditional with the more contemporary and delivers many layers of flavour – the lamb dishes and breads are particularly good. The restaurant is always busy yet service remains courteous and unhurried.

Menu £ 19 (lunch) – Carte £ 23/44

Town plan: 21K7-a – *236 King St. ✉ W6 0RF – ⊖ Ravenscourt Park – ✆ 020 8748 5959 – www.indianzing.co.uk*

Azou

NORTH AFRICAN • NEIGHBOURHOOD Silks, lanterns and rugs add to the atmosphere of this personally run, North African restaurant. Most come for the very filling tajines, served with triple steamed couscous. Many of the dishes are designed for sharing.

Carte £ 20/37

Town plan: 21J7-u - *375 King St ✉ W6 9NJ - ⊖ Stamford Brook - ✆ 020 8563 7266 (booking essential) - www.azou.co.uk - dinner only - Closed 1 January and 25 December*

Brackenbury

MEDITERRANEAN CUISINE • NEIGHBOURHOOD A much loved neighbourhood restaurant given a new lease of life. The kitchen looks to Italy, France and the Med for inspiration and doesn't waste time on presentation; dishes feel instinctive and flavours marry well.

Menu £ 18 (weekday lunch)
- Carte £ 23/35

Town plan: 15K6-c - *129 - 131 Brackenbury Rd ✉ W6 0BQ - ⊖ Ravenscourt Park - ✆ 020 8741 4928 - www.brackenburyrestaurant.co.uk - Closed Christmas, New Year, Easter, August bank holiday, Sunday and Monday*

Anglesea Arms

MODERN BRITISH • NEIGHBOURHOOD One of the daddies of the gastropub movement. The seasonal menu gives the impression it's written by a Brit who occasionally holidays on the Med - along with robust dishes are some that display a pleasing lightness of touch.

Carte £ 24/36

Town plan: 15K6-e - *35 Wingate Rd ✉ W6 0UR - ⊖ Ravenscourt Park - ✆ 020 8749 1291 - www.angleseaarmspub.co.uk - Closed 24-26 December and lunch Monday-Thursday*

Shepherd's Bush

Shikumen

CHINESE • INTIMATE Impressive homemade dim sum at lunch and excellent Peking duck are the standouts at this unexpectedly sleek Cantonese restaurant in an otherwise undistinguished part of Shepherd's Bush.

Carte £ 22/63

Town plan: 15K6-s - *58 Shepherd's Bush Grn ✉ W12 8QE - ⊖ Shepherd's Bush - ✆ 020 8749 9978 - www.shikumen.co.uk - Closed 25 December*

HARINGEY

Crouch End

Bistro Aix

FRENCH • BISTRO Dressers, cabinets and contemporary artwork lend an authentic Gallic edge to this bustling bistro, a favourite with many of the locals. Traditionally prepared French classics are the highlights of an extensive menu.

Menu £ 25 (early dinner)
- Carte £ 23/49

Town plan: 3E2-v - *54 Topsfield Par, Tottenham Ln ✉ N8 8PT - ⊖ Crouch Hill - ✆ 020 8340 6346 - www.bistroaix.co.uk - dinner only and lunch Saturday-Sunday - Closed 24, 26 December and 1 January*

HEATHROW AIRPORT

Hilton London Heathrow Airport Terminal 5

BUSINESS • MODERN A feeling of light and space pervades this modern, corporate hotel. Soundproofed rooms are fitted to a good standard; the spa offers wide-ranging treatments. Open-plan Gallery for British comfort food.

350 rooms – †£ 99/149 ††£ 149/249 – 4 suites

Poyle Rd, Colnbrook ✉ SL3 OFF – West : 2.5 mi by A 3113 – ✆ 01753 686860 – www.hilton.com/heathrowt5

Sofitel

BUSINESS • CONTEMPORARY Smart and well-run contemporary hotel, designed around a series of atriums, with direct access to T5. Crisply decorated, comfortable bedrooms with luxurious bathrooms. Choice of restaurant: international or classic French cuisine.

605 rooms – †£ 165/329 ††£ 179/359 – 27 suites

Town plan: 5A4-a – *Terminal 5, Heathrow Airport ✉ TW6 2GD*
⊖ Heathrow Terminal 5 – ✆ 020 8757 5029 – www.sofitelheathrow.com

HOUNSLOW

Chiswick

Hedone (Mikael Jonsson)

MODERN CUISINE • DESIGN XX The content of lawyer-turned-chef Mikael Jonsson's surprise menus is governed entirely by which ingredients are in their prime – and it is this passion for produce that underpins the superlative and very flavoursome cooking. The open kitchen takes centre-stage and service is smooth and engaging.

→ Isle of Mull scallops with San Danielle consommé and Amontillado foam. Roast rack of lamb, Komatsuna leaves, seaweed and mustard jus. Warm chocolate mousse, passion fruit and mascarpone ice cream.

Menu £ 65/95 – surprise menu only

Town plan: 6C4-g – *301-303 Chiswick High Rd ✉ W4 4HH – ⊖ Chiswick Park – ✆ 020 8747 0377 (booking essential) – www.hedonerestaurant.com – dinner only – Closed 2 weeks Christmas-New Year*

La Trompette

MODERN BRITISH • NEIGHBOURHOOD XX A warm, relaxed neighbourhood restaurant with a loyal, local following – a perfect fit for Chiswick. While the influences are varied, its heart is French with occasional nods to the Med. The dishes themselves are free of unnecessary adornment, so the focus remains on the top quality ingredients.

→ Home-cured Mangalitsa with ricotta, celeriac and pear. Cod with pumpkin gnocchetti, chanterelles and hazelnut pesto. Muscovado custard tart with Earl Grey ice cream and dates.

Menu £ 35 (weekday lunch)/55

Town plan: 21J7-y – *3-7 Devonshire Rd ✉ W4 2EU – ⊖ Turnham Green – ✆ 020 8747 1836 (booking essential) – www.latrompette.co.uk – Closed 24-26 December and 1 January*

Charlotte's Bistro

MODERN CUISINE • NEIGHBOURHOOD XX A friendly, brightly decorated and unpretentious bistro, with a well-priced menu of flavoursome, well-prepared and quite rustic dishes of largely European provenance. Sister to Charlotte's W5 in Ealing.

Menu £ 25/35

Town plan: 21J7-a – *6 Turnham Green Terr ✉ W4 1QP – ⊖ Turnham Green – ✆ 020 8742 3590 – www.charlottes.co.uk*

Michael Nadra

MODERN CUISINE • NEIGHBOURHOOD XX Half way down a residential side street is this intimate little place where the closely set tables add to the bonhomie. Dishes are modern, colourful and quite elaborate in their make-up; it's worth going for the sensibly priced set menu and the chosen wines.

Menu £ 28/39

Town plan: 21J7-z - *6-8 Elliott Rd ✉ W4 1PE - ⊖ Turnham Green - ✆ 020 8742 0766 - www.restaurant-michaelnadra.co.uk - Closed 24-28 December, 1 January and Monday*

High Road House

TOWNHOUSE • MINIMALIST A cool, sleek hotel and club; the latter a slick place to lounge around or play games. Light, bright bedrooms come with crisp linen and good facilities. This is a carefully appointed and fairly-priced destination.

14 rooms - †£ 200/295 ††£ 200/295 - ☕ £ 22

Town plan: 21J7-e - *162-166 Chiswick High Rd ✉ W4 1PR - ⊖ Turnham Green - ✆ 020 8742 1717 - www.highroadhouse.co.uk*

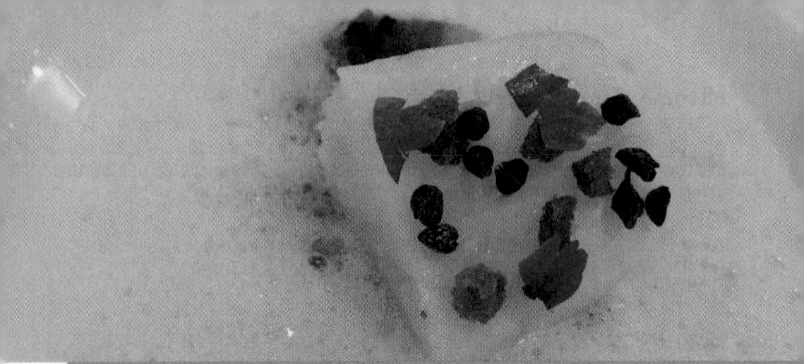

Michelin

ISLINGTON

Archway

🍴 St John's Tavern

MODERN CUISINE • PUB A Junction Road landmark with friendly service and a great selection of artisan beers. Tapas is served in the front bar; head to the vast, hugely appealing rear dining room for well-crafted British and Mediterranean dishes.

Carte £ 23/36

Town plan: 12Q1-s – *91 Junction Rd ✉ N19 5QU – ⊖ Archway. – ✆ 020 7272 1587 – www.stjohnstavern.com – Closed 25-26 December and Monday lunch*

Canonbury

Primeur

MODERN CUISINE • SIMPLE A relaxed neighbourhood restaurant whose concertina doors fold back to reveal a quirky interior with counter seating around the edges and a huge communal table. Plates are small and designed for sharing; understated but packed with flavour – simplicity is key, allowing the ingredients to really shine.

Carte £ 21/38

Town plan: 13T2-p – *116 Petherton Rd ✉ N5 2RT – ⊖ Canonbury – ✆ 020 7226 5271 – www.primeurn5.co.uk – Closed Christmas, Sunday dinner, Monday and lunch Tuesday-Thursday*

Trullo

ITALIAN • NEIGHBOURHOOD A neighbourhood gem split over two floors; its open kitchen serving an ingredient-led daily menu. Harmonious, tried-and-tested combinations create rustic, full-flavoured Italian dishes, including meats and fish cooked on the charcoal grill and delicious fresh pasta, hand-rolled before each service.

Carte £ 25/48

Town plan: 13S2-t – *300-302 St Paul's Rd ✉ N1 2LH – ⊖ Highbury & Islington – ✆ 020 7226 2733 (booking essential) – www.trullorestaurant.com – Closed 24 December-1 January and Sunday dinner*

🍴 Smokehouse

MODERN CUISINE • PUB You can smell the oak chips in the smoker as you approach this warm, modern pub. Meat is the mainstay – the peppered ox cheeks are a firm favourite – but whilst flavours are gutsy, the smoking and barbecuing is never overpowering.

Carte £ 29/35

Town plan: 13T3-h – *63-69 Canonbury Rd ✉ N1 2DG – ⊖ Highbury & Islington. – ✆ 020 7354 1144 – www.smokehouseislington.co.uk – Closed 24-26 December and lunch Monday-Thursday except bank holidays*

Clerkenwell

St John

TRADITIONAL BRITISH • SIMPLE A glorious celebration of British fare and a champion of 'nose to tail' eating. Utilitarian surroundings and a refreshing lack of ceremony ensure the food is the focus; it's appealingly simple, full of flavour and very satisfying.

→ Roast bone marrow with parsley salad. Grilled ox heart with beetroot, red cabbage and pickled walnut. Ginger loaf with butterscotch sauce.

Carte £ 26/63

Town plan: 33AU1-k - *26 St John St ✉ EC1M 4AY - ⊖ Farringdon - ✆ 020 7251 0848 (booking essential) - www.stjohnrestaurant.com - Closed 25-26 December, 1 January, Saturday lunch and Sunday dinner*

Comptoir Gascon

FRENCH • BISTRO A buzzy, well-priced restaurant; sister to Club Gascon. Rustic and satisfying specialities from the SW of France include wine, bread, cheese and plenty of duck, with cassoulet and duck rillettes perennial favourites and the duck burger popular at lunch. There's also produce on display to take home.

Carte £ 18/34

Town plan: 32AT1-a - *61-63 Charterhouse St. ✉ EC1M 6HJ - ⊖ Farringdon - ✆ 020 7608 0851 (booking essential) - www.comptoirgascon.com - Closed Christmas-New Year, Saturday lunch, Sunday, Monday and bank holidays*

Luca

ITALIAN • DESIGN Owned by the people behind The Clove Club, but less a little sister, more a distant cousin. There's a cheery atmosphere, a bar for small plates and a frequently changing menu of Italian dishes made with quality British ingredients.

Menu £ 19 (lunch and early dinner) - Carte £ 35/79

Town plan: 33AU1-c - *88 St. John St ✉ EC1M 4EH - ⊖ Farringdon - ✆ 020 3859 3000 (booking essential) - www.luca.restaurant - Closed Sunday*

Foxlow

MEATS AND GRILLS • NEIGHBOURHOOD From the clever Hawksmoor people comes this fun and funky place where the staff ensure everyone's having a good time. There are steaks available but plenty of other choices too, with influences from Italy, Asia and the Middle East.

Menu £ 18 (weekdays) - Carte £ 22/39

Town plan: 33AU1-b - *69-73 St John St ✉ EC1M 4AN - ⊖ Farringdon - ✆ 020 7680 2702 - www.foxlow.co.uk - Closed 24 December-1 January and bank holidays*

Palatino

ITALIAN • DESIGN Stevie Parle's airy, canteen-like, all-day restaurant has an open kitchen, yellow booths and an industrial feel. The seasonal Italian menu has a strong emphasis on Rome, with dishes like rigatoni with veal pajata.

Menu £ 16 (lunch and early dinner) - Carte £ 16/38

Town plan: 19T4-p - *71 Central St ✉ EC1V 8AB - ⊖ Old Street - ✆ 020 3481 5300 - www.palatino.london - Closed 23 December-3 January, Sunday and bank holidays*

Malmaison

TOWNHOUSE • MODERN Striking early 20C red-brick building overlooking a pleasant square. Stylish, comfy public areas. Bedrooms in vivid, bold colours, with plenty of extra touches. Modern brasserie with international menu; grilled meats a highlight.

97 rooms - †£ 129/309 ††£ 129/309 - ☕ £ 15

Town plan: 33AU1-q - *18-21 Charterhouse Sq ✉ EC1M 6AH - ⊖ Barbican - ✆ 020 7012 3700 - www.malmaison.com*

The Rookery

TOWNHOUSE • PERSONALISED A row of charmingly restored 18C houses which remain true to their roots courtesy of wood panelling, flagstone flooring, open fires and antique furnishings. Highly individual bedrooms have feature beds and Victorian bathrooms.

33 rooms – †£ 199 ††£ 230/499 – ☕£ 12 – 3 suites

Town plan: 33AU1-p – *12 Peters Ln, Cowcross St ✉ EC1M 6DS – ⊖ Farringdon – ✆ 020 7336 0931 – www.rookeryhotel.com*

Finsbury

Angler

SEAFOOD • ELEGANT XX As the name suggests, fish is the mainstay of the menu – mostly from Scotland and Cornwall. The kitchen has a light yet assured touch and understands that when fish is this good it doesn't need too much adornment. The ornate mirrored ceiling adds to the brightness of the room.

→ Roast octopus with taramasalata, potatoes and red wine bagna càuda. Cod with garlic, morels and squid. Rhubarb, Brillat-Savarin cream and stem ginger ice cream.

Menu £ 34 (weekday lunch) – Carte £ 50/72

Town plan: 33AW1-v – *South Place Hotel, 3 South Pl ✉ EC2M 2AF – ⊖ Moorgate – ✆ 020 3215 1260 – www.anglerrestaurant.com – Closed 26-30 December, Saturday lunch and Sunday*

Morito

SPANISH • TAPAS BAR X From the owners of next door Moro comes this authentic and appealingly down to earth little tapas bar. Seven or eight dishes between two should suffice but over-ordering is easy and won't break the bank.

Carte £ 14/29

Town plan: 19S4-b – *32 Exmouth Mkt ✉ EC1R 4QE – ⊖ Farringdon – ✆ 020 7278 7007 – www.morito.co.uk – Closed 24 December-2 January*

The Drunken Butler (N)

FRENCH • REGIONAL DÉCOR XX The chef-owner's quiet enthusiasm pervades every aspect of this small but bright restaurant. The cooking is classical French at heart but also informed by his travels and Persian heritage; dishes provide plenty of colour, texture and flavour.

Menu £ 24/49

Town plan: 19S4-k – *20 Rosebery Ave ✉ EC1R 4SX – ⊖ Farringdon – ✆ 020 7101 4020 (booking essential) – www.thedrunkenbutler.com – Closed 1 week August, Saturday lunch, Sunday and Monday*

Nuala (N)

MODERN BRITISH • RUSTIC XX The infectiously enthusiastic Northern Irish chef-owner trained as a butcher and much of the produce comes from the family farm. The main ingredients are cooked over an open flame with a mix of oak, apple, birch, ash and beech. The open kitchen allows the aromas to whet the appetite.

Menu £ 20 (lunch) – Carte £ 20/44

Town plan: 19T4-s – *70-74 City Rd ✉ EC1Y 2BJ – ⊖ Old Street – ✆ 020 3904 0462 – www.nualalondon.com – Closed Christmas-New Year, Sunday and Monday*

Quality Chop House

TRADITIONAL BRITISH • COSY X In the hands of owners who respect its history, this 'progressive working class caterer' does a fine job of championing gutsy British grub; game is best but steaks from the butcher next door are also worth ordering. The terrific little wine list has lots of gems. The Grade II listed room, with its trademark booths, has been an eating house since 1869.

Menu £ 25 (weekday lunch) – Carte £ 23/51

Town plan: 19S4-h – *92-94 Farringdon Rd ✉ EC1R 3EA – ⊖ Farringdon – ✆ 020 7278 1452 (booking essential) – www.thequalitychophouse.com – Closed 24-31 December, Sunday dinner and bank holidays*

Moro

MEDITERRANEAN CUISINE • FRIENDLY It's the stuff of dreams – pack up your worldly goods, drive through Spain, Portugal, Morocco and the Sahara, and then back in London, open a restaurant and share your love of Moorish cuisine. The wood-fired oven and chargrill fill the air with wonderful aromas and food is vibrant and colourful.

Carte £ 33/45

Town plan: 19S4-m – *34-36 Exmouth Mkt ✉ EC1R 4QE – ⊖ Farringdon – ✆ 020 7833 8336 (booking essential) – www.moro.co.uk – Closed 24 December-2 January*

South Place

BUSINESS • DESIGN Restaurant group D&D's first venture into the hotel business is a stylish affair; unsurprising as its interior was designed by Conran & Partners. Bedrooms are a treat for those with an eye for aesthetics and no detail has been forgotten. The ground floor hosts 3 South Place, a bustling bar and grill.

80 rooms – †£ 240/460 ††£ 240/460 – ☕ £ 15 – 1 suite

Town plan: 33AW1-v – *3 South Pl ✉ EC2M 2AF – ⊖ Moorgate – ✆ 020 3503 0000 – www.southplacehotel.com*

✿ **Angler** – See restaurant listing

Montcalm Royal London House

BUSINESS • MODERN A modern business hotel overlooking Finsbury Square, stylish bedrooms come with their own aromatherapy machines and smart phones. Burdock bar features craft beers and some unique shuffleboard tables. 10th floor Aviary serves classic grill dishes and has a superb panorama of the city skyline from its terrace.

253 rooms – †£ 160/367 ††£ 190/390 – ☕ £ 25 – 16 suites

Town plan: 33AW1-h – *22-25 Finsbury Sq ✉ EC2A 1DX – ⊖ Moorgate – ✆ 020 3873 4000 – www.montcalmroyallondoncity.co.uk*

Zetter

TOWNHOUSE • MODERN A trendy and discreet converted 19C warehouse with well-equipped bedrooms that come with pleasant touches, such as Penguin paperbacks. The more idiosyncratic Zetter Townhouse across the square is used as an overflow.

59 rooms – †£ 174/474 ††£ 174/474 – ☕ £ 16

Town plan: 19S4-s – *St John's Sq, 86-88 Clerkenwell Rd. ✉ EC1M 5RJ – ⊖ Farringdon – ✆ 020 7324 4444 – www.thezetter.com*

Highbury

Farang Ⓝ

THAI • FRIENDLY Seb and Dan had a series of pop-ups for their Thai street food before moving into this permanent home. Dishes have an authentic heart and use a mix of Thai and British produce. The small menu is supplemented by a number of specials, while the 'Feasting' menus are great for larger groups.

Carte £ 20/40

Town plan: 13T1-b – *72 Highbury Pk ✉ N5 2XE – ⊖ Arsenal – ✆ 020 7226 1609 – www.faranglondon.co.uk – dinner only and Saturday lunch – Closed Sunday and Monday*

Holloway

Westerns Laundry

MODERN BRITISH • FASHIONABLE Sister to Primeur and with the same industrial feel; set on the ground floor of a former laundry, with a pleasant front terrace. Sit at the kitchen counter or at one of the communal tables. The fish-focused menu is accompanied by natural wines and the confidently executed dishes are full of flavour.

Carte £ 26/35

Town plan: 13S2-w – *34 Drayton Pk ✉ N5 1PB – ⊖ Holloway Road – ✆ 020 7700 3700 (booking essential) – www.westernslaundry.com – Closed Monday, lunch Tuesday-Thursday and Sunday dinner*

Islington

Bellanger

FRENCH • BRASSERIE XX All-day brasserie, with the sumptuous style of an authentic grand café, modelled on those opened in Paris by the Alsatians at the turn of the century. Regional French and Alsatian-inspired fare is served from breakfast until late.

Menu £ 16 (lunch) - Carte £ 22/40

Town plan: 13S3-d - *9 Islington Grn ✉ N1 2XH - ⊖ Angel - ✆ 020 7226 2555 - www.bellanger.co.uk*

Plaquemine Lock

CREOLE • COSY A unique and very colourful pub named after a small city in Louisiana and with a menu centred around Creole and Cajun traditions. Dishes like gumbo with okra, blackened chicken, and crawfish with corn and potatoes are carefully cooked and packed with flavour. Big Easy style cocktails add to the fun.

Carte £ 21/35

Town plan: 13S3-e - *139 Graham St ✉ N1 8LB - ⊖ Angel - ✆ 020 7688 1488 - www.plaqlock.com - Closed 25 December*

Galley

SEAFOOD • BRASSERIE X A smart, colourful seafood restaurant with a brasserie feel; there's a bar at the front and a few prized booths, but the best seats in the house are at the kitchen counter. The hot or cold seafood platters are great to share.

Carte £ 27/42

Town plan: 13S3-a - *105-106 Upper St ✉ N1 1QN - ⊖ Highbury & Islington - ✆ 020 7684 2538 - www.galleylondon.co.uk - Closed 1 January*

Oldroyd

MODERN BRITISH • INTIMATE X The eponymous Oldroyd is Tom, who left his role with the Polpo group to open this busy little bistro. It's all about small plates - ingredients are largely British, influences are from within Europe and dishes are very easy to eat.

Menu £ 19 (weekday lunch) - Carte £ 16/35

Town plan: 13S3-w - *344 Upper St ✉ N1 0PD - ⊖ Angel - ✆ 020 8617 9010 - www.oldroydlondon.com - Closed 25-26 December and 1 January*

Radici

ITALIAN • RUSTIC X Its name means roots and cooking is based around hearty Southern Italian classics inspired by chef Francesco Mazzei's childhood. The room has a rustic look, a wood-fired oven for pizzas and a wine lounge packed with Italian bottles.

Menu £ 18 - Carte £ 28/36

Town plan: 13S3-r - *30 Almeida St ✉ N1 1AD - ⊖ Angel - ✆ 020 7354 4777 - www.radici.uk*

Drapers Arms

TRADITIONAL BRITISH • NEIGHBOURHOOD An imposing neighbourhood pub with warming fires, shabby-chic styling, a relaxed, unpretentious feel, a bevy of eager-to-please staff and a courtyard garden. They offer gutsy and satisfying seasonal British dishes, a great selection of regional ales and a well-thought-out wine list.

Carte £ 24/37

Town plan: 13S3-x - *44 Barnsbury St ✉ N1 1ER - ⊖ Highbury & Islington. - ✆ 020 7619 0348 - www.thedrapersarms.com - Closed 25-26 December*

Pig and Butcher

TRADITIONAL BRITISH • PUB Dating from the mid-19C, when cattle drovers taking livestock to Smithfield Market would stop for a swift one, and now fully restored. There's a strong British element to the daily menu; meat is butchered and smoked in-house.

Carte £ 28/50

Town plan: 13S3-e - *80 Liverpool Rd ✉ N1 0QD - ⊖ Angel - ✆ 020 7226 8304 - www.thepigandbutcher.co.uk - dinner only and lunch Friday-Sunday - Closed 24-26 December*

KENSINGTON and CHELSEA (ROYAL BOROUGH OF)

Chelsea

Gordon Ramsay

FRENCH • ELEGANT XxxX He may be one of the most famous chefs on the planet but Gordon Ramsay remains fiercely committed to maintaining the highest standards in his flagship restaurant. The charming Jean-Claude, who has run the restaurant since day one, oversees a team who get the service just right: yes, it's polished and professional, but it also has personality. This is the reason why every diner feels at ease and calmness rules.

Matt Abé, an Aussie who's spent over a decade working with Gordon Ramsay, is the chef. In 2018 he oversaw a kitchen redesign that resulted in a more ergonomic space and gave further proof that this restaurant never rests on its laurels. His large team create dishes that are classical in make-up but never backward-looking. The component parts marry perfectly, whether that's Isle of Skye scallops paired with apples, walnuts and cider, or Cornish turbot with celeriac and black truffle. The dishes are executed with great confidence yet also with an extraordinary lightness of touch.

→ Ravioli of lobster, langoustine and salmon with oxalis and sorrel. Herdwick lamb with spring vegetable 'navarin'. Lemonade parfait with honey, bergamot and sheep's milk yoghurt.

Menu £ 70/120

Town plan: 37AJ8-c - *68-69 Royal Hospital Rd. ✉ SW3 4HP - ⊖ Sloane Square - ✆ 020 7352 4441 (booking essential) - www.gordonramsayrestaurants.com/restaurant-gordon-ramsay/ - Closed 21-28 December, Sunday and Monday*

Claude Bosi at Bibendum

FRENCH • ELEGANT XxX Bibendum - on the first floor of the historic art deco building which was built as Michelin's London HQ in 1911 - now sports a clean, contemporary look, and its handsome interior cannot fail to impress. The iconic stained glass windows allow light to flood in - a fact best appreciated at lunch when the Michelin Man can be seen in all his glory; in fact, his presence is everywhere, from the butter dish to the salt and pepper pots. Service is smooth, well-paced and discreet; it's also not without humour.

Claude Bosi's cooking shows a man proud of his French heritage and confident of his abilities. His dishes are poised and well-balanced with bold, assured flavours. Choose the à la carte menu for classics like Brittany rabbit with langoustine and artichoke barigoule or turbot à la Grenobloise - and don't miss the soufflé for dessert, particularly if it's chocolate.

→ Duck jelly, Oscietra caviar, spring onion and smoked sturgeon. My mum's tripe and cuttlefish gratin with pig's ear and ham cake. Cep vacherin, banana and crème fraîche.

Menu £ 110 (dinner)/130– Carte lunch £ 53/109

Town plan: 37AH7-s - *Michelin House, 81 Fulham Rd ✉ SW3 6RD ⊖ South Kensington - ✆ 020 7581 5817 (booking essential) - www.bibendum.co.uk - Closed 24-26 December, 31 December-7 January, 26 August-5 September, Monday, lunch Tuesday-Wednesday and bank holidays*

Five Fields (Taylor Bonnyman)

MODERN CUISINE • NEIGHBOURHOOD XXX A formally run yet intimate restaurant, with a discreet atmosphere and a warm, comfortable feel. Modern dishes are skilfully conceived, quite elaborate constructions; attractively presented and packed with flavour. Produce is top-notch and often comes from the restaurant's own kitchen garden in East Sussex.

→ Foie gras with shimeji mushrooms and beetroot. Roe deer, morels, celeriac and sorrel. Apple with green shiso and jasmine.

Menu £ 65/90

Town plan: 37AJ7-s – *8-9 Blacklands Terr ✉ SW3 2SP – ⊖ Sloane Square – ✆ 020 7838 1082 (booking essential) – www.fivefieldsrestaurant.com – dinner only – Closed Christmas-mid-January, 2 weeks August, Saturday, Sunday and bank holidays*

Elystan Street (Philip Howard)

MODERN BRITISH • ELEGANT XX This elegant, understated restaurant is a joint venture between chef Philip Howard and experienced restaurateur Rebecca Mascarenhas. Cooking has a classical base yet displays a healthy lightness of touch; there's also a vigour and energy to it which suggests that it comes from the heart.

→ Ravioli of Orkney scallops and Cornish crab with spring onions, radish and chives. Fillet of cod with parmesan gnocchi, garlic leaf pesto and morels. Lemon tart with yoghurt ice cream.

Menu £ 43 (lunch) – Carte dinner £ 57/88

Town plan: 37AH7-e – *43 Elystan St ✉ SW3 3NT – ⊖ South Kensington – ✆ 020 7628 5005 (booking essential) – www.elystanstreet.com – Closed 25-26 December and 1 January*

Colbert

FRENCH • BRASSERIE XX With its posters, chessboard tiles and red leather seats, Colbert bears more than a passing resemblance to a Parisian pavement café. It's an all-day, every day operation with French classics from croque monsieur to steak Diane.

Carte £ 23/63

Town plan: 38AK7-t – *50-52 Sloane Sq ✉ SW1W 8AX – ⊖ Sloane Square – ✆ 020 7730 2804 – www.colbertchelsea.com – Closed 25 December*

Bluebird

MODERN BRITISH • DESIGN XX It boasts an épicerie, a café, a terrace and even a clothes shop, but the highlight is the first floor restaurant with its marble-topped horseshoe bar, bold print banquettes and abundance of foliage. A Mediterranean menu and super cocktails.

Menu £ 30 – Carte £ 32/70

Town plan: 36AF8-n – *350 King's Rd. ✉ SW3 5UU – ⊖ South Kensington – ✆ 020 7559 1000 – www.bluebird-restaurant.co.uk*

il trillo

ITALIAN • FRIENDLY XX The Bertuccelli family have been making wine and running a restaurant in the Tuscan Hills for over 30 years. Two of the brothers now run this smart local which showcases the produce and wine from their region. Delightful courtyard.

Menu £ 33 – Carte £ 35/58

Town plan: 36AE8-s – *4 Hollywood Rd ✉ SW10 9HY – ⊖ Earl's Court – ✆ 020 3602 1759 – www.iltrillo.net – dinner only and lunch Saturday-Sunday – Closed Monday*

The symbol guarantees a peaceful night's sleep.

Medlar

MODERN CUISINE • NEIGHBOURHOOD XX A charming, comfortable and very popular restaurant with a real neighbourhood feel, from two alumni of Chez Bruce. The service is engaging and unobtrusive; the kitchen uses good ingredients in dishes that deliver distinct flavours in classic combinations.

Menu £ 35/53

Town plan: 23N7-x – *438 King's Rd ✉ SW10 0LJ – ⊖ South Kensington – ✆ 020 7349 1900 – www.medlarrestaurant.co.uk – Closed 24-26 December, 1 January and Monday*

Outlaw's at The Capital

SEAFOOD • INTIMATE XX An elegant yet informal restaurant in a personally run hotel. The seasonal menus are all about sustainable seafood, with fish shipped up from Cornwall on a daily basis. The modern cooking is delicately flavoured, with the spotlight on the freshness of the produce.

Menu £ 33/69

Town plan: 37AJ5-a – *The Capital Hotel, 22-24 Basil St. ✉ SW3 1AT – ⊖ Knightsbridge – ✆ 020 7591 1202 (booking essential) – www.capitalhotel.co.uk – Closed 25-26 December, 1 January and Sunday*

Bandol

PROVENÇAL • DESIGN X Stylishly dressed restaurant with a 100 year old olive tree evoking memories of sunny days spent on the French Riviera. Sharing plates take centre stage on the Provençal and Niçoise inspired menu; seafood is a highlight.

Menu £ 15 (weekday lunch) – Carte £ 30/59

Town plan: 36AE8-b – *6 Hollywood Rd ✉ SW10 9HY – ⊖ Earl's Court – ✆ 020 7351 1322 – www.barbandol.co.uk*

Bo Lang

CHINESE • TRENDY X Come with friends for the cocktails and the dim sum at this diminutive and intimate spot, whose decorative style owes something to Hakkasan. The kitchen uses good quality ingredients and has a deft touch; the more traditional combinations often prove to be the best.

Menu £ 15 (lunch) – Carte £ 27/47

Town plan: 37AH7-a – *100 Draycott Ave ✉ SW3 3AD – ⊖ South Kensington – ✆ 020 7823 7887 – www.bolangrestaurant.co.uk*

Rabbit

MODERN BRITISH • RUSTIC X The Gladwin brothers have followed the success of The Shed with another similarly rustic and warmly run restaurant. Share satisfying, robustly flavoured plates; game is a real highlight, particularly the rabbit dishes.

Menu £ 15 (weekday lunch)/42 – Carte £ 26/40

Town plan: 37AH7-r – *172 King's Rd ✉ SW3 4UP – ⊖ Sloane Square – ✆ 020 3750 0172 (pre-book at weekends) – www.rabbit-restaurant.com – Closed 22 December-2 January*

Jumeirah Carlton Tower

BUSINESS • MODERN Imposing international hotel overlooking a leafy square and just yards from all the swanky boutiques. Well-equipped rooftop health club has great views. Generously proportioned bedrooms boast every conceivable facility.

216 rooms – †£ 333/479 ††£ 333/479 – ☕ £ 32 – 57 suites

Town plan: 37AJ6-r – *Cadogan Pl ✉ SW1X 9PY – ⊖ Knightsbridge – ✆ 020 7235 1234 – www.jumeirah.com*

The Capital

LUXURY • CLASSIC A fine, thoroughly British hotel, known for its discreet atmosphere and its conscientious and attentive service. Comfortable, immaculately kept bedrooms are understated in style. Enjoy afternoon tea in the intimate Sitting Room.

49 rooms – †£ 199/380 ††£ 349/420 – ☕ £ 20 – 1 suite

Town plan: 37AJ5-a – *22-24 Basil St.* ✉ *SW3 1AT* – ⊖ *Knightsbridge* – ✆ *020 7589 5171* – *www.capitalhotel.co.uk*

Outlaw's at The Capital – See restaurant listing

Draycott

TOWNHOUSE • PERSONALISED Charming 19C house with elegant sitting room overlooking tranquil garden for afternoon tea. Bedrooms are individually decorated in a country house style and are named after writers or actors.

35 rooms – †£ 150/200 ††£ 230/450 – ☕ £ 25 – 11 suites

Town plan: 37AJ7-c – *26 Cadogan Gdns* ✉ *SW3 2RP* – ⊖ *Sloane Square* – ✆ *020 7730 6466* – *www.draycotthotel.com*

Egerton House

TOWNHOUSE • CLASSIC Compact but comfortable townhouse in a very good location, well-maintained throughout and owned by the Red Carnation group. High levels of personal service make the hotel stand out.

28 rooms – †£ 315/630 ††£ 315/630 – ☕ £ 29

Town plan: 37AH6-e – *17-19 Egerton Terr* ✉ *SW3 2BX* – ⊖ *South Kensington* – ✆ *020 7589 2412* – *www.egertonhousehotel.com*

Franklin (N)

TOWNHOUSE • ELEGANT A discreet, elegant and charmingly run boutique hotel within a lovingly restored, red-brick Victorian townhouse. The quietest rooms are those that overlook the lovely communal garden at the back. Modern Italian menu.

35 rooms – †£ 176/347 ††£ 347/464 – ☕ £ 18 – 1 suite

Town plan: 37AH6-h – *24 Egerton Gdns* ✉ *SW3 2DB* – ⊖ *South Kensington* – ✆ *020 7584 5533* – *www.starhotelscollezione.com*

Knightsbridge

LUXURY • PERSONALISED Charming and attractively furnished townhouse in a Victorian terrace, with a very stylish, discreet feel. Every bedroom is immaculately appointed and has a style all of its own; fine detailing throughout.

44 rooms – †£ 295/418 ††£ 325/928 – ☕ £ 19

Town plan: 37AH6-s – *10 Beaufort Gdns* ✉ *SW3 1PT* – ⊖ *Knightsbridge* – ✆ *020 7584 6300* – *www.knightsbridgehotel.com*

The Levin

TOWNHOUSE • CLASSIC Little sister to The Capital next door. Impressive façade, contemporary interior and comfortable bedrooms in a subtle art deco style, with marvellous champagne mini bars. Simple dishes served all day down in the basement restaurant.

12 rooms – †£ 275/400 ††£ 300/450 – ☕ £ 13

Town plan: 37AJ5-c – *28 Basil St.* ✉ *SW3 1AS* – ⊖ *Knightsbridge* – ✆ *020 7589 6286* – *www.thelevinhotel.co.uk*

No.11 Cadogan Gardens

TOWNHOUSE • PERSONALISED Townhouse hotel fashioned out of four red-brick houses and exuberantly dressed in bold colours and furnishings. Theatrically decorated bedrooms vary in size from cosy to spacious. Intimate basement Italian restaurant with accomplished and ambitious cooking.

56 rooms – †£ 250/352 ††£ 250/395 – ☕ £ 24 – 7 suites

Town plan: 37AJ7-n – *11 Cadogan Gdns* ✉ *SW3 2RJ* – ⊖ *Sloane Square* – ✆ *020 7730 7000* – *www.11cadogangardens.com*

Earl's Court

K + K George

BUSINESS • MODERN In contrast to its period façade, this hotel's interior is stylish, colourful and contemporary. The hotel is on a quiet street, yet close to the Tube and has a large rear garden where you can enjoy breakfast in summer. Comfortable bar/lounge and a spacious restaurant serving a wide-ranging menu.

154 rooms – £ 190/280 £ 200/300

Town plan: 35AC7-s – *1-15 Templeton Pl ✉ SW5 9NB – Earl's Court – ✆ 020 7598 8700 – www.kkhotels.com*

Twenty Nevern Square

TOWNHOUSE • PERSONALISED Privately owned townhouse overlooking an attractive Victorian garden square. It's decorated with original pieces of hand-carved Indonesian furniture; breakfast in a bright conservatory. Some bedrooms have their own terrace.

22 rooms – £ 70 £ 70/215

Town plan: 35AC7-u – *20 Nevern Sq ✉ SW5 9PD – Earl's Court – ✆ 020 7565 9555 – www.mayflowercollection.com*

Kensington

Kitchen W8

MODERN CUISINE • NEIGHBOURHOOD XX A joint venture between Rebecca Mascarenhas and Philip Howard. Not as informal as the name suggests but still refreshingly free of pomp. The cooking has depth and personality and prices are quite restrained considering the quality of the produce and the kitchen's skill.

→ Smoked eel with grilled mackerel, golden beetroot and sweet mustard. Caramelised lamb shoulder with Pink Fir potatoes, pickles, Calçot onions and thyme. Poached Comice pear with spiced financier and honey ice cream.

Menu £ 28/30 (early weekday dinner) – Carte £ 41/54

Town plan: 35AC5-a – *11-13 Abingdon Rd ✉ W8 6AH – High Street Kensington – ✆ 020 7937 0120 – www.kitchenw8.com – Closed 24-26 December and bank holidays*

Launceston Place

MODERN CUISINE • NEIGHBOURHOOD XXX A favourite of many thanks to its palpable sense of neighbourhood, pretty façade and its nooks and crannies which make it ideal for trysts or tête-à-têtes. The menu is fashionably terse and the cooking is quite elaborate, with dishes big on originality and artfully presented.

Menu £ 28/60

Town plan: 36AE5-a – *1a Launceston Pl ✉ W8 5RL – Gloucester Road – ✆ 020 7937 6912 – www.launcestonplace-restaurant.co.uk – Closed 25-26 December, Monday and lunch Tuesday*

Clarke's

MODERN CUISINE • NEIGHBOURHOOD XX Its unhurried atmosphere, enthusiastic service and dedication to its regulars are just a few reasons why Sally Clarke's eponymous restaurant has instilled such unwavering loyalty for over 30 years. Her kitchen has a light touch and understands the less-is-more principle.

Menu £ 33/39 – Carte £ 42/64

Town plan: 27AC4-c – *124 Kensington Church St ✉ W8 4BH – Notting Hill Gate – ✆ 020 7221 9225 – www.sallyclarke.com – Closed 1 week August, Christmas-New Year and bank holidays*

Malabar

INDIAN • NEIGHBOURHOOD XX Still going strong in this smart residential Notting Hill street, having opened back in 1983. Refreshingly, the menu is a single page - order a curry and something charcoal-grilled. The buffet lunch on Sunday is a veritable institution in these parts.

Carte £ 18/38

Town plan: 27AC3-e - *27 Uxbridge St. ✉ W8 7TQ - ⊖ Notting Hill Gate - ✆ 020 7727 8800 - www.malabar-restaurant.co.uk - dinner only and lunch Saturday-Sunday - Closed 1 week Christmas*

Zaika

INDIAN • CONTEMPORARY DÉCOR XX The cooking focuses on the North of India and the influences of Mughal and Nawabi, so expect rich and fragrantly spiced dishes. The softly-lit room makes good use of its former life as a bank, with its wood-panelling and ornate ceiling.

Menu £ 23 (lunch) - Carte £ 28/65

Town plan: 36AD5-r - *1 Kensington High St. ✉ W8 5NP - ⊖ High Street Kensington - ✆ 020 7795 6533 - www.zaikaofkensington.com - Closed 25-26 December, 1 January and Monday lunch*

Mazi

GREEK • FRIENDLY X It's all about sharing at this simple, bright Greek restaurant where traditional recipes are given a modern twist to create vibrant, colourful and fresh tasting dishes. The garden terrace at the back is a charming spot in summer.

Menu £ 15 (weekday lunch) - Carte £ 28/43

Town plan: 27AC3-a - *12-14 Hillgate St ✉ W8 7SR - ⊖ Notting Hill Gate - ✆ 020 7229 3794 - www.mazi.co.uk - Closed 24-25 December, 1-2 January and Monday lunch*

The Shed

MODERN BRITISH • RUSTIC X It's more than just a shed but does have a higgledy-piggledy charm and a healthy dose of the outdoors. One brother cooks, one manages and the third runs the farm which supplies the produce for the earthy, satisfying dishes.

Carte £ 26/38

Town plan: 27AC3-s - *122 Palace Gardens Ter. ✉ W8 4RT - ⊖ Notting Hill Gate - ✆ 020 7229 4024 - www.theshed-restaurant.com - Closed Monday lunch and Sunday*

Royal Garden

BUSINESS • MODERN A tall, modern hotel with many of its rooms enjoying enviable views over the adjacent Kensington Gardens. All the modern amenities and services, with well-drilled staff. Bright, spacious Park Terrace offers an international menu as well as afternoon tea for which you're accompanied by a pianist.

394 rooms - †£ 195/514 ††£ 195/514 - ☕ £ 25 - 17 suites

Town plan: 36AD5-c - *2-24 Kensington High St ✉ W8 4PT ⊖ High Street Kensington - ✆ 020 7937 8000 - www.royalgardenhotel.co.uk*

The Milestone

LUXURY • PERSONALISED Elegant and enthusiastically run hotel with decorative Victorian façade and a very British feel. Charming oak-panelled sitting room is popular for afternoon tea; snug bar in former stables. Meticulously decorated bedrooms offer period detail. Ambitious cooking in discreet Cheneston's restaurant.

62 rooms ☕ - †£ 375/715 ††£ 415/755 - 6 suites

Town plan: 36AE5-u - *1-2 Kensington Ct ✉ W8 5DL - ⊖ High Street Kensington - ✆ 020 7917 1000 - www.milestonehotel.com*

Baglioni

LUXURY • PERSONALISED It's opposite Kensington Palace and there's no escaping the fact that this is an Italian-owned hotel. The interior is bold and ornate and comes with a certain swagger. Stylish bedrooms have a masculine feel and boast impressive facilities. Italian classics are served in the ground floor restaurant.

67 rooms – †£ 315/523 ††£ 315/523 – 15 suites

Town plan: 36AE5-e – *60 Hyde Park Gate ✉ SW7 5BB – ⊖ High Street Kensington – ✆ 020 7368 5718 – www.baglionihotels.com*

North Kensington

CORE by Clare Smyth Ⓝ (Clare Smyth)

MODERN BRITISH • CONTEMPORARY DÉCOR XXX Clare Smyth – for many years Gordon Ramsay's head chef in his flagship restaurant – has realised her ambition to open her own place. It comes with an understated elegance and includes a comfortable cocktail bar and a chef's table separated from the kitchen by a glass wall. Proof of her graduation from chef to consummate restaurateur is there to see in the service, which is highly professional but also warm and engaging.

All her staff are encouraged to develop relationships with the growers of the produce they prepare, and this passion for ingredients is evident in dishes that allow their natural flavours, subtly enhanced by carefully judged accompaniments, to shine. A dish like Charlotte potato with dulse beurre blanc, a nod to her Northern Ireland upbringing, illustrates how a seemingly simple ingredient can be elevated to something extraordinary and shows the real depth that her cooking delivers.

→ Isle of Mull scallop tartare, sea vegetables and consommé. Scottish venison, smoked bacon, pearl barley and whisky. 'Core apple'.

Menu £ 65/105

Town plan: 27AB2-e – *92 Kensington Park Rd ✉ W11 2PN – ⊖ Notting Hill Gate – ✆ 020 3937 5086 (booking essential) – www.corebyclaresmyth.com – Closed 24-26 December, 1 January, Sunday, Monday and lunch Tuesday-Wednesday*

Ledbury (Brett Graham)

MODERN CUISINE • NEIGHBOURHOOD XXX Look around the smart but unshowy Ledbury and you may catch sight of a chef or two having dinner – that's because Aussie Brett Graham is considered a "chef's chef" and it's easy to see why. His cooking is informed by the seasonal ingredients available and his deep-rooted knowledge of husbandry and the close relationships he has formed with his suppliers are revealed throughout his menu.

Game and in particular the Sika deer – raised on their own small estate in Oxfordshire – are always highlights. Other signature dishes, such as beetroot baked in clay with English caviar, and brown sugar tart demonstrate how adept the kitchen is at harnessing the true flavours of ingredients, often with complementing layers. Like a gifted sportsman, it can sometimes look effortlessly easy but it takes great skill to make something with some depth look so simple. The service is personable and free from affectation; the wine list is strong across all regions; and the atmosphere hospitable and grown up.

→ White beetroot baked in clay with English caviar and dried eel. Sika deer with smoked bone marrow, rhubarb, red leaves and vegetables. Brown sugar tart with stem ginger ice cream.

Menu £ 80/150

Town plan: 27AB2-c – *127 Ledbury Rd. ✉ W11 2AQ – ⊖ Notting Hill Gate – ✆ 020 7792 9090 – www.theledbury.com – Closed 25-26 December, August bank holiday and lunch Monday-Tuesday*

Flat Three

CREATIVE • DESIGN XX The open kitchen is the main feature of this roomy, basement restaurant. The flavours of Korea and Japan feature heavily in the elaborately constructed, original and creative dishes which deliver plenty of flavour. Service can be rather formal.

Menu £ 35/59

Town plan: 27AA4-k - *120-122 Holland Park Ave ✉ W11 4UA - ⊖ Holland Park - ✆ 020 7792 8987 - www.flatthree.london - dinner only and lunch Friday-Saturday - Closed 24 December-7 January, 20 August-3 September, Sunday and Monday*

108 Garage

MODERN BRITISH • NEIGHBOURHOOD X A daily changing 6 course menu is offered, with a choice of main course; the modern dishes offer plenty of contrasts and originality. This former garage has a utilitarian look that's all bare brick, exposed ducting and polished concrete. Sit at the counter if you want to chat with the chefs.

Menu £ 60 (dinner) - Carte £ 43/57

Town plan: 16L4-e - *108 Golborne Rd ✉ W10 5PS - ⊖ Westbourne Park - ✆ 020 8969 3769 (booking essential) - www.108garage.com - Closed 2 weeks August, 2 weeks Christmas, Sunday and Monday*

Granger and Co. Notting Hill

MODERN CUISINE • FRIENDLY X When Bill Granger moved from sunny Sydney to cool Notting Hill he opened a local restaurant too. He brought with him that delightful 'matey' service that only Aussies do, his breakfast time ricotta hotcakes and a fresh, zesty menu.

Carte £ 20/42

Town plan: 27AC2-x - *175 Westbourne Grove ✉ W11 2SB - ⊖ Bayswater - ✆ 020 7229 9111 (bookings not accepted) - www.grangerandco.com - Closed August bank holiday weekend and 25 December*

Six Portland Road

FRENCH • NEIGHBOURHOOD X An intimate and personally run neighbourhood restaurant owned by Oli Barker, previously of Terroirs. The menu changes frequently and has a strong French accent; dishes are reassuringly recognisable, skilfully constructed and very tasty.

Menu £ 17 (weekday lunch) - Carte £ 32/55

Town plan: 27AA4-n - *6 Portland Rd ✉ W11 4LA - ⊖ Holland Park - ✆ 020 7229 3130 - www.sixportlandroad.com - Closed Christmas-New Year, last 2 weeks August, Sunday dinner and Monday*

Zayane

MOROCCAN • NEIGHBOURHOOD X An intimate neighbourhood restaurant owned by Casablanca-born Meryem Mortell and evoking the sights and scents of North Africa. Carefully conceived dishes have authentic Moroccan flavours but are cooked with modern techniques.

Carte £ 25/42

Town plan: 16L4-z - *91 Golborne Rd ✉ W10 5NL - ⊖ Westbourne Park - ✆ 020 8960 1137 - www.zayanerestaurant.com - Closed 10 days January, 26 August-3 September, Sunday and Monday*

The Portobello

TOWNHOUSE • CLASSIC An attractive Victorian townhouse in a Kensington terrace. Its small, comfortable lounge has an honesty bar. Bedrooms are individually furnished in an English style with antique furniture; some have four-poster beds. Ask for a 'Signature' room overlooking a private garden at the back.

21 rooms - †£ 175/195 ††£ 195/455

Town plan: 27AB2-n - *22 Stanley Gdns. ✉ W11 2NG - ⊖ Notting Hill Gate - ✆ 020 7727 2777 - www.portobellohotel.com*

South Kensington

Bombay Brasserie

INDIAN • EXOTIC DÉCOR XXXX A well-run, well-established and comfortable Indian restaurant, featuring a very smart bar and conservatory. Creative dishes sit alongside more traditional choices on the various menus and vegetarians are well-catered for.

Menu £ 27 (weekday lunch) – Carte £ 32/53

Town plan: 36AE6-y – *Courtfield Rd. ✉ SW7 4QH – ⊖ Gloucester Road – ✆ 020 7370 4040 – www.bombayb.co.uk – Closed 25 December*

Cambio de Tercio

SPANISH • COSY XX A long-standing, ever-improving Spanish restaurant. Start with small dishes like the excellent El Bulli inspired omelette, then have the popular Pluma Iberica. There are super sherries and a wine list to prove there is life beyond Rioja.

Menu £ 24 (weekday lunch) – Carte £ 33/55 **s**

Town plan: 36AE7-a – *163 Old Brompton Rd. ✉ SW5 0LJ – ⊖ Gloucester Road – ✆ 020 7244 8970 – www.cambiodetercio.co.uk – Closed 2 weeks December and 2 weeks August*

Ognisko

POLISH • ELEGANT XX Ognisko Polskie – The Polish Hearth Club – was founded in 1940 in this magnificent townhouse; its elegant restaurant serves traditional dishes from across Eastern Europe and the cooking is without pretence and truly from the heart.

Menu £ 22 (lunch and early dinner) – Carte £ 27/37

Town plan: 37AG5-r – *55 Prince's Gate, Exhibition Rd ✉ SW7 2PN – ⊖ South Kensington – ✆ 020 7589 0101 – www.ogniskorestaurant.co.uk – Closed 24-26 December and 1 January*

Yashin Ocean House

JAPANESE • CHIC XX The USP of this chic Japanese restaurant is 'head to tail' eating, although, as there's nothing for carnivores, 'fin to scale' would be more precise. Stick with specialities like the whole dry-aged sea bream for the full umami hit.

Carte £ 20/55

Town plan: 36AF7-y – *117-119 Old Brompton Rd ✉ SW7 3RN – ⊖ Gloucester Road – ✆ 020 7373 3990 – www.yashinocean.com – Closed Christmas*

Capote y Toros

SPANISH • TAPAS BAR X Expect to queue at this compact and vividly coloured spot which celebrates sherry, tapas, ham... and bullfighting. Sherry is the star; those as yet unmoved by this most underappreciated of wines will be dazzled by the variety.

Carte £ 23/61

Town plan: 36AE7-v – *157 Old Brompton Road ✉ SW5 0LJ – ⊖ Gloucester Road – ✆ 020 7373 0567 – www.cambiodetercio.co.uk – dinner only – Closed 2 weeks Christmas, Sunday and Monday*

Go-Viet

VIETNAMESE • CONTEMPORARY DÉCOR X A Vietnamese restaurant from experienced chef Jeff Tan. Lunch concentrates on classics like pho and bun, while dinner provides a more sophisticated experience, offering interesting flavourful dishes with a distinct modern edge.

Carte £ 22/51

Town plan: 36AF7-v – *53 Old Brompton Rd ✉ SW7 3JS – ⊖ South Kensington – ✆ 020 7589 6432 – www.vietnamfood.co.uk – Closed 24-26 December*

Margaux

MEDITERRANEAN CUISINE • NEIGHBOURHOOD An earnestly run modern bistro with an ersatz industrial look.The classically trained kitchen looks to France and Italy for its primary influences and dishes are flavoursome and satisfying. The accompanying wine list has been thoughtfully compiled.

Menu £ 15 (weekday lunch) – Carte £ 28/58

Town plan: 36AE7-m – *152 Old Brompton Rd ✉ SW5 0BE – ⊖ Gloucester Road – ✆ 020 7373 5753 – www.barmargaux.co.uk – Closed 24-26 December, 1 January and lunch August*

Blakes

LUXURY • DESIGN Behind the Victorian façade is one of London's first 'boutique' hotels. Dramatic, bold and eclectic décor, with oriental influences and antiques from around the world. International dishes in the spacious ground floor restaurant.

45 rooms – †£ 225/325 ††£ 275/470 – 7 suites

Town plan: 36AF7-n – *33 Rowland Gdns ✉ SW7 3PF – ⊖ Gloucester Road – ✆ 020 7370 6701 – www.blakeshotels.com*

The Pelham

LUXURY • ELEGANT Great location if you're in town for museum visiting. It's a mix of English country house and city townhouse, with a panelled sitting room and library with honesty bar. Sweet and intimate basement restaurant with Mediterranean menu.

52 rooms – †£ 240/370 ††£ 240/370 – £ 15 – 2 suites

Town plan: 37AG6-z – *15 Cromwell Pl ✉ SW7 2LA – ⊖ South Kensington – ✆ 020 7589 8288 – www.pelhamhotel.co.uk*

Number Sixteen

TOWNHOUSE • ELEGANT Elegant 19C townhouses in a smart neighbourhood; well-run by charming, helpful staff. Tastefully furnished lounges feature attractive modern art. First floor bedrooms benefit from large windows and balconies; basement rooms are the quietest and two have their own terrace. Airy Orangery restaurant for afternoon tea and light meals overlooking the pretty garden.

41 rooms – †£ 180/240 ††£ 312/342 – £ 20

Town plan: 36AF7-d – *16 Sumner Pl. ✉ SW7 3EG – ⊖ South Kensington – ✆ 020 7589 5232 – www.firmdalehotels.com*

The Exhibitionist

TOWNHOUSE • DESIGN A funky, design-led boutique hotel fashioned out of several 18C townhouses. The modern artwork changes every few months and the bedrooms are individually furnished – several have their own roof terrace.

37 rooms – †£ 199/599 ††£ 199/899 – £ 20 – 3 suites

Town plan: 36AF6-b – *8-10 Queensberry Pl ✉ SW7 2EA ⊖ South Kensington – ✆ 020 7915 0000 – www.theexhibitionisthotel.com*

The Gore

TOWNHOUSE • PERSONALISED Idiosyncratic, hip Victorian house close to the Royal Albert Hall, whose charming lobby is covered with pictures and prints. Individually styled bedrooms have plenty of character and fun bathrooms. Bright and casual bistro.

50 rooms – †£ 190/250 ††£ 190/250 – £ 25

Town plan: 36AF5-n – *190 Queen's Gate ✉ SW7 5EX ⊖ Gloucester Road – ✆ 020 7584 6601 – www.gorehotel.com*

Be sure to read the section 'How to use this guide'.
It explains our symbols, classifications and abbreviations
and will help you make a more informed choice.

KING'S CROSS ST PANCRAS

Gilbert Scott

TRADITIONAL BRITISH • BRASSERIE XX Named after the architect of this Gothic masterpiece and run under the aegis of Marcus Wareing, this restaurant has the splendour of a Grand Salon but the buzz of a brasserie. The appealing menu showcases the best of British produce, whilst incorporating influences from further afield.

Menu £ 30 (lunch and early dinner) – Carte £ 28/61

Town plan: 18R4-d – *St Pancras Renaissance Hotel, Euston Rd ✉ NW1 2AR – ⊖ King's Cross St Pancras – ✆ 020 7278 3888 – www.thegilbertscott.co.uk*

St Pancras Renaissance

BUSINESS • ELEGANT This restored Gothic jewel was built in 1873 as the Midland Grand hotel and reopened in 2011 under the Marriott brand. A former taxi rank is now a spacious lobby and all-day dining is in the old booking office. Luxury suites in Chambers wing; Barlow wing bedrooms are a little more functional.

245 rooms – †£ 258/400 ††£ 290/500 – ☕ £ 18 – 10 suites

Town plan: 18R4-d – *Euston Rd ✉ NW1 2AR – ⊖ King's Cross St Pancras – ✆ 020 7841 3540 – www.stpancraslondon.com*

Gilbert Scott – See restaurant listing

Great Northern H. London

HISTORIC BUILDING • CONTEMPORARY Built as a railway hotel in 1854 and reborn as a stylish townhouse; it's connected to King's Cross' western concourse and just metres from the Eurostar check-in. Bespoke furniture features in each of the modern bedrooms. Classic British dishes in the intimate first floor bistro; start with a drink in the GNH bar.

91 rooms – †£ 279/299 ††£ 279/379 – ☕ £ 25 – 1 suite

Town plan: 12R3-n – *Pancras Rd ✉ N1C 4TB – ⊖ King's Cross St Pancras – ✆ 020 3388 0808 – www.gnhlondon.com*

KINGSTON UPON THAMES

Surbiton

The French Table

MEDITERRANEAN CUISINE • NEIGHBOURHOOD XX Husband and wife run this lively local: he cooks and she runs the show, assisted by her team of friendly staff. Expect zesty and satisfying French-Mediterranean cooking, as well as great bread, as they also run the bakery next door.

Menu £ 22/45

Town plan: 6C5-a – *85 Maple Rd ✉ KT6 4AW – ✆ 020 8399 2365 – www.thefrenchtable.co.uk – Closed 2 weeks August-September, Christmas-New Year, Sunday excluding December and Monday*

LAMBETH

Brixton

Nanban

JAPANESE • SIMPLE X A ramen-bar-cum-izakaya, tucked away at the back of Brixton Market and owned by former MasterChef winner, Tim Anderson. Food is fresh and full of flavour; the spicy, super-crispy chicken karaage will have you coming back for more.

Carte £ 21/35

Town plan: 25S9-n – *426 Coldharbour Ln ✉ SW9 8LF – ⊖ Brixton – ✆ 020 7346 0098 – www.nanban.co.uk – Closed 25 December and Monday lunch*

Clapham Common

Trinity

MODERN CUISINE • FASHIONABLE XX A bright, warmly run neighbourhood restaurant enthusiastically supported by the locals. Adam Byatt's cooking focuses on prime ingredients and classic flavour combinations. Don't miss crispy pig's trotter with sauce Gribiche and it's worth pre-ordering the tarte Tatin with prune and Armagnac ice cream for two.

→ Beef tartare with pickled mushrooms, smoked bone marrow and caviar. Brill cooked in sea urchin butter with asparagus and sauce Maltaise. Salt caramel custard tart with salt caramel ice cream.

Menu £ 40/68

Town plan: 24Q9-a – *4 The Polygon ✉ SW4 0JG – ⊖ Clapham Common – ✆ 020 7622 1199 – www.trinityrestaurant.co.uk – Closed 24-30 December and 1-2 January*

Bistro Union

MODERN BRITISH • NEIGHBOURHOOD X The little sister to Trinity restaurant is fun and affordable, with a welcoming feel and sweet staff. The menu is appealingly flexible, whether you're here for brunch or a full dinner; eschew starters in favour of their great 'snacks'.

Carte £ 23/49

Town plan: 7E4-s – *40 Abbeville Rd ✉ SW4 9NG – ⊖ Clapham South – ✆ 020 7042 6400 – www.bistrounion.co.uk – Closed 24-27 December*

Sorella (N)

ITALIAN • BISTRO X Cooking inspired by Italy's Amalfi region inspired this 'sister' to The Dairy. Expect a great buzz, fair prices and enthusiastic service. 4-5 sharing plates per couple should do it; be sure to include some pasta. Dishes may look simple but the kitchen infuses them with bags of flavour.

Carte £ 25/45

Town plan: 24Q9-b – *148 Clapham Manor St ✉ SW4 6BX – ⊖ Clapham Common – ✆ 020 7720 4662 (booking essential at dinner) – www.sorellarestaurant.co.uk – Closed 1 week Christmas, Sunday dinner, Monday and lunch Tuesday*

Upstairs (at Trinity)

MODERN BRITISH • FASHIONABLE X The open-plan kitchen is the focus of this more relaxed room upstairs from Trinity. It's all about sharing the visually appealing, flavoursome and reasonably priced plates, which bring a hint of the Mediterranean with them.

Carte £ 19/43

Town plan: 24Q9-a – *4 The Polygon ✉ SW4 0JG – ⊖ Clapham Common – ✆ 020 3745 7227 – www.trinityrestaurant.co.uk – dinner only – Closed 24-30 December, 1 January, Sunday and Monday*

Dairy

CREATIVE BRITISH • RUSTIC X The rustic, easy-to-eat food, which comes as small sharing plates, is driven by seasonality – some of the produce comes from their own farm. The higgledy-piggledy, homemade look of this fun, lively neighbourhood restaurant adds to its charm.

Menu £ 28 (weekday lunch)
– Carte £ 25/37

Town plan: 24Q9-d – *15 The Pavement ✉ SW4 0HY – ⊖ Clapham Common – ✆ 020 7622 4165 (booking essential at dinner) – www.the-dairy.co.uk – Closed 24-27 December, Sunday dinner and Monday*

Herne Hill

Llewelyn's

TRADITIONAL BRITISH • NEIGHBOURHOOD A neighbourhood restaurant in a village-like location. Cooking is British with Mediterranean influences and dishes to share are a feature. Expect quality ingredients in hearty portions, with no unnecessary elaboration.

Carte £ 24/33

Town plan: 7E4-n – *293-295 Railton Rd ✉ SE24 0JP – ⊖ Herne Hill – ✆ 020 7733 6676 – www.llewelyns-restaurant.co.uk – Closed 22 December-4 January, Sunday dinner and Monday*

Kennington

Kennington Tandoori

INDIAN • NEIGHBOURHOOD Kowsar Hoque runs this contemporary Indian restaurant with great pride and his eagerness and professionalism filters through to his staff. The food is prepared with equal care – try the seasonal specialities and the excellent breads.

Carte £ 20/34

Town plan: 40AS8-a – *313 Kennington Rd ✉ SE11 4QE – ⊖ Kennington – ✆ 020 7735 9247 – www.kenningtontandoori.com – dinner only and lunch Saturday-Sunday – Closed 25-26 December*

Southbank

Skylon

MODERN CUISINE • DESIGN Ask for a window table here at the Royal Festival Hall. Informal grill-style operation on one side, a more formal and expensive restaurant on the other, with a busy cocktail bar in the middle.

Menu £ 30 (weekdays) – Carte £ 38/52

Town plan: 32AR4-a – *1 Southbank Centre, Belvedere Rd ✉ SE1 8XX – ⊖ Waterloo – ✆ 020 7654 7800 – www.skylon-restaurant.co.uk – Closed 25 December*

London Marriott H. County Hall

BUSINESS • MODERN Occupying the historic County Hall building on the banks of the River Thames. Bedrooms are spacious, stylish and modern; many enjoy river and Parliament outlooks. Impressive leisure facilities. World famous views too from wood-panelled Gillray's, which specialises in steaks.

206 rooms – †£ 280/340 ††£ 290/350 – 5 suites

Town plan: 40AR5-a – *Westminster Bridge Rd ✉ SE1 7PB – ⊖ Westminster – ✆ 020 7928 5200 – www.marriottcountyhall.com*

Stockwell

Canton Arms

TRADITIONAL BRITISH • PUB An appreciative crowd of all ages come for the earthy, robust and seasonal British dishes which suit the relaxed environment of this pub so well. Staff are attentive and knowledgeable.

Carte £ 22/38

Town plan: 24R8-a – *177 South Lambeth Rd ✉ SW8 1XP – ⊖ Stockwell. – ✆ 020 7582 8710 (bookings not accepted) – www.cantonarms.com – Closed Monday lunch, Sunday dinner and bank holidays*

Don't expect guesthouses to provide the same level of service as a hotel. They are often characterised by a warm welcome and décor which reflects the owner's personality. Those shown in red are particularly charming.

LEWISHAM

Forest Hill

Babur

INDIAN • NEIGHBOURHOOD XX Good looks and innovative cooking make this passionately run and long-established Indian restaurant stand out. Influences from the south and north west feature most and seafood is a highlight - look out for the 'Treasures of the Sea' menu.

Menu £ 33/39 – Carte £ 27/36

Town plan: 7F4-s – *119 Brockley Rise ✉ SE23 1JP – ⊖ Honor Oak Park – ✆ 020 8291 2400 – www.babur.info – Closed 26 December*

Lewisham

Sparrow

MODERN BRITISH • FRIENDLY X A bright and buzzing neighbourhood spot whose name symbolises the culinary diversity of its globally influenced menus, as well as one of the owners' Sri Lankan heritage. Weekend brunches also offer an eclectic choice of dishes.

Carte £ 27/35

Town plan: 7F4-w – *2 Rennell St ✉ SE13 7HD – ⊖ Lewisham – ✆ 020 8318 6941 – www.sparrowlondon.co.uk – Closed Sunday dinner, Monday and lunch Tuesday*

MERTON

Wimbledon

Light House

MEDITERRANEAN CUISINE • NEIGHBOURHOOD X A neighbourhood favourite offering Mediterranean cooking in smart, comfortable surroundings. The food is wholesome and confident, with plenty of bold flavours; Italian dishes and puddings are the highlights and staff are calm and cheery.

Menu £ 23 (weekday dinner) – Carte £ 25/44

Town plan: 6D5-u – *75-77 Ridgway ✉ SW19 4ST – ⊖ Wimbledon – ✆ 020 8944 6338 – www.lighthousewimbledon.com – Closed 25-26 December, 1 January and Sunday dinner*

Takahashi

JAPANESE • FRIENDLY X The eponymous chef-owner of this sweet spot is a Nobu alumnus and his wife runs the service with a personal touch. Mediterranean ingredients bring a creative edge to the pure, delicately flavoured dishes. Sushi and sashimi are a highlight.

Menu £ 30/78

Town plan: 6D5-s – *228 Merton Rd ✉ SW19 1EQ – ⊖ South Wimbledon – ✆ 020 8540 3041 (booking essential) – www.takahashi-restaurant.co.uk – dinner only and lunch Saturday-Sunday – Closed Monday and Tuesday*

White Onion

MODERN CUISINE • BISTRO X A relaxed bistro deluxe with a handsome marble-topped bar and an attentive young team. Flavoursome classic French cooking has clever modern touches. Great value set lunch and a terrific selection of wine by the glass and carafe.

Menu £ 24 (lunch) – Carte dinner £ 32/46

Town plan: 6D5-w – *67 High St ✉ SW19 5EE – ⊖ Wimbledon – ✆ 020 8947 8278 – www.thewhiteonion.co.uk – Closed 5-14 August, 25 December-9 January, Monday, lunch Tuesday-Thursday and Sunday dinner*

Hotel du Vin

BUSINESS • CONTEMPORARY A charming part-Georgian house surrounded by over 30 acres of parkland. Dine in the light and airy Orangery or in the restaurant overlooking an Italian sunken garden; French-influenced menus offer something for everyone. Bedrooms are comfortable and well-equipped; ask for one with views of the park.

48 rooms - £139/525 £139/525 - 2 suites

Town plan: 6C5-x - *Cannizaro House, West Side, Wimbledon Common SW19 4UE - 0330 024 0706 - www.hotelduvin.com*

REDBRIDGE

South Woodford

Grand Trunk Road

INDIAN • CONTEMPORARY DÉCOR XX Named after one of Asia's oldest and longest routes, which provided inspiration for the menu. Dishes are well-balanced and original with a modern touch; breads come from a charcoal-fired tandoor and vegetable dishes are a highlight.

Menu £20 (weekday lunch) - Carte £30/57

Town plan: 4G2-w - *219 High Rd E18 2PB - South Woodford - 020 8505 1965 (booking essential at dinner) - www.gtrrestaurant.co.uk - Closed 25-26 December, 1 January and Monday*

Wanstead

Provender

FRENCH • BISTRO X A welcoming and busy neighbourhood bistro, courtesy of experienced restaurateur Max Renzland. The fairly priced French cooking is pleasingly rustic and satisfying; the classic dishes are the ones to go for. Look out for the good value menus during the week.

Menu £17 (lunch and early dinner) - Carte £20/45

Town plan: 4G2-x - *17 High St E11 2AA - Snaresbrook - 020 8530 3050 - www.provenderlondon.co.uk*

Five Fields

RICHMOND-UPON-THAMES

Barnes

Rick Stein

SEAFOOD • FASHIONABLE XX In a stunning spot beside the Thames; its glass extension offering the best views. Dishes from the celebrity chef's travels inform the menu, so expect Indonesian seafood curry alongside old favourites like cod and chips with mushy peas.

Menu £ 20 (weekday lunch) - Carte £ 28/91

Town plan: 21J8-r - *Tideway Yard, 125 Mortlake High St ✉ SW14 8SN - ✆ 020 8878 9462 - www.rickstein.com - Closed 25 December*

Sonny's Kitchen

MEDITERRANEAN CUISINE • NEIGHBOURHOOD X A longstanding and much-loved neighbourhood spot with a bright, relaxed feel and some striking art on the walls; co-owned by Barnes residents Rebecca Mascarenhas and Phil Howard. Menus are all-encompassing and portions generous.

Menu £ 23 (lunch and early dinner) - Carte £ 27/55

Town plan: 21K8-x - *94 Church Rd ✉ SW13 0DQ - ✆ 020 8748 0393 - www.sonnyskitchen.co.uk - Closed 25-26 December, 1 January and bank holiday Mondays*

Brown Dog

MODERN BRITISH • PUB Concealed in a maze of residential streets is this homely, relaxed pub with a lived-in feel. The balanced menu offers traditional and flavoursome fare like venison pie or haddock fishcake; all done 'properly'.

Carte £ 25/32

Town plan: 21J8-9-b - *28 Cross St ✉ SW13 0AP - ⊖ Barnes Bridge (Rail). - ✆ 020 8392 2200 - www.thebrowndog.co.uk - Closed 25 December*

East Sheen

Victoria

MODERN BRITISH • PUB A proper local, with a lived-in feel, especially in the bars; if you're here to eat head for the conservatory, which overlooks a terrace. The appealing menu offers a good range of dishes and comes with a distinct Mediterranean slant, with Middle Eastern influences never far away.

Menu £ 14 (weekday lunch) - Carte £ 25/41

7 rooms - £ 100/145 £ 100/145

Town plan: 6C4-h - *10 West Temple ✉ SW14 7RT - ⊖ Mortlake (Rail). - ✆ 020 8876 4238 - www.victoriasheen.co.uk*

Kew

✿ The Glasshouse

MODERN CUISINE • FASHIONABLE XX 2019 sees the 20th birthday of this very model of a modern neighbourhood restaurant. The quirkily-shaped room comes with textured walls and vibrant artwork and, as the name implies, it's a bright spot. The unfussy, natural style of cooking focuses on seasonal flavours that complement one another.

→ Salmon sashimi, with pickled rhubarb, ginger and white soy. Venison haunch and pie with smoked creamed potato, rainbow chard and pickled walnuts. Chocolate and hazelnut pavé with milk ice cream.

Menu £ 38/58

Town plan: 6C4-z – *14 Station Par. ✉ TW9 3PZ – ⊖ Kew Gardens*
– ✆ 020 8940 6777 – www.glasshouserestaurant.co.uk
– Closed 24-26 December, 1 January, Sunday dinner and Monday except bank holidays

Richmond

Dysart Petersham

MODERN CUISINE • INTIMATE XX A pub built in the 1900s as part of the Arts and Crafts movement but now run as quite a formal restaurant. The kitchen uses top-notch ingredients and adds subtle Asian tones to a classical base. Occasional music recital suppers.

Menu £ 28 (weekdays)
– Carte £ 40/75

Town plan: 6C4-d – *135 Petersham Rd ✉ TW10 7AA*
– ✆ 020 8940 8005 – www.thedysartpetersham.co.uk
– Closed Sunday dinner, Monday and Tuesday

Petersham Nurseries Café

MODERN CUISINE • RUSTIC X On a summer's day there can be few more delightful spots for lunch, whether that's on the terrace or in the greenhouse. The kitchen uses the freshest seasonal produce in unfussy, flavoursome dishes that have a subtle Italian accent.

Carte £ 39/51

Town plan: 6C4-k – *Church Ln (off Petersham Rd) ✉ TW10 7AB*
– ✆ 020 8940 5230 (booking essential) – www.petershamnurseries.com
– lunch only – Closed 24-27 December and Monday

Matsuba

JAPANESE • DESIGN X Family-run Japanese restaurant with just 11 tables; understated but well-kept appearance. Extensive menu offers wide range of Japanese dishes, along with bulgogi, a Korean barbecue dish.

Carte £ 30/45

Town plan: 6C4-n – *10 Red Lion St ✉ TW9 1RW – ⊖ Richmond*
– ✆ 020 8605 3513 – www.matsuba-restaurant.com
– Closed 25-26 December, 1 January, Sunday and Monday

Swagat

INDIAN • BISTRO X A very likeable little Indian restaurant, run by two friends who met while training with Oberoi hotels in India. One partner organises the warm service; the other prepares dishes with a pleasing degree of lightness and subtlety.

Carte £ 18/30

Town plan: 6C4-b – *86 Hill Rise ✉ TW10 6UB – ⊖ Richmond*
– ✆ 020 8940 7557 (booking essential) – www.swagatindiancuisine.co.uk
– dinner only – Closed 25 December

Petersham

HISTORIC · CLASSIC Extended over the years, a fine example of Victorian Gothic architecture, with Portland stone and self-supporting staircase. The most comfortable bedrooms overlook the Thames. Formal restaurant in which to enjoy a mix of classic and modern cooking; ask for a window table for terrific park and river views.

58 rooms ☕ – 👤£ 80/170 👥£ 130/220 – 1 suite

Town plan: 6C4-j – *Nightingale Ln* ✉ *TW10 6UZ* – ⊖ *Richmond* – ✆ *020 8940 7471* – *www.petershamhotel.co.uk* – *Closed 25-26 December*

Bingham

TOWNHOUSE · MODERN A pair of conjoined and restored Georgian townhouses; a short walk from Richmond centre. Ask for a room overlooking the river and garden. Contemporary bedrooms; some with four-posters.

15 rooms – 👤£ 144/289 👥£ 164/309 – ☕£ 17

Town plan: 6C4-c – *61-63 Petersham Rd* ✉ *TW10 6UT* – ⊖ *Richmond* – ✆ *020 8940 0902* – *www.thebingham.co.uk*

Twickenham

Crown

TRADITIONAL BRITISH · PUB Relaxed, stylish pub with parquet floors and feature fireplaces; sit in the airy, elegant rear restaurant, with its high vaulted ceiling and garden view. Global, bound-to-please menus offer fresh, tasty, amply-sized dishes.

Carte £ 16/44

Town plan: 5B4-c – *174 Richmond Rd, St Margarets* ✉ *TW1 2NH* – ⊖ *St Margarets (Rail).* – ✆ *020 8892 5896* – *www.crowntwickenham.co.uk* – *Closed 26 December*

Michelin

SOUTHWARK

Bermondsey

Story (Tom Sellers)

MODERN CUISINE • DESIGN XXX In 2018 the restaurant underwent more than just a major refit – it felt more like a rebirth. The huge picture window remains the dominant feature but the room now offers a greater level of comfort. You aren't given a menu; instead, chef Tom Sellers and his talented kitchen present a mixture of their classic dishes along with others informed by the seasons.

→ Bread and 'dripping'. Chicken, morels and truffle. Almond and dill.

Menu £ 80 (weekday lunch)/145 – surprise menu only

Town plan: 42AY5-s – *199 Tooley St ✉ SE1 2JX – ⊖ London Bridge – ✆ 020 7183 2117 (booking essential) – www.restaurantstory.co.uk – Closed 2 weeks Christmas-New Year, Sunday dinner and Monday lunch*

José

SPANISH • MINIMALIST X Standing up while eating tapas feels so right, especially at this snug, lively bar that packs 'em in like boquerones. The vibrant dishes are intensely flavoured – five per person should suffice; go for the daily fish dishes from the blackboard. There's a great list of sherries too.

Carte £ 16/34

Town plan: 42AX5-v – *104 Bermondsey St ✉ SE1 3UB – ⊖ London Bridge – ✆ 020 7403 4902 (bookings not accepted) – www.josepizarro.com – Closed 25-27 December and 1-2 January*

Le Pont de la Tour

FRENCH • ELEGANT XXX Few restaurants can beat the setting, especially when you're on the terrace with its breathtaking views of Tower Bridge. For its 25th birthday it got a top-to-toe refurbishment, resulting in a warmer looking room in which to enjoy the French-influenced cooking.

Menu £ 30 – Carte £ 35/75

Town plan: 34AY4-c – *36d Shad Thames, Butlers Wharf ✉ SE1 2YE – ⊖ London Bridge – ✆ 020 7403 8403 – www.lepontdelatour.co.uk – Closed 1 January*

Coal Shed (N)

MEATS AND GRILLS • DESIGN XX Coal Shed was established in Brighton before opening here in this modern development by Tower Bridge. It's set over two floors and specialises in steaks but there's also plenty of seafood on offer. Desserts are good too; try the various 'sweets'.

Menu £ 20 (lunch and early dinner) – Carte £ 27/54

Town plan: 34AX4-s – *Unit 3.1, One Tower Bridge, 4 Crown Sq ✉ SE1 2SE – ⊖ London Bridge – ✆ 020 3384 7272 – www.coalshed-restaurant.co.uk – Closed 25-26 December*

Duddell's

CHINESE • HISTORIC XX A former church, dating from 1703, seems an unlikely setting for a Cantonese restaurant but this striking conversion is the London branch of the Hong Kong original. Lunchtime dim sum is a highlight but be sure to order the Peking duck which comes with 8 condiments in two servings.

Menu £ 25 (weekday lunch) – Carte £ 36/69

Town plan: 33AW4-c – *9A St. Thomas St ✉ SE1 9RY – ⊖ London Bridge – ✆ 020 3957 9932 – www.duddells.co/london – Closed 25 December and 1 January*

Londrino

PORTUGUESE • DESIGN XX The chef-owner takes his influences from his home country of Portugal, from the various London restaurants in which he has worked and from his own extensive travels. The modern dishes are meant for sharing and the bright, open space has an easy-going feel.

Menu £ 22 (weekday lunch) – Carte £ 29/58

Town plan: 42AW5-o – *36 Snowsfields ✉ SE1 3SU – ⊖ London Bridge – ✆ 020 3911 4949 – www.londrino.co.uk – Closed Christmas-New Year, Sunday dinner and Monday*

Oblix

MEATS AND GRILLS • TRENDY XX A New York grill restaurant on the 32nd floor of The Shard; window tables for two are highly prized. Meats and fish from the rotisserie, grill and Josper oven are the stars of the show; brunch in the lounge bar at weekends.

Menu £ 38 (weekday lunch) – Carte £ 33/111

Town plan: 33AW4-e – *Level 32, The Shard, 31 St Thomas St. ✉ SE1 9RY – ⊖ London Bridge – ✆ 020 7268 6700 – www.oblixrestaurant.com*

Butlers Wharf Chop House

TRADITIONAL BRITISH • BRASSERIE X Grab a table on the terrace in summer and dine in the shadow of Tower Bridge. Rustic feel to the interior; noisy and fun. The menu focuses on traditional English ingredients and dishes; grilled meats a speciality.

Menu £ 30 – Carte £ 29/58

Town plan: 34AY4-n – *36e Shad Thames, Butlers Wharf ✉ SE1 2YE – ⊖ London Bridge – ✆ 020 7403 3403 – www.chophouse-restaurant.co.uk – Closed 1 January*

Casse Croûte

FRENCH • BISTRO X Squeeze into this tiny bistro and you'll find yourself transported to rural France. A blackboard menu offers three choices for each course but new dishes are added as others run out. The cooking is rustic, authentic and heartening.

Carte £ 31/37

Town plan: 42AX5-t – *109 Bermondsey St ✉ SE1 3XB – ⊖ London Bridge – ✆ 020 7407 2140 (booking essential) – www.cassecroute.co.uk – Closed Sunday dinner*

Flour & Grape

ITALIAN • SIMPLE X The clue's in the name – pasta and wine. A choice of 7 or 8 antipasti are followed by the same number of homemade pasta dishes, with a dessert menu largely centred around gelato. Add in a well-chosen wine list with some pretty low mark-ups and it's no wonder this place is busy.

Carte £ 15/28

Town plan: 42AX6-e – *214 Bermondsey St ✉ SE1 3TQ – ⊖ London Bridge – ✆ 020 7407 4682 (bookings not accepted) – www.flourandgrape.com – Closed Christmas and Monday lunch*

Pique-Nique

FRENCH • BISTRO Set in a converted 1920s park shelter is this fun French restaurant with a focus on rotisserie-cooked Bresse chicken. Concise menu of French classics; go for the 6 course 'Menu autour du poulet de Bresse' which uses every part of the bird.

Carte £ 24/44

Town plan: 42AX5-n - *Tanner St. Park ✉ SE1 3LD - ⊖ London Bridge - ✆ 020 7403 9549 (booking essential) - www.pique-nique.co.uk - Closed Sunday dinner*

Pizarro

MEDITERRANEAN CUISINE • NEIGHBOURHOOD José Pizarro has a refreshingly simple way of naming his establishments: after José, his tapas bar, comes Pizarro, a larger restaurant a few doors down. Go for the small plates, like prawns with piquillo peppers and jamón.

Carte £ 19/50

Town plan: 42AX6-r - *194 Bermondsey St ✉ SE1 3TQ - ⊖ London Bridge - ✆ 020 7378 9455 - www.josepizarro.com - Closed 25-27 December and 1-2 January*

Santo Remedio N

MEXICAN • COLOURFUL The cooking inspiration comes from the owner's time spent in Mexico City, the Yucatan and Oaxaca. Ingredients are a mix of imported - like grasshoppers to liven up the guacamole - and home-grown like Hertfordshire pork. Spread over two floors, the rooms are as colourful as the food.

Menu £ 20 (weekday lunch) - Carte £ 23/35

Town plan: 34AX4-r - *152 Tooley St ✉ SE1 2TU - ⊖ London Bridge - ✆ 020 7403 3021 - www.santoremedio.co.uk - Closed Christmas and Sunday dinner*

Tom Simmons N

MODERN CUISINE • SIMPLE The eponymous chef went from being a contestant on 'MasterChef: The Professionals' to having his name above the door of his own restaurant here in this modern development near Tower Bridge. His Welsh heritage comes through on the modern menu, with its use of Welsh lamb and beef.

Menu £ 24/27 - Carte £ 29/54

Town plan: 34AY4-c - *2 Still Walk ✉ SE1 2RA - ⊖ London Bridge - ✆ 020 3848 2100 - www.tom-simmons.co.uk - Closed Monday*

Garrison

MEDITERRANEAN CUISINE • PUB Known for its charming vintage look, booths and sweet-natured service, The Garrison boasts a warm, relaxed vibe. Open from breakfast until dinner, when a Mediterranean-led menu pulls in the crowds.

Carte £ 26/40

Town plan: 42AX5-z - *99-101 Bermondsey St ✉ SE1 3XB - ⊖ London Bridge. - ✆ 020 7089 9355 (booking essential at dinner) - www.thegarrison.co.uk - Closed 25 December*

Shangri-La

LUXURY • ELEGANT When your hotel occupies floors 34-52 of The Shard, you know it's going to have the wow factor. The pool is London's highest and north-facing bedrooms have the best views. An East-meets-West theme includes the restaurant's menu and afternoon tea when you have a choice of traditional English or Asian.

202 rooms - †£ 475/725 ††£ 475/725 - ☕ £ 32 - 17 suites

Town plan: 33AW4-s - *The Shard, 31 St Thomas St ✉ SE1 9QU - ⊖ London Bridge - ✆ 020 7234 8000 - www.shangri-la.com/london*

Bermondsey Square

BUSINESS • MODERN Cleverly designed hotel in a regenerated square, with subtle '60s influences and a hip feel. Relaxed public areas; well-equipped bedrooms include stylish loft suites.

90 rooms – £110/329 £110/329

Town plan: 42AX6-n – *Bermondsey Sq, Tower Bridge Rd SE1 3UN – London Bridge – 020 7378 2450 – www.bermondseysquarehotel.co.uk*

East Dulwich

Palmerston

MEDITERRANEAN CUISINE • PUB A brightly run Victorian pub that has a comfortable, lived-in feel and lies at the heart of the local community. The cooking has a satisfying, gutsy edge with meat dishes, especially game, being the highlight.

Menu £16 (weekday lunch) – Carte £27/44

Town plan: 26U9-x – *91 Lordship Ln SE22 8EP – East Dulwich (Rail). – 020 8693 1629 – www.thepalmerston.co.uk – Closed 25-26 December and 1 January*

Peckham

Kudu

MODERN CUISINE • NEIGHBOURHOOD Run by a young husband and wife team who have attracted a fun and young local clientele. Patrick's South African roots are evident in dishes like the mussel potjie and the 'braai' lamb neck; the brioche-style bread with bacon butter is memorable. Amy and her service team are delightful.

Carte £20/40

Town plan: 26V8-k – *119 Queen's Rd SE15 2EZ – Queens Road Peckham (Rail) – 020 3950 0226 – www.kudu-restaurant.com – Closed Monday, Tuesday and lunch Wednesday-Thursday.*

Artusi

ITALIAN • NEIGHBOURHOOD An enthusiastically run Italian restaurant which shows Peckham is on the rise. The kitchen displays clear respect for the seasonal ingredients, dishes are kept honest and the prices are more than fair.

Carte £21/35

Town plan: 26U9-a – *161 Bellenden Rd SE15 4DH – Peckham Rye – 020 3302 8200 (booking essential at dinner) – www.artusi.co.uk – Closed 1 week Christmas*

Southwark

Padella

ITALIAN • BISTRO This lively little sister to Trullo offers a short, seasonal menu where hand-rolled pasta is the star of the show. Sauces and fillings are inspired by the owners' trips to Italy and prices are extremely pleasing to the pocket. Sit at the ground floor counter overlooking the open kitchen.

Carte £12/22

Town plan: 33AW4-d – *6 Southwark St, Borough Market SE1 1TQ – London Bridge (bookings not accepted) – www.padella.co – Closed 25-26 December and bank holidays*

Roast

MODERN BRITISH • FRIENDLY Known for its British food and for promoting UK producers – not surprising considering the restaurant's in the heart of Borough Market. The 'dish of the day' is often a highlight; service is affable and there's live music at night.

Carte £35/63

Town plan: 33AV4-e – *The Floral Hall, Borough Market SE1 1TL – London Bridge – 020 3006 6111 (booking essential) – www.roast-restaurant.com – Closed 25-26 December, 1 January and Sunday dinner*

Union Street Café

ITALIAN • TRENDY XX Occupying a former warehouse, this Gordon Ramsay restaurant has been busy since day one and comes with a New York feel, a faux industrial look and a basement bar. The Italian menu keeps things simple and stays true to the classics.

Menu £26 - Carte £22/49

Town plan: 33AU4-u - *47-51 Great Suffolk St ✉ SE1 0BS - ⊖ London Bridge - ☎ 020 7592 7977 - www.gordonramsayrestaurants.com*

Bala Baya

MIDDLE EASTERN • DESIGN X A friendly, lively restaurant which celebrates the Middle Eastern heritage of its passionate owner. Dishes are fresh, vibrant and designed for sharing and the bright, modern interior is inspired by the Bauhaus architecture of Tel Aviv.

Menu £19 (lunch) - Carte £31/45

Town plan: 33AU4-a - *Arch 25, Old Union Yard Arches, 229 Union St ✉ SE1 0LR - ⊖ Southwark - ☎ 020 8001 7015 - www.balabaya.co.uk - Closed 25-26 December and Sunday dinner*

El Pastór

MEXICAN • TRENDY X A lively, informal restaurant under the railway arches at London Bridge; inspired by the taquerias of Mexico City. Flavours are beautifully fresh, fragrant and spicy; don't miss the Taco Al Pastór after which the restaurant is named.

Carte £14/32

Town plan: 33AV4-r - *7a Stoney St, Borough Market ✉ SE1 9AA - ⊖ London Bridge - ☎ 020 7440 1461 (bookings not accepted) - www.tacoselpastor.co.uk - Closed 25-26 December, 1 January, Sunday dinner and bank holidays*

Elliot's

MODERN CUISINE • RUSTIC X A lively, unpretentious café which sources its ingredients from Borough Market, in which it stands. The appealing menu is concise and the cooking is earthy, pleasingly uncomplicated and very satisfying. Try one of the sharing dishes.

Carte £21/41

Town plan: 33AV4-h - *12 Stoney St, Borough Market ✉ SE1 9AD - ⊖ London Bridge - ☎ 020 7403 7436 - www.elliotscafe.com - Closed Sunday and bank holidays*

Lobos

SPANISH • TAPAS BAR X A dimly lit, decidedly compact tapas bar under the railway arches - sit upstairs to enjoy the theatre of the open kitchen. Go for one of the speciality meat dishes like the leg of slow-roasted Castilian milk-fed lamb.

Carte £15/48

Town plan: 33AW4-a - *14 Borough High St ✉ SE1 9QG - ⊖ London Bridge - ☎ 020 7407 5361 - www.lobostapas.co.uk - Closed 25-26 December and 1 January*

Oxo Tower Brasserie

MODERN CUISINE • DESIGN X Less formal but more fun than the next-door restaurant. The open-plan kitchen produces modern, colourful and easy-to-eat dishes with influences from the Med. Great views too from the bar.

Menu £30 (lunch) - Carte £27/49

Town plan: 32AS3-a - *Oxo Tower Wharf (8th floor), Barge House St ✉ SE1 9PH - ⊖ Southwark - ☎ 020 7803 3888 - www.oxotower.co.uk - Closed 25 December*

Tapas Brindisa

SPANISH • TAPAS BAR X A blueprint for many of the tapas bars that subsequently sprung up over London. It has an infectious energy and the well-priced, robust dishes include Galician-style octopus and black rice with squid; try the hand-carved Ibérico hams.

Carte £ 14/38

Town plan: 33AV4-k - *18-20 Southwark St, Borough Market ✉ SE1 1TJ - ⊖ London Bridge - ✆ 020 7357 8880 (bookings not accepted) - www.brindisatapaskitchens.com*

Tate Modern (Restaurant)

MODERN BRITISH • DESIGN X A contemporary, faux-industrial style restaurant on the ninth floor of the striking Switch House extension. Modern menus champion British ingredients; desserts are a highlight and the wine list interesting and well-priced.

Menu £ 25 - Carte £ 26/36

Town plan: 33AU3-s - *Switch House (9th floor), Tate Modern, Bankside ✉ SE1 9TG - ⊖ Southwark - ✆ 020 7401 5621 - www.tate.org.uk - lunch only and dinner Friday-Saturday - Closed 24-26 December*

Wright Brothers

SEAFOOD • COSY X Originally an oyster wholesaler; now offers a wide range of oysters along with porter, as well as fruits de mer, daily specials and assorted pies. It fills quickly and an air of contentment reigns.

Carte £ 29/40

Town plan: 33AV4-m - *11 Stoney St, Borough Market ✉ SE1 9AD - ⊖ London Bridge - ✆ 020 7403 9554 - www.thewrightbrothers.co.uk - Closed 25-26 December and 1 January*

Anchor & Hope

MODERN BRITISH • PUB As popular as ever thanks to its congenial feel and lived-in looks but mostly because of the appealingly seasonal menu and the gutsy, bold cooking that delivers on flavour. No reservations so be prepared to wait at the bar.

Menu £ 17 (weekday lunch) - Carte £ 19/46

Town plan: 32AT4-n - *36 The Cut ✉ SE1 8LP - ⊖ Southwark. - ✆ 020 7928 9898 (bookings not accepted) - www.anchorandhopepub.co.uk - Closed Christmas-New Year, Sunday dinner, Monday lunch and bank holidays*

Hilton London Bankside

BUSINESS • MODERN A sleek, design-led hotel with faux industrial touches; ideally situated for visiting the attractions of the South Bank. Spacious, contemporary bedrooms are furnished in a minimalist style. Impressive pool in the basement. OXBO serves a range of British dishes including meats from the Josper grill.

292 rooms - †£ 249/379 ††£ 249/379 - ☕ £ 30 - 30 suites

Town plan: 33AU4-b - *2-8 Great Suffolk St ✉ SE1 0UG - ⊖ Southwark - ✆ 020 3667 5600 - www.londonbankside.hilton.com*

Mondrian London

BUSINESS • DESIGN The former Sea Containers house now has slick, stylish look evoking the golden age of the transatlantic liner. Rooms come with a bright splash of colour; Suites have balconies and Superiors, a river view. Globally influenced small plates in the smart restaurant, with meat and fish from the grill & clay oven.

359 rooms - †£ 218/507 ††£ 348/1111 - ☕ £ 16 - 5 suites

Town plan: 32AT3-x - *20 Upper Ground ✉ SE1 9PD - ⊖ Southwark - ✆ 020 3747 1000 - www.mondrianlondon.com*

TOWER HAMLETS

Bethnal Green

Brawn

MODERN CUISINE • NEIGHBOURHOOD Unpretentious and simply kitted out, with a great local atmosphere and polite, helpful service. The name captures the essence of the cooking perfectly: it is rustic, muscular and makes very good use of pig. Interesting wine list with a focus on natural and organic wines.

Carte £ 27/43

Town plan: 20U4-z - *49 Columbia Rd. ✉ E2 7RG - ⊖ Bethnal Green - ✆ 020 7729 5692 - www.brawn.co - Closed Christmas-New Year, Sunday dinner, Monday lunch and bank holidays*

Smokestak

MEATS AND GRILLS • RUSTIC A buzzing barbecue restaurant with an open kitchen and an industrial feel. Highlights include the brisket and ribs: these are brined, oak-smoked, coated with a sweet and sour BBQ sauce and chargrilled - the results being unctuous and incredibly satisfying. The charming staff are happy to guide you.

Carte £ 16/31

Town plan: 20U4-f - *35 Sclater St ✉ E1 6LB - ⊖ Shoreditch High Street - ✆ 020 3873 1733 - www.smokestak.co.uk*

Blanchette

FRENCH • BISTRO Sister to the Soho original with the same lively buzz, funky music and tasty French dishes, but this time the menu heads further south, with a few North African influences too. 3 or 4 plates per person should suffice.

Menu £ 20 (lunch) - Carte £ 23/36

Town plan: 20U4-h - *204 Brick Ln ✉ E1 6SA - ⊖ Shoreditch High Street - ✆ 020 7729 7939 - www.blanchettelondon.co.uk - Closed 24-26 December*

Sager + Wilde

MEDITERRANEAN CUISINE • RUSTIC Friendly neighbourhood restaurant - a former wine bar - set underneath a railway arch. Tasty, well-priced, creative dishes have a Mediterranean heart and an eye-catching modern style, with some interesting combinations.

Carte £ 21/30

Town plan: 20V4-s - *250 Paradise Row ✉ E2 9LE - ⊖ Bethnal Green - ✆ 020 7613 0478 - www.sagerandwilde.com - Closed Monday lunch*

Marksman

TRADITIONAL BRITISH • FRIENDLY With its quirky, brown-tiled façade, this pub has long been a local landmark; the wood-panelled bar retains the feel of a traditional boozer, while the first floor dining room is more modern. Simply cooked, seasonal British dishes are wonderfully fresh, well-balanced and full of flavour.

Menu £ 24 (weekday lunch) - Carte £ 28/39

Town plan: 20U3-m - *254 Hackney Rd ✉ E2 7SJ - ⊖ Hoxton. - ✆ 020 7739 7393 - www.marksmanpublichouse.com - dinner only and lunch Friday-Sunday - Closed 25-30 December*

Town Hall

LUXURY • DESIGN Grand Edwardian and Art Deco former council offices converted into a stylish, trendy hotel, whilst retaining many original features. Striking, individually decorated bedrooms come with retro furnishings and frequently changing art.

97 rooms - †£ 170/457 ††£ 190/532 - 57 suites

Town plan: 20V4-x - *Patriot Sq ✉ E2 9NF - ⊖ Bethnal Green - ✆ 020 7871 0460 - www.townhallhotel.com*

Spitalfields

Galvin La Chapelle (Jeff Galvin)

FRENCH • ELEGANT XXX With its vaulted ceiling, arched windows and marble pillars, this restaurant remains as impressive now as when it first opened nearly a decade ago. Service is professional and the atmosphere, relaxed and unstuffy. Cooking is assured, with a classical French foundation and a sophisticated modern edge.

→ Lasagne of Dorset crab with beurre Nantais & pea shoots. Roast loin and slow-cooked venison with butternut, chestnuts and sauce grand veneur. Banoffee cheesecake with chocolate ice cream.

Menu £ 34 (lunch and early dinner) – Carte £ 53/78

Town plan: 34AX1-v – *35 Spital Sq ✉ E1 6DY – ⊖ Liverpool Street – ✆ 020 7299 0400 – www.galvinrestaurants.com – Closed 25-26 December and 1 January*

Blixen

MEDITERRANEAN CUISINE • FASHIONABLE X A charmingly run and good-looking restaurant with lots of natural light; set in a former bank. The appealing European menu offers keenly priced modern dishes. Service is enthusiastic, the atmosphere's buzzing and you'll want to return for breakfast, or cocktails in the basement bar.

Carte £ 27/50

Town plan: 34AY1-w – *65a Brushfield St ✉ E1 6AA – ⊖ Liverpool Street – ✆ 020 7101 0093 – www.blixen.co.uk – Closed Sunday dinner*

Gunpowder

INDIAN • SIMPLE X A loud, buzzy restaurant with just ten tightly packed tables, serving vibrant small plates from across the Indian regions. The name is a reference to the chef's daily-made spice mix and his menu takes its influence from old family recipes. Standout dishes include deep-fried crab and crispy pork ribs.

Carte £ 16/39

Town plan: 34AY1-g – *11 White's Row ✉ E1 7NF – ⊖ Liverpool Street – ✆ 020 7426 0542 (bookings not accepted) – www.gunpowderlondon.com – Closed Sunday*

St John Bread and Wine

TRADITIONAL BRITISH • BISTRO X An appealing restaurant with a stripped back style. The highly seasonal menu offers starter-sized dishes perfect for sharing and the cooking is British, uncomplicated and very satisfying. Breakfast includes a wonderful rare breed bacon sandwich.

Carte £ 21/43

Town plan: 34AY1-a – *94-96 Commercial St ✉ E1 6LZ – ⊖ Liverpool Street – ✆ 020 7251 0848 – www.stjohngroup.uk.com – Closed 25-26 December and 1 January*

Hawksmoor

MEATS AND GRILLS • FRIENDLY X A buzzy, relaxed restaurant with friendly staff. It's not really about the starters or the puds here – the star is the great British beef, hung for 35 days, which comes from Longhorn cattle in the heart of the Yorkshire Moors.

Menu £ 25 (lunch and early dinner) – Carte £ 26/86

Town plan: 34AY1-s – *157a Commercial St ✉ E1 6BJ – ⊖ Shoreditch High Street – ✆ 020 7234 9940 (booking essential) – www.thehawksmoor.com – Closed 25-26 December and 1 January*

Don't expect guesthouses to provide the same level of service as a hotel. They are often characterised by a warm welcome and décor which reflects the owner's personality. Those shown in red are particularly charming.

Som Saa

THAI • RUSTIC Som Saa's success took it from pop-up to permanent restaurant, with a lively atmosphere and a rustic, industrial look. Menus showcase the diversity of Thai cuisine. 4 or 5 dishes between two are recommended – and do try a cocktail or two!

Carte £ 19/32

Town plan: 34AY1-t – *43a Commerical St ✉ E1 6BD – ⊖ Aldgate East – ✆ 020 7324 7790 – www.somsaa.com – Closed Christmas, bank holiday Mondays, Sunday and lunch Monday*

Batty Langley's

TOWNHOUSE • ELEGANT It looks and feels like a Georgian house, thanks to the antique furniture and attention to detail, yet even the façade was rebuilt. The luxurious rooms come with flowing drapes, reproduction fireplaces and lovely bathrooms. An oasis of composed elegance.

29 rooms – †£ 205/240 ††£ 240/340 – ☕ £ 12 – 3 suites

Town plan: 34AY1-y – *12 Folgate St ✉ E1 6BX – ⊖ Liverpool Street – ✆ 020 7377 4390 – www.battylangleys.com*

Whitechapel

Cafe Spice Namaste

INDIAN • NEIGHBOURHOOD Fresh, vibrant and fairly priced Indian cuisine from Cyrus Todiwala, served in a colourfully decorated room that was once a magistrate's court. Engaging service from an experienced team.

Menu £ 18 (lunch) – Carte £ 26/38

Town plan: 34AZ3-z – *16 Prescot St. ✉ E1 8AZ – ⊖ Tower Hill – ✆ 020 7488 9242 – www.cafespice.co.uk – Closed Saturday lunch, Sunday and bank holidays*

An important business lunch or dinner with friends?
The symbol ⇔ indicates restaurants with private rooms.

WANDSWORTH

Battersea

London House

MODERN BRITISH • NEIGHBOURHOOD One doesn't always associate neighbourhood restaurants with Gordon Ramsay but London House is an appealing place. It's comfortable and well run and the classically-based dishes come with modern touches and ingredients that marry well.

Menu £ 20 (weekdays)/30 – Carte £ 35/55

Town plan: 23N8-h – *7-9 Battersea Sq, Battersea Village ✉ SW11 3RA – ⊖ Clapham Junction – ✆ 020 7592 8545 – www.gordonramsayrestaurants.com/london-house*

Gastronhome

MODERN FRENCH • INTIMATE A cosy restaurant run by two young Frenchmen. Bi-monthly changing menus offer regional French dishes which come with a very modern, almost Scandic touch. The Gallic wine list has prices right across the scale.

Menu £ 35 (lunch) – Carte £ 44/55

Town plan: 24Q9-e – *59 Lavender Hill ✉ SW11 5QN – ✆ 020 3417 5639 (booking essential at dinner) – www.gastronhome.co.uk – Closed Monday-Wednesday lunch*

Hatched

MODERN BRITISH • NEIGHBOURHOOD X The large open kitchen is the focus of this relaxed and simply styled room. The ethos is about using quality ingredients, prepared with skill, and with the addition of some international flavours which reflect the chef-owner's travels. Gnocchi is a standout.

Carte £ 30/51

Town plan: 23N9-d – *189 St John's Hill ✉ SW11 1TH – ⊖ Clapham Junction – ✆ 020 7738 0735 – www.hatchedsw11.com – Closed 1 week January, 1 week June, 1 week August, Monday, Tuesday, Sunday dinner and lunch Wednesday-Thursday*

Nutbourne

MODERN BRITISH • NEIGHBOURHOOD X The 3rd restaurant from the Gladwin brothers; named after the family farm and vineyards in West Sussex. British produce drives the eclectic daily menu, with meats cooked on the open fire; dishes are hearty, wholesome and full of flavour.

Carte £ 25/45

Town plan: 23P8-n – *Unit 29, Ransomes Dock, 35-37 Parkgate Rd ✉ SW11 4NP – ✆ 020 7350 0555 – www.nutbourne-restaurant.com – Closed 23 December-2 January, Easter, Sunday dinner and Monday*

Sinabro

MODERN CUISINE • NEIGHBOURHOOD X The main room feels almost kitchen-like, courtesy of a wall of stainless steel; sit at the wooden counter – made by the chef-owner's father. Confidently prepared dishes rely largely on classic French flavours but are modern in style.

Menu £ 29/49

Town plan: 23P9-r – *28 Battersea Rise ✉ SW11 1EE – ⊖ Clapham Junction – ✆ 020 3302 3120 – www.sinabro.co.uk – Closed 12-27 August, 25-26 December, 1 January, Sunday and Monday*

Soif

FRENCH • NEIGHBOURHOOD X A busy bistro-cum-wine-shop with a great atmosphere. The satisfying French food takes regular excursions across the border into Italy and the thoughtfully compiled wine list includes plenty of natural wines from artisan winemakers.

Carte £ 29/39

Town plan: 23P9-c – *27 Battersea Rise ✉ SW11 1HG – ⊖ Clapham Junction – ✆ 020 7223 1112 (booking essential at dinner) – www.soif.co – Closed Christmas, New Year, Sunday dinner, Monday lunch and bank holidays*

Wandsworth

Chez Bruce (Bruce Poole)

FRENCH • BRASSERIE XX The longevity of this neighbourhood restaurant is no accident. Cooking techniques are kept unapologetically traditional; the base is largely classical French but with a pronounced Mediterranean influence and the food is all about flavour and balance. The atmosphere is clubby and the service sprightly.

→ Grilled tuna with lemon dressing, aioli and aubergine. Pig's cheek and pork belly with boudin noir, celeriac and mustard. Buttermilk pudding with rhubarb, lemon and pistachio.

Menu £ 38/58

Town plan: 6D5-e – *2 Bellevue Rd ✉ SW17 7EG – ⊖ Tooting Bec – ✆ 020 8672 0114 (booking essential) – www.chezbruce.co.uk – Closed 24-26 December and 1 January*

Benares

WESTMINSTER (City of)

Bayswater and Maida Vale

Hereford Road

TRADITIONAL BRITISH • NEIGHBOURHOOD Converted butcher's shop specialising in tasty British dishes without frills, using first-rate, seasonal ingredients; offal a highlight. Booths for six people are the prized seats. Friendly and relaxed feel.

Menu £ 16 (weekday lunch)
– Carte £ 25/32

Town plan: 27AC2-s – *3 Hereford Rd ✉ W2 4AB – ⊖ Bayswater – ✆ 020 7727 1144 (booking essential) – www.herefordroad.org – Closed 24 December-3 January and August bank holiday*

Kateh

MEDITERRANEAN CUISINE • NEIGHBOURHOOD Booking is imperative if you want to join the locals who have already discovered what a little jewel they have in the form of this buzzy, busy Persian restaurant. Authentic stews, expert chargrilling and lovely pastries and teas.

Carte £ 21/38

Town plan: 28AE1-a – *5 Warwick Pl ✉ W9 2PX – ⊖ Warwick Avenue – ✆ 020 7289 3393 (booking essential) – www.katehrestaurant.co.uk – dinner only and lunch Saturday-Sunday – Closed 25-26 December*

Angelus

FRENCH • BRASSERIE Hospitable owner has created an attractive French brasserie within a 19C former pub, with a warm and inclusive feel. Satisfying and honest French cooking uses seasonal British ingredients.

Menu £ 28/41 – Carte £ 39/54

Town plan: 29AG2-c – *4 Bathurst St ✉ W2 2SD – ⊖ Lancaster Gate – ✆ 020 7402 0083 – www.angelusrestaurant.co.uk – Closed 24-25 December and 1 January*

Marianne

FRENCH • COSY With just six tables, there are few more intimate restaurants that this one, set up by Marianne Lumb, a former finalist on MasterChef. The menus are changed daily and while the cooking is classically based, it also keeps things quite light.

Menu £ 48/75 – tasting menu only

Town plan: 27AC1-m – *104a Chepstow Rd ✉ W2 5QS – ⊖ Westbourne Park – ✆ 020 3675 7750 (booking essential) – www.mariannerestaurant.com – dinner only and lunch Friday-Sunday – Closed 22 December-7 January, 19 August-2 September, Monday and bank holidays*

Pomona's

WORLD CUISINE • NEIGHBOURHOOD X A large neighbourhood restaurant with bright décor, an airy, open feel and a fun, laid-back Californian vibe. All-day menus offer soulful, colourful cooking with breakfast, smoothies, salads, house specials and small plates.

Carte £ 23/51

Town plan: 27AC2-a - *47 Hereford Rd ✉ W2 5AH - ⊖ Bayswater - ✆ 020 7229 1503 - www.pomonas.co.uk - Closed 25-26 December*

Belgravia

Marcus

MODERN CUISINE • ELEGANT XXXX Marcus Wareing's eponymous restaurant inside the glamorous Berkeley Hotel is elegant and stylish, but also has a relaxed, easy-going feel. There's a steadfast Britishness to the menu which uses superlative produce like Isle of Gigha halibut, Cornish turbot and Galloway beef. The kitchen eschews complication and lets the main ingredient speak for itself.

→ Pheasant egg with short-rib ragu, wild garlic and asparagus. Middle White suckling pig with bacon broth and agnolotti. Salted milk chocolate aero with sorrel and clementine.

Menu £ 55/120

Town plan: 38AK5-e - *Berkeley Hotel, Wilton Pl ✉ SW1X 7RL - ⊖ Knightsbridge - ✆ 020 7235 1200 - www.marcusrestaurant.com - Closed Sunday*

Céleste

CREATIVE FRENCH • ELEGANT XXXX With its crystal chandeliers, immaculately dressed tables, Wedgwood blue friezes and fluted columns, this is a room in which you feel truly cosseted. The menu is overseen by Éric Fréchon, head chef of Le Bristol in Paris, so expect some of his specialities. However, the kitchen is unafraid of adding its own decidedly modern touches.

→ Fluffy organic Scotch egg. Lamb saddle with nori crust, kohlrabi purée and gnocchi. Coffee ice cream with caramelised pecan nuts and milk chocolate Chantilly.

Menu £ 39 (lunch) - Carte £ 72/100

Town plan: 38AK5-c - *The Lanesborough Hotel, Hyde Park Corner ✉ SW1X 7TA - ⊖ Hyde Park Corner - ✆ 020 7259 5599 - www.lanesborough.com*

Pétrus

FRENCH • ELEGANT XXX Gordon Ramsay's Belgravia restaurant is a sophisticated and elegant affair. The service is discreet and professional, and the cooking is rooted in classical techniques but isn't afraid of using influences from further afield. The superb wine list has Château Pétrus going back to 1928.

→ Steak tartare with crispy tendons, wasabi leaf and egg yolk. Fillet of Cornish brill with rouille, confit peppers and shellfish bisque. 'Black Forest' kirsch mousse with Amarena and Morello cherry sorbet.

Menu £ 45/105

Town plan: 38AK5-v - *1 Kinnerton St ✉ SW1X 8EA - ⊖ Knightsbridge - ✆ 020 7592 1609 - www.gordonramsayrestaurants.com/petrus - Closed 21-27 December and 1 January*

Amaya

INDIAN • DESIGN XXX London has many open kitchens but at this Indian restaurant the shooting flames and enticing aromas from the tawa, tandoor and sigri grills will instantly alert your tastebuds that something interesting is about to happen. The service is as bright and lively as the surroundings.

→ Turmeric and tarragon chicken tikka. Tandoori wild prawns. Lime tart with limoncello jelly and blackberry compote.

Menu £ 26/85 - Carte £ 33/82

Town plan: 37AJ5-k - *Halkin Arcade, 19 Motcomb St ✉ SW1X 8JT - ⊖ Knightsbridge - ✆ 020 7823 1166 - www.amaya.biz*

Zafferano

ITALIAN • FASHIONABLE XXX The immaculately coiffured regulars continue to support this ever-expanding, long-standing and capably run Italian restaurant. They come for the reassuringly familiar, if rather steeply priced dishes from all parts of Italy.

Menu £ 27 (weekday lunch) - Carte £ 36/85

Town plan: 37AJ5-f - *15 Lowndes St ✉ SW1X 9EY - ⊖ Knightsbridge - ✆ 020 7235 5800 (booking essential) - www.zafferanorestaurant.com - Closed 25 December*

Berkeley

GRAND LUXURY • ELEGANT A number of different designers have been used to update and modernise the bedrooms and the results are impressive. The Collins room remains a fine spot for afternoon tea with its Prêt-à-Portea theme and the Blue Bar enjoys a reputation as one of London's best. Great park views from the pool.

190 rooms - †£ 410/810 ††£ 425/960 - ☕ £ 38 - 27 suites

Town plan: 38AK5-e - *Wilton Pl ✉ SW1X 7RL - ⊖ Knightsbridge - ✆ 020 7235 6000 - www.the-berkeley.co.uk*

✿ **Marcus** - See restaurant listing

The Lanesborough

GRAND LUXURY • ELEGANT A multi-million pound refurbishment has restored this hotel's Regency splendour; its elegant Georgian-style bedrooms offering bespoke furniture, beautiful fabrics, tablet technologies and 24 hour butler service. Opulent Céleste serves rich French cooking under its domed glass roof.

93 rooms - †£ 525/795 ††£ 625/895 - ☕ £ 38 - 46 suites

Town plan: 38AK5-c - *Hyde Park Corner ✉ SW1X 7TA - ⊖ Hyde Park Corner - ✆ 020 7259 5599 - www.lanesborough.com*

✿ **Céleste** - See restaurant listing

COMO The Halkin

LUXURY • ELEGANT Opened in 1991 as one of London's first boutique hotels and still looking pretty sharp today. Stylish bedrooms come with silk walls and marble bathrooms; those overlooking the garden at the back are quiet. Creative and colourful cuisine in Ametsa, from the team behind Spain's Arzak restaurant.

41 rooms - †£ 385/760 ††£ 385/760 - ☕ £ 25 - 6 suites

Town plan: 38AK5-b - *5 Halkin St ✉ SW1X 7DJ - ⊖ Hyde Park Corner - ✆ 020 7333 1000 - www.comohotels.com/thehalkin*

The Wellesley

TOWNHOUSE • ART DÉCO Stylish, elegant townhouse inspired by the jazz age, with lovely art deco styling throughout. Impressive cigar lounge and bar with a super selection of whiskies and cognacs. Smart bedrooms have full butler service; those facing Hyde Park are the most prized. Modern Italian food in the discreet restaurant.

36 rooms - †£ 325/445 ††£ 375/505 - ☕ £ 35 - 14 suites

Town plan: 38AK5-w - *11 Knightsbridge ✉ SW1X 7LY - ⊖ Hyde Park Corner - ✆ 020 7235 3535 - www.thewellesley.co.uk*

Hari

BUSINESS • MODERN An elegant and fashionable boutique-style hotel with a relaxed atmosphere and a hint of bohemia. Uncluttered, decently proportioned bedrooms come with oak flooring and lovely marble bathrooms. Cigar bar and terrace featuring a retractable roof. Italian dishes are served in the stylish restaurant.

85 rooms - †£ 250/489 ††£ 250/489 - ☕ £ 21 - 9 suites

Town plan: 38AK6-c - *20 Chesham Pl ✉ SW1X 8HQ - ⊖ Knightsbridge - ✆ 020 3189 4850 - www.thehari.com*

Hyde Park and Knightsbridge

Dinner by Heston Blumenthal

TRADITIONAL BRITISH • DESIGN XXX Heston Blumenthal's international reputation was built on the multi-sensory alchemy performed at his Fat Duck restaurant in Bray but his restaurant at the Mandarin Oriental hotel is a different beast. Here, the menu celebrates British culinary triumphs through the ages, with the date of origin given to each dish along with information about its provenance.

An impressively well-manned kitchen works with obvious intelligence, calm efficiency and attention to detail to produce dishes that look deceptively simple but taste sublime. Many of them have already achieved near legendary status and so enjoy a permanent presence on the menu, like 'Meat Fruit' (c.1500) which is a thing of beauty, and 'Rice & Flesh' (c.1390) - a variation of risotto alla Milanese with oxtail.

The large, light room has quirky touches, like wall sconces shaped as jelly moulds, but the main focus is on the open kitchen, with its oversized watch mechanics powering the spit to roast the pineapple that goes with the Tipsy Cake (c.1810).

→ Mandarin, chicken liver parfait and grilled bread (c.1500). Hereford rib-eye with mushroom ketchup and triple cooked chips (c.1830). Tipsy cake with spit-roast pineapple (c.1810).

Menu £ 45 (weekday lunch) - Carte £ 58/121

Town plan: 37AJ5-x - *Mandarin Oriental Hyde Park Hotel, 66 Knightsbridge, SW1X 7LA - Knightsbridge - 020 7201 3833 - www.dinnerbyheston.com - Closed 17-31 October*

Bar Boulud

FRENCH • BRASSERIE XX Daniel Boulud's London outpost is fashionable, fun and frantic. His hometown is Lyon but he built his considerable reputation in New York, so charcuterie, sausages and burgers are the highlights.

Menu £ 19 (weekday lunch) - Carte £ 26/57

Town plan: 37AJ5-x - *Mandarin Oriental Hyde Park Hotel, 66 Knightsbridge SW1X 7LA - Knightsbridge - 020 7201 3899 - www.mandarinoriental.com/london*

Zuma

JAPANESE • FASHIONABLE XX Now a global brand but this was the original. The glamorous clientele come for the striking surroundings, bustling atmosphere and easy-to-share food. Go for the more modern dishes and those cooked on the robata grill.

Carte £ 31/150

Town plan: 37AH5-m - *5 Raphael St SW7 1DL - Knightsbridge - 020 7584 1010 (booking essential) - www.zumarestaurant.com - Closed 25 December*

Mandarin Oriental Hyde Park

GRAND LUXURY • CONTEMPORARY This celebrated hotel, dating from 1889, is a London landmark; to ensure it remains as such, improvements are constantly being made - this time to the spacious bedrooms, many of which have views of Hyde Park. Enjoy afternoon tea in the charming Rosebery salon or relax in the luxurious spa with its 17m pool. Service remains as strong as ever.

181 rooms - †£ 540/1080 ††£ 540/1080 - £ 36 - 25 suites

Town plan: 37AJ5-x - *66 Knightsbridge SW1X 7LA - Knightsbridge - 020 7235 2000 - www.mandarinoriental.com/london*

Dinner by Heston Blumenthal • **Bar Boulud** - See restaurant listing

Bulgari

LUXURY • ELEGANT Impeccably tailored hotel making stunning use of materials like silver, mahogany, silk and marble. Luxurious bedrooms with sensual curves, sumptuous bathrooms and a great spa - and there is substance behind the style. Down a sweeping staircase to the Alain Ducasse restaurant.

85 rooms - †£ 650/850 ††£ 650/850 - £ 34 - 23 suites

Town plan: 37AH5-k - *171 Knightsbridge SW7 1DW - Knightsbridge - 020 7151 1010 - www.bulgarihotels.com/london*

Mayfair

✿✿✿ Alain Ducasse at The Dorchester

FRENCH • ELEGANT XXXXX Alain Ducasse's elegant London outpost understands that it's all about making the diner feel at ease – as Coco Chanel said "Luxury must be comfortable, otherwise it is not luxury". Thanks to their charm and professionalism, the service team's attentiveness is never overbearing nor does their confidence ever cross the line into haughtiness.

The kitchen uses the best British or French produce to create visually striking dishes, including some that showcase the flavours of Southern France. Dishes like 'Sauté gourmand' of lobster are much loved perennials while others, such as Anjou pigeon with sardine, prove that the kitchen is not averse to taking risks. For dessert, it's hard to resist the signature Rum Baba.

The exemplary wine list includes an impressive selection of Domaine de la Romanée Conti and Château d'Yquem. The best tables are in the main room – those on the raised dais can feel a little detached from the action. Luminaries wanting a semi-private experience should book the 'Table Lumière' which is wrapped in a shimmering curtain.

→ Dorset crab, celeriac and caviar. Halibut with oyster and seaweed. 'Baba like in Monte Carlo'.

Menu £ 70/105

Town plan: 30AK4-a – *Dorchester Hotel, Park Ln ✉ W1K 1QA – ⊖ Hyde Park Corner – ✆ 020 7629 8866 (booking essential) – www.alainducasse-dorchester.com – Closed 3 weeks August, first week January, 26-30 December, Easter, Saturday lunch, Sunday and Monday*

✿✿✿ The Araki (Mitsuhiro Araki)

JAPANESE • INTIMATE XX It wasn't a straightforward move when Mitsuhiro Araki packed up his Three Star sushi restaurant in Tokyo's Ginza district and sailed for London in 2014. He wanted a challenge so instead of merely importing produce from Tsukiji fish market, he set himself the task of using largely European fish and shellfish and spent time adjusting his Edomae methods and techniques accordingly – the results are extraordinary.

There are two sittings at his 9-seater counter, at 18.00 and 20.30, and payment is taken in advance. Only an omakase menu is served – it doesn't come cheap, but the best things in life rarely do. His exquisite nigiri comes in manageable sizes and you can expect, for example, tuna and mackerel from Spanish waters, salmon from Scotland and caviar from Cornwall. The rice, grown by his father-in-law back in Japan, is extraordinary; it is served at near body temperature, with every grain discernible in the mouth.

→ Tuna tartare. Nigiri sushi. Wagashi.

Menu £ 300 – tasting menu only

Town plan: 30AM3-e – *12 New Burlington St ✉ W1S 3BF – ⊖ Oxford Circus – ✆ 020 7287 2481 (booking essential) – www.the-araki.com – dinner only – Closed last 2 weeks August, Christmas-first week January and Monday*

✿✿ Hélène Darroze at The Connaught

MODERN CUISINE • LUXURY XXXX When it's time to choose what you're going to eat you'll be handed a Solitaire board featuring 13 marbles, each bearing the name of a single ingredient – you choose 5, 7 or 9 (courses). The board is accompanied by a menu showing the other components of the dishes in question, which are delivered in any order you wish. Some will love this game, others will hate it, but at least it highlights the fact that the dishes are built around a stunning main ingredient and allows Hélène Darroze to shine a light on her wonderful French and British suppliers. Her cooking is largely informed by her homeland but she's not averse to using the occasional unexpected flavour, be it Asian or Indian, if she feels it brings something to the dish; she is also aware of the modern diners' preference for a lighter, less elaborate style of cooking.

The wood-panelled room is comfortable and elegant and credit must go to the service team who keep the atmosphere light, relaxed and never overbearingly formal.

→ Foie gras with black truffle, apple, celery and brioche. Venison with Sarawak pepper, butternut, grapes and Stichelton. Chocolate, cardamom and vanilla.

Menu £ 55/105

Town plan: 30AL3-e – *Connaught Hotel, Carlos Pl. ✉ W1K 2AL – ⊖ Bond Street – ✆ 020 7107 8880 (booking essential) – www.the-connaught.co.uk*

✿✿ Sketch (The Lecture Room & Library)

MODERN FRENCH • LUXURY XXXX We all need a little luxury in our lives from time to time – so praise be for Mourad Mazouz and Pierre Gagnaire's 18C fun-house. As you're whisked past the braided rope and up the stairs to the Lecture Room & Library, you'll feel your expectations rise with every step. The room is lavishly decorated in a kaleidoscope of colours and the impeccably set tables are so far apart they're virtually in different postcodes. The staff are unfailingly polite and professional and it appears that nothing is too much trouble.

The French cooking bears all the Pierre Gagnaire hallmarks: the main 'plate' comes surrounded by a number of complementary dishes and at first you don't quite know what to focus on – now is the time to relax into that comfortable armchair and just enjoy the variety of textures and tastes, the complexity and depth of flavours and the quality of the ingredients.

The wine list is a tome of epic proportions; take the sommeliers' advice; they know what they're talking about. And do make sure you order the array of treats that make up the 'grand dessert' – pudding it ain't.

→ Live langoustines. Organic rack of pork with sage, mango vinegar and seasonal fruit. Pierre Gagnaire's 'Grand Dessert'.

Carte £ 102/131

Town plan: 30AM2-h – *9 Conduit St (1st floor) ✉ W1S 2XG – ⊖ Oxford Circus – ✆ 020 7659 4500 (booking essential) – www.sketch.london – Closed 25 December, 1 January, 2 weeks late August-early September, Sunday, Monday and lunch Tuesday-Thursday.*

✿✿ Le Gavroche (Michel Roux Jnr)

FRENCH • INTIMATE XXXX You don't get to celebrate 50 years – as Le Gavroche did in 2017 – without doing something right. Anyone with any interest in Britain's post-war culinary history will be aware of this restaurant's significance, not just because of its celebration of French cuisine but also because of all the chefs who have passed through its kitchen over the years.

In an age of hectoring health-consciousness and tedious calorie counting there is something exhilarating about Michel Roux and head chef Rachel Humphrey's unapologetically extravagant French dishes. The ingredients are of the highest order, whether that's the huge scallops or the succulent Goosnargh duck. Everyone has their favourite dish but if the soufflé Suissesse or omelette Rothschild ever came off the menu there'd be riots, albeit polite ones, in Upper Brook Street. The cheese board is one of London's best. You're guided gracefully through the meal by a charming team and the hum of satisfaction that pervades the room says it all.

→ Artichoke with foie gras, truffles and chicken mousse. Butter poached lobster with white wine, asparagus and claw tart. Apricot and Cointreau soufflé.

Menu £ 70/175 **s** – Carte £ 68/197 **s**

Town plan: 30AK3-c – *43 Upper Brook St ✉ W1K 7QR – ⊖ Marble Arch – ✆ 020 7408 0881 (booking essential) – www.le-gavroche.co.uk – Closed 2 weeks Christmas, Saturday lunch, Sunday, Monday and bank holidays*

✿✿ Greenhouse

CREATIVE • FASHIONABLE XXX The Greenhouse has many charms and one of them is its setting. You enter via a mews, through a little bamboo garden, and this pastoral theme continues inside with a pale green colour scheme and leaf-etched glass. The restaurant is bright and airy during the day, and warm and intimate by night. If it wasn't for the fact that your fellow diners are an immaculately robed, international crowd, you would scarcely believe you were in the heart of the city.

The cooking here has always been underpinned by a sound classical French base. A variety of menus provide plenty of choice and the sourcing finds the best produce from around the UK, whether that's seafood from Cornwall and Scotland or lamb and venison from Wales. The wine list features the good and the great and an exceptional breadth of vintages: Château Lafite back to 1870, Château Latour to 1900, Château Haut Brion to 1945, 15 vintages of La Tâche and 37 of Penfolds Grange.

→ Native lobster with chicken, kohlrabi and cardamom leaf. Welsh lamb with aubergine, gomasio, harissa and soya. 'Ajuba Head' - chocolate with walnut and nutmeg.

Menu £ 45/100

Town plan: 30AL3-m - *27a Hay's Mews ✉ W1J 5NY - ⊖ Hyde Park Corner - ✆ 020 7499 3331 - www.greenhouserestaurant.co.uk - Closed Saturday lunch, Sunday and bank holidays*

✿✿ Umu

JAPANESE • FASHIONABLE XXX The kaiseki menu is the best way to truly experience chef Yoshinori Ishii's cuisine – he trained at Kitcho in Kyoto, a bastion of tradition where the central tenets and philosophy of kaiseki are preserved and celebrated. Here at Umu he has steadily been shifting the food away from a Western idea of Japanese food to a more authentic base, which means that flavours are more delicate and subtle than many expect. It hasn't always been easy: to get hold of fish in the right condition he went out with Cornish fishermen himself to teach them the ikejime method of killing fish – and you'll see the benefit in the firmer texture of the tsukuri. But that's not to say he's trying to replicate what happens in Kyoto – he wisely acknowledges that this is a London restaurant by incorporating the best of the UK's larder as well as dropping in an occasional playfulness.

Instead of tatami rooms you'll find a neatly laid out restaurant making good use of warm woods and natural materials.

→ Cornish cuttlefish with bottarga and tosazu sauce. Charcoal-grilled Wagyu tataki with vegetables and a sesame and ponzu sauce. Japanese seasonal tiramisu with matcha tea and ginjo sake.

Menu £ 45/155 – Carte £ 46/151

Town plan: 30AL3-k - *14-16 Bruton Pl. ✉ W1J 6LX - ⊖ Bond Street - ✆ 020 7499 8881 - www.umurestaurant.com - Closed Christmas, New Year and Sunday*

✿ Fera at Claridge's

CREATIVE BRITISH • ELEGANT XXXX Elegant without stuffiness, this is one of the most striking rooms in the capital and the attentive, personable service is a good match to the setting. There's an impressive purity and originality to the seasonal ingredients, and dishes are deftly executed and wonderfully balanced, with layers of texture and flavour. Tasting menus only, Thurs-Sat.

→ Roasted quail with hazelnut, carrot and juniper. Aged Dexter beef sirloin with ox cheek, salsify and thyme. Chocolate, whiskey and pine.

Menu £ 42 (lunch) – Carte £ 63/85

Town plan: 30AL2-c - *Claridge's Hotel, Brook St ✉ W1K 4HR - ⊖ Bond Street - ✆ 020 7107 8888 - www.feraatclaridges.co.uk*

✿ Alyn Williams at The Westbury

MODERN CUISINE • DESIGN XXXX Confident, cheery service ensures the atmosphere never strays into terminal seriousness; rosewood panelling and a striking wine display add warmth. The cooking is creative and even playful, but however elaborately constructed the dish, the combinations of flavours and textures always work.

→ Orkney scallop with yuzu caramel, white asparagus, morels and seaweed. Roasted halibut with fennel compote, cashews and coconut. Gariguette strawberry tartlet, lemon, vanilla curd and basil.

Menu £ 30/90

Town plan: 30AM3-z - *Westbury Hotel, 37 Conduit St ✉ W1S 2YF - ⊖ Bond Street - ✆ 020 7183 6426 - www.alynwilliams.com - Closed first 2 weeks January, last 2 weeks August, Sunday and Monday*

✿ The Square

CREATIVE FRENCH • ELEGANT XXXX A landmark restaurant that wasn't just refurbished and re-launched – you really sense that a new era begun. Chef Clément Leroy, a proud Frenchman, is keen to celebrate the UK's wonderful produce, albeit with imaginative or even playful twists. The room now has a sleeker, more contemporary look.

→ Orkney scallop with coffee and marsala. Aged Herdwick lamb 'earth and sea'. St John's Wood honey with grapefruit and sweet potato.

Menu £ 37/85

Town plan: 30AM3-v – *6-10 Bruton St.* ✉ *W1J 6PU*
– ⊖ *Green Park* – ✆ *020 7495 7100*
– *www.squarerestaurant.com – Closed 24-26 December and Sunday*

✿ Benares

INDIAN • CHIC XXX No Indian restaurant in London enjoys a more commanding location or expansive interior. The influences are many and varied, the spicing is deft and they make excellent use of British ingredients like Scottish scallops and New Forest venison. The Chef's Table has a window into the kitchen.

→ Crispy soft shell crab with puy lentil salad, kasundi and honey dressing. Venison, kale and chestnut mushroom biryani with butternut purée. Peanut butter parfait, with almond cake, cumin marshmallow and jaggery ice cream.

Menu £ 29 (lunch and early dinner)/98
– Carte £ 50/79

Town plan: 30AL3-q – *12a Berkeley Square House, Berkeley Sq.* ✉ *W1J 6BS*
– ⊖ *Green Park* – ✆ *020 7629 8886*
– *www.benaresrestaurant.com – Closed lunch 25 December,1 January and Sunday lunch*

✿ Galvin at Windows

MODERN CUISINE • FRIENDLY XXX The cleverly laid out room makes the most of the spectacular views across London from the 28th floor. Relaxed service takes the edge off the somewhat corporate atmosphere. The bold cooking uses superb ingredients and the classically based food comes with a pleasing degree of flair and innovation.

→ Cured Loch Fyne salmon with brown crab mousseline and celeriac remoulade. Fillet of beef and short-rib beignet with ox tongue and red wine jus. Pavlova with exotic fruit salsa and coconut ice cream.

Menu £ 37 (weekday lunch)/82

Town plan: 30AL4-e – *London Hilton Hotel, 22 Park Ln (28th floor)* ✉ *W1K 1BE*
– ⊖ *Hyde Park Corner* – ✆ *020 7208 4021*
– *www.galvinatwindows.com – Closed Saturday lunch and Sunday dinner*

✿ Kai

CHINESE • INTIMATE XXX Both the owner and his long-standing chef Alex Chow are Malaysian and, while the cooking features dishes from several provinces in China, it is the southern region of Nanyang which is closest to their hearts. The unashamedly glitzy look of the restaurant is as eclectic as the food and the service team are switched on and fully conversant with the menu.

→ Seared scallop with spicy XO sauce, lotus root crisp and stir-fried vegetables. Kagoshima Wagyu with foie gras, sesame ginger paste and Wagyu infused rice. Coconut parfait with chocolate and mango sorbet.

Carte £ 51/199

Town plan: 30AK3-n – *65 South Audley St* ✉ *W1K 2QU*
– ⊖ *Hyde Park Corner*
– ✆ *020 7493 8988 (booking essential)*
– *www.kaimayfair.co.uk – Closed 25-26 December and 1 January*

✿ Murano (Angela Hartnett)

ITALIAN • **FASHIONABLE** XXX Angela Hartnett's Italian-influenced cooking exhibits an appealing lightness of touch, with assured combinations of flavours, borne out of confidence in the ingredients. This is a stylish, elegant room run by a well-organised, professional and friendly team who put their customers at ease.

→ Scallops, whipped cod's roe, dill, cucumber and horseradish. Lamb saddle, crispy shoulder, morels and wild garlic. Blood orange polenta cake and cream cheese sorbet.

Menu £ 28/70

Town plan: 30AL4-b - *20 Queen St ✉ W1J 5PP - ⊖ Green Park - ✆ 020 7495 1127 - www.muranolondon.com - Closed Christmas and Sunday*

✿ Hide Ⓝ

MODERN BRITISH • **DESIGN** XX A collaboration between Hedonism Wines and chef Ollie Dabbous; the striking decor is inspired by the park opposite. 'Above' offers only tasting menus while 'Below' is an all-day operation. Both share the same commitment to producing immaculately drafted dishes that emphasise the natural flavours of ingredients.

→ Celeriac, avocado and angelica seed. Slow-roast goose with birch sap and kale. Jasmine and wild pea flower religieuse.

Menu £ 42/95 - Carte £ 42/72

Town plan: 30AL4-d - *85 Piccadilly ✉ W1J 7NB - ⊖ Green Park - ✆ 020 3146 8666 - www.hide.co.uk - Closed 25 December*

✿ Bonhams

MODERN CUISINE • **MINIMALIST** XX Established in 1793, Bonhams is now one of the world's largest fine art and antique auctioneers. Its restaurant is bright, modern and professionally run. Dishes are elegant and delicate and there is real clarity to the flavours. The wine list has also been very thoughtfully compiled by Bonhams' own wine department.

→ Devon crab with bone marrow royale, green apple and horseradish. Saddle of Welsh hogget with smoked pomme purée, artichoke and grelot onions. Gariguette strawberry, rice crème, rhubarb and rose meringue.

Menu £ 42/70

Town plan: 30AL2-n - *101 New Bond St ✉ W1S 1SR - ⊖ Bond Street - ✆ 020 7468 5868 - www.bonhamsrestaurant.com - Closed 2 weeks Christmas, 2 weeks mid-August, Saturday, Sunday, dinner Monday-Thursday and bank holidays*

✿ Gymkhana

INDIAN • **FASHIONABLE** XX If you enjoy Trishna then you'll love Karam Sethi's Gymkhana – that's if you can get a table. Inspired by Colonial India's gymkhana clubs, the interior is full of wonderful detail and plenty of wry touches; ask to sit downstairs. The North Indian dishes have a wonderful richness and depth of flavour.

→ Dosa, Chettinad duck and coconut. Wild muntjac biryani with pomegranate and mint raita. Saffron and pistachio kulfi falooda

Menu £ 25 (weekday lunch) - Carte £ 25/67

Town plan: 30AM3-a - *42 Albemarle St ✉ W1S 4JH - ⊖ Green Park - ✆ 020 3011 5900 (booking essential) - www.gymkhanalondon.com - Closed 1-3 January, 25-27 December and Sunday*

**Don't confuse the classification X with the Stars ✿!
The number of X denotes levels of comfort and service, while Stars are awarded solely for the cooking.**

Hakkasan Mayfair

CHINESE • MINIMALIST XX If coming for lunchtime dim sum then sit on the ground floor; for dinner ask for a table in the moodily lit and altogether sexier basement. The Cantonese cuisine uses top quality produce and can be delicate one minute; robust the next. There are also specialities specific to this branch.

→ Soft shell crab with red chilli. Pan-fried Wagyu beef in spicy Sichuan sauce. Apple and sesame croustillant.

Menu £ 42 (lunch and early dinner)/120 – Carte £ 38/115

Town plan: 30AL3-a – *17 Bruton St ✉ W1J 6QB – ⊖ Green Park – ✆ 020 7907 1888 (booking essential) – www.hakkasan.com – Closed 24-25 December*

Pollen Street Social (Jason Atherton)

CREATIVE • FASHIONABLE XX The restaurant where it all started for Jason Atherton when he went solo. Top quality British produce lies at the heart of the menu and the innovative dishes are prepared with great care and no little skill. The room has plenty of buzz, helped along by the 'dessert bar' and views of the kitchen pass.

→ Slow-cooked Copper Maran egg with turnip purée, parmesan, sage and kombu crumb. Lake District lamb loin & fillet with peas, broad beans and seaweed. Pistachio soufflé with 70% chocolate and vanilla ice cream.

Menu £ 37 (lunch) – Carte £ 64/78

Town plan: 30AM2-c – *8-10 Pollen St ✉ W1S 1NQ – ⊖ Oxford Circus – ✆ 020 7290 7600 (booking essential) – www.pollenstreetsocial.com – Closed Sunday and bank holidays*

Veeraswamy

INDIAN • DESIGN XX It may have opened in 1926 but this celebrated Indian restaurant keeps producing wonderfully authentic and satisfying dishes from all parts of the country; dishes inspired by royal recipes are worth exploring. The room is awash with colour and is run with charm and obvious pride; ask for a window table.

→ Venison mutta kebab with tamarind glaze. Goan roast duck vindaloo. Rasmalai with tandoori fruit.

Menu £ 26/45 – Carte £ 40/76

Town plan: 31AN3-t – *Victory House, 99 Regent St ✉ W1B 4RS – Entrance on Swallow St. – ⊖ Piccadilly Circus – ✆ 020 7734 1401 – www.veeraswamy.com*

Sabor (N) (Nieves Barragán Mohacho)

SPANISH • TAPAS BAR X A truly joyful and authentic tapas bar. Start with the pan con tomate at the ground floor counter. Bookings are only taken for El Asador upstairs, where succulent suckling pig and melt-in-the-mouth octopus are the must-haves. You'll be licking your lips for hours.

→ Pulpo a feira. Segovian suckling pig. Cuajada de turrón with oloroso cream.

Carte £ 24/40

Town plan: 30AM3-p – *35-37 Heddon St ✉ W1B 4BR – ⊖ Oxford Circus – ✆ 020 3319 8130 – www.saborrestaurants.co.uk – Closed 24-26 December, 1-2 January, Sunday dinner and Monday*

Park Chinois

CHINESE • EXOTIC DÉCOR XXX Old fashioned glamour, strikingly rich surroundings and live music combine to great effect at this sumptuously decorated restaurant. The menu traverses the length of China, with dim sum at lunchtimes and afternoon tea at weekends.

Menu £ 26 (lunch) – Carte £ 53/124

Town plan: 30AM3-f – *17 Berkeley St ✉ W1J 8EA – ⊖ Green Park – ✆ 020 3327 8888 (booking essential) – www.parkchinois.com – Closed 25 December*

Scott's

SEAFOOD • FASHIONABLE XXX Scott's is proof that a restaurant can have a long, proud history and still be fashionable, glamorous and relevant. It has a terrific clubby atmosphere and if you're in a two then the counter is a great spot. The choice of prime quality fish and shellfish is impressive.

Carte £ 39/66

Town plan: 30AK3-h – *20 Mount St ✉ W1K 2HE – ⊖ Bond Street – ✆ 020 7495 7309 – www.scotts-restaurant.com – Closed 25-26 December*

Corrigan's Mayfair

MODERN BRITISH • ELEGANT XXX Richard Corrigan's flagship celebrates British and Irish cooking, with game a speciality. The room is comfortable, clubby and quite glamorous and feels as though it has been around for years.

Menu £ 28 (lunch and early dinner) – Carte £ 42/76

Town plan: 30AK3-a – *28 Upper Grosvenor St. ✉ W1K 7EH – ⊖ Marble Arch – ✆ 020 7499 9943 – www.corrigansmayfair.com – Closed 25-26 December, 1 January, Saturday lunch, Sunday and bank holidays*

Ella Canta (N)

MEXICAN • DESIGN XXX Martha Ortiz is one of Mexico's most celebrated chefs and she now has a London outpost here at the InterContinental. The cooking draws on themes of history, philosophy and fantasy to create dishes that are colourful, creative and original. Great drinks list and charming staff.

Menu £ 25 (weekday lunch) – Carte £ 34/63

Town plan: 30AL4-k – *InterContinental London Park Lane Hotel, 1 Hamilton Pl, Park Ln ✉ W1J 7QY – ⊖ Hyde Park Corner – ✆ 020 7318 8715 – www.ellacanta.com – Closed Sunday dinner and Monday lunch*

Momo

MOROCCAN • EXOTIC DÉCOR XX An authentic Moroccan atmosphere comes courtesy of the antiques, kilim rugs, Berber artwork, bright fabrics and lanterns – you'll feel you're eating near the souk. Go for the classic dishes: zaalouk, briouats, pigeon pastilla, and tagines with mountains of fluffy couscous.

Menu £ 20 (weekday lunch) – Carte £ 32/49

Town plan: 30AM3-n – *25 Heddon St. ✉ W1B 4BH – ⊖ Oxford Circus – ✆ 020 7434 4040 – www.momoresto.com – Closed 25 December*

Sketch (The Gallery)

MODERN CUISINE • TRENDY XX The striking 'Gallery' has a smart look from India Mahdavi and artwork from David Shrigley. At dinner the room transmogrifies from art gallery to fashionable restaurant, with a menu that mixes the classic, the modern and the esoteric.

Carte £ 43/86

Town plan: 30AM2-h – *9 Conduit St ✉ W1S 2XG – ⊖ Oxford Circus – ✆ 020 7659 4500 (booking essential) – www.sketch.london – dinner only – Closed 25 December and 1 January*

Bentley's

SEAFOOD • TRADITIONAL DÉCOR XX This hundred year old seafood institution comes in two parts: upstairs is the more formal and smartly dressed Grill, with seafood classics and grilled meats; on the ground floor is the Oyster Bar which is more fun and does a good fish pie.

Carte £ 39/93

Town plan: 31AN3-c – *11-15 Swallow St. ✉ W1B 4DG – ⊖ Piccadilly Circus – ✆ 020 7734 4756 – www.bentleys.org – Closed 25 December, 1 January, Saturday lunch and Sunday*

Black Roe

WORLD CUISINE • TRENDY XX Poke, made famous in Hawaii, is the star here. You can choose traditional ahi over the sushi rice or something more original like scallop and octopus. Other options include dishes with assorted Pacific Rim influences, along with others cooked on the Kiawe wood grill.

Carte £ 26/66

Town plan: 30AM2-b - *4 Mill St ✉ W1S 2AX - ⊖ Oxford Circus - ✆ 020 3794 8448 - www.blackroe.com - Closed Sunday*

Bombay Bustle Ⓝ

INDIAN • FASHIONABLE XX Tiffin tin carriers on Mumbai's railways inspired Jamavar's second London restaurant. A charming train theme runs through it; the ground floor is the livelier; downstairs is more 'first class'. Before a curry, biryani or dish from the tandoor order some tasting plates, made from family recipes.

Menu £ 16 (lunch) - Carte £ 29/42

Town plan: 30AM2-k - *29 Maddox St ✉ W1S 2PA - ⊖ Oxford Circus - ✆ 020 7290 4470 - www.bombaybustle.com - Closed 25-25 December and 1-2 January*

Chucs Bar and Grill

ITALIAN • ELEGANT XX Like the shop to which it's attached, Chucs caters for those who summer on the Riviera and are not afraid of showing it. It's decked out like a yacht and the concise but not inexpensive menu offers classic Mediterranean dishes.

Carte £ 36/69

Town plan: 30AM3-r - *30b Dover St. ✉ W1S 4NB - ⊖ Green Park - ✆ 020 3763 2013 (booking essential) - www.chucsrestaurant.com - Closed 25-26 and dinner 24 and 31 December, 1 January and bank holidays*

Goodman Mayfair

MEATS AND GRILLS • BRASSERIE XX A worthy attempt at recreating a New York steakhouse; all leather and wood and macho swagger. Beef is dry or wet-aged in-house and comes with a choice of four sauces; rib-eye the speciality.

Carte £ 31/107

Town plan: 30AM2-e - *26 Maddox St ✉ W1S 1QH - ⊖ Oxford Circus - ✆ 020 7499 3776 (booking essential) - www.goodmanrestaurants.com - Closed Sunday and bank holidays*

Heddon Street Kitchen

MODERN CUISINE • BRASSERIE XX Gordon Ramsay's follow up to Bread Street is spread over two floors and is all about all-day dining: breakfast covers all tastes, there's weekend brunch, and an à la carte offering an appealing range of European dishes executed with palpable care.

Menu £ 23 (lunch and early dinner) - Carte £ 26/63

Town plan: 30AM3-y - *3-9 Heddon St ✉ W1B 4BE - ⊖ Oxford Circus - ✆ 020 7592 1212 - www.gordonramsayrestaurants.com*

Indian Accent Ⓝ

INDIAN • ELEGANT XX The third branch, after New Delhi and NYC, is set over two levels, with a bright, fresh look. The kitchen takes classic dishes from all regions of India and blends them with European and Asian notes and techniques. The resulting dishes are colourful, sophisticated and full of flavour.

Menu £ 30/55

Town plan: 30AM3-c - *16 Albemarle St ✉ W1S 4HW - ⊖ Green Park - ✆ 020 7629 9802 - www.indianaccent.com - Closed Christmas, New Year, Sunday and bank holidays*

Jamavar

INDIAN • EXOTIC DÉCOR XX Leela Palaces & Resorts are behind this smartly dressed Indian restaurant. The menus, including vegetarian, look to all parts of India, with a bias towards the north. The 'small plates' section includes Malabar prawns, and kid goat shami kebab; from the tandoor the stone bass tikka is a must; and biryanis are also good.

Menu £ 24 (lunch and early dinner) – Carte £ 32/54

Town plan: 30AL3-v – *8 Mount St ✉ W1K 3NF – ⊖ Bond Street – ✆ 020 7499 1800 (booking essential at dinner) – www.jamavarrestaurants.com – Closed 25-26 December, 1 January and Sunday*

Jean-Georges at The Connaught

MODERN CUISINE • INTIMATE XX Low-slung bespoke marble-topped tables and comfy sofas make this room at the front of The Connaught hotel somewhere between a salon and a restaurant. It has something for all tastes, from Asian-inspired dishes to fish and chips. The truffle-infused pizza is a best seller.

Carte £ 57/88

Town plan: 30AL3-e – *Connaught Hotel, Carlos Pl. ✉ W1K 2AL – ⊖ Bond Street – ✆ 020 7107 8861 – www.the-connaught.co.uk*

Nobu

JAPANESE • FASHIONABLE XX Nobu restaurants are now all over the world but this was Europe's first and opened in 1997. It retains a certain exclusivity and is buzzy and fun. The menu is an innovative blend of Japanese cuisine with South American influences.

Carte £ 24/73

Town plan: 30AL4-c – *Metropolitan by COMO Hotel, 19 Old Park Ln ✉ W1Y 1LB – ⊖ Hyde Park Corner – ✆ 020 7447 4747 (booking essential) – www.noburestaurants.com – Closed 25 December*

Nobu Berkeley St

JAPANESE • FASHIONABLE XX This branch of the glamorous chain is more of a party animal than its elder sibling at The Metropolitan. Start with cocktails then head upstairs for Japanese food with South American influences; try dishes from the wood-fired oven.

Carte £ 30/92

Town plan: 30AM3-b – *15 Berkeley St. ✉ W1J 8DY – ⊖ Green Park – ✆ 020 7290 9222 (booking essential) – www.noburestaurants.com – Closed 25 December*

Sakagura

JAPANESE • EXOTIC DÉCOR XX A contemporary styled Japanese restaurant part owned by the Japan Centre and Gekkeikan, a sake manufacturer. Along with an impressive drinks list is an extensive menu covering a variety of styles; highlights include the skewers cooked on the robata charcoal grill.

Carte £ 21/53

Town plan: 30AM3-s – *8 Heddon St ✉ W1B 4BS – ⊖ Oxford Circus – ✆ 020 3405 7230 – www.sakaguralondon.com – Closed 25 December*

Sexy Fish

SEAFOOD • DESIGN XX Everyone will have an opinion about the name but what's indisputable is that this is a very good looking restaurant, with works by Frank Gehry and Damien Hirst, and a stunning ceiling by Michael Roberts. The fish comes with various Asian influences but don't ignore the meat dishes like the beef rib skewers.

Carte £ 44/58

Town plan: 30AL3-w – *Berkeley Sq. ✉ W1J 6BR – ⊖ Green Park – ✆ 020 3764 2000 – www.sexyfish.com – Closed 25-26 December*

StreetXO

CREATIVE • TRENDY XX The menu at Madrid chef David Muñoz's London outpost is inspired by European, Asian and even South American cuisines. Dishes are characterised by explosions of colour and a riot of different flavours, techniques and textures. The quasi-industrial feel of the basement room adds to the moody, noisy atmosphere.

Menu £ 25 (weekday lunch) - Carte £ 45/68

Town plan: 30AM3-t - *15 Old Burlington St ✉ W1S 2JL - ⊖ Oxford Circus - ✆ 020 3096 7555 - www.streetxo.com - Closed 23-26 December, 1 January and Monday lunch*

Theo Randall

ITALIAN • CLASSIC DÉCOR XX There's an attractive honesty about Theo Randall's Italian food, which is made using the very best of ingredients. The somewhat corporate nature of the hotel in which it is located can sometimes seem a little at odds with the rustic style of food but the room is bright, relaxed and well run.

Menu £ 29 (weekday lunch) - Carte £ 35/63

Town plan: 30AL4-k - *InterContinental London Park Lane Hotel, 1 Hamilton Pl, Park Ln ✉ W1J 7QY - ⊖ Hyde Park Corner - ✆ 020 7318 8747 - www.theorandall.com - Closed 25 December*

Tokimeitē

JAPANESE • CHIC XX Yoshihiro Murata, one of Japan's most celebrated chefs, teamed up with the Zen-Noh group to open this good looking, intimate restaurant on two floors. Their aim is to promote Wagyu beef in Europe, so it's understandably the star of the show.

Menu £ 25 (lunch) - Carte £ 40/106

Town plan: 30AM3-k - *23 Conduit St ✉ W1S 2XS - ⊖ Oxford Circus - ✆ 020 3826 4411 - www.tokimeite.com - Closed Sunday and bank holidays*

Wild Honey

MODERN CUISINE • DESIGN XX The elegant wood panelling and ornate plasterwork may say 'classic Mayfair institution' but the personable service team keep the atmosphere enjoyably easy-going. The kitchen uses quality British ingredients and a French base but is not afraid of the occasional international flavour.

Menu £ 35 (lunch and early dinner) - Carte £ 33/59

Town plan: 30AM2-w - *12 St George St. ✉ W1S 2FB - ⊖ Oxford Circus - ✆ 020 7758 9160 - www.wildhoneyrestaurant.co.uk - Closed 25-26 December, 1 January, Sunday and bank holidays except Good Friday*

Le Boudin Blanc

FRENCH • RUSTIC X Appealing, lively French bistro in Shepherd Market, spread over two floors. Satisfying French classics and country cooking are the draws, along with authentic Gallic service. Good value lunch menu.

Menu £ 19 (lunch) - Carte £ 28/57

Town plan: 30AL4-q - *5 Trebeck St ✉ W1J 7LT - ⊖ Green Park - ✆ 020 7499 3292 - www.boudinblanc.co.uk - Closed 24-26 December and 1 January*

Little Social

FRENCH • BISTRO X Jason Atherton's lively French bistro, opposite his Pollen Street Social restaurant, has a clubby feel and an appealing, deliberately worn look. Service is breezy and capable and the food is mostly classic with the odd modern twist.

Menu £ 25 - Carte £ 38/65

Town plan: 30AM2-r - *5 Pollen St ✉ W1S 1NE - ⊖ Oxford Circus - ✆ 020 7870 3730 (booking essential) - www.littlesocial.co.uk - Closed Sunday and bank holidays*

Kitty Fisher's

MODERN CUISINE • BISTRO Warm, intimate and unpretentious restaurant – the star of the show is the wood grill which gives the dishes added depth. Named after an 18C courtesan, presumably in honour of the profession for which Shepherd Market was once known.

Carte £ 36/70

Town plan: 30AL4-s – *10 Shepherd Mkt ✉ W1J 7QF – ⊖ Green Park – ✆ 020 3302 1661 (booking essential) – www.kittyfishers.com – Closed Christmas, New Year, Easter, Sunday and bank holidays*

Magpie Ⓝ

MODERN CUISINE • FASHIONABLE From the same team as Hackney's Pidgin. Sharing plates using an eclectic array of ingredients make for some original flavour pairings. This former gallery has an open feel and benefits from a large glass roof at the back; ask for one of the side booths.

Menu £ 25 (lunch) – Carte £ 25/38

Town plan: 30AM3-x – *10 Heddon St ✉ W1B 4BX – ⊖ Oxford Circus – ✆ 020 3903 9096 – www.magpie-london.com – Closed Sunday dinner and bank holidays*

Mayfair Chippy

FISH AND CHIPS • VINTAGE There are chippies, and there is the Mayfair Chippy. Here you can get cocktails, wine, oysters, starters and dessert but, most significantly, the 'Mayfair Classic' – fried cod or haddock with chips, tartar sauce, mushy peas and curry sauce.

Carte £ 19/38

Town plan: 30AK2-e – *14 North Audley St ✉ W1K 6WE – ⊖ Marble Arch – ✆ 020 7741 2233 – www.eatbrit.com – Closed 25 December and 1 January*

Claridge's

GRAND LUXURY • CLASSIC Claridge's has a long, illustrious history dating back to 1812 and this iconic and very British hotel has been a favourite of the royal family over generations. Its most striking decorative feature is its art deco. The hotel also moves with the times, with its modern restaurant Fera proving a perfect fit.

197 rooms – †£ 510/1140 ††£ 510/1140 – ☕ £ 34 – 62 suites

Town plan: 30AL2-c – *Brook St ✉ W1K 4HR – ⊖ Bond Street – ✆ 020 7629 8860 – www.claridges.co.uk*

✿ **Fera at Claridge's** – See restaurant listing

Connaught

GRAND LUXURY • CLASSIC One of London's most famous hotels, the Connaught offers effortless serenity and exclusivity and an elegant British feel. All the luxurious bedrooms come with large marble bathrooms and butler service; some overlook a small oriental garden, others look down onto mews houses. Refined French cooking in Hélène Darroze; something for everyone in all-day Jean-Georges.

121 rooms – †£ 420/990 ††£ 420/990 – ☕ £ 38 – 25 suites

Town plan: 30AL3-e – *Carlos Pl. ✉ W1K 2AL – ⊖ Bond Street – ✆ 020 7499 7070 – www.the-connaught.co.uk*

✿✿ **Hélène Darroze at The Connaught** • **Jean-Georges at The Connaught** – See restaurant listing

Dorchester

GRAND LUXURY • CLASSIC One of the capital's iconic properties offering every possible facility and exemplary levels of service. The striking marbled and pillared promenade provides an elegant backdrop for afternoon tea. Bedrooms are eminently comfortable; some overlook Hyde Park. The Grill is for all things British; Alain Ducasse waves Le Tricolore; China Tang celebrates the cuisine of the Orient.

250 rooms – †£ 485/805 ††£ 580/900 – ☕ £ 45 – 51 suites

Town plan: 30AK4-a – *Park Ln ✉ W1K 1QA – ⊖ Hyde Park Corner – ✆ 020 7629 8888 – www.dorchestercollection.com*

✿✿✿ **Alain Ducasse at The Dorchester** – See restaurant listing

Four Seasons

GRAND LUXURY • MODERN It raised the bar for luxury hotels: a striking red and black lobby sets the scene, while the spacious, sumptuous and serenely coloured bedrooms have a rich, contemporary look and boast every conceivable comfort. Italian influenced menu in Amaranto, with its outdoor terrace. Great views from the stunning rooftop spa.

193 rooms – †£ 480/930 ††£ 480/930 – ☕ £ 30 – 33 suites

Town plan: 30AL4-v – *Hamilton Pl, Park Ln* ✉ *W1J 7DR* – ⊖ *Hyde Park Corner* – ✆ *020 7499 0888* – *www.fourseasons.com/london*

45 Park Lane

LUXURY • MODERN It was the original site of the Playboy Club and used to be a car showroom, before being reborn as The Dorchester's sister hotel. The bedrooms, all with views over Hyde Park, are wonderfully sensual and the marble bathrooms are beautiful.

46 rooms – †£ 650/1030 ††£ 650/1030 – ☕ £ 38 – 10 suites

Town plan: 30AK4-r – *45 Park Ln* ✉ *W1K 1PN* – ⊖ *Hyde Park Corner* – ✆ *020 7493 4545* – *www.45parklane.com*

The Beaumont

LUXURY • ART DÉCO From a 1926 former garage, restaurateurs Chris Corbin and Jeremy King fashioned their first hotel; art deco inspired, it's stunning, stylish and exudes understated luxury. The attention to detail is exemplary, from the undeniably masculine bedrooms to the lively, cool cocktail bar and busy brasserie.

73 rooms – †£ 450/605 ††£ 450/605 – ☕ £ 32 – 10 suites

Town plan: 30AK2-x – *Brown Hart Gdns* ✉ *W1K 6TF* – ⊖ *Bond Street* – ✆ *020 7499 1001* – *www.thebeaumont.com*

Brown's

LUXURY • CLASSIC Opened in 1837 by James Brown, Lord Byron's butler. This urbane and very British hotel with an illustrious past offers a swish bar with Terence Donovan prints, bedrooms in neutral hues and a classic English sitting room for afternoon tea. Heinz Beck oversees the Italian food in the wood-panelled dining room.

115 rooms – †£ 480/1000 ††£ 480/1000 – ☕ £ 36 – 33 suites

Town plan: 30AM3-d – *33 Albemarle St* ✉ *W1S 4BP* – ⊖ *Green Park* – ✆ *020 7493 6020* – *www.roccofortehotels.com*

Westbury

BUSINESS • MODERN As stylish now as when it opened in the 1950s. Smart, comfortable bedrooms with terrific art deco inspired suites. Elegant, iconic Polo bar and bright, fresh sushi bar. All the exclusive brands are outside the front door.

225 rooms – †£ 279/779 ††£ 279/779 – ☕ £ 26 – 13 suites

Town plan: 30AM3-z – *37 Conduit St* ✉ *W1S 2YF* – ⊖ *Bond Street* – ✆ *020 7629 7755* – *www.westburymayfair.com*

✿ **Alyn Williams at The Westbury** – See restaurant listing

Chesterfield

TOWNHOUSE • CLASSIC There's an assuredly English feel to this Georgian house. The discreet lobby leads to a clubby bar and wood panelled library. Individually decorated bedrooms, with some antique pieces. Intimate and pretty restaurant.

107 rooms – †£ 195/390 ††£ 220/510 – ☕ £ 22 – 4 suites

Town plan: 30AL3-f – *35 Charles St* ✉ *W1J 5EB* – ⊖ *Green Park* – ✆ *020 7491 2622* – *www.chesterfieldmayfair.com*

Flemings

TOWNHOUSE • CONTEMPORARY Made up of a series of conjoined townhouses, this hotel was re-launched in 2016 following a comprehensive refit. Bedrooms are very pleasantly decorated and the keen team provide charming and attentive service.

129 rooms – †£ 200/300 ††£ 250/500 – ☕ £ 20 – 10 suites

Town plan: 30AL4-m – *7-12 Half Moon St ✉ W1J 7BH – ⊖ Green Park – ✆ 020 7499 0000 – www.flemings-mayfair.co.uk*

Regent's Park and Marylebone

Locanda Locatelli (Giorgio Locatelli)

ITALIAN • FASHIONABLE XXX Giorgio Locatelli's Italian restaurant may be well into its second decade but it still looks as dapper as ever. The service is smooth and the room was designed with conviviality in mind. The hugely appealing menu covers all regions; unfussy presentation and superb ingredients allow natural flavours to shine.

→ Burrata with blood orange, black olive and fennel bread crisps. Tagliatelle with kid goat ragu, chilli and pecorino. Liquorice semifreddo with lime jelly, caviar and Branca Menta sauce.

Carte £ 49/74

Town plan: 29AJ2-r – *8 Seymour St. ✉ W1H 7JZ – ⊖ Marble Arch – ✆ 020 7935 9088 – www.locandalocatelli.com – Closed 24-26 December and 1 January*

Roganic (N)

CREATIVE BRITISH • MINIMALIST XX Simon Rogan's London outpost is certainly not a copy of his L'Enclume restaurant in the Lake District but is intended to deliver elements of it. Much of the produce, however, comes from their farm in Cartmel. The cuisine style – which uses plenty of techniques including pickling and curing – will leave you feeling closer to nature.

→ Cured mackerel with radishes and sorrel sauce. Cornish lamb with broad beans and courgettes. Caramelised apple tart with Douglas fir ice cream.

Menu £ 35/95 – tasting menu only

Town plan: 30AK1-d – *5-7 Blandford St ✉ W1U 3DB – ⊖ Bond Street – ✆ 020 3370 6260 (booking essential) – www.roganic.uk – Closed 22 December-7 January, 25 August-2 September, Sunday and Monday*

Texture (Agnar Sverrisson)

CREATIVE • DESIGN XX Technically skilled but light and invigorating cooking from an Icelandic chef-owner, who uses ingredients from his homeland. Bright restaurant with high ceiling and popular adjoining champagne bar. Pleasant service from keen staff, ready with a smile.

→ Salmon gravlax with Oscietra caviar, mustard and sorrel. Lightly salted cod with avocado, Jersey Royals, romanesco and wild garlic. Icelandic skyr with vanilla, Gariguette strawberries and rye bread crumbs.

Menu £ 29/95 – Carte £ 70/95

Town plan: 30AK2-p – *34 Portman St ✉ W1H 7BY – ⊖ Marble Arch – ✆ 020 7224 0028 – www.texture-restaurant.co.uk – Closed 2 weeks August, 1 week Easter, Christmas-New Year, Sunday, Monday and lunch Tuesday-Wednesday*

Portland

MODERN CUISINE • INTIMATE X The look is just the right side of austere, service is knowledgeable and wine is given equal billing to the food. One glance at the menu and you know you'll eat well: it changes daily and the combinations just sound right. The kitchen trusts the quality of the ingredients and lets natural flavours shine.

→ Asparagus, frozen egg yolk, nettles and ricotta gnudi. Gloucester Old Spot loin with braised treviso and lardo with quince. Bergamot custard, Douglas fir ice cream and burnt meringue.

Menu £ 30/75 – Carte dinner £ 43/61

Town plan: 30AM1-p – *113 Great Portland St ✉ W1W 6QQ – ⊖ Great Portland Street – ✆ 020 7436 3261 (booking essential) – www.portlandrestaurant.co.uk – Closed 23 December-3 January and Sunday*

Trishna (Karam Sethi)

INDIAN • NEIGHBOURHOOD A double-fronted, modern Indian restaurant dressed in an elegant, understated style. The coast of southwest India provides the influences and the food is vibrant, satisfying and executed with care – the tasting menus provide a good all-round experience, and much thought has gone into the matching wines.

→ Aloo tokri chaat. Dorset brown crab with butter, pepper, chilli and garlic. Baked yoghurt with apricot chutney.

Menu £ 28/65 – Carte £ 32/59

Town plan: 30AK1-r – *15-17 Blandford St. ✉ W1U 3DG – ⊖ Baker Street – ✆ 020 7935 5624 – www.trishnalondon.com – Closed 25-27 December and 1-3 January*

Picture Fitzrovia

MODERN BRITISH • SIMPLE An ex Arbutus and Wild Honey triumvirate created this cool, great value restaurant. The look may be a little stark but the delightful staff add warmth. The small plates are vibrant and colourful, and the flavours are assured.

Menu £ 23 (lunch) – Carte £ 23/33

Town plan: 30AM1-t – *110 Great Portland St. ✉ W1W 6PQ – ⊖ Oxford Circus – ✆ 020 7637 7892 – www.picturerestaurant.co.uk – Closed Sunday and bank holidays*

Orrery

MODERN CUISINE • NEIGHBOURHOOD The most recent redecoration left this comfortable restaurant, located in what were converted stables from the 19C, looking lighter and more contemporary; the bar and terrace are also smarter. Expect quite elaborate, modern European cooking, strong on presentation and with the occasional twist.

Menu £ 25/59

Town plan: 18Q4-a – *55 Marylebone High St ✉ W1U 5RB – ⊖ Regent's Park – ✆ 020 7616 8000 (booking essential) – www.orrery-restaurant.co.uk*

Les 110 de Taillevent

FRENCH • ELEGANT Ornate high ceilings and deep green banquettes create an elegant look for this French brasserie deluxe, which is more food orientated than the Paris original. It also offers 110 wines by the glass: 4 different pairings for each dish, in 4 different price brackets.

Menu £ 28 (lunch) – Carte £ 38/76

Town plan: 30AL2-f – *16 Cavendish Sq ✉ W1G 9DD – ⊖ Oxford Circus – ✆ 020 3141 6016 – www.les-110-taillevent-london.com*

Chiltern Firehouse

WORLD CUISINE • FASHIONABLE How appropriate – one of the hottest tickets in town is a converted fire station. The room positively bursts with energy but what makes this celebrity hangout unusual is that the food is rather good. Nuno Mendes' menu is full of vibrant North and South American dishes that are big on flavour.

Carte £ 37/63

Town plan: 30AK1-a – *Chiltern Firehouse Hotel, 1 Chiltern St ✉ WIU 7PA – ⊖ Baker Street – ✆ 020 7073 7676 – www.chilternfirehouse.com*

Fischer's

AUSTRIAN • BRASSERIE An Austrian café and konditorei that summons the spirit of old Vienna, from the owners of The Wolseley et al. Open all day; breakfast is a highlight – the viennoiserie are great. Schnitzels are also good; upgrade to a Holstein.

Carte £ 23/59

Town plan: 30AK1-b – *50 Marylebone High St ✉ W1U 5HN – ⊖ Baker Street – ✆ 020 7466 5501 – www.fischers.co.uk – Closed 25 December*

Lurra

BASQUE • DESIGN XX Its name means 'land' in Basque and reflects their use of the freshest produce, cooked over a charcoal grill. Choose tasty nibbles or sharing plates like 14 year old Galician beef, whole grilled turbot or slow-cooked shoulder of lamb.

Menu £ 25 (weekday lunch) – Carte £ 27/70

Town plan: 29AJ2-c – *9 Seymour Pl ✉ W1H 5BA – ⊖ Marble Arch – ✆ 020 7724 4545 – www.lurra.co.uk – Closed Sunday dinner and Monday lunch*

Meraki

GREEK • FASHIONABLE XX A lively Greek restaurant from the same owners as Roka and Zuma; its name a fitting reference to the passion put into one's work. Contemporary versions of classic Greek dishes; much of the produce is imported from Greece, including the wines.

Menu £ 20 (lunch) – Carte £ 25/60

Town plan: 30AM1-m – *80-82 Great Titchfield St ✉ W1W 7QT – ⊖ Goodge Street – ✆ 020 7305 7686 – www.meraki-restaurant.com – Closed Christmas and Sunday dinner*

The Providores

CREATIVE • TRENDY XX Tables and tapas are shared in the buzzing ground floor; head to the elegant, slightly more sedate upstairs room for innovative fusion cooking, with ingredients from around the world. New Zealand wine list; charming staff.

Carte £ 36/48

Town plan: 30AK1-y – *109 Marylebone High St. ✉ W1U 4RX – ⊖ Bond Street – ✆ 020 7935 6175 – www.theprovidores.co.uk – Closed Easter, dinner 24 and 31 December and 25-26 December*

Roux at The Landau

FRENCH • ELEGANT XX There's been a change to a more informal style for this restaurant run under the aegis of the Roux organisation – it's now more akin to a modern bistro in looks and atmosphere and is all the better for it. The cooking is classical French and informed by the seasons; shellfish is a highlight.

Menu £ 25 (weekday lunch) – Carte £ 33/71

Town plan: 30AM1-n – *Langham Hotel, 1c Portland Pl., Regent St. ✉ W1B 1JA – ⊖ Oxford Circus – ✆ 020 7965 0165 – www.rouxatthelandau.com – Closed Monday*

Royal China Club

CHINESE • ORIENTAL DÉCOR XX Service is fast-paced and to the point, which is understandable considering how busy this restaurant always is. The large menu offers something for everyone and the lunchtime dim sum is very good; at dinner try their more unusual Cantonese dishes.

Carte £ 35/80

Town plan: 30AK1-c – *40-42 Baker St ✉ W1U 7AJ – ⊖ Baker Street – ✆ 020 7486 3898 – www.royalchinagroup.co.uk – Closed 25-27 December*

Serge et Le Phoque (N)

MODERN CUISINE • DESIGN XX This outpost of the Hong Kong original may be in the Mandrake hotel but decoratively it's quite subdued compared to the rest of the building. Dishes, on the other hand, are quite dramatic; from the Earth, Sea and Land come some fine ingredients partnered with flavours and spices from around the world.

Menu £ 22 (lunch) – Carte £ 18/41

Town plan: 31AN1-r – *Mandrake Hotel, 20-21 Newman St ✉ W1T 1PG – ⊖ Tottenham Court Road – ✆ 020 3146 8880 – www.serge.london – Closed 24-27 December*

Bonnie Gull

SEAFOOD • SIMPLE Sweet Bonnie Gull calls itself a 'seafood shack' – a reference perhaps to its modest beginnings as a pop-up. Start with something from the raw bar then go for classics like Cullen skink, Devon cock crab or fish and chips. There's another branch in Soho.

Carte £ 31/45

Town plan: 30AM1-b – *21a Foley St ✉ W1W 6DS – ⊖ Goodge Street – ✆ 020 7436 0921 (booking essential) – www.bonniegull.com – Closed 25 December-3 January*

Clipstone

MODERN CUISINE • FASHIONABLE Another wonderful neighbourhood spot from the owners of Portland, just around the corner. The sharing menu is a lesson in flavour and originality; choose one charcuterie dish, one from the seasonal vegetable-based section, one main and a dessert. Cocktails and 'on-tap' wine add to the fun.

Menu £ 24 (lunch) – Carte £ 34/40

Town plan: 30AM1-n – *5 Clipstone St ✉ W1W 6BB – ⊖ Great Portland Street – ✆ 020 7637 0871 – www.clipstonerestaurant.co.uk – Closed Christmas, New Year and Sunday*

Dinings

JAPANESE • COSY It's hard not to be charmed by this sweet little Japanese place, with its ground floor counter and basement tables. Its strengths lie with the more creative, contemporary dishes; sharing is recommended but prices can be steep.

Carte £ 25/67

Town plan: 29AH1-c – *22 Harcourt St. ✉ W1H 4HH – ⊖ Edgware Road – ✆ 020 7723 0666 (booking essential) – www.dinings.co.uk – Closed Christmas*

Donostia

BASQUE • TAPAS BAR The two young owners were inspired by the food of San Sebastián to open this pintxos and tapas bar. Sit at the counter for Basque classics like cod with pil-pil sauce, chorizo from the native Kintoa pig and slow-cooked pig's cheeks.

Menu £ 20 (weekday lunch) – Carte £ 20/43

Town plan: 29AJ2-s – *10 Seymour Pl ✉ W1H 7ND – ⊖ Marble Arch – ✆ 020 3620 1845 – www.donostia.co.uk – Closed Christmas, New Year and lunch Sunday-Monday*

Jikoni

INDIAN • ELEGANT Indian tablecloths and colourful cushions create a homely feel at this idiosyncratic restaurant. Born in Kenya of Indian parents and brought up in London, chef Ravinder Bhogal takes culinary inspiration from these sources and more.

Menu £ 20 (weekday lunch) – Carte £ 24/48

Town plan: 30AK1-d – *19-21 Blandford St ✉ W1U 3DH – ⊖ Baker Street – ✆ 020 7034 1988 – www.jikonilondon.com – Closed Monday and lunch Tuesday*

Lima

PERUVIAN • NEIGHBOURHOOD Lima is one of those restaurants that just makes you feel good about life – and that's even without the pisco sours. The Peruvian food at this informal, fun place is the ideal antidote to times of austerity: it's full of punchy, invigorating flavours and fantastically vivid colours.

Menu £ 19 (weekday lunch) – Carte £ 30/59

Town plan: 31AN1-h – *31 Rathbone Pl ✉ W1T 1JH – ⊖ Goodge Street – ✆ 020 3002 2640 – www.limalondongroup.com – Closed 24-26 December, 1 January and bank holidays*

Mac & Wild

SCOTTISH • FRIENDLY The owner of this 'Highland restaurant' is the son of an Ardgay butcher - it is all about their wild venison and top quality game and seafood from Scotland. Don't miss the 'wee plates' like the deliriously addictive haggis pops. There's also a choice of over 100 whiskies.

Carte £ 21/62

Town plan: 30AM1-a - *65 Great Titchfield St ✉ W1W 7PS - ⊖ Oxford Circus - ✆ 020 7637 0510 - www.macandwild.com - Closed Sunday dinner*

Opso

GREEK • NEIGHBOURHOOD A modern Greek restaurant which has proved a good fit for the neighbourhood - and not just because it's around the corner from the Hellenic Centre. It serves small sharing plates that mix the modern with the traditional.

Carte £ 14/55

Town plan: 30AK1-s - *10 Paddington St ✉ W1U 5QL - ⊖ Baker Street - ✆ 020 7487 5088 - www.opso.co.uk - Closed 23 December-3 January*

Picture Marylebone

MODERN BRITISH • DESIGN This follow-up to Picture Fitzrovia hit the ground running. The cleverly created à la carte of flavoursome small plates lists 3 vegetable, 3 fish and 3 meat choices, followed by 3 desserts - choose one from each section.

Menu £ 23 (lunch) - Carte £ 27/33

Town plan: 30AL1-m - *19 New Cavendish St ✉ W1G 9TZ - ⊖ Bond Street - ✆ 020 7935 0058 - www.picturerestaurant.co.uk - Closed Sunday, Monday and bank holidays*

Riding House Café

MODERN CUISINE • RUSTIC It's less a café, more a large, quirkily designed, all-day New York style brasserie and cocktail bar. The small plates have more zing than the main courses. The 'unbookable' side of the restaurant is the more fun part.

Carte £ 25/49

Town plan: 30AM1-k - *43-51 Great Titchfield St ✉ W1W 7PQ - ⊖ Oxford Circus - ✆ 020 7927 0840 - www.ridinghousecafe.co.uk - Closed 25-26 December*

Zoilo

ARGENTINIAN • FRIENDLY It's all about sharing so plonk yourself at the counter and discover Argentina's regional specialities. Typical dishes include braised pig head croquettes or grilled scallops with pork belly, and there's an appealing all-Argentinian wine list.

Menu £ 19 (lunch) - Carte £ 29/53

Town plan: 30AK2-z - *9 Duke St. ✉ W1U 3EG - ⊖ Bond Street - ✆ 020 7486 9699 - www.zoilo.co.uk - Closed Sunday*

The Wigmore N

TRADITIONAL BRITISH • PUB The impressively high ceiling can only mean one thing - this was once a bank. Booths, high tables, a sizeable bar and bold emerald green tones lend a clubby feel to this addendum to The Langham. Classic, hearty British dishes are given an update.

Carte £ 26/40

Town plan: 30AM1-e - *Langham Hotel, 15 Langham Place, Upper Regent St ✉ W1B 1JA - ⊖ Oxford Circus - ✆ 020 7965 0198 - www.the-wigmore.co.uk*

Langham

LUXURY • ELEGANT Was one of Europe's first purpose-built grand hotels when it opened in 1865. Now back to its best, with its famous Palm Court for afternoon tea, its stylish Artesian bar and bedrooms that are not without personality and elegance.

380 rooms - †£ 325/700 ††£ 325/700 - ☕ £ 25 - 31 suites

Town plan: 30AM1-n - *1c Portland Pl, Regent St ✉ W1B 1JA - ⊖ Oxford Circus - ✆ 020 7636 1000 - www.langhamhotels.com/london*

Roux at The Landau • **The Wigmore** - See restaurant listing

Charlotte Street

LUXURY · CONTEMPORARY Stylish interior designed with a charming, understated English feel. Impeccably kept and individually decorated bedrooms. Popular in-house screening room. Colourful restaurant whose terrace spills onto Charlotte Street; grilled meats a highlight.

52 rooms – †£ 276/420 ††£ 480/552 – ☕ £ 18 – 5 suites

Town plan: 31AN1-e – *15 Charlotte St ✉ W1T 1RJ – ⊖ Goodge Street*
– *✆ 020 7806 2000 – www.charlottestreethotel.co.uk*

Chiltern Firehouse

TOWNHOUSE · CONTEMPORARY From Chateau Marmont in LA to The Mercer in New York, André Balazs' hotels are effortlessly cool. For his London entrance, he sympathetically restored and extended a Gothic Victorian fire station. The style comes with an easy elegance; it's an oasis of calm and hardly feels like a hotel at all.

26 rooms ☕ – †£ 460/720 ††£ 560/950 – 12 suites

Town plan: 30AK1-a – *1 Chiltern St ✉ W1U 7PA – ⊖ Baker Street*
– *✆ 020 7073 7676 – www.chilternfirehouse.com*

Chiltern Firehouse – See restaurant listing

Mandrake Ⓝ

LUXURY · DESIGN In a city with so many different hotels, The Mandrake still manages to stand out. It's filled with art and sculpture, has a great bar called Waeska and you can gaze up at the living walls or chill in the greenhouse in Jurema. No two bedrooms are the same but all are striking and luxurious.

33 rooms ☕ – †£ 290/1500 ††£ 330/1500

Town plan: 31AN1-r – *20-21 Newman St ✉ W1T 1PG – ⊖ Tottenham Court Road*
– *✆ 020 3146 7770 – www.themandrake.com*
– *Closed 24-27 December*

Serge et Le Phoque – See restaurant listing

The London Edition

BUSINESS · DESIGN Formerly Berners, a classic Edwardian hotel, strikingly reborn through a partnership between Ian Schrager and Marriott – the former's influence most apparent in the stylish lobby and bar. Ask for a bedroom with a balcony.

173 rooms – †£ 350/765 ††£ 350/765 – ☕ £ 26 – 5 suites

Town plan: 31AN2-b – *10 Berners St ✉ W1T 3NP – ⊖ Tottenham Court Road*
– *✆ 020 7781 0000 – www.editionhotels.com/london*

Sanderson

LUXURY · MINIMALIST Formerly home of Sanderson Textiles, this hotel was designed by Philippe Starck and his influence is still evident, especially in the large lobby. The Purple Bar is dark and moody; the stylish Long Bar has an equally popular terrace. Bedrooms are bright, light, pared-back and crisply decorated.

150 rooms – †£ 265/592 ††£ 265/592 – ☕ £ 22

Town plan: 31AN1-c – *50 Berners St ✉ W1T 3NG – ⊖ Oxford Circus*
– *✆ 020 7300 1400 – www.morganshotelgroup.com*

Zetter Townhouse Marylebone

TOWNHOUSE · ELEGANT Once home to Edward Lear, now a stylish Georgian townhouse full of character. It's crammed with furniture, has a rich red colour scheme and open fires. The comfortable bedrooms are equally quirky and very English in character; the best has a roll-top bath on its rooftop terrace.

24 rooms ☕ – †£ 330/450 ††£ 330/800

Town plan: 29AJ2-b – *28-30 Seymour St ✉ W1H 7JB – ⊖ Marble Arch*
– *✆ 020 7324 4544 – www.thezettertownhouse.com*

Dorset Square

TOWNHOUSE • CONTEMPORARY Having reacquired this Regency townhouse, Firmdale refurbished it fully before reopening it in 2012. It has a contemporary yet intimate feel and visiting MCC members will appreciate the cricketing theme, which even extends to the cocktails in their sweet little basement brasserie.

38 rooms – £ 180/288 £ 270/522

Town plan: 17P4-s – *39-40 Dorset Sq* ✉ *NW1 6QN*
– ⊖ *Marylebone* – ✆ *020 7723 7874*
– *www.firmdalehotels.co.uk*

Durrants

TRADITIONAL • CLASSIC Traditional, privately owned hotel with friendly, longstanding staff. Bedrooms are now brighter in style but still retain a certain English character. Clubby dining room for mix of British classics and lighter, European dishes.

92 rooms – £ 135/195 £ 155/250 – £ 15 – 6 suites

Town plan: 30AK1-e – *26-32 George St* ✉ *W1H 5BJ*
– ⊖ *Bond Street* – ✆ *020 7935 8131*
– *www.durrantshotel.co.uk*

Marble Arch London

TOWNHOUSE • CONTEMPORARY Conveniently located five storey Georgian townhouse, with an impressive original staircase. Bedrooms may be a little compact but they are stylishly designed and well looked after. The breakfast room benefits from having a glass roof.

42 rooms – £ 282/330 £ 300/330 – £ 20

Town plan: 29AJ2-a – *31 Great Cumberland Pl* ✉ *W1H 7TA*
– ⊖ *Marble Arch* – ✆ *020 7258 0777*
– *www.themarblearch.co.uk*

St James's

Ritz Restaurant

MODERN BRITISH • LUXURY XXXXX Executive Chef John Williams MBE and his team take classic dishes, including some Escoffier recipes, and add their own subtle touches of modernity. Needless, to say, the ingredients are luxurious. Thanks to the lavishness of its Louis XVI decoration, there is nowhere grander than The Ritz. The faultless service adds to the experience.

→ Artichoke royale with truffle, pear and Ragstone cheese. Native lobster with broad beans, almond and lemon verbena. Apple mousseline with marigold and buttermilk sorbet.

Menu £ 57/67 – Carte £ 73/123

Town plan: 30AM4-c – *Ritz Hotel, 150 Piccadilly* ✉ *W1J 9BR*
– ⊖ *Green Park* – ✆ *020 7300 2370*
– *www.theritzlondon.com*

Seven Park Place

MODERN CUISINE • COSY XXX 2019 sees William Drabble celebrate 10 years as head chef and it's a rare night if he's not at the stove. He starts with premier ingredients, most of which he sources himself; he then uses classic flavour combinations and tried-and-tested techniques. The gilded 9-table restaurant is intimate and discreet.

→ Lobster tail with cauliflower and truffle butter sauce. Fillet of turbot with chestnut purée and wild mushrooms. Dark chocolate ganache with caramelised banana.

Menu £ 28/95

Town plan: 30AM4-k – *St James's Hotel and Club, 7-8 Park Pl* ✉ *SW1A 1LS*
– ⊖ *Green Park* – ✆ *020 7316 1615 (booking essential)*
– *www.stjameshotelandclub.com* – *Closed Sunday and Monday*

Aquavit

SCANDINAVIAN • BRASSERIE XX Unlike the original in NYC, this Aquavit comes in the form of a warmly lit, relaxed brasserie. The Scandinavian cooking may also be less intricate but it's still immeasurably appealing. Kick things off by heading straight to the smörgåsbord section and some wonderful herring or shrimp.

→ Crab with rye brioche and fennel. Turbot with horseradish, beetroot and Sandefjord sauce. Douglas fir panna cotta with queen's sorbet and sorrel.

Menu £ 24 (lunch) – Carte £ 34/58

Town plan: 31AN3-d – *St James's Market, 1 Carlton St ✉ SW1Y 4QQ – ⊖ Piccadilly Circus – ✆ 020 7024 9848 – www.aquavitrestaurants.com – Closed 23-27 December*

Ikoyi (N) (Jeremy Chan)

CREATIVE • SIMPLE X The somewhat colourless development that is St James's Market is the unlikely setting for one of the most innovative and original restaurants to open in the capital in recent times. The two owners, friends since childhood, have put together a kitchen that uses home-grown ingredients enlivened with flavours from West Africa.

→ Mushroom suya, malted barley and pine. Duck, uda, candied bacon and bitter leaf. Black benne & blackcurrant.

Menu £ 35 (lunch and early dinner)/60 – Carte lunch £ 36/51

Town plan: 31AN3-b – *1 St. James's Market ✉ SW1Y 4AH – ⊖ Piccadilly Circus – ✆ 020 3583 4660 (booking essential) – www.ikoyilondon.com – Closed 25 -26 December, 1 January and Sunday*

Chutney Mary

INDIAN • ELEGANT XXX One of London's pioneering Indian restaurants, set in the heart of St James's. Elegant surroundings feature bold art and Indian artefacts. Spicing is understated, classics are done well, and some regional dishes have been subtly updated.

Menu £ 29 (lunch) – Carte £ 39/70

Town plan: 30AM4-c – *73 St James's St ✉ SW1A 1PH – ⊖ Green Park – ✆ 020 7629 6688 – www.chutneymary.com – Closed 25 December*

The Wolseley

MODERN CUISINE • FASHIONABLE XXX This feels like a grand and glamorous European coffee house, with its pillars and high vaulted ceiling. Appealing menus offer everything from caviar to a hotdog. It's open from early until late and boasts a large celebrity following.

Carte £ 25/76

Town plan: 30AM3-q – *160 Piccadilly ✉ W1J 9EB – ⊖ Green Park – ✆ 020 7499 6996 (booking essential) – www.thewolseley.com*

45 Jermyn St

TRADITIONAL BRITISH • BRASSERIE XX Style and comfort go hand in hand at this bright, contemporary brasserie. The menu is a mix of European and British classics; the beef Wellington and lobster spaghetti are finished off at your table. Sodas, coupes and floats pay tribute to its past as Fortnum's Fountain restaurant.

Menu £ 26 (early dinner) – Carte £ 30/67

Town plan: 31AN3-f – *45 Jermyn St. ✉ SW1 6DN – ⊖ Piccadilly Circus – ✆ 020 7205 4545 – www.45jermynst.com*

Franco's

ITALIAN • TRADITIONAL DÉCOR XX Have an aperitivo in the clubby bar before sitting down to eat at one of London's oldest yet rejuvenated Italian restaurants. The kitchen focuses on the classics and they live up to expectations; the regulars, of whom there are many, all have their favourites.

Menu £ 32 – Carte £ 36/64

Town plan: 30AM3-i – *61 Jermyn St ✉ SW1Y 6LX – ⊖ Green Park – ✆ 020 7499 2211 (booking essential) – www.francoslondon.com – Closed Sunday and bank holidays*

Cafe Murano

ITALIAN • **FASHIONABLE** XX Angela Hartnett and her chef have created an appealing and flexible menu of delicious North Italian delicacies – the lunch menu is very good value. It's certainly no ordinary café and its popularity means pre-booking is essential.

Menu £ 23 (lunch and early dinner) – Carte £ 30/42

Town plan: 30AM4-m – *33 St. James's St ✉ SW1A 1HD – ⊖ Green Park – ✆ 020 3371 5559 (booking essential) – www.cafemurano.co.uk – Closed Sunday dinner*

Ginza Onodera

JAPANESE • **ELEGANT** XX Re-fitted and re-launched in 2017 on the site of what was Matsuri for over 20 years. A staircase leads down to the smart restaurant and the three counters: for sushi, teppanyaki and the robata grill. The emphasis is on traditional Japanese cuisine and top-end ingredients.

Menu £ 23 (lunch) – Carte £ 29/70

Town plan: 31AN4-w – *15 Bury St ✉ SW1Y 6AL – ⊖ Green Park – ✆ 020 7839 1101 – www.onodera-group.com – Closed 25 December and 1 January*

Portrait

MODERN CUISINE • **CONTEMPORARY DÉCOR** XX Set on the top floor of National Portrait Gallery with views of local landmarks. Carefully prepared modern European food; dishes are sometimes created in celebration of current exhibitions. Good value pre-theatre and weekend set menus.

Menu £ 20/33 – Carte £ 37/87

Town plan: 31AP3-n – *National Portrait Gallery (3rd floor), St Martin's Pl. ✉ WC2H 0HE – ⊖ Charing Cross – ✆ 020 7312 2490 (booking essential) – www.npg.org.uk/portraitrestaurant – lunch only and dinner Thursday-Saturday – Closed 24-26 December*

Quaglino's

MODERN CUISINE • **DESIGN** XX This colourful, glamorous restaurant manages to be cavernous and cosy at the same time, with live music and a late night bar adding a certain sultriness to proceedings. The kitchen specialises in contemporary brasserie-style food.

Menu £ 33 – Carte £ 36/52

Town plan: 30AM4-j – *16 Bury St ✉ SW1Y 6AJ – ⊖ Green Park – ✆ 020 7930 6767 – www.quaglinos-restaurant.co.uk – Closed Easter Monday and Sunday dinner*

Sake No Hana

JAPANESE • **MINIMALIST** XX A modern Japanese restaurant within a Grade II listed '60s edifice – and proof that you can occasionally find good food at the end of an escalator. As with the great cocktails, the menu is best enjoyed when shared with a group.

Menu £ 34 (lunch and early dinner)/45 – Carte £ 39/123

Town plan: 30AM4-n – *23 St James's ✉ SW1A 1HA – ⊖ Green Park – ✆ 020 7925 8988 – www.sakenohana.com – Closed 25-26 December, Sunday and bank holiday Mondays*

Scully (N)

WORLD CUISINE • **FRIENDLY** X The eponymous chef-owner's travels and family heritage inform his style of food. The small plates feature an array of international influences and the bold, diverse flavours give them an appealing vitality. The kitchen makes good use of the shelves of pickles and spices.

Carte £ 21/46

Town plan: 31AN3-r – *4 St James's Market ✉ SW1Y 4AH – ⊖ Piccadilly Circus – ✆ 020 3911 6840 (booking essential) – www.scullyrestaurant.com – Closed dinner Sunday and bank holidays*

Ritz

GRAND LUXURY · CLASSIC Opened in 1906 as a fine example of Louis XVI architecture and decoration, The Ritz is one of London's most celebrated hotels. The Palm Court is famed for its afternoon tea and the Rivoli Bar is beautiful. Lavishly appointed bedrooms are constantly being refreshed and refurbished while respecting the hotel's heritage; many overlook the park.

136 rooms – £ 445/1200 £ 445/1200 – £ 40 – 24 suites

Town plan: 30AM4-c – *150 Piccadilly* ✉ *W1J 9BR* – *Green Park* – *020 7493 8181* – *www.theritzlondon.com*

Ritz Restaurant – See restaurant listing

Haymarket

LUXURY · PERSONALISED Housed in a John Nash Regency building, this hotel not only boasts a great location but is stylishly decorated with works of art and sculpture. Large, comfortable bedrooms come in soothing colours and there's an impressive basement pool. Brumus restaurant a good choice for pre-theatre dining.

50 rooms – £ 330/650 £ 330/650 – £ 18 – 3 suites

Town plan: 31AP3-x – *1 Suffolk Pl.* ✉ *SW1Y 4HX* – *Piccadilly Circus* – *020 7470 4000* – *www.haymarkethotel.com*

Sofitel London St James

LUXURY · ELEGANT Great location for this international hotel in a Grade II former bank. The triple-glazed bedrooms are classically styled and the bar was inspired by Coco Chanel; the lounge suggests an English rose garden. Balcon is a grand brasserie occupying the former banking hall.

183 rooms – £ 360/680 £ 360/700 – £ 22 – 18 suites

Town plan: 31AP3-a – *6 Waterloo Pl.* ✉ *SW1Y 4AN* – *Piccadilly Circus* – *020 7747 2200* – *www.sofitelstjames.com*

Stafford

LUXURY · ELEGANT Styles itself as a 'country house in the city'; its bedrooms are divided between the main house, converted 18C stables and a more modern mews. The legendary American bar is certainly worth a visit.

107 rooms – £ 348/678 £ 390/720 – £ 32 – 15 suites

Town plan: 30AM4-u – *16-18 St James's Pl.* ✉ *SW1A 1NJ* – *Green Park* – *020 7493 0111* – *www.thestaffordlondon.com*

Dukes

TOWNHOUSE · CLASSIC The wonderfully located Dukes has been steadily updating its image over the last few years, despite being over a century old. Bedrooms are now fresh and uncluttered and the atmosphere less starchy. GBR restaurant offers an all-day menu of British dishes and also serves afternoon tea.

90 rooms – £ 276/540 £ 276/540 – £ 24 – 6 suites

Town plan: 30AM4-f – *35 St James's Pl.* ✉ *SW1A 1NY* – *Green Park* – *020 7491 4840* – *www.dukeshotel.com*

St James's Hotel and Club

BUSINESS · MODERN 1890s house, formerly a private club, in a wonderfully central yet quiet location. Modern, boutique-style interior with over 300 European works of art from the '20s to the '50s. Fine finish to the compact but well-equipped bedrooms.

60 rooms – £ 340 £ 340/620 – £ 23 – 10 suites

Town plan: 30AM4-k – *7-8 Park Pl.* ✉ *SW1A 1LS* – *Green Park* – *020 7316 1600* – *www.stjameshotelandclub.com*

Seven Park Place – See restaurant listing

Soho

Yauatcha Soho

CHINESE • DESIGN XX 2019 is its 15th birthday but it still manages to feel fresh and contemporary, with its bright ground floor and moody basement, featuring low banquettes, an aquarium bar and a star-lit ceiling. Dishes are colourful with strong flavours and excellent texture contrasts; dim sum is the highlight – try the venison puff.

→ Scallop shu mai. Stir-fried rib-eye of beef. Chocolate pebble.

Carte £ 25/65

Town plan: 31AN2-k – *15 Broadwick St ✉ W1F 0DL – ⊖ Tottenham Court Road – ✆ 020 7494 8888 – www.yauatcha.com – Closed 25 December*

Barrafina

SPANISH • TAPAS BAR X In 2016 the original Barrafina moved to this brighter, roomier site fashioned out of what was previously a part of Quo Vadis restaurant. Dishes burst with flavour – do order some dishes from the blackboard specials – the staff are fun and the L-shaped counter fills up quickly, so be prepared to wait.

→ Ham croquetas. Chorizo, potato and watercress. Santiago tart.

Carte £ 20/40

Town plan: 31AP2-v – *26-27 Dean St ✉ W1D 3LL – ⊖ Tottenham Court Road – ✆ 020 7440 1456 (bookings not accepted) – www.barrafina.co.uk – Closed bank holidays*

Social Eating House

MODERN CUISINE • FASHIONABLE X The coolest joint in Jason Atherton's stable comes with distressed walls, moody lighting and a laid-back vibe – it also has a terrific speakeasy-style bar upstairs. The 'Sampler' menu is a good way of experiencing the full breadth of the kitchen's skill at producing dishes with punchy, well-judged flavours.

→ Truffled Royal Legbar egg, Iberico de Bellota with Jerusalem artichoke. Slow-cooked rump of salt marsh lamb with olive oil mash, pickled turnips and sauce niçoise. Peanut butter parfait with cherry sorbet, almond and griottine cherry.

Menu £ 27/36 – Carte £ 49/60

Town plan: 31AN2-t – *58 Poland St ✉ W1F 7NR – ⊖ Oxford Circus – ✆ 020 7993 3251 – www.socialeatinghouse.com – Closed Christmas, Sunday and bank holidays*

Brasserie Zédel

FRENCH • BRASSERIE XX A grand French brasserie, which is all about inclusivity and accessibility, in a bustling subterranean space restored to its original art deco glory. Expect a roll-call of classic French dishes and some very competitive prices.

Menu £ 11/20 – Carte £ 18/43

Town plan: 31AN3-q – *20 Sherwood St ✉ W1F 7ED – ⊖ Piccadilly Circus – ✆ 020 7734 4888 – www.brasseriezedel.com – Closed 25 December*

Bao

ASIAN • SIMPLE X There are some things in life worth queueing for – and that includes the delicious eponymous buns here at this simple, great value Taiwanese operation. The classic bao and the confit pork bao are standouts, along with 'small eats' like trotter nuggets. There's also another Bao in Windmill St.

Carte £ 17/27

Town plan: 31AN2-f – *53 Lexington St ✉ W1F 9AS – ⊖ Tottenham Court Road – ✆ 020 3011 1632 (bookings not accepted) – www.baolondon.com – Closed 24-26 December, 1 January and Sunday dinner*

Copita

SPANISH • TAPAS BAR X Perch on one of the high stools or stay standing and get stuck into the daily menu of small, colourful and tasty dishes. Staff add to the atmosphere and everything on the Spanish wine list comes by the glass or copita.

Carte £ 20/41

Town plan: 31AN2-h - *27 D'Arblay St ✉ W1F 8EP - ⊖ Oxford Circus - ☎ 020 7287 7797 (bookings not accepted) - www.copita.co.uk - Closed Sunday and bank holidays*

Hoppers

SOUTH INDIAN • SIMPLE X Street food inspired by the flavours of Tamil Nadu and Sri Lanka features at this fun little spot from the Sethi family (Trishna, Gymkhana). Hoppers are bowl-shaped pancakes made from fermented rice and coconut – ideal with a creamy kari. The 'short eats' are great too, as are the prices, so expect a queue.

Menu £ 20 (lunch) - Carte £ 15/30

Town plan: 31AP2-z - *49 Frith St ✉ W1D 4SG - ⊖ Tottenham Court Road - ☎ 020 3011 1021 (bookings not accepted) - www.hopperslondon.com - Closed 25-27 December and 1-3 January.*

Kiln

THAI • SIMPLE X Sit at the far counter to watch chefs prepare fiery Thai food in clay pots, woks and grills. The well-priced menu includes influences from Laos, Myanmar and Yunnan – all prepared using largely British produce. The counter is for walk-ins only but parties of four can book a table downstairs.

Carte £ 10/22

Town plan: 31AN3-k - *58 Brewer St ✉ W1F 9TL - ⊖ Piccadilly Circus (bookings not accepted) - www.kilnsoho.com*

Kricket

INDIAN • SIMPLE X From Brixton pop-up to a permanent spot in Soho; not many Indian restaurants have a counter, an open kitchen, sharing plates and cocktails. The four well-priced dishes under each heading of 'Meat, 'Fish' and 'Veg' are made with home-grown ingredients. Bookings are only taken for groups of 4 or more at the communal tables downstairs.

Carte £ 20/27

Town plan: 31AN3-t - *12 Denman St ✉ W1D 7HH - ⊖ Piccadilly Circus - ☎ 020 7734 5612 (bookings not accepted) - www.kricket.co.uk - Closed 25-26 December, 1 January and Sunday*

Palomar

WORLD CUISINE • TRENDY X A hip slice of modern-day Jerusalem in the heart of theatreland, with a zinc kitchen counter running back to an intimate wood-panelled dining room. Like the atmosphere, the contemporary Middle Eastern cooking is fresh and vibrant.

Carte £ 17/40

Town plan: 31AP3-s - *34 Rupert St ✉ W1D 6DN - ⊖ Piccadilly Circus - ☎ 020 7439 8777 - www.thepalomar.co.uk - Closed dinner 24-26 December*

Polpetto

ITALIAN • SIMPLE X Order a negroni at the bar then start ordering some of those Italian-inspired small plates. Look for the daily specials on the blackboard but don't forget old favourites like the pork and beef meatballs. It's fun, busy and great for a quick bite.

Carte £ 14/24

Town plan: 31AN2-u - *11 Berwick St ✉ W1F 0PL - ⊖ Tottenham Court Road - ☎ 020 7439 8627 - www.polpo.co.uk*

Gauthier - Soho

FRENCH • INTIMATE XXX Detached from the rowdier elements of Soho is this charming Georgian townhouse, with dining spread over three floors. Alex Gauthier offers assorted menus of his classically based cooking, with vegetarians particularly well looked after.

Menu £ 30/75

Town plan: 31AP2-k – *21 Romilly St ✉ W1D 5AF – ⊖ Leicester Square – ✆ 020 7494 3111 – www.gauthiersoho.co.uk – Closed Sunday, Monday and bank holidays except Good Friday*

Bob Bob Ricard

TRADITIONAL BRITISH • VINTAGE XX Small but perfectly formed, BBR actually sees itself as a glamorous grand salon; ask for a booth. The menu is all-encompassing – from pies and burgers to oysters and caviar. Prices are altered depending on how busy they are, with up to a 25 % reduction at off-peak times.

Carte £ 38/86

Town plan: 31AN2-s – *1 Upper James St ✉ W1F 9DF – ⊖ Oxford Circus – ✆ 020 3145 1000 – www.bobbobricard.com*

100 Wardour St

MODERN CUISINE • CONTEMPORARY DÉCOR XX For a night out with a group of friends, this D&D place is worth considering. At night, head downstairs for cocktails, live music (well, this was once The Marquee Club) and a modern, Med-influenced menu with the odd Asian touch. During the day, the ground floor offers an all-day menu.

Menu £ 42 – Carte £ 31/58

Town plan: 31AN2-v – *100 Wardour St ✉ W1F 0TN – ⊖ Tottenham Court Road – ✆ 020 7314 4000 – www.100wardourst.com – Closed 25-26 December and Sunday-Monday*

Tamarind Kitchen

INDIAN • EXOTIC DÉCOR XX A more relaxed sister to Tamarind in Mayfair, this Indian restaurant comes with endearingly earnest service and a lively buzz. There's a nominal Northern emphasis to the fairly priced menu, with Awadhi kababs a speciality, but there are also plenty of curries and fish dishes.

Menu £ 18 (lunch) – Carte £ 22/35

Town plan: 31AN2-m – *167-169 Wardour St ✉ W1F 8WR – ⊖ Tottenham Court Road – ✆ 020 7287 4243 – www.tamarindkitchen.co.uk – Closed 25-26 December, 1 January*

Temper

BARBECUE • CONTEMPORARY DÉCOR XX A fun, basement restaurant all about barbecue and meats. The beasts are cooked whole, some are also smoked in-house and there's a distinct South African flavour to the salsas that accompany them. Kick off with some tacos – they make around 1,200 of them every day.

Carte £ 20/40

Town plan: 31AN2-r – *25 Broadwick St ✉ W1F 0DF – ⊖ Oxford Circus – ✆ 020 3879 3834 – www.temperrestaurant.com – Closed 25-26 December and 1 January*

Vasco and Piero's Pavilion

ITALIAN • FRIENDLY XX Regulars and tourists have been flocking to this institution for over 40 years; its longevity is down to a twice daily changing menu of Umbrian-influenced dishes rather than the matter-of-fact service or simple decoration.

Carte £ 28/48

Town plan: 31AN2-q – *15 Poland St ✉ W1F 8QE – ⊖ Oxford Circus – ✆ 020 7437 8774 (booking essential at lunch) – www.vascosfood.com – Closed Saturday lunch, Sunday and bank holidays*

Nopi

MEDITERRANEAN CUISINE • DESIGN X The bright, clean look of Yotam Ottolenghi's charmingly run all-day restaurant matches the fresh, invigorating food. The sharing plates take in the Mediterranean, the Middle East and Asia and the veggie dishes stand out.

Carte £ 31/49

Town plan: 31AN3-g - *21-22 Warwick St ✉ W1B 5NE - ⊖ Piccadilly Circus - ✆ 020 7494 9584 - www.ottolenghi.co.uk - Closed 25-26 December, 1 January and Sunday dinner*

XU Ⓝ

ASIAN • CHIC X They've squeezed a lot into the two floors to create the feel of 1930s Taipei, including an emerald lacquered tea kiosk and mahjong tables. Don't miss the numbing beef tendon and classics like Shou Pa chicken. Tofu is made in-house and Chi Shiang rice is flown in from Taiwan.

Menu £ 18 (lunch) - Carte £ 22/38

Town plan: 31AP3-s - *30 Rupert St ✉ W1D 6DL - ⊖ Piccadilly Circus - ✆ 020 3319 8147 (booking essential) - www.xulondon.com - Closed 25-26 December*

Barshu

CHINESE • EXOTIC DÉCOR X The fiery and authentic flavours of China's Sichuan province are the draw here; help is at hand as the menu has pictures. It's well run and decorated with carved wood and lanterns; downstairs is better for groups.

Carte £ 19/53

Town plan: 31AP2-g - *28 Frith St. ✉ W1D 5LF - ⊖ Leicester Square - ✆ 020 7287 8822 - www.barshurestaurant.co.uk - Closed 24-25 December*

Beijing Dumpling

CHINESE • NEIGHBOURHOOD X This relaxed little place serves freshly prepared dumplings of both Beijing and Shanghai styles. Although the range is not as comprehensive as the name suggests, they do stand out, especially varieties of the famed Xiao Long Bao.

Menu £ 17/25 - Carte £ 14/38

Town plan: 31AP3-e - *23 Lisle St ✉ WC2H 7BA - ⊖ Leicester Square - ✆ 020 7287 6888 (bookings not accepted) - Closed 24-25 December*

Blanchette

FRENCH • SIMPLE X Run by three frères, Blanchette takes French bistro food and gives it the 'small plates' treatment. It's named after their mother – the ox cheek Bourguignon is her recipe. Tiles and exposed brick add to the rustic look.

Menu £ 20 (lunch and early dinner) - Carte £ 18/49

Town plan: 31AN2-c - *9 D'Arblay St ✉ W1F 8DR - ⊖ Oxford Circus - ✆ 020 7439 8100 (booking essential) - www.blanchettelondon.co.uk*

Bocca di Lupo

ITALIAN • TAPAS BAR X Atmosphere, food and service are all best when sitting at the marble counter, watching the chefs at work. Specialities from across Italy come in large or small sizes and are full of flavour and vitality. Try also their gelato shop opposite.

Carte £ 26/63

Town plan: 31AN3-e - *12 Archer St ✉ W1D 7BB - ⊖ Piccadilly Circus - ✆ 020 7734 2223 (booking essential) - www.boccadilupo.com - Closed 25 December and 1 January*

Casita Andina

PERUVIAN • RUSTIC X Respect is paid to the home-style cooking of the Andes at this warmly run and welcoming Peruvian picantería. Dishes are gluten-free and as colourful as the surroundings of this 200 year old house.

Carte £ 18/37

Town plan: 31AN3-n - *31 Great Windmill St ✉ W1D 7LP - ⊖ Piccadilly Circus - ✆ 020 3327 9464 - www.andinalondon.com/casita*

Cây Tre

VIETNAMESE • MINIMALIST Bustling Vietnamese restaurant offering specialities from all parts of the country. Dishes are generously sized and appealingly priced; their various versions of pho are always popular. Come in a group to compete with the noise.

Menu £ 25 – Carte £ 14/27

Town plan: 31AP2-m – *42-43 Dean St ✉ W1D 4PZ – ⊖ Tottenham Court Road – ✆ 020 7317 9118 – www.thevietnamesekitchen.co.uk – Closed 25 December*

Ceviche Soho

PERUVIAN • FRIENDLY This is where it all started for this small group that helped London discover Peruvian food. It's as loud and cramped as it is fun and friendly. Start with a pisco-based cocktail then order classics like tiradito alongside dishes from the grill such as ox heart anticuchos.

Carte £ 17/29

Town plan: 31AP2-w – *17 Frith St ✉ W1D 4RG – ⊖ Tottenham Court Road – ✆ 020 7292 2040 (booking essential) – www.cevicherestaurants.com – Closed 24-26 December and 1 January*

Darjeeling Express

INDIAN • BRASSERIE With Royal Mughlai ancestry and a great love of food gained from cooking traditional family recipes, the owner couldn't be better qualified. Her open kitchen is run by a team of housewives; the influences are mostly Bengali but there are also dishes from Kolkata to Hyderabad. Lively and great fun.

Carte £ 22/29

Town plan: 31AN2-x – *Top Floor, Kingly Ct. Carnaby St ✉ W1B 5PW – ⊖ Oxford Circus – ✆ 020 7287 2828 (booking essential) – www.darjeeling-express.com – Closed 25-26 and 31 December, 1 January and Sunday*

Dehesa

MEDITERRANEAN CUISINE • TAPAS BAR Repeats the success of its sister restaurant, Salt Yard, by offering flavoursome and appealingly priced Spanish and Italian tapas. Busy, friendly atmosphere in appealing corner location. Good drinks list too.

Menu £ 15 (weekday lunch) – Carte £ 20/35

Town plan: 30AM2-i – *25 Ganton St ✉ W1F 9BP – ⊖ Oxford Circus – ✆ 020 7494 4170 – www.dehesa.co.uk – Closed 25 December*

Duck & Rice

CHINESE • INTIMATE Something a little different – a converted pub with a Chinese kitchen – originally set up by Alan Yau. Beer and snacks are the thing on the ground floor; upstairs, with its booths and fireplaces, is for Chinese favourites and comforting classics.

Carte £ 21/49

Town plan: 31AN2-w – *90 Berwick St ✉ WIF 0QB – ⊖ Tottenham Court Road – ✆ 020 3327 7888 – www.theduckandrice.com – Closed 25 December*

Ember Yard

MEDITERRANEAN CUISINE • TAPAS BAR Those familiar with the Salt Yard Group will recognise the Spanish and Italian themed menus – but their 4th fun outlet comes with a focus on cooking over charcoal or wood. There's even a seductive smokiness to some of the cocktails.

Carte £ 29/48

Town plan: 31AN2-e – *60 Berwick St ✉ W1F 8DX – ⊖ Oxford Circus – ✆ 020 7439 8057 – www.emberyard.co.uk – Closed 25-26 December and 1 January*

Evelyn's Table

MODERN CUISINE • SIMPLE A former beer cellar of a restored 18C inn – much is made of the whole cramped, underground, speakeasy thing. Watching the chefs behind the counter is all part of the appeal; their modern European dishes are designed for sharing, with fish from Cornwall a highlight.

Carte £ 25/43

Town plan: 31AP3-u – *The Blue Posts, 28 Rupert St*
W1D 6DJ – Piccadilly Circus – www.theblueposts.co.uk – dinner only
– Closed 25-26 December and Sunday

Flavour Bastard

FUSION • BRASSERIE Here it's about "London on a plate" – food that celebrates our truly international capital. The 'Small' and 'Tiny' sharing plates fuse influences from Asia to the Caribbean, Europe to South America; in fact, nowhere is off-limits. Do try 'Cloud of curds' and 'TFC' (tandoori-fried chicken).

Menu £ 15 (lunch) – Carte £ 27/33

Town plan: 31AP2-a – *63-64 Frith St W1D 3JW – Tottenham Court Road*
– 020 7734 4545 – www.flavourbastard.com – Closed 25 December, Sunday and bank holidays

Jinjuu

ASIAN • DESIGN American-born celebrity chef Judy Joo's restaurant is a celebration of her Korean heritage. The vibrant dishes, whether Bibimbap bowls or Ssam platters, burst with flavour and are as enjoyable as the fun surroundings. There's another branch in Mayfair.

Menu £ 14 (weekday lunch) – Carte £ 27/57

Town plan: 31AN2-d – *15 Kingly St W1B 5PS – Oxford Circus*
– 020 8181 8887 – www.jinjuu.com – Closed 1 January and 25 December

Jugemu

JAPANESE • SIMPLE Like all the best izakaya, this one is tucked away down a side street and easy to miss. It has three small tables and a 9-seater counter from where you can watch the chef-owner at work. Popular with a homesick Japanese clientele, it keeps things traditional; the sashimi is excellent.

Carte £ 10/50

Town plan: 31AN2-3-a – *3 Winnett St W1D 6JY – Piccadilly Circus*
– 020 7734 0518 – dinner only – Closed Christmas, New Year and Sunday

Koya Bar

JAPANESE • SIMPLE A simple, sweet place serving authentic Udon noodles and small plates; they open early for breakfast. Counter seating means everyone has a view of the chefs; bookings aren't taken and there is often a queue, but the short wait is worth it.

Carte £ 14/32

Town plan: 31AP2-z – *50 Frith St W1D 4SQ – Tottenham Court Road*
– 020 7494 9075 (bookings not accepted) – www.koya.co.uk – Closed 25 December and 1 January

Mele e Pere

ITALIAN • FRIENDLY There's a small dining room on the ground floor but all the fun happens downstairs, where you'll find a large vermouth bar with vintage posters and plenty of seating in the buzzy vaulted room. The rustic Italian dishes hit the spot and the pre-theatre menu is great value.

Menu £ 20 (lunch and early dinner) – Carte £ 22/39

Town plan: 31AN3-h – *46 Brewer St W1F 9TF – Piccadilly Circus*
– 020 7096 2096 – www.meleepere.co.uk – Closed 25-26 December and 1 January

Pastaio

ITALIAN • OSTERIA Get ready to queue and even share a table – but at these prices who cares? This buzzy spot, a stone's throw from Carnaby Street, is all about pasta. It's made in-house daily by the all Italian team, with short and long semolina pasta extruded through bronze dies. The tiramisu is great too.

Carte £ 24/28

Town plan: 30AN2-p – *19 Ganton St ✉ W1F 9BN – ⊖ Oxford Circus – ✆ 020 3019 8680 (bookings not accepted) – www.pastaio.london – Closed 25 December and 1 January*

Rambla

SPANISH • TAPAS BAR The owner's childhood in Barcelona is celebrated here with an interesting range of Catalan-inspired dishes, which are punchy in flavour and designed to be shared. It's a simple unpretentious place dominated by an open kitchen; the best seats are at the counter.

Carte £ 22/39

Town plan: 31AP2-q – *64 Dean St ✉ W1D 4QQ – ⊖ Tottenham Court Road – ✆ 020 7734 8428 – www.ramblalondon.com – Closed Christmas*

Zelman Meats

MEATS AND GRILLS • RUSTIC Those clever Goodman people noticed a lack of affordable steakhouses and so opened this fun, semi-industrial space. They serve three cuts of beef: sliced picanha (from the rump), Chateaubriand, and a wonderfully smoky short rib.

Carte £ 18/49

Town plan: 31AN2-y – *2 St Anne's Ct ✉ W1F 0AZ – ⊖ Tottenham Court Rd – ✆ 020 7437 0566 – www.zelmanmeats.com – Closed Monday lunch and bank holidays*

Café Royal

GRAND LUXURY • HISTORIC One of the most famous names of the London social scene for the last 150 years is now a luxury hotel. The bedrooms are beautiful, elegant and discreet and the wining and dining options many and varied – they include the gloriously rococo Oscar Wilde lounge, once home to the iconic Grill Room.

160 rooms – †£ 380/700 ††£ 380/700 – ☕ £ 32 – 16 suites

Town plan: 31AN3-r – *68 Regent St ✉ W1B 4DY – ⊖ Piccadilly Circus – ✆ 020 7406 3333 – www.hotelcaferoyal.com*

Ham Yard

LUXURY • ELEGANT This stylish hotel from the Firmdale group is set around a courtyard – a haven of tranquillity in the West End. Each of the rooms is different but all are supremely comfortable. There's also a great roof terrace, a theatre, a fully stocked library and bar... and even a bowling alley.

91 rooms – †£ 380/460 ††£ 380/460 – ☕ £ 14 – 7 suites

Town plan: 31AN3-p – *1 Ham Yard ✉ W1D 7DT – ⊖ Piccadilly Circus – ✆ 020 3642 2000 – www.hamyardhotel.com*

Soho

LUXURY • PERSONALISED Stylish and fashionable hotel that mirrors the vibrancy of the neighbourhood. Boasts two screening rooms, a comfortable drawing room and up-to-the-minute bedrooms; some vivid, others more muted but all with hi-tech extras.

96 rooms ☕ – †£ 390/500 ††£ 390/500 – 6 suites

Town plan: 31AN2-n – *4 Richmond Mews ✉ W1D 3DH – ⊖ Tottenham Court Road – ✆ 020 7559 3000 – www.firmdalehotels.com*

Dean Street Townhouse

TOWNHOUSE • CONTEMPORARY In the heart of Soho and where bedrooms range from tiny to bigger; the latter have roll-top baths in the room. All are well designed and come with a good range of extras. Cosy ground floor lounge.

39 rooms – †£ 180/375 ††£ 180/510 – ☕ £ 15

Town plan: 31AP2-t – *69-71 Dean St.* ✉ *W1D 3SE* – ⊖ *Piccadily Circus* – ✆ *020 7434 1775* – *www.deanstreettownhouse.com*

Kettner's Townhouse (N)

HISTORIC • PERSONALISED Established by August Kettner in 1867 as one of London's first French restaurants. Edward VII courted Lillie Langtry here and Sir Winston Churchill, Agatha Christie and Oscar Wilde came through its doors. Now a fully restored, atmospheric townhouse with many original features.

33 rooms – †£ 155/300 ††£ 250/800 – ☕ £ 6

Town plan: 31AP2-z – *29 Romilly St* ✉ *W1D 5HP* – ⊖ *Leicester Square* – ✆ *020 7734 5650* – *www.kettnerstownhouse.com*

Hazlitt's

TOWNHOUSE • HISTORIC Dating from 1718, the former house of essayist and critic William Hazlitt still welcomes many a writer today in its role as a charming townhouse hotel. It has plenty of character and is warmly run. No restaurant so breakfast in bed really is the only option – and who is going to object to that?

30 rooms – †£ 235/265 ††£ 255/300 – ☕ £ 12

Town plan: 31AP2-u – *6 Frith St* ✉ *W1D 3JA* – ⊖ *Tottenham Court Road* – ✆ *020 7434 1771* – *www.hazlittshotel.com*

Strand and Covent Garden

L'Atelier de Joël Robuchon

FRENCH • ELEGANT X Ground floor L'Atelier, with counter dining and chefs on view; La Cuisine upstairs offers table dining in an intimate setting just a few nights a week. Assured, accomplished cooking with an emphasis on the Mediterranean; dishes are creative and well-balanced, with a pleasing simplicity to their presentation.

→ Langoustine and truffle ravioli with Savoy cabbage. Oxtail braised with chestnuts, bone marrow and black truffle. Exotic fruit soufflé with coconut ice cream.

Menu £ 45 (lunch and early dinner) – Carte £ 65/117

Town plan: 31AP2-n – *13-15 West St.* ✉ *WC2H 9NE* – ⊖ *Leicester Square* – ✆ *020 7010 8600* – *www.joelrobuchon.co.uk* – *Closed 25 December*

Cinnamon Bazaar

INDIAN • EXOTIC DÉCOR X Vivek Singh's latest venture provides relaxed, all-day contemporary Indian dining in the heart of Covent Garden, with a bright, colourful interior evoking a marketplace. Menus are influenced by the trade routes of the subcontinent, with twists that encompass Afghanistan, the Punjab and the Middle East.

Menu £ 17/24 – Carte £ 20/38

Town plan: 31AQ3-b – *28 Maiden Ln* ✉ *WC2E 7JS* – ⊖ *Leicester Square* – ✆ *020 7395 1400* – *www.cinnamon-bazaar.com*

Delaunay

MODERN CUISINE • ELEGANT XXX The Delaunay was inspired by the grand cafés of Europe but, despite sharing the same buzz and celebrity clientele as its sibling The Wolseley, is not just a mere replica. The all-day menu is more mittel-European, with great schnitzels and wieners.

Carte £ 31/70

Town plan: 32AR2-x – *55 Aldwych* ✉ *WC2B 4BB* – ⊖ *Temple* – ✆ *020 7499 8558 (booking essential)* – *www.thedelaunay.com* – *Closed 25 December*

The Ivy

TRADITIONAL BRITISH • FASHIONABLE XXX This landmark restaurant has had a facelift and while the glamorous clientele remain, it now has an oval bar as its focal point. The menu offers international dishes alongside the old favourites and personable staff anticipate your every need.

Menu £ 24 (weekday lunch) – Carte £ 32/74

Town plan: 31AP2-p – *9 West St ✉ WC2H 9NE – ⊖ Leicester Square – ✆ 020 7836 4751 – www.the-ivy.co.uk – Closed 25 December*

J.Sheekey

SEAFOOD • FASHIONABLE XX Festooned with photographs of actors and linked to the theatrical world since opening in 1890. Wood panels and alcove tables add famed intimacy. Accomplished seafood cooking.

Carte £ 40/72

Town plan: 31AP3-v – *28-32 St Martin's Ct ✉ WC2N 4AL – ⊖ Leicester Square – ✆ 020 7240 2565 (booking essential) – www.j-sheekey.co.uk – Closed 25-26 December*

Rules

TRADITIONAL BRITISH • TRADITIONAL DÉCOR XX London's oldest restaurant boasts a fine collection of antique cartoons, drawings and paintings. Tradition continues in the menu, specialising in game from its own estate.

Carte £ 39/70

Town plan: 31AQ3-n – *35 Maiden Ln ✉ WC2E 7LB – ⊖ Leicester Square – ✆ 020 7836 5314 (booking essential) – www.rules.co.uk – Closed 25-26 December*

Spring

ITALIAN • FASHIONABLE XX Spring occupies the 'new wing' of Somerset House that for many years was inhabited by the Inland Revenue. It's a bright, feminine space under the aegis of chef Skye Gyngell. Her cooking is Italian-influenced and ingredient-led.

Menu £ 32 (lunch) – Carte £ 41/63

Town plan: 32AR3-c – *New Wing, Somerset House, Strand ✉ WC2R 1LA – Entrance on Lancaster Pl – ⊖ Temple – ✆ 020 3011 0115 – www.springrestaurant.co.uk – Closed Sunday*

Balthazar

FRENCH • BRASSERIE XX Those who know the original Balthazar in Manhattan's SoHo district will find the London version of this classic brasserie uncannily familiar in looks, vibe and food. The Franglais menu keeps it simple and the cocktails are great.

Menu £ 23 (lunch and early dinner) – Carte £ 31/73

Town plan: 31AQ2-t – *4-6 Russell St. ✉ WC2B 5HZ – ⊖ Covent Garden – ✆ 020 3301 1155 (booking essential) – www.balthazarlondon.com – Closed 25 December*

Clos Maggiore

FRENCH • CLASSIC DÉCOR XX One of London's most romantic restaurants – but be sure to ask for the enchanting conservatory with its retractable roof. The sophisticated French cooking is joined by a wine list of great depth. Good value and very popular pre/post theatre menus.

Menu £ 30 (weekday lunch)/37 – Carte £ 44/64

Town plan: 31AQ3-a – *33 King St ✉ WC2E 8JD – ⊖ Leicester Square – ✆ 020 7379 9696 – www.closmaggiore.com – Closed 24-25 December*

Eneko Basque Kitchen & Bar

BASQUE • DESIGN XX Set in the One Aldwych Hotel, this stylish, ultra-modern restaurant features curved semi-private booths and a bar which seems to float above like a spaceship. Menus offer a refined reinterpretation of classic Basque dishes.

Menu £ 22 (lunch and early dinner) - Carte £ 26/89

Town plan: 32AR3-r - *One Aldwych Hotel, 1 Aldwych ✉ WC2B 4BZ - ⊖ Temple - ✆ 020 7300 0300 - www.eneko.london*

Frog by Adam Handling

MODERN CUISINE • FASHIONABLE XX The chef put his name in the title to signify that this is the flagship of his bourgeoning group. His dishes, which change regularly, are attractive creations and quite detailed in their composition. The well-run room is not without some understated elegance.

Menu £ 35 (lunch and early dinner) - Carte £ 48/61

Town plan: 31AQ3-z - *34-35 Southampton St ✉ WC2E 7HG - ⊖ Charing Cross - ✆ 020 7199 8370 - www.frogbyadamhandling.com - Closed Sunday*

Petersham

MEDITERRANEAN CUISINE • ELEGANT XX Along with a deli, shop and florist is this elegant restaurant with contemporary art, Murano glass and an abundance of fresh flowers. The Italian-based menu uses produce from their Richmond nursery and Devon farm. The lovely terrace is shared with La Goccia, their more informal spot for sharing plates.

Carte £ 42/73

Town plan: 31AQ3-p - *2 Floral Court ✉ WC2E 9FB - ⊖ Covent Garden - ✆ 020 7305 7676 - www.petershamnurseries.com*

Tredwells

MODERN BRITISH • BRASSERIE XX Chef-owner Chantelle Nicholson's contemporary cooking makes good use of British ingredients and also displays the occasional Asian twist. It's set over three floors, with a subtle art deco feel. A good choice for a Sunday roast.

Menu £ 30 (lunch and early dinner) - Carte £ 29/57

Town plan: 31AP2-s - *4a Upper St Martin's Ln ✉ WC2H 9EF - ⊖ Leicester Square - ✆ 020 3764 0840 - www.tredwells.com - Closed 24-26 December and 1 January*

J.Sheekey Atlantic Bar

SEAFOOD • INTIMATE X An addendum to J. Sheekey restaurant. Sit at the bar to watch the chefs prepare the same quality seafood as next door but at slightly lower prices; fish pie and fruits de mer are the popular choices. Open all day.

Carte £ 22/49

Town plan: 31AP3-v - *33-34 St Martin's Ct. ✉ WC2 4AL - ⊖ Leicester Square - ✆ 020 7240 2565 - www.jsheekeyatlanticbar.co.uk - Closed 25-26 December*

Barrafina

SPANISH • TAPAS BAR X The second Barrafina is not just brighter than the Soho original - it's bigger too, so you can wait inside with a drink for counter seats to become available. Try more unusual tapas like ortiguillas, frit Mallorquin or the succulent meats.

Carte £ 27/52

Town plan: 31AQ3-x - *10 Adelaide St ✉ WC2N 4HZ - ⊖ Charing Cross - ✆ 020 7440 1456 (bookings not accepted) - www.barrafina.co.uk - Closed Christmas, New Year and bank holidays*

Barrafina

SPANISH • TAPAS BAR The third of the Barrafinas is tucked away at the far end of Covent Garden; arrive early or prepare to queue. Fresh, vibrantly flavoured fish and shellfish dishes are a real highlight; tortillas y huevos also feature.

Carte £ 27/52

Town plan: 31AQ2-a - *43 Drury Ln ✉ WC2B 5AJ - ⊖ Covent Garden - ✆ 020 7440 1456 (bookings not accepted) - www.barrafina.co.uk - Closed 25-26 December, 27 May and 26 August*

Dishoom

INDIAN • TRENDY Expect long queues at this group's original branch. It's based on a Bombay café, of the sort opened by Iranian immigrants in the early 20C. Try vada pau (Bombay's version of the chip butty), a curry or grilled meats; and finish with kulfi on a stick. It's lively, a touch chaotic but great fun.

Carte £ 14/28

Town plan: 31AP2-j - *12 Upper St Martin's Ln ✉ WC2H 9FB - ⊖ Leicester Square - ✆ 020 7420 9320 (bookings not accepted) - www.dishoom.com - Closed dinner 24 December, 25-26 December and 1-2 January*

Frenchie

MODERN CUISINE • BISTRO A well-run modern-day bistro - younger sister to the Paris original, which shares the name given to chef-owner Greg Marchand when he was head chef at Fifteen. The adventurous, ambitious cooking is informed by his extensive travels.

Menu £ 27 (lunch) - Carte £ 45/60

Town plan: 31AQ3-c - *16 Henrietta St ✉ WC2E 8QH - ⊖ Covent Garden - ✆ 020 7836 4422 - www.frenchiecoventgarden.com - Closed 25-26 December and 1 January*

Oystermen (N)

SEAFOOD • RUSTIC Covent Garden isn't an area usually associated with independent restaurants but this bustling and modestly decorated little spot is thriving. From its tiny open kitchen come oysters, crabs and expertly cooked fish.

Carte £ 28/48

Town plan: 31AQ3-r - *32 Henrietta St ✉ WC2E 8NA - ⊖ Covent Garden - ✆ 020 7240 4417 - www.oystermen.co.uk - Closed 25 December-1 January*

Savoy

GRAND LUXURY • ART DÉCO One of the grande dames of London's hotel scene. Luxurious bedrooms come in Edwardian or Art Deco styles; many have magnificent views over the Thames and the stunning suites pay homage to past guests. Enjoy tea in the Thames Foyer; sip a cocktail in the iconic American Bar or elegant Beaufort bar. Dine in the famous Savoy Grill or enjoy seafood and steaks in Kaspar's.

267 rooms - †£ 580/1300 ††£ 580/1300 - ☕ £ 35 - 45 suites

Town plan: 31AQ3-s - *Strand ✉ WC2R 0EU - ⊖ Charing Cross - ✆ 020 7836 4343 - www.fairmont.com/savoy*

One Aldwych

GRAND LUXURY • MODERN A stylish hotel featuring over 400 pieces of contemporary artwork. Bedrooms are understated in style with fine linen and fresh fruit and flowers delivered daily. Charlie and the Chocolate Factory themed afternoon tea. Gluten and dairy-free British dishes in Indigo; Basque cooking in Eneko.

103 rooms - †£ 325/610 ††£ 325/610 - ☕ £ 21 - 13 suites

Town plan: 32AR3-r - *1 Aldwych ✉ WC2B 4BZ - ⊖ Temple - ✆ 020 7300 1000 - www.onealdwych.com*

Eneko Basque Kitchen & Bar - See restaurant listing

Waldorf Hilton

HISTORIC • ELEGANT Impressive curved and columned façade: an Edwardian landmark in a great location. Stylish, contemporary bedrooms in calming colours have superb bathrooms and all mod cons. Tea dances in the Grade II listed Palm Court Ballroom. Stylish 'Homage' is popular for afternoon tea and relaxed brasserie style dining.

298 rooms – †£ 219/425 ††£ 229/435 – ☕ £ 25 – 12 suites

Town plan: 32AR2-s – *Aldwych ✉ WC2B 4DD – ⊖ Temple – ✆ 020 7836 2400 – www.waldorf.hilton.com*

St Martins Lane

LUXURY • DESIGN The unmistakable hand of Philippe Starck is evident at this most contemporary of hotels. Unique and stylish, from the starkly modern lobby to the state-of-the-art bedrooms, which come in a blizzard of white.

204 rooms – †£ 254/411 ††£ 254/411 – ☕ £ 18 – 2 suites

Town plan: 31AP-AQ3-e – *45 St Martin's Ln ✉ WC2N 3HX – ⊖ Charing Cross – ✆ 020 7300 5500 – www.morganshotelgroup.com*

Henrietta

BOUTIQUE HOTEL • DESIGN Cosy boutique townhouse in the heart of Covent Garden; stylish, contemporary bedrooms offer good facilities including Bluetooth speakers and Nespresso machines. Ask for one of the quieter rooms at the back; 18, with its balcony and city views, is best. Cocktail bar and restaurant serving original modern dishes.

18 rooms – †£ 250/350 ††£ 250/350 – ☕ £ 60 – 1 suite

Town plan: 31AQ3-c – *14-15 Henrietta St ✉ WC2E 8QH – ⊖ Covent Garden – ✆ 020 3794 5313 – www.henriettahotel.com*

Victoria

Dining Room at The Goring

TRADITIONAL BRITISH • ELEGANT XXX A paean to all things British and the very model of discretion and decorum – the perfect spot for those who 'like things done properly' but without the stuffiness. The menu is an appealing mix of British classics and lighter, more modern dishes, all prepared with great skill and understanding.

→ Orkney scallop and kedgeree with shiso and lime. Salt-marsh lamb with haggis bun, shallot purée and seaweed tapenade. Brown sugar cake with poached pear, pine caramel and ginger ice cream.

Menu £ 52/64

Town plan: 38AL6-a – *Goring Hotel, 15 Beeston Pl ✉ SW1W 0JW – ⊖ Victoria – ✆ 020 7396 9000 – www.thegoring.com – Closed Saturday lunch*

Quilon

INDIAN • DESIGN XXX A meal here will remind you how fresh, vibrant, colourful and healthy Indian food can be. Chef Sriram Aylur and his team focus on India's southwest coast, so the emphasis is on seafood and a lighter style of cooking. The room is stylish and comfortable and the service team, bright and enthusiastic.

→ Lobster broth with coriander and coconut cream. Venison chilli fry with onions and curry leaves. Baked yoghurt with palm jaggery, orange, mango and lychee.

Menu £ 31/60 – Carte £ 42/57

Town plan: 39AN5-6-e – *St James' Court Hotel, 41 Buckingham Gate ✉ SW1E 6AF – ⊖ St James's Park – ✆ 020 7821 1899 – www.quilon.co.uk – Closed 25 December*

A. Wong (Andrew Wong)

CHINESE • NEIGHBOURHOOD X A modern Chinese restaurant with a buzzy ground floor and a sexy basement. The talented eponymous chef reinvents classic Cantonese dishes using creative, modern techniques; retaining the essence of a dish, whilst adding an impressive lightness and intensity of flavour. Service is keen, as are the prices.

→ Crab claw and cured scallop with wasabi mayonnaise. Roasted char sui with sausage and foie gras. Poached meringue, orange sorbet, pomelo and passion fruit tofu.

Carte £ 24/54

Town plan: 38AM7-w - *70 Wilton Rd ✉ SW1V 1DE - ⊖ Victoria - ✆ 020 7828 8931 (booking essential) - www.awong.co.uk - Closed 23 December-4 January, Monday lunch and Sunday*

The Cinnamon Club

INDIAN • HISTORIC XXX Locals and tourists, business people and politicians – this smart Indian restaurant housed in the listed former Westminster Library attracts them all. The fairly elaborate dishes arrive fully garnished and the spicing is quite subtle.

Menu £ 28 (weekday lunch) - Carte £ 37/84

Town plan: 39AP6-c - *30-32 Great Smith St ✉ SW1P 3BU - ⊖ St James's Park - ✆ 020 7222 2555 - www.cinnamonclub.com - Closed bank holidays except 25 December*

Roux at Parliament Square

MODERN CUISINE • ELEGANT XXX Light floods through the Georgian windows of this comfortable restaurant within the offices of the Royal Institute of Chartered Surveyors. Carefully crafted, elaborate and sophisticated cuisine, with some interesting flavour combinations.

Menu £ 42/79

Town plan: 39AP5-x - *Royal Institution of Chartered Surveyors, Parliament Sq. ✉ SW1P 3AD - ⊖ Westminster - ✆ 020 7334 3737 - www.rouxatparliamentsquare.co.uk - Closed 2 weeks August, Christmas, New Year, Saturday, Sunday and bank holidays*

Rex Whistler

MODERN CUISINE • CLASSIC DÉCOR XX A hidden gem, tucked away on the lower ground floor of Tate Britain; its most striking element is Whistler's restored mural, 'The Expedition in Pursuit of Rare Meats', which envelops the room. The menu is stoutly British and the remarkably priced wine list has an unrivalled 'half bottle' selection.

Menu £ 36

Town plan: 39AP7-w - *Tate Britain, Millbank ✉ SW1P 4RG - ⊖ Pimlico - ✆ 020 7887 8825 - www.tate.org.uk/visit/tate-britain/rex-whistler-restaurant - lunch only - Closed 24-26 December*

Aster

MODERN CUISINE • CONTEMPORARY DÉCOR XX Aster has a deli, a café, a bar and a terrace, as well the restaurant; a stylish, airy space on the first floor. The Finnish chef brings a Nordic slant to the modern French cuisine, with dishes that are light, refined and full of flavour.

Carte £ 36/55

Town plan: 38AM6-a - *150 Victoria St ✉ SW1E 5LB - ⊖ Victoria - ✆ 020 3875 5555 - www.aster-restaurant.com - Closed Sunday*

An important business lunch or dinner with friends?
The symbol ⇔ indicates restaurants with private rooms.

Enoteca Turi

ITALIAN • NEIGHBOURHOOD XX In 2016 Putney's loss was Pimlico's gain when, after 25 years, Giuseppe and Pamela Turi had to find a new home for their Italian restaurant. They brought their warm hospitality and superb wine list with them, and the chef has introduced a broader range of influences from across the country.

Menu £ 25 (lunch) – Carte £ 39/59

Town plan: 38AK7-s – *87 Pimlico Rd ✉ SW1W 8PU – ⊖ Sloane Square – ✆ 020 7730 3663 – www.enotecaturi.com – Closed 25-26 December, 1 January, Sunday and bank holiday lunch*

Osteria Dell' Angolo

ITALIAN • NEIGHBOURHOOD XX At lunch, this Italian opposite the Home Office is full of bustle and men in suits; at dinner it's a little more relaxed. Staff are personable and the menu is reassuringly familiar; homemade pasta and seafood dishes are good.

Menu £ 19 (lunch) – Carte £ 26/50

Town plan: 39AP6-n – *47 Marsham St ✉ SW1P 3DR – ⊖ St James's Park – ✆ 020 3268 1077 (booking essential at lunch) – www.osteriadellangolo.co.uk – Closed 1-4 January, 24-28 December, Easter, Saturday lunch, Sunday and bank holidays*

Lorne

MODERN CUISINE • SIMPLE X A small, simply furnished restaurant down a busy side street. The experienced chef understands that less is more and the modern menu is an enticing list of unfussy, well-balanced British and European dishes. Diverse wine list.

Menu £ 27 (lunch and early dinner) – Carte £ 34/52

Town plan: 38AM7-e – *76 Wilton Rd ✉ SW1V 1DE – ⊖ Victoria – ✆ 020 3327 0210 (booking essential) – www.lornerestaurant.co.uk – Closed 1 week Christmas, Sunday dinner, Monday lunch and bank holidays*

Olivo

ITALIAN • NEIGHBOURHOOD X A popular, pleasant and relaxed neighbourhood Italian with rough wooden floors, intimate lighting and contemporary styling. Carefully prepared, authentic and tasty dishes, with the robust flavours of Sardinia to the fore.

Menu £ 27 (weekday lunch) – Carte £ 34/51

Town plan: 38AL6-z – *21 Eccleston St ✉ SW1W 9LX – ⊖ Victoria – ✆ 020 7730 2505 (booking essential) – www.olivorestaurants.com – Closed lunch Saturday-Sunday and bank holidays*

Olivomare

SEAFOOD • DESIGN X Expect understated and stylish piscatorial decoration and seafood with a Sardinian base. Fortnightly changing menu, with high quality produce, much of which is available in the deli next door.

Carte £ 39/51

Town plan: 38AL6-b – *10 Lower Belgrave St ✉ SW1W 0LJ – ⊖ Victoria – ✆ 020 7730 9022 – www.olivorestaurants.com – Closed bank holidays*

The Other Naughty Piglet

MODERN CUISINE • SIMPLE X A light, spacious restaurant with friendly staff and a relaxed atmosphere, set on the first floor of The Other Palace theatre. Eclectic modern small plates are designed for sharing and accompanied by an interesting list of natural wines.

Menu £ 22 (lunch) – Carte £ 18/35

Town plan: 38AM5-t – *The Other Palace, 12 Palace St ✉ SW1E 5JA – ⊖ Victoria – ✆ 020 7592 0322 (booking essential) – www.theothernaughtypiglet.co.uk – Closed Christmas, Sunday and lunch Monday*

The Orange

MODERN CUISINE • FRIENDLY The old Orange Brewery is as charming a pub as its stucco-fronted façade suggests. Try the fun bar or book a table in the more sedate upstairs room. The menu has a Mediterranean bias; spelt or wheat-based pizzas are a speciality. Bedrooms are stylish and comfortable.

Carte £ 25/48

4 rooms - £ 205/240 £ 205/240

Town plan: 38AK7-k - *37 Pimlico Rd ✉ SW1W 8NE - ⊖ Sloane Square.* - *✆ 020 7881 9844 - www.theorange.co.uk*

Corinthia

GRAND LUXURY • ELEGANT The restored Victorian splendour of this grand, luxurious hotel cannot fail to impress. Tasteful and immaculately finished bedrooms are some of the largest in town; suites come with butlers. The stunning spa is over four floors. Opulent Massimo serves seasonal Italian fare.

294 rooms - £ 560/1015 £ 560/1015 - 23 suites

Town plan: 31AQ4-x - *Whitehall Pl. ✉ SW1A 2BD - ⊖ Embankment* - *✆ 020 7930 8181 - www.corinthia.com*

Goring

LUXURY • ELEGANT Under the stewardship of the founder's great grandson, this landmark hotel has been restored and renovated while maintaining its traditional atmosphere and pervading sense of Britishness. Expect first class service and immaculate, very comfortable bedrooms, many of which overlook the garden.

69 rooms - £ 300/615 £ 450/710 - £ 32 - 8 suites

Town plan: 38AL6-a - *15 Beeston Pl ✉ SW1W 0JW - ⊖ Victoria* - *✆ 020 7396 9000 - www.thegoring.com*

✿ **Dining Room at The Goring** - See restaurant listing

St James' Court

LUXURY • CLASSIC Built in 1897 as serviced accommodation for visiting aristocrats. Behind the impressive Edwardian façade lies an equally elegant interior. The quietest bedrooms overlook a courtyard. Relaxed, bright Bistro 51 comes with an international menu; Bank offers brasserie classics in a conservatory.

318 rooms - £ 250/480 £ 250/480 - £ 20 - 20 suites

Town plan: 39AN5-6-e - *45 Buckingham Gate ✉ SW1E 6BS - ⊖ St James's Park* - *✆ 020 7834 6655 - www.tajhotels.com/stjamescourt*

✿ **Quilon** - See restaurant listing

Artist Residence

TOWNHOUSE • PERSONALISED A converted pub made into a comfortable, quirky townhouse hotel, with stylish bedrooms featuring mini Smeg fridges, retro telephones, reclaimed furniture and pop art. Cool bar and sitting room beneath the busy Cambridge Street Kitchen.

10 rooms - £ 255/450 £ 380/450 - £ 15

Town plan: 38AL7-r - *52 Cambridge St ✉ SW1V 4QQ - ⊖ Victoria* - *✆ 020 7931 8946 - www.artistresidencelondon.co.uk*

Lord Milner

TOWNHOUSE • CLASSIC A four storey terraced house, with individually decorated bedrooms, three with four-poster beds and all with smart marble bathrooms. Garden Suite is the best room; it has its own patio. Breakfast served in your bedroom.

11 rooms - £ 127/224 £ 178/254 - £ 17

Town plan: 38AL6-k - *111 Ebury St ✉ SW1W 9QU - ⊖ Victoria* - *✆ 020 7881 9880 - www.lordmilner.com*

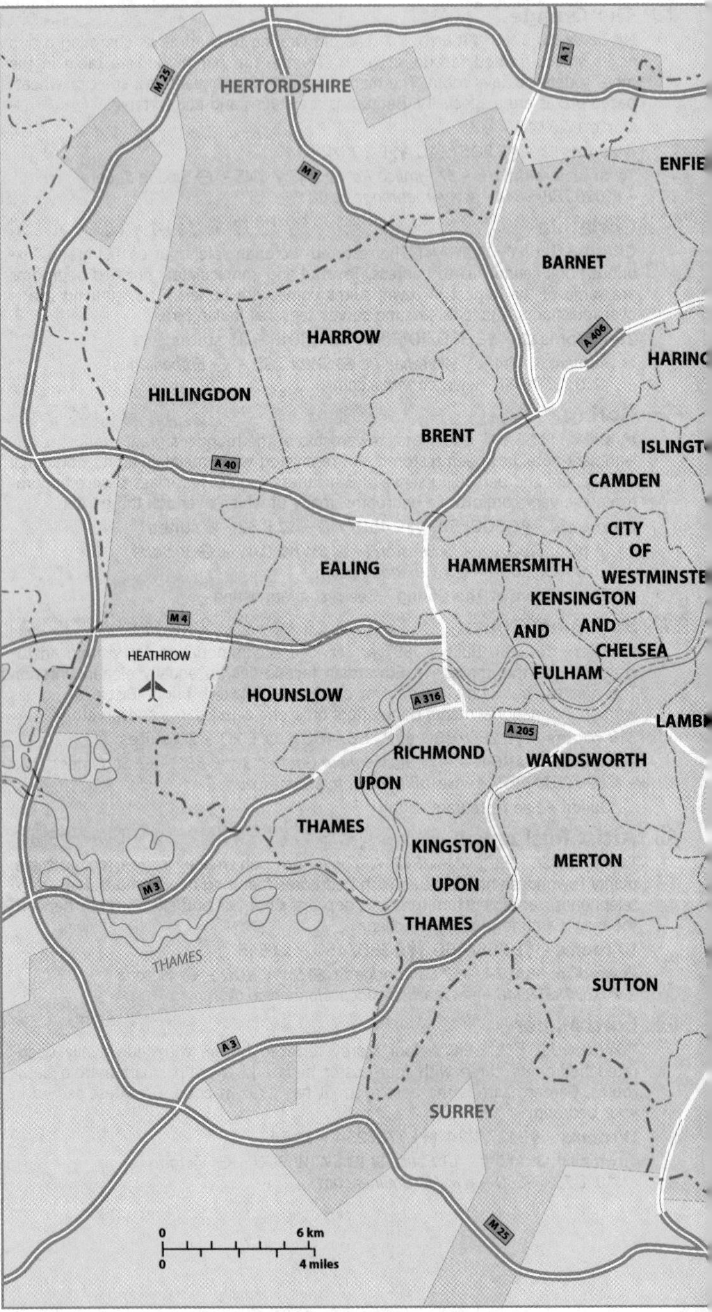
HERTORDSHIRE
M 25
M 1
A 1
ENFIE
BARNET
A 406
HARROW
HARING
HILLINGDON
BRENT
ISLINGT
A 40
CAMDEN
CITY
OF
WESTMINSTE
EALING
HAMMERSMITH
KENSINGTON
AND
AND
CHELSEA
FULHAM
M 4
HEATHROW
HOUNSLOW
A 316
LAMB
A 205
RICHMOND
UPON
THAMES
WANDSWORTH
KINGSTON
UPON
THAMES
MERTON
M 3
THAMES
SUTTON
A 3
SURREY
M 25
0
6 km
0
4 miles

GREATER LONDON
County Boundary
EALING
Borough Boundary
ESSEX
A 10
M 25
M 11
A 12
A 406
A 13
A 205
A 2
A 20
M 20
M 26
WALTHAM
FOREST
REDBRIDGE
HAVERING
BARKING
AND
DAGENHAM
HACKNEY
NEWHAM
TOWER
HAMLETS
THAMES
THWARK
GREENWICH
BEXLEY
LEWISHAM
BROMLEY
OYDON
KENT

GREATER LONDON
NORTH-WEST

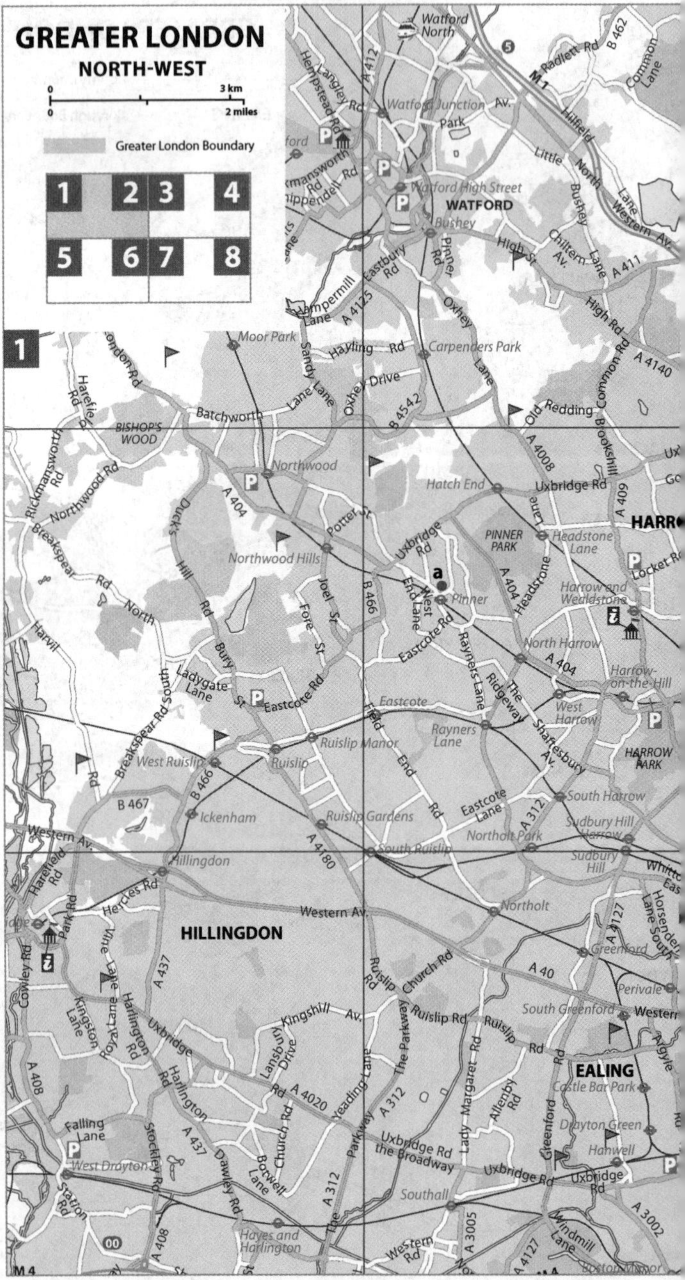

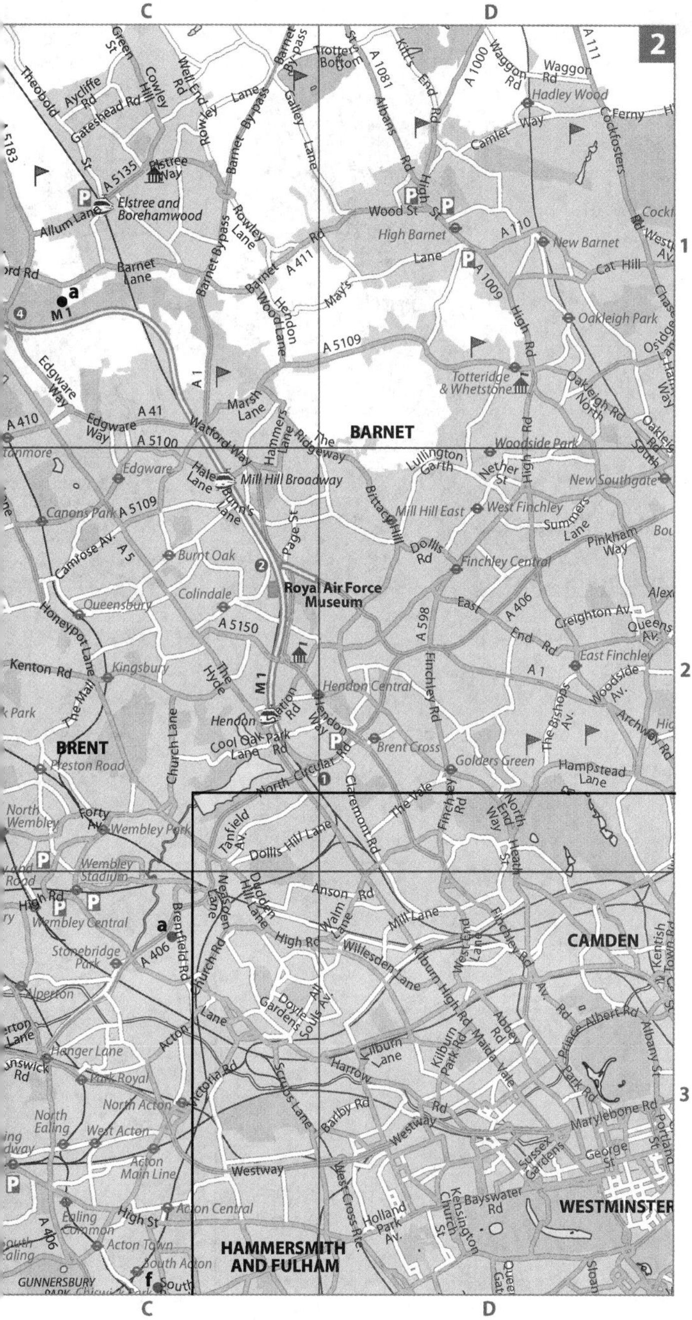
C
D
2
1
2
3
BARNET
BRENT
CAMDEN
WESTMINSTER
HAMMERSMITH AND FULHAM
Royal Air Force Museum
Elstree and Borehamwood
High Barnet
New Barnet
Hadley Wood
Oakleigh Park
Totteridge & Whetstone
Woodside Park
New Southgate
Mill Hill Broadway
Mill Hill East
West Finchley
Finchley Central
East Finchley
Edgware
Canons Park
Burnt Oak
Colindale
Queensbury
Kingsbury
Hendon
Hendon Central
Brent Cross
Golders Green
Preston Road
North Wembley
Wembley Park
Wembley Stadium
Wembley Central
Stonebridge Park
Alperton
Hanger Lane
Park Royal
North Acton
North Ealing
West Acton
Acton Main Line
Acton Central
Ealing Common
Acton Town
South Acton
GUNNERSBURY PARK
Theobold St
Aycliffe Rd
Gateshead Rd
Green St
Cowley Hill
Well End Rd
Rowley Lane
Barnet By-pass
Barnet Bypass
Galley Lane
Trotters Bottom
A 1081
Kitt's End Rd
A 1000
Waggon Rd
A 111
Ferny Hill
Camlet Way
Cockfosters Rd
Albans Rd
High St
Wood St
A 110
Cat Hill
Chase Side
A 5183
A 5135
Elstree Way
Allum Lane
Rowley Lane
Barnet Lane
Barnet Rd
A 411
Lane
May's Lane
A 1009
High Rd
Hendon Wood Lane
A 5109
M 1
Edgware Way
A 410
A 41
A 5100
A 1
Marsh Lane
Watford Way
Hammers Lane
The Ridgeway
Lullington Garth
Nether St
Oakleigh Rd North
Oakleigh Rd South
Osidge Lane
Hale Lane
Burn's Lane
Bittacy Hill
Page St
Summers Lane
Pinkham Way
Dollis Rd
Camrose Av.
A 5
A 5109
East End Rd
A 406
Creighton Av.
Queens Av.
A 598
A 5150
Honeypot Lane
Kenton Rd
The Mall
The Hyde
Station Rd
Hendon Way
Finchley Rd
The Bishops Av.
Woodside Av.
Archway Rd
Church Lane
Cool Oak Lane
Park Rd
North Circular Rd
Claremont Rd
The Vale
North End Way
Hampstead Lane
Forty Av.
Tanfield Av.
Dollis Hill Lane
Heath St
Neasden Lane
Dudden Hill Lane
Anson Rd
Walm Lane
Mill Lane
High Rd
Willesden Lane
Kilburn High Rd
West End Lane
Finchley Rd
Brentfield Rd
A 406
Church Rd
Doyle Gardens
All Souls Av.
Kilburn Lane
Kilburn Park Rd
Maida Vale
Abbey Rd
Av. Rd
Prince Albert Rd
Albany St
Kentish Town Rd
Acton Lane
Victoria Rd
Scrubs Lane
Harrow Rd
Barlby Rd
Westway
Park Rd
Marylebone Rd
Sussex Gardens
George St
Portland
West Cross Rte.
Holland Park Av.
Kensington Church St
Bayswater Rd
Queen's Gate
Sloane
High St
A 406

E F

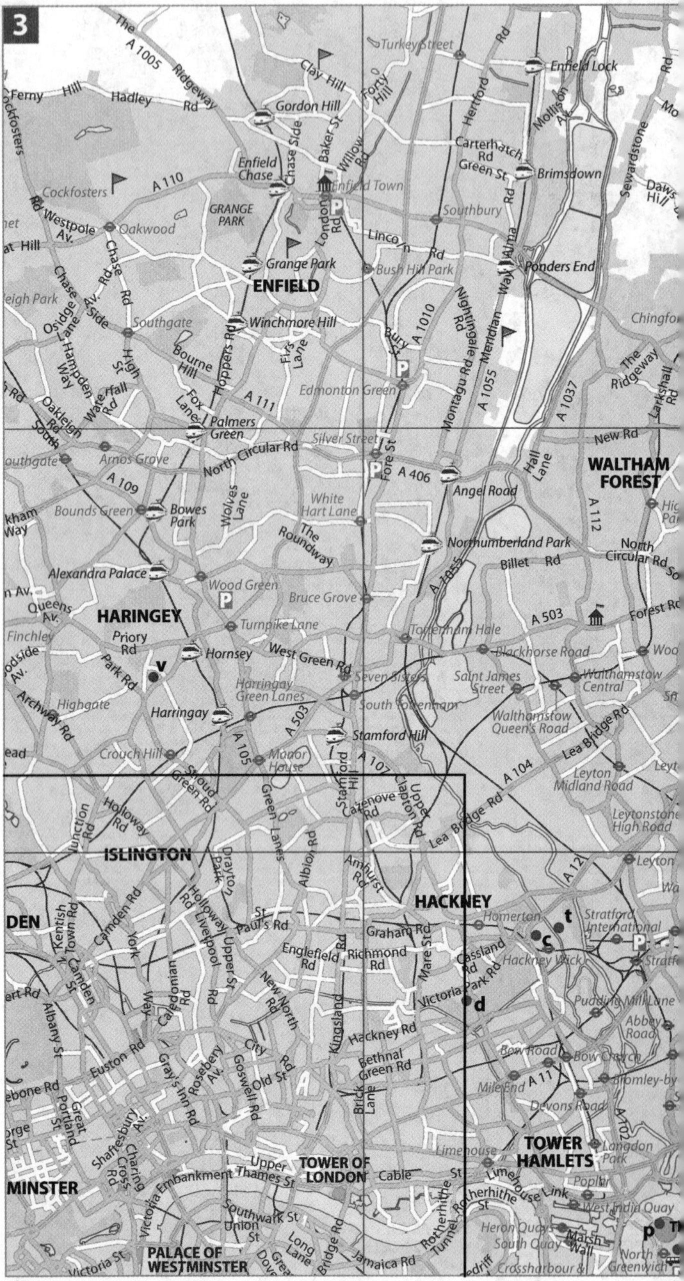
3
1
2
3
ENFIELD
HARINGEY
ISLINGTON
HACKNEY
WALTHAM FOREST
TOWER HAMLETS
TOWER OF LONDON
PALACE OF WESTMINSTER
Turkey Street
Enfield Lock
Clay Hill
Gordon Hill
Forty Hill
The Ridgeway
A 1005
Ferny Hill
Hadley Rd
Cockfosters
Enfield Chase
Chase Side
Baker St
Willow Rd
Enfield Town
Carterhatch Rd
Green St
Brimsdown
Hertford Rd
Mollison Av.
Sewardstone
Daws Hill
A 110
GRANGE PARK
London Rd
Southbury
Westpole Av.
Oakwood
Chase Rd
Lincoln Rd
Alma
Ponders End
Grange Park
Bush Hill Park
Winchmore Hill
Southgate
Osidge Lane
Hampden Way
High St
Bourne Hill
Hoppers Rd
Firs Lane
Bury St
A 1010
Nightingale Rd
Meridian Way
Chingford
The Ridgeway
Larkshall Rd
Oakleigh Rd South
Waterfall Rd
Fox Lane
Palmers Green
A 111
Edmonton Green
Montagu Rd
A 1055
A 1037
Silver Street
New Rd
North Circular Rd
Arnos Grove
Fore St
A 406
Angel Road
Hall Lane
A 109
Bounds Green
Bowes Park
Wolves Lane
White Hart Lane
A 112
The Roundway
Northumberland Park
North Circular Rd
Billet Rd
Alexandra Palace
Wood Green
Bruce Grove
Queens Av.
Turnpike Lane
Tottenham Hale
A 503
Forest Rd
Finchley
Priory Rd
Blackhorse Road
Park Rd
Hornsey
West Green Rd
Seven Sisters
Saint James Street
Walthamstow Central
Harringay Green Lanes
South Tottenham
Archway Rd
Highgate
Harringay
Walthamstow Queen's Road
Lea Bridge Rd
A 503
Stamford Hill
A 105
Crouch Hill
Manor House
A 107
A 104
Leyton Midland Road
Stroud Green Rd
Stamford Hill
Upper Clapton Rd
Cazenove Rd
Holloway Rd
Junction Rd
Lea Bridge Rd
Leytonstone High Road
Green Lanes
Drayton Park
Albion Rd
Amhurst Rd
A 12
Leyton
Kentish Town Rd
Camden Rd
Holloway Rd
Liverpool Rd
Homerton
Stratford International
St Paul's Rd
Graham Rd
York Way
Upper St
Englefield Rd
Richmond Rd
Mare St
Cassland Rd
Hackney Wick
Camden St
Caledonian Rd
Victoria Park Rd
Stratford
Albany St
New North Rd
Kingsland Rd
Pudding Mill Lane
Abbey Road
Hackney Rd
Euston Rd
Gray's Inn Rd
Rosebery Av.
City Rd
Goswell Rd
Old St
Bethnal Green Rd
Bow Road
Bow Church
Mile End
A 11
Bromley-by
Great Portland St
Brick Lane
Devons Road
A 102
Shaftesbury Av.
Charing Cross Rd
Upper Thames St
Victoria Embankment
Cable St
Limehouse
Langdon Park
Limehouse Link
Poplar
Rotherhithe St
Rotherhithe Tunnel
West India Quay
Southwark St
Union St
Heron Quays
South Quay
Marsh Wall
Long Lane
Bridge Rd
Jamaica Rd
Victoria St
Crossharbour
North Greenwich
v
t
c
d
p

E F

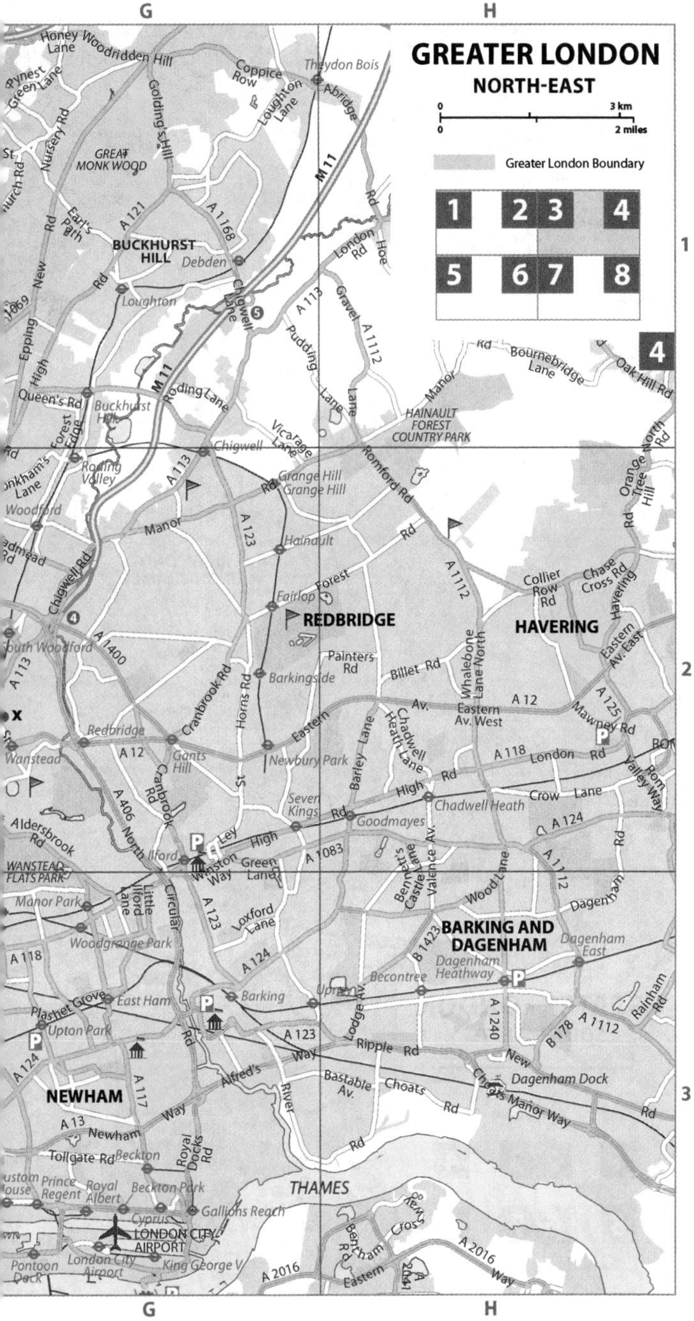
GREATER LONDON
NORTH-EAST
0
3 km
0
2 miles
Greater London Boundary
1
2
3
4
5
6
7
8
G
H
1
2
3
4
Honey Lane
Woodridden Hill
Pynest Green Lane
Coppice Row
Theydon Bois
Abridge
Loughton Lane
Nursery Rd
Golding's Hill
GREAT MONK WOOD
M 11
A 121
A 1168
Earl's Path
New Rd
BUCKHURST HILL
Debden
London Rd
Hoe
Loughton
Chigwell Lane
A 113
Gravel
A 1112
Pudding Lane
Epping
High
Rd
Bournebridge Lane
Oak Hill Rd
Manor
Queen's Rd
Buckhurst Hill
Roding Lane
HAINAULT FOREST COUNTRY PARK
Forest Edge
Vicarage Lane
Chigwell
Roding Valley
Grange Hill
Romford Rd
North Rd
Orange Tree Hill
Woodford
Manor
A 123
Hainault
Chigwell Rd
Forest
Fairlop
A 1112
Collier Row Rd
Chase Cross Rd
Havering
REDBRIDGE
HAVERING
South Woodford
A 1400
Painters Rd
Billet Rd
Whalebone Lane North
Eastern Av. East
A 113
Cranbrook Rd
Horns Rd
Barkingside
Av.
Eastern Av. West
A 12
A 125
Mawney Rd
Redbridge
Eastern
Barley Lane
Chadwell Heath Lane
Wanstead
A 12
Gants Hill
Newbury Park
A 118
London Rd
Rom Valley Way
A 406
Cranbrook Rd
Seven Kings
High Rd
Chadwell Heath
Crow Lane
Aldersbrook Rd
North
Ley
High
Rd
Goodmayes
A 124
Ilford
Winston Way
Green Lane
A 1083
Bennett's Castle Lane
Valence Av.
A 1112
WANSTEAD FLATS PARK
Manor Park
Little Ilford Lane
Circular
A 123
Loxford Lane
Wood Lane
Dagenham
BARKING AND DAGENHAM
Woodgrange Park
B 1423
Dagenham East
A 118
A 124
Dagenham Heathway
Becontree
Barking
Upney
Lodge Av.
A 1240
Rainham Rd
Plashet Grove
East Ham
Upton Park
A 123
Ripple Rd
B 178
A 1112
A 124
Way
New
Alfred's
River
Bastable Av.
Choats
Chequers
Dagenham Dock
NEWHAM
A 117
Way
Rd
Choats Manor Way
A 13
Newham
Royal Docks Rd
Tollgate Rd
Beckton
Custom House
Prince Regent
Royal Albert
Beckton Park
THAMES
Gallions Reach
Cyprus
LONDON CITY AIRPORT
Pontoon Dock
London City Airport
King George V
A 2016
Bentham Rd
Cross
A 2016 Way
Eastern
A 2041
G
H

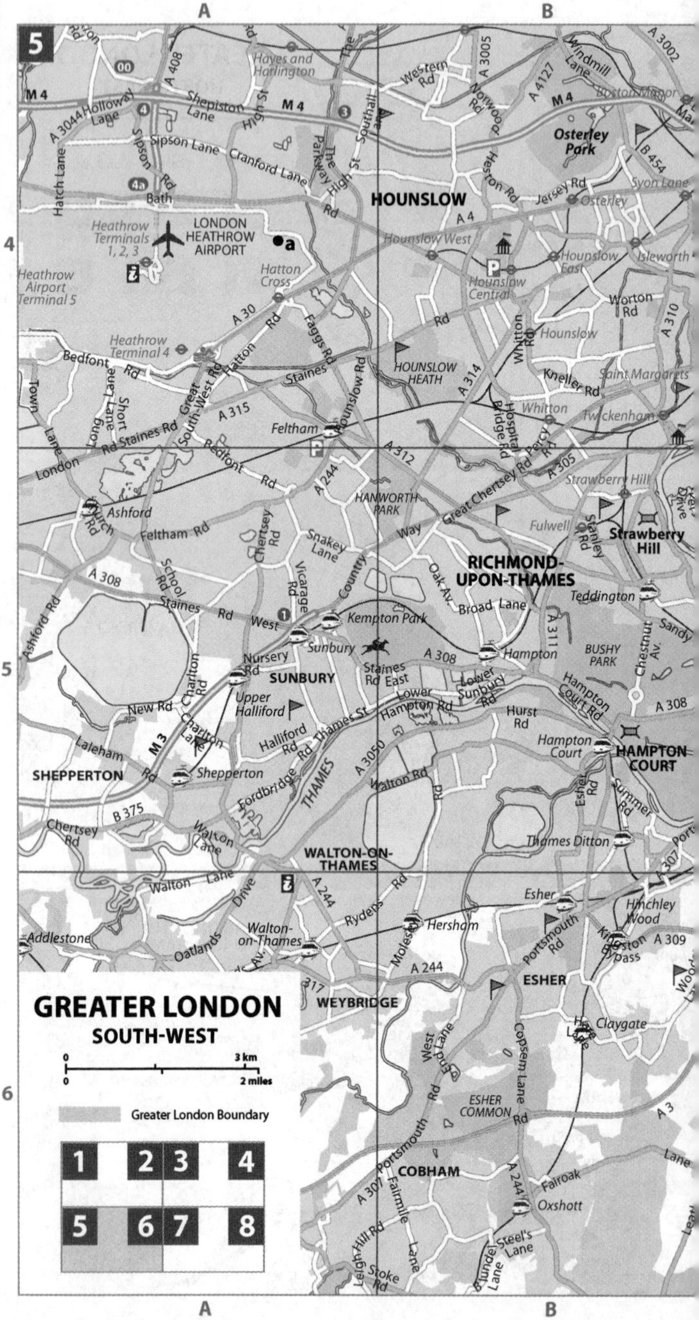
A
B
5
4
5
6
M 4
A 408
A 3044 Holloway Lane
Hatch Lane
Sipson Rd
Sipson Lane
Bath
Shepiston Lane
High St
Hayes and Harlington
Cranford Lane
The Parkway
Southall Lane
Western Rd
A 3005
Norwood Rd
A 4127
Windmill Lane
A 3002
Boston Manor
Osterley Park
B 454
Syon Lane
Jersey Rd
Osterley
Heston Rd
HOUNSLOW
A 4
Hounslow West
Hounslow East
Isleworth
Hounslow Central
Worton Rd
A 310
Heathrow Terminals 1, 2, 3
LONDON HEATHROW AIRPORT
a
Heathrow Airport Terminal 5
Hatton Cross
A 30
Hatton Rd
Faggs Rd
Heathrow Terminal 4
Bedfont Rd
Great South-West Rd
Staines Rd
Hounslow Rd
HOUNSLOW HEATH
A 314
Whitton Rd
Hounslow
Kneller Rd
Saint Margarets
Whitton
Twickenham
Hospital Bridge Rd
Percy Rd
Town Lane
Long Lane
Short Lane
Staines Rd
A 315
Feltham
London Rd
Bedfont Rd
A 312
A 244
A 305
Great Chertsey Rd
Strawberry Hill
HANWORTH PARK
Ashford
Church Rd
Feltham Rd
Chertsey Rd
Snakey Lane
Country Way
Fulwell
Stanley Rd
Strawberry Hill
RICHMOND-UPON-THAMES
Oak Av.
A 308
School Rd
Staines Rd West
Vicarage Rd
Kempton Park
Broad Lane
Teddington
Ashford Rd
Sunbury
A 308
Hampton
A 311
BUSHY PARK
Chestnut Av.
Sandy
Nursery Rd
Staines Rd East
SUNBURY
Charlton Rd
Upper Halliford
Lower Sunbury Rd
Lower Hampton Rd
Hampton Court Rd
A 308
New Rd
Charlton Lane
M 3
Laleham Rd
Halliford Rd
Thames St
Hurst Rd
Hampton Court
HAMPTON COURT
SHEPPERTON
Shepperton
Fordbridge Rd
THAMES
A 3050
Walton Rd
Esher Rd
Summer Rd
B 375
Chertsey Rd
Walton Lane
WALTON-ON-THAMES
Thames Ditton
A 307
Walton Lane
Drive
A 244
Rydens Rd
Esher
Hinchley Wood
Addlestone
Oatlands
Walton-on-Thames
Hersham
Molesey Rd
Portsmouth Rd
Kingston By-pass
A 309
A 244
ESHER
WEYBRIDGE
Claygate
GREATER LONDON
SOUTH-WEST
0
3 km
0
2 miles
Greater London Boundary
1
2
3
4
5
6
7
8
West End Lane
Copsem Lane
ESHER COMMON
Rd
A 3
Portsmouth Rd
A 307
COBHAM
A 244
Fairoak Lane
Oxshott
Fairmile Lane
Leigh Hill Rd
Stoke Rd
Steel's Lane
Blundel Lane
Lane

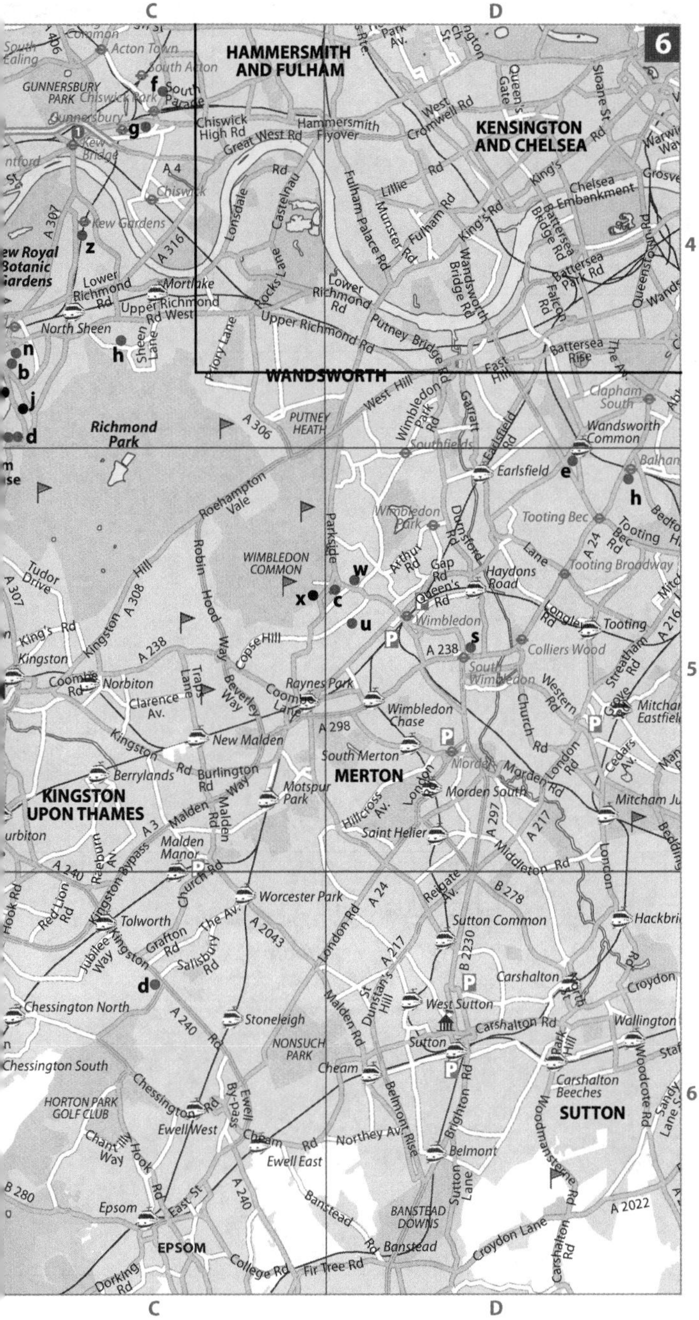
C
D
6
4
5
6
HAMMERSMITH AND FULHAM
KENSINGTON AND CHELSEA
WANDSWORTH
MERTON
KINGSTON UPON THAMES
SUTTON
EPSOM
Acton Town
South Acton
GUNNERSBURY PARK
Chiswick Park
South Parade
Gunnersbury
Kew Bridge
Chiswick High Rd
Great West Rd
Hammersmith Flyover
West Cromwell Rd
Queen's Gate
Sloane St
Chiswick
Kew Gardens
Kew Royal Botanic Gardens
Lower Richmond Rd
Mortlake
Upper Richmond Rd West
North Sheen
Sheen Lane
Lonsdale Rd
Castelnau
Rocks Lane
Priory Lane
Fulham Palace Rd
Lillie Rd
Munster Rd
Fulham Rd
King's Rd
Wandsworth Bridge Rd
Battersea Bridge Rd
Chelsea Embankment
Battersea Park Rd
Queenstown Rd
Falcon Rd
Lower Richmond Rd
Upper Richmond Rd
Putney Bridge Rd
East Hill
Battersea Rise
The Av.
Clapham South
Wandsworth Common
Richmond Park
PUTNEY HEATH
West Hill
A 306
Wimbledon Park Rd
Garratt Lane
Earlsfield Rd
Southfields
Earlsfield
Balham
Roehampton Vale
Wimbledon Park
Tooting Bec
Tooting Bec Rd
Durnsford Rd
WIMBLEDON COMMON
Parkside
Arthur Rd
Gap Rd
Haydons Road
Tooting Broadway
Queen's Rd
Wimbledon
Tooting
Tudor Drive
Kingston Hill
A 308
Robin Hood Way
Copse Hill
A 238
Colliers Wood
South Wimbledon
King's Rd
Kingston
Coombe Rd
Norbiton
Traps Lane
Beverley Way
Coombe Lane
Raynes Park
Clarence Av.
Wimbledon Chase
A 298
Western Rd
Church Rd
Streatham Rd
Mitcham Eastfields
New Malden
South Merton
Morden
Morden Rd
London Rd
Cedars Av.
Berrylands
Burlington Rd
Malden Way
Motspur Park
Hillcross Av.
Morden South
Mitcham Junction
Malden Rd
A 3
Surbiton
Saint Helier
A 297
A 217
Malden Manor
Kingston Bypass
Raeburn Av.
A 240
Church Rd
Worcester Park
A 24
Reigate Av.
Middleton Rd
B 278
Hook Rd
Red Lion Rd
Tolworth
The Av.
A 2043
Sutton Common
Hackbridge
London Rd
Jubilee Way
Kingston Rd
Grafton Rd
Salisbury Rd
B 2230
Carshalton
Croydon Rd
Chessington North
St Dunstan's Hill
West Sutton
Stoneleigh
NONSUCH PARK
Carshalton Rd
Wallington
Sutton
Chessington South
Cheam
Park Hill
Woodcote Rd
Carshalton Beeches
HORTON PARK GOLF CLUB
Chessington Rd
Ewell By-Pass
Belmont Rise
Brighton Rd
Woodmansterne Rd
Ewell West
Chantilly Way
Hook Rd
Cheam Rd
Northey Av.
Belmont
Ewell East
Sutton Lane
B 280
Epsom
East St
A 240
Banstead Rd
BANSTEAD DOWNS
A 2022
Banstead
Croydon Lane
Carshalton Rd
Dorking Rd
College Rd
Fir Tree Rd

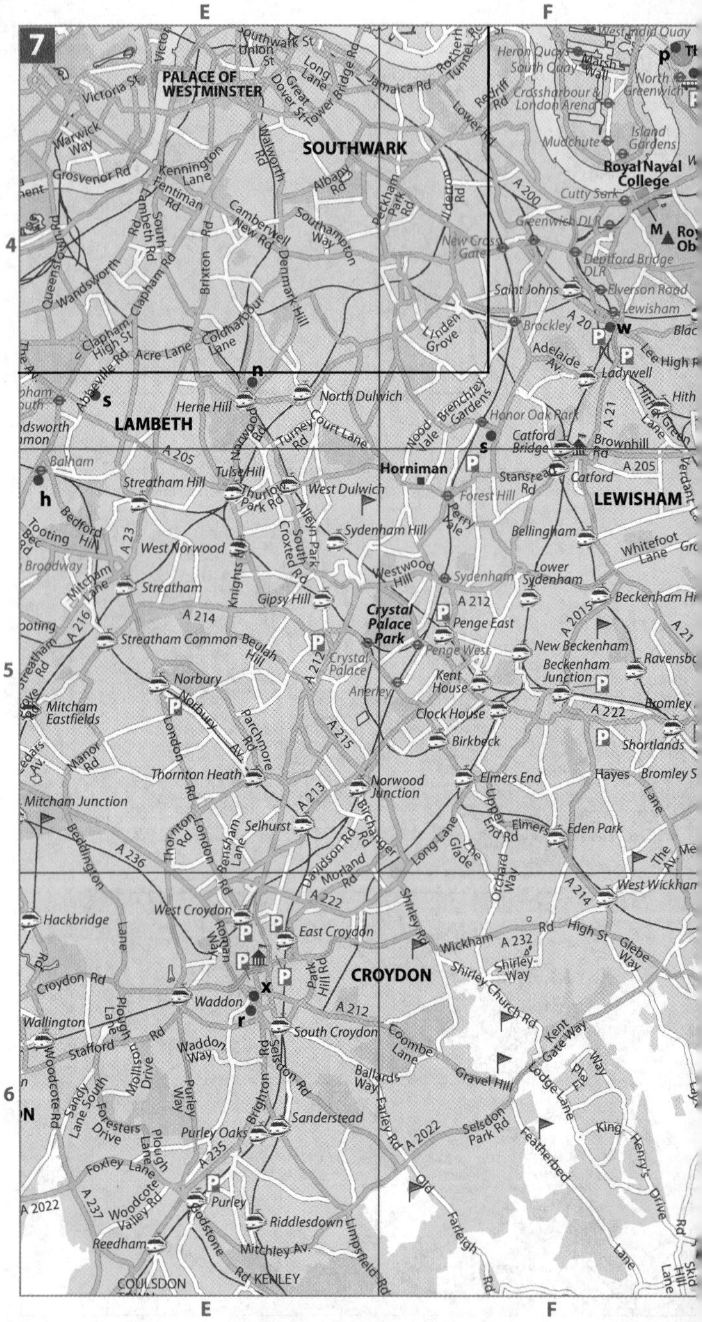
E
F
7
4
5
6
PALACE OF WESTMINSTER
SOUTHWARK
LAMBETH
LEWISHAM
CROYDON
Royal Naval College
Horniman
Crystal Palace Park
Southwark St
Union St
Long Lane
Great Dover St
Tower Bridge Rd
Jamaica Rd
Rotherhithe Tunnel
Redriff Rd
Lower Rd
Victoria St
Warwick Way
Grosvenor Rd
Kennington Lane
Fentiman Rd
Walworth Rd
Albany Rd
Camberwell New Rd
Southampton Way
Peckham Park Rd
Queenstown Rd
Wandsworth
Clapham Rd
South Lambeth Rd
Brixton Rd
Denmark Hill
Coldharbour Lane
Acre Lane
Clapham High St
Abbeville Rd
Linden Grove
West India Quay
Heron Quays
South Quay
Marsh Wall
Crossharbour & London Arena
North Greenwich
Mudchute
Island Gardens
Cutty Sark
Greenwich DLR
A 200
New Cross Gate
Deptford Bridge DLR
Saint Johns
Elverson Road
Lewisham
Brockley
A 20
Adelaide Av.
Ladywell
Lee High Rd
Hither Green Lane
A 21
Herne Hill
North Dulwich
Turney Rd
Court Lane
Norwood Rd
Nood Vale
Brenchley Gardens
Honor Oak Park
Catford Bridge
Brownhill Rd
Catford
A 205
Balham
Streatham Hill
Tulse Hill
Thurlow Park Rd
West Dulwich
Forest Hill
Stanstead Rd
Perry Vale
Bedford Hill
Tooting Bec Rd
A 23
West Norwood
Knights Hill
Alleyn Park
South Croxted Rd
Sydenham Hill
Bellingham
Whitefoot Lane
Tooting Broadway
Mitcham Lane
Streatham
Westwood Hill
Sydenham
Lower Sydenham
Gipsy Hill
A 212
Beckenham Hill
A 214
A 216
Penge East
A 2015
Streatham Common
Beulah Hill
Crystal Palace
Penge West
New Beckenham
Ravensbourne
Norbury
Anerley
Kent House
Beckenham Junction
Bromley
Mitcham Eastfields
Norbury Av.
London Rd
Parchmore Rd
A 215
Clock House
A 222
Birkbeck
Shortlands
Manor Rd
Cedars Av.
Thornton Heath
Norwood Junction
Elmers End
Hayes Lane
Bromley South
Mitcham Junction
A 213
Birchanger Rd
Upper Elmers End Rd
Eden Park
Beddington Lane
Selhurst
Thornton Rd
Bensham Lane
Davidson Rd
Morland Rd
Long Lane
The Glade
Orchard Way
The Av.
A 236
A 214
West Wickham
West Croydon
Roman Way
Shirley Rd
Wickham Rd
A 232
High St
Glebe Way
Hackbridge
East Croydon
Shirley Way
Croydon Rd
Park Hill Rd
Shirley Church Rd
Waddon
A 212
Kent Gate Way
Wallington
Plough Lane
Stafford Rd
Mollison Drive
Waddon Way
South Croydon
Coombe Lane
Woodcote Rd
Sandy Lane South
Foresters Drive
Purley Way
Brighton Rd
Selsdon Rd
Ballards Way
Gravel Hill
Lodge Lane
Sanderstead
Farley Rd
A 2022
Selsdon Park Rd
Featherbed Lane
King Henry's Drive
Purley Oaks
A 235
Foxley Lane
Plough Lane
A 237
Woodcote Valley Rd
Purley
Old Farleigh Rd
Riddlesdown
Limpsfield Rd
Godstone Rd
Reedham
Mitchley Av.
Skid Hill Lane
COULSDON
KENLEY

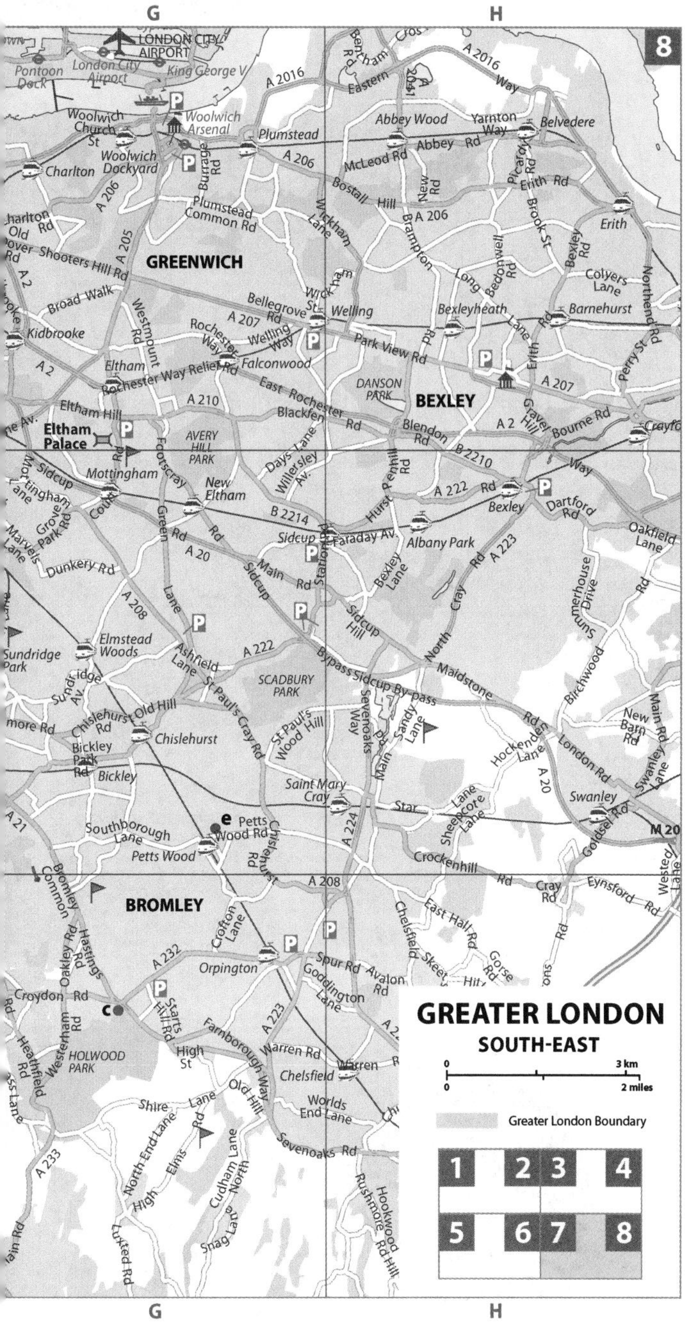
G
H
8
4
5
6
LONDON CITY AIRPORT
Pontoon Dock
London City Airport
King George V
A 2016
Eastern Way
Woolwich Church St
Woolwich Arsenal
Plumstead
Abbey Wood
Yarnton Way
Belvedere
Abbey Rd
Woolwich Dockyard
Charlton
A 206
McLeod Rd
Bostall Hill
Burrage Rd
Picardy Rd
Erith Rd
Plumstead Common Rd
Wickham Lane
Brampton
Brook St
Erith
Shooters Hill Rd
A 205
GREENWICH
Bexley Rd
Colyers Lane
Northend Rd
Broad Walk
Westmount Rd
Bellegrove Rd
Welling
Long Lane
Bexleyheath
Barnehurst
Kidbrooke
A 207
Rochester Way
Welling Way
Falconwood
Park View Rd
Erith Rd
Perry St
Eltham
Rochester Way Relief Rd
East Rochester
DANSON PARK
BEXLEY
A 207
A 2
Eltham Hill
A 210
Blackfen Rd
Blendon Rd
Gravel Hill
Bourne Rd
Crayford
Eltham Palace
AVERY HILL PARK
Footscray
Days Lane
Willersley Av.
Penhill Rd
B 2210
Way
Sidcup
Mottingham
New Eltham
A 222
Rd
Bexley
Dartford Rd
Court
Grove Park Rd
Green
B 2214
Hurst Rd
Oakfield Lane
Sidcup
Faraday Av.
Albany Park
A 223
Marvels Lane
Dunkery Rd
A 20
Main Rd
Station
Bexley Lane
Summerhouse Drive
A 208
Lane
Sidcup Hill
Cray
Elmstead Woods
North
Sundridge Park
Ashfield Lane
A 222
Bypass Sidcup By-pass
Maidstone
Birchwood
SCADBURY PARK
Sundridge Av.
Chislehurst Old Hill
St Paul's Cray Rd
Sevenoaks Way
Sandy Lane
Rd
New Barn Rd
Main Rd
Chislehurst
St Paul's Wood Hill
Main
Hockenden Lane
London Rd
Bickley Park Rd
Bickley
A 20
Swanley Lane
Saint Mary Cray
Star
Sheepcote Lane
Swanley
A 21
Southborough Lane
e
Petts Wood Rd
Chislehurst Rd
A 224
Goldsel Rd
M 20
Petts Wood
Crockenhill
Wested Lane
Bromley Common
A 208
Rd
Cray Rd
Eynsford Rd
BROMLEY
Crofton Lane
Chelsfield
East Hall Rd
Rd
Hastings Rd
Oakley Rd
A 232
Orpington
Spur Rd
Avalon Rd
Gorse Rd
Croydon Rd
c
Starts Hill Rd
Goddington Lane
Westerham Rd
Heathfield Rd
HOLWOOD PARK
High St
Farnborough Way
A 223
Warren Rd
Warren
Chelsfield
Old Hill
Shire Lane
Worlds End Lane
A 233
North End Lane
Elms Rd
Sevenoaks Rd
High
Cudham Lane North
Rushmore Hill
Hookwood Rd
Snag Lane
Luxted Rd
GREATER LONDON
SOUTH-EAST
0 3 km
0 2 miles
Greater London Boundary
1
2
3
4
5
6
7
8

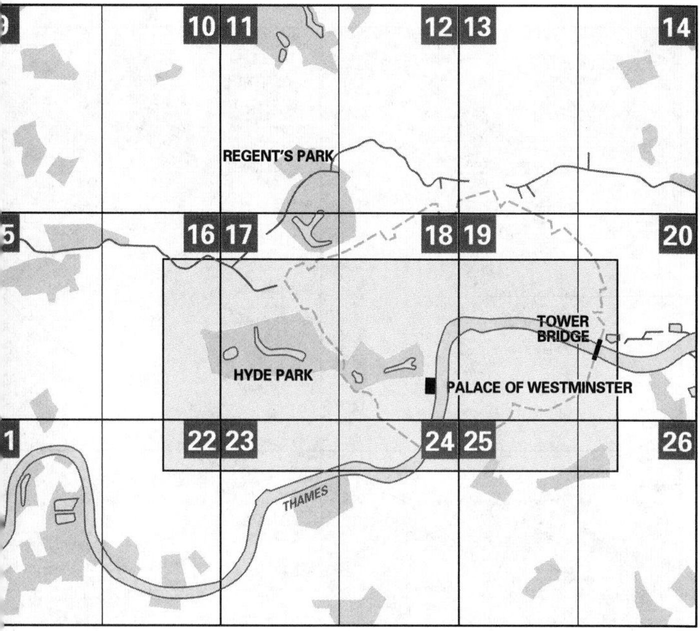
10 11
12 13
14
REGENT'S PARK
16 17
18 19
20
TOWER BRIDGE
HYDE PARK
PALACE OF WESTMINSTER
22 23
24 25
26
THAMES

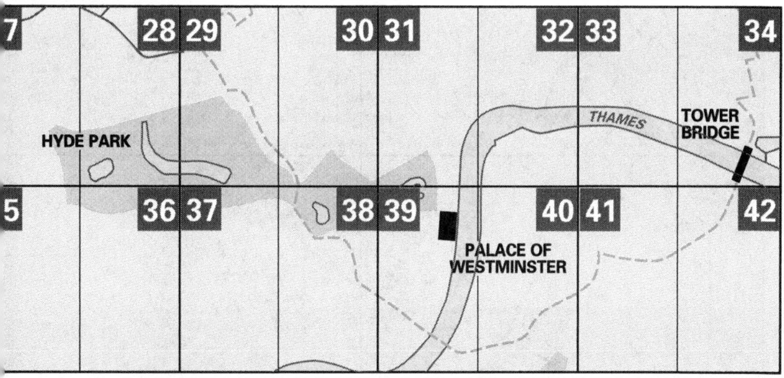
28 29
30 31
32 33
34
THAMES
TOWER BRIDGE
HYDE PARK
36 37
38 39
40 41
42
PALACE OF WESTMINSTER

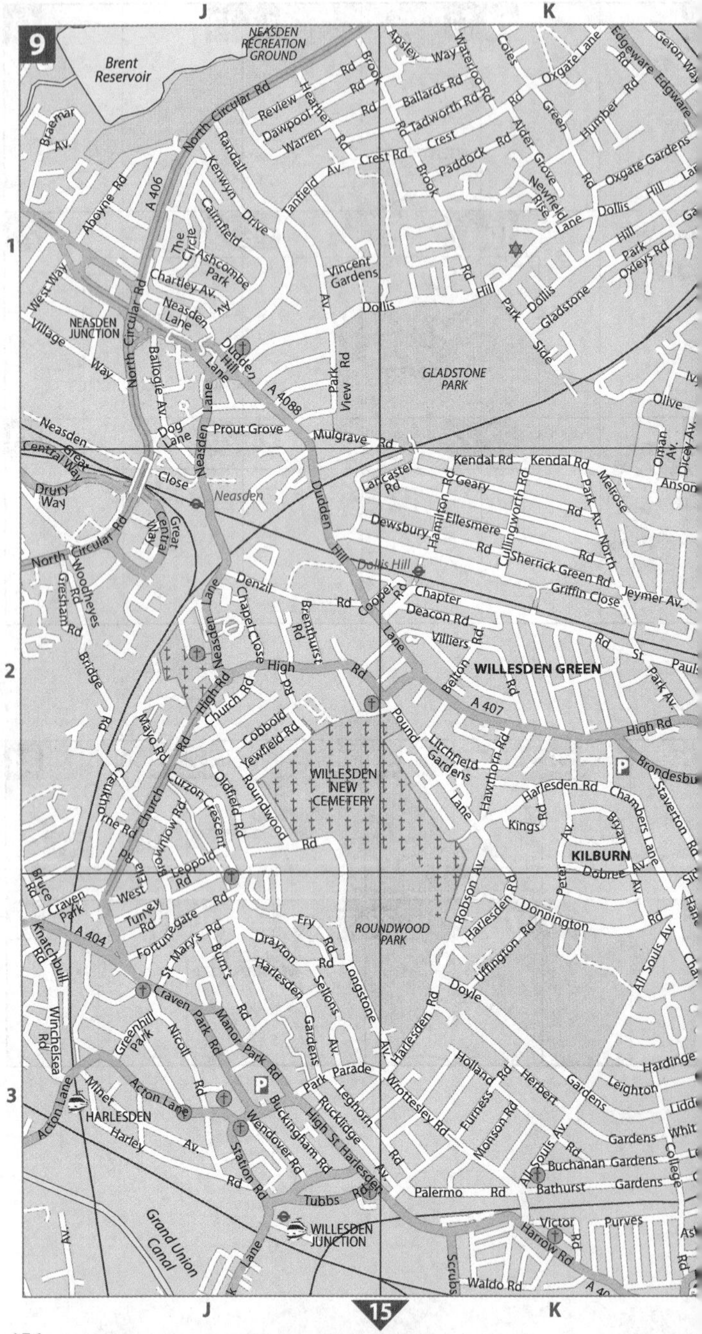
J
K
9
1
2
3
15
Brent Reservoir
NEASDEN RECREATION GROUND
NEASDEN JUNCTION
GLADSTONE PARK
WILLESDEN GREEN
WILLESDEN NEW CEMETERY
KILBURN
ROUNDWOOD PARK
HARLESDEN
WILLESDEN JUNCTION
Neasden
Dollis Hill
Grand Union Canal
A 406
A 4088
A 407
A 404
North Circular Rd
Braemar Av.
Aboyne Rd
West Way
Village Way
Neasden Lane
Chartley Av.
The Circle
Ashcombe Park
Cairnfield Av.
Kenwyn Drive
Randall Av.
Review Rd
Dawpool Rd
Heather Rd
Warren Rd
Brook Rd
Tanfield Av.
Crest Rd
Apsley Way
Waterloo Rd
Ballards Rd
Tadworth Rd
Paddock Rd
Coles Green Rd
Alder Grove
Oxgate Lane
Edgeware Rd
Geron Way
Humber Rd
Oxgate Gardens
Newfield Rise
Dollis Hill Lane
Park Rd
Oxleys Rd
Gladstone Park Gardens
Dollis Hill Av.
Vincent Gardens
Park View Rd
Dudden Hill Lane
Balogie Av.
Dog Lane
Prout Grove
Mulgrave Rd
Neasden Close
Great Central Way
Drury Way
Kendal Rd
Lancaster Rd
Geary Rd
Hamilton Rd
Cullingworth Rd
Ellesmere Rd
Dewsbury Rd
Sherrick Green Rd
Park Av. North
Melrose Av.
Griffin Close
Jeymer Av.
Olive Rd
Oman Av.
Dicey Av.
Anson Rd
Woodheyes Rd
Gresham Rd
Bridge Rd
Denzil Rd
Chapel Close
Brenthurst Rd
Cooper Rd
Chapter Rd
Deacon Rd
Villiers Rd
Belton Rd
St Paul's Av.
High Rd
Church Rd
Mayo Rd
Cobbold Rd
Yewfield Rd
Pound Lane
Litchfield Gardens
Hawthorn Rd
Brondesbury Park
Harlesden Rd
Chambers Lane
Staverton Rd
Kings Rd
Bryan Av.
Peter Av.
Dobree Av.
Creukhorne Rd
Curzon Crescent
Oldfield Rd
Roundwood Rd
Brownlow Rd
Leopold Rd
Bruce Rd
Craven Park
Tunley Rd
Fortunegate Rd
St Mary's Rd
Burn's Rd
Fry Rd
Drayton Rd
Harlesden Gardens
Sellons Av.
Longstone Av.
Robson Av.
Donnington Rd
Uffington Rd
Doyle Gardens
All Souls Av.
Knatchbull Rd
Winchelsea Rd
Greenhill Park
Nicoll Rd
Craven Park Rd
Manor Park Rd
Acton Lane
Harley Rd
Station Rd
Wendover Rd
Buckingham Rd
High St Harlesden
Park Parade
Leghorn Rd
Rucklidge Av.
Wrottesley Rd
Holland Rd
Furness Rd
Monson Rd
Herbert Gardens
Leighton Gardens
Hardinge Rd
Buchanan Gardens
Bathurst Gardens
College Rd
Palermo Rd
Tubbs Rd
Victor Rd
Purves Rd
Harrow Rd
Scrubs Lane
Waldo Rd

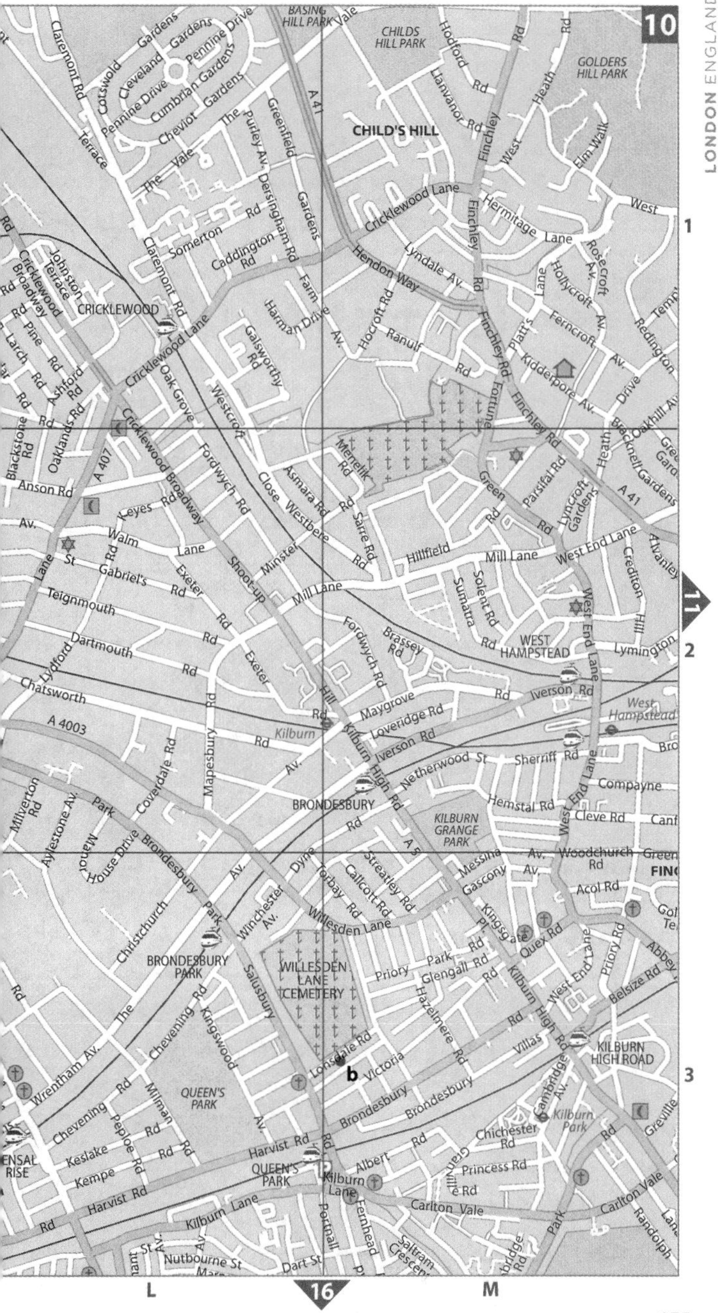
L
M
10
11
16
1
2
3
CHILD'S HILL
CHILDS HILL PARK
GOLDERS HILL PARK
BASING HILL PARK
CRICKLEWOOD
WEST HAMPSTEAD
West Hampstead
Kilburn
BRONDESBURY
KILBURN GRANGE PARK
BRONDESBURY PARK
WILLESDEN LANE CEMETERY
QUEEN'S PARK
KILBURN HIGH ROAD
Kilburn Park
KENSAL RISE
A 41
A 407
A 4003
A 5
Claremont Rd
Cotswold Gardens
Cleveland Gardens
Pennine Drive
Cumbrian Gardens
Cheviot Gardens
The Vale
Purley Av.
Greenfield Gardens
Dersingham Rd
Somerton Rd
Caddington Rd
Claremont Rd
Terrace
Hodford Rd
Llanvanor Rd
Finchley Rd
West Heath Rd
Elm Walk
Cricklewood Lane
Hermitage Lane
West Heath
Hendon Way
Lyndale Av.
Rosecroft Av.
Hollycroft Av.
Platt's Lane
Ferncroft Av.
Redington Rd
Kidderpore Av.
Fortune Green Rd
Farm Av.
Harman Drive
Hocroft Rd
Ranulf Rd
Galsworthy Rd
Johnston Terrace
Cricklewood Broadway
Pine Rd
Larch Rd
Ashford Rd
Oaklands Rd
Blackstone Rd
Anson Rd
Oak Grove
Westcroft Close
Fordwych Rd
Menelik Rd
Asmara Rd
Sarre Rd
Westbere Rd
Minster Rd
Hillfield Rd
Mill Lane
West End Lane
Parsifal Rd
Lyncroft Gardens
Heath Drive
Bracknell Gardens
Oakhill Av.
Alvanley Gardens
Crediton Hill
Solent Rd
Sumatra Rd
Lymington Rd
Keyes Rd
Walm Lane
St Gabriel's Rd
Exeter Rd
Shoot-up Hill
Teignmouth Rd
Dartmouth Rd
Lydford Rd
Chatsworth Rd
Brassey Rd
Maygrove Rd
Loveridge Rd
Iverson Rd
Netherwood St
Sherriff Rd
Compayne Gardens
Hemstal Rd
Cleve Rd
Woodchurch Rd
Acol Rd
Mapesbury Rd
Coverdale Rd
Kilburn High Rd
Milverton Rd
Aylestone Av.
Manor House Drive
Brondesbury Park
Christchurch Av.
Dyne Rd
Torbay Rd
Callcott Rd
Streatley Rd
Messina Av.
Gascony Av.
Kingsgate Pl.
Quex Rd
Priory Rd
Abbey Rd
Belsize Rd
Willesden Lane
Winchester Av.
Salusbury Rd
Priory Park Rd
Glengall Rd
Hazelmere Rd
Chevening Rd
Kingswood Av.
Wrentham Av.
Lonsdale Rd
Victoria Rd
Brondesbury Villas
Cambridge Av.
Milman Rd
Peploe Rd
Keslake Rd
Kempe Rd
Harvist Rd
Albert Rd
Chichester Rd
Princess Rd
Kilburn Lane
Carlton Vale
Fernhead Rd
Portnall Rd
Saltram Crescent
Randolph
Greville
Nutbourne St
Dart St
b

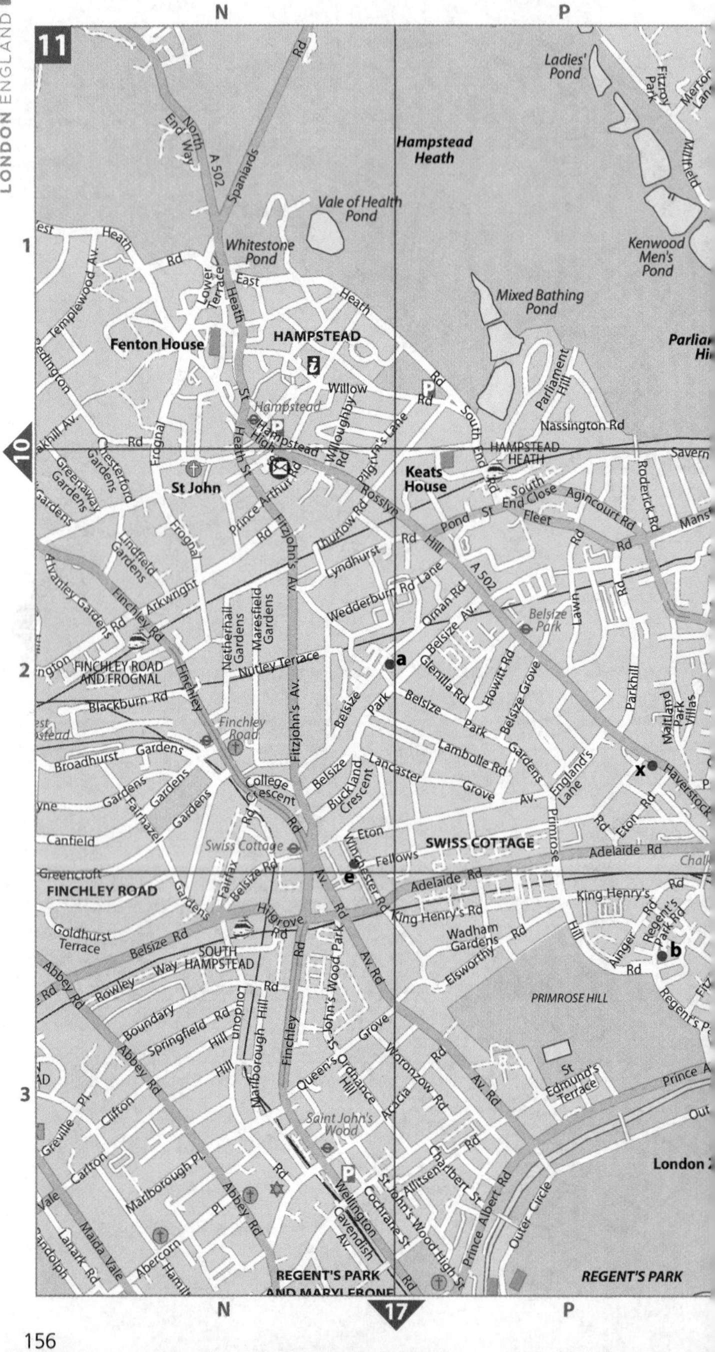
11
N
P
1
2
3
10
17
Hampstead Heath
Ladies' Pond
Fitzroy Park
Merton Lane
Millfield
Vale of Health Pond
Whitestone Pond
Kenwood Men's Pond
Mixed Bathing Pond
Spaniards Rd
North End Way
A 502
Heath Rd
Lower Terrace
East Heath Rd
Heath St
Templewood Av.
Fenton House
HAMPSTEAD
Willow Rd
Hampstead
Hampstead High St
Willoughby Rd
Pilgrim's Lane
South End Rd
Parliament Hill
Nassington Rd
HAMPSTEAD HEATH
Keats House
Rosslyn Hill
Frognal
Chesterford Gardens
Greenaway Gardens
St John
Prince Arthur Rd
Fitzjohn's Av.
Thurlow Rd
Lyndhurst Rd
Pond St
South End Close
Fleet Rd
Agincourt Rd
Roderick Rd
Lindfield Gardens
Arkwright Rd
Finchley Rd
Netherhall Gardens
Maresfield Gardens
Wedderburn Rd
Lyndhurst Gardens
Belsize Lane
Ornan Rd
Belsize Av.
A 502
Belsize Park
Lawn Rd
FINCHLEY ROAD AND FROGNAL
Nutley Terrace
a
Glenilla Rd
Howitt Rd
Belsize Grove
Parkhill Rd
Maitland Park Villas
Blackburn Rd
Finchley Road
Fitzjohn's Av.
Belsize Park
Belsize Park Gardens
Lamble Rd
Broadhurst Gardens
College Crescent
Belsize Crescent
Buckland Crescent
Lancaster Grove
Grove
England's Lane
x
Haverstock Hill
Fairhazel Gardens
Canfield Gardens
Eton Av.
Eton Rd
Swiss Cottage
Winchester Rd
Fellows Rd
SWISS COTTAGE
Primrose Hill
Adelaide Rd
Greencroft Gardens
FINCHLEY ROAD
Fairfax Rd
Belsize Rd
Adelaide Rd
King Henry's Rd
Regent's Park Rd
Hilgrove Rd
Avenue Rd
Goldhurst Terrace
Belsize Rd
SOUTH HAMPSTEAD
Rowley Way
Wadham Gardens
Elsworthy Rd
Ainger Rd
b
PRIMROSE HILL
Abbey Rd
Boundary Rd
Springfield Rd
Loudoun Rd
Marlborough Hill
Finchley Rd
St John's Wood Park
Grove End Rd
Queen's Grove
Ordnance Hill
Acacia Rd
Woronzow Rd
St Edmund's Terrace
Prince Albert Rd
Outer Circle
Clifton Hill
Greville Pl.
Carlton Hill
Marlborough Pl.
Saint John's Wood
Charlbert St
Allitsen Rd
Prince Albert Rd
London Zoo
Wellington Rd
Cochrane St
St John's Wood High St
Cavendish Av.
Maida Vale
Lanark Rd
Randolph
Abercorn Pl.
REGENT'S PARK AND MARYLEBONE
REGENT'S PARK

Q
R
12
13
18
1
2
3
Highgate
DARTMOUTH PARK
Archway
UPPER HOLLOWAY
WHITTINGTON PARK
Tufnell Park
KENTISH TOWN
KENTISH TOWN WEST
CALEDONIAN PARK
Caledonian Road
CAMDEN ROAD
Camden Town
Mornington Crescent
London Canal Museum
King's Cross
St Pancras
REGENT'S PARK
Cumberland Terrace
TERRACES
Highgate Hill
Archway Rd
Holloway Rd
Magdala Av.
Anatola Rd
Stoneleigh Terrace
Chester Rd
Bredgar Rd
Hargrave Park
Bickerton Rd
Swain's Lane
St Alban's Rd
Laurier Rd
Dartmouth Park Rd
Dartmouth Park Hill
Spencer Rise
Chetwynd Rd
Junction Rd
Station Rd
Foxham Rd
Tytherton Rd
Mercers Rd
Tufnell Park Rd
St George's Av.
Carleton Rd
Crayford Rd
Tabley Rd
St John's Way
Elthorne Rd
St John's Villas
Fairbridge Rd
Hatchard Rd
Marlborough Rd
Cornwallis Rd
Kingsdown Rd
Sussex Way
Alexander Rd
Tollington Way
Fairmead Rd
Manor Gardens
Windsor Rd
Hornsey Rd
Mitford Rd
Hanley Rd
Corbyn
Thorpedale
Wray Crescent
A 1
Lady Somerset Rd
Burghley Rd
Fortess Rd
Lupton St
Margaret Rd
Countess Rd
Falkland Rd
Lady Margaret Rd
Leighton Rd
Leighton Grove
Brecknock Rd
Anson Rd
Hilldrop Crescent
Hilldrop Rd
Dalmeny Av.
Camden Rd
Parkhurst Rd
Penn Rd
Beacon Hill
Hillmarton Rd
Hartham Rd
Sutterton Way
Regis Rd
Holmes Rd
Islip St
Gaisford St
Patshull Rd
Lawford Rd
Bartholomew Rd
Bartholomew Rd
Torriano Av.
Rowstock Gardens
Hungerford Rd
North Rd
Mews
A 503
Wales Rd
Grafton Rd
Castle Rd
Castlehaven Rd
Harmood St
Hartland Rd
Ferdinand St
Rochester Rd
Rochester Pl.
Royal St
Kentish Town Rd
Camden Mews
Murray Mews
St Augustine's Rd
York Way
Market Rd
Brewery Rd
Blundell St
Caledonian Rd
A 5203
Hawley Rd
Farm Rd
Agar Grove
Tileyard Rd
Bunning Way
Pancras Way
Jamestown Rd
Oval Rd
Georgiana St
College St
Freight Lane
Pembroke St
Carnoustie Drive
Havelock St
Bemerton St
Handyside St
Stable St
Parkway
Arlington Rd
Albert St
Bayham St
Camden High St
Pratt St
Delancey St
Plender St
Granary St
Camley St
Crowndale Rd
Goods Way
Wharfdale Rd
Charrington St
Chalton St
Eversholt St
Werrington St
Pancras Rd
Park Village East
Albany St
Barnby St
Calshot St
Pentonville
Gloucester Gate
Highgate Rd
Gordon House Rd

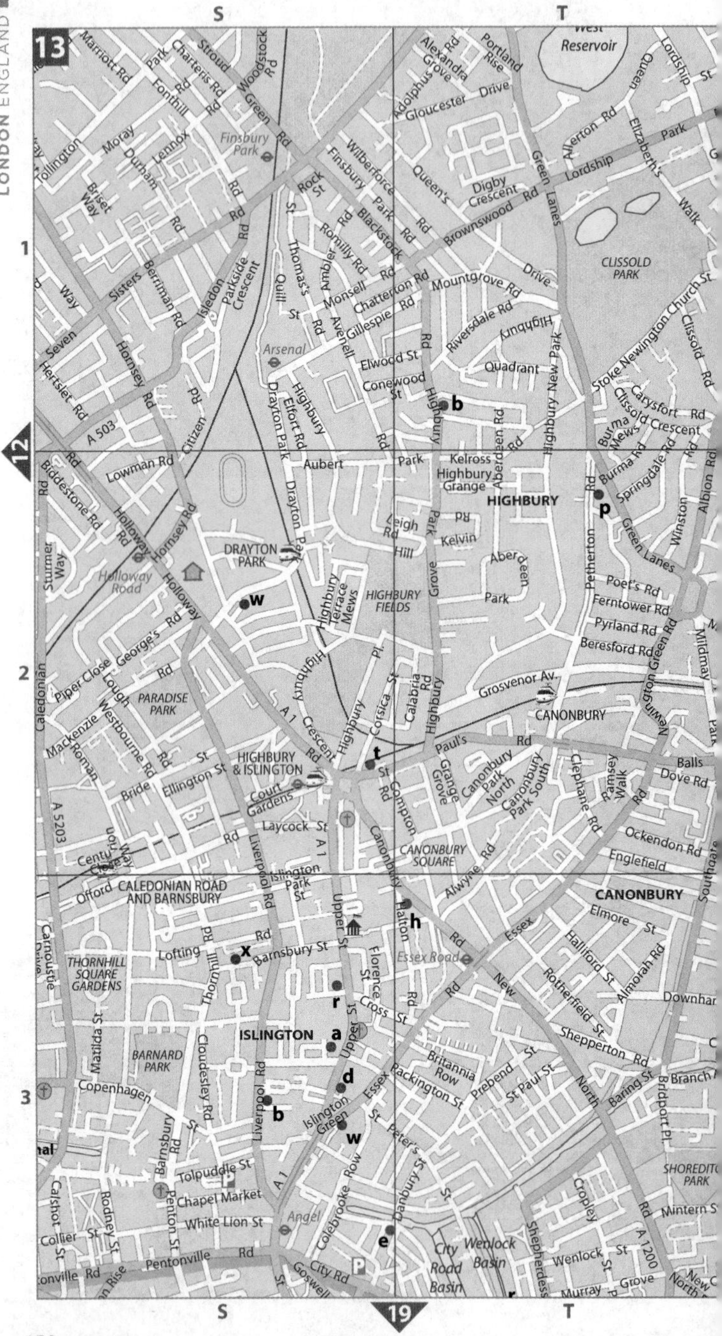
S
T
13
12
19
1
2
3
West Reservoir
Finsbury Park
Arsenal
Holloway Road
DRAYTON PARK
HIGHBURY FIELDS
HIGHBURY
CLISSOLD PARK
PARADISE PARK
HIGHBURY & ISLINGTON
CANONBURY
CANONBURY SQUARE
CALEDONIAN ROAD AND BARNSBURY
THORNHILL SQUARE GARDENS
BARNARD PARK
ISLINGTON
Essex Road
Angel
City Road Basin
Wenlock Basin
SHOREDITCH PARK
Seven Sisters Rd
Hornsey Rd
Holloway Rd
Blackstock Rd
Brownswood Rd
Green Lanes
Lordship Park
Highbury Grove
Highbury Park
Highbury New Park
Grosvenor Av.
St Paul's Rd
Canonbury Rd
Upper St
Liverpool Rd
Essex Rd
New North Rd
Caledonian Rd
Pentonville Rd
City Rd
Goswell St
A 1
A 503
A 5203
A 1200
b
p
w
t
h
x
r
a
d
e

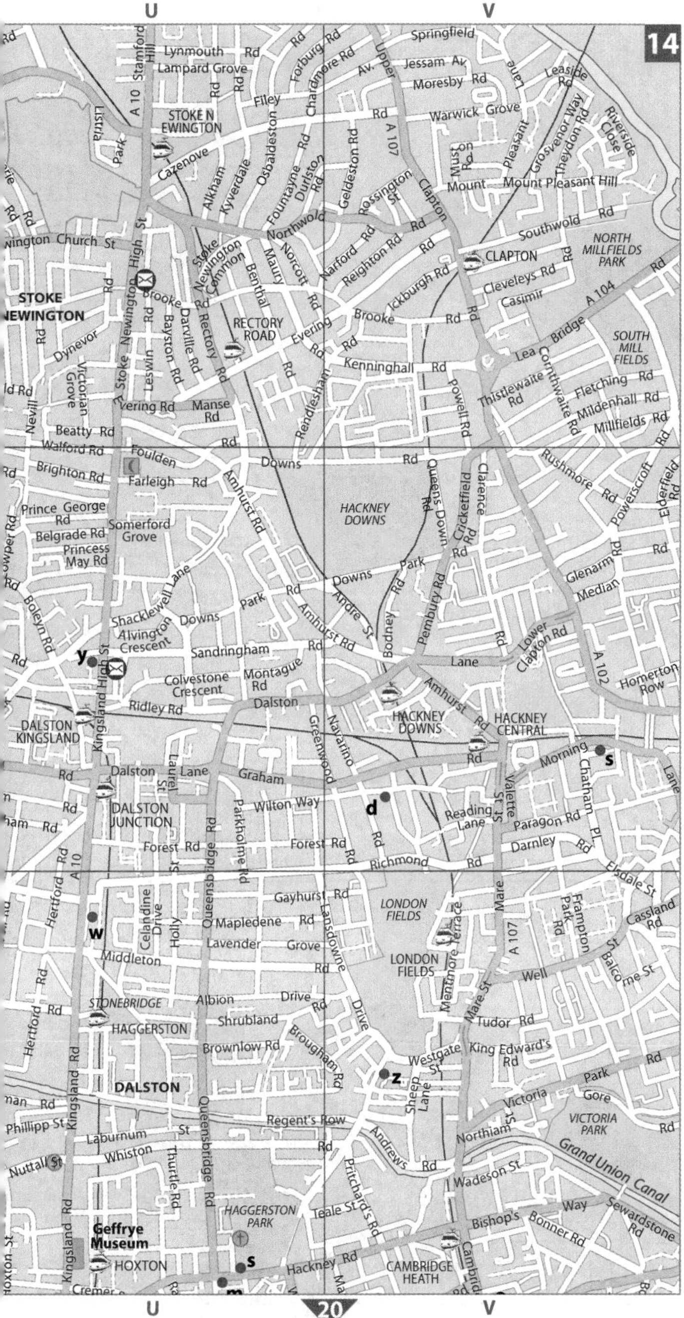
U
V
14
1
2
3
20
STOKE NEWINGTON
STOKE
NEWINGTON
CLAPTON
NORTH MILLFIELDS PARK
SOUTH MILL FIELDS
RECTORY ROAD
HACKNEY DOWNS
HACKNEY CENTRAL
DALSTON KINGSLAND
DALSTON JUNCTION
LONDON FIELDS
STONEBRIDGE
HAGGERSTON
DALSTON
VICTORIA PARK
HAGGERSTON PARK
Geffrye Museum
HOXTON
CAMBRIDGE HEATH
Grand Union Canal
Stamford Hill
A 10
A 107
A 104
A 102
Lynmouth Rd
Lampard Grove
Springfield
Upper Clapton Rd
Jessam Av.
Moresby Rd
Warwick Grove
Leaside Rd
Riverside Close
Mount Pleasant Hill
Southwold Rd
Northwold Rd
Cazenove Rd
Stoke Newington High St
Stoke Newington Common
Stoke Newington Church St
Kingsland High St
Kingsland Rd
Evering Rd
Brooke Rd
Kenninghall Rd
Lea Bridge Rd
Rushmore Rd
Amhurst Rd
Downs Park Rd
Dalston Lane
Graham Rd
Wilton Way
Richmond Rd
Mare St
Queensbridge Rd
Hackney Rd
Regent's Row
Victoria Park Rd
Bishop's Way
Wadeson St
Sewardstone Rd
Well St
Morning Lane
Homerton Row
Cassland Rd
Tudor Rd
Westgate St
Sheep Lane
Andrews Rd
Pritchard's Rd
Teale St
Whiston Rd
Laburnum St
Brownlow Rd
Shrubland Rd
Albion Drive
Middleton Rd
Lavender Grove
Mapledene Rd
Gayhurst Rd
Forest Rd
Darnley Rd
Paragon Rd
Reading Lane
Mentmore Terrace
Lansdowne Drive
Brougham Rd
Sandringham Rd
Shacklewell Lane
Somerford Grove
Farleigh Rd
Foulden Rd
Brighton Rd
Walford Rd
Beatty Rd
Manse Rd
Dynevor Rd
Rectory Rd
Powell Rd
Queens Down Rd
Cricketfield Rd
Clarence Rd
Pembury Rd
Bodney Rd
Andre St
Lower Clapton Rd
Glenarm Rd
Median Rd
Millfields Rd
Mildenhall Rd
Fletching Rd
Thistlewaite Rd
Cornthwaite Rd
Powerscroft Rd
Elderfield Rd
Chatham Pl.
Elsdale St
Balcorne St
King Edward's Rd
Northiam St
Bonner Rd
Nuttall St
Hertford Rd
Ridley Rd
Colvestone Crescent
Montague Rd
Alvington Crescent
Belgrade Rd
Prince George Rd
Princess May Rd
Boleyn Rd
Celandine Drive
Holly St
Parkholme Rd
Laurel St
Greenwood Rd
Navarino Rd
Valette St
Frampton Park Rd
Thurtle Rd
y
w
d
s
z
m

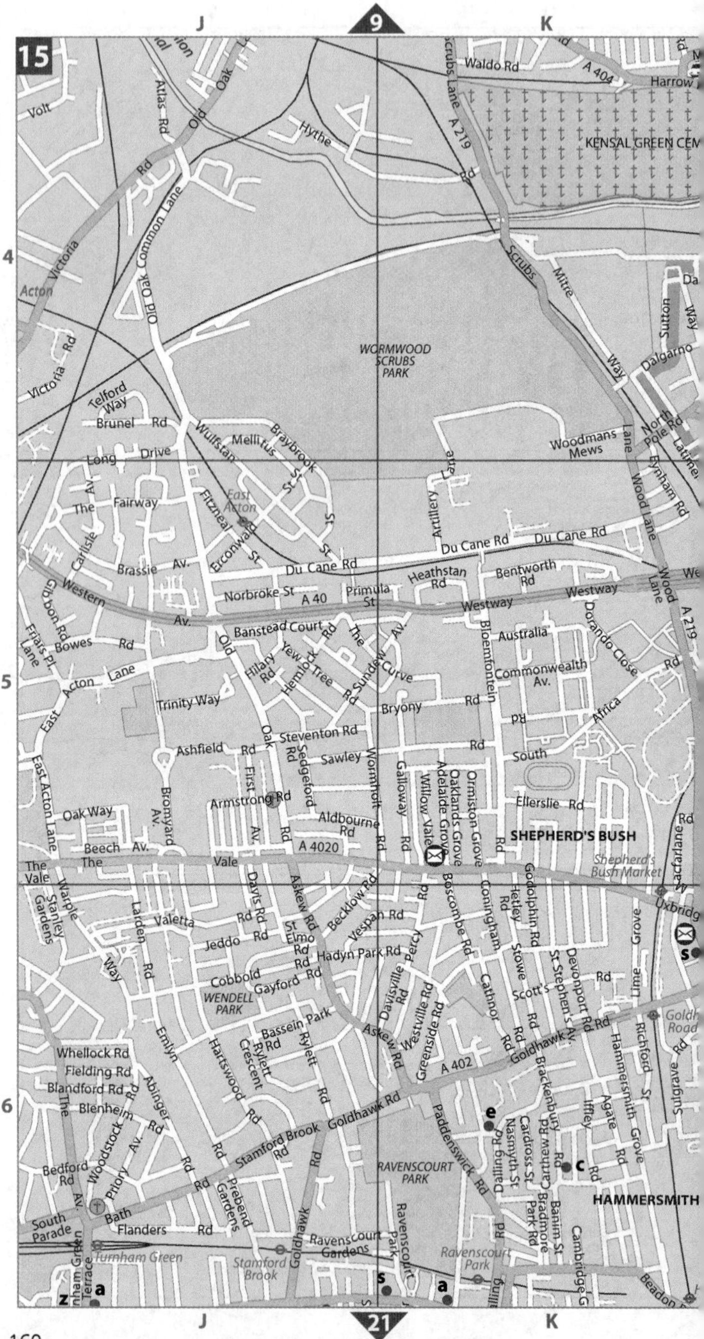
15
J
K
9
21
4
5
6
WORMWOOD SCRUBS PARK
KENSAL GREEN CEM
SHEPHERD'S BUSH
Shepherd's Bush Market
HAMMERSMITH
WENDELL PARK
RAVENSCOURT PARK
Acton
East Acton
Turnham Green
Stamford Brook
Ravenscourt Park
Goldhawk Road
Waldo Rd
A 404
Harrow
Scrubs Lane
A 219
Volt
Atlas Rd
Old Oak Rd
Hythe
Victoria Rd
Old Oak Common Lane
Telford Way
Brunel Rd
Long Drive
Wulfstan
Mellitus
Braybrook St
The Fairway
Carlisle Av.
Fitzneal
Erconwald St
Brassie Av.
Du Cane Rd
Artillery Lane
Heathstan Rd
Bentworth Rd
Woodmans Mews
Scrubs
Mitre Way
Dalgarno
Sutton Way
North Pole Rd
Latimer
Wood Lane
Eynham Rd
Western Av.
Gibbon Rd
Norbroke St
A 40
Primula St
Westway
Friars Pl. Lane
Bowes Rd
Banstead Court
The Curve
Sundew Av.
Hilary Rd
Yew Tree Rd
Hemlock Rd
Bloemfontein Rd
Australia Rd
Dorando Close
Commonwealth Av.
Africa
East Acton Lane
Trinity Way
Bryony Rd
Steventon Rd
Ashfield Rd
Sawley Rd
South Africa Rd
Sedgeford Rd
First Av.
Armstrong Rd
Bromyard Av.
Oak Way
Wormholt Rd
Galloway Rd
Willow Vale
Adelaide Grove
Oaklands Grove
Ormiston Grove
Ellerslie Rd
Aldbourne Rd
Beech Av.
The Vale
A 4020
Stanley Gardens
Warple Way
Larden Rd
Valetta Rd
Davis Rd
Askew Rd
Becklow Rd
Vespan Rd
Boscombe Rd
Coningham Rd
Hetley Rd
Godolphin Rd
Macfarlane Rd
Uxbridge
Jeddo Rd
St Elmo Rd
Hadyn Park Rd
Percy Rd
Stowe Rd
St Stephen's Av.
Devonport Rd
Lime Grove
Cobbold Rd
Gayford Rd
Davisville Rd
Westville Rd
Cathnor Rd
Scott's Rd
Greenside Rd
Emlyn
Hartswood Rd
Bassein Park Rd
Rylett Crescent
Rylett Rd
A 402
Goldhawk Rd
Hammersmith Grove
Richford St
Whellock Rd
Fielding Rd
Blandford Rd
The Av.
Blenheim Rd
Abinger Rd
Woodstock Av.
Bedford Rd
Priory
Stamford Brook Rd
Paddenswick Rd
Dalling Rd
Nasmyth St
Cardross St
Carthew Rd
Brackenbury Rd
Iffley Rd
Agate Rd
Sulgrave Rd
Bath Rd
South Parade
Flanders Rd
Prebend Gardens
Goldhawk Rd
Ravenscourt Gardens
Ravenscourt Park
Bradmore Park Rd
Banim St
Cambridge G
Beadon
Turnham Green Terrace
e
c
s
a
z

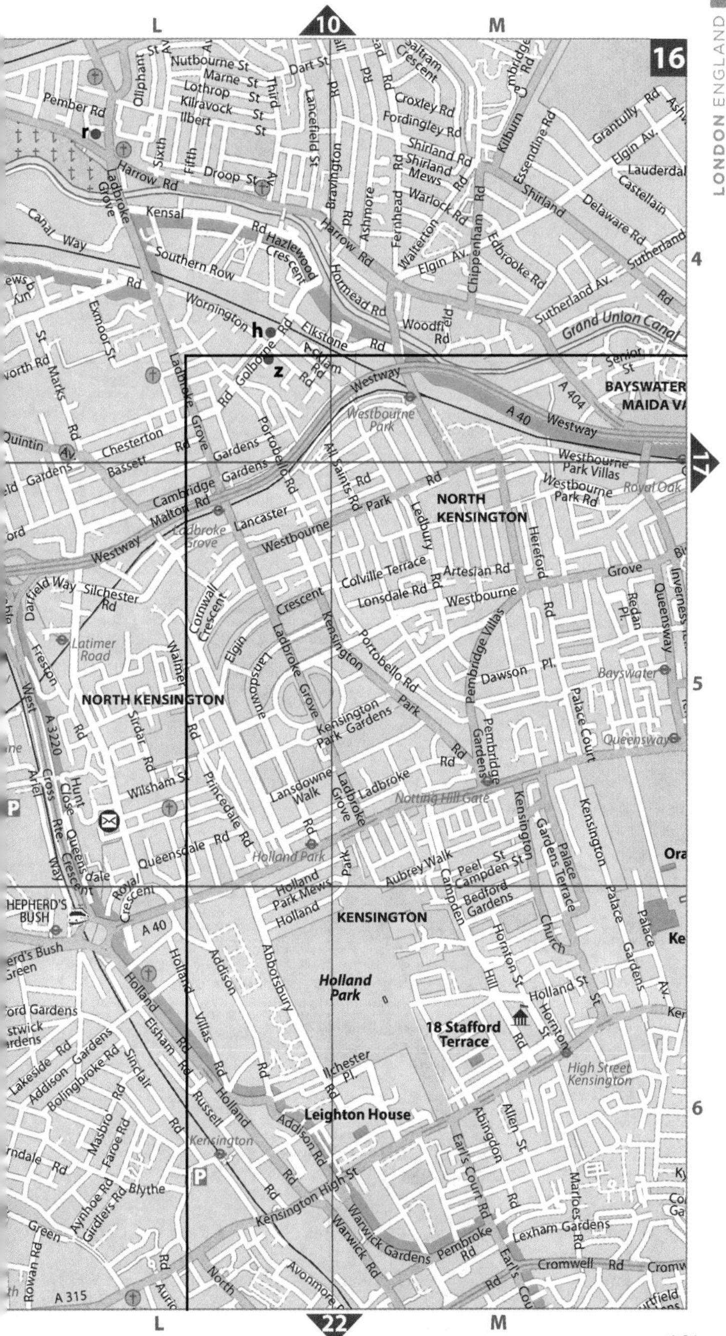
L
M
10
16
17
22
4
5
6
Harrow Rd
Kensal
Canal Way
Southern Row
Wornington Rd
Grand Union Canal
Westway
A 40
A 404
BAYSWATER
MAIDA VALE
Westbourne Park
NORTH KENSINGTON
Ladbroke Grove
Latimer Road
Portobello Rd
Kensington Park Rd
Notting Hill Gate
Holland Park
Queensway
Bayswater
Royal Oak
KENSINGTON
Holland Park
18 Stafford Terrace
Leighton House
High Street Kensington
Kensington High St
Kensington
Warwick Gardens
Earl's Court Rd
Cromwell Rd
Lexham Gardens
Shepherd's Bush Green
A 3220
A 315
Holland Rd
Addison Rd
Abbotsbury Rd
Campden Hill
Palace Gardens Terrace
Kensington Church St
Westbourne Grove
Ledbury Rd
Pembridge Villas
Ladbroke Grove
Lancaster Rd
Elgin Crescent
Cornwall Crescent
Lansdowne Rd
Chepstow

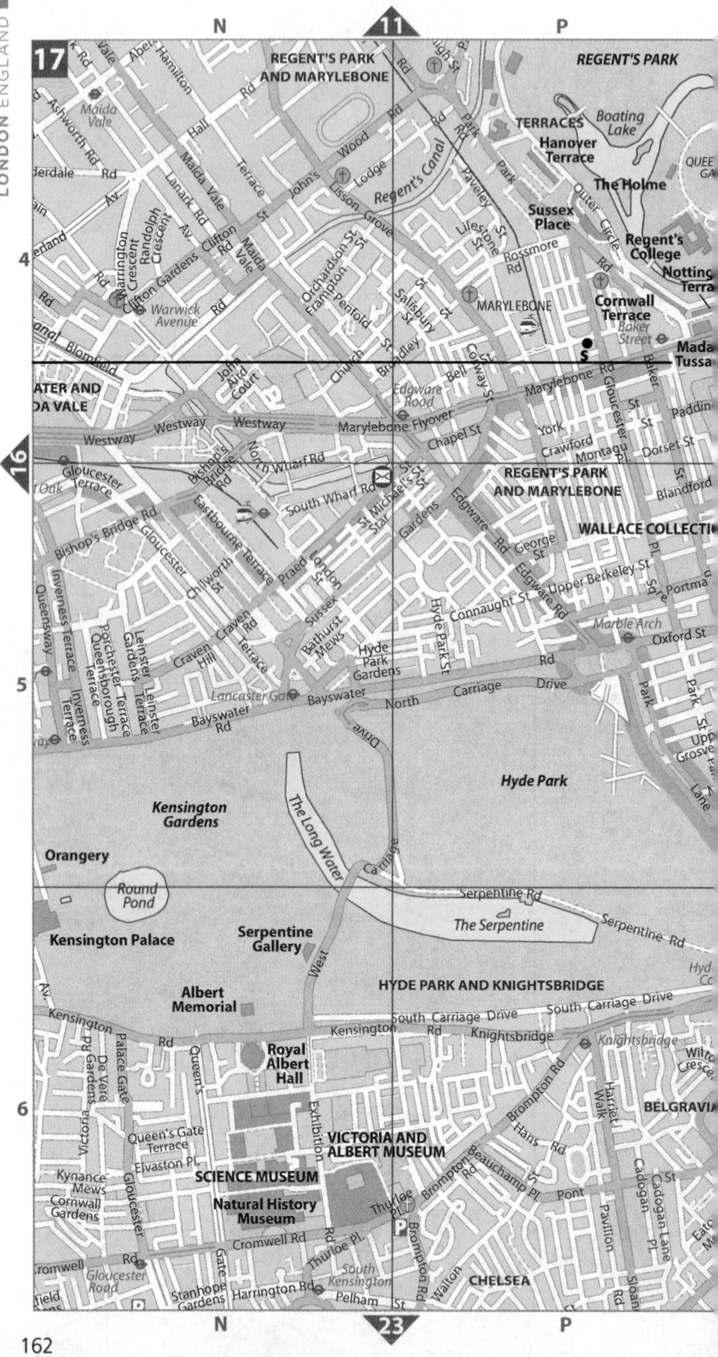
N
11
P
17
REGENT'S PARK AND MARYLEBONE
REGENT'S PARK
Maida Vale
Boating Lake
TERRACES
Hanover Terrace
The Holme
Sussex Place
Regent's College
Notting Terra
Cornwall Terrace
Baker Street
Mada Tussa
MARYLEBONE
Regent's Canal
Lisson Grove
Warwick Avenue
Edgware Road
Marylebone Flyover
Westway
ATER AND DA VALE
16
REGENT'S PARK AND MARYLEBONE
WALLACE COLLECTI
Marble Arch
Oxford St
Lancaster Gate
Bayswater Rd
North Carriage Drive
Hyde Park
Kensington Gardens
The Long Water
Orangery
Round Pond
Kensington Palace
Serpentine Gallery
The Serpentine
Serpentine Rd
Albert Memorial
HYDE PARK AND KNIGHTSBRIDGE
South Carriage Drive
Kensington Rd
Knightsbridge
Royal Albert Hall
BELGRAVI
VICTORIA AND ALBERT MUSEUM
SCIENCE MUSEUM
Natural History Museum
Cromwell Rd
Gloucester Road
South Kensington
CHELSEA
4
5
6
N
23
P

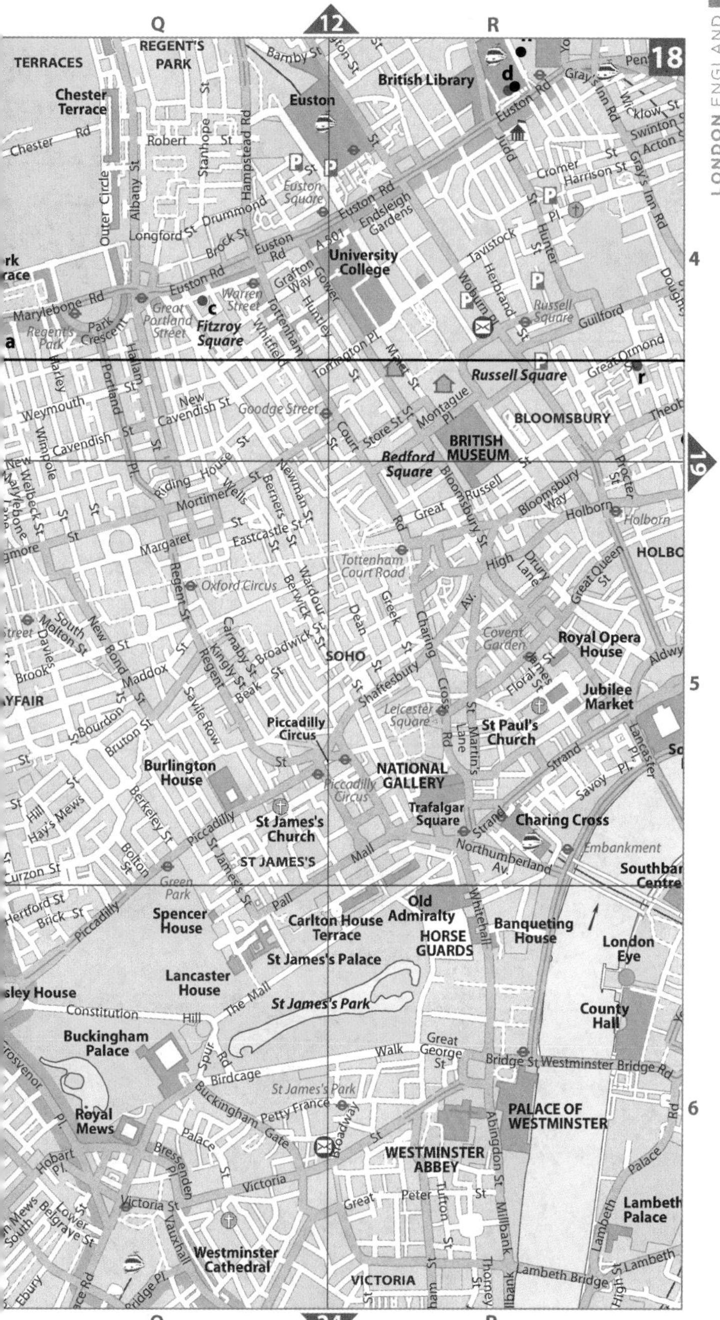
Q
12
R
18
TERRACES
REGENT'S PARK
Chester Terrace
Chester Rd
Outer Circle
Albany St
Robert St
Stanhope St
Hampstead Rd
Barmby St
Euston
Euston Square
Euston Rd
British Library
Gray's Inn Rd
Wicklow St
Swinton St
Acton St
Judd St
Cromer St
Harrison St
Hunter St
Tavistock Pl.
Herbrand St
Woburn Pl.
Russell Square
Guilford St
Great Ormond St
Doughty St
Longford St
Drummond St
Brock St
Endsleigh Gardens
Grafton Way
Gower St
University College
Warren Street
Great Portland Street
Fitzroy Square
Marylebone Rd
Regent's Park
Park Crescent
Whitfield St
Tottenham Ct Rd
Huntley St
Torrington Pl.
Malet St
Montague Pl.
BLOOMSBURY
BRITISH MUSEUM
Bedford Square
Store St
Goodge Street
New Cavendish St
Weymouth St
Harley St
Portland Pl.
Hallam St
Cavendish St
Wimpole St
New Cavendish St
Marylebone Lane
Welbeck St
Riding House St
Mortimer St
Wells St
Berners St
Newman St
Eastcastle St
Margaret St
Great Russell St
Bloomsbury St
Bloomsbury Way
Holborn
HOLBORN
Procter St
Theobalds Rd
Tottenham Court Road
High Holborn
Drury Lane
Great Queen St
Oxford Circus
Regent St
Wardour St
Berwick St
Dean St
Greek St
Charing Cross Rd
Covent Garden
Royal Opera House
Aldwych
South Molton St
Davies St
New Bond St
Brook St
MAYFAIR
Maddox St
Carnaby St
Kingly St
Broadwick St
Beak St
Savile Row
SOHO
Shaftesbury Av.
Leicester Square
Floral St
James St
Jubilee Market
St Martin's Lane
St Paul's Church
Lancaster Pl.
Strand
Savoy Pl.
Bourdon St
Bruton St
Piccadilly Circus
NATIONAL GALLERY
Burlington House
Berkeley St
Hay's Mews
Hill St
Piccadilly
St James's Church
Trafalgar Square
Charing Cross
Embankment
Northumberland Av.
Bolton St
St James's St
ST JAMES'S
Mall
Curzon St
Green Park
Southbank Centre
Hertford St
Brick St
Spencer House
Pall Mall
Carlton House Terrace
Old Admiralty
HORSE GUARDS
Whitehall
Banqueting House
London Eye
St James's Palace
Lancaster House
Apsley House
Constitution Hill
The Mall
St James's Park
County Hall
Buckingham Palace
Spur Rd
Birdcage Walk
Great George St
Bridge St
Westminster Bridge Rd
Grosvenor Pl.
Buckingham Gate
St James's Park
Petty France
Broadway
PALACE OF WESTMINSTER
Royal Mews
Palace St
Bressenden Pl.
WESTMINSTER ABBEY
Abingdon St
Hobart Pl.
Victoria St
Great Peter St
Tufton St
Millbank
Lambeth Palace
Lower Belgrave St
Vauxhall Bridge Rd
Westminster Cathedral
Lambeth Bridge
Lambeth High St
Thorney St
VICTORIA
Ebury Bridge Rd
Palace Rd
4
5
6
19
24

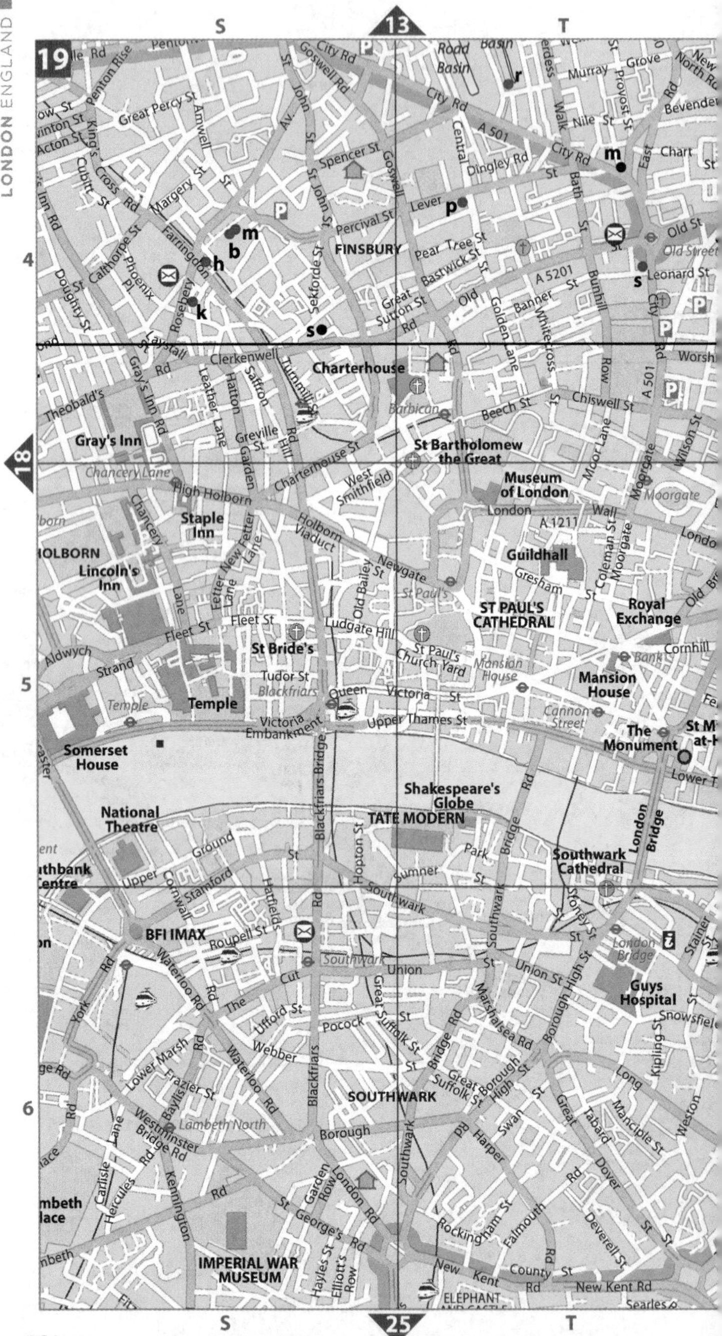
19
S
T
13
18
25
4
5
6
FINSBURY
Charterhouse
St Bartholomew the Great
Museum of London
Gray's Inn
Staple Inn
HOLBORN
Lincoln's Inn
Guildhall
ST PAUL'S CATHEDRAL
Royal Exchange
St Bride's
Mansion House
Temple
The Monument
Somerset House
Shakespeare's Globe
TATE MODERN
National Theatre
Southwark Cathedral
BFI IMAX
Guys Hospital
SOUTHWARK
IMPERIAL WAR MUSEUM

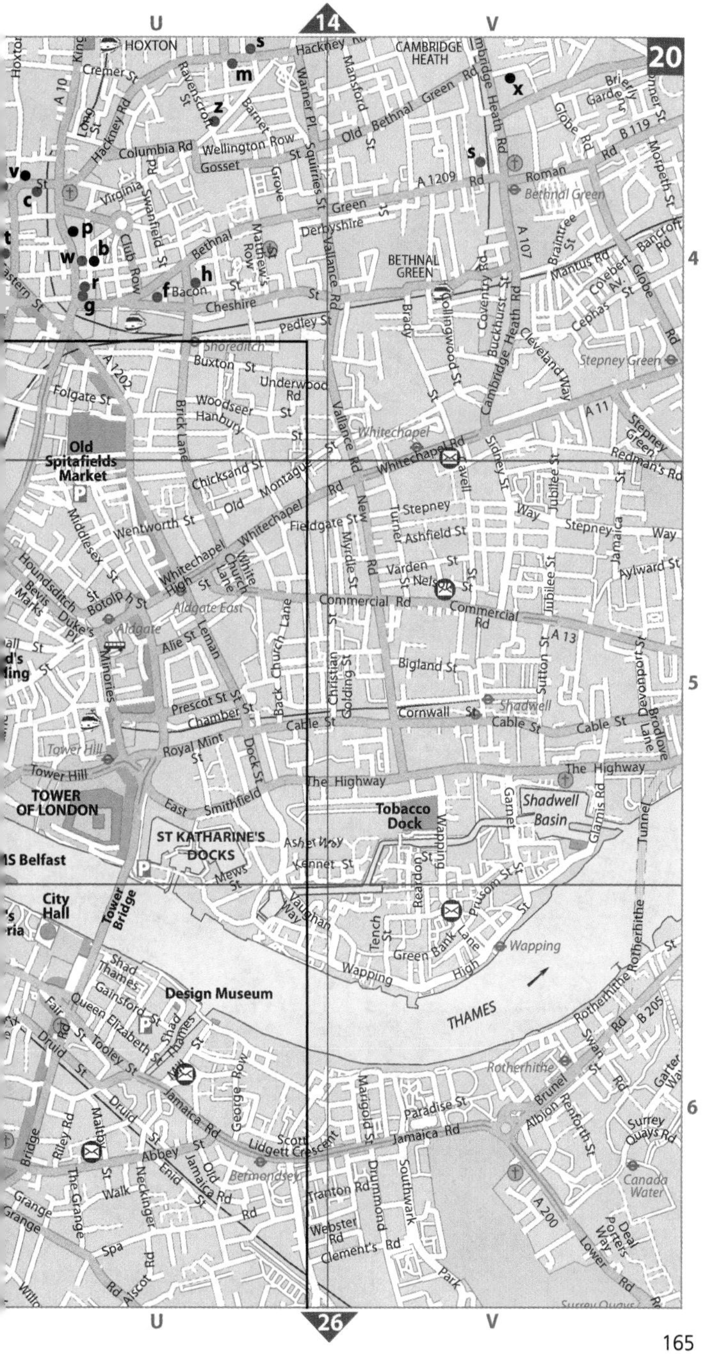
U
14
V
20
HOXTON
CAMBRIDGE HEATH
BETHNAL GREEN
Old Spitafields Market
TOWER OF LONDON
ST KATHARINE'S DOCKS
City Hall
Tower Bridge
Design Museum
Tobacco Dock
Shadwell Basin
THAMES
Hackney Rd
Cremer St
Columbia Rd
Wellington Row
Gosset St
Old Bethnal Green Rd
Roman Rd
A 1209
Derbyshire St
Bethnal Green Rd
Cheshire St
Pedley St
Buxton St
Folgate St
Brick Lane
Hanbury St
Chicksand St
Old Montague St
Wentworth St
Whitechapel Rd
Whitechapel High St
Commercial Rd
Cable St
The Highway
Royal Mint St
East Smithfield
Wapping High St
Wapping Lane
Tower Hill
Aldgate
Aldgate East
Shoreditch
Whitechapel
Bethnal Green
Stepney Green
Shadwell
Wapping
Rotherhithe
Bermondsey
Canada Water
Surrey Quays
Vallance Rd
Cambridge Heath Rd
Stepney Way
Jamaica Rd
Tooley St
Shad Thames
Lower Rd
Rotherhithe Tunnel
A 13
A 11
A 107
A 200
B 205
4
5
6
26

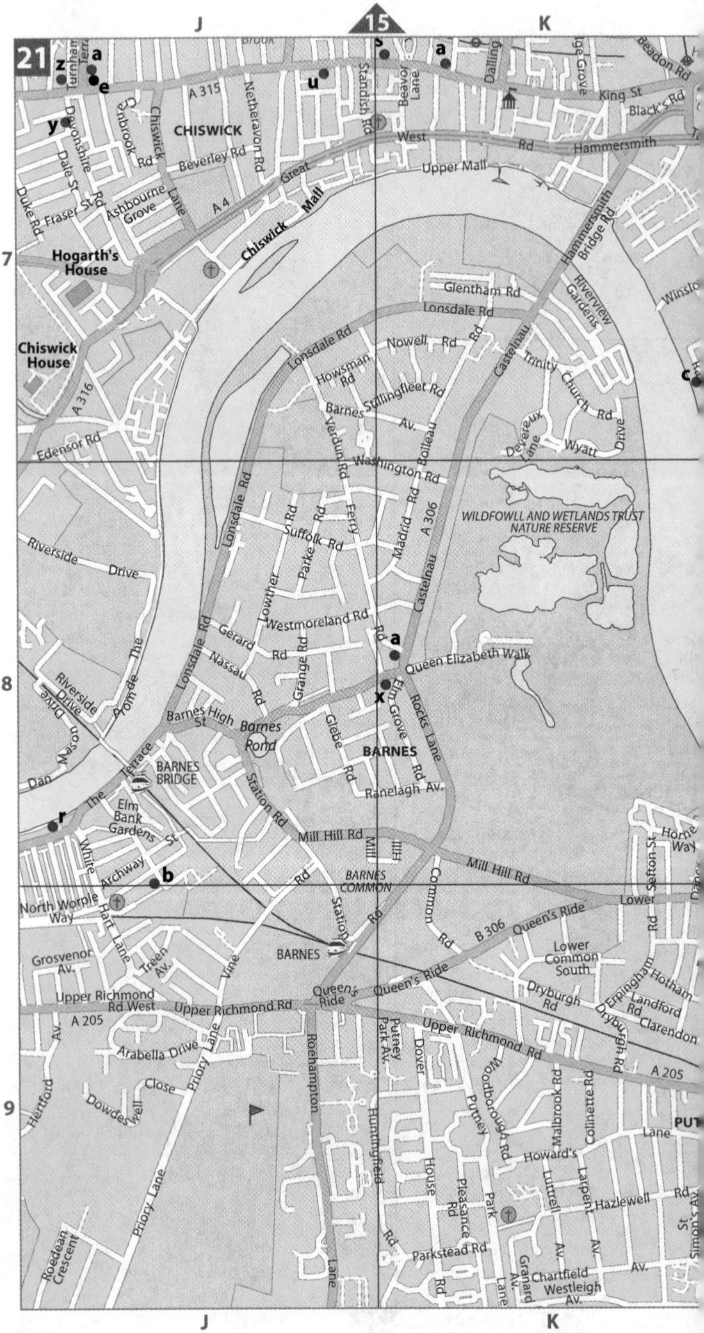
J
15
K
21
CHISWICK
Hogarth's House
Chiswick House
Chiswick Mall
Upper Mall
Hammersmith Bridge Rd
King St
Black's Rd
Great West Rd
Hammersmith
Beverley Rd
Ashbourne Grove
Devonshire Rd
Dale St
Duke Rd
Fraser St
Chiswick Lane
Netheravon Rd
Standish Rd
Beavor Lane
Dalling
Beadon Rd
Turnham
Edensor Rd
Riverside Drive
Glentham Rd
Lonsdale Rd
Riverview Gardens
Nowell Rd
Howsman Rd
Stillingfleet Rd
Barnes Av.
Castelnau
Trinity Church Rd
Devereux Lane
Wyatt Drive
Washington Rd
Verdun Rd
Boileau Rd
WILDFOWLL AND WETLANDS TRUST NATURE RESERVE
Suffolk Rd
Ferry Rd
Madrid Rd
A 306
Lowther Rd
Parke Rd
Westmoreland Rd
Gerard Rd
Nassau Rd
Grange Rd
Queen Elizabeth Walk
Elm Grove Rd
Rocks Lane
Barnes High St
Barnes Pond
BARNES
Glebe Rd
Ranelagh Av.
Prom de The
The Terrace
BARNES BRIDGE
Dan Mason Drive
Elm Bank Gardens
White Archway St
Station Rd
Mill Hill Rd
BARNES COMMON
Common Rd
B 306
Queen's Ride
Lower Common South
North Worple Way
Hart Lane
Grosvenor Av.
Treen Av.
Vine Rd
BARNES
Station Rd
Upper Richmond Rd West
A 205
Upper Richmond Rd
Dryburgh Rd
Erpingham Rd
Hotham Rd
Landford Rd
Clarendon
Sefton St
Horne Way
Lower
Arabella Drive
Priory Lane
Roehampton Lane
Putney Park Av.
Dover House Rd
Putney Park Lane
Woodborough Rd
Malbrook Rd
Colinette Rd
Hertford Av.
Close
Dowdeswell Close
Huntingfield Rd
Howard's Lane
Luttrell Av.
Larpent Av.
Hazlewell Rd
Pleasance Rd
Parkstead Rd
Granard Av.
Chartfield Av.
Westleigh Av.
Roedean Crescent
Simon's Av.
A 315
A 4
A 316
7
8
9

L
16
M
22
23
7
8
9
EARL'S COURT
Earl's Court
WEST KENSINGTON
West Kensington
Barons Court
West Brompton
BROMPTON CEMETERY
NORMAND PARK
FULHAM
Fulham Broadway
Parsons Green
EEL BROOK COMMON
BISHOPS PARK
Putney Bridge
HURLINGHAM PARK
SOUTH PARK
WANDSWORTH PARK
PUTNEY
East Putney
WANDSWORTH TOWN
A 315
A 304
A 308
A 217
A 219
Cromwell Rd
West Cromwell Rd
North End Rd
Lillie Rd
Old Brompton Rd
Warwick Rd
Philbeach Gardens
Trebovir Rd
Eardley Crescent
Finborough Rd
Ifield Rd
Redcliffe Gardens
Coleherne Rd
Bolton Gardens
Edith Rd
Gwendwr Rd
Comeragh Rd
Castletown Rd
Fairholme Rd
Perham Rd
Star Rd
Turneville Rd
Musard Rd
Margravine Gardens
Margravine Rd
Greyhound Rd
Claxton Grove
Everington St
Fulham Palace Rd
Brecon Rd
Chaldon Rd
Delaford St
Mendora Rd
Prothero Rd
Estcourt Rd
Dawes Rd
Racton Rd
Ongar Rd
Halford Rd
Walham Grove
Shorrolds Rd
Burnthwaite Rd
Barclay Rd
Harwood Rd
Britannia Rd
King's Rd
Fulham Rd
Homestead Rd
Kelvedon Rd
Orbain Rd
Wyfold Rd
Kingwood Rd
Filmer Rd
Lilyville Rd
Radipole Rd
Chesilton Rd
Rostrevor Rd
Felden St
Munster Rd
Purser's Cross Rd
Fulham Court
Wardo Av.
Gowan Av.
Vera Rd
Finlay St
Ellerby St
Doneraile St
Bishop's Av.
Fulham High St
Fulham Park Gardens
New King's Rd
Parsons Green
Clancarty Rd
Coniger Rd
Perrymead St
Imperial Rd
Bagley's Lane
Peterborough Rd
Settrington Rd
Broomhouse Lane
Hurlingham Rd
Napier Av.
Ranelagh Gardens
Putney Bridge Approach
Richmond Rd
Lacy Rd
Deodar Rd
Putney Bridge Rd
Chelverton Rd
Norroy Rd
Oxford Rd
Wadham Rd
Fawe Park Rd
Osiers Rd
Upper Richmond Rd
Putney Hill
St John's Av.
Carlton Drive
Keswick Rd
Oakhill Rd
Schubert Rd
Mexfield Rd
Cromford Rd
Santos Rd
Fiction Close
West Hill
Frogmore
The Causeway
Wandle
Ram St
Fairfield St
Wandsworth High St
Smugglers Way
Swandon Way
Sullivan Rd
Hugon Rd
Carnwath Rd
Stephendale Rd
Cranbury Rd
Hazlebury Rd
a
m
k
s
a
e
x
r
b

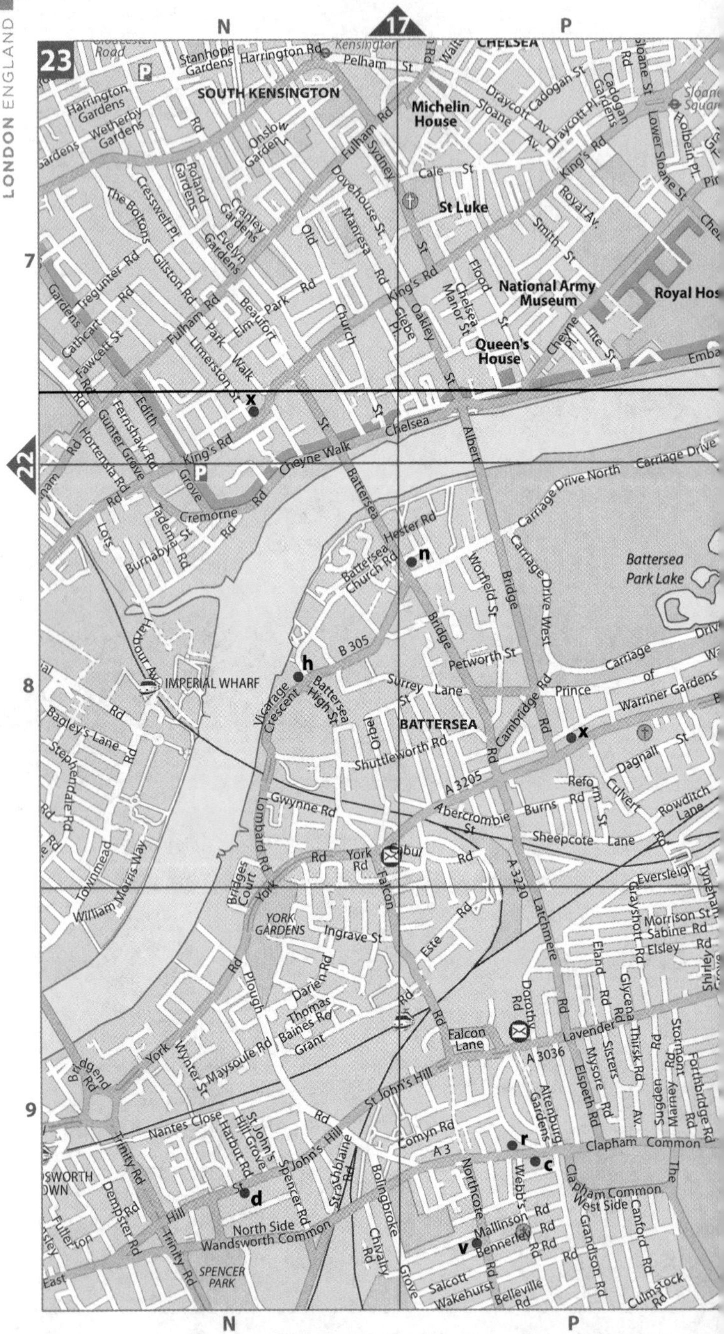
N
P
17
22
23
7
8
9
SOUTH KENSINGTON
CHELSEA
Michelin House
St Luke
National Army Museum
Queen's House
Royal Hos
Battersea Park Lake
IMPERIAL WHARF
BATTERSEA
YORK GARDENS
SPENCER PARK
Harrington Rd
Pelham St
Fulham Rd
King's Rd
Cheyne Walk
Chelsea
Battersea Bridge Rd
Albert Bridge Rd
Carriage Drive North
Carriage Drive West
Prince of Wales Dr
Battersea High St
Vicarage Crescent
Battersea Church Rd
Hester Rd
Surrey Lane
Shuttleworth Rd
Gwynne Rd
York Rd
Falcon Rd
Lombard Rd
Cremorne Rd
Lots Rd
Harbour Av
Bagley's Lane
Townmead Rd
William Morris Way
St John's Hill
Lavender Hill
Clapham Common North Side
Clapham Common West Side
Wandsworth Common North Side
Trinity Rd
Northcote Rd
Latchmere Rd
Cambridge Rd
Abercrombie St
Sheepcote Lane
Falcon Lane
A 3205
A 3220
A 3036
A 3
B 305
x
n
h
d
r
c
v
N
P

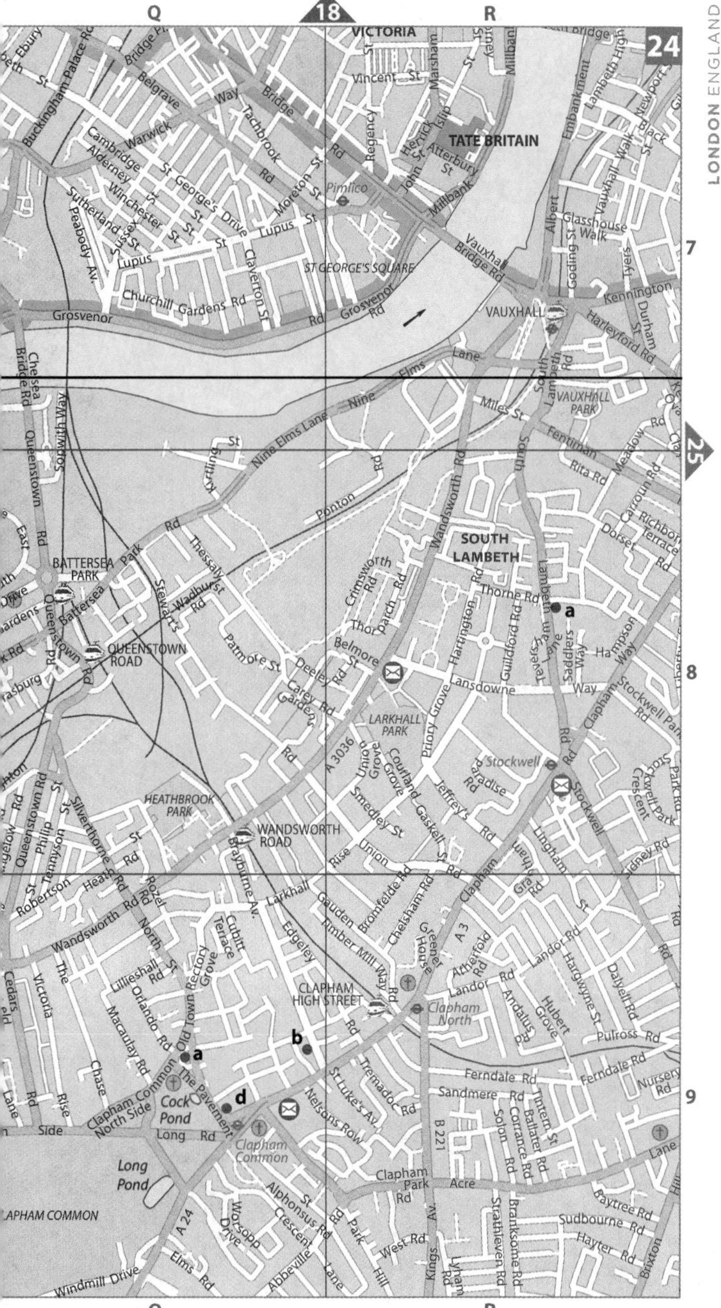

Q
18
R
24
VICTORIA
Vincent St
Marsham St
Millbank
Bridge Pl.
Buckingham Palace Rd
Eccleston
Belgrave Rd
Warwick Way
Vauxhall Bridge Rd
Tachbrook St
Cambridge St
Alderney St
Winchester St
St George's Drive
Sutherland St
Sussex St
Peabody Av.
Moreton St
Lupus St
Claverton St
Churchill Gardens Rd
Grosvenor Rd
Regency St
Herrick St
John Islip St
Atterbury St
TATE BRITAIN
Pimlico
ST GEORGE'S SQUARE
Albert Embankment
Lambeth High St
Newport St
Black Prince Rd
Vauxhall Walk
Glasshouse Walk
Goding St
Tyers St
Kennington Lane
Durham St
Harleyford Rd
VAUXHALL
Bridge Rd
Chelsea Bridge Rd
Nine Elms Lane
Miles St
South Lambeth Rd
VAUXHALL PARK
Fentiman Rd
Rita Rd
Meadow Rd
Carroun Rd
Richborne Terrace
Dorset Rd
25
Queenstown Rd
Sopwith Way
Kirtling St
Ponton Rd
Wandsworth Rd
SOUTH LAMBETH
Crimsworth Rd
Thorncroft
Thorparch Rd
Belmore St
Thorne Rd
Hartington Rd
Guildford Rd
Teversham Lane
Saddlers Way
Hampson Way
Lansdowne Way
Stockwell Park Rd
Clapham Rd
BATTERSEA PARK
Battersea Park Rd
QUEENSTOWN ROAD
Thessaly Rd
Stewart's Rd
Wadhurst Rd
Patmore St
Deeley Rd
Carey Gardens
LARKHALL PARK
Priory Grove
Stockwell
Paradise Rd
Jeffrey's Rd
Union Grove
Courland Grove
Smedley St
Gaskell St
A 3036
Stockwell Park Crescent
HEATHBROOK PARK
WANDSWORTH ROAD
Brayburne Av.
Union Rd
Rise
Bromfelde Rd
Chelsham Rd
Lingham St
Sidney Rd
Philip St
Tennyson St
Silverthorne Rd
Robertson St
Heath Rd
Rozel Rd
Larkhall
Gauden Rd
Timber Mill Way
Edgeley Rd
Cubitt Terrace
Wandsworth Rd
North St
Rectory Grove
Greener House
A 3
Atherfold Rd
Landor Rd
Hargwyne St
Dalyell Rd
Lilleshall Rd
Orlando Rd
Old Town
Macaulay Rd
Victoria Rise
The Chase
CLAPHAM HIGH STREET
Clapham North
Andalus Rd
Hubert Grove
Pulross Rd
a
b
d
Clapham Common North Side
The Pavement
Cock Pond
Long Rd
Tremadoc Rd
St Luke's Av.
Nelsons Row
Ferndale Rd
Sandmere Rd
Solon Rd
Corrance Rd
Tintern St
Ballater Rd
Nursery Rd
B 221
Clapham Common
Long Pond
CLAPHAM COMMON
A 24
Worsopp Drive
Alphonsus St
Crescent Rd
Park Hill
Clapham Park Rd
Acre Lane
Baytree Rd
Sudbourne Rd
Hayter Rd
Brixton Hill
West Rd
Kings Av.
Lyham Rd
Strathleven Rd
Branksome Rd
Abbeville Rd
Elms Rd
Windmill Drive
7
8
9

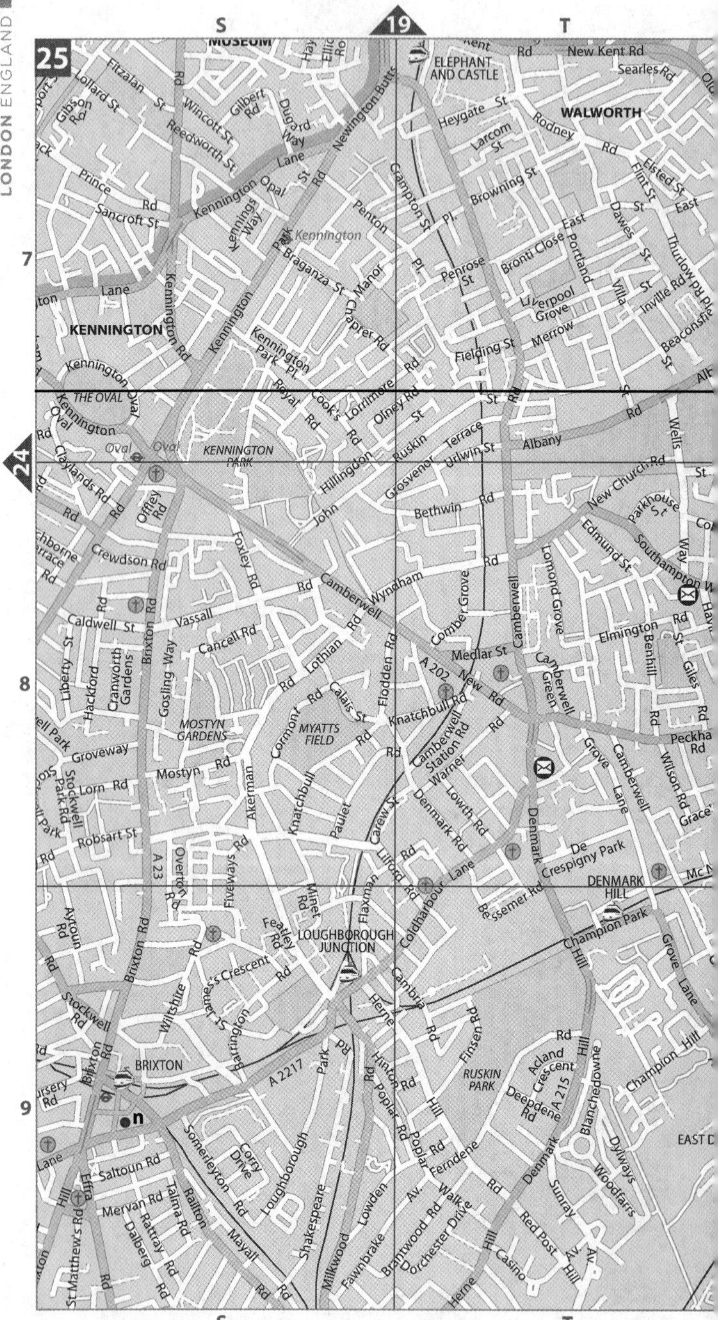
S
19
T
25
24
7
8
9
MUSEUM
ELEPHANT AND CASTLE
WALWORTH
KENNINGTON
THE OVAL
KENNINGTON PARK
MOSTYN GARDENS
MYATTS FIELD
LOUGHBOROUGH JUNCTION
DENMARK HILL
BRIXTON
RUSKIN PARK
EAST D
Kennington
New Kent Rd
Searles Rd
Heygate St
Larcom St
Rodney Rd
Elsted St
Flint St
East St
Browning St
Dawes St
Thurlow Park Rd
Bronti Close
East St
Portland St
Villa St
Inville Rd
Beaconsfield St
Penrose St
Liverpool Grove
Merrow St
Fielding St
Crampton St
Penton Pl.
Manor Pl.
Chapter Rd
Braganza St
Kennington Park Rd
Kennington Park Pl.
Newington Butts
Kennington Lane
Opal St
Kennings Way
Dugard Way
Gilbert Rd
Wincott St
Reedworth St
Fitzalan St
Lollard St
Gibson Rd
Prince Rd
Sancroft St
Kennington Rd
Kennington Oval
Royal Rd
Cook's Rd
Lorrimore Rd
Olney Rd
Ruskin St
Hillingdon St
John Ruskin St
Grosvenor Terrace
Urlwin St
Albany Rd
Wells Way
New Church Rd
Parkhouse St
Bethwin Rd
Edmund St
Southampton Way
Claylands Rd
Offley Rd
Crewdson Rd
Foxley Rd
Camberwell Rd
Wyndham Rd
Comber Grove
Lomond Grove
Elmington Rd
Benhill Rd
St Giles Rd
Caldwell St
Brixton Rd
Vassall Rd
Cancell Rd
Lothian Rd
Flodden Rd
Medlar St
Camberwell Green
Liberty St
Hackford Rd
Cranworth Gardens
Gosling Way
Calais St
Cormont Rd
Knatchbull Rd
A 202
Camberwell New Rd
Camberwell Station Rd
Warner Rd
Groveway
Mostyn Rd
Akerman Rd
Paulet Rd
Carew St
Denmark Rd
Lowth Rd
Grove Lane
Camberwell Grove
Wilson Rd
Peckham Rd
Lorn Rd
Stockwell Park Rd
Robsart St
A 23
Overton Rd
Fiveways Rd
Lilford Rd
Coldharbour Lane
De Crespigny Park
Denmark Hill
Bessemer Rd
Champion Park
Aytoun Rd
Minet Rd
Flaxman Rd
Featley Rd
St James's Crescent
Wiltshire Rd
Stockwell Rd
Barrington Rd
Cambria Rd
Herne Hill Rd
Finsen Rd
Acland Crescent
Blanchedowne
Champion Hill
A 2217
Hinton Rd
Poplar Rd
Deepdene Rd
A 215
Nursery Rd
Saltoun Rd
Somerleyton Rd
Corry Drive
Loughborough Rd
Ferndene Rd
Dylways
Woodfarrs
Sunray Av.
Effra Rd
Mervan Rd
Talma Rd
Railton Rd
Rattray Rd
Dalberg Rd
St Matthew's Rd
Mayall Rd
Shakespeare Rd
Milkwood Rd
Lowden Rd
Fawnbrake Av.
Brantwood Rd
Dorchester Drive
Red Post Hill
Casino Av.
Herne Hill

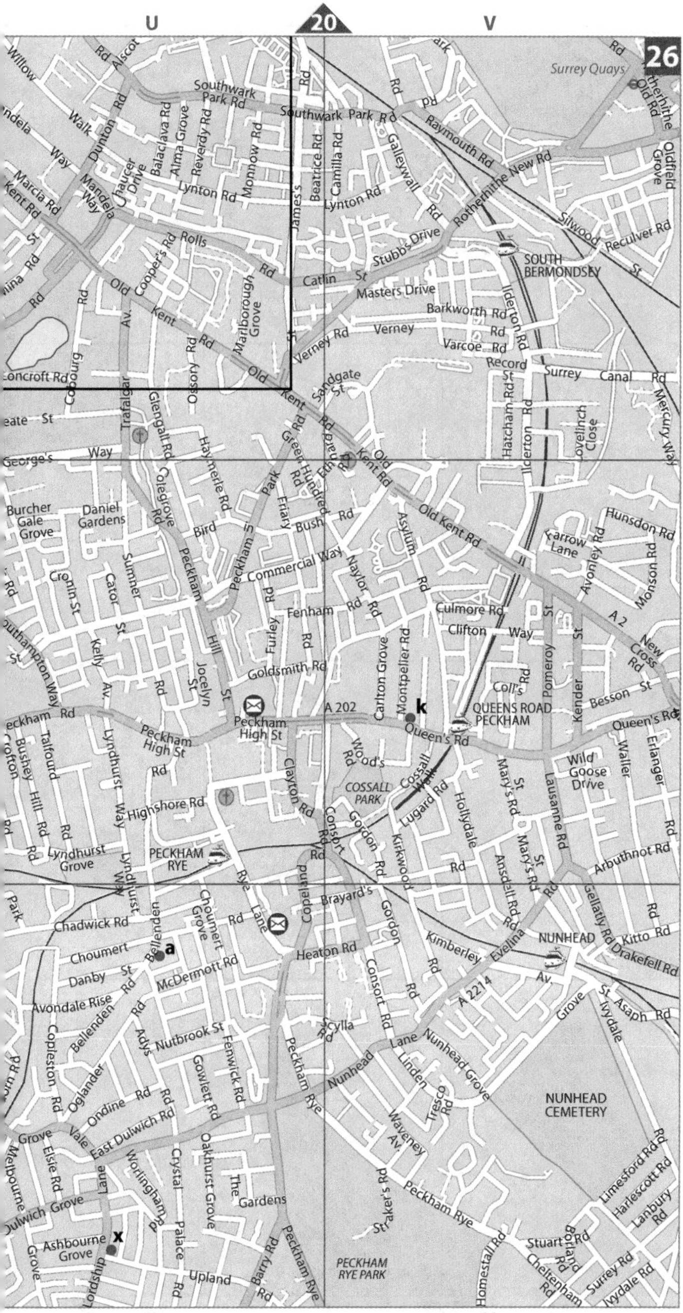
U
20
V
26
7
8
9
Surrey Quays
Southwark Park Rd
Southwark Park Rd
Raymouth Rd
Rotherhithe New Rd
Rotherhithe Old Rd
Oldfield Grove
Silwood St
Reculver Rd
Alscot Rd
Willow Walk
Mandela Way
Marcia Rd
Dunton Rd
Chaucer Drive
Balaclava Rd
Alma Grove
Reverdy Rd
Monnow Rd
Lynton Rd
Beatrice Rd
Camilla Rd
Galleywall Rd
James's
Rolls Rd
Catlin St
Stubbs Drive
SOUTH BERMONDSEY
Masters Drive
Barkworth Rd
Verney Rd
Varcoe Rd
Record St
Ilderton Rd
Surrey Canal Rd
Mercury Way
Old Kent Rd
Cooper's Rd
Marlborough Grove
Ossory Rd
Cobourg Rd
Trafalgar Av.
Glengall Rd
Sandgate St
Hatcham Rd
Lovelinch Close
St George's Way
Coleqrove Rd
Haymerle Rd
Green Hundred Rd
Ethnard Rd
Burcher Gale Grove
Daniel Gardens
Peckham Hill St
Bird in Bush Rd
Friary Rd
Asylum Rd
Hunsdon Rd
Farrow Lane
Avonley Rd
Monson Rd
Sumner Rd
Cator St
Cronin St
Commercial Way
Naylor Rd
Fenham Rd
Culmore Rd
Clifton Way
Pomeroy St
Kender St
A 2
New Cross Rd
Kelly Av.
Jocelyn St
Furley Rd
Goldsmith Rd
Carlton Grove
Montpelier Rd
Coll's Rd
Besson St
Southampton Way
Peckham Rd
Peckham High St
A 202
k
QUEENS ROAD PECKHAM
Queen's Rd
Crofton Rd
Bushey Hill Rd
Talfourd Rd
Lyndhurst Way
Wood's Rd
COSSALL PARK
Cossall Walk
Lugard Rd
Hollydale Rd
St Mary's Rd
Lausanne Rd
Wild Goose Drive
Waller Rd
Erlanger Rd
Clayton Rd
Highshore Rd
Consort Rd
Gordon Rd
Kirkwood Rd
Ansdell Rd
Arbuthnot Rd
Lyndhurst Grove
PECKHAM RYE
Rye Lane
Copeland Rd
Brayard's Rd
Gellatly Rd
Park
Chadwick Rd
Bellenden Rd
Choumert Grove
Choumert Rd
a
Kimberley Rd
Evelina Rd
NUNHEAD
Kitto Rd
Drakefell Rd
Danby St
McDermott Rd
Heaton Rd
A 2214
Avondale Rise
St Asaph Rd
Ivydale Rd
Copleston Rd
Adys Rd
Nutbrook St
Fenwick Rd
Scylla Rd
Nunhead Lane
Nunhead Grove
Oglander Rd
Gowlett Rd
Linden Grove
Ondine Rd
NUNHEAD CEMETERY
Grove Vale
East Dulwich Rd
Tresco Rd
Waveney Av.
Melbourne Grove
Elsie Rd
Worlingham Rd
Crystal Palace Rd
Oakhurst Grove
The Gardens
Limesford Rd
Harlescott Rd
Lanbury Rd
Dulwich Grove
Lordship Lane
x
Ashbourne Grove
Straker's Rd
Peckham Rye
Homestall Rd
Stuart Rd
Borland Rd
Cheltenham Rd
Surrey Rd
Ivydale Rd
Upland Rd
Barry Rd
PECKHAM RYE PARK

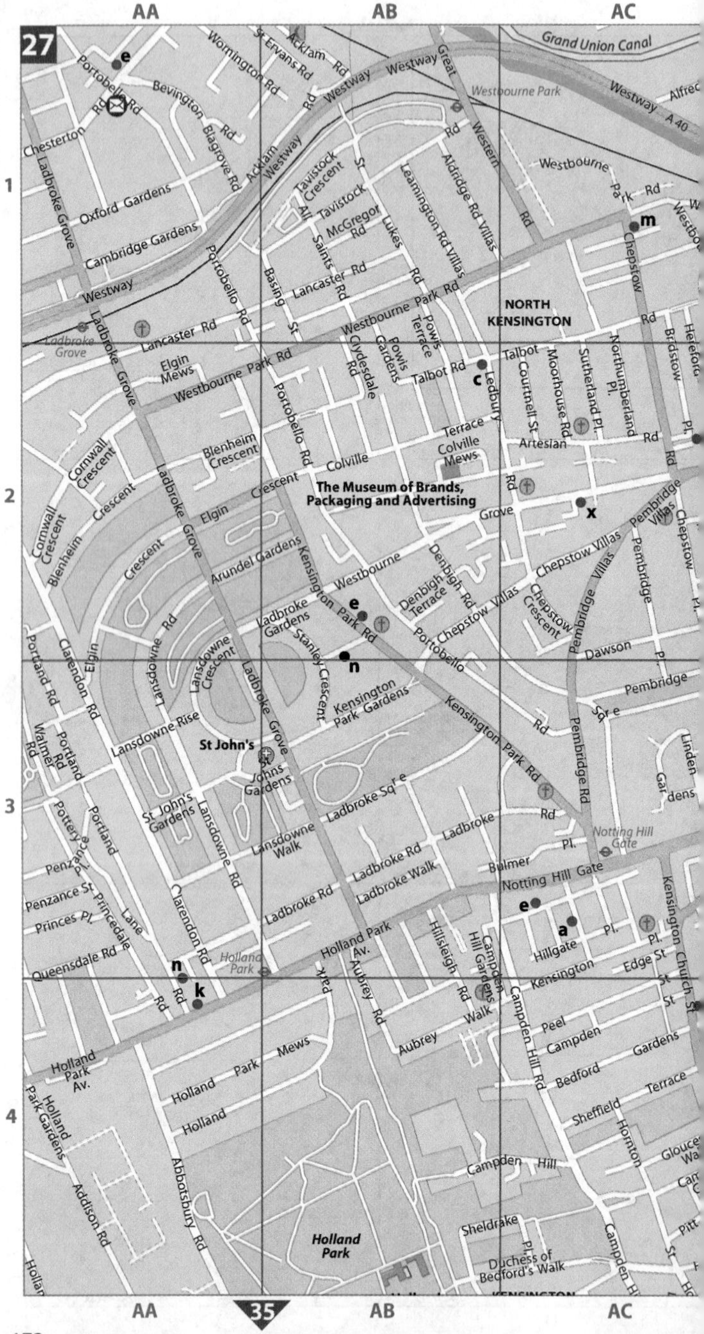
27
AA
AB
AC
1
2
3
4
35
Grand Union Canal
Westway
NORTH KENSINGTON
The Museum of Brands, Packaging and Advertising
St John's
Holland Park
Ladbroke Grove
Portobello Rd
Westbourne Park Rd
Kensington Park Rd
Notting Hill Gate
Holland Park Av.
Westbourne Park
Notting Hill Gate
Holland Park
Ladbroke Grove
Chepstow Villas
Pembridge Villas
Ledbury Rd
Talbot Rd
Elgin Crescent
Lansdowne Rd
Clarendon Rd
Campden Hill Rd
Kensington Church St
Abbotsbury Rd
Addison Rd

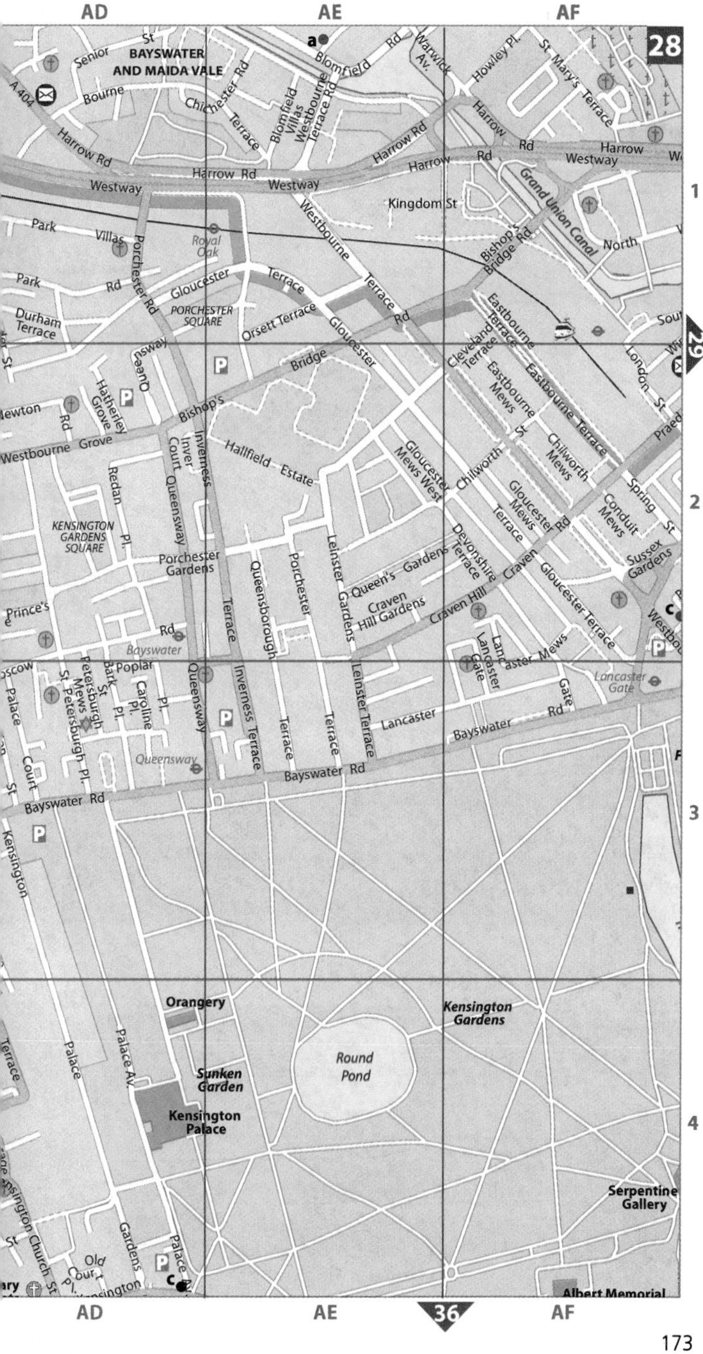
AD
AE
AF
28
29
36
1
2
3
4
BAYSWATER AND MAIDA VALE
A 404
Senior St
Bourne
Harrow Rd
Westway
Chichester Rd
Terrace
Blomfield
Blomfield Villas
Westbourne Terrace Rd
Warwick Av.
Howley Pl.
St Mary's Terrace
Harrow Rd
Harrow
Rd
Harrow
Westway
Grand Union Canal
Kingdom St
North
Park
Villas
Royal Oak
Porchester Rd
Park
Rd
Gloucester
Terrace
Westbourne
Terrace
Rd
Bishop's Bridge Rd
Durham Terrace
PORCHESTER SQUARE
Orsett Terrace
Gloucester
Eastbourne Terrace
Cleveland Terrace
Eastbourne Mews
Eastbourne Terrace
London St
Praed
Queensway
Bridge
Bishop's
Hatherley Grove
Newton Rd
Westbourne Grove
Inverness Court
Inver Court
Hallfield Estate
Gloucester Mews West
Chilworth
St
Chilworth Mews
Spring St
Conduit Mews
Gloucester Mews
Terrace
Rd
Sussex Gardens
Redan Pl.
KENSINGTON GARDENS SQUARE
Queensway
Porchester Gardens
Devonshire Terrace
Craven
Gloucester Terrace
Queensborough
Porchester
Leinster Gardens
Queen's Gardens
Craven Hill Gardens
Craven Hill
Prince's
Rd
Bayswater
Terrace
Lancaster Gate
Lancaster Mews
Westbourne
Poplar Pl.
Moscow
Palace
Court
St Petersburgh Mews
St Petersburgh Pl.
Caroline Pl.
Queensway
Inverness Terrace
Terrace
Terrace
Leinster Terrace
Lancaster
Bayswater
Rd
Gate
Lancaster Gate
Queensway
Bayswater Rd
Bayswater Rd
Kensington
Orangery
Kensington Gardens
Round Pond
Terrace
Palace
Palace Av.
Sunken Garden
Kensington Palace
Serpentine Gallery
Kensington Church St
St
Old Court Pl.
Gardens
Palace
Kensington
Albert Memorial

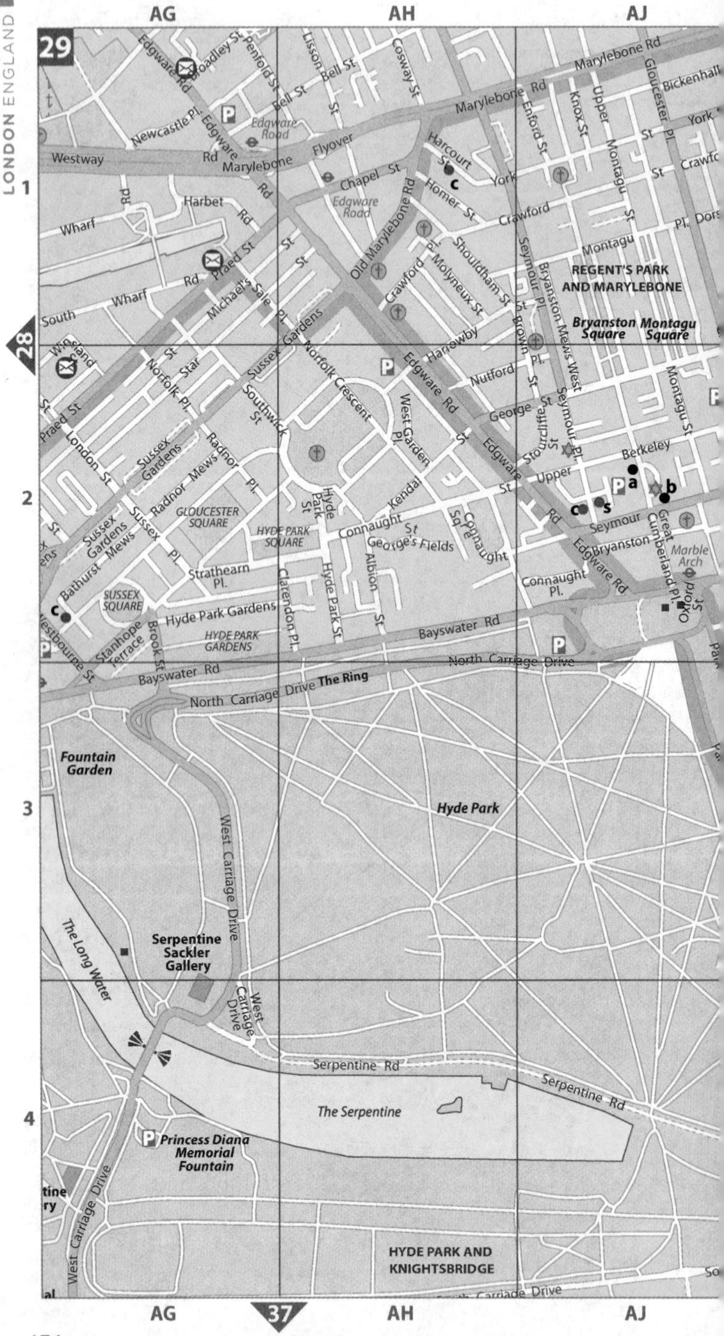
AG
AH
AJ
29
28
37
1
2
3
4
Edgware Rd
Broadley St
Penfold St
Lisson St
Bell St
Cosway St
Marylebone Rd
Gloucester Pl.
Bickenhall
Newcastle Pl.
Edgware Road
Marylebone Flyover
Westway
Harcourt St
Enford St
Knox St
Upper Montagu St
York St
Crawford St
Chapel St
Homer St
Harbet Rd
Wharf Rd
Old Marylebone Rd
Crawford
Shouldham St
Seymour Pl.
Bryanston Mews West
Montagu
Dorset
Praed St
Crawford Pl.
Molyneux St
REGENT'S PARK AND MARYLEBONE
South Wharf Rd
St Michael's St
Sale Pl.
Sussex Gardens
Norfolk Crescent
Harrowby St
Brown St
Bryanston Square
Montagu Square
Norfolk Pl.
Star St
Southwick St
Nutford Pl.
George St
Montagu St
West Garden Pl.
Stourcliffe St
Seymour Pl.
Berkeley
London St
Sussex Gardens
Radnor Pl.
Radnor Mews
Upper Berkeley St
Kendal St
GLOUCESTER SQUARE
HYDE PARK SQUARE
Hyde Park St
Connaught Sq
Connaught St
George's Fields
Connaught Pl.
Seymour
Bryanston
Great Cumberland Pl.
Marble Arch
Oxford St
Bathurst Mews
Sussex Pl.
Strathearn Pl.
Clarendon Pl.
Albion St
SUSSEX SQUARE
Hyde Park Gardens
HYDE PARK GARDENS
Westbourne St
Stanhope Terrace
Brook St
Bayswater Rd
North Carriage Drive
The Ring
Fountain Garden
West Carriage Drive
Hyde Park
The Long Water
Serpentine Sackler Gallery
Serpentine Rd
The Serpentine
Princess Diana Memorial Fountain
HYDE PARK AND KNIGHTSBRIDGE
South Carriage Drive

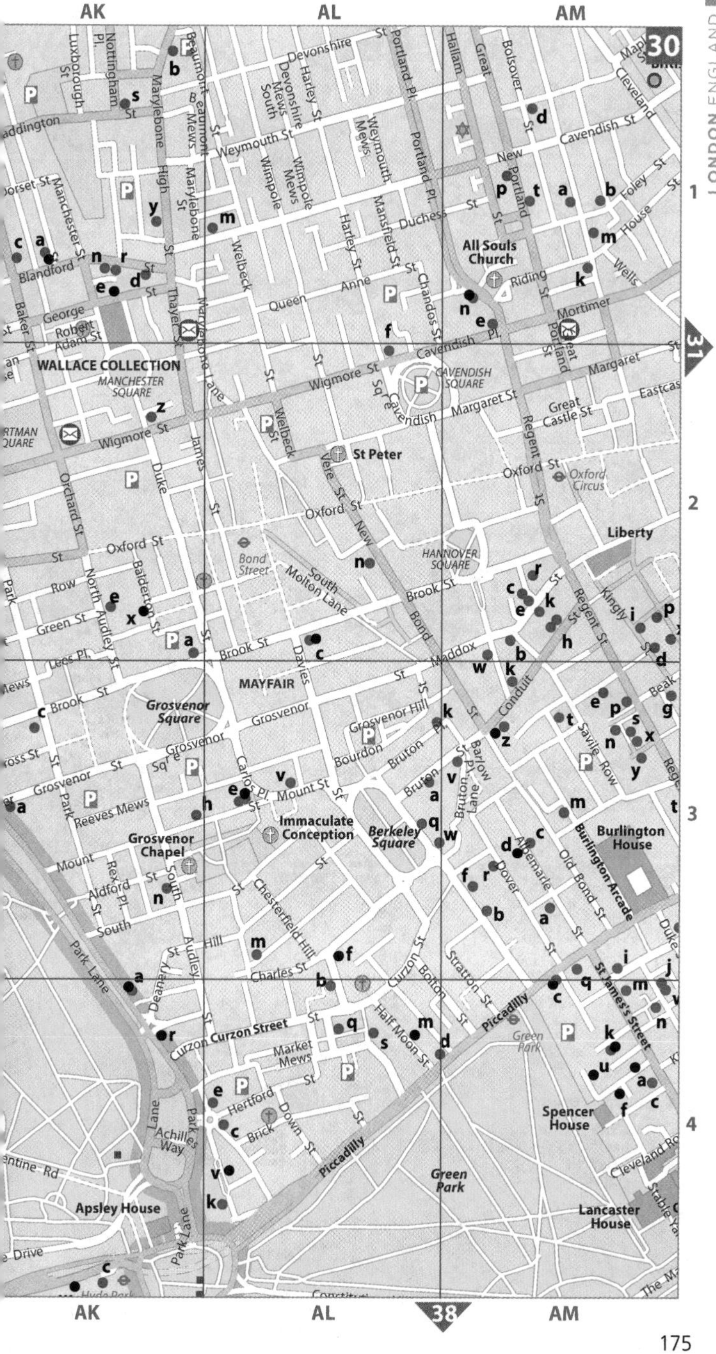
AK
AL
AM
30
31
38
1
2
3
4
WALLACE COLLECTION
MANCHESTER SQUARE
All Souls Church
CAVENDISH SQUARE
St Peter
Oxford Circus
Liberty
HANNOVER SQUARE
Bond Street
MAYFAIR
Grosvenor Square
Immaculate Conception
Berkeley Square
Grosvenor Chapel
Burlington House
Burlington Arcade
Green Park
Spencer House
Lancaster House
Apsley House
Devonshire St
Harley St
Portland Pl.
Weymouth St
Wimpole St
Welbeck St
Marylebone High St
Marylebone Lane
Baker St
Blandford St
George St
Wigmore St
Cavendish Pl.
Margaret St
Great Castle St
Oxford St
Regent St
New Bond St
Brook St
South Molton Lane
Davies St
Grosvenor St
Bruton St
Berkeley St
Conduit St
Maddox St
Savile Row
Old Bond St
Albemarle St
Dover St
Mount St
South Audley St
North Audley St
Park Lane
Park St
Curzon Street
Charles St
Half Moon St
Piccadilly
St James's Street
Cleveland Row
Duchess St
Queen Anne St
Mortimer St
Riding House St
New Cavendish St
Great Portland St
Carlos Pl.
Chesterfield Hill
Hertford St
Brick St
Down St
Achilles Way
Market Mews
Hyde Park

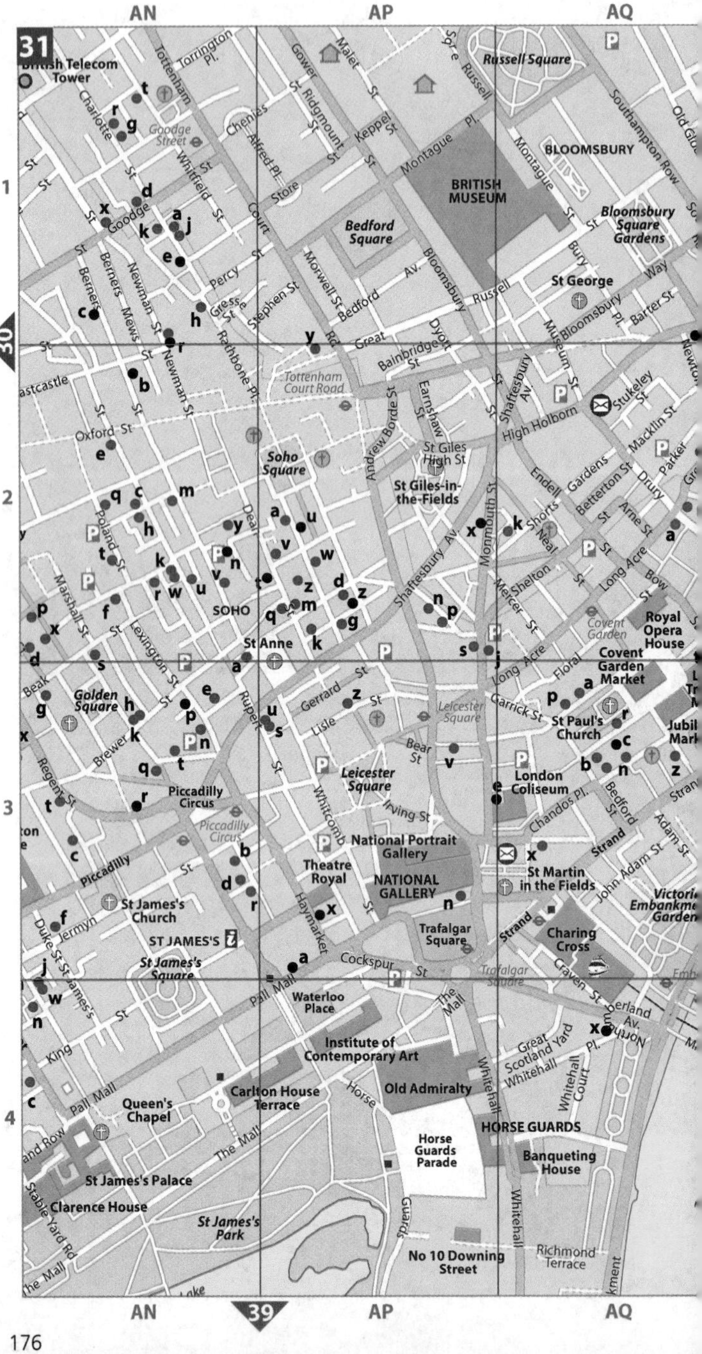
AN
AP
AQ
31
British Telecom Tower
Russell Square
BLOOMSBURY
BRITISH MUSEUM
Bedford Square
Bloomsbury Square Gardens
St George
Goodge Street
Tottenham Court Road
Soho Square
St Giles-in-the-Fields
St Giles High St
SOHO
St Anne
Royal Opera House
Covent Garden
Covent Garden Market
Golden Square
Leicester Square
St Paul's Church
London Coliseum
Piccadilly Circus
National Portrait Gallery
Theatre Royal
NATIONAL GALLERY
St Martin in the Fields
St James's Church
ST JAMES'S
St James's Square
Trafalgar Square
Charing Cross
Waterloo Place
Institute of Contemporary Art
Carlton House Terrace
Old Admiralty
Queen's Chapel
HORSE GUARDS
Horse Guards Parade
Banqueting House
St James's Palace
Clarence House
St James's Park
No 10 Downing Street
Richmond Terrace
Oxford St
Shaftesbury Av.
Charing Cross Rd
Long Acre
Strand
Piccadilly
Regent St
Haymarket
Pall Mall
The Mall
Whitehall
Horse Guards Rd
Great Russell St
High Holborn
39
30

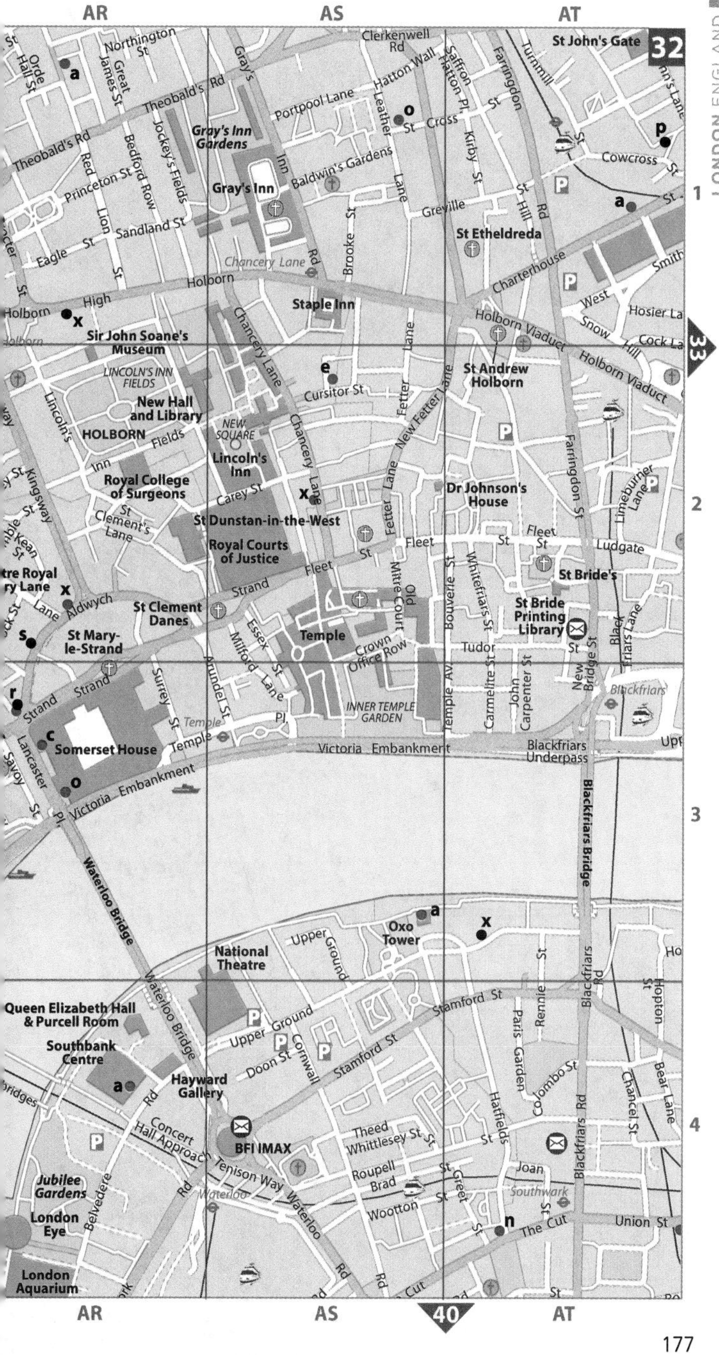
AR
AS
AT
32
33
40
1
2
3
4
St John's Gate
Northington St
Orde Hall St
Great James St
Theobald's Rd
Jockey's Fields
Bedford Row
Princeton St
Red Lion St
Sandland St
Eagle St
Gray's Inn Gardens
Gray's Inn
Gray's Inn Rd
Portpool Lane
Baldwin's Gardens
Clerkenwell Rd
Hatton Wall
Leather Lane
St Cross St
Saffron Hill
Hatton Pl
Kirby St
Farringdon Rd
Turnmill St
Cowcross St
Greville St
Brooke St
St Etheldreda
Chancery Lane
Holborn
High Holborn
Staple Inn
Charterhouse St
West Smithfield
Snow Hill
Hosier Lane
Cock Lane
Holborn Viaduct
St Andrew Holborn
Sir John Soane's Museum
LINCOLN'S INN FIELDS
New Hall and Library
HOLBORN
Lincoln's Inn Fields
NEW SQUARE
Lincoln's Inn
Cursitor St
Fetter Lane
New Fetter Lane
Chancery Lane
Royal College of Surgeons
Carey St
Kingsway
St Clement's Lane
Kean St
St Dunstan-in-the-West
Royal Courts of Justice
Dr Johnson's House
Farringdon St
Limeburner Lane
Fleet St
Ludgate
St Bride's
Aldwych
Drury Lane
St Clement Danes
St Mary-le-Strand
Strand
Essex St
Milford Lane
Arundel St
Surrey St
Temple
Mitre Court
Old Mitre Court
Crown Office Row
Bouverie St
Whitefriars St
St Bride Printing Library
Tudor St
New Bridge St
Black Friars Lane
Temple Av
Carmelite St
John Carpenter St
INNER TEMPLE GARDEN
Temple Pl
Blackfriars
Somerset House
Lancaster Pl
Savoy St
Victoria Embankment
Blackfriars Underpass
Blackfriars Bridge
Waterloo Bridge
Oxo Tower
National Theatre
Upper Ground
Stamford St
Rennie St
Hopton St
Queen Elizabeth Hall & Purcell Room
Southbank Centre
Hayward Gallery
Doon St
Cornwall Rd
Paris Garden
Colombo St
Blackfriars Rd
Chancel St
Bear Lane
Concert Hall Approach
BFI IMAX
Theed St
Whittlesey St
Hatfields
Roupell St
Brad St
Greet St
Joan St
Southwark
Jubilee Gardens
Belvedere Rd
Tenison Way
Waterloo
Waterloo Rd
Wootton St
The Cut
Union St
London Eye
London Aquarium

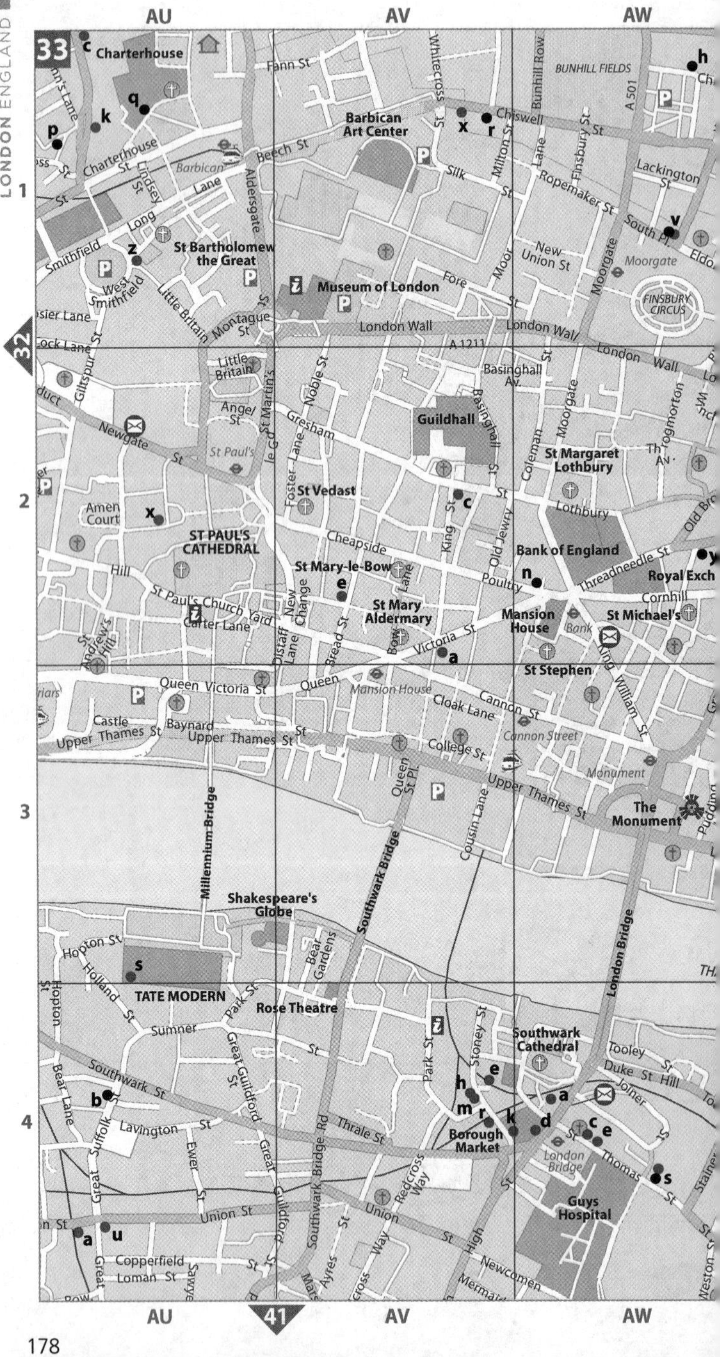
AU
AV
AW
33
32
41
1
2
3
4
Charterhouse
Fann St
Whitecross St
Bunhill Row
BUNHILL FIELDS
A 501
Barbican Art Center
Chiswell St
Charterhouse St
Beech St
Barbican
Lindsey St
Aldersgate
Silk St
Milton St
Ropemaker St
Finsbury St
Lackington St
Long Lane
Smithfield
St Bartholomew the Great
West Smithfield
Little Britain
Montague St
Museum of London
Fore St
Moor Lane
New Union St
Moorgate
South Pl.
Moorgate
FINSBURY CIRCUS
London Wall
A 1211
Basinghall Av.
Little Britain
Giltspur St
Noble St
St Martin's le Grand
Angel St
Gresham St
Newgate St
St Paul's
Foster Lane
Guildhall
Basinghall St
Coleman St
Moorgate
Throgmorton Av.
St Margaret Lothbury
Lothbury
St Vedast
Amen Court
ST PAUL'S CATHEDRAL
Cheapside
King St
Old Jewry
Bank of England
Threadneedle St
Royal Exch
Hill
St Mary-le-Bow
Bow Lane
Poultry
Cornhill
St Paul's Church Yard
New Change
St Mary Aldermary
Mansion House
St Michael's
Carter Lane
St Andrew's Hill
Distaff Lane
Bread St
Victoria St
Bank
King William St
St Stephen
Queen Victoria St
Queen
Mansion House
Cloak Lane
Cannon St
Castle Baynard St
Upper Thames St
Upper Thames St
College St
Cannon Street
Queen St Pl.
Monument
Upper Thames St
The Monument
Millennium Bridge
Cousin Lane
Southwark Bridge
Shakespeare's Globe
Bear Gardens
London Bridge
Hopton St
Holland St
TATE MODERN
Park St
Rose Theatre
Hopton St
Sumner St
Southwark Cathedral
Tooley St
Duke St Hill
Stoney St
Park St
Great Guildford St
Southwark St
Joiner St
Bear Lane
Lavington St
Thrale St
Borough Market
London Bridge
Suffolk
Ewer St
Great Guildford
Redcross Way
Southwark Bridge Rd
St Thomas St
Guys Hospital
Union St
Union St
High St
Copperfield St
Loman St
Ayres St
Newcomen
Great
Sawyer

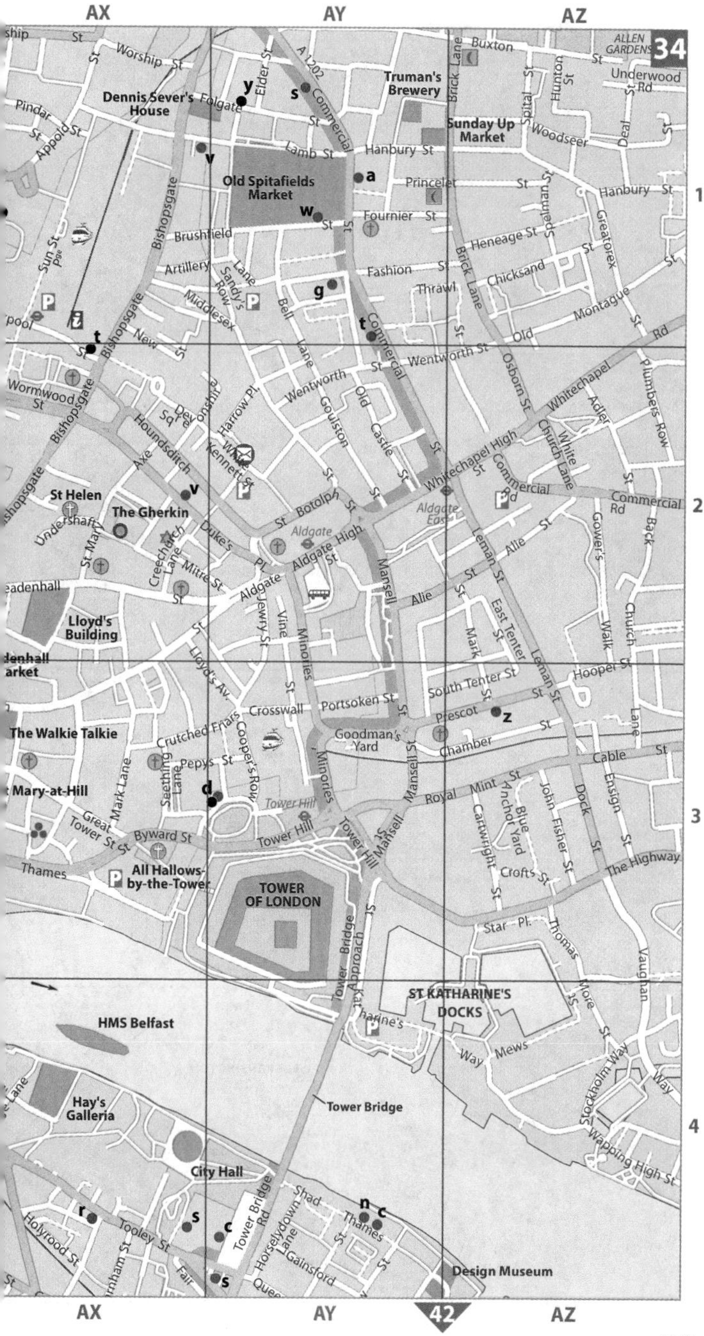
AX
AY
AZ
34
1
2
3
4
42
Dennis Sever's House
Truman's Brewery
Sunday Up Market
Old Spitafields Market
St Helen
The Gherkin
Lloyd's Building
The Walkie Talkie
All Hallows-by-the-Tower
TOWER OF LONDON
ST KATHARINE'S DOCKS
HMS Belfast
Hay's Galleria
City Hall
Tower Bridge
Design Museum
ALLEN GARDENS
Aldgate
Aldgate East
Tower Hill
Commercial St
Whitechapel High St
Whitechapel Rd
Bishopsgate
Brick Lane
Minories
Mansell St
Leman St
The Highway
Tooley St
Wapping High St
Royal Mint St
Cable St
Crutched Friars
Lamb St
Hanbury St
Fournier St
Fashion St
Wentworth St
Goulston St
Houndsditch
Aldgate High St
Alie St
Prescot St
Cartwright St
Thomas More St
Tower Bridge Approach
Tower Bridge Rd
Stockholm Way
Thames

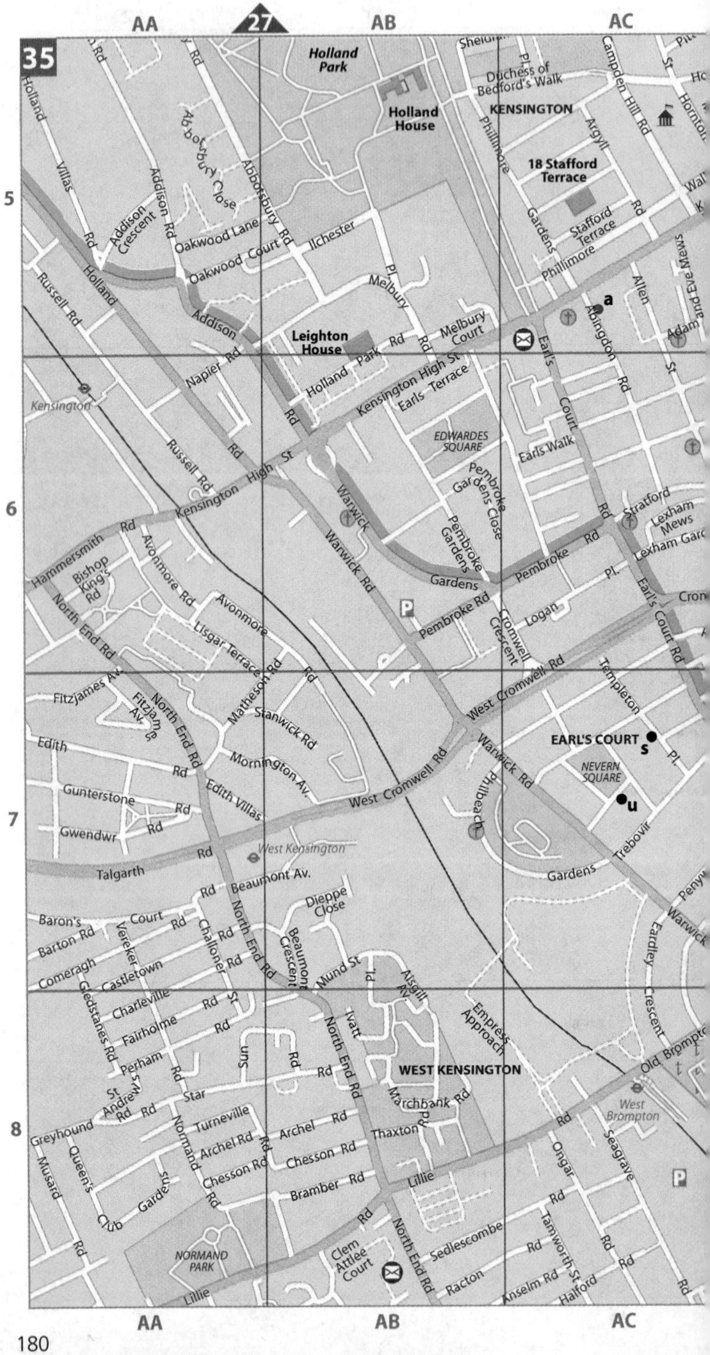

35
27
AA
AB
AC
5
6
7
8
Holland Park
Holland House
KENSINGTON
18 Stafford Terrace
Duchess of Bedford's Walk
Phillimore Gardens
Campden Hill Rd
Argyll Rd
Stafford Terrace
Phillimore
Holland Villas Rd
Addison Crescent
Addison Rd
Abbotsbury Close
Abbotsbury Rd
Oakwood Lane
Oakwood Court
Ilchester Pl.
Melbury Rd
Melbury Court
Holland Rd
Russell Rd
Leighton House
Holland Park Rd
Kensington High St
Earls Terrace
Abingdon Rd
Allen St
Adam and Eve Mews
Earl's Court Rd
Napier Rd
Kensington
EDWARDES SQUARE
Earls Walk
Pembroke Gardens Close
Pembroke Gardens
Pembroke Rd
Pembroke Pl.
Stratford Rd
Lexham Mews
Lexham Gardens
Warwick Gardens
Warwick Rd
Hammersmith Rd
Bishop King's Rd
Avonmore Rd
Avonmore
Lisgar Terrace
North End Rd
Logan Pl.
Cromwell Crescent
West Cromwell Rd
Templeton Pl.
EARL'S COURT
NEVERN SQUARE
Fitzjames Av.
Matheson Rd
Stanwick Rd
Mornington Av.
Edith Rd
Edith Villas
Gunterstone Rd
Gwendwr Rd
Talgarth Rd
West Kensington
Philbeach Gardens
Trebovir Rd
Beaumont Av.
Dieppe Close
Beaumont Crescent
Baron's Court Rd
Barton Rd
Vereker Rd
Challoner St
Comeragh Rd
Castletown Rd
Mund St
Aisgill Av.
Empress Approach
Eardley Crescent
Penywern Rd
Gledstanes Rd
Charleville Rd
Fairholme Rd
Perham Rd
Sun Rd
Ivatt Pl.
WEST KENSINGTON
Old Brompton Rd
West Brompton
St Andrew's Rd
Star Rd
Greyhound Rd
Turneville Rd
Archel Rd
Chesson Rd
Bramber Rd
Marchbank Rd
Thaxton Rd
Lillie Rd
Normand Rd
Musard Rd
Queen's Club Gardens
NORMAND PARK
Clem Attlee Court
Sedlescombe Rd
Racton Rd
Tamworth St
Anselm Rd
Halford Rd
Ongar Rd
Seagrave Rd

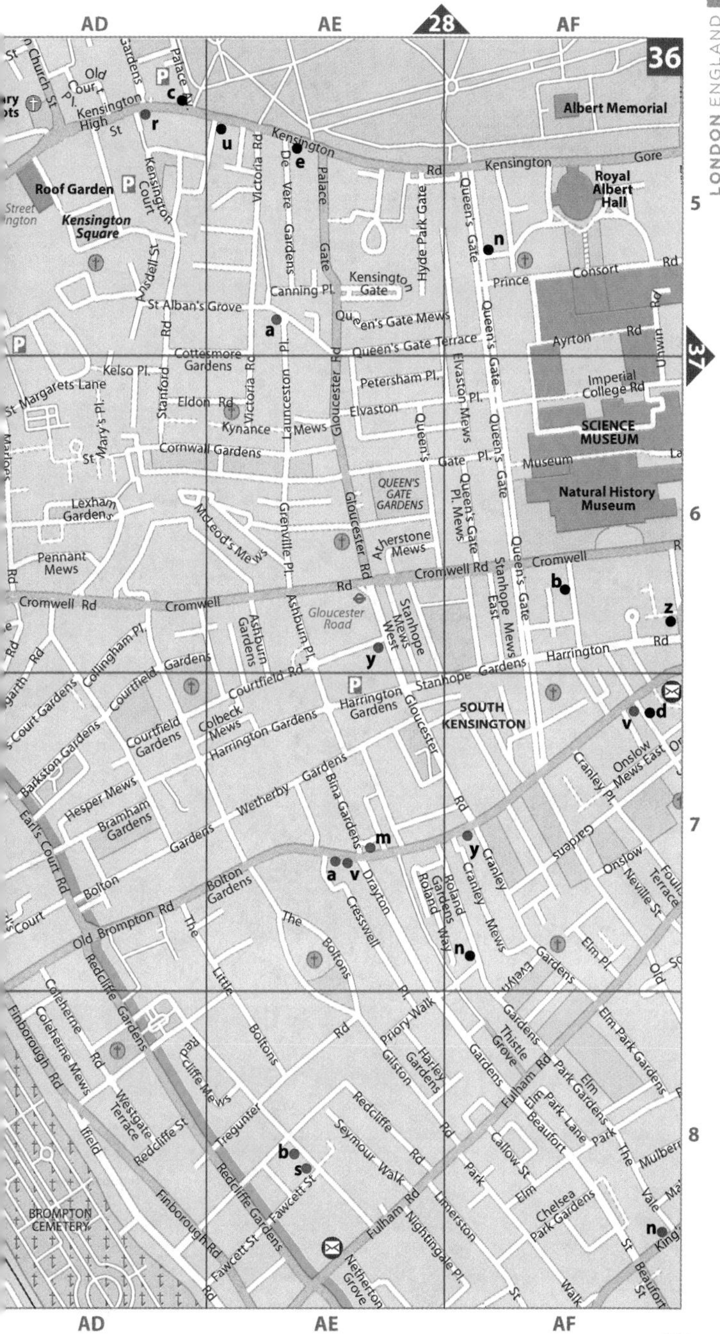
AD
AE
AF
28
36
37
5
6
7
8
Albert Memorial
Royal Albert Hall
Roof Garden
Kensington Square
Kensington High St
Kensington Gore
Kensington Rd
Old Court Pl.
Church St
Palace Gate
De Vere Gardens
Victoria Rd
Hyde Park Gate
Queen's Gate
Kensington Gate
Canning Pl.
Queen's Gate Mews
Queen's Gate Terrace
Prince Consort Rd
Ayrton Rd
Imperial College Rd
Unwin Rd
SCIENCE MUSEUM
Museum
Natural History Museum
St Alban's Grove
Ansdell St
Stanford Rd
Kelso Pl.
St Margarets Lane
St Mary's Pl.
Cottesmore Gardens
Eldon Rd
Kynance Mews
Launceston Pl.
Cornwall Gardens
Gloucester Rd
Petersham Pl.
Elvaston Pl.
Elvaston Mews
Queen's Gate Pl.
Queen's Gate Pl. Mews
QUEEN'S GATE GARDENS
Lexham Gardens
Pennant Mews
McLeod's Mews
Grenville Pl.
Atherstone Mews
Cromwell Rd
Gloucester Road
Ashburn Gardens
Ashburn Pl.
Stanhope Mews West
Stanhope Mews East
Stanhope Gardens
Harrington Rd
Harrington Gardens
Collingham Pl.
Courtfield Gardens
Courtfield Rd
Colbeck Mews
SOUTH KENSINGTON
Onslow Mews East
Cranley Pl.
Barkston Gardens
Hesper Mews
Bramham Gardens
Wetherby Gardens
Bina Gardens
Earl's Court Rd
Bolton Gardens
Old Brompton Rd
Drayton Gardens
Cresswell Pl.
Roland Gardens
Roland Way
Cranley Mews
Cranley Gardens
Onslow Gardens
Neville St
Foulis Terrace
Elm Pl.
Evelyn Gardens
The Boltons
The Little Boltons
Redcliffe Gardens
Coleherne Rd
Coleherne Mews
Finborough Rd
Westgate Terrace
Redcliffe St
Redcliffe Mews
Ifield Rd
Tregunter Rd
Priory Walk
Harley Gardens
Gilston Rd
Redcliffe Rd
Seymour Walk
Fawcett St
Fulham Rd
Nightingale Pl.
Limerston St
Netherton Grove
Thistle Grove
Elm Park Gardens
Elm Park Lane
Elm Park Rd
Beaufort St
Callow St
Chelsea Park Gardens
The Vale
Mulberry Walk
Old Church St
King's Rd
BROMPTON CEMETERY

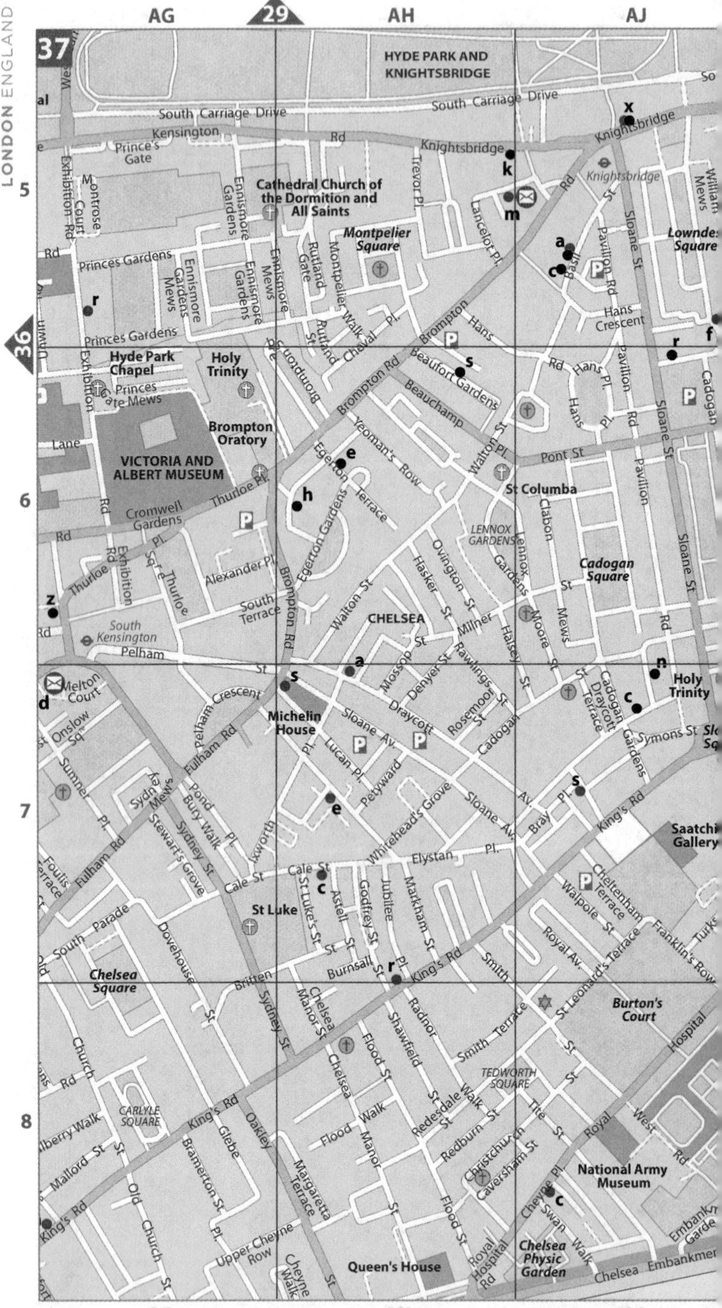
AG
AH
AJ
29
37
36
5
6
7
8
HYDE PARK AND KNIGHTSBRIDGE
South Carriage Drive
Kensington Rd
Knightsbridge
Prince's Gate
Exhibition Rd
Montrose Court
Ennismore Gardens
Cathedral Church of the Dormition and All Saints
Montpelier Square
Trevor Pl.
Lancelot Pl.
Knightsbridge
Basil St
Pavilion Rd
Sloane St
Lowndes Square
William Mews
Princes Gardens
Ennismore Gardens Mews
Ennismore Mews
Rutland Gate
Montpelier Walk
Hans Crescent
Hyde Park Chapel
Holy Trinity
Princes Gate Mews
Brompton Rd
Cheval Pl.
Beaufort Gardens
Hans Rd
Hans Pl.
Cadogan
Brompton Oratory
VICTORIA AND ALBERT MUSEUM
Beauchamp Pl.
Walton St
Pont St
Egerton Terrace
Yeoman's Row
St Columba
Thurloe Pl.
Cromwell Gardens
Egerton Gardens
LENNOX GARDENS
Lennox Gardens
Clabon Mews
Cadogan Square
Alexander Pl.
Thurloe Sq.
Thurloe St
South Terrace
Ovington St
Hasker St
CHELSEA
Milner St
Moore St
Halsey St
South Kensington
Pelham St
Mossop St
Denyer St
Rawlings St
Melton Court
Pelham Crescent
Michelin House
Draycott Av.
Rosemoor St
Cadogan St
Cadogan Gardens
Draycott Terrace
Holy Trinity
Symons St
Onslow Sq.
Sumner Pl.
Fulham Rd
Sloane Av.
Lucan Pl.
Petyward
Sydney Mews
Pond Pl.
Bury Walk
Whitehead's Grove
Bray Pl.
King's Rd
Saatchi Gallery
Stewart's Grove
Sydney St
Ixworth Pl.
Elystan Pl.
Foulis Terrace
Cale St
St Luke's St
Astell St
Godfrey St
Jubilee Pl.
Markham St
Cheltenham Terrace
Walpole St
Franklin's Row
St Luke
South Parade
Dovehouse St
Royal Av.
St Leonard's Terrace
Burnsall St
Smith St
Chelsea Square
Britten St
Chelsea Manor St
Radnor Walk
Burton's Court
Smith Terrace
Shawfield St
Flood St
Hospital Rd
Church St
TEDWORTH SQUARE
CARLYLE SQUARE
Glebe Pl.
Oakley St
Redesdale St
Tite St
Royal Hospital Rd
West Rd
Mulberry Walk
Mallord St
Bramerton St
Flood Walk
Chelsea Manor St
Redburn St
Christchurch St
National Army Museum
Old Church St
Margaretta Terrace
Caversham St
Cheyne Pl.
Swan Walk
King's Rd
Upper Cheyne Row
Cheyne Walk
Queen's House
Chelsea Physic Garden
Chelsea Embankment
Embankment Gardens

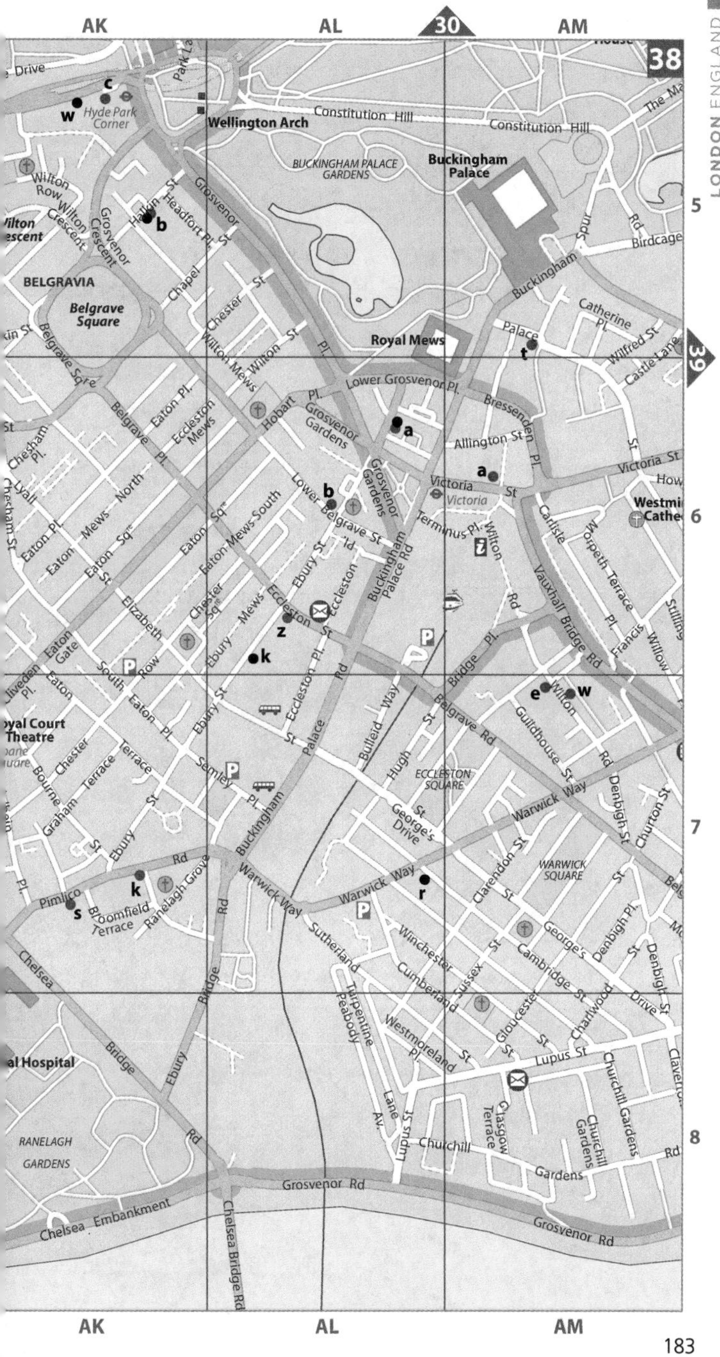
AK
AL
30
AM
38
39
5
6
7
8
Hyde Park Corner
Wellington Arch
Constitution Hill
BUCKINGHAM PALACE GARDENS
Buckingham Palace
Birdcage
Wilton Row
Wilton Crescent
Grosvenor Crescent
Halkin St
Headfort Pl.
Grosvenor Pl.
BELGRAVIA
Belgrave Square
Chapel St
Chester St
Wilton Mews
Wilton St
Royal Mews
Buckingham Gate
Catherine Pl.
Palace St
Wilfred St
Castle Lane
Lower Grosvenor Pl.
Bressenden Pl.
Hobart Pl.
Grosvenor Gardens
Allington St
Victoria St
Victoria
Westminster Cathedral
Eaton Pl.
Eccleston Mews
Belgrave Pl.
Chesham Pl.
Lyall St
Chesham St
Eaton Mews North
Eaton Sq.
Eaton Mews South
Lower Belgrave St
Terminus Pl.
Wilton Rd
Carlisle Pl.
Morpeth Terrace
Buckingham Palace Rd
Ebury St
Eccleston St
Elizabeth St
Chester Sq.
Ebury Mews
Eccleston Pl.
Vauxhall Bridge Rd
Francis St
Willow Pl.
Eaton Gate
South Eaton Pl.
Cliveden Pl.
Royal Court Theatre
Chester Row
Bridge Pl.
Belgrave Rd
Wilton Rd
Guildhouse St
Bulleid Way
Hugh St
ECCLESTON SQUARE
Semley Pl.
Chester Terrace
Bourne St
Graham Terrace
St George's Drive
Warwick Way
Denbigh St
Churton St
Clarendon St
WARWICK SQUARE
Pimlico
Bloomfield Terrace
Ranelagh Grove
Pimlico Rd
Sutherland St
Winchester St
Cumberland St
Sussex St
Cambridge St
Denbigh Pl.
Chelsea Bridge Rd
Turpentine Lane
Peabody Av.
Westmoreland Pl.
Gloucester St
Charlwood St
Lupus St
Claverton St
Royal Hospital
Ebury Bridge
Glasgow Terrace
Churchill Gardens
Churchill Gardens Rd
RANELAGH GARDENS
Grosvenor Rd
Chelsea Embankment
Chelsea Bridge Rd
AK
AL
AM

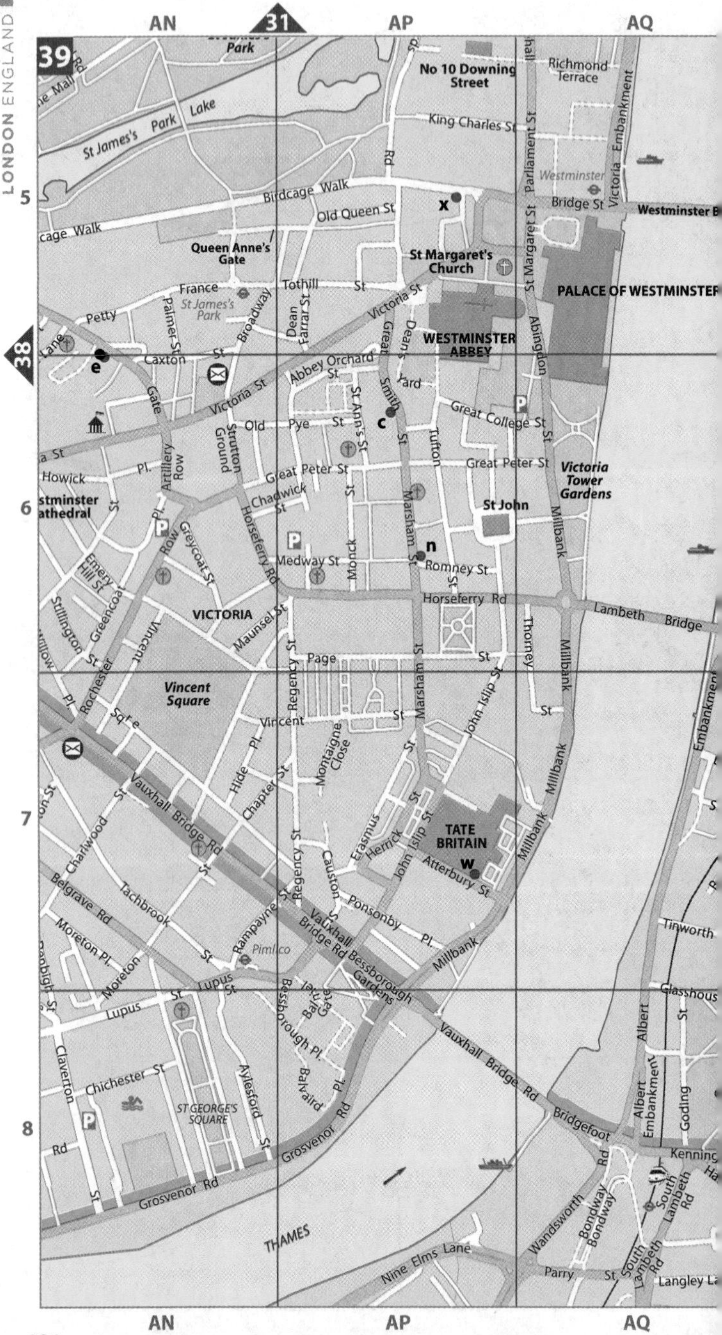
AN
31
AP
AQ
39
Park
No 10 Downing Street
Richmond Terrace
King Charles St
St James's Park Lake
Victoria Embankment
Parliament St
Westminster
5
Birdcage Walk
Bridge St
Westminster B
Old Queen St
x
Queen Anne's Gate
St Margaret's Church
St Margaret St
PALACE OF WESTMINSTER
France
Tothill St
St James's Park
Victoria St
Petty
Palmer St
Broadway
Dean Farrar St
Great Smith St
Dean's Yard
WESTMINSTER ABBEY
Abingdon
38
Caxton St
e
Abbey Orchard St
Gate
Victoria St
St Ann's St
c
Great College St
Old Pye St
Strutton Ground
Tufton
Howick Pl.
Artillery Row
Great Peter St
Great Peter St
Victoria Tower Gardens
6
Westminster Cathedral
Chadwick St
Marsham St
St John
Millbank
Horseferry Rd
n
Greycoat St
Medway St
Monck St
Romney St
Emery Hill St
Greencoat
Stillington St
VICTORIA
Maunsel St
Horseferry Rd
Lambeth Bridge
Vincent
Regency St
Page St
Thorney St
Millbank
Rochester
Vincent Square
John Islip St
Vincent St
Embankment
Hide Pl.
Montaigne Close
Chapter St
Vauxhall Bridge Rd
Millbank
7
Charlwood
Erasmus
Herrick
John Islip St
TATE BRITAIN
w
Atterbury St
Causton St
Tachbrook
Rampayne St
Ponsonby Pl.
Belgrave Rd
Moreton Pl.
Moreton
Pimlico
Vauxhall Bridge Rd
Bessborough Gardens
Millbank
Tinworth
Lupus St
Lupus St
Bessborough Pl.
Glasshous
Claverton
Vauxhall Bridge Rd
Albert Embankment
Chichester St
ST GEORGE'S SQUARE
Aylesford St
Balvaird Pl.
Grosvenor Rd
Bridgefoot
Goding
8
Rd
Kenning
South Lambeth Rd
Grosvenor Rd
Wandsworth Rd
Bondway
THAMES
Nine Elms Lane
Parry St
South Lambeth Rd
Langley La
AN
AP
AQ

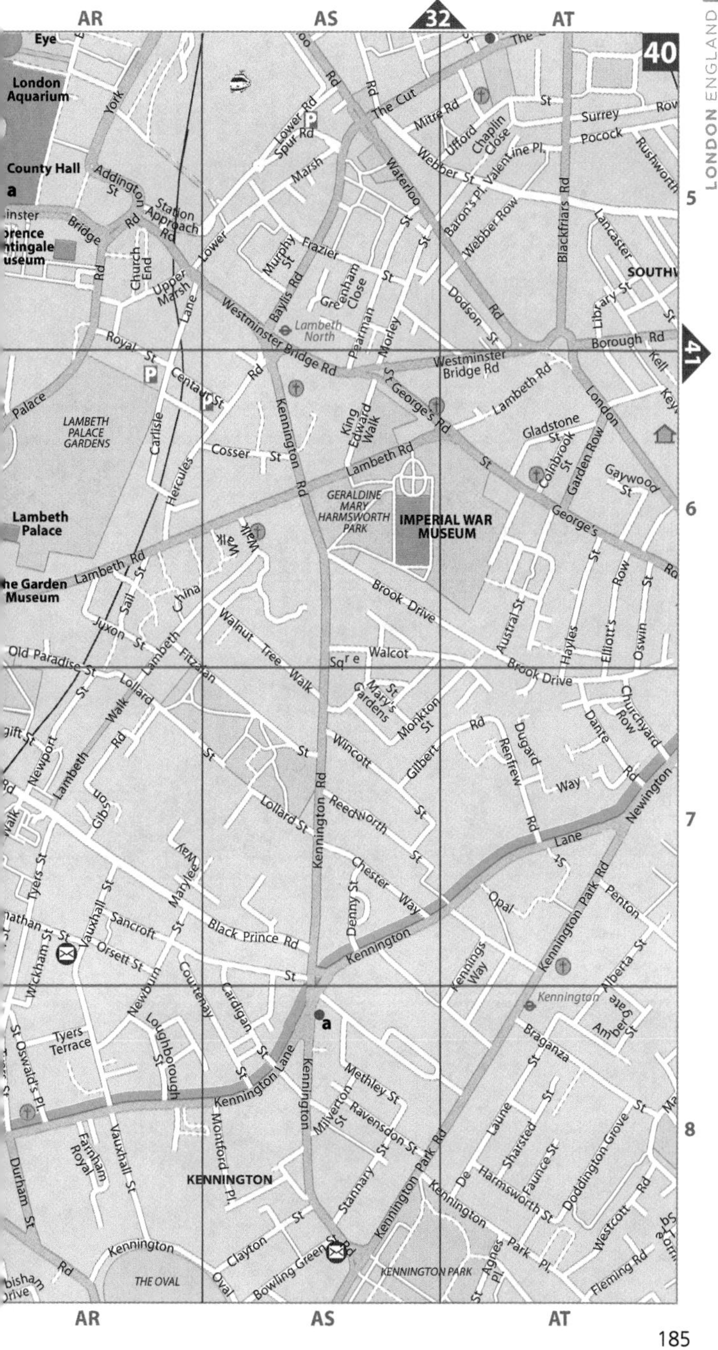
AR
AS
AT
32
40
41
5
6
7
8
Eye
London Aquarium
County Hall
a
Addington St
Station Approach Rd
Bridge Rd
Church End
Upper Marsh
Lower Marsh
Lower Rd
Spur Rd
York Rd
The Cut
Mitre Rd
Ufford St
Chaplin Close
Valentine Pl.
Surrey Row
Pocock St
Rushworth St
Webber St
Waterloo Rd
Baron's Pl.
Webber Row
Blackfriars Rd
Lancaster St
SOUTHW
Murphy St
Frazier St
Baylis Rd
Greenham Close
Pearman St
Morley St
Dodson St
Library St
Borough Rd
Lambeth North
Westminster Bridge Rd
Royal St
Centaur St
Lane
Palace
LAMBETH PALACE GARDENS
Carlisle
Hercules
Cosser St
Kennington Rd
King Edward Walk
St George's Rd
Lambeth Rd
Gladstone St
Colnbrook St
Garden Row
London Rd
Gaywood St
GERALDINE MARY HARMSWORTH PARK
IMPERIAL WAR MUSEUM
Lambeth Palace
The Garden Museum
Walk
Sail St
China Walk
Brook Drive
Austral St
Hayles St
Elliott's Row
Oswin St
Juxon St
Old Paradise St
Lambeth Walk
Fitzalan St
Walnut Tree Walk
Walcot Sq
St Mary's Gardens
Monkton St
Lollard St
Newport St
Gilbert Rd
Renfrew Rd
Dugard Way
Dante Rd
Churchyard Row
Newington
Wincott St
Reedworth St
Gibson Rd
Marylee Way
Chester Way
Denny St
Opal St
Kennington Park Rd
Penton St
Tyers St
Vauxhall St
Sancroft St
Black Prince Rd
Kennington Lane
Orsett St
Wickham St
Kennings Way
Alberta St
Kennington
Courtenay St
Cardigan St
Newburn St
Loughborough St
Tyers Terrace
St Oswald's Pl.
Amelia St
Braganza St
Methley St
Milverton St
Ravensdon St
Laune St
Sharsted St
Faunce St
Doddington Grove
Montford Pl.
Royal Fairham
Durham St
KENNINGTON
Stannary St
De Harmsworth St
Kennington Park Pl.
Westcott Rd
Clayton St
Bowling Green St
Kennington Rd
THE OVAL
Oval
KENNINGTON PARK
Agnes Pl.
Fleming Rd

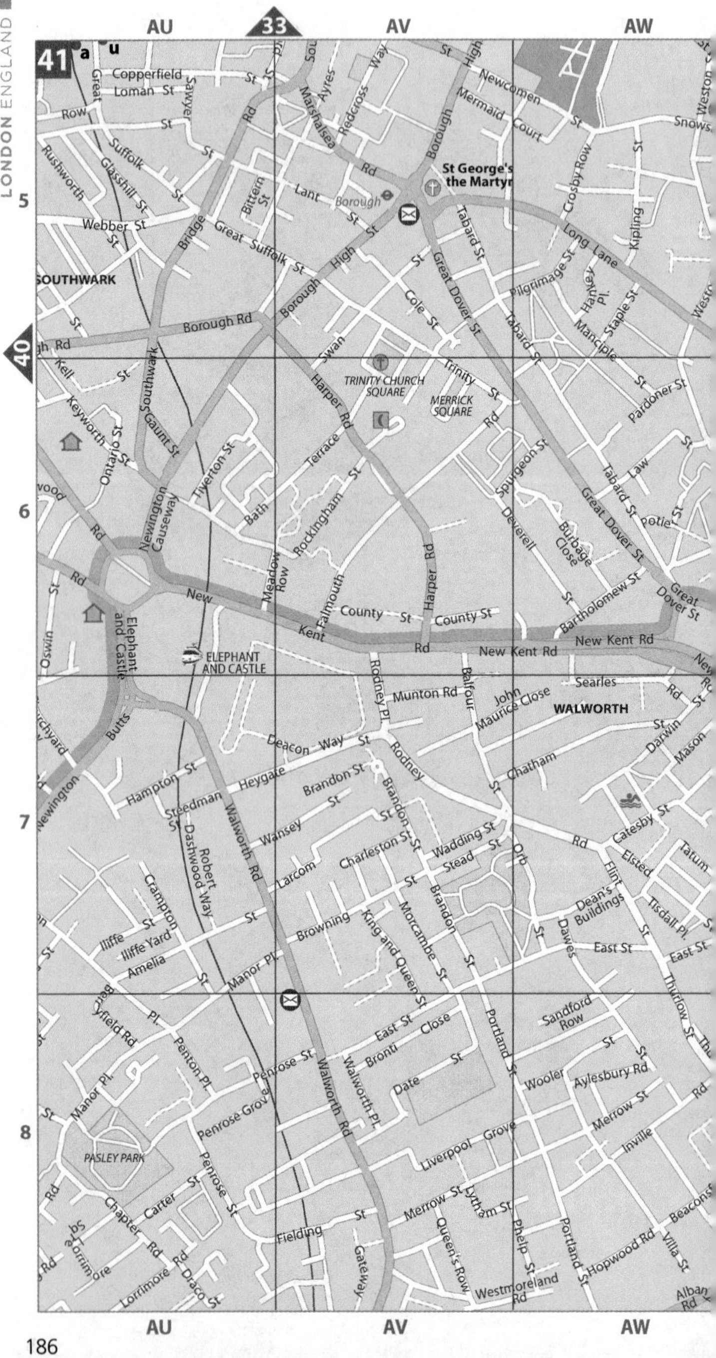
AU
33
AV
AW
41
5
6
7
8
40
SOUTHWARK
WALWORTH
St George's the Martyr
Borough
TRINITY CHURCH SQUARE
MERRICK SQUARE
ELEPHANT AND CASTLE
PASLEY PARK
Copperfield St
Loman St
Great Suffolk St
Suffolk St
Glasshill St
Rushworth St
Webber St
Sawyer St
Southwark Bridge Rd
Marshalsea Rd
Ayres St
Redcross Way
Bittern St
Lant St
Borough High St
Borough Rd
Newcomen St
Mermaid Court
Long Lane
Crosby Row
Kipling St
Snowsfields
Weston St
Tabard St
Great Dover St
Pilgrimage St
Manciple St
Staple St
Pardoner St
Cole St
Trinity St
Swan St
Harper Rd
Terrace
Rockingham St
Bath Terrace
Tiverton St
Gaunt St
Keyworth St
Ontario St
Kell St
Newington Causeway
Spurgeon St
Deverell St
Burbage Close
Law St
Bartholomew St
New Kent Rd
County St
Falmouth Rd
Meadow Row
Elephant and Castle
Oswin St
Rodney Pl
Munton Rd
Balfour St
John Maurice Close
Searles Rd
Darwin St
Mason St
Deacon Way
Heygate St
Hampton St
Brandon St
Rodney Rd
Chatham St
Catesby St
Tatum St
Elsted St
Flint St
Steedman St
Dashwood
Robert Dashwood Way
Walworth Rd
Wansey St
Larcom St
Charleston St
Wadding St
Stead St
Orb St
Crampton St
Iliffe St
Iliffe Yard
Amelia St
Browning St
King and Queen St
Morecambe St
Dean's Buildings
Dawes St
East St
Tisdall Pl.
Manor Pl.
Thurlow St
Penton Pl.
Penrose St
Penrose Grove
Bronti Close
Date St
Portland St
Sandford Row
Wooler St
Aylesbury Rd
Merrow St
Inville Rd
Liverpool Grove
Lytham St
Fielding St
Gateway
Queen's Row
Phelp St
Westmoreland Rd
Hopwood Rd
Villa St
Beaconsfield
Albany Rd
Carter St
Chapter Rd
Lorrimore Rd
Draco St
Butts
Newington Butts
Churchyard Row
Pasley Park

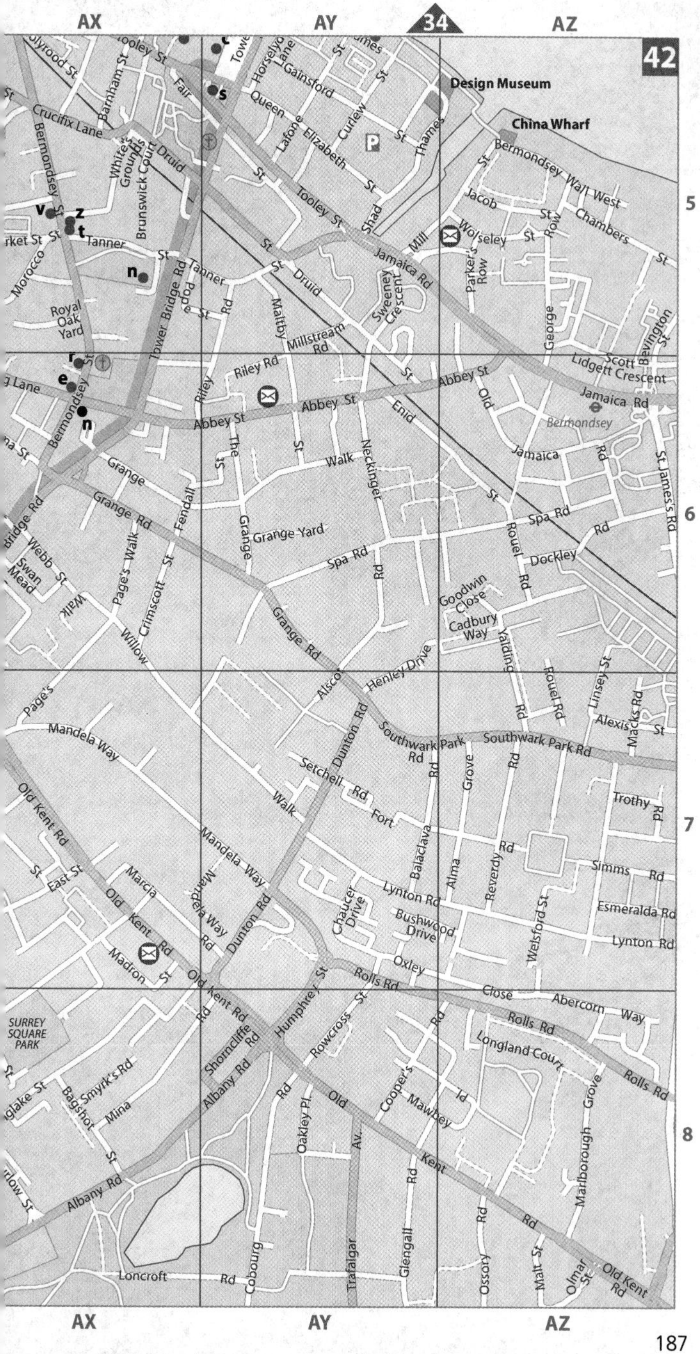
AX
AY
34
AZ
42
Design Museum
China Wharf
5
6
7
8
Crucifix Lane
Bermondsey St
Tooley St
Queen Elizabeth St
Gainsford St
Curlew St
Lafone St
Shad Thames
Horselydown Lane
Bermondsey Wall West
Jacob St
Chambers St
Wolseley St
Mill St
Jamaica Rd
Parker's Row
George Row
Bevington St
Scott Lidgett Crescent
Bermondsey
Tanner St
Druid St
Maltby St
Millstream Rd
Sweeney Crescent
Tower Bridge Rd
Royal Oak Yard
Morocco St
Brunswick Court
White's Grounds
Riley Rd
Abbey St
Enid St
Old Jamaica Rd
St James's Rd
Grange Walk
Neckinger
The Grange
Grange Rd
Grange Yard
Fendall St
Spa Rd
Rouel Rd
Dockley Rd
Page's Walk
Crimscott St
Webb St
Swan Mead
Willow Walk
Goodwin Close
Cadbury Way
Yalding Rd
Henley Drive
Alscot
Linsey St
Alexis St
Macks Rd
Southwark Park Rd
Mandela Way
Dunton Rd
Setchell Rd
Fort Rd
Balaclava Rd
Grove
Alma
Reverdy Rd
Trothy Rd
Simms Rd
Esmeralda Rd
Lynton Rd
Welsford St
Chaucer Drive
Bushwood Drive
Oxley Close
Rolls Rd
Abercorn Way
Longland Court
Old Kent Rd
East St
Marcia Rd
Madron St
SURREY SQUARE PARK
Humphrey St
Rowcross St
Shorncliffe Rd
Albany Rd
Smyrk's Rd
Bagshot St
Mina Rd
Oakley Pl.
Cooper's Rd
Mawbey Rd
Marlborough Grove
Trafalgar Av.
Glengall Rd
Cobourg Rd
Loncroft Rd
Ossory Rd
Malt St
Olmar St

ENGLAND

A vision of England sweeps across historic buildings and rolling landscapes, but from the rugged splendour of Cornwall's cliffs to pounding Northumbrian shores, this image seeks parity with a newer picture of Albion: refined cities whose industrial past has been reshaped by a shiny, interactive reality. The country's bones and bumps are a reassuring constant: the windswept moors of the south west and the craggy peaks of the Pennines, the summery orchards of the Kentish Weald, the constancy of East Anglian skies and the mirrored calm of Cumbria's lakes.

Renewed interest in all things regional means restaurants are increasingly looking to serve dishes rooted in their locality. Think Melton Mowbray pie in Leicestershire or Lancashire hotpot in the north west – and what better place to eat cheese than where it was made? Seafood is an important part of the English diet: try shrimps from Morecambe Bay, oysters from Whitstable, crab from Cromer and fish from Brixham. Sunday pub roasts are another quintessential part of English life – and a trip to the South West wouldn't be complete without a cream tea.

- Michelin Road maps
  n° 502, 503, 504 and 713
- Michelin Green Guide:
  Great Britain

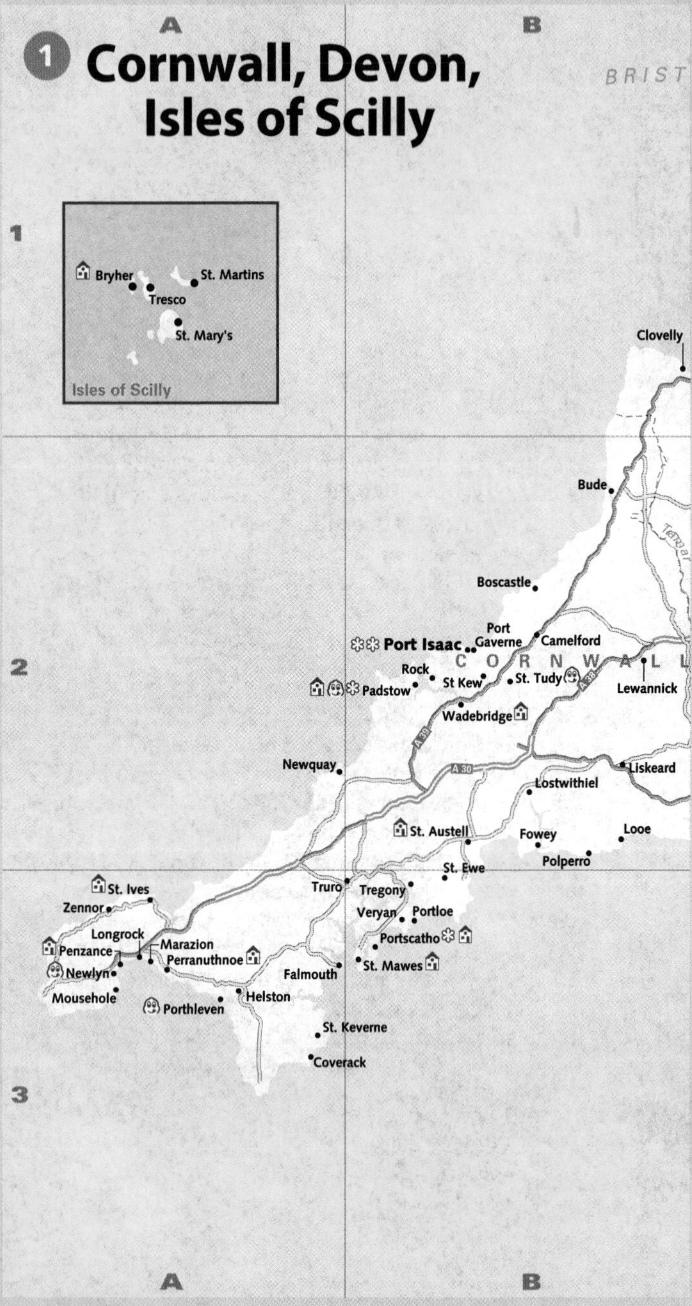
A
B
1
Cornwall, Devon,
Isles of Scilly
BRIST
1
Bryher
St. Martins
Tresco
St. Mary's
Isles of Scilly
Clovelly
Bude
Boscastle
Port
Gaverne
Camelford
Port Isaac
CORNWALL
2
Rock
St Kew
St. Tudy
Lewannick
Padstow
Wadebridge
A 39
A 38
Newquay
A 30
Liskeard
Lostwithiel
St. Austell
Fowey
Looe
Polperro
St. Ewe
St. Ives
Truro
Tregony
Zennor
Veryan
Portloe
Longrock
Portscatho
Penzance
Marazion
Perranuthnoe
St. Mawes
Newlyn
Falmouth
Mousehole
Helston
Porthleven
St. Keverne
Coverack
3
A
B

C
D
WALES
(plans 19)
Cardiff
Severn Estuary
BRISTOL CHANNEL
1
SOMERSET, DORSET, GLOUCESTERSHIRE, WILTSHIRE
(plans 2)
Ilfracombe
Martinhoe
Lynton
Woolacombe
Kentisbury
Bideford
Knowstone
Bampton
Taunton
Parrett
A 361
M 5
A 303
Taw
DEVON
Bow
Honiton
A 35
Axminster
Virginstow
Drewsteignton
A 30
Exeter
Lifton
Lewdown
Chagford
Dunsford
Lydford
Moretonhampstead
Topsham
Sidmouth
Chillaton
North Bovey
Lympstone
2
Milton Abbot
Postbridge
A 38
Kenton
Tavistock
Lyme Bay
Callington
Ashburton
St. Mellion
Plymouth
South Brent
Torquay
Antony
Ermington
Freathy
Dartmouth
Noss Mayo
Kingsbridge
Bigbury-on-Sea
Strete
Salcombe
South Pool
Place with at least:
a hotel or a restaurant
a starred establishment
a "Bib Gourmand" restaurant
a particularly pleasant accommodation
3
ENGLISH

2 Somerset, Dorset, Gloucestershire, Wiltshire

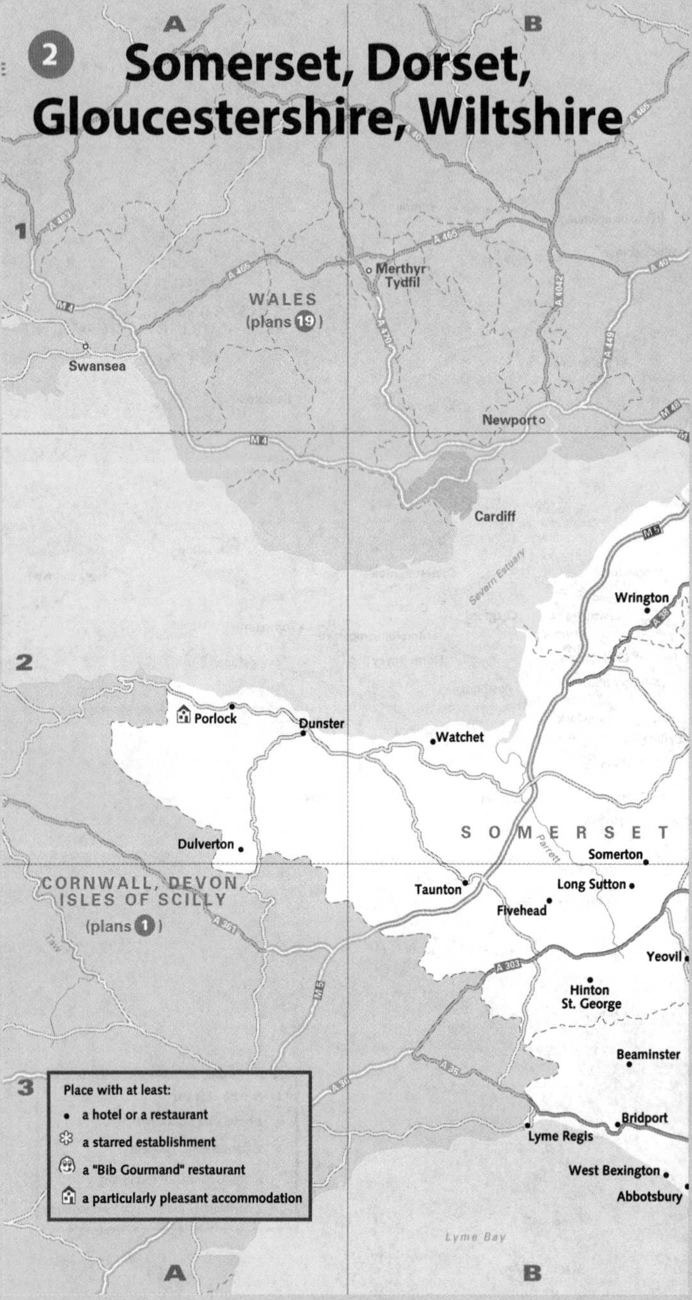

A
B
1
2
3
Merthyr Tydfil
WALES
(plans 19)
Swansea
Newport
Cardiff
Severn Estuary
Wrington
Porlock
Dunster
Watchet
Dulverton
SOMERSET
Somerton
Long Sutton
Taunton
Fivehead
CORNWALL, DEVON, ISLES OF SCILLY
(plans 1)
Yeovil
Hinton St. George
Beaminster
Lyme Regis
Bridport
West Bexington
Abbotsbury
Lyme Bay
Place with at least:
a hotel or a restaurant
a starred establishment
a "Bib Gourmand" restaurant
a particularly pleasant accommodation

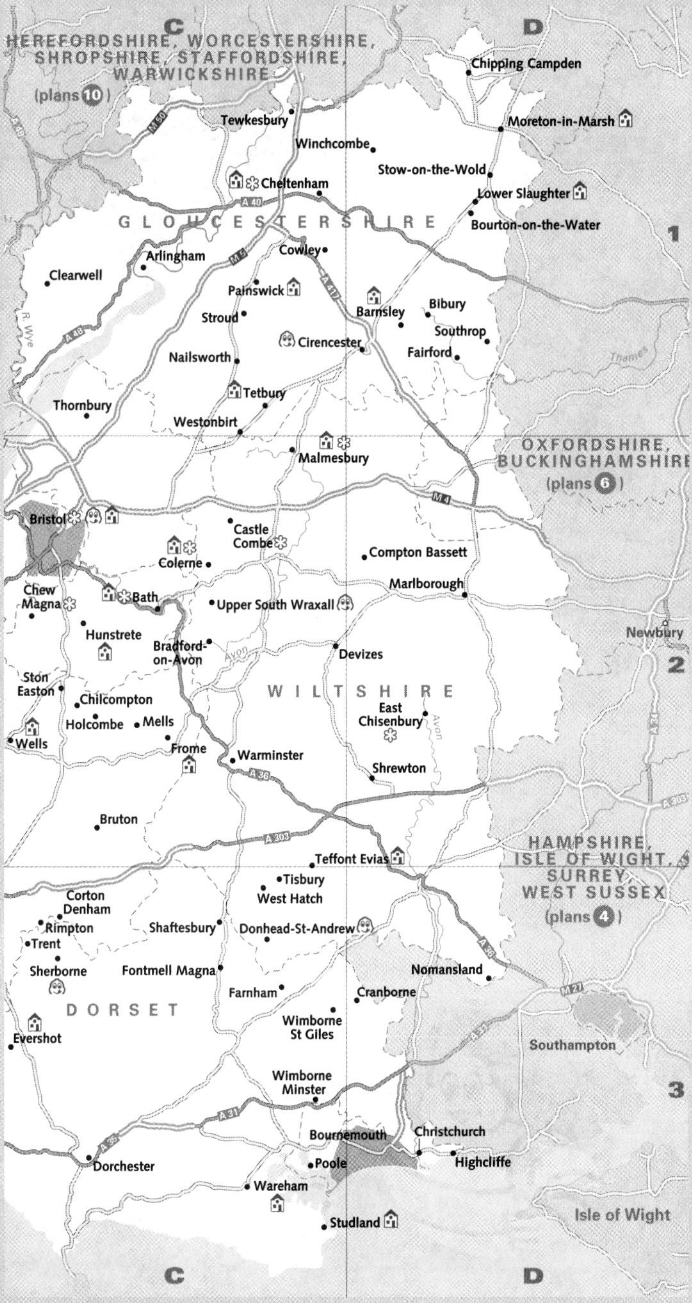
C
D
HEREFORDSHIRE, WORCESTERSHIRE, SHROPSHIRE, STAFFORDSHIRE, WARWICKSHIRE
(plans 10)
Chipping Campden
Tewkesbury
Moreton-in-Marsh
Winchcombe
Stow-on-the-Wold
Cheltenham
Lower Slaughter
GLOUCESTERSHIRE
Bourton-on-the-Water
1
Cowley
Arlingham
Clearwell
Painswick
Barnsley
Bibury
Stroud
Southrop
Cirencester
Fairford
Nailsworth
Thames
Tetbury
Thornbury
Westonbirt
OXFORDSHIRE, BUCKINGHAMSHIRE
Malmesbury
(plans 6)
Bristol
Castle Combe
Compton Bassett
Colerne
Marlborough
Chew Magna
Bath
Upper South Wraxall
Newbury
Hunstrete
Bradford-on-Avon
Devizes
2
Ston Easton
WILTSHIRE
Chilcompton
East Chisenbury
Holcombe
Mells
Wells
Frome
Warminster
Shrewton
Bruton
HAMPSHIRE, ISLE OF WIGHT, SURREY, WEST SUSSEX
Teffont Evias
Tisbury
Corton Denham
West Hatch
(plans 4)
Rimpton
Shaftesbury
Donhead-St-Andrew
Trent
Sherborne
Fontmell Magna
Nomansland
Farnham
Cranborne
DORSET
Wimborne St Giles
Evershot
Southampton
3
Wimborne Minster
Bournemouth
Christchurch
Highcliffe
Dorchester
Poole
Wareham
Studland
Isle of Wight
C
D

Channel Islands 3

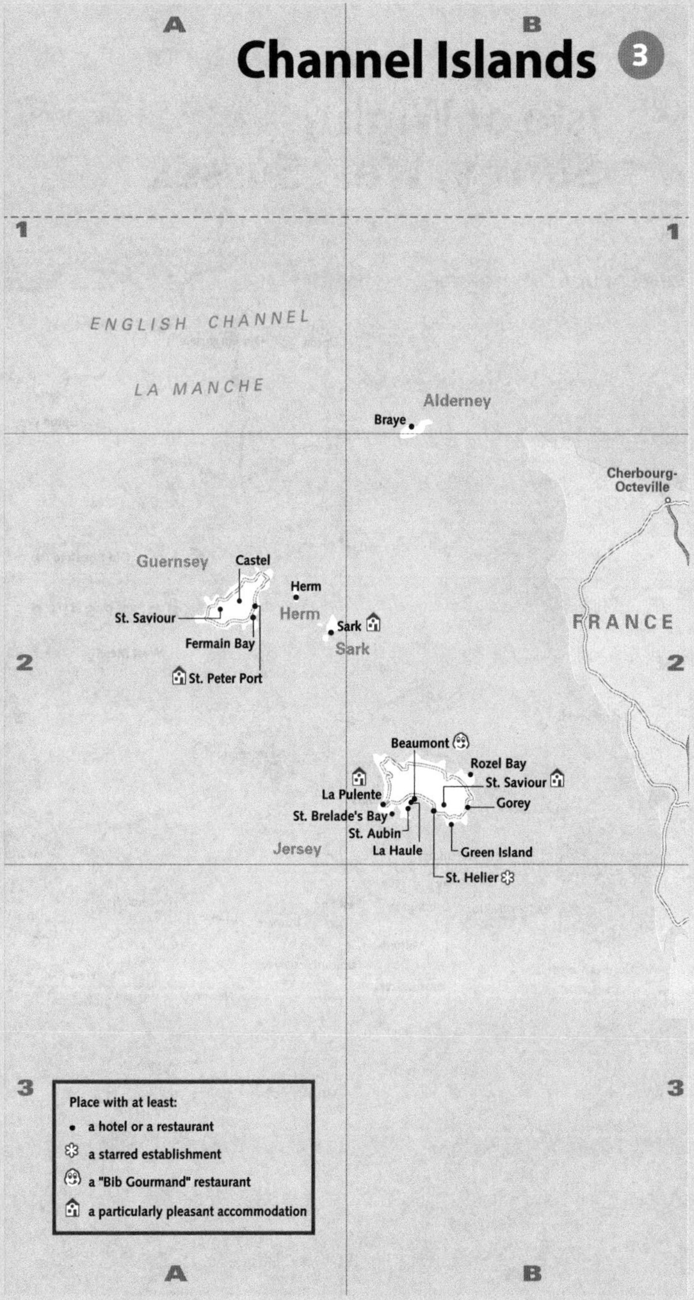
A
B
1
2
3
ENGLISH CHANNEL
LA MANCHE
Alderney
Braye
Cherbourg-Octeville
FRANCE
Guernsey
Castel
Herm
Herm
St. Saviour
Fermain Bay
St. Peter Port
Sark
Sark
Beaumont
Rozel Bay
St. Saviour
La Pulente
Gorey
St. Brelade's Bay
St. Aubin
Jersey
La Haule
Green Island
St. Helier
Place with at least:
a hotel or a restaurant
a starred establishment
a "Bib Gourmand" restaurant
a particularly pleasant accommodation

4 Hampshire, Isle of Wight, Surrey, West Sussex

A
B
1
2
3
Reading
Newbury
SOMERSET, DORSET, GLOUCESTERSHIRE, WILTSHIRE
(plans 2)
Upton
Old Burghclere
Baughurst
Hook
Upton Grey
Stockbridge
Old Alresford
Salisbury
Winchester
HAMPSHIRE
West Meon
Romsey
Fordingbridge
Southampton
Lyndhurst
Brockenhurst
Beaulieu
Emsworth
Sway
New Milton
Lymington
East End
Portsmouth
Gurnard
Cowes
Hayling Island
Milford-on-Sea
Bournemouth
Yarmouth
Freshwater
Seaview
Newport
St. Helens
Shanklin
Isle of Wight
Ventnor
A
B

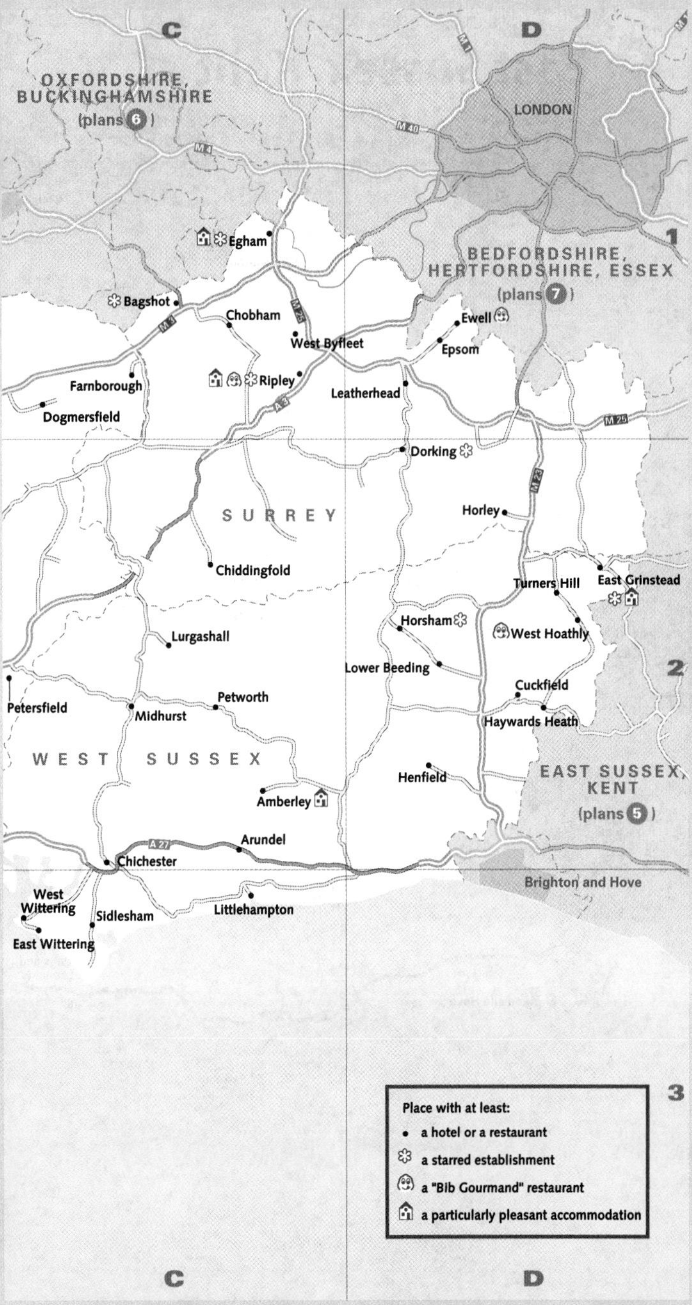
C
D
OXFORDSHIRE, BUCKINGHAMSHIRE
(plans 6)
LONDON
M 40
M 4
M 1
BEDFORDSHIRE, HERTFORDSHIRE, ESSEX
(plans 7)
1
Egham
Bagshot
Chobham
M 25
M 3
West Byfleet
Ewell
Epsom
Farnborough
Ripley
Leatherhead
Dogmersfield
A 3
M 25
Dorking
M 23
SURREY
Horley
Chiddingfold
East Grinstead
Turners Hill
Horsham
West Hoathly
Lurgashall
Lower Beeding
2
Cuckfield
Petersfield
Petworth
Midhurst
Haywards Heath
WEST SUSSEX
EAST SUSSEX, KENT
(plans 5)
Henfield
Amberley
Arundel
A 27
Chichester
Brighton and Hove
West Wittering
Sidlesham
Littlehampton
East Wittering
3
Place with at least:
• a hotel or a restaurant
a starred establishment
a "Bib Gourmand" restaurant
a particularly pleasant accommodation
C
D

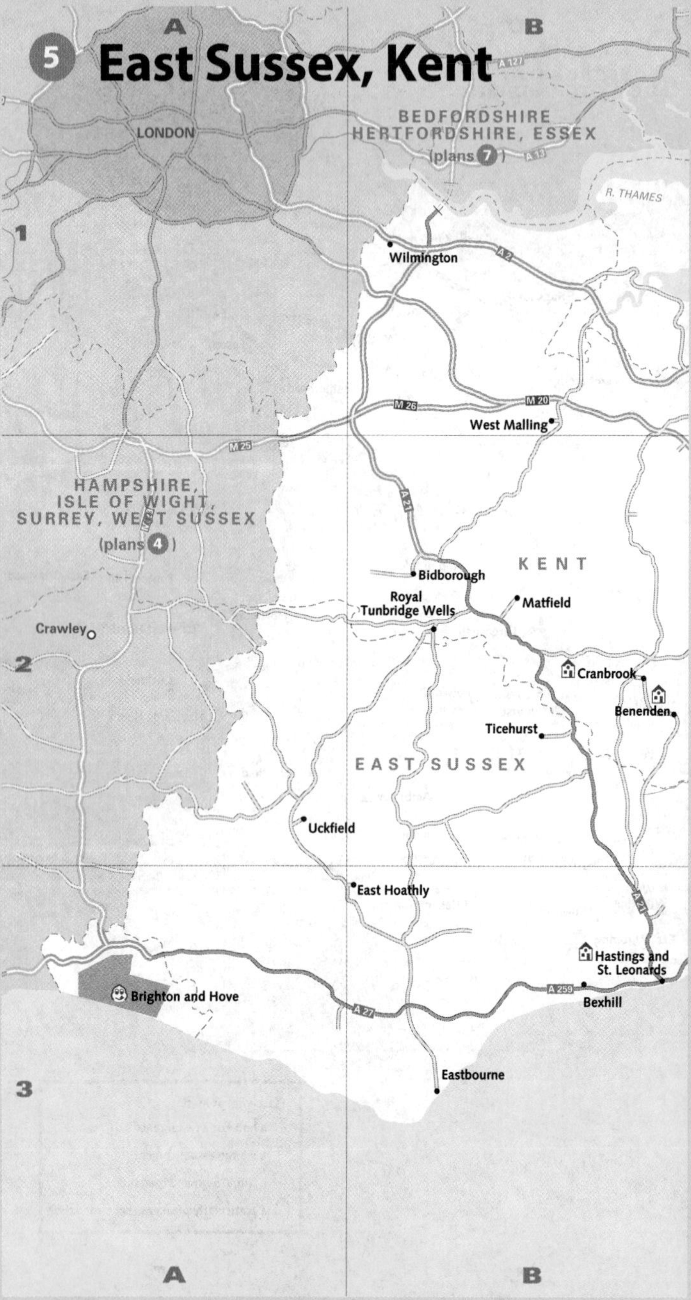

5 East Sussex, Kent
A
B
LONDON
BEDFORDSHIRE
HERTFORDSHIRE, ESSEX
(plans 7)
A 127
A 13
R. THAMES
1
Wilmington
A 2
M 26
M 20
West Malling
M 25
HAMPSHIRE,
ISLE OF WIGHT,
SURREY, WEST SUSSEX
(plans 4)
A 21
KENT
Bidborough
Royal
Tunbridge Wells
Matfield
Crawley
2
Cranbrook
Benenden
Ticehurst
EAST SUSSEX
Uckfield
East Hoathly
A 21
Hastings and
St. Leonards
Brighton and Hove
A 259
Bexhill
A 27
Eastbourne
3
A
B

C
D
BEDFORDSHIRE
HERTFORDSHIRE, ESSEX
(plans 7)
Southend-on-Sea
1
Margate
Whitstable
Seasalter
A 299
Broadstairs
Faversham
M 2
Fordwich
Doddington
Canterbury
Ickham
Sandwich
Hollingbourne
Leeds
Stalisfield
A 2
KENT
A 256
Deal
Egerton
Crundale
Wye
Alkham
Ashford
Biddenden
M 20
2
Tenterden
Folkestone
A 259
Rye
Camber
3
Place with at least:
a hotel or a restaurant
a starred establishment
a "Bib Gourmand" restaurant
a particularly pleasant accommodation
C
D

6 Oxfordshire, Buckinghamshire

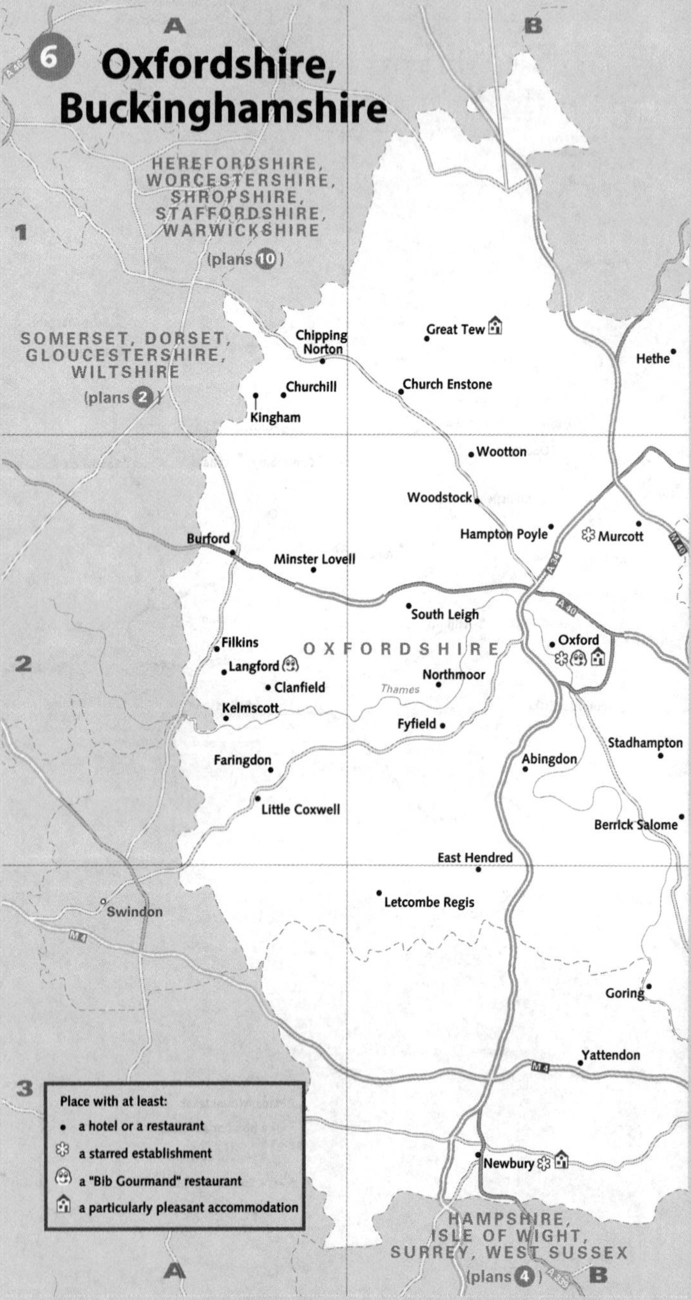

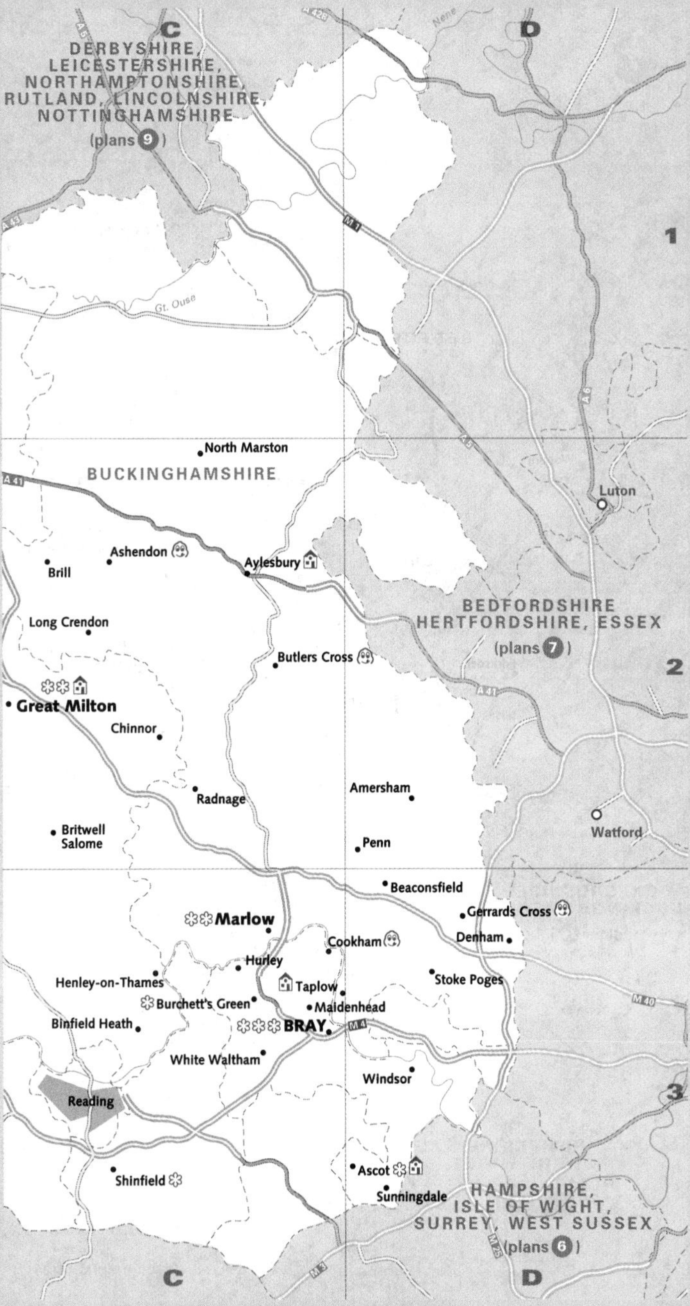
C
D
DERBYSHIRE,
LEICESTERSHIRE,
NORTHAMPTONSHIRE,
RUTLAND, LINCOLNSHIRE,
NOTTINGHAMSHIRE
(plans 9)
A 5
A 43
A 428
Nene
M 1
Gt. Ouse
1
A 6
A 5
North Marston
BUCKINGHAMSHIRE
A 41
Luton
Ashendon
Brill
Aylesbury
BEDFORDSHIRE
HERTFORDSHIRE, ESSEX
(plans 7)
Long Crendon
Butlers Cross
2
Great Milton
A 41
Chinnor
Radnage
Amersham
Watford
Britwell Salome
Penn
Beaconsfield
Marlow
Gerrards Cross
Cookham
Denham
Hurley
Henley-on-Thames
Taplow
Stoke Poges
Burchett's Green
Maidenhead
M 40
Binfield Heath
BRAY
M 4
White Waltham
Windsor
3
Reading
Shinfield
Ascot
Sunningdale
HAMPSHIRE,
ISLE OF WIGHT,
SURREY, WEST SUSSEX
(plans 6)
M 25
M 3
C
D

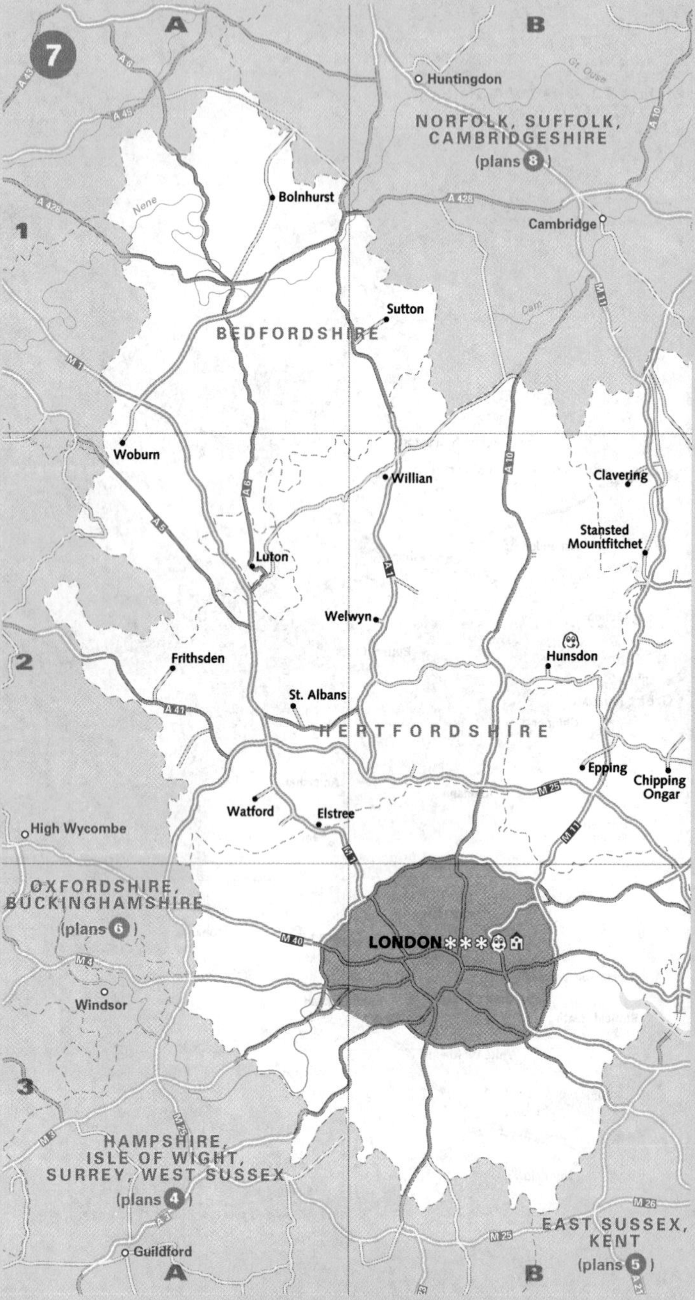
7
A
B
Huntingdon
Gr. Ouse
NORFOLK, SUFFOLK, CAMBRIDGESHIRE
(plans 8)
A 43
A 6
A 45
A 428
A 10
Nene
Bolnhurst
Cambridge
1
Cam
M 11
Sutton
BEDFORDSHIRE
M 1
Woburn
Willian
A 10
Clavering
A 6
A 5
Stansted Mountfitchet
Luton
A 1
Welwyn
Hunsdon
2
Frithsden
St. Albans
A 41
HERTFORDSHIRE
Epping
Chipping Ongar
M 25
Watford
Elstree
High Wycombe
M 11
M 1
OXFORDSHIRE, BUCKINGHAMSHIRE
(plans 6)
M 40
LONDON ***
M 4
Windsor
3
M 3
M 25
HAMPSHIRE, ISLE OF WIGHT, SURREY, WEST SUSSEX
(plans 4)
M 26
A 3
EAST SUSSEX, KENT
M 25
Guildford
(plans 5)
A
B

Bedfordshire, Hertfordshire, Essex

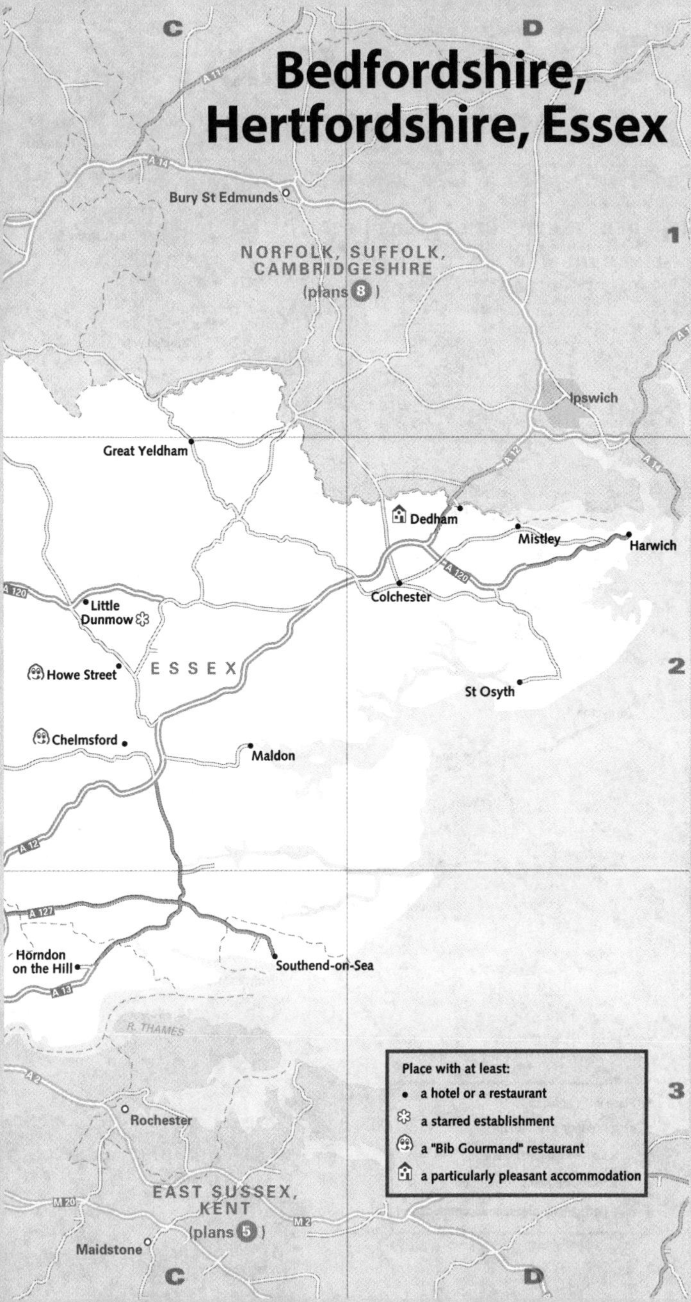

8 Norfolk, Suffolk, Cambridgeshire

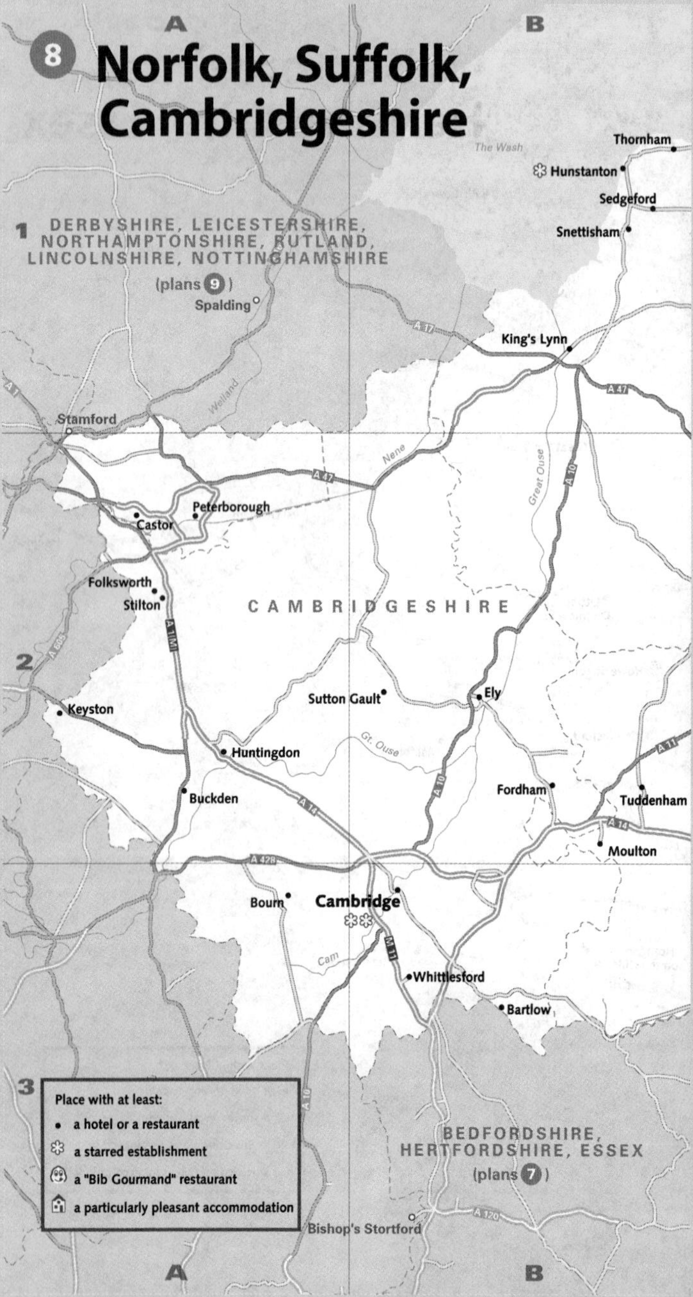

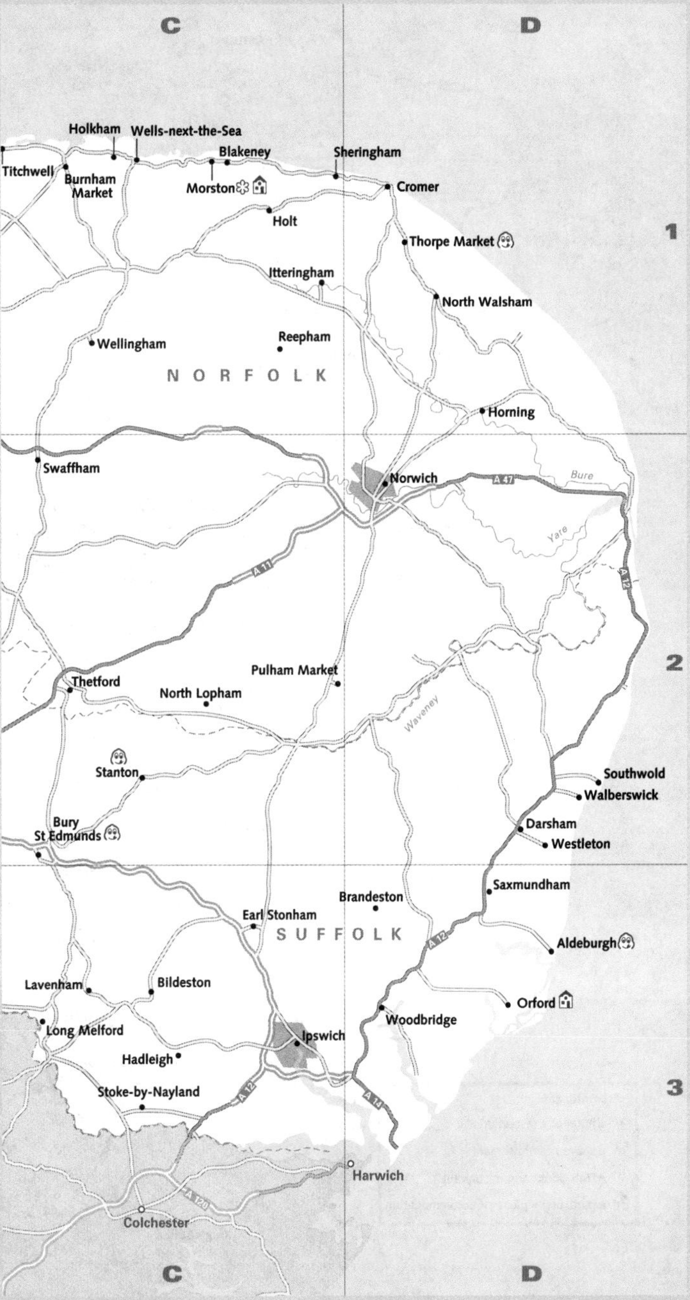
C
D
Holkham
Wells-next-the-Sea
Blakeney
Sheringham
Titchwell
Burnham Market
Morston
Cromer
Holt
1
Thorpe Market
Itteringham
North Walsham
Wellingham
Reepham
NORFOLK
Horning
Swaffham
Norwich
A 47
Bure
Yare
A 11
A 12
2
Pulham Market
Thetford
North Lopham
Waveney
Stanton
Southwold
Walberswick
Bury St Edmunds
Darsham
Westleton
Saxmundham
Brandeston
Earl Stonham
SUFFOLK
A 12
Aldeburgh
Lavenham
Bildeston
Orford
Woodbridge
Long Melford
Ipswich
Hadleigh
3
Stoke-by-Nayland
A 12
A 14
Harwich
A 120
Colchester
C
D

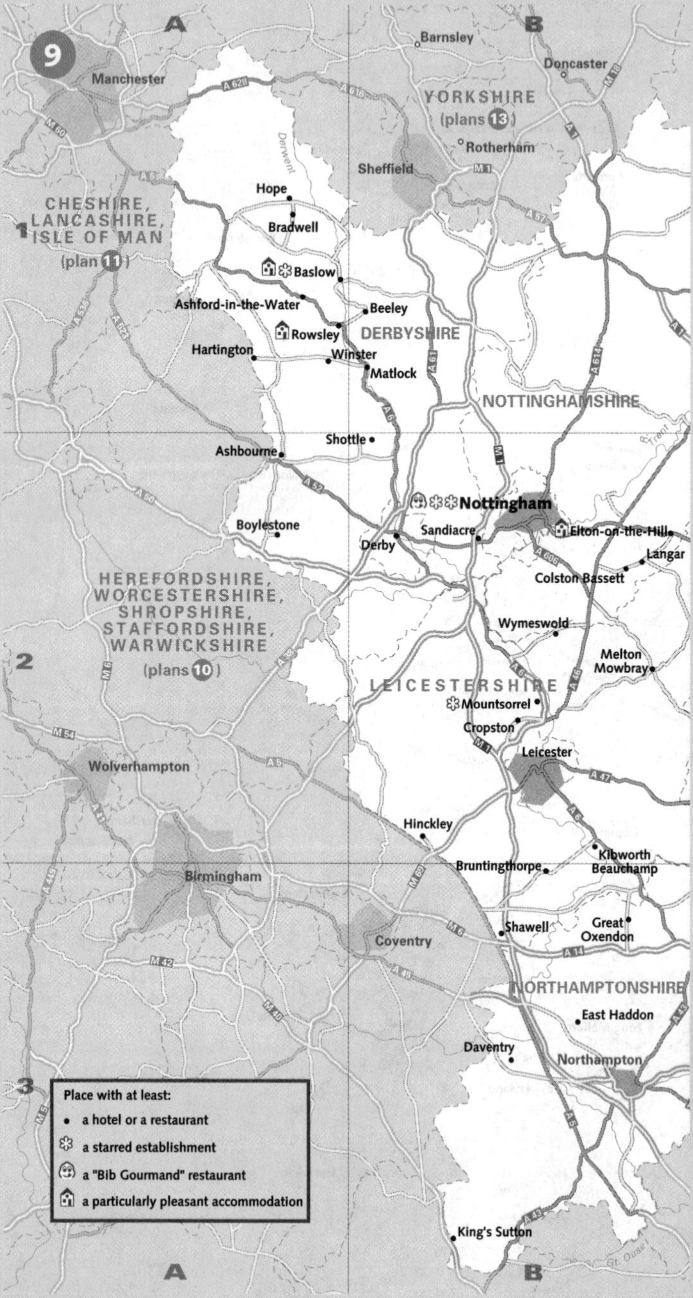

9
A
B
Manchester
Barnsley
Doncaster
YORKSHIRE
(plans 13)
Rotherham
Sheffield
Derwent
CHESHIRE,
LANCASHIRE,
ISLE OF MAN
(plan 11)
1
Hope
Bradwell
Baslow
Ashford-in-the-Water
Beeley
Rowsley
DERBYSHIRE
Hartington
Winster
Matlock
NOTTINGHAMSHIRE
Shottle
Ashbourne
Nottingham
Boylestone
Sandiacre
Derby
Elton-on-the-Hill
Langar
Colston Bassett
HEREFORDSHIRE,
WORCESTERSHIRE,
SHROPSHIRE,
STAFFORDSHIRE,
WARWICKSHIRE
(plans 10)
2
Wymeswold
Melton
Mowbray
LEICESTERSHIRE
Mountsorrel
Cropston
Leicester
Wolverhampton
Hinckley
Kibworth
Beauchamp
Bruntingthorpe
Birmingham
Shawell
Great
Oxendon
Coventry
NORTHAMPTONSHIRE
East Haddon
Daventry
Northampton
3
Place with at least:
• a hotel or a restaurant
a starred establishment
a "Bib Gourmand" restaurant
a particularly pleasant accommodation
King's Sutton
Gt. Ouse
R. Trent
A
B

Derbyshire, Leicestershire, Northamptonshire, Rutland, Lincolnshire, Nottinghamshire

10 Herefordshire, Worcestershire, Shropshire, Staffordshire, Warwickshire

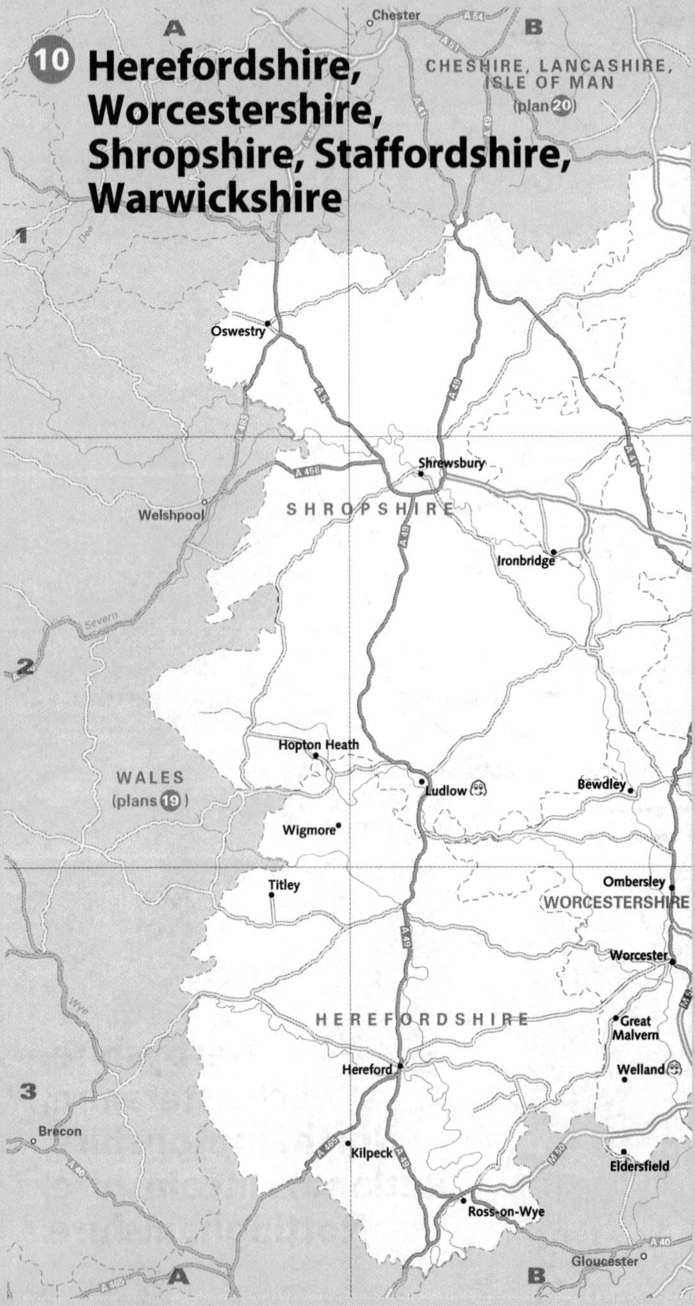

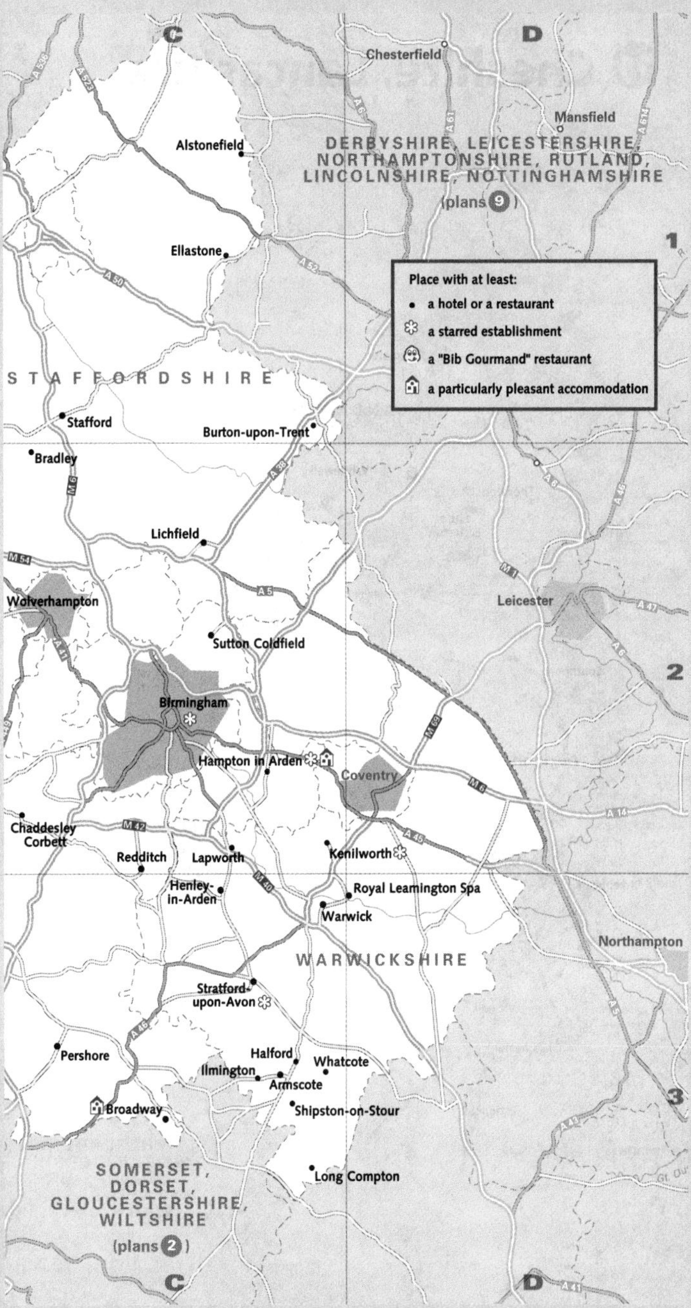

C
D
Chesterfield
Mansfield
DERBYSHIRE, LEICESTERSHIRE,
NORTHAMPTONSHIRE, RUTLAND,
LINCOLNSHIRE, NOTTINGHAMSHIRE
(plans 9)
1
2
3
Place with at least:
• a hotel or a restaurant
a starred establishment
a "Bib Gourmand" restaurant
a particularly pleasant accommodation
Alstonefield
Ellastone
STAFFORDSHIRE
Stafford
Bradley
Burton-upon-Trent
Lichfield
Wolverhampton
Sutton Coldfield
Leicester
Birmingham
Hampton in Arden
Coventry
Chaddesley Corbett
Redditch
Lapworth
Kenilworth
Henley-in-Arden
Royal Leamington Spa
Warwick
Northampton
WARWICKSHIRE
Stratford-upon-Avon
Pershore
Halford
Whatcote
Ilmington
Armscote
Broadway
Shipston-on-Stour
Long Compton
SOMERSET,
DORSET,
GLOUCESTERSHIRE,
WILTSHIRE
(plans 2)
C
D

11 Cheshire, Lancashire

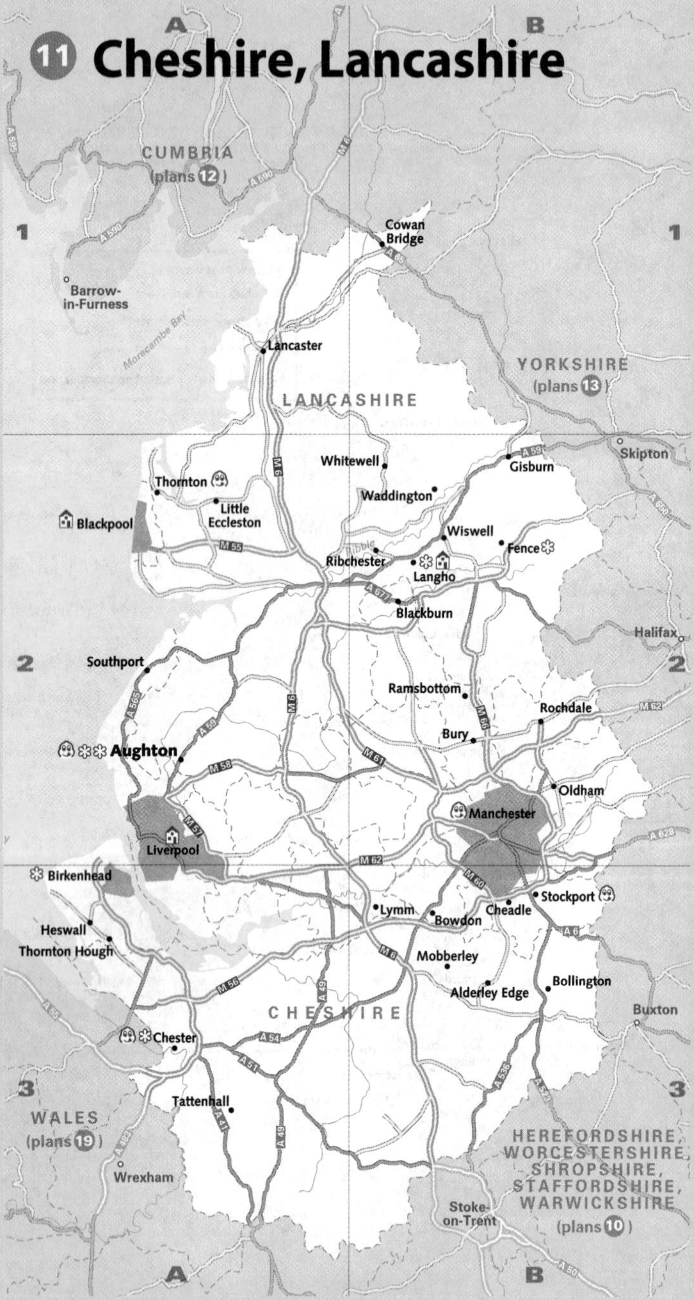

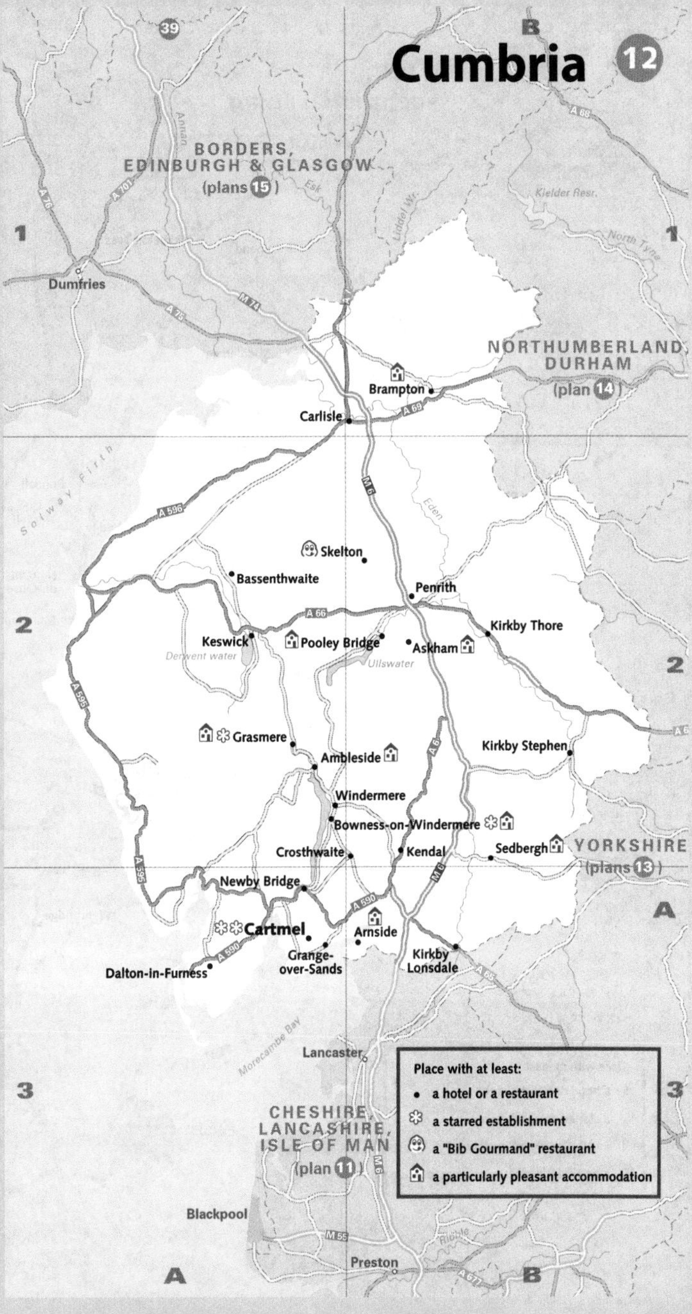
Cumbria
12
39
BORDERS,
EDINBURGH & GLASGOW
(plans 15)
NORTHUMBERLAND,
DURHAM
(plan 14)
YORKSHIRE
(plans 13)
CHESHIRE,
LANCASHIRE,
ISLE OF MAN
(plan 11)
Dumfries
Brampton
Carlisle
Skelton
Bassenthwaite
Penrith
Kirkby Thore
Keswick
Pooley Bridge
Askham
Derwent water
Ullswater
Grasmere
Ambleside
Kirkby Stephen
Windermere
Bowness-on-Windermere
Crosthwaite
Kendal
Sedbergh
Newby Bridge
Cartmel
Arnside
Grange-over-Sands
Kirkby Lonsdale
Dalton-in-Furness
Lancaster
Blackpool
Preston
Solway Firth
Morecambe Bay
Kielder Resr.
North Tyne
Eden
Esk
Liddel Wr.
Annan
Ribble
A 76
A 701
A 75
M 74
A 68
A 69
M 6
A 596
A 66
A 595
A 6
A 590
A 65
M 55
A 677
Place with at least:
a hotel or a restaurant
a starred establishment
a "Bib Gourmand" restaurant
a particularly pleasant accommodation

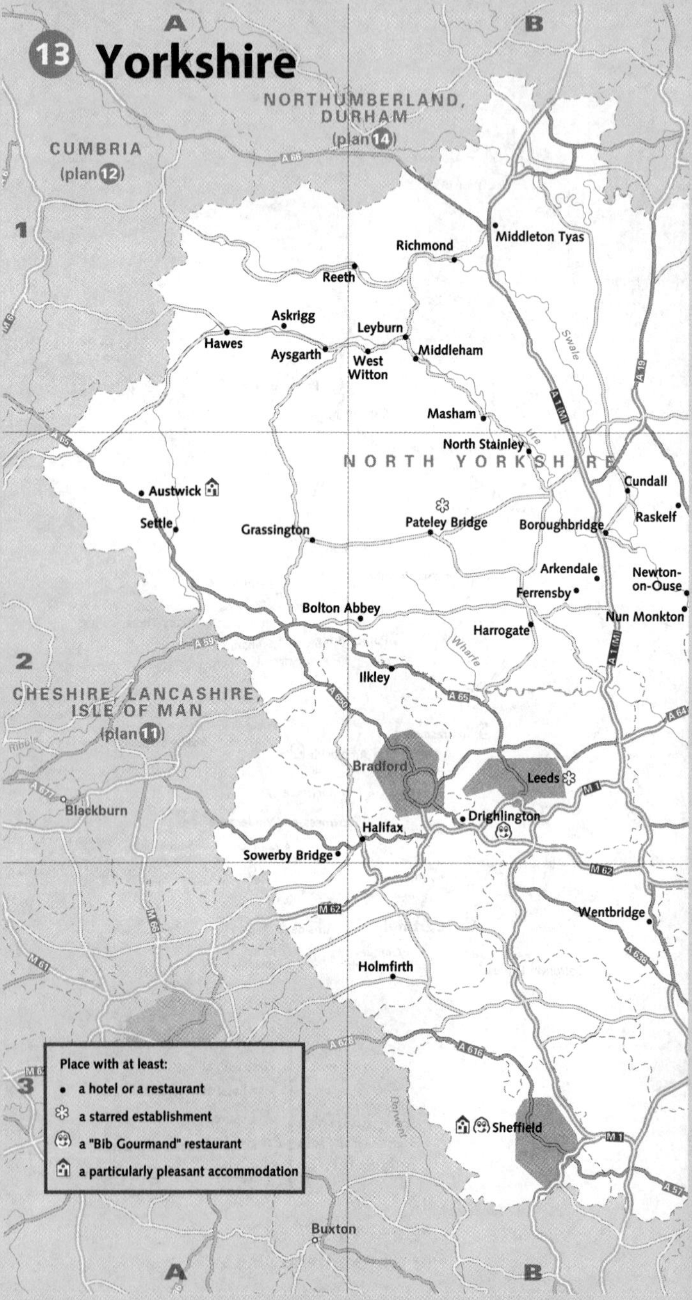
A
B
13 Yorkshire
NORTHUMBERLAND, DURHAM
(plan 14)
CUMBRIA
(plan 12)
1
A 66
Middleton Tyas
Richmond
Reeth
Askrigg
Leyburn
Hawes
Aysgarth
West Witton
Middleham
Swale
A 19
A 1 (M)
Masham
North Stainley
Ure
A 65
NORTH YORKSHIRE
Cundall
Austwick
Raskelf
Settle
Grassington
Pateley Bridge
Boroughbridge
Arkendale
Newton-on-Ouse
Ferrensby
Bolton Abbey
Nun Monkton
Harrogate
A 59
Wharfe
2
Ilkley
CHESHIRE, LANCASHIRE, ISLE OF MAN
(plan 11)
A 650
A 65
A 64
Ribble
Bradford
Leeds
M 1
A 677
Blackburn
Drighlington
Halifax
Sowerby Bridge
M 62
M 62
Wentbridge
M 66
M 61
A 638
Holmfirth
A 628
A 616
M 62
3
Place with at least:
a hotel or a restaurant
a starred establishment
a "Bib Gourmand" restaurant
a particularly pleasant accommodation
Derwent
Sheffield
M 1
A 57
Buxton
A
B

C
D
Middlesbrough
Whitby
1
Hawnby
Kirkbymoorside
Helmsley
Harome
Pickering
Scarborough
Oldstead
A 64
Wold Newton
Crayke
Malton
Stillington
Welburn
A 19
York
EAST RIDING
OF
YORKSHIRE
2
A 1079
South Dalton
A 19
Derwent
Sancton
Beverley
A 63
Kingston
upon Hull
A 164
R. Ouse
M 62
River Humber
Winteringham
South Ferriby
A 15
NORTH
LINCOLNSHIRE
NORTH EAST
LINCOLNSHIRE
M 180
M 18
3
A 1
R. Trent
DERBYSHIRE, LEICESTERSHIRE,
NORTHAMPTONSHIRE, RUTLAND,
LINCOLNSHIRE, NOTTINGHAMSHIRE
(plans 9)
Louth
C
A 57
A 158
D

Northumberland, Durham 14

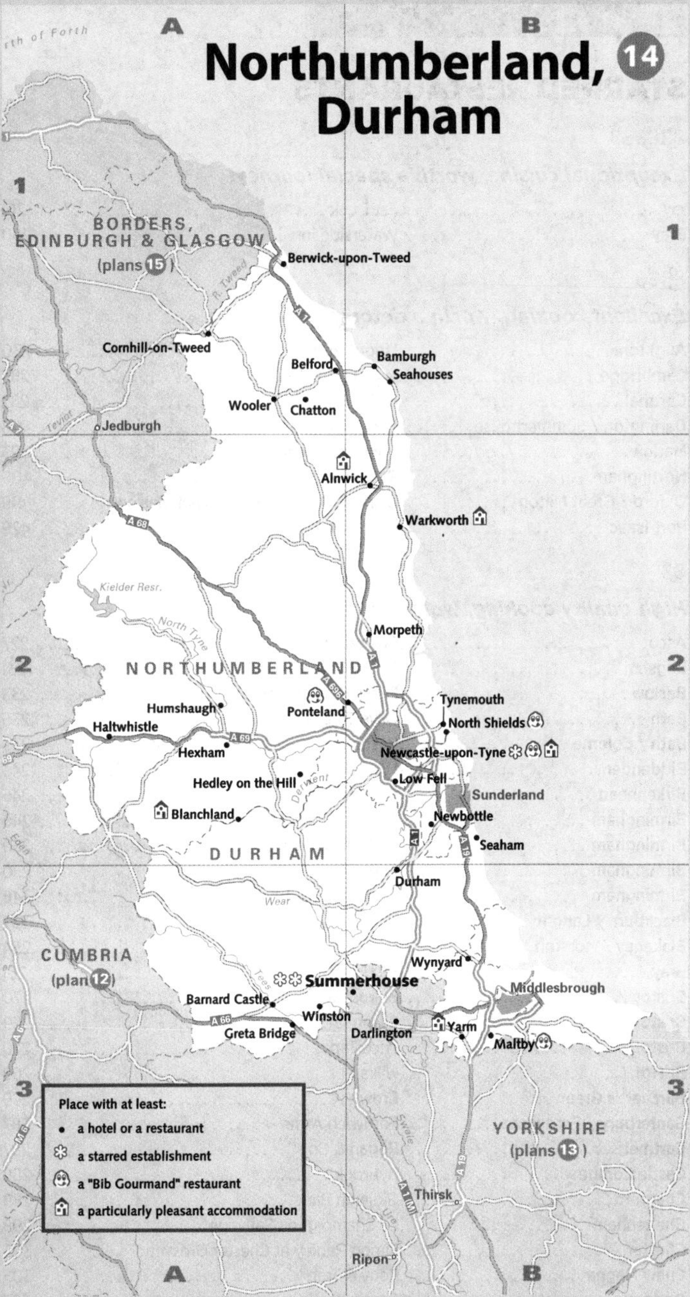
A
B
1
2
3
rth of Forth
BORDERS, EDINBURGH & GLASGOW (plans 15)
Berwick-upon-Tweed
R. Tweed
A 1
Cornhill-on-Tweed
Belford
Bamburgh
Seahouses
Wooler
Chatton
Teviot
Jedburgh
Alnwick
Warkworth
A 68
Kielder Resr.
North Tyne
Morpeth
NORTHUMBERLAND
A 696
Humshaugh
Ponteland
Tynemouth
North Shields
Haltwhistle
A 69
Hexham
Newcastle-upon-Tyne
Hedley on the Hill
Derwent
Low Fell
Sunderland
Blanchland
Newbottle
A 19
Seaham
DURHAM
Eden
Durham
Wear
CUMBRIA (plan 12)
Tees
Wynyard
Summerhouse
Middlesbrough
Barnard Castle
A 66
Winston
Greta Bridge
Darlington
Yarm
Maltby
A 6
M 6
Swale
YORKSHIRE (plans 13)
A 1(M)
Thirsk
Ure
Ripon
Place with at least:
a hotel or a restaurant
a starred establishment
a "Bib Gourmand" restaurant
a particularly pleasant accommodation

NOT TO BE MISSED

STARRED RESTAURANTS

✿✿✿

Exceptional cuisine, worth a special journey!

✿✿

Excellent cooking, worth a detour!

✿

High quality cooking, worth a stop!

Michelin

BIB GOURMAND RESTAURANTS

Good quality, good value cooking

Restaurant Nathan Outlaw, Port Isaac

OUR TOP PICKS

BOUTIQUE BOLTHOLES BY THE SEA

CHARMING CHOCOLATE BOX PUBS

REGIONAL STAND-OUTS

SOMETHING A LITTLE DIFFERENT

ICONIC COUNTRY HOUSES

THE ULTIMATE IN LUXURY

Bunch of Grapes

ABBOTSBURY

Dorset – Pop. 481 – Regional map n° **2**-B3

Abbey House

HISTORIC • COSY A characterful guesthouse-cum-tea-shop in a stunning location, with the ruins of an 11C abbey and a Benedictine watermill in its grounds. Well-kept, classical bedrooms have feature beds and one has its bathroom in an old monk's cell.

5 rooms – £ 90/140 £ 90/150

Church St ✉ DT3 4JJ – ✆ 01305 871330 – www.theabbeyhouse.co.uk

ABBOTS RIPTON – Cambridgeshire ➜ See Huntingdon

ABINGDON

Oxfordshire – Pop. 38 262 – Regional map n° **6**-B2

Rafters

FAMILY • MODERN A modest-looking house which belies its modern interior. Scandic-style bedrooms come with striking bathrooms and plenty of extra touches; the best boasts a small 'Zen Garden'. Local produce features at breakfast.

4 rooms – £ 62/114 £ 119/139

Abingdon Rd, Marcham ✉ OX13 6NU – West : 3 mi on A 415 – ✆ 01865 391298 – www.bnb-rafters.co.uk – Closed 2 weeks Christmas and New Year

ALDEBURGH

Suffolk – Pop. 2 341 – Regional map n° **8**-D3

Lighthouse

MEDITERRANEAN CUISINE • BISTRO X Popular, long-standing, split-level eatery with bright yellow décor, amiable service and a laid-back feel. Menus change constantly, featuring fish from the boats 200m away and local, seasonal meats and vegetables. Cooking is rustic and flavoursome, and dishes arrive generously proportioned.

Menu £ 17 (lunch and early dinner) – Carte £ 21/40

77 High St ✉ IP15 5AU – ✆ 01728 453377 (booking essential) – www.lighthouserestaurant.co.uk – Closed 26 December and lunch 1 January

Sea Spice

INDIAN • ELEGANT XX Hidden in a hotel is this dark, moody restaurant with period lighting and contrastingly bright, patterned crockery. Freshly ground spices and local fish, meat and game feature; try the muntjac vindaloo and the delicious rasmalai.

Menu £ 13 (lunch) – Carte £ 24/36

White Lion Hotel, Market Cross Pl ✉ IP15 5BJ – ✆ 01728 452720 – www.seaspice.co.uk – Closed Monday

Wentworth

TRADITIONAL • PERSONALISED The friendly, engaging team know all the regulars at this family-run seaside hotel. The conservatory and large front terrace are popular spots. Extremely comfortable bedrooms come with a copy of locally set 'Orlando the Marmalade Cat'. The formal dining room serves a traditional daily menu.

35 rooms (dinner included) – £ 83/124 £ 135/303

Wentworth Rd ✉ IP15 5BD – ✆ 01728 452312 – www.wentworth-aldeburgh.com – Closed January

Brudenell

FAMILY • MODERN A contemporary hotel right on the beachfront, with a relaxed ambience and superb sea views; take it all in from the large terrace. New England style bedrooms come with modern bathrooms and up-to-date facilities. The informal, split-level bar-cum-restaurant offers an accessible seafood-orientated menu.

44 rooms – £ 106/340 £ 126/360

The Parade IP15 5BU – 01728 452071 – www.brudenellhotel.co.uk

ALDERLEY EDGE

Cheshire East – Pop. 5 280 – Regional map n° **11**-B3

Alderley Edge

BUSINESS • CLASSIC This smartly refurbished, early Victorian country house sits in an affluent village. Bedrooms in the main house have a characterful country style; the more contemporary rooms at the back overlook the immaculate gardens. The brightly decorated brasserie offers a seasonally evolving modern British menu.

50 rooms – £ 110 £ 120/200 – 1 suite

Macclesfield Rd SK9 7BJ – 01625 583033 – www.alderleyedgehotel.com

ALKHAM

Kent – Pop. 351 – Regional map n° **5**-D2

Alkham Court

FAMILY • RURAL Set on a hill, surrounded by mature grounds, is this delightful guesthouse with a hot tub and sauna. Homely, well-equipped bedrooms come with complimentary sherry and stylish bathrooms. The large conservatory has lovely country views.

4 rooms – £ 80/100 £ 140/170

Meggett Ln CT15 7DG – Southwest : 1 mi by Alkham Valley Rd – 01303 892056 – www.alkhamcourt.co.uk

ALNWICK

Northumberland – Pop. 8 116 – Regional map n° **14**-B2

Cookie Jar (N)

TOWNHOUSE • DESIGN This former convent is now a stylish hotel. Every bedroom comes with a 'smart' speaker and a jar of homemade cookies; the Chapel Suite has original stained glass windows and a shower where the alter used to be. Enjoy afternoon tea in the beautifully secluded terraced garden. The bistro opens Thurs-Sat.

11 rooms – £ 160 £ 295

12 Bailiffgate NE66 1LU – 01665 510465 – www.cookiejaralnwick.com

Greycroft

TOWNHOUSE • PERSONALISED 19C house near the Castle, run by welcoming owners with good local knowledge. Bedrooms are well-equipped and have homely touches; the conservatory breakfast room overlooks a lovely walled garden.

6 rooms – £ 65/70 £ 95/135

Croft Pl NE66 1XU – via Prudhoe St – 01665 602127 – www.greycroftalnwick.co.uk – Closed mid-December-mid-January

West Acre House

TOWNHOUSE • PERSONALISED Proudly run Edwardian villa with a beautifully maintained 1 acre garden. Well-proportioned rooms come with bold wallpapers, Arts and Crafts features and a keen eye for detail; choose a Georgian, Edwardian, Oriental or Parisian theme.

4 rooms – £ 106/130 £ 106/130

West Acres NE66 2QA – East : 0.5 mi by A 1068 – 01665 510374 – www.westacrehouse.co.uk

ALSTONEFIELD

Staffordshire - Pop. 274 - Regional map n° **10**-C1

The George

TRADITIONAL CUISINE • PUB The moment you walk into this 18C pub on the village green, feel the warmth from the roaring fires and start to soak up the relaxed, cosy atmosphere, you just know it's going to be good. It's simply furnished, with stone floors and scrubbed wooden tables, and cooking is well-priced and down-to-earth.

Carte £ 27/49

DE6 2FX - 01335 310205 - www.thegeorgeatalstonefield.com - Closed 25 December and Sunday dinner

AMBERLEY

West Sussex - Arundel - Pop. 586 - Regional map n° **4**-C2

Queen's Room

MODERN BRITISH • ELEGANT XXX Within the walls of a stunning 12C castle is this elegant dining room with a barrel-vaulted ceiling, lancet windows and an open fire. Ambitious modern dishes arrive artfully presented. Henry VIII's wives all visited, hence its name.

Menu £ 35/68

Amberley Castle Hotel, BN18 9LT - Southwest : 0.5 mi on B 2139 - 01798 831992 (booking essential) - www.amberleycastle.co.uk

Amberley Castle

LUXURY • HISTORIC Stunning 12C castle displaying original stonework, battlements and evidence of a moat. The charming grounds consist of lovely gardens, lakes and a croquet lawn, and are matched inside by a characterful array of rooms. Sumptuous bedrooms have a palpable sense of history; those in the main castle are the best.

19 rooms - £ 175/640 £ 370/770 - 6 suites

BN18 9LT - 01798 831992 - www.amberleycastle.co.uk

Queen's Room - See restaurant listing

AMBLESIDE

Cumbria - Pop. 2 529 - Regional map n° **12**-A2

The Samling

MODERN CUISINE • DESIGN XXX A stunning glass and slate extension to a superbly set hotel - its full-length windows offer wonderful lake and country views. Elaborate modern cooking showcases garden ingredients in eye-catching dishes. Start with drinks on the terrace or in the stylish lounge.

Menu £ 45/100 - tasting menu only

The Samling Hotel, Ambleside Rd LA23 1LR - South : 1.5 mi on A 591 - 015394 31922 (booking essential) - www.thesamlinghotel.co.uk

Old Stamp House

MODERN CUISINE • INTIMATE XX A quirky little place hidden in the cellar of an old house and named after William Wordsworth. Two low-ceilinged rooms feature exposed beams and slate floors. The natural flavours of Cumbrian ingredients are championed in concise menus which showcase modern cooking.

Menu £ 25 (lunch) - Carte £ 34/51

Church St LA22 0BU - 015394 32775 (booking essential) - www.oldstamphouse.com - Closed Christmas, 3-25 January, Sunday and Monday

Lake Road Kitchen

CREATIVE • SIMPLE Wooden planks line the walls and fleeces cover the chairs at this intimate restaurant. The passionate chef-owner uses only ingredients grown in the same climate as The Lakes and his experience with preservation techniques allows him to use seasonal ingredients year-round. Creative dishes have natural flavours.

Menu £ 65 – tasting menu only

Lake Rd LA22 0AD – 015394 22012 (booking essential) – www.lakeroadkitchen.co.uk – dinner only – Closed Monday and Tuesday

Drunken Duck Inn

WORLD CUISINE • RURAL This picture-postcard pub sits in the heart of the beautiful Lakeland countryside. Simple lunches are followed by elaborate dinners with subtle global influences. Cooking is generous, service is attentive and the ales are brewed on-site. Some of the boutique country bedrooms have terraces with fell views.

Menu £ 38 – Carte lunch approx. £ 22

13 rooms – £ 94/244 £ 125/325

Barngates LA22 0NG – Southwest : 3 mi by A 593 and B 5286 on Tarn Hows rd – 015394 36347 (booking essential at dinner) – www.drunkenduckinn.co.uk – Closed 25 December

The Samling

COUNTRY HOUSE • CONTEMPORARY A former farmhouse and outbuildings perched on the hillside; the outdoor hot tub is the perfect spot to take in the stunning lake and fell views. Both the guest areas and the bedrooms have a stylish, contemporary look; the latter come in neutral tones and their bathrooms have underfloor heating.

7 rooms – £ 310/670 £ 310/670 – 5 suites

Ambleside Rd LA23 1LR – South : 1.5 mi on A 591 – 015394 31922 – www.thesamlinghotel.co.uk

The Samling – See restaurant listing

Nanny Brow

COUNTRY HOUSE • HISTORIC Charming Arts and Crafts house with views of the River Brathay and the Langdale Fells. Spacious, antique-furnished bedrooms sit above an elegant lounge. Original stained glass, wood panelling and impressive fireplaces feature.

14 rooms – £ 145/280 £ 160/280

Clappersgate LA22 9NF – Southwest : 1.25 mi on A 593 – 015394 33232 – www.nannybrow.co.uk – Closed 25-26 December

Riverside

TRADITIONAL • COSY A homely slate house in a peaceful riverside location; run by delightful owners. The steep, mature garden is filled with rhododendrons. Bedroom 2 has a four-poster, a whirlpool bath and water views. Breakfast is locally sourced.

6 rooms – £ 110/118 £ 110/118

Under Loughrigg LA22 9LJ – West : 1 mi by A 591 and A 593 – 015394 32395 – www.riverside-at-ambleside.co.uk – Closed 7 December-24 January

AMERSHAM (Old Town)

Buckinghamshire – Pop. 23 086 – Regional map n° **6**-D2

Artichoke

MODERN BRITISH • ELEGANT 16C red-brick house in a picturesque town. A narrow beamed room with polished tables leads through to a Scandic-style extension with a semi-open kitchen and glass screens etched with branches. Modern dishes are nicely presented.

Menu £ 28 (weekday lunch)/50 – Carte lunch £ 44/51

9 Market Sq HP7 0DF – 01494 726611 (booking essential at dinner) – www.artichokerestaurant.co.uk – Closed 2 weeks Christmas-New Year, 2 weeks late August, 1 week Easter, Sunday and Monday

Hawkyns

MODERN BRITISH • DESIGN XX Set within a 16C red-brick coaching inn, in a picturesque town, this heavily timbered restaurant has a warm, welcoming feel. Original modern dishes are artistically presented and have an Indian slant; the Green Egg is used to good effect.

Carte £ 31/48

Crown Inn, 16 High St ✉ HP7 0DH – ✆ 01494 721541 – www.hawkynsrestaurant.co.uk

AMPLEFORTH – North Yorkshire → See Helmsley

ANTONY

Cornwall – Regional map n° **1**-C2

Carew Arms

MODERN BRITISH • FRIENDLY A friendly little pub with a bright interior; they also operate the village shop from the next room. Pop in for a local beer and a scotch egg, a pub favourite or something more interesting like scallops with chorizo and apple jam.

Menu £ 16 (lunch) – Carte £ 24/38

Antony Hill ✉ PL11 3AB – ✆ 01752 814440 – www.carewarms.com – Closed 25 December, Monday except bank holidays and Tuesday.

ARKENDALE

North Yorkshire – Regional map n° **13**-B2

Blue Bell

TRADITIONAL BRITISH • COSY This might be a modern dining pub but it still has plenty of character, courtesy of hops hanging over the bar, sofas set in front of a wood burning stove and locals hanging out with their dogs. When it comes to the food, everything is homemade. Upstairs are four smart bedrooms with super king sized beds.

Carte £ 24/42

4 rooms – †£ 60/120 ††£ 60/120

Moor Ln ✉ HG5 0QT – ✆ 01423 369242 – www.thebluebellatarkendale.co.uk

ARLINGHAM

Gloucestershire – Pop. 459 – Regional map n° **2**-C1

Old Passage

SEAFOOD • FRIENDLY XX Sit out on the terrace or beside the window, surrounded by colourful art, and watch the famous Severn bore travel up the estuary. Concise seafood menus offer everything from a fish pie to a fruits de mer platter or lobster direct from their saltwater tank. Simply furnished modern bedrooms share the view.

Menu £ 19 (weekday lunch) – Carte £ 35/60

2 rooms – †£ 80/120 ††£ 100/140

Passage Rd ✉ GL2 7JR – West : 0.75 mi – ✆ 01452 740547 – www.theoldpassage.com – Closed 25-27 December, Sunday dinner, Monday and dinner Tuesday-Wednesday January-March

ARMSCOTE

Warwickshire – Regional map n° **10**-C3

Fuzzy Duck

TRADITIONAL CUISINE • PUB Siblings Adrian and Tania – also owners of toiletries company Baylis & Harding – took this place from boarded up boozer to welcoming, fashionably attired dining pub. Seasonal British dishes use great quality local and sustainable ingredients. Stylish boutique bedrooms complete the picture.

Carte £ 25/46

4 rooms – †£ 110/160 ††£ 110/160

Ilmington Rd ✉ CV37 8DD – ✆ 01608 682635 – www.fuzzyduckarmscote.com – Closed 26 December, Sunday dinner and Monday

ARNSIDE

Cumbria - Pop. 2 334 - Regional map n° **12**-A3

Number 43

LUXURY • CONTEMPORARY Stylishly converted Victorian townhouse boasting superb views over the estuary and fells. Contemporary bedrooms have smart bathrooms, quality furnishings, good facilities and plenty of extras. The comfortable open-plan lounge and dining room offers light meat and cheese sharing platters in the evening. Start the day with breakfast on the glass-enclosed terrace.

5 rooms - £ 125/185 £ 125/185

43 The Promenade ✉ LA5 0AA - 01524 762761 - www.no43.org.uk

ARUNDEL

West Sussex - Pop. 3 285 - Regional map n° **4**-C2

Parsons Table

MODERN BRITISH • FRIENDLY XX Tucked away in a little courtyard is this lovely restaurant with a fresh modern feel. Flavoursome dishes have a hint of modernity and are as seasonal and local as the quality of the produce will allow. Service comes with a smile.

Menu £ 18 (lunch) - Carte £ 30/41

2 & 8 Castle Mews, Tarrant St ✉ BN18 9DG - 01903 883477 - www.theparsonstable.co.uk - Closed 1 week February, 1 week late August, 24-28 December, Sunday and Monday

Town House

MODERN CUISINE • ELEGANT XX If you're a fan of Renaissance architecture, head for this early 17C townhouse, where you'll find a gilt walnut panelled ceiling which was originally installed in the Medici Palace in Florence. Cooking is assured; if there's local crab on the menu, be sure to choose it. Comfy bedrooms include four-posters.

Menu £ 23/33

5 rooms - £ 75/110 £ 110/150

65 High St ✉ BN18 9AJ - 01903 883847 - www.thetownhouse.co.uk - Closed 2 weeks November, 1 week March, 1 week August-September, 25-26 December, 1-2 January, Sunday and Monday

at Burpham Northeast: 3 mi by A27 ✉ Arundel

The George at Burpham

MODERN BRITISH • RUSTIC A local consortium headed by three local businessmen saved this pub from closure and it's since been given a smart new look, to which beams, fires and a smugglers' wheel add character. The seasonal menu is full of tasty, popular classics.

Carte £ 25/44

Main St ✉ BN18 9RR - 01903 883131 - www.georgeatburpham.co.uk - Closed 25 December and dinner Sunday-Monday in winter

ASCOT

Windsor and Maidenhead - Pop. 15 761 - Regional map n° **6**-D3

Coworth Park

MODERN CUISINE • ELEGANT XXX An elegant, intimate restaurant in a beautiful house, with a striking copper oak leaf chandelier matching the autumnal colours, and a lovely terrace overlooking manicured gardens. The assured, technically skilled cooking is modern yet respectful of classic combinations and displays real depth and finesse.

→ Marinated scallop, pickled strawberry, tarragon and hazelnut. Herb-crusted lamb, Yorkshire fettle cheese, peas and mint. Passion fruit and yuzu tart with coconut sorbet.

Menu £ 35/80 **s**

Coworth Park Hotel, Blacknest Rd ✉ SL5 7SE - East : 2.75 mi on A 329 - 01344 876600 (booking essential) - www.dorchestercollection.com - dinner only and lunch Friday-Sunday - Closed Sunday dinner, Monday and Tuesday

Ascot Grill

MEATS AND GRILLS • FASHIONABLE XX Neighbourhood restaurant with a slick, minimalistic interior featuring leather, silk and velvet; full-length windows open onto a pleasant pavement terrace. Wide-ranging modern grill menu offers steak and seafood. Good value lunches.

Carte £ 24/52

6 Hermitage Par, High St ✉ SL5 7HE – ✆ 01344 622285 – www.ascotgrill.co.uk – Closed first week January, Sunday dinner and Monday

Coworth Park

COUNTRY HOUSE • GRAND LUXURY A luxurious 18C property set in 246 acres, with stylish, contemporary guest areas and beautiful bedrooms featuring bespoke furniture, marble bathrooms and excellent facilities; those in main house are the largest. Dine in the elegant restaurant or more causal brasserie, overlooking their championship polo fields. The superb spa has a 'living roof' of herbs and flowers.

70 rooms – £ 350/750 £ 350/750 – 19 suites

Blacknest Rd ✉ SL5 7SE – East : 2.75 mi on A 329 – ✆ 01344 876600 – www.dorchestercollection.com

✿ **Coworth Park** – See restaurant listing

ASHBOURNE

Derbyshire – Pop. 8 377 – Regional map n° **9**-A2

Callow Hall

TRADITIONAL • PERSONALISED Traditional Victorian country house in 30 acres of gardens, fields and woodland. Individually styled bedrooms boast original features, spacious bathrooms, and traditional fabrics and furnishings. Seasonal menus showcase local produce in classically based dishes with the occasional modern touch.

16 rooms – £ 110/195 £ 150/250 – 1 suite

Mapleton Rd ✉ DE6 2AA – West : 0.75 mi by Union St (off Market Pl) – ✆ 01335 300900 – www.callowhall.co.uk

at Shirley Southeast: 5 mi by A515 and off A52

Saracen's Head

TRADITIONAL BRITISH • RUSTIC A rustic, open-plan dining pub opposite the village church, in a remote, picturesque village. Menus are chalked on blackboards above the open fire and offer an eclectic mix of generously portioned pub and restaurant-style classics.

Carte £ 23/44

Church Ln ✉ DE6 3AS – ✆ 01335 360330 – www.saracens-head-shirley.co.uk – Closed 25 December

ASHBURTON

Devon – Pop. 3 346 – Regional map n° **1**-C2

Agaric

TOWNHOUSE • THEMED Friendly owners welcome you to this rustic guesthouse on the main street with its comfortable, simply furnished bedrooms. The single is decorated in a Chinese style, while the best is Havana with its four-poster bed and roll top bath.

4 rooms – £ 58/90 £ 100/120

36 North St ✉ TQ13 7QD – ✆ 01364 654478 – www.agaricrestaurant.co.uk – Closed Christmas

ASHENDON

Buckinghamshire – Regional map n° **6**-C2

The Hundred of Ashendon

REGIONAL CUISINE • FRIENDLY In Saxon times, shires were divided into 'hundreds' for military and judicial purposes. This charming 17C inn keeps the concept alive by sourcing its produce from within its 'hundred'. Great value dishes arrive in hearty portions, packed full of flavour – and influences from Matt's time at St John are clear to see. Modest bedrooms are continually being upgraded.

Carte £ 24/36

5 rooms – £ 55/65 £ 70/105

Lower End ✉ HP18 0HE – ✆ 01296 651296 – www.thehundred.co.uk – Closed 25 December, Sunday dinner and Monday

ASHFORD

Kent – Pop. 67 528 – Regional map n° **5**-C2

Eastwell Manor

LUXURY • HISTORIC Impressive manor house with Tudor origins, surrounded by beautifully manicured gardens and extensive parkland. Rebuilt in 1926 following a fire but some superb plaster ceilings and stone fireplaces remain. Characterful guest areas and luxurious bedrooms. Sizeable spa and golf course. Choice of wood-panelled restaurant complete with pianist or more casual brasserie and terrace.

42 rooms – £ 160/450 £ 160/450 – 20 suites

Eastwell Park, Boughton Lees ✉ TN25 4HR – North : 3 mi by A 28 on A 251 – ✆ 01233 213000 – www.eastwellmanor.co.uk

ASHFORD-IN-THE-WATER

Derbyshire – Regional map n° **9**-A1

Riverside House

TRADITIONAL • COSY Charming former hunting lodge with gardens running down to the river. Comfy, individually styled bedrooms are named after flowers and birds: one is a four-poster and some have French doors opening onto garden terraces. Classical dining takes place over four different rooms. It has a homely feel throughout.

14 rooms – £ 125/155 £ 150/195

Fennel St ✉ DE45 1QF – ✆ 01629 814275 – www.riversidehousehotel.co.uk

ASKHAM – Cumbria → See Penrith

ASKRIGG

North Yorkshire – ✉ Leyburn – Pop. 1 002 – Regional map n° **13**-A1

Yorebridge House

MODERN BRITISH • DESIGN XX Romantic restaurant set within an old schoolmaster's house and offering lovely countryside views. Concise menus evolve with the seasons and feature locally sourced produce; dishes are modern, flavoursome and attractively presented.

Menu £ 60

Yorebridge House Hotel, Bainbridge ✉ DL8 3EE – West : 1.25 mi – ✆ 01969 652060 (bookings essential for non-residents) – www.yorebridgehouse.com – dinner only

Yorebridge House

COUNTRY HOUSE • CONTEMPORARY Stylish former schoolmaster's house in a lovely Dales setting, with a snug bar and great country views. Bold modern bedrooms are themed around the owner's travels; those in the old schoolhouse have riverside patios and hot tubs.

12 rooms – £ 195/270 £ 220/410

Bainbridge ✉ DL8 3EE – West : 1.25 mi – ✆ 01969 652060 – www.yorebridgehouse.com

Yorebridge House – See restaurant listing

AUGHTON

Lancashire - Pop. 8 342 - Regional map n° **11**-A2

✿✿ Moor Hall (Mark Birchall)

MODERN BRITISH • DESIGN XxX Charming grounds with a lake and a fountain lead up to this 16C house with Tudor origins and Victorian extensions. Inside it's an appealing mix of the old and the new: cosy lounges feature ornately carved dark wood panelling and squashy sofas set in front of roaring fires, which contrast with an ultra-modern glass-fronted restaurant with sleek blond wood furnishings and an impressive open kitchen.

Mark Birchall brings his knowledge and experience together in a style of his own, where skilfully executed dishes combine the classic flavours of the region with modern techniques and a light touch. The produce leads the menu and he only uses ingredients at their peak; as well as tasting delicious individually, each has its part to play when a dish is eaten as a whole, contributing maybe earthiness, acidity or herbal tones. Local gingerbread is often a feature and the pacing of the meal is well-judged.

Spacious bedrooms have a contemporary feel.

→ Turnip and crab with anise hyssop and sunflower seeds. Grilled Herdwick lamb, courgette, onion and anchovy. Gingerbread, roots and pine.

Menu £ 40/105

7 rooms - †£ 195/350 ††£ 195/350

Prescot Rd ✉ L39 6RT - On B 5197 - ☎ 01695 572511 (booking essential) - www.moorhall.com - Closed 3-16 January, 31 July-14 August, Wednesday lunch, Monday and Tuesday

The Barn - See restaurant listing

The Barn Ⓝ

TRADITIONAL BRITISH • RUSTIC XX In the grounds of Moor Hall you'll find this rustic barn and terrace overlooking the lake. The ground floor houses the aging rooms; head upstairs for a draught beer in the bar and a traditional meal while watching the chefs. Familiar British dishes showcase local ingredients and are cooked with care.

Menu £ 23 (lunch) - Carte £ 27/54

Moor Hall, Prescot Rd ✉ L39 6RT - On B 5197 - ☎ 01695 572511 - www.moorhall.com - Closed 3-16 January, 31 July-14 August, Monday-Wednesday lunch

AUSTWICK

North Yorkshire - Pop. 463 - Regional map n° **13**-A2

Traddock

COUNTRY HOUSE • PERSONALISED Unusually named after a horse trading paddock; a Georgian country house with Victorian additions - once a private residence. Inside it's traditional with bright, airy lounges and bedrooms boasting feature beds and country views. Dine formally from a menu of local produce and expect the odd global touch.

12 rooms - †£ 99/170 ††£ 99/300

✉ LA2 8BY - ☎ 015242 51224 - www.thetraddock.co.uk - Closed 3 days early January

Austwick Hall

HISTORIC BUILDING • PERSONALISED Set in a delightful village on the edge of the Dales and surrounded by tiered gardens, is this characterful house built in 1590 for the Master of the Mint. The flagged hall has an impressive stained glass window framed by two columns and antiques abound. Nothing is too much trouble for the friendly owners.

4 rooms - †£ 110/140 ††£ 125/155

Townhead Ln ✉ LA2 8BS - ☎ 015242 51794 - www.austwickhall.co.uk

AXMINSTER

Devon - Pop. 5 761 - Regional map n° **1**-D2

River Cottage Canteen

REGIONAL CUISINE • RUSTIC Busy restaurant, deli and coffee shop owned by Hugh Fearnley-Whittingstall. The slightly stark rear room was once a dance hall. Menus change twice-daily and offer gutsy, flavoursome country dishes which showcase local produce.

Menu £ 12 (weekday lunch) - Carte £ 25/39

Trinity Sq EX13 5AN - 01297 631715 - www.rivercottage.net/restaurants/axminster - Closed 25 December, Sunday dinner and Monday dinner except July-August

AYLESBURY

Buckinghamshire - Pop. 71 977 - Regional map n° **6**-C2

Hartwell House

HISTORIC • CLASSIC An impressive palatial house set in 90 acres of parkland: the erstwhile residence of Louis XVIII, exiled King of France, and now owned by the National Trust. It boasts ornate furnishings, luxurious lounges, an intimate spa and magnificent antique-filled bedrooms. The formal restaurant offers traditional country house cooking and afternoon tea is a speciality.

48 rooms - †£ 200/750 ††£ 240/750 - 10 suites

Oxford Rd HP17 8NR - Southwest : 2 mi on A 418 - 01296 747444 - www.hartwell-house.com

AYOT GREEN - Hertfordshire → See Welwyn

AYSGARTH

North Yorkshire - Regional map n° **13**-A1

Stow House

COUNTRY HOUSE • PERSONALISED A Gothic-style residence built in 1876 for the Rev Stow, which sits in an enviable position looking down the valley. The owners have an extensive art collection and the smart retro bedrooms are named after pictures on their walls.

7 rooms - †£ 100/175 ††£ 110/175

DL8 3SR - East : 0.5 mi on A 684 - 01969 663635 - www.stowhouse.co.uk

BABBACOMBE - Torbay → See Torquay

BAGSHOT

Surrey - Pop. 5 430 - Regional map n° **4**-C1

Matt Worswick at The Latymer

MODERN CUISINE • CLASSIC DÉCOR Traditional dark wood panels and beams are offset by colourful, boldly printed fabrics, which give this formal hotel dining room an elegant, contemporary feel. Choose between two set menus of deceptively simple-looking dishes, which have superb depth and show a great understanding of complementary flavours.

→ Salt-baked celeriac with remoulade, lovage and truffle. Rack of hogget, heritage potato, wild garlic and smoked goat's curd. Chocolate délice with milk crumble and yoghurt sorbet.

Menu £ 69/95 - tasting menu only

Pennyhill Park Hotel, London Rd GU19 5EU - Southwest : 1 mi on A 30 - 01276 471774 - www.exclusivehotels.co.uk - dinner only and lunch Saturday-Sunday - Closed 1-16 January, Monday and Tuesday

Pennyhill Park

LUXURY • CLASSIC An impressive 19C manor house set in 123 acres and boasting one of Europe's best spas. Both the guest areas and the bedrooms are spacious, with period furnishings and modern touches; feature bathrooms come with rain showers or glass baths. Dine in the elegant restaurant or stylish brasserie.

124 rooms – £ 250/295 £ 440/485 – £ 22 – 12 suites

London Rd ✉ GU19 5EU – ✆ 01276 471774 – www.exclusivehotels.co.uk

Matt Worswick at The Latymer – See restaurant listing

BAMBURGH

Northumberland – Pop. 279 – Regional map n° **14**-B1

Potted Lobster

SEAFOOD • FRIENDLY A sweet, homely bistro hung with dramatic local seascapes; sit outside for a view of the majestic castle. Classic dishes come in large portions. Check the blackboard for the latest catch; the squid and oysters are must-tries.

Carte £ 24/58

3 Lucker Rd ✉ NE69 7BS – ✆ 01668 214088 – www.thepottedlobsterbamburgh.co.uk – Closed 25-26 December and 1 January

Lord Crewe Arms

INN • COSY Smart 17C former coaching inn, privately owned and superbly set in the shadow of a famous Norman castle. Comfy, cosy bedrooms have a modern feel, yet are in keeping with the age of the building. Characterful stone-walled bar and New England style restaurant serve brasserie dishes. Efficient service.

7 rooms – £ 60/90 £ 105/135

Front St ✉ NE69 7BL – ✆ 01668 214243 – www.lord-crewe.co.uk – Closed 25 December

at Waren Mill West: 2.75 mi on B1342 ✉ Belford

Waren House

FAMILY • CLASSIC Personally run, antique-furnished country house set in beautiful, tranquil gardens. Bedrooms – some named after the owners' family members – mix classic and modern styles: some have four-posters and coastal views. Formal dining room boasts an ornate ceiling; traditional menus showcase local ingredients.

13 rooms – £ 95/145 £ 100/170 – 2 suites

✉ NE70 7EE – ✆ 01668 214581 – www.warenhousehotel.co.uk

BAMPTON

Devon – Pop. 1 260 – Regional map n° **1**-D1

Swan

TRADITIONAL BRITISH • INN The Swan's history can be traced back to 1450, when it provided accommodation for craftsmen working on the village church – and its original inglenook fireplace and bread oven still remain. Neatly presented, unfussy pub classics showcase local farm produce. Smart, modern bedrooms are on the 2nd floor.

Carte £ 25/39

3 rooms – £ 85/100 £ 90/100

Station Rd ✉ EX16 9NG – ✆ 01398 332248 – www.theswan.co – Closed 25 December

BARNARD CASTLE

Durham – Pop. 7 040 – Regional map n° **14**-A3

at Greta Bridge Southeast: 4.5 mi off A66 ✉ Barnard Castle

Morritt

INN • PERSONALISED Attractive 19C inn on the site of an old Roman fort. The characterful interior cleverly blends the old and the new, with antiques and feature bedsteads offset by contemporary décor. The superb spa has a car garage theme. All-day snacks are served in the bar-bistro and there's a modern menu in the restaurant.

26 rooms – †£ 95/145 ††£ 115/155 – 1 suite

✉ DL12 9SE – ✆ 01833 627232 – www.themorritt.co.uk

at Hutton Magna Southeast: 7.25 mi by A66

Oak Tree Inn

TRADITIONAL BRITISH • COSY Small but charming whitewashed pub with six tables flanked by green settles and a bench table for drinkers. It's run by a husband and wife team; he cooks, while she serves. Cooking is hearty and flavoursome with a rustic British style.

Carte £ 34/47

✉ DL11 7HH – ✆ 01833 627371 (booking essential) – www.theoaktreehutton.co.uk – dinner only – Closed 24-27 and 31 December, 1-2 January and Monday

BARNSLEY – Gloucestershire → See Cirencester

BARTLOW

Cambridgeshire – Regional map n° **8**-B3

The Three Hills

MODERN BRITISH • INN It's named after a nearby Roman burial site and has 15C origins but it wasn't until the 1840s that The Three Hills first opened as an ale house. Seasonal modern menus mix pub and restaurant style dishes and there's a pizza oven on the charming terrace. Bedrooms are chic and comfy.

Menu £ 17 (lunch) – Carte £ 25/37

6 rooms – †£ 85/130 ††£ 85/130

Dean Rd ✉ CB21 4PW – ✆ 01223 890500 – www.thethreehills.co.uk – Closed Monday lunch and Sunday dinner

BARWICK – Somerset → See Yeovil

BASLOW

Derbyshire – Pop. 1 178 – Regional map n° **9**-A1

Fischer's at Baslow Hall

MODERN CUISINE • ELEGANT A fine Edwardian manor house with a country house feel, impressive formal grounds and a walled vegetable garden. The two dining rooms, with their ornate ceilings, offer a mix of classic and original modern dishes, prepared using skilful techniques; sit at the 'Kitchen Tasting Bench' to be part of the action. Bedrooms are charming – the Garden Rooms are the largest.

→ Tandoori quail with mango, lime and Ceylon sauce. Sirloin of beef with snails, wild garlic and Lyonnaise potatoes. Chocolate with passion fruit, hazelnut whiskey and orange ice cream.

Menu £ 34/79

11 rooms – †£ 185/225 ††£ 260/325 – 1 suite

Calver Rd ✉ DE45 1RR – on A 623 – ✆ 01246 583259 (booking essential) – www.fischers-baslowhall.co.uk – Closed dinner 24-26 and 31 December, 1 January

The Gallery

MODERN BRITISH • ELEGANT XXX A striking modern restaurant in an elegant hotel – sit below antique oil paintings looking out over the grounds. Well-presented, contemporary British dishes use estate produce; for a ringside seat book the chef's table.

Menu £ 53

Cavendish Hotel, Church Ln ✉ DE45 1SP – on A 619 – ✆ 01246 582311 – www.cavendish-hotel.net

Rowley's

MODERN BRITISH • BRASSERIE X Stone-built former blacksmith's; now a contemporary bar-restaurant with a small terrace and friendly service. Dine in the buzzy ground floor bar or more intimate upstairs rooms. Hearty, satisfying dishes have classic French roots.

Menu £ 17/31 – Carte £ 24/33

Church Ln ✉ DE45 1RY – ✆ 01246 583880 – www.rowleysrestaurant.co.uk – Closed 25 December and Sunday dinner

Cavendish

TRADITIONAL • PERSONALISED Set on the edge of the Chatsworth Estate is this fine stone building with superb parkland views. Delightful bedrooms are full of period charm and many are styled by national designers and the Duchess of Devonshire herself. Enjoy drinks in the plush bar-cum-sitting room or afternoon tea in the Garden Room.

28 rooms – †£ 175/232 ††£ 230/360 – ☕ £ 20 – 1 suite

Church Ln ✉ DE45 1SP – on A 619 – ✆ 01246 582311 – www.cavendish-hotel.net

The Gallery – See restaurant listing

Heathy Lea

COUNTRY HOUSE • PERSONALISED 17C farmhouse owned by the Chatsworth Estate – which has access to the grounds through its garden gate. Cosy, comfortable bedrooms have views over the farmland. The estate farm shop provides much of the produce used at breakfast.

3 rooms ☕ – †£ 60/75 ††£ 90/120

✉ DE45 1PQ – East : 0.75 mi on A 619 – ✆ 01246 583842 – www.heathylea.co.uk – Closed Christmas

BASSENTHWAITE

Cumbria – Pop. 433 – Regional map n° **12**-A2

Pheasant

INN • CLASSIC Characterful 16C coaching inn with comfy lounges and welcoming open fires. Bedrooms are spacious and retain a classic look appropriate to the building's age; some have lovely country outlooks. Have drinks amongst polished brass in the bar then make for the rustic oak-furnished bistro or more formal restaurant.

15 rooms ☕ – †£ 95/125 ††£ 130/200

✉ CA13 9YE – Southwest : 3.25 mi by B 5291 on Wythop Mill Rd – ✆ 017687 76234 – www.the-pheasant.co.uk – Closed 25 December

T. Bagnall/age fotostock

GOOD TIPS!

Known for its Georgian architecture and its Roman Baths, this city is one in which to relax and rejuvenate, so keep a look out for the spa symbol when choosing a hotel. Locally produced Bath Buns are the star of the show at afternoon tea in the **Royal Crescent** hotel, in the centre of the famous terrace designed by John Wood the Younger.

BATH

Bath and North East Somerset – Pop. 94 782 – Regional map n° **2**-C2

Restaurants

Olive Tree

MODERN CUISINE • INTIMATE XX Have a drink in the cool hotel bar or on the enclosed rear terrace, then head down to this surprisingly airy basement restaurant spread over three modern rooms. Dishes may appear simple but that's all part of their skilful make-up. Refined, creative cooking use colours, textures and flavours to full effect.

→ Asparagus with smoked eel, spring onion and Exmoor caviar. Lamb rump with aubergine, garlic and mint. Gariguette strawberry with meringue, mascarpone, orange blossom and basil.

Menu £ 48/82

Town plan: C1-x – *Queensberry Hotel, Russel St ✉ BA1 2QF – ✆ 01225 447928 – www.olivetreebath.co.uk – dinner only and lunch Friday-Sunday*

Menu Gordon Jones

MODERN CUISINE • INTIMATE XX A tiny restaurant comprising 8 tables and an open kitchen. Surprise daily changing tasting menus showcase some unusual British ingredients such as beef tendons or rabbit kidneys. Complex modern dishes have interesting texture and flavour combinations.

Menu £ 50/55 – surprise menu only

Town plan: A2-e – *2 Wellsway ✉ BA2 3AQ – ✆ 01225 480871 (booking essential at dinner) – www.menugordonjones.co.uk – Closed 1-16 January, 20-25 April, 28 May-5 June, 2-17 September, 28 October-5 November, Christmas-New Year, Sunday and Monday*

Acorn

VEGETARIAN • INTIMATE X A sweet, intimate, split-level restaurant set within one of Bath's oldest buildings. Modern vegetarian dishes are full of colour and show a great understanding of flavours. Wines are carefully chosen to match the food.

Menu £ 25/38

Town plan: D2-a – *2 North Parade Passage ✉ BA1 1NX – ✆ 01225 446059 – www.acornrestaurant.co.uk – Closed Christmas*

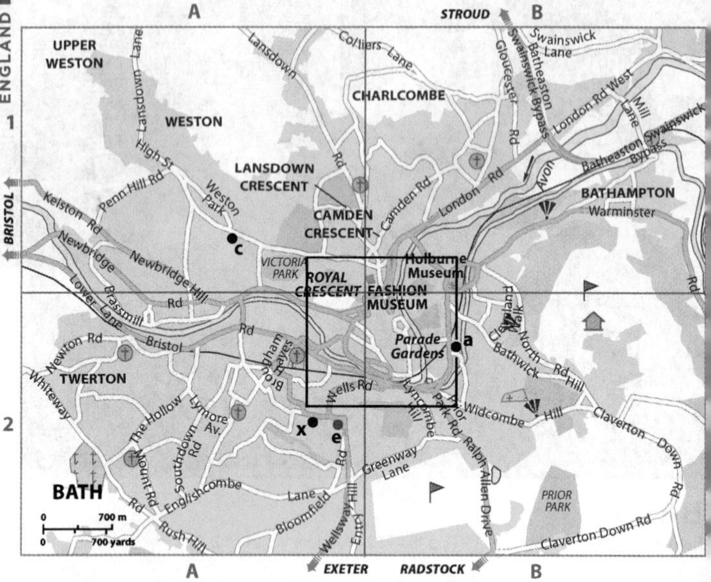

Circus

TRADITIONAL BRITISH • NEIGHBOURHOOD The small pavement terrace of this neighbourhood bistro is the perfect spot for people-watching in the historic heart of the city. Unfussy dishes use West Country produce and have a Mediterranean bias. Wines come from small growers.

Carte £ 23/33

Town plan: C1-c – *34 Brock St ✉ BA1 2LN*
– *✆ 01225 466020 – www.thecircusrestaurant.co.uk*
– *Closed 23 December-14 January and Sunday*

Henry's

MODERN BRITISH • NEIGHBOURHOOD A laid-back bistro in a pretty pedestrianised street. It's simple yet appealing, with wooden furnishings and pictures of local scenes. Original modern dishes include some interesting vegetarian options.

Menu £ 50 – Carte £ 31/42

Town plan: C1-n – *4 Saville Row ✉ BA1 2QP*
– *✆ 01225 780055 – www.henrysrestaurantbath.com*
– *Closed first week January, last 2 weeks July, 25-26 December, Sunday and Monday*

Marlborough Tavern

TRADITIONAL BRITISH • NEIGHBOURHOOD This 18C pub sits on the edge of Victoria Park, surrounded by grand terraced properties. Despite its traditional appearance, it's surprisingly chic and fashionable inside, with boldly patterned wallpapers and contemporary art. Carefully sourced ingredients feature in pub classics and interesting specials.

Carte £ 27/41

Town plan: C1-z – *35 Marlborough Buildings ✉ BA1 2LY*
– *✆ 01225 423731 – www.marlborough-tavern.com*
– *Closed dinner 25-26 December*

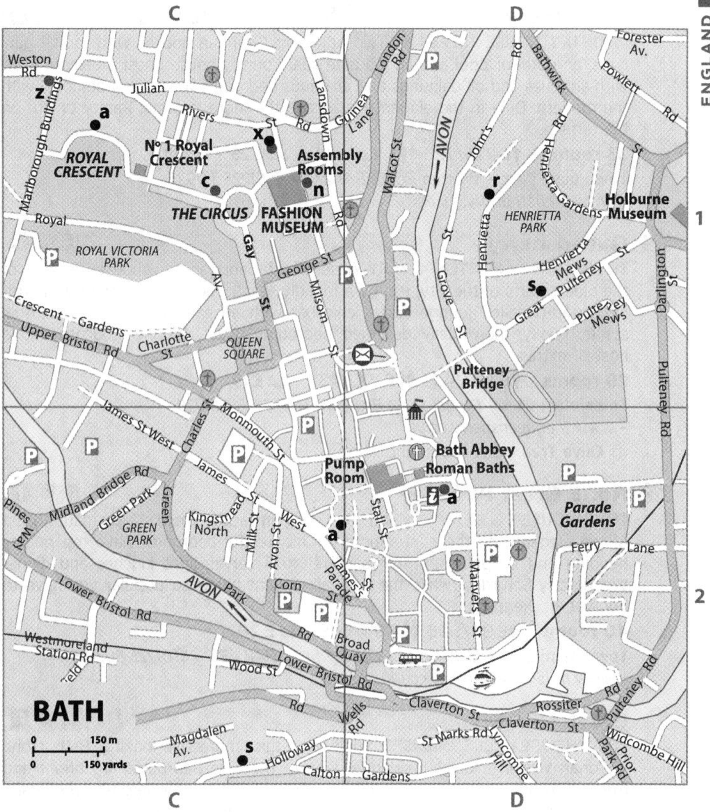

Hotels

Royal Crescent

HISTORIC • ELEGANT An elegantly refurbished Grade I listed building in a magnificent sweeping terrace. Ornate plasterwork, pastel shades and gilt-framed portraits evoke feelings of the Georgian era, and bedrooms are plush and luxurious. The lovely spa is in the old gothic chapel. Dine on attractive modern dishes.

45 rooms – £ 330/700 £ 330/700 – 12 suites

Town plan: C1-a – *16 Royal Cres* ✉ *BA1 2LS* – *01225 823333* – *www.royalcrescent.co.uk*

Gainsborough Bath Spa

THERMAL SPA • ELEGANT Set within two listed buildings, this hotel boasts a state-of-the-art spa whose three thermal pools tap into the city's original springs. Bedrooms are elegantly understated and three have thermal water piped directly to their baths. Enjoy afternoon tea in the Canvas Room and seasonal dishes in the restaurant.

99 rooms – £ 260/450 £ 260/450 – £ 30

Town plan: C2-a – *Beau St* ✉ *BA1 1QY* – *01225 358888* – *www.thegainsboroughbathspa.co.uk*

Bath Priory

COUNTRY HOUSE • ELEGANT Two adjoining Georgian houses with formal gardens, an outdoor pool and an intimate spa. Country house guest areas are filled with antiques and oil paintings and luxurious bedrooms blend the traditional with the modern. Dine in the elegant restaurant, the more informal Pantry or out on the terrace.

33 rooms – £ 225/725 £ 225/725 – £ 25 – 6 suites

Town plan: A1-c – *Weston Rd BA1 2XT – 01225 331922 – www.thebathpriory.co.uk*

Queensberry

TOWNHOUSE • CONTEMPORARY A series of Georgian townhouses in one of the oldest parts of the city, run by a friendly team. Guest areas include a charming wood-panelled lounge and a chic bar with an extensive array of unusual spirits. Funky, individually designed bedrooms boast designer touches and a host of extras.

29 rooms – £ 100/435 £ 100/435 – £ 19

Town plan: C1-x – *Russel St BA1 2QF – 01225 447928 – www.thequeensberry.co.uk*

Olive Tree – See restaurant listing

No.15 Great Pulteney

TOWNHOUSE • ELEGANT Behind the Georgian façade there's a dramatic fusion of the elegant and the contemporary. Chic, restful bedrooms have top quality bedding and bespoke furnishings. Café No.15 serves light lunches and dinner Wednesday-Saturday, while the cocktail elegant bar is so popular you have to book at weekends.

40 rooms – £ 94/506 £ 94/506 – £ 20

Town plan: D1-s – *13-15 Great Pulteney St BA2 4BS – 01225 807015 – www.no15greatpulteney.co.uk*

Grays

TOWNHOUSE • PERSONALISED You'll find this impressive-looking Bath stone Victorian villa in a quiet residential area of the city. Bedrooms are bright and fresh, with good facilities – the ground floor rooms are the largest, with cosier rooms cleverly fitted into the eaves; many have views over the city rooftops.

12 rooms – £ 99/205 £ 99/205

Town plan: A2-x – *9 Upper Oldfield Pk BA2 3JX – 01225 403020 – www.graysbath.co.uk – Closed 24-26 December*

Paradise House

TOWNHOUSE • PERSONALISED Elegant 18C house with award-winning gardens, set on Beechen Cliff, overlooking the city. The interior is charming and homely, with a cosy, classical lounge and bedrooms ranging from traditional four-posters to more modern styles.

12 rooms – £ 75/201 £ 75/210

Town plan: C2-s – *86-88 Holloway BA2 4PX – 01225 317723 – www.paradise-house.co.uk – Closed 24-25 December*

Roseate Villa

TOWNHOUSE • CONTEMPORARY In summer, enjoy afternoon tea in the garden of this attractive Victorian villa beside Henrietta Park. Bedrooms come in pastel colours, with eye-catching feature walls and shuttered windows. They have a night baker, so you awake to the aroma of freshly baked breads and pastries filling the house.

21 rooms – £ 130/400 £ 140/400

Town plan: D1-r – *Henrietta Rd BA2 6LX – 01225 466329 – www.roseatevillabath.com*

Brindleys

TOWNHOUSE • DESIGN Tucked away on a residential street is this cosy, comfy, immaculately kept Victorian villa, which is owned and run by a friendly team. Bedrooms come in contemporary pastel or monochrome themes but also give a nod to the villa's age and heritage. Local produce is a feature at breakfast.

6 rooms – £ 99/205 £ 99/205

Town plan: B2-a – *14 Pulteney Gdns ✉ BA2 4HG – ✆ 01225 310444 – www.brindleysbath.co.uk – Closed Christmas*

at Colerne Northeast: 6.5 mi by A4 ✉ Chippenham

Restaurant Hywel Jones by Lucknam Park

MODERN BRITISH • ELEGANT XXXX A meal in this opulent country house dining room is not one you'll soon forget. Expertly crafted, sophisticated dishes rely on classic techniques but have a light, modern style. The chef is a proud Welshman, so ingredients from his homeland sit alongside British and kitchen garden produce.

→ Roast scallops with smoked eel, apple and horseradish. Brecon lamb with carrots, yoghurt and cumin granola. Banana parfait, warm raisin sponge with banana and passion fruit sorbet.

Menu £ 87 (weekdays)/110

Lucknam Park Hotel, ✉ SN14 8AZ – North : 0.5 mi on Marshfield rd – ✆ 01225 742777 (booking essential) – www.lucknampark.co.uk – dinner only and Sunday lunch – Closed Monday and Tuesday

Brasserie

INTERNATIONAL • FASHIONABLE XX A stylish brasserie in a beautiful courtyard within Lucknam Park's state-of-the-art spa. There's a spacious bar-lounge and an airy dining room with full-length windows. Precise, modern cooking arrives in well-judged combinations and many healthy options are available. Dine on the charming terrace in summer.

Carte £ 26/59

Lucknam Park Hotel, ✉ SN14 8AZ – North : 0.5 mi on Marshfield rd – ✆ 01225 742777 – www.lucknampark.co.uk

Lucknam Park

GRAND LUXURY • ELEGANT A grand Palladian mansion with a mile-long tree-lined drive, rich, elegant décor, luxurious furnishings and sumptuous fabrics. Bedrooms are classically appointed and extremely comfortable. Top class facilities include an impressive spa and well-being centre, a renowned equestrian centre and a cookery school.

42 rooms – £ 275/650 £ 275/650 – £ 32 – 5 suites

✉ SN14 8AZ – North : 0.5 mi on Marshfield rd – ✆ 01225 742777 – www.lucknampark.co.uk

Restaurant Hywel Jones by Lucknam Park • **Brasserie** – See restaurant listing

BAUGHURST

Hampshire – Regional map n° **4**-B1

Wellington Arms

TRADITIONAL CUISINE • PUB At this smart cream pub they have their own herb and vegetable beds, keep sheep, pigs, chickens and bees, and source the rest of their meats from within 20 miles. Menus feature 6 dishes per course – supplemented by a selection of specials – and cooking is generous and satisfying. Smart, rustic bedrooms come with slate floors, sheepskin rugs and big, comfy beds.

Menu £ 18 (weekday lunch) – Carte £ 22/47

4 rooms – £ 110/200 £ 110/200

Baughurst Rd ✉ RG26 5LP – Southwest : 0.5 mi – ✆ 0118 982 0110 (booking essential) – www.thewellingtonarms.com – Closed Sunday dinner

BEACONSFIELD

Buckinghamshire - Pop. 13 797 - Regional map n° **6**-D3

No 5 London End

MODERN BRITISH • BISTRO A welcoming, modern-day bistro with a faux-distressed interior and a mix of banquettes and burnished leather seats. Creative menus are highly seasonal and textures and flavours are well thought out; influences are wide-ranging with a Mediterranean slant. Service is friendly and passionate.

Carte £ 26/40

London End ✉ HP9 2HN - ✆ 01494 355500 - www.no5londonend.co.uk - Closed 25 December and Sunday dinner

Crazy Bear

LUXURY • DESIGN A unique hotel with sumptuous, over-the-top styling. Moody, masculine bedrooms blend original features with rich fabrics and idiosyncratic furnishings (some slightly less flamboyant bedrooms are located over the road). The lavishly styled 'English' restaurant uses produce from their farm shop, while sexy, extravagant 'Thai' serves Asian cuisine.

45 rooms - †£ 199/289 ††£ 199/289

75 Wycombe End ✉ HP9 1LX - ✆ 01494 673086 - www.crazybeargroup.co.uk

BEAMINSTER

Dorset - Pop. 2 957 - Regional map n° **2**-B3

Brassica

MEDITERRANEAN CUISINE • BISTRO Two pretty little 16C houses on the small town square: one is a homeware shop and the other a laid-back restaurant. Tasty, rustic cooking is full of flavour; influences are Mediterranean, with a particular focus on Spain and Italy.

Menu £ 20 (weekday lunch) - Carte £ 27/42

3-4 The Square ✉ DT8 3AS - ✆ 01308 538100 (booking essential) - www.brassicarestaurant.co.uk - Closed 25-26 December, Sunday dinner, Monday and Tuesday

BEAULIEU

Hampshire - ✉ Brockenhurst - Pop. 726 - Regional map n° **4**-B2

The Terrace

MODERN BRITISH • TRADITIONAL DÉCOR This elegant dining room is found at the heart of an alluring 18C inn; sit on the terrace for views across the lovely gardens. Classically based dishes have a modern touch; fish is from the Solent and game from the New Forest.

Menu £ 30 (weekday lunch) - Carte £ 47/81

Montagu Arms Hotel, Palace Ln ✉ SO42 7ZL - ✆ 01590 612324 - www.montaguarmshotel.co.uk - Closed Monday and lunch Tuesday

Montagu Arms

INN • CLASSIC With its characterful parquet floors and wood panelling, this 18C inn has a timeless elegance. Traditional country house bedrooms marry antique furniture with modern facilities, and the conservatory and terrace overlook the lovely gardens. Dine on updated classics in the dining room or pub classics in Monty's.

22 rooms - †£ 215/335 ††£ 229/349 - 4 suites

Palace Ln ✉ SO42 7ZL - ✆ 01590 612324 - www.montaguarmshotel.co.uk

The Terrace - See restaurant listing

BEAUMONT - Saint Peter → See Channel Islands (Jersey)

BEELEY

Derbyshire - Pop. 165 - Regional map n° **9**-B1

Devonshire Arms

TRADITIONAL BRITISH • INN This stone inn boasts both a hugely characterful low-beamed bar and a modern glass extension with views of the stream. A small selection of pub favourites sit alongside some more interesting dishes and estate produce is used to the full. Choose a cosy bedroom in the inn or a modern room in the old dovecote.

Carte £ 25/41

14 rooms – †£ 101/117 ††£ 221/237

Devonshire Sq ✉ DE4 2NR – ✆ 01629 733259 – www.devonshirebeeley.co.uk

BELFORD

Northumberland – Pop. 1 258 – Regional map n° **14**-A1

Market Cross

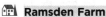

TOWNHOUSE • PERSONALISED 200 year old stone townhouse, set close to the medieval cross in the market square and run by friendly, welcoming owners. Bright modern bedrooms come in neutral hues and feature complimentary sherry and Lindisfarne Mead. Local produce features at breakfast and dinner is served by arrangement.

4 rooms – †£ 65/105 ††£ 85/115

1 Church St ✉ NE70 7LS – ✆ 01668 213013 – www.marketcrossbelford.co.uk – Closed 1-28 December

BENENDEN

Kent – Pop. 787 – Regional map n° **5**-B2

Ramsden Farm

COUNTRY HOUSE • CONTEMPORARY This pretty clapboard house sits in a delightful spot; in summer, have breakfast on the terrace, overlooking the lovely garden and the Kent Weald. Nothing is too much trouble for the charming owner and the place has a refreshingly laid-back air. Bright, stylishly understated bedrooms have country views.

3 rooms – †£ 90/115 ††£ 95/120

Dingleden Ln ✉ TN17 4JT – Southeast : 1 mi by B 2086 – ✆ 01580 240203 – www.ramsdenfarmhouse.co.uk

BEPTON - West Sussex ➜ See Midhurst

BERRICK SALOME

Oxfordshire – Pop. 326 – Regional map n° **6**-B2

Chequers

TRADITIONAL BRITISH • FRIENDLY Delightful 17C pub with a spacious garden and a warm, welcoming interior with fresh flowers and candles on the tables and warming open fires. Hearty menus list British classics and at lunchtime they offer a good value 2 course menu.

Menu £ 12 (weekday lunch) – Carte £ 24/43

✉ OX10 6JN – ✆ 01865 891118 – www.chequersberricksalome.co.uk – Closed 25 December and Tuesday

BERWICK-UPON-TWEED

Northumberland – Pop. 13 265 – Regional map n° **14**-A1

Granary

TOWNHOUSE • PERSONALISED Discreet Georgian house on a side street near the river. Guest areas are on the first floor; breakfast features organic and Fairtrade produce. The 2nd floor bedrooms are bright and modern with eye-catching art and thoughtful extras.

3 rooms – †£ 90/96 ††£ 108/138

11 Bridge St ✉ TD15 1ES – ✆ 01289 304403 – www.granaryguesthouse.co.uk

BEVERLEY

East Riding of Yorkshire – ✉ Kingston-Upon-Hull – Pop. 30 587 – Regional map n° **13**-D2

Westwood

MODERN BRITISH • BRASSERIE XX The twins who own this smart modern brasserie clearly share the same vision. Appealing menus offer unfussy, recognisable dishes and the meats cooked 'a la plancha' are a hit. It sits in the wing of an impressive Georgian courthouse.

Menu £ 20 (weekdays) – Carte £ 27/51

New Walk ✉ HU17 7AE – ✆ 01482 881999 – www.thewestwood.co.uk – Closed 24 December-8 January, Sunday dinner and Monday

Whites

CREATIVE • NEIGHBOURHOOD XX An enthusiastic chef-owner runs this small restaurant beside the old city walls, where black furnishings and eye-catching art stand out against a plain backdrop. Ambitious modern cooking is delivered in 4 and 9 course surprise menus.

Menu £ 28/58 – surprise menu only

12a North Bar Without ✉ HU17 7AB – ✆ 01482 866121 – www.whitesrestaurant.co.uk – dinner only and Saturday lunch – Closed 1 week Christmas, 1 week August, Sunday and Monday

at Tickton Northeast: 3.5 mi by A1035✉ Kingston-Upon-Hull

Tickton Grange

COUNTRY HOUSE • CLASSIC A warm, welcoming, family-run hotel in an extended Georgian house – a popular wedding venue. Bedrooms are stylish and up-to-date, and the spacious sitting room looks out over the immaculately kept gardens. Ambitious, modern cooking is served in the contemporary restaurant.

21 rooms – †£ 100/165 ††£ 140/210

✉ HU17 9SH – on A 1035 – ✆ 01964 543666 – www.ticktongrange.co.uk

BEWDLEY

Worcestershire – Pop. 8 571 – Regional map n° **10**-B2

Kateshill House

TOWNHOUSE • PERSONALISED This elegant Georgian manor house is surrounded by beautiful gardens; where you'll find a tree from the reign of King Henry VIII. Sumptuous, contemporary furnishings provide a subtle contrast to the house's original features.

8 rooms – †£ 75/85 ††£ 100/110

Redhill ✉ DY12 2DR – South : 0.25 mi on B 4194 – ✆ 01299 401563 – www.kateshillhouse.co.uk

BEXHILL

East Sussex – Pop. 42 369 – Regional map n° **5**-B3

The Driftwood (N)

ASIAN • CONTEMPORARY DÉCOR X Not far from the De La Warr pavilion is this surprisingly stylish little high street bistro. Together with her husband, the chef-owner creates authentic, vibrantly flavoured dishes that span Asia – including Chinese dumplings, Thai curries and Malaysian rendang. Above, comfy boutique bedrooms await.

Carte £ 21/29

6 rooms – †£ 80 ††£ 90/135

40 Sackville Rd ✉ TN39 3JE – ✆ 01424 732584 – www.thedriftwoodbexhill.co.uk – Closed Sunday dinner and Monday

BIBURY

Gloucestershire – ✉ Cirencester – Pop. 570 – Regional map n° **2**-D1

Swan

INN • PERSONALISED Set in a delightful village, this ivy-clad coaching inn has a trout stream running through the garden and a cosy, characterful interior. Bedrooms mix cottagey character with contemporary touches; the best are in the annexes. The brasserie opens onto a lovely flag-stoned courtyard and has an appealing menu.

22 rooms - £ 120/220 £ 140/240 - 4 suites

GL7 5NW - 01285 740695 - www.cotswold-inns-hotels.co.uk/swan

Cotteswold House

FAMILY • PERSONALISED This pleasant guesthouse is set on the edge of picturesque Bibury and provides an ideal base for exploring the area. The Victorian façade conceals traditional, spotlessly kept bedrooms and the friendly owner offers a warm welcome.

3 rooms - £ 70 £ 95

Arlington GL7 5ND - on B 4425 - 01285 740609 - www.cotteswoldhouse.net

BIDBOROUGH

Kent - Regional map n° **5**-B2

Kentish Hare

MODERN CUISINE • PUB Behind a grey and white clapboard façade are walls adorned with old photos of the village, which attest to the pub's history. Head through stylish rooms to the extension to watch the chefs cooking steaks on two Big Green Eggs. Care is taken both in sourcing and cooking, and dishes are tasty and well-presented.

Menu £ 24 (lunch and early dinner) - Carte £ 27/49

95 Bidborough Ridge TN3 0XB - 01892 525709 - www.thekentishhare.com - Closed Sunday dinner and Monday except bank holidays

BIDDENDEN

Kent - Pop. 1 303 - Regional map n° **5**-C2

West House (Graham Garrett)

MODERN BRITISH • RUSTIC Two 16C cottages in a picturesque village; the heavily timbered interior hung with modern art is a mirror of the food, where classically based dishes are given a modern twist. Cooking is assured and everything is on the plate for a reason. Service is refreshingly unpretentious and bedrooms have stylish themes.

→ Roast Jerusalem artichoke with sherry vinegar and cured foie gras. Pork collar with butter roast turnip and calvados sauce. Salt-baked pineapple, chilli and rum syrup and yoghurt sorbet.

Menu £ 29/65

4 rooms (dinner included) - £ 265 £ 340/440

28 High St TN27 8AH - 01580 291341 (booking essential) - www.thewesthouserestaurant.co.uk - Closed Christmas, Saturday lunch, Sunday dinner, Monday and Tuesday

The Three Chimneys

CLASSIC CUISINE • PUB A delightful pub which dates back to 1420 and boasts dimly lit low-beamed rooms with an old world feel, a contrastingly airy conservatory and a charming terrace. Traditional British dishes are accompanied by local wines, ciders and ales. Bedrooms are at the end of the garden and open onto a private terrace.

Carte £ 25/39

5 rooms - £ 90 £ 130/150

Hareplain Rd TN27 8LW - West : 1.5 mi by A 262 - 01580 291472 (booking essential) - www.thethreechimneys.co.uk

Barclay Farmhouse

TRADITIONAL • CLASSIC A converted farmhouse and barn in an acre of neatly kept gardens, complete with a duck pond. Comfortable bedrooms feature French oak furniture and characterful beams; extra touches include chocolate truffles on your pillow.

3 rooms – £ 75/80 £ 95/100

Woolpack Corner ✉ TN27 8BQ – South : 0.5 mi by A 262 on Benenden rd – ✆ 01580 292626 – www.barclayfarmhouse.co.uk

BIDEFORD

Devon – Pop. 18 029 – Regional map n° **1**-C1

Yeoldon House

COUNTRY HOUSE • PERSONALISED A delightfully run 19C house featuring original stained glass and wood-panelling. It's set in a peaceful riverbank location and the landscaped gardens offer lovely walks. Some of the cosy bedrooms have balconies with river views.

10 rooms – £ 125/145 £ 125/145

Durrant Ln, Northam ✉ EX39 2RL – North : 1.5 mi by B 3235 off A 386 – ✆ 01237 474400 – www.yeoldonhouse.co.uk – Closed Christmas and February

BIGBURY-ON-SEA

Devon – ✉ Kingsbridge – Pop. 220 – Regional map n° **1**-C3

Burgh Island

HISTORIC • ART DÉCO Grade II listed house on its own island, accessed using the hotel's Land Rover (or tractor at high tide!). It has classic art deco styling throughout, from the guest areas to the individually designed bedrooms; some rooms have small balconies and most have excellent bay views. 1930s themed 'black tie' dinners take place in the ballroom; there's live music Weds and Sat.

25 rooms (dinner included) – £ 320/700 £ 440/700 – 12 suites

✉ TQ7 4BG – South : 0.5 mi by hotel transport – ✆ 01548 810514 – www.burghisland.com

Henley

TRADITIONAL • PERSONALISED Not only is this extended cottage very personally run by its welcoming owners but it also affords superb views over Burgh Island and towards Bolt Tail. Charming bedrooms mix antique and modern furnishings and all share the wonderful view. Home-cooked meals are taken in the wicker-furnished conservatory.

5 rooms – £ 95/100 £ 127/166

Folly Hill ✉ TQ7 4AR – ✆ 01548 810240 – www.thehenleyhotel.co.uk – Closed November-mid-March

BILDESTON

Suffolk – Regional map n° **8**-C3

Bildeston Crown

MODERN BRITISH • INTIMATE XX Sit in the bar or one of several dining rooms in this historic inn, where you'll find thick walls, heavy beams and vast open fires. Choose from the 'Classic' or more complex 'Select' menu which, in season, has game at its heart.

Menu £ 15 (weekday lunch) – Carte £ 30/42

Bildeston Crown Hotel, 104 High St ✉ IP7 7EB – ✆ 01449 740510 (booking essential) – www.thebildestoncrown.co.uk – Closed dinner 25-26 December, 1 January and Sunday

Bildeston Crown

INN • CONTEMPORARY A hugely characterful 15C wool merchant's with a lovely rear courtyard. The stylish interior has warm colours and open fires. Luxurious bedrooms vary from florally feminine to bright and bold - all have designer furnishings.

12 rooms - £ 70/175 £ 90/175

104 High St IP7 7EB - 01449 740510 - www.thebildestoncrown.com

Bildeston Crown - See restaurant listing

BINFIELD HEATH

Oxfordshire - Pop. 709 - Regional map n° **6**-C3

Bottle & Glass Inn

MODERN BRITISH • PUB This pretty thatched pub sits in a lovely rural spot. The original part is the most characterful, while the restaurant is more up-to-date. Modern British cooking is refined but unfussy and has an appealing simplicity.

Menu £ 25 (weekday lunch) - Carte £ 30/44

Bones Ln RG9 4JT - North : 0.5 mi by Arch Hill and Common Ln. - 01491 412625 - www.bottleandglassinn.com - Closed 25-26 December and Sunday dinner

BIRKENHEAD

Merseyside - Pop. 142 968 - Regional map n° **11**-A3

Fraiche (Marc Wilkinson)

CREATIVE • INTIMATE Enter into the cosy bar, where seasonal images are projected onto the wall, then head through to the boldly decorated restaurant which seats just 10 diners. Cooking is innovative and presentation is key - both the colours of the ingredients and the shape and style of the crockery play their part.

→ Cured scallop with pea consommé and verjus. Mangalitza pork loin with cabbage textures and tarragon juice. 'Fallen leaves'.

Menu £ 88 - tasting menu only

11 Rose Mount, Oxton CH43 5SG - Southwest : 2.25 mi by A 552 and B 5151 - 0151 652 2914 (booking essential) - www.restaurantfraiche.com - dinner only and Sunday lunch - Closed 25 December, 1-7 September, Sunday dinner, Monday and Tuesday

Michelin

GOOD TIPS!

Known as a city of cars, canals and chocolate, the 'Second City of the Kingdom' is also a centre for culinary excellence, boasting four Michelin-starred restaurants. 21C Brum is a major convention and retail destination, and redevelopment continues apace; hotels like **Malmaison** and **Hotel Indigo** provide luxury accommodation for its many visitors.

BIRMINGHAM

West Midlands - Pop. 1 085 810 - Regional map n° **10**-C2

Restaurants

✿ **Simpsons** (Andreas Antona and Luke Tipping)

MODERN CUISINE • FASHIONABLE XXX Behind the walls of this suburban Georgian house is a sleek dining room, a cookery school and three contemporary bedrooms. Cooking has a clean, Scandic style and the visually appealing dishes are packed with flavour. Lunch sees a 2-choice set price menu; dinner a 4-course set price menu and a tasting option - some courses are served by the chefs themselves.

→ Nori-cured salmon with kohlrabi, buttermilk and dill oil. Chicken with artichokes, morels, wild garlic and an anchovy cream. Fermented blueberries with skyr and almonds.

Menu £ 45/75

3 rooms - †£ 110 ††£ 110

Town plan: A2-e - *20 Highfield Rd, Edgbaston ✉ B15 3DU*
- ✆ 0121 454 3434
- www.simpsonsrestaurant.co.uk - Closed Sunday dinner, Monday and bank holidays

✿ **Adam's** (Adam Stokes)

MODERN CUISINE • ELEGANT XXX Enjoy a drink in the smart cocktail bar then move on to the bright, elegant restaurant with a subtle retro feel. Choose from a concise set menu or an 8 course tasting menu: top notch produce is used in carefully prepared dishes which have wonderfully bold complementary flavours and contrasting textures.

→ Orkney scallop, mussel, sea purslane and smoked caviar. Loin of venison, faggot, celeriac and black garlic. Passe-Crassane pear, toasted hay and praline.

Menu £ 40 (weekdays)/65

Town plan: E2-c - *New Oxford House, 16 Waterloo St ✉ B2 5UG*
- ✆ 0121 643 3745 (booking essential)
- www.adamsrestaurant.co.uk - Closed 2 weeks Christmas-New Year, Sunday and Monday

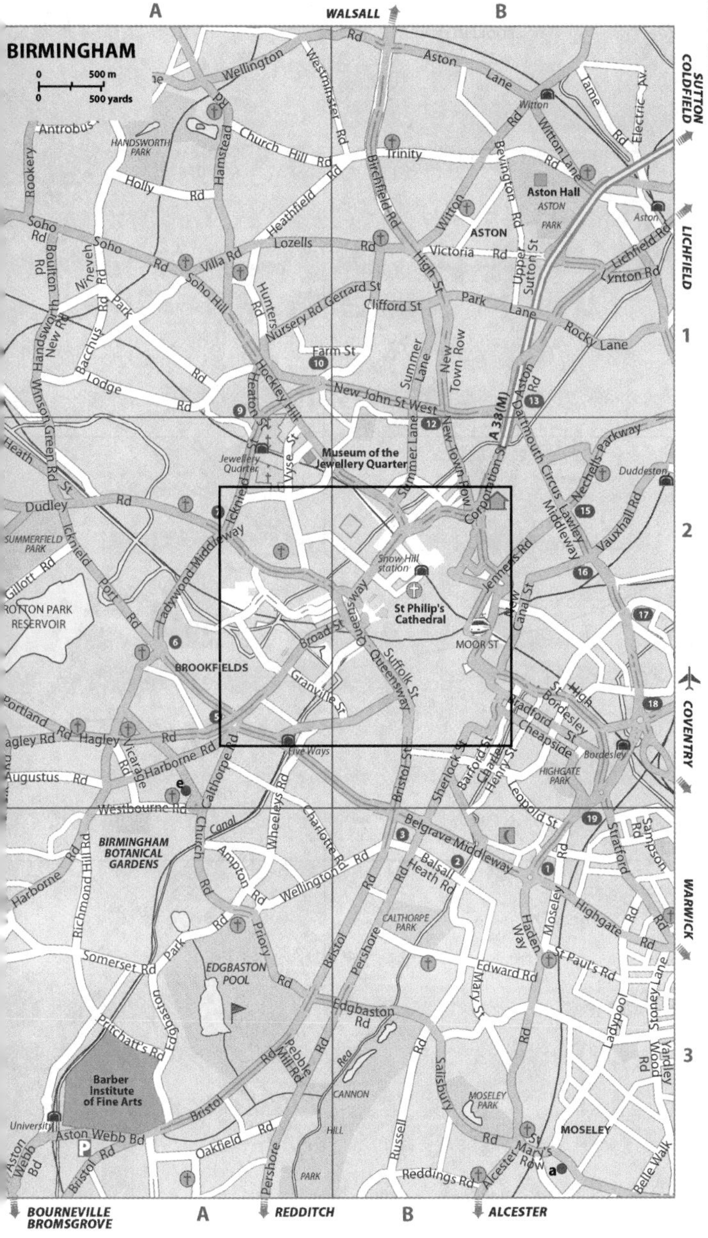
BIRMINGHAM
0 500 m
0 500 yards
A
B
WALSALL
SUTTON COLDFIELD
LICHFIELD
COVENTRY
WARWICK
BOURNEVILLE BROMSGROVE
REDDITCH
ALCESTER
1
2
3
Wellington Rd
Aston Lane
Westminster Rd
Antrobus
HANDSWORTH PARK
Church Hill Rd
Hamstead Rd
Holly Rd
Rookery
Trinity
Birchfield Rd
Heathfield Rd
Witton
Tame Rd
Electric Av
Witton Rd
Witton Lane
Bevington Rd
Aston Hall
ASTON PARK
ASTON
Aston
Lichfield Rd
Lynton Rd
Soho Rd
Boulton Rd
Nineveh Rd
Lozells Rd
Villa Rd
Soho Hill
Victoria Rd
Upper Sutton St
High St
Park
Hunters Rd
Nursery Rd
Gerrard St
Clifford St
Park Lane
Rocky Lane
Handsworth New Rd
Bacchus Rd
Lodge Rd
Farm St
Summer Lane
New Town Row
Hockley Hill
Heaton St
New John St West
A 38(M)
Aston Rd
Dartmouth Circus
Winson Green Rd
Heath St
Jewellery Quarter
Vyse St
Museum of the Jewellery Quarter
Corporation St
Nechells Parkway
Duddeston
Dudley Rd
Icknield St
Lawley Middleway
Vauxhall Rd
SUMMERFIELD PARK
Ladywood Middleway
Snow Hill station
Jennens Rd
Gillott Rd
Icknield Port Rd
Queensway
St Philip's Cathedral
New Canal St
ROTTON PARK RESERVOIR
Broad St
MOOR ST
BROOKFIELDS
Suffolk St Queensway
Granville St
High St Bordesley
Bradford St
Cheapside
Portland Rd
Hagley Rd
Vicarage Rd
Harborne Rd
Calthorpe Rd
Five Ways
Bristol St
Sherlock St
Barford St
Charles Henry St
Bordesley
HIGHGATE PARK
Augustus Rd
Wheeleys Rd
Charlotte Rd
Leopold St
Westbourne Rd
Canal
Belgrave Middleway
Sampson Rd
Stratford Rd
BIRMINGHAM BOTANICAL GARDENS
Church Rd
Ampton Rd
Wellington Rd
Balsall Heath Rd
Harborne Rd
Richmond Hill Rd
Priory Rd
Pershore Rd
CALTHORPE PARK
Haden Way
Moseley Rd
Highgate Rd
St Paul's Rd
Somerset Rd
Park Rd
EDGBASTON POOL
Edward Rd
Mary St
Edgbaston Rd
Pritchatt's Rd
Edgbaston Rd
Rea
Pebble Mill Rd
Salisbury Rd
Ladypool Rd
Stoney Lane
Yardley Wood Rd
Barber Institute of Fine Arts
CANNON HILL PARK
MOSELEY PARK
University
Aston Webb Bd
Bristol Rd
Oakfield Rd
Russell Rd
St Mary's Row
MOSELEY
Reddings Rd
Alcester Rd
Belle Walk
Trafalgar Rd

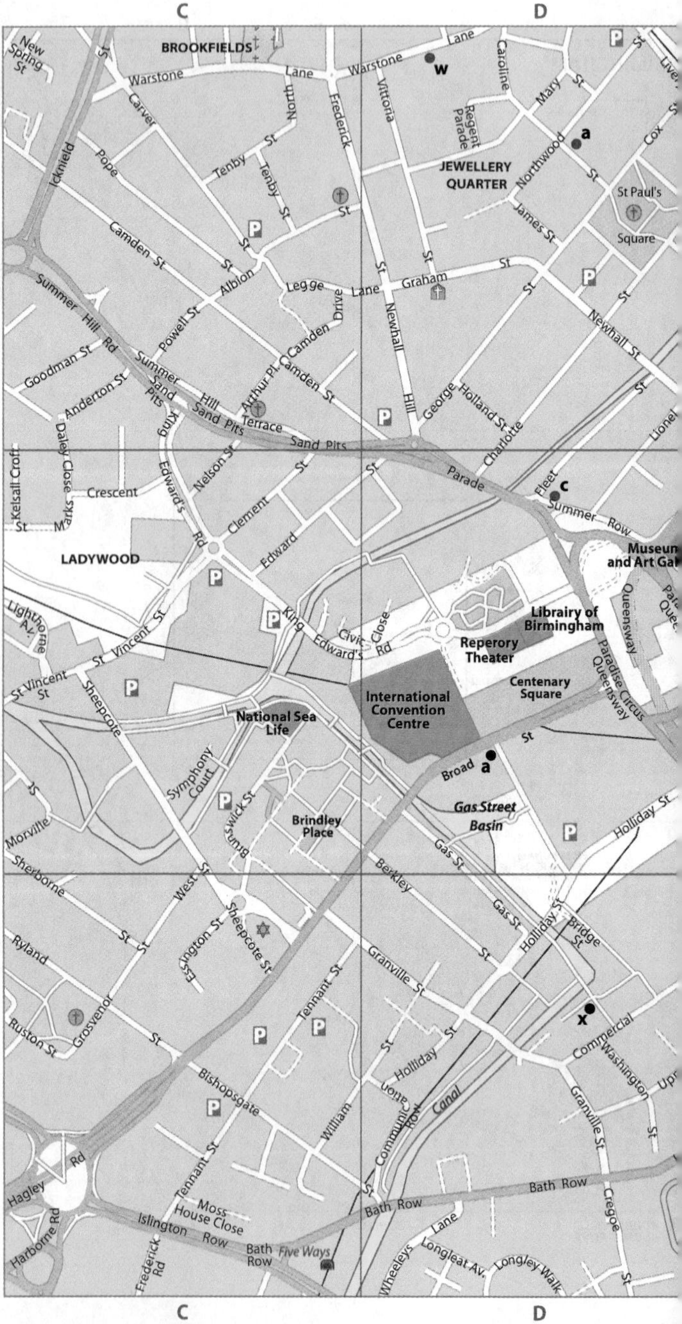
C
D
1
2
3
BROOKFIELDS
JEWELLERY QUARTER
LADYWOOD
Warstone Lane
New Spring St
Carver St
Pope St
Icknield St
Camden St
Tenby St
North St
Frederick St
Vittoria St
Regent Parade
Caroline St
Mary St
Northwood St
James St
Cox St
St Paul's Square
Legge Lane
Graham St
Albion St
Newhall St
Newhall Hill
Charlotte St
George St
Holland St
Lionel St
Summer Hill Rd
Summer Hill Terrace
Goodman St
Anderton St
Powell St
Camden Drive
Arthur Pl.
Sand Pits
Sand Pits Parade
Daley Close
Kelsall Croft
Marks St
Crescent
King Edward's Rd
Nelson St
Clement St
Edward St
Fleet St
Summer Row
Museum and Art Gallery
Civic Close
Library of Birmingham
Reperory Theater
Centenary Square
Paradise Circus Queensway
Queensway
Lighthorne Av.
St Vincent St
Sheepcote St
National Sea Life
International Convention Centre
Broad St
Symphony Court
Brunswick St
Brindley Place
Gas Street Basin
Gas St
Holliday St
Morville St
Sherborne St
West St
Berkley St
Bridge St
Ryland St
Essington St
Sheepcote St
Granville St
Tennant St
Ruston St
Grosvenor St
Bishopsgate St
William St
Commercial St
Washington St
Communication Row
Canal
Granville St
Hagley Rd
Harborne Rd
Moss House Close
Islington Row
Bath Row
Five Ways
Frederick Rd
Wheeleys Lane
Longleat Av.
Longley Walk
Cregoe St
w
a
c
x

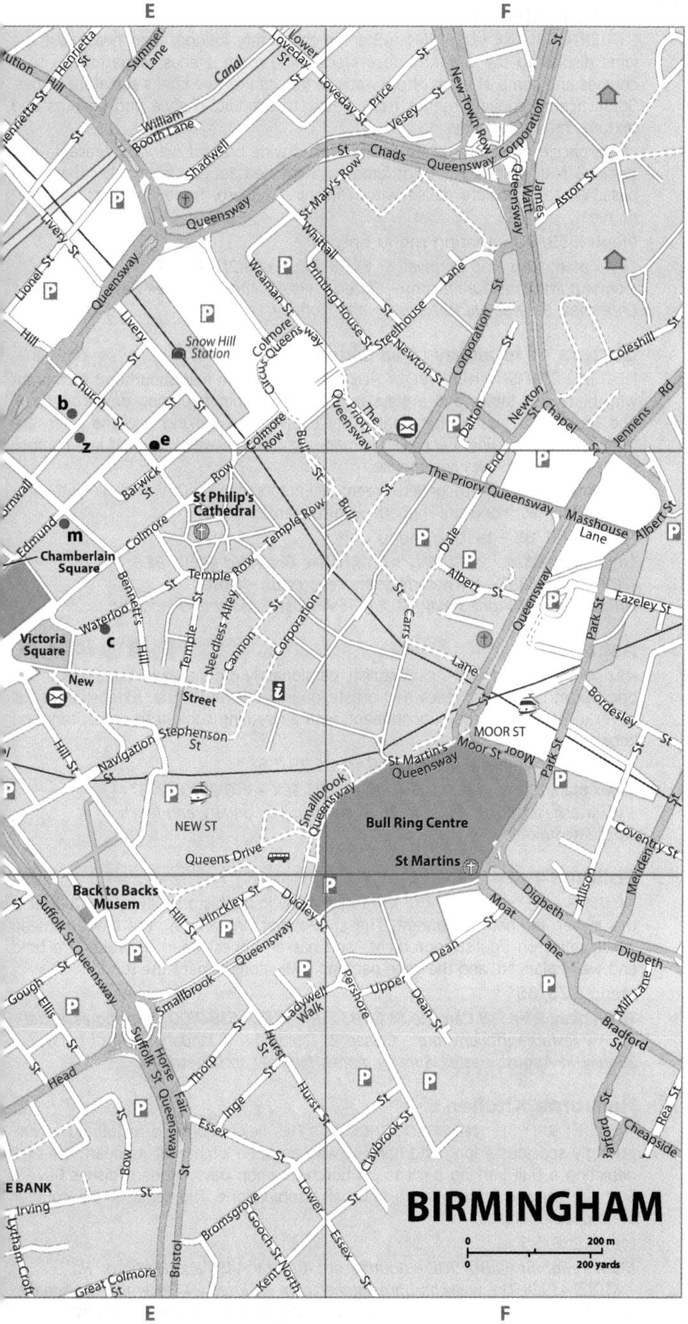
E
F
1
2
3
BIRMINGHAM
200 m
200 yards
Snow Hill Station
St Philip's Cathedral
Chamberlain Square
Victoria Square
New Street
NEW ST
MOOR ST
Bull Ring Centre
St Martins
Back to Backs Musem
Queens Drive
Queensway
St Chads Queensway
Corporation St
Colmore Row
Colmore Circus Queensway
Temple Row
Waterloo St
Bennett's Hill
Needless Alley
Cannon St
Stephenson St
Navigation St
Hill St
Smallbrook Queensway
St Martin's Queensway
Moor St Queensway
The Priory Queensway
Masshouse Lane
Albert St
Dale End
Carrs Lane
Bull St
Dalton St
Newton St
Steelhouse Lane
Printing House St
Whittall St
Weaman St
St Mary's Row
Livery St
Lionel St
Church St
Barwick St
Edmund St
Summer Lane
Henrietta St
Loveday St
Lower Loveday St
Price St
Vesey St
New Town Row
James Watt Queensway
Aston St
Coleshill St
Chapel St
Jennens Rd
Fazeley St
Park St
Bordesley St
Coventry St
Meriden St
Allison St
Digbeth
Moat Lane
Dean St
Upper Dean St
Pershore St
Ladywell Walk
Hurst St
Hinckley St
Dudley St
Smallbrook Queensway
Suffolk St Queensway
Horse Fair
Thorp St
Inge St
Essex St
Claybrook St
Bromsgrove St
Gooch St North
Kent St
Bristol St
Great Colmore St
Lower Essex St
Bow St
Irving St
Lytham Croft
Gough St
Ellis St
Holloway Head
Mill Lane
Bradford St
Barford St
Cheapside
Rea St
Shadwell St
William Booth Lane
Canal
b
z
e
m
c

Purnell's (Glynn Purnell)

MODERN CUISINE • DESIGN XXX Start in the comfy lounge, then head past the wine display to the vibrantly decorated dining room. Menus range from 3 to 9 courses and some of them offer swaps so you can try the chef's signature dishes. Sophisticated cooking ranges from classic to Scandic in style and flavours and textures marry perfectly.

→ Carpaccio of Herefordshire beef with red wine braised octopus, bresaola and sweet & sour onions. Rump of lamb with smoked aubergine tartlet, capers and basil. White chocolate délice with Yorkshire rhubarb, frozen yoghurt and meringue.

Menu £ 39/90 – tasting menu only

Town plan: E1-b – *55 Cornwall St ✉ B3 2DH – ✆ 0121 212 9799 – www.purnellsrestaurant.com – Closed 2 weeks August, 1 week Easter, 1 week Christmas, Saturday lunch, Sunday and Monday*

Carters of Moseley (Brad Carter)

MODERN BRITISH • NEIGHBOURHOOD XX Lovely little neighbourhood restaurant with black ash tables and a glass-fronted wine cabinet running down one wall. The passionate young chef continually evolves his cooking and the team are friendly and engaging. Each dish is made up of three well-balanced key components and the flavours are intense.

→ Orkney scallop with grilled cream & Exmoor caviar. Devon duck with preserved cherries. Yorkshire rhubarb with fermented rice.

Menu £ 40/85 – tasting menu only

Town plan: B3-a – *2c St Mary's Row, Wake Green Rd ✉ B13 9EZ – ✆ 0121 449 8885 – www.cartersofmoseley.co.uk – Closed 1-18 January, 24 April-3 May, 31 July-16 August, Sunday and Monday*

Asha's

INDIAN • EXOTIC DÉCOR XX A stylish, passionately run Indian restaurant with exotic décor; owned by renowned artiste/gourmet Asha Bhosle. Extensive menus cover most parts of the Subcontinent, with everything cooked to order. Tandoori kebabs are a speciality.

Menu £ 13 (weekday lunch) – Carte £ 29/55

Town plan: E2-m – *12-22 Newhall St ✉ B3 3LX – ✆ 0121 200 2767 – www.ashasuk.co.uk – Closed 26 December, 1-2 January and lunch Saturday-Sunday*

Folium (N)

MODERN BRITISH • INTIMATE XX Hidden away in the historic Jewellery Quarter is this sweet, intimate restaurant. The chef-owner prepares a very modern menu which relies on English ingredients and has an honest heart. Flavours are bold and well-balanced, and the wine pairings really complement the food.

Menu £ 33/65

Town plan: D1-a – *8 Caroline St ✉ B3 1TR – ✆ 0121 638 0100 (booking essential) – www.restaurantfolium.com – Closed 23 December-9 January, 21 April-1 May, 28 July-14 August, Easter, Sunday dinner, Monday and Tuesday*

Harborne Kitchen (N)

MODERN BRITISH • NEIGHBOURHOOD XX This neighbourhood restaurant is surprisingly spacious – long and narrow, with an open kitchen at its heart; the tiles depicting a bull harking back to its butcher's shop days. Modern dishes have a Scandic feel and feature some unusual combinations. The seats at the counter are a popular choice.

Menu £ 18/55

175-179 High St ✉ B17 9QE – Southwest : 4 mi by A456 and Harborne Rd – ✆ 0121 439 9150 – www.harbornekitchen.com – Closed 24 December-6 January, 28 October-5 November, Sunday, Monday and lunch Tuesday-Wednesday

Opheem

INDIAN • FASHIONABLE XX Experienced chef Aktar Islam owns this luxuriously-appointed restaurant in the heart of Birmingham. He set out to explore India's culinary heritage and move it on a level with his unique modern approach. He grinds his own spices and sometimes pickles them to intensify their flavours.

Menu £ 24 (weekday lunch) – Carte £ 35/42

Town plan: D2-c – *48 Summer Row ✉ B3 1JJ – ✆ 0121 201 3377 – www.opheem.com – Closed 24-25 December, 1 January and Monday*

Opus

MODERN CUISINE • DESIGN XX A very large and popular restaurant with floor to ceiling windows; enjoy an aperitif in the cocktail bar before dining in the stylish main room or at the chef's table in the kitchen. The daily menu offers modern brasserie dishes.

Menu £ 35

Town plan: E1-z – *54 Cornwall St ✉ B3 2DE – ✆ 0121 200 2323 – www.opusrestaurant.co.uk – Closed 24 December-7 January, Sunday and bank holidays*

The Wilderness

MODERN BRITISH • FASHIONABLE XX Birmingham's Jewellery Quarter plays host to this dark, moody restaurant with a rustic look and pumping music. Interesting set menus have a playful approach and could open with snacks such as a 'Big Mac' or 'Custard Cream', followed by lamb and charcoal with cucumber.

Menu £ 40/90 – tasting menu only

Town plan: D1-w – *27 Warstone Ln, Unit B ✉ B18 6JQ – ✆ 0121 233 9425 – www.wearethewilderness.co.uk – Closed Sunday-Tuesday*

Hotels

Hyatt Regency

BUSINESS • CONTEMPORARY An eye-catching, mirror-fronted, tower block hotel in a prime city centre location, with a covered link to the International Convention Centre. Spacious bedrooms have floor to ceiling windows and an excellent level of facilities. Aria restaurant, in the atrium, offers modern European menus.

319 rooms – †£ 117/250 ††£ 159/275 – ☕ £ 19 – 11 suites

Town plan: D2-a – *2 Bridge St ✉ B1 2JZ – ✆ 0121 643 1234 – www.birmingham.regency.hyatt.com*

Hotel Du Vin

BUSINESS • DESIGN A characterful former eye hospital with a relaxed, shabby-chic style. Bright bedrooms are named after wine companies and estates; one suite boasts an 8 foot bed, two roll-top baths and a gym. Kick-back in the small cellar pub or comfy champagne bar; the classical bistro has a lively buzz and a French menu.

66 rooms ☕ – †£ 89/224 ††£ 89/224

Town plan: E1-e – *25 Church St ✉ B3 2NR – ✆ 0121 794 3005 – www.hotelduvin.com*

Malmaison

BUSINESS • MODERN A stylish hotel with dark, moody décor, set on the site of the old Royal Mail sorting office beside designer clothing and homeware shops. Bedrooms are spacious and the boldly decorated Nirvana suite comes with a mirror-tiled jacuzzi. Dine from an accessible British menu in the bustling brasserie.

192 rooms – †£ 99/189 ††£ 100/199 – ☕ £ 17 – 2 suites

Town plan: E2-e – *Mailbox, 1 Wharfside St ✉ B1 1RD – ✆ 0121 246 5000 – www.malmaison.com*

Hotel Indigo

BUSINESS • DESIGN A stylish hotel located on the top three floors of the eye-catching 'Cube' building. Both the appealingly styled guest areas and vividly decorated bedrooms have floor to ceiling windows. Dine on Italian dishes or in the smart steakhouse which boasts a champagne bar, a terrace and a view from every table.

52 rooms – £ 165/200 £ 165/200 – £ 16

Town plan: D3-x – *The Cube* ✉ *B1 1PR* – *✆ 0121 643 2010 – www.hotelindigobirmingham.com*

at National Exhibition Centre Southeast : 9.5 mi on A 45 ✉ Birmingham

Andy Waters

TRADITIONAL BRITISH • CHIC XX Unusually set in a shopping centre, beside a multiplex cinema, is this smart, formal restaurant run by an experienced chef – ask for one of the booths around the edge of the room. Traditional cooking sees classically based combinations given a personal touch.

Menu £ 40

Floor One, Resorts World, Pendigo Way ✉ *B40 1PU* – *✆ 020 1273 1238 – www.watersrestaurant.co.uk – dinner only and Sunday lunch – Closed 25 December*

BLACKBURN

Blackburn with Darwen – Pop. 117 963 – Regional map n° **11**-B2

at Langho North: 4.5 mi on A666 ✉ Whalley

Northcote

MODERN BRITISH • CONTEMPORARY DÉCOR XXX An elegant restaurant set within an impressive Victorian house. Refined, sophisticated cooking shows real depth of flavour and a lightness of touch. Produce is either biodynamic or organic, with as much as possible coming from the kitchen garden. Watch the chefs close-up from the glass-walled kitchen table.

→ "Scampi" Scottish langoustine with cucumber tartare and burnt lemon. Wagyu oyster blade with smoked mustard, sour cream and carrots. Warm Bramley "Apple Pie" with nuts, maple and caramelised milk.

Menu £ 35 (lunch) – Carte £ 46/73

Northcote Hotel, Northcote Rd ✉ *BB6 8BE – North : 0.5 mi on A 59 at junction with A 666 – ✆ 01254 240555 (booking essential) – www.northcote.com*

Northcote

COUNTRY HOUSE • ELEGANT This well-run Victorian house sits on the edge of the Ribble Valley. Individually designed bedrooms are spacious, stylish and sophisticated – all have queen or king-sized beds and some have garden terraces. Enjoy afternoon tea beside the fire in the lounge, followed by drinks in the bright, glitzy bar.

26 rooms – £ 240/585 £ 280/650 – 1 suite

Northcote Rd ✉ *BB6 8BE – North : 0.5 mi on A 59 at junction with A 666 – ✆ 01254 240555 – www.northcote.com*

Northcote – See restaurant listing

at Mellor Northwest: 3.25 mi by A677 ✉ Blackburn

Stanley House

LUXURY • DESIGN Attractive part-17C manor house boasting superb country views and a smart spa with four types of sauna. Bedrooms in the main house are elegant and feature original beams and mullioned windows; the 'Woodland Rooms' are more contemporary. Stylish 'Grill on the Hill' offers modern favourites and views over the garden towards the coast; 'Mr Fred's' serves simpler fare.

30 rooms – £ 155/225 £ 155/225

✉ *BB2 7NP – Southwest : 0.75 mi by A 677 and Further Ln – ✆ 01254 769200 – www.stanleyhouse.co.uk*

BLACKPOOL

Blackpool - Pop. 147 663 - Regional map n° **11**-A2

Number One St Lukes

TOWNHOUSE • DESIGN A boutique guesthouse set close to the promenade and the Pleasure Beach and run by a very charming owner. Bedrooms are named after the town's piers: 'North' has an African feel and 'Central' has a white half-tester and a more feminine touch. There's also an outdoor hot tub and a mini pitch and putt green!

3 rooms - £ 75/130 £ 110/140

1 St Lukes Rd ✉ FY4 2EL - ✆ 01253 343901 - www.numberoneblackpool.com

at Thornton Northeast: 5.5 mi by A584 - on B5412 ✉ Blackpool

Twelve

MODERN BRITISH • DESIGN XX This passionately run cocktail bar and restaurant sits beside one of Europe's tallest working windmills. Dine in the main room, on the mezzanine or in the bar, surrounded by brick walls, reclaimed wood and graffiti art. Hearty, wholesome cooking has a refined edge; the à la carte menu is the most innovative.

Menu £ 22/28 - Carte £ 24/46

Marsh Mill, Fleetwood Rd North ✉ FY5 4JZ - ✆ 01253 821212 - www.twelve-restaurant.co.uk - dinner only and Sunday lunch - Closed first 2 weeks January and Monday

BLAKENEY

Norfolk - ✉ Holt - Pop. 801 - Regional map n° **8**-C1

Wiveton Farm Café

REGIONAL CUISINE • FRIENDLY X An extension of a farm shop, set down a dusty track and run by a smiley young team. Light breakfasts and tasty, salad-based lunches; weekends see 'Norfolk' tapas in the evenings. Take in glorious farm and sea views from the terrace.

Carte £ 22/32

✉ NR25 7TE - East : 0.75 mi on A 149 - ✆ 01263 740515 - www.wivetonhall.co.uk - lunch only and dinner Friday-Saturday May-September - Closed 12 November-20 March

Blakeney

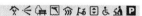

FAMILY • CONTEMPORARY This privately run flint-built property is set in a bustling coastal town. The surroundings might be modern but the service is pleasingly traditional and personalised. Bedrooms are stylish; those in the old granary are the quietest. The bar and dining room have great views over the salt marshes to the estuary.

64 rooms - £ 117/187 £ 234/374

The Quay ✉ NR25 7NE - ✆ 01263 740797 - www.blakeneyhotel.co.uk

at Cley next the Sea East: 1.5 mi on A149 ✉ Holt

Cley Windmill

HISTORIC • COSY With its views over the marshes and river, this restored 18C windmill is a birdwatcher's paradise. Snug, characterful bedrooms are split between the mill, the stables and the boatshed. The flagstoned dining room offers a set menu of homemade country dishes and the tea room opens in the summer months.

9 rooms - £ 159/245 £ 159/245

The Quay ✉ NR25 7RP - ✆ 01263 740209 - www.cleywindmill.co.uk

at Wiveton South: 1 mi by A149 on Wiveton Rd

Wiveton Bell

TRADITIONAL BRITISH • INN Modernised pub featuring beams, stripped floors and wood-burning stoves; with picnic tables out the front and a beautifully landscaped rear terrace. Seasonal menu offers pub classics, carefully crafted from quality local ingredients. Stylish, cosy bedrooms have smart bathrooms; continental breakfasts.

Carte £ 23/41

6 rooms – †£ 95/180 ††£ 95/180

Blakeney Rd ✉ NR25 7TL – ✆ 01263 740101 (booking essential)
– www.wivetonbell.com
– Closed 25 December

at Morston West: 1.5 mi on A149 ✉ Holt

Morston Hall (Galton Blackiston)

MODERN BRITISH • ELEGANT XX Set in an attractive country house surrounded by landscaped gardens: choose between a traditionally furnished room or a beautiful conservatory. The set 7 course daily menu (served at 8pm), offers well-balanced seasonal dishes. Cooking is classically based, sophisticated and exhibits a delicate modern touch.

→ Langoustine with endive, curry and sauternes jus. Suckling pig with a burnt apple sauce Robert. Baked crème fraîche and Gariguette strawberries.

Menu £ 80 – tasting menu only

Morston Hall Hotel, The Street ✉ NR25 7AA – ✆ 01263 741041 (booking essential)
– www.morstonhall.com – dinner only and Sunday lunch
– Closed 1-25January and 24-26 December

Morston Hall

COUNTRY HOUSE • PERSONALISED An attractive, personally run country house with manicured gardens, set in a small coastal hamlet. Comfy guest areas feature antiques and paintings. Bedrooms are split between the main house and an annexe – the latter are larger and have subtle contemporary touches. Service is keen and friendly.

13 rooms (dinner included) – †£ 215/305 ††£ 250/410

The Street ✉ NR25 7AA – ✆ 01263 741041 – www.morstonhall.com
– Closed 1-25 January and 24-26 December

Morston Hall – See restaurant listing

BLANCHLAND

Northumberland – Regional map n° **14**-A2

Lord Crewe Arms

TRADITIONAL • CONTEMPORARY A 12C abbot's priory, which has also spent time as a hunting lodge and a lead miners' hostelry. Its hugely characterful guest areas don't disappoint and the delightful garden offers commanding country views. Bespoke-furnished bedrooms have a modern country charm; many are located around the village square.

21 rooms – †£ 99/200 ††£ 119/224 – 2 suites

The Square ✉ DH8 9SP – ✆ 01434 675469 – www.lordcrewearmsblanchland.co.uk

BLEDINGTON – Gloucestershire → See Stow-on-the-Wold

BOLLINGTON

Cheshire East – ✉ Cheshire – Pop. 7 373 – Regional map n° **11**-B3

Tapa

MODERN CUISINE • RUSTIC As its name suggests, this appealing restaurant serves small plates designed for sharing. Interesting cooking uses a diverse range of ingredients and has global influences; the fish dishes are usually a highlight.

Menu £ 22

22 High St SK10 5PH - 01625 575058 - www.tapawinebar.co.uk - dinner only and Sunday lunch - Closed 25-26 December, 1 January and Sunday dinner

BOLNHURST

Bedford - Regional map n° **7**-A1

Plough at Bolnhurst

MODERN BRITISH • INN Charming whitewashed pub with a rustic bar, a modern restaurant, a lovely garden and a bustling atmosphere. Menus change with the seasons but always feature 28-day aged Aberdeenshire steaks, dishes containing Mediterranean ingredients like Sicilian black olives, and a great selection of wines and cheeses.

Menu £ 25 (weekdays) - Carte £ 31/50

Kimbolton Rd MK44 2EX - South : 0.5 mi on B 660 - 01234 376274 - www.bolnhurst.com - Closed 2 weeks January, Sunday dinner and Monday

BOLTON ABBEY

North Yorkshire - Skipton - Pop. 117 - Regional map n° **13**-B2

The Burlington

MODERN BRITISH • ELEGANT An antique-filled hotel dining room hung with impressive oils; sit in the conservatory overlooking the Italian garden. Restrained modern dishes utilise just a handful of complementary ingredients, with many coming from the kitchen garden and estate. The wine cellar is one of the best in northern England.

Menu £ 70/95 - tasting menu only

Devonshire Arms Hotel & Spa, BD23 6AJ - 01756 718100 - www.thedevonshirearms.co.uk - dinner only - Closed Monday

Devonshire Arms H. & Spa

LUXURY • ELEGANT A charming coaching inn and spa on the Duke and Duchess of Devonshire's 30,000 acre estate in the Yorkshire Dales. Comfy lounges display part of the owners' vast art collection and dogs are welcome. Bedrooms in the wing are bright, modern and compact; those in the inn are more characterful.

40 rooms - £ 140/420 £ 159/439 - 2 suites

BD23 6AJ - 01756 718100 - www.thedevonshirearms.co.uk

The Burlington - See restaurant listing

BOROUGHBRIDGE

North Yorkshire - Pop. 3 610 - Regional map n° **13**-B2

thediningroom

MODERN BRITISH • INTIMATE Characterful bow-fronted cottage concealing an opulent bar-lounge and an intimate beamed dining room. Wide-ranging menus offer boldly flavoured, Mediterranean-influenced dishes and chargrilled meats. In summer, head for the terrace.

Menu £ 22 (weekdays) - Carte £ 27/47

20 St James's Sq YO51 9AR - 01423 326426 - www.thediningroomonline.co.uk - dinner only and Sunday lunch - Closed 26 December, 1 January, Sunday dinner and Monday

BORROWDALE - Cumbria → See Keswick

BOSCASTLE

Cornwall - Regional map n° **1**-B2

Boscastle House

FAMILY · PERSONALISED Modern styling in a detached Victorian house with a calm, relaxing air. Bedrooms are light and spacious, with roll-top baths and walk-in showers. Hearty breakfasts feature home-baked muffins and banana bread. Tea and cake on arrival.

5 rooms - £ 90 £ 115/128

Tintagel Rd ✉ PL35 OAS - South : 0.75 mi on B 3263
- ✆ 01840 250654 - www.boscastlehouse.com
- Closed November-February

BOURN

Cambridgeshire - Pop. 669 - Regional map n° **8**-A3

Willow Tree

MODERN BRITISH · CONTEMPORARY DÉCOR Named after the vast tree in the garden, this quirky restaurant comes complete with gilt mirrors, chandeliers, Louis XV style furniture, a heated terrace and even a tepee. Contemporary European dishes include some small plates.

Carte £ 24/54

29 High St ✉ CB23 2SQ
- ✆ 01954 719775 - www.thewillowtreebourn.com

BOURNEMOUTH

Bournemouth - Pop. 187 503 - Regional map n° **2**-D3

Arbor

MODERN CUISINE · CONTEMPORARY DÉCOR Located in an eco-friendly hotel, Arbor comes complete with a feature tree, FSC timbered floors, low energy induction cookers and honey bees on the roof. Modern menus display innovative touches and produce is local and sustainable.

Menu £ 23 (lunch and early dinner) - Carte dinner £ 23/48

Green House Hotel, 4 Grove Rd ✉ BH1 3AX
- ✆ 01202 498900 - www.arbor-restaurant.co.uk

Neo

MODERN BRITISH · BRASSERIE Have a cocktail on the ground floor of this unusual round building then head up to the restaurant for views of the gardens and pier. Appetising dishes change with the seasons; the Josper-grilled meats and Dorset lobster are hits.

Menu £ 19 (lunch and early dinner) - Carte £ 31/51

Hermitage Hotel, Exeter Rd ✉ BH2 5AH -
✆ 01202 203610 - www.neorestaurant.co.uk

Green House

BUSINESS · DESIGN Bright, eco-friendly hotel set in a small Grade II listed property. Furnishings are reclaimed and wallpapers are printed using vegetable ink. They generate their own electricity and even use old cooking oil to power their car!

32 rooms - £ 89/160 £ 99/180

4 Grove Rd ✉ BH1 3AX
- ✆ 01202 498900 - www.thegreenhousehotel.com

Arbor - See restaurant listing

at Southbourne East : 3.75 mi. by A 35 on B 3059

Roots

MODERN BRITISH • NEIGHBOURHOOD XX In an ordinary-looking parade of shops, behind frosted glass, is this bright, modern restaurant with 9 tables and a jovial, laid-back feel. Dishes are attractively prepared, delicately constructed and encompass a contrast of textures, temperatures and flavours; some even mix savoury and sweet.

Menu £ 40/60

141 Belle Vue Rd ✉ BH6 3EN
- ✆ 01202 430005 (booking essential) - www.restaurantroots.co.uk - dinner only and Friday-Saturday lunch - Closed 23 December-mid-January, 2 weeks May-June, Sunday and Monday

Bed & Breakfast by the Beach Ⓝ

TRADITIONAL • COSY The experienced owners of this unassuming-looking guesthouse - set just a stone's throw from 8 miles of golden sands - will give you a truly warm welcome. Spacious, immaculately kept bedrooms provide all you could want. Watch the birds and squirrels while enjoying a delicious breakfast in the conservatory.

4 rooms - £ 70/95 £ 85/115

Burtley Manor, 7 Burtley Rd, ✉ BH6 4AP
- ✆ 01202 433632 - www.bedandbreakfastbythebeach.co.uk

BOURTON-ON-THE-WATER

Gloucestershire - Pop. 3 296 - Regional map n° **2**-D1

Coombe House

TRADITIONAL • PERSONALISED You'll be warmly welcomed at this homely, immaculately kept house in a charming Cotswold village. The breakfast room boasts full-length leaded windows and overlooks the attractive garden, and the first floor terrace is perfect for sunny days. Aga-cooked breakfasts use local ingredients.

5 rooms - £ 110/150 £ 110/150

Rissington Rd ✉ GL54 2DT
- ✆ 01451 821966 - www.coombehousecotswolds.co.uk - Closed 19 December-30 January

at Lower Slaughter Northwest: 1.75 mi by A429 ✉ Cheltenham

Slaughters Manor House

MODERN CUISINE • CHIC XXX An elegant dining room in a bright, airy extension of a fine manor house hotel, overlooking its lovely gardens. Immaculately laid tables have beautiful floral displays. Menus offer accomplished modern dishes with a classical base.

Menu £ 30/68

Slaughters Manor House Hotel, ✉ GL54 2HP
- ✆ 01451 820456 - www.slaughtersmanor.co.uk

Slaughters Manor House

LUXURY • CLASSIC A beautiful part-17C manor house built from warm Cotswold stone and surrounded by delightful grounds. Elegant bedrooms are split between the house and the stables: the former are individually styled, while the latter are more up-to-date - and two have private hot tubs. Guest areas are modern and stylish.

19 rooms - £ 150/240 £ 150/285

✉ GL54 2HP
- ✆ 01451 820456 - www.slaughtersmanor.co.uk

Slaughters Manor House - See restaurant listing

Slaughters Country Inn

INN • CONTEMPORARY Originally a crammer school for Eton College, this stone-built manor house is a good choice for families – and they welcome dogs too! It's relaxed and understated, with modern styling; the cosy bedrooms have feature walls and up-to-date facilities. The pub and restaurant serve British classics.

31 rooms – †£ 99/185 ††£ 99/195 – 7 suites

GL54 2HS – 01451 822143 – www.theslaughtersinn.co.uk

at Upper Slaughter Northwest: 2.5 mi by A429 Bourton-On-The-Water

Lords of the Manor

LUXURY • CLASSIC A charming 17C rectory in a pretty Cotswold village, with beautiful gardens, a superb outlook and a real sense of tranquility. Country house style bedrooms have subtle contemporary touches. Enjoy an aperitif on one of two luxurious sitting rooms then dine from a concise modern menu in the traditional dining room.

26 rooms – †£ 195/510 ††£ 195/510 – 3 suites

GL54 2JD – 01451 820243 – www.lordsofthemanor.com

BOW

Devon – Pop. 1 095 – Regional map n° **1**-C2

Paschoe House (N)

COUNTRY HOUSE • ELEGANT This elegant 19C country house blends classic and contemporary styles. It has a lovely tiled reception room and a modern bar offering far-reaching views over the well-tended grounds. Bedrooms come with hot water bottles and a map of local walks – and wellies are in the boot room. Cooking is modern and refined.

9 rooms – †£ 150/220 ††£ 290/360

EX17 6JT – East : 2.5 mi off A3072 on Coleford/ Colebrook rd – 01363 84244 – www.paschoehouse.co.uk

BOWDON

Greater Manchester – Greater Manchester – Pop. 6 079 – Regional map n° **11**-B3

Borage

MODERN CUISINE • NEIGHBOURHOOD XX An airy neighbourhood restaurant in a pleasant village. Well-presented, colourful European dishes showcase Polish ingredients and are full of flavour. The homemade breads are a highlight, as is the chocolate mousse.

Carte £ 28/34

7 Vale View, Vicarage Ln WA14 3BD – 0161 929 4775 – www.boragebowdon.co.uk – dinner only and Sunday lunch – Closed 24-26 December, 1-15 January, Sunday dinner, Monday and Tuesday

BOWNESS-ON-WINDERMERE – Cumbria

→ See Windermere

BOYLESTONE

Derbyshire – Regional map n° **9**-A2

Lighthouse

MODERN BRITISH • DESIGN XX It may not be near the coast but the Lighthouse does attract your attention. The self-taught chef prepares ambitious dishes with great combinations of flavours and textures; a good selection of keenly priced wines accompanies.

Menu £ 45/55 – tasting menu only

New Rd DE6 5AA – behind Rose & Crown public house – 01335 330658 – www.the-lighthouse-restaurant.co.uk – dinner only – Closed Sunday-Tuesday

BRADFORD-ON-AVON

Wiltshire – Pop. 9 149 – Regional map n° **2**-C2

Bunch of Grapes

FRENCH • PUB A collaboration between 5 friends who love the food and wine of South West France. Rustic cooking focuses on the wood-fired Bertha oven and wines are imported directly from France. The place has an appealingly bijou, brocante feel.

Menu £ 18 (lunch) – Carte £ 25/49

14 Silver St ✉ BA15 1JY
– ✆ 01225 938088 – www.thebunchofgrapes.com – Closed lunch Monday-Wednesday

Timbrell's Yard

INN • CONTEMPORARY This Grade II listed riverside inn was once part of the old dye works. Bedrooms come in muted tones and feature reclaimed furnishings, quirky contemporary art and vintage touches; ask for a duplex room with river and church views. Enjoy appealing modern day classics in the rustic bar or restaurant.

17 rooms – †£ 95/150 ††£ 95/150

49 St Margaret's St ✉ BA15 1DE
– ✆ 01225 869492 – www.timbrellsyard.com

Woolley Grange

COUNTRY HOUSE • CLASSIC Fine Jacobean manor house that's geared towards families, with a crèche, a kids' club, a games room and outdoor activities. For adults, there's a chic spa and some lovely country views. Smart bedrooms come in many styles. Accomplished, classical cooking is served in the restaurant and more relaxed orangery.

25 rooms – †£ 105/130 ††£ 120/170 – 6 suites

Woolley Green ✉ BA15 1TX – Northeast : 0.75 mi by B 3107 on Woolley St
– ✆ 01225 864705 – www.woolleygrangehotel.co.uk

BRADLEY

Staffordshire – Pop. 513 – Regional map n° **10**-C2

The Red Lion

TRADITIONAL CUISINE • PUB An airy bar and conservatory opens onto a dining room hung with photos of the pub through the ages. Menus offer plenty of choice, with hearty, flavoursome dishes ranging from whole roast witch sole to curried chicken Kiev.

Carte £ 24/42

Smithy Ln ✉ ST18 9DZ
– ✆ 01785 780297 – www.redlionbradley.co.uk – Closed 25 December

BRADWELL

Derbyshire – Pop. 1 416 – Regional map n° **9**-A1

Samuel Fox Country Inn

MODERN BRITISH • PUB An attractive, light-stone pub with smart, cosy bedrooms and a dramatic, hilly backdrop: named after the inventor of the steel-ribbed umbrella, who was born in the village. Flavourful classic dishes have modern touches and make good use of seasonal local produce. Popular 7 course tasting menu.

Menu £ 36

4 rooms – †£ 80/115 ††£ 100/140

Stretfield Rd ✉ S33 9JT
– ✆ 01433 621562 – www.samuelfox.co.uk – dinner only and Sunday lunch – Closed 2-18 January, Sunday dinner, Monday and Tuesday

BRAITHWAITE - Cumbria → See Keswick

BRAMPFORD SPEKE - Devon → See Exeter

BRAMPTON

Cumbria - Pop. 4 229 - Regional map n° **12**-B1

Farlam Hall

TRADITIONAL • PERSONALISED A well-run, family-owned country house, whose origins can be traced back to the 1600s. Bedrooms are furnished with antiques but also have modern touches like Bose radios. The sumptuous dining room has a traditional daily menu and romantic views across a lake, while afternoon tea is served in the curio-filled lounges, overlooking the immaculate ornamental gardens.

12 rooms (dinner included) - †£ 145/155 ††£ 310/370

CA8 2NG - Southeast : 2.75 mi on A 689
- 016977 46234 - www.farlamhall.co.uk - Closed 7-26 January and 25-30 December

BRANDESTON

Suffolk - Pop. 296 - Regional map n° **8**-D3

The Queen

TRADITIONAL BRITISH • RUSTIC A rustic, shabby-chic pub with snug corners. Veg comes from the huge kitchen garden and whole beasts are brought in from a farm nearby. Puddings are delightful, there's an amazing array of cheeses and it's worth getting up early for breakfast. If you're a fan of glamping, they have some lovely shepherd's huts.

Carte £ 23/33

The Street IP13 7AD - 01728 685307 - www.thequeenatbrandeston.co.uk - Closed Sunday dinner and Monday

BRAY

Windsor and Maidenhead - Pop. 8 121 - Regional map n° **6**-C3

Waterside Inn (Alain Roux)

CLASSIC FRENCH • ELEGANT XXXX This illustrious restaurant sits in a glorious spot on a bank of the River Thames. It was opened in 1972 by brothers Michel and Albert Roux and is now in the hands of Michel's son Alain. It remains the longest-standing Starred restaurant in the UK, having been awarded One Star in 1974, Two Stars in 1977 and Three Stars in 1985.

Michel, one of the forefathers of classical French cuisine, set the bar high, and luxury is at every turn. Tables are superbly laid with the finest crockery and glassware, an abundance of staff cater for guests every whim, and menus are packed with top quality ingredients. Carefully considered classical French menus are a calendar for the seasons and dishes arrive in perfectly judged, sophisticated combinations. The lobster and rabbit are specialities, the Challandais duck for 2 is a seminal dish and the cheese trolley and the soufflé of the day are not to be missed.

Bedrooms are fittingly chic and sumptuous.

→ Tronçonnettes de homard poêlées minute au porto blanc. Filets de lapereau grillés sur un fondant de céleri-rave, sauce à l'armagnac et aux marrons glacés. Soufflé chaud aux mirabelles.

Menu £ 64 (weekday lunch)/168 - Carte £ 127/175

11 rooms - †£ 275/585 ††£ 275/585 - 2 suites

Ferry Rd SL6 2AT - 01628 620691 (booking essential)
- www.waterside-inn.co.uk - Closed dinner 25 December-31 January, Monday and Tuesday

✿✿✿ Fat Duck (Heston Blumenthal)

CREATIVE • ELEGANT XXX Tables at this iconic restaurant are released 3 months in advance and it is then that your journey begins... First you will be contacted to see which flavours evoke memories of your childhood – as Heston's aim is to recreate moods from your formative years – then once you arrive a dedicated Story Teller will guide you through your journey from 'breakfast' through to 'dinner'.

Both the décor and the table settings are understated, allowing you to fully immerse yourself in the theatrical, multi-sensory experience. The innovative cooking is detailed, playful and perfectly judged, and the textures and flavours are harmonious. Elaborate, interactive presentation and an truly engaging service team further heighten the experience and every dish will leave you eagerly anticipating the next.

→ Hot and cold tea. Duck à l'orange. Botrytis cinerea.

Menu £ 325 – tasting menu only

High St ✉ SL6 2AQ – ✆ 01628 580333 (booking essential) – www.thefatduck.co.uk – Closed 2 weeks Christmas-New Year, Sunday and Monday

✿ Hinds Head

TRADITIONAL BRITISH • HISTORIC X Start with a cocktail in The Royal Lounge – surrounded by unusual taxidermy – before heading for the characterful 15C restaurant of this quintessentially English inn. Sophisticated dishes celebrate time-honoured British recipes but Heston Blumenthal's creative influences are also evident.

→ Lapsang souchong tea-smoked salmon with sour cream butter and soda bread. Oxtail and kidney pudding. Rhubarb trifle with saffron custard and hazelnut praline.

Menu £ 25 (weekday lunch) – Carte £ 38/72

High St ✉ SL6 2AB – ✆ 01628 626151 (booking essential) – www.hindsheadbray.com – Closed 25 December and Sunday dinner

Caldesi in Campagna

ITALIAN • INTIMATE XX Sister of Café Caldesi in London, is this chic, sophisticated restaurant with a cosy conservatory and a lovely covered terrace – complete with a wood-fired oven. Flavoursome Italian dishes feature Tuscan and Sicilian specialities.

Menu £ 20 (weekday lunch) – Carte £ 35/57

Old Mill Ln ✉ SL6 2BG – ✆ 01628 788500 – www.caldesi.com – Closed Sunday dinner and Monday

Crown

TRADITIONAL BRITISH • PUB Charmingly restored 16C building; formerly two cottages and a bike shop! Drinkers mingle with diners, and dark columns, low beams and roaring fires create a cosy atmosphere. Carefully prepared British dishes are robust and flavoursome.

Carte £ 32/40

High St ✉ SL6 2AH – ✆ 01628 621936 – www.thecrownatbray.com – Closed Sunday dinner

Royal Oak

TRADITIONAL BRITISH • DESIGN It might be a pub but the Royal Oak is a place with an air of formality and a sense of occasion. Classic British dishes follow the seasons – and you definitely won't leave hungry! In summer, pick a spot in the tranquil garden; in winter, cosy up by the fire in the characterful bar.

Carte £ 34/61

Paley Street ✉ SL6 3JN – Southwest : 3.5 mi by A 308 and A 330 on B 3024 – ✆ 01628 620541 – www.theroyaloakpaleystreet.com – Closed Sunday dinner

BRAYE
→ See Channel Islands (Alderney)

BRIDPORT

Dorset - Pop. 13 737 - Regional map n° **2**-B3

Dorshi

ASIAN • FRIENDLY A bohemian-style restaurant with a laid-back feel: the ground floor is lively while upstairs it's more intimate. Asian street food inspired small plates are perfect for sharing and their flavours pack a punch; the dumplings are a highlight. Cocktails are creative and at weekends there's a house party vibe.

Carte £ 20/30

Bartholomews Hall, 6 Chancery Ln. ✉ DT6 3PX - Off East St. - ✆ 01308 423221 (booking essential) - www.dorshi.co.uk - Closed Christmas, 1 January, Sunday-Tuesday and bank holidays

at Burton Bradstock Southeast: 2 mi by B3157

Seaside Boarding House

TRADITIONAL BRITISH • CONTEMPORARY DÉCOR Stunningly located on the clifftop, this old hotel has a fresh, new look. The bright, airy restaurant has a subtle maritime theme and there's a lovely terrace with sea views. Menus offer everything from fish soup to plaice with lemon and caper butter. Classically understated bedrooms come with claw-foot baths and there's a pleasant bar and library for residents.

Menu £ 15 (weekday lunch) - Carte £ 24/42

9 rooms - †£ 185/205 ††£ 210/230

Cliff Rd ✉ DT6 4RB - Southeast : 0.5 mi - ✆ 01308 897205 - www.theseasideboardinghouse.com

Michelin

GOOD TIPS!

The jewel of the south coast knows how to have a good time and has plenty of cool, quirky hotels and restaurants. Enjoy views out over the Channel from a bedroom at **Drakes** or **A Room with a View**. **Terre à Terre** is a vegetarian's dream, pescatarians should head for **Little Fish Market** and those on a budget should try Bib Gourmand awarded **64°**, **Chilli Pickle** or **Cin Cin**.

BRIGHTON AND HOVE

Brighton and Hove – Pop. 229 700 – Regional map n° **5**-A3

Restaurants

Chilli Pickle

INDIAN • SIMPLE X A laid-back restaurant with a buzzy vibe and friendly service. The passionate chef uses good quality ingredients to create authentic Indian dishes with vibrant colours and flavours. Go for a thali at lunch and a kebab, grill or curry at dinner. Beside the terrace they also have a cart selling street food.

Menu £ 25 (dinner) – Carte £ 22/34

Town plan: C2-z – *17 Jubilee St ✉ BN1 1GE – ✆ 01273 900383 – www.thechillipickle.com – Closed 25-26 December*

Cin Cin (N)

ITALIAN • SIMPLE X This former single-car garage is hidden away in the North Laine area. It's a modest, quirky little place and seats 21 around a horseshoe counter. The food is Italian, with fresh ingredients cooked simply and natural flavours allowed to shine. Enjoy tasty small plates and delicious homemade pastas.

Carte £ 23/31

Town plan: C2-n – *13-16 Vine St ✉ BN1 4AG – ✆ 01273 698813 (booking essential) – www.cincin.co.uk – Closed 25-26 December, 1 January, Sunday and Monday.*

64°

MODERN BRITISH • SIMPLE X Hidden away in The Lanes is this stylish, laid-back restaurant comprising 3 tables and a kitchen counter where you can interact with the chefs. The pared back menu offers 'Fish', 'Meat' and 'Veg' small plates. Fresh, flavoursome dishes use just a handful of ingredients and deliver well-judged contrasts.

Carte £ 23/30

Town plan: B2-c – *53 Meeting House Ln. ✉ BN1 1HB – ✆ 01273 770115 (booking essential) – www.64degrees.co.uk – Closed 25-26 December and 1 January*

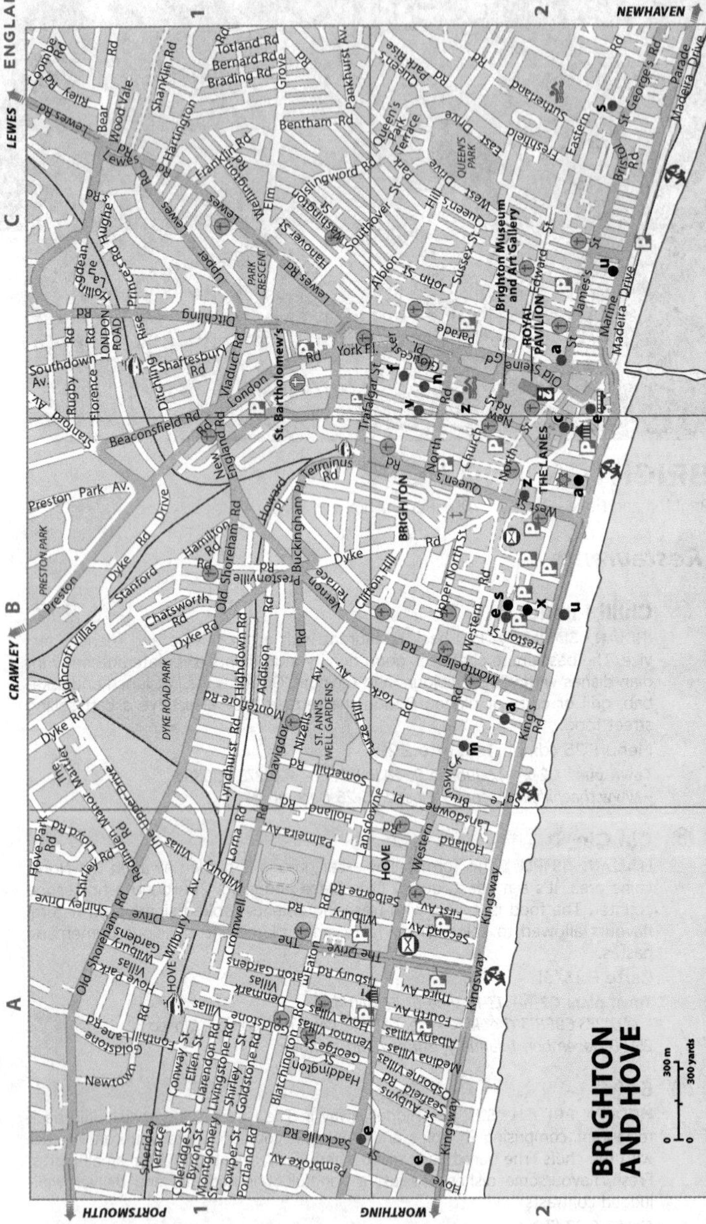
BRIGHTON AND HOVE
300 m
300 yards
LEWES
NEWHAVEN
CRAWLEY
PORTSMOUTH
WORTHING
A
B
C
1
2
BRIGHTON
HOVE
THE LANES
ROYAL PAVILION
Brighton Museum and Art Gallery
St. Bartholomew's
QUEEN'S PARK
PRESTON PARK
DYKE ROAD PARK
ST. ANN'S WELL GARDENS
PARK CRESCENT
LONDON ROAD
Kingsway
King's Rd
Marine Drive
Madeira Drive
Western Rd
Church St
North St
Queen's Rd
Dyke Rd
Lewes Rd
Ditchling Rd
Preston Park Av.
Old Shoreham Rd
New England Rd
Sackville Rd
The Drive
Montpelier Rd
Edward St
Eastern Rd
St. George's Rd

Pascere

MODERN BRITISH • CHIC XX One of Brighton's oldest buildings sits within The Lanes and is home to this chic, cosy restaurant set over two floors; head upstairs to the kitchen counter to really get in on the action. Sophisticated cooking sees a mix of small plates, seasonal British dishes and a tasting menu.

Carte £ 35/42

Town plan: B2-z - *8 Duke St ✉ BN1 1AH - ✆ 01273 917949 - www.pascere.co.uk - Closed Sunday and Monday*

Pike & Pine

MODERN BRITISH • FASHIONABLE XX A smart, light-filled restaurant filled with plants and trees; sit on comfy banquettes and watch the chefs in action. Punchy, eye-catching dishes blend classic and modern techniques - some have playful touches.

Carte £ 25/49

Town plan: C2-a - *1D St James's ✉ BN2 1RE - ✆ 01273 686668 - www.pikeandpine.co.uk - dinner only - Closed 25 December, Sunday-Tuesday*

etch. by Steven Edwards

MODERN BRITISH • NEIGHBOURHOOD X This compact restaurant is a hit with the locals. Ask to sit in one of the bay window booths then choose between two weekly set menus - go for 6 courses at lunch or 8 courses at dinner. Cooking captures flavours to the full.

Menu £ 50/70 - tasting menu only

Town plan: A1-e - *216 Church Rd, Hove ✉ BN3 2DJ - ✆ 01273 227485 (booking essential) - www.etchfood.co.uk - dinner only and Saturday lunch - Closed last week December, first week January and Sunday-Tuesday*

Gingerman

MODERN CUISINE • NEIGHBOURHOOD X There's a smart Scandic feel to the decoration and an intimacy to the atmosphere at this long-standing neighbourhood restaurant. Lunch is fairly classical while dinner features more elaborate, innovative combinations.

Menu £ 20 (weekday lunch)/40

Town plan: B2-a - *21a Norfolk Sq ✉ BN1 2PD - ✆ 01273 326688 (booking essential at dinner) - www.gingermanrestaurants.com - Closed 2 weeks winter, 25 December and Monday*

Isaac At

MODERN BRITISH • SIMPLE X You have to buy a 'ticket' in advance for dinner at this modest little 20-seater restaurant. Watch the young kitchen team on the TV screen or from the two counter spaces. Sussex produce is showcased in 8 daily changing dishes which have an understated modern style and rely on natural flavours.

Menu £ 35/55 - tasting menu only

Town plan: C2-f - *2 Gloucester St ✉ BN1 4EW - ✆ 07765 934740 (booking essential) - www.isaac-at.com - dinner only and Saturday lunch - Closed Sunday and Monday*

Little Fish Market

SEAFOOD • SIMPLE X Fish is the focus at this simple restaurant, set in a converted fishmonger's opposite the old Victorian fish market. The owner cooks alone and his set 5 course menu offers refined, interesting modern seafood dishes.

Menu £ 65 - tasting menu only

Town plan: B2-m - *10 Upper Market St, Hove ✉ BN3 1AS - ✆ 01273 722213 (booking essential) - www.thelittlefishmarket.co.uk - dinner only and Saturday lunch - Closed 1 week April, 2 weeks September, 1 week December, Sunday and Monday*

Murmur

MODERN BRITISH • BISTRO The sister of 64° sits in a pleasant spot on the seafront. It's a colourful, laid-back place, built into the arches of the promenade, and has a lovely beachside terrace for sunny days. Modern classics are supplemented by blackboard specials; the lobster croquettes are a signature dish.

Menu £ 20 (weekday lunch) - Carte £ 27/40

Town plan: B2-u - *91-96 Kings Road Arches* *BN1 2FN*
- *01273 711900 - www.murmur-restaurant.co.uk*
- *Closed Sunday dinner*

The Set

MODERN BRITISH • RUSTIC A quirky little hotel eatery with two distinct parts: to the front, a café serving small plates; to the rear a restaurant and kitchen counter, where they offer a choice of seasonal modern British set menus. Exposed wood, brick, iron and reclaimed furnishings set the scene.

Menu £ 40/45 (dinner) - Carte £ 18/27

Town plan: B2-e - *Artist Residence Hotel, 33 Regency Sq* *BN1 2GG*
- *01273 324302 (booking essential) - www.thesetrestaurant.com*

Silo

MODERN CUISINE • RUSTIC The UK's first zero-waste restaurant: furnishings are made from reclaimed materials, plates are recycled from carrier bags and food waste is sent back to the farm where their ingredients are grown. Brunch and dinner comprise of small plates - the latter a mix of 'plant' and 'omnivore'.

Menu £ 38 (dinner) - Carte £ 24/35

Town plan: C2-v - *39 Upper Gardner St* *BN1 4AN*
- *01273 674259 (booking essential at dinner) - www.silobrighton.com*
- *dinner only and lunch Friday-Sunday*

Terre à Terre

VEGETARIAN • NEIGHBOURHOOD Relaxed, friendly restaurant decorated in warm burgundy colours. Appealing menu of generous, tasty, original vegetarian dishes which include items from Japan, China and South America. Mini épicerie sells wine, pasta and chutney.

Menu £ 35 - Carte £ 32/35

Town plan: C2-e - *71 East St* *BN1 1HQ*
- *01273 729051 (booking essential) - www.terreaterre.co.uk*
- *Closed 25-26 December and Monday in winter*

Ginger Dog

MODERN BRITISH • PUB A charming Victorian pub with a pleasingly shabby-chic feel. Ornately carved woodwork sits comfortably alongside more recent additions like bowler hat lampshades. Menus list pub staples alongside some more interesting dishes with a subtle modern style. The dessert cocktails are worth a try.

Carte £ 28/42

Town plan: C2-s - *12 College Pl* *BN2 1HN*
- *01273 620990 - www.gingermanrestaurants.com*
- *Closed 25 December*

Don't expect guesthouses to provide the same level of service as a hotel. They are often characterised by a warm welcome and décor which reflects the owner's personality. Those shown in red are particularly charming.

Ginger Pig

TRADITIONAL BRITISH • PUB A striking mock-Tudor building with a beautiful antique revolving door and a charming wooden bar counter. The original, highly seasonal menu has a distinct European accent and gives the odd nod to North Africa. Modern, loft-style bedrooms have Hypnos beds - BBQs and picnic hampers are available to borrow.

Menu £ 18 (lunch) - Carte £ 27/44

11 rooms - †£ 100/200 ††£ 100/200 - ☕ £ 11

Town plan: A2-e - *3 Hove St, Hove ✉ BN3 2TR*
- ✆ 01273 736123 - www.gingermanrestaurants.com
- Closed 25 December

Hotels

Hotel du Vin

BUSINESS • CONTEMPORARY Made up of various different buildings; the oldest being a former wine merchant's. Kick-back in the cavernous, gothic-style bar-lounge or out on the terrace. Bedrooms are richly decorated and have superb monsoon showers. The relaxed brasserie, with its hidden courtyard, serves French bistro classics.

49 rooms ☕ - †£ 75/399 ††£ 89/399

Town plan: B2-a - *2-6 Ship St ✉ BN1 1AD*
- ✆ 01273 718588 - www.hotelduvin.com

Drakes

TOWNHOUSE • DESIGN These two Georgian houses sit in a perfect position on the promenade, with the pier just a stone's throw away. Character comes in the form of original hanging staircases, while the bedrooms are chic and contemporary; some have fantastic sea views and one has a bath in the bay window! Eclectic art hangs in the lounge-bar and dinner takes place in the stylish basement.

20 rooms - †£ 120/200 ††£ 120/360 - ☕ £ 15

Town plan: C2-u - *43-44 Marine Par ✉ BN2 1PE*
- ✆ 01273 696934 - www.drakesofbrighton.com

Artist Residence (N)

TOWNHOUSE • QUIRKY These two townhouses look over Regency Square to the West Pier. Their style is shabby-chic, with bedrooms featuring reclaimed furnishings and named after the artists who furnished them; choose one with a balcony and a sea view. Unwind with a game of table tennis or a drink in the cocktail shack.

25 rooms - †£ 135/310 ††£ 135/310 - ☕ £ 11

Town plan: B2-e - *33 Regency Sq ✉ BN1 2GG*
- ✆ 01273 324302 - www.artistresidence.co.uk

The Set - See restaurant listing

Hotel Una (N)

TOWNHOUSE • UNIQUE An architect and a designer own this townhouse in Regency Square, which results in an interior which is not only comfortable but stylish and unique. Oak and mahogany feature extensively in the bedrooms - choose a room with a balcony, a sauna or even a private cinema!

17 rooms ☕ - †£ 85/95 ††£ 115/310

Town plan: B2-a - *55-56 Regency Sq ✉ BN1 2FF*
- ✆ 01273 820464 - www.hotel-una.co.uk
- Closed 22-26 December

A Room with a View

TOWNHOUSE · PERSONALISED Snuggle into a Hungarian goose down duvet and, if your room is at the front of this Regency townhouse on the promenade, enjoy a view out over the Channel. All of the rooms are contemporary and come with coffee machines – and Room 10 has a rooftop terrace. At breakfast, all guests can share the vista.

10 rooms – £ 59/89 £ 74/295

Town plan: C2-u – *41 Marine Par. ✉ BN2 1PE – 01273 682885 – www.aroomwithaviewbrighton.com*

BRILL

Buckinghamshire – Pop. 1 141 – Regional map n° **6**-C2

The Pointer

MODERN BRITISH · INN Sit in one of two beamed dining rooms or beside the fire in one of the smaller rooms and take time to read the menu, which explains what they are currently growing in the gardens and using in the cooking. Rare breed meats come from their 240 acre farm – take something home from their adjoining butcher's shop. Stylish, contemporary bedrooms are in the cottage opposite.

Menu £ 18 (weekday lunch) – Carte £ 31/54

4 rooms – £ 130/185 £ 130/185

27 Church St ✉ HP18 9RT – 01844 238339 – www.thepointerbrill.co.uk – Closed first week of January and Monday

GOOD TIPS!

The unofficial capital of the West Country has a vibrant cultural and recreational scene, yet retains the friendly feel of a smaller town. Alongside Starred restaurants such as **Casamia** and **wilks** are great value Bib Gourmand restaurants like **Bell's Diner & Bar Rooms**, **Root** and **Tare**, and the continued development of Wapping Wharf looks set to bring more exciting new openings.

BRISTOL

City of Bristol – Pop. 535 907 – Regional map n° **2**-C2

Restaurants

✿ Casamia (Peter Sanchez-Iglesias) ♿

CREATIVE • **DESIGN** XX Casamia sits in an impressive listed Victorian hospital overlooking Bathurst Basin. You enter through double glass doors, under an arch and through into a pared down, Scandic-style room. The team are charming and the passionate chefs personally deliver the skilfully prepared, highly creative, seasonal dishes.

→ Parmesan tartlet. Turbot with champagne sabayon. Passion fruit and tarragon.

Menu £ 98 – tasting menu only

Town plan: C2-e – *The General, Lower Guinea St* ✉ *BS1 6FU*
– *✆ 0117 959 2884 (booking essential)* – *www.casamiarestaurant.co.uk*
– *dinner only and lunch Friday-Saturday*
– *Closed 1-4 January, 24-27 April, 26-29 June, 25-28 September, 25-28 December and Sunday-Tuesday*

✿ wilks (James Wilkins)

MODERN BRITISH • **FRIENDLY** XX Vibrant modern art hangs on grey walls at this appealing neighbourhood restaurant. The experienced chef is well-travelled and skilfully balances different textures with flavours from around the globe. French and British ingredients jostle with one another on the menu and all of the fish is wild.

→ Langoustine tartare, wasabi, apple & ginger. Squab with liver parfait, cocoa jus. Kaffir lime leaf meringue sphere, marinated pineapple & crème fraîche sorbet.

Menu £ 29 (weekday lunch) – Carte £ 52/62

Town plan: A1-d – *1 Chandos Rd* ✉ *BS6 6PG*
– *✆ 0117 973 7999 (booking essential)* – *www.wilksrestaurant.co.uk*
– *Closed 24 December-16 January, 5-28 August, Wednesday lunch, Monday and Tuesday*

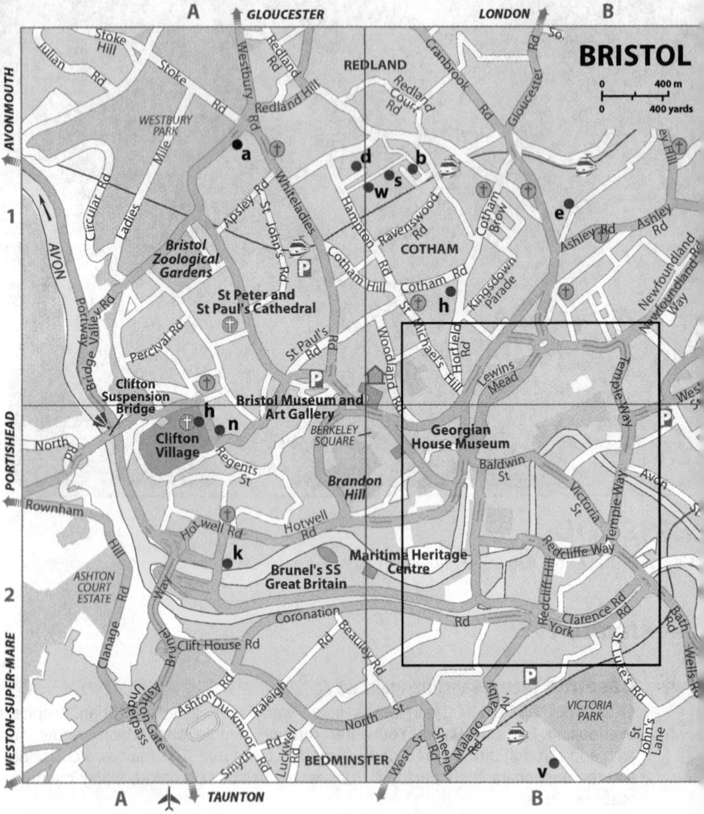

Bulrush

MODERN BRITISH • NEIGHBOURHOOD A sweet neighbourhood restaurant run by a friendly team; stay downstairs to soak up the atmosphere from the kitchen. Seasonal ingredients are foraged or organic, and preserving and pickling play a key role. The imaginative, well-balanced and deftly prepared tasting menus are a popular choice.

→ Heritage tomato, sheep's milk ice cream and nettle sauce. Bream, white asparagus and turnip. Truffle ice cream, croissant mousse, caramel apples.

Menu £ 50 – Carte £ 34/41

Town plan: B1-h – *21 Cotham Rd South ✉ BS6 5TZ – ✆ 0117 329 0990 (booking essential) – www.bulrushrestaurant.co.uk – Closed 24 December-1 January, 2 weeks August, Sunday, Monday and lunch Tuesday-Wednesday*

Paco Tapas

SPANISH • TAPAS BAR This buzzy tapas bar is the sister to Casamia. Sit on the terrace for nibbles accompanied by one of their fine Spanish wines or head for the 8-seater counter set around the large open grill. Authentic, skilfully prepared dishes are packed with flavour; try the "Chef's Menu" for a best-of-the-best tour of Spain.

→ Tortilla Española. Stuffed quail, Sobrassada and dates. Crema Catalana.

Menu £ 50 – Carte £ 20/38

Town plan: C2-t – *The General, 3A Lower Guinea St ✉ BS1 6FU – ✆ 0117 925 7021 (booking essential) – www.pacotapas.co.uk – dinner only and lunch Friday-Saturday – Closed 24-26 December, Sunday and Monday*

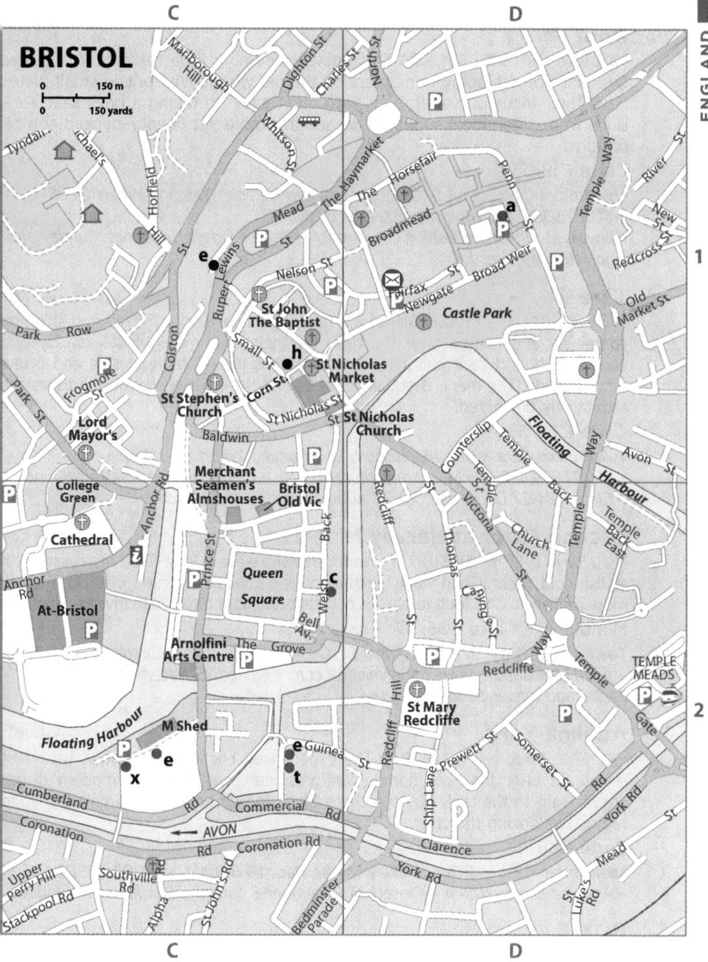

Bell's Diner & Bar Rooms

MEDITERRANEAN CUISINE • BISTRO X A bustling city institution with an über-cool bohemian feel; its décor retains evidence of its grocer's shop days. Mediterranean cooking shows a good understanding of ingredients and dishes are full of colour and flavour. Try the charred carrot, mint and hazelnut salad or the glistening boquerones.

Menu £ 33 – Carte £ 23/36

Town plan: B1-e – *1-3 York Rd, Montpelier ✉ BS6 5QB – ✆ 0117 924 0357*
– www.bellsdiner.com – dinner only and lunch Saturday and Sunday
– Closed 24-26 December, 1 January, Monday and Tuesday lunch, Wednesday and Thursday lunch October-April

The symbol 🍇 denotes a particularly interesting wine list.

Root

MODERN BRITISH • SIMPLE This busy, welcoming little restaurant occupies five first floor shipping containers on the old wharf. Well-priced small plates have their focus on vegetables, with meat and fish taking a back seat. Produce from small local suppliers is used in simple yet flavour-packed combinations.

Carte £ 19/33

Town plan: C2-x – *Unit 9, Cargo 1, Gaol Ferry Steps, Wapping Wharf ✉ BS1 6WP – ✆ 0117 930 0260 (booking essential at dinner) – www.eatdrinkbristolfashion.co.uk/root/ – Closed 3 days Christmas, Sunday and lunch Monday-Tuesday*

Tare

MODERN BRITISH • FASHIONABLE Tare is set in a block of converted shipping containers and named after the term for their empty weight. It's run by two young chefs and their charming team, and has just 10 tables inside and a few more outside. The menu is equally concise and the creative, flavourful dishes are attractively presented.

Carte £ 28/33

Town plan: C2-e – *Unit 14, Museum St, Wapping Wharf ✉ BS1 6ZA – ✆ 0117 929 4328 – www.tarerestaurant.co.uk – dinner only and Saturday lunch – Closed 24-27 December, 20-26 August, Sunday and Monday*

Second Floor at Harvey Nichols

MODERN CUISINE • DESIGN A spacious and elegant light-filled restaurant with stylish gold décor. Good value lunch menu and concise à la carte offering original, modern dishes. Chic lounge bar for cocktails and light bites. Attentive service.

Menu £ 25 – Carte £ 36/47

Town plan: D1-a – *27 Philadelphia St, Quakers Friars, Cabot Circus ✉ BS1 3BZ – ✆ 0117 916 8898 – www.harveynichols.com – Closed 25 December, 1 January, Easter and dinner Sunday-Monday*

Adelina Yard

MODERN CUISINE • INTIMATE The experienced chef-owners named their first restaurant after their old home. Well-presented, well-balanced modern dishes are brought to the tables by the chefs. Sit at the far end of the simple L-shaped room, overlooking the quay.

Carte £ 38/44

Town plan: C2-c – *3 Queen Quay, Welsh Back ✉ BS1 4SL – ✆ 0117 911 2112 – www.adelinayard.com – Closed 23 December-8 January, Sunday and Monday*

BOX-E

MODERN BRITISH • SIMPLE Wapping Wharf is home to Cargo, a retail yard made of converted shipping containers, and on the first floor is intimate BOX-E, a compact restaurant clad in chipboard. Dishes are modern and colourful; the panna cotta is a must.

Carte £ 27/38

Town plan: C2-x – *Unit 10, Cargo 1, Wapping Wharf ✉ BS1 6WP – www.boxebristol.com – Closed Sunday-Tuesday lunch*

No Man's Grace

MODERN BRITISH • NEIGHBOURHOOD A simple, stripped-back restaurant with a decked terrace; proudly run by an experienced young chef. To the regulars this is both their local and a special occasion place, which gives it an atmospheric neighbourhood feel. Unfussy cooking relies on just a few ingredients, allowing their flavours to shine.

Menu £ 22/45

Town plan: AB1-w – *6 Chandos Rd ✉ BS6 6PE – ✆ 0117 974 4077 – www.nomansgrace.com – dinner only and lunch Friday-Sunday – Closed 24 December-2 January, Sunday dinner, Monday and Tuesday*

Nutmeg

INDIAN • NEIGHBOURHOOD A long, narrow restaurant with a boldly stencilled wall. The à la carte covers all 29 states of India, while the tasting menu rotates through the regions. Cooking is vibrant, spices are ground daily and the breads are delicious.

Carte £ 19/31

Town plan: A2-n – *10 The Mall ✉ BS8 4DR – ✆ 0117 360 0288 – www.nutmegbristol.com – Closed Monday and lunch Tuesday-Wednesday*

Wellbourne

MODERN BRITISH • BISTRO Two friends run this small restaurant in charming Clifton Village. Lunch sees a selection of brunch-style dishes, including eggs Benedict made with homemade muffins and bacon, while the concise evening à la carte offers modern dishes with a British heart. Their vol au vents are something of a speciality.

Carte £ 16/35

Town plan: A2-h – *25 The Mall, Clifton Village ✉ BS8 4JG – ✆ 0117 239 0683 (booking essential at dinner) – https://wellbourne.restaurant*

Wilsons

MODERN BRITISH • RUSTIC Wilsons really fits the bill of being a proper neighbourhood restaurant. Vodkas infused with various fruits sit on the bar and large blackboards list the day's dishes. Highly seasonal cooking is gutsy, generous and flavoursome and some of the ingredients come from their own smallholding.

Carte £ 30/35

Town plan: B1-s – *24 Chandos Road ✉ BS6 6PF – ✆ 0117 973 4157 – www.wilsonsrestaurant.co.uk – Closed 2 weeks August, Easter, Christmas, Sunday, Monday and Tuesday lunch.*

Kensington Arms

MODERN BRITISH • PUB It might be painted 'stealth' grey but this smart Victorian-style pub stands out a mile for its warm neighbourhood atmosphere. The menu evolves throughout the week and is a curious mix of the traditional and the modern.

Menu £ 15 (weekday lunch) – Carte £ 22/37

Town plan: B1-b – *35-37 Stanley Rd ✉ BS6 6NP – ✆ 0117 944 6444 – www.thekensingtonarms.co.uk*

Victoria Park

MODERN BRITISH • NEIGHBOURHOOD This neighbourhood pub is named after the nearby park and its jewel in the crown is its spacious terrace and tiered gardens which offer lovely views over the rooftops. Menus list a great mix of dishes that you'll know and love.

Carte £ 18/34

Town plan: B2-v – *66 Raymend Rd ✉ BS3 4QW – ✆ 0117 330 6043 – www.thevictoriapark.co.uk – Closed 26 December and 1 January*

Hotels

Bristol Harbour

HISTORIC BUILDING • ELEGANT Located within two listed 1840s banks with stunning facades. Bedrooms are spacious and modern, the ballroom is an impressive space and the old vault now hides a delightful spa. The 'Gold Bar' comprises 4 intimate, ornately decorated rooms, while the large, bustling brasserie specialises in seafood.

42 rooms – †£ 170/200 ††£ 170/200

Town plan: C1-h – *55 Corn St ✉ BS1 1HT – ✆ 0117 203 4456 – www.bristol-harbour-hotel.co.uk*

Hotel du Vin

BUSINESS • DESIGN Characterful 18C former sugar refinery with classical Hotel du Vin styling and a wine-theme running throughout. Dark-hued bedrooms and duplex suites boast Egyptian cotton linen – one room has twin roll-top baths. Cosy lounge-bar; French brasserie with a pleasant courtyard terrace for bistro classics.

40 rooms – £ 99/189 £ 99/289

Town plan: C1-e – *The Sugar House ✉ BS1 2NU – ✆ 0117 403 2979 – www.hotelduvin.com*

Berwick Lodge

COUNTRY HOUSE • PERSONALISED A former private home, run by gregarious, hands-on owners. It's 18 acres of grounds offer views over Avonmouth and the Severn Bridge. Inside, original features combine with Eastern furnishings and mosaic tiles, and impressive bedrooms boast vintage beds. The intimate restaurant serves modern fare.

14 rooms – £ 85/115 £ 125/145 – £ 15

Berwick Dr ✉ BS10 7TD – Northwest : 5 mi by A 4018 – ✆ 0117 958 1590 – www.berwicklodge.co.uk

Number 38 Clifton

TOWNHOUSE • PERSONALISED Built in 1820, this substantial townhouse overlooks both the city and the Clifton Downs. Boutique bedrooms have coloured wood-panelled walls, Roberts radios and smart bathrooms with underfloor heating; the most luxurious are the loft suites, complete with copper baths. The rear terrace makes a great suntrap.

11 rooms – £ 115/240 £ 130/255

Town plan: A1-a – *38 Upper Belgrave Rd ✉ BS8 2XN – ✆ 0117 946 6905 – www.number38clifton.com*

at Long Ashton Southwest: 2.5 mi by A370 off B3128

Bird in Hand

TRADITIONAL BRITISH • COSY A tiny country pub with three small but smartly decorated rooms. Quirky touches include an antelope's head and a wall covered in pages from Mrs Beeton's Book of Household Management. British dishes let local and foraged ingredients speak for themselves.

Carte £ 28/68

17 Weston Rd ✉ BS41 9LA – ✆ 01275 395222 – www.bird-in-hand.co.uk

BRITWELL SALOME

Oxfordshire – Pop. 187 – Regional map n° **6**-C2

Olivier at The Red Lion

FRENCH • TRADITIONAL DÉCOR Grab one of just a few tables by the bar to enjoy snacks like breaded pigs' trotters or head through to the dining room for carefully prepared classical French dishes like 12-hour Aga-cooked oxtail in pastry or Cornish fish with champagne sauce. Cooking is rich and delicious, from an experienced hand.

Menu £ 21 (lunch) – Carte £ 30/40

✉ OX49 5LG – ✆ 01491 613140 – www.olivierattheredlionbritwellsalome.co.uk – Closed Sunday dinner-Tuesday

BROADSTAIRS

Kent – Pop. 23 632 – Regional map n° **5**-D1

Stark

MODERN BRITISH • SIMPLE X Their slogan 'Good food, laid bare', sums up this bijou restaurant, where ladders and rope lights hang beside rustic wood-panelled walls. The modern 6 course tasting menu is highly seasonal and dishes are beautifully presented.

Menu £ 45 – tasting menu only

1 Oscar Rd ✉ CT10 1QJ – ✆ 01843 579786 (booking essential) – www.starkfood.co.uk – dinner only – Closed 23-30 December and Sunday-Tuesday

Wyatt & Jones

MODERN BRITISH • BISTRO X Follow the narrow road under the arch and towards the beach. Here you'll find 3 old fishermen's cottages with pleasant sea views; watch the boats landing their speciality, lobster. Appealing menus keep things regional – start with some tempting nibbles and finish with a traditional pudding.

Carte £ 25/39

23-27 Harbour St ✉ CT10 1EU – ✆ 01843 865126 – www.wyattandjones.co.uk – Closed 25-26 December, Monday except bank holiday and Tuesday

Belvidere Place

TOWNHOUSE • QUIRKY Centrally located Georgian house with a charming owner, green credentials and an eclectic, individual style. Bohemian, shabby-chic lounge boasts a retro football table. Spacious bedrooms mix modern facilities with older antique furnishings.

5 rooms – £ 140/160 £ 160/200

Belvedere Rd ✉ CT10 1PF – ✆ 01843 579850 – www.belvidereplace.co.uk – Closed 25-26 December

BROADWAY

Worcestershire – Pop. 2 496 – Regional map n° **10**-C3

Buckland Manor

MODERN BRITISH • INTIMATE XX A formal restaurant set within a country house hotel. The elegant room has wood-clad walls hung with oil paintings and offers views over the gardens and there are cosy lounges in which to begin and end your meal. Time-honoured dishes have clean flavours and are brought up-to-date in their presentation.

Menu £ 30/70

Buckland Manor Hotel, Buckland ✉ WR12 7LY – Southwest : 2.25 mi by B 4632 – ✆ 01386 852626 (booking essential) – www.bucklandmanor.com

Garden Room

MODERN BRITISH • ELEGANT XX A stylish hotel houses this chic, understated restaurant, which offers great country views from its full-length windows. The knowledgeable team offer a choice of set or à la carte menus and the cooking is delicate, exacting and full of flavour. Unique combinations are well-balanced and complementary.

Carte £ 60/82

Dormy House Hotel, Willersey Hill ✉ WR12 7LF – ✆ 01386 852711 (booking essential) – www.dormyhouse.co.uk – dinner only and Sunday lunch – Closed Monday and Tuesday

Lygon Bar & Grill N

TRADITIONAL BRITISH • BISTRO XX The Lygon Arms' Great Hall houses this spacious dining room and smart cocktail bar. Dramatic stag antler chandeliers hang above well-spaced marble-topped tables and faux-leather banquettes. The appealing menu lists everything from quinoa salad to well-hung steaks, and the ingredients are top quality.

Carte £ 31/60

Lygon Arms Hotel, High St ✉ WR12 7DU – ✆ 01386 852255 – www.lygonarmshotel.co.uk

Russell's

MODERN BRITISH • FASHIONABLE XX An attractive Cotswold stone house in the centre of the village, with a smart brasserie-style interior and both a front and rear terrace. Choose from a constantly evolving selection of modern British dishes. Service is relaxed and friendly and bedrooms are stylish – there's even a spacious suite!

Menu £ 20 (weekdays) – Carte £ 29/57

7 rooms – £ 130/300 £ 130/300

20 High St WR12 7DT – 01386 853555 – www.russellsofbroadway.co.uk
– Closed Sunday dinner and bank holidays

Buckland Manor

HISTORIC • CLASSIC With its 13C origins, beautiful gardens and peaceful setting, this is one of England's most charming country houses. The elegant interior comprises tastefully appointed country house bedrooms and traditionally furnished guest areas featuring parquet floors, wood panelling and big open fires.

15 rooms – £ 205/580 £ 215/655

Buckland WR12 7LY – Southwest : 2.25 mi by B 4632 – 01386 852626
– www.bucklandmanor.com

Buckland Manor – See restaurant listing

Dormy House

LUXURY • CONTEMPORARY Behind the original farmhouse façade you'll find a modern interior and a luxurious spa. The odd beam and fireplace remain but bold contemporary fabrics and designer furnishings now feature too; wood and stone play a big part and the atmosphere is laid-back. The Potting Shed has an informal bistro feel, while the stylish Garden Room offers a sophisticated alternative.

38 rooms – £ 269 £ 269/545 – 10 suites

Willersey Hill WR12 7LF – East : 4 mi by A 44 – 01386 852711
– www.dormyhouse.co.uk

Garden Room – See restaurant listing

Lygon Arms N

HISTORIC • ROMANTIC A sympathetic refurbishment has retained this historical hotel's period charm, which comes courtesy of open fires, wonky ceilings and antique furnishings. The small wine bar serves Italian small plates and afternoon tea is popular in the pretty Russell Room. Bedrooms in the courtyard are the most spacious.

86 rooms – £ 195/235 £ 195/460 – 27 suites

High St WR12 7DU – 01386 852255 – www.lygonarmshotel.co.uk

Lygon Bar & Grill – See restaurant listing

The Fish

TRADITIONAL • PERSONALISED Up until the 16C the Benedictine monks kept their fish stocks in the local hillside caves – hence its name. Guest areas are set in a wood-clad building and include a British brasserie specialising in meats and grills. Scandinavian-style bedrooms are set in various outbuildings and have lovely country views.

63 rooms – £ 150/420 £ 150/420 – 3 suites

Farncombe Estate WR12 7LJ – East : 4 mi by A 44 – 01386 858000
– www.thefishhotel.co.uk

Foxhill Manor

COUNTRY HOUSE • DESIGN Once home to Henry Maudslay, who died in the Dam Busters raid; a Grade II listed Arts and Crafts house, where guests are made to feel as if they're staying in a private home. Striking bedrooms have first class facilities – 'Oak' has his and hers baths with a view. Modern 4 course menus are discussed with the chef; after dinner, relax on bean bags in front of the 74" TV.

8 rooms – £ 399/699 £ 399/699 – 2 suites

Farncombe Estate WR12 7LJ – East : 3.75 mi by A 44 – 01386 852711
– www.foxhillmanor.com

East House

HISTORIC • PERSONALISED Beautifully furnished, 18C former farmhouse in lovely mature gardens, with wood-burning stoves and a welcoming feel. Sumptuous beamed bedrooms mix antique furniture with modern technology; superb bathrooms have underfloor heating. The Jacobean Suite is the biggest room, with a four-poster and garden views.

4 rooms – †£ 185/225 ††£ 185/225

162 High St ✉ WR12 7AJ – ✆ 01386 853789 – www.easthouseuk.com

Mill Hay House

HISTORIC • ELEGANT This lovely 17C house, tucked away on the edge of the village, comes with beautiful gardens overlooking a lake. With just three individually furnished bedrooms, the atmosphere is intimate, and guests are treated as family friends.

3 rooms – †£ 175/225 ††£ 195/255

Snowshill Rd ✉ WR12 7JS – South : 0.5 mi – ✆ 01386 852498 – www.millhay.co.uk – Closed Christmas-New Year

Olive Branch

TOWNHOUSE • COSY Welcoming guesthouse run by an experienced husband and wife team. Pleasantly cluttered bedrooms with thoughtful extras; one has a small veranda. Rustic, characterful dining room with homemade cakes, breads and muesli at breakfast.

8 rooms – †£ 85/95 ††£ 117/125

78 High St ✉ WR12 7AJ – ✆ 01386 853440 – www.theolivebranch-broadway.com

Windrush House

FAMILY • COSY Welcoming guesthouse in a pretty village. Individually decorated bedrooms have bold feature walls: some use Laura Ashley designs and have wrought iron beds; four-poster 'Snowshill' is the best. Homemade jams feature at breakfast.

5 rooms – †£ 77/92 ††£ 87/112

Station Rd ✉ WR12 7DE – ✆ 01386 853577 – www.windrushhouse.com

BROCKENHURST

Hampshire – Pop. 3 552 – Regional map n° **4**-A2

The Pig

TRADITIONAL BRITISH • BRASSERIE A delightful conservatory with plants dotted about, an eclectic collection of old tables and chairs, and a bustling atmosphere. The forager and kitchen gardener supply what's best and any ingredients they can't get themselves are sourced from within 25 miles. Cooking is unfussy, wholesome and British-based.

Carte £ 32/45

The Pig Hotel, Beaulieu Rd ✉ SO42 7QL – East : 1 mi on B 3055 – ✆ 01590 622354 – www.thepighotel.com

The Pig

COUNTRY HOUSE • PERSONALISED This smart manor house hotel follows a philosophy of removing barriers and bringing nature indoors. Characterful bedrooms are divided between the house and a stable block, and boast distressed wood floors, chunky furnishings and large squashy beds. The comfy lounges and dining room have a shabby-chic style.

31 rooms – †£ 155/430 ††£ 155/430 – £ 15 – 3 suites

Beaulieu Rd ✉ SO42 7QL – East : 1 mi on B 3055 – ✆ 01590 622354 – www.thepighotel.com

The Pig – See restaurant listing

Daisybank Cottage

LUXURY • PERSONALISED This charming Arts and Craft house was inspired by Charles Rennie Mackintosh. Contemporary, boutique-style bedrooms boast extras such as robes and coffee machines; one room has a small inner courtyard terrace and there's a shepherd's hut in the garden with a terrace and luxury 'Private Privvy'.

8 rooms - £ 95/135 £ 110/160

Sway Rd ✉ SO42 7SG - South : 0.5 mi on B 3055 - ☎ 01590 622086 - www.bedandbreakfast-newforest.co.uk - Closed 10 days Christmas

BROMESWELL - Suffolk → See Woodbridge

BRUNTINGTHORPE

Leicestershire - Regional map n° **9**-B3

The Joiners

TRADITIONAL BRITISH • RUSTIC Beams and a tiled floor bring 17C character to this dining pub but designer wallpaper and fresh flower displays give it a chic overall feel. There's plenty of choice on the menus, with the likes of pork rillettes or pot-roast pheasant.

Menu £ 17 (weekday lunch) - Carte £ 26/40

Church Walk ✉ LE17 5QH - ☎ 0116 247 8258 (booking essential) - www.thejoinersarms.co.uk - Closed Sunday dinner and Monday

BRUTON

Somerset - Pop. 2 984 - Regional map n° **2**-C2

Roth Bar & Grill

TRADITIONAL BRITISH • DESIGN The converted outbuildings of a working farm now house this charming restaurant with its striking modern art exhibitions. Beef, pork and lamb from the farm are aged in their salting room. Be sure to try the caramelised lemonade.

Menu £ 25 (dinner) - Carte £ 23/47

Durslade Farm, Dropping Ln ✉ BA10 0NL - Southeast : 0.5 mi on B 3081 - ☎ 01749 814700 - www.rothbarandgrill.co.uk - lunch only and dinner Thursday-Saturday - Closed first week January, 25-27 December and Monday except bank holidays

At The Chapel

MEDITERRANEAN CUISINE • DESIGN A stylish, informal restaurant in a former 18C chapel, with a bakery to one side and a wine shop to the other. Daily menus offer rustic Mediterranean-influenced dishes; specialities include wood-fired breads, pizzas and cakes. Bedrooms are luxurious - Room 8 even has its own terrace.

Carte £ 22/44

8 rooms - £ 125/150 £ 125/250 - £ 12

High St ✉ BA10 0AE - ☎ 01749 814070 - www.atthechapel.co.uk - Closed 25 December

BRYHER → See Scilly (Isles of)

BUCKDEN

Cambridgeshire - Pop. 2 385 - Regional map n° **8**-A2

George

HISTORIC • PERSONALISED Delightfully restored part black and white, part red-brick coaching inn. Original flag floors mix with modern furnishings, creating a stylish, understated feel. The simple yet tastefully decorated bedrooms are named after famous 'Georges'. Classic brasserie dishes feature in the restaurant.

12 rooms - £ 95/150 £ 120/150

High St ✉ PE19 5XA - ☎ 01480 812300 - www.thegeorgebuckden.com

BUDE

Cornwall - Pop. 5 091 - Regional map n° **1**-B2

Beach

BOUTIQUE HOTEL • CONTEMPORARY A spacious New England style hotel with views over the Atlantic Ocean and a pleasingly laid-back feel. Contemporary bedrooms have limed oak furnishings and the latest mod cons; 'Deluxe' boast roll-top baths and either a terrace or balcony. The smart restaurant and bar offers classic dishes and grills.

18 rooms - £ 138/240 £ 150/254

Summerleaze Cres. ✉ EX23 8HL - ✆ 01288 389800 - www.thebeachatbude.co.uk - Closed 24-26 December

BURCHETT'S GREEN

Windsor and Maidenhead - Pop. 306 - Regional map n° **6**-C3

Crown (Simon Bonwick)

REGIONAL CUISINE • RUSTIC The Crown is very personally and passionately run by the Bonwick family and comes with a small bar and two intimate, open-fired dining rooms. The refined, deftly prepared dishes - six per course - are decided upon daily; the options are diverse and appealing, with flavours clearly defined.

→ Salcombe crab with apple, passion fruit, cashew. Roast rump of Texel lamb, confit garlic and sarriette. Coffee and walnut bavarois, brittle bitter chocolate.

Carte £ 24/42

✉ SL6 6QZ - ✆ 01628 824079 - www.thecrownburchettsgreen.com - Closed Monday, Tuesday and Sunday dinner

BURFORD

Oxfordshire - Pop. 1 171 - Regional map n° **6**-A2

Lamb Inn

TRADITIONAL BRITISH • COSY This charming 15C inn is a place of two halves: the cosy, antique-furnished bar serves old favourites, while the more romantic, crisply-laid candlelit restaurant offers skilfully prepared, creative modern dishes. The garden is a must in warmer weather and the bijoux country bedrooms offer plenty of extras.

Carte £ 28/51

17 rooms - £ 110/200 £ 120/210

Sheep St ✉ OX18 4LR - ✆ 01993 823155 - www.cotswold-inns-hotels.co.uk/the-lamb-inn

Burford House

TRADITIONAL • PERSONALISED The welcome is warm at this delightful part-timbered 17C house, where spacious, comfy bedrooms - including 3 four-posters - mix traditional styling with contemporary touches. Cosy sitting rooms and a lovely terrace for afternoon tea.

6 rooms - £ 100/180 £ 100/220

99 High St ✉ OX18 4QA - ✆ 01993 823151 - www.burford-house.co.uk

at Swinbrook East: 2.75 mi by A40 ✉ Burford

Swan Inn

MODERN BRITISH • PUB Wisteria-clad, honey-coloured pub on the riverbank, boasting a lovely garden filled with fruit trees. The charming interior displays an open oak frame and exposed stone walls hung with old lithographs and handmade walking sticks. The daily menu showcases the latest local produce and features modern takes on older recipes. Well-appointed bedrooms have a luxurious feel.

Carte £ 24/35

11 rooms - £ 85 £ 125/195

✉ OX18 4DY - ✆ 01993 823339 - www.theswanswinbrook.co.uk - Closed 25-26 December

BURNHAM MARKET

Norfolk - Pop. 877 - Regional map n° **8**-C1

Socius

MODERN BRITISH • DESIGN XX One meaning of the Latin word Socius is 'sharing' - and it is all about sharing at this smart, Scandic-style restaurant. Sit up on the steel-framed mezzanine level or on the ground floor to watch the chefs hard at work. Unfussy modern small plates feature on a flexible, constantly evolving menu.

Carte £ 22/37

11 Foundry Pl ✉ PE31 8LG - ✆ 01328 738307 - www.sociusnorfolk.co.uk - Closed 2 weeks January, 25-26 December, Sunday dinner, Monday and Tuesday

North Street Bistro

TRADITIONAL BRITISH • BISTRO X An old flint chapel set just off the village green; inside it's small and simply decorated, with high ceilings and a bistro feel. Cooking is fresh and unfussy, with local produce well used. Flavours are clear and textures are complementary. It's proudly run by Dan, Holly and their charming young team.

Menu £ 15 (lunch) - Carte £ 24/37

20 North St ✉ PE31 8HG - ✆ 01328 730330 (booking essential at dinner) - www.20northstreet.co.uk - Closed 24-27 December and Sunday dinner-Wednesday lunch

Hoste

INN • PERSONALISED At the heart of a pretty village you'll find this greatly extended inn with two annexes: one a townhouse; the other an old station master's house which comprises three cottages and a railway carriage. It also has a small museum, cinema and spa. Bedrooms range from traditional to luxurious and one even has a weekend butler service. The brasserie serves British favourites.

62 rooms - †£ 165/260 ††£ 195/340

The Green ✉ PE31 8HD - ✆ 01328 738777 - www.thehoste.com

BURPHAM - West Sussex → See Arundel

BURTON BRADSTOCK → See Bridport

BURTON-UPON-TRENT

Staffordshire - Pop. 72 299 - Regional map n° **10**-C1

99 Station Street

TRADITIONAL BRITISH • NEIGHBOURHOOD X Amongst the vast brewing towers is this bright, boldly decorated neighbourhood restaurant, run by two experienced locals. They make everything on the premises daily and showcase regional ingredients; try the mature rare breed meats.

Menu £ 15 (weekday lunch) - Carte £ 24/38

99 Station St ✉ DE14 1BT - ✆ 01283 516859 - www.99stationstreet.com - Closed Sunday dinner-Wednesday lunch

BURY

Greater Manchester - Pop. 77 211 - Regional map n° **11**-B2

Bird at Birtle

TRADITIONAL BRITISH • BISTRO X A very popular restaurant in a modernised pub. Start with a cocktail on a comfy sofa or out on the terrace then head upstairs to the stylish dining room with its balcony and fell views. Classic dishes are given a modern touch.

Carte £ 24/35

293 Bury and Rochdale Old Rd, Birtle ✉ OL10 4BQ - East : 2.25 mi on B 6222 - ✆ 01706 540500 - www.thebirdatbirtle.co.uk

BURY ST EDMUNDS

Suffolk - Pop. 41 113 - Regional map n° **8**-C2

Pea Porridge

MODERN BRITISH • BISTRO X A charming former bakery in two 19C cottages, with its original bread oven still in situ. Tasty country cooking is led by the seasons and has a Mediterranean bias; many dishes are cooked in the wood-fired oven. It has a stylish, rustic look and a homely feel - its name is a reference to the old town green.

Menu £ 19 (lunch) - Carte dinner £ 28/35

28-29 Cannon St ✉ IP33 1JR - ✆ 01284 700200 - www.peaporridge.co.uk - Closed first week January, 2 weeks summer, last week December, Sunday-Monday and lunch Tuesday-Wednesday

Maison Bleue

FRENCH • NEIGHBOURHOOD XX A passionately run town centre restaurant in a converted 17C house, complete with wooden panelling and impressive fish sculptures. Cooking is classically French at heart but has modern and Asian touches. Seafood is a strength and you must try the excellent French cheeses.

Menu £ 26 (weekday lunch)/37 - Carte £ 39/57

30-31 Churchgate St ✉ IP33 1RG - ✆ 01284 760623 - www.maisonbleue.co.uk - Closed 23 December-16 January, first 2 weeks September Sunday and Monday

1921

MODERN CUISINE • INTIMATE XX A fine period house located at 19-21 Angel Hill; its smart, modern facelift complements the original beams and red-brick inglenook fireplace. Cooking displays a modern flair and features some interesting combinations.

Menu £ 18 (lunch) - Carte £ 32/49

19-21 Angel Hill ✉ IP33 1UZ - ✆ 01284 704870 - www.nineteen-twentyone.co.uk - Closed 2 weeks Christmas-New Year, Sunday and Monday

Eaterie

TRADITIONAL BRITISH • BRASSERIE X An airy two-roomed bistro set within an attractive 15C coaching inn where Dickens once stayed. There's an impressive modern chandelier and a display of the owner's contemporary art. Tasty British brasserie dishes use local produce.

Carte dinner £ 22/49

Angel Hotel, 3 Angel Hill ✉ IP33 1LT - ✆ 01284 714000 - www.theangel.co.uk

Angel

HISTORIC • PERSONALISED The creeper-clad Georgian façade hides a surprisingly stylish hotel. Relax in the atmospheric bar or smart lounges. Individually designed bedrooms offer either classic four-poster luxury or come with funky décor and iPod docks.

77 rooms - †£ 139/189 ††£ 139/189

3 Angel Hill ✉ IP33 1LT - ✆ 01284 714000 - www.theangel.co.uk

Eaterie - See restaurant listing

Northgate

TOWNHOUSE • CONTEMPORARY Stylish, elegantly understated bedrooms give this fine period townhouse a luxurious feel. Try something from the extensive cocktail list in the cosy bar or head through to the pleasant terrace. The two dining rooms have impressive ceilings and serve flavoursome modern dishes; there's also a chef's table.

9 rooms - †£ 120/210 ††£ 135/210

Northgate St ✉ IP33 1HP - ✆ 01284 339604 - www.thenorthgate.com

at Horringer Southwest: 3 mi on A143 ✉ Bury St Edmunds

Ickworth

HISTORIC • CLASSIC This family-orientated hotel occupies the east wing of a grand 200 year old mansion set in 1,800 acres: former home of the 7th Marquess of Bristol and now owned by the National Trust. It features huge art-filled lounges, antique-furnished bedrooms and luxurious suites. Dine in the formal restaurant or in the impressive orangery, which serves relaxed meals and high teas.

39 rooms – †£ 150/395 ††£ 250/595 – 12 suites

✉ IP29 5QE – ✆ 01284 735350 – www.ickworthhotel.co.uk

BUTLERS CROSS

Buckinghamshire – Regional map n° **6**-C2

Russell Arms

TRADITIONAL BRITISH • INN You'll find walkers relaxing at the tables to the side and a large terrace to the rear. Daily coffee mornings are followed by a great value lunchtime 'plat du jour' and on Fridays they host children's tea parties. The chef knows how to get the best out of his ingredients and dishes are packed with flavour.

Carte £ 27/35

2 Chalkshire Rd ✉ HP17 0TS – ✆ 01296 624411 – www.therussellarms.co.uk – Closed 25-26 December and Monday

CALLINGTON

Cornwall – Pop. 4 698 – Regional map n° **1**-C2

Langmans

MODERN BRITISH • INTIMATE XX Langmans is run by a husband and wife and dining here is an all-night affair. Pre-dinner drinks with your fellow guests are followed by a tasting menu in the formal dining room; cooking is refined and they have a great cheese selection.

Menu £ 48 – tasting menu only

3 Church St ✉ PL17 7RE – ✆ 01579 384933 (booking essential) – www.langmansrestaurant.co.uk – dinner only – Closed Sunday-Wednesday

Cadson Manor

WORKING FARM • PERSONALISED Welcoming guesthouse on a 600 year old working farm, with views over an iron age settlement. Cosy, individually furnished bedrooms feature antiques, fresh flowers and a decanter of sherry. Rayburn-cooked breakfasts include weekly specials.

3 rooms – †£ 85 ††£ 120/125

✉ PL17 7HW – Southwest : 2.75 mi by A 390 – ✆ 01579 383969 – www.cadsonmanor.co.uk – Closed Christmas

CAMBER

East Sussex – Pop. 1 265 – Regional map n° **5**-C2

Gallivant

BOUTIQUE HOTEL • SEASIDE A laid-back hotel opposite set opposite the beach and run by a friendly team. Relax by the fire in the New England style lounge. Bedrooms come in blues and whites, with distressed wood furniture, bespoke beds and modern facilities – those to the rear have decked terraces.

20 rooms – †£ 115/230 ††£ 125/240

New Lydd Rd. ✉ TN31 7RB – ✆ 01797 225057 – www.thegallivant.co.uk

GOOD TIPS!

This thriving city has stood on the banks of the River Cam since Roman times, with the world-famous university appearing relatively recently in the 13C. Where better to celebrate obtaining a first-class degree than Michelin Two-Starred Midsummer House? Wherever you find students, you'll also find pubs; try Pint Shop for gutsy, satisfying fare.

CAMBRIDGE

Cambridgeshire - Pop. 123 867 - Regional map n° **8**-B3

Restaurants

✿✿ Midsummer House (Daniel Clifford)

MODERN CUISINE • ELEGANT XXX A beautiful Victorian house with a lovely conservatory extension plays host to this stylish restaurant. It's set in an idyllic location overlooking Midsummer Common and the first floor lounge and terrace make the perfect spot for drinks and canapés, as they look over the garden and the River Cam.

Experienced chef-owner Daniel Clifford offers a good-sized fixed price menu - which could include a dish to share - alongside a multi-course tasting menu. Creative, highly accomplished cooking has a classic base but also comes with plenty of personality. Dishes may seem quite simple at first but their appearance belies their complex composition, as they have great depth of flavour and well-balanced textures. Colours are vibrant, produce is top quality and the main ingredient of each dish is allowed to shine.

→ Scallop with Granny Smith apple, celeriac and truffle purée. Braised turbot, cuttlefish, clams and seaweed with gnocchi and jus de cuisson. Tarte Tatin with garlic and bay foam and vanilla ice cream.

Menu £ 69/118

Town plan: B1-a - *Midsummer Common ✉ CB4 1HA - ✆ 01223 369299 - www.midsummerhouse.co.uk - Closed last week December, first week January, Sunday, Monday and lunch Tuesday*

Alimentum

BRITISH MODERN • MINIMALIST XX Alimentum is unusually located on the ground floor of a suburban apartment block but, inside, has a smart, modern feel. Combinations are original and flavours are clearly defined. Ask for a table by the kitchen window.

Menu £ 28 (lunch and early dinner)/55

152-154 Hills Rd ✉ CB2 8PB - Southeast : 1.5 mi by Regent St on Hills Rd - ✆ 01223 413000 - www.restaurantalimentum.co.uk - Closed 24-30 December and Monday-Tuesday

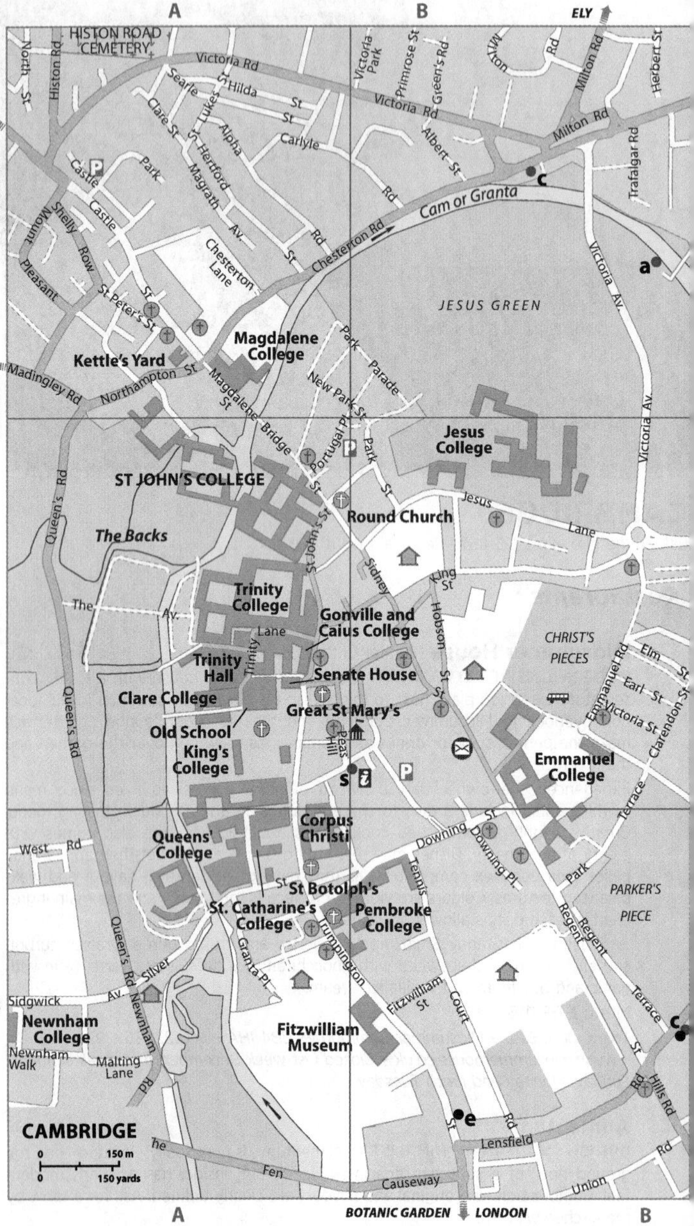
CAMBRIDGE
150 m
150 yards
A
B
1
2
3
ELY
HUNTINGDOW
BEDFORD
BOTANIC GARDEN
LONDON
HISTON ROAD CEMETERY
Victoria Rd
Histon Rd
North St
Searle St
Hilda St
Clare St
St Lukes St
Alpha Rd
Carlyle Rd
Hertford St
Magrath Av.
Castle St
Castle St
Shelly Row
Mount Pleasant
Chesterton Lane
Chesterton Rd
Cam or Granta
St Peter's St
Kettle's Yard
Madingley Rd
Northampton St
Magdalene College
Magdalene St
Magdalene Bridge St
Park Parade
New Park St
Portugal Pl.
Park St
Victoria Park
Primrose St
Green's Rd
Milton Rd
Milton Rd
Herbert St
Albert St
Trafalgar Rd
Victoria Av.
JESUS GREEN
Jesus College
Jesus Lane
ST JOHN'S COLLEGE
St John's St
Round Church
Sidney St
King St
Hobson St
The Backs
Queen's Rd
The Av.
Trinity College
Trinity Lane
Gonville and Caius College
Trinity Hall
Senate House
Clare College
Great St Mary's
Old School
King's College
Peas Hill
CHRIST'S PIECES
Emmanuel Rd
Elm St
Earl St
Victoria St
Clarendon St
Emmanuel College
Corpus Christi
Queens' College
West Rd
Downing St
Downing Pl.
Tennis Court Rd
St Botolph's
Pembroke College
St. Catharine's College
Trumpington St
Granta Pl.
Silver St
Fitzwilliam St
Fitzwilliam Museum
Park Terrace
Regent St
Regent Terrace
PARKER'S PIECE
Sidgwick Av.
Newnham College
Newnham Walk
Malting Lane
Newnham Rd
The Fen Causeway
Lensfield Rd
Hills Rd
Union Rd
a
c
c
e
s

Cotto

MODERN CUISINE • INTIMATE XX A stylish, sophisticated hotel restaurant set in a modern glass extension. The experienced chef skilfully prepares a wide range of dishes which are made up of many different components; the chocolate desserts are a highlight.

Menu £70/75

Town plan: B3-c - *Gonville Hotel, Gonville Pl. ✉ CB1 1LY - ✆ 01223 302010 (booking essential) - www.cottocambridge.co.uk - dinner only - Closed 2 weeks August, Easter, Sunday and Monday*

Navadhanya

INDIAN • CONTEMPORARY DÉCOR XX This former pub is home to a well-regarded restaurant with white décor and a contemporary look. Dishes take their influences from around India and exhibit a modern style, while at the same time respecting tradition.

Carte £20/49

73 Newmarket Rd ✉ CB5 8EG - East : 0.75 mi on A 1134 - ✆ 01223 300583 - www.navadhanya.co.uk - dinner only - Closed Monday

Restaurant 22

MODERN CUISINE • INTIMATE XX This long-standing restaurant in a converted Victorian townhouse is now run by a young couple, Sam and Alex, who have given it a contemporary makeover with a monochrome theme. Ambitious modern cooking features plenty of contrasting textures and tastes; most diners opt for the tasting menus.

Menu £20/45 - Carte £30/42

Town plan: B1-c - *22 Chesterton Rd ✉ CB4 3AX - ✆ 01223 351880 (booking essential) - www.restaurant22.co.uk - dinner only - Closed 24 December-2 January, Sunday and Monday*

Pint Shop

BRITISH TRADITIONAL • PUB 'MEAT. BEER. BREAD.' is written on the window - and that pretty much sums this place up. Cooking is gutsy and satisfying and the charcoal grill takes centre stage. To accompany are 10 keg beers, 6 cask beers and over 70 different gins.

Menu £13 (lunch and early dinner) - Carte £19/32

Town plan: B2-s - *10 Peas Hill ✉ CB2 3NP - ✆ 01223 352293 - www.pintshop.co.uk - Closed 25-26 December and 1 January*

Hotels

Hotel du Vin

TOWNHOUSE • DESIGN Stylish hotel set over a row of 16C and 17C ex-university owned buildings. Original quarry tiled floors and wood-panelled walls feature, along with plenty of passages, nooks and crannies. Chic, modern bedrooms include one with its own cinema. The appealing bistro has a Gallic-led menu.

41 rooms - †£120/400 ††£120/400 - ☕ £17

Town plan: B3-e - *15-19 Trumpington St ✉ CB2 1QA - ✆ 01223 928991 - www.hotelduvin.com*

Tamburlaine

BUSINESS • CONTEMPORARY This modern business hotel is named after Christopher Marlowe's play and is well-located for those travelling by train. Bedrooms are spacious, light and well-equipped, and make good use of different textures in their furnishings. The pretty restaurant has a botanical theme and a laid-back feel.

155 rooms - †£200/340 ††£200/340 - ☕ £10 - 2 suites

27-29 Station Rd ✉ CB1 2FB - Southeast : 0.75 mi by Regent St off Hills Rd - ✆ 01223 792888 - www.thetamburlaine.co.uk

Gonville

BUSINESS • CONTEMPORARY A well-located hotel with the city's main attractions just a stroll away across the common. Bedrooms have smart black and red colour schemes and come with iPads; the rear rooms are quieter. Enjoy a cocktail in the chic bar followed by a casual meal in the brasserie or dinner in the sophisticated restaurant.

84 rooms – £ 165/255 £ 165/255

Town plan: B3-c – *Gonville Pl ✉ CB1 1LY – ✆ 01223 366611 – www.gonvillehotel.co.uk*

Cotto – See restaurant listing

at Horningsea Northeast: 4 mi by A1303 and B1047 ✉ Cambridge

Crown & Punchbowl

MODERN BRITISH • PUB Watch your head on the beams as you enter the bar, then take you pick from several different seating areas. Start with rustic bread and zingy olive oil then move on to modern seasonal dishes or one of the wide-ranging specials chalked on the fish board. Cosy, welcoming bedrooms are named after local writers.

Menu £ 22 (weekdays) – Carte £ 27/43

5 rooms – £ 85/120 £ 85/120 – £ 10

High St ✉ CB25 9JG – ✆ 01223 860643 – www.cambscuisine.com

CAMELFORD

Cornwall – Pop. 2 335 – Regional map n° **1**-B2

Pendragon Country House

COUNTRY HOUSE • PERSONALISED This former vicarage is run by an extremely enthusiastic couple and offers views across the fields to the church it once served. There's always a jigsaw on the go in the period furnished drawing room and Cornish artwork features throughout. Home-baked breads, homemade cake and local produce feature.

7 rooms – £ 65/75 £ 95/150

Davidstow ✉ PL32 9XR – Northeast : 3.5 mi by A 39 on A 395 – ✆ 01840 261131 – www.pendragoncountryhouse.com – Closed 23-27 December

CANTERBURY

Kent – Pop. 54 880 – Regional map n° **5**-D2

Corner House

MODERN BRITISH • BISTRO A characterful former pub on the edge of the city; reputedly Charles Dickens' local, with underground passages leading to the cathedral. Appealing modern British dishes make good use of Kentish produce and everything is made on-site. Bedrooms are comfy – the rate includes a continental breakfast in your room.

Menu £ 16 (lunch) – Carte £ 27/42

3 rooms – £ 79/150 £ 79/150

1 Dover St ✉ CT1 3HD – ✆ 01227 780793 – www.cornerhouserestaurants.co.uk

The Goods Shed

TRADITIONAL BRITISH • RUSTIC Daily farmers' market and food hall in an early Victorian locomotive shed, selling an excellent variety of organic, free range and homemade produce. Hearty, rustic, daily changing dishes are served at scrubbed wooden tables.

Carte £ 24/37

Station Rd West, St Dunstans ✉ CT2 8AN – ✆ 01227 459153 – www.thegoodsshed.co.uk – Closed 25-26 December, 1-2 January, Sunday dinner and Monday

at Fordwich Northeast : 2.75 mi by A28

Fordwich Arms (Daniel Smith)

MODERN CUISINE • COSY England's smallest town plays host to this elegant Arts and Crafts style pub, which boasts an impressive bar and a wood-panelled dining room by the river. The provenance of ingredients is key and they butcher beasts, cure meats, churn butter and bake bread on-site. Pared-down dishes are perfectly balanced.

→ Pheasant dumplings, roasted onion and herb broth. Cornish hake, wild garlic, girolles and Gusborne lees. Brioche with fruit cake ice cream and caramel apple.

Menu £ 35 (weekdays) - Carte £ 38/52

King St ✉ CT2 0DB - ✆ 01227 710444 - www.fordwicharms.co.uk - Closed Sunday dinner and Monday

CARBIS BAY - Cornwall → See St Ives

CARLISLE

Cumbria - Pop. 75 306 - Regional map n° **12**-A1

The Halston

HISTORIC BUILDING • MODERN An impressive Georgian building - the city's old Post Office - houses this stylish aparthotel. Well-furnished suites come with a lounge and a fully equipped kitchen but you can also enjoy small plates in the bar or modern dishes in the brasserie. It makes a great base for exploring northern Cumbria.

22 suites - ††£ 110/300 - ☕ £ 12

20-34 Warwick Rd ✉ CA1 1AB - ✆ 01228 210240 - www.thehalston.com

CARTMEL

Cumbria - Regional map n° **12**-A3

L'Enclume (Simon Rogan)

CREATIVE • HISTORIC XXX Opened in 2002 by Simon Rogan and his wife, L'Enclume has become as synonymous with this sleepy little Lakeland village as sticky toffee pudding and horse racing. Indeed, it's been so successful, that the couple also opened the more relaxed Rogan & Co restaurant, as well as stylish bedrooms which are spread about various houses in the village.

The characterful old building still displays evidence of its 'smithy' days and its location next to a brook makes it a truly charming spot on a warm summer's evening. 20 or so courses make up the well-balanced, perfectly paced tasting menu and produce from their 12 acre farm guides the fiercely seasonal dishes, which are passionately prepared, innovative and full of interest. Flavours are natural and harmonious and an array of textures stimulates the palate. For those wanting to immerse themselves further, the development kitchen, Aulis, opens at weekends.

→ Smoked eel with fermented sweetcorn. Herdwick lamb with stout and black garlic. Compressed pear with eucalyptus from our farm.

Menu £ 59/155 - tasting menu only

16 rooms ☕ - †£ 130/315 ††£ 180/435

Cavendish St ✉ LA11 6PZ - ✆ 015395 36362 (booking essential) - www.lenclume.co.uk - Closed 1 week January and Monday

Rogan & Co

CREATIVE BRITISH • COSY XX L'Enclume's more laid-back cousin is housed within a pretty cottage by a stream and its cosy, rustic interior is hung with Lakeland photography. Simon Rogan's influence is clear to see in skilfully prepared, understated dishes which make use of creative flavour combinations. The set lunch is great value.

→ Terrine of our farm pork, apricot and pork fat. Halibut in mussel broth, sea beets & black garlic. Baked cheesecake with lightly spiced pineapple.

Menu £ 25 (lunch) - Carte £ 33/45

Devonshire Sq ✉ LA11 6QD - ✆ 015395 35917 - www.roganandco.co.uk - Closed 2 weeks January

CASTLE COMBE

Wiltshire – Pop. 347 – Regional map n° **2**-C2

✿ Bybrook

MODERN BRITISH • ELEGANT XXX Spacious dining room within a charming 14C manor house. Large, well-spaced oak tables are immaculately laid. Menus offer refined, carefully prepared dishes with a classical base and modern overtones. Local and kitchen garden produce plays a pivotal role, with cooking following the seasons.

→ Fillet of mackerel with crab, Exmoor caviar and avocado. Wiltshire lamb, asparagus, morels and sweetbread foam. Egg custard tart with poached rhubarb and nougatine.

Menu £ 75/95

Manor House Hotel and Golf Club, ✉ SN14 7HR – ✆ 01249 782206 – www.exclusive.co.uk – dinner only

Manor House H. and Golf Club

LUXURY • ELEGANT Fine period manor house in 365 acres of formal gardens and parkland. The interior exudes immense charm, with characterful oak panelling and a host of open-fired lounges. Luxurious bedrooms are split between the main house and mews cottages. Book ahead for one of the event days.

50 rooms – £ 220/460 £ 220/460 – 8 suites

✉ SN14 7HR – ✆ 01249 782206 – www.exclusive.co.uk

✿ **Bybrook** – See restaurant listing

Castle Inn

HISTORIC • COSY A delightful 12C inn set in a charming village. A sympathetic refurbishment has retained its original rustic features but added contemporary touches; ask for a room with a four-poster bed. There are two cosy lounges, an atmospheric bar and a pubby dining room. Menus cover all the old favourites.

12 rooms – £ 65/95 £ 145/235

✉ SN14 7HN – ✆ 01249 783030 – www.thecastleinn.co.uk – Closed 25 December

CASTOR

Peterborough – Pop. 1 393 – Regional map n° **8**-A2

Chubby Castor (N)

MODERN BRITISH • INTIMATE XX Having spent most of his life in London, Adebola Adeshina found a new home in this 400 year old thatched pub. Inside it's surprisingly modern, with a smart lounge and an intimate linen-laid dining room. Time-honoured recipes are reworked, with flavourful dishes presented in a restrained modern vein.

Menu £ 28 (lunch) – Carte £ 31/62

Fitzwilliam Arms, 34 Peterborough Rd ✉ PE5 7AX – ✆ 01733 380801 – www.thechubbycastor.com

CATEL/CASTEL → See Channel Islands (Guernsey)

CHADDESLEY CORBETT

Worcestershire – Pop. 1 440 – Regional map n° **10**-C2

Brockencote Hall

COUNTRY HOUSE • CONTEMPORARY Follow the long drive, past a lake and grazing cattle, to this 19C mansion with the feel of a French château. Period features blend well with contemporary country house furnishings and bold colour schemes, and bedrooms are spacious and well-equipped. The elegant restaurant overlooks the gardens.

21 rooms – £ 130/320 £ 170/370

✉ DY10 4PY – On A 448 – ✆ 01562 777876 – www.brockencotehall.com

CHAGFORD

Devon – Pop. 1 020 – Regional map n° **1**-C2

Gidleigh Park

MODERN CUISINE • ELEGANT XXXX Within a grand Edwardian house you'll find these three intimate dining rooms, where produce from the kitchen garden is showcased in understatedly elegant dishes comprising just 2 or 3 ingredients. Cooking has a traditional base but displays a lightness of touch and some modern twists.

→ Anjou squab with parsnip, bacon and an onion dressing. Monkfish, Jerusalem artichoke, chicken dressing and seaweed. Passion fruit mousse with mango, coconut and lime granité

Menu £ 65/125

Gidleigh Park Hotel, ✉ TQ13 8HH – Northwest : 2 mi by Gidleigh Rd – ✆ 01647 432367 (booking essential) – www.gidleigh.co.uk

Gidleigh Park

LUXURY • ELEGANT A stunningly located and truly impressive Arts and Crafts house with lovely tiered gardens and Teign Valley views. Luxurious sitting and drawing rooms have a classic country house feel but a contemporary edge; wonderfully comfortable bedrooms echo this, with their appealing mix of styles.

24 rooms – †£ 248/945 ††£ 248/945 – 1 suite

✉ TQ13 8HH – Northwest : 2 mi by Gidleigh Rd – ✆ 01647 432367 – www.gidleigh.co.uk

Gidleigh Park – See restaurant listing

at Sandypark Northeast: 2.25 mi on A382 ✉ Chagford

Mill End

TRADITIONAL • PERSONALISED Whitewashed former mill off a quiet country road: once home to Frank Whittle, inventor of the jet engine. Comfy, cosy lounges with beams and open fires. Contemporary bedrooms have bold feature walls and colourful throws. Bright dining room offers classical dishes prepared using local produce.

15 rooms – †£ 90/105 ††£ 110/130 – 1 suite

✉ TQ13 8JN – On A 382 – ✆ 01647 432282 – www.millendhotel.com – Closed 5-21 January

Michelin

CHANNEL ISLANDS

Regional map n° **3**-B2

ALDERNEY

Alderney - Pop. 2 400 - Regional map n° **3**-B1

Braye

Braye Beach

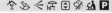

COUNTRY HOUSE · MODERN Stylish hotel on Braye beach, just a stone's throw from the harbour. The vaulted basement houses two lounges and a 19-seater cinema; above is a modern bar with a delightful terrace. Bedrooms are beech-furnished, and some have balconies and bay views. The formal restaurant showcases local island seafood.

27 rooms - £ 100/180 £ 120/240

Braye St. ✉ GY9 3XT - ☎ 01481 824300 - www.brayebeach.com

GUERNSEY

Guernsey - Pop. 58 867 - Regional map n° **3**-A2

Castel

Cobo Bay

FAMILY · MODERN Modern hotel set on the peaceful side of the island and well run by the 3rd generation of the family. Bright, stylish bedrooms come with fresh fruit, irons, safes and bathrobes - some have large balconies overlooking the sandy bay. Smart dining room; sit on the spacious terrace for lovely sunset views.

34 rooms - £ 49/219 £ 79/219

Cobo Coast Rd ✉ GY5 7HB
- ☎ 01481 257102 - www.cobobayhotel.com
- Closed 1 January-28 March

Fermain Bay

Fermain Valley

COUNTRY HOUSE · MODERN Stylish hotel with beautiful gardens, hidden in a picturesque valley and affording pleasant bay views through the trees. Well-equipped bedrooms are widely dispersed; the 'Gold' rooms have balconies. Dine with a view in Ocean or from a steakhouse menu - accompanied by cocktails - in contemporary Rock Garden.

45 rooms - £ 60/150 £ 100/175

Fermain Ln ✉ GY1 1ZZ - ☎ 01481 235666 - www.fermainvalley.com

St Peter Port

Le Nautique

CLASSIC CUISINE • MEDITERRANEAN DÉCOR XX An old sailmaker's warehouse on the quayside, with a stylish nautical interior and a pleasant marina view - ask for a window seat. The large menu offers classic dishes and the fish specials are worth considering.

Menu £ 19 (weekday lunch) - Carte £ 32/59

Quay Steps ✉ GY1 2LE - ✆ 01481 721714 - www.lenautiquerestaurant.co.uk - Closed Sunday

The Hook

MEATS AND GRILLS • FASHIONABLE X Start with a cocktail on the 3rd floor then head for the sushi bar or the buzzy restaurant with harbour views. Dishes arrive in satisfying portions - steaks are a speciality, with larger 'sharing' cuts featured on the blackboard.

Menu £ 19 (lunch and early dinner) - Carte £ 22/49

North Plantation (1st floor) ✉ GY1 2LQ - ✆ 01481 701373 - www.thehook.gg - Closed Sunday lunch January-May and Sunday dinner

Slaughterhouse

TRADITIONAL BRITISH • FASHIONABLE X Old meat hooks hanging from the ceiling of this chic, buzzy bar and brasserie, hint at its past as the island's former slaughterhouse. Dine on the mezzanine for the best views. Extensive menus list fresh, tasty dishes.

Carte £ 24/50

Castle Pier ✉ GY1 1AU - ✆ 01481 712123 - www.slaughterhouse.gg

Old Government House H. & Spa

HISTORIC BUILDING • CLASSIC Fine, classically furnished 18C building, with many of its original features restored, including a glorious ballroom. Individually styled bedrooms have padded walls, modern bathrooms and a personal touch. Relax in the well-equipped spa or outdoor pool. Authentic Indian cooking in The Curry Room. The smart yet informal brasserie has a delightful terrace.

62 rooms - †£ 193/404 ††£ 193/404 - 1 suite

St Ann's Pl ✉ GY1 2NU - ✆ 01481 724921 - www.theoghhotel.com

Duke of Richmond

BUSINESS • CONTEMPORARY Contemporary hotel with a bright reception area and a stylish lounge ideal for afternoon tea. Smart, modern bedrooms; some with balconies. Relax in the secluded pool or on the patio overlooking the 19C Candie Gardens. A chic bar with leopard print furnishings leads to the restaurant and terrace.

73 rooms - †£ 165/378 ††£ 165/378 - 1 suite

Cambridge Pk. ✉ GY1 1UY - ✆ 01481 726221 - www.dukeofrichmond.com

Duke of Normandie

BUSINESS • MODERN A former German HQ during the WW2 invasions; superbly located in the centre of town. Brightly coloured designer bedrooms have a cosy feel and some are set in the courtyard. The characterful bar is decorated with historical island memorabilia and offers traditional pub dishes.

37 rooms - †£ 49/84 ††£ 79/169 - £ 13

Lefebvre St ✉ GY1 2JP - ✆ 01481 721431 - www.dukeofnormandie.com

La Frégate

HISTORIC BUILDING • CONTEMPORARY Greatly extended 18C property offering stunning panoramic views across the harbour and out towards the island of Herm. Bedrooms have a clean contemporary style; go for one with a balcony or terrace. Extensive menus feature modern international dishes. Breakfast on the terrace is hard to beat.

22 rooms - †£ 100/110 ††£ 205/265 - 1 suite

Beauregard Ln, Les Cotils ✉ GY1 1UT - ✆ 01481 724624 - www.lafregatehotel.com

Ziggurat

TOWNHOUSE • MEDITERRANEAN A relaxed, boutique townhouse with a slightly bohemian style. The North African décor focuses on warm colours and ornate furnishings and the restaurant has a North African menu to match. A lovely terrace overlooks the harbour and the castle, and luxury sheds in the garden are great for small gatherings.

14 rooms – £ 70/110 £ 120/150

5 Constitution Steps ✉ *GY1 2PN – ✆ 01481 723008 – www.hotelziggurat.com*

St Saviour

Farmhouse

TRADITIONAL • MODERN Former farm restyled in a boutique vein. Stylish, sumptuous bedrooms come with hi-tech amenities and the bathrooms have heated floors. The pleasant garden features a pool, a terrace and a kitchen garden. Contemporary cooking has an international edge and uses the island's finest produce in eclectic ways.

14 rooms – £ 139/239 £ 139/239

Route des Bas Courtils ✉ *GY7 9YF – ✆ 01481 264181 – www.thefarmhouse.gg*

HERM

Herm – Pop. 60 – Regional map n° **3**-A2

White House

COUNTRY HOUSE • TRADITIONAL The only hotel on this tranquil, car-free island. The lounge offers bay views and the vast tropical gardens come with tennis courts and a pool. Airy bedrooms are split between the house and various cottages. Enjoy classically prepared local produce in the Conservatory or more modern fare in the Ship Inn.

40 rooms – £ 45/117 £ 90/234

✉ *GY1 3HR – ✆ 01481 750075 – www.herm.com – Closed mid-week October-March*

JERSEY

C.I. – Pop. 85 150 – Regional map n° **3**-B2

Beaumont

Mark Jordan at the Beach

MEDITERRANEAN CUISINE • NEIGHBOURHOOD XX Modern brasserie with a small lounge and bar; a paved terrace with bay views; and a dining room with heavy wood tables, modern seashore paintings and animal ornaments. Menus showcase island produce and fish from local waters. Cooking is refined but hearty, mixing tasty brasserie and restaurant style dishes.

Menu £ 25 (weekdays)/28 – Carte £ 30/50

La Plage, La Route de la Haule ✉ *JE3 7YD – ✆ 01534 780180 – www.markjordanatthebeach.com – Closed 1-15 January and Monday in winter*

Gorey

Sumas

MODERN CUISINE • FRIENDLY XX A well-known restaurant in a whitewashed house, with a smart heated terrace affording lovely harbour views. Modern European dishes feature island produce. The monthly changing lunch and midweek dinner menus represent good value.

Menu £ 26 (weekdays) – Carte £ 27/49

Gorey Hill ✉ *JE3 6ET – ✆ 01534 853291 (booking essential) – www.sumasrestaurant.com – Closed 21 December-19 January and Sunday dinner*

Walker's

TRADITIONAL CUISINE • TRADITIONAL DÉCOR XX Formal hotel restaurant with a modern lounge, harbour views and local artwork on display. Good value menus offer well-prepared, unashamedly traditional dishes in tried-and-tested combinations and feature the odd personal twist.

Carte £ 33/65

Moorings Hotel, Gorey Pier ✉ JE3 6EW - ✆ 01534 853633 - www.themooringshotel.com - dinner only and Sunday lunch - Closed lunch Easter-September

Bass and Lobster

TRADITIONAL CUISINE • BISTRO X This simply furnished 'Foodhouse' sits close to the beach. Menus offer plenty of choice and you can watch fresh seafood, meats and vegetables from around the island being prepared through the kitchen window.

Menu £ 20 (weekdays) - Carte £ 28/48

Gorey Coast Rd ✉ JE3 6EU - ✆ 01534 859590 - www.bassandlobster.com - Closed 26 December and Sunday-Monday April-September

Moorings

TRADITIONAL • PERSONALISED Keenly run hotel below the ramparts of Mont Orgueil castle, overlooking the harbour. Leather-furnished first floor lounge. Modern bedrooms in cream, brown and purple colour schemes; some have small balconies. Formal restaurant or casual bistro and terrace for comfort dishes and seafood specials.

15 rooms - £ 110/180 £ 140/200

Gorey Pier ✉ JE3 6EW - ✆ 01534 853633 - www.themooringshotel.com

Walker's - See restaurant listing

Green Island

Green Island

MEDITERRANEAN CUISINE • FRIENDLY X Friendly, personally run restaurant with a terrace and beachside kiosk; the southernmost restaurant in the British Isles. Mediterranean-influenced dishes and seafood specials showcase island produce. Flavours are bold and perfectly judged.

Menu £ 19 (lunch) - Carte £ 33/50

St Clement ✉ JE2 6LS - ✆ 01534 857787 (booking essential) - www.greenisland.je - Closed 31 December-early February, Sunday dinner and Monday

La Haule

La Haule Manor

TOWNHOUSE • ELEGANT Attractive Georgian house overlooking the fort and bay, with a lovely terrace, a good-sized pool and neat lawned gardens. Stylish guest areas and spacious bedrooms mix modern and antique furnishings; those in the wing are the largest.

16 rooms - £ 81/217 £ 107/217

St Aubin's Bay ✉ JE3 8BS - ✆ 01534 741013 - www.lahaulemanor.com

La Pulente

Ocean

MODERN CUISINE • LUXURY XXX Perched in a hotel high above St Ouen's Bay, is this smart, understated restaurant with crisply laid tables; ceiling fans and shuttered windows add a slightly colonial feel. The experienced chef creates modern menus which showcase the best of the island's produce - seafood is a highlight.

Menu £ 25/80

Atlantic Hotel, Le Mont de la Pulente ✉ JE3 8HE - on B 35 - ✆ 01534 744101 (booking essential) - www.theatlantichotel.com - Closed 2 January-8 February

Atlantic

LUXURY · CONTEMPORARY Set in a superb spot overlooking St Ouen's Bay, this understatedly elegant hotel strikes the perfect balance with its service, which is polished and professional yet warm and welcoming. Stone and wood feature in the laid-back guest areas and many bedrooms look out over the lovely pool and terrace to the sea.

50 rooms - £ 120/320 £ 140/340 - 1 suite

Le Mont de la Pulente JE3 8HE - on B 35 - 01534 744101 - www.theatlantichotel.com - Closed 2 January-8 February

Ocean - See restaurant listing

Rozel Bay

Rozel

TRADITIONAL CUISINE · PUB A cosy pub in small coastal hamlet. The upstairs dining room has distant sea views but, come summer, the terraced garden is the place to be. Cooking is traditional and homely and ales are from the island's Liberation Brewery.

Carte £ 20/40

Rozel Valley JE3 6AJ - 01534 863438 - www.rozelpubanddining.co.uk - Closed Sunday dinner

Chateau La Chaire

HISTORIC · CLASSIC An attractive, traditionally styled 19C house surrounded by peaceful gardens and mature woodland. Bedrooms are well-equipped - the 1st floor rooms are the largest and some also have balconies. The formal restaurant leads through to a conservatory and terrace and offers classic dishes with a twist.

12 rooms - £ 85/155 £ 120/255 - 1 suite

Rozel Valley JE3 6AJ - 01534 863354 - www.chateau-la-chaire.co.uk

St Aubin

Panorama

TRADITIONAL · PERSONALISED An immaculately-kept house with Georgian origins, colourful gardens and stunning views over the fort and bay. It's run by welcoming owners and has a traditional feel. Over 1,400 teapots are displayed about the place.

14 rooms - £ 50/90 £ 100/200

La Rue du Crocquet JE3 8BZ - 01534 742429 - www.panoramajersey.com - Closed mid-October-early April

St Brelade's Bay

Oyster Box

SEAFOOD · BRASSERIE Glass-fronted eatery with pleasant heated terrace, set on the promenade and affording superb views over St Brelade's Bay. Stylish, airy interior hung with sail cloths and fishermen's floats. Laid-back, friendly service. Accessible seasonal menu features plenty of fish and shellfish; oysters are a speciality.

Carte £ 25/53

La Route de la Baie JE3 8EF - 01534 850888 - www.oysterbox.co.uk - Closed 25-26 December, 1 January, dinner Sunday-Monday October-March and Monday lunch

L'Horizon Beach H & Spa

LUXURY · SEASIDE Long-standing hotel located right on the beachfront and boasting stunning views over the bay. Luxurious interior with extensive guest areas and subtle modern styling. Choose a deluxe bedroom, as they come with balconies and sea views. Stylish, formal restaurant; modern British menus focus on local seafood.

106 rooms - £ 70/240 £ 160/315 - 4 suites

La Route de la Baie JE3 8EF - 01534 743101 - www.handpickedhotels.co.uk

St Brelade's Bay

FAMILY • SEASIDE Smart seafront hotel with charming tropical gardens and panoramic bay views. Modern guest areas, an excellent leisure club and contemporary bedrooms fit well alongside original parquet floors and ornate plaster ceilings. The formal restaurant offers impressive sea views and a classic menu.

74 rooms - £100/150 £150/300 - 5 suites

La Route de la Baie JE3 8EF - 01534 746141 - www.stbreladesbayhotel.com

St Helier

Bohemia

MODERN CUISINE • FASHIONABLE XXX A marble-fronted hotel restaurant with a chic cocktail bar and an intimate dining room. The emphasis is on tasting menus, with both pescatarian and vegetarian options available. Cooking is modern, vibrant and has a lightness of touch; original texture and flavour combinations feature.

→ Foie gras with duck salad, sea buckthorn and kumquat. Veal with artichoke, coffee, apple and hazelnut. Sour cherry with dark chocolate and kirsch.

Menu £30/65

Club Hotel & Spa, Green St JE2 4UH - 01534 880588
- www.bohemiajersey.com - Closed 24-30 December, Sunday and bank holidays

Samphire

MODERN CUISINE • DESIGN XX This buzzy all-day brasserie deluxe comes with blue banquettes, yellow leather chairs and a pavement terrace. Lee Smith employs a modern approach with global influences and alongside the à la carte offers a 'Casual Dining' menu. Presentation is sharp, flavours are well-judged and local seafood is a highlight.

→ Crab, pomelo, Jersey Royals and chervil. Pork rib eye with cauliflower cheese, apple ketchup. Duck egg custard, almond streusel, rhubarb and ginger.

Menu £29 (weekdays) - Carte £32/67

7-11 Don St JE2 4TQ - 01534 725100 - www.samphire.je - Closed 25 December, 1 January, Sunday and bank holidays

Banjo

INTERNATIONAL • BRASSERIE X Substantial former gentlemen's club with an ornate façade; the banjo belonging to the owner's great grandfather is displayed in a glass-fronted wine cellar. The appealing, wide-ranging menu features everything from brasserie classics to sushi. Stylish bedrooms have Nespresso machines and Bose sound systems.

Carte £23/51

4 rooms - £80/185 £80/185 - £10

8 Beresford St JE2 4WN - 01534 850890 - www.banjojersey.com - Closed 25-26 December, 1 January and Sunday

Grand Jersey

LUXURY • MODERN Welcoming hotel with a large terrace overlooking the bay. The stylish interior incorporates a chic champagne bar, a well-equipped spa and a corporate cinema. Contemporary bedrooms come in bold colours; some have balconies and sea views. Watch TV footage from the kitchen in intimate Tassili; Victoria's serves brasserie dishes.

123 rooms - £99/155 £120/245

The Esplanade JE2 3QA - 01534 722301 - www.handpickedhotels.co.uk

Club Hotel & Spa

BUSINESS • MODERN A modern hotel with stylish guest areas, an honesty bar and a split-level breakfast room. Contemporary bedrooms have floor to ceiling windows and good facilities. Relax in the smart spa or on the terrace beside the small outdoor pool.

46 rooms - £99/245 £99/445 - 4 suites

Green St JE2 4UH - 01534 876500 - www.theclubjersey.com - Closed 24-30 December

Bohemia - See restaurant listing

St Saviour

Longueville Manor

MODERN CUISINE • ELEGANT XXX Set within a charming manor house; dine in the characterful 15C oak-panelled room, the brighter Garden Room or on the terrace. Daily menus champion island produce; seafood is a feature and many ingredients come from the impressive kitchen garden. Classic dishes have a modern edge.

Menu £ 25/110 **s** - Carte £ 63/71

Longueville Manor Hotel, Longueville Rd ✉ JE2 7WF - on A 3 - ✆ 01534 725501 - www.longuevillemanor.com - Closed 3-31 January

Longueville Manor

LUXURY • CONTEMPORARY An iconic 13C manor house, which is very personally and professionally run. Comfy, country house guest areas have a modern edge and the well-equipped bedrooms are a mix of classic and contemporary styles. Relax in the lovely pool, on the charming terrace or in the delightful gardens.

28 rooms - £ 175/550 ££ 195/595 - 2 suites

Longueville Rd ✉ JE2 7WF - on A 3 - ✆ 01534 725501 - www.longuevillemanor.com - Closed 2-23 January

Longueville Manor - See restaurant listing

SARK

Sark - Pop. 550 - Regional map n° **3**-A2

La Sablonnerie

SEAFOOD • COSY XX A charming 16C whitewashed farmhouse with beautiful gardens and a cosy beamed interior; start with an aperitif in the comfy lounge. The regularly changing 5 course dinner menu displays a classic style of cooking and uses produce from the island and their own farm. Lunch is best enjoyed on the terrace. Bedrooms are neat and tidy - No.14, in the old stables, is the best.

Carte £ 30/52

22 rooms - £ 50/98 ££ 100/195 - 2 suites

Little Sark ✉ GY9 OSD - ✆ 01481 832061 (booking essential) - www.lasablonnerie.com - Closed mid-October-mid-April

Stocks

COUNTRY HOUSE • PERSONALISED A personally run former farmhouse whose formal gardens boast a split-level swimming pool and a jacuzzi. Bedrooms are sleek, contemporary and well-equipped. Dine on garden and island produce in the panelled dining room, the bistro or out on the terrace. The fantastic wine cellar was built during the war and the harbourmaster also brews country wines and liqueurs here.

23 rooms - £ 253/273 ££ 283/305 - 5 suites

✉ GY10 1SD - ✆ 01481 832001 - www.stockshotel.com - Closed January-February

CHARWELTON - Northamptonshire

→ See Daventry

CHATTON

Northumberland - Pop. 438 - Regional map n° **14**-A1

Chatton Park House

TRADITIONAL • PERSONALISED Charming 1730s house in 6 acres of formal gardens. It has a smart parquet-floored hallway, a huge open-fired sitting room and spacious bedrooms which blend modern décor and original features. Excellent breakfasts use local produce.

5 rooms - £ 99/199 ££ 99/225

✉ NE66 5RA - East : 1 mi on B 6348 - ✆ 01688 215507 - www.chattonpark.com - Closed November-March

CHEADLE

Greater Manchester - Pop. 13 467 - Regional map n° **11**-B3

Oddfellows on the Park

HISTORIC BUILDING • PERSONALISED Set close to Manchester Airport, in the middle of a park; a Victorian mansion which blends original features with modern furnishings. Opt for a suite in the tower above the front door; the Douglas tartan is a nod to house's original owners. Modern British dishes are served in the stunningly restored ballroom.

22 rooms - †£ 120/369 ††£ 130/369

Bruntwood Hall, Bruntwood Park ✉ SK8 1RS - South : 1.25 mi by A 560 and Wilmslow Rd off Cheadle Rd - ✆ 0161 697 3066 - www.oddfellowsonthepark.com

CHELMONDISTON - Suffolk

→ See Ipswich

CHELMSFORD

Essex - Pop. 99 962 - Regional map n° **7**-C3

The Windmill Chatham Green (N)

CLASSIC CUISINE • PUB Friendly young couple Mick and Lydia have transformed this whitewashed inn into a smart dining pub. Concise menus constantly evolve as the latest seasonal produce arrives; dishes are refined versions of British and pub classics. You can also enjoy afternoon tea in the base of the village's old windmill!

Menu £ 24 (weekdays) - Carte £ 27/40

Chatham Green ✉ CM3 3LE - North : 6 mi by A 130 off A 131 - ✆ 01245 910910 (booking essential) - www.thewindmillchathamgreen.com - dinner only and Sunday lunch - Closed 1 week January and Monday-Tuesday

GOOD TIPS!

This pretty spa town on the edge of the Cotswolds is renowned for its splendid Regency buildings, such as the elegant Grade II listed **Malmaison** hotel and the chic **Hotel du Vin**. There's a profusion of Indian restaurants, which include **Bhoomi**, **Curry Corner**, **East India Cafe** and **Prithvi.** For a bit of fun try **Daffodil**, which is set in a converted cinema.

CHELTENHAM

Gloucestershire - Pop. 116 447 - Regional map n° **2**-C1

Restaurants

✿ Le Champignon Sauvage (David Everitt-Matthias) A/C

MODERN CUISINE • INTIMATE XXX For over 30 years, David Everitt-Matthias and his wife Helen's brightly decorated restaurant has been the first choice of those looking to celebrate that special occasion. David seeks out the best of British ingredients for his contemporary dishes; he uses modern techniques and adds his own original touches.

→ Scallop and salsify with milk crumbs, cured jowl and onion dashi. Loin of lamb, wild garlic pesto, sheep's curd and an anchovy emulsion. Bitter chocolate and pistachio délice.

Menu £ 35/70

Town plan: A2-a - *24-28 Suffolk Rd ✉ GL50 2AQ - ✆ 01242 573449 - www.lechampignonsauvage.co.uk - Closed 3 weeks June, 10 days Christmas, Sunday and Monday*

Lumière A/C

MODERN CUISINE • INTIMATE XXX Friendly, personally run restaurant; its unassuming exterior concealing a long, stylish room decorated with mirrors. Seasonal dishes are modern and intricate with the occasional playful twist - desserts are often the highlight.

Menu £ 35/70

Town plan: AB1-z - *Clarence Par ✉ GL50 3PA - ✆ 01242 222200 (booking essential) - www.lumiere.cc - dinner only and lunch Friday-Saturday - Closed 2 weeks January, 2 weeks summer and Sunday-Tuesday*

Daffodil A/C

MODERN BRITISH • BRASSERIE XX A delightful 1920s art deco cinema: the tables are in the old stalls, the kitchens are in the screen area and the stylish lounge is up on the balcony. A slick team serve classic brasserie dishes, including steaks from the Josper grill. At weekends lunch is accompanied by live jazz.

Menu £ 16 (early dinner) - Carte £ 31/59

Town plan: A2-u - *18-20 Suffolk Par ✉ GL50 2AE - ✆ 01242 700055 - www.thedaffodil.com - Closed 25-26 December, Sunday dinner and lunch Monday-Thursday*

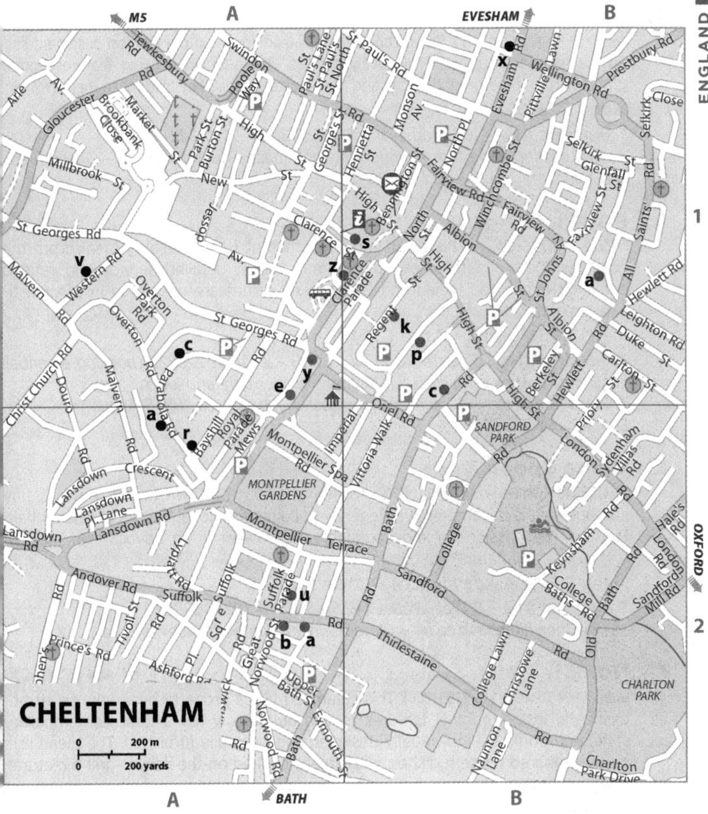

Bhoomi

INDIAN • ROMANTIC XX You'll receive a warm welcome at his luxurious restaurant. You won't find all the usual curries but you will discover original, refined, modern dishes with a focus on southeast India. They also offer a tasting menu and wine pairings.

Menu £ 49 (dinner)
- Carte £ 33/42

Town plan: A2-b – *52 Suffolk Rd ✉ GL50 2AQ*
– ✆ 01242 222010 – www.bhoomi.co.uk
– Closed 25 December-9 January, Easter Sunday, Monday and lunch Tuesday-Thursday

Curry Corner

BANGLADESHI • NEIGHBOURHOOD XX Long-standing, family-run restaurant in a smart Regency townhouse. Authentic, flavoursome dishes take their influences from across Bangladesh, India and Persia. Imported spices are ground and roasted every morning.

Carte £ 27/44

Town plan: B1-a – *133 Fairview Rd ✉ GL52 2EX*
– ✆ 01242 528449 – www.thecurrycorner.com
– dinner only – Closed 25 December and Monday

East India Cafe

INDIAN • FRIENDLY XX Steep candlelit steps leads down into a magical basement setting, where you're greeted by lovely aromas. Anglo-Indian cooking features home-grown herbs, home-ground spices and prime local meats. They also make their own gin.

Menu £ 33/55

Town plan: A1-y - *103 Promenade ✉ GL50 1NW - ✆ 01242 300850 - www.eastindiacafe.com - dinner only and lunch Friday-Saturday - Closed first week January, Sunday and Monday*

Prithvi

INDIAN • DESIGN XX This smart Indian restaurant is a refreshing break from the norm, with its ambitious owner, designer décor, detailed service and refined cooking. Reinvented Indian and Bangladeshi dishes are presented in a sophisticated manner.

Menu £ 25 (lunch) - Carte £ 36/46

Town plan: B1-c - *37 Bath Rd ✉ GL53 7HG - ✆ 01242 226229 (booking essential at dinner) - www.prithvirestaurant.com - dinner only and lunch Thursday-Saturday - Closed 24 December-7 January, 28 July-5 August, Sunday and Monday*

White Spoon

MODERN BRITISH • ELEGANT XX Hidden away in the town centre, down a tiny passageway, is this impressive Regency building with lovely views of Cheltenham Minster. The passionate, knowledgeable chef-owner is an advocate of modern techniques and natural flavours.

Menu £ 12 (weekday lunch) - Carte £ 34/43

Town plan: B1-s - *8 Well Walk ✉ GL50 3JX - ✆ 01242 228555 - www.thewhitespoon.co.uk - Closed Sunday dinner, Monday and Tuesday*

No. 131

MODERN CUISINE • BISTRO X This columned 1820s property overlooks an attractive park. Inside, original features remain but it now has a cool, contemporary style. Bedrooms are individually designed and tastefully furnished. The menu lists deftly-prepared modern dishes, with steaks cooked on the Josper grill a feature.

Carte £ 24/57

11 rooms - †£ 150/450 ††£ 150/450

Town plan: A1-e - *131 Promenade ✉ GL50 1NW - ✆ 01242 822939 (booking essential) - www.no131.com*

Koj (N)

JAPANESE • SIMPLE X This intimate little restaurant is both fun and great value. There's no sushi, just a selection of authentic appetisers, buns and grazing plates. Accompany these with Japanese beers, sake and cocktails and you will leave with a smile.

Carte £ 20/30

Town plan: B1-k - *3 Regent St ✉ GL50 1HE - ✆ 01242 580455 - www.kojcheltenham.co.uk - Closed Christmas-New Year, Tuesday lunch, Sunday and Monday*

Purslane

MODERN BRITISH • INTIMATE X A stylishly minimalistic neighbourhood restaurant with relaxed, efficient service. Fresh seafood from Cornwall and Scotland is combined with good quality, locally sourced ingredients to produce interesting, original dishes.

Menu £ 15 (lunch and early dinner)/41

Town plan: B1-p - *16 Rodney Rd ✉ GL50 1JJ - ✆ 01242 321639 - www.purslane-restaurant.co.uk - Closed 2 weeks January, 2 weeks August-September, Sunday and Monday*

Hotels

Ellenborough Park

LUXURY • ELEGANT A part-15C timbered manor house with stone annexes, an Indian-themed spa and large grounds stretching down to the racecourse. Beautifully furnished guest areas have an elegant classical style. Nina Campbell designed bedrooms have superb bathrooms, the latest mod cons and plenty of extras. Dine on elaborate dishes in the restaurant or pub fare in the brasserie.

61 rooms - £ 134/679 £ 134/679

Southam Rd GL52 3NJ - Northeast : 2.75 mi on B 4632 - 01242 545454 - www.ellenboroughpark.com

Hotel du Vin

TOWNHOUSE • THEMED Attractive Regency house in an affluent residential area. Inside it's chic and laid-back, with a leather-furnished bar and a comfy lounge. Some of the individually designed, well-equipped, wine-themed bedrooms have baths in the room. The French bistro features an eye-catching wine glass chandelier.

49 rooms - £ 99/200 £ 99/200 - 1 suite

Town plan: A1-c - *Parabola Rd GL50 3AQ - 01242 588450 - www.hotelduvin.com*

Malmaison

TOWNHOUSE • MODERN Chic Regency townhouse, where stylish modern guest areas are hung with an impressive collection of contemporary art. Light wood furnished bedrooms come with Nespresso machines, complimentary mini bars and in-room info on an iPod touch. Dine on British dishes at marble-topped tables or on one of two terraces.

61 rooms - £ 110/195 £ 110/195 - £ 15

Town plan: A2-r - *Bayshill Rd GL50 3AS - 01242 527788 - www.malmaison.com*

No 38 The Park

TOWNHOUSE • DESIGN Behind the attractive Georgian façade is a very original, tastefully designed hotel with a relaxed atmosphere and supremely comfortable furnishings. Bedrooms come with coffee machines and vast walk-in showers or feature baths.

13 rooms - £ 110/315 £ 120/325

Town plan: B1-x - *38 Eversham Rd GL52 2AH - 01242 248656 - www.no38thepark.com*

Beaumont House

TOWNHOUSE • CONTEMPORARY Your hosts here are warm and welcoming, just like the hotel. The lounge and breakfast room are comfortably and classically furnished, while the bedrooms are more contemporary; there are two themed rooms - Africa and Asia.

16 rooms - £ 75/239 £ 109/298

56 Shurdington Rd GL53 0JE - South : 1.5 mi on A 46 - 01242 223311 - www.bhhotel.co.uk

Wyastone Townhouse

TOWNHOUSE • ART DÉCO Nothing is too much trouble for the charming young owner of this attractive townhouse. Inside, contemporary décor blends with period features. Bedrooms - split between the house and the courtyard - are surprisingly spacious.

16 rooms - £ 75/98 £ 110/165

Town plan: A1-a - *Parabola Rd GL50 3BG - 01242 245549 - www.wyastonehotel.co.uk - Closed 23 December-1 January*

Butlers

TOWNHOUSE • PERSONALISED The bedrooms of this tastefully furnished Victorian townhouse are named after famous butlers – a theme which continues in the classical lounge and breakfast room. There's also an interesting collection of hats about the place!

9 rooms – £ 80/120 £ 99/180

Town plan: A1-v – *Western Rd ✉ GL50 3RN – ✆ 01242 570771 – www.butlers-hotel.co.uk*

Detmore House

COUNTRY HOUSE • CONTEMPORARY Peace and tranquility reign at this 1840s country house, which is accessed via a private drive and offers pleasant rural views. Bedrooms are modern and comfortable – 'Oak' is the best. Breakfast is served at a fine oak table.

4 rooms – £ 85/95 £ 100/125

London Rd, Charlton Kings ✉ GL52 6UT – Southeast : 2.5 mi by A 40 – ✆ 01242 582868 – www.detmorehouse.com – Closed Christmas and New Year

at Shurdington Southwest: 3.75 mi on A46✉ Cheltenham

Greenway

COUNTRY HOUSE • CLASSIC 16C ivy-clad manor house, set in 8 acres of peaceful grounds and offering pleasant views over the hills. Comfy drawing rooms and well-equipped bedrooms have a pleasant country house style. Enjoy a laid-back brasserie-style lunch on the terrace of the lovely spa. The oak-panelled restaurant offers classic dishes with modern overtones and overlooks the lily pond.

21 rooms – £ 110/325 £ 135/375 – 1 suite

✉ GL51 4UG – ✆ 01242 862352 – www.thegreenwayhotelandspa.com

GOOD TIPS!

There is evidence of Chester's Roman origins all around the city; not least, its two miles of ancient walls. It is also known for its black & white half-timbered buildings, like the Grade II listed **Chester Grosvenor** hotel – home to Simon Radley's Michelin Starred restaurant. Carnivores will appreciate the quality of the meat on offer **Upstairs at the Grill**.

CHESTER

Cheshire West and Chester – Pop. 86 011 – Regional map n° **11**-A3

Restaurants

Simon Radley at Chester Grosvenor

MODERN CUISINE • LUXURY XXXX This hotel restaurant has a classically elegant feel, a stylish cocktail lounge and an impressive wine cellar. Confident cooking shows respect for ingredients, bringing together clean, clear flavours in sophisticated dishes that display interesting, innovative touches. Service is detailed.

→ Ragout of all things duck with soaked Pedro Ximénez brioche. Turbot with chicken wing dumplings and asparagus. Turkish Delight and sweet curd with Cheshire saffron cake, lemon and rose.

Menu £ 75/99

Town plan: B2-a – *Chester Grosvenor Hotel, Eastgate ✉ CH1 1LT – ✆ 01244 895618 – www.chestergrosvenor.com – dinner only – Closed dinner 24-25 December, Sunday and Monday*

Joseph Benjamin

MODERN CUISINE • BISTRO X This personally and passionately run bistro is named after its owners, Joe and Ben. The light, simple décor mirrors the style of cooking and the monthly menu offers tasty, well-judged dishes. They serve breakfast, lunch, coffee and homemade pastries and, from Thursday to Saturday, intimate candlelit dinners.

Carte £ 20/35

Town plan: A1-u – *134-140 Northgate St ✉ CH1 2HT – ✆ 01244 344295 – www.josephbenjamin.co.uk – lunch only and dinner Thursday-Saturday – Closed 25 December-1 January and Monday*

Upstairs at the Grill

MEATS AND GRILLS • INTIMATE XX Smart restaurant offering prime quality steaks – including porterhouse and bone-in fillet or rib-eye; the 5 week dry-aged cuts are from premium Welsh beef. Eat in the moody cocktail bar or downstairs amongst the cow paraphernalia.

Carte £ 27/60

Town plan: A2-n – *70 Watergate St ✉ CH1 2LA – ✆ 01244 344883 – www.upstairsatthegrill.co.uk – dinner only and lunch Thursday-Sunday – Closed 25 December and 1 January*

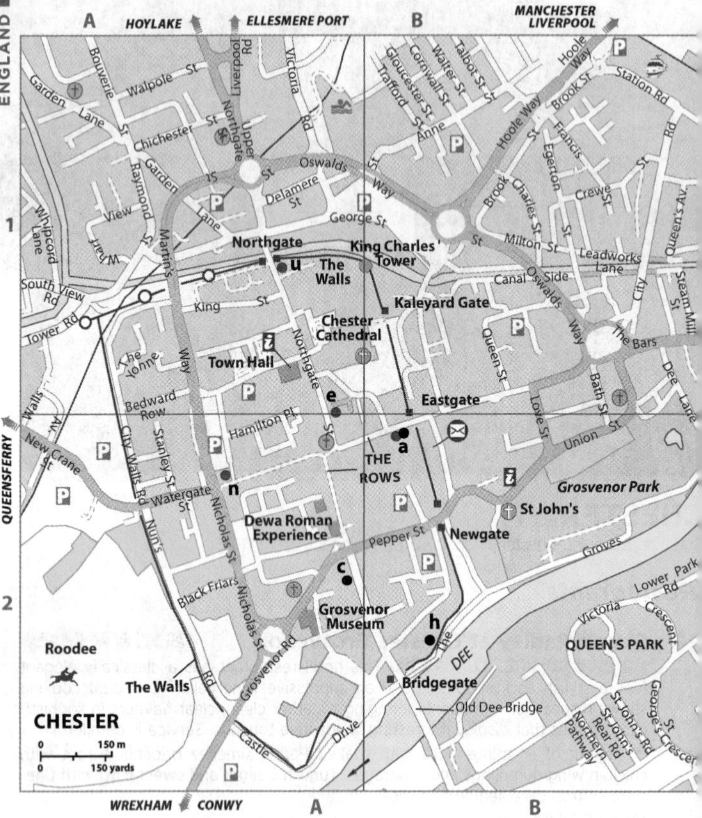

Chef's Table

MODERN BRITISH • SIMPLE A cosy, intimate city centre bistro tucked away down a narrow street; it has a loyal following and a pleasingly laid-back vibe. Monthly menus list colourful, artfully presented dishes. Vegetables are from a local grower who cultivates one of the oldest organic fields in England.

Menu £ 18 (lunch) – Carte £ 29/41

Town plan: A1-2-e – *4 Music Hall Passage ✉ CH1 2EU – ✆ 01244 403040 (booking essential) – www.chefstablechester.co.uk – Closed Monday lunch*

Porta

SPANISH • TAPAS BAR Close to the city wall, behind a narrow terrace, is this cosy, characterful little tapas bar. It has no phone number or reservation system, but it does offer generous, tasty dishes which are served by a friendly young team.

Carte £ 11/20

Town plan: A1-u – *140 Northgate St ✉ CH1 2HT – ✆ 01244 344295 (bookings not accepted) – www.portatapas.co.uk – dinner only – Closed 25 December-1 January*

Hotels

Chester Grosvenor

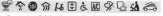

LUXURY • CLASSIC Behind this 19C hotel's grand black and white timbered façade are a buzzy lounge and stylish bedrooms which blend traditional furnishings with contemporary fabrics. Unwind in the lovely spa, then dine on French classics in the appealing brasserie or more sophisticated fare in the restaurant.

80 rooms – £ 135/400 £ 155/420 – 12 suites

Town plan: B2-a – *Eastgate ✉ CH1 1LT – ✆ 01244 324024 – www.chestergrosvenor.com – Closed 24-25 December*

Simon Radley at Chester Grosvenor – See restaurant listing

Oddfellows

TOWNHOUSE • DESIGN This was originally an Oddfellows Hall built in 1676 to help the poor but its name now perfectly suits its unique, quirky styling. Well-equipped bedrooms include duplex suites: some have circular beds or double roll-top baths. The garden-themed restaurant offers a flexible menu of creative British dishes.

22 rooms – £ 100/290 £ 100/290 – £ 14

Town plan: A2-c – *20 Lower Bridge St ✉ CH1 1RS – ✆ 01244 345454 – www.oddfellowschester.com – Closed 25 December*

Edgar House

TOWNHOUSE • ELEGANT A charming 17C house by the city walls, in the historic heart of Chester. The delightful garden overlooks the River Dee and the bright, modern bedrooms have raised beds so you can see the water. An honesty bar is housed in an old telephone box and the rustic dining room offers a British-inspired tasting menu.

7 rooms – £ 179/269 £ 189/339

Town plan: B2-h – *22 City Walls ✉ CH1 1SB – ✆ 01244 347007 – www.edgarhouse.co.uk*

CHEW MAGNA

Bath and North East Somerset – Pop. 1 149 – Regional map n° **2**-C2

Pony & Trap (Josh Eggleton)

MODERN BRITISH • COSY Sit in the characterful front bar, the rustic rear room or out on the terrace – the latter two afford wonderful country views. The daily menu sees herbs and fruits from the garden come together with West Country meats and fish. Precisely prepared dishes range from appealing snacks to more refined main courses.

→ Seaweed cured salmon with dill mayonnaise & crispy oyster. Lamb rump with ragu, sweetbread, malted rye & wild garlic. Hazelnut & chocolate éclair with malt ice cream.

Carte £ 33/48

Knowle Hill, New Town ✉ BS40 8TQ – South : 1.25 mi on Bishop Sutton rd – ✆ 01275 332627 (booking essential) – www.theponyandtrap.co.uk – Closed 25-26 December, dinner 31 December, 1 January and bank holidays

CHICHESTER

West Sussex – Pop. 28 657 – Regional map n° **4**-C2

Chichester Harbour

BUSINESS • MODERN This charming Grade II listed property was once home to one of Nelson's men. It boasts a sweeping wrought iron Georgian staircase and contrastingly stylish bedrooms with boldly designed soft furnishings. Unwind in the chic spa before enjoying unfussy seafood dishes in the bright, laid-back restaurant.

37 rooms – £ 90/150 £ 130/355

57 North St ✉ PO19 1NH – ✆ 01243 778000 – www.chichester-harbour-hotel.co.uk

at Mid Lavant North: 2 mi on A286

Earl of March

TRADITIONAL CUISINE • PUB This 18C inn offers the perfect blend of contemporary styling and relaxed country character. Good quality seasonal produce is showcased in British-based dishes. Find a spot on the terrace to take in the amazing South Downs views.

Menu £ 25 (lunch and early dinner) - Carte £ 34/53

PO18 0BQ - 01243 533993 - www.theearlofmarch.com

Rooks Hill

COUNTRY HOUSE • PERSONALISED Grade II listed house with a pleasant view across to the Goodwood estate. Relax on the charming courtyard terrace or next to the wood burner in the cosy sitting room. Individually decorated bedrooms have contemporary touches.

4 rooms - £ 105/125 £ 125/175

Lavant Rd PO18 0BQ - 01243 528400 - www.rookshill.co.uk

at Tangmere East: 2 mi by A27 Chichester

Cassons

MODERN CUISINE • RUSTIC XX Passionately run restaurant with exposed brick, wooden beams and a rustic feel. Boldly flavoured dishes are generously proportioned. Cooking is classically based but employs modern techniques. The regular gourmet evenings are a hit.

Menu £ 43

Arundel Rd PO18 0DU - Northwest : 0.25 mi off A 27 (westbound) - 01243 773294 - www.cassonsrestaurant.co.uk - dinner only and Sunday lunch - Closed 25-30 December and Sunday dinner

at West Ashling Northwest: 4.5 mi by B2178 and B2146

Richmond Arms

INTERNATIONAL • RUSTIC Appealing, laid-back country pub opposite a duck pond in a lovely little village. The menu offers an appealing mix, from freshly sliced hams and local steaks to game from the family estate in Anglesey; many meats are cooked on the rotisserie or the Japanese robata grill. Two luxurious bedrooms are above.

Carte £ 25/47

2 rooms - £ 125/165 £ 125/165

Mill Rd PO18 8EA - 01243 572046 - www.therichmondarms.co.uk - Closed Sunday dinner, Monday and Tuesday

at Funtington Northwest: 4.75 mi by B2178 on B2146 Chichester

Hallidays

CLASSIC CUISINE • INTIMATE XX Characterful thatched cottage comprising a series of interconnecting rooms with low beams. The chef knows a thing or two about sourcing good ingredients and his menu changes regularly. Cooking is skilful and classically based.

Menu £ 22 (weekday lunch) - Carte £ 32/41

Watery Ln PO18 9LF - 01243 575331 - www.hallidays.info.co.uk - Closed 2 weeks August, 1 week March, 1 week Christmas-New Year, Saturday lunch, Sunday dinner, Monday and Tuesday

CHIDDINGFOLD

Surrey - Pop. 2 211 - Regional map n° **4**-C2

Swan Inn

MODERN CUISINE • INN It might be over 200 years old but the Swan has a modern feel and its 11 comfy bedrooms are equally stylish. The extensive menu changes a little each day and offers a mix of pub and restaurant style dishes. Unsurprisingly, on sunny days, the stepped rear terrace is a popular spot.

Carte £ 27/41

11 rooms - £ 74/134 £ 74/134

Petworth Rd GU8 4TY - 01428 684688 - www.theswaninnchiddingfold.com

CHILCOMPTON

Somerset - Pop. 2 062 - Regional map n° **2**-C2

Redan Inn

MODERN BRITISH • PUB This smartly refurbished pub displays an impressive selection of old curios. The concise weekly menu offers an enticing mix of accomplished dishes. They cure their own meats, make their own sausages and use apples from the garden for their chutney. Service is relaxed and engaging and bedrooms are stylish.

Carte £ 26/43

7 rooms - £ 85/140 £ 100/170

Fry's Well BA3 4HA - 01761 258560 - www.theredaninn.co.uk

CHILLATON - Devon → See Tavistock

CHINNOR

Oxfordshire - Pop. 5 473 - Regional map n° **6**-C2

at Sprigg's Alley Southeast: 2.5 mi by Bledlow Ridge rd Chinnor

Sir Charles Napier

MODERN BRITISH • COSY XX Enjoy an aperitif in the delightful garden or beside the log fire in this quirky restaurant, where animal sculptures peer out from every corner. British cooking is modern yet unfussy and the wine list is a labour of love.

Menu £ 22 (weekdays) - Carte £ 40/58

Sprigs Holly OX39 4BX - 01494 483011 - www.sircharlesnapier.co.uk
- Closed 24-26 December, Sunday dinner and Monday except bank holidays

CHIPPING CAMPDEN

Gloucestershire - Pop. 2 037 - Regional map n° **2**-D1

Cotswold House H. and Spa

TOWNHOUSE • CONTEMPORARY A set of stylish Regency townhouses with lovely gardens, boldly decorated lounges hung with eclectic modern art, and a beautiful staircase winding upwards towards luxurious modern bedrooms. Relax in the spa our outdoor hot tub then enjoy sophisticated modern dishes amongst Regency columns.

28 rooms - £ 140/240 £ 150/250 - 3 suites

The Square GL55 6AN - 01386 840330 - www.cotswoldhouse.com

Kings

TOWNHOUSE • CLASSIC A beautiful Cotswold stone townhouse with a stylish boutique interior. Bedrooms in the main house mix antiques - including sleigh beds - with modern facilities. Rooms in the cottage at the end of the garden are more up-to-date. The appealingly rustic restaurant serves modern British dishes.

18 rooms - £ 95/355 £ 95/355 - 1 suite

The Square GL55 6AW - 01386 840256 - www.kingscampden.co.uk

at Ebrington East: 2 mi by B4035

Ebrington Arms

MODERN CUISINE • COSY Set in a charming chocolate box village, a proper village local with a beamed, flag-floored bar at its hub. Choose from pub classics on the blackboard or more elaborate dishes on the à la carte. Be sure to try one of the ales brewed to their own recipe. Bedrooms have country views and thoughtful extras.

Carte £ 22/37

5 rooms – £ 139/169 £ 139/169

GL55 6NH – 01386 593223 – www.theebringtonarms.co.uk – Closed 25 December

at Paxford Southeast : 3 mi by B 4035

Churchill Arms

TRADITIONAL BRITISH • COSY This charming 17C inn sits in a residential spot in a delightful Cotswold village and the intimate bar is hung with photos of local scenes taken by the owner himself. A bewildering array of menus offers everything from unfussy classics to more modern dishes. Bedrooms are comfy and well-appointed.

Carte £ 29/49

4 rooms – £ 120 £ 120

GL55 6XH – 01386 593159 – www.churchillarms.co.uk

CHIPPING NORTON

Oxfordshire – Pop. 5 719 – Regional map n° **6**-A1

Wild Thyme

TRADITIONAL BRITISH • COSY A keen husband and wife team run this cosy restaurant with rustic tables; number 10, in the window, is the best. Wholesome regional British cooking has Mediterranean influences, with tasty homemade breads and game in season.

Menu £ 20 (weekdays)/40

10 New St OX7 5LJ – 01608 645060 – www.wildthymerestaurant.co.uk – dinner only and lunch Thursday-Saturday – Closed first week January, Sunday and Monday

CHIPPING ONGAR

Essex – Pop. 6 093 – Regional map n° **7**-B2

Smith's

SEAFOOD • BRASSERIE Long-standing, locally acclaimed seafood restaurant with a buzzy atmosphere. The à la carte and extensive daily set menu offer dishes ranging from Cornish squid to Scottish smoked salmon. Lobster, cooked several ways, is a speciality.

Menu £ 24/32 – Carte £ 35/79

Fyfield Rd CM5 0AL – 01277 365578 (booking essential) – www.smithsrestaurants.com – Closed 25-26 December, 1 January and Monday lunch

CHOBHAM

Surrey – Pop. 2 771 – Regional map n° **4**-C1

Stovell's

MODERN BRITISH • INTIMATE The owner of this characterful 16C farmhouse has put Chobham firmly on the culinary map. Creative, often intricate dishes use top quality ingredients. Highlights include the bespoke tasting menu and dishes from the wood-fired grill.

Menu £ 26/48

125 Windsor Rd GU24 8QS – North : 0.75 mi on B 383 – 01276 858000 (booking essential) – www.stovells.com – Closed 1-10 January, Sunday dinner, Monday and lunch Tuesday-Wednesday

CHRISTCHURCH

Dorset - Pop. 54 210 - Regional map n° **2**-D3

Jetty

MODERN BRITISH • DESIGN XX Set within the grounds of the Christchurch Harbour hotel, this contemporary, eco-friendly restaurant offers fantastic water views. Appealing menus reflect what's available locally, with fish from nearby waters and game from the forest.

Menu £ 25 (weekdays) - Carte £ 36/52

Christchurch Harbour Hotel, 95 Mudeford ✉ BH23 3NT - East : 2 mi by B 3059 - ✆ 01202 400950 - www.thejetty.co.uk

Captain's Club

BUSINESS • CONTEMPORARY A striking modern building with nautical and art deco influences; it's set in a lovely riverside spot and offers fantastic views from its floor to ceiling windows. Bedrooms are sleek and contemporary - the largest are three-roomed suites. Relax in the stylish spa or out on the water on their boat before dining on modern brasserie classics in the restaurant.

29 rooms - †£ 179/289 ††£ 199/299 - 12 suites

Wick Ferry, Wick Ln ✉ BH23 1HU - ✆ 01202 475111 - www.captainsclubhotel.com

Christchurch Harbour

BUSINESS • CONTEMPORARY Don't be fooled by the unassuming exterior; inside is a cool, chic hotel with a smart basement spa - its waterside location reflected in the modern, nautical-inspired décor. Some bedrooms have waterfront terraces or balconies. Both of the restaurants open onto delightful terraces with far-reaching views.

64 rooms - †£ 150/245 ††£ 150/245

95 Mudeford ✉ BH23 3NT - East : 2 mi by B 3059 - ✆ 01202 483434 - www.christchurch-harbour-hotel.co.uk

Jetty - See restaurant listing

Kings Arms

TOWNHOUSE • PERSONALISED This lovingly restored Georgian inn stands opposite the bowling green and castle ruins, and has been given a smart modern makeover. Guest areas have a chic yet characterful feel and the boutique-style bedrooms are well-appointed.

20 rooms - †£ 105/125 ††£ 125/185

18 Castle St ✉ BH23 1DT - ✆ 01202 588933 - www.thekings-christchurch.co.uk

CHURCHILL

Oxfordshire - Pop. 502 - Regional map n° **6**-A1

Chequers

TRADITIONAL CUISINE • PUB Welcoming limestone pub in the heart of the village; it's a vital part of the community and the owners have got the formula just right. The bar is stocked with local ales; gutsy, traditional dishes include steaks cooked on the Josper grill.

Carte £ 23/36

Church Rd ✉ OX7 6NJ - ✆ 01608 659393 - www.thechequerschurchill.com

CHURCH ENSTONE

Oxfordshire - Regional map n° **6**-B1

Crown Inn

TRADITIONAL BRITISH • PUB 17C inn set among pretty stone houses in a picturesque village. Sit in the slate-floored conservatory, the beamed dining room or the rustic bar. Meat, fruit and veg come from local farms; seafood is a speciality, as is the steak pie.

Carte £ 20/32

Mill Ln ✉ OX7 4NN - ✆ 01608 677262 - www.crowninnenstone.co.uk - Closed 25-26 December, 1 January and Sunday dinner

CIRENCESTER

Gloucestershire - Pop. 16 325 - Regional map n° **2**-D1

Made by Bob

MEDITERRANEAN CUISINE • FASHIONABLE The name says it all: Bob makes most of the products himself - be it for the informal eatery or the crammed deli; and the rest of the ingredients are organic and locally sourced. It's open for breakfast, lunch and Sunday brunch, and service is bright and breezy. If you can't find a seat, they also do takeaway.

Carte £ 22/42

The Corn Hall, 26 Market Pl ✉ GL7 2NY - ✆ 01285 641818 (bookings not accepted) - www.foodmadebybob.com - lunch only - Closed 25-26 December and 1 January

Jesse's Bistro

TRADITIONAL CUISINE • COSY This rustic bistro is hidden away in a little courtyard behind the Jesse Smith butcher's shop. Local meat and veg feature alongside Cornish fish and good use is made of the wood-fired oven. Beams and flagstones give it a cosy feel.

Menu £ 15 (lunch) - Carte £ 29/50

14 Blackjack St ✉ GL7 2AA - ✆ 01285 641497 - www.jessesbistro.co.uk - Closed Sunday-Monday dinner

Kings Head

HISTORIC • DESIGN A former coaching inn built from local stone, set overlooking the Market Place. Original features attest to its age but it's now a stylish, modern hotel offering spacious bedrooms with all the latest mod cons. The popular restaurant offers hearty seasonal classics.

52 rooms - †£ 119/279 ††£ 119/409 - ☕ £ 18

24 Market Pl ✉ GL7 2NR - ✆ 01285 700900 - www.kingshead-hotel.co.uk

No 12

TOWNHOUSE • PERSONALISED This 16C townhouse provides plenty of contrasts: its façade is Georgian yet it hides a modern interior, and the large bedrooms blend original features with stylish furnishings. In summer, breakfast on local, organic and homemade products in the delightful walled garden.

4 rooms ☕ - †£ 100 ††£ 130/150

12 Park St ✉ GL7 2BW - ✆ 01285 640232 - www.no12cirencester.co.uk

Old Brewhouse

TOWNHOUSE • PERSONALISED 17C former brewhouse in busy central spot, with a characterful cluttered interior and two stone-walled breakfast rooms. Choose between cottage-style bedrooms - most with wrought iron beds - or more modern rooms set around a small courtyard.

10 rooms ☕ - †£ 95/110 ††£ 110/120

7 London Rd ✉ GL7 2PU - ✆ 01285 656099 - www.theoldbrewhouse.com - Closed 24 December-2 January

at Barnsley Northeast: 4 mi by A429 on B4425 ✉ Cirencester

Village Pub

TRADITIONAL BRITISH • COSY With an interior straight out of any country homes magazine, this place has the cosy, open-fired, village pub vibe down to a tee. It has four intimate rooms and a carefully manicured terrace. Appealing modern British dishes and irresistible nibbles feature locally sourced meats, charcuterie from Highgrove and comforting desserts. Bedrooms are tastefully styled.

Carte £ 26/44

6 rooms ☕ - †£ 99/179 ††£ 109/189

✉ GL7 5EF - ✆ 01285 740421 (booking essential) - www.thevillagepub.co.uk

Barnsley House

HISTORIC • PERSONALISED A 17C Cotswold manor house with a wonderfully relaxed vibe, set in the midst of beautiful gardens styled by Rosemary Verey. The chic interior blends original features with modern touches; there's also a spa and even a cinema in the grounds. The kitchen gardens inform what's on the menu.

18 rooms – £ 299/498 £ 309/557 – 8 suites

GL7 5EE – 01285 740000 – www.barnsleyhouse.com

at Sapperton West: 5 mi by A419 Cirencester

The Bell

TRADITIONAL CUISINE • RUSTIC Charming and characterful Cotswold pub with flagged floors, exposed stone, an abundance of beams and warming log fires. Menus offer the expected burger or fish and chips, as well as dishes which show off more of the chef's skills.

Carte £ 24/42

GL7 6LE – 01285 760298 – www.bellsapperton.co.uk – Closed 25 December, Sunday dinner and Monday November-March

CLANFIELD

Oxfordshire – Pop. 1 709 – Regional map n° **6**-A2

Cotswold Plough

TRADITIONAL BRITISH • FRIENDLY XX Set within a 16C hotel, a lovely three-roomed restaurant with relaxed service, a gin pantry and a comfortingly traditional feel. Classic menus provide plenty of appeal and all wines are available by the glass or carafe.

Carte £ 25/45

Cotswold Plough Hotel, Bourton Rd OX18 2RB – on A 4095 – 01367 810222 – www.cotswoldploughhotel.com – Closed 24-27 December

Cotswold Plough

TRADITIONAL • CLASSIC Charming 16C wool merchant's house in the heart of a pretty village, with an antique-furnished lounge and a characterful bar boasting two open fires and over 500 types of gin. Bedrooms in the main house are cosy with mullioned windows; those in the extension are more spacious.

11 rooms – £ 89/115 £ 115/150

Bourton Rd OX18 2RB – on A 4095 – 01367 810222 – www.cotswoldploughhotel.com – Closed 24-27 December

Cotswold Plough – See restaurant listing

CLAVERING

Essex – Pop. 882 – Regional map n° **7**-B2

Cricketers

MEDITERRANEAN CUISINE • INN This long-standing pub has built up quite a name for itself. The characterful main bar has extremely low ceilings and timbers hung with horse brasses. Menus offer plenty of choice and include lots of British classics. Bedrooms are set over three different buildings (the keys come attached to cricket balls!)

Carte £ 28/44

20 rooms – £ 70/120 £ 95/130

CB11 4QT – 01799 550442 – www.thecricketers.co.uk – Closed 25-26 December

CLEARWELL
Gloucestershire - Regional map n° **2**-C1

Tudor Farmhouse

COUNTRY HOUSE • CONTEMPORARY A group of converted farm buildings set on the roadside in the centre of the village. Two cosy dining rooms serving appealing dishes are found in the old farmhouse and, above them, characterful bedrooms with old beams and wonky floors; more modern bedrooms are housed in two of the outbuildings.

20 rooms - £ 130/250 £ 130/250 - 5 suites

High St ✉ GL16 8JS - ✆ 01594 833046 - www.tudorfarmhousehotel.co.uk

CLEESTANTON - Shropshire ➜ See Ludlow

CLEY-NEXT-THE-SEA - Norfolk ➜ See Blakeney

CLIPSHAM
Rutland - Pop. 120 - Regional map n° **9**-C2

Olive Branch & Beech House

TRADITIONAL BRITISH • INN Characterful village pub made up of a series of small rooms which feature open fires and exposed beams. The selection of rustic British dishes changes daily, reflecting the seasons and keeping things fiercely local. These are accompanied by real ales, homemade lemonade and vodka made from hedgerow berries. Bedrooms are cosy and thoughtfully finished.

Menu £ 23 (weekday lunch) - Carte £ 30/58

6 rooms - £ 103/160 £ 140/190

Main St ✉ LE15 7SH - ✆ 01780 410355 (booking essential)
- www.theolivebranchpub.com

CLOVELLY
Devon - Pop. 439 - Regional map n° **1**-B1

Red Lion

TRADITIONAL • COSY Traditional inn set in a wonderful location under the cliffs, right on the harbourfront. Good-sized, comfortable bedrooms all have sea views; the newest and largest rooms are in the converted sail loft. Enjoy classic dishes and a superb vista in the dining room; lighter snacks are served in the bar.

17 rooms - £ 135/190 £ 135/190

The Quay ✉ EX39 5TF - ✆ 01237 431237 - www.stayatclovelly.co.uk/red-lion

COLCHESTER
Essex - Pop. 119 441 - Regional map n° **7**-D2

Church Street Tavern

TRADITIONAL BRITISH • BRASSERIE Set down a narrow city centre street, this modern brasserie sits within an attractive 18C building and is run in a relaxed, efficient manner. The trendy, shabby-chic bar serves cocktails and light bites, while the upstairs restaurant offers British classics with Mediterranean influences.

Carte £ 25/40

3 Church St ✉ CO1 1NF - ✆ 01206 564325 - www.churchstreettavern.co.uk
- Closed 25-26 December, first week January, Sunday dinner, Monday and Tuesday

Greyfriars

HISTORIC • ELEGANT It took five years to convert this former monastery into the fine hotel that it is today. Stunning public areas include beautiful rooms hung with Murano chandeliers, and the bedrooms are a curious mix of the simple and the ostentatious. Dine on complex dishes in the old chapel, under stained glass windows.

26 rooms - £ 95/115 £ 115/250 - 17 suites

High St ✉ CO1 1UG - ✆ 01206 575913 - www.greyfriarscolchester.co.uk

COLERNE - Wiltshire → See Bath

COLSTON BASSETT
Nottinghamshire - Pop. 239 - Regional map n° **9**-B2

The Martins Arms
TRADITIONAL CUISINE • TRADITIONAL DÉCOR Creeper-clad pub in a charming village, with a cosy fire-lit bar and period furnished dining rooms. The menu has a meaty, masculine base, with a mix of classical and more modern dishes - and plenty of local game in season.

Carte £ 36/54

School Ln ✉ NG12 3FD - ✆ 01949 81361 - www.themartinsarms.co.uk - Closed dinner 25 and 26 December and Sunday dinner

COMPTON BASSETT
Wiltshire - Regional map n° **2**-C2

White Horse Inn
TRADITIONAL BRITISH • FRIENDLY The White Horse dates back over a century: the cosy bar is where you'll find the regulars, while most diners head for the rustic room next door. For traditionalists there are pub classics; for those with more adventurous tastes there's the à la carte. Beyond the large garden are 8 snug bedrooms.

Menu £ 15 (weekday lunch) - Carte £ 23/52

8 rooms - £ 85/110 £ 95/120

✉ SN11 8RG - ✆ 01249 813118 - www.whitehorse-comptonbassett.co.uk

CONDOVER - Shropshire → See Shrewsbury

COOKHAM
Windsor and Maidenhead - ✉ Maidenhead - Pop. 5 304 - Regional map n° **6**-C3

White Oak
TRADITIONAL BRITISH • FRIENDLY One could argue whether this is a contemporary pub or a pubby restaurant, as it's set up quite formally, but what is in no doubt is the warmth of the welcome and the affection in which the place is held by its regulars. Cooking is carefully executed and full of flavour; the set menu is great value.

Menu £ 19 (weekdays) - Carte £ 26/40

Pound Ln ✉ SL6 9QE - ✆ 01628 523043 - www.thewhiteoak.co.uk - Closed Sunday dinner

CORNHILL-ON-TWEED
Northumberland - Pop. 347 - Regional map n° **14**-A1

Tillmouth Park
COUNTRY HOUSE • HISTORIC Late Victorian country house set in 15 acres of prime shooting and fishing country. The welcoming interior comes with grand staircases, wood panelling and characterful stained glass. Traditional guest areas have lovely views; the most popular bedrooms boast four-poster beds. Cooking is fittingly classical.

14 rooms - £ 79/170 £ 190/280

✉ TD12 4UU - Northeast : 2.5 mi on A 698 - ✆ 01890 882255 - www.tillmouthpark.co.uk - Closed 1 February-12 April

CORSE LAWN - Worcestershire → See Tewkesbury (Glos.)

CORTON DENHAM

Somerset – ✉ Sherborne – Pop. 210 – Regional map n° **2**-C3

Queens Arms

MODERN BRITISH • PUB This hub-of-the-village pub hosts plenty of events and comes with plush bedrooms. The menu lists food 'metres' and much of the produce is from their smallholding; choose from small plates, pub classics and more elaborate dishes. The bar is topped with tempting treats and they do a great trade in afternoon tea.

Menu £ 17 (weekday lunch) – Carte £ 30/49

8 rooms – †£ 80/109 ††£ 99/150

✉ DT9 4LR – ✆ 01963 220317 – www.thequeensarms.com

COVERACK

Cornwall – Regional map n° **1**-A3

Bay

COUNTRY HOUSE • COSY Imposing, family-run country house located in a pretty fishing village and boasting views over the bay. Homely lounge and bar. Spotless, modern bedrooms with a slight New England edge. Dining room and conservatory offer a classical daily menu and local seafood specials.

14 rooms (dinner included) – †£ 95/220 ††£ 130/280

North Corner ✉ TR12 6TF – ✆ 01326 280464 – www.thebayhotel.co.uk – Closed November-25 March

COWAN BRIDGE

Lancashire – Regional map n° **11**-B1

Hipping Hall

MODERN CUISINE • ROMANTIC XX A charming part-15C blacksmith's named after the stepping stones over the beck. The elegant restaurant has a superb beamed ceiling, a minstrel's gallery and a medieval feel. Creative, original dishes feature on two tasting menus and come with wine pairings. The best bedrooms are in the outbuildings.

Menu £ 55/75

15 rooms – †£ 152/252 ††£ 169/269 – 3 suites

on A 65 ✉ LA6 2JJ – ✆ 015242 71187 (booking essential) – www.hippinghall.com – dinner only and lunch Saturday-Sunday

COWLEY

Gloucestershire – Regional map n° **2**-C1

Cowley Manor

LUXURY • CONTEMPORARY Impressive Regency house in 55 acres, with beautiful formal gardens, a superb spa, and lake views from some of the bedrooms. Original features and retro furnishings mix with bold colours and modern fittings to create a laid-back, understated vibe. The carved wood panelling in the restaurant is a feature.

30 rooms – †£ 205/565 ††£ 205/675 – 8 suites

✉ GL53 9NL – ✆ 01242 870900 – www.cowleymanor.com

CRANBORNE

Dorset – Pop. 606 – Regional map n° **2**-D3

10 Castle Street

HISTORIC BUILDING • ELEGANT A listed Queen Anne house with a lovely terrace looking out over beautiful gardens. The stunning interior has a relaxed, contemporary country house style and bedrooms are supremely comfortable. Laid-back dining features fresh, unfussy flavours. The first floor comprises a residents' and private members' club.

9 rooms – £ 155/350 £ 195/450

10 Castle St BH21 5PZ – 01725 551133 – www.10castlestreet.com – Closed 25 and 31 December

CRANBROOK

Kent – Pop. 4 225 – Regional map n° **5**-B2

Cloth Hall Oast

HISTORIC • PERSONALISED A superbly restored oast house in a charming countryside spot. Antiques, family photos and fine artwork fill the drawing room and bedrooms are traditional and well-equipped; one boasts a splendid four-poster bed. Communal breakfasts are taken at an antique table in the galleried hall.

3 rooms – £ 65/130 £ 95/130

Coursehorn Ln TN17 3NR – East : 1 mi by Tenterden rd – 01580 712220 – www.clothhalloast.co.uk – Closed Christmas

CRAYKE

North Yorkshire – Regional map n° **13**-C2

Durham Ox

TRADITIONAL BRITISH • PUB A 300 year old pub in a sleepy hamlet; in summer, head for the lovely courtyard. Menus focus on honest, homely cooking, with everything made on-site; choose a blackboard special – often game or seafood accompanied by something 'wild'. Cosy bedrooms feature original brickwork and quarry tiling.

Menu £ 17 (weekday lunch) – Carte £ 25/48

6 rooms – £ 100/150 £ 120/150

Westway YO61 4TE – 01347 821506 – www.thedurhamox.com

CROCKERTON – Wiltshire → See Warminster

CROMER

Norfolk – Pop. 7 949 – Regional map n° **8**-D1

No1 Cromer

FISH AND CHIPS • SIMPLE This is fish and chips with a difference: looking out over the beach and pier and offering everything from fresh fish and battered local sausages to cockle popcorn and mushy pea fritters. Potatoes are from their farm and the varieties change throughout the year. Head up to the bistro for some tasty fish tapas.

Carte £ 19/29

1 New St NR27 9HP – 01263 515983 (bookings not accepted) – www.no1cromer.com – Closed 2 weeks January, 1 week November and 24-25 December

CROPSTON

Leicestershire – Pop. 1 197 – Regional map n° **9**-B2

Horseshoe Cottage Farm

FAMILY • CLASSIC Well-run, extended farmhouse and outbuildings, beside Bradgate Country Park. Traditional bedrooms with beams, exposed stonework and coordinating fabrics. Small breakfast room and a larger, high-ceilinged drawing room, with a solid oak table where communal dinners are served; local and garden produce features.

3 rooms – £ 70 £ 110

Roecliffe Rd, Hallgates LE7 7HQ – Northwest : 1 mi on Woodhouse Eaves rd – 0116 235 0038 – www.horseshoecottagefarm.com

CROSTHWAITE

Cumbria - Regional map n° **12**-A2

Punch Bowl Inn

TRADITIONAL BRITISH • INN The picturesque Lyth valley plays host to this charming 17C inn, where a cosy beamed bar doubles as the village post office. Have a pint of local beer and some homemade pork scratchings or fresh, carefully cooked classics like cheese soufflé or coq au vin. Bedrooms are luxurious - one even has twin baths!

Carte £ 29/48

9 rooms - £ 85/240 £ 110/320

LA8 8HR - 015395 68237 - www.the-punchbowl.co.uk

CRUDWELL - Wiltshire → See Malmesbury

CRUNDALE

Kent - Regional map n° **5**-C2

Compasses Inn

MODERN CUISINE • TRADITIONAL DÉCOR This hugely characterful 1420s pub is run by an enthusiastic young couple who have a genuine desire to please. The small front bar has hop-hung beams and inglenook fireplaces and the dining room opens out onto the garden. Menus mix well-prepared comfort dishes with those with a little more finesse.

Menu £ 17 (weekday lunch) - Carte £ 34/42

Sole Street CT4 7ES - Northwest : 1.25 mi - 01227 700300 - www.thecompassescrundale.co.uk - Closed Sunday dinner, Monday and Tuesday

CUCKFIELD

West Sussex - Pop. 3 500 - Regional map n° **4**-D2

Ockenden Manor

HISTORIC • CLASSIC A part-Elizabethan manor house in 9 acres of parkland. Kick-back in the cosy panelled bar or beside the grand fireplace in the elegant drawing room, then stay the night in either a characterful period bedroom or one of the modern rooms above the chic spa. Classical seasonal cooking is served in the orangery.

28 rooms - £ 149/529 £ 189/569 - 3 suites

Ockenden Ln RH17 5LD - 01444 416111 - www.ockenden-manor.co.uk

CUNDALL

North Yorkshire - Regional map n° **13**-B2

Cundall Lodge Farm

COUNTRY HOUSE • RURAL A Grade II listed Georgian farmhouse on a working arable farm; its 150 acres include a stretch of the River Swale. Country bedrooms come with homemade flapjack and Roberts radios. The breakfast room looks out over the Vale of York towards the Hambleton Hills. The friendly owners have great local knowledge.

3 rooms - £ 75/110 £ 90/110

YO61 2RN - Northwest : 0.5 mi on Asenby rd - 01423 360203 - www.cundall-lodgefarm.co.uk - Closed Christmas-New Year

DALTON-IN-FURNESS

Cumbria - Pop. 7 827 - Regional map n° **12**-A3

Clarence House

MODERN BRITISH • TRADITIONAL DÉCOR XX This is a proper country house hotel restaurant with luxurious furnishings and willing service. Dishes are traditionally based but are modern in their execution. They use the finest Cumbrian meats, so steak is always a good bet.

Carte £ 27/52

Clarence House Hotel, Skelgate ✉ LA15 8BQ - ✆ 01229 462508 - www.clarencehouse-hotel.co.uk - Closed 25-26 December

Clarence House

FAMILY • CLASSIC The majority of guests here are repeat customers – which says a lot about the way the family run it. Relax in the peaceful, mature gardens or in one of the plush sitting rooms. Some bedrooms come with jacuzzis or four-posters.

28 rooms ☕ - †£ 95/130 ††£ 115/160

Skelgate ✉ LA15 8BQ - ✆ 01229 462508 - www.clarencehouse-hotel.com - Closed 25-26 December

Clarence House – See restaurant listing

DARLEY ABBEY - Derby → See Derby

DARLINGTON

Darlington – Pop. 92 363 – Regional map n° **14**-B3

Clow Beck House

FAMILY • COSY A collection of converted farm buildings not far from the River Tees, with welcoming owners and a homely interior. Immaculately kept, tastefully furnished bedrooms come with bathrobes and chocolates; the larger ones have dressing rooms. Dinners are home-cooked, with puzzles supplied while you wait.

10 rooms ☕ - †£ 90 ††£ 140

Monk End Farm, Croft-on-Tees ✉ DL2 2SP - South : 5.25 mi by A 167 off Barton rd - ✆ 01325 721075 - www.clowbeckhouse.co.uk - Closed 24 December-3 January

Houndgate Townhouse

TOWNHOUSE • CONTEMPORARY This smart Georgian townhouse – formerly a registry office – is set on a quiet square in the heart of town. Inside, stylish colour schemes and contemporary furnishings create a boutique feel; bedroom Two has a bath in the room. The bistro has comfy booths, a terrace and a menu of modern classics.

8 rooms ☕ - †£ 90/140 ††£ 100/150

11 Houndgate ✉ DL1 5RF - ✆ 01325 486011 - www.houndgatetownhouse.co.uk - Closed 25-26 December

at Hurworth-on-Tees South: 5.5 mi by A167

The Orangery

MODERN CUISINE • INTIMATE XXX An elegant glass extension in a country house hotel. Set menus include vegetarian, pescatarian and surprise options. Dishes are carefully crafted and eye-catching, with contrasting textures and flavours.

Menu £ 65

Rockcliffe Hall Hotel, ✉ DL2 2DU - ✆ 01325 729999 (booking essential) - www.rockliffehall.com - dinner only - Closed Sunday and Monday

Bay Horse

MODERN CUISINE • PUB A good-looking pub with a smart, elegant feel; the jewel in its crown is a lovely garden and terrace. Appealing modern menus include the likes of rabbit ballotine with creamed polenta and confit rabbit lasagne.

Menu £ 20 (weekday lunch) - Carte £ 35/59

45 The Green ✉ DL2 2AA - ✆ 01325 720663 - www.thebayhorsehurworth.com - Closed 25-26 December

Rockliffe Hall

LUXURY • MODERN An impressive manor house set in 376 acres of grounds, complete with a championship golf course, extensive leisure facilities and an Alice in Wonderland outdoor adventure area. The original Victorian house has grand guest areas and characterful bedrooms; rooms in the extensions are more modern. Dining options range from classics and grills to ambitious modern dishes.

61 rooms – £ 200/250 £ 230/505

DL2 2DU – 01325 729999 – www.rockliffehall.com

The Orangery – See restaurant listing

at Summerhouse Northwest: 6.5 mi by A68 on B6279

Raby Hunt (James Close)

MODERN BRITISH • INTIMATE XX This former drovers' inn in a rural hamlet was originally part of the Raby Estate and its name refers to it being a favourite finishing point for the old hunt. It's owned by the Close family, with son James – a self-taught chef – heading up the kitchen. His interest in food was sparked as a youngster, when he would ask his parents to order certain dishes in restaurants so that he could try new things – and even at such a young age kept notebooks of his discoveries.

Now inspired by the landscape around him, he favours a classic base with modern overtones and a European style, and his drive and ambition – along with his travels – lead him to continually refine and enhance his dishes. Ingredients are first-class and, whilst his ethos is one of simplicity, every dish is original and flavours are sublime, leaving you impatient for the next.

Stay the night in a contemporary bedroom.

→ Tempura langoustine. Raw beef and caviar. Mango, yuzu and coconut tart.

Menu £ 120/150 – tasting menu only

3 rooms – £ 180/200 £ 180/200

DL2 3UD – 01325 374237 (booking essential) – www.rabyhuntrestaurant.co.uk – dinner only and Friday-Saturday lunch – Closed 1 week spring, 1 week summer, 1 week autumn, 2 weeks Christmas and Sunday-Tuesday

at Headlam Northwest: 8 mi by A67 ✉ Gainford

Headlam Hall

FAMILY • HISTORIC A family-run manor house with delightful walled gardens, set in a secluded country spot. Spacious sitting rooms are furnished with antiques and the well-equipped bedrooms are a mix of the traditional and the modern.

38 rooms – £ 115/205 £ 145/235 – 4 suites

DL2 3HA – 01325 730238 – www.headlamhall.co.uk – Closed 24-27 December

DARSHAM

Suffolk – Regional map n° **8**-D2

Darsham Nurseries Café

COUNTRY • SIMPLE X In 2014 the owners of this nursery opened a smart gift shop and this sweet little café. Expect colourful, richly flavoured small plates of locally sourced organic and garden produce, with vegetarian and vegan dishes making up a large proportion of the menu. On Sundays they only serve brunch.

Carte £ 17/27

Main Rd ✉ IP17 3PW – (on A 12) – 01728 667022 (booking essential) – www.darshamnurseries.co.uk – lunch only and dinner Friday-Saturday – Closed 25-26 December

DARTMOUTH

Devon – Pop. 6 008 – Regional map n° **1**-C3

Seahorse

SEAFOOD • CHIC XX A smart restaurant in a lovely spot on the embankment; sit outside looking over the estuary or inside beside the glass-walled kitchen. Seafood-orientated menus have a Mediterranean bias, with Josper-grilled whole fish and fresh pastas the favourites. Start with a cocktail in the lovely Joe's Bar.

Menu £ 20 (lunch and early dinner) – Carte £ 39/64

5 South Embankment ✉ TQ6 9BH – ✆ 01803 835147 (booking essential) – www.seahorserestaurant.co.uk – Closed 4 days Christmas, Sunday dinner and Monday

Dart Marina

TRADITIONAL • DESIGN Once an old boat works and chandlery, now a relaxed, modern hotel with a small spa and leisure centre. Smart, contemporary bedrooms have lovely outlooks over either the river or marina – many also boast balconies. The stylish, formal restaurant offers up-to-date versions of British classics.

53 rooms – £ 115/160 £ 180/470 – 4 suites

Sandquay Rd ✉ TQ6 9PH – ✆ 01803 832580 – www.dartmarina.com

at Strete Southwest: 4.5 mi on A379 ✉ Dartmouth

Strete Barton House

HISTORIC • PERSONALISED Attractive part-16C manor house in a quiet village, with partial views over the rooftops to the sea. The contemporary interior has a personal style; bedrooms come with bold feature walls and modern facilities. Homemade cake is served on arrival and top quality local ingredients feature at breakfast.

6 rooms – £ 82/175 £ 82/175

Totnes Rd ✉ TQ6 0RU – ✆ 01803 770364 – www.stretebarton.co.uk – Closed January

DAVENTRY

Northamptonshire – Pop. 23 879 – Regional map n° **9**-B3

Fawsley Hall

COUNTRY HOUSE • PERSONALISED Set in 2,000 peaceful acres, a luxurious Tudor manor house with Georgian and Victorian extensions. Have afternoon tea in the Great Hall or unwind in the exclusive spa. Smart, well-appointed bedrooms vary from wing to wing. Have lunch in the courtyard and dinner in the atmospheric restaurant.

60 rooms – £ 152/282 £ 152/282 – 2 suites

Fawsley ✉ NN11 3BA – South : 6.5 mi by A 45 off A 361 – ✆ 01327 892000 – www.handpicked.co.uk/fawsley

at Staverton Southwest: 2.75 mi by A45 off A425 ✉ Daventry

Colledges House

TRADITIONAL • PERSONALISED Lovely 17C thatched cottage and barn run by a charming owner. The cosy lounge is filled with antiques and curios; the conservatory is a pleasant spot in summer. Bedrooms have floral fabrics and good extras.

4 rooms – £ 68/70 £ 95/99

Oakham Ln ✉ NN11 6JQ – off Glebe Ln – ✆ 01327 702737 – www.colledgeshouse.co.uk

at Charwelton South : 6.25 mi by A 45 on A 361

Fox & Hounds

TRADITIONAL BRITISH • PUB The Fox & Hounds has been a fixture in Charwelton since 1871 and is now owned by the villagers themselves. Lunch sees pub classics, while at dinner the chef's Italian heritage really shines through in confidently prepared dishes such as coley with caponata, walnut gnocchi and sage pesto.

Menu £ 18 (weekdays) – Carte £ 25/45

Banbury Rd ✉ NN11 3YY – ✆ 01327 260611 – www.foxandhoundscharwelton.co.uk – Closed 1-7 January and Sunday dinner

DAYLESFORD - Gloucestershire ➜ See Stow-on-the-Wold

DEAL

Kent - Pop. 30 555 - Regional map n° **5**-D2

Frog and Scot

MODERN BRITISH • BISTRO A quirky bistro with yellow canopies and mismatched furnishings; its unusual name refers to its French and Scottish owners. Large blackboard menus list refined, innately simple dishes which let the ingredients do the talking.

Menu £ 15 (lunch) - Carte dinner £ 30/46

86 High St ✉ CT14 6EG - ✆ 01304 379444 - www.frogandscot.co.uk - Closed 25 December, 1 January and Sunday dinner-Tuesday

Victuals & Co

MODERN BRITISH • BISTRO You'll find this enthusiastically run restaurant down a narrow passageway - its name a reference to the victuallers who once supplied the local ships. Classic dishes are given modern twists; the set menu represents good value.

Carte £ 30/49

St Georges Passage ✉ CT14 6TA - ✆ 01304 374389 - www.victualsandco.com - Closed January-February, Monday-Tuesday except bank holiday Mondays and lunch Wednesday-Friday

Bear's Well (N)

TOWNHOUSE • PERSONALISED Set in the shadow of St George's Church, this Georgian house takes its name from an old freshwater well which was sited beneath the property and used to supply passing vessels. Tastefully decorated, understated bedrooms are hung with attractive local art. Local and homemade produce features at breakfast.

3 rooms - †£ 110/120 ††£ 120/130

10 St George's Rd ✉ CT14 6BA - ✆ 01304 694144 - www.bearswell.co.uk

at Worth Northwest: 5 mi by A258

Solley Farm House

FAMILY • PERSONALISED Attractive 300 year old house overlooking the duck pond and run by a charming owner. In the beamed lounge, a vast inglenook fireplace takes centre stage; colour-themed bedrooms come with great extras. Have breakfast on the terrace.

3 rooms - †£ 115 ††£ 160

The Street ✉ CT14 0DG - ✆ 01304 613701 - www.solleyfarmhouse.co.uk - Closed December

DEDHAM

Essex - ✉ Colchester - Pop. 719 - Regional map n° **7**-D2

Le Talbooth

MODERN BRITISH • RUSTIC This superbly characterful property on the riverbank is the restaurant of a charming hotel; if you're staying the night, you can be chauffeured over by Bentley. Inside it has a stylish rustic-chic design and most tables have a river view. Cooking has classic roots and subtle modern touches.

Menu £ 36 (weekday lunch) - Carte £ 47/65

Maison Talbooth Hotel, Gun Hill ✉ CO7 6HN - West : 0.75 mi - ✆ 01206 323150 - www.milsomhotels.com - Closed Sunday dinner October-May

Sun Inn

ITALIAN • INN Characterful yellow inn with an appealing shabby-chic style, located in a picturesque spot in the heart of Constable Country. The monthly menu offers generous Italian-inspired dishes and the well-chosen wine list offers plenty by the glass. Bedrooms are cosy – two have a modern New England style.

Carte £ 24/40

7 rooms – £ 90/130 £ 145

High St ✉ CO7 6DF – ✆ 01206 323351 – www.thesuninndedham.com – Closed 25-26 December

Maison Talbooth

LUXURY • CONTEMPORARY A charming part-Georgian house in rolling countryside, with a modern country house feel and views over the river valley. Luxurious bedrooms boast quality furnishings and come in a mix of classic and contemporary styles. Seek out the tennis court and the year-round heated outdoor pool and hot tub.

12 rooms – £ 300/499 £ 300/499

Stratford Rd ✉ CO7 6HN – West : 0.5 mi – ✆ 01206 322367 – www.milsomhotels.com

Le Talbooth – See restaurant listing

Milsoms

COUNTRY HOUSE • MODERN A late 19C country house with modern additions, overlooking Dedham Vale; its interior is stylish and contemporary, and its bedrooms are luxurious and well-equipped. The airy bar-restaurant with its covered terrace is a popular spot – it's open all day and offers an appealing menu.

15 rooms – £ 145/190 £ 145/190

Stratford Rd ✉ CO7 6HW – West : 0.75 mi – ✆ 01206 322795 – www.milsomhotels.com

DENHAM

Buckinghamshire – Pop. 1 432 – Regional map n° **6**-D3

Swan Inn

TRADITIONAL BRITISH • PUB Located in a picture postcard village; a wisteria-clad, red-brick Georgian pub with a pleasant terrace and mature gardens. Alongside well-executed pub classics you'll find more interesting dishes such as twice-baked pumpkin soufflé. Puddings are traditional – choose 'Coffee & Pud' for a smaller treat.

Carte £ 24/44

Village Rd ✉ UB9 5BH – ✆ 01895 832085 – www.swaninndenham.co.uk

DERBY

Derby – Pop. 255 394 – Regional map n° **9**-B2

at Darley Abbey North : 2.5 mi off A6 ✉ Derby

Darleys

MODERN CUISINE • FRIENDLY XX A popular weir-side restaurant, located in the old canteen of a 19C silk mill. Start with drinks in the modern bar-lounge or on the attractive terrace. Good value lunches are followed by more ambitious European dishes in the evening.

Menu £ 25 (lunch and early dinner) – Carte £ 34/47

Darley Abbey Mill ✉ DE22 1DZ – ✆ 01332 364987 – www.darleys.com – Closed 25 December-10 January, Sunday dinner and bank holidays

DEVIZES

Wiltshire – Pop. 18 064 – Regional map n° **2**-C2

Blounts Court Farm

COUNTRY HOUSE · PERSONALISED Delightfully run farmhouse on a 150 acre working farm; the village cricket team play in one of their fields! The snug interior consists of a cosy lounge and a spacious breakfast room filled with clocks and curios. Warm, well-kept bedrooms show good attention to detail. Pastel artwork and country photos abound.

3 rooms – £ 62/68 £ 94/110

Coxhill Ln, Potterne ✉ SN10 5PH – South : 2.25 mi by A 360 – ✆ 01380 727180 – www.blountscourtfarm.co.uk

DIDSBURY – Greater Manchester → See Manchester

DODDINGTON

Kent – Regional map n° **5**-C2

Old Vicarage

FAMILY · CLASSIC Grade II listed former vicarage with 16C origins, where wood and stone blend with modern furnishings. There's an impressive galleried hall and a striking antique breakfast table. Bedrooms feature coffee machines and Bose sound systems.

5 rooms – £ 75/90 £ 105/120

Church Hill ✉ ME9 0BD – ✆ 01795 886136 – www.oldvicaragedoddington.co.uk – Closed 24 December-2 January

DOGMERSFIELD

Hampshire – Regional map n° **4**-C1

Four Seasons

LUXURY · CLASSIC An attractive part-Georgian house in 350 acres of parkland where, along with relaxing in the superb spa, you can try your hand at all manner of outdoor pursuits. Luxurious bedrooms are well-equipped and boast marble bathrooms. Rotisserie meats are a speciality in the stylish bar and brasserie.

133 rooms – £ 340/350 £ 340/350 – £ 30 – 21 suites

Dogmersfield Park, Chalky Ln ✉ RG27 8TD – ✆ 01252 853000 – www.fourseasons.com/hampshire

DONHEAD-ST-ANDREW

Wiltshire – Regional map n° **2**-C3

The Forester

TRADITIONAL BRITISH · RUSTIC A gloriously rustic 13C thatched pub, hidden down narrow lanes in a delightful village. Exposed stone walls and vast open fires feature throughout. Daily changing menus showcase well-prepared, flavoursome dishes with a classical country base and a refined edge; Brixham fish features highly.

Menu £ 27 (weekdays) – Carte £ 24/40

Lower St ✉ SP7 9EE – ✆ 01747 828038 – www.theforesterdonheadstandrew.co.uk – Closed Sunday dinner and Monday except bank holidays

DORCHESTER

Dorset – Pop. 19 060 – Regional map n° **2**-C3

Sienna

MODERN CUISINE • COSY XX This unassuming high street restaurant is run by a keen young chef who cooks alone in the kitchen. Concise menu descriptions belie the complexity of the dishes, which are modern and ambitious both in flavour and presentation. It has just five tables, so book ahead.

Menu £ 25/35

36 High West St ✉ DT1 1UP - ✆ 01305 250022 (booking essential) - www.siennadorchester.co.uk - Closed 25-26 December, 1 January and Sunday dinner-Tuesday

Yalbury Cottage

TRADITIONAL BRITISH • RUSTIC XX This very proudly and personally run restaurant is set within an old thatched cottage and has a snug beamed interior. Cooking is traditional, gutsy and flavoursome. Produce is sourced from within 9 miles and the menu evolves as new ingredients become available. Well-kept cottagey bedrooms are located in a wing.

Menu £ 40

8 rooms - †£ 75/85 ††£ 99/125

Lower Bockhampton ✉ DT2 8PZ - East : 3.75 mi by A 35 - ✆ 01305 262382 (booking essential) - www.yalburycottage.com - dinner only and Sunday lunch - Closed 23 December-18 January

Little Court

TRADITIONAL • CLASSIC Lutyens-style house boasting Edwardian wood and brickwork, leaded windows and mature gardens with a pool and tennis court. Bedrooms display original features and modern furnishings; one has a four-poster bed.

8 rooms - †£ 79/119 ††£ 89/129

5 Westleaze, Charminster ✉ DT2 9PZ - North : 1 mi by B3147, turning right at Loders garage - ✆ 01305 261576 - www.littlecourt.net - Closed 22 December-2 January

DORKING

Surrey - Pop. 17 098 - Regional map n° **4**-D2

Sorrel (Steve Drake)

MODERN BRITISH • ELEGANT XX Steve Drake knows the area well and understands what the locals want. The main room is intimate, understated and packed with period charm - and the glass-walled kitchen provides a modern contrast. Precisely prepared dishes are original, colourful and sometimes playful. You'll leave planning your next visit.

→ Scallop, smoked cauliflower, curried granola and cucumber ketchup. Herdwick lamb with artichoke, smoked paprika, sherry and miso aubergine. Ginger, blueberry, oregano and lavender.

Menu £ 35/95

77 South St ✉ RH4 2JU - ✆ 01306 889414 (booking essential) - www.sorrelrestaurant.co.uk - Closed 2 weeks Christmas, 2 weeks August and Sunday-Tuesday

DREWSTEIGNTON

Devon - Pop. 668 - Regional map n° **1**-C2

Old Inn

MODERN BRITISH • INTIMATE XX An old 17C pub in the centre of a lovely village. It has two small, cosy dining rooms, and a parquet-floored lounge with a woodburning stove in its inglenook fireplace and modern art for sale on the walls. The concise menu offers assured, seasonal modern dishes. Bedrooms are simply furnished.

Menu £ 55

3 rooms - †£ 80/90 ††£ 100/110

✉ EX6 6QR - ✆ 01647 281276 (booking essential) - www.old-inn.co.uk - dinner only - Closed 2 weeks January, 1-5 June and Sunday-Tuesday

DRIGHLINGTON

West Yorkshire – Regional map n° **13**-B2

Prashad

INDIAN VEGETARIAN • NEIGHBOURHOOD XX Stylish former pub with wooden panels from India fronting the bar; head upstairs to admire the huge picture of a Mumbai street scene. Authentic vegetarian dishes range from enticing street food to more original creations, with influences from Southern India and Gujarat; be sure to try the dosas.

Menu £ 17 (weekdays) – Carte £ 25/40

137 Whitehall Rd ✉ BD11 1AT – ✆ 0113 285 2037 – www.prashad.co.uk – dinner only and lunch Saturday-Sunday – Closed 25 December

DULVERTON

Somerset – Pop. 1 052 – Regional map n° **2**-A2

Woods

MODERN BRITISH • PUB Former bakery, with a cosy, hugely characterful interior. Tasty, carefully prepared dishes offer more than just the usual pub fare. Provenance is taken seriously, with quality local ingredients including meat from the owner's farm.

Carte £ 25/41

4 Banks Sq ✉ TA22 9BU – ✆ 01398 324007 – www.woodsdulverton.co.uk – Closed 25 December, dinner 26 December and 1 January

DUNSFORD

Devon – Regional map n° **1**-C2

Weeke Barton

HISTORIC • CONTEMPORARY The owners of this 15C Devonshire longhouse are friendly and laid-back, and the place itself has a funky yet cosy feel. The interior combines old world character with stylish furnishings, and bedrooms are modern and minimalistic. Rustic, home-cooked dishes feature in the communal dining room.

5 rooms – †£ 115/135 ††£ 125/145

✉ EX6 7HH – Southeast : 1.5 mi by B 3212 and Christow rd, turning right up unmarked road after river bridge – ✆ 01647 253505 – www.weekebarton.com – Closed Christmas and New Year

DUNSTER

Somerset – Pop. 408 – Regional map n° **2**-A2

Luttrell Arms

HISTORIC • PERSONALISED A stone built 15C inn – once a hostelry for monks – with open fires, period features and a small medieval courtyard. Bedrooms are named after local landmarks: one has an ornate plaster fireplace; another a four-poster and an impressive timbered ceiling. Traditional dishes are served in the formal restaurant.

28 rooms – †£ 105/140 ††£ 150/220

32-36 High St ✉ TA24 6SG – ✆ 01643 821555 – www.luttrellarms.co.uk

DURHAM

Durham – Pop. 47 785 – Regional map n° **14**-B3

Finbarr's

MODERN BRITISH • BISTRO XX Finbarr's has relocated to a converted farm building on the edge of the city – it's a place familiar to the owners, who both worked here previously. Menus offer plenty of choice and the hearty brasserie cooking suits the area well.

Menu £ 18/25 (weekdays) – Carte £ 29/54

Aykley Heads House, Aykley Heads ✉ DH1 5TS – Northwest : 1.5 mi by A 691 and B 6532. – ✆ 0191 307 7033 – www.finbarrsrestaurant.co.uk – Closed first week January, 25-26 December and bank holidays

Castle View

TOWNHOUSE • COSY An attractive Georgian townhouse set beside a Norman castle on a steep cobbled hill. Large bedrooms have modern monochrome colour schemes and smart bathrooms. Enjoy breakfast on the terrace in summer.

5 rooms – £ 90 £ 110

4 Crossgate ✉ DH1 4PS
– ✆ 0191 386 8852 – www.castle-view.co.uk
– Closed 16 December-10 January

EARL STONHAM

Suffolk – Regional map n° **8**-C3

Bays Farm

FAMILY • PERSONALISED A delightful 17C farmhouse run by charming hosts and surrounded by 4 acres of beautifully landscaped gardens. Smart, modern bedrooms are individually styled – 'The Hayloft' is the most luxurious and the stand-alone wooden Shepherd's Hut has its own decked terrace. Breakfast features homemade bread and jam.

5 rooms – £ 80/135 £ 90/145

Forward Grn ✉ IP14 5HU – Northwest : 1 mi by A 1120 on Broad Green rd
– ✆ 01449 711286 – www.baysfarmsuffolk.co.uk

EAST CHISENBURY

Wiltshire – Regional map n° **2**-D2

Red Lion Freehouse (Guy Manning)

CLASSIC CUISINE • SIMPLE Set on the edge of Salisbury Plain, this charming thatched pub and its pretty garden immediately draw you in. The daily à la carte is a roll-call of carefully prepared classics, which arrive fully garnished and packed with flavour; the midweek lunch is great value. Smart, well-equipped bedrooms are set opposite and have private terraces overlooking the river.

→ Foie gras and wood pigeon terrine. Roast turbot with mussels, saffron potatoes and shellfish beurre blanc. New York cheesecake with Yorkshire rhubarb and iced Hendrick's & tonic.

Menu £ 24 (lunch and early dinner) – Carte £ 36/54

5 rooms – £ 160/245 £ 160/245

✉ SN9 6AQ
– ✆ 01980 671124 – www.redlionfreehouse.com
– Closed Sunday dinner except bank holidays, Monday and Tuesday

EAST END

Hampshire – Regional map n° **4**-A3

East End Arms

TRADITIONAL BRITISH • RUSTIC This traditional country pub is owned by John Illsley of Dire Straits and boasts a great display of photos from his personal collection in its shabby bar and pine-furnished dining room. Concise menus feature local produce in satisfying British dishes. Modern cottage-style bedrooms provide a smart contrast.

Carte £ 23/46

5 rooms – £ 110/120 £ 120/140

Lymington Rd ✉ SO41 5SY
– ✆ 01590 626223 – www.eastendarms.co.uk
– Closed dinner Sunday

EAST GRINSTEAD

West Sussex – Pop. 29 084 – Regional map n° **4**-D2

✿ Gravetye Manor

MODERN BRITISH • TRADITIONAL DÉCOR XXX This contemporary extension sits on the side of a Grade 1 listed country house. The architect has been a regular guest at the hotel for over 30 years and his design brings the wonderful gardens inside by using natural colours and glass. Local and garden produce informs the highly visual dishes.

→ Crab and cucumber with crab emulsion and caviar. Lamb with new potatoes, peas and mint jellies. Guanaja chocolate bar, lovage and cocoa nibs.

Menu £ 40/75

Gravetye Manor Hotel, Vowels Ln ✉ RH19 4LJ
– ✆ 01342 810567 (booking essential) – www.gravetyemanor.co.uk

Gravetye Manor

LUXURY • CLASSIC A quintessential English country house set in a forest and surrounded by 35 acres of glorious gardens. Ornate Elizabethan ceilings and fireplaces dominate beautifully furnished lounges, which provide the perfect spot for afternoon tea. Bedrooms are luxurious and the service is personalised and detailed.

17 rooms – †£ 275/595 ††£ 275/595 – 1 suite

Vowels Ln ✉ RH19 4LJ – Southwest : 4.5 mi by B 2110 taking second turn left towards West Hoathly
– ✆ 01342 810567 – www.gravetyemanor.co.uk

✿ **Gravetye Manor** – See restaurant listing

EAST HADDON

Northamptonshire – Pop. 643 – Regional map n° **9**-B3

Red Lion

TRADITIONAL CUISINE • PUB A thatched, honey-stone inn at the heart of an attractive village, with a pleasing mix of exposed wood, brick and slate, a pretty garden and chic, cosy bedrooms. The good value, seasonal menu offers generously proportioned dishes; the scotch egg is a favourite. Service is smiley and enthusiastic.

Carte £ 22/44

7 rooms – †£ 85/95 ††£ 95/110

Main St ✉ NN6 8BU
– ✆ 01604 770223 – www.redlioneasthaddon.co.uk – Closed 25 December

EAST HENDRED

Oxfordshire – Pop. 1 116 – Regional map n° **6**-B3

Eyston Arms

TRADITIONAL CUISINE • PUB A series of cosy, low-beamed rooms centre around an inglenook fireplace at this charming pub, and candles and caricatures of the locals add a modern touch. The menu draws on many cuisines, from Italian to Asian.

Carte £ 25/38

High St ✉ OX12 8JY
– ✆ 01235 833320 – www.eystonarms.co.uk – Closed 25 December

EAST HOATHLY

East Sussex – Pop. 893 – Regional map n° **5**-B3

Old Whyly

TRADITIONAL • PERSONALISED A traditional red-brick house built in 1760, set in beautiful grounds and very personally run by a delightful owner. Guest areas mix the classic and the contemporary; the lovely dining room offers daily 3 course dinners. Bedrooms are designed around subtle themes: choose Tulip, French or Chinese.

4 rooms – £ 85/150 £ 98/150

London Rd ✉ BN8 6EL – ✆ 01825 840216 – www.oldwhyly.co.uk

EAST WITTERING

West Sussex – Pop. 5 647 – Regional map n° **4**-C3

Samphire

TRADITIONAL BRITISH • SIMPLE A brightly decorated bistro with a shabby-chic beach café style, set 100 metres from the sea. Freshly caught seafood comes from the local day boats and meats are from the surrounding countryside. Cooking is unfussy and good value.

Menu £ 16 (weekday lunch) – Carte £ 27/38

57 Shore Rd ✉ PO20 8DY – ✆ 01243 672754 – www.samphireeastwittering.co.uk – Closed 2 weeks January, Christmas and Sunday

EASTBOURNE

East Sussex – Pop. 109 185 – Regional map n° **5**-B3

Grand

GRAND LUXURY • CLASSIC Built in 1875 and offering all its name promises, the Grand retains many original features including ornate plasterwork, columned corridors and a Great Hall. The delightful gardens feature a superb outdoor pool and sun terrace. Bedrooms are spacious and classical – it's worth paying extra for a sea view. Dine in formal Mirabelle or the more accessible Garden Restaurant.

152 rooms – £ 120 £ 150/345 – 14 suites

King Edward's Par. ✉ BN21 4EQ – ✆ 01323 412345 – www.grandeastbourne.com

Ocklynge Manor

HISTORIC • PERSONALISED Sit in the small summerhouse and admire the beautiful gardens of this charming 18C guesthouse, where Mabel Lucie Attwell (illustrator of Peter Pan and Wendy) once lived. Homemade cake is served on arrival and homemade bread, jam and yoghurt feature at breakfast. Bedrooms are comfy and traditional.

3 rooms – £ 60/120 £ 100/130

Mill Rd ✉ BN21 2PG – Northwest : 2 mi by A 259 and A 2270 – ✆ 01323 734121 – www.ocklyngemanor.co.uk

EBRINGTON – Gloucestershire → See Chipping Campden

ECKINGTON – Worcestershire → See Pershore

EGERTON

Kent – Regional map n° **5**-C2

The Barrow House

TRADITIONAL BRITISH • PUB This stylishly modernised inn was built in 1576 using timbers from old sailing ships. Wide-ranging menus appeal to all, with flavoursome small plates and satisfying mains. Meats are free-range and all ingredients are sourced from within 20 miles. Bedrooms blend modern décor with heavy beams.

Carte £ 23/43

3 rooms – £ 80/140 £ 80/140

The Street ✉ TN21 9DJ – ✆ 01233 756599 – www.thebarrowhouse.co.uk – Closed 25 December

EGHAM

Surrey - Pop. 25 996 - Regional map n° **4**-C1

Tudor Room

MODERN CUISINE • INTIMATE XxX An intimate hotel dining room with mullioned windows, burgundy décor and large tapestries on the walls. The menu might be concise but dishes are interesting, accomplished and full of flavour. Cooking is sophisticated but not over-complicated and the kitchen garden provides many of the ingredients.

→ Anjou pigeon with walnut, pomegranate and celeriac. Turbot with gnocchi and sprouts. Manjari chocolate with blood orange sorbet.

Menu £ 39/72 - tasting menu only

Great Fosters Hotel, Stroude Rd ✉ TW20 9UR - South : 1.25 mi by B 388 - ✆ 01784 433822 (booking essential) - www.greatfosters.co.uk - dinner only and lunch Thursday-Friday - Closed 2 weeks January, 2 weeks Easter, 2 weeks summer, Sunday-Tuesday

Great Fosters

BUSINESS • ELEGANT A striking Elizabethan manor built as a hunting lodge for Henry VIII, boasting 50 acres of gardens, a beautiful parterre and an amphitheatre. The charming interior displays characterful original detailing. Bedrooms come with feature beds and a flamboyant touch; those in the annexes are more modern. Dine on steaks from the Josper grill or more formally in the Tudor Room.

43 rooms - †£ 165/550 ††£ 225/550 - ☕ £ 20 - 3 suites

Stroude Rd ✉ TW20 9UR - South : 1.25 mi by B 388 - ✆ 01784 433822 - www.greatfosters.co.uk

Tudor Room - See restaurant listing

ELDERSFIELD

Worcestershire - Regional map n° **10**-B3

Butchers Arms

MODERN BRITISH • RUSTIC A thick wooden door salvaged from an old ship leads you into this sweet rural inn where hop bines vie for space with the locals' tankards on low exposed beams. Food is a mix of the classical and the modern, flavours are honest and portions are satisfying. Ales are served straight from the keg.

Menu £ 25 (weekday dinner) - Carte £ 35/49

Lime Street ✉ GL19 4NX - Southeast : 1 mi - ✆ 01452 840381 (booking essential) - www.thebutchersarms.net - dinner only and lunch Friday-Sunday - Closed last 2 weeks August, 1 week early January, Sunday dinner, Monday and bank holidays

ELLASTONE

Staffordshire - Regional map n° **10**-C1

Duncombe Arms

TRADITIONAL BRITISH • COSY A stylish dining pub owned by the Hon. Johnny Greenall - of the famous brewing family - and his wife, a descendant of the Duncombe family after which the pub is named. There are several cosy rooms to choose from, each with their own identity. Menus mix pub classics with more ambitious restaurant-style dishes.

Menu £ 22 (weekdays) - Carte £ 30/45

Main Road ✉ DE6 2GZ - ✆ 01335 324275 - www.duncombearms.co.uk - Closed 1 week January

ELSTREE

Hertfordshire - Pop. 1 986 - Regional map n° **7**-A2

Laura Ashley-The Manor H. Elstree

HISTORIC • PERSONALISED An eye-catching, timbered Edwardian house which showcases the latest fabrics, furnishings and fittings from the famous company. Well-equipped bedrooms: the largest and most characterful are in the main house. The intimate, formal restaurant offers modern cooking and views over the extensive gardens.

49 rooms - £ 110/205 £ 130/285

Barnet Ln ✉ WD6 3RE - ✆ 020 8327 4700 - www.lauraashleyhotels.com/elstree

ELTON-ON-THE-HILL

Nottinghamshire - Regional map n° **9**-B2

The Grange

FAMILY • COSY What better way to start your holiday than in this charming Georgian farmhouse with a slice of homemade cake? The owners are lovely, the gardens are delightful and the country views are superb. Bedrooms are homely and come with good facilities and thoughtful touches; one is accessed via a spiral staircase.

3 rooms - £ 55/59 £ 85/89

Sutton Ln. ✉ NG13 9LA - ✆ 07887 952181
- www.thegrangebedandbreakfastnotts.co.uk

ELY

Cambridgeshire - Pop. 19 090 - Regional map n° **8**-B2

Poets House

BUSINESS • MODERN A series of 19C townhouses set opposite the cathedral. Spacious, boutique bedrooms come with beautiful bathrooms, good extras and a moody feel. The modern bar overlooks the pretty walled garden and also offers afternoon tea. Dine on ambitious dishes, which include plenty of vegetarian options.

21 rooms - £ 150/230 £ 170/280

St Mary's St ✉ CB7 4EY - ✆ 01353 887777 - www.poetshouse.uk.com

EMSWORTH

Hampshire - Pop. 18 777 - Regional map n° **4**-B2

36 on the Quay

MODERN BRITISH • ELEGANT XX Long-standing, intimate restaurant and conservatory bar-lounge in a quayside cottage with pleasant harbour views. Concise menus offer elaborate modern dishes in some unusual combinations and foraged ingredients feature highly. Stylish bedrooms have good comforts; be ready to order breakfast at check-in.

Menu £ 29/58

4 rooms - £ 75/90 £ 100/150

47 South St, The Quay ✉ PO10 7EG - ✆ 01243 375592 - www.36onthequay.co.uk - Closed 2 weeks January, 1 week May, 1 week October, 23-29 December, Sunday and Monday

Fat Olives

MODERN BRITISH • RUSTIC X This sweet 17C fisherman's cottage sits in a characterful coastal town, in a road leading down to the harbour. It's run by a charming couple and has a rustic modern feel, courtesy of locally crafted tables and upholstered chairs. Classic British dishes have a modern edge and rely on small local suppliers.

Menu £ 25 (lunch) - Carte £ 31/46

30 South St ✉ PO10 7EH - ✆ 01243 377914 (booking essential)
- www.fatolives.co.uk - Closed 2 weeks late June, Christmas, New Year, Tuesday after bank holiday, Sunday and Monday

EPPING

Essex - Pop. 10 289 - Regional map n° **7**-B2

Haywards

MODERN CUISINE • INTIMATE XX This proudly run restaurant is the realisation of a couple's dream. It's set in the old stables of their family's pub and boasts a hammerbeam ceiling, cherry wood tables and canvases of local forest scenes. Appealing dishes follow the seasons and flavours are well-balanced. Service is extremely welcoming.

Menu £ 28 (weekdays)/49

111 Bell Common ✉ CM16 4DZ - Southwest : 1 mi by B 1393 and Theydon Rd - ✆ 01992 577350 - www.haywardsrestaurant.co.uk - Closed 1-22 January and Sunday dinner-Wednesday lunch

EPSOM

Surrey - Pop. 31 474 - Regional map n° **4**-D1

Le Raj

BANGLADESHI • ELEGANT XXX This passionately-run restaurant has been welcoming guests since 1989 and has become a local institution. Dine on freshly made, authentic Bangladeshi dishes and superb breads, surrounded by wooden panels picked out in gold leaf.

Menu £ 38 (weekdays) - Carte £ 26/48

211 Fir Tree Rd, Epsom Downs ✉ KT17 3LB - Southeast : 2 mi by B 289 and B 284 on B 291 - ✆ 01737 371371 - www.lerajrestaurant.co.uk

ERMINGTON

Devon - Regional map n° **1**-C2

Plantation House

MODERN CUISINE • INTIMATE XX Georgian former rectory in a pleasant country spot, with a small drinks terrace, an open-fired lounge and two dining rooms: one formal, with black furnishings; one more relaxed, with polished wood tables. Interesting modern menus feature local produce. Stylish bedrooms come with fresh milk and homemade cake.

Menu £ 40 **s**

8 rooms - †£ 70/185 ††£ 125/230

Totnes Rd ✉ PL21 9NS - Southwest : 0.5 mi on A 3121 - ✆ 01548 831100 (bookings essential for non-residents) - www.plantationhousehotel.co.uk - dinner only

ESHOTT - Northd. ➔ See Morpeth

EVERSHOT

Dorset - Pop. 225 - Regional map n° **2**-C3

Summer Lodge

LUXURY • ELEGANT An attractive former dower house in mature gardens, featuring a smart wellness centre, a pool and a tennis court. Plush, individually designed bedrooms come with marble bathrooms and country house guest areas display heavy fabrics and antiques - the drawing room was designed by Thomas Hardy. Dine formally from a classic menu, which is accompanied by a superb wine list.

24 rooms - †£ 215/475 ††£ 215/475 - 4 suites

9 Fore St ✉ DT2 0JR - ✆ 01935 482000 - www.summerlodgehotel.com - Closed 3 weeks January

Acorn Inn

INN • CLASSIC The historic Acorn Inn was mentioned in 'Tess of the d'Urbervilles' and to this day is the hub of the village. Cosy, individually appointed bedrooms have fabric-covered walls – some have four-posters and the attic is perfect for families. Dine in the classic restaurant or the locals bar with its skittle alley.

10 rooms – £ 95/165 £ 105/230

28 Fore St DT2 0JW
– 01935 83228 – www.acorn-inn.co.uk

Wooden Cabbage

COUNTRY HOUSE • COSY The unusual name comes from the local term for a stunted oak tree. An attractive former gamekeeper's cottage, it sits in a quiet spot and has lovely countryside views from its pretty bedrooms and tropical plant filled orangery.

4 rooms – £ 105/120 £ 115/145

East Chelborough DT2 0QA – Northwest : 3.25 mi by Beaminster rd and Chelborough rd on East Chelborough rd
– 01935 83362 – www.woodencabbage.co.uk
– Closed November-mid-March

EWELL

Surrey – Pop. 51 727 – Regional map n° **4**-D1

See Greater London Plan 6

Dastaan

INDIAN • NEIGHBOURHOOD Two friends who worked in London's Gymkhana own this simple restaurant in a parade of shops. Its name means 'story' – their story – and they even made the tables and benches themselves! Great value cooking is mainly northern Indian and ranges from street food and classics to some more unusual choices.

Carte £ 18/38

Town plan: C6-d – *447 Kingston Rd KT19 0DB*
– 020 8786 8999 – www.dastaan.co.uk
– dinner only and lunch Saturday-Sunday – Closed Monday

EXETER

Devon – Pop. 113 507 – Regional map n° **1**-D2

Southernhay House

TOWNHOUSE • CONTEMPORARY Attractive Georgian townhouse with original ceiling roses and ornate coving. Smart, compact guest areas include a stylish lounge and a bar with bright blue furniture. Warmly decorated bedrooms have sumptuous beds, luxurious fabrics and chic bathrooms. The small dining room offers British-based menus.

10 rooms – £ 100/170 £ 100/260 – £ 14

36 Southernhay East EX1 1NX
– 01392 435324 – www.southernhayhouse.com

Don't expect guesthouses to provide the same level of service as a hotel. They are often characterised by a warm welcome and décor which reflects the owner's personality. Those shown in red are particularly charming.

ENGLAND

at Brampford Speke North: 5 mi by A377

Lazy Toad Inn

REGIONAL CUISINE • COSY Follow winding lanes to this sweet Grade II listed pub in a pretty village near the river. In winter, sit under a lovely oak-beamed ceiling beside an inviting log fire; in summer, head for the beautiful walled garden or charming cobbled courtyard. Hearty British dishes showcase garden produce.

Menu £ 17 (weekdays) - Carte £ 19/40

EX5 5DP

- 01392 841591 - www.thelazytoad.com - Closed 1 week January, Sunday dinner and Monday

FAIRFORD

Gloucestershire - Pop. 2 960 - Regional map n° **2**-D1

The Bull

TRADITIONAL CUISINE • INN The 14C Bull sits in the marketplace of an attractive little town and is a hit with fishermen courtesy of its mile of fishing rights. The main bar is characterful and cosy, while the two smaller dining rooms have a quirky feel. Menus offer plenty of choice, from antipasti, pizza and pasta to hearty British dishes. Bedrooms come with exposed timbers and designer touches.

Menu £ 17 (weekday lunch) - Carte £ 30/40

21 rooms - †£ 75 ††£ 100/220

Market Pl GL7 4AA

- 01285 712535 - www.thebullhotelfairford.co.uk

FALMOUTH

Cornwall - Pop. 22 686 - Regional map n° **1**-A3

Oliver's

TRADITIONAL CUISINE • NEIGHBOURHOOD Although it's just a few paces from the water, Oliver's is known more for its game than anything else. Good value lunches are followed by more ambitious dinners. It's a simple place, run with plenty of passion, and a hit with the locals.

Menu £ 23 (lunch) - Carte dinner £ 29/39

33 High St TR11 2AD

- 01326 218138 - www.oliversfalmouth.com - Closed 10 December-7 January, Sunday, Monday and bank holidays

Chelsea House

TOWNHOUSE • PERSONALISED An imposing Edwardian house in a quiet residential street close to the beaches. It's a trendy spot where retro furnishings fuse with vibrant fabrics to create a modish, boutique feel. Bedrooms on the top floors have good sea views.

9 rooms - †£ 80/99 ††£ 99/170

2 Emslie Rd TR11 4BG

- 01326 212230 - www.chelseahousefalmouth.com

Highcliffe

TOWNHOUSE • PERSONALISED The owner has put her Design degree to good use at this homely Victorian house between the town and the sea. Room 8 runs the length of the house and has stunning views. Locally roasted coffee and a daily special feature at breakfast.

8 rooms - †£ 45/70 ††£ 72/160

22 Melvill Rd TR11 4AR

- 01326 314466 - www.highcliffefalmouth.com - Closed December

at Maenporth Beach South: 3.75 mi by Pennance Rd

Cove

MODERN CUISINE • ROMANTIC X A bright, stylish restaurant in a smart glass-fronted building overlooking the beach, the cove and St Anthony's Head. The modern dining room leads through to a lovely split-level terrace with a retractable roof. Menus are contemporary, with a strong seafood base and some Asian influences.

Menu £ 22 – Carte £ 28/37

Maenporth Beach ✉ TR11 5HN – ✆ 01326 251136 – www.thecovemaenporth.co.uk – Closed 25 December

FARINGDON

Oxfordshire – Pop. 7 121 – Regional map n° **6**-A2

Restaurant 56

MODERN CUISINE • ELEGANT XXX A Georgian manor house in the grounds of a corporate hotel – its wood-panelling and red fabrics give it a smart, formal feel. Attractive dishes are crafted from good quality produce; cooking is classically based with a modern edge.

Menu £ 55

Sudbury House Hotel, 56 London St ✉ SN7 7AA – ✆ 01367 245389 – www.restaurant56.co.uk – dinner only – Closed 2-16 January, Sunday and Monday

Sudbury House

BUSINESS • FUNCTIONAL A corporate hotel in 9 acres of grounds, not far from the Folly Tower. The eight meeting rooms include a 100-seater tiered lecture theatre. Bedrooms are modern and functional with smart bathrooms. Have snacks in the bar, stone-baked pizzas in relaxed Magnolia or more elaborate dishes in Restaurant 56.

50 rooms – †£ 104/200 ††£ 130/210 – ☕ £ 13 – 1 suite

56 London St. ✉ SN7 7AA – ✆ 01367 241272 – www.sudburyhouse.co.uk – Closed 2-16 January

Restaurant 56 – See restaurant listing

FARNBOROUGH

Hampshire – Pop. 65 034 – Regional map n° **4**-C1

Aviator

BUSINESS • MODERN Eye-catching modern hotel overlooking Farnborough Airport with a striking circular atrium, a stylish cocktail bar and an American burger joint. Sleek, good-sized bedrooms feature light wood and modern facilities. The contemporary restaurant serves modern British dishes and steaks from the Josper grill.

168 rooms – †£ 125/250 ††£ 125/250 – ☕ £ 18

55 Farnborough Rd ✉ GU14 6EL – Southwest : 1 mi on A 325 – ✆ 01252 555890 – www.aviatorbytag.com

FARNHAM

Dorset – Regional map n° **2**-C3

Farnham Farm House

FAMILY • COSY Welcoming farmhouse on a 300 acre working farm, complete with a swimming pool and a holistic therapy centre. Homely, immaculately kept bedrooms have country views. Enjoy tea and cake on arrival; the eggs are from their own hens.

3 rooms ☕ – †£ 90/100 ††£ 90/100

✉ DT11 8DG – North : 1 mi by Shaftesbury rd – ✆ 01725 516254 – www.farnhamfarmhouse.co.uk – Closed 25-26 December

FAVERSHAM

Kent - Pop. 19 829 - Regional map n° **5**-C1

Read's

MODERN BRITISH • ELEGANT XxX An elegant Georgian manor house in landscaped grounds, with traditional country house styling, antique furnishings and lovely oil paintings. Classically based dishes have subtle modern touches and make use of seasonal produce from the walled kitchen garden and the nearby quay. Comfortable bedrooms are full of period charm and thoughtful extras provide a sense of luxury.

Menu £ 32/65

6 rooms - £ 140/195 £ 180/210

Macknade Manor, Canterbury Rd ✉ ME13 8XE - East : 1 mi on A 2
- ✆ 01795 535344 - www.reads.com
- Closed 2 weeks early September, 1 week early January, 25-26 December, Sunday and Monday

FENCE

Lancashire - Pop. 1 459 - Regional map n° **11**-B2

White Swan (Tom Parker)

MODERN BRITISH • SIMPLE A traditional pub leased from Timothy Taylor's brewery: you're guaranteed a great pint - and the food is just as good. Well-crafted dishes have considerable depth of flavour; the tasting menu best demonstrates the kitchen's skill. To finish, the cheeseboard with homemade crackers and truffle honey is a must.

→ Sticky lamb 'cottage pie', potato, curd cheese and crackling. Wild turbot with white asparagus, smoked haddock and wild garlic. Blackberry crumble soufflé with organic yoghurt sorbet.

Menu £ 28/45

300 Wheatley Lane Rd ✉ BB12 9QA - ✆ 01282 611773
- www.whiteswanatfence.co.uk - Closed Sunday dinner and Monday

FERMAIN BAY → See Channel Islands (Guernsey)

FERRENSBY

North Yorkshire - Regional map n° **13**-B2

General Tarleton

TRADITIONAL BRITISH • INN XX Characterful 18C coaching inn with low beams and exposed stone walls; most sit in the main room but there's also a glass-roofed courtyard and a large terrace for warmer days. Hearty dishes champion Yorkshire produce. Bedrooms feature solid oak furnishings and come with home-baked biscuits.

Menu £ 19 (lunch and early dinner) - Carte £ 25/44

13 rooms - £ 75/85 £ 129/150

Boroughbridge Rd ✉ HG5 0PZ
- ✆ 01423 340284 - www.generaltarleton.co.uk

FILKINS

Oxfordshire - Pop. 434 - Regional map n° **6**-A2

Five Alls

TRADITIONAL BRITISH • PUB Like its curious logo, this pub has it all: an open-fired bar where they serve snacks and takeaway burgers, a locals bar stocked with fine ales, three antique-furnished dining rooms, and a lovely terrace and garden. The menu is satisfyingly traditional and bedrooms are modern and cosy.

Menu £ 26 (weekdays) - Carte £ 21/44

9 rooms - £ 95/180 £ 95/180

✉ GL7 3JQ - ✆ 01367 860875 - www.thefiveallsfilkins.co.uk
- Closed 25 December and Sunday dinner

FIVEHEAD

Somerset - Pop. 609 - Regional map n° **2**-B3

Langford Fivehead

MODERN CUISINE • INTIMATE XX A beautiful, personally run country house with 13C origins, set in 7 acres of well-tended gardens - with its antique panelling, old stone fireplaces and mullioned windows, it conveys a real sense of history. Well-balanced modern menus are highly seasonal and feature lots of kitchen garden ingredients. Bedrooms are tastefully furnished and many have four-poster beds.

Menu £ 28/43

6 rooms - £ 150/275 £ 195/290

Lower Swell ✉ TA3 6PH - East : 0.5 mi by Westport rd on Swell rd
- ✆ 01460 282020 (booking essential) - www.langfordfivehead.co.uk
- dinner only and lunch Wednesday-Friday
- Closed 1-15 January, 22 July-6 August, 25-26 December, Sunday and Monday

FOLKESTONE

Kent - Pop. 51 337 - Regional map n° **5**-D2

Rocksalt

SEAFOOD • DESIGN XX An impressive harbourfront eco-building with a curvaceous wood façade. Full-length windows give every table a view and the terrace extends over the water. Seafood-orientated menus also offer local meats. The semi-open upstairs bar serves lighter dishes. Stylish bedrooms - in an annexe - have a loft-like feel.

Menu £ 25 (weekday lunch) - Carte £ 33/43

4 rooms - £ 85/115 £ 85/115

4-5 Fish Market ✉ CT19 6AA
- ✆ 01303 212070 - www.rocksaltfolkestone.co.uk
- Closed Sunday dinner

FOLKSWORTH

Cambridgeshire - Pop. 881 - Regional map n° **8**-A2

The Fox at Folksworth

MODERN CUISINE • CONTEMPORARY DÉCOR The Fox's dining room is hung with chandeliers and its light, bright bar is filled with designer furniture and has sliding doors which open onto a huge terrace. Dine on pub favourites or more creative modern dishes.

Menu £ 15 (weekday lunch) - Carte £ 25/38

34 Manor Rd ✉ PE7 3SU - ✆ 01733 242867 - www.foxatfolksworth.co.uk

FONTMELL MAGNA

Dorset - Pop. 333 - Regional map n° **2**-C3

Fontmell

MODERN CUISINE • PUB A stylish dining pub in a delightfully rural spot, with a cosy bar and a restaurant straddling the beck - keep an eye out for otters. The eclectic modern menu offers something for all tastes, from British to Mediterranean and Asian; try their own rare breed Old Spot pork. Bedrooms are chic and well-appointed.

Carte £ 24/50

6 rooms - £ 75/165 £ 85/175

Crown Hill ✉ SP7 0PA - ✆ 01747 811441 - www.thefontmell.com - Closed 1-15 January

FORDHAM

Cambridgeshire - Regional map n° **8**-B2

White Pheasant

MODERN CUISINE • SIMPLE An enthusiastic chef-owner runs this cosy former pub in the centre of the village. Cooking is all-encompassing, including everything from well-presented classics to creative modern dishes.

Carte £ 29/45

21 Market St ✉ CB7 5LQ - ✆ 01638 720414 - www.whitepheasant.com - Closed first week January, Sunday dinner and Monday

FORDINGBRIDGE

Hampshire - Pop. 4 474 - Regional map n° **4**-A2

Three Lions

FAMILY • COSY A former farmhouse and pub in a small hamlet. Homely bedrooms are split between this and various outbuildings; those in the garden come with French windows and outdoor seating and the self-catering 3-bedroom Lions Retreat sits by the river. Blackboard menus offer classically inspired Anglo-French dishes.

7 rooms - †£ 80/125 ††£ 80/125

Stuckton Rd, Stuckton ✉ SP6 2HF - Southeast : 1 mi by B 3078 - ✆ 01425 652489 - www.thethreelionsrestaurant.co.uk - Closed last 2 weeks February

FORDWICH

→ See Canterbury

FOWEY

Cornwall - Pop. 2 131 - Regional map n° **1**-B2

Q

MODERN CUISINE • INTIMATE Ask for a window seat or head to the terrific waterside terrace of this romantic hotel restaurant. Dinner is the main event, with modern takes on old classics: presentation is colourful and provenance is key.

Menu £ 25/45

Old Quay House Hotel, 28 Fore St ✉ PL23 1AQ - ✆ 01726 833302 - www.theoldquayhouse.com - Closed lunch October-April except 24 December-2 January

Fowey Hall

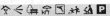

COUNTRY HOUSE • PERSONALISED A striking 19C manor house with an ornate lounge and a mix of traditional and modern bedrooms. It's set high above the village and has lovely views. Families are well-catered for and an informal feel pervades. There's an oak-panelled restaurant reserved for adults and a conservatory for those with children.

36 rooms - †£ 125/695 ††£ 140/710

Hanson Dr ✉ PL23 1ET - West : 0.5 mi off A 3082 - ✆ 01726 833866 - www.foweyhallhotel.co.uk

Old Quay House

TOWNHOUSE • CONTEMPORARY A 19C seamen's mission in a pretty harbour village; now a boutique hotel with a laid-back feel and a lovely riverside terrace. Bedrooms have an understated modern style; most have balconies and water views.

11 rooms - †£ 170/200 ††£ 200/340

28 Fore St ✉ PL23 1AQ - ✆ 01726 833302 - www.theoldquayhouse.com

Q - See restaurant listing

FREATHY

Cornwall - Regional map n° **1**-C2

The View

MODERN BRITISH • SIMPLE A charming converted café perched on the clifftop and affording commanding coastal views; if the weather's right, find a spot on the terrace. It has a relaxed daytime vibe and is more atmospheric in the evening. Assured, confident, cooking arrives in generous portions; the homemade bread is tasty.

Menu £ 20 (lunch) – Carte £ 33/45

PL10 1JY – East : 1 mi
– 01752 822345 (booking essential) – www.theview-restaurant.co.uk
– Closed 1-14 February, Monday and Tuesday

FRILSHAM – West Berkshire → See Yattendon

FRITHSDEN

Hertfordshire – Regional map n° **7**-A2

Alford Arms

TRADITIONAL BRITISH • INN An attractive Victorian pub beside the village green. The menu follows the seasons and offers a broad array of dishes, so alongside British classics you'll find dishes with more global leanings such as imam bayildi.

Carte £ 24/40

HP1 3DD
– 01442 864480 – www.alfordarmsfrithsden.co.uk
– Closed 25-26 December

FROME

Somerset – Pop. 26 203 – Regional map n° **2**-C2

Babington House

LUXURY • TRENDY Behind this country house's classic Georgian façade is a cool, fashionable hotel with bold colour schemes, understated bedrooms and a bohemian feel. Unwind in the luxurious lounges or in the beautiful spa with its superb fitness area and pool. The Orangery offers an accessible menu of Mediterranean-influenced dishes which showcase ingredients from the walled garden.

33 rooms – †£ 255/380 ††£ 350/615 – £ 17 – 11 suites

Babington BA11 3RW – Northwest : 6.5 mi by A 362 on Vobster rd
– 01373 812266 – www.babingtonhouse.co.uk

FUNTINGTON – West Sussex → See Chichester

FYFIELD

Oxfordshire – Regional map n° **6**-B2

White Hart

TRADITIONAL BRITISH • PUB An intriguing 15C chantry house with a cosy open-fired bar, a minstrels' gallery and an impressive three-storey high vaulted dining room; not forgetting a pleasant terrace. The diverse range of dishes is guided by produce from the vegetable plot. Save room for one of the excellent desserts.

Menu £ 20 (weekday lunch) – Carte £ 31/45

Main Rd OX13 5LW
– 01865 390585 – www.whitehart-fyfield.com
– Closed Monday except bank holidays and Sunday lunch

GERRARDS CROSS

Buckinghamshire - Pop. 20 633 - Regional map n° **6**-D3

Three Oaks

MODERN BRITISH • PUB An appealing, well-run pub in a rural location, comprising several different areas: dine in the brighter room overlooking the terrace and pretty garden. Cooking is tasty, satisfying and seasonal, and they offer particularly good value set lunch and dinner menus. The bright young staff are eager to please.

Menu £ 19 (weekdays) - Carte £ 26/40

Austenwood Ln ✉ SL9 8NL - Northwest : 0.75 mi by A 413 on Gold Hill rd
- ✆ 01753 899016 - www.thethreeoaksgx.co.uk
- Closed Sunday dinner

GISBURN

Lancashire - Pop. 521 - Regional map n° **11**-B2

La Locanda

ITALIAN • NEIGHBOURHOOD A charming low-beamed, flag-floored restaurant run by a keen couple: a little corner of Italy in Lancashire. Extensive menu of hearty homemade dishes; try the tasty pastas. Top quality local and imported produce; well-chosen wine list.

Carte £ 23/36

Main St ✉ BB7 4HH - ✆ 01200 445303 - www.lalocanda.co.uk
- Closed 25 December, 1 January, Monday and lunch Tuesday-Wednesday

Park House

TOWNHOUSE • CLASSIC Imposing Victorian house with a classical open-fired drawing room and a small library leading to a hidden stepped garden. Bedrooms mix antique and more modern furnishings. Good breakfast selection; tea and homemade cake served on arrival.

5 rooms - †£ 55/110 ††£ 70/125

13 Church View ✉ BB7 4HG - ✆ 01200 445269 - www.parkhousegisburn.co.uk
- Closed 26 November-14 February

GLINTON - Peterborough → See Peterborough

GOREY → See Channel Islands (Jersey)

GORING

Oxfordshire - Pop. 4 193 - Regional map n° **6**-B3

Miller of Mansfield

MODERN BRITISH • FRIENDLY Large 18C inn close to the Thames; sit in the cosy bar rooms, the dining room or out on the terrace. Dishes range from homemade sausage rolls to poached lobster salad; the homemade bread and desserts are a highlight. Bedrooms blend modern furnishings with original features.

Carte £ 35/46

13 rooms - †£ 109/119 ††£ 119/189

High St ✉ RG8 9AW
- ✆ 01491 872829 - www.millerofmansfield.com

GRANGE-OVER-SANDS

Cumbria - Pop. 4 788 - Regional map n° **12**-A3

Clare House

FAMILY • PERSONALISED Enjoy afternoon tea in a sitting room of this superbly set Victorian house, overlooking lovely gardens and out across Morecambe Bay. It's keenly run by an experienced family and blends the traditional and the contemporary. Ask for a bedroom with a balcony. Classic dishes are served in a stylish setting.

18 rooms (dinner included) – £ 100/110 £ 200/220

Park Rd LA11 7HQ – 015395 33026 – www.clarehousehotel.co.uk – Closed mid-December-March

GRANTHAM

Lincolnshire – Pop. 41 998 – Regional map n° **9**-C2

Harry's Place

TRADITIONAL BRITISH • COSY XX Long-standing, intimate restaurant in a former farmhouse: it consists of just 3 tables and is personally run by a dedicated and delightful husband and wife team. Warm, welcoming feel, with fresh flowers, candles and antiques. Classically based menus offer 2 choices per course. Good cheese selection.

Carte £ 59/73

17 High St, Great Gonerby NG31 8JS – Northwest : 2 mi on B 1174 – 01476 561780 (booking essential) – Closed 2 weeks August, Christmas-New Year, Sunday and Monday

GRASMERE

Cumbria – Regional map n° **12**-A2

Forest Side

MODERN BRITISH • DESIGN XX Sit in deep leather armchairs and take in the view over the 23 acre hotel grounds. With produce originating from the walled garden and foraged from the surrounding area, their strapline 'inspired by the Cumbrian landscape' is spot on. Scandic-style dishes are creative and modern with a deceptive simplicity.

→ Lemon sole, celeriac, mussels and savoury. Aged shorthorn rib, smoked squash with scurvy grass. Apple, buttermilk and lovage.

Menu £ 35/95

Forest Side Hotel, Keswick Rd LA22 9RN – On A 591 – 015394 35250 (bookings essential for non-residents) – www.theforestside.com – Closed Monday and Tuesday

Dining Room

MODERN CUISINE • INTIMATE XX The owner of this unassuming hotel has a passion for gastronomy, and the pleasant conservatory restaurant looking out over the garden has a light, airy feel. Lakeland ingredients underpin accomplished dishes, which have a modern style yet respect their classic roots.

Carte £ 32/44 – bar lunch

Oak Bank Hotel, Broadgate LA22 9TA – 015394 35217 (booking essential) – www.lakedistricthotel.co.uk – Closed 16-26 December, 6-25 January and 21 July-1 August

Rothay Garden

COUNTRY HOUSE • CONTEMPORARY Slate-built Lakeland house with modern extensions, which include a spa and a copper-roofed conservatory restaurant with a lovely outlook and a classically based menu. Bedrooms are stylish and contemporary – many have king-sized beds and some have balconies or patios; the Loft Suites are the best.

30 rooms – £ 120/150 £ 160/310

Broadgate LA22 9RJ – 015394 35334 – www.rothaygarden.com

Forest Side

COUNTRY HOUSE • CONTEMPORARY Enjoy afternoon tea in the elegant fire-lit lounge while admiring the view over the deer-filled grounds towards the mountains. Both the guest areas and bedrooms have a modern country house style and there's a laid back feel throughout.

20 rooms - £ 139/279 £ 229/369

Keswick Rd ✉ LA22 9RN - On A 591
- ✆ 015394 35250 - www.theforestside.com

Forest Side - See restaurant listing

Grasmere

COUNTRY HOUSE • CONTEMPORARY This Victorian country house is run very personally run, with mum designing, dad cooking and the daughters playing hand-on roles. Original features remain and the décor is fittingly traditional. The bright dining room offers a British menu with modern touches and overlooks the garden and river.

11 rooms - £ 69/74 £ 126/148

Broadgate ✉ LA22 9TA
- ✆ 015394 35277 - www.grasmerehotel.co.uk - Restricted opening in winter

Oak Bank

TRADITIONAL • PERSONALISED A cosy Victorian hotel built of traditional Lakeland slate and set in the middle of a busy little village. Cosy bedrooms come in bold modern designs and those at the top of the house have superb views of the surrounding fells. It's very personally run by its passionate owners.

13 rooms - £ 75/135 £ 90/170

Broadgate ✉ LA22 9TA
- ✆ 015394 35217 - www.lakedistricthotel.co.uk - Closed 16-26 December, 6-25 January and 21 July-1 August

Dining Room - See restaurant listing

GRASSINGTON

North Yorkshire - Pop. 1 126 - Regional map n° **13**-A2

Grassington House

MODERN BRITISH • BRASSERIE XX This attractive Grade II listed Georgian house sits overlooking a cobbled square in the heart of the Yorkshire Dales. Home-bred pork and many other home-smoked items feature on the Mediterranean-inspired menu, and afternoon tea has become something of a feature. Bedrooms are smart and modern.

Menu £ 18 (lunch and early dinner) - Carte £ 27/42

9 rooms - £ 118 £ 135/155

5 The Square ✉ BD23 5AQ
- ✆ 01756 752406 - www.grassingtonhouse.co.uk - Closed 25 December

GREAT MALVERN

Worcestershire - Pop. 36 770 - Regional map n° **10**-B3

Cotford

TOWNHOUSE • CONTEMPORARY The owners of this 1851 Gothic-style house (built for the Bishop of Worcester), put a lot of effort into getting things right. It mixes the traditional and the contemporary and has stylish bedrooms and a chic black and pink bar.

15 rooms - £ 80/95 £ 150/165

51 Graham Rd ✉ WR14 2HU
- ✆ 01684 572427 - www.cotfordhotel.co.uk

at Welland Southeast: 5 mi on B4208

The Inn at Welland

TRADITIONAL BRITISH • CONTEMPORARY DÉCOR Take in delightful views of the Malvern Hills from the terrace of this remotely set inn or sit on plush chairs at large wooden tables, surrounded by flower-filled vases. The menu has something for one and all, with carefully prepared dishes packed full of flavour. The experienced owner runs a tight ship.

Carte £ 26/46

Hook Bank ✉ WR13 6LN - East : 1 mi on A 4104 - ✆ 01684 592317 - www.theinnatwelland.co.uk - Closed 25-26 December, 31 December-2 January, Sunday dinner and Monday

GREAT MILTON - Oxfordshire ➔ See Oxford

GREAT OXENDON

Northamptonshire - Regional map n° **9**-B3

The George

MODERN BRITISH • FASHIONABLE XX An experienced chef has transformed this roadside inn by creating a modern country house lounge and a lovely New England style dining room complete with glass doors opening onto the pretty terrace and garden. Classically based British dishes have an unfussy modern style. Bedrooms are bright and contemporary.

Carte £ 27/38

7 rooms - †£ 75/90 ††£ 110/120

Harborough Rd ✉ LE16 8NA - ✆ 01858 452286 - www.thegeorgegreatoxendon.co.uk - Closed Christmas

GREAT TEW

Oxfordshire - Pop. 145 - Regional map n° **6**-B1

Soho Farmhouse

RESORT • DESIGN Set in 100 acres of rolling countryside, this exclusive resort offers everything you could want. Luxurious self-contained cabins are dotted about the estate and come with wellies and bikes. There's a range of different restaurants and breakfast is transported on a milk float and cooked outside your door. Unwind in the stunning spa or the outside pool set within a lake.

44 rooms - †£ 400/2000 ††£ 400/2000 - £ 13 - 18 suites

✉ OX7 4JS - South 0.75 mi by New Rd and Ledwell Ln. - ✆ 01608 691000 - www.sohofarmhouse.com - Members only June, July and Friday-Saturday August-May

GREAT YELDHAM

Essex - Pop. 1 844 - Regional map n° **7**-C2

White Hart

MODERN BRITISH • ROMANTIC XX Charming 16C house with a characterful interior. The open-fired bar with its wonky floors and exposed beams serves unfussy favourites, while the elegant restaurant (open later in the week) offers a refined modern menu of skilfully prepared dishes. Bedrooms are stylish and comfortable.

Carte £ 35/52

13 rooms - †£ 70 ††£ 90/210

Poole St ✉ CO9 4HJ - ✆ 01787 237250 - www.whitehartyeldham.co.uk - Closed 1-18 January, dinner 24-31 December, Monday, Tuesday and lunch Wednesday

GREEN ISLAND → See Channel Islands (Jersey)

GREETHAM

Rutland - Regional map n° **9**-C2

Wheatsheaf Inn

TRADITIONAL BRITISH • FAMILY The aroma of fresh bread greets you at this simple, family-friendly country pub. Cooking is unfussy and traditional; cheaper cuts keep prices sensible and desserts are a must. It's run by a charming couple.

Carte £ 26/34

1 Stretton Rd ✉ LE15 7NP - ✆ 01572 812325 - www.wheatsheaf-greetham.co.uk - Closed first 2 weeks January, Sunday dinner and Monday except bank holidays

GRETA BRIDGE - Durham → See Barnard Castle

GRIMSTON - Norfolk → See King's Lynn

GULWORTHY - Devon → See Tavistock

GURNARD → See Wight (Isle of)

HADLEIGH

Suffolk - Pop. 8 150 - Regional map n° **8**-C3

Hadleigh Ram

MODERN CUISINE • RUSTIC Smart, modern pub with a formal feel. Brunch is served from 10am-2pm, while the extensive à la carte covers everything from interesting bar snacks and sharing boards to Shetland mussels several ways and 21 day dry-aged local steaks. Fish dishes are a strength and desserts keep things pleasingly traditional.

Carte £ 27/43

5 Market Pl ✉ IP7 5DL - ✆ 01473 822880 - www.thehadleighram.co.uk - Closed Sunday dinner

Edge Hall

TOWNHOUSE • CLASSIC A lovely Queen Anne style house with a Georgian brick façade, dating from 1453 and supposedly the oldest house in town. Bedrooms are spacious and furnished with antiques. The breakfast room overlooks the delightful garden.

6 rooms - †£ 70/100 ††£ 110/160

2 High St ✉ IP7 5AP - ✆ 01473 822458 - www.edgehall.co.uk - Closed 23-29 December

HALFORD

Warwickshire - Pop. 301 - Regional map n° **10**-C3

Old Manor House

COUNTRY HOUSE • HISTORIC Characterful part-timbered house in a pleasant spot next to the River Stour. Well-appointed drawing room with garden views and an antique-furnished breakfast room with a large inglenook. Appealing period style bedrooms have rich fabrics.

3 rooms - †£ 85/110 ††£ 110/120

Queens St ✉ CV36 5BT - ✆ 01789 740264 - www.oldmanor-halford.co.uk

HALIFAX

West Yorkshire - Pop. 88 134 - Regional map n° **13**-B2

Holdsworth House

HISTORIC • COSY Attractive 17C property with beautiful gardens and a parterre within its old stone walls. Characterful rooms feature original wood panelling and mullioned windows; bedrooms are contemporary. The three-roomed restaurant offers a mix of homely classics and more refined dishes – all use local produce.

38 rooms – £ 89/250 £ 99/275

Holdsworth Rd ✉ HX2 9TG – North : 3 mi by A 629 and Shay Ln – ✆ 01422 240024 – www.holdsworthhouse.co.uk

HALTWHISTLE

Northumberland – Pop. 3 791 – Regional map n° **14**-A2

Ashcroft

FAMILY • CLASSIC A family-run early Victorian vicarage, with beautiful award-winning gardens. The spacious interior retains many of its original features and smoothly blends the classic with the contemporary. Some of the bedrooms have roof terraces.

9 rooms – £ 72/90 £ 84/110

Lantys Lonnen ✉ NE49 0DA – ✆ 01434 320213 – www.ashcroftguesthouse.co.uk – Closed 25 December

HAMBLETON – Rutland

➜ See Oakham

HAMPTON IN ARDEN

West Midlands – Pop. 1 678 – Regional map n° **10**-C2

Peel's

CREATIVE BRITISH • ELEGANT XXX This elegant dining room is situated within an impressive manor house and features beautiful plasterwork, oak panelling and hand-painted Chinoiserie wallpaper. Modern dishes come from a confident kitchen and feature refined, original combinations with some playful elements. Service is pitched perfectly.

→ Asparagus with burrata & chicken. Wagyu with celeriac & truffle. Chocolate with sherry & vanilla.

Menu £ 70/85

Hampton Manor Hotel, Shadowbrook Ln ✉ B92 0DQ – ✆ 01675 446080 (booking essential) – www.hamptonmanor.com – dinner only – Closed 1-4 January, Sunday and Monday

Hampton Manor

HISTORIC • GRAND LUXURY An early Victorian Gothic-style manor house set in 45 acres of mature grounds – it was built for Sir Robert Peel's son. Contemporary décor blends with characterful original plasterwork and wood panelling in various lounges and drawing rooms. Spacious bedrooms have a smart modern style and superb bathrooms.

15 rooms – £ 135/365 £ 150/380 – 3 suites

Shadowbrook Ln ✉ B92 0DQ – ✆ 01675 446080 – www.hamptonmanor.com – Closed 1-4 January

Peel's – See restaurant listing

HAMPTON POYLE

Oxfordshire – Pop. 106 – Regional map n° **6**-B2

Bell at Hampton Poyle

MEDITERRANEAN CUISINE • PUB A passionately run pub with several comfy lounge areas and a chic restaurant. The open kitchen adds a buzz and the pizza oven and glass meat ageing fridge draw your eye. The menu covers many bases and has strong Mediterranean undertones. Stylish bedrooms are located above the bar and in a cottage.

Menu £ 10 (weekdays) – Carte £ 20/45

9 rooms – £ 95/150 £ 120/175

11 Oxford Rd ✉ OX5 2QD – ✆ 01865 376242 – www.thebellathamptonpoyle.co.uk

HAROME - North Yorkshire ➜ See Helmsley

HARROGATE

North Yorkshire - Pop. 73 576 - Regional map n° **13**-B2

Horto

MODERN BRITISH • DESIGN XX This smart restaurant is set in Rudding Park's spa and has floor to ceiling windows overlooking the hotel's grounds. Choose between three different tasting menus, where classic dishes are made up of just a few complementary ingredients; much of the produce is picked from the garden each morning.

Menu £ 40 - Carte £ 51/62

Rudding Park Hotel, Rudding Park, Follifoot ✉ HG3 1JH - Southeast : 3.75 mi by A 661 - ✆ 01423 871350 (booking essential) - www.ruddingpark.co.uk - dinner only - Closed Monday and Tuesday

Restaurant 92

MODERN BRITISH • FASHIONABLE XX A large bay-windowed Victorian property in the town centre plays host to this modern restaurant with eye-catching chandeliers and marble-topped sewing machine tables. Ambitious dishes feature many different ingredients.

Menu £ 30 (lunch and early dinner) - Carte £ 32/48

92-94 Station Par ✉ HG1 1HQ - ✆ 01423 503027 - www.restaurant92.co.uk - Closed 1-17 January, Sunday dinner, Monday and Tuesday

Stuzzi

ITALIAN • RUSTIC X A great little place comprising a deli, a café and an osteria, and serving homemade cakes, topped focaccia and fresh, authentic Italian small plates. It's run with passion by a young but experienced team and it's great value too.

Carte £ 20/43

46b King's Rd ✉ HG1 5JW - ✆ 01423 705852 - www.stuzzi.co.uk - Closed 25-26 December, 1 January, Monday and Tuesday

Rudding Park

LUXURY • CONTEMPORARY A substantial hotel set in 250 acres; its listed manor house is popular for events. The superb spa has outdoor hot tubs, rooftop terraces and an infinity pool, while the best of the sleek bedrooms have their own jacuzzis or saunas. Dine on modern British dishes in Clocktower or those crafted from garden produce in Horto.

90 rooms - £ 175/574 £ 203/686 - 6 suites

Rudding Park, Follifoot ✉ HG3 1JH - Southeast : 3.75 mi by A 661 - ✆ 01423 871350 - www.ruddingpark.co.uk

Horto - See restaurant listing

Hotel du Vin

TOWNHOUSE • DESIGN Smart hotel with a small basement spa, set in a terrace of Georgian houses overlooking the green. Inside it has a stylish, boutique-style feel; the attic rooms boast huge bathrooms with 'his and hers' roll-top baths. Have a drink at the smart zinc bar before dinner in the chic French bistro or the courtyard.

49 rooms - £ 110/350 £ 110/350 - £ 17

Prospect Pl ✉ HG1 1LB - ✆ 01423 856800 - www.hotelduvin.com

West Park

INN • CONTEMPORARY It might still look like a pub but once inside you'll find a stylish, contemporary hotel. Bedrooms have the latest mod cons, including coffee machines; the suites overlook the park and have small balconies. The lively open-plan bar and modern restaurant serve an extensive list of brasserie favourites.

25 rooms - £ 79/215 £ 79/215 - £ 15 - 2 suites

19 West Park Rd ✉ HG1 1BJ - ✆ 01423 524471 - www.thewestparkhotel.com

Ascot House

TOWNHOUSE • PERSONALISED A family-run Victorian property – once home to W H Baxter, inventor of the 'knapping' machine (used in road-making). Original features include ornate plasterwork, coving and an impressive stained glass window; contemporary fabrics and king-sized beds feature. The traditional restaurant offers a classic menu.

19 rooms – £ 49/100 £ 79/150

53 King's Rd ✉ HG1 5HJ – ✆ 01423 531005 – www.ascothouse.com

Brookfield House

TOWNHOUSE • CONTEMPORARY A well-run, three-storey Victorian townhouse on a quiet street. Modern bedrooms come in light hues: the first floor rooms are bright and airy, while the top floor rooms are cosy and intimate – all have fridges and ironing boards.

4 rooms – £ 65/85 £ 75/95

5 Alexandra Rd ✉ HG1 5JS – ✆ 01423 506646 – www.brookfieldhousehotel.co.uk – Closed Christmas-New Year

at Kettlesing West: 6.5 mi by A 59 ✉ Harrogate

Cold Cotes

TRADITIONAL • PERSONALISED A remotely located former farmhouse bordered by colourful gardens. Bedrooms are in the old outbuildings: some are suites with lounges and private terraces, and Room 6 has an impressive exposed timber truss. Local produce features at breakfast – try the bacon and onion relish sandwich.

7 rooms – £ 79/109 £ 89/119

Cold Cotes Rd, Felliscliffe ✉ HG3 2LW – West : 1 mi by A 59 – ✆ 01423 770937 – www.coldcotes.com – Closed mid-December-mid-February

HARTINGTON

Derbyshire – Pop. 1 604 – Regional map n° **9**-A1

Biggin Hall

TRADITIONAL • COSY Characterful house with traditional, rustic appeal. Many guests follow the Tissington and High Peak Trails: bike storage and picnics are offered. Classical, low-beamed bedrooms in the main house; brighter rooms in the barns. Pleasant garden views and homely cooking in the dining room .

21 rooms – £ 70/185 £ 80/185

Biggin ✉ SK17 0DH – Southeast : 2 mi by B 5054 – ✆ 01298 84451 – www.bigginhall.co.uk

HARWICH

Essex – Pop. 19 738 – Regional map n° **7**-D2

The Pier

SEAFOOD • CONTEMPORARY DÉCOR XX This stylish 1st floor hotel brasserie boasts a terrific balcony with North Sea views. Seafood forms the foundation of the menu, with much landed locally. The chic bar has an impressive gin library.

Carte £ 28/50 **s**

The Pier Hotel, The Quay ✉ CO12 3HH – ✆ 01255 241212 – www.milsomhotels.com

The Pier

TOWNHOUSE • CONTEMPORARY A striking Victorian hotel by the quayside, built for rail travellers waiting to board their cruise liners and ideal if you're catching the ferry. Some of the stylish New England style bedrooms have views of the port. Dine on seafood dishes or Nordic-inspired snacks overlooking the pier.

14 rooms – £ 135/215 £ 135/215

The Quay ✉ CO12 3HH – ✆ 01255 241212 – www.milsomhotels.com

The Pier – See restaurant listing

HASTINGS and ST LEONARDS

East Sussex – Pop. 91 053 – Regional map n° **5**-B3

Old Rectory

TOWNHOUSE • QUIRKY A delightful Georgian house with beautiful tiered gardens, set next to the church at the bottom of the hill, not far from the sea. No expense has been spared inside, with hand-painted feature walls, bespoke designer furnishings and luxurious styling. They cure the bacon and make their own sausages on-site.

8 rooms – †£ 90/115 ††£ 110/175

Harold Rd, Old Town ✉ TN35 5ND – ✆ 01424 422410 – www.theoldrectoryhastings.co.uk – Closed 1 week January and 1 week Christmas

HAWES

North Yorkshire – Pop. 887 – Regional map n° **13**-A1

Stone House

COUNTRY HOUSE • COSY Characterful stone house built in 1908. Guest areas include a pleasant drawing room with an oak-panelled fireplace and a small billiard-room-cum-library. Bedrooms vary in size and décor; some have conservatories and are ideal for those with dogs. The traditional beamed dining room offers a classical menu.

24 rooms – †£ 80/210 ††£ 80/210

Sedbusk ✉ DL8 3PT – North : 1 mi by Muker rd – ✆ 01969 667571 – www.stonehousehotel.co.uk – Closed January and mid-week December

HAWNBY

North Yorkshire – Regional map n° **13**-C1

Laskill Country House

TRADITIONAL • PERSONALISED A delightful stone house draped with wisteria. It's remotely set and very personally run, with a welcoming house party atmosphere. There's a cosy open-fired lounge and a communal dining room where they serve meat from the family farm. Bedrooms have eye-catching modern wallpapers and country views.

3 rooms – †£ 50/90 ††£ 100/150

Easterside, Laskill ✉ YO62 5NB – Northeast : 2.25 mi by Osmotherley rd – ✆ 01439 798265 – www.laskillcountryhouse.co.uk – Closed 24-25 December

HAYDON BRIDGE – Northumberland ➜ See Hexham

HAYWARDS HEATH

West Sussex – Pop. 33 845 – Regional map n° **4**-D2

Jeremy's at Borde Hill

MODERN CUISINE • FRIENDLY XX Converted stable block with exposed rafters, contemporary sculptures, vivid artwork and delightful views towards the Victorian walled garden. Interesting, modern European dishes and a good value 'menu of the day'. Regular gourmet nights.

Menu £ 29 (weekdays) – Carte £ 35/55

Borde Hill Gdns ✉ RH16 1XP – North : 1.75 mi by B 2028 and Balcombe Rd on Borde Hill Ln. – ✆ 01444 441102 – www.jeremysrestaurant.co.uk – Closed 2-15 January, Monday except bank holidays and Sunday dinner

HEADLAM – Durham ➜ See Darlington

HEATHROW AIRPORT – Greater London ➜ See London

HEDLEY ON THE HILL

Northumberland – Regional map n° **14**-A2

Feathers Inn

TRADITIONAL BRITISH · PUB Traditional stone inn set on a steep hill in the heart of a rural village. Daily changing menu of hearty British classics, cooked using carefully sourced regional produce, with meat and game to the fore. Relaxed, friendly atmosphere.

Carte £ 20/32

✉ NE43 7SW – ✆ 01661 843607 – www.thefeathers.net – Closed first 2 weeks January, Sunday dinner, Monday, Tuesday except bank holidays and lunch Wednesday

HELMSLEY

North Yorkshire – Pop. 1 515 – Regional map n° **13**-C1

Gallery

MODERN BRITISH · BRASSERIE XX Bright, modern restaurant within a historic 15C coaching inn; its walls are filled with artwork for sale and at dinner, the plate becomes the canvas. Attractive, modern dishes have a classical base; the tasting menu is a highlight.

Carte £ 37/55

Black Swan Hotel, Market Pl ✉ YO62 5BJ – ✆ 01439 770466 – www.blackswan-helmsley.co.uk – dinner only and Sunday lunch

The Weathervane

MODERN CUISINE · BRASSERIE XX Modern hotel restaurant with a pleasingly laid-back style. In summer, have lunch in the garden or on the poolside terrace. Dishes feature the latest local produce and cooking is refined and accurate; the tasting menu is worth a try.

Menu £ 50 – bar lunch Monday-Saturday

Feversham Arms Hotel, 1-8 High St ✉ YO62 5AG – ✆ 01439 770766 – www.fevershamarmshotel.com

Black Swan

HISTORIC · PERSONALISED Set overlooking the historic marketplace, The Black Swan is one of the country's best known coaching inns. The charming interior features beamed lounges, a modern bar and a tea shop. Bedrooms are a mix of characterful and contemporary. On Friday and Saturday nights, dinner is included in the rate.

45 rooms – †£ 120/235 ††£ 155/250 – 1 suite

Market Pl ✉ YO62 5BJ – ✆ 01439 770466 – www.blackswan-helmsley.co.uk

Gallery – See restaurant listing

Feversham Arms H. & Verbena Spa

TRADITIONAL · CONTEMPORARY 19C former coaching inn with a lovely stone façade. Relax on the terrace beside the outdoor pool; the spa is superb and boasts a salt vapour room and an ice cave. Be sure to book one of the stylish newer bedrooms; many have stoves or fires.

33 rooms – †£ 100/300 ††£ 120/400 – 20 suites

1-8 High St ✉ YO62 5AG – ✆ 01439 770766 – www.fevershamarmshotel.com

The Weathervane – See restaurant listing

at Harome Southeast: 2.75 mi by A170 ✉ York

Star Inn at Harome (Andrew Pern)

MODERN BRITISH · INN 14C thatched pub with a delightful terrace, a low-ceilinged bar and a brasserie-like restaurant with a chef's table. Dishes have assured flavours and a skilled, classical style; they use the very best of local produce, including veg from the kitchen garden and meats from their own pigs and chickens.

→ Black pudding and foie gras with apple & vanilla chutney. Wild turbot with garlic butter pie and garden alliums. Buttermilk and Yorkshire rhubarb.

Menu £ 25 (weekdays) – Carte £ 36/60

High St ✉ YO62 5JE – ✆ 01439 770397 (booking essential) – www.thestaratharome.co.uk – Closed Monday lunch except bank holidays

ENGLAND

Pheasant

MODERN BRITISH • ELEGANT XX Elegant hotel dining room with both classical and contemporary touches – along with a less formal conservatory and a lovely terrace overlooking the village duck pond. Appealing menus of seasonal dishes with a classical base and a modern touch. Skilful, knowledgeable cooking; smooth, assured service.

Carte £ 35/58

Pheasant Hotel, Mill St ✉ YO62 5JG – ✆ 01439 771241 – www.thepheasanthotel.com

Pheasant

TRADITIONAL • PERSONALISED An attractive hotel in a picturesque hamlet, with a delightful duck pond and a mill stream close by. Beautiful, very comfortable lounges and spacious, well-furnished bedrooms; Rudland – running the width of the building and with views of the pond – is one of the best. Pleasant service. Excellent breakfasts.

16 rooms – †£ 95/240 ††£ 180/270

Mill St ✉ YO62 5JG – ✆ 01439 771241 – www.thepheasanthotel.com

Pheasant – See restaurant listing

Cross House Lodge

COUNTRY HOUSE • DESIGN These sympathetically converted farm buildings have a rustic ski-chalet style and ultra-stylish, individually decorated bedrooms; one boasts a snooker table; another, a bed suspended on ropes. Relax in the open-plan, split-level lounge; excellent breakfasts are taken in the dramatic beamed 'Wheelhouse'.

9 rooms – †£ 135/245 ††£ 150/260

High St ✉ YO62 5JE – ✆ 01439 770397 – www.thestaratharome.co.uk

Star Inn at Harome – See restaurant listing

at Ampleforth Southwest: 4.5 mi by A170 off B1257 ✉ Helmsley

Shallowdale House

TRADITIONAL • CLASSIC A remotely set, personally run house with a well-tended garden and stunning views of the Howardian Hills. Charming, antique-furnished interior, with an open-fired sitting room and good-sized bedrooms decorated in bright, Mediterranean tones. Four course set menu of home-cooked fare.

3 rooms – †£ 125/140 ††£ 145/170

✉ YO62 4DY – West : 0.5 mi – ✆ 01439 788325 – www.shallowdalehouse.co.uk – Closed Christmas-New Year

at Scawton West : 5 mi. by B 1257 ✉ Helmsley

The Hare Inn

MODERN CUISINE • COSY XX Exposed bricks and wooden beams give this passionately run, part-13C inn a characterful pubby feel but, despite its appearance, this is a restaurant through and through. The self-taught chef offers 2 set menus of creative, accomplished dishes which are attractively presented and full of flavour.

Menu £ 55 (weekdays)/70 – tasting menu only

✉ YO7 2HG – ✆ 01845 597769 (booking essential) – www.thehare-inn.com – dinner only – Closed 2-27 January, 1 week June, 1 week November and Sunday-Tuesday

HELSTON

Cornwall – Pop. 11 311 – Regional map n° **1**-A3

at Trelowarren Southeast: 4 mi by A394 and A3083 on B3293 ✉ Helston

New Yard

MODERN BRITISH • RUSTIC Converted 17C stable building adjoining a craft gallery. Spacious, rustic room with timbered walls and doors opening onto the terrace. Seasonal menu uses quality Cornish produce; breads and ice creams are homemade. Friendly service.

Menu £ 25 - Carte £ 29/50

Trelowarren Estate ✉ TR12 6AF - ✆ 01326 221595 - www.newyardrestaurant.co.uk - Closed 3 weeks January, Monday and Tuesday October-Easter

HEMINGFORD GREY - Cambridgeshire → See Huntingdon

HENFIELD

West Sussex - Pop. 4 527 - Regional map n° **4**-D2

Ginger Fox

CLASSIC CUISINE • PUB Look out for the thatched fox running across the roof of this long-standing pub, then head under the fruiting vine into a lovely garden with hidden bee hives. Menus mix refined, delicate dishes with those of a more hearty nature; the vegetarian tasting plate is a hit and the playful desserts are a must.

Menu £ 18 (weekday lunch) - Carte £ 28/45

Muddleswood Rd, Albourne ✉ BN6 9EA - Southwest : 3 mi on A 281 - ✆ 01273 857888 - www.gingermanrestaurants.com - Closed 25 December

HENLEY - West Sussex → See Midhurst

HENLEY-IN-ARDEN

Warwickshire - Pop. 2 846 - Regional map n° **10**-C3

Cheal's of Henley

MODERN CUISINE • ELEGANT A 400 year old house on the high street, which has been smartly refurbished yet retains plenty of character - it's owned by a local couple and run by their son. Complex modern cooking relies on classic flavour combinations.

Menu £ 33/55

65 High St ✉ B95 5BX - ✆ 01564 793856 - www.chealsofhenley.co.uk - Closed 25-26 December, 1-9 January, 1 week Easter, Sunday dinner, Monday and Tuesday

Bluebell

MODERN BRITISH • NEIGHBOURHOOD This early 16C pub in a busy market town is run by a brother and sister: he cooks and she looks after the service. Modern dishes have bold, distinctive flavours - the Aubrey Allen steaks are popular and desserts are a highlight.

Menu £ 19 (weekday lunch) - Carte £ 24/34

93 High St ✉ B95 5AT - ✆ 01564 793049 - www.thebluebell-henley.co.uk

HENLEY-ON-THAMES

Oxfordshire - Pop. 11 494 - Regional map n° **6**-C3

Shaun Dickens at The Boathouse

MODERN BRITISH • FRIENDLY This modern restaurant is sure to please with its floor to ceiling glass doors and decked terrace overlooking the Thames. The young chef-owner offers an array of menus; attractively presented dishes centre around local ingredients.

Menu £ 26 (lunch) - Carte £ 39/49

Station Rd ✉ RG9 1AZ - ✆ 01491 577937 - www.shaundickens.co.uk - Closed 25-26 December, Monday and Tuesday

Luscombes at The Golden Ball

TRADITIONAL CUISINE • FRIENDLY A pretty former pub – now a cosy restaurant popular with the locals. Appealing menus offer well-executed modern classics; the afternoon tea with homemade preserves is a hit. Service is friendly and attentive.

Menu £ 17 (weekday lunch) – Carte £ 33/43

Lower Assendon ✉ RG9 6AH – Northwest : 1.5 mi by A 4130 on B 480 – ✆ 01491 574157 – www.luscombes.co.uk – Closed Sunday dinner and Monday

Hotel du Vin

BUSINESS • MODERN Characterful 1857 building that was formerly the Brakspear Brewery. Stylish bedrooms include airy doubles and duplex suites: one features two roll-top tubs and a great view of the church; others boast heated balconies and outdoor baths. Choose from a list of brasserie classics and over 400 wines in the bistro.

43 rooms – †£ 119/300 ††£ 119/300 – ☕ £ 17 – 2 suites

New St. ✉ RG9 2BP – ✆ 01491 848400 – www.hotelduvin.com

at Shiplake South: 2 mi on A4155

Orwells

MODERN BRITISH • RUSTIC XX This 18C building may look like a rural inn but inside it has a modern, formal feel. Creative cooking uses top quality produce and flavours are pronounced. It's named after George Orwell, who spent his childhood in the area.

Menu £ 25/35 (weekdays) – Carte £ 42/61

Shiplake Row ✉ RG9 4DP – West 0.5 mi on Binfield Heath rd. – ✆ 0118 940 3673 – www.orwellsrestaurant.co.uk – Closed first 2 weeks January, 1 week April, last week August, first week September, Sunday dinner, Tuesday and Monday except bank holidays

HEREFORD

Herefordshire – Pop. 60 415 – Regional map n° **10**-B3

Castle House

MODERN CUISINE • ELEGANT XX This elegant restaurant looks out over the hotel gardens and across the old moat of Hereford Castle. Classic dishes are reinvented in a modern manner and ingredients from Herefordshire feature highly. Menus offer plenty of choice.

Menu £ 23 (weekday lunch) – Carte £ 23/46

Castle House Hotel, Castle St ✉ HR1 2NW – ✆ 01432 356321 – www.castlehse.co.uk

Castle House

TOWNHOUSE • CONTEMPORARY This elegant Georgian house sits close to the cathedral. An impressive staircase leads to warmly furnished bedrooms of various sizes; some overlook the old castle moat. More contemporary rooms can be found in nearby 'Number 25'.

24 rooms ☕ – †£ 125/140 ††£ 155/260

Castle St ✉ HR1 2NW – ✆ 01432 356321 – www.castlehse.co.uk

Castle House – See restaurant listing

HESWALL

Mersey. – Pop. 29 977 – Regional map n° **11**-A3

Burnt Truffle

MODERN BRITISH • BISTRO A friendly team run this sweet modern bistro. Menus offer a good range of original dishes with global influences. Start with the sourdough bread with truffle and walnut butter and be sure to save room for the delicious desserts.

Menu £19 (lunch and early dinner) – Carte dinner £24/39

106 Telegraph Rd ✉ CH60 0AQ – ✆ 0151 342 1111 – www.burnttruffle.net – Closed 25-26 December

HETHE

Oxfordshire – Regional map n° **6**-B1

Muddy Duck

MODERN CUISINE • FRIENDLY It might have been modernised but this welcoming local retains plenty of rustic character. Choose from pub staples or more adventurous dishes, with steaks hung in a unique salt-ageing chamber and specials from the wood-fired oven in summer. The friendly team always welcome you with a smile.

Carte £24/52

Main St ✉ OX27 8ES – ✆ 01869 278099 – www.themuddyduckpub.co.uk – Closed 25 December and Sunday dinner

HEXHAM

Northumberland – Pop. 11 388 – Regional map n° **14**-A2

Rat Inn

TRADITIONAL BRITISH • PUB Set in a small hillside hamlet is this traditional 18C drovers' inn with wooden beams, an open range and a multi-level garden boasting arbours and Tyne Valley views. The daily changing menu showcases good quality produce in interesting dishes; the Northumberland rib of beef 'for two or more' is a must.

Menu £18 (weekdays) – Carte £24/44

Anick ✉ NE46 4LN – Northeast : 1.75 mi by A 6079 – ✆ 01434 602814 – www.theratinn.com – Closed 25 December and Sunday dinner

at Haydon Bridge West: 7.5 mi on A69 ✉ Hexham

Langley Castle

HISTORIC BUILDING • CLASSIC Impressive 14C castle in 12 acres; its charming guest areas feature stone walls, tapestries and heraldic shields. Characterful bedrooms, some with four-posters; Castle View rooms are more uniform in style. Modern, international menus in the romantic dining room or in the glass cube overlooking the gardens.

27 rooms – †£130/230 ††£170/290

Langley-on-Tyne ✉ NE47 5LU – South : 2 mi by Alston rd on A 686 – ✆ 01434 688888 – www.langleycastle.com

HIGHCLIFFE

Dorset – Regional map n° **2**-D3

Lord Bute

BUSINESS • PERSONALISED Some of the suites in this elegant hotel stand where the original 18C entrance lodges to Highcliffe Castle (home of Lord Bute), were once located. Bedrooms are well-appointed and decorated in a contemporary style. The smart restaurant and courtyard offer classical menus and host jazz and cabaret evenings.

13 rooms – †£130/140 ††£130/140 – 2 suites

179-185 Lymington Rd ✉ BH23 4JS – ✆ 01425 278884 – www.lordbute.co.uk

HINCKLEY

Leicestershire - Pop. 45 249 - Regional map n° **9**-B2

34 Windsor St

MODERN CUISINE • FASHIONABLE XX This stylish modern restaurant is well-run by an experienced, hands-on owner. It has a relaxed feel and a smart chill-out terrace to the rear. Cooking is also contemporary; the 8 course tasting menu shows the kitchen's ambition.

Carte £ 28/43

34 Windsor St, Burbage ✉ LE10 2EF - Southeast : 2.25 mi by B 4669 off B 578 - ✆ 01455 234342 - www.34windsorst.com - Closed 27-28 December, 1-3 January, Sunday dinner, Monday and Tuesday

HINTLESHAM - Suffolk → See Ipswich

HINTON ST GEORGE

Somerset - Pop. 442 - Regional map n° **2**-B3

Lord Poulett Arms

MODERN BRITISH • INN Characterful pub with open fires and beams fringed with hop bines; outside it's just as charming, with a lavender-framed terrace, a boules pitch and a secret garden. Creative cooking has a British base but also displays a wide range of influences. Stylish bedrooms come with feature beds and Roberts radios.

Menu £ 20 (lunch and early dinner) - Carte £ 27/42

4 rooms - †£ 65/85 ††£ 90/120

High St ✉ TA17 8SE - ✆ 01460 73149 - www.lordpoulettarms.com - Closed 25-26 December and 1 January

HOLCOMBE

Somerset - Regional map n° **2**-C2

Holcombe Inn

INN • CONTEMPORARY This modernised 17C inn set deep in the heart of the Somerset countryside, provides all the charm you'd expect of a building its age, with exposed beams, flagged floors and cosy open fires. Bedrooms are luxuriously appointed and some boast views over Downside Abbey. Hearty comfort dishes feature on the menu.

11 rooms - †£ 75/85 ††£ 100/145

Stratton Rd ✉ BA3 5EB - West : 0.25 mi on Stratton-on-the-Fosse rd - ✆ 01761 232478 - www.holcombeinn.co.uk

HOLKHAM

Norfolk - Regional map n° **8**-C1

Victoria

INN • COSY An extended flint inn with a relaxed, modern style, large lawned gardens and pleasant country views, set close to the beach at the gates of Holkham Hall. Stylish bedrooms - some in 'Ancient House' across the road. Dine on traditional British dishes overlooking the marshes of the adjacent nature reserve.

20 rooms - †£ 125/155 ††£ 155/255

Park Rd ✉ NR23 1RG - ✆ 01328 711008 - www.holkham.co.uk/victoria

Be sure to read the section 'How to use this guide'. It explains our symbols, classifications and abbreviations and will help you make a more informed choice.

HOLLINGBOURNE

Kent - Regional map n° **5**-C2

The Windmill

TRADITIONAL BRITISH • PUB With its giant inglenook fireplace and low-slung beams, the Windmill is as characterful as they come. You'll find tempting bar snacks, sharing roasts on Sundays and, alongside the hearty British classics, some more refined dishes too.

Menu £13 (weekday lunch)/28 - Carte £27/54

32 Eyhorne St ✉ ME17 1TR - ✆ 01622 889000 - www.thewindmillhollingbourne.co.uk

HOLMFIRTH

West Yorkshire - Pop. 21 706 - Regional map n° **13**-B3

Sunnybank

TOWNHOUSE • ELEGANT Attractive Victorian house with lovely gardens and great views; hidden up a narrow road in the village where 'Last of the Summer Wine' was filmed. Cosy bedrooms have a personal touch. Look out for the original stained glass window.

6 rooms - †£75/115 ††£85/125

78 Upperthong Ln ✉ HD9 3BQ - Northwest : 0.5 mi by A 6024 - ✆ 01484 684065 - www.sunnybankguesthouse.co.uk

HOLT

Norfolk - Pop. 3 550 - Regional map n° **8**-C1

Byfords

TOWNHOUSE • PERSONALISED A Grade II listed 15C flint house whose stunning bedrooms come with feature beds, underfloor heating and plenty of extras. Numerous characterful rooms are home to a deli, café and restaurant. Extensive menus include grazing dishes, sharing platters and afternoon tea. It's a real hit with the locals.

17 rooms - †£135/155 ††£165/215

Shirehall Plain ✉ NR25 6BG - ✆ 01263 711400 - www.byfords.org.uk

HONITON

Devon - Pop. 11 483 - Regional map n° **1**-D2

The Pig

TRADITIONAL BRITISH • RUSTIC A bubbly team welcome you to the Pig hotel's laid-back restaurant. The '25 mile' menu showcases produce from the beautiful kitchen gardens and local suppliers. Appealing, classical dishes have an unfussy style and rely on fresh, natural flavours to do the talking. A comprehensive range of wines accompanies.

Carte £31/43

The Pig Hotel, Gittisham ✉ EX14 3AD - Southwest : 5 mi by A 30 and B 3177 - ✆ 01404 540400 (booking essential) - www.thepighotel.com

Holt

REGIONAL CUISINE • PUB A rustic, family-run pub, where their passion for food is almost palpable. The regularly changing menu features regional and homemade produce, with meats and fish smoked and cured on-site. Try the 3 or 5 ale tasting rack - thirds of pints of Otter Brewery ales from their nearby family brewery.

Carte £30/38

178 High St ✉ EX14 1LA - ✆ 01404 47707 - www.theholt-honiton.com - Closed 25 December-2 January, Sunday and Monday

The Pig

COUNTRY HOUSE • CONTEMPORARY A hugely impressive Elizabethan mansion at the end of a winding drive. Its traditional interior has been stylishly redesigned (the historic entrance hall is now a bar) and service is relaxed. Bedrooms in the house boast wonderful country views; those in the old stables still have their original partitions.

30 rooms - †£145/325 ††£145/325 - ☕£11

Gittisham ✉ EX14 3AD - Southwest : 5 mi by A 30 and B 3177 - ✆ 01404 540400 - www.thepighotel.com

The Pig - See restaurant listing

HOOK

Hampshire - Pop. 7 934 - Regional map n° **4**-B1

Tylney Hall

LUXURY • CLASSIC Impressively restored 19C mansion full of period grandeur. Bedrooms are split between the main house and courtyard: the former are traditionally furnished with period features; the latter benefit from views over the delightful gardens, designed by Jekyll. The formal panelled restaurant offers classic dishes.

113 rooms ☕ - †£150/235 ††£170/255 - 12 suites

Rotherwick ✉ RG27 9AZ - Northwest : 2.5 mi by A 30 and Newnham Rd on Ridge Ln - ✆ 01256 764881 - www.tylneyhall.com

HOPE

Derbyshire - Regional map n° **9**-A1

Losehill House

COUNTRY HOUSE • PERSONALISED Peacefully located former walkers' hostel affording wonderful views up to Win Hill; in summer it's a popular wedding venue. It has an airy open-plan lounge-bar and bright modern bedrooms. Unwind in the spa or in the hot tub on the terrace. The formally laid restaurant offers classic dishes with a modern edge.

22 rooms ☕ - †£150/225 ††£185/295

Lose Hill Ln, Edale Rd ✉ S33 6AF - North : 1 mi by Edale Rd - ✆ 01433 621219 - www.losehillhouse.co.uk

HOPTON HEATH

Shropshire - Regional map n° **10**-A2

Hopton House

COUNTRY HOUSE • PERSONALISED Take in views over the Shropshire Hills from this charming guesthouse. Spacious open-plan bedrooms boast super king sized beds, Smart TVs, silent fridges and double-ended baths. A freshly baked cake is a pleasing extra.

2 rooms ☕ - †£125/135 ††£125/135

✉ SY7 0QD - On Clun rd - ✆ 01547 530885 - www.shropshirebreakfast.co.uk

HORLEY

Surrey - Pop. 22 693 - Regional map n° **4**-D2

Langshott Manor

HISTORIC • PERSONALISED Characterful 16C manor house set amidst roses, vines and ponds. The traditional exterior contrasts with contemporary furnishings and many of the bedrooms have fireplaces, four-posters or balconies. Afternoon tea is a feature.

22 rooms - †£99/315 ††£99/315 - ☕£17 - 1 suite

Langshott ✉ RH6 9LN - North : 0.5 mi by A 23 turning right at Chequers Hotel onto Ladbroke Rd - ✆ 01293 786680 - www.alexanderhotels.com

HORNDON ON THE HILL

Thurrock – Pop. 1 596 – Regional map n° **7**-C3

Bell Inn

TRADITIONAL BRITISH • **INN** The Bell was built in the first half of the 15C and positively oozes history; keep an eye out for the hot cross bun collection! Cooking has a pleasingly classical edge and a modern touch. Two neighbouring Georgian buildings house contemporary bedrooms and the Ostlers restaurant (open Fri and Sat nights).

Carte £ 25/49

26 rooms – †£ 75/140 ††£ 80/145 – £ 9

High Rd ✉ SS17 8LD – ✆ 01375 642463 – www.bell-inn.co.uk – Closed 25-26 December and dinner on bank holidays

HORNING

Norfolk – Pop. 1 098 – Regional map n° **8**-D1

Bure River Cottage

SEAFOOD • **FRIENDLY** X Friendly restaurant tucked away in a lovely riverside village that's famed for its boating. Informal, L-shaped room with modern tables and chairs. Blackboard menu features fresh, carefully cooked fish and shellfish; much from Lowestoft.

Carte £ 26/51

27 Lower St ✉ NR12 8AA – ✆ 01692 631421
– www.burerivercottagerestaurant.co.uk – dinner only – Closed 25 December-13 February, Sunday and Monday

HORNINGSEA – Cambridgeshire → See Cambridge

HORRINGER – Suffolk → See Bury St Edmunds

HORSHAM

West Sussex – Pop. 48 041 – Regional map n° **4**-D2

Restaurant Tristan (Tristan Mason)

MODERN BRITISH • **RUSTIC** X A characterful beamed dining room on the first floor of a 16C town centre property. Carefully crafted, creative dishes are delivered with a modern touch; ingredients are excellent and flavours, distinct and well-matched. Service is enthusiastic and friendly and the atmosphere, refreshingly relaxed.

→ Orkney scallop with cauliflower, Westcombe cheddar and black truffle. Fillet of turbot with carrot, mussels, buckwheat and sea buckthorn. Rhubarb soufflé with cardamom-poached rhubarb.

Menu £ 30 (weekdays)/50

3 Stans Way, East St ✉ RH12 1HU – ✆ 01403 255688
– www.restauranttristan.co.uk – Closed 25-26 December,1-2 January, Sunday and Monday

at Rowhook Northwest: 4 mi by A264 and A281 off A29 ✉ Horsham

Chequers Inn

TRADITIONAL BRITISH • **COSY** Part-15C inn with a charming open-fired, stone-floored bar and an unusual dining room extension. The chef-owner grows, forages for or shoots the majority of his produce. Classical menus.

Carte £ 30/43

✉ RH12 3PY – ✆ 01403 790480 – www.thechequersrowhook.com – Closed 25 December and Sunday dinner

HOUGH-ON-THE-HILL - Lincolnshire → See Grantham

HOWE STREET

Essex – Regional map n° **7**-C2

Green Man

TRADITIONAL BRITISH • FRIENDLY The Galvin brothers couldn't resist buying this pub in their native county. The original 14C building offers all the rustic charm you'd expect and they've added a beautiful, modern barn extension. Classic British dishes are carefully cooked and full of flavour; flatbreads from the wood oven are a speciality.

Menu £ 13/19 – Carte £ 25/41

Main Rd ✉ CM3 1BG – ✆ 01245 408820 – www.galvingreenman.com

HUMSHAUGH

Northumberland – Regional map n° **14**-A2

Carraw

FAMILY • PERSONALISED A converted stone farmhouse and barn built on the foundations of Hadrian's Wall. Stay here in beamed bedrooms or in the more modern lodge which has a delightful lounge with full-length windows and panoramic country views.

9 rooms – †£ 69/105 ††£ 89/125

Carraw Farm, Military Rd ✉ NE46 4DB – West : 5 mi on B 6318 – ✆ 01434 689857 – www.carraw.co.uk

HUNSDON

Hertfordshire – Regional map n° **7**-B2

Fox & Hounds

TRADITIONAL BRITISH • PUB A welcoming high street pub with contemporary styling. The chef's ethos is to let good quality ingredients speak for themselves. Alongside homemade pasta dishes you'll find meats cooked on the Josper grill and plenty of local game. Flavours are pronounced, combinations are classical and portions are hearty.

Menu £ 20 (weekdays) – Carte £ 24/40

2 High St ✉ SG12 8NH – ✆ 01279 843999 – www.foxandhounds-hunsdon.co.uk – Closed 25-26 December, Sunday dinner and Monday

HUNSTANTON

Norfolk – Pop. 8 704 – Regional map n° **8**-B1

The Neptune (Kevin Mangeolles)

MODERN CUISINE • INTIMATE XX A passionate couple have transformed this old roadside inn into a smart destination restaurant with stylishly understated bedrooms. Start with a drink and canapés in the bar while choosing from the ever-evolving menu. Kevin cooks alone and his skilfully crafted, unfussy dishes allow the natural flavours of top quality produce from the nearby waters and countryside to shine.

→ Soused mackerel with shaved fennel and beetroot mayonnaise. 250-day aged rump of Dexter beef with braised short rib, blue cheese purée and heritage carrots. Colombian milk chocolate mousse with Horlicks ice cream and honeycomb.

Menu £ 62

4 rooms – †£ 120/150 ††£ 160/200

85 Old Hunstanton Rd, Old Hunstanton ✉ PE36 6HZ – Northeast : 1.5 mi on A 149 – ✆ 01485 532122 – www.theneptune.co.uk – dinner only and Sunday lunch – Closed 3 weeks January, 1 week May, 1 week November and Monday

Lodge

FAMILY • PERSONALISED After a day at the beach head for this laid-back hotel and one of its modern, well-equipped bedrooms; go for a suite for views over the rooftops to the sea. Dine in the smart, cosy bar or head through to the more formal, intimate dining room; the menu offers a mix of pub classics and Italian-based dishes.

16 rooms – £ 75/125 £ 120/170

Old Hunstanton Rd ✉ PE36 6HX – Northeast : 1.5 mi on A 149
– ✆ 01485 532896 – www.thelodgehunstanton.co.uk

No. 33

LUXURY • DESIGN A Victorian house with an unusual façade, set in a peaceful street. Designer touches feature throughout, from the cosy open-fired lounge to the boutique bedrooms with their creative feature walls; some even have baths in the room.

5 rooms – £ 85/140 £ 95/190

33 Northgate ✉ PE36 6AP
– ✆ 01485 524352 – www.33hunstanton.co.uk

HUNSTRETE

Bath and North East Somerset – Regional map n° **2**-C2

The Pig

TRADITIONAL CUISINE • BRASSERIE XX This rustic hotel conservatory takes things back to nature with pots of fresh herbs placed on wooden tables and chimney pots filled with flowering shrubs. The extremely knowledgeable team serve dishes which showcase ingredients from their extensive gardens, along with produce sourced from within 25 miles.

Carte £ 32/45

The Pig Hotel, Hunstrete House ✉ BS39 4NS
– ✆ 01761 490490 (booking essential)
– www.thepighotel.com

The Pig

COUNTRY HOUSE • PERSONALISED Nestled in the Mendip Hills, with deer roaming around the parkland, this Grade II listed house is all about getting back to nature. It has a relaxed, friendly atmosphere and extremely comfortable bedrooms which feature handmade beds and fine linens; some are in converted sheds in the walled vegetable garden.

29 rooms – £ 155/330 £ 155/330 – £ 18

Hunstrete House ✉ BS39 4NS
– ✆ 01761 490490 – www.thepighotel.com

The Pig – See restaurant listing

HUNTINGDON

Cambridgeshire – Pop. 23 937 – Regional map n° **8**-A2

Old Bridge

TOWNHOUSE • CONTEMPORARY Attractive 18C former bank next to the River Ouse; its bright, contemporary décor cleverly blended with the property's original features. Individually styled, up-to-date bedrooms; some with four-poster beds. Cosy oak-panelled bar, conservatory restaurant with a lovely terrace and a superbly stocked wine shop.

24 rooms – £ 95/150 £ 139/250

1 High St ✉ PE29 3TQ
– ✆ 01480 424300 – www.huntsbridge.com

HUNTINGDON

Abbots Ripton North: 6.5 mi by B1514 and A141 on B1090

Abbot's Elm

TRADITIONAL BRITISH • INN A modern reconstruction of an attractive 17C pub, with a spacious open-plan layout, homely touches and a vaulted, oak-beamed roof. Extensive menus offer hearty, flavoursome cooking; the wine list is a labour of love and the cosy, comfy bedrooms come with fluffy bathrobes and complimentary mineral water.

Menu £ 14 (weekday lunch) - Carte £ 24/48

4 rooms - £ 70/75 £ 85/95

Moat Lane PE28 2PA - 01487 773773 - www.theabbotselm.co.uk - Closed Sunday dinner

HURLEY

Windsor and Maidenhead - Pop. 1 712 - Regional map n° **6**-C3

Hurley House

MODERN BRITISH • PUB Hurley House is a stylish place: outside you'll find a charming canopied terrace with patio heaters and its own bar, while inside smart furnishings sit amongst exposed bricks, beams and flagstones. Well-sourced ingredients underpin modern British dishes, which confidently blend contrasting tastes and textures. Well-appointed bedrooms pay great attention to detail.

Menu £ 19 (weekday lunch) - Carte £ 30/54

10 rooms - £ 160/270 £ 170/280

Henley Rd SL6 5LH - East : 1 mi on A 4130 - 01628 568500 - www.hurleyhouse.co.uk

HURWORTH-ON-TEES - Darlington ➜ See Darlington

HUTTON MAGNA - Durham ➜ See Barnard Castle

ICKHAM

Kent - Regional map n° **5**-D2

Duke William

MODERN BRITISH • PUB The smart exterior of this pub has more of a city than a country look but inside it has a good old neighbourhood vibe. Keenly priced menus list time-honoured classics everyone knows and loves. Cosy up on fur throw covered benches by the fire, then stay the night in one of the smart yet casual bedrooms.

Carte £ 23/49

4 rooms - £ 60/120 £ 60/120

The Street CT3 1QP - 01227 721308 - www.thedukewilliamickham.com

ILFRACOMBE

Devon - Pop. 11 184 - Regional map n° **1**-C1

Thomas Carr @ The Olive Room

SEAFOOD • RUSTIC A simple, homely restaurant set in a 19C townhouse and run by an experienced local chef. Ultra-fresh seafood is the focus, with dishes only confirmed once the day boat deliveries come in. Cooking is creative, with distinct flavours, and each dish comprises just 4 or 5 complementary ingredients. Bedrooms have a pleasant period feel and some have great views over the town.

→ Fennel cured salmon with oyster cream and apple. Hake, crab, golden beetroot, orange and basil. Chocolate tart, mousse and rum and raisin ice cream.

Menu £ 55 (weekdays)/95 - tasting menu only

5 rooms - £ 55/65 £ 90/130

56 Fore St EX34 9DJ - 01271 867831 (booking essential) - www.thomascarrdining.co.uk - dinner only and lunch Friday-Saturday - Closed January, Sunday and Monday

Antidote (N)

MODERN BRITISH • FRIENDLY X A sweet glass-fronted former shop set just off the quayside and run by a friendly couple; brown paper covered tables contribute the cool, modish feel. Thoughtfully prepared menus list well-judged dishes with plenty of flavour and prices are kept low. Bedrooms are modern – one even has a small terrace.

Carte £ 24/30

3 rooms – †£ 85/105 ††£ 89/160

20 St James Pl ✉ EX34 9BJ
– ✆ 01271 865339 – www.theantidoteilfracombe.co.uk – dinner only – Closed Sunday and Monday

Quay

MODERN BRITISH • DESIGN XX

A long-standing restaurant on the harbourside, overlooking the sea. Downstairs they serve snacks, while upstairs the menus focus on local fish and Devon beef. It's owned by local lad Damien Hirst, which explains the art – he also designed everything from the uniform to the crockery.

Menu £ 30 – Carte £ 28/47

11 The Quay ✉ EX34 9EQ
– ✆ 01271 868090 – www.11thequay.co.uk
– Closed 2 weeks January

Thomas Carr Seafood and Grill (N)

MODERN BRITISH • NEIGHBOURHOOD X A crowd-funding campaign kicked off the conversion of this old town centre pub into a simple brasserie. The rustic downstairs room has a casual feel and the more elegant upstairs room is open Friday and Saturday evenings. Cooking is unfussy, with dishes divided into 'Small Bites' and 'Bigger Bites'.

Menu £ 24 (weekday lunch) – Carte £ 25/40

59 High St ✉ EX34 9QB
– ✆ 01271 555005 – www.thomascarrdining.co.uk – Closed Sunday dinner, Monday and Tuesday

Westwood

FAMILY • DESIGN Perched on the hillside overlooking the rooftops, this appealingly styled Victorian house offers warm décor and an eclectic mix of modern and retro furniture. Spacious bedrooms boast bold feature wallpaper; those to the front are the best.

5 rooms – †£ 85/125 ††£ 85/125

Torrs Pk ✉ EX34 8AZ
– ✆ 01271 867443 – www.west-wood.co.uk

ILKLEY

West Yorkshire – Pop. 14 809 – Regional map n° **13**-B2

Box Tree

MODERN BRITISH • CLASSIC DÉCOR XXX This iconic Yorkshire restaurant was established back in 1962. It's set in two charming sandstone cottages and has a plush, antique-furnished lounge and two luxurious dining rooms. Cooking has a classical French base with subtle modern touch and dishes are light and delicate.

Menu £ 40/70

37 Church St ✉ LS29 9DR
– ✆ 01943 608484 – www.theboxtree.co.uk
– dinner only and lunch Friday-Sunday – Closed 26-30 December, 1-7 January, Sunday dinner, Monday and Tuesday

ILMINGTON

Warwickshire – Pop. 712 – Regional map n° **19**-C3

Howard Arms

MODERN BRITISH • PUB Built from golden stone quarried in the village itself, The Howard Arms really is part of the local community. Hearty flavours are the order of the day and pub favourites are listed alongside more global dishes. Bedroom styles vary between the pub and the extension: 'Village' overlooks the village green.

Carte £ 25/40

8 rooms – †£ 104/130 ††£ 110/150

Lower Green ✉ CV36 4LT – ✆ 01608 682226 – www.howardarms.com – Closed 6-10 January

IPSWICH

Suffolk – Pop. 144 957 – Regional map n° **8**-C3

Trongs

CHINESE • FRIENDLY XX Loyal locals are always a good sign, and this sweet little restaurant has plenty. One brother cooks and the other looks after the service. Authentic dishes include spicy Hunanese specialities – ask and they will adjust the heat.

Menu £ 26/30 – Carte £ 14/37

23 St Nicholas St ✉ IP1 1TW – ✆ 01473 256833 – dinner only – Closed 3 weeks August and Sunday

Salthouse Harbour

BUSINESS • PERSONALISED A stylish former salt warehouse – its trendy lobby-lounge boasts floor to ceiling windows and great marina views. Boutique bedrooms have well-appointed bathrooms; some feature chaise longues, copper slipper baths or balconies. The chic brasserie has a zinc-topped bar, gold pillars and padded booths.

70 rooms – †£ 120/190 ††£ 150/250 – £ 14

1 Neptune Quay ✉ IP4 1AX – ✆ 01473 226789 – www.salthouseharbour.co.uk

Kesgrave Hall

HISTORIC • MODERN An impressive house built in 1812, with a delightful terrace overlooking large lawned gardens to a 38 acre wood. Stylish lounges have a relaxed, urban-chic feel. Luxurious bedrooms boast quality furnishings, modern facilities and stylish bathrooms. The busy brasserie offers a European menu.

23 rooms – †£ 145/330 ††£ 145/330

Hall Rd, Kesgrave ✉ IP5 2PU – East : 4.75 mi by A 1214 on Bealings rd – ✆ 01473 333471 – www.kesgravehall.com

at Chelmondiston Southeast : 6 mi by A 137 on B 1456

Red Lion

TRADITIONAL CUISINE • BISTRO X Smartly refurbished former pub with a few comfy chairs in the bar and two dining rooms furnished with dark wood tables and Lloyd Loom chairs. Menus offer a broad range of dishes and daily specials. The bubbly owner leads the service.

Carte £ 23/38

Main St ✉ IP9 1DX – ✆ 01473 780400 – www.chelmondistonredlion.co.uk – Closed Sunday and Monday

IRONBRIDGE

Telford and Wrekin – Pop. 1 560 – Regional map n° **10**-B2

Library House

TOWNHOUSE • PERSONALISED Attractive former library, just a stone's throw from the famous bridge. It has a farmhouse-style breakfast room and a homely lounge where books sit on the old library shelves. Tastefully furnished bedrooms are named after poets.

3 rooms – £75/95 £100/125

11 Severn Bank ✉ TF8 7AN – ✆ 01952 432299 – www.libraryhouse.com

ITTERINGHAM

Norfolk – Regional map n° **8**-C1

Walpole Arms

MODERN BRITISH • PUB Pretty 18C pub in a sleepy village, with a surprisingly modern yet sympathetically designed interior. Refined dishes champion local ingredients and feature produce from their own farm; rare breed beef is a speciality.

Carte £19/42

The Common ✉ NR11 7AR – ✆ 01263 587258 – www.thewalpolearms.co.uk – Closed 25 December and Sunday dinner in winter

IXWORTH – Suffolk → See Bury St Edmunds

KELMSCOTT

Oxfordshire – Regional map n° **6**-A2

Plough

TRADITIONAL CUISINE • RURAL The 16C Plough has all the character you would expect of a pub its age, with rough stone walls, open fires and a cottage-style garden. Traditional menus list dishes you'll know and love, from buck rarebit to devilled lambs' kidneys.

Carte £25/35

8 rooms – £100/120 £110/130

✉ GL7 3HG – ✆ 01367 253543 – www.theploughinnkelmscott.com – Closed dinner Sunday and Monday

KENDAL

Cumbria – Pop. 28 586 – Regional map n° **12**-B2

Castle Dairy N

MODERN BRITISH • HISTORIC XX Kendal's oldest inhabited building dates back to 1402 and has a cobbled Roman road running through its centre and several delightfully timbered little rooms. College apprentices are guided by an experienced chef-manager and cooking is modern and sophisticated.

Menu £25/40

Wildman St ✉ LA9 6EN – ✆ 01539 814756 – www.castledairy.co.uk – Closed 3 weeks January, 2 weeks June, 2 weeks September, 25-26 December and Sunday-Tuesday

KENILWORTH

Warwickshire – Pop. 22 413 – Regional map n° **10**-C2

The Cross at Kenilworth (Adam Bennett)

CLASSIC CUISINE • ELEGANT A smartly furnished pub with eager, welcoming staff. Skilfully executed, classical cooking uses prime seasonal ingredients, and dishes not only look impressive but taste good too. Sit in the back room to watch the kitchen team in action. The bright, airy room next door used to be a classroom.

→ Crispy duck egg, cured ham, with celeriac purée, chicken jus. Slow-cooked beef cheek & sirloin, carrots, Yukon Gold mash, Bordelaise sauce. Hazelnut praline soufflé, blood orange ice cream, caramelised white chocolate sauce.

Menu £30 (lunch) – Carte £50/70

16 New St ✉ CV8 2EZ – ✆ 01926 853840 – www.thecrosskenilworth.co.uk – Closed 25-26 December, 1 January, Sunday dinner, Monday and bank holidays

KENTISBURY

Devon – Regional map n° **1**-C1

Coach House by Michael Caines

MODERN CUISINE • DESIGN XX This smart hotel restaurant has a lovely walnut and marble bar counter, a funky lounge under the eaves and an elegant dining room featuring plush blue velvet booths. Flavoursome modern dishes use local meats and south coast fish.

Menu £ 24/50

Kentisbury Grange Hotel, ✉ EX31 4NL – Southeast : 1 mi by B 3229 on A39 – ✆ 01271 882295 – www.kentisburygrange.co.uk

Kentisbury Grange

COUNTRY HOUSE • DESIGN This Victorian country house may have a Grade II listing but it's been smartly decked out with designer fabrics and furnishings in the colours of its original stained glass windows. Go for one of the chic, detached Garden Suites.

21 rooms – £ 110/150 ££ 150/225

✉ EX31 4NL – Southeast : 1 mi by B 3229 on A39 – ✆ 01271 882295 – www.kentisburygrange.co.uk

Coach House by Michael Caines – See restaurant listing

KENTON

Devon – Regional map n° **1**-D2

Rodean

TRADITIONAL BRITISH • NEIGHBOURHOOD XX This family-run restaurant sits overlooking a tiny village green and started life as a butcher's shop. The two characterful dining rooms come with wooden beams, exposed stone, dark wood panelling and traditional furnishings. Constantly evolving menus have a classic base and modern overtones.

Menu £ 26 – Carte £ 31/51

The Triangle ✉ EX6 8LS – ✆ 01626 890195 – www.rodeanrestaurant.co.uk – dinner only and Sunday lunch – Closed Sunday dinner and Monday

KESWICK

Cumbria – Pop. 4 984 – Regional map n° **12**-A2

Inn on the Square

TOWNHOUSE • CONTEMPORARY This 19C former coaching inn stands proudly on the town square. Inside it's surprisingly modern, with bright, bold furnishings, a chic bar, a steakhouse and a cosy pub. Stylish bedrooms have top facilities and locally made beds; ask for a quieter 'Herdwick' room, which comes with a sheep mural!

34 rooms – £ 190/220 ££ 200/230

Market Sq ✉ CA12 5JF – ✆ 017687 73333 – www.innonthesquare.co.uk

Howe Keld

TOWNHOUSE • CONTEMPORARY These two unassuming-looking slate cottages stand in the centre of town – but if you have a room with a view down the valley, you might find that hard to believe. Bedrooms are striking, courtesy of vibrantly coloured furnishings. Breakfast is a must and comes with a Swiss accent.

12 rooms – £ 70/90 ££ 115/140

5-7 The Heads ✉ CA12 5ES – ✆ 017687 72417 – www.howekeld.co.uk – Closed January-mid-February

at Borrowdale South : 5.5 mi on B 5289 ✉ Keswick

Leathes Head

MODERN BRITISH • CONTEMPORARY DÉCOR XX Enjoy an aperitif on the terrace of this Lakeland hotel and take in magnificent mountain views; in colder weather the Graphite Bar with its impressive slate-topped counter provides a stylish alternative. The constantly evolving modern menu sees natural flavours feature in well-judged combinations.

Menu £ 35/45

Leathes Head Hotel, Borrowdale ✉ CA12 5UY – ✆ 017687 77247 (bookings essential for non-residents) – www.leatheshead.co.uk – Closed 3-25 January

Leathes Head

COUNTRY HOUSE • CONTEMPORARY The beautiful fells and mountains of Borrowdale provide the backdrop for this traditional slate-built hotel and its attractive gardens. Both the bedrooms and guest areas mix the classic and the contemporary; an original tiled floor contrasts with a stylish bar and an attractive modern dining room.

11 rooms (dinner included) – †£ 110/115 ††£ 180/195

✉ CA12 5UY – ✆ 017687 77247 – www.leatheshead.co.uk – Closed 3-25 January

Leathes Head – See restaurant listing

at Braithwaite West: 2 mi by A66 on B5292 ✉ Keswick

Cottage in the Wood

MODERN BRITISH • ROMANTIC XX This cosy little cottage sits in an elevated forest setting and is run by a friendly team. In winter sit in the dining room; in summer take in views over the fells and valley from the conservatory. Carefully sourced ingredients feature in beautifully presented, well-balanced dishes. Bedrooms are contemporary.

Menu £ 30/65 **s**

9 rooms – †£ 96 ††£ 130/220

Magic Hill, Whinlatter Forest ✉ CA12 5TW – Northwest : 1.75 mi on B 5292 – ✆ 017687 78409 (bookings essential for non-residents) – www.thecottageinthewood.co.uk – dinner only and lunch Thursday-Saturday – Closed 6-22 January and Sunday-Monday

KETTERING

Northamptonshire – Pop. 56 226 – Regional map n° **9**-C3

at Rushton Northwest : 3.5 mi by A 14 and Rushton Rd

Rushton Hall

COUNTRY HOUSE • HISTORIC An imposing 15C house with stunning architecture, set in 28 acres of countryside. The Grand Hall features huge stained glass windows and an impressive fireplace, and the classically furnished bedrooms are luxurious. Dine in the brasserie or on more elaborate dishes in the grand restaurant.

51 rooms – †£ 150/380 ††£ 170/400 – 3 suites

✉ NN14 1RR – ✆ 01536 713001 – www.rushtonhall.com

KETTLESING – North Yorkshire → See Harrogate

KEYSTON

Cambridgeshire – ✉ Huntingdon – Pop. 257 – Regional map n° **8**-A2

Pheasant

TRADITIONAL BRITISH • PUB Hidden away in a sleepy hamlet is this big pub with enormous character; think exposed beams, hunting scenes and John Bull wallpaper. The wide-ranging menu includes a section of classics and there's an excellent value set menu. Staff are warm and attentive and there's a delightful rear terrace too.

Menu £ 20 (lunch and early dinner) – Carte £ 23/42

Village Loop Rd ✉ PE28 0RE – ✆ 01832 710241 (booking essential) – www.thepheasant-keyston.co.uk – Closed 2-15 January, Sunday dinner and Monday

KIBWORTH BEAUCHAMP

Leicestershire – Pop. 3 550 – Regional map n° **9**-B2

Lighthouse

SEAFOOD • NEIGHBOURHOOD With its array of nautical knick-knacks, the Lighthouse is a fitting name. The flexible menu has a seafood emphasis and offers many dishes in two different sizes; the 'Nibbles' are a popular choice.

Menu £ 15 (weekdays) – Carte £ 16/39

9 Station St ✉ LE8 0LN – ✆ 0116 279 6260 (booking essential) – www.lighthousekibworth.co.uk – dinner only – Closed Sunday, Monday and bank holidays

KILPECK

Herefordshire – Regional map n° **10**-A3

Kilpeck Inn

TRADITIONAL CUISINE • PUB A popular pub which narrowly escaped being turned into private housing thanks to the villagers' valiantly fought 'Save Our Pub' campaign. Its spacious interior and bedrooms are smart, modern and characterful, with impressive green credentials. Menus offer locally sourced meat and old fashioned puddings.

Carte £ 23/33

4 rooms – £ 85/115 £ 85/115

✉ HR2 9DN – ✆ 01981 570464 – www.kilpeckinn.com – Closed 25 December, Monday lunch except bank holidays and Sunday dinner

KINGHAM

Oxfordshire – Pop. 547 – Regional map n° **6**-A1

Kingham Plough

MODERN BRITISH • PUB Set on the green of an unspoilt village, this pub delivers all the rusticity you'd hope for along with some subtle modern touches. Sit out on the terrace, in the stylish dining room or beside locals and their dogs in the bar. Fiercely seasonal British dishes exude freshness and simplicity. Bedrooms are comfy.

Carte £ 31/43

6 rooms – £ 110/150 £ 145/195

The Green ✉ OX7 6YD – ✆ 01608 658327 – www.thekinghamplough.co.uk – Closed 25 December and dinner Sunday

The Wild Rabbit

MODERN BRITISH • CHIC Just down the road from the Daylesford Farm Shop is the Bamford family's stylishly modernised country pub. Accomplished modern dishes have plenty of appeal, with the natural flavours of their farm's superb organic ingredients underpinning the menu. Luxurious bedrooms are delightfully understated.

Carte £ 44/66

15 rooms – £ 140/335 £ 140/350

Church St ✉ OX7 6YA – ✆ 01608 658389 – www.thewildrabbit.co.uk – Closed 1-4 January

KING'S LYNN

Norfolk – Pop. 46 093 – Regional map n° **8**-B1

Market Bistro

MODERN BRITISH • BISTRO Sit in the front room if you want more character, as although its 17C beams and a fireplace still remain, this relaxed bistro is more up-to-date than its exterior suggests. Complex cooking uses passionately sourced local produce and modern techniques. The chef's wife looks after the service.

Menu £ 22 (weekday lunch) – Carte £ 25/41

11 Saturday Market Pl ✉ PE30 5DQ – ✆ 01553 771483 – www.marketbistro.co.uk – Closed 26 December, 1 and 7-14 January, Sunday, Monday and lunch Tuesday

at Grimston East: 6.25 mi by A148

Congham Hall

COUNTRY HOUSE • ELEGANT A part-Georgian house set in 30 acres of peaceful grounds. Guest areas include a spacious drawing room with a subtle modern edge. Bedrooms have a contemporary country house style; opt for a Garden Room next to the spa, overlooking the flower or herb gardens. The formal restaurant offers classic fare.

26 rooms – †£ 135/260 ††£ 135/260 – ☕£ 15 – 2 suites

Lynn Rd. ✉ PE32 1AH – ✆ 01485 600250 – www.conghamhallhotel.co.uk

KINGS MILLS → See Channel Islands (Guernsey)

KING'S SUTTON

Northamptonshire – Pop. 2 069 – Regional map n° **9**-B3

White Horse

MODERN BRITISH • PUB Pretty sandstone pub run by a keen young couple. The self-taught chef makes everything from scratch and always tries to exceed his guests' expectations. Produce is fresh and local and follows a 'when it's gone, it's gone' approach.

Menu £ 14 (weekday lunch) – Carte £ 25/54

2 The Square ✉ OX17 3RF – ✆ 01295 812440 – www.whitehorseks.co.uk – Closed 25 December, Monday and Tuesday

KINGSBRIDGE

Devon – Pop. 6 116 – Regional map n° **1**-C3

Buckland-Tout-Saints

HISTORIC • CLASSIC Appealing Queen Anne mansion set in large, peaceful grounds. Traditional, antique-furnished interior with wood-panelling in many rooms. Bedrooms vary in shape and size; some have a classic country house feel and others are more contemporary. Choice of two dining rooms offering accomplished dishes.

16 rooms ☕ – †£ 89/289 ††£ 89/289 – 2 suites

Goveton ✉ TQ7 2DS – Northeast : 3 mi by A 381 – ✆ 01548 853055 – www.tout-saints.co.uk

KINGSTON-UPON-HULL

Kingston upon Hull – Pop. 284 321 – Regional map n° **13**-D2

Tapasya

INDIAN • DESIGN XX White banquettes set under chandeliers, a glass wine cellar, and a wall of water behind the bar set the scene for some sophisticated cooking. Carefully spiced dishes use good ingredients and are presented in a modern manner.

Menu £ 10 (lunch) – Carte £ 19/33

590-582 Beverley High Rd ✉ HU6 7LH – North : 1.5 mi on A 1079 – ✆ 01482 242606 – www.tapasyarestaurants.co.uk

KIRKBY LONSDALE

Cumbria – Pop. 1 843 – Regional map n° **12**-B3

Sun Inn

TRADITIONAL BRITISH • PUB After a stroll by the river head for this charming 17C pub. Enjoy a local beer in the characterful bar with exposed stone walls then dine in the smart restaurant. Lunch sees 'small bites' and pub classics, while dinner steps up a gear with much more elaborate dishes. Cosy bedrooms feature Swaledale wool carpets.

Carte £ 28/35

11 rooms ☕ – †£ 107/128 ††£ 117/138

6 Market St ✉ LA6 2AU – ✆ 015242 71965 – www.sun-inn.info – Closed Monday lunch

Royal

INN • CONTEMPORARY A well-run Georgian hotel overlooking the town square. The décor is a mix of modern and boutique and the owner has a keen eye for detail; some of the spacious bedrooms have free-standing baths in the room. Relax in the snug open-fired lounge then dine on classics or wood-fired pizzas in the all-day brasserie.

14 rooms – £ 85/185 £ 95/210

Main St ✉ LA6 2AE – ✆ 015242 71966 – www.royalhotelkirkbylonsdale.co.uk

at Lupton Northwest: 4.75 mi on A65

Plough

TRADITIONAL BRITISH • PUB A homely former coaching inn with exposed beams and open fires, set on the main road from the Lake District to North Yorkshire. Sit in the shabby-chic bar or smarter pink-hued restaurant and choose from an appealing menu with a modern touch. Stylish, individually styled bedrooms boast roll-top baths.

Carte £ 19/43

6 rooms – £ 85/225 £ 85/225

Cow Brow ✉ LA6 1PJ – ✆ 015395 67700 – www.theploughatlupton.co.uk

KIRKBY STEPHEN

Cumbria – Pop. 1 522 – Regional map n° **12**-B2

Augill Castle

FAMILY • QUIRKY This carefully restored, castellated country house is set in 15 acres of countryside. It's a quirky, characterful place with antiques and a Victorian Gothic style, but it's also surprisingly laid-back, and offers bedrooms and facilities geared towards families. Dine at huge communal tables from cheese or meat platters on weekdays or from a set menu at weekends.

17 rooms – £ 160/240 £ 160/320

Leacetts Lane ✉ CA17 4DE – Northeast : 4.25 mi by A 685 – ✆ 017683 41937 – www.stayinacastle.com

KIRKBY THORE

Cumbria – Pop. 758 – Regional map n° **12**-B2

Bridge

TRADITIONAL CUISINE • BISTRO A remodelled roadside pub set on the A66 which cuts across the country from East to West. Its owners – a husband and wife team – have given it a makeover and it now has a modern bistro feel. The menu is a roll-call of tasty classics and ingredients are well-sourced and carefully cooked.

Carte £ 22/45

✉ CA10 1UZ – on A66 – ✆ 017683 62766 – www.thebridgebistro.co.uk – Closed 25 December, Tuesday in winter and Sunday dinner

KIRKBYMOORSIDE

North Yorkshire – Pop. 2 751 – Regional map n° **13**-C1

Cornmill

HISTORIC • TRADITIONAL Charming 18C cornmill with a pleasant courtyard and gardens; look for the mill race running beneath the glass panel in the characterful breakfast room. The cosy lounge and elegant bedrooms are set in the old farmhouse and stables.

5 rooms – £ 60/115 £ 90/115

Kirby Mills ✉ YO62 6NP – East : 0.5 mi by A 170 – ✆ 01751 432000 – www.kirbymills.co.uk

KNOWSTONE

Devon – Regional map n° **1**-C1

Masons Arms (Mark Dodson)

CLASSIC FRENCH • **PUB** This pretty 13C inn sits in a secluded village. Dine in the cosy bar or take in delightful country views from beneath a Grecian ceiling mural in the bright rear dining room. Cooking is refined, ingredients are top class and flavours are pronounced and assured. Charming service is a perfect match for the food.

→ Langoustine and scallop with truffled Jerusalem artichoke and bisque sauce. Loin of lamb with boulangère potatoes, aubergine purée and toasted cumin seed jus. Passion fruit tart with gorse flower ice cream.

Menu £ 25 (lunch) - Carte £ 44/53

✉ EX36 4RY - ✆ 01398 341231 (booking essential) - www.masonsarmsdevon.co.uk - Closed first week January, 10 days August-September, Sunday and Monday

LETCOMBE REGIS

Oxfordshire - Pop. 578 - Regional map n° **6**-B3

Greyhound Inn

MODERN BRITISH • **RUSTIC** Two villagers stepped in to save this 18C pub from redevelopment and the locals are clearly thankful. Its original character is still visible through its beams and lovely inglenook fireplace but it's also been subtly modernised. Menus range from pub favourites to more sophisticated dishes. Bedrooms are cosy.

Menu £ 23 (lunch) - Carte £ 26/33

8 rooms - †£ 80 ††£ 95/145

Main St ✉ OX12 9JL - ✆ 01235 771969 - www.thegreyhoundletcombe.co.uk - Closed 7-18 January, 25 December and Monday lunch except bank holidays

LA HAULE → See Channel Islands (Jersey)

LA PULENTE → See Channel Islands (Jersey)

LANCASTER

Lancashire - Pop. 48 085 - Regional map n° **11**-A1

Ashton

TRADITIONAL • **MODERN** This stylishly decorated Georgian house surrounded by lawned gardens is very personally run by its friendly owner. Good-sized, boldly coloured bedrooms blend modern and antique furnishings; one room has a double shower, another, a roll-top bath. Simple weekday dinners are offered by arrangement.

6 rooms ☕ - †£ 115/135 ††£ 125/195

Wyresdale Rd ✉ LA1 3JJ - Southeast : 1.25 mi by A 6 on Clitheroe rd - ✆ 01524 68460 - www.theashtonlancaster.com

LANGAR

Nottinghamshire - Regional map n° **9**-B2

Langar Hall

COUNTRY HOUSE • **QUIRKY** Characterful Georgian manor surrounded by over 20 acres of pastoral land and ponds; its antique-furnished bedrooms named after those who've featured in the house's history. Dine by candlelight in the elegant, pillared dining room; classically based cooking features veg from the kitchen garden and local game.

12 rooms ☕ - †£ 110/180 ††£ 125/225 - 1 suite

Church Ln ✉ NG13 9HG - ✆ 01949 860559 - www.langarhall.co.uk

LANGFORD
Oxfordshire – Regional map n° **6**-A2

㊎ Bell Inn Ⓝ

TRADITIONAL BRITISH • RUSTIC The Bell Inn's rustic charm is hard to resist with its cosy bar, impressive inglenook fireplace and 16C origins. The large menu offers everything from a homemade burger to a muntjac, cep and bacon pie, and the wood-fired garlic, parsley and bone marrow flatbread is a must. Bedrooms are nicely furnished.

Carte £ 15/37

8 rooms – †£ 72/139 ††£ 72/139

✉ GL7 3LF – ✆ 01367 860249 (booking essential) – www.thebelllangford.com

LANGHO – Lancashire ➜ See Blackburn

LANGTHWAITE – North Yorkshire ➜ See Reeth

LAPWORTH
Warwickshire – Pop. 2 100 – Regional map n° **10**-C2

Boot Inn

TRADITIONAL BRITISH • PUB A big, buzzy pub boasting a large terrace, a traditional quarry-floored bar and a modern restaurant. Dishes range from sandwiches, picnic boards and sharing plates to more sophisticated specials. You can eat in a tepee in the summer!

Menu £ 16 (lunch and early dinner) – Carte £ 25/43

Old Warwick Rd ✉ B94 6JU – ✆ 01564 782464 (booking essential) – www.lovelypubs.co.uk

Enjoy good food without spending a fortune!
Look out for the Bib Gourmand ㊎ symbol to find restaurants offering good food at great prices!

LAVENHAM
Suffolk – ✉ Sudbury – Pop. 1 413 – Regional map n° **8**-C3

Great House

CLASSIC FRENCH • ELEGANT XXX Passionately run restaurant on the main square of an attractive town; its impressive Georgian façade concealing a timbered house with 14C origins. Choose between two dining rooms and a smart enclosed terrace. Concise menus offer ambitious dishes with worldwide influences and a French heart. Stylish, contemporary décor blends well with the old beams in the bedrooms.

Menu £ 26/37 – Carte £ 41/54

5 rooms – †£ 99/215 ††£ 99/215 – ☕ £ 12

Market Pl ✉ CO10 9QZ – ✆ 01787 247431 – www.greathouse.co.uk – Closed 3 weeks January, 2 weeks September, Sunday dinner, Monday and lunch Tuesday

The Swan at Lavenham H. & Spa

HISTORIC • PERSONALISED Numerous 15C cottages make up this characterful property, which has several delightful lounges, a hugely atmospheric bar and a smart spa with a terrace. Choose either a classic beamed or more contemporary bedroom. Dine on classics beneath the minstrels' gallery or more modern dishes in the brasserie.

45 rooms ☕ – †£ 107 ††£ 115/205

High St ✉ CO10 9QA – ✆ 01787 247477 – www.theswanatlavenham.co.uk

LEATHERHEAD

Surrey – Pop. 32 522 – Regional map n° **4**-D1

Dining Room

JAPANESE • HISTORIC XX Have a drink in the elegant Parrot Bar of this historic country house before heading for the delightful dining room with its bold décor, impressive ceiling and huge windows overlooking the estate. Extensive Japanese menus mix the classic with the modern and the flavours provide plenty of interest.

Carte £ 22/83

Beaverbrook Hotel, Reigate Rd ✉ KT22 8QX – ✆ 01372 375532 – www.beaverbrook.co.uk – Closed Sunday dinner and Monday

Beaverbrook

HISTORIC BUILDING • HISTORIC This neo-classical Victorian mansion set in 400 acres was once the country home of Lord Beaverbrook – a close friend of Churchill. Take in delightful country views from the many terraces or relax in huge guest areas which evoke memories of yesteryear. Bedrooms are charming. Enjoy British and Italian cooking in the Garden Room or Japanese dishes in the Dining Room.

18 rooms – †£ 225/400 ††£ 225/400 – ☕ £ 25 – 3 suites

Reigate Rd ✉ KT22 8QX – ✆ 01372 571300 – www.beaverbrook.co.uk

Dining Room – See restaurant listing

LEEDS

Kent – Regional map n° **5**-C2

Leeds Castle

HISTORIC BUILDING • PERSONALISED This unique accommodation is found in the grounds of 900 year old Leeds Castle. Stay in smart, modern bedrooms in the 1920s stable block or in a more historic room in the Maiden's Tower (an old Tudor bakehouse beside the castle). The timbered café morphs into a candlelit restaurant in the evening.

22 rooms ☕ – †£ 85/100 ††£ 110/170

Broomfield Gate ✉ ME17 1PL – Southeast: 3 mi by A 20 – ✆ 01622 767823 – www.leeds-castle.co.uk – Closed 25 December

GOOD TIPS!

This former mill town is now known as the 'Knightsbridge of the North', so it comes as no surprise to find restaurants located in both old industrial buildings and newer retail spaces: from **Ox Club** in an old mill, **HOME** in a Victorian former fish market and Michelin Starred **The Man Behind the Curtain** in a shop basement to **Crafthouse** in the Trinity shopping centre.

LEEDS

West Yorkshire – Pop. 751 485 – Regional map n° **13**-B2

Restaurants

✿ The Man Behind The Curtain (Michael O'Hare) A/C

CREATIVE • FASHIONABLE XX An idiosyncratic basement restaurant comprising black marble, mirrors and polished concrete. Accomplished, highly skilled cooking showcases some very original, creative combinations and the artful presentation is equally striking. Choose 10 courses at lunch or 14 at dinner from a 'collection' of dishes.

→ Veal sweetbread slider and XO. Squab pigeon, crispy leg with rhubarb hoisin. Cardamom and lemongrass soup, chilli sorbet.

Menu £ 65/95 – surprise menu only

Town plan: B2-c – *68-78 Vicar Ln* ✉ *LS1 7JH – (Lower ground floor) – ✆ 0113 243 2376 (booking essential) – www.themanbehindthecurtain.co.uk – dinner only and lunch Thursday-Saturday – Closed 23 December-4 January and Sunday-Monday*

Crafthouse A/C

MODERN CUISINE • DESIGN XX A bright, chic restaurant in the Trinity shopping centre, with great rooftop views and a wraparound terrace. Creative, elaborate dishes showcase a huge array of ingredients. The open kitchen and marble counter take centre stage. Start with a cocktail in all-day Angelica.

Menu £ 24 (lunch and early dinner) – Carte £ 27/44

Town plan: A2-a – *Trinity Leeds (5th Floor), 70 Boar Ln* ✉ *LS1 6HW – ✆ 0113 897 0444 – www.crafthouse-restaurant.co.uk – Closed 25 December and 1 January*

HOME Ⓝ A/C

MODERN BRITISH • FASHIONABLE XX HOME is a buzzy place with a stylish feel. It's unusually set in an old Victorian fish market, above the shops on a pedestrianised street; ascend the original stairs and emerge in a spacious lounge-bar. Pre-paid tasting menus see interesting combinations of British ingredients full of texture contrasts.

Menu £ 50/70 – tasting menu only

Town plan: B2-z – *16/17 Kirkgate* ✉ *LS1 6BY – ✆ 0113 430 0161 (booking essential) – www.homeleeds.co.uk – dinner only and lunch Friday-Sunday – Closed first 2 weeks January, first 2 weeks August, Sunday dinner-Tuesday*

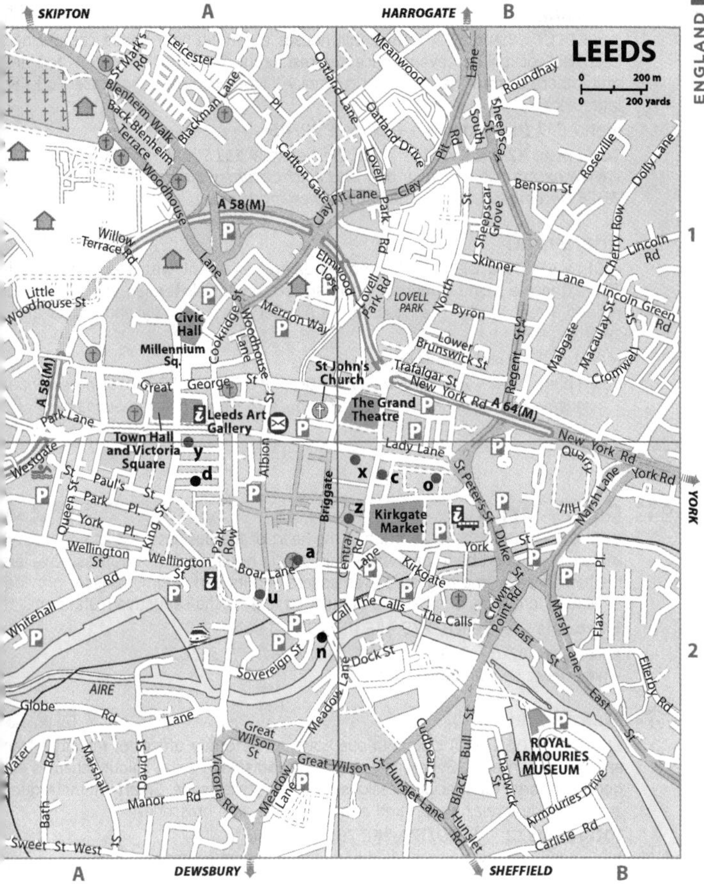

Issho

JAPANESE • FASHIONABLE XX This chic eatery in Victoria Gate serves modern Japanese cooking in a stylish setting, including sushi, tempura and dishes from the robata grill. Enjoy cocktails in the bar and city skyline views from the roof-top terrace.

Menu £ 25 (early dinner) – Carte £ 22/57

Town plan: B2-o – *Victoria Gate ✉ LS2 7AU – ✆ 0113 426 5000 – www.issho-restaurant.com – Closed Sunday dinner and Monday*

Stockdales of Yorkshire

MEATS AND GRILLS • CLASSIC DÉCOR XX Here, it's is all about showcasing the county's best ingredients in attractively presented dishes, with Josper-cooked beef – including Yorkshire Wagyu – a speciality. Sit in the comfy lounge-bar or attractive basement restaurant.

Menu £ 23 (weekday lunch) – Carte £ 27/66

Town plan: A1-2-y – *8 South Par ✉ LS1 5QX – ✆ 0113 204 2460 – www.stockdales-restaurant.com – Closed 24-26 December, 1 January and Sunday dinner*

Ox Club

BARBECUE • SIMPLE A former mill houses this multi-floor venue comprising a beer hall, cocktail bar, event space and restaurant. The latter boasts a wood-fired grill imported from the USA; rustic, smoky-flavoured dishes showcase Yorkshire ingredients.

Menu £ 17 (early dinner) - Carte £ 22/45

Town plan: B2-x - *Bramleys Yard, The Headrow ✉ LS1 6PU - ✆ 07470 359961 - www.oxclub.co.uk - dinner only and lunch Saturday-Sunday - Closed 25-26 December, 1 January, Sunday dinner and Monday*

Tharavadu

INDIAN • EXOTIC DÉCOR A simple-looking restaurant with seascape murals. The extensive menu offers superbly spiced, colourful Keralan specialities and refined street food - the dosas are a hit. Service is friendly and dishes arrive swiftly.

Menu £ 28 - Carte £ 18/36

Town plan: A2-u - *7-8 Mill Hill ✉ LS1 5DQ - ✆ 0113 244 0500 (booking essential) - www.tharavadurestaurants.com - Closed 23-26 December and Sunday*

Hotels

Dakota Deluxe

BUSINESS • MODERN Its location in the heart of the business district and its stylish, well-equipped bedrooms make this design hotel ideal for business travellers. It's tucked away in a pedestrianised square and its dark, intimate décor provides a calming influence. The bar is a popular spot, as is the seductive restaurant.

84 rooms - †£ 101/275 ††£ 115/293 - 1 suite

Town plan: A2-d - *8 Russell St ✉ LS1 5RN - ✆ 0113 322 6261 - www.leeds.dakotahotels.co.uk*

Malmaison

BUSINESS • DESIGN A chic boutique hotel in the former offices of the city's tram and bus department. Generously sized bedrooms have warm colour schemes and good comforts; for special occasions book the stylish suite. Smart, intimate guest areas include a relaxing bar and a modern take on a brasserie.

100 rooms - †£ 79/179 ††£ 79/179 - 1 suite

Town plan: A2-n - *1 Swinegate ✉ LS1 4AG - ✆ 0113 426 0047 - www.malmaison.com*

LEICESTER

Leicester - Pop. 443 760 - Regional map n° **9**-B2

Hotel Maiyango

BUSINESS • MODERN Privately owned city centre hotel in a 150 year old shoe factory. The interior is stylish and the trendy bar boasts a terrace overlooking the rooftops. Spacious, individually designed bedrooms have bespoke wood furnishings and a colonial feel. The oriental restaurant serves global dishes with Indian spicing.

14 rooms - †£ 99/139 ††£ 99/139 - £ 10 - 1 suite

13-21 St Nicholas Pl ✉ LE1 4LD - ✆ 0116 251 8898 - www.maiyango.com - Closed 25-26 December

LEWANNICK

Cornwall - Regional map n° **1**-B2

Coombeshead Farm

MODERN CUISINE • RUSTIC Set on a working farm, in 66 acres of meadows and woodland, this former farmhouse and dairy offers the ultimate field to fork experience. Techniques include curing, pickling and cooking over wooden embers. The home-bred Mangalitsa pork and home-baked sourdough are hits. Bedrooms have a cosy farmhouse style.

Menu £ 65 - surprise menu only

5 rooms - £ 120/130 £ 175/185

PL15 7QQ - Southeast 0.7mi by Callington/ North Hill rd and Trelaske rd on Congdons Shop rd - 01566 782009 (bookings essential for non-residents) - www.coombesheadfarm.co.uk - dinner only and Sunday lunch - Closed January, 24-26 December, Monday-Wednesday

LEWDOWN

Devon - Regional map n° **1**-C2

Lewtrenchard Manor

HISTORIC • ELEGANT Hugely impressive Grade II listed Jacobean manor house in mature grounds. The characterful antique-furnished interior features huge fireplaces, ornate oak panelling, intricately designed ceilings and mullioned windows. Bedrooms are spacious and well-equipped; those in the coach house are the most modern.

14 rooms - £ 145/235 £ 180/280 - 1 suite

EX20 4PN - South : 0.75 mi by Lewtrenchard rd - 01566 783222 - www.lewtrenchard.co.uk

LEYBURN

North Yorkshire - Pop. 2 183 - Regional map n° **13**-B1

Sandpiper Inn

TRADITIONAL BRITISH • PUB A friendly Yorkshire welcome is extended at this characterful, stone-built, part-16C pub just off the main square. Subtle, refined cooking offers a modern take on the classics and the skilled kitchen prides itself on the provenance of its ingredients. Two country-chic style bedrooms offer excellent comforts.

Carte £ 28/38 **s**

2 rooms - £ 80/90 £ 90/100

Market Pl DL8 5AT - 01969 622206 - www.sandpiperinn.co.uk - Closed 2 weeks January, Tuesday in winter and Monday

Clyde House

TOWNHOUSE • PERSONALISED 18C former coaching inn on the main market square, run by an experienced owner and immaculately kept throughout. Small, cosy sitting room and cottagey breakfast room. Smart, comfortable bedrooms with good quality soft furnishings, hair dryers and bathrobes. Extensive buffet and 'full Yorkshire' breakfasts.

5 rooms - £ 60/65 £ 90/100

5 Railway St DL8 5AY - 01969 623941 - www.clydehouse.com

LICHFIELD

Staffordshire - Pop. 32 877 - Regional map n° **10**-C2

The Boat Inn

MODERN BRITISH • PUB This old roadside hostelry was once backed by a canal and its walls are filled with black and white photos of the area's locks. Refined modern dishes are colourful and eye-catching, and the chef likes to make local, organic ingredients the stars of the show - including their home-raised chickens and pigs.

Menu £ 16/20 (weekdays) - Carte £ 27/51

Walsall Rd WS14 0BU - Southwest : 4 mi on A 461 - 01543 361692 - www.theboatinnlichfield.com - Closed 26 December-1 January, 10 days August, Monday, Tuesday and Sunday dinner

Wine House

TRADITIONAL CUISINE • NEIGHBOURHOOD X This smart red-brick house has an open-fired bar at one end and a dining room at the other. Lunch sees good value comfort dishes, while dinner puts steaks and seafood to the fore. It's named after its impressive glass wine cellar.

Carte £ 21/52

27 Bird St ✉ WS13 6PW – ✆ 01543 419999 – www.thewinehouselichfield.co.uk – Closed Sunday dinner

Swinfen Hall

COUNTRY HOUSE • HISTORIC Grade II listed Georgian mansion with an impressive façade, set in 100 acres. Original features abound, including a stucco ceiling in the magnificent foyer. Individually styled bedrooms; extras include fruit and freshly baked shortbread.

17 rooms – †£ 160/350 ††£ 180/375 – 1 suite

✉ WS14 9RE – Southeast : 2.75 mi by A 5206 on A 38 – ✆ 01543 481494 – www.swinfenhallhotel.co.uk – Restricted opening Christmas-New Year

Netherstowe House

COUNTRY HOUSE • CLASSIC An extensively restored 19C country house, professionally run by a family team. Period lounges and luxurious bedrooms come with antique furnishings and original fireplaces; modern apartments complete with kitchenettes are located in the grounds. Afternoon tea is comprehensive, with macaroons a speciality.

24 rooms – †£ 90/200 ††£ 110/200 – 10 suites

Netherstowe Ln ✉ WS13 6AY – Northeast : 1.75 mi following signs for A 51 and A 38, off Eastern Ave – ✆ 01543 254270 – www.netherstowehouse.com

St Johns House

TOWNHOUSE • CONTEMPORARY Impressive Regency townhouse fronted by large columns. Enter through a beautiful tiled hallway into a contemporary drawing room with ornate cornicing and chandeliers. Individually styled bedrooms have a modern, understated feel.

12 rooms – †£ 75/140 ††£ 120/250

28 St John St ✉ WS13 6PB – ✆ 01543 252080 – www.stjohnshouse.co.uk – Closed 25-30 December

LICKFOLD - West Sussex

→ See Petworth

LIFTON

Devon – Pop. 1 180 – Regional map n° **1**-C2

Arundell Arms

TRADITIONAL • COSY Family-run roadside coaching inn with cosy, traditional bedrooms and access to 20 miles of private fishing on the River Tamar and its tributaries. The characterful lounge and bar serve a brasserie menu, while the restaurant – which overlooks the terrace and gardens – offers classical fare.

25 rooms – †£ 99/125 ††£ 145/185

Fore St ✉ PL16 0AA – ✆ 01566 784666 – www.arundellarms.com

LINCOLN

Lincolnshire – Pop. 100 160 – Regional map n° **9**-C1

Jews House

MODERN CUISINE • COSY XX At the bottom of a steep cobbled hill is this cosy stone house dating from 1150; reputedly Europe's oldest surviving dwelling. Bold, ambitious dishes display an eclectic mix of influences – the tasting menu is a hit. Service is charming.

Menu £ 24 (lunch) – Carte £ 35/49

15 The Strait ✉ LN2 1JD – ✆ 01522 524851 – www.jewshouserestaurant.co.uk – Closed 2 weeks January, 2 weeks July, 1 week November, Sunday, Monday and lunch Tuesday

The Rest

TOWNHOUSE • CONTEMPORARY With direct access to the bedrooms from the street, guests can come and go freely at this laid-back hotel. Breakfast is served in the coffee shop-cum-bar. Chic bedrooms feature bespoke furnishings and bathrooms with heated floors.

10 rooms – £ 88/150 £ 88/150

55A Steep Hill ✉ LN2 1LR
– ☎ 01522 247888 – www.theresthotellincoln.co.uk

LISKEARD

Cornwall – Pop. 9 237 – Regional map n° **1**-B2

Pencubitt Country House

TRADITIONAL • PERSONALISED Sympathetically restored Victorian property with delightful views over the gardens and countryside – take it all in from the veranda or from the balcony in bedroom 3. Look out too for the original windows and staircase in the lovely hall. They offer home-cooked dinners, cream teas and picnics by arrangement.

9 rooms – £ 65/75 £ 79/120

Station Rd ✉ PL14 4EB – South : 0.5 mi by B 3254 on Lamellion rd
– ☎ 01579 342694 – www.pencubitt.com – Closed January and February

LITTLE BEDWYN – Wiltshire → See Marlborough

LITTLE COXWELL

Oxfordshire – Pop. 132 – Regional map n° **6**-A2

Eagle Tavern

TRADITIONAL BRITISH • TRADITIONAL DÉCOR This welcoming pub was built in 1901 for the farmers of this sleepy hamlet and, although it might look a little different now, a convivial atmosphere still reigns. The self-taught chef cooks the kind of food he likes to eat, including dishes from his homeland, Slovakia. Spacious bedrooms are spotlessly kept.

Menu £ 26

6 rooms – £ 80/90 £ 90/100

✉ SN7 7LW
– ☎ 01367 241879 – www.eagletavern.co.uk – Closed Sunday dinner, Monday and Tuesday-Thursday lunch

LITTLE DUNMOW

Essex – Pop. 2 190 – Regional map n° **7**-C2

Tim Allen's Flitch of Bacon

MODERN BRITISH • NEIGHBOURHOOD XX For classics in an informal setting find a seat in the bar. For a greater sense of occasion head for the dining room, where concise menus showcase top quality produce – from Cornish fruit to Scottish scallops – and modern dishes have a refined yet unfussy style. Three Big Green Eggs cater for summer BBQs and the old Citroën van is a bar. Bedrooms are boldly decorated.

→ Flitch of bacon, maple glaze, cauliflower, apple and scallop. Monkfish, buttered potato, brown shrimps, capers and browned lemon butter. Forced rhubarb, caramelised sourdough ice cream and candied ginger.

Menu £ 25 (weekday lunch) – Carte £ 39/61

3 rooms – £ 80/120 £ 90/130

The Street ✉ CM6 3HT
– ☎ 01371 821660 – www.flitchofbacon.co.uk – Closed Sunday dinner-Tuesday

LITTLE ECCLESTON

Lancashire - Regional map n° **11**-A2

Cartford Inn

TRADITIONAL CUISINE • PUB The Cartford Inn stands next to small toll bridge on the River Wyre and comes complete with a deli and farm shop. Cooking is gutsy and satisfying and many of the tried-and-tested classics come with a twist. The owner played a big part in the interior design, particularly the bold, boutique bedrooms.

Carte £ 28/44

17 rooms - £ 75/130 £ 110/250

Cartford Ln PR3 0YP - 01995 670166 - www.thecartfordinn.co.uk - Closed 25 December and Monday lunch except bank holidays

LITTLEHAMPTON

West Sussex - Pop. 55 706 - Regional map n° **4**-C3

Bailiffscourt H. & Spa

COUNTRY HOUSE • HISTORIC Charming, reconstructed medieval manor in immaculately kept gardens. Bedrooms are split between the main house and the outbuildings; the newer rooms are in the grounds and are more suited to families. Beautiful spa facility. Classic country house cooking served in the formal dining room.

39 rooms - £ 215/675 £ 245/705

Climping St, Climping BN17 5RW - West : 2.75 mi by A 259 - 01903 723511 - www.hshotels.co.uk

LIVERPOOL

Merseyside - Pop. 552 267 - Regional map n° **11**-A3

The Art School

MODERN BRITISH • ELEGANT XXX Bright red chairs contrast with crisp white tablecloths at this elegant restaurant, where a huge glass roof floods the room with light. The experienced local chef carefully prepares a bewildering array of colourful modern dishes.

Menu £ 25/69

1 Sugnall St L7 7DX - 0151 230 8600 - www.theartschoolrestaurant.co.uk - Closed 25-26 December, 1-7 January, 6-12 August, Sunday and Monday

Panoramic 34

MODERN BRITISH • FASHIONABLE XXX On the 34th floor of the city's highest skyscraper you'll find this elegant restaurant with under-lit tables and fabulous 360° views. Ambitious dishes arrive swiftly and are attractively presented; the lunch menu offers good value.

Menu £ 34 (lunch) - Carte £ 35/52

West Tower (34th floor), Brook St L3 9PJ - 0151 236 5534 - www.panoramic34.com - Closed 25-26 December, 1 January and Monday

Röski N

MODERN CUISINE • COSY XX An amalgamation of the owners' names, Röski is a small modern restaurant decorated in grey tones. Modern tasting menus list complex, carefully crafted dishes which feature many different ingredients and are eye-catchingly presented. Local produce is cleverly used to give dishes a regional slant.

Menu £ 25/75 - tasting menu only

16 Rodney St L1 2TE - 0151 708 8698 - www.roskirestaurant.com - Closed Sunday, Monday and lunch Tuesday

60 Hope Street

REGIONAL CUISINE • **BRASSERIE** XX This long-standing restaurant might be located in a Grade II listed house but it certainly moves with the times, with its modern brasserie and chic basement wine bar. Local produce is used in refined versions of classic comfort dishes.

Menu £ 30 (lunch and early dinner) - Carte £ 30/63

60 Hope St ✉ L1 9BZ - ✆ 0151 707 6060 - www.60hopestreet.com - Closed 26 December

Neon Jamón

SPANISH • **TAPAS BAR** X In the bustling Penny Lane, you'll find this equally buzzy, industrial-style tapas bar. Service is friendly and obliging, and dishes are carefully prepared and full of flavour. Sit in the livelier downstairs room.

Carte £ 15/27

12 Smithdown Pl ✉ L15 9EH - Southeast : 3.5 mi by Upper Parliament St (A 562) - ✆ 0151 734 3840 (bookings not accepted) - www.neonjamon.com - Closed 25 December

Spire

MODERN BRITISH • **BISTRO** X Two experienced, enthusiastic brothers run this homely neighbourhood restaurant in the Penny Lane area of the city. Well-priced menus list modern British dishes which are full of flavour and rely on regional ingredients.

Menu £ 15/19 - Carte £ 26/43

1 Church Rd ✉ L15 9EA - Southeast : 3.5 mi by Upper Parliament St (A 562) - ✆ 0151 734 5040 - www.spirerestaurant.co.uk - Closed 25-26 December, 1-7 January, Sunday and lunch Saturday and Monday

Aloft Liverpool

HISTORIC • **DESIGN** An uber-cool hotel in the Grade II listed Royal Insurance building in the centre of the city. It features stunning original panelling and ornate plasterwork, alongside colourful contemporary décor and the latest mod cons. An open lounge with pool and football tables leads to the New York style restaurant.

116 rooms - £ 69/399 £ 69/399

1 North John St ✉ L2 5QW - ✆ 0151 294 4050 - www.aloftliverpool.com

Hard Days Night

LUXURY • **DESIGN** The world's only Beatles-themed hotel sits adjacent to the Cavern Club - in a Grade II listed building dating from 1884 - and is packed to the rafters with photos, memorabilia and specially commissioned artwork; the two suites are themed around Lennon and McCartney. Modern brasserie fare is served in Blakes.

110 rooms - £ 99/290 £ 99/290 - 2 suites

Central Buildings, North John St ✉ L2 6RR - ✆ 0151 236 1964 - www.harddaysnighthotel.com

Hope Street

TOWNHOUSE • **DESIGN** A minimalist hotel set over two adjoining buildings: bedrooms in the old carriage works have a rustic edge, while those in the former police station are more contemporary - and the top floor suites afford stunning skyline views. Large shards of glass divide the spacious restaurant, which offers modern fare.

89 rooms - £ 89/295 £ 89/295 - £ 19

40 Hope St ✉ L1 9DA - ✆ 0151 709 3000 - www.hopestreethotel.co.uk

2 Blackburne Terrace

LUXURY • **ELEGANT** A delightful Georgian house with plenty of personality - the owners are charming and there is a playful element to the place. Individually styled bedrooms come with top quality beds, free-standing baths and extras such as fresh fruit and cut flowers. Modern art features in the large sitting room.

4 rooms - £ 140/300 £ 160/300

2 Blackburne Terr ✉ L8 7PJ - ✆ 0151 708 5474 - www.2blackburneterrace.com

LONG ASHTON - North Somerset → See Bristol

LONG COMPTON

Warwickshire - ✉ Shipston-On-Stour - Pop. 705 - Regional map n° **10**-C3

Red Lion

TRADITIONAL BRITISH • FRIENDLY 18C former coaching inn with flag floors, log fires and a warm, modern feel. Seasonal menu of tasty, home-cooked pub classics, with more adventurous daily specials. Keen service. Good-sized garden and children's play area. Stylish bedrooms have a contemporary, country-chic feel and a good level of facilities.

Menu £ 15 (lunch and early dinner) - Carte £ 27/35

5 rooms - †£ 65/70 ††£ 100/160

Main St ✉ CV36 5JS - ✆ 01608 684221 - www.redlion-longcompton.co.uk

LONG CRENDON

Buckinghamshire - ✉ Aylesbury - Pop. 2 335 - Regional map n° **6**-C2

Mole & Chicken

TRADITIONAL BRITISH • RURAL A charming pub built in 1831 as part of a local farm workers' estate, with low wonky ceilings, open fires and a large garden offering commanding country views. The menu features classic British dishes and heartwarming puddings. Staff are friendly and there are five cosy bedrooms in the adjoining house.

Menu £ 14 (lunch) - Carte £ 27/46

5 rooms - †£ 95 ††£ 125

Easington ✉ HP18 8EY - North 0.5 mi by Dorton rd - ✆ 01844 208387 - www.themoleandchicken.co.uk - Closed 25 December

LONG MELFORD

Suffolk - Pop. 2 898 - Regional map n° **8**-C3

Swan

MODERN CUISINE • INN A stylish dining pub in a characterful old wool town. Dad oversees the finances, his daughter is the interior designer and his son is the chef. Appealing menus provide plenty of choice, from tasty pub classics to restaurant-style dishes. The eye-catching modern décor extends through to the bedrooms.

Carte £ 30/52

10 rooms - †£ 95/120 ††£ 155/210

Hall St ✉ CO10 9JQ - ✆ 01787 464545 - www.longmelfordswan.co.uk

LONG ROCK

Cornwall - Pop. 570 - Regional map n° **1**-B2

Mexico Inn

TRADITIONAL CUISINE • FRIENDLY This roadside inn is run by an experienced local couple, who host regular quiz and live music nights. It has a touch of the shabby-chic about it, with a wood-burner in the bar and a sunnier room to the rear - and there's a lovely suntrap terrace too. Classic pub dishes are gutsy and flavourful.

Carte £ 23/33

4 Riverside ✉ TR20 8JD - ✆ 01736 710625 - www.themexicoinn.com

LONG SUTTON

Somerset - ✉ Langport - Regional map n° **2**-B3

Devonshire Arms

REGIONAL CUISINE • INN A striking Grade II listed hunting lodge overlooking the green. Wing-back chairs sit by an open fire and panelled walls are broken up by bold wallpaper; there's also a lovely split-level garden. Appealing menus follow the seasons and keep refined pub classics to the fore. Modern bedrooms are well-furnished.

Carte £ 25/38

9 rooms - £ 90/160 £ 100/160

TA10 9LP - 01458 241271 - www.thedevonshirearms.com - Closed 25-26 December

LONGHORSLEY - Northumberland → See Morpeth

LOOE

Cornwall - Pop. 5 112 - Regional map n° **1**-B2

Beach House

FAMILY • PERSONALISED A personally run, detached house in a fantastic spot on the edge of town, looking out to sea. Bedrooms are immaculately kept; Fistral, with its balcony, is the best. The breakfast room is on the first floor and offers super views.

5 rooms - £ 85/135 £ 85/135

Marine Dr, Hannafore PL13 2DH - Southwest : 0.75 mi by Quay Rd - 01503 262598 - www.thebeachhouselooe.co.uk - Closed Christmas

at Talland Bay Southwest : 4 m. by A 387

Talland Bay N

COUNTRY HOUSE • PERSONALISED In an elevated clifftop position, a short stroll from the beach, is this old manor house offering stunning sea views. The décor is eye-catching with quirky touches and eclectic art. Ask for a sea-facing room or Garden Suite. Dine on Cornish produce in the intimate restaurant or bright conservatory.

23 rooms - £ 150/240 £ 160/350

PL13 2JB - 01503 272667 - www.tallandbayhotel.com - Closed January

LOSTWITHIEL

Cornwall - Pop. 2 659 - Regional map n° **1**-B2

Asquiths

MODERN CUISINE • INTIMATE XX Smartly converted shop with exposed stone walls hung with modern Cornish art, funky lampshades and contemporary styling. Confidently executed dishes feature some original flavour combinations. The atmosphere is relaxed and intimate.

Carte £ 31/40

19 North St PL22 0EF - 01208 871714 - www.asquithsrestaurant.co.uk - dinner only - Closed first 2 weeks January, Sunday and Monday

LOUTH

Lincolnshire - Pop. 16 419 - Regional map n° **9**-D1

14 Upgate

MODERN CUISINE • INTIMATE XX This elegantly converted townhouse seats just 12 diners at 6 tables. Service is engaging. The modern tasting menus change weekly and present some unusual twists and turns along the way. Start with a drink in the first floor sitting room.

Menu £ 27/47 - tasting menu only

14 Upgate LN11 9ET - 01507 610610 - www.14upgate.co.uk - dinner only - Closed 25 December-1 February and Sunday-Tuesday

LOW FELL

Tyne and Wear – Regional map n° **14**-B2

Eslington Villa

TRADITIONAL CUISINE • BISTRO XX This bright, airy hotel dining room feels like a conservatory and offers pleasant views over the tiered gardens. Menus are based on dishes people know and love and come with a few unusual twists along the way. Service is chatty.

Carte £ 27/42

Eslington Villa Hotel, 8 Station Rd ✉ NE9 6DR – West : 0.75 mi by Belle Vue Bank.
– ✆ 0191 487 6017 – www.eslingtonvilla.co.uk – Closed 25-26 December and 1 January

Eslington Villa

TRADITIONAL • PERSONALISED This Victorian villa has been keenly run by the same family since 1987. Bedrooms come in various shapes and sizes and most have feature walls and colourful fabrics. The large lawned garden is a lovely place to relax in summer.

18 rooms – †£ 88/100 ††£ 105/125

8 Station Rd ✉ NE9 6DR – West : 0.75 mi by Belle Vue Bank.
– ✆ 0191 487 6017 – www.eslingtonvilla.co.uk – Closed 25-26 December and 1 January

Eslington Villa – See restaurant listing

LOWER BEEDING

West Sussex – Regional map n° **4**-D2

Crabtree

TRADITIONAL CUISINE • PUB A family-run affair with a cosy, lived-in feel, warming fires and cheery, helpful staff. Traditional English dishes come with a touch of refinement and plenty of flavour, and the wine list is well-priced and full of helpful information.

Menu £ 16 (weekday lunch) – Carte £ 25/47

Brighton Rd ✉ RH13 6PT – South : 1.5 mi by B 2110 on A 281 – ✆ 01403 892666 – www.crabtreesussex.com – Closed Sunday dinner

South Lodge

LUXURY • HISTORIC Intricate carved fireplaces and ornate ceilings are proudly displayed in this Victorian mansion, which affords superb South Downs views from its 93 acres. Bedrooms are beautifully appointed – some are traditional, while others are more modern. Relax in the luxurious spa with its lovely pool, then dine in the grand restaurant or in the kitchen itself.

85 rooms – †£ 185/365 ††£ 195/365 – 4 suites

Brighton Rd ✉ RH13 6PS – South : 1.5 mi by B 2110 on A 281 – ✆ 01403 891711 – www.exclusive.co.uk/south-lodge – Closed 1-17 January

LOWER ODDINGTON – Gloucestershire → See Stow-on-the-Wold

LOWER SLAUGHTER – Gloucestershire → See Bourton-on-the-Water

LUDLOW

Shropshire – Pop. 10 515 – Regional map n° **10**-B2

Charlton Arms

TRADITIONAL BRITISH • RUSTIC This pub sits in a commanding position on the banks of the River Teme and is owned by Claude Bosi's brother Cedric and Cedric's wife, Amy. Menus offer something for everyone and the carefully prepared dishes are good value and full of flavour. Most of the bedrooms have river outlooks.

Carte £ 23/34

9 rooms – †£ 90/100 ††£ 100/160

Ludford Bridge ✉ SY8 1PJ – ✆ 01584 872813 – www.thecharltonarms.co.uk – Closed 25-26 December

Forelles

MODERN CUISINE • INTIMATE XX An appealing conservatory restaurant offering lovely views over the hotel gardens and named after the pear tree just outside. Attractively presented dishes use local produce and modern techniques, and feature some unusual flavour and texture combinations.

Menu £ 35/55

Fishmore Hall Hotel, Fishmore Rd ✉ SY8 3DP - North : 1.5 mi by B 4361 and Kidderminster rd on Fishmore Rd
- ✆ 01584 875148 - www.fishmorehall.co.uk
- Closed Sunday dinner and Monday lunch

Mortimers

MODERN BRITISH • ELEGANT XX A local forest gives this 16C townhouse restaurant its name. It has plenty of character, courtesy of exposed stone, sloping floors and lovely wood panelling. Concise set menus offer classically rooted dishes with a personal touch.

Menu £ 26/63

17 Corve St ✉ SY8 1DA
- ✆ 01584 872325 - www.mortimersludlow.co.uk
- Closed 1 week January, 1 week October, Sunday and Monday

Old Downton Lodge

MODERN CUISINE • RURAL XX Set on a 5,500 acre estate, these supremely characterful farm buildings date from medieval to Georgian times. Dining takes place in the 13C stone and timber barn and cooking is contemporary and original with a Scandic style. Bedrooms combine period features with modern amenities.

Menu £ 50/75 - tasting menu only

10 rooms - †£ 155/215 ††£ 155/345

Downton on the Rock ✉ SY8 2HU - West : 7.5 mi by A 49, off A 4113
- ✆ 01568 771826 (booking essential) - www.olddowntonlodge.com
- dinner only - Closed 23-27 December, Sunday and Monday

Fishmore Hall

COUNTRY HOUSE • DESIGN A whitewashed Georgian mansion in half an acre of mature gardens, set just out of town. Original features mix with modern fittings to create a boutique country house feel. Smart bedrooms have bold wallpapers, stylish bathrooms and good views. The lovely spa features an outdoor hot tub.

15 rooms - †£ 110/240 ††£ 175/275

Fishmore Rd ✉ SY8 3DP - North : 1.5 mi by B 4361 and Kidderminster rd on Fishmore Rd
- ✆ 01584 875148 - www.fishmorehall.co.uk

Forelles - See restaurant listing

at Cleestanton Northeast: 5.5 mi by A4117 and B4364

Timberstone

COUNTRY HOUSE • PERSONALISED This pair of cosy 17C cottages offer a wonderfully peaceful atmosphere and lovely rural views. Beamed bedrooms come with stylish modern bathrooms; one room even has its own balcony. Dine around the large farmhouse table - there's always a good selection, which includes many organic or home-grown options.

4 rooms - †£ 70/85 ††£ 98/100

✉ SY8 3EL
- ✆ 01584 823519 - www.timberstoneludlow.co.uk

LUPTON - Cumbria → See Kirkby Lonsdale

LURGASHALL
West Sussex - Regional map n° **4**-C2

Noah's Ark Inn
TRADITIONAL CUISINE • COSY A quintessentially English pub in a picturesque village green location; its garden overlooks the cricket pitch. The gloriously rustic interior features a bar, a baronial-style room with cosy sofas and 'The Restaurant' with its large inglenook fireplace. Generous dishes keep things in the traditional vein.

Carte £ 24/40

The Green ✉ GU28 9ET - ✆ 01428 707346 - www.noahsarkinn.co.uk

LUTON
Luton - Pop. 211 228 - Regional map n° **7**-A2

Luton Hoo
GRAND LUXURY • HISTORIC Stunning 18C house in over 1,000 acres of gardens; some designed by Capability Brown. The main mansion boasts an impressive hallway, numerous beautifully furnished drawing rooms and luxurious bedrooms. The marble-filled Wernher restaurant offers sophisticated classic cuisine. The old stable block houses the smart spa and casual, contemporary brasserie.

228 rooms - †£ 180/300 ††£ 200/320 - 23 suites

The Mansion House ✉ LU1 3TQ - Southeast : 2.5 mi by A 505 on A 1081 - ✆ 01582 734437 - www.lutonhoo.com

LYDDINGTON - Rutland → See Uppingham

LYDFORD
Devon - ✉ Okehampton - Pop. 1 734 - Regional map n° **1**-C2

Dartmoor Inn
MODERN BRITISH • PUB A rustic roadside pub with spacious bedrooms and a shabby-chic style; low ceilings add a cosy feel, while the artwork provides a modern touch. Satisfying classics are full of flavour and there's an emphasis on local produce. Specialities include Devon Ruby Red beef and dishes from the charcoal grill.

Carte £ 28/52

3 rooms - †£ 65/100 ††£ 100/140

Moorside ✉ EX20 4AY - East : 1 mi on A 386 - ✆ 01822 820221 - www.dartmoorinn.com - Closed Sunday dinner and Monday

LYME REGIS
Dorset - Pop. 4 712 - Regional map n° **2**-B3

HIX Oyster & Fish House
SEAFOOD • SIMPLE Superbly located on the clifftop, this modern, Scandic-style restaurant offers breathtaking views over Lyme Bay and the Cobb. Menus focus on the latest catch brought in by the day boats and the place has a relaxed, buzzy vibe.

Menu £ 20 (weekdays) - Carte £ 24/67

Lister Gdns, Cobb Rd ✉ DT7 3JP - ✆ 01297 446910 (booking essential) - www.hixoysterandfishhouse.co.uk - Closed 25-26 December and Monday-Tuesday November-March except half-term holidays

Alexandra

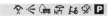

BOUTIQUE HOTEL • CONTEMPORARY An 18C dower house with super views over the Cobb and out to sea. There's a small heated terrace and a lookout tower (for hire) in the lovely gardens. The lounges and bedrooms are contemporary; No.12 has a large bay window to take in the view. Modern menus are served in the formal restaurant and conservatory.

23 rooms - £ 95/350 £ 180/350

Pound St DT7 3HZ
- 01297 442010 - www.hotelalexandra.co.uk - Closed 30 December-1 February

HIX Townhouse

TOWNHOUSE • QUIRKY This Georgian townhouse has a quirky, bohemian style. Bedrooms are themed around owner Mark Hix's interests - including hunting, sailing, shooting and fishing - and come with thoughtful extras. Breakfast is delivered in a wicker hamper.

8 rooms - £ 115/155 £ 125/165

1 Pound St DT7 3HZ
- 01297 442499 - www.hixtownhouse.co.uk

LYMINGTON

Hampshire - Pop. 15 218 - Regional map n° **4**-A3

Elderflower

MODERN CUISINE • FAMILY XX Their motto is 'quintessentially British, with a sprinkling of French', and that's just what you'll find at this proudly run restaurant. Cooking is playful and imaginative - as well as an à la carte they also serve small plates. Bedrooms are simply appointed and the quay is just a stone's throw away.

Carte £ 40/57

2 rooms - £ 99 £ 110

4-5 Quay St SO41 3AS
- 01590 676908 - www.elderflowerrestaurant.co.uk - Closed Sunday dinner, Monday and Tuesday

Stanwell House

TOWNHOUSE • PERSONALISED An attractive 18C house whose tastefully designed bedrooms are comfy and well-equipped: those in the original house are the most characterful; those in the extension are more contemporary. Dine on creative British dishes in Etain or grazing dishes/small plates in informal Burcher & Co. The trendy wine bar is themed around Sir Ben Ainslie, who once lived here.

29 rooms - £ 99/145 £ 99/145 - 7 suites

14-15 High St SO41 9AA
- 01590 677123 - www.stanwellhouse.com

LYMM

Warrington - Pop. 11 608 - Regional map n° **11**-B3

Church Green

MODERN BRITISH • PUB A double-fronted pub beside Lymm Dam, with an attractive decked terrace. Choose from small plates, popular sharing platters, an appealing set selection or a grill menu where you choose a cut, then add a sauce and extras. If the village is hosting an event, then this pub is sure to be involved.

Menu £ 24/30 - Carte £ 28/48

Higher Ln WA13 0AP - on A 56
- 01925 752068 (booking essential) - www.thechurchgreen.co.uk - Closed 25 December

LYMPSTONE

Devon – Pop. 1 763 – Regional map n° **1**-D2

✿ Lympstone Manor (Michael Caines)

MODERN CUISINE • ELEGANT XXX This elegant restaurant sits within a luxurious country house hotel owned by local chef Michael Caines. Accomplished cooking has classical undertones and is superbly balanced, sophisticated and packed with flavour. The 8 course tasting menu best demonstrates the team's abilities.

→ Millefeuille of tuna with soused vegetables, wasabi, honey and soy vinaigrette. Cornish duckling, braised chicory, anise and orange scented jus. Hot pistachio soufflé with pistachio ice cream.

Menu £ 60/145

Lympstone Manor Hotel, Courtlands Ln. ✉ EX8 3NZ – Southeast : 1.75 mi by A 376
– ✆ 01395 202040 (booking essential)
– www.lympstonemanor.co.uk

Lympstone Manor

COUNTRY HOUSE • ELEGANT A tastefully restored Georgian country house set in peaceful grounds which stretch down to the estuary – the pretty veranda is the perfect spot to admire the view. Luxurious bedrooms are beautifully furnished and have a stylish, modern feel; opt for a Garden Room with a fire and hot tub on the terrace.

21 rooms – †£ 300/1095 ††£ 325/1120

Courtlands Ln. ✉ EX8 3NZ – Southeast : 1.75 mi by A 376
– ✆ 01395 202040
– www.lympstonemanor.co.uk

✿ **Lympstone Manor** – See restaurant listing

LYNDHURST

Hampshire – Pop. 2 347 – Regional map n° **4**-A2

Hartnett Holder & Co

ITALIAN • ELEGANT XX Elegant restaurant in an impressive Georgian mansion, offering a relaxed, clubby feel and views over the delightful grounds. The main menu lists Italian favourites like pizzetta, pastas and risottos as well as authentic fish and meat dishes. The sharing menu offers the likes of whole duck 'family-style'.

Menu £ 22 (weekday lunch) – Carte £ 36/58

Lime Wood Hotel, Beaulieu Rd ✉ SO43 7FZ – Southeast : 1 mi by A 35 on B 3056
– ✆ 023 8028 7177 – www.limewood.co.uk

Lime Wood

LUXURY • ELEGANT Impressive Georgian mansion with a stunning spa topped by a herb garden roof. Stylish guest lounges have quality fabrics and furnishings; one is set around a courtyard and features a retractable glass roof. Beautifully furnished bedrooms boast luxurious marble-tiled bathrooms, and many have New Forest views.

33 rooms – †£ 385/510 ††£ 385/510 – £ 25 – 14 suites

Beaulieu Rd ✉ SO43 7FZ – Southeast : 1 mi by A 35 on B 3056
– ✆ 023 8028 7177 – www.limewoodhotel.co.uk

Hartnett Holder & Co – See restaurant listing

Don't expect guesthouses to provide the same level of service as a hotel. They are often characterised by a warm welcome and décor which reflects the owner's personality. Those shown in red are particularly charming.

LYNTON

Devon - Pop. 1 157 - Regional map n° **1**-C1

at Martinhoe West: 4.25 mi via Coast rd (toll) ✉ Barnstaple

Old Rectory

COUNTRY HOUSE • ELEGANT Built in the 19C for a rector of Martinhoe's 11C church, this quiet country retreat is in a charming spot, with a well-tended 3 acre garden and a cascading brook. Fresh, bright bedrooms are modern, yet retain period touches: Heddon and Paddock are two of the best. Comfortable dining room; simple home-cooking.

11 rooms (dinner included) - †£ 160/230 ††£ 205/275

✉ EX31 4QT - ✆ 01598 763368 - www.oldrectoryhotel.co.uk - Closed November-March

MAENPORTH BEACH - Cornwall → See Falmouth

MAIDENCOMBE - Torbay → See Torquay

MAIDENHEAD

Windsor and Maidenhead - Pop. 63 580 - Regional map n° **6**-C3

Fredrick's

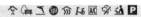

BUSINESS • CLASSIC It's hard to imagine that this smart red-brick hotel - with its stylish spa - was once an inn. It's classically styled, with a marble reception, a clubby bar and a formal restaurant serving modern French dishes. Bedrooms have panelled walls and bespoke wooden furnishings, and most overlook the gardens.

37 rooms - †£ 129/194 ††£ 139/204 - 2 suites

Shoppenhangers Rd ✉ SL6 2PZ - ✆ 01628 581000 - www.fredricks-hotel.co.uk

MALDON

Essex - Pop. 21 462 - Regional map n° **7**-C3

Rubino Kitchen

MODERN BRITISH • COSY XX Hidden away on Chigborough Farm is this tiny restaurant, where you can come for a meal at any time of day. Cooking mixes English and Italian influences; at dinner choose 2-5 courses from 9 tasty weekly dishes.

Menu £ 20 - Carte dinner approx. £ 32

Chigborough Farm, Chigborough Rd, Heybridge ✉ CM9 4RE - East : 2.5 mi by B 1022 off B 1026 - ✆ 01621 855579 (booking essential) - www.rubinokitchen.co.uk - Closed Sunday dinner, Monday and Tuesday

MALMESBURY

Wiltshire - Pop. 6 318 - Regional map n° **2**-C2

The Dining Room

ASIAN INFLUENCES • ELEGANT XXX This country house hotel's intimate dining room has a serene feel and its neutral décor keeps the focus on the food. Modern cooking has a well-measured playfulness and many Asian elements feature in the appealing multi-course set menu; the chefs often present and explain the dishes themselves.

→ Mackerel tart. Pigeon with gem lettuce and allium. Honey, caramel and custard.

Menu £ 120 **s** - tasting menu only

Whatley Manor Hotel, Easton Grey ✉ SN16 0RB - West : 2.25 mi on B 4040 - ✆ 01666 822888 (booking essential) - www.whatleymanor.com - dinner only - Closed 6 January-7 February, Monday and Tuesday

Grey's Brasserie

MODERN BRITISH • BRASSERIE XX The slightly less formal alternative to Whatley Manor's 'Dining Room' is this elegant grey-hued brasserie; ask for a booth or dine in the garden in the summer months. Salad and vegetables from the kitchen garden feature on modern menus with a Mediterranean edge. Brunch is served on Sundays.

Menu £ 25 (weekday lunch) - Carte £ 31/40 **s**

Whatley Manor Hotel, Easton Grey ✉ SN16 0RB - West : 2.25 mi on B 4040 - ✆ 01666 822888 - www.whatleymanor.com - Closed 6 January-7 February

Whatley Manor

LUXURY • CONTEMPORARY A charming Cotswold stone house built in 1802 and set in 12 acres of formal gardens. Guest areas include a delightful wood-panelled sitting room, a stunning spa, a top class business centre and a cinema. Luxurious, individually decorated bedrooms have sumptuous bathrooms and a contemporary feel.

23 rooms - †£ 249/849 ††£ 249/849 - 8 suites

Easton Grey ✉ SN16 0RB - West : 2.25 mi on B 4040 - ✆ 01666 822888 - www.whatleymanor.com - Closed 6 January-7 February

The Dining Room • **Grey's Brasserie** - See restaurant listing

at Crudwell North: 4 mi on A429 ✉ Malmesbury

Potting Shed

REGIONAL CUISINE • COSY Spacious, light-filled pub with contemporary décor, exposed beams and a relaxing feel. Monthly changing menus offer wholesome, satisfying dishes, with vegetables and herbs from their garden.

Carte £ 23/35

The Street ✉ SN16 9EW - ✆ 01666 577833 - www.thepottingshedpub.com - Closed dinner 25 December

The Rectory

COUNTRY HOUSE • CONTEMPORARY An attractive 18C rectory with a surprisingly stylish interior. Contemporary country house guest areas are hung with eye-catching art and the bar leads out to a lovely walled garden. Understated bedrooms are a pleasing mix of the old and the new. Dine on unfussy modern British dishes in the conservatory.

15 rooms - †£ 120 ††£ 140/400

✉ SN16 9EP - ✆ 01666 577194 - www.therectoryhotel.com

MALTBY

Stockton-on-Tees - Regional map n° **14**-B3

Chadwicks Inn

MODERN CUISINE • COSY This 19C pub was a favourite haunt of the Spitfire pilots before their missions. The à la carte features ambitious, intricate dishes and is supplemented by a simpler early evening bistro menu and a good value set selection. The live acoustic sessions and wine tasting evenings are popular.

Menu £ 18 (weekday lunch)/28 - Carte £ 34/51

High Ln ✉ TS8 0BG - ✆ 01642 590300 - www.chadwicksinnmaltby.co.uk - Closed 26 December, 1 January and Monday except bank holidays

Take note of the classification: you should not expect the same level of service in a X or 🏠 as in a XXXXX or 🏰.

MALTON

North Yorkshire - Pop. 4 888 - Regional map n° **13**-C2

New Malton

TRADITIONAL BRITISH • PUB 18C stone pub with open fires, reclaimed furniture and photos of old town scenes. A good-sized menu offers hearty pub classics with the odd more adventurous dish thrown in; cooking is unfussy and flavoursome with an appealing Northern bias.

Carte £ 18/36

2-4 Market Pl YO17 7LX - 01653 693998 - www.thenewmalton.co.uk - Closed 25-26 December and 1 January

Talbot

HISTORIC • CLASSIC An early 17C hunting lodge owned by the Fitzwilliam Estate, featuring an impressive wooden staircase and country house style rooms filled with family artefacts. Traditional bedrooms have smart marble bathrooms. Dine in the grand restaurant or the rustic modern brasserie in the glass-enclosed courtyard.

26 rooms - £ 90/410 £ 90/410

Yorkersgate YO17 7AJ - 01653 639096 - www.talbotmalton.co.uk

GOOD TIPS!

The Manchester dining scene has exploded in recent years and now offers a vibrancy and diversity unrivalled outside of London. Sample tasty, authentic tapas at the three-storey **El Gato Negro** or try modern Indian cuisine at glamorous **Asha's**; enjoy artisan beers and street food in the lively basement restaurant **Bundobust** or sail up 19 floors to take in the view from **20 Stories**.

MANCHESTER

Greater Manchester – Pop. 510 746 – Regional map n° **11**-B2

Restaurants

El Gato Negro

SPANISH • TAPAS BAR X 'The Black Cat' sits in a three storey building in a pedestrianised street. The ground floor houses a bar, the first floor plays host to an industrial-style dining room and the third floor boasts a cocktail bar with a retractable roof. Appealing tapas dishes include meats from the Josper grill.

Menu £ 15 (weekday lunch) - Carte £ 23/36

Town plan: A2-e – *52 King St ✉ M2 4LY*
– ✆ 0161 694 8585 (booking essential) – www.elgatonegrotapas.com – Closed 25 December

Adam Reid at The French

MODERN BRITISH • ELEGANT XXX An intimate hotel restaurant created in the Belle Époque age and brought up-to-date with a moody colour scheme, striking chandeliers and booths down the centre of the room. Boldly flavoured modern dishes focus on one main ingredient. Bread is served as a course in itself and desserts are playful.

Menu £ 45 (weekday dinner)/85

Town plan: A2-x – *Midland Hotel. Peter St. ✉ M60 2DS*
– ✆ 0161 932 4780 (booking essential) – www.the-french.co.uk – dinner only
– Closed 2 weeks August, 1 week Christmas, Sunday and Monday

Asha's

INDIAN • ELEGANT XX Start in the intimately lit basement cocktail bar then move up to the exotic, glamorous restaurant. The modern Indian menu offers both 'Classic' and 'Creative' curries; kebabs are a specialty, as is the traditional masala recipe.

Menu £ 20 (weekday lunch) - Carte £ 28/39

Town plan: A2-c – *47 Peter St ✉ M2 3NG*
– ✆ 0161 832 5309 – www.ashasrestaurant.co.uk – Closed 25 December

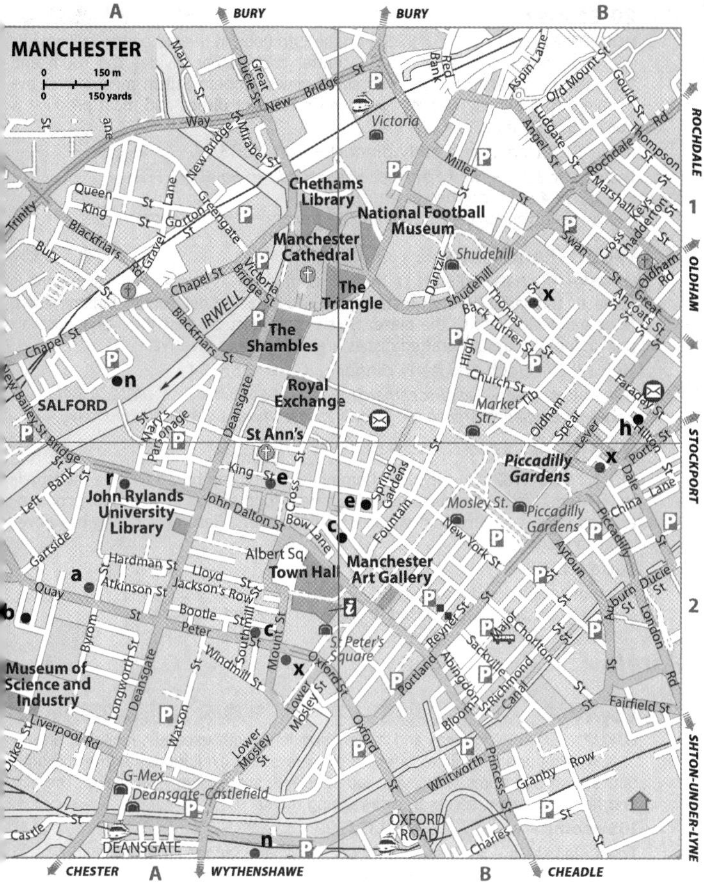

Manchester House

MODERN CUISINE • FASHIONABLE XX Step out the lift into this cool, industrial style restaurant with floor to ceiling windows. The large team of chefs prepare inventive, playful dishes which feature lots of different ingredients; they serve only a tasting menu Sat eve.

Menu £ 30 (lunch) – Carte £ 41/63

Town plan: A2-r – *Tower 12, 18-22 Bridge St ✉ M3 3BZ – ✆ 0161 835 2557 – www.manchesterhouse.uk.com – Closed 2 weeks January, 2 weeks August, 25-26 December, Sunday and Monday*

63 Degrees

FRENCH • NEIGHBOURHOOD XX The bustling Northern Quarter is home to this family-run restaurant. The experienced owner-chef hails from France and his classic dishes are cooked with pride and passion using both local and imported French produce. The set lunch represents good value.

Menu £ 20 (lunch) – Carte £ 33/65

Town plan: B1-x – *104 High St. ✉ M4 1HQ – ✆ 0161 832 5438 – www.63degrees.co.uk – Closed Monday*

20 Stories

MODERN BRITISH • DESIGN XX Set on the 19th floor, in the old cotton mill area, is this huge design-led restaurant. A central cocktail bar divides the room and there's a glass-walled terrace with super views. Modern British menus offer everything from homely classics to refined restaurant dishes and most produce is from within 50 miles.

Menu £ 28 (lunch and early dinner) - Carte £ 33/55

Town plan: A2-a - *No. 1 Spinningfields, 1 Hardman Sq ✉ M3 3EB - ✆ 0161 204 3333 (booking essential) - www.danddlondon.com/restaurant/20-stories/ - Closed Sunday dinner*

Wood Manchester

MODERN BRITISH • DESIGN XX The old Gaythorn Gas Works redevelopment is home to this large modern restaurant run by MasterChef winner Simon Wood. There's a lively buzz to the place, which could best be described as 'industrial-chic' in looks. Carefully crafted dishes are modern and creative.

Menu £ 28 (lunch and early dinner) - Carte £ 35/64

Town plan: A2-n - *Jack Rosenthal St, First St ✉ M15 4RA - ✆ 0161 236 5211 - www.woodmanchester.com - Closed 25 December, Sunday and Monday*

Bundobust

INDIAN VEGETARIAN • SIMPLE X Communal tables and booths fill the industrial-style interior, fresh, flavoursome Indian street food arrives in disposable containers and there's an amazing variety of artisan beers. Basement dining has never been so much fun!

Carte £ 12/18

Town plan: B2-x - *61 Piccadilly ✉ M1 2AG - ✆ 0161 359 6757 - www.bundobust.com - Closed 25-26 December and 1 January*

Hotels

Lowry

LUXURY • DESIGN Modern and hugely spacious, with excellent facilities, an impressive spa and a minimalist feel: art displays and exhibitions feature throughout. Stylish bedrooms with oversized windows; some have river views. The airy first floor restaurant serves a wide-ranging menu.

165 rooms - †£ 139/399 ††£ 139/399 - ☕ £ 22 - 7 suites

Town plan: A1-n - *50 Dearmans Pl, Chapel Wharf, Salford ✉ M3 5LH - ✆ 0161 827 4000 - www.thelowryhotel.com*

Hotel Gotham

LUXURY • ELEGANT This Grade II listed former bank has something of a Manhattan-style exterior, hence its name. Stylish modern bedrooms have black and white prints of Manchester and New York on the walls and some have projected 'wonderwalls' instead of windows. The delightful all-day dining room serves English classics.

60 rooms - †£ 250/450 ††£ 250/450 - ☕ £ 15

Town plan: B2-e - *100 King St ✉ M2 4WU - ✆ 0161 413 0000 - www.hotelgotham.co.uk*

King Street Townhouse

TOWNHOUSE • CONTEMPORARY A boutique townhouse in an impressive Italianate building designed by local architect Edward Salomons in 1872. Stylish bedrooms are individually styled by the owner and have top quality furnishings. Relax in the infinity plunge pool looking out over the rooftops or enjoy a film in the 20-seater cinema.

40 rooms - †£ 230/400 ††£ 250/450 - ☕ £ 18

Town plan: B2-c - *10 Booth St ✉ M2 4AW - ✆ 0161 667 0707 - www.kingstreettownhouse.co.uk*

Great John Street

HISTORIC • CONTEMPORARY This stylish, boutique hotel was once a wonderful Victorian schoolhouse; you can hold a meeting in the old Headmaster's study! All of the bedrooms are duplex suites with roll-top baths. Relax on the roof terrace with its cocktail bar and hot-tub. There's no restaurant but they do offer room service.

30 rooms – †£ 210/450 ††£ 250/450 – ☕ £ 18

Town plan: A2-b – *Great John St ✉ M3 4FD – ✆ 0161 831 3211 – www.greatjohnstreet.co.uk*

Cow Hollow

TOWNHOUSE • CONTEMPORARY Set in an old Northern Quarter textile mill is this very individual urban-chic townhouse, run a relaxed but appealing manner. The décor has Asian influences but the local heritage isn't forgotten, with exposed brick walls, wooden beams and metal staircases. Bedrooms are stylish; breakfast arrives in a bag.

16 rooms ☕ – †£ 100/150 ††£ 130/190

Town plan: B1-h – *57 Newton St ✉ M1 1ET – ✆ 0161 228 7277 – www.cowhollow.co.uk*

at Didsbury South: 5.5 mi by A5103 on A5145 ✉ Manchester

Hispi

MODERN BRITISH • NEIGHBOURHOOD With its bright green façade, this simple yet stylish neighbourhood restaurant certainly stands out. Good value dishes are a pleasing mix of the classic and the modern and the concise wine list features some lesser-known producers.

Menu £ 16 (lunch and early dinner) – Carte £ 27/48

1c School Ln ✉ M20 6RD – ✆ 0161 445 3996 – www.hispi.net – Closed 25-26 December

Didsbury House

BOUTIQUE HOTEL • PERSONALISED A whitewashed Victorian villa with original features and a boutique feel – look out for the impressive stained glass window. Stylish, well-appointed bedrooms include duplex suites. There's no designated restaurant area but you can dine from an accessible menu in the bar and lounges or in your room. They also own similarly styled Eleven Didsbury Park, just down the road.

27 rooms – †£ 99/150 ††£ 99/220 – ☕ £ 17 – 4 suites

Didsbury Pk ✉ M20 5LJ – South : 1.5 mi on A 5145 – ✆ 0161 448 2200 – www.didsburyhouse.com

MARAZION

Cornwall – Pop. 1 294 – Regional map n° **1**-A3

Ben's Cornish Kitchen

MODERN CUISINE • SIMPLE Rustic family-run eatery; sit upstairs for views over the rooftops to St Michael's Mount. Unfussy lunches are followed by sophisticated dinners, which feature some interesting flavour combinations. They offer 25 wines by the glass.

Menu £ 24/35

West End ✉ TR17 0EL – ✆ 01736 719200 – www.benscornishkitchen.com – Closed 23-31 December, 1 January, Sunday and Monday

Mount Haven

BOUTIQUE HOTEL • PERSONALISED Lord and Lady St Levan own this stylish hotel looking out over the bay to St Michael's Mount – their family seat. 'Garden Haven' bedrooms have terraces and 'Blissful Bay' rooms have balconies and stunning views. Appealing menus use local produce in creative ways. Relax on the terrace with a cocktail at sunset.

19 rooms ☕ – †£ 80/280 ††£ 90/290

Turnpike Rd ✉ TR17 0DQ – East : 0.25 mi – ✆ 01736 719937 – www.mounthaven.co.uk – Closed 1 January-28 February

at Perranuthnoe Southeast: 1.75 mi by A394 ✉ Penzance

Victoria Inn

CLASSIC CUISINE • PUB A well-established, bright pink pub, in a small village close to the sea; the owner is a local returned home. Menus stick mainly to the classics and fish, landed at nearby Newlyn, is in abundance. Be sure to save room for one of the tasty puddings! Cosy, unfussy bedrooms have a seaside feel.

Menu £ 18 – Carte £ 27/43

2 rooms – †£ 75 ††£ 95

✉ TR20 9NP – ✆ 01736 710309 – www.victoriainn-penzance.co.uk – Closed 25 December and 1 January

Ednovean Farm

FAMILY • PERSONALISED 17C granite barn in a tranquil spot overlooking the bay and surrounded by 22 acres of sub-tropical gardens and paddocks. Individually styled bedrooms feature local toiletries; the Blue Room has a French bed, a roll-top bath and a terrace. Complimentary sherry is left in the hall. Have a range-cooked breakfast at the oak table or a continental selection in bed.

3 rooms – †£ 90/140 ††£ 90/150

✉ TR20 9LZ – ✆ 01736 711883 – www.ednoveanfarm.co.uk – Closed Christmas

MARGATE

Kent – Pop. 61 223 – Regional map n° **5**-D1

Hantverk & Found N

SEAFOOD • SIMPLE The owner of this tiny, bohemian café is passionate about art, so you'll find an exhibition by local artists in the cellar. Choose from the blackboard or have the daily menu, where seafood from the Kent coast features in unfussy dishes bursting with freshness and flavour.

Carte £ 24/44

16-18 King St ✉ CT9 1DA – ✆ 01843 280454 (booking essential) – www.hantverk-found.co.uk – Closed 23 December-11 January, Sunday dinner-Wednesday

Sands

BOUTIQUE HOTEL • CONTEMPORARY Set between the high street and the sea – a smartly refurbished hotel, with extremely stylish bedrooms. Have a cocktail in the white leather furnished lounge-bar overlooking the beach before watching the sun go down from the roof terrace. The brasserie serves modern British dishes and also shares the view.

20 rooms – †£ 100/210 ††£ 130/210

16 Marine Dr ✉ CT9 1DH – (entrance on High St) – ✆ 01843 228228 – www.sandshotelmargate.co.uk

Reading Rooms

TOWNHOUSE • PERSONALISED Passionately run guesthouse with original plaster walls and worn woodwork. Three bedrooms – one per floor – boast distressed furniture, super-comfy beds, huge bathrooms and Square views. Extensive breakfasts are served in your room.

3 rooms – †£ 95/160 ††£ 170/190

31 Hawley Sq ✉ CT9 1PH – ✆ 01843 225166 – www.thereadingroomsmargate.co.uk

MARLBOROUGH

Wiltshire – Pop. 8 092 – Regional map n° **2**-D2

Rick Stein

SEAFOOD • ELEGANT An attractive double-fronted townhouse where 5 charming rooms spread over 2 floors make you feel like you're dining privately. The daily menu offers the best value; for those pushing the boat out, try the turbot on the bone.

Menu £ 20 (weekday lunch) – Carte £ 25/57

Lloran House, 42a High St ✉ SN8 1HQ – ✆ 01672 233333 – www.rickstein.com

at Little Bedwyn East: 9.5 mi by A4 ✉ Marlborough

Harrow at Little Bedwyn

MODERN CUISINE • INTIMATE XX This former pub is tucked away in a small village and has an intimate, understated, neighbourhood style. Cooking has a classical base but exhibits some modern elements; choose between several set menus. The comprehensive wine list champions the New World and there's a good selection by the glass.

Menu £ 40/85 – tasting menu only

✉ SN8 3JP – ✆ 01672 870871 – www.theharrowatlittlebedwyn.com – Closed 25 December-8 January and Sunday-Tuesday

at West Overton West: 4 mi on A4

Bell

MODERN BRITISH • PUB A simple, friendly pub, rescued from oblivion by a local couple, who hired an experienced pair to run it. The menu mixes pub classics with Mediterranean-influenced dishes; presentation is modern but not at the expense of flavour.

Carte £ 26/45

Bath Rd ✉ SN8 1QD – ✆ 01672 861099 – www.thebellwestoverton.co.uk – Closed Sunday dinner and Monday except bank holidays

MARLOW

Buckinghamshire – Pop. 14 823 – Regional map n° **6**-C3

Hand and Flowers (Tom Kerridge)

MODERN BRITISH • FRIENDLY Norfolk-born Tom Kerridge has successfully turned this characterful beamed pub into a world-renowned destination that sets the benchmark for pub dining UK-wide; as such, you'll need to book well in advance. Arrive early for a drink beside the log-burning stove in the appealing bar, then head through to the smart, rustic restaurant with low beams, flagged floors and nooks and crannies aplenty.

Refined British dishes are elevated to new heights yet remain reassuringly familiar, and the chefs aren't afraid to push the boundaries while at the same time knowing when to hold back; as a result, the main ingredient is never overwhelmed. Sourcing of ingredients is given due reverence, execution is confident and presentation is first-rate. The desserts in particular are a highlight. For an extra-special occasion book The Shed, an intimate dining space with a special menu cooked by a dedicated team.

Luxurious bedrooms are dotted around Marlow and they can arrange for a driver to drop you off.

→ Lamb chorizo and haggis tart with carrot and fennel. Turbot with roast alliums, cheese mash, caviar and sauce bonne femme. Choux à la crème with lime Chantilly and banana sorbet

Menu £ 30 (weekday lunch) – Carte £ 56/73

11 rooms – †£ 195/295 ††£ 195/295

126 West St. ✉ SL7 2BP – ✆ 01628 482277 (booking essential) – www.thehandandflowers.co.uk – Closed 24-26 December, dinner 1 January and Sunday dinner

The Coach

MODERN BRITISH • FRIENDLY Tom Kerridge's second pub is a pleasingly unpretentious kind of a place, with studded red leather chairs and a comfortingly traditional air. The menu of small plates is headed 'Meat', 'No Meat' and 'Sweet', allowing you to compose your meal however you wish. Dishes are refined, detailed and packed with flavour.

→ Mushroom 'risotto' Claude Bosi. Venison chilli with red wine, chocolate and toasted rice cream. Tonka bean panna cotta with mango and ginger wine jelly.

Carte £ 20/33

3 West St ✉ SL7 2LS – ✆ 01628 481704 (bookings not accepted) – www.thecoachmarlow.co.uk – Closed 25 December

Sindhu

INDIAN • CONTEMPORARY DÉCOR XX Styled after the Sindhu restaurants on each of P&O's cruise liners, this hotel restaurant, rather appropriately, is named after the Indus River and sits in a great spot beside the gushing weir. South Indian recipes are given a sophisticated modern makeover to create refined, subtly spiced dishes.

Menu £ 22 (weekday lunch) – Carte £ 22/35

Compleat Angler Hotel, Marlow Bridge, Bisham Rd ✉ SL7 1RG – ☎ 01628 405405 – www.sindhurestaurant.co.uk

Vanilla Pod

FRENCH • INTIMATE XX An intimate, well-established restaurant in T. S. Eliot's former home, featuring a plush interior and smartly laid tables. The chef works alone, cooking ambitious dishes with classical French foundations and original touches.

Menu £ 20/45 **s**

31 West St ✉ SL7 2LS – ☎ 01628 898101 (booking essential) – www.thevanillapod.co.uk – Closed 30 March-10 April, 29 May-6 June, 27 August-5 September, 23 December-10 January, Sunday, Monday and bank holidays.

Royal Oak

MODERN BRITISH • PUB Part-17C, country-chic pub with a herb garden, a petanque pitch and a pleasant terrace. Set close to the M40 and M4, it's an ideal London getaway. Cooking is British-led; wash down an ox cheek pasty with a pint of local Rebellion ale.

Carte £ 23/40

Frieth Rd, Bovingdon Green ✉ SL7 2JF – West : 1.25 mi by A 4155 – ☎ 01628 488611 – www.royaloakmarlow.co.uk – Closed 25-26 December

Compleat Angler

TRADITIONAL • CLASSIC A well-kept hotel in an idyllic spot on the Thames, with views of the weir and the chain bridge. Comfy, corporate-style bedrooms blend classic furnishings with contemporary fabrics and some have balconies; go for a Feature Room. The restaurants offer modern British and Indian cooking overlooking the river.

64 rooms – †£ 170/290 ††£ 170/380 – 3 suites

Marlow Bridge, Bisham Rd ✉ SL7 1RG – ☎ 0344 879 9128 – www.macdonald-hotels.co.uk/compleatangler

Sindhu – See restaurant listing

MARTINHOE – Devon → See Lynton

MASHAM

North Yorkshire – ✉ Ripon – Pop. 1 205 – Regional map n° **13**-B1

Vennell's

TRADITIONAL BRITISH • INTIMATE XX This personally run restaurant has purple walls, boldly patterned chairs and a striking feature wall – at weekends, sit downstairs surrounded by local art. Seasonal menus offer 4 choices per course and cooking has a modern edge.

Menu £ 38 **s**

7 Silver St ✉ HG4 4DX – ☎ 01765 689000 (booking essential) – www.vennellsrestaurant.co.uk – dinner only and Sunday lunch – Closed first 2 weeks January, 1 week Easter, 1 week August, Sunday dinner and Monday

Swinton Park

HISTORIC • CLASSIC A 17C castle with Georgian and Victorian additions, set on a 22,000 acre estate; try your hand at shooting, riding or falconry or relax in the state-of-the-art spa. The grand interior features open fires, ornate plasterwork, oil portraits and antiques. Dine in the relaxed brasserie or impressive dining room.

32 rooms – †£ 170/470 ††£ 195/470 – 6 suites

Swinton ✉ HG4 4JH – Southwest : 1 mi – ☎ 01765 680900 – www.swintonestate.com

MATFIELD

Kent - Regional map n° **5**-B2

The Poet at Matfield

MODERN CUISINE • **RUSTIC** This unassuming-looking dining pub (named after local resident and war poet Siegfried Sassoon), has a modest rustic style and an atmospheric little dining room with an inglenook fireplace. 'Flavoursome, fresh and careful' is the South African chef's mantra and his dishes are modern and sophisticated.

Menu £ 23 (weekdays) - Carte £ 33/50

Maidstone Rd ✉ TN12 7JH
- ✆ 01892 722416 - www.thepoetatmatfield.co.uk - Closed Sunday dinner and Monday

MATLOCK

Derbyshire - Pop. 14 956 - Regional map n° **9**-B1

Stones

MODERN BRITISH • **NEIGHBOURHOOD** XX Negotiate the steep steps down to this small riverside restaurant and head for the front room with its floor to ceiling windows. Unfussy, modern British dishes are attractively presented and display the odd Mediterranean touch.

Menu £ 25/36

1c Dale Rd ✉ DE4 3LT
- ✆ 01629 56061 - www.stones-restaurant.co.uk - Closed 23 December-3 January, Sunday, Monday and lunch Tuesday

MAWGAN PORTH - Cornwall → See Newquay

MELLOR - Lancashire → See Blackburn

MELLS

Somerset - Pop. 2 222 - Regional map n° **2**-C2

Talbot Inn

TRADITIONAL BRITISH • **RUSTIC** This 15C coaching inn's cobbled courtyard leads through to a series of rustic rooms: there's a cosy open-fired sitting room, a snug bar offering real ales and an elegant Grill Room which opens at weekends. Gutsy cooking is seasonal, modern and full of flavour. Comfy bedrooms have an understated style

Carte £ 27/38

8 rooms - †£ 100/160 ††£ 100/160

Selwood St ✉ BA11 3PN
- ✆ 01373 812254 - www.talbotinn.com

MELTON MOWBRAY

Leicestershire - Pop. 27 158 - Regional map n° **9**-B2

Stapleford Park

COUNTRY HOUSE • **PERSONALISED** Beautiful stately home in 500 acres of landscaped grounds, with grand drawing rooms, exceedingly comfortable bedrooms and an ornate rococo dining room. British designers have styled the rooms in keeping with their original features; look out for the impressive Grinling Gibbons wood carvings.

55 rooms - †£ 170/300 ††£ 190/300 - 3 suites

✉ LE14 2EF - East : 5 mi by B 676 on Stapleford rd
- ✆ 01572 787000 - www.staplefordpark.com

MID LAVANT - West Sussex ➜ See Chichester

MIDDLEHAM

North Yorkshire – Pop. 754 – Regional map n° **13**-B1

The Saddle Room

TRADITIONAL BRITISH • RUSTIC Located within an area of parkland close to the 'Forbidden Corner', is this converted stable decked out with equine paraphernalia – ask for a table in a stall! Unfussy menus offer the usual pub favourites alongside more interesting dishes like sticky pig cheeks. Stylish bedrooms are named after racehorses.

Carte £ 22/54

9 rooms – †£ 90/130 ††£ 90/130

Tupgill Park, Coverdale ✉ DL8 4TJ – Southwest : 2.5 mi by Coverham rd – ✆ 01969 640596 – www.thesaddleroom.co.uk – Closed Sunday dinner

MIDDLETON TYAS

North Yorkshire – Pop. 581 – Regional map n° **13**-B1

The Coach House at Middleton Lodge

MODERN BRITISH • DESIGN XX A stylishly converted coach house to the Georgian mansion where the owner grew up. The dining area is in the former stables and the bar is where the coaches once parked. Concise, constantly evolving menus feature produce from within 40 miles. Contemporary bedrooms come with roll-top baths and Roberts radios.

Carte £ 26/46

29 rooms – †£ 190/225 ††£ 220/270

Kneeton Ln ✉ DL10 6NJ – Northwest : 1 mi on Barton rd – ✆ 01325 377977 – www.middletonlodge.co.uk

MIDHURST

West Sussex – Pop. 4 914 – Regional map n° **4**-C2

Spread Eagle

HISTORIC • TRADITIONAL Part-15C coaching inn retaining plenty of its original character and decked out with antiques, tapestries and gleaming brass – although there's also a modern, well-equipped spa. Bedrooms are traditional. Dine next to an inglenook fireplace under wooden beams and look out for the Christmas puddings too!

39 rooms – †£ 99/419 ††£ 119/419 – 3 suites

South St ✉ GU29 9NH – ✆ 01730 816911 – www.hshotels.co.uk

Church House

TOWNHOUSE • PERSONALISED An enthusiastically run townhouse; the main part dates from 1383 and features low beams and oak pillars. Bedrooms are quirky and luxurious; the best are 'Silver', with its slipper bath and 'Gaudi', with its vaulted ceiling and sleigh bed.

5 rooms – †£ 70/100 ††£ 140/165

Church Hill ✉ GU29 9NX – ✆ 01730 812990 – www.churchhousemidhurst.com – Closed Christmas

at Henley North: 4.5 mi by A286

Duke of Cumberland Arms

TRADITIONAL BRITISH • COSY A hidden gem, nestled in pretty tiered gardens with trickling streams, trout ponds and splendid South Downs views. Sit in the cosy bar or more modern dining area which opens onto a terrace. Appealing menus offer carefully prepared seasonal dishes: lunch sees pub classics and dinner shifts things up a gear.

Carte £ 32/53

✉ GU27 3HQ – ✆ 01428 652280 – www.dukeofcumberland.com – Closed 25-26 December and dinner Sunday-Monday

at Bepton Southwest: 2.5 mi by A286 on Bepton rd ✉ Midhurst

Park House

COUNTRY HOUSE • CONTEMPORARY Family-run country house with a light modern style and smart spa and leisure facilities. Spacious, homely bedrooms are split between this and South Downs Cottage; they come in neutral hues and most have views of the well-tended gardens and golf course. The stylish conservatory restaurant serves modern menus.

21 rooms – †£ 115/280 ††£ 130/295 – 1 suite

✉ GU29 0JB – ✆ 01730 819000 – www.parkhousehotel.com – Closed 23-27 December

MILFORD-ON-SEA

Hampshire – ✉ Lymington – Pop. 4 348 – Regional map n° **4**-A3

Verveine

SEAFOOD • FRIENDLY Behind this attractive-looking fishmonger's is a bright and airy New England style restaurant with an open kitchen. Breads are baked twice-daily, veg is from the raised beds and smoking takes place on-site. The focus is on wonderfully fresh fish and cooking is original with the odd playful twist.

Menu £ 18 (lunch) – Carte £ 41/56

98 High St ✉ SO41 0QE – ✆ 01590 642176 – www.verveine.co.uk – Closed Sunday and Monday

MILTON ABBOT - Devon ➜ See Tavistock

MINSTER LOVELL

Oxfordshire – Pop. 1 236 – Regional map n° **6**-A2

Old Swan

TRADITIONAL CUISINE • INN A quintessential country inn set in a lovely riverside village. Dine in the charming garden or in one of the open-fired front rooms with their beams and flagged floors. Menus blend hearty pub favourites with more restaurant-style dishes. Characterful bedrooms have a romantic feel.

Carte £ 27/47

15 rooms – †£ 100/240 ††£ 110/250

✉ OX29 0RN – ✆ 01993 774441 – www.oldswanminstermill.co.uk

Minster Mill

HISTORIC BUILDING • ELEGANT Charming 17C Cotswold stone mill on the riverbank, with admirable eco-credentials and a modern mini-spa. The open-fired lounge has a minstrels' gallery. Well-appointed bedrooms come with robes and sloe gin and the best boast riverside terraces. Meals are at the Old Swan, their sister pub.

38 rooms – †£ 100/240 ††£ 110/250

✉ OX29 0RN – ✆ 01993 774441 – www.oldswanminstermill.co.uk

MISTLEY

Essex – Pop. 1 696 – Regional map n° **7**-D2

Mistley Thorn

SEAFOOD • FRIENDLY An appealing bistro with a homeware shop and cookery school. The focus is on sourcing local, seasonal ingredients and then showing them off. Local seafood is to the fore and most of the fish and meat is grilled over wood. Bedrooms are stylishly understated; some have river views.

Menu £ 16 (weekday lunch) – Carte £ 25/40

12 rooms – †£ 75/85 ††£ 95/130

High St ✉ CO11 1HE – ✆ 01206 392821 – www.mistleythorn.co.uk – Closed 25 December

MOBBERLEY

Cheshire East - ✉ Knutsford - Regional map n° **11**-B3

Church Inn

TRADITIONAL CUISINE • COSY 18C brick pub beside the bowling green, offering lovely views of the 12C church from its terrace. Regularly changing menus reflect the seasons, with light dishes in summer and hearty stews in winter. Hand-pumped local beers feature.

Carte £ 24/45

Church Ln ✉ WA16 7RD - ✆ 01565 873178 - www.churchinnmobberley.co.uk

MORETONHAMPSTEAD

Devon - ✉ Newton Abbot - Pop. 1 339 - Regional map n° **1**-C2

The Horse

MEDITERRANEAN CUISINE • PUB Behind its unassuming façade, this rustic pub conceals an appealing flag-floored dining room and a sunny Mediterranean-style courtyard. The unfussy cooking has more than a hint of the Mediterranean about it, with authentic thin-crust pizzas baked in a custom-built oven and tapas served in the evening.

Carte £ 21/42

7 George St ✉ TQ13 8PG - ✆ 01647 440242 - www.thehorsedartmoor.co.uk
- Closed 25 December, Sunday lunch and Monday

MORETON-IN-MARSH

Gloucestershire - Pop. 3 493 - Regional map n° **2**-D1

Mulberry

MODERN BRITISH • DESIGN XXX A formal restaurant with an enclosed walled garden, set within a part-16C manor house. Cooking is modern and adventurous and features some challenging combinations - choose between a 4 course set menu and an 8 course tasting menu.

Carte £ 28/48

Manor House Hotel, High St ✉ GL56 0LJ - ✆ 01608 650501
- www.cotswold-inns-hotels.co.uk - dinner only and Sunday lunch

Manor House

INN • ELEGANT A part-16C manor house with a smart interior which mixes old beams and inglenook fireplaces with modern fabrics and contemporary art. Chic, stylish bedrooms boast bold décor and feature walls - those in the main house are the most characterful. Dine in the sophisticated restaurant or relaxed conservatory.

35 rooms - †£ 180/220 ††£ 200/240 - 1 suite

High St ✉ GL56 0LJ - ✆ 01608 650501 - www.cotswold-inns-hotels.co.uk

Mulberry - See restaurant listing

Old School

COUNTRY HOUSE • PERSONALISED Change pace at this laid-back, stone-built former school, where you can relax in the gardens over a game of boules or croquet. The impressive upstairs lounge features an exposed A-frame ceiling and original ecclesiastical-style windows; bright, modern bedrooms offer a high level of facilities.

4 rooms - †£ 120/135 ††£ 135/160

Little Compton ✉ GL56 0SL - East : 3.75 mi on A 44 - ✆ 01608 674588
- www.theoldschoolbedandbreakfast.com

MORPETH

Northumberland - Pop. 14 403 - Regional map n° **14**-B2

at Eshott North: 8.5 mi by A1 ✉ Morpeth

Eshott Hall

COUNTRY HOUSE • CLASSIC Attractive Georgian manor house in a quiet, rural location - yet only 5min from the A1. Classically stylish guest areas. Smart, modern bedrooms boast warm fabrics, antique furniture and good facilities. Formal dining room offers contemporary menus; local produce includes fruit and veg from the kitchen garden.

17 rooms - £ 150/250 £ 200/250

✉ NE65 9EN
- ✆ 01670 787454 - www.eshotthall.co.uk

at Longhorsley Northwest: 6.5 mi by A192 on A697 ✉ Morpeth

Thistleyhaugh Farm

FAMILY • COSY Attractive Georgian farmhouse, set off the beaten track on a 750 acre organic farm, with the River Coquet flowing through its grounds. Cosy, open-fired lounge and antique-filled dining room. Spacious, comfortable bedrooms - most have luxurious bathrooms with feature baths. Communal dinners; home-cooking features beef and lamb from the farm. Charming owners.

4 rooms - £ 90 £ 110

✉ NE65 8RG - Northwest : 3.75 mi by A 697 and Todburn rd taking first right turn
- ✆ 01665 570629 - www.thistleyhaugh.co.uk - Closed Christmas-1 February

MORSTON - Norfolk → See Blakeney

MOULTON

Suffolk - Regional map n° **8**-B2

Packhorse Inn

MODERN CUISINE • INN A smart modern pub set near the green in a pretty village and named after the 15C flint bridge which spans the river. Cooking keeps things classical, with the focus firmly on the ingredients' natural flavours. Ultra-stylish bedrooms have plush furnishings and roll-top baths.

Menu £ 16 (weekday lunch) - Carte £ 26/50

8 rooms - £ 85/225 £ 100/225

Bridge St ✉ CB8 8SP
- ✆ 01638 751818 - www.thepackhorseinn.com

MOUNTSORREL

Leicestershire - Pop. 12 120 - Regional map n° **9**-B2

John's House (John Duffin)

MODERN CUISINE • RUSTIC XX A 16C farmhouse where the eponymous and talented John was born and now cooks; his family also own the surrounding farm with its shop, café, petting farm and motor museum. Produce from the surrounding fields is used to create original, interesting dishes which show a real understanding of textures and flavours.

→ Chilled cream of Lincolnshire smoked eel, frozen horseradish and lovage. Gloucester Old Spot piglet, peanut, kalamansi and Thai spices. Carrot sorbet, yoghurt, liquorice and mint.

Menu £ 30/79

Stonehurst Farm, 141 Loughborough Rd ✉ LE12 7AR
- ✆ 01509 415569 (booking essential) - www.johnshouse.co.uk - Closed Sunday and Monday

MOUSEHOLE

Cornwall - ✉ Penzance - Regional map n° **1**-A3

Old Coastguard

MEDITERRANEAN CUISINE • BISTRO Old coastguard's cottage in a small fishing village, with a laid-back, open-plan interior, a sub-tropical garden and views towards St Clement's Isle. Well-presented brasserie dishes display a Mediterranean edge; great wine selection. Individually styled bedrooms – some with balconies, most with sea views.

Menu £25 – Carte £27/34 **s**

14 rooms – †£105/185 ††£140/245

The Parade ✉ TR19 6PR – ✆ 01736 731222 – www.oldcoastguardhotel.co.uk – Closed 25 December and 1 week January

2 Fore Street

SEAFOOD • FRIENDLY Friendly café-cum-bistro with a delightful courtyard terrace and garden. All-day menus offer everything from coffee and cake to a full meal, with brunch a feature at weekends. Tasty, unfussy dishes are guided by the day's catch.

Carte £29/39

2 Fore St ✉ TR19 6PF – ✆ 01736 731164 (booking essential at dinner) – www.2forestreet.co.uk – Closed 4 January-8 February

MURCOTT

Oxfordshire - ✉ Kidlington - Pop. 1 293 - Regional map n° **6**-B2

Nut Tree (Mike North)

TRADITIONAL BRITISH • RUSTIC With its 15C origins and smartly thatched roof it looks like a typical English pub but this is no ordinary village local. Menus comprise mainly of satisfying, full-flavoured restaurant-style dishes; for a quick snack try the Bar & Garden menu or for the full experience, go for the 7 course tasting menu.

→ Pan-fried scallops with mango salsa, purée and coriander. Saddle of lamb, braised shoulder with confit onion and creamed spinach. Vanilla custard soufflé and green apple sorbet.

Carte £40/64

Main St ✉ OX5 2RE – ✆ 01865 331253 – www.nuttreeinn.co.uk – Closed Sunday dinner

NAILSWORTH

Gloucestershire - Pop. 7 728 - Regional map n° **2**-C1

Wilder

MODERN CUISINE • INTIMATE Everyone arrives at 7.30pm for a 3-hour surprise menu accompanied by optional matching wines. Humble ingredients are used in well-balanced, ambitious combinations. Service is structured but passionate.

Menu £70 – surprise menu only

Market St ✉ GL6 0BX – ✆ 01453 835483 (booking essential) – www.dinewilder.co.uk – dinner only – Closed Sunday-Tuesday

Wild Garlic

MODERN BRITISH • INTIMATE This attractive little restaurant has a friendly, laid-back feel. Modern bistro dishes include artisan pastas, which are something of a speciality – the 5 spice pulled pork tagliatelle is a hit. Enjoy lunch on the south-facing terrace and brunch at weekends. Bedrooms are stylish and well-equipped.

Carte £24/46

5 rooms – †£80/160 ††£85/160

3 Cossack Sq ✉ GL6 0DB – ✆ 01453 832615 – www.wild-garlic.co.uk – Closed first week January and Sunday dinner-Monday

NATIONAL EXHIBITION CENTRE - W. Mids. ➔ See Birmingham

NETHER WESTCOTE - Gloucestershire ➔ See Stow-on-the-Wold

NETLEY MARSH - Hampshire ➔ See Southampton

NEW MILTON

Hampshire - Pop. 19 969 - Regional map n° **4**-A3

The Kitchen

MODERN BRITISH • FASHIONABLE A striking new build with an impressive kitchen garden and a greenhouse beside it; set at the entrance of the Chewton Glen hotel. Brasserie dishes showcase local and garden produce. The glass-fronted cookery school is popular.

Carte £ 17/44

Chewton Glen Hotel, Christchurch Rd ✉ BH25 6QS - West : 2 mi by A 337 and Ringwood Rd on Chewton Farm Rd - ✆ 01425 282212 - www.chewtonglen.com/the-kitchen - Closed Sunday dinner

Chewton Glen

GRAND LUXURY • CLASSIC A professionally run country house with an impressive spa, set in 130 acres of New Forest parkland - try a host of outdoor pursuits, including croquet, archery and clay pigeon shooting. Luxurious bedrooms range from classic to contemporary; opt for one with a balcony or terrace, or try a unique Treehouse suite. Dine in the traditional restaurant or modern brasserie.

72 rooms - £ 370/725 £ 370/725 - 18 suites

Christchurch Rd ✉ BH25 6QS - West : 2 mi by A 337 and Ringwood Rd on Chewton Farm Rd - ✆ 01425 275341 - www.chewtonglen.com

The Kitchen - See restaurant listing

NEWBOTTLE

Tyne and Wear - Regional map n° **14**-B2

Hideaway at Herrington Hill

FAMILY • REGIONAL The charming owners really look after their guests at this spacious former shooting lodge, built in 1838 for the Earl of Durham. Bedrooms blend period features and modern amenities. The Garden Room is largest, with views of the grounds.

5 rooms - £ 75/110 £ 75/130

High Ln ✉ DH4 4NH - West : 1 mile - ✆ 07730 957795 - www.hideawayatherringtonhill.com - Closed 23 December-2 January

NEWBURY

West Berkshire - Pop. 38 762 - Regional map n° **6**-B3

Woodspeen (John Campbell)

MODERN CUISINE • FASHIONABLE Despite being set in an old pub, this smart neighbourhood eatery has more of a bistro feel, courtesy of its Scandic styling and bright, modern thatched extension. Mouth-watering seasonal dishes feature local and garden produce; flavour is paramount and dishes have a comforting, modern classic style.

➔ Pork ballotine with glazed cheek, burnt apple, celeriac and mustard. Roast cod with salsify, braised onion and potted shrimps. Caramelised white chocolate crémeux with kiwi, grapes and mint.

Menu £ 29 (lunch and early dinner) - Carte £ 38/60

Lambourn Rd, Bagnor ✉ RG20 8BN - Northwest : 2 mi by A 4 and Station Rd - signed Watermill Theatre - ✆ 01635 265070 - www.thewoodspeen.com - Closed Sunday dinner

Blackbird (Dom Robinson)

CLASSIC CUISINE • NEIGHBOURHOOD This delightful inn sits in an equally charming hamlet and is a backbone of the local community. Freshly baked loaves sit on the bar and service is amiable. Top-notch ingredients feature in precisely prepared yet unfussy dishes with a classical French base and flavours are superb.

→ Salad of Wye Valley asparagus with Kennet crayfish and pistachio. Poached halibut, creamed leeks and sauce Veronique. Prune and Armagnac tart, Armagnac ice cream.

Menu £ 19 (weekday lunch) – Carte £ 36/53

Bagnor ✉ RG20 8AQ – Northwest : 2 mi by A 4 and Station Rd - signed Watermill Theatre – ✆ 01635 40005 – www.theblackbird.co.uk
– Closed 26-26 December, first week August, Sunday dinner, Monday and Tuesday

The Vineyard

MODERN CUISINE • ELEGANT XxX Smart hotel restaurant split over two levels. Accomplished dishes are attractively presented; choose between a set and two tasting menus. They offer over 100 wines by the glass – some from their own Californian vineyard.

Menu £ 29/69

Vineyard Hotel, Stockcross ✉ RG20 8JU – Northwest : 2 mi by A 4 on B 4000 – ✆ 01635 528770 – www.the-vineyard.co.uk
– Closed Sunday and Monday

Henry & Joe's

MODERN BRITISH • FRIENDLY X What started as a pop-up and a dream is now an appealing modern bistro that's winning everyone's hearts. Joe is a charmer and works the room with aplomb, while Henry conjures up interesting, adventurous dishes. The lunch and early evening menu is great value; don't miss the freshly baked bread.

Menu £ 21 – Carte £ 33/48

17 Cheap St ✉ RG14 5DD – ✆ 01635 581751 – www.henryandjoes.co.uk
– Closed 2 weeks January, 2 weeks September, Christmas and Sunday-Tuesday

The Vineyard

BUSINESS • CLASSIC Extended former hunting lodge with over 1,000 pieces of art and a striking fire and water feature. Some bedrooms have a country house style, while others are more contemporary; all boast smart marble bathrooms. The owner also has a vineyard in California, hence the stunning wine vault and the wine-themed bar.

49 rooms – †£ 275/350 ††£ 275/350 – ☕ £ 21 – 32 suites

Stockcross ✉ RG20 8JU – Northwest : 2 mi by A 4 on B 4000 – ✆ 01635 528770 – www.the-vineyard.co.uk

The Vineyard – See restaurant listing

NEWBY BRIDGE

Cumbria – Regional map n° **12**-A3

Lakeside

LUXURY • CLASSIC A superbly situated hotel on the water's edge; the Windermere Steamers run from the neighbouring pier. Guest areas are extremely comfortable and bedrooms are mix of the classic and the contemporary – some have great views. Dine in the stylish brasserie or traditional dining room, and be sure to find time for afternoon tea in the conservatory, overlooking the lake.

74 rooms ☕ – †£ 150/190 ††£ 190/250 – 7 suites

Lakeside ✉ LA12 8AT – Northeast : 1 mi on Hawkshead rd – ✆ 015395 30001 – www.lakesidehotel.co.uk
– Closed 3-18 January

Knoll

COUNTRY HOUSE • COSY You'll be warmly welcomed into this comfy, cosy slate house. Chesterfield sofas sit by the open fire in the lounge and there's a pleasant little dining room for home-cooked bistro-style dishes. Individually decorated bedrooms have bold décor; 'The Retreat' has a private entrance and a hot tub.

9 rooms – £ 85/160 £ 95/160

Lakeside LA12 8AU – Northeast : 1.25 mi on Hawkshead rd – 015395 31347 – www.theknoll-lakeside.co.uk – Closed 22-27, 31 December and 1 January

NEWCASTLE UPON TYNE

Tyne and Wear – Pop. 268 064 – Regional map n° **14**-B2

House of Tides (Kenny Atkinson)

MODERN CUISINE • INTIMATE XX A characterful 16C merchant's house on the quayside. Flagged floors, cast iron pillars and exposed bricks feature in the bar, while the upstairs restaurant boasts carved beams and a stone fireplace. Tasting menus list accomplished, creative dishes which are well-balanced and attractively presented.

→ Sea bass with chicken wings, white asparagus, lemon and thyme. Smoked lamb with hen of the woods and hazelnuts. Banana and coconut with kalamansi and sesame.

Menu £ 70/95 – tasting menu only

28-30 The Close NE1 3RF – 0191 230 3720 (booking essential) – www.houseoftides.co.uk – Closed 23 December-8 January, 27 May-2 June, 26-31 August, Sunday, Monday and lunch Tuesday-Wednesday

Route (N)

COUNTRY • BISTRO X This simple bistro sits on a steep city centre street that once formed the route from the castle to the quayside. It has a concrete floor, a breeze block wall and an open kitchen to the rear. Regularly changing menus offer well-priced, gutsy small plates with punchy flavours and a British heart.

Carte £ 23/33

35 Side NE1 3JE – 0191 222 0973 – www.routenewcastle.co.uk – Closed first 2 weeks January, 25-26 December and Sunday dinner-Wednesday lunch

Broad Chare

TRADITIONAL BRITISH • PUB Sit in the snug ground floor bar or more comfortable upstairs dining room of this quayside pub. Choose from a snack menu of 'Geordie Tapas', an appealing 'on toast' selection, hearty daily specials and tasty nursery puddings. They also offer over 40 ales, including some which are custom-made for the pub.

Carte £ 21/39

25 Broad Chare NE1 3DQ – 0191 211 2144 – www.thebroadchare.co.uk – Closed 25-26 December, 1 January and Sunday dinner

Dobson & Parnell

MODERN CUISINE • DESIGN XX An iconic address in the city, this elegant restaurant is named after Victorian architects John Dobson and William Parnell. Cooking has a Nordic style, with plenty of drying, pickling and curing. Dishes are colourful and satisfying.

Menu £ 19 (lunch and early dinner) – Carte £ 27/49

21 Queen St NE1 3UG – 0191 221 0904 – www.dobsonandparnell.co.uk – Closed Sunday dinner, Monday and bank holidays

Peace & Loaf

MODERN CUISINE • NEIGHBOURHOOD XX Found in a smart suburban parade, this fashionable restaurant and bar is set over three levels and has a lively atmosphere. Attractively presented modern dishes are ambitious, complex and employ many different cooking techniques.

Menu £ 25 (lunch and early dinner) – Carte £ 38/65

217 Jesmond Rd, Jesmond NE2 1LA – Northeast : 1.5 mi by A 1058 – 0191 281 5222 – www.peaceandloaf.co.uk – Closed 25-26 December, 1 January and Sunday dinner

21

MODERN BRITISH • BRASSERIE XX Start with a gin from the large selection behind the zinc-topped counter then head through to the smart red and black brasserie. Menus offer a comprehensive array of confidently cooked classics; the 'menu du jour' is good value.

Menu £ 23/24 – Carte £ 30/60

Trinity Gardens ✉ NE1 2HH – ✆ 0191 222 0755 – www.21newcastle.co.uk – Closed 25-26 December and 1 January

Bistro Forty Six

MODERN BRITISH • NEIGHBOURHOOD X A refreshingly honest bistro with a homely interior. The self-taught chef hunts and forages, using the local larder to full effect. Passionately seasonal dishes will appeal to one and all; check the blackboard for the daily specials.

Menu £ 19 (early dinner) – Carte £ 26/34

46 Brentwood Ave, Jesmond ✉ NE2 3DH – Northeast : 1.25 mi by B 1318 and Forsyth Rd – ✆ 0191 281 8081 – www.bistrofortysix.co.uk – Closed Sunday dinner, Monday and lunch Tuesday-Wednesday

The Patricia

MODERN BRITISH • NEIGHBOURHOOD X This simply furnished bistro sits in the vibrant suburb of Jesmond and is named after the owner's grandmother. Tasty cooking displays Mediterranean influences and the wine list is good value. They also open at the weekend for lunch – Saturday sees a selection of well-priced small plates.

Menu £ 20 – Carte £ 31/47

139 Jesmond Rd, Jesmond ✉ NE2 1JY – Northeast : 1.5 mi by A 1058 – ✆ 0191 281 4443 (booking essential) – www.the-patricia.com – dinner only and lunch Saturaday-Sunday – Closed Sunday dinner, Monday and Tuesday

Jesmond Dene House

LUXURY • MODERN Stone-built Arts and Crafts house in a peaceful city dene; originally owned by the Armstrong family. Characterful guest areas with wood panelling, local art and striking original fireplaces. Individually furnished bedrooms have bold feature walls, modern facilities and smart bathrooms with underfloor heating.

40 rooms – †£ 89/159 ††£ 89/159 – ☕ £ 18

Jesmond Dene Rd ✉ NE2 2EY – Northeast : 1.5 mi by B 1318 off A 189 – ✆ 0191 212 3000 – www.jesmonddenehouse.co.uk

Hotel du Vin

BUSINESS • CONTEMPORARY Extended red-brick building overlooking the river – formerly home to the Tyne Tees Steam Shipping Company. Characterful lounge with gas fire and zinc-topped bar. Chic, stylish, wine-themed bedrooms; some boast feature baths or terraces. Classical brasserie features a glass-fronted wine tasting room.

42 rooms – †£ 84/184 ††£ 100/184 – ☕ £ 17

Allan House, City Rd ✉ NE1 2BE – East : 0.75 mi on A 186 – ✆ 0191 229 2200 – www.hotelduvin.com/newcastle

The Townhouse

TOWNHOUSE • CONTEMPORARY End of terrace Victorian house in a residential area. All-day café serves breakfast, snacks, cakes and the like. Smart, stylish bedrooms offer bold, contemporary décor and extra touches such as iPod docks; Room 10 has a bath in the bedroom.

10 rooms ☕ – †£ 95/120 ††£ 95/120

1 West Ave, Gosforth ✉ NE3 4ES – North : 2.5 mi by B 1318 – ✆ 0191 285 6812

at Ponteland Northwest: 8.25 mi by A167 on A696 ✉ Newcastle Upon Tyne

Haveli

INDIAN • FASHIONABLE XX Haveli means 'grand house' and this neighbourhood restaurant is certainly very smart. Influences come from all over India; try one of the chef's signature curries. Staff combine personality with professionalism.

Menu £ 25 (early dinner) – Carte £ 19/34

3-5 Broadway, Darras Hall ✉ NE20 9PW – Southwest : 1.5 mi by B 6323 off Darras Hall Estate rd – ✆ 01661 872727 – www.haveliponteland.com – dinner only – Closed 25 December and Monday except bank holidays

NEWLYN

Cornwall – Pop. 3 536 – Regional map n° 1-A3

Tolcarne Inn

SEAFOOD • TRADITIONAL DÉCOR An unassuming, family-run pub behind the sea wall. Inside it's narrow and cosy, with 18C beams, a wood-burning stove and a long bar. The experienced chef offers appealing, flavoursome dishes which centre around fresh, locally landed fish and shellfish – go for the turbot if it's on the menu.

Carte £ 26/36

Tolcarne Pl ✉ TR18 5PR – ✆ 01736 363074 (booking essential at dinner) – www.tolcarneinn.co.uk – Closed 25-26 December

NEWPORT – Isle of Wight

→ See Wight (Isle of)

NEWQUAY

Cornwall – Pop. 20 189 – Regional map n° 1-A2

at Watergate Bay Northeast: 3 mi by A3059 on B3276 ✉ Newquay

Fifteen Cornwall

ITALIAN • TRENDY XX A lively beachfront restaurant with fabulous bay views; the profits go towards training disengaged adults to become chefs. Unfussy Italian menus have a Cornish twist and feature homemade pastas and steaks from the Josper grill. At lunch they also serve antipasti at the unbookable bar counter.

Carte dinner £ 28/52

On The Beach ✉ TR8 4AA – ✆ 01637 861000 (booking essential) – www.fifteencornwall.co.uk – Closed 2 weeks January

Watergate Bay

FAMILY • CONTEMPORARY A long-standing seaside hotel where fresh, contemporary bedrooms range from standards to family suites; some have freestanding baths with sea outlooks. The beautiful infinity pool and hot tub share the view and there's direct beach access, beach changing rooms and even a surfboard store. Dine in the bar, the laid-back sandy-floored café or the smart modern brasserie.

71 rooms – †£ 139/338 ††£ 185/450

On The Beach ✉ TR8 4AA – ✆ 01637 860543 – www.watergatebay.co.uk

at Mawgan Porth Northeast: 6 mi by A3059 on B3276

Scarlet

BOUTIQUE HOTEL • PERSONALISED Eco-centric, adults only hotel set high on a cliff and boasting stunning coastal views. Modern bar and lounges, and a great spa offering extensive treatments. Bedrooms range from 'Just Right' to 'Indulgent' and have unusual open-plan bathrooms and a cool, Scandic style – every room has a terrace and sea view.

37 rooms – †£ 200/330 ††£ 220/350

Tredragon Rd ✉ TR8 4DQ – ✆ 01637 861800 – www.scarlethotel.co.uk – Closed 3-31 January

NEWTON-ON-OUSE

North Yorkshire - Regional map n° **13**-B2

Dawnay Arms

MODERN BRITISH · PUB A handsome pub with stone floors, low beams, open fires and all manner of bric-a-brac – its delightful dining room has views over the garden and down to the river. Gutsy, well executed British dishes include plenty of local game.

Menu £ 18 (lunch and early dinner) – Carte £ 26/44

YO30 2BR – 01347 848345 – www.thedawnayatnewton.co.uk – Closed Sunday dinner and Monday except bank holidays

NOMANSLAND

Hampshire - Regional map n° **4**-D3

Les Mirabelles

CLASSIC FRENCH · FRIENDLY XX This bright, modern restaurant overlooks the common and is enthusiastically run by a welcoming Frenchman. The well-balanced menu features unfussy, classic Gallic dishes and the superb wine selection lists over 3,000 bins!

Menu £ 24 (weekdays) – Carte £ 31/50

Forest Edge Rd SP5 2BN – 01794 390205 – www.lesmirabelles.co.uk – Closed 22 December-13 January, 1 week May, 1 week September, Sunday and Monday

NORTH BOVEY

Devon - Newton Abbot - Pop. 254 - Regional map n° **1**-C2

Bovey Castle

HISTORIC · CLASSIC An impressive manor house on an extensive country estate beautifully set within the Dartmoor National Park. Bedrooms have contemporary touches but still retain their traditional edge, and there's a relaxed, homely feel throughout. Dine on either seasonal modern dishes or British classics.

60 rooms – £ 120/200 £ 190/800 – 6 suites

TQ13 8RE – Northwest : 2 mi by Postbridge rd, bearing left at fork just out of village – 01647 445000 – www.boveycastle.com

NORTH LOPHAM

Norfolk - Regional map n° **8**-C2

Church Farm House

FAMILY · PERSONALISED Characterful thatched farmhouse in the shadow of the village church, with lovely gardens and a terrace for summer breakfasts. The comfy conservatory and spacious beamed lounge are filled with antiques and musical curios; bedrooms are traditional. The charming owners prepare homely meals of local produce.

3 rooms – £ 75 £ 110

Church Rd IP22 2LP – 01379 687270 – www.churchfarmhouse.org – Closed January-mid-February

NORTH MARSTON

Buckinghamshire - Pop. 781 - Regional map n° **6**-C2

The Pilgrim

MODERN CUISINE · FRIENDLY A friendly community pub filled with heavy timbers; find a spot by the wood-burning stove in the cosy bar-lounge. Proper home-cooking relies on local, sustainable produce. Every Tuesday the menu changes for 'Village Night'.

Carte £ 21/31

25 High St MK18 3PD – 01296 670969 – www.thepilgrimpub.co.uk – Closed 26 December, 1 January , Sunday dinner, Monday and Tuesday lunch

NORTH SHIELDS

Tyne and Wear – Pop. 39 042 – Regional map n° **14**-B2

River Cafe on the Tyne

TRADITIONAL BRITISH • BISTRO Laid-back restaurant run by a friendly local team, set above a pub in the North Shields fish quay. The daily changing à la carte offers unfussy, bistro-style dishes of fresh local produce, including fish from the market on the quayside. The 3 course set lunch and early dinner menu is a steal.

Menu £ 8 (lunch and early dinner) – Carte £ 20/35

51 Bell St, Fish Quay ✉ NE30 1HF – ☎ 0191 296 6168 – www.rivercafeonthetyne.co.uk – Closed 25-26 December, 1-2 January, Monday, Sunday dinner and Tuesday lunch

Staith House

TRADITIONAL BRITISH • PUB A stone's throw from market stalls overflowing with crab, lobster and Craster kippers, is this smart quayside pub. Photos of the old docks line the walls of numerous dining areas and it has a pleasingly cluttered feel. Daily changing dishes showcase Northumberland's latest yield; the fish is smoked on-site.

Carte £ 23/43

57 Low Lights ✉ NE30 1JA – ☎ 0191 270 8441 (booking essential at dinner) – www.thestaithhouse.co.uk – Closed 25-26 December and 1-16 January

NORTH WALSHAM

Norfolk – Pop. 12 463 – Regional map n° **8**-D1

Beechwood

HISTORIC BUILDING • CLASSIC A part-Georgian, red-brick property with classical furnishings and bright, eye-catching colour schemes. Period bedrooms vary in size and comfort – many have feature beds and the best have terraces opening onto the lovely gardens. Seasonal menus have Mediterranean-influences.

18 rooms – †£ 100 ††£ 130/175

20 Cromer Rd ✉ NR28 0HD – ☎ 01692 403231 – www.beechwood-hotel.co.uk

NORTHMOOR

Oxfordshire – Regional map n° **6**-B2

Red Lion

TRADITIONAL BRITISH • FRIENDLY Extremely welcoming pub owned by the villagers and run by an experienced young couple and a friendly team. Low beams, open fires and fresh flowers abound and the menu is a great mix of pub classics and more modern daily specials.

Carte £ 18/36

Standlake Rd ✉ OX29 5SX – ☎ 01865 300301 – www.theredlionnorthmoor.com – Closed Sunday dinner and Monday

NORTH STAINLEY

North Yorkshire – Regional map n° **13**-B2

Old Coach House

TOWNHOUSE • ELEGANT Smart 18C coach house nestled between the Dales and the Moors. Bedrooms differ in size but all have a bright modern style and are furnished by local craftsmen. The breakfast room overlooks the fountain in the courtyard garden.

8 rooms – †£ 80/105 ††£ 90/120

✉ HG4 3HT – Southeast : 1 mi on A 6108 – ☎ 07912 634900 – www.oldcoachhouse.info – Closed 24-25 December

NORWICH

Norfolk - Pop. 186 682 - Regional map n° **8**-D2

Roger Hickman's

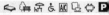

MODERN CUISINE • TRADITIONAL DÉCOR XX Personally run restaurant in a historic part of the city, with soft hues, modern art and romantic corners. Service is attentive yet unobtrusive. Cooking is modern, intricate and displays respect for ingredients' natural flavours.

Menu £ 26/48

79 Upper St Giles St ✉ NR2 1AB
- ✆ 01603 633522 - www.rogerhickmansrestaurant.com
- Closed 2 weeks Christmas, Sunday and Monday

Benedicts

MODERN CUISINE • BISTRO X A huge window lets in lots of light and white wood panelling keep things suitably down-to-earth. Tried-and-tested combinations are given subtle modern touches and show respect for good quality Norfolk ingredients.

Menu £ 22/39

9 St Benedicts Street ✉ NR2 4PE
- ✆ 01603 926080 - www.restaurantbenedicts.com
- Closed 23 December-8 January, 30 July-13 August, Sunday and Monday

Georgian Townhouse

TRADITIONAL CUISINE • NEIGHBOURHOOD Laid-back pub with a flexible menu: choose small plates to start or to share; dishes 'for the table' for 2 or 4 or something for yourself 'from the store'. Fruit and veg is home-grown and they home-smoke cheese and spit-roast and flame-grill meats. Bold, retro-style bedrooms have fridges and coffee machines.

Carte £ 24/40

22 rooms - †£ 85/120 ††£ 95/130

30-34 Unthank Rd ✉ NR2 2RB - West : 0.75 mi off A 147 and Convent Rd
- ✆ 01603 615655 - www.thegeorgiantownhousenorwich.com

38 St Giles

TOWNHOUSE • PERSONALISED City centre townhouse where boutique styling blends with original features. Elegant, uncluttered bedrooms boast high ceilings and wood panelling, along with silk curtains, handmade mattresses and quality linen. Excellent breakfasts.

8 rooms - †£ 95/195 ††£ 130/245

38 St Giles St ✉ NR2 1LL
- ✆ 01603 662944 - www.38stgiles.co.uk
- Closed 24-27 December

Catton Old Hall

HISTORIC • PERSONALISED Tucked away on the edge of the city is this attractive former merchant's house which was built in 1632 using reclaimed Caen stone, local flint and oak timbers. Characterful, individually designed bedrooms include 5 feature rooms; Anna Sewell, with exposed beams and a vast four poster, is the best.

7 rooms - †£ 99/150 ††£ 99/150

Lodge Ln, Old Catton ✉ NR6 7HG - North : 3.5 mi by Catton Grove Rd off St Faiths Rd
- ✆ 01603 419379 - www.catton-hall.co.uk
- Closed Christmas

Good quality cooking at a great price?
Look out for the Bib Gourmand.

at Stoke Holy Cross South: 5.75 mi by A140 ✉ Norwich

Stoke Mill

TRADITIONAL CUISINE • HISTORIC XX Characterful 700 year old mill spanning the River Tas; the adjoining building is where the Colman family started making mustard in 1814. Confidently prepared, classically based dishes use good ingredients and flavours are distinct.

Menu £ 16 (weekdays) – Carte £ 30/53

Mill Rd ✉ NR14 8PA – ☎ 01508 493337 – www.stokemill.co.uk – Closed Sunday dinner, Monday and Tuesday

NOSS MAYO

Devon – Regional map n° **1**-C3

Ship Inn

TRADITIONAL BRITISH • PUB Large, busy, well-run pub with characterful, nautical décor and wonderful waterside views from its peaceful spot on the Yealm Estuary. Appealing menu of unfussy pub classics. Bright, friendly service. Keep an eye on the tide!

Carte £ 25/37

✉ PL8 1EW – ☎ 01752 872387 – www.nossmayo.com – Closed 25 December

NOTTINGHAM

Nottingham – Pop. 289 301 – Regional map n° **9**-B2

Restaurant Sat Bains

CREATIVE • INTIMATE XXX The location beneath a flyover on the fringes of the city might be a little incongruous but don't let that put you off, as once at your table, the world outside will be forgotten. Flagged floors and deer skin covered tables blend with contemporary artwork and the atmosphere is smart yet casual.

At lunch a 7 course menu is offered in 3 intimate locations: the 'Chef's Table', the 'Kitchen Bench' or the development kitchen 'Nucleus'. In the latter, the Head Chef cooks for you personally, precisely preparing premium ingredients in dishes with plenty of originality; all the while answering your questions.

At night, the main room comes alive. 7 and 10 course tasting menus incorporate the five tastes – salt, sweet, sour, bitter and umami. Cooking is highly technical with good balance and a delicate style, and presentation is creative. Their urban kitchen garden provides many of the herbs and leaves.

Spacious modern bedrooms complete the picture.

→ Scallops roasted in garam masala with puy lentil dahl velouté. Monkfish XO with lettuce and cabbage. Gariguette strawberries with olive oil cake and Earl Grey tea.

Menu £ 95/110 – tasting menu only

7 rooms – †£ 140/285 ††£ 140/285 – 2 suites

Trentside, Lenton Ln ✉ NG7 2SA – Southwest : 3.5 mi by A 6005 (Castle Bd.) and A 52 – ☎ 0115 986 6566 (booking essential) – www.restaurantsatbains.com – Closed 2 weeks late December-early January, 2 weeks August, 1 week May and Sunday-Tuesday

Ibérico World Tapas

MEDITERRANEAN CUISINE • FASHIONABLE X A well-run restaurant with a vaulted ceiling, colourful Moorish tiles and ornate fretwork, hidden in the basement of the old city law courts and jail. Tapas-style sharing dishes are listed under 'Nibbles', 'Meat', 'Fish' and 'Veg'. Skilful cooking is full of flavour and displays some Japanese influences.

Menu £ 12 (weekdays) – Carte £ 14/25

The Shire Hall, High Pavement ✉ NG1 1HN – ☎ 0115 941 0410 (booking essential at dinner) – www.ibericotapas.com – Closed 1-5 January and Sunday

Alchemilla

MODERN BRITISH · RUSTIC XX Alchemilla occupies six red-brick vaulted arches of a Victorian carriage house set beneath properties once owned by wealthy lace merchants. Despite its rustic look, it's a modern place, with a living wall and a focus on vegetables and plants. Original dishes cleverly blend varying textures and flavours.

Menu £ 40/65 – tasting menu only

192 Derby Rd ✉ NG7 1NF – ✆ 0115 941 3515 – www.alchemillarestaurant.uk – Closed 2 weeks Christmas, 2 weeks August, Sunday, Monday and lunch Tuesday

Hart's

MODERN BRITISH · FASHIONABLE XX A contemporary restaurant in the A&E department of the old city hospital; colourful abstract artwork adorns the walls of the bright, airy room. British brasserie dishes feature on the well-priced daily menu, which follows the seasons and often sees many different flavours on the plate.

Menu £ 28 (weekday lunch) – Carte £ 33/55

Hart's Hotel, Standard Ct., Park Row ✉ NG1 6GN – ✆ 0115 988 1900 – www.hartsnottingham.co.uk – Closed 1 January and dinner 25-26 December

MemSaab

INDIAN · EXOTIC DÉCOR XX Professionally run restaurant with eye-catching artwork and a wooden 'Gateway of India'. Original, authentic cooking has a distinct North Indian influence. Spicing is well-judged and dishes from the charcoal grill are a highlight.

Carte £ 19/43

12-14 Maid Marian Way ✉ NG1 6HS – ✆ 0115 957 0009 – www.mem-saab.co.uk – dinner only – Closed 25 December

World Service

MODERN CUISINE · EXOTIC DÉCOR XX Hidden in the extension of a Georgian property and accessed via an Indonesian-inspired courtyard garden. It has a clubby, colonial feel, with panelled walls and cases of archaeological artefacts. Appealing dishes have global influences.

Menu £ 27 (lunch) – Carte £ 30/49

Newdigate House, Castlegate ✉ NG1 6AF – ✆ 0115 847 5587 – www.worldservicerestaurant.com – Closed 1-5 January and Sunday dinner

Bar Ibérico

MEDITERRANEAN CUISINE · TAPAS BAR X A buzzy, laid-back tapas bar with a large pavement terrace. The wide-ranging menu is designed for sharing, from charcuterie and cheese to pintxos from the Josper grill and tapas inspired by Spain and the Mediterranean.

Menu £ 11 (lunch and early dinner) – Carte £ 14/22

17-19 Carlton St ✉ NG1 1NL – ✆ 0115 988 1133 (bookings not accepted) – www.baribericotapas.com – Closed 25-26 December and 1 January

Larder on Goosegate

TRADITIONAL BRITISH · RUSTIC X This appealing restaurant sits on the first floor a listed Victorian building. It was the first branch of Boots the Chemists and the floor to ceiling windows displayed their wares; ask to sit beside them for a view of the street below. Dishes are unfussy, good value and tasty; the steaks are a hit.

Menu £ 16 (lunch and early dinner) – Carte £ 22/37

1st Floor, 16-22 Goosegate ✉ NG1 1FE – ✆ 0115 950 0111 – www.thelarderongoosegate.co.uk – dinner only and lunch Friday-Sunday – Closed Monday

Hart's

BUSINESS • DESIGN A sophisticated boutique-style hotel built on the ramparts of a medieval castle. Compact bedrooms have modern bathrooms and a high level of facilities; ask for one with a garden terrace. Unwind in the cosy bar or out in the courtyard. Breakfast includes bread and pastries from their own bakery.

32 rooms – £ 139/279 £ 139/279 – £ 15 – 2 suites

Standard Hill, Park Row ✉ NG1 6FN

– ✆ 0115 988 1900 – www.hartsnottingham.co.uk

Hart's – See restaurant listing

at West Bridgford Southeast: 1.75 mi by A60 ✉ Nottingham

escabeche

MEDITERRANEAN CUISINE • FRIENDLY X Informal, modern, Mediterranean-inspired restaurant with a sunny front terrace. The broad main menu lists vibrant, well-presented tapas dishes, offering a great variety of flavours. Excellent value set menu.

Menu £ 11 (lunch and early dinner) **s** – Carte £ 15/23

27 Bridgford Rd ✉ NG2 6AU

– ✆ 0115 981 7010 – www.escabeche.co.uk – Closed 25-26 December and 1 January

at Plumtree Southeast: 5.75 mi by A60 off A606 ✉ Nottingham

Perkins Bar & Bistro

MODERN BRITISH • FRIENDLY XX This red-brick Victorian railway station is now a bright family-run bistro; pick a seat overlooking the railway line. Modern British menus evolve daily and feature home-smoked fish, game and cheese; their Sleeper Boards are a hit. Stay in a cosy shepherd's hut overlooking the fields – one has a roll-top bath!

Menu £ 17 (weekday lunch) – Carte £ 23/45

3 rooms – £ 120/150 £ 120/150

Old Railway Station, Station Rd ✉ NG12 5NA

– ✆ 0115 937 3695 – www.perkinsrestaurant.co.uk – Closed Sunday dinner

at Ruddington South : 5.5 mi on A 60 ✉ Nottinghamshire

Ruddington Arms

TRADITIONAL CUISINE • NEIGHBOURHOOD This dramatically refurbished, faux-industrial style pub is found in a sleepy village. Flavoursome dishes cater for one and all, with everything from pub classics to more adventurous offerings. Tasty marmalades and chutneys are for sale.

Carte £ 23/36

56 Wilford Rd ✉ NG11 6EQ

– ✆ 0115 984 1628 – www.theruddingtonarms.com

NUN MONKTON

North Yorkshire – Regional map n° **13**-B2

Alice Hawthorn Inn

REGIONAL CUISINE • PUB This smart, stylish pub sits on a picturesque village green complete with a duck pond, grazing cattle and the country's tallest maypole. Well-presented dishes have classical roots and showcase local and garden produce.

Carte £ 24/47

The Green ✉ YO26 8EW

– ✆ 01423 330303 – www.thealicehawthorn.com – Closed Sunday dinner, Monday except bank holidays and Tuesday

OAKHAM

Rutland – Pop. 10 922 – Regional map n° **9**-C2

at Hambleton East: 3 mi by A606 ✉ Oakham

✿ Hambleton Hall

CLASSIC CUISINE • COUNTRY HOUSE XXX A traditional dining room in a lovely Victorian manor house, boasting superb views over Rutland Water. Accomplished cooking marries together a host of top quality seasonal ingredients. Gallic dishes are classically based but display the occasional modern touch; the delicious bread is from their artisan bakery.

→ Cornish crab with yuzu, apple, and ginger. Presa Ibérica pork, salt-baked swede, apple and crackling. Golden chocolate and blood orange sorbet.

Menu £ 38 (weekday lunch)/73

Hambleton Hall Hotel, ✉ LE15 8TH – ✆ 01572 756991 (booking essential) – www.hambletonhall.com

Hambleton Hall

LUXURY • CLASSIC A beautiful Victorian manor house in a peaceful location, with mature grounds sloping down to Rutland Water. Classical country house drawing rooms boast heavy drapes, open fires and antiques. Good-sized bedrooms are designed by the owner herself and come with a host of thoughtful extras. Service is engaging.

16 rooms – †£ 200/220 ††£ 290/415 – 1 suite

✉ LE15 8TH – ✆ 01572 756991 – www.hambletonhall.com

✿ **Hambleton Hall** – See restaurant listing

OLD ALRESFORD

Hampshire – Pop. 577 – Regional map n° **4**-B2

Pulpo Negro

SPANISH • TAPAS BAR X A characterful, laid-back restaurant in an old townhouse; its name translates as 'Black Octopus'. The stylish interior features exposed brick, rough floorboards and an open kitchen. The chef-owner hails from Barcelona and his tasty, authentic tapas is accompanied by a good choice of Spanish wines.

Carte £ 16/44

28 Broad St ✉ SO24 9AQ – ✆ 01962 732262 (booking essential) – www.pulponegro.co.uk – Closed 25-26 December, 1 January, Sunday, Monday and bank holidays

OLD BURGHCLERE

Hampshire – ✉ Newbury – Regional map n° **4**-B1

Dew Pond

CLASSIC FRENCH • COSY XX A part-16C farmhouse with well-tended gardens leading down to a dew pond. The longstanding restaurant is family owned and run and serves classic French cooking; enjoy an aperitif on the terrace, overlooking the real Watership Down.

Menu £ 36

✉ RG20 9LH – ✆ 01635 278408 – www.dewpond.co.uk – dinner only – Closed 2 weeks Christmas-New Year, Sunday and Monday

OLDHAM

Greater Manchester – Pop. 96 555 – Regional map n° **11**-B2

White Hart Inn

MODERN BRITISH • **CLASSIC DÉCOR** The original part of this stone-built inn dates from 1788 but there's always something new going on here. With its formal restaurant, private dining room, large function room and smart bedrooms, it can be a busy place. The menu offers a good range of refined pub classics, many with a Mediterranean slant.

Menu £ 18 (lunch and early dinner)
- Carte £ 27/49

16 rooms – £ 108/145 £ 175/185

51 Stockport Rd, Lydgate ✉ OL4 4JJ – East : 3 mi by A 669 on A 6050
– 01457 872566 – www.thewhitehart.co.uk
– Closed 1 January and 26 December

OLDSTEAD

North Yorkshire – Regional map n° **13**-C2

Black Swan (Tommy Banks)

MODERN BRITISH • **FAMILY** XX The Black Swan is owned by a family who've farmed in the area for generations. Enjoy an aperitif in the characterful bar, then head upstairs to the restaurant. Modern menus are driven by meats from their farm and produce grown in the garden; cooking is highly skilled and dishes are carefully presented. Antique-furnished bedrooms have smart bathrooms and private patios.

→ Crapaudine beetroot slow-cooked in beef fat. Venison and smoked sloes. Blackened apple with rye ice cream.

Menu £ 98 – tasting menu only

9 rooms – £ 150/260 £ 150/260

✉ YO61 4BL
– 01347 868387 (bookings essential for non-residents)
– www.blackswanoldstead.co.uk
– dinner only and Saturday lunch

OMBERSLEY

Worcestershire – Pop. 623 – Regional map n° **10**-B3

Venture In

TRADITIONAL BRITISH • **COSY** XX A hugely characterful black and white timbered house with 15C origins and a large inglenook fireplace in the bar. Cooking is classically based but has modern overtones and there's always a good choice of specials available.

Menu £ 30/49

Main St ✉ WR9 0EW
– 01905 620552 – www.theventurein.co.uk
– Closed 2 weeks August, 1 week March, 1 week June, 1 week Christmas, Monday and dinner Sunday

ORFORD

Suffolk – ✉ Woodbridge – Pop. 1 153 – Regional map n° **8**-D3

Crown and Castle

HISTORIC • **PERSONALISED** It is thought that the original 12C inn which stood on this site was built into the walls of Orford Castle. The latest incarnation, a Tudor-style house, is run in a pleasantly laid-back manner. Most bedrooms are in chalets and many have terraces and distant sea views. The bistro offers seasonal fare.

21 rooms – £ 140/160 £ 180/200 – 1 suite

✉ IP12 2LJ
– 01394 450205 – www.crownandcastle.co.uk

OSWESTRY

Shropshire – Pop. 16 660 – Regional map n° **10**-A1

Sebastians

TRADITIONAL CUISINE • COSY XX Housed in three characterful 17C cottages, Sebastians is a long-standing restaurant with an open fire, lots of beams and bags of charm. Cooking uses good ingredients and is classically based, and you'll be well looked after by the team. Many of the cosy, characterful bedrooms are set around a courtyard.

Menu £ 48

6 rooms – †£ 75/85 ††£ 85/105 – ☕£ 12

45 Willow St ✉ SY11 1AQ – ✆ 01691 655444 – www.sebastians-hotel.com – dinner only – Closed 25-26 December, 1 January, Sunday-Tuesday and bank holidays except Good Friday

Townhouse

MODERN BRITISH • FASHIONABLE XX Contemporary restaurant in a Georgian townhouse. There's a flamboyant cocktail bar, a sunny terrace and an airy dining room featuring glitzy chandeliers. Classical cooking has a modern edge and dishes are attractively presented.

Carte £ 19/29

35 Willow St ✉ SY11 1AQ – ✆ 01691 659499 – www.townhouseoswestry.com – Closed Sunday dinner

at Rhydycroesau West: 3.5 mi on B4580 ✉ Oswestry

Pen-Y-Dyffryn

TRADITIONAL • COSY An early Victorian rectory in a peaceful countryside setting, with a pretty garden and a lovely outlook. Classical lounges feature antique furnishings and roaring fires. Bedrooms have subtle modern touches and the Coach House rooms come with private terraces. Daily menus use local and organic produce.

12 rooms ☕ – †£ 99 ††£ 140/210

✉ SY10 7JD – ✆ 01691 653700 – www.peny.co.uk – Closed 14 December-15 January

GOOD TIPS!

England's oldest university city has a rich architectural heritage and this is reflected in our hotel selection, with **Malmaison**, for example, offering the opportunity to sleep in a former prison cell. A global restaurant scene sees British, Italian, Spanish and Thai restaurants all featured, with a couple of Bib Gourmands and plenty of pubs too.

OXFORD

Oxfordshire – Pop. 159 994 – Regional map n° **6**-B2

Restaurants

Oxford Kitchen

MODERN BRITISH • MINIMALIST XX Hidden away in trendy Summertown is this bright, modern neighbourhood restaurant; sit downstairs in one of the booths. The chef's knowledge and experience shows in assured, well-balanced, skilfully prepared dishes. Classical flavour combinations are given innovative modern touches and sourcing is top-notch.

→ Pressed tomato terrine with goat's curd, avocado and puffed rice. Roast halibut with apple dashi, kohlrabi and brown shrimps. Pineapple soufflé with coconut sorbet and Malibu sauce.

Menu £ 28/45

Town plan: A1-e – *215 Banbury Rd, Summertown ✉ OX2 7HQ – ✆ 01865 511149 – www.theoxfordkitchen.co.uk – Closed 2-16 January, Sunday and Monday*

Oli's Thai

THAI • FRIENDLY X This lovely little restaurant is set off the beaten track, in an up-and-coming residential area. Start with a drink on the patio then make for the cool, relaxed restaurant; if you haven't booked, try for a seat at the counter. The concise menu offers fresh, meticulously prepared, vibrantly flavoured dishes.

Carte £ 19/28

Town plan: B2-r – *38 Magdalen Rd ✉ OX4 1RB – ✆ 01865 790223 (booking essential) – www.olisthai.com – Closed Saturday dinner, Sunday and Monday*

Magdalen Arms

TRADITIONAL BRITISH • PUB Locals and visitors flock to this large pub to enjoy the lively, easy-going atmosphere. It opens at 10am for tea and cake and even hosts a monthly flea market. The experienced chef-owner creates gutsy, flavoursome dishes with wide-ranging influences and the menu can change up to twice a day.

Carte £ 22/31

Town plan: B2-s – *243 Iffley Rd ✉ OX4 1SJ – ✆ 01865 243159 – www.magdalenarms.co.uk – Closed 24-26 December, 1 January and Monday lunch*

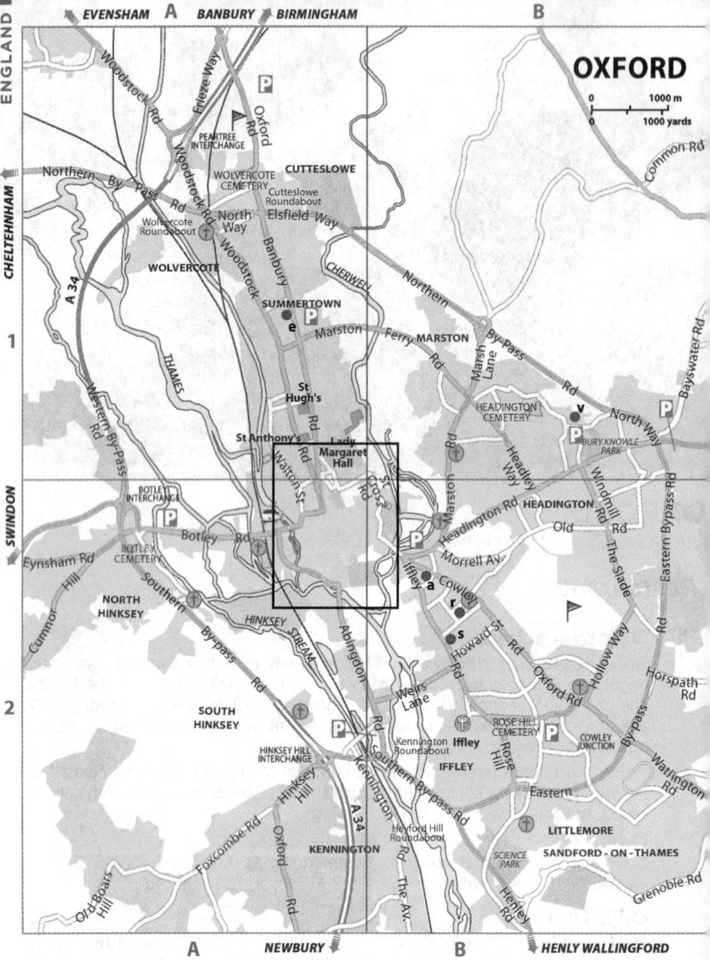

Arbequina

SPANISH • NEIGHBOURHOOD A simply furnished, bohemian tapas bar: sit downstairs by the vintage stainless steel counter or upstairs in the bay window. The concise menu offers tasty, authentic, filling tapas dishes; 3 plus dessert is about right.

Carte £14/26

Town plan: B2-a – *74 Cowley Rd ✉ OX4 1JB*
– ✆ 01865 792777 – www.arbequina.co.uk – dinner only and lunch Friday-Saturday
– Closed Christmas-New Year and Sunday

An important business lunch or dinner with friends?
The symbol ⛭ indicates restaurants with private rooms.

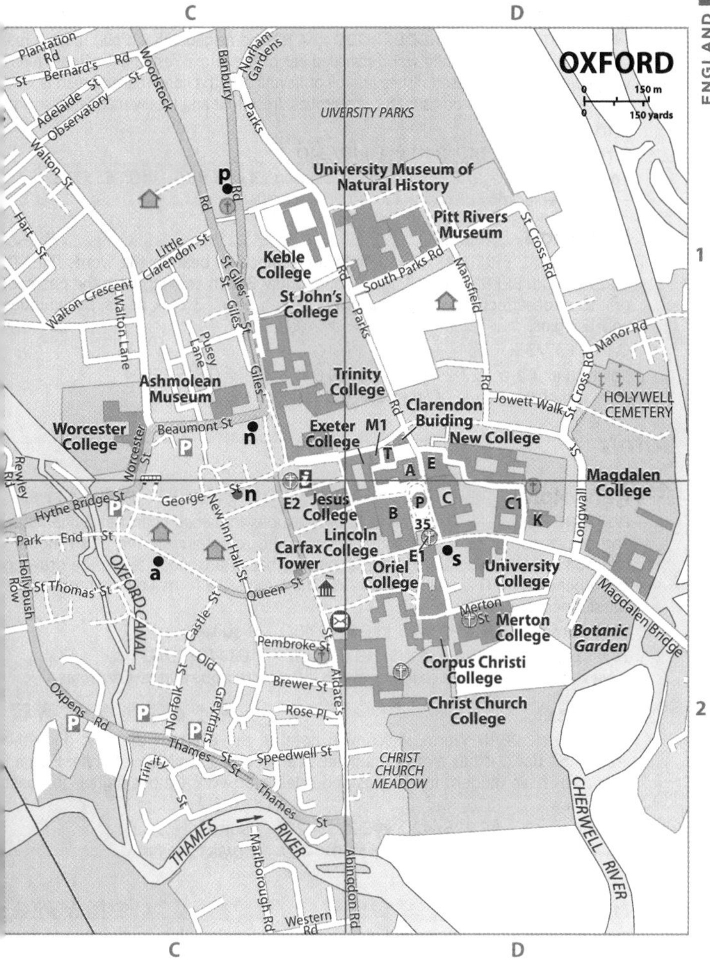

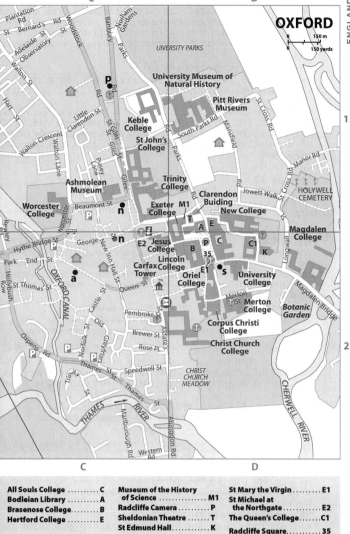

All Souls College	C	Museum of the History of Science	M1	St Mary the Virgin	E1
Bodleian Library	A	Radcliffe Camera	P	St Michael at the Northgate	E2
Brasenose College	B	Sheldonian Theatre	T	The Queen's College	C1
Hertford College	E	St Edmund Hall	K	Radcliffe Square	35

Black Boy

INTERNATIONAL • NEIGHBOURHOOD A relaxed neighbourhood pub that's a real social hub. Dine in the white wood-panelled bar or the formal restaurant with its funky wallpaper. Classically based dishes are full of flavour and the home-baked bread is hard to resist. Boutique bedrooms feature bathrobes, fresh fruit and locally made furnishings.

Carte £21/49

5 rooms – £140/240 £140/240

Town plan: B1-v – *91 Old High St, Headington ✉ OX3 9HT – 01865 741137 – www.theblackboy.uk.com – Closed 26 December*

Pint Shop

TRADITIONAL BRITISH • PUB Plate glass windows bearing the words 'MEAT', 'BREAD' and 'BEER' say it all. Interesting, gutsy British cooking uses the charcoal grill to good effect. The large bar offers 18 keg beers, 3 cask beers, 80 whiskies and 120 gins.

Carte £17/33

Town plan: C2-n – *27-29 George St ✉ OX1 2AU – 01865 251194 – www.pintshop.co.uk – Closed 25-26 December and 1 January*

Hotels

Randolph

HISTORIC • CLASSIC This grand old lady exudes immense charm and character, and comes complete with an intricate wrought iron staircase and plush modern bedrooms. Have a cocktail in the magnificent bar or afternoon tea in the drawing room beneath Sir Osbert Lancaster oils. The impressive formal dining room offers classic menus.

151 rooms – £292/375 £324/480 – 9 suites

Town plan: C1-n – *Beaumont St. ✉ OX1 2LN – 0344 879 9132 – www.macdonaldhotels.co.uk/randolph – Restricted opening at Christmas*

Old Bank

LUXURY • MODERN Warm, welcoming hotel in the heart of the city: once the area's first bank. It has a smart neo-classical façade and plenty of style. Elegant bedrooms have modern furnishings and eclectic artwork – those higher up boast great views.

43 rooms – £225/420 £225/420 – 1 suite

Town plan: D2-s – *92-94 High St ✉ OX1 4BJ – 01865 799599 – www.oldbank-hotel.co.uk*

Malmaison

BUSINESS • HISTORIC Unique hotel in the 13C castle prison, where a pleasant rooftop terrace contrasts with a moody interior. The most characterful bedrooms are in the old A Wing cells; feature rooms are in the Governor's House and House of Correction. The basement brasserie serves an accessible menu, with steaks a speciality.

95 rooms – £169/440 £169/440 – £14 – 3 suites

Town plan: C2-a – *Oxford Castle, 3 New Rd ✉ OX1 1AY – 01865 268400 – www.malmaison.com*

Old Parsonage

TOWNHOUSE • PERSONALISED This ivy-clad sandstone parsonage sits in the historic town centre and dates from the 1660s. Enter into the original house via a pretty terrace; inside it's chic and modern – bold greys and purples feature in the bedrooms, along with the latest mod cons. Appealing menus offer classic British comfort food.

35 rooms – £225/420 £225/420

Town plan: C1-p – *1 Banbury Rd ✉ OX2 6NN – 01865 310210 – www.oldparsonage-hotel.co.uk*

at Great Milton Southeast: 12 mi by A40 off A329 ✉ Oxford

Belmond Le Manoir aux Quat' Saisons (Raymond Blanc)

FRENCH • LUXURY XXXX Legendary French chef Raymond Blanc presides over this iconic restaurant set within a quintessentially English country house. You cannot help but fall in love with it: the setting is divine, the house is graciously elegant and a feeling of luxury envelops you. Enjoy a fine array of canapés in a sumptuous lounge then head through to the magical beamed restaurant comprising several interconnecting rooms - the perfect place to celebrate an occasion. In summer, be sure to sit in the conservatory for views over the manicured gardens (and ask for a garden tour after your meal!)

Top quality seasonal ingredients and beautifully fresh produce from the kitchen garden underpin the skilfully executed cooking - which has a classical French base and a light, modern touch - and the main menu is fittingly entitled 'Spécialités du Moment'. Flavours are intense, combinations are sophisticated and the presentation shows an eye for detail. Desserts are always a highlight and the service is polished.

→ Risotto of spring garden vegetables and chervil cream. Roasted fillet of Aberdeen Angus beef, braised Jacob's ladder, alliums, red wine essence. Exotic fruit ravioli with kaffir limes and coconut jus.

Menu £ 95/170

Church Rd ✉ OX44 7PD - ✆ 01844 278881 (booking essential) - www.belmond.com - Closed Monday lunch

Belmond Le Manoir aux Quat' Saisons

GRAND LUXURY • PERSONALISED This quintessential English country house part-dates from the 15C and is surrounded by majestic gardens. Guest areas are sumptuous, bedrooms are luxurious (ask for one in the Garden Wing) and service is top-class. Enjoy afternoon tea in the conservatory or on the delightful terrace overlooking the grounds.

32 rooms ☕ - †£ 695/1050 ††£ 695/1050 - 14 suites

Church Rd ✉ OX44 7PD - ✆ 01844 278881 - www.belmond.com/lemanoir

Belmond Le Manoir aux Quat' Saisons - See restaurant listing

PADSTOW

Cornwall - Pop. 2 449 - Regional map n° **1**-B2

Paul Ainsworth at No.6

MODERN CUISINE • INTIMATE X A delightful Georgian townhouse on a harbour backwater, with a clubby lounge and a funky dining room. Original modern cooking uses first class ingredients, flavours are clearly defined and there are lots of Cornish references. Service is friendly and enthusiastic and diners are encouraged to talk to the chefs.

→ Smoked haddock quiche Lorraine. Aged soy-glazed duck with clear Peking tea and 'pyo' salad. Bread and butter pudding and roast vanilla ice cream.

Menu £ 29 (lunch) - Carte £ 56/76

6 Middle St ✉ PL28 8AP - ✆ 01841 532093 - www.paul-ainsworth.co.uk - Closed 14 January-7 February, Sunday and Monday

Rick Stein's Café

INTERNATIONAL • BISTRO X A deceptively large café hidden behind a tiny shop front on a side street. The concise, seasonally changing menu offers tasty, unfussy dishes which display influences from Thailand, Morocco and the Med. The homemade bread is worth a try, as are the good value set dinner menu. Bedrooms are comfy and simply furnished; have breakfast in the café or small courtyard garden.

Menu £ 24 (dinner) - Carte £ 22/38

3 rooms ☕ - †£ 120/165 ††£ 120/165

10 Middle St ✉ PL28 8AP - ✆ 01841 532700 (booking essential at dinner) - www.rickstein.com - Closed 24-26 December and 1 May

Seafood

SEAFOOD • ELEGANT XxX Stylish, laid-back, local institution – dominated by a large pewter-topped bar. Daily menus showcase fresh fish and shellfish. Classic dishes sit alongside those influenced by Rick Stein's travels; perhaps Singapore chilli crab or Madras fish curry. New England style bedrooms boast good quality furnishings; some have terraces or balconies and estuary views.

Menu £ 41 – Carte £ 42/86

22 rooms – †£ 165/300 ††£ 165/300

Riverside ✉ PL28 8BY
– ✆ 01841 532700 (booking essential) – www.rickstein.com
– Closed 25-26 December

Appleton's

MEDITERRANEAN CUISINE • FRIENDLY X An old mill plays host to a winery with over 11,000 vines and this bright, spacious, first floor restaurant. Enjoy wines, ciders and apple juices made on-site while gazing down the valley and dining on fresh, unfussy Italian-influenced dishes. On warmer days have Sunday brunch on the terrace.

Carte £ 27/46

Trevibban Mill, Dark Ln ✉ PL27 7SE – South : 3.5 mi by A 389 off B 3274
– ✆ 01841 541355 – www.appletonsatthevineyard.com – Closed January and Sunday dinner-Tuesday

Prawn on the Lawn

SEAFOOD • TAPAS BAR X If you like seafood then you'll love this modern fishmongers-cum-seafood bar with its beautiful display of super-fresh fish out front and its tasty tapas-style sharing plates of shellfish and fish. It's cosy, with some counter seating.

Carte £ 30/61

11 Duke St ✉ PL28 8AB
– ✆ 01841 532223 – www.prawnonthelawn.com – Closed 1 January-4 February, Sunday October-Easter and Monday

Rojano's in the Square

ITALIAN • BRASSERIE X A bright, modern restaurant geared up to family dining, with a small cocktail bar, two floors for dining and a glass-enclosed terrace. Italian dishes are hearty and full of flavour and Cornish ingredients are to the fore.

Menu £ 19 – Carte £ 19/47

9 Mill Sq ✉ PL28 8AE
– ✆ 01841 532796 – www.paul-ainsworth.co.uk – Closed 24-26 December and 6-16 January

St Petroc's

SEAFOOD • BISTRO X Attractive house on a steep hill, with an oak-furnished bistro and terraces to both the front and rear. The menu offers simply prepared classics with an emphasis on seafood and grills. Smart, well-appointed bedrooms are split between the house and an annexe – where you'll also find a small lounge and library.

Menu £ 20 (lunch) – Carte £ 30/53

14 rooms – †£ 165/260 ††£ 165/260

4 New St ✉ PL28 8EA
– ✆ 01841 532700 (booking essential) – www.rickstein.com – Closed 24-26 December

Is breakfast included? If it is, the cup symbol appears after the number of rooms.

Padstow Townhouse

TOWNHOUSE • ELEGANT Everything's been thought of at this beautiful 18C townhouse. Six luxurious, individually styled suites come with top quality linens and bespoke toiletries made by local company St Kitts. There's an honesty bar in the kitchen pantry; breakfast is taken in your room or at their nearby restaurant.

6 rooms – £ 280/300 £ 320/380

16-18 High St PL28 8BB – 01841 550950 – www.paul-ainsworth.co.uk – Closed 23-26 December

Paul Ainsworth at No.6 – See restaurant listing

Treverbyn House

TOWNHOUSE • PERSONALISED A charming Edwardian house built for a wine merchant and run by a delightful owner. Comfy bedrooms feature interesting furniture from local sale rooms, along with roll-top baths and harbour views – the Turret Room is the best. Have breakfast in your bedroom, the dining room or the garden.

3 rooms – £ 100 £ 130/135

Station Rd PL28 8DA – 01841 532855 – www.treverbynhouse.com – Closed November-March

PAINSWICK

Gloucestershire – Pop. 1 762 – Regional map n° **2**-C1

The Painswick

HISTORIC • PERSONALISED A wonderful Regency house in the heart of a delightful village. A lovely inner hall leads to a relaxed, stylish sitting room but the jewel in the crown is the magnificent wisteria-clad stone terrace with valley views – the perfect spot for afternoon tea. Immaculate bedrooms have an understated designer feel.

16 rooms – £ 139 £ 139/319 – £ 16 – 1 suite

Kemps Ln GL6 6YB – 01452 813688 – www.thepainswick.co.uk

PATELEY BRIDGE

North Yorkshire – Harrogate – Pop. 1 432 – Regional map n° **13**-B2

Yorke Arms

MODERN CUISINE • FRIENDLY XXX This charming 17C inn sits on the green of a small hamlet and champions all things Yorkshire. Choose between the laid-back 'Little Dining Room' and the more formal 'Restaurant', where top quality local ingredients inform creative modern cooking. Stylish bedrooms also display Yorkshire themes.

→ Langoustine with crab and saltwater. Nidderdale beef fillet, rump and tongue with hyssop and fig. Rhubarb with strawberry, meringue and buckwheat.

Menu £ 75/105 – Carte £ 36/55

18 rooms (dinner included) – £ 275/300 £ 375/600 – 6 suites

Ramsgill-in-Nidderdale HG3 5RL – Northwest : 5 mi by Low Wath Rd – 01423 755243 – www.yorke-arms.co.uk – Closed Sunday and Monday

PENN

Buckinghamshire – Pop. 3 779 – Regional map n° **6**-D2

Old Queens Head

TRADITIONAL BRITISH • PUB Legend has it that Lord Penn inherited this characterful country pub when he won a game of cards against Charles II. Robust, satisfying dishes follow the seasons and have a British heart. The sunny terrace is a popular spot.

Carte £ 23/46

Hammersley Ln HP10 8EY – 01494 813371 – www.oldqueensheadpenn.co.uk

PENRITH

Cumbria – Pop. 15 181 – Regional map n° **12**-B2

Brooklands

TOWNHOUSE • PERSONALISED A friendly, welcoming couple run this Victorian terraced guesthouse; they've been here for years and have lots of regular guests. Stylish bedrooms are furnished to a high standard and come with smart modern bathrooms – although some subtle Victorian influences still remain. Breakfast is a feast.

6 rooms – £ 45/75 £ 88/98

2 Portland Pl ✉ CA11 7QN – ✆ 01768 863395 – www.brooklandsguesthouse.com – Closed Christmas and New Year

at Temple Sowerby East: 6.75 mi by A66 ✉ Penrith

Temple Sowerby House

COUNTRY HOUSE • CLASSIC An attractive, enthusiastically run, red-brick Georgian mansion with spacious, classically styled guest areas. Traditional country house bedrooms boast antique furnishings and contemporary facilities. Ambitious, modern menus of local, seasonal produce are served overlooking the enclosed lawned gardens.

12 rooms – £ 100/120 £ 130/170

✉ CA10 1RZ – ✆ 017683 61578 – www.templesowerby.com

at Askham South: 6 mi by A6

Allium at Askham Hall

MODERN BRITISH • INTIMATE XX Relax by the fire in the sitting room then head through to the modish country house restaurant with its unique tiled floor and elegant private room. Accomplished modern dishes showcase meats from their farm and veg from the kitchen garden. Dishes are stimulating and flavour contrasts are well judged.

Menu £ 50/65

✉ CA10 2PF – ✆ 01931 712350 (booking essential) – www.askhamhall.co.uk – dinner only – Closed 3 January-mid-February, Christmas, Sunday and Monday

Askham Hall

COUNTRY HOUSE • CONTEMPORARY At the edge of the Lowther Estate you'll find this fine, family-run castle dating from the 1200s and surrounded by beautiful gardens. It's been stylishly yet sympathetically refurbished and its spacious rooms are full of original features and old family furnishings. Opt for a bedroom in the Pele Tower.

18 rooms – £ 138/308 £ 150/320

✉ CA10 2PF – ✆ 01931 712350 – www.askhamhall.co.uk – Closed January-mid-February and Christmas

Allium at Askham Hall – See restaurant listing

PENZANCE

Cornwall – Pop. 16 336 – Regional map n° **1**-A3

Harris's

CLASSIC CUISINE • INTIMATE XX Long-standing, split-level restaurant with a spiral staircase and an unusual Welsh black metal plate ceiling; run by a keen husband and wife. Classical cooking uses seasonal Cornish produce; try the steamed lobster when it's in season.

Carte £ 34/43

46 New St ✉ TR18 2LZ – ✆ 01736 364408 – www.harrissrestaurant.co.uk – Closed 3 weeks winter, 25-26 December, Sunday and Monday

Shore

SEAFOOD • INTIMATE XX The name refers to the cooking rather than the location of this small bistro. The experienced chef works alone: his produce is ethically sourced and many of his precisely prepared dishes have Mediterranean or Asian influences.

Menu £ 45/63 – Carte approx. £ 42

13-14 Alverton St ✉ TR18 2QP
– ✆ 01736 362444 (booking essential at lunch)
– www.theshorerestaurant.uk
– Closed 2 weeks January, Sunday and Monday

Chapel House

GRAND TOWNHOUSE • CONTEMPORARY A smartly refurbished 18C house with a pretty walled garden. Sumptuous lounges are filled with modern art and there's a fabulous basement dining room where they serve breakfast and pre-booked weekend meals. Bedrooms have a cool, understated elegance and sea views: all feature fresh flowers and hand-crafted oak furnishings and one has a bathroom with a retractable roof!

6 rooms – £ 125/150 £ 150/210

Chapel St ✉ TR18 4AQ
– ✆ 01736 362024 – www.chapelhouse.pz.co.uk

Chy-An-Mor

TOWNHOUSE • PERSONALISED This fine Georgian townhouse overlooks the promenade; fittingly, its name means 'House of the Sea'. Bedrooms have lovely soft furnishings – two have 6ft cast iron beds. In the evening, twinkling garden lights welcome you home and at breakfast they offer homemade muffins, Scotch pancakes and granola sundaes.

9 rooms – £ 49/75 £ 85/99

15 Regent Terr ✉ TR18 4DW
– ✆ 01736 363441 – www.chyanmor.co.uk
– Closed November-March

PERRANUTHNOE - Cornwall → See Marazion

PERSHORE

Worcestershire – Pop. 7 125 – Regional map n° **10**-C3

Belle House

TRADITIONAL BRITISH • TRADITIONAL DÉCOR XX A pleasantly restored Georgian house in the centre of town, offering classically based cooking with modern touches; be sure to try the homemade bread. The well-stocked 'traiteur' selling freshly prepared takeaway dishes is a hit.

Menu £ 27/35 **s**

Bridge St ✉ WR10 1AJ
– ✆ 01386 555055 – www.belle-house.co.uk
– Closed first 2 weeks January, 25-30 December, Sunday-Tuesday

Barn

TRADITIONAL • COSY A hugely characterful series of hillside outbuildings, run by a charming owner. There's a homely beamed lounge and three warmly decorated bedrooms; one even boasts a sauna. The apple juice comes from the fruit trees in the garden.

3 rooms – £ 70 £ 95

Pensham Hill House, Pensham ✉ WR10 3HA
– Southeast : 1 mi by B 4084
– ✆ 01386 555270 – www.pensham-barn.co.uk

at Eckington Southwest: 4 mi by A4104 on B4080

Eckington Manor

MODERN CUISINE • DESIGN XX You'll find this proudly run 13C manor house and its characterful, converted barns on a 300 acre farm. In the restaurant, a husband and wife duo offer a constantly evolving set priced menu of refined, classical dishes which feature plenty of farm produce. For those who want to get involved there's a cookery school, along with stylish bedrooms for those wishing to stay.

Menu £ 28/48

17 rooms – †£ 95/169 ††£ 119/279

Manor Farm, Hammock Rd ✉ WR10 3BH – (via Drakes Bridge Rd) – ✆ 01386 751600 – www.eckingtonmanor.co.uk – dinner only and lunch Thursday-Sunday – Closed 25-26 December, 2-16 January, Sunday dinner, Monday and Tuesday

PETERBOROUGH

Peterborough – Pop. 161 707 – Regional map n° **8**-A2

Prévost

CREATIVE BRITISH • DESIGN XX You enter via an alleyway into a bright, spacious room, where local artists' work is displayed on the walls and the tables overlook a small kitchen garden. Lunch sees a good value 3 course set menu, while dinner offer 3, 5 or 9 courses. Attractive dishes have a creative Scandic style.

Menu £ 20/75 – tasting menu only

20 Priestgate ✉ PE1 1JA – ✆ 01733 313623 (booking essential) – www.prevostpeterborough.co.uk – Closed 1-14 January, 25 December and Sunday-Tuesday

PETERSFIELD

Hampshire – Pop. 14 974 – Regional map n° **4**-C2

JSW

MODERN BRITISH • INTIMATE XXX A smart 17C former inn on the main road, with heavy beams and a modern rustic style. Classical cooking uses recognisable combinations of ingredients and displays French influences. An impressive, well-priced wine list accompanies. Simply furnished bedrooms come with a continental breakfast.

Menu £ 45/55 **s**

4 rooms – †£ 95/115 ††£ 125/145

20 Dragon St ✉ GU31 4JJ – ✆ 01730 262030 (booking essential) – www.jswrestaurant.com – Closed 2 weeks January, 2 weeks April, 2 weeks August, Sunday dinner, Monday, Tuesday and lunch Wednesday

PETWORTH

West Sussex – Pop. 2 544 – Regional map n° **4**-C2

Old Railway Station

HISTORIC • PERSONALISED The perfect place for train enthusiasts: 8 of the 10 bedrooms are sited in wonderfully restored, genuine Pullman carriages which display impressive marquetry. They are sited at what was the platform; check in at the ticket booth.

10 rooms – †£ 90/128 ††£ 120/210

✉ GU28 0JF – South : 1.5 mi by A 285 – ✆ 01798 342346 – www.old-station.co.uk – Closed 23-26 December

at Tillington West: 1 mi on A272

Horse Guards Inn

REGIONAL CUISINE • RUSTIC In the heart of a quiet village sits this charming mid-17C inn, with views over the valley from its lavender-filled garden. Cooking mixes the rustic and the more elaborate and local seafood stands out. Service is chatty and willing. Bedrooms are charmingly understated; families can book the cottage next door.

Carte £ 23/38

3 rooms – £ 95/130 £ 110/170

Upperton Rd ✉ GU28 9AF – ✆ 01798 342332 – www.thehorseguardsinn.co.uk – Closed 25-26 December

at Lickfold Northwest : 6 mi by A 272 ✉ Petworth

Lickfold Inn

MODERN BRITISH • COSY XX A pretty Grade II listed brick and timber pub with a characterful lounge-bar serving small plates and a formal first floor restaurant. Terse descriptions hide the true complexities of the innovative dishes, which echo the seasons and are given a touch of theatre. Staff are friendly and eager to please.

Menu £ 19 (weekday lunch)/45 – Carte £ 34/50

Highstead Ln ✉ GU28 9EY – ✆ 01789 532535 (booking essential) – www.thelickfoldinn.co.uk – Closed 2 weeks January, Sunday dinner, Monday except bank holidays and Tuesday

PICKERING

North Yorkshire – Pop. 6 588 – Regional map n° **13**-C1

White Swan Inn

HISTORIC • COSY A characterful 17C coaching inn – its cosy bar and lounge decorated in modern hues. Bedrooms are appealing and come with smart bathrooms; the Hideaway rooms in the old stables have heated stone floors, and one even has a bath in the lounge. The brasserie-style restaurant specialises in meats and grills.

21 rooms – £ 121/131 £ 151/161 – 2 suites

Market Pl ✉ YO18 7AA – ✆ 01751 472288 – www.white-swan.co.uk

PLUMTREE – Nottinghamshire

→ See Nottingham

PLYMOUTH

Plymouth – Pop. 234 982 – Regional map n° **1**-C2

Greedy Goose

MODERN BRITISH • ELEGANT XX Smart restaurant housed in a delightful building dating from 1482 and named after the children's book 'Chocolate Mousse for Greedy Goose'. Cooking is modern and flavoursome and the local beef is superb. Sit in the 'quad' in summer.

Menu £ 20 (lunch and early dinner) – Carte £ 27/59

Prysten House, Finewell St ✉ PL1 2AE – ✆ 01752 252001 – www.thegreedygoose.co.uk – Closed Christmas and Monday

Barbican Kitchen

INTERNATIONAL • BRASSERIE X An informal eatery in the Plymouth Gin Distillery (where gin was once distilled for the Navy). Brasserie menus offer a good choice of simply cooked dishes, with classic comfort food to the fore; vegetarians are well catered for.

Menu £ 19 (lunch and early dinner) – Carte £ 26/52 **s**

Plymouth Gin Distillery, 60 Southside St ✉ PL1 2LQ – ✆ 01752 604448 – www.barbicankitchen.com – Closed 23-26 December, 30 December-3 January and Sunday

ENGLAND

Fig Tree @ 36

MODERN BRITISH • FRIENDLY X A young local couple run this inviting neighbourhood restaurant near Royal William Yard; it's named after a tree they found in the small rear courtyard. Alongside these fruits, you'll find regional produce and fish landed just down the road. Fresh, unfussy cooking lets the ingredients speak for themselves.

Menu £ 18 - Carte £ 27/40

36 Admiralty St ✉ PL1 3RU - ✆ 01752 253247 - www.thefigtreeat36.co.uk - closed 25-26 December, 1 January, Sunday dinner, Monday and lunch Tuesday

at Plympton St Maurice East: 6 mi by A374 on B3416✉ Plymouth

St Elizabeth's House

TRADITIONAL • PERSONALISED This former convent is now a cosy family-run hotel. Eye-catching fabrics add splashes of colour to the spacious bedrooms and many come with feature bathrooms; you can even watch TV from the spa bath in the St Elizabeth's Suite. Have a drink at the pewter-topped bar then dine formally overlooking the gardens.

15 rooms - £ 99/129 £ 109/159 - 1 suite

Longbrook St ✉ PL7 1NJ - ✆ 01752 344840 - www.stelizabeths.co.uk - Closed 24-26 December

PLYMPTON ST MAURICE Devon - Plymouth ➜ See Plymouth

POLPERRO

Cornwall - ✉ Looe - Regional map n° **1**-B2

Trenderway Farm

FAMILY • RURAL 16C farmhouse and outbuildings set in 206 acres of working farmland. Well-appointed bedrooms come in a mix of styles and some have seating areas and kitchenettes. A cream tea is served on arrival and breakfast is cooked on the Aga.

7 rooms - £ 109/175 £ 109/175

✉ PL13 2LY - Northeast : 2 mi by A 387 - ✆ 01503 272214 - www.trenderwayfarm.co.uk

PONTELAND - Northumberland ➜ See Newcastle upon Tyne

POOLE

Poole - Pop. 154 718 - Regional map n° **2**-C3

Rick Stein

SEAFOOD • FASHIONABLE XX Rick may be expanding his empire but he's keeping his fishy theme. The large menu offers everything from cod and chips to seafood platters and all his classics are there, including turbot hollandaise and plaice alla carlina. Start with a drink in the sleek bar then enjoy superb sea views from the restaurant.

Menu £ 25 (weekday lunch) - Carte £ 30/58

10-14 Banks Rd, Sandbanks ✉ BH13 7QB - Southeast : 4.75 mi by B 3068 and Sandbanks Rd - ✆ 01202 283000 (booking essential) - www.rickstein.com

Guildhall Tavern

SEAFOOD • BISTRO XX Proudly run restaurant opposite the Guildhall, with a bright, cheery interior and a nautical theme. Tasty, classical French dishes are generously proportioned and largely seafood-based. They also host monthly gourmet evenings.

Menu £ 21/30 (weekdays) - Carte £ 29/73

15 Market St ✉ BH15 1NB - ✆ 01202 671717 - www.guildhalltavern.co.uk - Closed 25 December-6 January, 2 weeks April, 2 weeks July, Sunday and Monday

Hotel du Vin

TOWNHOUSE • MODERN A strikingly extended Queen Anne property in the old town. Smart guest areas have eye-catching wine-themed murals; stylish, modern bedrooms are named after wine or champagne houses – one boasts an 8ft bed and twin roll-top baths. Local produce features in classic French dishes and there's a 300 bin wine list.

38 rooms – £ 119/234 £ 119/249

7-11 Thames St. BH15 1JN – 01305 819027 – www.hotelduvin.com

POOLEY BRIDGE

Cumbria – Regional map n° **12**-B2

Sharrow Bay Country House

CLASSIC CUISINE • ELEGANT XXX A charming country house in an idyllic lakeside location. Enjoy an aperitif by the fire in the sitting room then head through to one of two dining rooms – Lakeside offers stunning views. Well-judged dishes have a classical base and subtle modern touches; save room for their renowned sticky toffee pudding.

Menu £ 25/68

Sharrow Bay Country House Hotel, Ullswater CA10 2LZ – South : 2 mi on Howtown Rd – 017684 86301 (booking essential) – www.sharrowbay.co.uk

Sharrow Bay Country House

COUNTRY HOUSE • CLASSIC This iconic English country house sits in a stunning spot on the shore of Lake Ullswater and has the Lakeland hills as its backdrop. It has a charmingly traditional style and a tranquil feel; take in views of the water while enjoying afternoon tea. Bedrooms are elegant and luxurious.

17 rooms – £ 155/395 £ 165/395

Ullswater CA10 2LZ – South : 2 mi on Howtown Rd – 017684 86301 – www.sharrowbay.co.uk

Sharrow Bay Country House – See restaurant listing

at Watermillock Southwest 2.5 mi by B5320 on A592 Penrith

Another Place, The Lake

FAMILY • TRENDY A stunning spot on the shore of Lake Ullswater plays host to this stylishly understated, activity-led hotel, which has a laid-back atmosphere and caters well for children. The Living Space is ideal for an informal drink and a pub-style dish, while more sophisticated Rampsbeck serves a menu of classics.

40 rooms – £ 128/289 £ 170/289 – 2 suites

CA11 0LP – 017684 86442 – www.another.place/the-lake/

PORLOCK

Somerset – Minehead – Pop. 1 395 – Regional map n° **2**-A2

Cross Lane House

HISTORIC • PERSONALISED A very stylishly restored farmhouse and outbuildings dating from 1484; a short walk from the South West Coastal Path. Inside the old and the new have been cleverly blended, with great attention paid to detail. Cake is served on arrival and afternoon tea is a feature; there is even a small gift shop! The intimate formal restaurant offers a concise menu of modern dishes.

4 rooms – £ 145/200 £ 145/200

Allerford TA24 8HW – East : 1.25 mi on A 39 – 01643 863276 – www.crosslanehouse.com – Closed 3 January-12 February and 1 week mid-November

Oaks

TRADITIONAL • CLASSIC An imposing Edwardian house with great views over the weir and bay – the builder quarried the stone used to build it himself. The antique-filled entrance hall boasts a beautiful parquet floor and large bedrooms come with fresh flowers and sherry. Dine from a classic daily menu; every table has a view.

7 rooms – †£ 140 ††£ 150/180

TA24 8ES – 01643 862265 – www.oakshotel.co.uk – Closed November-April

PORT GAVERNE

Regional map n° **1**-B2

Pilchards (N)

SEAFOOD • SIMPLE X Park in Port Isaac and walk over to this modern timber and glass building with a large terraced garden, which overlooks the bay where the famous Cornish pilchards were once landed. The seafood-orientated menu offers both small and large plates, with whole fish grilled over charcoal a speciality.

Carte £ 25/31

PL29 3SQ – 01208 880891 (booking essential)
– www.pilchardsatportgaverne.co.uk – Restricted opening November-March

PORTHLEVEN

Cornwall – Pop. 3 059 – Regional map n° **1**-A3

Kota

ASIAN INFLUENCES • RUSTIC XX Welcoming harbourside granary with thick stone walls, a tiled floor and an array of wood furnishings; its name means 'shellfish' in Maori. Menus mix unfussy and more elaborate dishes and display subtle Asian influences courtesy of the owner's Chinese and Malaysian background. Many of the ingredients are foraged. Bedrooms are simply furnished – one overlooks the harbour.

Menu £ 28 (dinner) – Carte £ 27/45

2 rooms – †£ 75/105 ††£ 85/120

Harbour Head TR13 9JA – 01326 562407 – www.kotarestaurant.co.uk
– dinner only and lunch Friday-Saturday – Closed January, 25-26 December and Sunday

Rick Stein

SEAFOOD • FASHIONABLE XX This old harbourside clay store has been transformed into a smart restaurant with floor to ceiling windows and a first floor terrace. Top quality seafood small plates are inspired by Rick Stein's travels and sharing is encouraged.

Menu £ 22 (lunch) – Carte £ 25/41

Mount Pleasant Rd TR13 9JS – 01326 565636 – www.rickstein.com – Closed 25 December, Sunday dinner and Monday in winter

Square

MODERN CUISINE • SIMPLE X In summer, bag a table on the terrace of this small harbourside bistro; in winter, cosy up and watch the waves crash on the harbour wall. Coffee and cakes give way snacks and sharing platters, followed by well-prepared modern classics with punchy flavours. They have a deli and ice cream shop next door.

Menu £ 20/23 – Carte £ 27/36

7 Fore St TR13 9HQ – 01326 573911 – www.thesquareatporthleven.co.uk
– Closed Sunday dinner in winter

PORT ISAAC

Cornwall – Regional map n° **1**-B2

✿✿ Restaurant Nathan Outlaw (Nathan Outlaw)

SEAFOOD • INTIMATE XX He might not be Cornish by birth but Nathan Outlaw has certainly made Cornwall his home and he has been warmly welcomed by the locals. His smart yet relaxed restaurant sits in a great position on the headland, just a stone's throw from the harbour, and the views from the first floor dining room are stunning. If you'd rather keep your focus on the food though, there's also a Chef's Table opposite the open kitchen on the ground floor.

There is no other chef in the country who understands and executes seafood cookery so well and his name has become synonymous with ultra-fresh fish and shellfish. His no-choice set menus focus on seafood landed just down the road at Port Isaac harbour and his carefully crafted dishes feature classical combinations which keep the focus firmly on the main ingredient.

→ Raw scallops with peas and mint. John Dory, hazelnuts and red wine dressing. Strawberry ice cream sandwich.

Menu £ 130 – tasting menu only

6 New Rd ✉ PL29 3SB – ✆ 01208 880896 (booking essential) – www.nathan-outlaw.com – dinner only and lunch Thursday-Saturday – Closed January and Sunday-Tuesday

✿ Outlaw's Fish Kitchen

SEAFOOD • INTIMATE X This intimate 15C building has low ceilings and wonky walls and is found in the heart of this famous harbourside fishing village. The day boats guide the menu, which offers a delicious mix of old favourites and appealing small plates – 3 or 4 dishes should suffice. Cornish gins, beers and wines also feature.

→ Cured brill, basil, pistachio and anchovy mayonnaise. Lemon sole with crispy oyster and cucumber chutney. Rhubarb and custard 'baked Alaska'.

Carte £ 25/36

1 Middle St ✉ PL29 3RH – ✆ 01208 881183 (booking essential at dinner) – www.nathan-outlaw.com/outlaws-fish-kitchen/ – Closed 22 December-31 January, Sunday and Monday

PORTLOE

Cornwall – Regional map n° **1**-B3

Lugger

INN • COSY This 17C smugglers' inn sits in a picturesque fishing village and affords dramatic views over the rugged bay. It's snug and cosy, with open fires, low ceilings and friendly service. Have a drink on the terrace and dinner in the clean-lined, Scandic-style dining room, which serves seafood fresh from the bay.

24 rooms – †£ 145/295 ††£ 155/320

✉ TR2 5RD – ✆ 01872 501322 – www.luggerhotel.co.uk

PORTSCATHO

Cornwall – ✉ Truro – Regional map n° **1**-B3

✿ Driftwood

MODERN CUISINE • DESIGN XX A bright New England style restaurant set in an attractive hotel, in a peaceful clifftop setting; it's delightfully run by a friendly team and boasts superb views out to sea. Unfussy, modern, seasonally pertinent dishes display technical adroitness and feature excellent flavour and texture combinations.

→ Scallops with cauliflower, vanilla and lime. Roast cod with mussels, pickled cucumber and dill. Poached rhubarb and blood orange meringue with shortbread crumb.

Menu £ 75

Driftwood Hotel, Rosevine ✉ TR2 5EW – North : 2 mi by A 3078 – ✆ 01872 580644 (booking essential) – www.driftwoodhotel.co.uk – dinner only – Closed 10 December-31 January

Driftwood

COUNTRY HOUSE · PERSONALISED A charming clifftop hotel looking out over mature grounds, which stretch down to the shore and a private beach. Stylish, contemporary guest areas are decorated with pieces of driftwood. Smart bedrooms – in the main house and annexed cottages – have a good level of modern facilities; some have decked terraces.

15 rooms – £ 179/226 £ 210/295

Rosevine ✉ TR2 5EW – North : 2 mi by A 3078
– ✆ 01872 580644 – www.driftwoodhotel.co.uk – Closed 11 December-1 February

✿ **Driftwood** – See restaurant listing

PORTSMOUTH and SOUTHSEA

Portsmouth – Pop. 238 137 – Regional map n° **4**-B3

Restaurant 27

MODERN BRITISH · NEIGHBOURHOOD XX This elegant restaurant is professionally and passionately run. Attractively presented, contemporary dishes have a slight Scandic style; they only serve tasting menus, supplemented by a set priced Sunday lunch.

Menu £ 45/55 – tasting menu only

27a South Par, Southsea ✉ PO5 2JF – ✆ 023 9287 6272
– www.restaurant27.com – dinner only and Sunday lunch
– Closed 25-26 December, Sunday dinner, Monday and Tuesday

The symbol guarantees a peaceful night's sleep.

POSTBRIDGE

Devon – Regional map n° **1**-C2

Lydgate House

TRADITIONAL · COSY Personally run whitewashed house, set in a secluded spot high on the moors and accessed via a narrow track. Homely, cosy lounge and conservatory restaurant offering home-cooked local produce. Bedrooms are named after birds; many offer lovely views over the 36 acre grounds and the East Dart River.

7 rooms – £ 47/63 £ 95/132

✉ PL20 6TJ – ✆ 01822 880209
– www.lydgatehouse.co.uk – Closed January

PULHAM MARKET

Norfolk – ✉ Diss – Pop. 722 – Regional map n° **8**-C2

Old Bakery

TOWNHOUSE · CLASSIC Just off the green is this old 16C bakery: a sweet, characterful place with heavy beams and open fires – where neat bedrooms mix modern furnishings with antiques. Breakfast features local eggs, sausages and preserves and the charming suntrap garden is the perfect spot to enjoy Theresa's homemade cake.

5 rooms – £ 75 £ 95

Church Walk ✉ IP21 4SL – ✆ 01379 676492
– www.theoldbakery.net – Closed Christmas-New Year

PAXFORD → See Chipping Camden

RADNAGE

Buckinghamshire – Regional map n° **6**-C2

The Mash Inn

MODERN BRITISH • INN Characterful 18C pub with flagged floors, exposed timbers, hand-crafted oak tables, and great country views from the terrace. Top quality local and garden ingredients lead the handwritten daily menu and the bespoke wood-fired chargrill is used to great effect. Bedrooms are modern and simply furnished.

Menu £ 23/60

5 rooms - £ 110/210 £ 110/210

Horseshoe Rd, Bennett End HP14 4EB - North : 1.25 mi by Town End rd - 01494 482440 - www.themashinn.com - Closed Sunday-Tuesday

RAMSBOTTOM

Greater Manchester - Pop. 17 872 - Regional map n° **11**-B2

Levanter

SPANISH • TAPAS BAR Joe has a passion for all things Spanish – he's even a trained flamenco guitarist – so, unsurprisingly, his sweet little tapas bar has an authentic feel. The menu is dictated by market produce; be sure to try some of the freshly sliced Iberico ham. He also owns the nearby Basque-style Baratxuri pintxo bar.

Menu £ 15 (weekdays) - Carte £ 19/29

10 Square St BL0 9BE - 01706 551530 (bookings not accepted) - www.levanterfinefoods.co.uk - Closed Monday, Tuesday and lunch Wednesday

RASKELF

North Yorkshire - Pop. 519 - Regional map n° **13**-B2

Rascills

TRADITIONAL BRITISH • FRIENDLY Experienced husband and wife team, Richard and Lindsey, run this welcoming restaurant with pride. It's set on a working farm in a charming village and has a welcoming feel. Dishes are honest, unfussy and prepared with care.

Menu £ 20/45

Village Farm, Howker Ln YO61 3LF - 01347 822031 - www.rascillsrestaurant.co.uk - Closed first 10 days January and Sunday-Tuesday

READING

Reading - Pop. 218 705 - Regional map n° **6**-C3

Forbury's

MODERN CUISINE • FASHIONABLE In a city centre square near the law courts, with a pleasant terrace, a leather-furnished bar-lounge and a smart, spacious dining room decorated with wine paraphernalia. Menus offer French-inspired dishes. Popular monthly wine events.

Menu £ 28 - Carte £ 31/58

1 Forbury Sq RG1 3BB - 0118 957 4044 - www.forburys.co.uk - Closed 1-5 January and Sunday

Holiday Inn

BUSINESS • MODERN Conveniently located for the M4, with spacious open-plan guest areas, smart function facilities and a well-equipped leisure club. Stylish, uniform bedrooms come with good facilities and compact, up-to-date bathrooms. Have snacks in the comfy lounge or dine in the formal split-level restaurant.

174 rooms - £ 89/209 £ 89/209

Wharfedale Rd, Winnersh Triangle RG41 5TS - Southeast : 4.5 mi by A 4 and A 3290 off Winnerish rd - 0118 944 0444 - www.hireadinghotel.com

ENGLAND

Roseate

TOWNHOUSE • DESIGN An impressive former civic hall overlooking Forbury Square Gardens; now a smart townhouse hotel where contemporary designs meet with original features. Luxurious bedrooms come with coffee machines, fridges and top electronics. The chic bar and restaurant offer modern menus.

55 rooms - £150/250 £150/250

26 Forbury ✉ RG1 3EJ
- ✆ 0118 952 7770 - www.roseatehotels.com

at Sonning-on-Thames Northeast: 4.25 mi by A4 on B4446

French Horn

TRADITIONAL BRITISH • ELEGANT XXX A beautifully located, 200 year old coaching inn, set on a bank of the Thames fringed by weeping willows; on sunny days head for the splendid terrace. The formal dining room has delightful views over the river and gardens and offers a classical menu of dishes from yesteryear - a gueridon trolley adds to the theatre. Cosy bedrooms are also traditionally appointed.

Menu £ 33 (weekdays) - Carte £ 57/78 **s**

21 rooms - £ 135/180 £ 170/225 - 4 suites

✉ RG4 6TN - ✆ 0118 969 2204 - www.thefrenchhorn.co.uk
- Closed 2-5 January and dinner 25 December and 1 January

at Shinfield South: 4.25 mi on A327 ✉ Reading

L'Ortolan

FRENCH • INTIMATE XXX Beautiful, red-brick former vicarage with stylish, modern décor, several private dining rooms and a conservatory-lounge overlooking a lovely garden. Cooking is confident and passionate, with well-crafted, classically based dishes showing flair, originality and some playful, artistic touches.

→ Ponzu dressed crab. Loin of hogget, sweetbread and asparagus. Blood orange soufflé with chocolate and mint.

Menu £ 30/69

Church Ln ✉ RG2 9BY - ✆ 0118 988 8500 - www.lortolan.com
- Closed 25 December-3 January, Sunday and Monday

Follow our inspectors @MichelinGuideUK

REDDITCH

Worcestershire - Pop. 81 919 - Regional map n° **10**-C2

Old Rectory House

TRADITIONAL • PERSONALISED A part-Elizabethan, part-Georgian former rectory in well-tended gardens. Guest areas have a cosy country house feel. Bedrooms are split between the house and the characterful beamed stables. Enjoy a cocktail in the lounge, then dine in the bright conservatory restaurant where local steaks are to the fore.

10 rooms - £ 89/149 £ 89/149

Ipsley Ln, Ipsley ✉ B98 0AP - Southeast : 2.5 mi by A 4023 off B 4497
- ✆ 01527 523000 - www.oldrectoryhouse.co.uk
- Closed 25 December

REEPHAM

Norfolk - Pop. 2 405 - Regional map n° **8**-C1

Dial House

HISTORIC BUILDING • PERSONALISED This attractive Georgian townhouse sits overlooking a small marketplace in a delightful village; in a unique twist, all of its furniture, fabrics and antiques are for sale. Bedrooms are charming – one occupies the whole top floor and another has a roof terrace. The restaurant is open from morning 'til night,

8 rooms – £ 95/160 £ 125/190

7 Market Pl NR10 4JJ – 01603 879900 – www.thedialhouse.org.uk

REETH

North Yorkshire – Pop. 724 – Regional map n° **13**-B1

Burgoyne

TRADITIONAL • CLASSIC A late Georgian house with a cosy, comforting feel, set in a lovely spot overlooking the village green and the Yorkshire Dales. The two lounges are filled with antiques and vases of flowers. Bedrooms are individually styled and traditionally appointed. The elegant dining room offers an all-encompassing menu.

11 rooms – £ 82/223 £ 99/240

On The Green DL11 6SN – 01748 884292 – www.theburgoyne.co.uk – Closed 3-31 January

RHYDYCROESAU – Shropshire → See Oswestry

RIBCHESTER

Lancashire – Pop. 888 – Regional map n° **11**-B2

Angels

MODERN CUISINE • INTIMATE XXX Smartly converted roadside pub with a cocktail bar and comfy lounge seating. Two formally dressed dining rooms offer a comfortable, intimate dining experience. Classic dishes with a modern edge are tasty, well-balanced and good value.

Menu £ 23 (weekdays) – Carte £ 36/47

Fleet Street Ln PR3 3ZA – Northwest : 1.5 mi by B 6245 (Longridge Rd) – 01254 820212 – www.angelsribchester.co.uk – dinner only and Sunday lunch – Closed Monday

RICHMOND

North Yorkshire – Pop. 8 413 – Regional map n° **13**-B1

Easby Hall

COUNTRY HOUSE • PERSONALISED The views of the church, the abbey ruins and the hills are as stunning as this part-18C hall itself. There are two gardens, an orchard, a kitchen garden and a paddock – and even stables for your horse! Inside it's elegant and luxurious. Tea and scones or cocktails are served on arrival, depending on the time.

3 rooms – £ 150 £ 180

Easby DL10 7EU – Southeast : 2.5 mi by A 6108 off B 6271 – 01748 826066 – www.easbyhall.com

at Whashton Northwest : 4.5 mi by A 6108 off Ravensworth rd

Hack & Spade

HISTORIC • PERSONALISED The unusual name is a reference to the copper and lead mines that used to operate in the area. Extremely spacious bedrooms are tastefully done out with traditional furnishings and modern comforts. The beamed, open-fired restaurant has a homely feel; a short menu of home-cooked favourites is served Thurs-Sat.

5 rooms – £ 125/140 £ 125/140

DL11 7JL – 01748 823721 – www.hackandspade.com – Closed January and 24-26 and 31 December

RIMPTON

Somerset - Pop. 235 - Regional map n° **2**-C3

White Post

CLASSIC CUISINE • **PUB** A smart dining pub set on the Dorset/Somerset border and affording stunning West Country views. Pub classics sit alongside more imaginative dishes, some with quirky touches like the piggy nibbles and, every carnivore's dream, the Sunday roast board. Bedrooms are comfortable - 'Dorset' has the best views.

Menu £ 25 (weekdays) - Carte £ 26/50

3 rooms - †£ 80 ††£ 95

BA22 8AR

- 01935 851525 - www.thewhitepost.com - Closed Sunday dinner and Monday

RIPLEY

Surrey - Pop. 2 041 - Regional map n° **4**-C1

Clock House

MODERN CUISINE • **INTIMATE** XXX A beautiful Georgian building with a double-sided clock above the door. The panelled bar leads to an elegant timbered dining room overlooking a delightful garden. Creative cooking has a refined, understated style and displays plenty of finesse. Bold flavours come together in well-balanced combinations.

→ Isle of Wight tomatoes and smoked eel. Beef with sweetbreads, kohlrabi and morels. Hibiscus, apple, blackberry and shortbread.

Menu £ 35/75

High St GU23 6AQ

- 01483 224777 - www.theclockhouserestaurant.co.uk - Closed 2 weeks August, 1 week Easter, Christmas, 1 week January, Sunday, Monday and Tuesday

Anchor

CLASSIC CUISINE • **CONTEMPORARY DÉCOR** A smart yet rustic pub with a 400 year history, polished slate floors and on-trend grey walls. Despite its name, it's nowhere near the water, but it is close to a famous cycle route, which explains the bicycle-themed interior. Restaurant-style dishes are carefully executed and bursting with flavour.

Menu £ 28 - Carte £ 30/43

High St GU23 6AE

- 01483 211866 - www.ripleyanchor.co.uk - Closed 25-26 December, 1st January

Broadway Barn

TOWNHOUSE • **DESIGN** This charming double-fronted house spent time as an antiques shop before being converted into a guesthouse. The large open-fired lounge leads to a conservatory breakfast room which overlooks a well-tended garden. Bedrooms display good attention to detail and come with thoughtful extras.

4 rooms - †£ 120 ††£ 120

High St GU23 6AQ

- 01483 223200 - www.broadwaybarn.com

ROCHDALE

Greater Manchester - Pop. 107 926 - Regional map n° **11**-B2

Nutters

MODERN BRITISH • **FRIENDLY** XX Enthusiastically run restaurant in a beautiful old manor house - a popular spot for afternoon tea. Appealing menus list modern British dishes with international influences. Can't decide? Go for the 6 course 'Surprise' menu.

Menu £ 20 (weekday lunch) - Carte £ 34/45

Edenfield Rd, Norden OL12 7TT - West : 3.5 mi on A 680

- 01706 650167 - www.nuttersrestaurant.com

- Closed 27-28 December, 2-3 January and Monday

ROCK

Cornwall – ✉ Wadebridge – Pop. 4 593 – Regional map n° **1**-B2

Dining Room

MODERN BRITISH • NEIGHBOURHOOD XX Immaculately kept, understated restaurant with modern seascapes on the walls; run by a friendly, family-led team. Flavoursome, classically based cooking features local seasonal produce. Everything is homemade, including the butter.

Carte £ 45/51

Pavilion Buildings, Rock Rd ✉ PL27 6JS – ✆ 01208 862622 (booking essential) – www.thediningroomrock.co.uk – dinner only – Closed 6 weeks January-February, Sunday in winter, Monday except bank holidays and Tuesday

St Enodoc

BOUTIQUE HOTEL • PERSONALISED A beautifully located hotel boasting stunning bay views. The eye-catching décor comprises vibrantly coloured soft furnishings and pastel coloured woodwork, and the service is refreshingly friendly and relaxed. Most of the contemporary, well-appointed bedrooms have a sea outlook.

20 rooms – †£ 167/185 ††£ 185/300

✉ PL27 6LA – ✆ 01208 863394 – www.enodoc-hotel.co.uk – Closed 17 December-14 January

ROMSEY

Hampshire – Pop. 16 998 – Regional map n° **4**-A2

Three Tuns

TRADITIONAL BRITISH • PUB Cosy 300 year old pub off the market square. Original features include oak beams and a central bar which divides the place in two – head left if you want to dine. Classic pub dishes are generously proportioned and full of flavour.

Carte £ 22/36

58 Middlebridge St ✉ SO51 8HL – ✆ 01794 512639 – www.the3tunsromsey.co.uk – Closed 25 December

White Horse

INN • CONTEMPORARY Smartly refurbished coaching inn; one of only 12 in the country to have continuously served as a hotel since the 14C – maybe even earlier! Guest areas feature beams, exposed brick and inglenook fireplaces. Well-equipped modern bedrooms include two duplex suites. The extensive brasserie menu suits all tastes.

29 rooms – †£ 95/115 ††£ 145/295

Market Pl ✉ SO51 8ZJ – ✆ 01794 512431 – www.thewhitehorseromsey.co.uk

ROSS-ON-WYE

Herefordshire – Pop. 10 582 – Regional map n° **10**-B3

Wilton Court

HISTORIC • COSY An attractive part-Elizabethan house just out of town, on the banks of the River Wye. Comfortable bedrooms have a subtle modern style – those to the front have river views. Tasty breakfasts feature homemade preserves. For dinner there's a choice of two different rooms; classic menus utilise local produce.

11 rooms – †£ 110/160 ††£ 135/195

Wilton Ln, Wilton ✉ HR9 6AQ – West : 0.75 mi by B 4260 – ✆ 01989 562569 – www.wiltoncourthotel.com – Closed 2-22 January

Bridge House

TOWNHOUSE • ELEGANT You get a lot more than you bargained for at this 18C townhouse: original features combine with chic, stylish furnishings; there's a superb view of the town and the River Wye; and the ruins of Castle Wilton border the grounds.

8 rooms – £ 95/115 £ 105/130

Wilton ✉ HR9 6AA – West : 0.75 mi by B 4260 – 01989 562655 – www.bridgehouserossonwye.co.uk – Closed 15 December-31 January, minimum 2 nights stay at weekends

at Upton Bishop Northeast: 3 mi by A40 on B4221

Moody Cow

TRADITIONAL BRITISH • FRIENDLY A traditional country pub serving classic dishes to match the surroundings. What the food may lack in originality, it makes up for with quality ingredients, careful cooking and distinct flavours. Friendly owners run the place with passion.

Menu £ 30 (weekday lunch) – Carte £ 30/44

✉ HR9 7TT – 01989 780470 – www.moodycowpub.co.uk – Closed 1-17 January, Sunday dinner, Monday and Tuesday in winter

ROWHOOK – West Sussex ➔ See Horsham

ROWSLEY

Derbyshire – ✉ Matlock – Pop. 451 – Regional map n° **9**-A1

Peacock

MODERN CUISINE • INTIMATE XX An elegant hotel restaurant where old mullioned stone windows, oak 'Mousey Thompson' furnishings and antique oil paintings are juxtaposed with modern lighting and contemporary art. Modern cooking is ingredient-led and has fresh, clean flavours; alongside, they offer some more traditional 'Classics'.

Menu £ 25 (lunch) – Carte £ 43/66

Peacock Hotel, Bakewell Rd ✉ DE4 2EB – 01629 733518 – www.thepeacockatrowsley.com – Closed first 2 weeks January

Peacock

COUNTRY HOUSE • PERSONALISED A characterful 17C Dower House of the Duchess of Rutland, with gardens leading down to the river. There's a snug open-fired sitting room and a characterful bar with stone walls, wood-panelling and a large peacock mural. Bedrooms mix antique furnishings with modern facilities and service is top-notch.

15 rooms – £ 130/145 £ 225/310

Bakewell Rd ✉ DE4 2EB – 01629 733518 – www.thepeacockatrowsley.com – Closed first 2 weeks January

Peacock – See restaurant listing

East Lodge

TRADITIONAL • PERSONALISED A 17C hunting lodge surrounded by 10 acres of landscaped gardens which are dotted with ponds. Guest areas are elegant and well-appointed and bedrooms are individually styled – many have great views and two come with four-poster beds. The formal dining room boasts a delightful chef's table.

12 rooms – £ 110/250 £ 150/325

Main St ✉ DE4 2EF – 01629 734474 – www.eastlodge.com

ROYAL LEAMINGTON SPA

Warwickshire – Pop. 55 733 – Regional map n° **10**-D3

Oscar's

CLASSIC FRENCH • **BISTRO** Friendly French bistro with two rustic rooms downstairs and a third above. There's a buzzy atmosphere, especially on the good value 'Auberge' nights, and the classic Gallic dishes are truly satisfying.

Menu £ 25/32

39 Chandos St ✉ CV32 4RL - ✆ 01926 452807 (booking essential) - www.oscarsfrenchbistro.co.uk - Closed Sunday and Monday

Mallory Court

COUNTRY HOUSE • **PERSONALISED** A part-Edwardian house in Lutyens' style, with lovely gardens, a smart spa and classical lounges displaying fine antiques. Fresh flowers feature in the bedrooms: those in the main house are characterful, those in Orchard House are contemporary and those in the Knight's Suite have a more corporate feel. Dine from modern menus in the elegant dining room or brasserie.

42 rooms - †£ 146/306 ††£ 193/368

Harbury Ln, Bishop's Tachbrook ✉ CV33 9QB - South : 2.25 mi by B 4087 (Tachbrook Rd) - ✆ 01926 330214 - www.mallory.co.uk

ROYAL TUNBRIDGE WELLS

Kent - Pop. 57 772 - Regional map n° **5**-B2

Thackeray's

MODERN BRITISH • **INTIMATE** A softly illuminated clapboard house; the oldest in town and once home to the eponymous author. Classic dishes have modern elements and feature lots of different ingredients. The moody first floor private rooms showcase local art.

Menu £ 20/55

85 London Rd ✉ TN1 1EA - ✆ 01892 511921 - www.thackerays-restaurant.co.uk - Closed Sunday dinner and Monday

The Warren

MODERN BRITISH • **INTIMATE** This large, multi-roomed restaurant is set above the High Street shops and its eclectic décor includes gold walls, brightly coloured linen and objets d'art. Well-judged modern cooking showcases meats from their 650 acre estate.

Menu £ 20 (weekday lunch) - Carte £ 24/50

5a High St (1st Floor) ✉ TN1 1UL - ✆ 01892 328191 - www.thewarren.restaurant - Closed Sunday dinner and Monday

The Old Fishmarket

SEAFOOD • **SIMPLE** This small black and white building in The Pantiles was once the town's fish market, so it's fitting that it's now an intimate seafood restaurant. The menu focuses on oysters, fruits de mer platters and the daily catch.

Menu £ 15 (weekday lunch) - Carte £ 30/65

19 The Upper Pantiles ✉ TN2 5TN - ✆ 01892 511422 (booking essential) - www.sankeys.co.uk - Closed 25-26 December, 1 January, Sunday October-March and Monday

Black Pig

MODERN BRITISH • **FRIENDLY** The black façade may feel quite austere but inside it's quite the opposite, courtesy of a friendly team, a laid-back vibe and rustic shabby-chic styling. Dishes are gutsy and full-flavoured and there's even a 'PIG Heaven' section.

Carte £ 26/34

18 Grove Hill Rd ✉ TN1 1RZ - ✆ 01892 523030 - www.theblackpig.net - Closed 26 December and 1 January

Hotel du Vin

BUSINESS • CONTEMPORARY Take in views over Calverley Park from this fine Georgian property built by the Duke and Duchess of Kent in 1740. Many original features remain, including an impressive staircase; bedrooms are contrastingly stylish. Relax on the veranda overlooking the gardens. The laid-back bistro offers Gallic fare.

34 rooms – †£ 114/394 ††£ 114/394 – ☕ £ 17

Crescent Rd ✉ TN1 2LY
– ✆ 01892 320749 – www.hotelduvin.com

One Warwick Park

BOUTIQUE HOTEL • DESIGN A smart, centrally located hotel comprising a townhouse, an old brewhouse and a former school. Crisply decorated bedrooms have dark wood furnishings, silver fabrics and state-of-the-art bathrooms. Sleek guest areas include an underground art gallery.

39 rooms ☕ – †£ 80/300 ††£ 85/300

1 Warwick Pk ✉ TN2 5TA
– ✆ 01892 520587 – www.onewarwickpark.co.uk

Danehurst

TRADITIONAL • PERSONALISED Attractive Edwardian house with a pleasant terrace and koi carp pond; set in a peaceful residential area. Furnishings are top quality and show good attention to detail. The charming owners make the tasty bread and jam for breakfast.

4 rooms ☕ – †£ 135/199 ††£ 135/199

41 Lower Green Rd, Rusthall ✉ TN4 8TW – West : 1.75 mi by A 264
– ✆ 01892 527739 – www.danehurst.net – Closed 20 December-2 January

at Southborough North : 2 mi on A 26

The Twenty Six

CREATIVE • RUSTIC X A very homely, rustic restaurant with a welcoming woodburning stove, set overlooking the village green; it has 26 seats and 26 light bulbs hanging from the ceiling. They style themselves as a 'Test Kitchen'. Menus change daily and creative modern cooking offers stimulating contrasts in texture and flavour.

Menu £ 40/55 – tasting menu only

15a Church Rd ✉ TN4 0RX – ✆ 01892 544607 – www.thetwenty-six.co.uk – dinner only and lunch Saturday – Closed Sunday and Monday

ROZEL BAY → See Channel Islands (Jersey)

RUDDINGTON – Nottinghamshire → See Nottingham

RUSHTON – Northamptonshire → See Kettering

RYE

East Sussex – Pop. 3 708 – Regional map n° **5**-C2

Tuscan Kitchen

ITALIAN • RUSTIC X Owner Franco hails from Tuscany, which is the inspiration for everything in this sweet little house. It resembles an osteria and the walls are filled with Florentine artefacts. Cooking too is based on recipes of the region; homemade pasta is a strength and olive oil comes from their farm in San Gimignano.

Carte £ 22/35

8 Lion St ✉ TN31 7LB – ✆ 01797 223269 – www.tuscankitchenrye.co.uk – dinner only and Sunday lunch – Closed Monday and Tuesday

George in Rye

INN • DESIGN A deceptively large, centrally located coaching inn offering an attractive blend of the old and the new. Stylish bedrooms have bold colour schemes and good facilities. There's a characterful beamed bar, a cosy wood-panelled lounge and a modern grill restaurant where Josper-cooked steaks are a highlight.

34 rooms - †£ 100/325 ††£ 125/325

98 High St. ✉ TN31 7JT - ✆ 01797 222114 - www.thegeorgeinrye.com

Mermaid Inn

INN • HISTORIC The Mermaid sits on a beautiful cobbled street and offers all the charm you'd expect from one of England's oldest coaching inns, with its heavy beams, carved wood, false stairways and priests' holes. For the full experience, book the Elizabethan Bed Chamber. The formal candlelit dining room offers accomplished modern dishes.

31 rooms - †£ 90 ††£ 140/220

Mermaid St. ✉ TN31 7EY - ✆ 01797 223065 - www.mermaidinn.com

Jeake's House

TOWNHOUSE • ELEGANT Set on a lovely cobbled lane, Jeake's House comprises three 17C properties which have merged over time. It's hugely characterful, with beams and a genteel ambiance, and is run with passion by the charming owner and her long-standing team. Breakfast is in the old Quakers meeting hall - have the daily special.

11 rooms - †£ 95/150 ††£ 95/150

Mermaid St. ✉ TN31 7ET - ✆ 01797 222828 - www.jeakeshouse.com

RYHALL

Rutland - Pop. 1 459 - Regional map n° **9**-C2

Wicked Witch

CLASSIC CUISINE • NEIGHBOURHOOD XX A smart former pub with dark wood panelling, purple walls and a relaxed formality; one owner cooks and the other serves. Seasonal menus have a classic base but combinations are original and there's a real emphasis on presentation.

Menu £ 15/30

Bridge St ✉ PE9 4HH - ✆ 01780 763649 - www.thewickedwitchexperience.co.uk - Closed Sunday dinner and Monday

ST ALBANS

Hertfordshire - Pop. 82 146 - Regional map n° **7**-A2

Galvin at Centurion Club

FRENCH • FASHIONABLE XX A stylish golf clubhouse provides the setting for this comfy bar, lounge and restaurant. Carefully prepared modern classics look to France for their foundation. The fixed price lunch and dinner menu offers good value.

Menu £ 20 (weekdays) - Carte £ 31/59

Hemel Hempstead Rd ✉ HP3 8LA - West : 3.75 mi by A 5183 on A 4147 - ✆ 01442 510520 - www.galvinatcenturionclub.co.uk - Closed Sunday dinner

THOMPSON St Albans

MODERN CUISINE • INTIMATE XX Come on a Sunday for 'lobster and steak' night or any day of the week for refined, tasty dishes with a modern edge. Three contemporary dining rooms feature bold artwork from the local gallery. Try the lesser-known wines by the glass.

Menu £ 23/25 - Carte £ 45/58

2 Hatfield Rd ✉ AL1 3RP - ✆ 01727 730777 - www.thompsonstalbans.co.uk - Closed 2-10 January, Sunday dinner, Monday and lunch Tuesday

St Michael's Manor

HISTORIC BUILDING • CONTEMPORARY A part-16C William and Mary manor house with well-kept gardens and lake views. Characterful guest areas display contemporary touches. Bedrooms are well-appointed; those located in the Garden Wing are the most contemporary and some have terraces. The orangery restaurant offers a modern menu.

30 rooms – £ 115/230 £ 155/245 – 1 suite

St Michael's Village, Fishpool St ✉ AL3 4RY – ✆ 01727 864444 – www.stmichaelsmanor.com

ST AUBIN → See Channel Islands (Jersey)

ST AUSTELL

Cornwall – Pop. 23 864 – Regional map n° **1**-B2

Anchorage House

TOWNHOUSE • PERSONALISED A contemporary guesthouse run by lovely owners – one is an ex-American Naval Commander! Charming, antique-filled bedrooms boast modern fabrics, state-of-the-art bathrooms and plenty of extras. There's a lovely indoor pool with a sauna and a hot tub, along with a chill-out lounge. Afternoon tea is a hit.

4 rooms – £ 110/130 £ 130/155

Nettles Corner, Boscundle ✉ PL25 3RH – East : 2.75 mi by A 390 – ✆ 01726 814071 – www.anchoragehouse.co.uk – Closed 15 November-15 March

ST BRELADE'S BAY → See Channel Islands (Jersey)

ST EWE

Cornwall – Regional map n° **1**-B3

Lower Barns

FAMILY • PERSONALISED The gregarious owner extends a warm welcome at this stylishly converted 18C granite barn (formerly part of the Heligan Estate). Quirky, vibrantly decorated bedrooms are spread about the place and a hot tub on the decking overlooks the garden. Dinners are home-cooked. It's a popular place for small weddings.

6 rooms – £ 85/95 £ 130/180

Bosue ✉ PL26 6ET – North : 1.25 mi by Crosswyn rd, St Austell rd and signed off St Mawes rd – ✆ 01726 844881 – www.lowerbarns.co.uk

ST HELENS → See Wight (Isle of)

ST HELIER → See Channel Islands (Jersey)

ST IVES

Cornwall – Pop. 9 966 – Regional map n° **1**-A3

Porthgwidden Beach Café

MODERN CUISINE • NEIGHBOURHOOD Tucked away by the beach, this super-friendly all-day café offers fantastic views over the bay to the lighthouse. The appealing menu comprises unfussy Mediterranean-influenced dishes, including plenty of seafood from St Ives, Looe and Mevagissey; be sure to have the Panang curry if it's on the specials list.

Carte £ 23/34

Porthgwidden Beach ✉ TR26 1PL – ✆ 01736 796791 (booking essential) – www.porthgwiddencafe.co.uk – Closed Monday-Wednesday dinner November-Easter

Porthminster Beach Café

SEAFOOD • FASHIONABLE X A charming 1930s beach house in a superb location overlooking Porthminster Sands. It's hung with Cornish artwork, has a nautical style and leads out onto a glass-walled heated terrace. The seasonal seafood menu offers unfussy, vibrantly flavoured dishes with Asian influences. Service is relaxed and friendly.

Carte £ 28/50

Porthminster Beach ✉ TR26 2EB
- ✆ 01736 795352 - www.porthminstercafe.co.uk
- Closed 1-13 January

Porthmeor Café Bar

MODERN CUISINE • NEIGHBOURHOOD X A popular beachfront café where you can sit inside, on the terrace or in heated pods. They offer breakfast, cakes, Mediterranean small plates and a few more substantial dishes too. Every table has a great view, especially at sunset.

Carte £ 22/34

Porthmeor Beach ✉ TR26 1JZ
- ✆ 01736 793366 (booking essential at dinner) - www.porthmeor-beach.co.uk
- Closed dinner Sunday-Thursday November-February

Porthminster Kitchen

MODERN CUISINE • NEIGHBOURHOOD X Follow the narrow staircase up to this contemporary bistro and you'll be rewarded with glorious harbour views from both the restaurant and terrace. The all-day menu offers light, fresh, global cuisine with a focus on local seafood.

Carte £ 20/40

The Wharf ✉ TR26 1LG
- ✆ 01736 799874 - www.porthminster.kitchen - Closed 25 December

Blue Hayes

TOWNHOUSE • PERSONALISED A charmingly run hotel built in 1922 for a surgeon friend of Edward VIII. The spacious interior is immaculately kept but it's the lovely terrace overlooking the town and bay that's the biggest draw and makes the perfect spot for summer breakfasts or evening drinks. Cold suppers are available on request.

6 rooms - †£ 150/240 ††£ 220/300

Trelyon Ave ✉ TR26 2AD
- ✆ 01736 797129 - www.bluehayes.co.uk - Closed November-February

No 27

HISTORIC • PERSONALISED Unusually for St Ives, this stylishly restored Georgian house has its own car park... even more unusually, it also owns the beach beneath it! Bedrooms are modern and appealing. Take in a view of the bay from the airy breakfast room.

11 rooms - †£ 115/175 ††£ 115/175

27 The Terrace ✉ TR26 2BP - ✆ 01736 797450 - www.27theterrace.co.uk - Closed January and Christmas

Trevose Harbour House

TOWNHOUSE • CONTEMPORARY The experienced owners have decorated this stylish townhouse themselves, so you'll find lots of personal touches alongside an unusual mix of designer and upcycled furnishings. Breakfast features local produce and is a real highlight. They have 3 parking spaces reserved at the nearby station.

6 rooms - †£ 175/280 ††£ 185/290

22 The Warren ✉ TR26 2EA - ✆ 01736 793267 - www.trevosehouse.co.uk
- Closed mid-November-March

at Carbis Bay South: 1.75 mi on A3074 ✉ St Ives

Boskerris

FAMILY • CONTEMPORARY A passionately run hotel with a light and airy feel. The French-style lounge-bar leads out onto a huge terrace with panoramic views of Carbis Bay. Uncluttered bedrooms come in cool modern designs – ask for one which looks out over the sea.

15 rooms – †£ 120/222 ††£ 160/295

Boskerris Rd ✉ TR26 2NQ – ✆ 01736 795295 – www.boskerrishotel.co.uk – Closed mid-November-March

Beachcroft

TRADITIONAL • PERSONALISED Set in an elevated position, with stunning views across the bay. Contemporary interior with subtle 1920s touches. Comfy, understated bedrooms have bespoke furnishings and luxurious bathrooms. Have your breakfast on the delightful terrace.

4 rooms – †£ 150/200 ††£ 150/200

Valley Rd ✉ TR26 2QS – ✆ 01736 794442 – www.beachcroftstives.co.uk – Closed November-March except New Year

ST KEVERNE

Cornwall – Pop. 939 – Regional map n° **1**-A3

Old Temperance House

TOWNHOUSE • CONTEMPORARY This pretty pink-washed cottage framed by olive trees was once a 15C temperance house. The interior is contemporary and immaculately kept. Bright bedrooms are named after alcoholic drinks and display thoughtful touches. Fresh fruit and produce from the local butcher features at breakfast.

4 rooms – †£ 75 ††£ 90/95

The Square ✉ TR12 6NA – ✆ 01326 280986 – www.oldtemperancehouse.co.uk

ST KEW

Cornwall – Regional map n° **1**-B2

St Kew Inn

TRADITIONAL BRITISH • PUB A characterful country pub with flagged floors and wooden beams, set in a quintessentially English location. Menus offer a wide range of appealing, good value dishes and on summer Sundays joints are cooked in the garden on the Big Green Egg. Be sure to order a beer from the wooden casks behind the bar.

Carte £ 24/41

✉ PL30 3HB – ✆ 01208 841259 – www.stkewinn.co.uk – Closed 25-26 December

ST MARTIN → See Channel Islands (Guernsey)

ST MARTIN'S → See Scilly (Isles of)

ST MARY'S → See Scilly (Isles of)

ST MAWES

Cornwall – ✉ Truro – Regional map n° **1**-B3

Idle Rocks (N)

MODERN BRITISH • BRASSERIE XX This relaxed restaurant – running the entire length of the Idle Rocks hotel – offers superb bay views, and the water laps at its fabulous terrace. Refined, eye-catching dishes exhibit a wealth of flavours and textures, and the vegetarian dish of the day showcases produce from the Lost Gardens of Heligan.

Menu £ 35/58

Idle Rocks Hotel, Harbourside ✉ TR2 5AN – ✆ 01326 270270 (bookings essential for non-residents) – www.idlerocks.com – Closed 6-18 January

Watch House

MEDITERRANEAN CUISINE • SIMPLE Old Customs and Excise watch house on the quayside, with a nautically styled interior, friendly service and harbour views. Light lunches and substantial dinners; unfussy cooking follows a Mediterranean theme – try the tasty fish specials.

Menu £ 25 (lunch) – Carte £ 28/48

1 The Square ✉ TR2 5DJ – ✆ 01326 270038 – www.watchhousestmawes.co.uk – Closed 25-26 December and Sunday dinner, Monday-Tuesday October-Easter

Hotel Tresanton

GRAND LUXURY • SEASIDE Set in a collection of old fishermen's cottages and a former yacht club. Elegant, nautically themed guest areas include an intimate bar and a movie room. Understated bedrooms – some in cottages – have a high level of facilities and superb sea views. The lovely split-level terrace shares the outlook.

30 rooms – †£ 198/257 ††£ 220/285 – 4 suites

27 Lower Castle Rd ✉ TR2 5DR – ✆ 01326 270055 – www.tresanton.com

Idle Rocks

BOUTIQUE HOTEL • SEASIDE This boutique hotel sits on the water's edge and affords fabulous views over the harbour and estuary. The décor is personalised and local art is displayed throughout. Comfy modern bedrooms are well-equipped and have pleasing subtle touches; ask for one at the front.

19 rooms – †£ 150/210 ††£ 200/405

Harbourside ✉ TR2 5AN – ✆ 01326 270270 – www.idlerocks.com – Closed 6-18 January

Idle Rocks – See restaurant listing

St Mawes

BOUTIQUE HOTEL • CONTEMPORARY A smart refurbishment has given this classic harbourside hotel a cool and trendy vibe. Bedrooms are understated and immaculately kept, the restful lounge boasts squashy sofas and opens onto a small balcony, and there's even a small cinema. The lively restaurant serves fresh seafood and wood-fired pizzas.

7 rooms – †£ 150/215 ††£ 150/295

Harbourside ✉ TR2 5DN – ✆ 01326 270270 – www.stmaweshotel.com

ST MELLION

Cornwall – Regional map n° **1**-C2

Pentillie Castle

COUNTRY HOUSE • PERSONALISED A 17C house which was later transformed into a castle, set in 2,000 acres of stunning grounds overlooking the river. Spacious, elegant bedrooms have antique furnishings, luxurious bathrooms and offer some great views. Guest areas have a classical feel. It's a popular haunt for shooting parties in the winter.

9 rooms – †£ 115/240 ††£ 115/240

✉ PL12 6QD – Southeast : 1 mi by A 388 on Cargreen rd – ✆ 01579 350044 – www.pentillie.co.uk

ST OSYTH

Essex – Pop. 2 118 – Regional map n° **7**-D2

Park Hall

HISTORIC • PERSONALISED Charming 14C former monastery with a homely feel, surrounded by 400 acres of arable farmland. The characterful Garden Suites come with many extras. Seek out the hidden seating areas in the large grounds.

5 rooms – †£ 120/220 ††£ 140/220

Bypass Rd ✉ CO16 8HG – East : 1.5 mi on B 1027 – ✆ 01255 820922 – www.romanticbreaksfortwo.com

ST PETER PORT → See Channel Islands (Guernsey)

ST SAVIOUR → See Channel Islands (Jersey)

ST SAVIOUR → See Channel Islands (Guernsey)

ST TUDY

Cornwall - Pop. 604 - Regional map n° **1**-B2

St Tudy Inn

MODERN BRITISH • FRIENDLY A lovingly restored pub in a pretty village - inside there's a labyrinth of cosy rooms with fresh flowers, open fires and rustic modish overtones. Beautifully presented dishes are unfussy, seasonal and satisfying; meats are from Launceston and seafood is from Padstow. The chef is passionate, service is friendly and modern bedrooms complete the picture.

Menu £ 15 (weekday lunch) - Carte £ 27/41

4 rooms - £ 135/150 £ 135/150

Churchtown ✉ PL30 3NN - ✆ 01208 850656 - www.sttudyinn.com - Closed lunch 25-26 December

SALCOMBE

Devon - Pop. 1 893 - Regional map n° **1**-C3

Salcombe Harbour

LUXURY • CONTEMPORARY Take in views of the estuary from this contemporary seaside hotel, with its sleek, nautical edge. Stylish bedrooms come with Nespresso machines and tablets; many also have balconies. For relaxation there's a chic spa and even a cinema! The restaurant offers modern menus, with local seafood a feature.

50 rooms - £ 157/290 £ 166/350 - 1 suite

Cliff Rd ✉ TQ8 8JH - ✆ 01548 844444 - www.salcombe-harbour-hotel.co.uk

South Sands

FAMILY • DESIGN Stylish hotel by the water's edge, with a subtle New England theme running throughout and South Sands views. Small, modern bar and lounges. Smart bedrooms have heavy wood furnishings and good facilities; opt for one with a balcony.

27 rooms - £ 185/350 £ 195/395 - 5 suites

Bolt Head ✉ TQ8 8LL - Southwest : 1.25 mi - ✆ 01548 845900 - www.southsands.com

at Soar Mill Cove Southwest: 4.25 mi by A381 ✉ Salcombe

Soar Mill Cove

FAMILY • PERSONALISED Family-run hotel built from local slate and stone; delightfully set above a secluded cove. Relax in the modern lounge or smart bar. Spacious bedrooms come in bright, contemporary styles; half have private patios and sea views. Blue-hued restaurant offers a modern menu and a lovely outlook from every table.

22 rooms - £ 149/209 £ 199/319

✉ TQ7 3DS - ✆ 01548 561566 - www.soarmillcove.co.uk - Closed 2 January-10 February

SANCTON

East Riding of Yorkshire - Pop. 286 - Regional map n° **13**-C2

Star

MODERN CUISINE • FRIENDLY Personally run pub in a small village, with a cosy bar, two smart dining rooms and a smiley team. The bar menu offers hearty, boldly flavoured dishes, while the à la carte has some imaginative twists.

Menu £ 18 (weekday lunch) – Carte £ 26/55

King St ✉ YO43 4QP – ✆ 01430 827269 – www.thestaratsancton.co.uk – Closed Monday

SANDIACRE

Derbyshire – Pop. 9 600 – Regional map n° **9**-B2

La Rock

MODERN BRITISH • RUSTIC XX Charming, personally run restaurant with an airy feel – it was once a butcher's. Exposed brick walls and antler chandeliers feature. Cooking combines classical flavours with modern techniques; home-grown fruits are well utilised.

Menu £ 32 (lunch) – Carte £ 38/57

4 Bridge St ✉ NG10 5QT – ✆ 0115 939 9833 – www.larockrestaurant.co.uk – Closed 24 December-mid-January, Monday, Tuesday and lunch Wednesday

SANDSEND – North Yorkshire ➔ See Whitby

SANDWICH

Kent – Pop. 4 398 – Regional map n° **5**-D2

The Salutation N

MODERN BRITISH • CONTEMPORARY DÉCOR XX Book a table in the 'Tasting Room' – in the old servants' quarter of this impressive Lutyens-designed house – to watch the chefs through a glass wall. Modern dishes comprise many different ingredients and provide plenty of contrasts. A surprise tasting menu is available at both lunch and dinner.

Menu £ 32/70 – Carte £ 44/59

The Salutation Hotel, Knightrider St ✉ CT13 9EW – ✆ 01304 619919 (bookings essential for non-residents) – www.the-salutation.com

The Salutation N

HISTORIC BUILDING • CONTEMPORARY Behind high walls hides one of the town's finest properties – a Georgian-style house designed by Lutyens in 1912, with 4 acres of stunning gardens. Original features include beautiful wood panelling and striking barley sugar columns. Bedrooms are spacious and stylish; most have lovely garden views.

17 rooms – †£ 163/335 ††£ 163/335

Knightrider St ✉ CT13 9EW – ✆ 01304 619919 – www.the-salutation.com

The Salutation – See restaurant listing

SANDYPARK – Devon ➔ See Chagford

SAPPERTON – Gloucestershire ➔ See Cirencester

SAXMUNDHAM

Suffolk – Pop. 2 712 – Regional map n° **8**-D3

The Bell at Sax'

TRADITIONAL BRITISH • TRADITIONAL DÉCOR X The Bell sits at the centre of the community: it's a favourite haunt of the Rotary Club and the market takes place next door. It's comfy and cosy inside, from the well-kept bedrooms to the homely dining rooms. The experienced chef has a great understanding of flavours and his dishes are carefully priced.

Carte £ 20/45

10 rooms – †£ 80/100 ††£ 100

31 High St ✉ IP17 1AF – ✆ 01728 602331 – www.thebellatsax.co.uk

SCARBOROUGH

North Yorkshire – Pop. 61 749 – Regional map n° **13**-D1

Jeremy's

MODERN CUISINE • NEIGHBOURHOOD This smart, buzzy bistro started life as a 1930s butcher's shop and its original wall and floor tiles still remain. Tasty modern British dishes have subtle Italian and Asian touches and come courtesy of a confident chef.

Carte £ 33/57

33 Victoria Park Ave ✉ YO12 7TR – ✆ 01723 363871 (booking essential) – www.jeremys.co – dinner only and Sunday lunch – Closed first week January, Sunday dinner, Tuesday except mid-July-August and Monday

Alexander

TOWNHOUSE • COSY You're greeted with homemade shortbread at this double-fronted hotel near the sea. Contemporary bedrooms come with robes and seaside rock and provide a contrast to the more traditional lounge and cocktail bar. Local seafood is a highlight of the 3-choice dinner menu. (At times, there's a min. 2 night stay.)

8 rooms – †£ 74/104 ††£ 84/114

33 Burniston Rd ✉ YO12 6PG – ✆ 01723 363178 – www.alexanderhotelscarborough.co.uk – Closed mid-October-mid-March

SCAWTON – North Yorkshire → See Helmsley

→ See Helmsley

SCILLY (Isles of)

Cornwall – Regional map n° **1**-A3

Bryher

Cornwall – Pop. 78

Hell Bay

BOUTIQUE HOTEL • PERSONALISED Several charming, New England style buildings arranged around a central courtyard, with a contemporary, nautical-style interior displaying an impressive collection of modern art. Immaculately kept bedrooms come with plenty of thoughtful extras. The fabulous coastal location allows for far-reaching views.

25 rooms (dinner included) – †£ 175/450 ††£ 280/720 – 14 suites

✉ TR23 0PR – ✆ 01720 422947 – www.hellbay.co.uk – Closed November-February

St Martin's

Cornwall – Pop. 113 – Regional map n° **1**-A3

Karma St Martin's

FAMILY • PERSONALISED The owner of Karma Resorts spent time on the Isles of Scilly when he was young and its sandy white beaches and clear blue waters fit the group's ethos perfectly. The hotel resembles a row of cottages and has a bright, calming feel; Indonesian-style furniture is a feature. The modern menu is all-encompassing.

30 rooms – †£ 135/350 ††£ 135/350 – 3 suites

Lower Town ✉ TR25 0QW – ✆ 01720 422368 – www.karmastmartins.com – Closed November-March

St Mary's

Cornwall – Pop. 1 607

Atlantic

INN • FUNCTIONAL Former Customs Office in a charming bay setting, affording lovely views across the harbour. Bedrooms – accessed through twisty passages – are well-equipped, and many share the view. There's a comfortable lounge and a small bar, along with a wicker-furnished restaurant which offers an accessible menu.

25 rooms – †£ 135/240 ††£ 135/240

Hugh St, Hugh Town ✉ TR21 0PL – ✆ 01720 422417 – www.atlantichotelscilly.co.uk – Closed November-February

Star Castle

HISTORIC BUILDING • TRADITIONAL Elizabethan castle in the shape of an 8-pointed star. Well-appointed, classical bedrooms and brighter garden suites - some with harbour or island views. 17C staircase leads from the stone ramparts to the charming Dungeon bar. Fabulous fireplace and kitchen garden produce in the dining room. Seafood menus in the conservatory.

38 rooms - £ 80/157 £ 160/368 - 4 suites

The Garrison TR21 0JA - 01720 422317 - www.star-castle.co.uk - Closed November-mid-February

Evergreen Cottage

FAMILY • COSY 300 year old captain's cottage with colourful window boxes, set in the heart of town. The interior is cosy, with a small, low-ceilinged lounge and breakfast room. The modest oak-furnished bedrooms are compact but spotlessly kept.

5 rooms - £ 40/45 £ 80/90

Parade, Hugh Town TR21 0LP - 01720 422711 - www.evergreencottageguesthouse.co.uk - Closed 1 week February and Christmas-New Year

Tresco

Cornwall – Pop. 167

Ruin Beach Café

MEDITERRANEAN CUISINE • RUSTIC Relaxed beachside restaurant in an old smugglers cottage - part of an aparthotel. The rustic room is decorated with striking Cornish art and opens onto a terrace with superb St Martin views. Colourful Mediterranean dishes have big, bold flavours; seafood and pizzas from the wood-burning oven are a hit.

Carte £ 21/37

Sea Garden Cottages Hotel, Old Grimsby TR24 0QQ - 01720 424849 (booking essential) - www.tresco.co.uk - Closed November-mid-March

Sea Garden Cottages

A smart aparthotel divided into New England style 'cottages'. Each has an open-plan kitchen and lounge with a terrace; the first floor bedroom opens onto a balcony offering stunning views over Old Grimsby Quay and Blockhouse Point.

9 rooms - £ 260/337 £ 350/450

Old Grimsby TR24 0QQ - 01720 422849 - www.tresco.co.uk - Closed November-mid-March

Ruin Beach Café – See restaurant listing

New Inn

INN • COSY Stone-built inn boasting a large terrace, an appealing outdoor pool and pleasant coastal views. Bedrooms are bright, fresh and very comfy. Regular live music events attract guests from near and far. The hugely characterful bar and restaurant offer accessible menus.

16 rooms - £ 70/130 £ 70/130

New Grimsby TR24 0QQ - 01720 422849 - www.tresco.co.uk - Restricted opening November-February

SEAHAM

Durham – Pop. 22 373 – Regional map n° **14**-B2

Seaham Hall

LUXURY • CONTEMPORARY An imposing part-18C mansion which combines grand original features with striking modern styling. Spacious, contemporary bedrooms have luxurious touches and comfy sitting areas - and many have coastal views. There's also a chic lounge; a grill restaurant with velour booths and a zinc-topped bar; and a stylish Asian restaurant set within the impressively equipped spa.

21 rooms - £ 185/295 £ 185/295 - 5 suites

Lord Byron's Walk SR7 7AG - 0191 516 1400 - www.seaham-hall.com

SEAHOUSES

Northumberland - Pop. 1 959 - Regional map n° **14**-B1

St Cuthbert's House

HISTORIC • MODERN Former Georgian Presbyterian chapel, with comfortabl modern bedrooms, a homely lounge and a wood-furnished breakfast room; larg arched windows and many original features remain. The friendly, welcomin owners often host music nights.

6 rooms - £ 110/130 £ 110/130

192 Main St ✉ NE68 7UB - Southwest : 0.5 mi by Beadnell rd on North Sunderland rd - ✆ 01665 720456 - www.stcuthbertshouse.com - Restricted opening in winter

SEASALTER - Kent → See Whitstable

SEAVIEW - Isle of Wight → See Wight (Isle of)

SEDBERGH

Cumbria - Pop. 2 171 - Regional map n° **12**-B2

The Malabar

FAMILY • PERSONALISED A stylishly converted stone barn surrounded by rollin hills. The hands-on owners provide a warm welcome: Graham previously lived o an Indian tea plantation, so there's always a good choice of teas. Smart bed rooms mix antique furnishings with modern facilities. Cumbrian produce feature at breakfast.

6 rooms - £ 140/220 £ 160/240

Garths ✉ LA10 5ED - West : 1.75 mi on A 684 - ✆ 015396 20200 - www.themalabar.co.uk - Closed January

SEDGEFORD

Norfolk - Pop. 613 - Regional map n° **8**-B1

Magazine Wood

FAMILY • CONTEMPORARY Stylish guesthouse on a family farm beside the Ped dars Way. Luxuriously appointed bedrooms come with dining areas, continenta breakfasts and terraces overlooking the fields; you can order a newspaper or a cooked breakfast online.

3 rooms - £ 115/144 £ 115/144

Peddars Way ✉ PE36 5LW - East : 0.75 mi on B 1454 - ✆ 01485 750740 - www.magazinewood.co.uk - Closed Christmas (minimum two night stay at weekends)

SETTLE

North Yorkshire - Pop. 3 621 - Regional map n° **13**-A2

Falcon Manor

COUNTRY HOUSE • DESIGN Just out of town is this fine stone manor house with partial Fell views. It's owned by an interior designer, who has added some flamboyant touches to its Gothic Victorian architecture; it's worth paying the extra to stay in the huge Rafters Suite. Dine on modern classics in the snug bar or bright brasserie.

16 rooms - £ 75/125 £ 95/275 - 3 suites

Skipton Rd ✉ BD24 9BD - South : 0.25 mi on B 6479 - ✆ 01729 823814 - www.falconmanor.co.uk

SHAFTESBURY

Dorset - Pop. 7 314 - Regional map n° **2**-C3

Fleur de Lys

TRADITIONAL • CLASSIC A keenly run, creeper-clad stone house in a lovely market town. Comfy, well-kept bedrooms are named after grape varieties and each comes with its own laptop. The cosy lounge features a mahogany bar. Dine from traditional menus in the L-shaped restaurant and enjoy drinks on the wood-furnished terrace.

8 rooms – £ 85/150 £ 100/175

Bleke St ✉ SP7 8AW – ✆ 01747 853717 – www.lafleurdelys.co.uk – Closed 2 weeks January

Retreat

TRADITIONAL • CLASSIC Pretty Georgian house on a narrow street in a delightful market town; built for a local doctor on the old site of a school for poor boys. Wood-furnished breakfast room and immaculately kept bedrooms with good facilities. Charming owner.

9 rooms – £ 65/75 £ 95/99

47 Bell St ✉ SP7 8AE – ✆ 01747 850372 – www.the-retreat.co.uk – Closed 28 December-January

SHANKLIN – Isle of Wight → See Wight (Isle of)

SHAWELL

Leicestershire – Regional map n° **9**-B3

White Swan

MODERN BRITISH • PUB This welcoming village pub consists of a bar and two cosy rooms at the front and a contrastingly smart restaurant extension to the rear. Dishes are modern and sophisticated; come on a Saturday for their champagne breakfast.

Menu £ 22 (lunch) – Carte dinner £ 38/57

Main St ✉ LE17 6AG – ✆ 01788 860357 – www.whiteswanshawell.co.uk – Closed Sunday dinner and Monday

SHEFFIELD

South Yorkshire – Pop. 518 090 – Regional map n° **13**-B3

Jöro

SCANDINAVIAN • SIMPLE A simple but stylish place housed in the Krynkl shipping container development; book the Chef's Bench to feel part of the action. Daily changing small plates with unusual flavour combinations draw on New Nordic cuisine.

Menu £ 22 (lunch) – Carte £ 26/29

0.2-0.5 Krynkl, 294 Shalesmoor ✉ S3 8US
– ✆ 0114 299 1539 – www.jororestaurant.co.uk
– Closed 1-15 January, 15-21 April, 22-28 July, 16-22 September, Sunday-lunch Wednesday

Old Vicarage

MODERN CUISINE • FAMILY A delightful former vicarage in a semi-rural spot on the city's edge. Two fixed price menus offer sophisticated dishes with assured flavours and subtle modern influences; the 'Prestige' best showcases the chef's abilities.

Menu £ 40/70

Ridgeway Moor ✉ S12 3XW – Southeast : 6.75 mi by A 6135 (signed Hyde Park) and B 6054 on Marsh Lane rd.
– ✆ 0114 247 5814 – www.theoldvicarage.co.uk
– Closed 26 December-4 January, 23 July-6 August, Easter, Saturday lunch, Sunday and Monday

Rafters

MODERN BRITISH · CLASSIC DÉCOR XX A long-standing city institution; the owners stamped their own identity on it by using Sheffield cutlery and Yorkshire tweed covered chairs. Refined cooking sees well-judged flavour combinations presented in an attractive manner.

Menu £ 35/55

220 Oakbrook Rd, Nether Green ✉ S11 7ED – West : 2.5 mi by A 57 and Fulwood rd, turning left onto Hangingwater Rd
– ☎ 0114 230 4819 – www.raftersrestaurant.co.uk
– dinner only and Saturday lunch
– Closed 1-8 January, 26 August-3 September, 23-27 December, Sunday and Monday

Kitchen

TRADITIONAL BRITISH · BISTRO X A bright, laid-back 'urban kitchen' in a stylish hotel. It's open for breakfast, coffee and cakes, lunch and dinner, and offer some great salads and small plates, followed by more ambitious modern dishes in the evening.

Carte £ 30/44

Brocco on the Park Hotel, 92 Brocco Bank ✉ S11 8RS – Southwest : 2 mi by B 6547 and Clarkehouse Rd
– ☎ 0114 266 1233 – www.brocco.co.uk/kitchen
– Closed 25 December

Brocco on the Park

TOWNHOUSE · MODERN Broccos's claim to fame is that Picasso once stayed here! It's a compact place, overlooking a park, and has plenty of style and individuality, albeit set by a roundabout. Bedrooms have a chic modern feel courtesy of light colour schemes, quality furnishings and great attention to detail.

8 rooms – †£ 120/250 ††£ 120/250 – ☕ £ 10

92 Brocco Bank ✉ S11 8RS – Southwest : 2 mi by B 6547 and Clarkehouse Rd
– ☎ 0114 266 1233 – www.brocco.co.uk

Kitchen – See restaurant listing

SHERBORNE

Dorset – Pop. 9 523 – Regional map n° **2**-C3

The Green

MODERN CUISINE · BISTRO X A pretty listed stone property with an enclosed garden terrace. Mediterranean-style dishes are full of flavour; the 'Zakuski' (snacks) are great for sharing and the menu du jour (Tues-Thurs) is a steal. The chef-owner hails from the Russian foothills of the Caucasus Mountains and the team are super-friendly.

Menu £ 22 (weekdays) – Carte £ 30/43

3 The Green ✉ DT9 3HY – ☎ 01935 813821 – www.greenrestaurant.co.uk
– Closed 1-16 January, Sunday dinner and Monday

SHERINGHAM

Norfolk – Pop. 7 367 – Regional map n° **8**-C1

Ashbourne House

TOWNHOUSE · PERSONALISED Well-appointed guesthouse in an elevated position; its large, landscaped garden has access to the clifftop. Two of the homely comfortable bedrooms have coastal views. Local bacon and sausages feature at breakfast, which is taken beside an impressive fireplace in the wood-panelled breakfast room.

3 rooms ☕ – †£ 65/70 ††£ 85/90

1 Nelson Rd ✉ NR26 8BT – ☎ 01263 821555
– www.ashbournehousesheringham.co.uk – Closed 15 December-3 January

SHINFIELD - Wokingham → See Reading

SHIPLAKE - Oxfordshire → See Henley-on-Thames

SHIPSTON-ON-STOUR

Warwickshire - Pop. 5 038 - Regional map n° **10**-C3

Bower House

MODERN BRITISH • BRASSERIE This smart brasserie occupies two former shops in the heart of a small but characterful town. Appealing dishes are attractively presented and have a modern edge. Sit in the larger room with its comfy banquettes and copper-topped tables. Spacious bedrooms come with Hungarian-tiled bathrooms.

Menu £ 25

5 rooms - £ 130/185 £ 130/185

Market Pl ✉ CV36 4AG - ✆ 01608 663333 - www.thebowerhouseshipston.com - Closed dinner 24- lunch 31 December, Sunday dinner, Monday and Tuesday

SHIRLEY - Derbyshire → See Ashbourne

SHOTTLE

Derbyshire - Regional map n° **9**-B2

Dannah Farm Country House

TRADITIONAL • PERSONALISED 18C stone farmhouse on a 154 acre working farm owned by the Chatsworth Estate; its outbuildings converted into spacious, well-equipped bedrooms. Many rooms have spa baths and the Granary and Studio Suites have hot tubs and terraces.

8 rooms - £ 95/110 £ 185/295

Bowmans Ln. ✉ DE56 2DR - North : 0.25 mi by Alport rd - ✆ 01773 550273 - www.dannah.co.uk - Closed 24-26 December

SHREWSBURY

Shropshire - Pop. 71 715 - Regional map n° **10**-B2

Lion and Pheasant

HISTORIC • CONTEMPORARY A collection of adjoining 16C and 18C townhouses on a famous medieval street; inside the look is contrastingly modern, quirky and understated. Chic bedrooms, designed by the owner's daughter, have a boutique French feel - those to the rear are the quietest. Modern dishes are served in the bar and restaurant.

22 rooms - £ 99/165 £ 129/230

49-50 Wyle Cop ✉ SY1 1XJ - ✆ 01743 770345 - www.lionandpheasant.co.uk - Closed 25-26 December

at Upton Magna East : 6 mi by A 5064 off B 4380

The Haughmond

TRADITIONAL CUISINE • PUB A stylish dining pub complete with a 'Village Shop', smart modern bedrooms and a recurring stag theme. Lunchtime sees a good value selection of pub classics, the evening menus are more ambitious and Weds-Sat they open Basil's - an 18-seater restaurant offering a sophisticated 5 course set menu.

Menu £ 23 - Carte £ 26/42

5 rooms - £ 80/110 £ 90/120

✉ SY4 4TZ - ✆ 01743 709918 - www.thehaughmond.co.uk - Closed 25 December and 1 January

ENGLAND

at Condover South: 5 mi by A49

Grove Farm House

COUNTRY HOUSE • PERSONALISED The friendly owners of this 18C stone farmhouse have opened up their family home. Bedrooms are pleasantly furnished and come with well-equipped bathrooms and country views. Extensive breakfasts showcase local ingredients along with homemade bread and jam, and eggs from their chickens in the garden.

4 rooms - £ 75 £ 100

SY5 7BH - South : 0.75 mi on Dorrington rd - 01743 718544 - www.grovefarmhouse.com - Closed Christmas-New Year

SHREWTON

Wiltshire - Pop. 1 723 - Regional map n° **2**-D2

Rollestone Manor

COUNTRY HOUSE • PERSONALISED A Grade II listed house on a part-working farm just outside the village; reputedly once the home of Jane Seymour's family. Good-sized, antique-furnished bedrooms offer modern facilities; one even has a bath mounted on top of a plinth in the room. The contemporary restaurant serves traditional dishes.

7 rooms - £ 85/110 £ 95/125

SP3 4HF - Southeast : 0.5 mi on A 360 - 01980 620216 - www.rollestonemanor.com - Closed 24-26 December

SHURDINGTON - Gloucestershire → See Cheltenham

SIDFORD - Devon → See Sidmouth

SIDLESHAM

West Sussex - Regional map n° **4**-C3

Crab & Lobster

SEAFOOD • PUB This sympathetically modernised inn is superbly located within the striking landscape of Pagham Harbour Nature Reserve. Well-presented, seafood-focused dishes are at the restaurant end of the scale, although lunch also sees sandwiches and salads. Comfortable bedrooms have a modern, minimalist style.

Menu £ 23 (weekday lunch) - Carte £ 32/71

5 rooms - £ 95/150 £ 185/310

Mill Ln PO20 7NB - 01243 641233 - www.crab-lobster.co.uk

Landseer House

FAMILY • ELEGANT Tastefully furnished guesthouse, with numerous antiques and pleasant views of the surrounding wetlands. Contemporary bedrooms; go for Room 1 - the most luxurious. Those in the garden have their own terraces and kitchens.

6 rooms - £ 105/130 £ 125/195

Cow Ln PO20 7LN - South : 1.5 mi by B 2145 and Keynor Ln - 01243 641525 - www.landseerhouse.co.uk - Closed 23-28 December

SIDMOUTH

Devon - Pop. 12 569 - Regional map n° **1**-D2

Riviera

TRADITIONAL • PERSONALISED This characterful Regency hotel stands proudly on the promenade and has been family run for over 40 years. The elegant entrance hall leads through to modern guest areas. Classical bedrooms come in blues and golds and many have bay windows and sea views. Menus are traditional and cream teas are a speciality.

26 rooms (dinner included) - £ 116/208 £ 232/464

The Esplanade EX10 8AY - 01395 515201 - www.hotelriviera.co.uk - Closed 2 January-mid February

Sidmouth Harbour

BOUTIQUE HOTEL • CONTEMPORARY This Victorian property sits in an elevated position and offers great views out over the bay – head for the sleek seafood-orientated restaurant or cocktail bar for some of the finest views. Bright, nautically inspired bedrooms have a New England style; the best have balconies and sea outlooks.

57 rooms – £ 120/300 £ 120/300

The Westcliff, Manor Rd EX10 8RU – 01395 513252 – www.sidmouth-harbour-hotel.co.uk

at Sidford North: 2 mi

Salty Monk

REGIONAL CUISINE • INTIMATE XX Set in an old 16C salt house, a proudly run restaurant which pleasantly blends the old and the new. Dine from a menu of refined, classically based dishes in the Abbots Den or the Garden Room; or come for coffee and cake or afternoon tea. Bedrooms have good extras and there's a gym and hot tub in the garden.

Carte £ 28/50

7 rooms – £ 85/145 £ 135/200

Church St EX10 9QP – on A 3052 – 01395 513174 (booking essential) – www.saltymonk.com – dinner only – Closed January, Sunday and Monday

SKELTON

Cumbria – Regional map n° **12**-A2

Dog and Gun Inn

TRADITIONAL BRITISH • FRIENDLY Beams, an open fire and Lizzie's greeting give this modest pub a welcoming feel. Ben is an experienced hand in the kitchen and recognises that the locals want hearty, familiar dishes, so he takes pub classics, refines them and elevates them to new heights; they're not only delicious but good value too.

Carte £ 23/34

CA11 9SE – 017684 84301 – www.dogandgunskelton.co.uk – dinner only and Sunday lunch – Closed Monday-Tuesday

SNETTISHAM

Norfolk – Pop. 2 570 – Regional map n° **8**-B1

The Old Bank

MODERN BRITISH • BISTRO X A friendly young couple run this laid-back restaurant that has a café-like feel. Cooking is contrastingly modern and sophisticated, with well-crafted dishes keeping local produce to the fore, from Norfolk asparagus to Cromer crab. Lunch is good value and dinner sees the use of more luxurious ingredients.

Menu £ 20 (lunch) – Carte dinner £ 28/35

10 Lynn Rd PE31 7LP – 01485 544080 (booking essential) – www.theoldbankbistro.co.uk – Closed 2 weeks January, 1 week May, 1 week November, Sunday dinner, Monday and Tuesday

Rose and Crown

TRADITIONAL CUISINE • PUB 14C pub featuring a warren of rooms with uneven floors and low beamed ceilings. Gutsy cooking uses locally sourced produce, with globally influenced dishes alongside trusty pub classics. Impressive children's adventure fort. Modern bedrooms are decorated in sunny colours, and offer a good level of facilities.

Carte £ 24/39

16 rooms – £ 100 £ 120

Old Church Rd PE31 7LX – 01485 541382 – www.roseandcrownsnettisham.co.uk

SOAR MILL COVE - Devon → See Salcombe

SOMERTON

Somerset - Pop. 4 133 - Regional map n° **2**-B2

White Hart

MEDITERRANEAN CUISINE • RUSTIC A 16C inn on the village's main marke[t] square; its beautiful parquet-floored entrance leads to six characterful rooms, in[-]cluding 'the barn' where you can watch the chefs at work. Seasonal food centre[s] around the wood burning oven. Bedrooms are cosy and modern; Room 3, with bath centre stage, is the best.

Carte £ 27/35

8 rooms - £ 85/125 £ 85/125 - £ 6

Market Pl TA11 7LX - 01458 272273 - www.whitehartsomerton.com

SONNING-ON-THAMES - Wokingham → See Reading

SOUTH BRENT

Devon - Pop. 2 559 - Regional map n° **1**-C2

Glazebrook House

COUNTRY HOUSE • PERSONALISED A stunning 150 year old property set in [4] acres. It's been delightfully refurbished and features an eclectic mix of décor, lovely teak parquet floor and 'British' collections. Beautifully appointed, boutiqu[e] bedrooms are named after characters from Alice in Wonderland. Menus offer sea[-]sonal British dishes.

9 rooms - £ 134/234 £ 159/259

TQ10 9JE - Southwest : 0.5 mi by Exeter Rd - 01364 73322 - www.glazebrookhouse.com - Closed 7-20 January

SOUTH DALTON

East Riding of Yorkshire - Regional map n° **13**-C2

Pipe and Glass (James Mackenzie)

MODERN BRITISH • RUSTIC This charming 15C pub was originally the gate house of Dalton Park and its passionate owners have nurtured it from scruff[y] pub to destination dining inn. James champions regional ingredients in unfussy instantly recognisable dishes which are packed with flavour and exhibit subtl[e] modern touches. Bedrooms are luxurious and have private patios overlookin[g] the estate.

→ Crab with pickled carrot and coriander salad, roast lemon purée and hazelnuts Parkin-crusted loin of deer with haunch pasty and sticky red cabbage. Cinnamo[n] baked rice pudding with blood orange curd and doughnuts.

Carte £ 27/60

5 rooms - £ 170/210 £ 200/260

West End HU17 7PN - 01430 810246 - www.pipeandglass.co.uk - Closed 2 weeks January, Sunday dinner and Monday except bank holidays

SOUTH FERRIBY

North Lincolnshire - Pop. 651 - Regional map n° **13**-C3

Hope & Anchor

TRADITIONAL BRITISH • PUB A rustic, nautically-themed pub with Humbe[r] views. Tasty British dishes display touches of originality and showcase fish fro[m] Grimsby, fruit and veg from their smallholding and meats from the Lake Distric[t] - which are aged in a glass-fronted drying cabinet. Bedrooms are modern; som[e] have estuary views.

Carte £ 19/36

5 rooms - £ 95/115 £ 95/115 - £ 10

Sluice Rd DN18 6JQ - 01652 635334 - www.thehopeandanchorpub.co.uk - Closed first week January and Monday except bank holidays

SOUTH POOL

Devon - Regional map n° **1**-C3

Millbrook Inn

TRADITIONAL CUISINE • **PUB** You'll find this appealingly worn pub squeezed in between the houses on a narrow street. It really is a part of the village and hosts various events such as good value 'Village Table' nights and BBQs (which coincide with the tides). It also has two pleasant terraces and a lovely boutique apartment.

Carte £ 20/72

TQ7 2RW - 01548 531581 - www.millbrookinnsouthpool.co.uk

SOUTHAMPTON

Southampton - Pop. 253 651 - Regional map n° **4**-B2

Jetty

MODERN BRITISH • **DESIGN** The sister of the Jetty in Christchurch sits within a striking glass hotel. It's a stylish, elegant place with floor to ceiling windows and a great terrace offering spectacular views of the Ocean Village marina. Boldly flavoured, generously proportioned modern classics have a seafood bias.

Menu £ 20 (lunch and early dinner)
- Carte £ 37/46

Southampton Harbour Hotel, 5 Maritime Walk, Ocean Village SO14 3QT - 023 8110 3456 (booking essential) - www.southampton-harbour-hotel.co.uk

Southampton Harbour

LUXURY • MODERN This sleek harbourside property has an impressive super-yacht inspired design and its profusion of glass makes the most of the views. Luxurious bedrooms come with binoculars, coffee machines and Egyptian cotton linen, and the suites boast large balconies. Kick-back in the smart spa, the cinema room, the lively rooftop cocktail-bar-cum-brasserie or the chic restaurant.

85 rooms - †£ 190/290 ††£ 190/290 - 2 suites

5 Maritime Walk, Ocean Village SO14 3QT - 023 8110 3456 - www.southampton-harbour-hotel.co.uk

Jetty - See restaurant listing

Pig in the Wall

TOWNHOUSE • PERSONALISED A delightfully run, early 19C property that's been lovingly restored. Smart, boutique bedrooms come with antiques, super-comfy beds and Egyptian cotton linen. The rustic café-cum-deli serves light meals; for something more substantial they will chauffeur you to their sister restaurant.

12 rooms - †£ 135/190 ††£ 135/190 - £ 18

8 Western Esplanade SO14 2AZ - 023 8063 6900 - www.thepighotel.co.uk

at Netley Marsh West: 6.5 mi by A33 off A336

Spot in the Woods

BUSINESS • MODERN Inside, brown and orange tones give this red-brick Victorian house a relaxed Mediterranean feel. Boutique bedrooms have good facilities and thoughtful extras - ask for one with a roof terrace. The airy café overlooks the garden and offers everything from all day breakfasts and cake to pub-style dishes.

11 rooms - †£ 85/145 ††£ 95/155

174 Woodlands Rd SO40 7GL - 023 8029 3784 - www.spotinthewoods.co.uk

SOUTHBOROUGH - Kent ➔ See Royal Tunbridge Wells

SOUTHBOURNE - Bournemouth ➔ See Bournemouth

SOUTHEND-ON-SEA

Southend-on-Sea - Pop. 175 547 - Regional map n° **7**-C3

Seven (N)

BOUTIQUE HOTEL • DESIGN Take in views over the beach and the Thames Estuary from this purpose-built property at the end of a period terrace. Inside it's a rather blingy, courtesy of a polished copper gin bar, a kitsch brasserie servin modern British dishes and stylish bedrooms; the 4th floor rooms all come wit gold hues.

37 rooms - †£ 105/125 ††£ 200/300 - ☕ £ 10

7 Clifton Terr ✉ SS1 1DT - ☎ 01702 900010 - www.thesevenhotel.co.uk

SOUTH LEIGH

Oxfordshire - Regional map n° **6**-B2

Mr Hanbury's Mason Arms

MODERN CUISINE • INN This attractive thatched pub might look traditiona but inside it's as quirky and idiosyncratic as its name implies. Flagged floors an antique signs are juxtaposed with intriguing modern art. Lunch features ba snacks and classics, while dinner menus are modern and creative. Bedrooms ar stylishly furnished.

Carte £ 28/42

7 rooms - †£ 100/165 ††£ 120/425 - ☕ £ 15

Station Rd ✉ OX29 6XF - ☎ 01993 656238 - www.hanburysmasonarms.co.uk

SOUTHPORT

Merseyside - Pop. 91 703 - Regional map n° **11**-A2

Bistrot Vérité

CLASSIC FRENCH • FRIENDLY A friendly, experienced husband and wife tean run this bustling neighbourhood bistro in a pretty parade. Expect gutsy Frenc dishes with a classic base, punchy flavours and the occasional British touch; th 2 course lunch is good value.

Menu £ 19 (lunch) - Carte dinner £ 26/46

7 Liverpool Rd, Birkdale ✉ PR8 4AR - South : 1.5 mi by A 565 - ☎ 01704 564199 (booking essential) - www.bistrotverite.co.uk - Closed 1 week summer, 1 week winter, 25-26 December, 1 January, Sunday, Monday and lunch Tuesday

Vincent

BUSINESS • DESIGN A striking glass, steel and stone hotel set beside the gardens and bandstand. It has a stylish, boutique look, a chic bar and a fitnes room and spa. Sleek, modern bedrooms come in dark colours and boast Ne spresso machines and deep Japanese soaking tubs.

59 rooms ☕ - †£ 109/289 ††£ 119/299 - 2 suites

98 Lord St ✉ PR8 1JR - ☎ 01704 883800 - www.thevincenthotel.com

SOUTHROP

Gloucestershire - Pop. 245 - Regional map n° **2**-D1

Swan

TRADITIONAL BRITISH • NEIGHBOURHOOD A delightful Virginia creeper clad inn set in a quintessential Cotswold village in the Leach Valley. With its characterful low-beamed rooms and charming service, it's popular with locals and visitors alike. Dishes are mainly British-based and feature garden produce; try the delicious homemade bread.

Carte £ 24/41

✉ GL7 3NU - ☎ 01367 850205 - www.theswanatsouthrop.co.uk - Closed 25 December

SOUTHWOLD

Suffolk - Pop. 1 098 - Regional map n° **8**-D2

Swan

HISTORIC BUILDING • CONTEMPORARY This iconic coaching inn sits in the heart of town beside the Adnams Brewery, who own the place. Its origins may be 17C but its brightly furnished interior brings it into the 21C; ask for a bedroom in the lovely garden wing. The restaurant serves refined British classics; start with an Adnams ale in the bar.

42 rooms - £ 120/160 £ 200/295 - 2 suites

Market Pl IP18 6EG
- 01502 722186 - www.adnams.co.uk

Crown

INN • CONTEMPORARY A few doors down from its sister, the Swan, is this appealingly laid-back 17C coaching inn. Bedrooms have a modern 'coastal chic' style; those to the rear are the quietest. Have a pint of Adnams in the tiny nautically-themed bar, a stone's throw from their brewery. Daily menus keep things traditional.

14 rooms - £ 99/149 £ 165/265

90 High St IP18 6DP
- 01502 722275 - www.adnams.co.uk

Take note of the classification: you should not expect the same level of service in a X or as in a XXXXX or .

SOWERBY BRIDGE

West Yorkshire - Pop. 4 601 - Regional map n° **13**-A2

Moorcock Inn

CREATIVE BRITISH • RUSTIC A substantial yet cosy stone pub in the industrial heartland. Blackboards list homemade charcuterie and appealing snacks, while the 6 course daily set menu focuses on ingredients from Yorkshire's fields and coasts. They use lots of preservation techniques and the age of the produce informs the accompaniments.

Menu £ 35 - Carte £ 16/24

Moorbottom Lane, Norland HX6 3RP - Southwest : 2 mi off B 6113
- 01422 832103 (booking essential) - www.themoorcock.co.uk
- dinner only and lunch Saturday-Sunday - Closed Sunday dinner, Monday and Tuesday

SPARSHOLT - Hampshire ➜ See Winchester

SPRIGG'S ALLEY - Oxfordshire ➜ See Chinnor

STADHAMPTON

Oxfordshire - Pop. 702 - Regional map n° **6**-B2

Crazy Bear

LUXURY • MODERN Wacky converted pub with a London bus reception, a characterful bar, a smart glasshouse and even a Zen garden. Sumptuous, quirky bedrooms are spread about the place; some have padded walls and infinity baths. Eat in 'Thai' or flamboyant 'English', with its mirrored walls and classic British and French dishes.

18 rooms - £ 249/449 £ 249/449

Bear Ln OX44 7UR - Off Wallingford rd
- 01865 890714 - www.crazybeargroup.co.uk

STAFFORD

Staffordshire – Pop. 68 472 – Regional map n° **10**-C1

Moat House

BUSINESS • CLASSIC The original 15C farmhouse is now a pub and the sympathetically added extensions house characterful wood-panelled lounges, attractively furnished modern bedrooms and an orangery restaurant. There's a duck pond to the front and a canal to the rear. It's been owned and run by the same family for many years.

41 rooms – £ 90/125 £ 110/145 – 1 suite

Lower Penkridge Rd, Acton Trussell ✉ ST17 0RJ – South : 3.75 mi by A 449 – ✆ 01785 712217 – www.moathouse.co.uk

The Swan

INN • CONTEMPORARY This 17C coaching inn is found among some impressive old buildings, including a neighbouring Jacobean townhouse. Inside it's stylish and contemporary with up-to-date bedrooms. The brasserie offers a large menu of modern classics and there's also a coffee shop and two bars which share a pleasant terrace.

31 rooms – £ 75/100 £ 80/150

46 Greengate St ✉ ST16 2JA – ✆ 01785 258142 – www.theswanstafford.co.uk – Closed 24-25 December

STALISFIELD

Kent – Regional map n° **5**-C2

Plough Inn

TRADITIONAL BRITISH • RUSTIC The term 'rustic' could have been invented for this 15C pub, with its thick walls, farming implements, exposed beams and hop bines. You'll find the usual suspects on the bar menu and more ambitious dishes on the à la carte – along with an impressive range of Kentish real ales. Bedrooms are modern and stylish.

Carte £ 24/34

6 rooms – £ 90/150 £ 100/150

✉ ME13 0HY – ✆ 01795 890256 – www.theploughinnstalisfield.co.uk – Closed Sunday dinner and Monday in winter

STAMFORD

Lincolnshire – Pop. 22 574 – Regional map n° **9**-C2

The Oak Room

TRADITIONAL BRITISH • CLASSIC DÉCOR XXX Smart dress is required in this lovely oak-panelled dining room, which is found at the heart of an equally charming 16C coaching inn. Classical menus are largely British based with a few international influences. Alongside their speciality beef carving trolley, there are also 'cheese' and 'sweet' trolleys.

Menu £ 30 (weekday lunch) – Carte £ 37/86

George of Stamford Hotel, 71 St Martins ✉ PE9 2LB – ✆ 01780 750750 – www.georgehotelofstamford.com

George of Stamford

INN • ELEGANT This characterful coaching inn dates back over 500 years and, despite its bedrooms having a surprisingly contemporary feel, it still offers good old-fashioned hospitality. There are plenty of places to relax, with various bars, lounges and a walled garden. Dine in the laid-back Garden Room or the more formal restaurant – both spill out into the lovely courtyard in summer.

45 rooms – £ 130/180 £ 215/360 – 1 suite

71 St Martins ✉ PE9 2LB – ✆ 01780 750750 – www.georgehotelofstamford.com

The Oak Room – See restaurant listing

William Cecil

COUNTRY HOUSE • HISTORIC This 17C stone Plantation House is named after the 1st Baron Burghley and is where they filmed Pride and Prejudice. Inside it's shabby-chic, with Colonial-style bedrooms featuring wood carvings and pastoral scene wallpaper. The restaurant has intimate, Regency-style booths; take afternoon tea on the terrace.

27 rooms – £ 85/190 £ 95/190 – 1 suite

High St, St Martins ✉ PE9 2LJ – ✆ 01780 750070 – www.thewilliamcecil.co.uk

STANSTED MOUNTFITCHET

Essex – Pop. 6 669 – Regional map n° **7**-B2

Linden House

TOWNHOUSE • ROMANTIC This part-timbered former antique shop is now a smart hotel. Bedrooms have a pleasing mix of classic and modern elements and most come with a bath in the room. The bar has a shabby-chic, masculine feel and the rustic restaurant offers a menu of classic dishes given a modern twist.

9 rooms – £ 90/150 £ 125/180

1-3 Silver St ✉ CM24 8HA – ✆ 01279 813003 – www.lindenhousestansted.co.uk

Chimneys

TOWNHOUSE • COSY Charming 17C house with low-beamed ceilings and cosy guest areas. Pine-furnished bedrooms have a modern cottagey style and come with homely touches. Tasty breakfasts include Manx kippers and smoked haddock with poached eggs.

3 rooms – £ 62 £ 90

44 Lower St ✉ CM24 8LR – on B 1351 – ✆ 01279 813388
– www.chimneysguesthouse.co.uk

STANTON

Suffolk – Pop. 2 073 – Regional map n° **8**-C2

Leaping Hare

MODERN BRITISH • RUSTIC This beautiful 17C timber-framed barn sits at the centre of a 7 acre vineyard. Carefully judged cooking relies on well-sourced seasonal ingredients – many from their own farm. Sit on the lovely terrace and choose from the good value Vintners menu or pick something more refined from the à la carte.

Menu £ 21/28 – Carte £ 24/38

Wyken Vineyards ✉ IP31 2DW – South : 1.25 mi by Wyken Rd
– ✆ 01359 250287 (booking essential) – www.wykenvineyards.co.uk
– lunch only and dinner Friday-Saturday – Closed 25 December-5 January

STAVERTON – Northamptonshire → See Daventry

STILLINGTON

North Yorkshire – Regional map n° **13**-C2

Bay Tree

TRADITIONAL BRITISH • FRIENDLY Enthusiastic couple Ed and Harri run this homely village pub. Sit by the fire, in the cosy snug or in the conservatory dining room and enjoy a traditional pub dish or more adventurous daily special. They have a real passion for gin, with 110 varieties offered, along with the likes of gin-cured salmon.

Carte £ 15/44

Main St ✉ YO61 1JU
– ✆ 01347 811394 – www.theybaytreeyork.co.uk
– Closed Monday and Tuesday

STILTON

Cambridgeshire – ✉ Peterborough – Pop. 2 455 – Regional map n° **8**-A2

Bell Inn

INN • COSY This historic coaching inn on the Great North Road is where the first stilton cheese was sold. Most of the bedrooms have a traditional fee and two have four-posters and jacuzzi baths. The characterful lounge and bar feature exposed brick and beams, and the Galleried Restaurant offer a modern menu.

22 rooms – £ 90/126 £ 115/150

Great North Rd ✉ PE7 3RA
– ✆ 01733 241066 – www.thebellstilton.co.uk
– Closed 25 December

STOCKBRIDGE

Hampshire – Pop. 570 – Regional map n° **4**-B2

Greyhound on the Test

MODERN BRITISH • PUB Mustard-coloured pub with over a mile of River Test fishing rights to the rear. Low beams and wood burning stoves abound and elegant décor gives it a French bistro feel. The appealing range of dishes includes modern small plates, a selection 'on toast' and a classical daily menu; the chef will also cook your catch. Homely bedrooms have large showers and quality bedding.

Menu £ 20 (weekday lunch) – Carte £ 28/48

10 rooms – £ 90/150 £ 150/220

31 High St ✉ SO20 6EY
– ✆ 01264 810833 – www.thegreyhoundonthetest.co.uk
– Closed 25-26 December

STOCKPORT

Greater Manchester – Pop. 105 878 – Regional map n° **11**-B3

brassicagrill

MODERN BRITISH • NEIGHBOURHOOD The walls of this neighbourhood restaurant are filled with old lithographs of brassica plants and tea lights twinkle on the tables in the evening. Modern British cooking is honest, flavoursome and good value – and the homity pie is a hit. The team have worked together for many years and it shows.

Menu £ 17 – Carte £ 18/44

27 Shaw Rd ✉ SK4 4AG – Northwest : 2.5 mi by A 6 off B 5169 – ✆ 0161 442 6730 – www.brassicagrill.com – Closed 25-26 December, 1 January, Sunday dinner and Monday

Where The Light Gets In

MODERN BRITISH • RUSTIC This large, loft-style restaurant is located on the top floor of a Victorian coffee warehouse and its open kitchen forms part of the room. The surprise menu is formed from whatever they have foraged that day and beasts are brought in whole and fully utilised. Matching wine flights focus on natural wines.

Menu £ 80 – surprise menu only

7 Rostron Brow ✉ SK1 7JY – ✆ 0161 477 5744 (booking essential) – www.wtlgi.co – dinner only – Closed Christmas-New Year, 2 weeks Easter, last week August, first week September and Sunday-Tuesday

STOKE BY NAYLAND

Suffolk – Regional map n° **8**-C3

Crown

REGIONAL CUISINE • PUB Smart, relaxed pub in a great spot overlooking the Box and Stour river valleys. Globally influenced menus feature produce from local farms and estates, with seafood from the east coast. Well-priced wine list with over 25 wines by the glass. Large, luxurious, superbly equipped bedrooms with king or super king sized beds; some have French windows and terraces.

Carte £ 19/44

11 rooms – £ 110/150 £ 145/295

CO6 4SE – 01206 262001 – www.crowninn.net – Closed 25-26 December

STOKE HOLY CROSS – Norfolk → See Norwich

STOKE POGES

Buckinghamshire – Pop. 3 962 – Regional map n° **6**-D3

Stoke Park

LUXURY • CLASSIC Grade I listed Palladian property – once home to the Penn family, who created England's first country club. Extensive sporting activities, impressive spa and characterful guest areas. Mix of chic and luxurious 'Feature' bedrooms.

49 rooms – £ 190/350 £ 190/350 – £ 25 – 2 suites

Park Rd SL2 4PG – Southwest : 0.75 mi on B 416 – 01753 717171 – www.stokepark.com – Closed 2-4 January and 25-26 December

Stoke Place

HISTORIC • MODERN A 17C Queen Anne mansion set by a large lake and surrounded by delightful gardens and parkland. Quirky guest areas feature bold wallpapers and original furnishings and the uniquely styled bedrooms are spread about the house and the grounds. Modern menus use herbs, veg and fruit from the kitchen garden.

39 rooms – £ 95/200 £ 95/300 – £ 16

Stoke Green SL2 4HT – South : 0.5 mi by B 416 – 01753 534790 – www.stokeplace.co.uk

STON EASTON

Somerset – Pop. 579 – Regional map n° **2**-C2

Ston Easton Park

LUXURY • ELEGANT Striking Palladian mansion in 36 acres of delightful grounds. Fine rooms of epic proportions are filled with antiques, curios and impressive flower arrangements. Many of the bedrooms have coronet or four-poster beds; three are set in a cottage. Classic menus showcase produce from the Victorian kitchen garden.

23 rooms – £ 120/190 £ 195/345 – 2 suites

BA3 4DF – 01761 241631 – www.stoneaston.co.uk

STOW-ON-THE-WOLD

Gloucestershire – Pop. 2 042 – Regional map n° **2**-D1

Old Butchers

CLASSIC CUISINE • FRIENDLY XX An old butcher's shop with quirky décor, colourful chairs and ice bucket and colander lampshades. The menu offers plenty of choice from old favourites to dishes with a Mediterranean slant. The 'bin end' wine list is worth a look.

Carte £ 23/56

7 Park St GL54 1AQ – 01451 831700 – www.theoldbutchers.com – Closed 25-26 December

Number Four at Stow

BUSINESS • CONTEMPORARY Contemporary, open-plan hotel; so named as it' the fourth this experienced family own. The comfy lounge boasts bold brushe velvet seating, while the bright, compact bedrooms feature smart leather head boards, cream furniture and modern facilities. The comfortable brasserie offers classical menu.

18 rooms - £ 100/145 £ 145/170 - 3 suites

Fosseway GL54 1JX - South : 1.25 mi by A 429 on A 424 - 01451 830297 - www.hotelnumberfour.co.uk - Closed 23 December-27 January

Number Nine

FAMILY • COSY Expect a warm welcome at this ivy-clad, 18C stone house close to the historic town square. The cosy lounge and breakfast room boas exposed stone walls, open fireplaces and dark wood beams. A winding stair case leads up to the pleasant wood-furnished bedrooms, which come wit plenty of extras.

3 rooms - £ 55/65 £ 85/90

9 Park St GL54 1AQ - 01451 870333 - www.number-nine.info

at Lower Oddington East: 3 mi by A436 Stow-On-The-Wold

The Fox at Oddington

MODERN BRITISH • PUB A creeper-clad, quintessentially English pub at th heart of a peaceful Cotswold village, with beamed ceilings, solid stone walls flagged floors and plenty of cosy nooks and crannies. The menu focuses on care fully prepared, tasty British and European dishes. Comfy bedrooms are individu ally furnished.

Menu £ 20 (weekday lunch)
- Carte £ 29/47

3 rooms - £ 95/125 £ 95/125

GL56 0UR - 01451 870555 (booking essential) - Closed 25 December

at Daylesford East: 3.5 mi by A436 Stow-On-The-Wold

Café at Daylesford Organic

MODERN BRITISH • FASHIONABLE Stylish café attached to a farm shop; it rustic interior boasting an open charcoal grill and a wood-fired oven. During th day tuck into light dishes and small plates; at night you can book and candle-li suppers step things up a gear. Everything is organic, with much of the produc coming from the farm.

Carte £ 24/44

GL56 0YG - 01608 731700 (bookings not accepted) - www.daylesford.com - Closed 25-26 December and Sunday dinner

at Bledington Southeast: 4 mi by A436 on B4450

Kings Head Inn

TRADITIONAL BRITISH • INN A charming 16C former cider house on a pictur esque village green, bisected by a stream filled with bobbing ducks. Choos from appealing bar snacks, pub classics or some more interesting modern dishes The large bar has a vast inglenook fireplace and bedrooms are cosy; ask for on in the courtyard.

Carte £ 28/47

12 rooms - £ 80/110 £ 110/140

The Green OX7 6XQ - 01608 658365 - www.kingsheadinn.net - Closed 25-26 December

at Nether Westcote Southeast: 4.75 mi by A429 and A424

Feathered Nest

MODERN CUISINE • INN XX This 17C former malt house sits in an idyllic spot overlooking the valley and boasts a characterful flag-floored bar with leather saddle stools and two timbered dining rooms. Refined modern cooking is full of colour and beautifully presented. Well-appointed bedrooms are furnished with antiques.

Menu £ 38 (weekday lunch)/65

4 rooms - †£ 255/310 ††£ 255/310

OX7 6SD - 01993 833030 - www.thefeatherednestinn.co.uk - Closed last week February, first week March, last week July, first week August, last week October, 25 December and Monday-Wednesday

STRATFORD-UPON-AVON

Warwickshire - Pop. 27 830 - Regional map n° **10**-C3

Salt (Paul Foster)

MODERN BRITISH • RUSTIC X A lovely little restaurant with whitewashed walls and flagged floors; the simple look is in perfect harmony with the purity of the cooking. Unfussy, precisely prepared dishes show restrained originality. The weekday lunch is great value and the weekend tasting menus show the chefs' creativity to the full.

→ Cured turbot with cucumber, grapes, almonds and dill emulsion. BBQ Norfolk quail with peas and broad beans à la française, shallot purée. Sea buckthorn millefeuille with fig and goat's milk dulce de leche.

Menu £ 24/65

8 Church St CV37 6HB - 01789 263566 - www.salt-restaurant.co.uk - Closed 2 weeks Christmas-New Year, 1 week August, Sunday dinner, Monday and Tuesday

No 9 Church St.

MODERN BRITISH • BISTRO XX A friendly, cosy restaurant in a 400 year old townhouse a little off the main streets. The experienced chef-owner offers flavoursome British cooking with an original modern twist. Dishes are attractive and use lots of ingredients.

Menu £ 20 (lunch and early dinner)
- Carte dinner £ 27/54 **s**

9 Church St CV37 6HB - 01789 415522 - www.no9churchst.com - Closed 25 December-3 January, Sunday, Monday and bank holidays

Lambs

TRADITIONAL CUISINE • RUSTIC X Attractive 16C house with an interesting history; dine on one of several intimate levels, surrounded by characterful beams and original features. The classic bistro menu lists simply, carefully prepared favourites and daily fish specials.

Menu £ 15 (lunch and early dinner)
- Carte £ 25/43

12 Sheep St CV37 6EF - 01789 292554 - www.lambsrestaurant.co.uk - Closed 25-26 December and lunch Monday except bank holidays

Rooftop

MODERN BRITISH • DESIGN X Set atop the RSC Theatre; a curvaceous restaurant with a superb terrace and lovely views from its window tables. Come for a light lunch, afternoon tea, cocktails and snacks, or the pre-theatre set menu.

Menu £ 26 (early dinner)
- Carte £ 26/36

Royal Shakespeare Theatre, Waterside CV37 6BB - 01789 403449 - www.rsc.org.uk/eat - Closed 25 December and Sunday dinner

Arden

BUSINESS • MODERN Set in a great location opposite the RSC theatre, with a split-level terrace overlooking the river. It has a smart bar-lounge and also a second plush lounge for afternoon tea. Stylish bedrooms have bold wallpapers and vibrant colour schemes. The brasserie opens onto a landscaped riverside terrace.

45 rooms – †£ 133/255 ††£ 165/430

Waterside ✉ CV37 6BA – ✆ 01789 298682 – www.theardenhotelstratford.com

White Sails

LUXURY • PERSONALISED Keep an eye out for the tall wooden signs, which will help you locate this Edwardian guesthouse. Comfy bedrooms have smart bathrooms and come with good extras. Breakfast features a daily special and good veggie options.

4 rooms – †£ 90/115 ††£ 105/130

85 Evesham Rd ✉ CV37 9BE – Southwest : 1 mi on B 439 – ✆ 01789 550469 – www.white-sails.co.uk – Closed Christmas-New Year

STRETE – Devon → See Dartmouth

STRETTON

Rutland – Regional map n° **9**-C2

Jackson Stops Inn

TRADITIONAL BRITISH • RUSTIC A lovely stone and thatch pub comprising several different areas, including a small open-fired bar, a cosy barn and several beamed rooms. Choose from classics and pub favourites; the sharing boards are a hit.

Menu £ 16 (weekday lunch) – Carte £ 25/39

Rookery La ✉ LE15 7RA – ✆ 01780 410237 – www.thejacksonstops.com – Closed Monday except bank holidays and Sunday dinner

STROUD

Gloucestershire – Pop. 32 670 – Regional map n° **2**-C1

The Bear of Rodborough

INN • TRADITIONAL There's plenty of character to this 17C coaching inn, which stands on Rodborough Common and affords pleasant country views. The cosy beamed lounge and bar provide an atmospheric setting for a casual meal, while the more formal library offers modern cuisine. Bedrooms are stylish and contemporary.

45 rooms – †£ 80/110 ††£ 100/190

Rodborough Common ✉ GL5 5DE – Southeast : 2 mi by A 419 on Butterow Hill rd – ✆ 01453 878522 – www.cotswold-inns-hotels.co.uk

STUDLAND

Dorset – Pop. 299 – Regional map n° **2**-C3

Pig on the Beach

REGIONAL CUISINE • FRIENDLY Set within a large, plant-filled conservatory in a delightful country house; a rustic, shabby-chic restaurant where the wonderful kitchen garden informs the menu and additional produce comes from within 25 miles. Cooking is light and fresh and is accompanied by superb views over the lawns to Old Harry Rocks.

Carte £ 35/56

Pig on the Beach Hotel, Manor Rd ✉ BH19 3AU – ✆ 01929 450288 – www.thepighotel.com

Shell Bay

SEAFOOD • BISTRO Every table has a view at this superbly located restaurant on the water's edge, overlooking Brownsea Island. It started life as a shack and retains an appealingly rustic feel – and the terrace is a real hit come summer. The twice daily menu showcases local seafood in a mix of modern and classic dishes.

Carte £ 23/47

Ferry Rd ✉ BH19 3BA – North : 3 mi or via car ferry from Sandbanks – ✆ 01929 450363 (booking essential) – www.shellbay.net – Closed November-early February

Pig on the Beach

COUNTRY HOUSE • SEASIDE A delightful country house with commanding coastal views and lovely gardens leading down to the sea. It has a relaxed, shabby-chic style and the furnishings are a pleasing mix of the old and the new. For something a little different, stay in an old gardener's bothy or dovecote. Staff are extremely welcoming.

23 rooms – †£ 155/360 ††£ 155/360 – ☕ £ 18

Manor Rd ✉ BH19 3AU – ✆ 01929 450288 – www.thepighotel.com

Pig on the Beach – See restaurant listing

SUMMERHOUSE – Darlington → See Darlington

SUNNINGDALE

Windsor and Maidenhead – Regional map n° **6**-D3

Bluebells

MODERN CUISINE • INTIMATE The smart façade of this smoothly run restaurant is matched by an understatedly elegant interior furnished with white leather. Beautifully presented, delicate dishes are crafted using modern techniques and the fixed price menus offer great value.

Menu £ 29/40

Shrubbs Hill, London Rd ✉ SL5 0LE – Northeast : 0.75 mi on A 30 – ✆ 01344 622722 – www.bluebells-restaurant.com – Closed 1-12 January, 25-26 December, Sunday dinner, Monday and Tuesday

SUTTON

Central Bedfordshire – Pop. 299 – Regional map n° **7**-B1

John O'Gaunt Inn

TRADITIONAL CUISINE • COSY Well-run by experienced owners, this is a cosy, honest village inn with a fire-warmed bar, a smart dining room and delightful gardens overlooking wheat fields. The tried-and-tested menu includes some tasty 'Crumps Butchers' steaks.

Carte £ 26/42

30 High St ✉ SG19 2NE – ✆ 01767 260377 – www.johnogauntsutton.co.uk – Closed Monday except bank holidays and Sunday dinner

SUTTON GAULT

Cambridgeshire – Regional map n° **8**-B2

Anchor Inn

MODERN CUISINE • RUSTIC A pretty little cottage built in 1650; its history can be felt in its 3 cosy, rustic dining rooms. You'll find the odd pub classic but in the main cooking has more of a restaurant style, with some ambitious modern dishes thrown in.

Menu £ 15 (weekday lunch) – Carte dinner £ 26/48

4 rooms ☕ – †£ 60/112 ††£ 80/155

✉ CB6 2BD – ✆ 01353 778537 – www.anchor-inn-restaurant.co.uk – Closed 25-26 December

SUTTON COLDFIELD

West Midlands – Pop. 109 015 – Regional map n° **10**-C2

New Hall

HISTORIC • ELEGANT Despite its name, this is one of the oldest inhabite moated houses in England, dating back to the 13C. Mature, topiary-fille grounds give way to a characterful interior of wood panelling and staine glass. Bedrooms are luxurious. A mix of classic and modern dishes are offere in the restaurant.

60 rooms – £ 175/335 £ 185/235 – 5 suites

Walmley Rd ✉ B76 1QX – Southeast : 2.5 mi by A 5127 off Wylde Green Rd – ✆ 0121 378 2442 – www.handpickedhotels.co.uk/newhall

SWAFFHAM

Norfolk – Pop. 6 734 – Regional map n° **8**-C2

Strattons

TOWNHOUSE • PERSONALISED A laid-back, eco-friendly hotel in an eye-catcl ing 17C villa with Victorian additions. Quirky, individually styled bedrooms a spread about the place: some are duplex suites and some have terraces or cou yards. The rustic basement restaurant serves modern British dishes; breakfast taken in their deli.

14 rooms – £ 94/234 £ 99/254

4 Ash Cl ✉ PE37 7NH – ✆ 01760 723845 – www.strattonshotel.com – Closed 21-27 December

SWAY

Hampshire – Pop. 2 294 – Regional map n° **4**-A3

Manor at Sway

FAMILY • PERSONALISED The Manor sits in the centre of a busy New Forest villag Inside it's bold and bright with an appealing modern style; cosy bedrooms have Hypn beds – ask for one overlooking the delightful garden. The showy dining room has flo paisley wallpaper, black tables and a Mediterranean-influenced menu.

15 rooms – £ 90/240 £ 90/240

Station Rd ✉ SO41 1QE – ✆ 01590 682754 – www.themanoratsway.com

SWINBROOK – Oxfordshire ➜ See Burford

TALLAND BAY – Cornwall ➜ See Looe

TANGMERE – West Sussex ➜ See Chichester

TAPLOW

Buckinghamshire – Pop. 518 – Regional map n° **6**-C3

André Garrett at Cliveden House

MODERN CUISINE • LUXURY XXX A grand hotel dining room with views over th parterre garden. Classic recipes are brought up-to-date in refined, well-presente dishes where local and seasonal produce feature highly. These are accompanie by a superb wine list.

Menu £ 36 (lunch)
– Carte £ 48/115

Cliveden House, ✉ SL6 0JF – North : 2 mi by Berry Hill – ✆ 01628 607100 – www.clivedenhouse.co.uk

Cliveden House

HISTORIC • CLASSIC Stunning Grade I listed, 19C stately home in a superb location, boasting views over the formal parterre and National Trust gardens towards the Thames. The opulent interior boasts sumptuous antique-filled lounges and luxuriously appointed bedrooms. Unwind in the smart spa then take a picnic or afternoon tea hamper and kick-back in style on one of their vintage launches.

47 rooms - £ 495/750 £ 495/750 - 6 suites

SL6 0JF - North : 2 mi by Berry Hill - 01628 668561 - www.clivedenhouse.co.uk

André Garrett at Cliveden House - See restaurant listing

TATTENHALL

Cheshire West and Chester - Pop. 1 950 - Regional map n° **11**-A3

Allium by Mark Ellis

MODERN BRITISH • DESIGN XX You can't miss the bow-fronted façade of this former village shop, where you can come for everything from a light lunch or afternoon tea to a tasting menu and cocktails. Some dishes have a playful element and you can even cook your own steak on a lava stone at your table. Bedrooms are fresh and modern.

Carte £ 24/37

5 rooms - £ 45/65 £ 55/135

Lynedale House, High St CH3 9PX - 01829 771477 - www.theallium.co.uk - Closed Monday and Tuesday

TAUNTON

Somerset - Pop. 60 479 - Regional map n° **2**-B3

Castle Bow

MODERN CUISINE • ELEGANT XX Elegant, art deco style restaurant in the old snooker room of a Norman castle. Regularly changing menus showcase top quality regional produce. Well-balanced dishes are classically based yet refined, and feature some playful modern touches.

Carte £ 35/52

Castle Hotel, Castle Grn TA1 1NF - 01823 328328 - www.castlebow.com - dinner only - Closed January and Sunday-Tuesday

Augustus

MODERN BRITISH • BISTRO X An experienced chef and a bright, breezy team run this welcoming little bistro. Sit in the cosy, intimate dining room or the bright conservatory with sliding glass doors and a retractable roof. Hearty, unfussy cooking mixes French-influenced dishes with updated British classics.

Carte £ 25/46

3 The Courtyard, St James St. TA1 1JR - 01823 324354 (booking essential) - www.augustustaunton.co.uk - Closed 23 December-2 January, Sunday and Monday

Castle

HISTORIC BUILDING • CLASSIC Part-12C, wisteria-clad Norman castle with impressive gardens, a keep and two wells. It's been run by the Chapman family for three generations and retains a fittingly traditional style. Well-kept, individually decorated bedrooms. Castle Bow serves modern dishes; relaxed Brazz offers brasserie classics.

44 rooms - £ 115/130 £ 145/160

Castle Green TA1 1NF - 01823 272671 - www.the-castle-hotel.com

Castle Bow - See restaurant listing

TAVISTOCK

Devon – Pop. 12 280 – Regional map n° **1**-C2

Cornish Arms

TRADITIONAL CUISINE • COSY A fine selection of St Austell ales sit behir the bar, which provide a clue as to the owners. The knowledgeable team are ge uinely warm and welcoming and the mix of drinkers and diners make for a gre atmosphere. Appealing dishes mix classic elements with some unusual moder twists – and you'll have to go a long way to beat the sorbets! Bedrooms a bold and modern.

Menu £ 20 (weekday lunch) – Carte £ 21/48

7 rooms – †£ 110/220 ††£ 110/220

15 West St ✉ PL19 8AN – ✆ 01822 612145 – www.thecornisharmstavistock.co.uk – Closed dinner 24 December

Rockmount

TOWNHOUSE • CONTEMPORARY A 1920s house with a contrastingly contemp rary interior; set on a hill beside the Tavistock viaduct and overlooking the town rooftops. The sleek, individually furnished bedrooms might be compact but the come with extremely comfy beds and plenty of extras.

6 rooms – †£ 55/110 ††£ 65/130

Drake Rd ✉ PL19 0AX – ✆ 07445 009880 – www.rockmount-tavistock.com

Tavistock House

TOWNHOUSE • CONTEMPORARY This attractive 1820s townhouse has bee carefully restored by its passionate owners and, whilst some original features r main, it now has a stylish boutique appearance. There's an honesty bar in the ch lounge and light snacks are offered at lunch and dinner.

6 rooms – †£ 81/125 ††£ 99/144

50 Plymouth Rd ✉ PL19 8BU – ✆ 01822 481627 – www.tavistockhousehotel.co.u

at Gulworthy West: 3 mi on A390 ✉ Tavistock

Horn of Plenty

COUNTRY HOUSE • PERSONALISED This creeper-clad house sits on the hillsic overlooking the Tamar Valley and was originally built for the Duke of Bedford mine captain. Bedrooms are decorated with bright, eye-catching fabrics ar many have balconies or terraces; the Coach House rooms are the best. Moder menus utilise local produce.

16 rooms – †£ 110/335 ††£ 120/345

Gulworthy ✉ PL19 8JD – Northwest : 1 mi by B 3362 – ✆ 01822 832528 – www.thehornofplenty.co.uk

at Milton Abbot Northwest: 6 mi on B3362 ✉ Tavistock

Hotel Endsleigh

HISTORIC • CLASSIC Restored Regency lodge in an idyllic rural setting; spaciou guest areas offer wonderful countryside views and have a warm, classical sty with a contemporary edge. Comfortable, antique-furnished bedrooms boast a understated elegance; choose one overlooking the magnificent gardens.

18 rooms – †£ 180/405 ††£ 200/525 – 5 suites

✉ PL19 0PQ – Southwest : 1 mi – ✆ 01822 870000 – www.hotelendsleigh.com

at Chillaton Northwest: 6.25 mi by Chillaton rd ✉ Tavistock

Tor Cottage

TRADITIONAL • CLASSIC Remotely set cottage in 28 hillside acres, with peacef gardens and a lovely outdoor pool. Bedrooms, most in converted outhouse boast small kitchenettes and wood burning stoves. Breakfast is taken on the te race or in the conservatory. Charming owner.

5 rooms – †£ 98 ††£ 150/170

✉ PL16 0JE – Southwest : 0.75 mi by Tavistock rd, turning right at bridle path – ✆ 01822 860248 – www.torcottage.co.uk – Closed mid-December-1 February (minimum 2 night stay)

TEFFONT EVIAS

Wiltshire - Regional map n° **2**-C2

Howard's House

COUNTRY HOUSE • COSY This charming Grade II listed dower house stands in a beautiful English village; 'Howard' was a tenant here for 20yrs. Bright, understated bedrooms have village or garden views. The dining room has a sophisticated menu and opens onto a terrace. Good old-fashioned hospitality is provided by the friendly team.

9 rooms - £ 95/120 £ 150/225

SP3 5RJ - 01722 716392 - www.howardshousehotel.co.uk - Closed 23-26 December

TEMPLE SOWERBY - Cumbria → See Penrith

TENTERDEN

Kent - Pop. 7 118 - Regional map n° **5**-C2

Swan Wine Kitchen

MODERN BRITISH • FRIENDLY XX This rustic modern restaurant sits above the shop in the Chapel Down vineyard and boasts a cosy lounge and a lovely rooftop terrace with views over the vines; naturally, wines from the vineyard feature. Refined cooking is full of flavour and relies on just a few ingredients to do the talking.

Menu £ 29

Swan Chapel Down, Small Hythe Rd TN30 7NG - South : 2.75 mi by A 28 on B 2082 - 01580 761616 - www.swanchapeldown.co.uk - Closed dinner Sunday-Wednesday

TETBURY

Gloucestershire - Pop. 5 250 - Regional map n° **2**-C1

Conservatory

MODERN BRITISH • CHIC XX Next to the hotel's main entrance is this beautiful conservatory with a chic rustic style. One room overlooks the kitchen and its wood-fired oven; the other looks over the fields. Concise menus offer flavoursome modern dishes which showcase local ingredients - many from their own organically certified farm.

Menu £ 25 - Carte £ 30/56

Calcot Manor Hotel, Calcot GL8 8YJ - West : 3.5 mi on A 4135 - 01666 890391 - www.calcot.co

Gumstool Inn

TRADITIONAL CUISINE • CONTEMPORARY DÉCOR Set in the grounds of Calcot Manor; an attractive outbuilding with a contemporary 'Country Living' style. A flexible menu offers snacks, two sizes of starter and hearty British main courses - the open fire with a chargrill is a feature.

Carte £ 27/40

Calcot Manor Hotel, Calcot GL8 8YJ - West : 3.5 mi on A 4135 - 01666 890391 - www.calcot.co

Calcot Manor

FAMILY • CONTEMPORARY An impressive collection of converted farm buildings in a peaceful countryside setting, comprising ancient barns, old stables and a characterful farmhouse. Comfy lounges and stylish bedrooms have good mod cons; the outbuildings house a kids club, conference rooms and a superb spa complex.

35 rooms - £ 209/394 £ 209/394 - 1 suite

Calcot GL8 8YJ - West : 3.5 mi on A 4135 - 01666 890391 - www.calcot.co

Conservatory • **Gumstool Inn** - See restaurant listing

The Close

TOWNHOUSE • CONTEMPORARY The rear garden and courtyard of this 16C townhouse provide the perfect spot on a warm summer's day. Bold colours and contemporary furnishings blend well with the building's period features; look out for the superb cupola ceiling in the bar. The sophisticated restaurant serves refined modern dishes.

19 rooms – †£ 130/190 ††£ 200/370

Long St ✉ GL8 8AQ – ✆ 01666 502272 – www.cotswold-inns-hotels.co.uk

TEWKESBURY

Gloucestershire – Pop. 19 778 – Regional map n° **2**-C1

at Corse Lawn Southwest: 6 mi by A38 and A438 on B4211 ✉ Gloucester

Corse Lawn House

COUNTRY HOUSE • CLASSIC Elegant Grade II listed Queen Anne house, just off the village green and fronted by a pond. The traditionally appointed interior features open fires and antiques; some of the spacious bedrooms have four-poster or half-tester beds. Dine from classical menus in the formal restaurant or characterful bistro-bar.

18 rooms – †£ 90/110 ††£ 160/210 – 3 suites

✉ GL19 4LZ – ✆ 01452 780771 – www.corselawn.com – Closed 24-26 December

THETFORD

Norfolk – Pop. 24 833 – Regional map n° **8**-C2

The Mulberry

MEDITERRANEAN CUISINE • NEIGHBOURHOOD A bell tinkles as you enter this delightful stone property and the charming owner welcomes you in. The dining room leads through to a conservatory and a walled garden complete with a mulberry tree. Cooking is gutsy and boldly flavoured.

Carte £ 26/38

11 Raymond St ✉ IP24 2EA – ✆ 01842 824122 – www.mulberrythetford.co.uk – dinner only – Closed 6-18 August, 22-26 December, Sunday and Monday

THORNBURY

South Gloucestershire – ✉ Bristol – Pop. 11 687 – Regional map n° **2**-C1

Romy's Kitchen

INDIAN • SIMPLE In the centre of a medieval market town, in a listed stone building which was once part of the castle, is this sweet, friendly restaurant. The bubbly chef-owner freshly prepares everything from the naan to the chai-spiced ice cream.

Carte £ 17/33

2 Castle St ✉ BS35 1HB – ✆ 01454 416728 – www.romyskitchen.co.uk – Closed 25-28 December and Sunday-Tuesday

Thornbury Castle

HISTORIC • CLASSIC An impressive 16C castle with a long and illustrious history; Henry VIII stayed here on his honeymoon with Anne Boleyn! Characterful, baronial style bedrooms feature mullioned windows, wall tapestries, beams and huge fireplaces. The circular restaurant – sited in a tower – serves an elaborate modern menu.

27 rooms – †£ 145/230 ††£ 195/275 – 4 suites

Castle St ✉ BS35 1HH – ✆ 01454 281182 – www.thornburycastle.co.uk

Large towns and cities have detailed maps showing restaurant and hotel locations. Use the coordinates (eg.6CX-u) to find them.

THORNHAM

Norfolk - Regional map n° **8**-B1

Chequers Inn

TRADITIONAL CUISINE • FASHIONABLE Sit on the terrace or hire a wooden pavilion and take in the view. Cooking makes use of the local bounty; alongside the main menu there's tapas, such as tempura mussels, and pizzas which are stone-baked using local ingredients.

Carte £ 27/54

11 rooms - £ 120/195 £ 120/195

High St ✉ PE36 6LY - ✆ 01485 512229 - www.chequersinnthornham.com

THORNTON - Lancashire ➜ See Blackpool

THORNTON HOUGH

Merseyside - Regional map n° **11**-A3

Thornton Hall

BUSINESS • CONTEMPORARY A substantial manor house which has been added to over the years. Stained glass, carved wood reliefs and an oak-panelled restaurant with a ceiling crafted from leather and mother of pearl contrast with an impressive spa. The comfortable bedrooms are also a mix of the classic and contemporary.

62 rooms - £ 90/199 £ 90/350 - £ 17 - 1 suite

Neston Rd ✉ CH63 1JF - On B 5136 - ✆ 0151 336 3938
- www.thorntonhallhotel.com

THORPE MARKET

Norfolk - ✉ North Walsham - Regional map n° **8**-D1

Gunton Arms

TRADITIONAL BRITISH • INN This charming inn overlooks the 1,000 acre Gunton Estate deer park. Enjoy a tasty homemade snack over a game of pool or darts in the bar or make for a gnarled wood table by the fireplace in the flag-floored Elk Room. Dishes are fiercely seasonal; some - such as the Aberdeen Angus steaks - are cooked over the fire. Well-equipped bedrooms have a stylish country house feel.

Carte £ 20/46

16 rooms - £ 85/310 £ 95/320

Gunton Park ✉ NR11 8TZ - South : 1 mi on A 149
- ✆ 01263 832010 - www.theguntonarms.co.uk
- Closed 25 December and dinner 1 January

TICEHURST

East Sussex - ✉ Wadhurst - Pop. 1 705 - Regional map n° **5**-B2

Bell

TRADITIONAL BRITISH • INN With top hats as lampshades, tubas in the loos and a dining room called 'The Stable with a Table', quirky is this 16C coaching inn's middle name. Seasonal menus offer proper pub food and the rustic bedrooms and luxurious lodges in the garden share the pub's idiosyncratic charm.

Carte £ 23/42

11 rooms - £ 75/299 £ 75/299

High St ✉ TN5 7AS - ✆ 01580 200300 - www.thebellinticehurst.com

TICKTON - East Riding of Yorkshire → See Beverley

TILLINGTON - West Sussex → See Petworth

TISBURY

Wiltshire – Pop. 2 178 – Regional map n° **2**-C3

Beckford Arms

TRADITIONAL CUISINE • FRIENDLY Charming 18C inn with a beamed dining room, a rustic bar and a lovely country house sitting room – where films are screened on Sundays. There's a delightful terrace and garden with hammocks, a petanque pitch and even a dog bath. Tasty, unfussy classics and country-style dishes. Tasteful bedrooms provide thoughtful comforts. Smart duplex suites, a 3min drive away.

Carte £ 24/39

10 rooms – £ 95/130 £ 95/195

Fonthill Gifford SP3 6PX – Northwest : 2 mi by Greenwich Rd
– 01747 870385 (booking essential) – www.beckfordarms.com
– Closed 25 December

The Compasses Inn (N)

TRADITIONAL BRITISH • RUSTIC Hidden down narrow lanes in the Nadder Valley is this laid-back thatched inn. With 14C origins it's a hugely characterful place and it also has a pleasant terrace and garden. Fresh, tasty dishes have a mix of regional and Mediterranean influences. Bedrooms mix modern and antique furnishings.

Carte £ 24/36

5 rooms – £ 100 £ 110

Lower Chicksgrove SP3 6NB – East : 2.25 mi by Chicksgrove Rd
– 01722 714318 – www.thecompassesinn.com
– Closed 25 December

The sun's out? Enjoy eating outside on the terrace.

TITCHWELL

Norfolk – Pop. 99 – Regional map n° **8**-C1

The Conservatory

MODERN CUISINE • FASHIONABLE XX A smart hotel restaurant with views over the garden. Dinner offers two choices – a modern set price menu and a an à la carte of classics – and you can mix and match. Alternatively you can dine to sea views in the more informal, funky Eating Rooms, where they serve also light lunches.

Menu £ 42 – Carte £ 24/50 **s**

Titchwell Manor Hotel, PE31 8BB
– 01485 210221 – www.titchwellmanor.com
– dinner only

Titchwell Manor

COUNTRY HOUSE • PERSONALISED This attractive brick farmhouse has a stylish interior, where bare floorboards, Chesterfield sofas and seaside photos feature. Bedrooms in the main house have a quirky retro feel, while those in the grounds are modern and colourful. The Potting Shed – a stand-alone room – is a popular choice.

26 rooms – £ 75/240 £ 99/305

PE31 8BB – 01485 210221 – www.titchwellmanor.com

The Conservatory – See restaurant listing

Briarfields

TRADITIONAL • MODERN In winter, sink into a sofa by the cosy fire; in summer, relax in the secluded courtyard beside the pond or on the deck overlooking the salt marshes and the sea. Bedrooms are modern and immaculately kept; some open onto the garden.

23 rooms - †£ 85/140 ††£ 140/180

Main Street ✉ PE31 8BB
- ✆ 01485 210742 - www.briarfieldshotelnorfolk.co.uk

TITLEY

Herefordshire - ✉ Kington - Regional map n° **10**-A3

Stagg Inn

MODERN BRITISH • PUB Deep in rural Herefordshire, at the meeting point of two drover's roads, sits this part-medieval, part-Victorian pub. Seasonal menus offer tried-and-tested combinations; be sure to open with the home-salted crisps with vinegar dipping foam. The pub bedrooms can be noisy; opt for one in the old vicarage.

Carte £ 32/40

6 rooms - †£ 80/140 ††£ 100/140

✉ HR5 3RL - ✆ 01544 230221 (booking essential) - www.thestagg.co.uk
- Closed 30 January-8 February, 26 June-5 July, 6-22 November, 25-27 December, Monday and Tuesday

TOOT BALDON - Oxfordshire

→ See Oxford

TOPSHAM

Devon - ✉ Exeter - Pop. 3 730 - Regional map n° **1**-D2

Salutation Inn

MODERN CUISINE • DESIGN XX A 1720s coaching inn with a surprisingly contemporary interior. The glass-covered courtyard serves breakfast, a fixed price lunch and afternoon tea, while the stylish dining room offers nicely balanced weekly 4, 6 and 8 course menus of well-judged modern dishes. Bedrooms are up-to-date and understated.

Menu £ 25/43 - Carte lunch £ 22/31

6 rooms - †£ 115/205 ††£ 150/225

68 Fore St ✉ EX3 0HL - ✆ 01392 873060 (booking essential at dinner)
- www.salutationtopsham.co.uk - Closed 26 December and 1 January

TORQUAY

Torbay - Pop. 49 094 - Regional map n° **1**-C-D2

Elephant (Simon Hulstone)

MODERN BRITISH • FRIENDLY X Just across from the harbour is this brightly decorated bistro, which set out to prove that good food can be enjoyed in simple surroundings. Much of the produce comes from their 96 acre farm and the confidently crafted, eye-catching dishes are full of flavour; the seafood dishes are particularly accomplished.

→ Brixham crab with kohlrabi, apple, dulse and dashi gel. Fillet of cod with parsnip purée and spring onion butter. Rhubarb with baked custard, blood orange sorbet and pepper meringue.

Menu £ 22 (lunch) - Carte £ 33/47

3-4 Beacon Terr ✉ TQ1 2BH - ✆ 01803 200044 - www.elephantrestaurant.co.uk
- Closed 1-19 January, Sunday and Monday

Orange Tree

CLASSIC FRENCH · NEIGHBOURHOOD XX A homely, split-level restaurant se down a narrow town centre backstreet. The seasonally evolving menu is mad up of classically based, French-influenced dishes, which are carefully prepare and rely on fresh, local produce.

Carte £ 28/47

14-16 Parkhill Rd ✉ TQ1 2AL – ✆ 01803 213936 (booking essential) – www.orangetreerestaurant.co.uk – dinner only – Closed 2 weeks January, 2 weeks October-November, Sunday and Monday

Number 7

SEAFOOD · BISTRO X A personally run bistro in a terrace of Regency houses Fish-related photos and artefacts sit alongside extensive blackboard menus c seafood fresh from the Brixham day boats. The simplest dishes are the best They offer all of their 80+ wines – including some top vintages – by the glass.

Carte £ 25/47

7 Beacon Terr. ✉ TQ1 2BH – ✆ 01803 295055 – www.no7-fish.com – dinner only and lunch Wednesday-Saturday – Closed 2 weeks February, 1 week November, Christmas-New Year, Monday November-May and Sunday October-June

Somerville

TOWNHOUSE · PERSONALISED Set on the hillside, a short stroll from town, a traditional-looking hotel with a warm, welcoming interior. Bedrooms have good mod cons – Room 12 has direct garden access and is the only room to have breakfast served on the terrace.

8 rooms – £ 70/100 ££ 80/150

515 Babbacombe Rd. ✉ TQ1 1HJ – ✆ 01803 294755 – www.somervilletorquay.co.uk – Closed 25 November-26 December

Kingston House

FAMILY · CONTEMPORARY This enthusiastically run Victorian guesthouse comes with plenty of thoughtful touches, like fresh flowers displayed in the hallway homemade scones served by the fire on arrival and locally made chocolates lef in the bedrooms.

5 rooms – £ 85 £ 95/105

75 Avenue Rd ✉ TQ2 5LL – ✆ 01803 212760 – www.kingstonhousetorquay.co.uk – Closed December-February

Marstan

TOWNHOUSE · PERSONALISED Keenly run Victorian villa in a quiet part of town with an opulent lounge, a pool, a hot tub and a lovely suntrap terrace. Comfy bedrooms have warm red décor and sumptuous fabrics. Substantial breakfasts include homemade granola.

9 rooms – £ 65/155 £ 79/155

Meadfoot Sea Rd ✉ TQ1 2LQ – ✆ 01803 292837 – www.marstanhotel.co.uk – Closed November-15 March except 30 December-2 January

at Maidencombe North: 3.5 mi by A379 ✉ Torquay

Orestone Manor

TRADITIONAL · PERSONALISED A characterful house set amongst thick shrubbery and mature trees; dark wood furnishings and Oriental and African artefacts give it a colonial feel. Most of the individually designed bedrooms have sea or country views and some have hot tubs. Dine in the restaurant, the conservatory or on the terrace.

14 rooms – £ 90/110 £ 110/350

Rockhouse Ln ✉ TQ1 4SX – ✆ 01803 897511 – www.orestonemanor.com – Closed 3-30 January

at Babbacombe Northeast: 2 mi on A379

Cary Arms

INN • UNIQUE Built into the cliffside, this inn is wonderfully located and has great views out to sea. Sumptuous, well-equipped bedrooms have a New England style and include garden suites and duplex beach huts. There's a nautically-themed residents' lounge, a characterful bar and a terrace reaching down to the shore.

12 rooms - £ 196 £ 245

Babbacombe Beach TQ1 3LX - East : 0.25 mi by Beach Rd. - 01803 327110 - www.caryarms.co.uk - Closed 8-16 January

TREGONY

Cornwall - Pop. 768 - Regional map n° **1**-B3

Hay Barton

COUNTRY HOUSE • COSY The owner has lived in this warm, cosy farmhouse since the 1960s and still keeps some cattle. Country-style bedrooms come with Roberts radios and plenty to read; two have antique bath tubs. Cornish produce features at breakfast.

3 rooms - £ 70/80 £ 90/100

TR2 5TF - South : 1 mi on A 3078 - 01872 530288 - www.haybarton.com

TRELOWARREN - Cornwall → See Helston

TRENT

Dorset - Regional map n° **2**-C3

Rose & Crown

MODERN CUISINE • RUSTIC Sit in the characterful 'Buffs Bar' or the bright conservatory of this part-thatched 14C pub. Tasty country cooking is the order of the day - bypass the pub classics and go for the likes of pig's head with apple purée or calves' liver with sage fritters. Bedrooms come with patios overlooking the countryside.

Carte £ 25/40

3 rooms - £ 75/100 £ 85/120

DT9 4SL - 01935 850776 - www.theroseandcrowntrent.co.uk - Closed 25-26 December

TRESCO → See Scilly (Isles of)

TRING

Hertfordshire - Pop. 11 835 - Regional map n° **7**-A2

Crockers Chef's Table

MODERN BRITISH • DESIGN XX Arrive early for a cocktail in the smart bar before being shown through to a copper-walled room where orange leather stools are set at a large U-shaped counter. Lunch is at 12.30 and dinner at 7.30. Seasonal tasting menus feature creative, eye-catching modern dishes with distinct flavours and textures.

Menu £ 35/80 - tasting menu only

74 High St HP23 4AF - 01442 828971 (booking essential) - www.crockerstring.co.uk - Closed 2 weeks Christmas-New Year, 2 weeks summer, 1 week Easter, Sunday and Monday

TRURO

Cornwall - Pop. 20 332 - Regional map n° **1**-B3

Tabb's

MODERN BRITISH · NEIGHBOURHOOD XX Tucked away in the backstreets you'll find this unassuming former pub which comprises a series of homely cream and lilac rooms. The owner works alone in the kitchen, cooking refined, classically based dishes with masculine flavours. Sauces are a strength and the deep-fried courgettes are a must.

Menu £ 25 (lunch and early dinner) - Carte dinner £ 29/39

85 Kenwyn St ✉ TR1 3BZ - ✆ 01872 262110 (booking essential at lunch) - www.tabbs.co.uk - Closed 1 week January, 1 week October, Saturday lunch, Sunday and Monday

Mannings

BUSINESS · MODERN Imposing hotel located in the city centre, close to the cathedral. Boutique bedrooms are bright, modern and stylish; spacious apartment-style rooms - in the neighbouring mews - boast over-sized beds and galley kitchens. There's a chic cocktail bar and a stylish restaurant offering an eclectic all-day menu.

43 rooms - †£ 65/115 ††£ 125/145 - ☕ £ 11

Lemon St ✉ TR1 2QB - ✆ 01872 270345 - www.manningshotels.co.uk - Closed Christmas

TUDDENHAM

Suffolk - Pop. 400 - Regional map n° **8**-B2

Tuddenham Mill

MODERN BRITISH · CONTEMPORARY DÉCOR XX A delightful 18C watermill overlooking a millpond; the old workings are still in situ in the stylish bar, above which is a beamed restaurant with black furnishings. Cooking features quality seasonal produce in unusual, innovative combinations. Some of the modern bedrooms are in the attractive outbuildings.

Menu £ 26 (weekday lunch) - Carte dinner £ 36/54

20 rooms ☕ - †£ 145/475 ††£ 145/475

High St ✉ IP28 6SQ - ✆ 01638 713552 - www.tuddenhammill.co.uk

TURNERS HILL

West Sussex - Pop. 885 - Regional map n° **4**-D2

Alexander House

COUNTRY HOUSE · ELEGANT A stunning 18C country house in extensive grounds - once owned by Percy Shelley's family. The superb spa has 21 treatment rooms and a Grecian pool. Spacious bedrooms are well-equipped; the contemporary Cedar Lodge Suites have mood lighting and either a balcony or terrace. Dine in the brasserie or formal AG's.

58 rooms ☕ - †£ 179/359 ††£ 199/750 - 3 suites

East St ✉ RH10 4QD - East : 1 mi on B 2110 - ✆ 01342 714914 - www.alexanderhouse.co.uk

TYNEMOUTH

Tyne and Wear - Pop. 67 519 - Regional map n° **14**-B2

Grand

TRADITIONAL · CLASSIC A Victorian hotel with superb sea views: the Duchess of Northumberland's one-time holiday home. Original features include an impressive staircase. Bedrooms are either spacious and traditional or smaller and more modern - Room 222 has a four-poster and jacuzzi. The brasserie serves a modern menu.

46 rooms ☕ - †£ 69/120 ††£ 79/200

14 Grand Par. ✉ NE30 4ER - ✆ 0191 293 6666 - www.grandhoteltynemouth.co.uk/

Martineau

TOWNHOUSE • COSY Attractive 18C red-brick house named after Harriet Martineau. Cosy, individually furnished bedrooms come with thoughtful extras; two offer pleasant Tyne views. Superb communal breakfasts or a pre-ordered hamper in your room.

4 rooms – £ 80/100 £ 100/110

57 Front St NE30 4BX – 0191 257 9038 – www.martineau-house.co.uk – Closed 23-29 December

UCKFIELD

East Sussex – Pop. 15 213 – Regional map n° **5**-A2

Horsted Place

HISTORIC • CLASSIC A striking country house built in a classic Victorian Gothic style. The tiled entrance hall leads to an impressive main gallery where ornate sitting rooms are furnished with fine antiques. Luxurious bedrooms are well-equipped and most have views over the parkland. The formal dining room offers a classic menu.

17 rooms – £ 155/385 £ 155/385 – 5 suites

Little Horsted TN22 5TS – South : 2.5 mi by B 2102 and A 22 on A 26 – 01825 750581 – www.horstedplace.co.uk – Closed first week January

UPPER SLAUGHTER – Gloucestershire ➔ See Bourton-on-the-Water

UPPER SOUTH WRAXALL

Wiltshire – Regional map n° **2**-C2

Longs Arms

TRADITIONAL BRITISH • PUB Handsome, bay-windowed, Bath stone pub opposite a medieval church in a sleepy village. Traditional British dishes are full-flavoured, hearty and satisfying; everything is homemade and they smoke their own meats and fish. Dine in the characterful area in front of the bar. Warm, friendly service.

Carte £ 20/38

BA15 2SB – 01225 864450 (booking essential) – www.thelongsarms.com – Closed 3 weeks January, 2 weeks September, Sunday dinner, Monday and Tuesday

UPPINGHAM

Rutland – Pop. 4 745 – Regional map n° **9**-C2

Lake Isle

CLASSIC CUISINE • FRIENDLY XX Characterful 18C town centre property accessed via a narrow passageway and very personally run by experienced owners. It has a cosy lounge and a heavy wood-furnished dining room. Light lunches are followed by much more elaborate modern dinners. Bedrooms come with good extras and some have whirlpool baths.

Carte £ 28/50

12 rooms – £ 70/95 £ 90/120

16 High St East LE15 9PZ – 01572 822951 – www.lakeisle.co.uk – Closed Sunday dinner and Monday lunch

at Lyddington South: 2 mi by A6003 Uppingham

Old White Hart

TRADITIONAL CUISINE • PUB Sit in low-beamed bar or the larger dining room and conservatory. Well-hung steaks and homemade sausages are a feature, however, fish isn't overlooked, with the chef visiting Birmingham market twice a week. Prices are reasonable, especially from Monday-Thursday, and you can book for a game of petanque too. Bedrooms are smart and modern; some are in roadside cottages.

Menu £ 14 (weekdays) – Carte £ 23/32

14 rooms – £ 75/85 £ 100/110

51 Main St LE15 9LR – 01572 821703 – www.oldwhitehart.co.uk – Closed 25 December and Sunday dinner September-May

UPTON

Hampshire – Regional map n° **4**-B1

Crown Inn

MODERN BRITISH · FRIENDLY Set amidst narrow lanes and lush farmland is this truly welcoming pub. It has an open-fired bar with comfy sofas, an antique chess table and a farm shop, and an airy conservatory restaurant. Flavour-packed menus champion the county's produce, following the ethos of 'what grows together, goes together'.

Carte £ 26/46

SP11 0JS – 01264 736044 – www.thecrowninnupton.co.uk – Closed Monday and Tuesday

UPTON BISHOP – Herefordshire → See Ross-on-Wye

UPTON GREY

Hampshire – Pop. 449 – Regional map n° **4**-B1

Hoddington Arms

TRADITIONAL BRITISH · RUSTIC Find a sofa in the wonderfully atmospheric former barn – which has plenty of rustic character and a laid-back feel – bag a spot in the smart cabana or find a seat in the lovely garden beside the wood-burning oven. Menus mix pub classics and sharing boards with more adventurous dishes.

Menu £ 28 (weekday lunch) – Carte £ 25/44

Bidden Rd RG25 2RL – 01256 862371 – www.hoddingtonarms.co.uk – Closed 26 December, 1 January and Sunday dinner

UPTON MAGNA – Shropshire → See Shrewsbury

VENTNOR – Isle of Wight → See Wight (Isle of)

VERYAN

Cornwall – Truro – Pop. 877 – Regional map n° **1**-B3

Nare

COUNTRY HOUSE · CLASSIC Personally run, classic country house with a stunning bay outlook; take it in from the pool or hot tub. Most bedrooms have views and some have patios or balconies. Have afternoon tea in the drawing room followed by canapés in the bar, then choose from either a traditional daily menu in the dining room or more modern fare in Quarterdeck.

37 rooms – †£ 155/290 ††£ 295/560 – 7 suites

Carne Beach TR2 5PF – Southwest : 1.25 mi – 01872 501111 – www.narehotel.co.uk

VIRGINSTOW

Devon – Regional map n° **1**-C2

Percy's

TRADITIONAL · COSY Stone house in 130 acres of fields and woodland. The owners grow veg, breed racehorses, rear pigs and sheep, and sell wool, skins and produce. Spacious, comfy bedrooms in the former barn – some have jacuzzi baths. Set menu of traditional dishes in the formal dining room; ingredients are from the estate.

7 rooms – †£ 125/215 ††£ 140/230

Coombeshead Estate EX21 5EA – Southwest : 1.75 mi on Tower Hill rd – 01409 211236 – www.percys.co.uk

WADDINGTON

Lancashire – Pop. 3 992 – Regional map n° **11**-B2

Higher Buck

TRADITIONAL CUISINE • INN A smartly refurbished pub with pastel-painted wood panelling and modern furnishings, in a lovely Ribble Valley village. Bag a spot at one of the U-shaped banquettes or on the sunny terrace overlooking the Square and dine on reassuringly robust, seasonal dishes. Service is friendly and stylish bedrooms await.

Carte £ 21/41

7 rooms - £ 65/125 £ 100/125

The Square BB7 3HZ - 01200 423226 - www.higherbuck.com

WADEBRIDGE

Cornwall - Pop. 6 599 - Regional map n° **1**-B2

Trewornan Manor

COUNTRY HOUSE • ELEGANT Stunning Grade II listed 13C manor house set in 25 acres beside the River Amble, with over 8 acres of delightfully manicured gardens. Sumptuous, ultra-chic bedrooms all have views of the grounds. Welcoming young owners offer cream tea by the fire in the restful sitting room and fresh home-cooked breakfasts.

7 rooms - £ 117/225 £ 130/250

Trewornan Bridge, St Minver PL27 6EX - North : 1.75 mi on B3314 (Rock rd) - 01208 812359 - www.trewornanmanor.co.uk

WALBERSWICK

Suffolk - Pop. 380 - Regional map n° **8**-D2

Anchor

TRADITIONAL CUISINE • PUB A welcoming pub in an Arts and Crafts building; its sizeable garden features a wood-fired oven and leads down to the beach. Dishes are prepared with real care and global flavours punctuate the menu. If you're staying the night, choose a wood-clad chalet in the garden; breakfasts are impressive.

Carte £ 23/45

10 rooms - £ 95/115 £ 105/165

Main St IP18 6UA - 01502 722112 - www.anchoratwalberswick.com - Closed 25 December

WAREHAM

Dorset - Pop. 5 496 - Regional map n° **2**-C3

Priory

HISTORIC BUILDING • CLASSIC A delightfully located part-16C priory, which is proudly and personally run – this is a characterful place where peace and tranquility reign. Enjoy afternoon tea on the terrace overlooking the beautifully manicured gardens and on towards the river. Bedrooms have a charming country house style; those in the 'Boathouse' are the most luxurious. Dress smartly for dinner.

17 rooms - £ 176/304 £ 220/380 – 2 suites

Church Grn BH20 4ND - 01929 551666 - www.theprioryhotel.co.uk

Gold Court House

HISTORIC BUILDING • CLASSIC Charmingly run Georgian house in a small square off the high street; which stands on the foundations of a 13C goldsmith's house. It has a fire-lit lounge, a lovely breakfast room with garden views and traditional, restful bedrooms.

3 rooms - £ 70/85 £ 70/85

St John's Hill BH20 4LZ - 01929 553320 - www.goldcourthouse.co.uk - Closed 25 December-2 January

WAREN MILL - Northumberland ➜ See Bamburgh

WARKWORTH

Northumberland - Regional map n° **14**-B2

Roxbro House

TOWNHOUSE • GRAND LUXURY 'Elegant' and 'opulent' are suitable adjectives t describe these two houses in the shadow of Warkworth Castle, where boutique bed rooms mix modern facilities with antique furniture. Choose between two comfy lounge - one with an honesty bar; tasty breakfasts are served in a conservatory-style room.

6 rooms - £ 99/150 £ 99/150

5 Castle Terr NE65 0UP - 01665 711416 - www.roxbrohouse.co.uk - Closed 24-28 December

WARMINSTER

Wiltshire - Pop. 17 490 - Regional map n° **2**-C2

Weymouth Arms

TRADITIONAL BRITISH • NEIGHBOURHOOD Grade II listed building with plent of history. It's immensely characterful, with wood panelling, antiques and lithograph as well as two fireplaces originally intended for nearby Longleat House. Cooking is fres and fittingly traditional. Cosy bedrooms have charming original fittings.

Carte £ 21/45

8 rooms - £ 90/95 £ 100/110

12 Emwell St BA12 8JA - 01985 216995 - www.weymoutharms.co.uk - dinne only and lunch Friday-Sunday - Closed bank holiday Mondays

at Crockerton South: 2 mi by A350

Bath Arms

TRADITIONAL BRITISH • RUSTIC This down-to-earth pub was once part of the Longleat Estate. The daily menu features snacks, grills and classic pub dishes along with a selection of specials; try the legendary sticky beef with braised re cabbage. The two ultra-spacious, contemporary bedrooms are amusingly name 'Left' and 'Right'.

Carte £ 23/32

2 rooms - £ 80/110 £ 80/110

Clay St BA12 8AJ - On Shearwater rd - 01985 212262 - www.batharmscrockerton.co.uk - Closed Sunday dinner in autumn and winter

WARWICK

Warwickshire - Pop. 31 345 - Regional map n° **10**-C3

Tailors

MODERN CUISINE • INTIMATE X As well as a tailor's, this intimate restaurant was once a fishmonger's, a butcher's and a casino! It's run by two ambitious chefs who offer good value modern lunches, and elaborate dinners which feature unusual flavour combinations.

Menu £ 21/60

22 Market Pl CV34 4SL - 01926 410590 - www.tailorsrestaurant.co.uk - Closed Christmas, Sunday and Monday

WATCHET

Somerset - Pop. 3 581 - Regional map n° **2**-B2

Swain House

TOWNHOUSE • PERSONALISED In the characterful high street of this coasta town, you'll find this super smart guesthouse with spacious bedrooms and a sleek yet cosy feel. Parts of famous paintings make up feature walls and all have roll-top baths and rain showers.

4 rooms - £ 115/135 £ 115/135

48 Swain St TA23 0AG - 01984 631038 - www.swain-house.com

WATERGATE BAY - Cornwall ➔ See Newquay

WATFORD

Hertfordshire - Pop. 131 982 - Regional map n° **7**-A2

Colette's

MODERN CUISINE • DESIGN XXX A sleek, contemporary hotel restaurant with high ceilings and large windows overlooking the grounds. Complex modern dishes feature imaginative combinations; choose from a 3 course fixed price menu or a 5 course set menu.

Menu £ 65

Grove Hotel, Chandler's Cross ✉ WD3 4TG - Northwest : 2 mi on A 411 - ✆ 01923 296010 - www.thegrove.co.uk - dinner only and Sunday lunch - Closed 7 July-14 September, Sunday dinner except bank holidays and Monday

Grove

BUSINESS • GRAND LUXURY An impressive Grade II listed country house in 300 acres, with elegant lounges and smart, contemporary bedrooms - some with balconies. There's a superb spa and an outdoor pool, as well as tennis, croquet, golf and volleyball facilities. Enjoy fine dining in Colette's, casual meals in Stables or buffets in Glasshouse.

214 rooms ☕ - 👤£ 290/650 👥£ 290/650 - 6 suites

Chandler's Cross ✉ WD3 4TG - Northwest : 2 mi on A 411 - ✆ 01923 807807 - www.thegrove.co.uk

Colette's - See restaurant listing

WELBURN

North Yorkshire - Regional map n° **13**-C2

Crown and Cushion

CLASSIC CUISINE • FRIENDLY Well run 18C pub two miles from Castle Howard. The menu champions local meats and the kitchen's pride and joy is its charcoal-fired rotisserie. Dishes are hearty, sandwiches are doorstops, and puddings are of the nursery variety.

Carte £ 23/39

✉ YO60 7DZ - ✆ 01653 618777 - www.thecrownandcushionwelburn.com

WELLAND - Worcestershire ➔ See Great Malvern

WELLINGHAM

Norfolk - Regional map n° **8**-C1

Manor House Farm

WORKING FARM • CLASSIC Attractive, wisteria-clad farmhouse with large gardens, set by a church in a beautifully peaceful spot. Spacious, airy bedrooms are located in the former stables. Home-grown and home-reared produce is served at breakfast.

5 rooms ☕ - 👤£ 75/85 👥£ 130/145

✉ PE32 2TH - ✆ 01328 838227 - www.manor-house-farm.co.uk - Closed Christmas

WELLS

Somerset - Pop. 10 536 - Regional map n° **2**-C2

Swan

INN • CONTEMPORARY 15C former coaching inn with a good outlook onto the famous cathedral; its charming interior has subtle contemporary touches, particularly in the lounge and bar. Comfortable, stylish, well-equipped bedrooms and an opulent 'Cathedral Suite'. The formal, wood-panelled restaurant serves classic dishes.

48 rooms ☕ - 👤£ 104/116 👥£ 140/202 - 1 suite

11 Sadler St ✉ BA5 2RX - ✆ 01749 836300 - www.swanhotelwells.co.uk

ENGLAND

Beryl

COUNTRY HOUSE • CLASSIC A fine 19C country house in 11 acres of mature gardens, complete with a pond and a swimming pool. It's proudly run by a mother and her daughter and the delightful drawing rooms are packed with antiques and curios from her late husband's antique shop. Go for one of the four-poster bedrooms.

13 rooms - £ 75/100 £ 100/170

BA5 3JP - East : 1.25 mi by B 3139 off Hawkers Lane
- 01749 678738 - www.beryl-wells.co.uk - Closed 23-28 December

Stoberry House

TRADITIONAL • PERSONALISED 18C coach house with a delightful walled garden, overlooking Glastonbury Tor. Large lounge with a baby grand piano and antique furniture. Breakfast is an event, with 7 homemade breads, a porridge menu and lots of cooked dishes. Immaculately kept bedrooms come with fresh flowers, chocolates and a pillow menu.

7 rooms - £ 85/155 £ 128/225

Stoberry Park BA5 3LD - Northeast : 0.5 mi by A 39 on College Rd
- 01749 672906 - www.stoberryhouse.co.uk - Closed Christmas and New Year.

WELLS-NEXT-THE-SEA

Norfolk - Pop. 2 165 - Regional map n° **8**-C1

Crown

INN • CONTEMPORARY Set in the centre of town, overlooking the green, is this unassuming-looking old coaching inn. Guest areas are characterful and bedrooms blend classic furniture with some quirky modern touches; Room 23 has a copper bath on its roof terrace! Dine from an accessible menu in the charming bar or dining room.

20 rooms - £ 80/250 £ 100/270

The Buttlands NR23 1EX
- 01328 710209 - www.crownhotelnorfolk.co.uk

at Wighton Southeast: 2.5 mi by A149

Meadowview

FAMILY • MODERN Set in the centre of a peaceful village, this smart, modern guesthouse is the perfect place to unwind, as its neat garden boasts a hot tub and a comfy seating area overlooking a meadow. Breakfast is cooked on the Aga in the country kitchen.

5 rooms - £ 115/125 £ 115/125

53 High St NR23 1PF
- 01328 821527 - www.meadow-view.net - Closed January

WELWYN

Hertfordshire - Pop. 3 497 - Regional map n° **7**-B2

Tewin Bury Farm

BUSINESS • RURAL A collection of converted farm buildings set on a 400 acre working farm next to a nature reserve. Comfy oak-furnished bedrooms are located in various wings and the function room is in an impressive tithe barn beside the old mill race. In the old chicken shed, menus mix classic dishes with the more adventurous.

36 rooms - £ 120/125 £ 145/175

AL6 0JB - Southeast : 3.5 mi by A 1000 on B 1000
- 01438 717793 - www.tewinbury.co.uk

at Ayot Green Southwest: 2.5 mi by B 197

Waggoners

FRENCH • PUB A popular 17C Gallic-themed pub. Join local drinkers in the cosy bar for dishes such as crispy monkfish cheeks; the restaurant offers more ambitious modern fare, including the likes of beef short rib with treacle-cured bacon.

Menu £ 15 (weekday lunch) - Carte £ 27/46

Brickwall Cl ✉ AL6 9AA - ✆ 01707 324241 - www.thewaggoners.co.uk - Closed Sunday dinner

WENTBRIDGE

West Yorkshire - ✉ Pontefract - Regional map n° **13**-B3

Wentbridge House

INN • CONTEMPORARY An attractive, creeper-clad Georgian coaching inn on the Great North Road; its pretty grounds make it a popular place for weddings. Bedrooms are spacious and modern, with good facilities - the two four-poster rooms have an elegant feel and some outside can accommodate dogs. Dine from a mix of classics and elaborate modern dishes in the brasserie or formal restaurant.

41 rooms - †£ 90/130 ††£ 120/160

Old Great North Rd. ✉ WF8 3JJ - ✆ 01977 620444
- www.wentbridgehouse.co.uk

WEST ASHLING - West Sussex → See Chicester

WEST BRIDGFORD - Nottinghamshire → See Nottingham

WEST BYFLEET

Surrey - Regional map n° **4**-C1

London House

MODERN BRITISH • FASHIONABLE XX A pleasant neighbourhood restaurant set in a busy parade of shops. White walls are hung with modern art and equally colourful modern dishes take their influences from Britain and the Med. Top quality ingredients include local rare breed pork and their superb deli stocks some great cheeses.

Menu £ 19/44

30 Station Approach ✉ KT14 6NF - ✆ 01932 482026
- www.restaurantlondonhouse.co.uk - dinner only and lunch Thursday, Friday and Sunday - Closed first 2 weeks August, first week January, Sunday dinner and Monday

WEST BEXINGTON

Dorset - Regional map n° **2**-B3

Club House

SEAFOOD • BISTRO X This old clubhouse sits in a superb location atop Chesil Beach, so when the sun's out, head for the terrace. Inside, contemporary décor blends with period nautical touches such as lifebelts and sepia prints. Unfussy modern dishes showcase Exmouth oysters, Weymouth lobster, Portland crab and Brixham fish.

Carte £ 30/76

Beach Rd ✉ DT2 9NG - ✆ 01308 898302
- www.theclubhousewestbexington.co.uk - Closed 24-26 December, Sunday dinner, Monday and restricted opening November-Easter

WEST HATCH

Wiltshire – Regional map n° **2**-C3

Pythouse Kitchen Garden

TRADITIONAL BRITISH • SIMPLE A delightful red-brick potting shed with a glass extension, which sits inside an 18C walled garden. The terrace leads down to the kitchen garden and there's a fire-pit where many of the rustic, flavour-packed dishes are cooked. They serve breakfast, lunch, afternoon tea, and dinner on a Friday and Saturday.

Carte £ 23/43

SP3 6PA
– 01747 870444 – www.pythousekitchengarden.co.uk
– lunch only and dinner Friday-Saturday – Closed 25-26 December and 1 January

WEST HOATHLY

West Sussex – Pop. 709 – Regional map n° **4**-D2

Cat Inn

TRADITIONAL BRITISH • COSY Popular with the locals and very much a village pub, with beamed ceilings, pewter tankards, open fires and plenty of cosy corners. Carefully executed, good value cooking focuses on tasty pub classics like locally smoked ham, egg and chips or steak, mushroom and ale pie. Service is friendly and efficient – and four tastefully decorated bedrooms complete the picture.

Carte £ 25/37

4 rooms – £ 100/115 £ 125/165

North Ln. RH19 4PP
– 01342 810369 – www.catinn.co.uk
– Closed 25 December and dinner 26 December and 1 January

WEST MALLING

Kent – Pop. 2 266 – Regional map n° **5**-B1

Swan

MODERN CUISINE • FASHIONABLE A 15C coaching inn plays host to this stylish yet characterful restaurant. Start in the chic cocktail bar, then dine in the relaxed front or rear room or on the terrace. Modern day classics feature on an appealing menu and the experienced, hands-on owners keep things running smoothly from morning to night.

Menu £ 22 (lunch and early dinner) – Carte £ 29/50

35 Swan St. ME19 6JU
– 01732 521910 (booking essential) – www.theswanwestmalling.co.uk
– Closed 1 January and Sunday dinner

WEST MEON

Hampshire – Regional map n° **4**-B2

Thomas Lord

TRADITIONAL CUISINE • PUB This smart, early 19C pub is named after the founder of Lord's Cricket Ground and decorated with cricketing memorabilia. The atmosphere is warm and welcoming and the menu perfectly balances the classics with some more adventurous offerings. The lovely garden is home to a wood-burning stove, as well as to 4 delightful wooden lodges for those who wish to stay.

Carte £ 27/39

5 rooms – £ 74/159 £ 99/174

High St GU32 1LN
– 01730 829244 – www.thethomaslord.co.uk
– Closed dinner 25 December

VEST OVERTON - Wiltshire → See Marlborough

VEST WITTERING

/est Sussex – Pop. 875 – Regional map n° **4**-C3

Beach House

TOWNHOUSE It might be 10 minutes' from the beach but the Beach House is fittingly named, as with its large veranda and shuttered windows it has a real seaside feel. Bedrooms are bright and modern with a New England Style and breakfast is a treat. It's run by an enthusiastic, passionate owner.

7 rooms – £ 85 £ 120/130

Rookwood Rd PO20 8LT
– 01243 514800 – www.beachhse.co.uk
– Closed Monday-Wednesday in winter

VEST WITTON

orth Yorkshire – Leyburn – Regional map n° **13**-B1

Wensleydale Heifer

TRADITIONAL • PERSONALISED A whitewashed former pub in the heart of the Wensleydale Valley. Quirky bedrooms offering something a little different, with themes such as Champagne or James Bond. Relax by the fire in the characterful low-beamed lounge, then dine from an extensive menu where steaks and lobster are a feature.

13 rooms – £ 90 £ 120/220

DL8 4LS – 01969 622322 – www.wensleydaleheifer.co.uk

VESTONBIRT

iloucestershire – Regional map n° **2**-C1

Hare & Hounds

COUNTRY HOUSE • CONTEMPORARY Attractive former farmhouse with lovely gardens, set between Highgrove House and the National Arboretum. The country house style interior features several lounges and a small library; bedrooms blend modern fabrics with period furniture – half are located in the old outbuildings. Formal Beaufort offers classical dishes with a modern edge, while Jack Hare's serves a pub-style menu and real ales.

42 rooms – £ 95/185 £ 110/270 – 3 suites

GL8 8QL – on A 433 – 01666 881000 – www.cotswold-inns-hotels.co.uk

VESTLETON

uffolk – Saxmundham – Pop. 349 – Regional map n° **8**-D2

Westleton Crown

TRADITIONAL CUISINE • PUB Good-looking, 17C former coaching inn with an appealing terrace and garden, set in a pretty little village. Welcoming beamed bar with open fires; more modern conservatory. Seasonal menu, with special diets well-catered for. Uncluttered bedrooms are named after birds found on the adjacent RSPB nature reserve.

Carte £ 26/40

34 rooms – £ 100/110 £ 110/215

The Street IP17 3AD – 01728 648777 – www.westletoncrown.co.uk

Symbols shown in red XXX indicate particularly charming establishments.

WHASHTON - N. Yorks. → See Richmond

WHITBY

North Yorkshire - Pop. 13 213 - Regional map n° **13**-C1

The Star Inn The Harbour

MODERN BRITISH • BRASSERIE XX Andrew Pern has fulfilled a dream by openin this modern brasserie by the harbour in his home town. The extensive menu of fers classic British brasserie dishes from the 'Harbourside', the 'Countryside' an the 'Ice Cream Parlour'.

Carte £ 22/50

1 Langborne Rd ✉ YO21 1YN - ✆ 01947 821900 - www.starinntheharbour.co.uk - Closed 7-24 January except weekends

Raithwaite Hall

LUXURY • CONTEMPORARY A modern resort hotel with a smart spa, set in 93 acre of delightful parkland. Stylish bedrooms are spread about the place: some are in a moc ern mock-castle, some are in cottages and others are in a house overlooking the lak Dine on brasserie classics or from an accessible menu in the restaurant.

71 rooms - †£ 121/521 ††£ 133/533 - 9 suites

Sandsend Rd ✉ YO21 3ST - West : 2 mi on A 197 - ✆ 01947 661661 - www.raithwaiteestate.com

Dillons of Whitby

TOWNHOUSE • DESIGN Charming Victorian townhouse built for a sea captair set opposite the beautiful Pannett Park. Immaculately kept bedrooms are individ ually themed and feature Egyptian cotton linens. Extensive breakfasts are some thing of an event.

5 rooms - †£ 75/125 ††£ 85/145

14 Chubb Hill Rd ✉ YO21 1JU - ✆ 01947 600290 - www.dillonsofwhitby.co.uk - Closed 6-27 January

at Sandsend Northwest: 3 mi on A174✉ Whitby

Estbek House

SEAFOOD • FRIENDLY XX A personally run Regency house close to the beach, with lovely front terrace and an elegant dining room. The basement bar overlooks th kitchen and doubles as a breakfast room. Menus offer unfussy dishes of sustainabl wild fish from local waters. Smart bedrooms come with stylish bathrooms.

Carte £ 39/76

5 rooms - †£ 100/200 ††£ 135/250

East Row ✉ YO21 3SU - ✆ 01947 893424 - www.estbekhouse.co.uk - dinner onl - Closed January-9 February

WHITE WALTHAM

Windsor and Maidenhead - Pop. 349 - Regional map n° **6**-C3

Beehive

CLASSIC CUISINE • PUB A traditional English pub overlooking the cricke pitch, where you'll find local drinkers in the bar and a comfy, light-filled dinin room. Eye-catching daily dishes are full of flavour and exhibit a staunch sense c Britishness.

Menu £ 25 (weekday lunch) - Carte £ 30/50

Waltham Rd ✉ SL6 3SH - ✆ 01628 822877 - www.thebeehivewhitewaltham.com - Closed 25-26 December and Sunday dinner

WHITEWELL

Lancashire - ✉ Clitheroe - Pop. 5 617 - Regional map n° **11**-B2

Inn at Whitewell

INN • PERSONALISED A 14C creeper-clad inn set high on the banks of the river and affording stunning valley views. Spacious bedrooms are split between the inn and a nearby coach house - some are traditional, with four-posters and antique baths; others more contemporary. Classic menus offer wholesome, regionally inspired dishes.

23 rooms - £ 99/218 £ 137/270

Forest of Bowland ✉ BB7 3AT - ✆ 01200 448222 - www.innatwhitewell.com

WHITSTABLE

Kent - Pop. 32 100 - Regional map n° **5**-C1

Whitstable Oyster Company

SEAFOOD • RUSTIC A lovely old oyster warehouse with a tremendous view over the estuary. It has a large terrace, two capacious wood-panelled rooms and a trendy first floor lounge-bar. The hand-written menu changes daily depending on the latest catch; the oysters from their own beds are a must-try.

Carte £ 29/60

Royal Native Oyster Stores, Horsebridge ✉ CT5 1BU - ✆ 01227 276856 (booking essential) - www.whitstableoystercompany.com - Closed 25-26 December and November-January

at Seasalter Southwest: 2 mi by B2205 ✉ Whitstable

The Sportsman (Stephen Harris)

MODERN BRITISH • PUB It's long been about food at this wind-blown spot by the sea wall of the Thames Estuary, which has hosted an inn since the 17C and farmland since the 12C. This might look like a classic pub but the cooking diverts from the norm, with top local and garden ingredients featuring in carefully prepared dishes which follow a 'less is more' philosophy. Bedrooms are in garden cabins.

→ Slip sole grilled in seaweed butter. Roast saddle of lamb with mint sauce. Plum soufflé with plum ripple ice cream.

Menu £ 55/70 - Carte £ 40/48

6 rooms - £ 150 £ 150

Faversham Rd ✉ CT5 4BP - West : 2 mi following coast rd - ✆ 01227 273370 (booking essential) - www.thesportsmanseasalter.co.uk - Closed 25-27 December, 1 January, Sunday dinner and Monday

WHITTLESFORD

Cambridgeshire - Regional map n° **8**-B3

Tickell Arms

MODERN BRITISH • PUB Sit in the orangery-style extension overlooking the pond. Fish is delivered 6 days a week, on Tuesdays you can select your own cut for Steak Night, and on Sundays they leave fresh roasties on the bar.

Menu £ 22 (weekdays) - Carte £ 25/41

1 North Rd ✉ CB22 4NZ - ✆ 01223 833025 - www.cambscuisine.com

WIGHT (Isle of)

Isle of Wight - Pop. 138 500 - Regional map n° **4**-A/B 3

Cowes

North House

BOUTIQUE HOTEL • PERSONALISED A Grade II listed townhouse in the heart of the Old Town; now a boutique hotel where bedrooms blend original fireplaces with bold wallpapers, Egyptian cotton linen and coffee machines. Dine on seafood or steaks cooked over the charcoal grill either in the rustic bistro or on the sunny terrace.

14 rooms - £ 95/245 £ 95/245

30-32 Sun Hill ✉ PO31 7HY - ✆ 01983 209453 - www.northhousecowes.co.uk

Freshwater

The Hut

MODERN CUISINE • FRIENDLY This laid-back, beach shack style restaurant i superbly set among colourful beach huts and looks over the sea to Hurst Castle Sit on the terrace or under retractable roofs and enjoy anything from fish taco to a fruits de mer platter. Most diners arrive by boat (they'll even collect yo from your mooring).

Carte £ 26/62

Colwell Chine Rd, Colwell Bay ✉ PO40 9NP - Northwest : 1.25 mi by Tennyson R off A 3054 - ✆ 01983 893637 (booking essential) - www.thehutcolwell.co.uk - Closed November-Easter

Gurnard

Little Gloster

TRADITIONAL CUISINE • RUSTIC Set in a great spot among the beach huts with lovely views over The Solent. Have a cocktail on the terrace then head insid to the tables by the kitchen or the relaxed, shabby chic dining room. Unfussy, fla voursome cooking uses island produce. Stylish bedrooms have a fresh nautica theme and superb views.

Carte £ 19/40

3 rooms - †£ 130/175 ††£ 130/245

31 Marsh Rd ✉ PO31 8JQ - ✆ 01983 298776 - www.thelittlegloster.com - Closed January-mid-February, Christmas, Sunday and Monday-Wednesday in winter

Newport

Thompson's

MODERN BRITISH • TRENDY A stylish yet relaxed restaurant in the centre o town; try to book one of the three tables in front of the open kitchen. Origina cooking makes good use of island ingredients and exhibits some interesting fla vour combinations.

Menu £ 29 (lunch) - Carte £ 36/56

11 Town Ln ✉ PO30 1JU - ✆ 01983 526118 - www.robertthompson.co.uk - Closed 2 weeks February-March, 2 weeks November, 1 week Christmas, Sunday-Monday and Tuesday September-May

St Helens

Dans Kitchen

TRADITIONAL CUISINE • FRIENDLY Old corner shop in a lovely location over looking the village green. Simple wood furnishings, scatter cushions and nautica pictures feature. Traditional, hearty dishes showcase island produce; blackboar specials include the daily catch.

Menu £ 24 (lunch) - Carte £ 25/48

Lower Green Rd ✉ PO33 1TS - ✆ 01983 872303 - www.danskitcheniow.co.uk - Closed 3 weeks January, 1 week June, 1 week October, Sunday, Monday and lunch Tuesday-Wednesday

Seaview

Seaview

MODERN BRITISH • CLASSIC DÉCOR The seafaring décor gives a clue as t the focus at this boldly decorated hotel restaurant. Classically based seafoo dishes are well-prepared and come in a choice of two sizes. The 'Naval Mess and 'Pump Room' provide simpler alternatives and the crab ramekin has becom something of an institution.

Menu £ 18/28

Seaview Hotel, High St ✉ PO34 5EX - ✆ 01983 612711 (booking essential) - www.seaviewhotel.co.uk - Closed 24-25 December and Sunday dinner October-April

Seaview

TRADITIONAL • QUIRKY A long-standing seaside hotel with a laid-back feel – its interesting interior filled with nautical charts, maritime photos and model ships. Bright, comfy bedrooms come in various styles; some are in annexes and several are suites.

24 rooms – £ 95/210 £ 95/210 – 3 suites

High St PO34 5EX – 01983 612711 – www.seaviewhotel.co.uk – Closed 25 December

Seaview – See restaurant listing

Shanklin

Rylstone Manor

COUNTRY HOUSE • CLASSIC This attractive part-Victorian house sits in the town's historic gardens and was originally a gift from the Queen to one of her physicians. The classical interior has a warm, cosy feel and is furnished with antiques. Carefully prepared dishes are served in the formally laid dining room.

9 rooms – £ 70/130 £ 140/170

Rylstone Gdns PO37 6RG – 01983 862806 – www.rylstone-manor.co.uk – Closed 3 November-9 February

Ventnor

Ale and Oyster

TRADITIONAL BRITISH • BISTRO This relaxed little bistro sits in a super spot on the esplanade, looking out to sea, and is run by a friendly, experienced team. Enjoy a light lunch on the terrace or come in the evening for the likes of local lobster linguine.

Carte £ 35/48

The Esplanade PO38 1JX – 01983 857025 – www.thealeandoyster.co.uk – Closed 3 weeks January, 1 week November, Monday and Tuesday

Royal

TRADITIONAL • CLASSIC A sympathetically restored Victorian house with mature gardens and a heated outdoor pool. The interior has a bygone elegance with hints of modernity and some of the bedrooms offer sea views. Afternoon tea is an event, the bar serves light lunches, and sophisticated dinners take place under chandeliers.

51 rooms (dinner included) – £ 100/120 £ 160/275

Belgrave Rd PO38 1JJ – 01983 852186 – www.royalhoteliow.co.uk

Hillside

COUNTRY HOUSE • UNIQUE Set high above the town, this wonderful thatched Georgian house has a beautiful terrace and superb sea views. The Danish owner has fused period furnishings with clean-lined Scandinavian styling, and displays over 350 pieces of CoBrA and Scandinavian art. Everything is immaculate and the linens are top quality. Frequently changing menus use local and garden produce.

14 rooms – £ 78/93 £ 156/206

151 Mitchell Ave PO38 1DR – 01983 852271 – www.hillsideventnor.co.uk

Yarmouth

Isla's

MODERN CUISINE • DESIGN At the heart of an old inn you'll find this stylishly understated restaurant with large linen-laid tables and detailed service. Menus change with the seasons and cooking is modern and ambitious with bold flavours. Presentation is elaborate.

Menu £ 45 – tasting menu only

The George Hotel, Quay St PO41 0PE – 01983 760331 (booking essential) – www.thegeorge.co.uk – dinner only – Closed Tuesday in Winter, Sunday and Monday

Isla's Conservatory

TRADITIONAL BRITISH • BRASSERIE Hidden at the back of the George hotel i this airy brasserie with a sizeable terrace offering views over a lovely garde which leads down to the water's edge. It opens all day and offers everythin from breakfast, snacks and afternoon tea to modern brasserie classics featurin island produce.

Carte £ 28/54

The George Hotel, Quay St ✉ PO41 0PE – ✆ 01983 760331 – www.thegeorge.co.u

The George

INN • CLASSIC Set in the shadow of the castle, this cosy 17C inn blends subtl modern touches with characterful period features. Bedrooms vary in shape an style: some are wood-panelled, some have luxurious bathrooms, some ope onto the garden or have spacious balconies – and many have excellent Solen views.

17 rooms – †£ 145/380 ††£ 145/385

Quay St ✉ PO41 0PE – ✆ 01983 760331 – www.thegeorge.co.uk

Isla's • **Isla's Conservatory** – See restaurant listing

WIGHTON – Norfolk → See Wells-Next-The-Sea

WIGMORE

Herefordshire – Regional map n° **10**-A2

The Oak Wigmore

MODERN BRITISH • CONTEMPORARY DÉCOR The charming, hands-on owne spent 3 years transforming this 16C coaching inn and outbuildings into the smart contemporary pub you see before you today. The experienced local chef reall knows how to get the best out of his ingredients. Simple, comfortable bedroom complete the picture.

Carte £ 28/47

2 rooms – †£ 90/95 ††£ 100/120

Ford St ✉ HR6 9UJ – ✆ 01568 770424 – www.theoakwigmore.com – Closed Sunday dinner, Monday and Tuesday

WILLIAN

Hertfordshire – Pop. 326 – Regional map n° **7**-B2

Fox

MODERN BRITISH • FRIENDLY The Fox is set in the heart of the village an also plays host to the local Post Office and general store. Monthly menus presen carefully constructed, classic dishes which keep natural flavours to the fore There's a sheltered terrace for warmer days and very comfy, contemporary country bedrooms await.

Carte £ 23/40

8 rooms – †£ 65/115 ††£ 65/115

✉ SG6 2AE – ✆ 01462 480233 – www.foxatwillian.co.uk

WILMINGTON

Regional map n° **5**-B1

Rowhill Grange

COUNTRY HOUSE • MODERN An early 19C house set in 15 acres of pretty gardens, with smart modern bedrooms in dark, bold hues. The fantastic spa has 9 treatment rooms, a large gym and a superb swimming pool, along with a separate infinity pool with a waterfall. RG's serves fresh seasonal dishes – try the grills

38 rooms – †£ 177/427 ††£ 189/439

✉ DA2 7QH – Southwest : 2 mi on Hextable rd (B 258) – ✆ 01322 615136 – www.alexanderhotels.co.uk/rowhill-grange/

WIMBORNE MINSTER

Dorset – Pop. 15 174 – Regional map n° **2**-C3

Tickled Pig

MODERN BRITISH • BISTRO Charmingly run restaurant in the heart of a pretty market town, with a modern country interior, a lovely terrace and a laid-back feel. Daily brown paper menus feature home-grown veg and home-reared pork; their mantra is 'taking food back to its roots'. Cooking is vibrant, flavourful and unfussy.

Menu £ 23 (weekdays) – Carte £ 30/42

26 West Borough BH21 1NF – 01202 886778 – www.thetickledpig.co.uk – Closed 25-26 December, Sunday and Monday

WIMBORNE ST GILES

Dorset – Pop. 366 – Regional map n° **2**-C3

Home Farm House

COUNTRY HOUSE • PERSONALISED A pretty part-17C creamwashed farmhouse with a red-tiled roof; set surrounded by farm buildings, on the Shaftesbury Estate. Inside it has a 'Country Living' style. Bedrooms come with Lush toiletries, robes and home-baked cookies.

5 rooms – £ 65/95 £ 90/120

Butts Cl. BH21 5NB – Southeast : 0.5 mi by Salisbury rd – 01725 517338 – www.homefarmhousewsg.com – Closed Christmas and New Year

WINCHCOMBE

Gloucestershire – Pop. 4 538 – Regional map n° **2**-D1

5 North St

MODERN BRITISH • COSY This long-standing neighbourhood restaurant, run by a husband and wife, is a hit with the locals; it might be small inside but it's big on character. Concise menus feature regional ingredients in classic combinations.

Menu £ 32/54

5 North St GL54 5LH – 01242 604566 – www.5northstreetrestaurant.co.uk – Closed 2 weeks January, 1 week August, Monday, Tuesday lunch and Sunday dinner

WINCHESTER

Hampshire – Pop. 45 184 – Regional map n° **4**-B2

Black Rat

MODERN CUISINE • RUSTIC You can't help but love this rustic candlelit restaurant with its quirky, bohemian-style interior and lovely heated huts on the terrace. Refined, original cooking arrives in hearty portions and the flavours really pack a punch. A small bar offers cocktails and a selection of over 30 different gins.

→ Cod cheek and tongue with bouillabaisse. Duck breast with heritage beetroot and gooseberries. Chocolate pavé with dark fruits and pig's blood ice cream.

Menu £ 26 (lunch) – Carte £ 36/51

88 Chesil St. SO23 0HX – 01962 844465 – www.theblackrat.co.uk – dinner only and lunch Saturday-Sunday – Closed 2 weeks December-January

Chesil Rectory

MODERN CUISINE • HISTORIC This double-gabled wattle and daub house dates from the 15C and its characterful interior takes in heavily beamed ceilings and a large inglenook fireplace. Appealing menus offer classic British dishes with the odd Mediterranean touch.

Menu £ 22 (lunch and early dinner) – Carte £ 30/44

Chesil St. SO23 0HU – 01962 851555 – www.chesilrectory.co.uk – Closed 25 December

Kyoto Kitchen

JAPANESE • INTIMATE XX This sweet little restaurant is a hit with the locals. Authentic Japanese dishes are prepared with care and there's good detail in the execution. The tempura, sushi and sashimi are highlights but don't overlook the small plates.

Carte £ 21/49

70 Parchment St ✉ SO23 8AT
- ✆ 01962 890895 - www.kyotokitchen.co.uk - Closed 25-26 December

River Cottage Kitchen

TRADITIONAL BRITISH • RUSTIC X A delightful restaurant set within a 200 year old silk mill in the Abbey Gardens. The lower floor has an open kitchen and the upper floor has exposed timbers and rope lights. Seasonal regional produce is at the core of the menu and dishes are hearty and rustic; the small plates and sharing boards are popular.

Menu £ 17 (weekday lunch) - Carte £ 25/35

Abbey Mill, Abbey Mill Gdns. The Broadway ✉ SO23 9GH
- ✆ 01962 457747 (booking essential) - www.rivercottage.net - Closed 25 December, Sunday dinner

Hotel du Vin

TOWNHOUSE • CONTEMPORARY Attractive Georgian house dating from 1715 and the first ever Hotel du Vin. Wine-themed bedrooms, split between the house and garden, are stylish and well-equipped; some have baths in the room. The characterful split-level bistro offers unfussy French cooking and - as hoped - an excellent wine selection.

24 rooms - †£ 119/429 ††£ 119/429 - ☕ £ 13

14 Southgate St ✉ SO23 9EF
- ✆ 01962 841414 - www.hotelduvin.com

Giffard House

TOWNHOUSE • CLASSIC Imposing Victorian house in a quiet road. Spacious classically styled guest areas include a comfy drawing room, modern bar and formal breakfast room. Individually styled bedrooms boast quality furnishings and good facilities.

13 rooms ☕ - †£ 83/146 ††£ 109/166 - 1 suite

50 Christchurch Rd ✉ SO23 9SU
- ✆ 01962 852628 - www.giffardhotelwinchester.co.uk - Closed 24 December-2 January

Black Hole

TOWNHOUSE • PERSONALISED This three-storey guesthouse is fashioned on an 18C prison - the Black Hole of Calcutta - and comes with heavy prison doors, framed mugshots of history's villains and themed wallpapers. The top floor terrace has city rooftop views.

10 rooms ☕ - †£ 85/120 ††£ 85/120

Wharf Hill ✉ SO23 9NP
- ✆ 01962 807010 - www.theblackhole.co.uk

at Sparsholt Northwest: 3.5 mi by B3049 ✉ Winchester

Avenue

MODERN BRITISH • ELEGANT XX Start with a drink in the cedar wood panelled bar of this country house, then sit amongst oil paintings overlooking the avenue of lime trees which have stood here since 1716. Modern menus champion British produce, with scallops from Orkney, fish from Lymington and game from the New Forest.

Menu £ 62

Lainston House Hotel, Woodman Ln ✉ SO21 2LT
- ✆ 01962 776088 - www.exclusive.co.uk/lainston-house - dinner only and Sunday lunch

Lainston House

COUNTRY HOUSE • CONTEMPORARY An impressive 17C William and Mary manor house with attractive gardens and a striking mile-long avenue of lime trees. Enjoy a game of tennis, croquet or boules, try your hand at falconry, or brush up on your culinary skills at the superb cookery school. Bedrooms are spacious and contemporary.

50 rooms – £ 143/285 £ 143/285 – 3 suites

Woodman Ln SO21 2LT – 01962 776088
– www.exclusive.co.uk/lainston-house

Avenue – See restaurant listing

WINDERMERE

Cumbria – Pop. 5 243 – Regional map n° **12**-A2

Holbeck Ghyll

MODERN BRITISH • CLASSIC DÉCOR XX A three-roomed restaurant in a traditional stone Arts and Crafts house; its elegant oak-panelled front room offers superb views over Lake Windermere and the mountains. Concise, fixed price menus utilise good quality local ingredients in modern dishes; at dinner there's also an 8 course tasting menu.

Menu £ 45/72

Holbeck Ghyll Hotel, Holbeck Ln LA23 1LU – Northwest : 3.25 mi by A 591
– 015394 32375 – www.holbeckghyll.com – Closed first 2 weeks January

Holbeck Ghyll

TRADITIONAL • CLASSIC A charming Arts and Crafts house boasting stunning views over the lake and mountains. Well-equipped bedrooms are spread about the place and range from classical to contemporary; Miss Potter, complete with a hot tub, is the best.

32 rooms – £ 140/230 £ 170/420 – 4 suites

Holbeck Ln LA23 1LU – Northwest : 3.25 mi by A 591 – 015394 32375
– www.holbeckghyll.com – Closed first 2 weeks January

Holbeck Ghyll – See restaurant listing

Cedar Manor

TRADITIONAL • PERSONALISED Victorian house with a cedar tree in the garden; it was built by a former minister and has ecclesiastical influences. Contemporary country house bedrooms display locally made furniture – some have spa baths or views and the Coach House suite has a private terrace. Appealing menus use local produce.

10 rooms – £ 125 £ 145/475 – 2 suites

Ambleside Rd LA23 1AX – 015394 43192 – www.cedarmanor.co.uk – Closed 16-26 December and 2-18 January

Windermere Suites

LUXURY • DESIGN Spacious Edwardian house with a seductive interior. Funky, sexy bedrooms boast bold modern décor, iPod docks and walk-in wardrobes. Huge bathrooms feature TVs and colour-changing lights. Breakfast is served in your room.

8 rooms – £ 150/220 £ 180/270

New Rd LA23 2LA – 015394 47672 – www.windermeresuites.co.uk – Closed 24-25 December

Jerichos

TOWNHOUSE • CONTEMPORARY Victorian slate house in the town centre, with a contrastingly contemporary interior. The lounge is decorated in silver and the smart modern bedrooms have bold feature walls and good facilities; first floor rooms are the largest.

10 rooms – £ 75/84 £ 120/158

College Rd LA23 1BX – 015394 42522 – www.jerichos.co.uk

at Bowness-on-Windermere South: 1 mi ✉ Windermere

✿ HRiSHi

MODERN CUISINE · ELEGANT XXX A series of intimate dining rooms in a charming country house hotel; start with an aperitif in the comfy lounge or chic bar. Precisely prepared, original dishes are very attractively presented and provide a fitting sense of occasion; some make interesting use of spices. Service is excellent.

➜ Gravadlax of salmon loin with piccalilli, cucumber and puffed rice. Slow-roast pork belly, wild mushroom raviolo and Chinese 5 spice. Dark chocolate délice and lime leaf panna cotta with honeycomb and lemon balm.

Menu £ 70/90

Gilpin Hotel & Lake House Hotel, Crook Rd ✉ LA23 3NE – Southeast : 2.5 mi by A 5074 on B 5284 – ✆ 015394 88818 (booking essential) – www.thegilpin.co.uk – dinner only and Sunday lunch

Linthwaite House

MODERN CUISINE · ROMANTIC XXX Contemporary country house restaurant – sit in the intimate Mirror Room or the airy former billiard room. Seasonally evolving menus showcase Lakeland produce; deceptively simple modern cooking is packed with flavour.

Carte £ 40/71

Linthwaite House Hotel, Crook Rd ✉ LA23 3JA – South : 0.75 mi by A 5074 on B 5284 – ✆ 015394 88600 – www.leeucollection.com – dinner only

Gilpin Spice

ASIAN · EXOTIC DÉCOR XX Cumbria was a key player in the spice trade and this slate-built restaurant in the grounds of Gilpin Hotel is inspired by that history. Extensive menus follow the Silk Road from Cumbria to Asia and dishes are designed for sharing. Enter the colourful rooms via wooden walkways built over stone-filled pools.

Menu £ 38 – Carte £ 22/38

Gilpin Hotel & Lake House Hotel, Crook Rd ✉ LA23 3NE – Southeast : 2.5 mi by A 5074 on B 5284 – ✆ 015394 88818 – www.thegilpin.co.uk

Gilpin Hotel & Lake House

LUXURY · PERSONALISED A delightful country house hotel run by a charming experienced family. Bedrooms range from contemporary country doubles to spacious garden suites with outdoor hot tubs. There are even more peaceful, luxurious suites a mile down the road beside a tarn – stay here for exclusive use of the smart spa.

31 rooms (dinner included) – †£ 215/625 ††£ 275/625

Crook Rd ✉ LA23 3NE – Southeast : 2.5 mi by A 5074 on B 5284 – ✆ 015394 88818 (booking essential) – www.thegilpin.co.uk

✿ **HRiSHi** • **Gilpin Spice** – See restaurant listing

Linthwaite House

TRADITIONAL · CONTEMPORARY Linthwaite House reopened in June 2018 following an extensive refurbishment. It sits in a peaceful spot overlooking the lake and fells and is surrounded by 14 acres of beautiful grounds. Go for one of the suites: six are in the grounds, one has a telescope for star-gazing and another a hot tub with garden views. Cumbrian produce features in Italian-influenced dishes.

36 rooms – †£ 190/350 ††£ 190/350

Crook Rd ✉ LA23 3JA – South : 0.75 mi by A 5074 on B 5284 – ✆ 015394 88600 – www.leeucollection.com

Linthwaite House – See restaurant listing

Lindeth Howe

TRADITIONAL • CONTEMPORARY This charming arts and crafts house sits in an elevated spot and has a view down to Lake Windermere. It was once owned by Beatrix Potter and the strikingly contemporary lounge and bar draw on this theme. Bedrooms are a mix of classic and contemporary. Lunch is in the bar; dinner is in the formal dining room.

34 rooms - £ 90/136 £ 106/212

Lindeth Dr. Longtail Hill LA23 3JF - South : 1.25 mi by A 5074 on B 5284 - 015394 45759 - www.lindeth-howe.co.uk - Closed 2-12 January

Storrs Hall

HISTORIC • CONTEMPORARY The gardens of this striking part-Georgian country house sweep down to the lake shore and their private jetty. The décor combines the old and the new, while a striking cupola adds a touch of grandeur – as does the dark wood and stained glass bar which formerly resided in Blackpool Tower. Dine in the elegant dining room or bright conservatory.

30 rooms - £ 125/200 £ 125/480 - 1 suite

LA23 3LG - South : 2 mi on A 592 - 015394 47111 - www.storrshall.com

Ryebeck

FAMILY • ELEGANT Have afternoon tea on the terrace, looking over the delightful gardens and down to the famous lake. Some of the bright, airy bedrooms share the view and some have patios or Juliet balconies. Kick-back in one of the cosy modern lounges then head to the dining room for brasserie classics of Cumbrian produce.

24 rooms - £ 85/115 £ 119/159

Lyth Valley Rd LA23 3JP - South : 0.75 mi on A 5074 - 015394 88195 - www.ryebeck.com - Closed 1 week in January

WINDSOR

Windsor and Maidenhead - Pop. 31 225 - Regional map n° **6**-D3

Greene Oak

MODERN CUISINE • DESIGN The Greene Oak's modern, open-plan bar has a laid-back feel and its large terrace is a real suntrap. Menus mix pub classics with more interesting dishes - start with some 'Tasters' and finish with mini 'Jam Jar' desserts.

Carte £ 26/44

Oakley Green SL4 5UW - West : 3 mi by A 308 on B 3024 - 01753 864294 - www.thegreeneoak.co.uk - Closed Sunday dinner

Oxford Blue

MODERN CUISINE • INTIMATE With its contemporary look and smart landscaped grounds, you'd be forgiven for thinking this is a new-build, but it started life as two 19C gamekeepers' cottages and has been a pub for over 100 years. Accomplished classics offer more than their descriptions imply and come with the occasional modern twist.

Menu £ 25 (lunch) - Carte £ 42/62

10 Crimp Hill, Old Windsor SL4 2QY - Southeast : 2.75 mi by A 308 off B 3021 - 01753 861954 - www.oxfordbluepub.co.uk - Closed 23-29 December, 24 July-2 August, Sunday dinner, Monday and Tuesday

Macdonald Windsor

BUSINESS • DESIGN Set in a former department store opposite the Guildhall. Pass through attractive open-plan guest areas up to contemporary bedrooms with a high level of facilities and bold masculine hues; two have balconies overlooking the castle. The modern brasserie specialises in mature Scottish beef from the Josper grill.

120 rooms - £ 157/347 £ 157/347 - £ 20

23 High St. SL4 1LH - 01753 483100 - www.macdonald-hotels.co.uk/windsor

Sir Christopher Wren's House

HISTORIC • CONTEMPORARY Impressive house on the riverbank, built by Wren in 1676 as his family home. Characterful guest areas have high ceilings, panelled walls and bold modern furnishings. Some of the stylish bedrooms are beamed and some have balconies and river views. The modern restaurant has a lovely Thames outlook.

98 rooms - £ 140/190 £ 150/350 - 3 suites

Thames St SL4 1PX - 01753 442400 - www.sarova.com

Christopher

INN • CONTEMPORARY 18C brick-built coaching inn close to Eton College; cross the footbridge over the Thames to reach the castle. Contemporary bedrooms are spread about the main building and a mews; guest areas have an informal feel. The brightly coloured bistro offers international menus with subtle North African influences.

34 rooms - £ 126/155 £ 160/220 - £ 13

110 High St, Eton SL4 6AN - 01753 852359 - www.thechristopher.co.uk

WINSTER

Derbyshire – Pop. 1 787 – Regional map n° **9**-A1

Old Shoulder of Mutton

TOWNHOUSE • PERSONALISED This old village pub closed in 1916 but its name and character have been kept and it's been transformed into a stylish, cosy guesthouse. Beams and handmade furniture abound and local produce features at breakfast. (Min 2 nights stay).

3 rooms - £ 110/145 £ 125/160

West Bank DE4 2DQ - 01629 650005 - www.oldshoulderofmutton.co.uk - Closed December-April

WINSTON

Durham – Regional map n° **14**-A3

Bridgewater Arms

SEAFOOD • COSY This traditional pub spent the first hundred years of its life as a school; look out for the copperplate alphabet. The chef is known for his seafood and dishes are unashamedly classic, accurately executed and extremely satisfying.

Carte £ 25/66

DL2 3RN - 01325 730302 - www.thebridgewaterarms.com - Closed 25-26 December, 1 January, Sunday and Monday

WINTERINGHAM

North Lincolnshire – Scunthorpe – Pop. 1 000 – Regional map n° **13**-C3

Winteringham Fields (Colin McGurran)

MODERN CUISINE • INTIMATE XXX This 16C former farmhouse sits in a sleepy village in an area rich in agriculture and the long-standing owners also have their own smallholding. Their impeccable ingredients are married with classic techniques, resulting in refined, flavoursome dishes with bags of flavour. Dinner is a multi-course surprise menu. Bedrooms mix classic character with modern comforts.

→ Seared Cornish mackerel with kohlrabi, ponzu and nori emulsion. BBQ rump of Herdwick lamb with braised gem, goat's curd and mint. Bex's iced honey parfait with apricot sorbet and honeycomb crumb.

Menu £ 65/89 - Carte lunch £ 45/72

15 rooms - £ 150/180 £ 180/220

1 Silver St DN15 9ND - 01724 733096 (booking essential) - www.winteringhamfields.co.uk - Closed 3 weeks August, 1 week January, Christmas, Tuesday lunch, Sunday and Monday

WISWELL

Lancashire - Regional map n° **11**-B2

Freemasons

MODERN BRITISH • PUB A delightful pub hidden away on a narrow lane. The antique-furnished upstairs has an elegant feel, while downstairs, with its flagged floors, low beams and open fires is more rustic. The interesting menu features modern versions of traditional pub dishes and cooking is refined and skilful. Bedrooms are set to open at the start of 2019.

Menu £ 23 (lunch and early dinner) - Carte £ 44/72

8 Vicarage Fold ✉ BB7 9DF - ✆ 01254 822218 - www.freemasonsatwiswell.com - Closed 2-9 January and Monday-Tuesday except bank holidays

WITHAM ON THE HILL

Lincolnshire - Pop. 260 - Regional map n° **9**-C2

Six Bells

TRADITIONAL CUISINE • FRIENDLY This pub's spacious courtyard is an obvious draw and the bright, stylish interior keeps things cheery whatever the weather. Choose hand-crafted pizzas cooked in the wood-burning oven in the bar or something more sophisticated from the main menu. Bedrooms are very stylishly appointed; Hayloft is the best.

Menu £ 14 (weekday lunch) - Carte £ 21/39

5 rooms - £ 75/130 £ 90/150

✉ PE10 0JH - ✆ 01778 590360 - www.sixbellswitham.co.uk - Closed 25-31 December and 1 January

WIVETON - Norfolk → See Blakeney

WOBURN

✉ Milton Keynes - Pop. 1 534 - Regional map n° **7**-A2

Paris House

CREATIVE • INTIMATE XX A beautiful mock-Tudor house, built in Paris and reassembled in this idyllic location; enjoy an aperitif on the terrace while watching the deer. Cooking is a mix of Asian dishes and British classics given ambitious modern makeovers.

Menu £ 49/96

Woburn Park ✉ MK17 9QP - Southeast : 2.25 mi on A 4012 - ✆ 01525 290692 (booking essential) - www.parishouse.co.uk - Closed 24 December-3 January and Sunday dinner-Wednesday

The Woburn

HISTORIC • CONTEMPORARY The Woburn Estate comprises a 3,000 acre deer park, an abbey and this 18C coaching inn. Charming guest areas include a cosy bar and brasserie-style Olivier's. This is where afternoon tea was popularised in the 1840s. The best of the bedrooms are the themed suites and those in the 300yr old beamed Cottages.

55 rooms - £ 125/155 £ 157/187 - 9 suites

1 George St ✉ MK17 9PX - ✆ 01525 290441 - www.thewoburnhotel.co.uk - Closed 1-7 January

WOLD NEWTON

East Riding of Yorkshire - Regional map n° **13**-D2

Wold Cottage

COUNTRY HOUSE • CONTEMPORARY A fine Georgian manor house in 300 acres of tranquil farmland, which guests are encouraged to explore. Enjoy cakes by the fire on arrival and feast on local produce at breakfast. Sizeable bedrooms boast luxurious soft furnishings and antiques and some have feature beds; the courtyard rooms are simpler.

6 rooms - £ 70/90 £ 100/140

✉ YO25 3HL - South : 0.5 mi on Thwing rd - ✆ 01262 470696 - www.woldcottage.com

WOLVERHAMPTON

West Midlands - Pop. 210 319 - Regional map n° **10**-C2

Bilash

INDIAN • FAMILY XX This smart contemporary restaurant is well-established and has several generations of the same family involved. Appealing, original menus offer South Indian and Bangladeshi dishes, crafted only from local and home made produce.

Menu £ 14 (lunch)/20 - Carte £ 25/55

No 2 Cheapside WV1 1TU - 01902 427762 - www.thebilash.co.uk - Closed 25-27 December, 1 January and Sunday

WOODBRIDGE

Suffolk - Pop. 11 341 - Regional map n° **8**-D3

Turk's Head

MODERN BRITISH • FAMILY Charming pub with a petanque pitch, lovely gardens and a great terrace with country views. As well as pub classics, the Indian chef creates interesting, cleverly spiced dishes such as paneer steak with curry butter.

Menu £ 15 (lunch) - Carte £ 25/44

Low Rd, Hasketon IP13 6JGB - Northwest : 2 mi by Burkitt Rd, B 1079 and Shrubbery Rd. - 01394 610343 - www.theturksheadhasketon.co.uk - Closed Sunday dinner

Seckford Hall

HISTORIC BUILDING • CONTEMPORARY This part-Tudor country house in attractive gardens was reputedly once visited by Elizabeth I - she would hardly recognise it now, with its bold champagne bar, stylish sitting rooms and creatively designed modern bedrooms. The linen-laid restaurant offers a seasonal menu of modern classics.

34 rooms - †£ 90/150 ††£ 100/200 - 6 suites

IP13 6NU - Southwest : 1.25 mi by A 12 - 01394 385678 - www.seckford.co.uk

at Bromeswell Northeast: 2.5 mi by B1438 off A1152

Unruly Pig

MODERN CUISINE • PUB This modern dining pub is far from unruly, its owner - a former lawyer - sees to that; and the wood panelling, interesting art and friendly team add a warm feel. The Mediterranean-inspired cooking offers plenty of choice, the set menus are good value and the vegetarian and gluten free options are a hit.

Menu £ 19 (weekdays) - Carte £ 27/45

Orford Rd IP12 2PU - 01394 460310 - www.theunrulypig.co.uk - Closed Sunday dinner and Monday

WOODSTOCK

Oxfordshire - Pop. 2 389 - Regional map n° **6**-B2

Kitchen by Dominic Chapman

MODERN CUISINE • INTIMATE XX This two-roomed hotel restaurant juxtaposes the old and new, with wood-panelling, bold fabrics and contemporary artwork. Concise menus are highly seasonal and dishes are unfussy with a classic British base.

Menu £ 21 (lunch) - Carte dinner £ 25/51

Feathers Hotel, Market St OX20 1SX - 01993 812291 (booking essential) - www.feathers.co.uk

Crown

MEDITERRANEAN CUISINE • FRIENDLY It might have 18C origins but the Crown is not your typical coaching inn, with its bright, almost greenhouse-style dining room complete with an attractive Belgian tiled floor. Fresh, light cooking takes its influences from the Med and makes good use of the wood-fired oven. Bedrooms are beautifully appointed.

Carte £ 20/40

5 rooms – †£ 125/175 ††£ 125/275

31 High St ✉ OX20 1TE – ✆ 01993 813339 – www.thecrownwoodstock.com – Closed dinner 25-26 December and 1 January

Feathers

TOWNHOUSE • ELEGANT It might date from the 17C but this townhouse has a stylish modern interior. Bedrooms blend bold fabrics and wallpapers with antique furnishings. The bar offers over 400 gins and the courtyard terrace is a great spot for lunch.

21 rooms – †£ 89/219 ††£ 99/229 – 5 suites

Market St ✉ OX20 1SX – ✆ 01993 812291 – www.feathers.co.uk

Kitchen by Dominic Chapman – See restaurant listing

WOOLACOMBE

Devon – Pop. 840 – Regional map n° **1**-C1

Noel Corston

MODERN BRITISH • INTIMATE A rustic restaurant consisting of just 8 seats set around an open kitchen counter. Dinner is served at 7pm and the multi-course tasting menu evolves daily, with skilfully prepared modern dishes showcasing ingredients largely from North Devon's UNESCO Biosphere Reserve. Go for the wine pairings.

Menu £ 105 – tasting menu only

South St ✉ EX34 7BB – ✆ 01271 871187 (booking essential) – www.noelcorston.com – dinner only – Closed October-Easter and Sunday-Tuesday

WOOLER

Northumberland – Pop. 1 983 – Regional map n° **14**-A1

Firwood

TRADITIONAL • COSY Bay-windowed dower house in a peaceful setting, with a beautiful tiled hall, a comfy lounge and lovely countryside views. Spacious bedrooms are furnished in a simple period style. The friendly owners are a font of local knowledge.

3 rooms – †£ 60/90 ††£ 60/90

Middleton Hall ✉ NE71 6RD – South : 1.75 mi by Earle rd on Middleton Hall rd – ✆ 01668 283699 – www.firwoodhouse.co.uk – Closed 1 December-13 February

WOOTTON

Oxfordshire – Regional map n° **6**-B2

Killingworth Castle

TRADITIONAL BRITISH • RUSTIC A welcoming roadside inn dating from the 16C, set just outside the village centre. The chatty staff know what they're doing and food is great value, especially the dish of the day. Interesting menus champion local produce; here they bake their own breads, butcher their own meats and brew their own beers. Retire to one of the spacious bedrooms feeling suitably fortified.

Carte £ 21/35

8 rooms – †£ 139/169 ††£ 139/169

Glympton Rd ✉ OX20 1EJ – ✆ 01993 811401 – www.thekillingworthcastle.com – Closed 25 December

WORCESTER

Worcestershire – Pop. 100 153 – Regional map n° **10**-B3

Old Rectifying House

TRADITIONAL BRITISH • PUB With shabby-chic décor, young chefs hard at work in the open kitchen, a cocktail list and a soundtrack of jazz, blues and soul, this mock-Tudor building overlooking the river brings a hipster vibe to Worcester. Appealing dishes have a British slant and there's a well-thought-out vegan menu too.

Carte £ 21/42

North Par. ✉ WR1 3NN – ✆ 01905 619622 – www.theoldrec.co.uk – Closed Monday except bank holidays and 25 December

WORTH – Kent ➔ See Deal

WRINGTON

North Somerset – Pop. 1 918 – Regional map n° **2**-B2

The Ethicurean

MODERN BRITISH • SIMPLE Two rustic, informal glasshouses in a beautifully restored Victorian walled garden; fresh produce leads the daily menu and they strive to be 'ethical' and 'epicurean'. They serve everything from coffee and cake to 5 set courses.

Menu £ 30/44 (dinner) – Carte lunch £ 27/42

Barley Wood Walled Garden, Long Ln ✉ BS40 5SA – East : 1.25 mi by School Rd on Redhill rd – ✆ 01934 863713 (booking essential) – www.theethicurean.com – Closed Sunday dinner and Monday

WYE

Kent – ✉ Ashford – Pop. 2 066 – Regional map n° **5**-C2

Wife of Bath

SPANISH • DESIGN An attractive red-brick house plays host to this understated restaurant where a Spanish tiled floor marries with a wooden bar counter and old timbers. The menu champions northern Spain, with colourful, vibrant dishes including sharing plates and a small range of tapas. Stylish bedrooms come with lots of extras.

Menu £ 25 (weekday lunch) – Carte £ 30/44

6 rooms – †£ 95/140 ††£ 95/140

4 Upper Bridge St ✉ TN25 5AF – ✆ 01233 812232 – www.thewifeofbath.com – Closed Sunday dinner and Monday

WYMESWOLD

Leicestershire – Pop. 1 296 – Regional map n° **9**-B2

Hammer & Pincers

MODERN BRITISH • ELEGANT Formerly the village forge (the old water pump can still be seen at the back), then a pub, and now a stylish, intimate restaurant. Modern menus have classic British roots; the 7 and 10 course grazing menus are the most creative.

Menu £ 29 (weekdays) – Carte dinner £ 34/50

5 East Rd ✉ LE12 6ST – ✆ 01509 880735 – www.hammerandpincers.co.uk – Closed 25 December, Sunday dinner and Monday

WYMONDHAM

Leicestershire – Pop. 600 – Regional map n° **9**-C2

Berkeley Arms

TRADITIONAL BRITISH • PUB Attractive 16C village pub run by an experienced local couple; turn left for the low-beamed bar or right for the dining room. Appealing, gutsy dishes rely on seasonal local produce and are constantly evolving; alongside British favourites you'll find the likes of mallard with poached pears. Service is relaxed.

Menu £ 16/19 - Carte £ 26/49

59 Main St ✉ LE14 2AG - ✆ 01572 787587 (booking essential) - www.theberkeleyarms.co.uk - Closed first 2 weeks January, 2 weeks summer, Sunday dinner and Monday

WYNYARD

Stockton-on-Tees - Pop. 2 462 - Regional map n° **14**-B3

Wynyard Hall

COUNTRY HOUSE • ELEGANT An impressive Georgian mansion built for the Marquis of Londonderry; its smart spa overlooks a lake. Bedrooms in the main house are traditional, while those in the lodges are more modern. Classic guest areas feature stained glass, open fires and antiques. The formal dining room offers modern classics.

24 rooms - †£ 205 ††£ 290 - 3 suites

✉ TS22 5NF - ✆ 01740 644811 - www.wynyardhall.co.uk

WHATCOTE

Warwickshire - Regional map n° **10**-C3

The Royal Oak

MODERN BRITISH • PUB Originally a 12C workmen's drinks shelter, this is reputedly one of the oldest pubs in the country; Oliver Cromwell supposedly stayed here before the Battle of Edgehill in 1642. It has plenty of character, a lovely atmosphere and a strong 'farm to fork' ethos. Dishes are creative and attractively presented.

Carte £ 32/46

The Orchard ✉ CV36 5EF - ✆ 01295 688100 (booking essential) - www.theroyaloakwhatcote.co.uk - Closed 14-31 January and Sunday dinner -Wednesday lunch

YARM

Stockton-on-Tees - Pop. 19 184 - Regional map n° **14**-B3

Judges Country House

MODERN CUISINE • TRADITIONAL DÉCOR A formal two-roomed restaurant in a traditional country house hotel; the conservatory extension has a lovely outlook over the lawns. Modern, well-prepared dishes are straightforward yet full of flavour.

Menu £ 25 - Carte £ 28/57

Judges Country House, Kirklevington Hall, Kirklevington ✉ TS15 9LW - South : 1.5 mi on A 67 - ✆ 01642 789000 - www.judgeshotel.co.uk

Muse

INTERNATIONAL • BRASSERIE A smart continental café with a bright modern interior and a popular pavement terrace. Extensive international menus list everything from a bacon sandwich to salads, pastas and grills; they also offer a good value set price menu.

Menu £ 16 (lunch and early dinner) - Carte £ 25/55

104b High St ✉ TS15 9AU - ✆ 01642 788558 - www.museyarm.com - Closed 25 December, 1 January and Sunday dinner

Judges Country House

COUNTRY HOUSE • CLASSIC A charming Victorian judge's house with a welcoming atmosphere, filled with wood panelling, antiques and ornaments and set within impressive grounds. Traditional country house bedrooms come with a high level of facilities, bright modern bathrooms and extra touches such as fresh fruit and flowers.

21 rooms - £ 99/205 £ 145/225

Kirklevington Hall, Kirklevington ✉ TS15 9LW - South : 1.5 mi on A 67 - ✆ 01642 789000 - www.judgeshotel.co.uk

Judges Country House - See restaurant listing

YARMOUTH - Isle of Wight ➜ See Wight (Isle of)

YATTENDON

West Berkshire - ✉ Newbury - Pop. 288 - Regional map n° **6**-B3

Royal Oak

TRADITIONAL BRITISH • INN A red-brick pub bursting with country charm, set in a picture postcard village; you'll find a heavily beamed bar with a roaring fire at its hub and plenty of local ales on offer. Menus offer honest British dishes and traditional puddings. Country house style bedrooms come with their own gun cabinets.

Menu £ 20 (weekday lunch) - Carte £ 31/49

10 rooms - £ 99/140 £ 99/140

The Square ✉ RG18 0UF - ✆ 01635 201325 - www.royaloakyattendon.co.uk

at Frilsham South: 1 mi by Frilsham rd on Bucklebury rd ✉ Yattendon

Pot Kiln

TRADITIONAL BRITISH • COSY Head for the cosy bar and order a pint of Brick Kiln beer then follow the delicious aromas through to the dining area, where flavoursome British dishes arrive in gutsy portions. On summer Sundays they fire up the outdoor pizza oven.

Carte £ 30/47

✉ RG18 0XX - ✆ 01635 201366 - www.potkiln.org

YEOVIL

Somerset - Pop. 45 784 - Regional map n° **2**-B3

at Barwick South: 2 mi by A30 off A37 ✉ Yeovil

Little Barwick House

MODERN BRITISH • INTIMATE XX Attractive Georgian dower house on the outskirts of town, run by a hospitable husband and wife team. Relax on deep sofas before heading into the elegant dining room with its huge window and heavy drapes. Cooking is classical, satisfying and full of flavour - a carefully chosen wine list accompanies. Charming, comfortably furnished bedrooms, each with its own character.

Menu £ 32/49

7 rooms - £ 85/155 £ 121/190

✉ BA22 9TD - ✆ 01935 423902 (booking essential) - www.littlebarwickhouse.co.uk - Closed 26 December-27 January, Sunday, Monday and lunch Tuesday

GOOD TIPS!

In the tourist capital of the North, every cobbled twist and turn reveals another historic building. A stone's throw from the magnificent York Minster cathedral is the **Judge's Lodging**; once a doctor's house and now a characterful hotel. Follow the ancient city walls to the Museum Gardens and the **Star Inn The City**, where chargrilled meats are a highlight.

YORK

York - Pop. 198 900 - Regional map n° **13**-C2

Restaurants

Skosh

MODERN BRITISH • FASHIONABLE X Skosh sits in a glass-fronted Grade II listed building close to the 12C Micklegate Bar. Both the décor and the cooking are bright and colourful; sit at the counter to really get involved. Constantly evolving small plates keep Yorkshire produce at their heart but have global – especially Indian – influences.

Carte £ 17/34

Town plan: A2-s – *98 Micklegate ✉ YO1 6JX – ✆ 01904 634849 (booking essential at dinner) – www.skoshyork.co.uk – Closed 1 week January, 1 week May, 2 weeks September, Sunday dinner, Monday and Tuesday*

Arras

MODERN CUISINE • DESIGN XX A red-brick former coach house with a bright, contemporary interior. Well-priced modern menus offer creative cooking. The bar boasts an unusual white-fronted counter and there's a lovely enclosed terrace hidden to the rear.

Menu £ 20/45

Town plan: B1-x – *The Old Coach House, Peasholme Green ✉ YO1 7PW – ✆ 01904 633737 – www.arrasrestaurant.co.uk – Closed Christmas-mid-January, late August-early September, Sunday, Monday and lunch Tuesday*

Hudsons by Craig Atchinson (N)

MODERN BRITISH • ELEGANT XX If you're after a sense of occasion, this intimate hotel restaurant with its feature parquet floor is the answer. Choose from two seasonally evolving tasting menus which showcase Yorkshire ingredients. Cooking employs modern techniques and dishes are bold and gutsy with clearly defined flavours.

Menu £ 50/80 – tasting menu only

Town plan: A2-v – *Grand Hotel & Spa York, Station Rise ✉ YO1 6GD – ✆ 01904 380038 – www.thegrandyork.co.uk/drinking-and-dining/hudsons/ – dinner only – Closed Sunday and Monday*

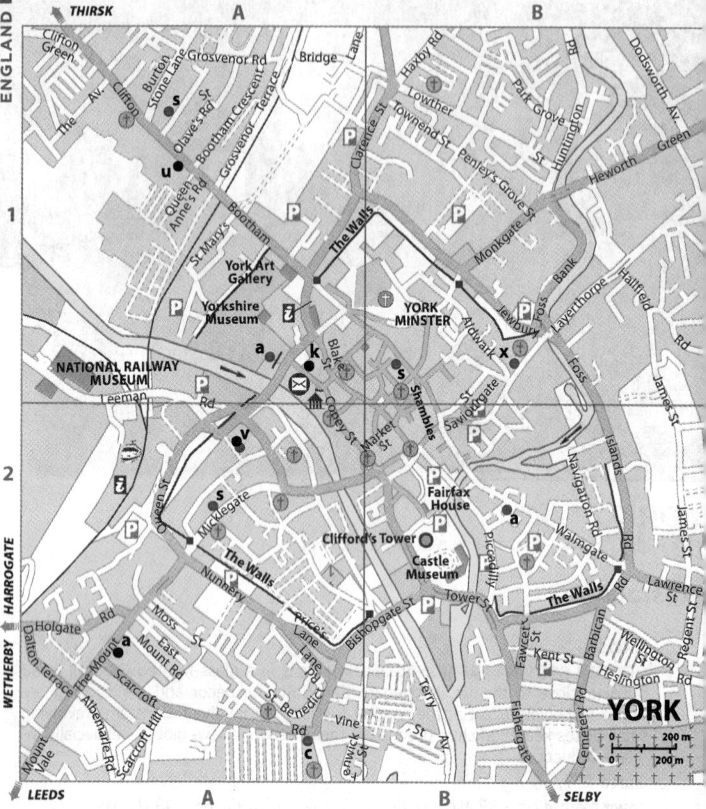

Melton's

MODERN BRITISH • NEIGHBOURHOOD XX A cosy-looking shop conversion in the suburbs. The walls are covered in murals of ingredients and happy diners, which is fitting as local produce features highly and the restaurant is well-regarded. Cooking is fresh and flavoursome.

Menu £ 32 (lunch and early dinner)/42

Town plan: A2-c – *7 Scarcroft Rd ✉ YO23 1ND*
– ✆ 01904 634341 (booking essential) – www.meltonsrestaurant.co.uk
– Closed 3 weeks Christmas, Sunday, Monday and lunch Tuesday

The Park

MODERN CUISINE • INTIMATE XX Adam Jackson has moved his restaurant to a quiet residential suburb of York; it's set within a hotel and is run by a chatty, knowledgeable team. The seasonal set menus feature complex, eye-catching dishes comprising many flavours.

Menu £ 35/60 – tasting menu only

Town plan: A1-s – *Marmadukes Hotel, 4-5 St Peters Grove, Bootham ✉ YO30 6AQ – ✆ 01904 540903 – www.theparkrestaurant.co.uk – dinner only – Closed 2 weeks January, 2 weeks summer, 24-26 December, Sunday and Monday*

Star Inn The City

MODERN BRITISH • DESIGN A buzzy all-day brasserie set in an old brick engine house, in a delightful riverside spot beside the Museum Gardens. Well-judged dishes are modern yet gutsy and showcase top Yorkshire produce – the chargrilled meats are a highlight.

Menu £ 17 (weekday lunch) – Carte £ 22/59

Town plan: A1-a – *Lendal Engine House, Museum St ✉ YO1 7DR – ✆ 01904 619208 – www.starinnthecity.co.uk – Closed 25-26 December and 1 January*

Le Cochon Aveugle

MODERN CUISINE • BISTRO A charming, rustic bistro with striking chequer-board flooring and a homely style. The 'surprise' set menu offers original modern dishes and although the ingredients are firmly British, the cooking is French to the core.

Menu £ 60 – tasting menu only

Town plan: B2-a – *37 Walmgate ✉ YO1 9TX – ✆ 01904 640222 (booking essential) – www.lecochonaveugle.uk – dinner only and Saturday lunch – Closed Christmas-New Year and Sunday-Tuesday*

Mr P's Curious Tavern

TRADITIONAL BRITISH • BISTRO This is indeed a curious place, with a fun, bohemian style and a lively buzz. Well-priced small plates are full of personality and keep local suppliers to the fore. It's set in a Grade I listed house in the shadow of the Minster.

Carte £ 24/41

Town plan: B1-s – *71 Low Petergate ✉ YO1 7HY – ✆ 01904 521177 – www.mrpscurioustavern.co.uk – Closed Sunday dinner*

Hotels

Grand H. & Spa York

BUSINESS • CONTEMPORARY Choose a bedroom in the grand William and Mary style former offices of the North Eastern Railway Company or a brighter, more contemporary room with great city views in the adjoining building; all are well-equipped. Relax in the impressive basement spa then enjoy some of the 110 whiskies on offer in the Whisky Lounge. Dine in the smart brasserie or formal restaurant.

208 rooms – †£ 170/280 ††£ 190/320 – 13 suites

Town plan: A2-v – *Station Rise ✉ YO1 6GD – ✆ 01904 380038 – www.thegrandyork.co.uk*

Hudsons by Craig Atchinson – See restaurant listing

Hotel du Vin

TOWNHOUSE • CONTEMPORARY An 18C former orphanage with a Georgian-style annexe, set on the edge of city. The stylish interior features two snug lounges, a chic champagne bar and a glass-roofed courtyard for afternoon tea. Well-equipped bedrooms are wine-themed and they offer an imaginative wine list in the popular French bistro.

44 rooms – †£ 109/320 ††£ 109/320

Town plan: A2-a – *89 The Mount ✉ YO24 1AX – ✆ 01904 557350 – www.hotelduvin.com*

Middlethorpe Hall

HISTORIC • CLASSIC A William and Mary House dating from 1699, set in 20 acres of impressive parkland. The elegant sitting room has French-style furnishings, oil paintings and flower displays. Antique-filled bedrooms are split between the house and the courtyard. Classic cooking uses luxury ingredients and kitchen garden produce.

29 rooms – †£ 149/159 ††£ 219/299 – 9 suites

Bishopthorpe Rd ✉ YO23 2GB – South : 1.75 mi – ✆ 01904 641241 – www.middlethorpe.com

Grange

TOWNHOUSE • ELEGANT Well-run, Grade II listed Regency hotel with a grand portico entrance. Inside, flower arrangements and horse racing memorabilia abound. Choose between traditional bedrooms – some with four-posters – or more up-to-date rooms with TVs in the bathrooms. The informal basement brasserie serves a classical menu.

41 rooms – £ 125/254 £ 145/264 – 1 suite

Town plan: A1-u – *1 Clifton ✉ YO30 6AA – ☎ 01904 644744*
– www.grangehotel.co.uk

Judge's Lodging

HISTORIC • CONTEMPORARY Built for a doctor in 1706 and later used by judges sitting at the nearby court. Rooms in the main building have high ceilings and antique furnishings; the terrace rooms are more modern with smart shower rooms. It also has a wonderfully characterful barrel-ceilinged bar and a stylish brasserie and terrace.

21 rooms – £ 110/170 £ 110/185

Town plan: A1-k – *9 Lendal ✉ YO1 8AQ – ☎ 01904 638733*
– www.judgeslodgingyork.co.uk

ZENNOR

Cornwall – Regional map n° **1**-A3

Gurnard's Head

MODERN BRITISH • INN Surrounded by nothing but fields and livestock; a dog-friendly pub with shabby-chic décor, blazing fires and a relaxed, cosy feel. Menus rely on regional and foraged produce and the wine list offers some interesting choices by the glass. Compact bedrooms feature good quality linen and colourful throws.

Menu £ 20 – Carte £ 24/36

7 rooms – £ 105/177 £ 125/245

Treen ✉ TR26 3DE – West : 1.5 mi on B 3306 – ☎ 01736 796928
– www.gurnardshead.co.uk – Closed 25 December and 1 week in January

SCOTLAND

Scotland may be small, but its variety is immense. The vivacity of Glasgow can seem a thousand miles from the vast peatland wilderness of Caithness; the arty vibe of Georgian Edinburgh a world away from the remote and tranquil Ardnamurchan peninsula. Wide golden sands trim the Atlantic at South Harris, and the coastline of the Highlands boasts empty islands and turquoise waters. Meantime, Fife's coast draws golf fans to St Andrews and the more secretive delights of East Neuk, an area of fishing villages and stone harbours. Wherever you travel, a sense of a dramatic history prevails in the shape of castles, cathedrals and rugged lochside monuments to the heroes of old.

Food and drink embraces the traditional too, typified by Speyside's famous Malt Whisky Trail. And what better than Highland game, fresh fish from the Tweed or haggis, neeps and tatties to complement a grand Scottish hike? The country's glorious natural larder yields such jewels as Spring lamb from the Borders, Perthshire venison, fresh fish and shellfish from the Western Highlands and Aberdeen Angus beef.

- Michelin Road maps n° 501, 502 and 713
- Michelin Green Guide: Great Britain

IOB/Loop Images/age fotostock

15 Borders, Edinburgh & Glasgow

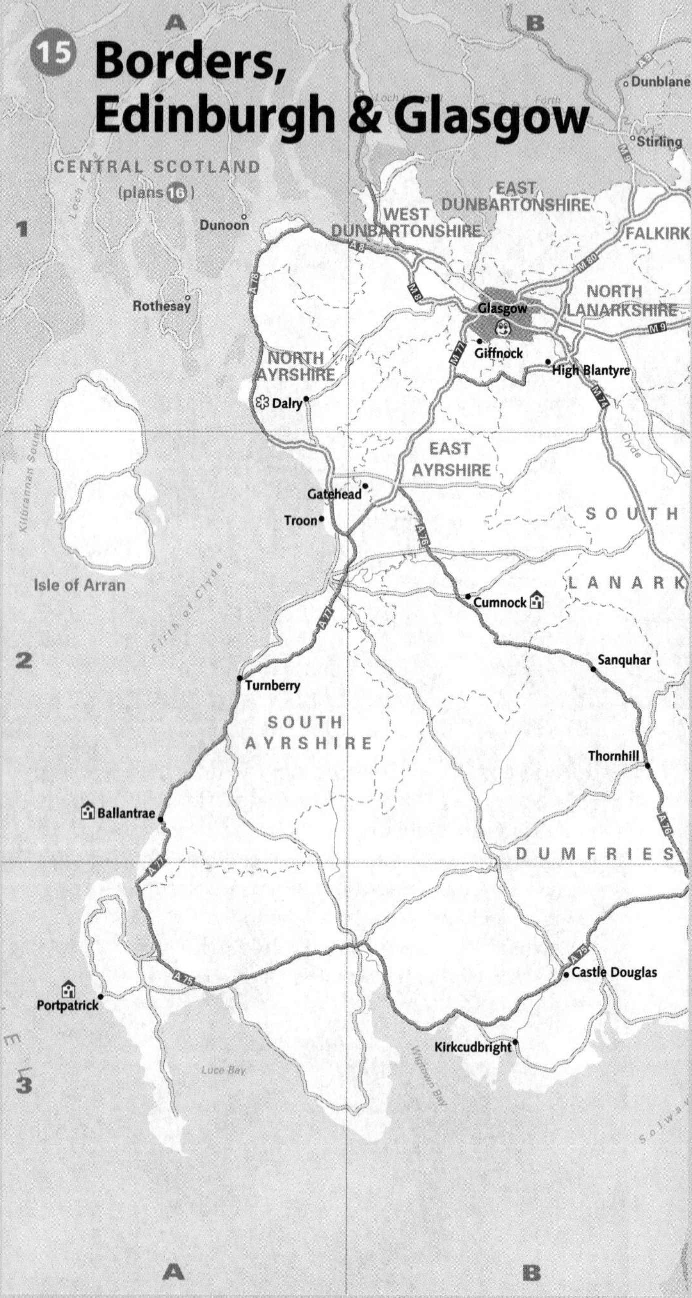
A
B
1
2
3
CENTRAL SCOTLAND
(plans 16)
Dunoon
Rothesay
Loch Fyne
Dunblane
Stirling
Forth
WEST DUNBARTONSHIRE
EAST DUNBARTONSHIRE
FALKIRK
NORTH LANARKSHIRE
Glasgow
Giffnock
High Blantyre
NORTH AYRSHIRE
Dalry
EAST AYRSHIRE
Gatehead
Troon
Kilbrannan Sound
Isle of Arran
Firth of Clyde
SOUTH LANARK
Clyde
Cumnock
Sanquhar
Turnberry
SOUTH AYRSHIRE
Thornhill
Ballantrae
DUMFRIES
Castle Douglas
Portpatrick
Kirkcudbright
Luce Bay
Wigtown Bay
Solway
A 8
M 8
A 78
M 77
M 80
M 9
M 74
A 76
A 71
A 77
A 75

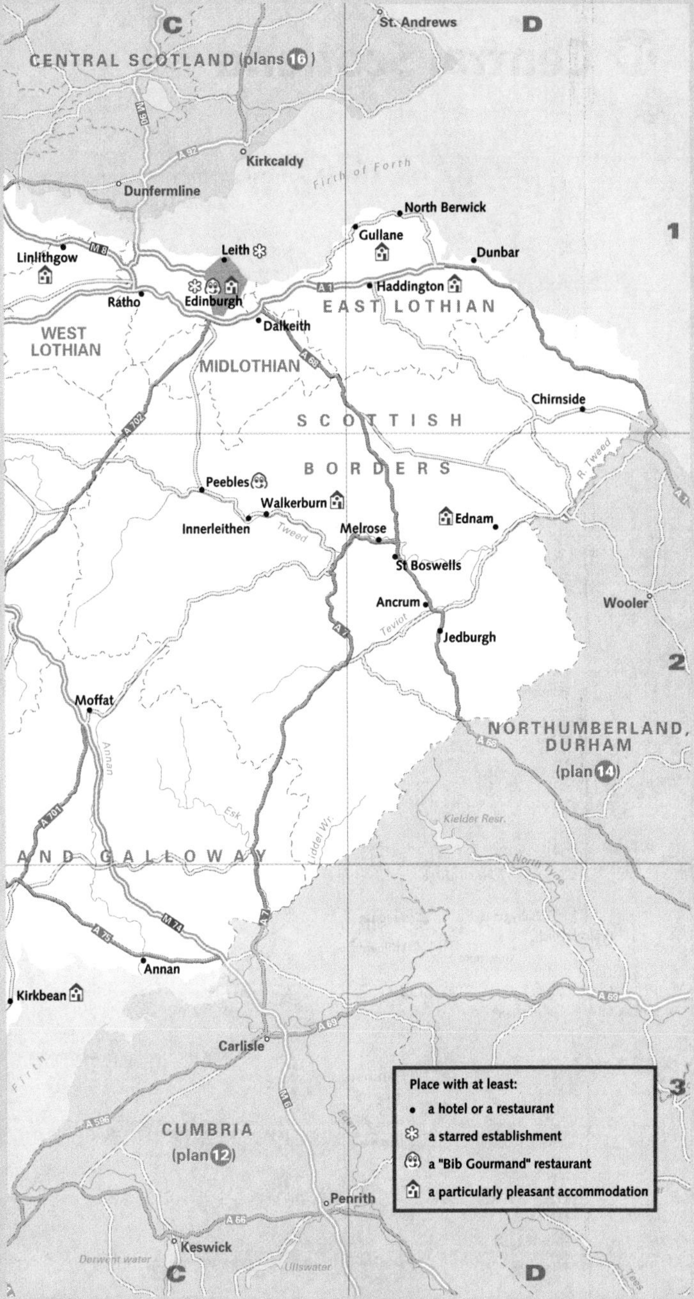

C
D
St. Andrews
CENTRAL SCOTLAND (plans 16)
M 90
A 92
Kirkcaldy
Firth of Forth
Dunfermline
North Berwick
Gullane
1
Dunbar
Linlithgow
M 8
Leith
Edinburgh
Ratho
A 1
Haddington
EAST LOTHIAN
Dalkeith
WEST LOTHIAN
MIDLOTHIAN
A 68
Chirnside
SCOTTISH BORDERS
A 702
R. Tweed
Peebles
Walkerburn
Innerleithen
Tweed
Melrose
Ednam
St Boswells
Ancrum
Wooler
Jedburgh
A 7
Teviot
2
Moffat
NORTHUMBERLAND, DURHAM
(plan 14)
A 68
Annan
Esk
Liddel Wr.
Kielder Resr.
A 701
AND GALLOWAY
North Tyne
M 74
A 75
Annan
Kirkbean
A 69
Carlisle
M 6
3
CUMBRIA
(plan 12)
A 595
Eden
Penrith
A 66
Keswick
Derwent water
Ullswater
Tees
Place with at least:
• a hotel or a restaurant
a starred establishment
a "Bib Gourmand" restaurant
a particularly pleasant accommodation

16 Central Scotland

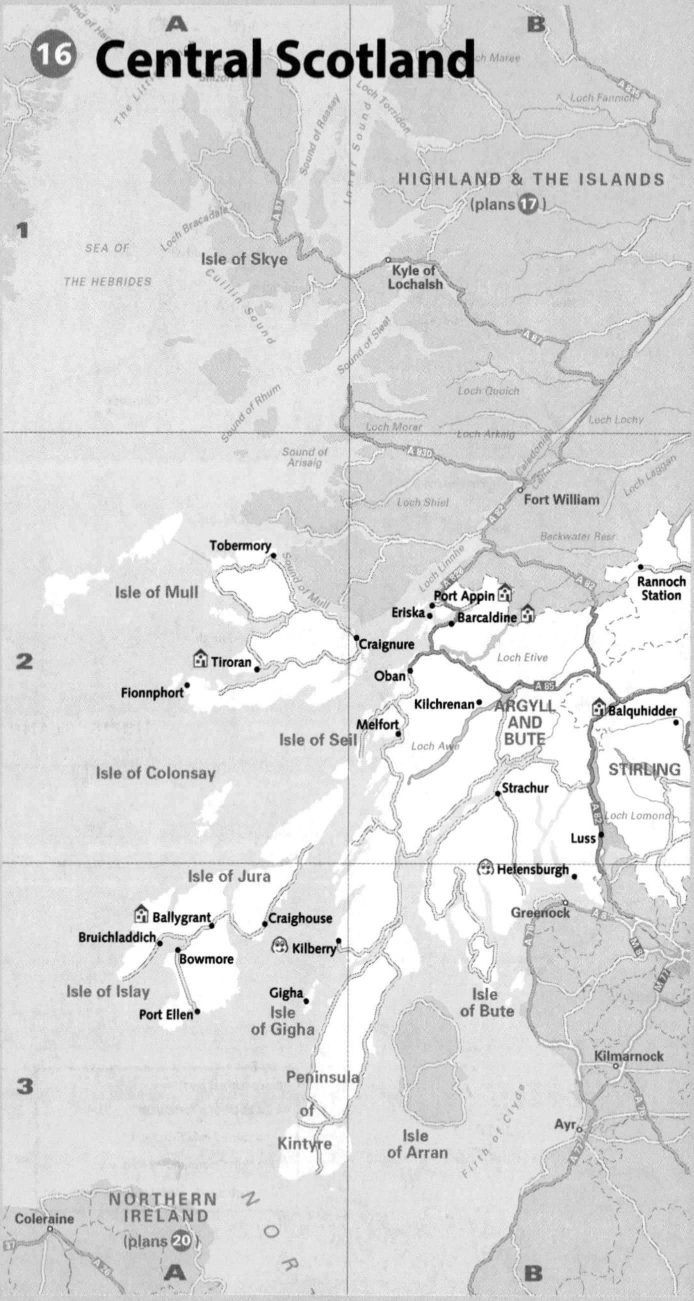

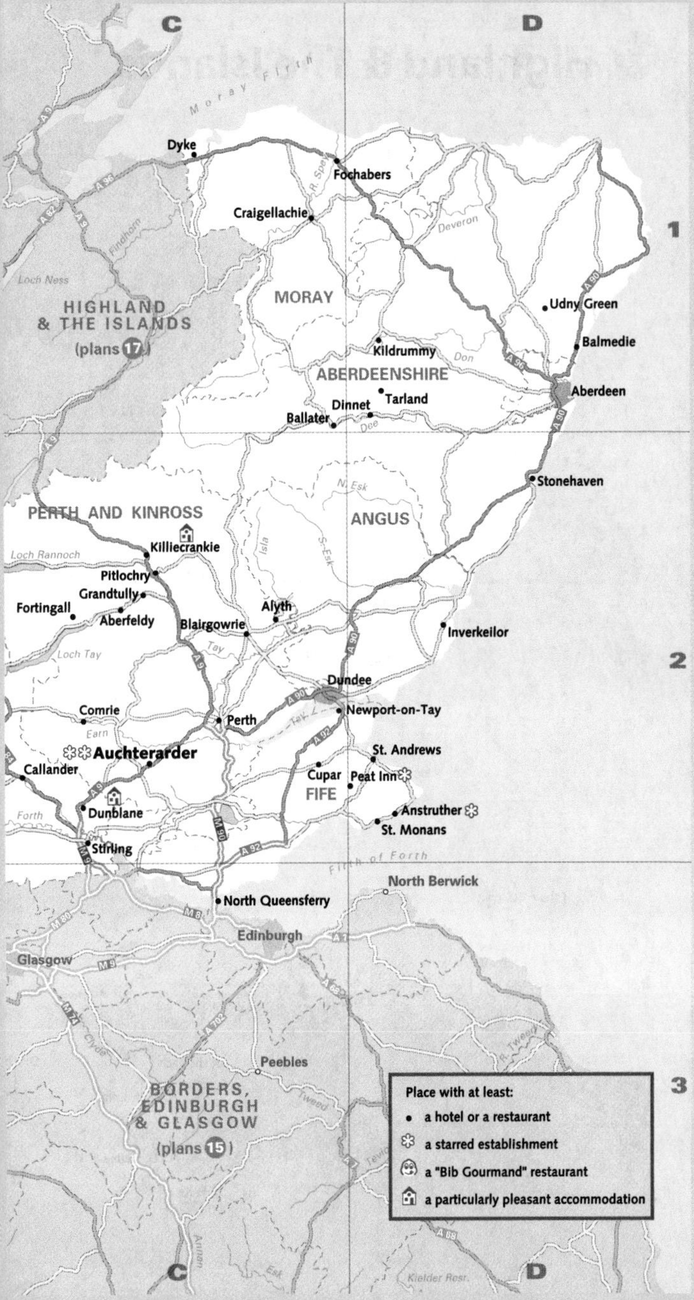
C
D
Moray Firth
Dyke
Fochabers
Craigellachie
1
HIGHLAND & THE ISLANDS
(plans 17)
Loch Ness
MORAY
Udny Green
Balmedie
Kildrummy
ABERDEENSHIRE
Aberdeen
Tarland
Dinnet
Ballater
Stonehaven
PERTH AND KINROSS
ANGUS
Killiecrankie
Loch Rannoch
Pitlochry
Grandtully
Fortingall
Aberfeldy
Alyth
Blairgowrie
Inverkeilor
Loch Tay
2
Dundee
Newport-on-Tay
Comrie
Perth
Auchterarder
St. Andrews
Callander
Cupar
Peat Inn
FIFE
Dunblane
Anstruther
St. Monans
Stirling
Firth of Forth
North Berwick
North Queensferry
Edinburgh
Glasgow
Peebles
3
BORDERS, EDINBURGH & GLASGOW
(plans 15)
Place with at least:
a hotel or a restaurant
a starred establishment
a "Bib Gourmand" restaurant
a particularly pleasant accommodation
Kielder Resr.
C
D

17 Highland & The Islands

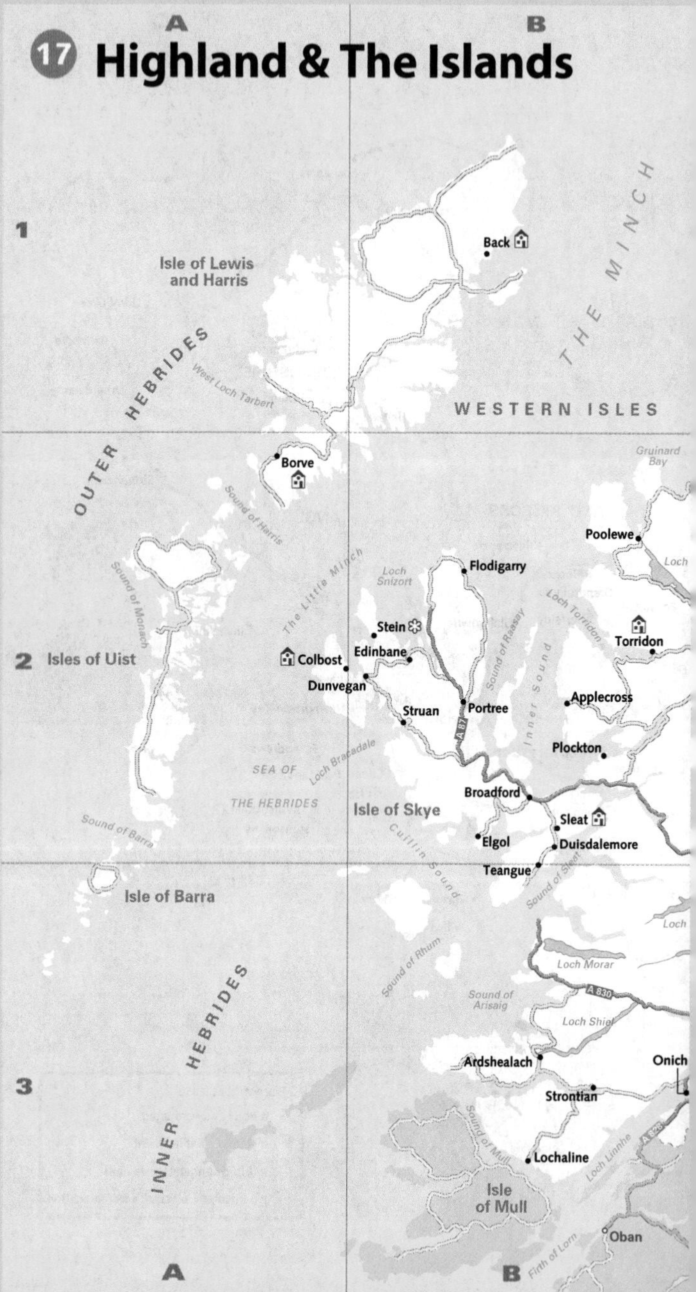

A
B
1
2
3
Isle of Lewis and Harris
Back
THE MINCH
OUTER HEBRIDES
West Loch Tarbert
WESTERN ISLES
Gruinard Bay
Borve
Sound of Harris
Poolewe
Loch
Sound of Monach
The Little Minch
Loch Snizort
Flodigarry
Loch Torridon
Torridon
Stein
Sound of Raasay
Isles of Uist
Colbost
Edinbane
Dunvegan
Inner Sound
Applecross
Struan
Portree
A 87
Plockton
SEA OF THE HEBRIDES
Loch Bracadale
Broadford
Isle of Skye
Sleat
Sound of Barra
Elgol
Duisdalemore
Cuillin Sound
Teangue
Sound of Sleat
Isle of Barra
Loch
Loch Morar
Sound of Rhum
A 830
Sound of Arisaig
Loch Shiel
HEBRIDES
Ardshealach
Onich
Strontian
INNER
Sound of Mull
A 828
Loch Linnhe
Lochaline
Isle of Mull
Oban
Firth of Lorn

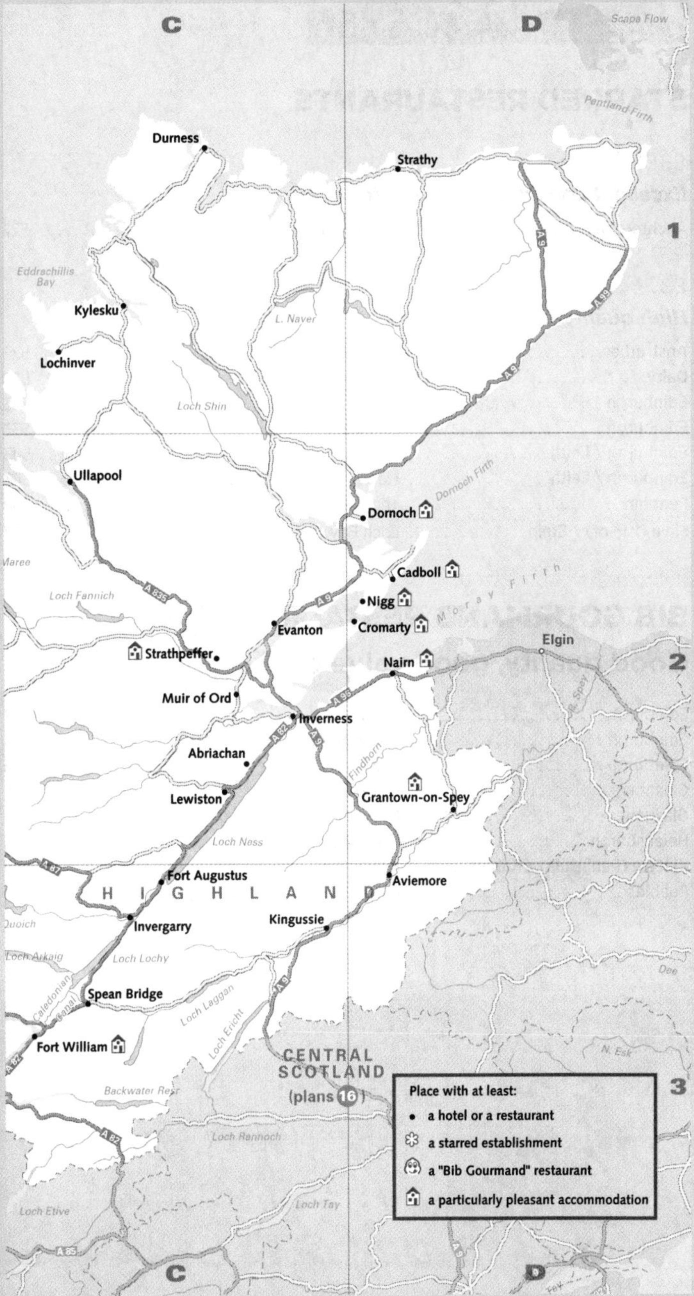
C
D
Scapa Flow
Pentland Firth
1
2
3
Durness
Strathy
Eddrachillis Bay
Kylesku
Lochinver
L. Naver
Loch Shin
A 9
A 99
Ullapool
Dornoch Firth
Dornoch
Maree
Cadboll
Loch Fannich
A 835
Nigg
Moray Firth
Cromarty
Evanton
Elgin
Strathpeffer
Nairn
Muir of Ord
A 96
R. Spey
Inverness
A 82
Abriachan
Findhorn
Lewiston
Grantown-on-Spey
Loch Ness
A 87
Fort Augustus
Aviemore
HIGHLAND
Quoich
Invergarry
Kingussie
Loch Arkaig
Loch Lochy
Dee
Caledonian Canal
Spean Bridge
Loch Laggan
Loch Ericht
Fort William
N. Esk
CENTRAL SCOTLAND
(plans 16)
Backwater Res.
Place with at least:
a hotel or a restaurant
a starred establishment
a "Bib Gourmand" restaurant
a particularly pleasant accommodation
Loch Rannoch
Loch Etive
Loch Tay
A 85
Tay

NOT TO BE MISSED

STARRED RESTAURANTS

✿✿

Excellent cooking, worth a detour!

✿

High quality cooking, worth a stop!

BIB GOURMAND RESTAURANTS

Good quality, good value cooking

OUR TOP PICKS

A SENSE OF GOLFING HISTORY

CHARMING GUESTHOUSES

Michelin

KNOWN FOR THEIR WELCOME

SOMETHING A LITTLE DIFFERENT

HIDEAWAYS

THE ULTIMATE IN LUXURY

ABERDEEN

Aberdeen City – Pop. 195 021 – Regional map n° **16**-D1

IX

MODERN BRITISH • DESIGN XX Pass through The Chester Hotel's moody cocktail bar and up to the chic split-level restaurant. Creative cooking champions Scottish produce, with Aberdeenshire steaks from the Josper grill a highlight. Brunch is served on Sundays.

Carte £ 35/72

The Chester Hotel, 59-63 Queens Rd ✉ AB15 4YP – ✆ 01224 327777 – www.chester-hotel.com – dinner only – Closed Sunday

Silver Darling

SEAFOOD • FRIENDLY XX Attractively set at the port entrance, on the top floor of the castellated former customs house. Floor to ceiling windows make the most of the superb view. Neatly presented dishes showcase excellent quality seafood.

Carte £ 28/48

Pocra Quay, North Pier ✉ AB11 5DQ – Southeast : 1.5 mi by Milner St, St Clement St and York St – ✆ 01224 576229 – www.thesilverdarling.co.uk – Closed Sunday lunch

Moonfish Cafe

MODERN BRITISH • BISTRO X A high ceiling and mirrored walls give this former toy shop an airy feel. Concise menus change every 6 weeks and the 2 course lunch is a bargain. Descriptions are terse, presentation is colourful and flavours are well-defined.

Menu £ 17 (weekday lunch)/36

9 Correction Wynd ✉ AB10 1HP – ✆ 01224 644166 – www.moonfishcafe.co.uk – Closed first 2 weeks January, 24-26 December, Sunday and Monday

Yorokobi by CJ

JAPANESE • INTIMATE X Its name means 'joyous bliss'; C is for chef and J is for Jang, who takes on that role. Good value Japanese and Korean dishes are flavourful and authentic; try one of the sizzling platters or a Korean pot dish.

Carte £ 21/43

51 Huntly St ✉ AB10 1TH – ✆ 01224 566002 – www.yorokobibycj.co.uk – dinner only and lunch Friday-Saturday – Closed 2 weeks summer, 2 weeks Christmas-New Year, Sunday and Monday

The Chester

TOWNHOUSE • CONTEMPORARY This smart boutique townhouse fits perfectly in this wealthy residential area. Sleek, contemporary bedrooms come with the latest mod cons and show a keen eye for detail. The cocktail bar and restaurant are set over three levels.

50 rooms – †£ 99/219 ††£ 119/229 – 2 suites

59-63 Queens Rd ✉ AB15 4YP – ✆ 01224 327777 – www.chester-hotel.com

IX – See restaurant listing

Malmaison

BUSINESS • DESIGN Set in a smart city suburb and built around a period property; its funky, modern bedrooms are the height of urban chic. The black, slate-floored reception is adorned with bagpipes and kilts and there's a stylish bar with a whisky cellar. The brasserie serves modern dishes, with steaks a speciality.

79 rooms – †£ 79/350 ††£ 81/362 – £ 16

49-53 Queens Rd ✉ AB15 4YP – ✆ 01224 327370 – www.malmaison.com

bauhaus

BUSINESS • MINIMALIST Set just off the main street, this hotel's functional, minimalist style is in keeping with the Bauhaus school of design. Stylish, colour-coded bedrooms have sharp, clean lines and an uncluttered feel – 'Gropius' and 'Kandinsky' are the best. The first floor restaurant offers a pizza menu.

39 rooms – †£ 65 ††£ 65/120 – 1 suite

52-60 Langstane Pl. ✉ AB11 6EN – ✆ 01224 212122 – www.thebauhaus.co.uk

ABERFELDY

Perth and Kinross – Pop. 1 986 – Regional map n° **16**-C2

Errichel

WORKING FARM • PERSONALISED An 18C stone cottage set on a 500 acre working farm. Stylish bedrooms feature locally made, contemporary wooden furnishings with Asian touches. They rear Shetland cattle and rare breed pigs, which feature on the ambitious Middle-Eastern influenced menu in the striking circular restaurant.

4 rooms – £ 100/120 £ 120/149

Crieff Rd ✉ PH15 2EL – Southeast : 2 mi on A 826 – ✆ 01887 820850 – www.errichel.co.uk – Closed 24-26 December

ABRIACHAN

Highland – Pop. 120 – Regional map n° **17**-C2

Loch Ness Lodge

LUXURY • CONTEMPORARY Passionately run modern country house, set in 18 acres of immaculately kept grounds overlooking Loch Ness. A classic-contemporary style features throughout. Spacious bedrooms have a high level of facilities and come with extras such as sherry and Penhaligon's toiletries. Afternoon tea is served on arrival.

9 rooms – £ 180/245 £ 180/350

Brachla ✉ IV3 8LA – on A 82 – ✆ 01456 459469 – www.loch-ness-lodge.com – Closed weekends in November, Christmas and New Year

ALYTH

Perth and Kinross – Pop. 2 403 – Regional map n° **16**-C2

Tigh Na Leigh

LUXURY • MODERN An imposing Victorian house run in a relaxed yet professional manner. The interior is surprisingly modern – guest areas are inviting and contemporary bedrooms boast feature beds and great bathrooms with spa baths. The kitchen garden informs the unfussy modern menu; enjoy the lovely garden view while dining.

5 rooms – £ 57/85 £ 97/136

22-24 Airlie St ✉ PH11 8AJ – ✆ 01828 632372 – www.tighnaleigh.co.uk – Closed December-January

ANCRUM

The Scottish Borders – Regional map n° **15**-D2

Ancrum Cross Keys

TRADITIONAL BRITISH • PUB Set beside the River Ale and run by the owner of the nearby Born in the Borders Brewery. It's not all about the beer here though, as the cooking is fittingly satisfying too, with local produce used in hearty dishes.

Carte £ 22/34

The Green ✉ TD8 6XH – ✆ 01835 830242 – www.ancrumcrosskeys.com – dinner only and lunch Saturday-Sunday – Closed Monday and Tuesday

ANNAN

Dumfries and Galloway – Pop. 8 960 – Regional map n° **15**-C3

Del Amitri

MODERN BRITISH • BRASSERIE Set within a coastal hotel, a cleanly decorated restaurant with views out over the Solway Firth. The extensive menu has a Scottish bias and focuses on classically based dishes which have a modern edge.

Carte £ 25/34

Powfoot Hotel, Links Ave, Powfoot ✉ DG12 5PN – Southwest : 4 mi by B 721 and B 724 – ✆ 01461 700300 – www.thepowfoothotel.com – dinner only and Sunday lunch – Closed 26 December

ANSTRUTHER

Fife – Pop. 3 446 – Regional map n° **16**-D2

✿ The Cellar (Billy Boyter)

MODERN CUISINE • RUSTIC XX Previously a smokehouse and a cooperage – now an iconic restaurant with exposed beams, stone walls and a cosy, characterful feel; pleasingly run by a local lad. Delicious, deftly prepared dishes are light, well-balanced and have subtle modern influences. Service is friendly and the atmosphere is relaxed.

→ Ox tongue with parmesan and pickled onion. Halibut with baby gem, mussels, bacon jam and charcoal oil. Barley pudding with blood orange and milk & hay sorbet.

Menu £ 35/60

24 East Green ✉ KY10 3AA – ✆ 01333 310378 (booking essential) – www.thecellaranstruther.co.uk – Closed first 3 weeks January, 10 days May, 10 days September, 24-26 December, lunch Wednesday-Thursday October-March and Monday-Tuesday

APPLECROSS

Highland – Regional map n° **17**-B2

Applecross Walled Garden

TRADITIONAL CUISINE • FRIENDLY X Set in an old potting shed in a 17C walled garden – where much of the produce is grown. In the daytime come for home-made cake, local langoustines or fresh crab lasagne; at night come for boldly flavoured, original dishes.

Carte £ 22/38

✉ IV54 8ND – North : 0.5 mi – ✆ 01520 744440 – www.applecrossgarden.co.uk – Closed November-February

Applecross Inn

SEAFOOD • INN Unpretentious inn with friendly service and a bustling atmosphere; take the scenic route over the hair-raising, single-track Bealach na Ba, with its stunning views and hairpin bends to reach it. Dine on the freshest of seafood, often caught within sight of the door. Simple bedrooms have marvellous sea views.

Carte £ 22/45

7 rooms – †£ 95/100 ††£ 140/150

Shore St ✉ IV54 8LR – ✆ 01520 744262 (booking essential) – www.applecross.uk.com – Closed 25 December and 1-2 January

ARDSHEALACH

Highland – Regional map n° **17**-B3

Ardshealach Lodge

TRADITIONAL • PERSONALISED Smart Victorian former hunting lodge in 22 acres of grounds; in a fabulous location on the Ardnamurchan Peninsula overlooking Loch Sheil. Traditional bedrooms; ask for one at the front. Wide range of classic dishes served in the restaurant, with fruit, veg and herbs from the garden. Non-resident diners welcome.

3 rooms – †£ 55/65 ††£ 110/130

✉ PH36 4JL – On A 861 – ✆ 01967 431399 – www.ardshealach-lodge.co.uk

AUCHTERARDER

Perth and Kinross – Pop. 4 206 – Regional map n° **16**-C2

✿✿ Andrew Fairlie at Gleneagles

CREATIVE FRENCH • LUXURY XXXX You'll find this elegant restaurant concealed within the world-famous Gleneagles hotel. It may be windowless, but the classically dressed room is an intimate spot, with neatly spot-lit contemporary still-life paintings on the wall along with the odd portrait of the eponymous chef. Tables are immaculately laid and an air of real comfort pervades the room. That's not to say the atmosphere is in any way stilted or solemn as the customers here are a largely confident bunch who know how to enjoy themselves.

The kitchen works well with the seasons and when you're in this part of the world you don't lack for prime ingredients, whether that's scallops from Mull, Highland lamb or local venison. These ingredients form the focus of the French-based menu and add a luxury element and a genuine sense of indulgence. The chefs also make great use of their own Victorian walled garden which provides plenty of leaves, vegetables and fruits.

→ Home-smoked lobster, lime and herb butter. Poached fillet of turbot with razor clams and langoustine bisque. Passion fruit soufflé with piña colada sorbet.

Menu £110/155

Gleneagles Hotel, ✉ PH3 1NF – Southwest : 2 mi by A 824 on A 823
– ✆ 01764 694267 – www.andrewfairlie.co.uk – dinner only
– Closed 3 weeks January, 25-26 December and Sunday

Gleneagles

GRAND LUXURY • ART DÉCO This iconic resort hotel boasts a world-famous golf course, a state-of-the-art spa, an equestrian centre and even a gun-dog school.Guest areas are majestic and have lovely art deco touches. Bedrooms are elegant - the best are luxurious with top class comforts. Dining options include a laid-back brasserie, a classical restaurant and intimate Andrew Fairlie.

232 rooms – †£ 360/565 ††£ 360/565 – 26 suites

✉ PH3 1NF – Southwest : 2 mi by A 824 on A 823
– ✆ 01764 662231 – www.gleneagles.com

✿✿ **Andrew Fairlie at Gleneagles** – See restaurant listing

AVIEMORE

Highland – Pop. 3 147 – Regional map n° **17**-D3

Old Minister's Guest House

TRADITIONAL • PERSONALISED A 19C stone-built manse with unusual carved wood animals out the front and pretty gardens leading down to the river. The smart lounge has deep sofas and an honesty bar and the stylish bedrooms are spacious and well-appointed.

5 rooms – †£ 145/160 ††£ 155/170

Rothiemurchus ✉ PH22 1QH – Southeast : 1 mi on B 970
– ✆ 01479 812181 – www.theoldministershouse.co.uk
– Closed October-April

BACK – Western Isles → See Lewis and Harris (Isle of)

BALLANTRAE

South Ayrshire – ✉ Girvan – Pop. 672 – Regional map n° **15**-A2

Glenapp Castle

HISTORIC BUILDING • CLASSIC A long wooded drive leads to this stunning baronial castle with beautifully manicured gardens and Ailsa Craig views; it's personally run and the service is charming. The grand antique-filled interior has oak-panelled hallways, luxurious, impressively proportioned lounges and handsomely appointed bedrooms. The elegant dining room showcases local and garden ingredients.

18 rooms (dinner included) – †£ 315/545 ††£ 395/675 – 2 suites

✉ KA26 0NZ – South : 1 mi by A 77 taking first right turn after bridge
– ✆ 01465 831212 – www.glenappcastle.com
– Closed 2-17 January

BALLATER

Aberdeenshire - Pop. 1 533 - Regional map n° **16**-C1

Rothesay Rooms

MODERN BRITISH • COSY XX The Prince of Wales' restaurant sits beside the Highgrove shop and has the look of a Baronial dining room, with its green walls, tartan fabrics and antique furnishings. Seasonal dishes are classically executed and full of flavour.

Carte £ 34/56

3 Netherley Pl ✉ AB35 5EQ - ✆ 01339 753816 - www.rothesay-rooms.co.uk - Closed 25 December and Sunday dinner-Tuesday

BALLYGRANT - Argyll and Bute → See Islay (Isle of)

BALMEDIE

Aberdeenshire - Pop. 2 534 - Regional map n° **16**-D1

Cock and Bull

TRADITIONAL BRITISH • RUSTIC Quirky pub with a profusion of knick-knacks; dine in the cosy open-fired lounge, the formal dining room or the airy conservatory. Menus offer a mix of well-presented pub classics and more modern restaurant-style dishes. Spacious, contemporary bedrooms are located in the next door bungalow.

Carte £ 17/38

6 rooms - †£ 58/95 ††£ 60/95

Ellon Rd, Blairton ✉ AB23 8XY - North : 1 mi on A 90 - ✆ 01358 743249 - www.thecockandbull.co.uk - Closed 26-27 December and 1-2 January

Trump International Golf Links Scotland

LUXURY • MODERN Intimate hotel with a Championship links golf course, set on a 2,200 acre estate. The hotel is split between an 18C stone house and a lodge and features plush fabrics and opulent furnishings. Large bedrooms have arabesque furnishings and offer all you could want. The intimate restaurant serves a modern menu.

16 rooms - †£ 265/365 ††£ 295/395

MacLeod House and Lodge, Menie Estate ✉ AB23 8YE - North : 2 mi on A 90 - ✆ 01358 743300 - www.trumpgolfscotland.com - Closed November-March

BALQUHIDDER

Stirling - Regional map n° **16**-B2

Monachyle Mhor

TRADITIONAL • PERSONALISED A former farmhouse set in a beautiful, very remote glen. Contemporary furnishings blend with original features in the reception, lounge and cosy bar. Bedrooms boast slate-tiled bathrooms with underfloor heating; those in the main house afford great views over the Braes of Balquhidder.

18 rooms - †£ 195/285 ††£ 195/285

✉ FK19 8PQ - West : 3.75 mi - ✆ 01877 384622 (booking essential) - www.mhor.net - Closed 5-25 January

BARCALDINE

Argyll and Bute - Regional map n° **16**-B2

Ardtorna

LUXURY • CONTEMPORARY An ultra-modern guesthouse in a stunning spot, with lovely views of the lochs and mountains - and amazing sunsets. Immaculate bedrooms have plenty of space in which to relax, perhaps with a complimentary glass of whisky. Home-baked scones are served on arrival. The charming owners also offer archery lessons.

6 rooms - †£ 150/190 ††£ 150/190

Mill Farm ✉ PA37 1SE - West : 1.5 mi on A 828 - ✆ 01631 720125 - www.ardtorna.co.uk - Closed mid-November-mid-March

Barcaldine Castle

HISTORIC BUILDING • PERSONALISED This lochside castle, built in 1609, simply oozes history. Charming bedrooms have period furnishings – one has an antique four-poster bed, one has a dressing area in a turret, and another a roll-top bath with a terrific view. Breakfast is served in the Great Hall, complete with stags' heads and cannons.

6 rooms – £170/255 £200/285

PA37 1SA – West : 3.5 mi by A 828 – 01631 720598 – www.barcaldinecastle.co.uk – Closed 1 November-15 December and 5 January-7 March

BLAIRGOWRIE

Perth and Kinross – Pop. 8 954 – Regional map n° **16**-C2

Dalmore Inn

TRADITIONAL CUISINE • PUB A traditional-looking pub with a surprisingly stylish interior, where brightly coloured walls are juxtaposed with old stonework. Unfussy, good value cooking is full of flavour; everything is freshly prepared using Scottish produce.

Menu £18 (weekdays) – Carte £17/60

Perth Rd PH10 6QB – Southwest : 1.5 mi on A 93 – 01250 871088 – www.dalmoreinn.com – Closed 25 December and 1-2 January

Kinloch House

FAMILY • PERSONALISED Imposing ivy-clad country house in a tranquil, elevated setting, with beautiful walled gardens to the rear and 25 acres of grounds. Smart oak-panelled hall and a vast array of welcoming guest areas complete with log fires and antiques. Classical bedrooms are well-appointed and immaculately maintained.

15 rooms – £185/275 £185/340 – 1 suite

PH10 6SG – West : 3 mi on A 923 – 01250 884237 – www.kinlochhouse.com – Closed 14-29 December

BORVE – Western Isles → See Lewis and Harris (Isle of)

BOWMORE – Argyll and Bute → See Islay (Isle of)

BROADFORD – Highland → See Skye (Isle of)

BROUGHTY FERRY – Dundee City → See Dundee

BRUICHLADDICH – Argyll and Bute → See Islay (Isle of)

BUNCHREW – Highland → See Inverness

CADBOLL – Highland → See Tain

CALLANDER

Stirling – Pop. 3 077 – Regional map n° **16**-C2

Roman Camp

COUNTRY HOUSE • CLASSIC Pretty pink house – a 17C former hunting lodge – set by the river among well-tended gardens. Traditional bedrooms have a subtle contemporary edge and there's a characterful panelled library and chapel.

15 rooms – £110/165 £160/290 – 3 suites

Main St FK17 8BG – 01877 330003 – www.romancamphotel.co.uk

Westerton

TOWNHOUSE • PERSONALISED Homely stone house run by delightful owners with a colourful garden sweeping down to the river - take it all in from the terrace. Spotless bedrooms have wrought iron beds and good mod cons; some have mountain views.

3 rooms - £ 90/135 £ 90/135

Leny Rd ✉ FK17 8AJ - ✆ 01877 330147 - www.westertonhouse.co.uk - Closed November-April

CASTLE DOUGLAS

Dumfries and Galloway - Pop. 4 174 - Regional map n° **15**-B3

Douglas House

TOWNHOUSE • PERSONALISED An attractive 19C townhouse run by experienced owners. Comfy, individually decorated bedrooms have a modern edge. The lounge-cum-breakfast-room is light and airy; breakfast offers plenty of choice and features only local produce.

4 rooms - £ 41/56 £ 79/87

63 Queen St ✉ DG7 1HS - ✆ 01556 503262 - www.douglas-house.com

CHIRNSIDE

The Scottish Borders - ✉ Duns - Pop. 1 459 - Regional map n° **15**-D1

Chirnside Hall

COUNTRY HOUSE • CLASSIC Sizeable 1834 country house with a lovely revolving door and beautiful views over the Cheviots. Grand lounges have original cornicing and huge fireplaces. Bedrooms are cosy and classical; some have four-poster beds. Local, seasonal dishes are served in the traditional dining room.

10 rooms - £ 100/180 £ 160/180

✉ TD11 3LD - East : 1.75 mi on A 6105 - ✆ 01890 818219 - www.chirnsidehallhotel.com - Closed March

COLBOST - Highland

→ See Skye (Isle of)

COMRIE

Perth and Kinross - Pop. 1 927 - Regional map n° **16**-C2

Royal

TRADITIONAL • PERSONALISED Charming coaching inn dating back to the 18C and set at the heart of a riverside town. Cosy bar and lovely open-fired library with squashy sofas. Well-appointed bedrooms; some with four-posters and antiques. Relaxed, personable service.

11 rooms - £ 105/120 £ 135/170

Melville Sq ✉ PH6 2DN - ✆ 01764 679200 - www.royalhotel.co.uk - Closed 25-26 December

CRAIGELLACHIE

Moray - Regional map n° **16**-C1

Craigellachie

HISTORIC • PERSONALISED Set in the heart of Speyside, this characterful Victorian hotel is perfectly located for those following the Whisky Trail. Stylish, understated bedrooms have a 'Country Living' style. The bar serves over 700 whiskies and the rustic restaurant serves Scottish pub classics with a modern twist.

26 rooms - £ 135/175 £ 150/270

Victoria St ✉ AB38 9SR - ✆ 01340 881204 - www.craigellachiehotel.co.uk

CRAIGHOUSE - Argyll and Bute

→ See Jura (Isle of)

CROMARTY

Highland - Pop. 726 - Regional map n° **17**-D2

Sutor Creek Cafe

TRADITIONAL CUISINE • FRIENDLY A great little eatery hidden away by the harbour in a well-preserved coastal town. Wonderfully seasonal cooking features seafood from the local boats and pizzas from the wood-fired oven. It's run by a friendly, experienced couple.

Carte £ 25/47

21 Bank St ✉ IV11 8YE – ✆ 01381 600855 (booking essential) – www.sutorcreek.co.uk – Closed January and Monday-Wednesday September-April

Factor's House

LUXURY • PERSONALISED This late Georgian house is very passionately run by a charming owner. It sits in a peaceful spot on the edge of an attractive town and offers pleasant sea views from its mature gardens. Bedrooms have a subtle contemporary style and good extras. Breakfast and dinner are taken around a farmhouse table; the latter is four courses and features accomplished home cooking.

3 rooms – †£ 120/125 ††£ 140/150

Denny Rd ✉ IV11 8YT – ✆ 01381 600394 – www.thefactorshouse.com – Closed 18 December-31 January

CUMNOCK

East Ayrshire – Pop. 9 039 – Regional map n° **15**-B2

Dumfries House Lodge

COUNTRY HOUSE • PERSONALISED Set at the entrance to the 2,000 acre Dumfries Estate is this stylish country house hotel, formerly a factor's house and steading. There are two cosy lounges and a billiard room and some of the furniture is from the original manor house. Bedrooms are designed by the Duchess of Cornwall's sister.

22 rooms – †£ 120/140 ††£ 120/140

Dumfries House ✉ KA18 2NJ – West : 1.5 mi on A 70 – ✆ 01290 425959 – www.dumfries-house.org.uk – Closed 23-27 December and 31-December-3 January

CUPAR

Fife – Pop. 9 339 – Regional map n° **16**-C2

Ferrymuir Stables

LUXURY • CONTEMPORARY The old stables of Ferrymuir House date from 1800 – but you'd never know. The hub of the house is a light, spacious orangery overlooking the stable yard. Modern bedrooms come with designer furnishings, smart wet rooms and Netbooks.

3 rooms – †£ 55/80 ††£ 110/120

Beechgrove Rise ✉ KY15 5DT – West : 1 mi by Bonnygate (A91) and West Park Rd off Westfield Rd – ✆ 01334 657579 – www.ferrymuirstables.co.uk

DALKEITH

Midlothian – Pop. 12 342 – Regional map n° **15**-C1

Sun Inn

TRADITIONAL CUISINE • PUB A 17C blacksmith's with two open-fired rooms and a rustic modern extension, where bright wallpapers sit beside stone walls. Extensive menus feature top local produce – lunch keeps things simple but appealing, while dinner is more ambitious. Smart bedrooms boast handmade furniture and Egyptian cotton linen.

Menu £ 16 (early dinner) – Carte £ 24/32

7 rooms – †£ 75/125 ††£ 110/165

Lothian Bridge ✉ EH22 4TR – Southwest : 2 mi by A 6094 and B 6392 on A 7 – ✆ 0131 663 2456 – www.thesuninnedinburgh.co.uk – Closed 26 December and 1 January

DALRY

North Ayrshire – Regional map n° **15**-A1

Braidwoods (Keith Braidwood)

CLASSIC CUISINE • INTIMATE Just 40mins from Glasgow is this whitewashed crofter's cottage surrounded by fields and mountains. It's run in an unassuming manner by Mr and Mrs Braidwood and has a cosy, intimate feel. Menus show-case tried-and-tested classics where the true flavour of each ingredient is allowed to shine.

→ Hand-dived scallops with baby leeks and an Arran mustard butter sauce. Roast loin of roe deer with spinach, wild garlic and chanterelles. Dark Valrhona chocolate truffle cake with espresso and caramelised pecan nut ice cream.

Menu £ 32/55

Drumastle Mill Cottage ✉ KA24 4LN – Southwest : 1.5 mi by A 737 on Saltcoats ro – ✆ 01294 833544 (booking essential) – www.braidwoods.co.uk – Closed 25 December-January, 2 weeks September, Sunday dinner-Tuesday lunch and Sunday May-mid-September

DERVAIG – Argyll and Bute → See Mull (Isle of)

DINNET

Aberdeenshire – Regional map n° **16**-D1

Glendavan House

FAMILY • CLASSIC Set in 9 lochside acres, this former shooting lodge is somewhere to get away from it all. Two of the three bedrooms are very large suites; all are tastefully furnished with antiques and memorabilia. Delicious communal breakfasts.

3 rooms – †£ 90/130 ††£ 130/170

✉ AB34 5LU – Northwest : 3 mi by A 97 on B 9119 – ✆ 01339 881610 – www.glendavanhouse.com

DORNOCH

Highland – Pop. 1 208 – Regional map n° **17**-D2

Links House

LUXURY • CONTEMPORARY This restored 19C manse sits opposite the first tee of the Royal Dornoch Golf Club. Enjoy a dram from the honesty bar in the pine-panelled library or have tea and cake in the antique-furnished sitting room. Some of the beautifully furnished bedrooms feature bespoke tweed fabrics. The elegant orangery boasts an impressive stone fireplace and an elaborate 4 course menu.

15 rooms – †£ 270/325 ††£ 270/325

Golf Rd ✉ IV25 3LW – ✆ 01862 810279 – www.linkshousedornoch.com – Closed 4 January-31 March

2 Quail

TOWNHOUSE • PERSONALISED A bijou terraced house built in 1898 for a sea captain. Intimate bedrooms are furnished with antiques – in a Victorian style – and one has a wrought iron bedstead. The small open-fired library-lounge boasts a large array of vintage books. Daily changing set dinners are offered by arrangement.

3 rooms – †£ 75/130 ††£ 85/140

Castle St ✉ IV25 3SN – ✆ 01862 811811 – www.2quail.com

DUISDALEMORE – Highland → See Skye (Isle of)

DUNBAR

East Lothian – Pop. 8 486 – Regional map n° **15**-D1

Creel

TRADITIONAL CUISINE • **BISTRO** An unassuming, cosy former pub with wood-panelling on the walls and ceiling. The experienced chef creates good value, full-flavoured dishes using seafood fresh from the adjacent harbour. Service is friendly.

Menu £ 19/30

The Harbour, 25 Lamer St ✉ EH42 1HG - ✆ 01368 863279 (booking essential) - www.creelrestaurant.co.uk - Closed Sunday dinner-Wednesday lunch

DUNBLANE

Stirling - Pop. 8 811 - Regional map n° **16**-C2

Chez Roux

FRENCH • **BRASSERIE** Light and spacious conservatory restaurant in a magnificent country house hotel. Smart, yet relaxed, it's a hit with locals and tourists alike thanks to the enthusiastic service and good value, flavoursome cooking. Classic French dishes might include soufflé Suissesse, chateaubriand or tarte au citron.

Menu £ 37/40 - Carte £ 43/52

Cromlix Hotel, Kinbuck ✉ FK15 9JT - North : 3.5 mi on B 8033 - ✆ 01786 822125 - www.cromlix.com

Cromlix

COUNTRY HOUSE • **MODERN** This grand house, owned by Sir Andy Murray, has elegant sitting rooms, a whisky room, a chapel and a superb games room, as well as a tennis court in its 30 acre grounds. Luxurious, antique-furnished bedrooms display modern touches while also respecting the house's original style.

16 rooms - £ 235/295 £ 280/395 - 5 suites

Kinbuck ✉ FK15 9JT - North : 3.5 mi on B 8033 - ✆ 01786 822125 - www.cromlix.com

Chez Roux - See restaurant listing

DUNDEE

Dundee City - Pop. 147 285 - Regional map n° **16**-C2

Castlehill

MODERN CUISINE • **INTIMATE** Both its name and its décor celebrate the city's history. Choose from a set price or tasting menu; at dinner, every dish from the former can be ordered as either a starter or main course. Cooking is complex and elaborate.

Menu £ 18/38

22 Exchange St ✉ DD1 3DL - ✆ 01382 220008 - www.castlehillrestaurant.co.uk - Closed Sunday-Tuesday

Malmaison

BUSINESS • **CONTEMPORARY** The best feature of this lovingly restored hotel is the wrought iron cantilevered staircase topped by a domed ceiling. Contemporary bedrooms come in striking bold colours and have a masculine feel. The all-day bar serves cocktails and nibbles and there's a DJ at weekends; the brasserie offers a grill menu.

91 rooms - £ 69/367 £ 79/367

44 Whitehall Cres ✉ DD1 4AY - ✆ 01382 339715 - www.malmaison.com

Balmuirfield House

COUNTRY HOUSE • **COSY** A double-fronted stone dower house built in 1904; Dighty Water runs past the bottom of the garden. Inside it's spacious and homely, with a cosy open-fired lounge. Two of the bedrooms have four-posters and one has an antique bath.

4 rooms - £ 60/85 £ 85/120

Harestane Rd ✉ DD3 0NU - North : 3.5 mi by A 929, A 90, Claverhouse Rd and Old Glamis Rd - ✆ 01382 819655 - www.balmuirfieldhouse.com

at Broughty Ferry East : 4.5 mi by A 930

Collinsons

CLASSIC CUISINE • FRIENDLY XX You can't miss the name etched in large letters across the floor to ceiling windows of this bright modern restaurant. Cooking is classic to the core, with unfussy, wholesome dishes presented in a refined, eye-catching manner.

Menu £ 23/36

122-124 Brown St ✉ DD5 1EN – ✆ 01382 776000 – www.collinsonsrestaurant.com – Closed 1-10 January, 25-26 December, Sunday and Monday

Tayberry

MODERN BRITISH • FRIENDLY XX An unassuming roadside property overlooking the mouth of the Tay. The keen young chef offers fresh, tasty cooking with original modern touches and local and foraged ingredients play a key role. Service is engaging and attentive.

Menu £ 36

594 Brook St ✉ DD5 2EA – ✆ 01382 698280 – www.tayberryrestaurant.com – Closed 25-28 December, Sunday and Monday

DUNVEGAN - Highland → See Skye (Isle of)

DURNESS

Highland – Regional map n° **17**-C1

Mackay's

FAMILY • MODERN This smart grey stone house sits at the most north-westerly point of the mainland. It has a light, airy lounge and a cosy open-fired snug. The owner is a textile designer and this shows in the bedrooms, which have a stylish rustic feel.

7 rooms – †£ 119/129 ††£ 129/169

✉ IV27 4PN – ✆ 01971 511202 – www.visitdurness.com – Closed October-April

DYKE

Moray – Regional map n° **16**-C1

Old Kirk

HISTORIC • DESIGN A peacefully set, converted 1856 church, surrounded by grain fields. It has an airy interior, a cosy library and a comfortable open-fired lounge with a pretty stained glass window. Charming, individually decorated bedrooms boast original stonework and arched windows; one has a carved four-poster bed.

3 rooms – †£ 85/95 ††£ 85/95

✉ IV36 2TL – Northeast : 0.5 mi – ✆ 01309 641414 – www.oldkirk.co.uk – Closed October-March

EDINBANE - Highland → See Skye (Isle of)

GOOD TIPS!

A cool, cosmopolitan city with stunning scenery and a colourful history, Scotland's capital is home to Michelin-Starred restaurants as well as busy wine bars and bistros, with global flavours including Korean, Italian and Thai. The famous Royal Mile is the location of the luxurious **Radisson Collection Hotel**, while the **Sheraton Grand** has views of the iconic castle.

EDINBURGH

City of Edinburgh - Pop. 459 366 - Regional map n° **15**-C1

Restaurants

✿ Number One

MODERN CUISINE • INTIMATE XXXX A stylish, long-standing restaurant with a chic cocktail bar, set in the basement of a grand hotel. Richly upholstered banquettes and red lacquered walls give it a plush, luxurious feel. Cooking is modern and intricate and prime Scottish ingredients are key. Service is professional and has personality.

→ Hand-dived scallop, 'Cullen Skink' with smoked haddock and baby leeks. Guinea fowl with coco bean cassoulet, hispi cabbage and girolles. Raspberry soufflé, with white chocolate and crème fraîche ice cream.

Menu £ 80

Town plan: G2-n - *Balmoral Hotel, 1 Princes St ✉ EH2 2EQ - ✆ 0131 557 6727 - www.roccofortehotels.com - dinner only - Closed first 2 weeks January*

✿ 21212 (Paul Kitching)

CREATIVE • ELEGANT XXX Stunningly refurbished Georgian townhouse designed by William Playfair. The glass-fronted kitchen is the focal point of the stylish, high-ceilinged dining room. Cooking is skilful and innovative and features quirky combinations; '21212' reflects the number of dishes per course at lunch - at dinner it's '31313'. Some of the luxurious bedrooms overlook the Firth of Forth.

→ Haggis risotto with caramelised onion and aubergine sauce. Chicken with fig, black garlic and smoked cheese. Chocolate & rhubarb.

Menu £ 28/85 **s**

4 rooms ☕ - †£ 115/325 ††£ 115/325

Town plan: H1-c - *3 Royal Terr ✉ EH7 5AB - ✆ 0345 222 1212 (booking essential) - www.21212restaurant.co.uk*
- Closed 10 days January, 10 days September, Sunday and Monday

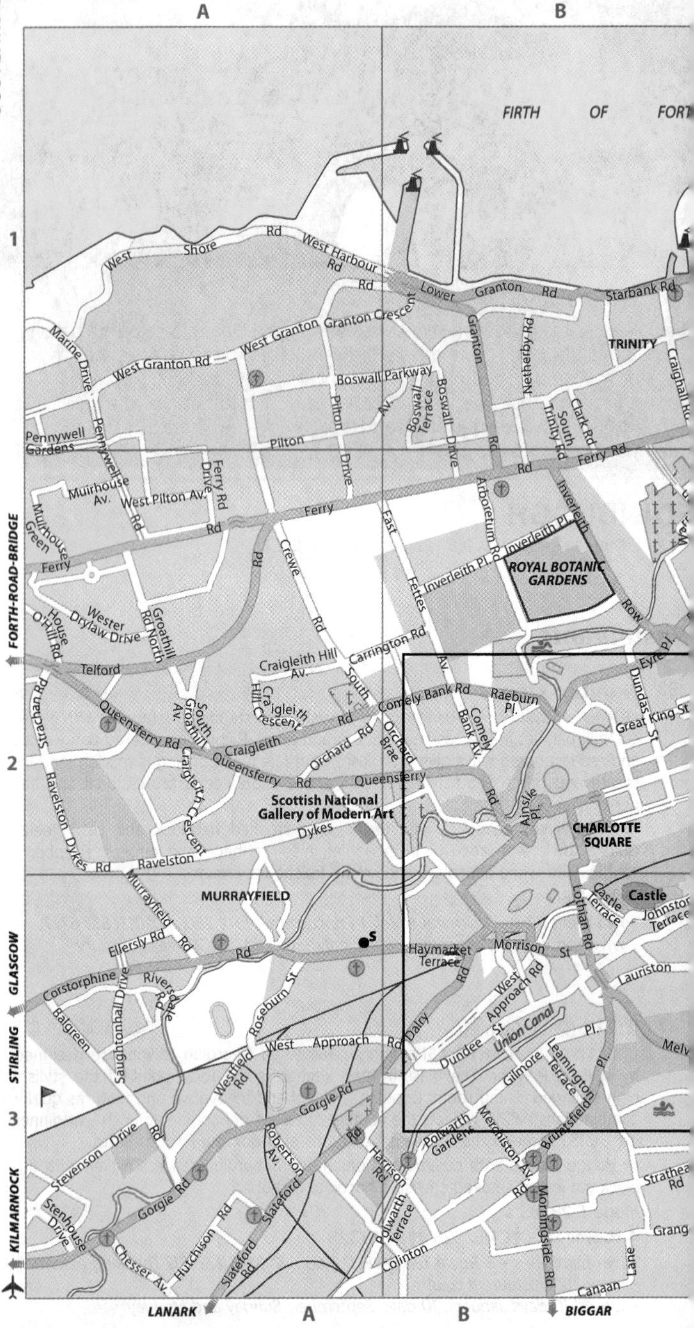
A
B
1
2
3
FIRTH OF FORT
West Shore Rd
West Harbour Rd
Rd
Lower Granton Rd
Starbank Rd
Marine Drive
West Granton Rd
West Granton Granton Crescent
Boswall Parkway
Boswall Terrace
Boswall Drive
Granton Rd
Netherby Rd
TRINITY
Craighall Rd
Pennywell Gardens
Pennywell Rd
Pilton
Pilton Drive
Av.
South Trinity Rd
Clark Rd
Ferry Rd
Muirhouse Av.
West Pilton Av.
Ferry Rd Drive
Muirhouse Green
Ferry Rd
East Fettes Av.
Arboretum Rd
Inverleith Pl.
Inverleith Row
ROYAL BOTANIC GARDENS
Crewe Rd
Wester Drylaw Drive
Groathill Rd North
House O'Hill Rd
Telford
Craigleith Hill Av.
Carrington Rd
Craigleith Hill Crescent
South
Comely Bank Rd
Raeburn Pl.
Comely Bank Av.
Eyre Pl.
Dundas St
Great King St
Strachan Rd
Queensferry Rd
South Groathill Av.
Craigleith Rd
Orchard Rd
Orchard Brae
Queensferry Rd
Craigleith Crescent
Scottish National Gallery of Modern Art
Ainslie Pl.
CHARLOTTE SQUARE
Ravelston Dykes Rd
Ravelston Dykes
MURRAYFIELD
Murrayfield Rd
Castle
Castle Terrace
Johnston Terrace
Lothian Rd
Ellersly Rd
Corstorphine Rd
Haymarket Terrace
Morrison St
Lauriston
Riversdale Rd
West Approach Rd
Balgreen
Saughtonhall Drive
Roseburn St
Dalry Rd
Union Canal
West Approach Rd
Dundee St
Pl.
Melv
Westfield Rd
Gilmore
Leamington Terrace
Bruntsfield Pl.
Gorgie Rd
Stevenson Drive
Robertson Av.
Polwarth Gardens
Merchiston Av.
Rd
Harrison Rd
Stenhouse Drive
Gorgie Rd
Slateford Rd
Strathea Rd
Polwarth Terrace
Morningside Rd
Grang
Chesser Av.
Hutchison Rd
Slateford Rd
Colinton
Lane
Canaan
FORTH-ROAD-BRIDGE
GLASGOW
STIRLING
KILMARNOCK
LANARK
BIGGAR

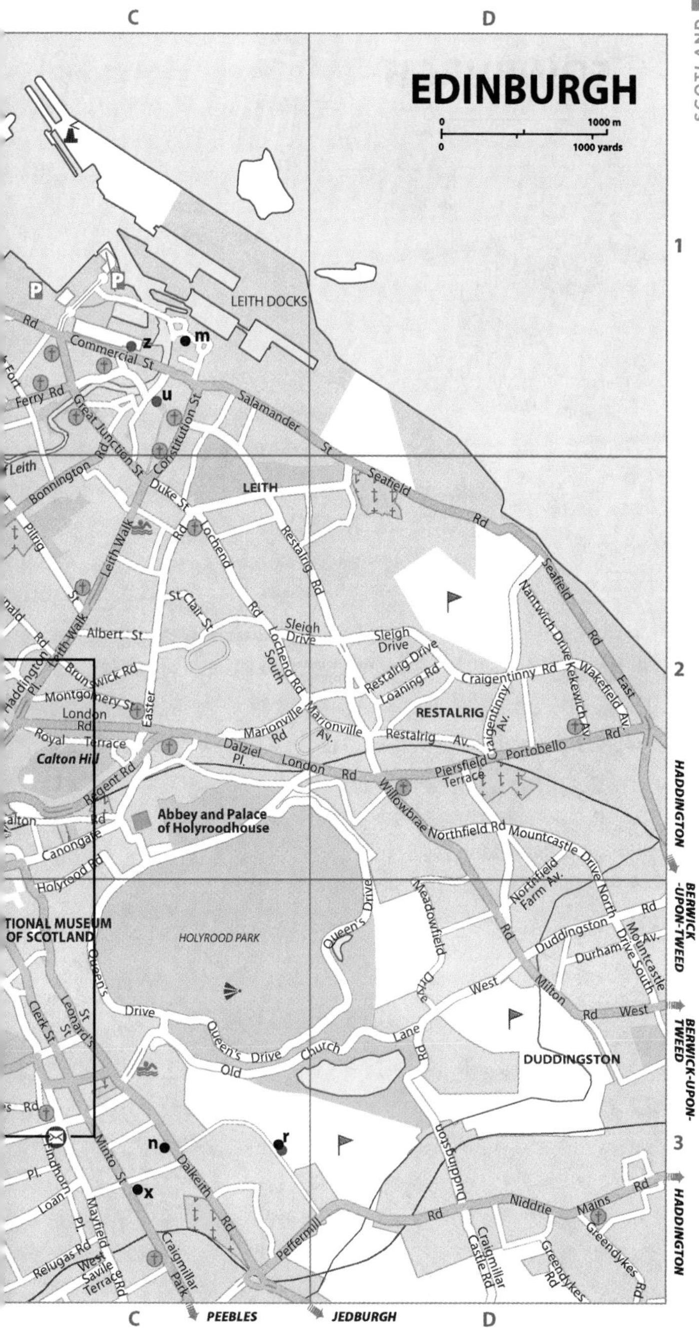
EDINBURGH
0
1000 m
0
1000 yards
C
D
1
2
3
LEITH DOCKS
LEITH
RESTALRIG
Calton Hill
Abbey and Palace of Holyroodhouse
NATIONAL MUSEUM OF SCOTLAND
HOLYROOD PARK
DUDDINGSTON
Commercial St
Ferry Rd
Great Junction St
Constitution St
Salamander St
Seafield Rd
Bonnington Rd
Duke St
Pilrig St
Leith Walk
Lochend Rd
Restalrig Rd
Easter Rd
St Clair St
Albert St
Sleigh Drive
Lochend Rd South
Restalrig Drive
Loaning Rd
Craigentinny Rd
Craigentinny Av.
Nantwich Drive
Kekewich Av.
Wakefield Av.
Seafield Rd East
Brunswick Rd
Montgomery St
London Rd
Royal Terrace
Haddington Pl.
Regent Rd
Marionville Rd
Marionville Av.
Restalrig Av.
Portobello Rd
Dalziel Pl.
London Rd
Piersfield Terrace
Willowbrae Rd
Northfield Rd
Mountcastle Drive North
Northfield Farm Av.
Canongate
Holyrood Rd
Queen's Drive
Meadowfield Drive
Duddingston Rd
Durham Av.
Mountcastle Drive South
Milton Rd West
West
Lane
Church
Old
Clerk St
St Leonard's St
Minto St
Dalkeith Rd
Peffermill Rd
Duddingston
Niddrie Mains Rd
Greendykes Rd
Craigmillar Castle Rd
Craigmillar Park
Mayfield Pl.
West Savile Terrace
Relugas Rd
Findhorn Pl.
Loan
Pl.
HADDINGTON
BERWICK-UPON-TWEED
PEEBLES
JEDBURGH
m
z
u
n
r
x

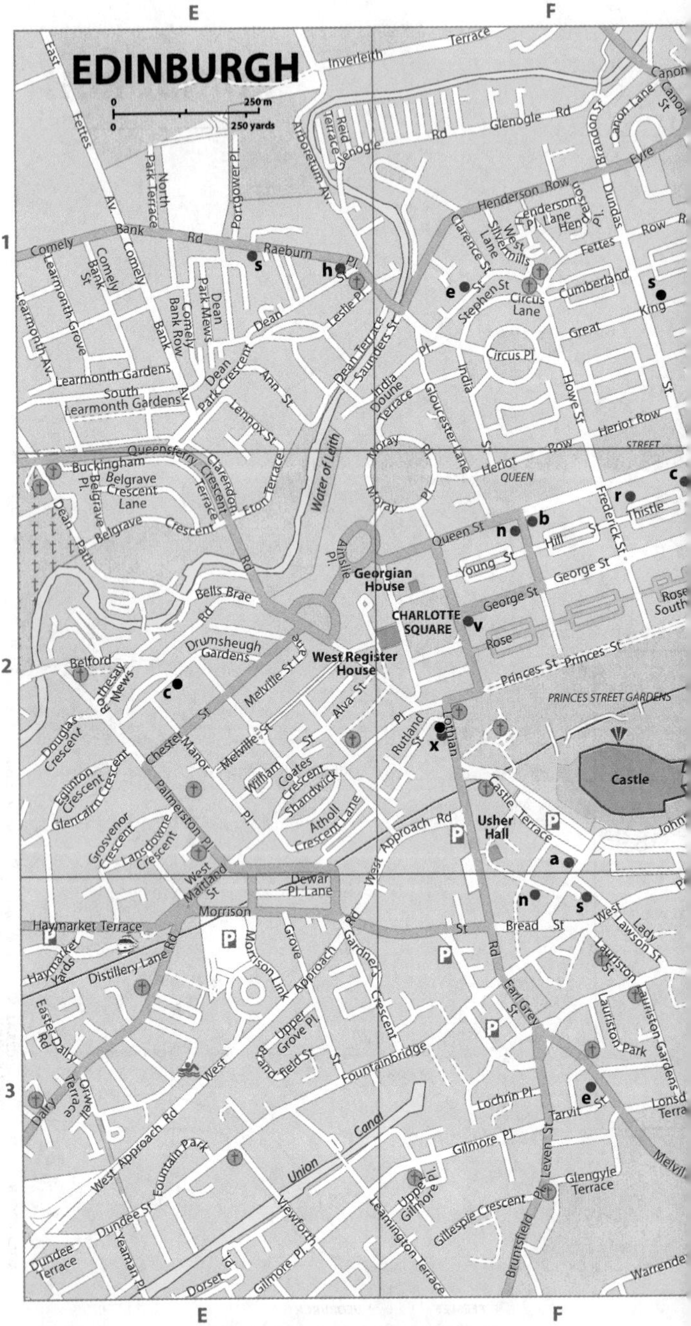
EDINBURGH
0 250 m
0 250 yards
E
F
1
2
3
Inverleith
Terrace
Glenogle Rd
Reid Terrace
Arboretum Av.
Brandon St
Canon Lane
Canon St
Eyre
Henderson Row
Henderson Pl. Lane
Dundas
Fettes Row
Clarence St
West Silvermills Lane
Cumberland
King
Great
Circus Lane
Circus Pl.
Stephen St
India Pl.
Saunders St
Dean Terrace
Leslie Pl.
Raeburn Pl.
Comely Bank Rd
Fettes Av.
East
North Park Terrace
Portgower Pl.
Comely Bank St
Comely Bank Av.
Comely Bank Row
Dean Park Mews
Learmonth Grove
Learmonth Av.
Learmonth Gardens
South Learmonth Gardens
Dean Park Crescent
Ann St
Lennox St
Doune Terrace
Gloucester Lane
Howe St
Heriot Row
QUEEN STREET
Moray Pl.
Queensferry Rd
Buckingham Pl.
Belgrave Crescent Lane
Belgrave Crescent
Clarendon Crescent
Eton Terrace
Water of Leith
Dean Path
Ainslie Pl.
Queen St
Frederick St
Thistle St
Hill St
Young St
George St
Georgian House
CHARLOTTE SQUARE
Rose St
Rose St South
Princes St
PRINCES STREET GARDENS
Castle
Bells Brae
Drumsheugh Gardens
Melville St Lane
West Register House
Belford
Rothesay Mews
Chester St
Manor Pl.
Melville St
Alva St
William St
Coates Crescent
Shandwick Pl.
Rutland St
Lothian Rd
Douglas Crescent
Eglinton Crescent
Glencairn Crescent
Palmerston Pl.
Grosvenor Crescent
Lansdowne Crescent
Atholl Crescent Lane
West Approach Rd
Castle Terrace
Usher Hall
Johnst
West Maitland St
Dewar Pl. Lane
Morrison St
Haymarket Terrace
Haymarket Yards
Distillery Lane
Morrison Link
Grove St
Approach Rd
Gardner's Crescent
Bread St
West Port
Lady Lawson St
Lauriston St
Lauriston Park
Lauriston Gardens
Earl Grey St
Easter Dalry Rd
Dalry Rd
Orwell Terrace
Upper Grove Pl.
Brandfield St
Fountainbridge
Lochrin Pl.
Tarvit St
Lonsdale Terrace
Melville
Gilmore Pl.
Leven St
Glengyle Terrace
Union Canal
Fountain Park
Dundee St
Dundee Terrace
Yeaman Pl.
Viewforth
Upper Gilmore Pl.
Leamington Terrace
Gillespie Crescent
Bruntsfield Pl.
Warrender
Dorset Pl.
Gilmore Pl.
P

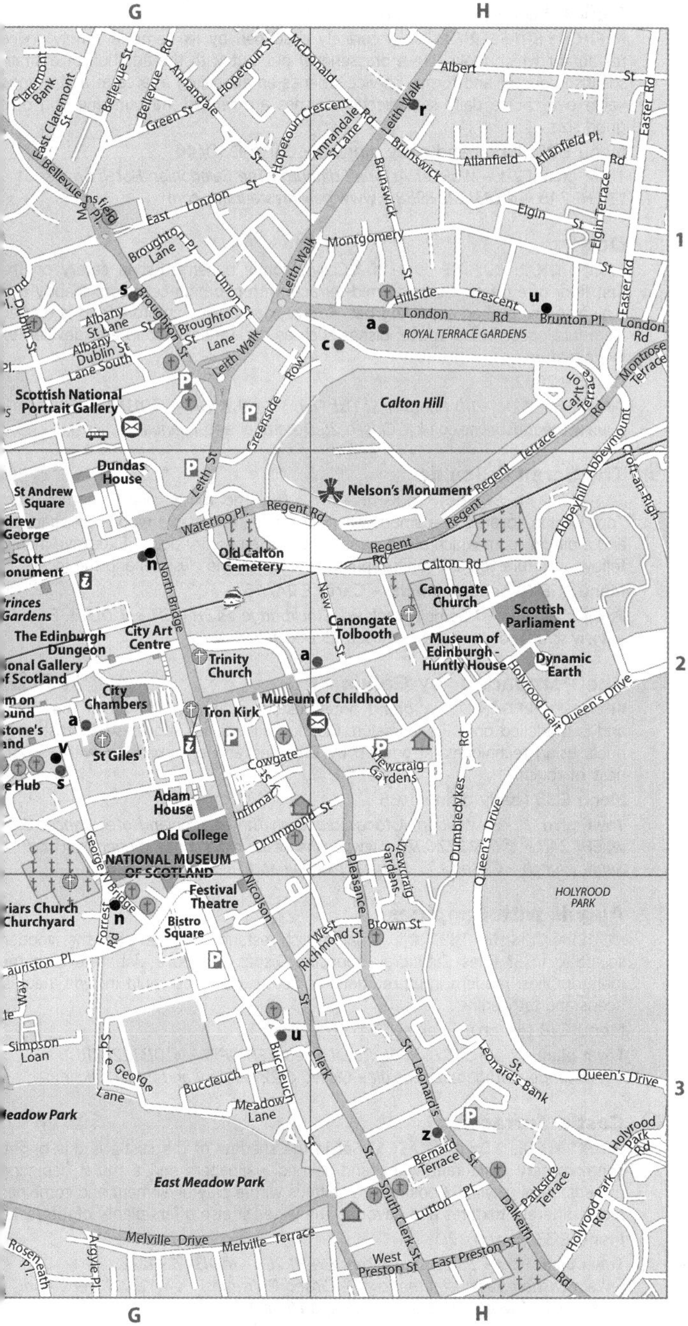
G
H
1
2
3
Claremont Bank
East Claremont St
Bellevue St
Bellevue Rd
Bellevue
Annandale
Green St
Hopetoun St
McDonald
Hopetoun Crescent
Annandale St Lane
Annandale Rd
Leith Walk
Albert
St
Easter Rd
Brunswick
Allanfield
Allanfield Pl.
Elgin
Elgin Terrace
Mansfield Pl.
East London St
Broughton Pl.
Broughton Lane
Montgomery
Hillside
Crescent
London
Rd
Brunton Pl.
London Rd
ROYAL TERRACE GARDENS
Dublin St
Albany St Lane
Albany
Dublin St Lane South
Broughton St
Union St
Broughton St Lane
Greenside Row
Calton Hill
Carlton Terrace
Montrose Terrace
Scottish National Portrait Gallery
Dundas House
St Andrew Square
Leith St
Nelson's Monument
Regent Terrace
Waterloo Pl.
Regent Rd
Abbeyhill
Abbeymount
Croft-an-Righ
Scott Monument
Old Calton Cemetery
Calton Rd
North Bridge
Princes Gardens
New St
Canongate Church
Scottish Parliament
The Edinburgh Dungeon
City Art Centre
Canongate Tolbooth
Museum of Edinburgh - Huntly House
Dynamic Earth
National Gallery of Scotland
Trinity Church
Holyrood Galt
Queen's Drive
City Chambers
Museum of Childhood
Tron Kirk
St Giles'
Cowgate
Newcraig Gardens
Dumbiedykes Rd
Hub
Adam House
Infirmary St
Drummond St
Old College
Queen's Drive
Viewcraig Gardens
NATIONAL MUSEUM OF SCOTLAND
George IV Bridge
Pleasance
Festival Theatre
Nicolson
HOLYROOD PARK
Friars Church Churchyard
Forrest Rd
Bistro Square
West Richmond St
Brown St
Lauriston Pl.
Simpson Loan
Sq're George
Lane
Buccleuch Pl.
Buccleuch
Meadow Lane
Clerk St
St Leonard's
St Leonard's Bank
Queen's Drive
Meadow Park
Bernard Terrace
Holyrood Park Rd
East Meadow Park
South Clerk St
Lutton Pl.
Dalkeith Rd
Parkside Terrace
Holyrood Park Rd
Melville Drive
Melville Terrace
West Preston St
East Preston St
Rosebeath Pl.
Argyle Pl.
r
u
a
c
n
s
v
z

Galvin Brasserie De Luxe

FRENCH • BRASSERIE XX It's accurately described by its name: a simply styled restaurant which looks like a brasserie of old, but with the addition of a smart shellfish counter and formal service. There's an appealing à la carte and a good value two-choice daily set selection; dishes are refined, flavoursome and of a good size.

Menu £ 25 (lunch and early dinner) – Carte £ 30/46

Town plan: F2-x – *Waldorf Astoria Edinburgh The Caledonian Hotel, Princes St ✉ EH1 2AB – ✆ 0131 222 8988 – www.galvinrestaurants.com*

Dogs

TRADITIONAL CUISINE • BISTRO X Cosy, slightly bohemian-style eatery on the first floor of a classic Georgian mid-terrace, with two high-ceilinged, shabby chic dining rooms and an appealing bar. Robust, good value comfort food is crafted from local, seasonal produce; dishes such as cock-a-leekie soup and devilled ox livers feature.

Carte £ 20/28

Town plan: F2-c – *110 Hanover St (1st Floor) ✉ EH2 1DR – ✆ 0131 220 1208 – www.thedogsonline.co.uk – Closed 25 December and 1 January*

The Scran & Scallie

TRADITIONAL BRITISH • NEIGHBOURHOOD The more casual venture from Tom Kitchin, located in a smart, village-like suburb. It has a wood-furnished bar and a dining room which blends rustic and contemporary décor. Extensive menus follow a 'Nature to Plate' philosophy and focus on the classical and the local.

Menu £ 18 (weekday lunch) – Carte £ 24/46

Town plan: E1-s – *1 Comely Bank Rd, Stockbridge ✉ EH4 1DT – ✆ 0131 332 6281 – www.scranandscallie.com – Closed 25 December*

The Pompadour by Galvin

FRENCH • ELEGANT XXX A grand hotel restaurant which opened in the 1920s and is modelled on a French salon. Classic Gallic dishes showcase Scottish produce, using techniques introduced by Escoffier, and are executed with a lightness of touch.

Menu £ 35 (early dinner)/65

Town plan: F2-x – *Waldorf Astoria Edinburgh The Caledonian Hotel, Princes St ✉ EH1 2AB – ✆ 0131 222 8975 – www.galvinrestaurants.com – dinner only and Sunday lunch – Closed 1-15 January, Monday and Tuesday*

Angels with Bagpipes

MODERN CUISINE • BISTRO XX Small, stylish restaurant named after the wooden sculpture in St Giles Cathedral, opposite. Dishes are more elaborate than the menu implies; modern interpretations of Scottish classics could include 'haggis neeps and tattiesgine'.

Menu £ 18 (lunch) – Carte £ 34/56

Town plan: G2-a – *343 High St, Royal Mile ✉ EH1 1PW – ✆ 0131 220 1111 – www.angelswithbagpipes.co.uk – Closed 6-22 January and 24-27 December*

Castle Terrace

MODERN CUISINE • INTIMATE XX Set in the shadow of the castle is this bright contemporary restaurant with hand-painted wallpapers and a mural depicting the Edinburgh skyline. Cooking is ambitious with a playful element and combines many different textures and flavours. The wine list also offers plenty of interest.

Menu £ 33 (lunch)/70

Town plan: F2-a – *33-35 Castle Terr ✉ EH1 2EL – ✆ 0131 229 1222 – www.castleterracerestaurant.com – Closed Christmas, New Year, 1 week April, 1 week July, 1 week October, Sunday and Monday*

The Honours

CLASSIC CUISINE • **BRASSERIE** XX Bustling brasserie with a smart, stylish interior and a pleasingly informal atmosphere. Classical brasserie menus have French leanings but always offer some Scottish dishes too; meats cooked on the Josper grill are popular.

Menu £ 23 (lunch and early dinner) – Carte £ 33/63

Town plan: F2-n – *58A North Castle St ✉ EH2 3LU – ✆ 0131 220 2513 – www.thehonours.co.uk – Closed 25-26 December, 1-2 January, Sunday and Monday*

Mark Greenaway

MODERN CUISINE • **INTIMATE** XX Smart restaurant located in an old Georgian bank – they store their wine in the old vault. The well-travelled chef employs interesting texture and flavour combinations. Dishes are modern, ambitious and attractively presented.

Menu £ 30 (lunch and early dinner)/50

Town plan: F2-b – *69 North Castle St ✉ EH2 3LJ – ✆ 0131 226 1155 – www.markgreenaway.com – Closed 25-26 December, 1-2 January, Sunday and Monday*

Ondine

SEAFOOD • **BRASSERIE** XX Smart, lively restaurant dominated by an impressive horseshoe bar and a crustacean counter. Classic menus showcase prime Scottish seafood in tasty, straightforward dishes which let the ingredients shine. Service is well-structured.

Menu £ 19 (lunch and early dinner) – Carte £ 35/78

Town plan: G2-s – *2 George IV Bridge (1st floor) ✉ EH1 1AD – ✆ 0131 226 1888 – www.ondinerestaurant.co.uk – Closed 1 week early January and 24-26 December*

Timberyard

MODERN CUISINE • **RUSTIC** X Trendy warehouse restaurant; its spacious, rustic interior incorporating wood-burning stoves. The Scandic-influenced menu offers 'bites', 'small' and 'large' sizes, with some home-smoked ingredients and an emphasis on distinct, punchy flavours. Cocktails are made with vegetable purées and foraged herbs.

Menu £ 25 (lunch and early dinner)/55

Town plan: F3-s – *10 Lady Lawson St ✉ EH3 9DS – ✆ 0131 221 1222 (booking essential at dinner) – www.timberyard.co – Closed 1-7 January,1 week April, 1 week October, Christmas, Sunday and Monday*

Aizle

MODERN CUISINE • **SIMPLE** X Modest little suburban restaurant whose name means 'ember' or 'spark'. Well-balanced, skilfully prepared dishes are, in effect, a surprise, as the set menu is presented as a long list of ingredients – the latest 'harvest'.

Menu £ 55 – tasting menu only

Town plan: H3-z – *107-109 St Leonard's St ✉ EH8 9QY – ✆ 0131 662 9349 – www.aizle.co.uk – dinner only – Closed 22 December-23 January, 7-23 July, Sunday except August and December, Monday and Tuesday*

Baba (N)

MIDDLE EASTERN • **MEDITERRANEAN DÉCOR** X Follow a long bar with cosy booths through to the lively dining room decorated in bright colours and hung with kilims. A mix of small and large Middle-Eastern sharing dishes show vibrancy in both their colours and flavours, and can be accompanied by some lesser-known wines from Lebanon and Greece.

Carte £ 17/26

Town plan: F2-v – *Principal Hotel, 38 Charlotte Sq ✉ EH2 4HQ – (entrance 130 George St) – ✆ 0131 527 4999 – www.baba.restaurant*

Café St Honoré

CLASSIC FRENCH • BISTRO Long-standing French bistro, tucked away down side street. The interior is cosy, with wooden marquetry, mirrors on the wal and tightly packed tables. Traditional Gallic menus use Scottish produce an they even smoke their own salmon.

Menu £ 19/26 – Carte £ 34/50

Town plan: F2-r – *34 North West Thistle Street Ln. ✉ EH2 1EA – ✆ 0131 226 221 (booking essential) – www.cafesthonore.com – Closed 24-26 December and 1-2 January*

Fhior

CREATIVE • DESIGN A husband and wife team run this appealing Scandic-styl restaurant whose name means 'True'. Creative modern cooking showcases Sco tish produce, including foraged and home-preserved ingredients. Lunch sees sma plates which are ideal for sharing, while dinner offers two surprise tasting menu

Menu £ 40/65 – Carte lunch £ 14/20

Town plan: G1-s – *36 Broughton St ✉ EH1 3SB – ✆ 0131 477 5000 (booking essential) – Closed 1 week Christmas, Sunday-Tuesday and lunch Wednesday-Thursday*

Gardener's Cottage

TRADITIONAL CUISINE • RUSTIC This quirky little eatery was once home to royal gardener. Two cosy, simply furnished rooms have long communal table Lunch is light and dinner offers a multi-course set menu; much of the pro duce comes from the kitchen garden.

Menu £ 40/60 (dinner) – Carte lunch £ 20/39

Town plan: H1-a – *1 Royal Terrace Gdns ✉ EH7 5DX – ✆ 0131 677 0244 – www.thegardenerscottage.co – Closed 25-26 December*

Kanpai

JAPANESE • SIMPLE Uncluttered, modern Japanese restaurant with a sma sushi bar and cheerful service. Colourful, elaborate dishes have clean, well-de fined flavours; the menu is designed to help novices feel confident and expert feel at home.

Carte £ 12/40

Town plan: F3-n – *8-10 Grindlay St ✉ EH3 9AS – ✆ 0131 228 1602 – www.kanpaisushiedinburgh.co.uk – Closed Sunday and Monday*

Kim's Mini Meals

KOREAN • SIMPLE A delightfully quirky little eatery filled with bric-a-brac an offering good value, authentic Korean home cooking. Classic dishes like bulgog dolsot and jjigae come with your choice of meat or vegetables as the main ir gredient.

Menu £ 18

Town plan: G3-u – *5 Buccleuch St ✉ EH8 9JN – ✆ 0131 629 7951 (booking essential at dinner) – www.kimsminimeals.com*

The Little Chartroom

MODERN BRITISH • SIMPLE There's a lively buzz to this laid-back little restau rant on Leith Walk, which is run by an experienced young couple and filled wit nautical charts. Cooking is fresh and flavoursome. Simple small plates and sharin dishes are followed by a modern menu with a Scottish edge; at weekends the serve brunch.

Carte £ 20/37

Town plan: H1-r – *30-31 Albert Pl ✉ EH7 5HN – ✆ 0131 556 6600 (booking essential) – www.thelittlechartroom.com – Closed first 2 weeks January, 1 week March, 1 week June, 1 week October, Monday and Tuesday*

Passorn

THAI • FRIENDLY The staff are super-friendly at this popular neighbourhood restaurant whose name means 'Angel'. Authentic menus feature Thai classics and old family recipes; the seafood dishes are a highlight and everything is attractively presented. Spices and other ingredients are flown in from Thailand.

Menu £ 16 (lunch and early dinner) – Carte £ 23/38

Town plan: F3-e – *23-23a Brougham Pl ✉ EH3 9JU – ☎ 0131 229 1537 (booking essential) – www.passornthai.com – Closed 25-26 December, 1-2 January, Sunday and lunch Monday*

Purslane

MODERN CUISINE • NEIGHBOURHOOD A cosy, atmospheric basement restaurant made up of just 9 tables. The young chef-owner creates ambitious modern dishes which mix tried-and-tested flavours with modern techniques. Lunch is particularly good value.

Menu £ 15/35

Town plan: F1-e – *33a St Stephen St ✉ EH3 5AH – ☎ 0131 226 3500 (booking essential) – www.purslanerestaurant.co.uk – Closed 25-26 December, 1 January and Monday*

Taisteal

MODERN BRITISH • NEIGHBOURHOOD Taisteal is Irish Gaelic for 'journey' and is the perfect name: photos from the chef's travels line the walls and dishes have global influences, with Asian flavours to the fore. The wine list even has a sake section.

Menu £ 16 (lunch and early dinner) – Carte £ 27/39

Town plan: E1-h – *1-3 Raeburn Pl, Stockbridge ✉ EH4 1HU – ☎ 0131 332 9977 – www.taisteal.co.uk – Closed first 2 weeks September, 1 week January, Sunday and Monday*

Wedgwood

MODERN CUISINE • FRIENDLY Atmospheric bistro hidden away at the bottom of the Royal Mile. Well-presented dishes showcase produce foraged from the surrounding countryside and feature some original, modern combinations. It's personally run by a friendly team.

Menu £ 20 (lunch) – Carte dinner £ 36/52

Town plan: H2-a – *267 Canongate ✉ EH8 8BQ – ☎ 0131 558 8737 – www.wedgwoodtherestaurant.co.uk – Closed 1-24 January and 25-26 December*

Hotels

Balmoral

GRAND LUXURY • CLASSIC A renowned Edwardian hotel which provides for the 21C traveller whilst retaining its old-fashioned charm. Bedrooms are classical with a subtle contemporary edge; JK Rowling completed the final Harry Potter book in the top suite! Live harp music accompanies afternoon tea in the Palm Court and 'Scotch' offers over 460 malts. Dine on modern dishes or brasserie classics.

188 rooms – †£ 200/725 ††£ 225/845 – ☕ £ 27 – 20 suites

Town plan: G2-n – *1 Princes St ✉ EH2 2EQ – ☎ 0131 556 2414 – www.roccofortehotels.com*

✿ **Number One** – See restaurant listing

Sheraton Grand H. & Spa

GRAND LUXURY • MODERN A spacious hotel with castle views from some rooms – an impressive four-storey glass cube houses the stunning spa. Sleek, stylish bedrooms have strong comforts, the latest mod cons and smart bathrooms with mood lighting. The casual restaurant serves an all-encompassing menu and the bar offers over 50 gins.

269 rooms – †£ 160/675 ††£ 160/675 – ☕ £ 22 – 11 suites

Town plan: F2-v – *1 Festival Sq ✉ EH3 9SR – ☎ 0131 229 9131 – www.sheratonedinburgh.co.uk*

Waldorf Astoria Edinburgh The Caledonian

HISTORIC • DESIGN Smart hotel in the old railway terminus: have afternoon tea on the former forecourt or cocktails where the trains onc pulled in. Sumptuous modern bedrooms have excellent facilities; ask for a cast' view. Unwind in the UK's first Guerlain spa, then dine in the grand French salon c luxurious brasserie.

241 rooms – £ 249/619 £ 269/639 – £ 23 – 6 suites

Town plan: F2-x – *Princes St* ✉ *EH1 2AB* – *0131 222 8888* – *www.waldorfastoriaedinburgh.com*

Galvin Brasserie De Luxe • **The Pompadour by Galvin** – See restaurant lis ing

Prestonfield

LUXURY • PERSONALISED 17C country house in a pleasant rural spot, with a opulent, dimly lit interior displaying warm colours, fine furnishings and old tape tries – it's hugely atmospheric and is one of the most romantic hotels aroun Luxurious bedrooms boast a high level of facilities and service is excellent.

23 rooms – £ 345/405 £ 345/405 – 5 suites

Town plan: C3-r – *Priestfield Rd* ✉ *EH16 5UT* – *0131 225 7800* – *www.prestonfield.com*

Hotel du Vin

LUXURY • DESIGN Boutique hotel located close to the Royal Mile, featuring u ique murals and wine-themed bedrooms furnished with dark wood. Guest area include a whisky snug and a mezzanine bar complete with glass-fronted cella and a wine tasting room. The traditional bistro offers classic French cooking.

47 rooms – £ 174/344 £ 174/344

Town plan: G3-n – *11 Bristo Pl* ✉ *EH1 1EZ* – *0131 247 4900* – *www.hotelduvin.com/edinburgh*

Radisson Collection H. Royal Mile Edinburgh

LUXURY • DESIGN Set in a great central location on the historic Royal Mile, a striking hotel with bold colour schemes, stylish furnishings an clever design features. Bedrooms on the upper floors have impressive city skylir views. Enjoy Italian dinners and breakfasts featuring honey from the bees the keep on the roof.

136 rooms – £ 150/300 £ 200/400 – 7 suites

Town plan: G2-v – *1 George IV Bridge* ✉ *EH1 1AD* – *0131 220 6666* – *www.radissoncollection.com*

Chester Residence

TOWNHOUSE • CONTEMPORARY A series of peacefully located Georgian towr houses. The luxurious suites come with kitchens and state-of-the-art facilities ir cluding video entry and integrated sound systems; the Mews apartments are th best.

23 rooms – £ 160/340 £ 160/340 – £ 12

Town plan: E2-c – *9 Rothesay Pl* ✉ *EH3 7SL* – *0131 226 2075* – *www.chester-residence.com* – *Closed 23-26 December*

The Dunstane

TOWNHOUSE • CONTEMPORARY An impressive house which used to be a trair ing centre for the Royal Bank of Scotland. Guest areas retain original Victoria features and the smart bedrooms have designer touches; some are locate across a busy road. Light snacks are served all day in the lounge.

35 rooms – £ 129/259 £ 139/319

Town plan: A3-s – *4 West Coates* ✉ *EH12 5JQ* – *0131 337 6169* – *www.thedunstane.com*

23 Mayfield

TOWNHOUSE • CLASSIC Lovingly restored Victorian house with a helpful owner, an outdoor hot tub and a rare book collection. Sumptuous bedrooms come with coordinated soft furnishings, mahogany features and luxurious bathrooms. Breakfast is extravagant.

7 rooms – †£ 99/160 ††£ 120/230

Town plan: C3-x – *23 Mayfield Gdns ✉ EH9 2BX – ☎ 0131 667 5806 – www.23mayfield.co.uk*

Six Brunton Place

TOWNHOUSE • CONTEMPORARY This late Georgian townhouse – run by a charming owner – was once home to Frederick Ritchie, who designed the One O'Clock Gun and Time Ball. Inside you'll find flagged floors, columns, marble fireplaces and a cantilevered stone staircase; these contrast with contemporary furnishings and vibrant modern art.

4 rooms – †£ 139/159 ††£ 159/179

Town plan: H1-u – *6 Brunton Pl ✉ EH7 5EG – ☎ 0131 622 0042 – www.sixbruntonplace.com – Closed 20-28 December*

94 DR

TOWNHOUSE • PERSONALISED Charming owners welcome you to this very stylish and individual hotel in a Victorian terraced house. Bedrooms are well-equipped, there's a retro lounge with an honesty bar and breakfast is served in the conservatory with its decked terrace.

6 rooms – †£ 120/220 ††£ 120/220

Town plan: C3-n – *94 Dalkeith Rd ✉ EH16 5AF – ☎ 0131 662 9265 – www.94dr.com – Closed 24-25 December and 4-18 January*

at Leith

Martin Wishart

MODERN CUISINE • ELEGANT XXX This elegant, modern restaurant is becoming something of an Edinburgh institution. Choose between three 6 course menus – Classic, Seafood and Vegetarian – and a concise à la carte. Top ingredients are used in well-judged, flavourful combinations; dishes are classically based but have elaborate, original touches.

→ Scallop, Jerusalem artichoke, hazelnut and truffle pesto. Wild sea bass, cauliflower and shrimp gratin, caviar and champagne velouté. Buttermilk mousse, fennel sorbet and sorrel parfait.

Menu £ 32 (weekday lunch)/95

Town plan: C1-u – *54 The Shore ✉ EH6 6RA – ☎ 0131 553 3557 (booking essential) – www.martin-wishart.co.uk – Closed one week July, 25-26 December, 2 weeks in January, Sunday and Monday*

Kitchin (Tom Kitchin)

MODERN CUISINE • DESIGN XX A smartly converted whisky warehouse provides the perfect setting for this patriotic restaurant, where the windswept highlands are brought indoors courtesy of tartan tweed, tree bark, whisky barrels and dry stone walls. Menus mix boldly flavoured classics with fresh modern dishes. Each ingredient has a purpose and is allowed to shine; vegetables are the chef's passion.

→ Seafood with sea vegetables, ginger and shellfish consommé. Roasted loin and braised haunch of roe deer with root vegetable mash and a red wine sauce. Warm apple tart, vanilla ice cream and calvados sauce.

Menu £ 33 (lunch)/75

Town plan: C1-z – *78 Commercial Quay ✉ EH6 6LX – ☎ 0131 555 1755 (booking essential) – www.thekitchin.com – Closed 25 December-14 January, 2-6 April, 16-20 August, 15-19 October, Sunday and Monday*

SCOTLAND

Malmaison

BUSINESS • CONTEMPORARY An impressive former seamen's mission locate on the quayside – the first of the Malmaison hotels. The décor is a mix of bol stripes and contrasting black and white themes. Bedrooms are well-equippe and one has a tartan roll-top bath! The restaurant serves grills and European far

100 rooms – £ 65/275 £ 65/275

Town plan: C1-m – *1 Tower Pl* ✉ *EH6 7BZ* – ✆ *0131 285 1478* – *www.malmaison.com*

EDNAM – The Scottish Borders ➜ See Kelso

ELGOL – Highland ➜ See Skye (Isle of)

ERISKA (Isle of)

Argyll and Bute – ✉ Oban – Regional map n° **16**-B2

Isle of Eriska

COUNTRY HOUSE • CONTEMPORARY An impressive 19C baronial mansion set i an idyllic spot on a private island and boasting fantastic views. A contempora style contrasts with original features in the main house and there are luxuriou hilltop lodges in the grounds. Dine on modern dishes featuring garden ingred ents in the restaurant or bistro; the latter has stunning views from its balcony.

29 rooms – £ 239/329 £ 266/550 – 13 suites

Benderloch ✉ *PA37 1SD* – ✆ *01631 720371* – *www.eriska-hotel.co.uk* – *Closed January*

EVANTON

Highland – Regional map n° **17**-C2

Kiltearn House

COUNTRY HOUSE • CONTEMPORARY This large sandstone former manse sits i a quiet spot, yet is only a few minutes from the A9. It has a classical sitting roo and a conservatory breakfast room; bedrooms are more modern – two hav views over Cromarty Firth.

5 rooms – £ 72/100 £ 96/200

✉ *IV16 9UY* – *South : 1 mi by B 817 on Kiltearn Burial Ground rd* – ✆ *01349 8306* – *www.kiltearn.co.uk* – *Closed 25 December*

FIONNPHORT – Argyll and Bute ➜ See Mull (Isle of)

FLODIGARRY – Highland ➜ See Skye (Isle of)

FOCHABERS

Moray – Pop. 1 728 – Regional map n° **16**-C1

Trochelhill Country House

COUNTRY HOUSE • CLASSIC Whitewashed Victorian house; well-run by friend owners who serve tea and cake on arrival. Spacious bedrooms feature moder bathrooms with walk-in showers; two have roll-top baths. Breakfast includes hag gis, black pudding and homemade bread.

3 rooms – £ 100/110 £ 100/110

✉ *IV32 7LN* – *West : 2.75 mi by A 96 off B 9015* – ✆ *01343 821267* – *www.trochelhill.co.uk*

FORT AUGUSTUS

Highland – Pop. 621 – Regional map n° **17**-C3

The Lovat

TRADITIONAL • PERSONALISED A professionally run Victorian house which has been given a bold, stylish makeover. Bedrooms are a mix of the classic – with feature beds and antique furnishings – and the contemporary, with vibrant colours and feature wallpapers.

28 rooms – £ 122/340 £ 136/432

PH32 4DU – 01456 459250 – www.thelovat.com – Closed 3 January-7 February and Monday-Tuesday February-Easter

FORT WILLIAM

Highland – Pop. 5 883 – Regional map n° **17**-C3

Inverlochy Castle

MODERN CUISINE • LUXURY Set within a striking castle in the shadow of Ben Nevis is this grand restaurant offering stunning loch views. Choose between two candlelit dining rooms where period sideboards are filled with polished silver. Richly flavoured classic dishes showcase luxurious Scottish produce.

Menu £ 67 – tasting menu only

Inverlochy Castle Hotel, Torlundy PH33 6SN – Northeast : 3 mi on A 82 – 01397 702177 (booking essential) – www.inverlochycastlehotel.com – dinner only

blas

MODERN CUISINE • SIMPLE 'Blas' can be translated as 'taste', 'savour', 'gusto' or 'relish' – and this laid-back restaurant's subtly modernised cooking is certainly packed with flavour. Lunch is light, so come for dinner. Its cellar is already home to the Lochaber Gin Distillery, which will soon be joined by a nano-brewery.

Carte £ 26/34

147 High St PH33 6EA – 01397 702726 (booking essential at dinner) – www.blasfortwilliam.co.uk – Closed Sunday dinner and Monday

Lime Tree An Ealdhain

MODERN CUISINE • RUSTIC Attractive 19C manse – now an informally run restaurant and art gallery, where the owner's pieces are displayed and two public exhibitions are held each year. Rustic dining room with exposed beams and an open kitchen; cooking is fresh and modern. Simply furnished bedrooms – ask for one with a view of Loch Linnhe.

Carte £ 29/36

9 rooms – £ 70/135 £ 100/150

Achintore Rd PH33 6RQ – 01397 701806 (booking essential) – www.limetreefortwilliam.co.uk – dinner only – Closed November, last 3 weeks January and 24-28 December

Inverlochy Castle

GRAND LUXURY • CLASSIC A striking castellated house in beautiful grounds, boasting stunning views over the loch to Glenfinnan. The classical country house interior comprises sumptuous open-fired lounges and a grand hall with an impressive ceiling mural. Elegant bedrooms offer the height of luxury; mod cons include mirrored TVs.

18 rooms – £ 310/455 £ 350/725 – 1 suite

Torlundy PH33 6SN – Northeast : 3 mi on A 82 – 01397 702177 – www.inverlochycastlehotel.com

Inverlochy Castle – See restaurant listing

Grange

TOWNHOUSE • PERSONALISED Take in loch and hills views from this delightful Victorian house and its attractive gardens. Spacious bedrooms are luxuriously appointed. Two are suites; one has a beautiful copper bath in the room and the other is a timber bothy in the garden. The charming owner really knows how to look after her guests.

4 rooms – £155/198 £155/198

Grange Rd. ✉ PH33 6JF – South : 0.75 mi by A 82 and Ashburn Ln – ✆ 01397 705516 – www.grangefortwilliam.com – Closed November-mid-March

FORTINGALL

Perth and Kinross – Regional map n° **16**-C2

Fortingall

TRADITIONAL • PERSONALISED Stylish Arts and Crafts house on a tranquil private estate, boasting lovely country views. The interior is delightful, with its snug open-fired bar and cosy sitting rooms filled with Scottish country knick knacks. Bedrooms are modern but in keeping with the building's age. Dining is formal and classical.

10 rooms – £100/150 £190/230

✉ PH15 2NQ – ✆ 01887 830367 – www.fortingall.com

GATEHEAD

East Ayrshire – ✉ East Ayrshire – Regional map n° **15**-B2

Cochrane Inn

TRADITIONAL CUISINE • PUB This ivy-covered pub is surprisingly bright and modern inside, with its copper lampshades, coal-effect gas fires and striking contemporary art. It offers a good range of tasty, generously priced dishes; the Express Menu is a steal.

Menu £14 (lunch and early dinner)/21 – Carte £19/41

45 Main Rd ✉ KA2 0AP – ✆ 01563 570122 – www.costley-hotels.co.uk

GATTONSIDE – The Scottish Borders ➜ See Melrose

GIFFNOCK

East Renfrewshire – Pop. 12 156 – Regional map n° **15**-B1

Catch

FISH AND CHIPS • SIMPLE Modern fish and chip shop with exposed bricks and nautical styling; sit in a booth to take in the action from the open kitchen. Fresh sustainably sourced fish comes in crisp batter and is accompanied by twice-cooked chips.

Carte £18/29

186 Fenwick Rd ✉ G46 6XF – ✆ 0141 638 9169 – www.catchfishandchips.co.uk – Closed 25 December and 1 January

GIGHA (Isle of)

Argyll and Bute – Regional map n° **16**-A3

The Boathouse

SEAFOOD • RUSTIC This 300 year old boathouse is set on a small community-owned island, overlooking the water. Whitewashed stone walls and beamed ceilings enhance the rustic feel. Menus cater for all, centring around fresh seafood and local meats.

Carte £24/58

Ardminish Bay ✉ PA41 7AA – ✆ 01583 505123 – www.boathouseongigha.com – Closed November-April

GOOD TIPS!

This former industrial powerhouse has been reborn as a cultural and commercial hub, with a lively dining scene to boot. History is all around: enjoy a stay in the stunning **Blythswood Square** hotel – once the RAC HQ. Modernity comes in the form of creative, cutting-edge restaurants like **Cail Bruich** and Bib Gourmand awarded neighbourhood bistro **Monadh Kitchen**.

GLASGOW

Glasgow City – Pop. 590 507 – Regional map n° **15**-B1

Restaurants

Monadh Kitchen N

MODERN BRITISH • FRIENDLY X This delightful neighbourhood restaurant has a modern bistro style and is very personally run by a husband and wife. The experienced chef creates a series of appealing, seasonally evolving menus, where classic Scottish cooking is given a contemporary twist; the 2 course lunch is particularly good value.

Menu £ 23 – Carte £ 29/40

19 New Kirk Rd, Bearsden ✉ G61 3SJ – Northwest : 5.75 mi by A81 off A809 – ✆ 0141 258 6420 – www.monadhkitchen.co.uk – Closed 1-17 January, 15-31 July, 25 December, Sunday dinner, Tuesday lunch and Monday

Ox and Finch

MODERN BRITISH • DESIGN X A bright, breezy team run this likeable rustic restaurant, with its tile-backed open kitchen and wines displayed in a huge metal cage. The international small plates tempt one and all: cooking centres around old favourites but with added modern twists – and the flavours really shine through.

Carte £ 17/30

Town plan: A2-c – *920 Sauchiehall St ✉ G3 7TF – ✆ 0141 339 8627 – www.oxandfinch.com – Closed 25-26 December and 1-2 January*

Brian Maule at Chardon d'Or

MODERN CUISINE • ELEGANT XXX Georgian townhouse in the city's heart, with original pillars, ornate carved ceilings and white walls hung with vibrant modern art. Generously proportioned, classical dishes have a modern edge and showcase luxurious ingredients.

Menu £ 25 (lunch and early dinner) – Carte £ 40/59

Town plan: C2-b – *176 West Regent St. ✉ G2 4RL – ✆ 0141 248 3801 – www.brianmaule.com – Closed 25 December, 1-2 January, Sunday, Monday and bank holidays*

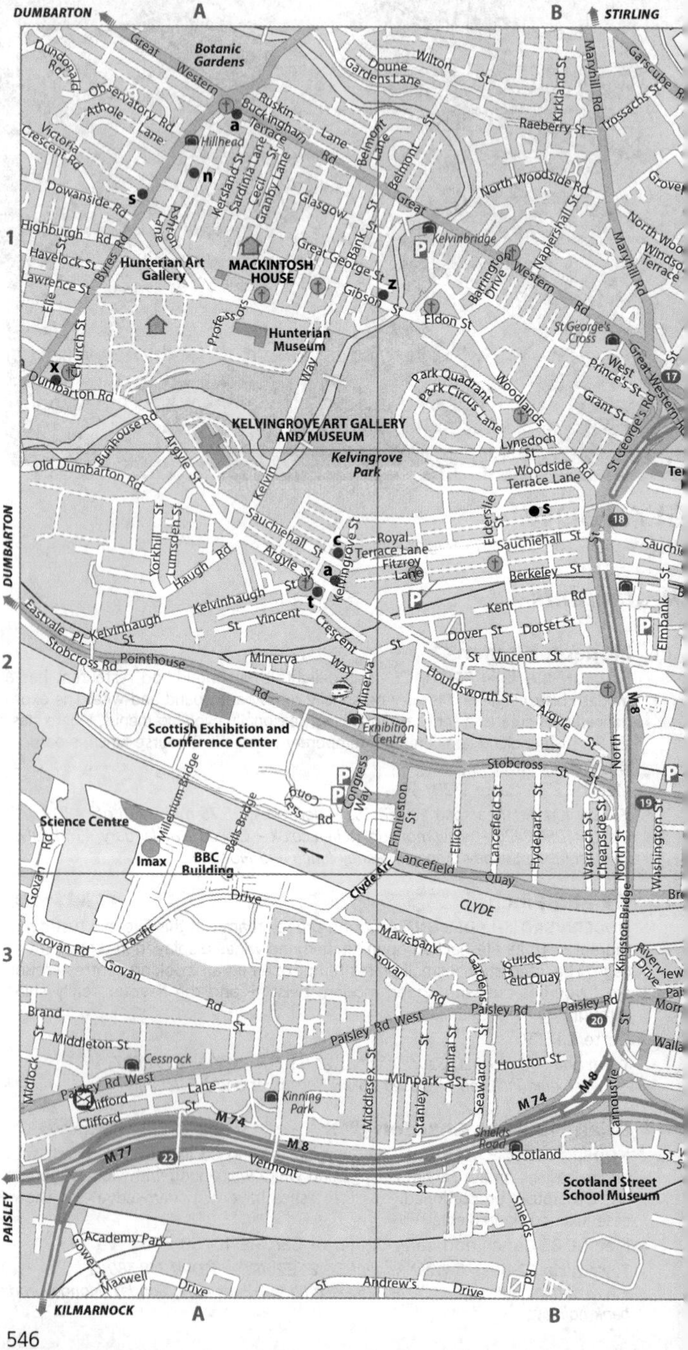
DUMBARTON
STIRLING
A
B
1
2
3
Botanic Gardens
Great Western Rd
Dundonald Rd
Observatory Rd
Athole Lane
Victoria Crescent Rd
Dowanside Rd
Highburgh Rd
Havelock St
Lawrence St
Byres Rd
Hillhead
Ashton Lane
Ruskin Lane
Buckingham Terrace
Kersland St
Sardinia Lane
Cecil St
Granby Lane
Glasgow
Great George St
Gibson St
Hunterian Art Gallery
MACKINTOSH HOUSE
Hunterian Museum
Professors
Church St
Dumbarton Rd
Doune Gardens Lane
Wilton St
Belmont Lane
Belmont St
Bank St
Kelvinbridge
Barrington Drive
Eldon St
Kirkland St
Raeberry St
North Woodside Rd
Napiershall St
Maryhill Rd
Garscube Rd
Trossachs St
St George's Cross
West Prince's St
Grant St
Great Western Rd
St George's Rd
Park Quadrant
Park Circus Lane
Woodlands
Lynedoch St
Woodside Terrace Lane
KELVINGROVE ART GALLERY AND MUSEUM
Kelvingrove Park
Kelvin Way
Bunhouse Rd
Old Dumbarton Rd
Argyle St
Sauchiehall St
Kelvingrove St
Royal Terrace Lane
Fitzroy Lane
Elderslie St
Sauchiehall St
Berkeley St
Kent Rd
Dover St
Dorset St
St Vincent St
Elmbank
Yorkhill St
Lumsden St
Haugh Rd
Kelvinhaugh St
Vincent St
Crescent
Eastvale Pl.
Stobcross Rd
Pointhouse Rd
Minerva Way
Minerva St
Houldsworth St
Argyle St
Scottish Exhibition and Conference Center
Exhibition Centre
Stobcross St
North St
M 8
Millennium Bridge
Bells Bridge
Congress Rd
Congress Way
Finnieston St
Elliot St
Lancefield St
Hydepark St
Warroch St
Cheapside St
Washington St
Science Centre
Imax
BBC Building
Lancefield Quay
Clyde Arc
CLYDE
Kingston Bridge
Govan Rd
Pacific Drive
Mavisbank
Govan Rd
Springfield Quay
River view Drive
Brand St
Middleton St
Cessnock
Paisley Rd West
Paisley Rd
Gardens
Middlesex St
Stanley St
Admiral St
Seaward St
Houston St
Milnpark St
Kinning Park
Midlock St
Clifford St
Clifford Lane
M 74
M 8
M 77
Vermont St
Shields Road
Scotland St
Carnoustie St
Scotland Street School Museum
Shields Rd
PAISLEY
Academy Park
Gower St
Maxwell Drive
St Andrew's Drive
KILMARNOCK
17
18
19
20
22

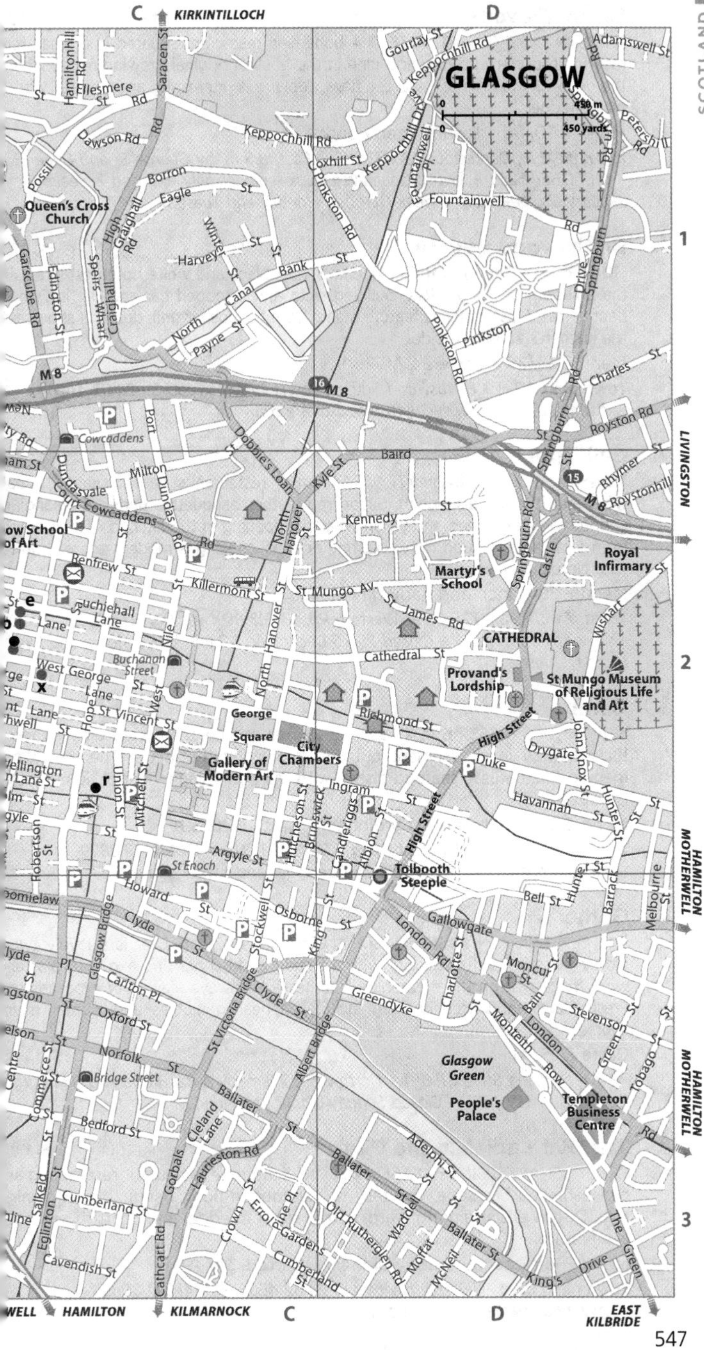
GLASGOW
0
450 m
0
450 yards
C
D
KIRKINTILLOCH
LIVINGSTON
HAMILTON MOTHERWELL
HAMILTON MOTHERWELL
HAMILTON
KILMARNOCK
EAST KILBRIDE
1
2
3
Queen's Cross Church
Royal Infirmary
Martyr's School
CATHEDRAL
Provand's Lordship
St Mungo Museum of Religious Life and Art
George Square
City Chambers
Gallery of Modern Art
Tolbooth Steeple
Glasgow Green
People's Palace
Templeton Business Centre
Cowcaddens
Buchanan Street
St Enoch
Bridge Street
M 8
16
15
Saracen St
Keppochhill Rd
Pinkston Rd
Springburn Rd
High Street
Duke St
Gallowgate
London Rd
Argyle St
Clyde St
Glasgow Bridge
St Victoria Bridge
Albert Bridge
Ballater St
Gorbals St
Cathcart Rd
Eglinton St
Dobbie's Loan
North Hanover St
Cathedral St
Ingram St
Kyle St
Royston Rd

Bilson Eleven

MODERN CUISINE • INTIMATE XX A bohemian restaurant situated in a small ter race in an eastern suburb; you dine in the house's original drawing room, wher the décor blends the old and the new. Cooking is interesting and original with playful edge.

Menu £ 50/60 – tasting menu only

10 Annfield Pl, Dennistoun ✉ G31 2XQ – East : 1.5 mi by George St and Duke St – ✆ 0141 554 6259 – www.bilsoneleven.co.uk – dinner only – Closed 2 weeks January, 2 weeks July, 1 week October, Monday and Tuesday

Blythswood Square

MODERN CUISINE • FASHIONABLE XX Stylish black and white hotel restaurant i the ballroom of the old RAC building, with a zinc-topped bar and Harris Twee banquettes. Classic menus feature meats from the Josper grill; desserts showcas the kitchen's ambitious side.

Menu £ 23/25 – Carte £ 27/52

Town plan: C2-n – *Blythswood Square Hotel, 11 Blythswood Sq ✉ G2 4AD – ✆ 0141 248 8888 – www.blythswoodsquare.com*

Cail Bruich

MODERN CUISINE • INTIMATE XX This smart restaurant's name means 'to ea well', and it won't disappoint. Sit on red leather banquettes under low-hanging copper lights and keep an eye on what's happening in the kitchen. Menus rang from a market selection to two tasting options; cooking is modern and elaborat with Nordic touches.

Menu £ 28 (lunch and early dinner)/55

Town plan: A1-a – *725 Great Western Rd. ✉ G12 8QX – ✆ 0141 334 6265 – www.cailbruich.co.uk – Closed 25-26 December, 1-2 and 7-15 January and lunch Monday-Tuesday*

Gamba

SEAFOOD • BRASSERIE XX A cosy bar-lounge and contemporary dining room tucked away in a basement but well-known by the locals. The appealing menu offers unfussy seafood dishes with the odd Asian influence; lemon sol is a speciality.

Menu £ 22 (lunch and early dinner) – Carte £ 26/59

Town plan: C2-x – *225a West George St. ✉ G2 2ND – ✆ 0141 572 0899 – www.gamba.co.uk – Closed 25-26 December and 1 week January*

Gather N

MODERN CUISINE • FASHIONABLE XX Cafezique's bigger sister is a lovely two storey glass-fronted restaurant with a trendy cocktail bar and exquisite plaster work friezes; sit on the mezzanine level for a bird's eye view over proceedings Fresh, Italian-influenced cooking includes appealing nibbles and vibrant mai courses.

Carte £ 25/41

70-72 Hyndland St ✉ G11 5PT – Northwest : 2.5 mi by A 82, B 808 and Highburgh Rd – ✆ 0141 339 2000 – Closed Sunday dinner and Monday

Two Fat Ladies in the City

TRADITIONAL CUISINE • CLASSIC DÉCOR XX Intimate restaurant resembling ar old-fashioned brasserie, courtesy of its wooden floor, banquettes and mirrors. Dishes are straightforward, with a modern edge, and Scottish seafoo is a feature.

Menu £ 16 (lunch and early dinner) – Carte £ 30/49

Town plan: C2-e – *118a Blythswood St ✉ G2 4EG – ✆ 0141 847 0088 – www.twofatladiesrestaurant.com*

Ubiquitous Chip (Mezzanine 'Brasserie')

MODERN CUISINE • BISTRO XX A quirky, iconic establishment on a cobbled street; the son of the original owner runs it with passion. The mezzanine brasserie serves Scottish favourites but it's the ground floor restaurant with its ponds, fountains and greenery that is the place to eat. Interesting modern classics showcase local produce.

Menu £ 24 (lunch and early dinner) – Carte £ 22/51

Town plan: A1-n – *12 Ashton Ln ✉ G12 8SJ – ✆ 0141 334 5007 – www.ubiquitouschip.co.uk – Closed 25 December and 1 January*

Alchemilla

MEDITERRANEAN CUISINE • SIMPLE X A bright, friendly restaurant offering Mediterranean-inspired dishes in a range of sizes. There's a basement level but the place to sit is on the ground floor – either in the window, on the mezzanine or at the counter watching the chefs. Ingredients are kept to a minimum but flavours have maximum impact.

Menu £ 10 (weekday lunch) – Carte £ 19/36

Town plan: A2-a – *1126 Argyle St ✉ G3 8TD – ✆ 0141 337 6060 – www.thisisalchemilla.com*

Cafezique

MODERN CUISINE • BISTRO X Underneath the old Hargan's Dairy sign is a cosy, shabby-chic eatery, where striking black and white screen prints hang on stone walls and a relaxed, buzzy vibe pervades. All-day breakfasts and Mediterranean light bites are followed by vibrant dishes in two sizes at dinner.

Carte £ 18/35

66 Hyndland St ✉ G11 5PT – Northwest : 2.5 mi by A 82, B 808 and Highburgh Rd – ✆ 0141 339 7180 – www.delizique.com – Closed 25-26 December, 1 January and Sunday dinner.

The Gannet

MODERN BRITISH • RUSTIC X This appealingly rustic restaurant makes passionate use of Scotland's larder and as such, its menus are constantly evolving. Classic dishes are presented in a modern style and brought to the table by a charming team. The chefs have a good understanding of flavour combinations.

Carte £ 33/45

Town plan: A2-t – *1155 Argyle St ✉ G3 8TB – ✆ 0141 204 2081 – www.thegannetgla.com – Closed 24-27 December, Monday and lunch Tuesday-Wednesday*

Hanoi Bike Shop

VIETNAMESE • SIMPLE X Relaxed Vietnamese café; head to the lighter upstairs room with its fine array of lanterns. Simple, classic Vietnamese dishes include street food like rice paper summer rolls. The charming, knowledgeable team offer recommendations.

Carte £ 20/28

Town plan: A1-s – *8 Ruthven Ln ✉ G12 9BG – Off Byres Rd – ✆ 0141 334 7165 – www.hanoibikeshop.co.uk – Closed 25 December and 1 January*

Julie's Kopitiam (N)

MALAYSIAN • SIMPLE X The young owner has kept the décor simple and the focus firmly on the food at this traditional Malaysian coffee shop; she even visits Malaysia regularly to gather new ideas. Good value street food dishes are vibrant and flavoursome and service is sweet and cheerful. Watch the chefs in the open kitchen.

Carte £ 15/24

1109 Pollokshaws Rd ✉ G41 3YG – Southwest : 2.5 mi on A77 – ✆ 0141 237 9560 (bookings not accepted) – Closed Monday and lunch Tuesday-Wednesday

Six by Nico

MODERN CUISINE • FRIENDLY It's all in the name: the good value 6 course tasting menu changes every 6 weeks and is designed by Italian owner Nico along with his team. Themes are announced on the website and could be anything from 'Picnic' to 'Vietnamese Street Food'. Dishes are well-executed and a vegetarian menu runs in parallel.

Menu £ 28 – tasting menu only

Town plan: A2-a – *1132 Argyle St ✉ G3 8TD – ✆ 0141 334 5661 (pre-book at weekends) – www.sixbynico.co.uk – Closed 25-26 December, 1-2 January and Monday*

Stravaigin

INTERNATIONAL • SIMPLE Their motto here is 'think global, eat local'. On the ground floor, the shabby-chic café-bar serves international and subtly spiced Asian-influenced dishes; the intimate downstairs restaurant opens in the evenings and serves more classical fare. They make their own haggis and host regular theme nights.

Carte £ 30/48

Town plan: B1-z – *28 Gibson St. ✉ G12 8NX – ✆ 0141 334 2665 (booking essential at dinner) – www.stravaigin.co.uk – Closed 25 December and 1 January*

Two Fat Ladies West End

SEAFOOD • NEIGHBOURHOOD Quirky neighbourhood restaurant with red velour banquettes, bold blue and gold décor, and a semi open plan kitchen in the window. Cooking is simple and to the point, and focuses on classical fish dishes.

Menu £ 22 (lunch and early dinner) – Carte £ 30/45

Town plan: A1-x – *88 Dumbarton Rd ✉ G11 6NX – ✆ 0141 339 1944 – www.twofatladiesrestaurant.com – Closed 1-2 January*

Hotels

Blythswood Square

HISTORIC • DESIGN Stunning property on a delightful Georgian square. Modern décor contrasts with original fittings; bedrooms are dark and moody and the Penthouse Suite features a bed adapted from a snooker table. Afternoon tea is a hit.

100 rooms – £ 150/282 £ 150/282 – 3 suites

Town plan: C2-n – *11 Blythswood Sq ✉ G2 4AD – ✆ 0141 248 8888 – www.blythswoodsquare.com*

Blythswood Square – See restaurant listing

Hotel du Vin at One Devonshire Gardens

TOWNHOUSE • ELEGANT A collection of adjoining townhouses boasting original 19C stained glass, wood panelling and a labyrinth of corridors. It's furnished in dark, opulent shades but has a contemporary country house air. Dine on modern dishes in the elegant oak-panelled restaurant; they also offer wine tastings in the cellar.

49 rooms – £ 110/550 £ 110/550 – £ 18 – 3 suites

1 Devonshire Gdns ✉ G12 OUX – Northwest : 2.5 mi by A 82 (Great Western Rd) – ✆ 0141 378 0385 – www.hotelduvin.com

Dakota Deluxe

BUSINESS • CONTEMPORARY With its black brick façade and box hedges, this boutique hotel wouldn't look out of place in NYC. Sleek, spacious bedrooms have good comforts and the professional staff make it feel like a home-from-home. On the first floor there's a champagne bar; in the basement, classics and grills are brought up-to-date.

83 rooms – £ 125/300 £ 135/310 – 1 suite

Town plan: B2-h – *179 West Regent St ✉ G2 4DP – ✆ 0141 404 3680 – www.glasgow.dakotahotels.co.uk*

Malmaison

BUSINESS • CONTEMPORARY An impressive-looking former Greek Orthodox Church, with moody, masculine décor. Stylish, boldly coloured bedrooms offer good facilities; the best are the brighter duplex suites. The lively glass-roofed basement bar specialises in craft beers and the vaulted brasserie offers a wide-ranging global menu.

72 rooms – †£ 90/320 ††£ 90/320 – ☕ £ 15 – 8 suites

Town plan: C2-c – *278 West George St ✉ G2 4LL – ✆ 0141 572 1000 – www.malmaison.com*

Grasshoppers

BUSINESS • DESIGN Located on the 6th floor of the Victorian railway station; its lounge overlooks the largest glass roof in Europe. Stylish, well-designed bedrooms have bespoke Scandinavian-style furnishings, Scottish art and smart, compact shower rooms. Three course suppers are served Mon-Thurs (residents only).

29 rooms ☕ – †£ 68/108 ††£ 78/138

Town plan: C2-r – *Caledonian Chambers (6th Floor), 87 Union St ✉ G1 3TA – ✆ 0141 222 2666 – www.grasshoppersglasgow.com – Closed 3 days Christmas*

15 Glasgow

TOWNHOUSE • PERSONALISED Delightful Victorian townhouse on a quiet square. Characterful original features include mosaic floors and ornate cornicing. Spacious bedrooms have top-class furnishings and a subtle Scottish theme. Breakfast is served in your room.

5 rooms ☕ – †£ 90/150 ††£ 120/160

Town plan: B2-s – *15 Woodside Pl. ✉ G3 7QL – ✆ 0141 332 1263 – www.15glasgow.com*

GRANDTULLY

Perth and Kinross – Pop. 750 – Regional map n° **16**-C2

Inn on the Tay

TRADITIONAL CUISINE • FRIENDLY A smart, modern inn on the banks of the Tay. It has a snug bar and a large dining room with superb views over the water. Burgers and gourmet sandwiches fill the lunch menu, while in the evening, satisfying tried-and-tested classics feature. The owners are cheery and welcoming and the bedrooms, comfy and cosy.

Carte £ 21/41

6 rooms ☕ – †£ 55/70 ††£ 110/130

✉ PH9 0PL – ✆ 01887 840760 – www.theinnonthetay.co.uk – Closed 25-26 December

GRANTOWN-ON-SPEY

Highland – Pop. 2 428 – Regional map n° **17**-D2

Dulaig

TRADITIONAL • CLASSIC Small, detached, personally run guesthouse, built in 1910 and tastefully furnished with original Arts and Crafts pieces. Modern fabrics and an uncluttered feel in the comfortable bedrooms. Tea and homemade cake on arrival. Communal breakfasts include home-baked bread and muffins.

3 rooms ☕ – †£ 130/150 ††£ 170/190

Seafield Av ✉ PH26 3JF – ✆ 01479 872065 – www.thedulaig.com – Closed 15 December-6 January

GULLANE

East Lothian – Pop. 2 568 – Regional map n° **15**-D1

Chez Roux

FRENCH • INTIMATE XX Formal restaurant in a classic country house hotel; enjoy an aperitif in the lounge or delightful Jekyll-designed gardens before dining with a view over the Muirfield golf course. Classical French menus have a Roux signature style and feature tried-and-tested classics with a modern edge.

Menu £ 37/40 – Carte £ 43/69

Greywalls Hotel, Duncur Rd, Muirfield ✉ EH31 2EG – Northeast : 0.75 mi by A 198 – ✆ 01620 842144 (bookings essential for non-residents) – www.greywalls.co.uk

La Potinière

TRADITIONAL CUISINE • COSY XX Sweet little restaurant where the two owners share the cooking. The regularly changing menu lists two carefully prepared dishes per course; produce is local or home-grown and their homemade bread is renowned.

Menu £ 22/39

Main St ✉ EH31 2AA – ✆ 01620 843214 (booking essential) – www.lapotiniere.co.uk – Closed January, 24-26 December, Sunday dinner, Monday, Tuesday and bank holidays

Greywalls

COUNTRY HOUSE • CLASSIC A long-standing Edwardian country house by Lutyens, in a superb location beside the Muirfield golf course, overlooking the Firth of Forth. Compact bedrooms are furnished with antiques and the library is particularly cosy. The stunning formal gardens were designed by Jekyll.

23 rooms – †£ 95/400 ††£ 300/420

Duncur Rd, Muirfield ✉ EH31 2EG – Northeast : 0.75 mi by A 198 – ✆ 01620 842144 – www.greywalls.co.uk

Chez Roux – See restaurant listing

HADDINGTON

East Lothian – Pop. 9 064 – Regional map n° **15**-D1

Letham House

COUNTRY HOUSE • CLASSIC A classically proportioned former laird's house dating from 1645. It's been lovingly restored by its current owners in a style which enhances its original features. Luxurious bedrooms have antique furnishings, beautiful fabrics and well-equipped modern bathrooms. Dine communally around a large table: 3 courses of seasonal local produce are tailored to requirements.

5 rooms – †£ 100/150 ††£ 130/215

✉ EH41 3SS – West : 1.25 mi on B 6471 – ✆ 01620 820055 – www.lethamhouse.com

HARRIS

– Highland → See Lewis and Harris (Isle of)

HELENSBURGH

Argyll and Bute – Pop. 14 220 – Regional map n° **16**-B3

Sugar Boat

MODERN BRITISH • BISTRO X This appealing all-day bistro is named after the nearby shipwreck. To the front is a café-style area with a marble-topped island bar; behind is the dining room and an enclosed courtyard. Pared-down dishes feature just a handful of carefully prepared ingredients. Flavours are clear and contrasts well-judged.

Menu £ 14 (weekday lunch) – Carte £ 25/36

30 Colquhoun Sq ✉ G84 8AQ – ✆ 01436 647522 – www.sugarboat.co.uk – Closed 25 December

HIGH BLANTYRE

outh Lanarkshire - Regional map n° **15**-B1

Crossbasket Castle

HISTORIC BUILDING • PERSONALISED With its 15C origins and sumptuous furnishings, this beautiful castle is a popular spot for weddings. There are elegant drawing rooms, a baronial-style library and an ornately decorated dining room. Bedrooms vary in size and are named after former custodians; the Tower Suite is set over numerous floors.

9 rooms - £ 286/300 £ 286/560 - 2 suites

Stoneymeadow Rd ✉ G72 9UE - Southwest : 1 mi by B 7012
- ✆ 01698 829461 - www.crossbasketcastle.com

NNERLEITHEN

he Scottish Borders - Pop. 3 031 - Regional map n° **15**-C2

Caddon View

TOWNHOUSE • PERSONALISED Substantial Victorian house with a large garden and cosy lounge; run by a hospitable couple. Individually decorated bedrooms have modern touches - 'Yarrow' is the most spacious and 'Moorfoot' has the best views. The bright, airy dining room offers a daily set menu of Tweed Valley produce.

8 rooms - £ 50/60 £ 65/120

14 Pirn Rd. ✉ EH44 6HH
- ✆ 01896 830208 - www.caddonview.co.uk
- Closed 24-27 December

NVERGARRY

ighland - Regional map n° **17**-C3

Glengarry Castle

COUNTRY HOUSE • HISTORIC Family-run Victorian house built in a baronial style and named after the ruined castle in its 60 acre grounds. Two large, open-fired sitting rooms are filled with stuffed wild animals. Classical bedrooms are individually designed; some come with four-poster beds. Dine formally, from a 3 course Scottish menu.

26 rooms - £ 85/100 £ 130/270

✉ PH35 4HW - South : 0.75 mi on A 82
- ✆ 01809 501254 - www.glengarry.net
- Closed 5 November-29 March

NVERKEILOR

ngus - Pop. 902 - Regional map n° **16**-D2

Gordon's

MODERN CUISINE • INTIMATE XX A long-standing, passionately run restaurant with stone walls, open fires and exposed beams. The son works in the kitchen and his mother oversees the service. The concise menu lists carefully prepared classics which use local seasonal produce. Bedrooms are smart, modern and well-kept.

Menu £ 65

5 rooms - £ 110 £ 110/165

32 Main St ✉ DD11 5RN
- ✆ 01241 830364 (booking essential) - www.gordonsrestaurant.co.uk - dinner only and Sunday lunch
- Closed January, Monday and Sunday dinner October-April

INVERNESS

Highland – Pop. 48 201 – Regional map n° **17**-C2

Chez Roux

FRENCH • MINIMALIST XX Smart modern restaurant consisting of three rooms their walls hung with photos of the Roux brothers' early days. Polished table are well-spaced and service is professional. The French-inspired menu offers ro bust, flavoursome dishes.

Menu £ 35/38 – Carte £ 35/55

Rocpool Reserve Hotel, 14 Culduthel Rd ✉ IV2 4AG – ✆ 01463 240089 – www.rocpool.com

Rocpool

MODERN BRITISH • FRIENDLY XX Well-run restaurant on the banks of the Rive Ness; close to town and popular with the locals. Wide-ranging menus offer vi brant, colourful dishes that are full of flavour and have a distinct Mediterranea edge. The room has a modish feel.

Menu £ 17 (weekday lunch) – Carte £ 27/48

1 Ness Walk ✉ IV3 5NE – ✆ 01463 717274 – www.rocpoolrestaurant.com – Close 25-26 December, 1-3 January and Sunday

Rocpool Reserve

BUSINESS • DESIGN Stylish boutique hotel with a chic lounge and a sexy split-leve bar. Minimalist bedrooms come with emperor-sized beds and are graded 'Hip', 'Chic 'Decadent' and 'Extra Decadent'; some have terraces, hot tubs or saunas.

11 rooms – †£ 290/595 ††£ 290/595

14 Culduthel Rd ✉ IV2 4AG – ✆ 01463 240089 – www.rocpool.com

Chez Roux – See restaurant listing

Trafford Bank

HISTORIC • PERSONALISED 19C house with a modern, bohemian style. Origina features include a tiled entrance and cast iron banister. Bedrooms come wit iPod docks and decanters of sherry. Breakfast arrives on local china and include haggis and tattie scones.

5 rooms – †£ 100/125 ††£ 110/150

96 Fairfield Rd ✉ IV3 5LL – West : 0.75 mi by A 82 and Harrowden Rd – ✆ 01463 241414 – www.traffordbankguesthouse.co.uk – Closed 13 February-16 March

at Bunchrew West: 3 mi on A862 ✉ Inverness

Bunchrew House

HISTORIC • CLASSIC Impressive 17C Scottish mansion, in a beautiful spot on th shore of Beauly Firth. Clubby, cosy, open-fired bar and intimate, wood-panelled draw ing room. Good-sized, traditionally styled bedrooms; one with a four-poster, anothe with estuary views. Classical restaurant, with a menu to match and garden views.

16 rooms – †£ 145/345 ††£ 145/345

✉ IV3 8TA – ✆ 01463 234917 – www.bunchrewhousehotel.com

ISLAY (Isle of)

Argyll and Bute – Regional map n° **16**-A3

Ballygrant

Kilmeny Country House

TRADITIONAL • PERSONALISED You won't find a warmer welcome than at thi lovely 18C whitewashed house which sits on a 300 acre working farm. After noon tea is served in the antique-furnished sitting room on arrival and the clas sical bedrooms come with thoughtful extras like binoculars, home-baked biscuit and whisky.

5 rooms – †£ 90/125 ††£ 145/175

✉ PA45 7QW – Southwest : 0.5 mi on A 846 – ✆ 01496 840668 – www.kilmeny.co.uk – Closed Christmas-New Year

Bowmore

Harbour Inn

INN • CONTEMPORARY The owners of this pretty inn also run the neighbouring Bowmore Distillery, so the seafood-orientated menus also come with whisky pairings. Stylish bedrooms blend the classic and the contemporary and come with wood panelling, tartan throws and Islay slate bathrooms - some have views over the harbour.

12 rooms - £ 115/135 £ 145/175

The Square PA43 7JR - 01496 810330 - www.harbour-inn.com - Closed 15 November-15 February

Bruichladdich

Kentraw Farmhouse

FAMILY • CONTEMPORARY An 18C former croft with panoramic loch views; the owner was a local gamekeeper for many years and now runs tours around the island. Spacious bedrooms feature solid oak furnishings - ask for one at the front to wake up to the view.

3 rooms - £ 85/120 £ 85/140

PA49 7UN - North : 1 mi on A 847 - 01496 850643 - www.kentraw.com

Port Ellen

Glenegedale House

TRADITIONAL • PERSONALISED This passionately run former factor's house is handy for the airport. It has a boldly decorated lounge, a sunny morning room and stylish bedrooms with funky feature walls. Breakfast is an event - try the porridge with Laphroaig whisky!

4 rooms - £ 100/195 £ 110/195

PA42 7AS - Northwest : 4.75 mi on A 846 - 01496 300400 - www.glenegedalehouse.co.uk - Closed Christmas-New Year

The symbol guarantees a peaceful night's sleep.

JEDBURGH

The Scottish Borders - Pop. 4 030 - Regional map n° **15**-D2

Willow Court

FAMILY • PERSONALISED Contemporary guesthouse overlooking the rooftops. Comfortable ground floor bedrooms offer a light, stylish space and smart bathrooms. Communal breakfasts feature eggs from their hens. Relax in the conservatory or out on the patio.

3 rooms - £ 80/90 £ 80/90

The Friars TD8 6BN - 01835 863702 - www.willowcourtjedburgh.co.uk

JURA (Isle of)

Argyll and Bute - Regional map n° **16**-A3

Craighouse

Jura

FAMILY • CLASSIC An 18C drover's cottage on an unspoilt island, which sits in a beautiful spot beside the distillery, looking out over the bay. Bedrooms are simply furnished and those to the front have the view. Menus are traditional (go for the local lobster or langoustines) - and keep an eye out for the murals in the bar.

17 rooms - £ 70/105 £ 105/135

PA60 7XU - 01496 820243 - www.jurahotel.co.uk - Closed 1 week Christmas

KELSO
The Scottish Borders - Pop. 5 639 - Regional map n° **15**-D2

at Ednam North: 2.25 mi on B6461 ✉ Kelso

Edenwater House
HISTORIC • CLASSIC This delightful house is run by an equally charming couple. Relax in the lovely garden beside the stream or in one of the antique-filled lounges. Bedrooms are individually styled and tastefully furnished. Dine on traditional dishes overlooking the garden or more informally in the wine cellar.

4 rooms - †£ 85/120 ††£ 85/120

✉ *TD5 7QL - Off Stichill rd - ✆ 01573 224070 - www.edenwaterhouse.co.uk - Closed 1 December-22 March*

KILBERRY - Argyll and Bute ➜ See Kintyre (Peninsula)

KILCHRENAN
Argyll and Bute - ✉ Taynuilt - Regional map n° **16**-B2

Roineabhal
COUNTRY HOUSE • COSY This charming stone and log house was built by the owners themselves. Relax in the open-fired lounge or lovely riverside garden. Bedrooms are immaculate - two are up a spiral staircase and all have access to a roll-top bath with views. Local produce is served in the homely breakfast room. (Min. 2 night stay.)

3 rooms - †£ 90/120 ††£ 90/120

✉ *PA35 1HD - ✆ 01866 833207 - www.roineabhal.com - Closed November-Easter*

KILDRUMMY
Aberdeenshire - Regional map n° **16**-D1

Kildrummy Inn
MODERN BRITISH • COSY X Cosy up beside the fire and sample some local whiskies before enjoying dinner in the intimate dining room or bright conservatory. Dishes are original and creative and the sourcing of ingredients is given top priority. Bedrooms have country views and are popular with fishermen, as the inn has a private beat.

Menu £ 35

4 rooms - †£ 89/99 ††£ 89/99

✉ *AB33 8QS - Northeast : 0.5 mi on A 97 - ✆ 01975 571227 (booking essential) - www.kildrummyinn.co.uk - dinner only and Sunday lunch - Closed January and Tuesday*

KILLIECRANKIE - Perth and Kinross ➜ See Pitlochry

KINGUSSIE
Highland - Pop. 1 476 - Regional map n° **17**-C3

Cross at Kingussie
MODERN BRITISH • RUSTIC XX 19C tweed mill in four acres of wooded grounds. Enjoy drinks on the terrace or in the first floor lounge then head to the dining room with its low beams, antiques and ornaments. Attractively presented cooking is modern British/Scottish. Pleasant, pine-furnished bedrooms have thoughtful extras.

Menu £ 30/55

8 rooms - †£ 90/160 ††£ 100/210

Tweed Mill Brae, Ardbroilach Rd ✉ PH21 1LB - ✆ 01540 661166 (booking essential at lunch) - www.thecross.co.uk - Closed January and Christmas

KINTILLO - Perth and Kinross ➜ See Perth

KINTYRE (Peninsula)
Argyll and Bute - Regional map n° **16**-B3

Kilberry

Kilberry Inn

REGIONAL CUISINE • INN A remotely set former croft house whose striking red roof stands out against whitewashed walls. Inside you'll find wooden beams, open fires and a mix of bare and linen-laid tables. Classic dishes are crafted from carefully sourced local produce and meat and fish are smoked in-house. Modern bedrooms are named after nearby islands; one has an outdoor hot tub.

Carte £ 27/39

5 rooms (dinner included) - £ 140 £ 230/235

PA29 6YD - 01880 770223 (booking essential) - www.kilberryinn.com - dinner only and lunch Friday-Sunday - Closed January-mid-March, weekends only November-December, Christmas and Monday

KIRKBEAN

Dumfries and Galloway – Regional map n° **15**-C3

Cavens

TRADITIONAL CUISINE • ELEGANT Start with drinks by the fire in the sitting room of this 18C country house, before dinner in the elegant candle-lit dining room. Classic dishes are full of flavour and prepared with care. Seafood is from the Dumfriesshire coast, meat from the surrounding fields and game from the local hills.

Menu £ 35

Cavens Hotel DG2 8AA - 01387 880234 (bookings essential for non-residents) - www.cavens.com - dinner only - Closed January-February

Cavens

COUNTRY HOUSE • PERSONALISED A wealthy merchant built this attractive country house in 1752, which sits in an enviable position, with views stretching over 20 acres to the Solway Firth. The owners welcome you with afternoon tea beside the fire in the cosy, elegant lounge. Choose from a luxurious 'Estate' or simpler 'Country' bedroom.

6 rooms (dinner included) - £ 150 £ 180/350

DG2 8AA - 01387 880234 - www.cavens.com - Closed January-February

Cavens - See restaurant listing

KIRKCUDBRIGHT

Dumfries and Galloway – Pop. 3 352 – Regional map n° **15**-B3

Selkirk Arms

TRADITIONAL • PERSONALISED This well-run 18C inn sits in a pretty harbour town and is where Robert Burns wrote the Selkirk Grace in 1794 (in what is now Room 9). Comfy bedrooms have boldly coloured fabrics and throws; some are located in the courtyard. The busy bar is hung with paintings of local scenes and menus are extensive.

16 rooms - £ 84/98 £ 98/125 - 2 suites

High St DG6 4JG - 01557 330402 - www.selkirkarmshotel.co.uk - Closed 24-26 December

Gladstone House

TOWNHOUSE • COSY An attractive 18C former merchant's house run by friendly owners. There's a comfy antique-furnished lounge and simple pastel-hued bedrooms with seating areas by the windows where you can take in the rooftop views. Three course dinners use local produce and are tailored around guests' preferences.

3 rooms - £ 70 £ 80

48 High St DG6 4JX - 01557 331734 - www.kirkcudbrightgladstone.com - Closed 2 weeks January-February and Christmas

Glenholme Country House

COUNTRY HOUSE • CLASSIC Take in mountain views from this stone house spacious garden. Inside, it has a cosy, eye-catching style and there's a larg book and music library in place of TVs. Bedrooms are themed around Victoria political figures. The dining room features Chinese furnishings and meals are ta lored to guests' tastes.

4 rooms - £ 110/135 £ 120/135

Tongland Rd DG6 4UU - Northeast : 1 mi on A 711
- 01557 339422 - www.glenholmecountryhouse.com - Closed Christmas-New Year

KYLESKU

Highland - Regional map n° **17**-C1

Kylesku

REGIONAL CUISINE • INN Breathtaking views of Loch Glendhu and the moun tains make this 17C coaching inn an essential stop-off point. Fresh seafood is th way to go, with langoustines and mussels landed 200 yards away. Relax on th waterside terrace then make for one of the cosy bedrooms; two have balconie with panoramic views.

Carte £ 24/93

11 rooms - £ 79/110 £ 120/190

IV27 4HW - 01971 502231 - www.kyleskuhotel.co.uk - Closed late November-mid-February

LEITH - City of Edinburgh

➜ See Edinburgh

nage source/hemis.fr

LEWIS AND HARRIS (ISLE OF)

Vestern Isles - Regional map n° **17**-B1

.EWIS

Vestern Isles - Regional map n° **17**-B1

3ack

Broad Bay House

LUXURY • CONTEMPORARY Delightful guesthouse with a decked terrace and a garden leading down to the beach. Luxurious interior features an open-plan, Scandinavian-style lounge and a dining area with panoramic views. Modern, oak-furnished bedrooms come with super king sized beds, great extras and sliding doors onto private terraces.

4 rooms - £ 139/149 £ 179/189

HS2 0LQ - Northeast : 1 mi on B 895 - 01851 820990 - www.broadbayhouse.co.uk - Closed October-March

HARRIS

Vestern Isles - Regional map n° **17**-A2

3orve

Pairc an t-Srath

FAMILY • PERSONALISED Welcoming guesthouse on a working croft, with views out over the Sound of Taransay. Comfy, open-fired lounge has a chaise longue; the intimate dining room offers delicious home-cooked meals and wonderful vistas. Extremely friendly owners serve tea and homemade cake on arrival. Immaculate bedrooms feature smart oak furniture and brightly coloured Harris Tweed fabrics.

4 rooms - £ 54/84 £ 108

HS3 3HT - 01859 550386 - www.paircant-srath.co.uk - Closed 2 weeks October-November and Christmas-New Year

LEWISTON

Highland - Regional map n° **17**-C2

Loch Ness Inn

TRADITIONAL CUISINE • INN There are two parts to this pub: the small Brewery Bar, home to locals and walkers fresh from the Great Glen Way; and the open-plan Lewiston restaurant with its wood burning stove and bright timbered beams. Hearty, robust, flavoursome dishes champion Scottish produce. Bedrooms are spacious and comfortable.

Menu £ 17 (lunch and early dinner) - Carte £ 19/42

11 rooms - £ 89/130 £ 112/150

IV63 6UW - 01456 450991 - www.staylochness.co.uk - Closed 25 December

LINLITHGOW

West Lothian – Pop. 13 462 – Regional map n° **15**-C1

Champany Inn

MEATS AND GRILLS • INTIMATE XXX Set in a collection of whitewashed cottage – the traditional restaurant was once a flour mill, hence its unusual shape. The fo cus is on meat and wine, with 21-day aged Aberdeen Angus beef a speciality There's also a well-stocked wine shop, a more laid-back 'Chop and Ale House and 16 tartan-themed bedrooms.

Menu £ 28/45 – Carte £ 48/76

16 rooms – £ 99/149 £ 109/149

Champany ✉ EH49 7LU – Northeast : 2 mi on A 803 at junction with A 904 – ✆ 01506 834532 – www.champany.com – Closed 25-26 December, 1-2 January, Saturday lunch and Sunday

Arden House

LUXURY • MODERN The welcoming owner pays great attention to detail at thi purpose-built guesthouse beside a 105 acre sheep farm. Spacious, tastefull styled bedrooms boast modern slate-floored bathrooms and plenty of extras lik fresh flowers and magazines. The wide-ranging breakfasts are a highlight.

3 rooms – £ 78/120 £ 96/126

Belsyde ✉ EH49 6QE – Southwest : 2.25 mi on A 706 – ✆ 01506 670172 – www.ardencountryhouse.com – Closed 25-26 December and restricted opening in winter

LOCHALINE

Highland – Regional map n° **17**-B3

Whitehouse

MODERN BRITISH • COSY X Adjoining the village shop in a remote coastal hamle is this unassuming restaurant decorated with nautical memorabilia. A blackboar lists 6 constantly evolving dishes – at lunch pick 2, at dinner 4 or 6. Dishes ar accomplished and beautifully presented; ingredients are from the surrounding es tate and coast.

Menu £ 25/65

✉ PA80 5XT – ✆ 01967 421777 – www.thewhitehouserestaurant.co.uk – Closed November-Easter, Sunday and Monday

LOCHINVER

Highland – Pop. 470 – Regional map n° **17**-C1

Chez Roux

FRENCH • INTIMATE XX Romantic restaurant hung with photos of the eponymou brothers, where well-spaced tables take in fantastic bay and mountain views Regularly changing, classical French menus make use of the wealth of produc on their doorstep.

Menu £ 47 – bar lunch Monday-Saturday

Inver Lodge Hotel, Iolaire Rd ✉ IV27 4LU – ✆ 01571 844496 (bookings essential for non-residents) – www.inverlodge.com – Closed November-April

Caberfeidh

SEAFOOD • COSY Its name means stag's antlers and in the early 1900s it wa once Mrs McKenzie's House and Shop (see the plans on the walls). Local drinker occupy the rustic bar, while the waterside restaurant is filled with diners. The twic daily blackboard menu is guided largely by what the local fishermen have landed

Carte £ 25/43

Main St ✉ IV27 4JY – ✆ 01571 844321 (booking essential) – www.thecaberfeidh.co.uk – Closed January, 25 December, Monday in winter and lunch Tuesday-Wednesday

Inver Lodge

TRADITIONAL • PERSONALISED Superbly located on a hillside, overlooking a quiet fishing village. Smart bedrooms have good mod cons and great bay and island views. Relax in the open-fired lounge or billiard room - or try one of their whiskies in the elegant bar.

21 rooms - £ 180/225 £ 260/560

Iolaire Rd IV27 4LU - 01571 844496 - www.inverlodge.com - Closed November-April

Chez Roux - See restaurant listing

Albannach

TRADITIONAL • PERSONALISED Curl up with a book in the cosy snug or enjoy views over the mature grounds from the sun lounge of this 19C gabled house, which looks out over both the mountains and the bay. Modern bedrooms are a contrast to the more traditional guest areas; the best room boasts a private terrace and a hot tub.

5 rooms - £ 115/130 £ 155/170

Baddidarroch IV27 4LP - West : 1 mi by Baddidarroch rd - 01571 844407 - www.thealbannach.co.uk - Restricted opening in winter

LUSS

Argyll and Bute - Pop. 402 - Regional map n° **16**-B2

Loch Lomond Arms

INN • COSY Retaining the warmth and character of an old inn, this hotel offers individual, contemporary bedrooms. 'Lomond' and 'Colquhoun' are the most luxurious: the former has a four-poster bed; the latter, superb views. Wide-ranging menu: dine in the open-fired bar, the relaxed dining room or the more formal library.

15 rooms - £ 79/150 £ 89/250

Main Rd G83 8NY - 01436 860420 - www.lochlomondarmshotel.com

MELFORT

Argyll and Bute - Regional map n° **16**-B2

Melfort House

COUNTRY HOUSE • PERSONALISED Enjoy homemade cake in the splendid sitting room or out on the lovely terrace looking over the loch. Bedrooms are furnished with antiques and rich fabrics and one has wonderful water views. The impressive Victorian gardens include two 150yr old monkey puzzle trees. Communal dinners are served by arrangement.

3 rooms - £ 70/100 £ 120/140

PA34 4XD - 01852 200326 - www.melforthouse.co.uk - Closed Christmas and New Year

MELROSE

The Scottish Borders - Pop. 2 307 - Regional map n° **15**-D2

Burts

INN • CONTEMPORARY Characterful 18C coaching inn on the main square; run by the same family for two generations. Appealing bedrooms blend contemporary furnishings with original features. The cosy bar serves old classics and is a hit with the locals, while the formal dining room offers a mix of modern and traditional dishes.

20 rooms - £ 78/89 £ 130/165

Market Sq. TD6 9PL - 01896 822285 - www.burtshotel.co.uk - Closed 7-21 February and 25-26 December

at Gattonside North: 2 mi by B6374 on B6360 ✉ Melrose

Seasons

TRADITIONAL CUISINE • NEIGHBOURHOOD X A small Borders village plays hos to this friendly restaurant. As its name suggests, cooking is driven by the season – the chef works closely with local suppliers and even forages himself. Alongside the ever-changing blackboards they offer a menu of perennial favourites such a chargrilled steaks.

Menu £ 24 (lunch and early dinner) – Carte £ 19/47

Main St ✉ TD6 9NP – ✆ 01896 823217 – www.seasonsborders.co.uk – Closed January, Monday-Tuesday and lunch Wednesday-Thursday

Fauhope House

HISTORIC • PERSONALISED Charming 19C house by the Tweed, overlooking Melrose – its delightful gardens stretch for 15 acres. The quirkily decorated room display an eclectic mix of art and antiques. Bedrooms are very different; som have bold colour schemes.

3 rooms – £ 90/113 £ 140/160

✉ TD6 9LU – East : 0.25 mi by B 6360 taking unmarked lane to the right of Monkswood Rd at edge of village – ✆ 01896 823184 – www.fauhopehouse.com

MOFFAT

Dumfries and Galloway – Pop. 2 582 – Regional map n° **15**-C2

Brodies

REGIONAL CUISINE • NEIGHBOURHOOD XX Large, laid-back, modern eatery tha caters for all appetites – serving snacks, light lunches, afternoon tea, more substantial dinners and all-day brunch on Sundays. Cooking has a traditional bas and features fresh, local ingredients.

Carte £ 24/39

1-2 Altrive Pl, Holm St ✉ DG10 9EB – ✆ 01683 222870 – www.brodiesofmoffat.co.uk – Closed 25-27 December

Lime Tree

TRADITIONAL CUISINE • COSY XX Small hotel restaurant with a feature fireplace attractive marquetry and a bay window looking down the valley. Good value menus feature well-judged, attractively presented classics packed with flavour.

Menu £ 30

Hartfell House Hotel, Hartfell Cres. ✉ DG10 9AL – ✆ 01683 220153 (booking essential) – www.hartfellhouse.co.uk – dinner only – Closed 1 week January, 1 week October, Christmas, Sunday and Monday

Hartfell House

TOWNHOUSE • CLASSIC Keenly run house built in 1866 and located in a peacefu crescent. Original features include parquet floors and ornate cornicing. Bedroom are spacious and traditional and the comfy first floor drawing room has a southerly aspect.

7 rooms – £ 50/53 £ 75/80

Hartfell Cres. ✉ DG10 9AL – ✆ 01683 220153 – www.hartfellhouse.co.uk – Closed 1 week January, 1 week October and Christmas

Lime Tree – See restaurant listing

Bridge House

TRADITIONAL • PERSONALISED A classic-looking bay-windowed house in a quiet residential area – the front rooms have views over the hills and valley. Spotlessly-kept bedrooms boast comfy Hypnos mattresses; Munro has a four-poster bed and a great outlook.

7 rooms – £ 60/65 £ 80/115

Well Rd ✉ DG10 9JT – East : 0.75 mi by Selkirk rd (A 708) taking left hand turn before bridge – ✆ 01683 220558 – www.bridgehousemoffat.scot

MUIR OF ORD

Highland – Pop. 2 555 – Regional map n° **17**-C2

Dower House

TRADITIONAL • CLASSIC Personally run, part-17C house with charming mature gardens. Characterful guest areas include an antique-furnished dining room and a small, open-fired lounge with fresh flowers and shelves crammed with books. Comfy bedrooms; one with a bay window overlooking the garden. Traditional, daily set menu.

3 rooms – £ 120/135 £ 145/165

Highfield ✉ IV6 7XN – North : 1 mi on A 862 – ☎ 01463 870090 – www.thedowerhouse.co.uk – Closed November-March

MULL (Isle of)

Argyll and Bute – Pop. 2 800 – Regional map n° **16**-A2

Craignure

Pennygate Lodge

MODERN BRITISH • CONTEMPORARY DÉCOR XX Those arriving on the island by ferry should head straight for this 19C former manse on the shore-side. Island ingredients features on an ambitious modern menu where dishes deliver contrasting flavours, textures and temperatures. Most of the stylishly understated bedrooms have a sea view.

Carte £ 32/52

6 rooms – £ 95/160 £ 115/190

✉ PA65 6AY – ☎ 01680 812333 (bookings essential for non-residents) – www.pennygatelodge.scot – dinner only – Closed January and Christmas-New Year

Fionnphort

Ninth Wave

SEAFOOD • CONTEMPORARY DÉCOR XX This remotely set modern restaurant started life as a crofter's bothy and both the décor and the cooking reflect the owners' travels. Seafood plays a key role, with crab, lobster and other shellfish caught by Mr Lamont himself.

Menu £ 48/68

Bruach Mhor ✉ PA66 6BL – East : 0.75 mi by A 849 – ☎ 01681 700757 (booking essential) – www.ninthwaverestaurant.co.uk – dinner only – Closed November-April, Monday and Tuesday

Tiroran

Tiroran House

COUNTRY HOUSE • PERSONALISED The beautiful drive over to this remotely set, romantic Victorian house is all part of the charm. Stylish, antique-furnished bedrooms come with plenty of extras and two lovely lounges look out over 56 acres of grounds which lead down to a loch. Dine from a concise à la carte in the conservatory or cosy dining room. The welcoming owner encourages a house party atmosphere.

10 rooms – £ 170 £ 195/235

✉ PA69 6ES – ☎ 01681 705232 – www.tiroran.com – Closed November-mid-March

Tobermory

Highland Cottage

TRADITIONAL CUISINE • FAMILY XX Long-standing, personally run restaurant in an intimate cottage, where family antiques and knick-knacks abound. Classical linen-laid dining room and a homely lounge. Traditional daily menu with a seafood base features plenty of local produce. Bedrooms are snug and individually styled.

Menu £ 48

6 rooms – £ 125/180 £ 150/180

Breadalbane St ✉ PA75 6PD – via B 8073 – ☎ 01688 302030 (bookings essential for non-residents) – www.highlandcottage.co.uk – dinner only – Closed 15 October-1 April

MUTHILL

Perth and Kinross – Pop. 747 – Regional map n° **16**-2

Barley Bree

CLASSIC CUISINE • RUSTIC The concise, daily changing menu champions loca Scottish produce and creative dishes have a classical base and a modern twist Have pre-dinner drinks in the modern lounge-bar before dining in the rustic restaurant decorated with fishing memorabilia. Bedrooms are bright and modern.

Menu £ 18 (weekday lunch) – Carte £ 43/50 **s**

6 rooms – £ 70/110 £ 99/160

6 Willoughby St PH5 2AB – 01764 681451 – www.barleybree.com – Closed 1 week July, Christmas, Monday and Tuesday

NAIRN

Highland – Pop. 9 773 – Regional map n° **17**-D2

Boath House

HISTORIC • PERSONALISED An elegant 1825 neo-classical mansion framed by Corinthian columns. Inside it cleverly blends original features and contemporary furnishings, and most of the modern art is for sale. Bedrooms are elegant and intimate and some have views over the lake. Traditional Scottish menus showcase garden produce and wood-fired pizzas are a speciality in Kale Yard.

9 rooms – £ 190/260 £ 260/365

Auldearn IV12 5TE – East : 2 mi on A 96 – 01667 454896 – www.boath-house.com – Closed 23-27 December

Cawdor House

TOWNHOUSE • PERSONALISED 19C former manse run by friendly, knowledgeable owners. The cosy lounge has a marble fireplace and bedrooms are clean and uncluttered; original features blend with contemporary styling. Enjoy local bacon and sausages at breakfast.

6 rooms – £ 72/95 £ 85/120

7 Cawdor St IV12 4QD – 01667 455855 – www.cawdorhousenairn.co.uk

NEWPORT-ON-TAY

Fife – Pop. 4 250 – Regional map n° **16**-C2

The Newport

MODERN BRITISH • COSY The Newport is the place to come for cheery, upbeat service in a great waterside location. It serves colourful, imaginative small plates themed around 'land', 'sea', 'garden' and 'ground', which display modern techniques and are presented in a attractive manner.

Carte £ 18/36

4 rooms – £ 119/160 £ 119/160

1 High St. DD6 8AB – 01382 541449 (booking essential at dinner) – www.thenewportrestaurant.co.uk – Closed 24-26 December, 1-8 January, Sunday dinner, Monday and lunch Tuesday and in winter dinner Tuesday and lunch Wednesday

NIGG → See Tain

NORTH BERWICK

East Lothian – Pop. 6 605 – Regional map n° **15**-D1

Glebe House

FAMILY • PERSONALISED Spacious, welcoming Georgian house with attractive walled gardens and views over the town and sea. It's beautifully furnished inside with good quality fabrics and antiques. Classically styled bedrooms have lots of extra touches.

3 rooms – £ 95/140 £ 95/140

Law Rd EH39 4PL – 01620 892608 – www.glebehouse-nb.co.uk – Closed Christmas-New Year and restricted opening in winter

NORTH QUEENSFERRY

ife - Pop. 1 076 - Regional map n° **16**-C3

Wee Restaurant

TRADITIONAL CUISINE • BISTRO A likeable quarry-floored restaurant in the shadow of the Forth Rail Bridge; as its name suggests, it's small and cosy. Fresh Scottish ingredients are served in neatly presented, classical combinations. Lunch represents the best value.

Menu £ 20 (weekdays)/36 **s**

17 Main St ✉ KY11 1JT - ✆ 01383 616263 - www.theweerestaurant.co.uk - Closed 25-26 December, 1-2 January and Monday

OBAN

Argyll and Bute - Pop. 8 574 - Regional map n° **16**-B2

Etive

MODERN BRITISH • COLOURFUL Run by two passionate young owners, this brightly coloured restaurant takes its name from the loch where the business was originally located. Ingredients from the Scottish land and lochs underpin dishes that are carefully cooked, full of flavour and classically based with a subtle modernity.

Carte £ 26/48

43 Stevenson St ✉ PA34 5NA - ✆ 01631 564899 - www.etiverestaurant.co.uk - Closed Monday and Tuesday

Manor House

TRADITIONAL • CLASSIC Take in stunning bay views from this charmingly old world dower house, which was once part of the Argyll Estate. It's classically furnished throughout, with a gentile feel; choose a Superior room with a view. Enjoy afternoon tea on the terrace, a drink in the cosy bar and dinner in the intimate restaurant.

11 rooms - †£ 125/185 ††£ 135/270

Gallanach Rd. ✉ PA34 4LS - ✆ 01631 562087 - www.manorhouseoban.com - Closed 25-26 December

Glenburnie House

TOWNHOUSE • PERSONALISED A bay-windowed house on the main esplanade, affording great bay and island views. Period features include a delightful staircase and etched glass windows, and antiques abound. Good-sized bedrooms have a subtle contemporary style.

12 rooms - †£ 45/75 ††£ 100/150

Corran Esplanade ✉ PA34 5AQ - ✆ 01631 562089 - www.glenburnie.co.uk - Closed December-February

ONICH

Highland - Regional map n° **17**-B3

Lochleven Seafood Café

SEAFOOD • SIMPLE This laid-back seafood restaurant is part of a family business that started with the shellfish shop next door. It's superbly set on the loch shore and offers stunning water and mountain views. West Coast fish is listed on the blackboards and shellfish comes from the seawater tanks next door.

Carte £ 21/47 **s**

Lochleven ✉ PH33 6SA - Southeast : 6.5 mi by A 82 on B 863 - ✆ 01855 821048 - www.lochlevenseafoodcafe.co.uk - Closed November-March

SCOTLAND

PEAT INN

Fife – Regional map n° **16**-D2

The Peat Inn (Geoffrey Smeddle)

CLASSIC CUISINE • CONTEMPORARY DÉCOR XXX Whitewashed former pub; now a contemporary restaurant run by a charming team. The smart lounge still has its original log fireplace; ask for a table overlooking the floodlit gardens. Accomplished, classical cooking has subtle modern touches and local ingredients are to the fore. Stylish, split-level bedrooms have plenty of extras and breakfast is served in your room.

→ Kedgeree of Arbroath smokie with pearl barley, Exmoor caviar and poached quail's egg. Roast loin of venison with grapes and celeriac & hazelnut purée. Croustillant of rhubarb & custard with stem ginger ice cream.

Menu £ 25/50 – Carte £ 35/64

8 rooms – †£ 205/225 ††£ 225/250

KY15 5LH – 01334 840206 (booking essential) – www.thepeatinn.co.uk – Closed 10 days January, 4 days Christmas, Sunday and Monday

PEEBLES

The Scottish Borders – Pop. 8 376 – Regional map n° **15**-C2

Osso

MODERN CUISINE • FRIENDLY X By day, this is a bustling coffee shop serving a bewildering array of light snacks and daily specials; come evening, it transforms into a more sophisticated restaurant offering a great value, regularly changing menu of well-presented, flavoursome dishes. Service is friendly and attentive.

Menu £ 28 (dinner) – Carte lunch £ 29/49

Innerleithen Rd EH45 8BA – 01721 724477 – www.ossorestaurant.com – Closed 1 January, 25 December, dinner Tuesday-Wednesday in winter except December and dinner Sunday-Monday

PERTH

Perth and Kinross – Pop. 46 970 – Regional map n° **16**-C2

Deans

TRADITIONAL CUISINE • FRIENDLY XX This is a real family affair, with the father and one son in the kitchen and the mother and the other son out front. It's a smart, modern place with red furnishings and a cocktail bar. Ambitious dishes feature many ingredients.

Menu £ 19/22 – Carte £ 27/46

77-79 Kinnoull St PH1 5EZ – 01738 643377 – www.letseatperth.co.uk – Closed 2 weeks January, 1 week November and Monday

63@Parklands

MODERN BRITISH • INTIMATE XX An intimate, conservatory-style hotel restaurant decorated in muted shades, with fish-eye mirrors and stag antler lights. Creative dishes are well-presented and showcase the best of Scottish ingredients.

Menu £ 40 – Carte £ 26/52

Parklands Hotel, 2 St Leonard's Bank PH2 8EB – 01738 622451 – www.63atparklands.com – dinner only – Closed 26 December-7 January and Monday-Wednesday

63 Tay Street

MODERN BRITISH • INTIMATE XX A well-established riverside restaurant with grey tongue and groove panelling, burgundy chairs and striking exposed stone effect wallpaper. Tersely described modern dishes take their influences from around the globe.

Menu £ 26 (lunch and early dinner)/35

63 Tay St PH2 8NN – 01738 441451 – www.63taystreet.com – Closed 1-8 January, 1-9 July, 26-31 December, Sunday, Monday and lunch Tuesday-Wednesday

Pig Halle

FRENCH • BISTRO X Lively bistro; its square, marble-floored room tightly packed with tables and dominated by a mirror stencilled with a Paris Metro map. Menus list Gallic favourites. The adjoining deli serves wood-fired pizzas and tasty pastries.

Menu £ 17 (lunch) – Carte £ 25/37

38 South St ✉ PH2 8PG – ✆ 01738 248784 – www.pighalle.co.uk – Closed 26 December and 1 January

Parklands

BUSINESS • MODERN A personally run, extended Georgian house with a contemporary interior. Spacious bedrooms have good facilities and sizeable bathrooms; those to the front have pleasant views over the park. Dine in informal No.1 The Bank or in intimate 63@Parklands.

15 rooms – †£ 95/165 ††£ 125/210

2 St Leonard's Bank ✉ PH2 8EB – ✆ 01738 622451 – www.theparklandshotel.com – Closed 26 December-7 January

63@Parklands – See restaurant listing

Townhouse

TOWNHOUSE • ELEGANT This creamwashed terraced house overlooks the park and is well-run by two experienced owners. Ornate 1830s coving and marble fireplaces still remain and bedrooms are furnished in a period style, with plenty of antiques.

5 rooms – †£ 65/95 ††£ 90/165

17 Marshall Pl ✉ PH2 8AG – ✆ 01738 446179 – www.thetownhouseperth.co.uk – Closed 20-26 December

at Kintillo Southeast: 4.5 mi off A912

Roost

MODERN BRITISH • INTIMATE XX A converted brick hen house in the heart of the village, with a smart modern interior and galline references in its décor. Service is engaging and eager to please. The experienced chef prepares refined, classical dishes with some restrained modern touches; meats are local and veg is from the garden.

Carte £ 30/65

Forgandenny Rd ✉ PH2 9AZ – ✆ 01738 812111 – www.theroostrestaurant.co.uk – Closed 1-16 January, 25-26 December, Monday, Tuesday and dinner Sunday

PITLOCHRY

Perth and Kinross – Pop. 2 776 – Regional map n° **16**-C2

Sandemans

MODERN CUISINE • INTIMATE XXX This intimate wood-panelled hotel restaurant comprises just 8 tables and is the perfect place for celebrating an occasion. A tasting menu showcases top Scottish ingredients from mountain to coast and cooking is clean and precise.

Menu £ 75 – tasting menu only

Fonab Castle Hotel, Foss Rd ✉ PH16 5ND – ✆ 01796 470140 (booking essential) – www.fonabcastlehotel.com – dinner only – Closed Sunday and Monday

Fonab Brasserie

MODERN CUISINE • BRASSERIE XX Start with a cocktail in the 'Bar in the Air', then head back down to the chic hotel restaurant and terrace with their panoramic loch views. The concise menu offers modern classics and grills. Service is friendly.

Carte £ 27/79

Fonab Castle Hotel, Foss Rd ✉ PH16 5ND – ✆ 01796 470140 – www.fonabcastlehotel.com

East Haugh House

REGIONAL CUISINE • INTIMATE XX Appealing dishes use top Scottish produc and there's a focus on fish, game and steak. Dine amongst fishing memorabilia i the charming bar or in the bright, slightly more formal restaurant of this 17C hote

Carte £ 22/47

East Haugh House Hotel, ✉ PH16 5TE – Southeast : 1.75 mi off A 924 (Perth Rd) – ✆ 01796 473121 – www.easthaugh.co.uk – dinner only and lunch Saturday-Sunday – Closed 1 week Christmas

Fonab Castle

HISTORIC • CONTEMPORARY This 19C baronial castle offers superb views ove the loch to the hills beyond. Bedrooms have a subtly traditional feel and smal bathrooms; the 'Woodland' rooms are more modern and have terraces or balco nies.

42 rooms – †£ 185/350 ††£ 195/375 – 4 suites

Foss Rd ✉ PH16 5ND – ✆ 01796 470140 – www.fonabcastlehotel.com

Fonab Brasserie • **Sandemans** – See restaurant listing

Green Park

TRADITIONAL • CLASSIC Long-standing, family-run hotel on the shore of Loc Faskally; many of its guests return year after year. Well-appointed lounges offe stunning loch and countryside views. Bedrooms vary in style; the largest an most modern are in the newer wing. A traditional dinner is included in the pric of the room.

51 rooms (dinner included) – †£ 89/99 ††£ 178/198

Clunie Bridge Rd ✉ PH16 5JY – ✆ 01796 473248 – www.thegreenpark.co.uk – Closed 17-27 December

Craigmhor Lodge and Courtyard

COUNTRY HOUSE • MODERN Spacious, cosy house just out of town, with an air breakfast room where local fruits, bacon and sausages are served. Well-kep modern bedrooms are set in the courtyard – some have balconies. Supper ham pers can be delivered to your room.

12 rooms – †£ 110/160 ††£ 125/175

27 West Moulin Rd ✉ PH16 5EF – ✆ 01796 472123 – www.craigmhorlodge.co.uk – Closed Christmas

East Haugh House

TRADITIONAL • PERSONALISED A family-run, 17C turreted stone house in tw acres of gardens. Cosy, traditionally appointed bedrooms are named after fishin flies and are split between the house, a former bothy and the old gatehouse.

14 rooms – †£ 85/200 ††£ 85/200

✉ PH16 5TE – Southeast : 1.75 mi off A 924 (Perth Rd) – ✆ 01796 473121 – www.easthaugh.co.uk – Closed 1 week Christmas

East Haugh House – See restaurant listing

Craigatin House and Courtyard

TOWNHOUSE • MODERN Built in 1820 as a doctor's house; now a stylish boutiqu hotel. The stunning open-plan lounge and breakfast room centres around a woo burning stove and overlooks the garden. Bedrooms are modern and minimalist.

14 rooms – †£ 100/128 ††£ 110/138

165 Atholl Rd ✉ PH16 5QL – ✆ 01796 472478 – www.craigatinhouse.co.uk – Closed Christmas

Northlands

TOWNHOUSE • PERSONALISED This guesthouse, set high above the town, wa originally named after the large sentinel stone in its grounds. You'll receive a warm welcome and no detail is forgotten; it's tastefully furnished with antique and Laura Ashley fabrics.

3 rooms – †£ 95/110 ††£ 105/120

Lettoch Rd ✉ PH16 5AZ – ✆ 01796 474131 – www.northlandsbandb.com – Closed January-February

t Killiecrankie Northwest: 4 mi by A924 and B8019 on B8079 ✉ Pitlochry

Killiecrankie

TRADITIONAL • CLASSIC A whitewashed former vicarage built in 1840 and set in 4.5 acres of mature rhododendron-filled grounds, with a small kitchen garden to the rear. There's a charming open-fired lounge, a snug bar and well-appointed bedrooms which offer everything you might want, including a hot water bottle. Choose between light suppers and traditional dinners. Service is excellent.

10 rooms (dinner included) – †£ 165 ††£ 280/335

✉ PH16 5LG – ✆ 01796 473220 – www.killiecrankiehotel.co.uk – Closed 3 January-22 March

PLOCKTON

ighland – Regional map n° **17**-B2

Plockton Hotel

TRADITIONAL CUISINE • INN A one-time ships' chandlery with a distinctive black exterior and stunning views over Loch Carron to the mountains beyond. Cooking is honest and hearty with a strong Scottish influence, so expect herring in oatmeal or haggis with whisky – and don't miss the Plockton prawns. Simple, comfortable bedrooms.

Carte £ 15/42

15 rooms – †£ 50/100 ††£ 100/150

41 Harbour St ✉ IV52 8TN – ✆ 01599 544274 – www.plocktonhotel.co.uk

POOLEWE

ighland – Regional map n° **17**-B2

Pool House

FAMILY • PERSONALISED This family-run former fishing lodge sits in a lovely spot on the water's edge and was the naval HQ of the arctic convoys in WWII; take in the view from the delightful lounge. Bedrooms are all uniquely themed suites – 'Ashanti' features a 19C Chinese marriage bed. Light suppers are served by arrangement.

3 rooms – †£ 175/270 ††£ 200/295

✉ IV22 2LD – ✆ 01445 781272 – www.pool-house.co.uk – Closed November-March

PORT CHARLOTTE - Argyll and Bute → See Islay (Isle of)

PORT ELLEN - Argyll and Bute → See Islay (Isle of)

PORTPATRICK

Dumfries and Galloway – ✉ Stranraer – Pop. 534 – Regional map n° **15**-A3

Knockinaam Lodge

CLASSIC CUISINE • INTIMATE XX Located within a delightful lodge, a traditionally furnished, smartly dressed dining room with delightful sea views (ask for table 5). The four course set menu evolves with the seasons and offers good quality produce – often from their own gardens – cooked in classic combinations.

Menu £ 33/70 – tasting menu only

Knockinaam Lodge Hotel, ✉ DG9 9AD – Southeast : 5 mi by A 77 off B 7042 – ✆ 01776 810471 (bookings essential for non-residents) – www.knockinaamlodge.com

Knockinaam Lodge

COUNTRY HOUSE · PERSONALISED A charming former hunting lodge in a delightfully secluded private cove, with gardens leading down to the sea. Sample their malts in the wood-panelled bar or relax in the country house style drawing room. Bedrooms are furnished with antiques – 'Churchill' boasts a century-old bathtub. Service is detailed.

10 rooms (dinner included) – £ 155/295 £ 240/390

DG9 9AD – Southeast : 5 mi by A 77 off B 7042 – 01776 810471 – www.knockinaamlodge.com

Knockinaam Lodge – See restaurant listing

PORT APPIN

Argyll and Bute – Appin – Regional map n° **16**-B2

Airds

MODERN BRITISH · ELEGANT XX An intimate, candlelit country house restaurant with superb loch and mountain views. Classic dishes are presented with a modern edge and much use is made of west coast seafood and local meats, with game a highlight. Don't miss the Mallaig crab or the scallops – and ensure you ask for a table in the window!

Menu £ 58 (dinner) – Carte lunch £ 21/48

Airds Hotel, PA38 4DF – 01631 730236 (bookings essential for non-residents) – www.airds-hotel.com – Closed 28 November-13 December and Monday-Tuesday November-January

Airds

LUXURY · PERSONALISED A characterful former ferryman's cottage fronted by colourful planters and offering lovely loch and mountain views. Two sumptuous antique-furnished sitting rooms are filled with fresh flowers and magazines. Bedrooms offer understated luxury – ask for one at the front with a waterside view.

11 rooms – £ 175/365 £ 189/379

PA38 4DF – 01631 730236 – www.airds-hotel.com – Closed 28 November-13 December and Monday-Tuesday November-January

Airds – See restaurant listing

PORTREE – Highland → See Skye (Isle of)

RANNOCH STATION

Perth and Kinross – Regional map n° **16**-B2

Moor of Rannoch

FAMILY · COSY This 19C hotel is perched high on the moor and is the ultimate in hiking getaways. The views are delightful, the whole place has a serene feel and wildlife is in abundance. Bedrooms are cosy and the open-fired guest areas come with jigsaws instead of TVs. Rustic home cooking utilises Scottish ingredients.

5 rooms – £ 125/180 £ 125/180

PH17 2QA – 01882 633238 – www.moorofrannoch.co.uk – Closed November-mid-February

RATHO

City of Edinburgh – Pop. 1 634 – Regional map n° **15**-C1

Bridge Inn

MODERN CUISINE · PUB A friendly pub on the tow path between Edinburgh and the Falkirk Wheel. The fruit and veg comes from their walled garden, the pork is from their pigs and the eggs are from their chickens and ducks. For a treat, book the private room on their restaurant barge. All of the cosy bedrooms have water views.

Carte £ 19/45

4 rooms – £ 80/170 £ 80/180

27 Baird Rd EH28 8RU – 0131 333 1320 – www.bridgeinn.com – Closed 25 December

ST ANDREWS

Fife – Pop. 16 870 – Regional map n° **16**-D2

Adamson

MEATS AND GRILLS • **BRASSERIE** XX A stylish brasserie and cocktail bar set within a house once owned by eminent photographer John Adamson (it was also later the town's Post Office). The wide-ranging menu of tasty dishes includes steaks from the Josper grill.

Menu £ 13 (lunch and early dinner) – Carte £ 23/55

127 South St ✉ KY16 9UH – ✆ 01334 479191 – www.theadamson.com – Closed 25-26 December and 1 January

Seafood Ristorante

SEAFOOD • **DESIGN** XX This striking glass cube offers commanding bay views and is perfect for watching the setting sun. The experienced team bring a modern Italian twist to seafood: choose from cicchetti, fish platters, hearty stews and homemade pastas.

Menu £ 20 (lunch) – Carte £ 38/64

Bruce Embankment, The Scores ✉ KY16 9AB – ✆ 01334 479475 – www.theseafoodristorante.com – Closed 24-26 December, 1 and 7-14 January

Grange Inn

TRADITIONAL CUISINE • **COSY** X A former pub, atop a hill, with great views over the bay. Have an aperitif beside the fire, then head for the stone-walled restaurant with its huge stag's head. The experienced chef serves a menu of tasty, well-prepared classics.

Menu £ 20/45

Grange Rd ✉ KY16 8LJ – Southeast : 1.75 mi by A 917 – ✆ 01334 472670 (booking essential) – www.thegrangeinn.com – Closed 3 weeks January, Sunday dinner and Monday

Old Course H. Golf Resort & Spa

LUXURY • **CLASSIC** A vast resort hotel with an impressive spa, set on a world-famous golf course overlooking the bay. Luxurious guest areas have a subtle Scottish theme and bedrooms are chic, sumptuous and well-equipped. Try their bespoke ales in the Jigger Inn then dine on modern-classics, Josper-grilled meats or seafood.

144 rooms – †£ 197/380 ††£ 292/427 – 15 suites

Old Station Rd ✉ KY16 9SP – West : 0.75 mi off A 91 – ✆ 01334 474371 – www.oldcoursehotel.co.uk

Rusacks

LUXURY • **PERSONALISED** The oldest hotel in St Andrews sits in a commanding position overlooking the 18th green of the Old Course. Original 1846 columns feature in the lobby and a huge array of paintings pay homage to golfing greats. Bedrooms are stylish; choose one with a view. Dine in the pub or formal restaurant.

70 rooms – †£ 199/299 ††£ 199/299 – 4 suites

Pilmour Links ✉ KY16 9JQ – ✆ 0344 879 9136 – www.macdonaldhotels.co.uk

Rufflets Country House

COUNTRY HOUSE • **PERSONALISED** This country house hotel is surrounded by well-tended gardens and has been owned by the same family since 1952. Inside it's a mix of the old and the new, with original Arts and Crafts features sitting alongside stylish, contemporary bedrooms. Menus offer modern interpretations of classic dishes.

23 rooms – †£ 125/275 ††£ 150/375 – 2 suites

Strathkinness Low Rd ✉ KY16 9TX – West : 1.5 mi on B 939 – ✆ 01334 472594 – www.rufflets.co.uk – Closed 3-21 January

Fairways

TOWNHOUSE • CONTEMPORARY This tall Victorian building is the closest gues house to the Old Course – ask for Room 3 and sit on the balcony overlooking th 18th hole. Bedrooms are contemporary and of a good size. Nothing is too muc trouble for the owners.

3 rooms – £ 85/110 £ 90/150

8a Golf Pl. KY16 9JA
– 01334 479513 – www.fairwaysofstandrews.co.uk

Five Pilmour Place

TOWNHOUSE • CONTEMPORARY Victorian terraced house with a surprising stylish interior. There's a bright, clubby lounge and a locker room with underfloc heating. Bedrooms have bold feature walls and smart walk-in showers; Room also has a claw-foot bath.

7 rooms – £ 70/85 £ 95/170

5 Pilmour Pl. KY16 9HZ
– 01334 478665 – www.5pilmourplace.com
– Closed 12 December-15 January

ST BOSWELLS

The Scottish Borders – Melrose – Pop. 1 279 – Regional map n° **15**-D2

Buccleuch Arms

INN • QUIRKY A smart, long-standing coaching inn which offers popular golfing fishing and shooting breaks. Guest areas have a quirky, shabby-chic style an cosy bedrooms have co-ordinated headboards and soft furnishings. The relaxe shabby chic bistrot offers classics, grills and afternoon tea.

19 rooms – £ 79/95 £ 95/125

The Green TD6 0EW
– 01835 822243 – www.buccleucharms.com –
Closed 24-25 December

Whitehouse

TRADITIONAL • PERSONALISED Built in 1872 by the Duke of Sutherland, thi cosy dower house is equally popular with romantic couples as with walkers, hun ters and fishermen. Traditionally furnished bedrooms boast excellent views ove the estate and have contrastingly modern bathrooms. Wild salmon and loca game feature at dinner.

3 rooms – £ 108 £ 144/160

TD6 0ED – Northeast : 3 mi on B 6404
– 01573 460343 – www.whitehousecountryhouse.com

ST MONANS

Fife – Pop. 1 265 – Regional map n° **16**-D2

Craig Millar @ 16 West End

MODERN CUISINE • FRIENDLY XX A former pub with an attractive interior anc a small terrace affording harbour views. 'Land' and 'Sea' tasting menus fea ture at dinner and cooking is refined and flavoursome. It's run by a charmin team.

Menu £ 22/45

16 West End KY10 2BX
– 01333 730327 (booking essential) – www.16westend.com
– Closed 1-15 January, 1 week October and Monday-Tuesday

SANQUHAR

Dumfries and Galloway – Pop. 2 021 – Regional map n° **15**-B2

Blackaddie House

MODERN BRITISH • TRADITIONAL DÉCOR XX A stone-built former manse with 16C origins, set by the river. Lunch offers good value classics, while dinner is more elaborate and features original modern cooking; ingredients are luxurious and dishes are well-presented. Bedrooms are named after game birds - ask for 'Grouse', which has a four-poster bed.

Menu £ 40/63

7 rooms - £ 115/230 £ 130/250

Blackaddie Rd DG4 6JJ - 01659 50270 (booking essential at lunch) - www.blackaddiehotel.co.uk

SKYE (Isle of)

Highland – Pop. 10 008 – Regional map n° **17**-B2

Broadford

Tigh an Dochais

BOUTIQUE HOTEL • MODERN Striking house with award-winning architecture, overlooking Broadford Bay and the Applecross Peninsula. Comfy lounge has well-stocked bookshelves. Modern, minimalist bedrooms boast superb views and good facilities, including underfloor heating and plenty of extras. Communal, home-cooked meals by arrangement.

3 rooms - £ 85/90 £ 105/110

13 Harrapool IV49 9AQ - on A 87 - 01471 820022 - www.skyebedbreakfast.co.uk - Closed November-February

Colbost

Three Chimneys & The House Over-By

MODERN CUISINE • RUSTIC XX Immaculately kept crofter's cottage in a stunning lochside setting. Contemporary art hangs on exposed stone walls in the characterful low-beamed dining rooms. Modern Scottish menus showcase good regional ingredients and seafood from local waters is a highlight. Spacious, split-level bedrooms are stylishly understated and the residents' lounge has a great outlook.

Menu £ 40/68

6 rooms - £ 360 £ 360

IV55 8ZT - 01470 511258 (booking essential) - www.threechimneys.co.uk - dinner only and lunch April-November - Closed mid-December-mid-January

Hillstone Lodge

COUNTRY HOUSE • DESIGN A delightfully located modern house: lots of windows and a pleasant terrace make the most of the fantastic loch and island views, and the immaculately kept bedrooms share the outlook. Breakfast features local bacon and sausages; dinner is served as and when requested, and showcases market seafood and meats.

3 rooms - £ 100/155 £ 120/185

IV55 8ZT - 01470 511434 - www.hillstonelodge.com - Closed December and January

Duisdalemore

Duisdale House

TRADITIONAL • PERSONALISED Stylish, up-to-date hotel with lawned gardens, a hot tub and coastal views. Comfortable bedrooms boast bold décor, excellent bathrooms and a pleasing blend of contemporary and antique furniture. Modern cooking makes good use of local produce. Smart uniformed staff.

18 rooms - £ 99/238 £ 125/388 - 1 suite

Sleat IV43 8QW - on A 851 - 01471 833202 - www.duisdale.com

Dunvegan

Roskhill House

COUNTRY HOUSE • CONTEMPORARY Welcoming 19C croft house, in a peacefu location close to the water. Formerly the old post office, the lounge boasts ex posed stone, wooden beams and an open fire. Fresh, bright bedrooms have contemporary edge and smart bathrooms.

5 rooms – £ 80/90 £ 90/105

Roskhill IV55 8ZD – Southeast : 2.5 mi by A 863 – 01470 521317 – www.roskhillhouse.co.uk – Closed mid-October-mid-March

Edinbane

Edinbane Inn

TRADITIONAL CUISINE • COSY This traditional-looking former farmhouse i the perfect place to cosy up by the fire on a misty night. Choose a pub favourit or one of the appealing specials. Come on a Wednesday, Friday or Sunday fc the popular music sessions, then stay the night in one of the comfy, cosy, Scot tish-themed bedrooms.

Carte £ 25/41

6 rooms – £ 75/135 £ 75/155

IV51 9PW – 01470 582414 – www.edinbaneinn.co.uk – Closed 2 January-2 February

Elgol

Coruisk House

TRADITIONAL CUISINE • SIMPLE This traditional croft house is very remotel set on the west of the island and offers superb views over the hills to the moun tains. It's very personally run and seats just 16. Skye produce features in fresh flavoursome daily dishes. Two simply furnished bedrooms share the stunning outlook.

Menu £ 39/68

5 rooms – £ 150/280 £ 150/280

IV49 9BL – 01471 866330 (booking essential) – www.coruiskhouse.com – Closed November-February

Flodigarry

Flodigarry

COUNTRY HOUSE • PERSONALISED This 19C house was once Jacobite heroin Flora MacDonald's home. Lawned gardens lead down to the coast and it has ex cellent panoramic views; stylish designer décor features throughout. The bar is i the old billiard room – look out for the original round windows in the ceiling Cooking is modern and Scottish.

19 rooms – £ 175/355 £ 175/355

IV51 9HZ – 01470 552203 – www.hotelintheskye.co.uk – Restricted opening in winter

Portree

Scorrybreac

MODERN CUISINE • BISTRO Simply furnished restaurant with distant mountai views and just 8 tables; named after the chef's parents' house, where he ran hi first pop-up. Creative modern cooking uses meats from the hills and seafooc from the harbour below.

Menu £ 36/42

7 Bosville Terr IV51 9DG – 01478 612069 (booking essential) – www.scorrybreac.com – dinner only – Closed Monday

Cuillin Hills

TRADITIONAL • CLASSIC Set in 15 acres of grounds, a 19C hunting lodge offering stunning views over Portree Bay towards the Cuillin Mountains; enjoy top Scottish produce in the restaurant, which shares the outlook. Bedrooms have good facilities – the best are to the front. The stylish open-plan bar serves over 100 malt whiskies.

34 rooms – †£ 120/250 ††£ 120/250

✉ IV51 9QU – Northeast : 0.75 mi by A 855
– ✆ 01478 612003 – www.cuillinhills-hotel-skye.co.uk

Bosville

INN • CONTEMPORARY The Bosville sits in an elevated spot overlooking the harbour and the Cuillin Mountains. Stylish bedrooms have locally woven throws and dramatic Skye scenes on the walls. Enjoy a dram by the fire in the lively bar then head for the bistro-style dining room, which showcases the best of Skye's natural larder.

20 rooms – †£ 110/210 ††£ 110/210

Bosville Terr ✉ IV51 9DG
– ✆ 01478 612846 – www.bosvillehotel.co.uk
– Closed Christmas

Marmalade

HISTORIC • ELEGANT Pretty gardens front this elegant 1817 house on the edge of town, which has been returned to its former glory. Stylish bedrooms come in grey hues, with contrastingly colourful throws made by the island's weavers. The comfy bar leads through to a smart brasserie specialising in steak and oysters.

11 rooms – †£ 110/210 ††£ 110/210

Home Farm Rd ✉ IV51 9LX
– ✆ 01478 611711 – www.marmaladehotel.co.uk

Sleat

Kinloch Lodge

COUNTRY HOUSE • CLASSIC With a loch in front and heather-strewn moorland behind, this 17C hunting lodge affords fantastic panoramic views. It has a traditional country house feel, with antique-filled lounges hung with photos of the Macdonald clan and contemporary bedrooms each themed around a different tartan. Menus mix traditional Scottish elements with some more unusual flavour combinations.

19 rooms (dinner included) – †£ 220/290 ††£ 280/440 – 3 suites

✉ IV43 8QY – ✆ 01471 833214 – www.kinloch-lodge.co.uk

Stein

Loch Bay (Michael Smith)

MODERN CUISINE • SIMPLE This pretty little crofter's cottage sits in an idyllic hamlet and is a pleasingly simple place with a wood-burning stove and Harris Tweed covered chairs. The experienced chef skilfully prepares intensely flavoured Scottish dishes with French overtones; opt for the well-judged Loch Bay Seafood tasting menu.

→ Smoky shellfish bree. Highland venison with seasonal vegetables, cep and cocoa. Clootie dumpling with whisky cream and custard.

Menu £ 30/70

1 Macleods Terr, ✉ IV55 8GA
– ✆ 01470 592235 (booking essential) – www.lochbay-restaurant.co.uk
– Closed January, February, Monday, Sunday dinner and lunch Tuesday, Saturday, November and December

On a budget? Take advantage of lunchtime prices.

Struan

Ullinish Country Lodge

MODERN CUISINE • CLASSIC DÉCOR XX Formal hotel dining room with a tradi tional, masculine style and a house party atmosphere. The daily changing, 2 choice set menu uses good quality local ingredients; dishes are modern and in ventive and combinations are well-judged.

Menu £ 65

Ullinish Country Lodge Hotel, ✉ IV56 8FD - West : 1.5 mi by A 863 - ✆ 01470 572214 (bookings essential for non-residents) - www.theisleofskye.co.uk - dinner only - Closed January and Christmas-New Year

Ullinish Country Lodge

TRADITIONAL • CLASSIC Personally run, 18C former hunting lodge in a wind swept location, affording lovely loch and mountain views. The lounge is fille with ornaments and books about the area. Warmly decorated bedrooms boas good facilities and extras.

6 rooms - £ 105/155 £ 145/205

✉ IV56 8FD - West : 1.5 mi by A 863 - ✆ 01470 572214 - www.theisleofskye.co.u - Closed January and Christmas-New Year

Ullinish Country Lodge - See restaurant listing

Teangue

Toravaig House

COUNTRY HOUSE • CONTEMPORARY Stylish whitewashed house with neat gar dens, set on the road to the Mallaig ferry. Cosy, open-fired lounge with a bab grand piano and heavy fabrics. Individually designed bedrooms boast quality ma terials and furnishings. The two-roomed restaurant offers a concise, classica menu of island produce.

9 rooms - £ 90/278 £ 230/398

Knock Bay ✉ IV44 8RE - on A 851 - ✆ 01471 820200 - www.skyehotel.co.uk

SLEAT - Highland → See Skye (Isle of)

SPEAN BRIDGE

Highland - Regional map n° **17**-C3

Russell's at Smiddy House

TRADITIONAL BRITISH • INTIMATE XX A friendly, passionately run restauran with a smart ornament-filled lounge and two intimate dining rooms. Tasty dishe showcase local ingredients, with old Scottish recipes taking on a modern style Cosy, well-equipped bedrooms come with comfy beds and fine linens; home made cake is served on arrival.

Menu £ 35

5 rooms - £ 95/125 £ 115/220

Roybridge Rd ✉ PH34 4EU - ✆ 01397 712335 (booking essential) - www.smiddyhouse.com - dinner only - Closed Monday and restricted opening in winter

STEIN - Highland → See Skye (Isle of)

STIRLING

Stirling - Pop. 36 142 - Regional map n° **16**-C2

Victoria Square

TOWNHOUSE • ELEGANT Many original features remain in this 19C house, fron stained glass to ornate cornicing. Spacious bedrooms have William Morris styl wallpapers; some have seating areas, feature beds or views over Victoria Square

10 rooms - £ 70/85 £ 94/145

12 Victoria Sq. ✉ FK8 2QZ - ✆ 01786 473920 - www.victoriasquareguesthouse.com - Closed 22-28 December and 1-5 January

West Plean House

TRADITIONAL • PERSONALISED An attractive house on a working farm, with a long history and a very welcoming owner. It has two classic lounges and warm, traditional bedrooms. Eggs come from their hens and the fruits for the jams, from the garden.

5 rooms – £ 85/95 £ 95/115

FK7 8HA - South : 3.5 mi on A 872 (Denny rd) - 01786 812208 - www.westpleanhouse.com - Closed 20 December-8 January

STONEHAVEN

Aberdeenshire – Pop. 11 431 – Regional map n° **16**-D2

Tolbooth

SEAFOOD • RUSTIC XX Stonehaven's oldest building, located on the harbourside: formerly a store, a sheriff's courthouse and a prison. Classic dishes have modern touches; the emphasis being on local seafood, with langoustine and crab the highlights.

Menu £ 23 (weekday lunch) - Carte £ 32/57

Old Pier, Harbour AB39 2JU - 01569 762287 - www.tolbooth-restaurant.co.uk - Closed 1-24 January, 16-22 October, 25-26 December and Monday

STRACHUR

Argyll and Bute – Pop. 628 – Regional map n° **16**-B2

Inver

MODERN BRITISH • VINTAGE X A former crofter's cottage and boat store in a beautifully isolated spot on the loch shore. Enjoy afternoon tea sitting in sheepskin covered armchairs in the lounge-bar or take in the view from the vintage-style restaurant, where concise modern menus are led by the finest local and foraged ingredients. Luxurious bothy-style bedrooms in the grounds complete the picture.

Carte £ 27/42

4 rooms – £ 135 £ 160

Strathlaclan PA27 8BU - Southwest : 6.5 mi by A 886 on B 8000 - 01369 860537 (booking essential) - www.inverrestaurant.co.uk - Closed January-mid-March, Christmas, Thursday November-December and Monday-Tuesday except bank holidays

STRATHPEFFER

Highland – Pop. 1 109 – Regional map n° **17**-C2

Craigvar

TRADITIONAL • CLASSIC Proudly run by a charming owner, an attractive Georgian house overlooking the main square of a delightful spa village. Traditional guest areas include a comfy lounge and an antique-furnished breakfast room. Spacious bedrooms have a modern edge and plenty of personal touches. Good breakfast selection.

3 rooms – £ 105/110 £ 105/110

The Square IV14 9DL - 01997 421622 - www.craigvar.com - Closed 18 December-14 January

STRATHY

Highland – Regional map n° **17**-D1

Sharvedda

FAMILY • PERSONALISED You won't find a warmer welcome than at this remotely located guesthouse on a working croft. Homemade fudge and cake are served on arrival and breakfast is taken in the sunny conservatory, with its wild views over the Pentland Firth.

3 rooms – £ 65/70 £ 85/90

Strathy Point KW14 7RY - North : 1.5 mi on Strathy Point rd - 01641 541311 - www.sharvedda.co.uk - Closed 25-26 December

STRONTIAN

Highland - Regional map n° **17**-B3

Kilcamb Lodge

COUNTRY HOUSE • TRADITIONAL A charming lochside hunting lodge in an idyllic location, where 22 acres of meadows and woodland run down to a private shore. The traditional interior boasts rich fabrics and log fires yet has a modern edge. Bedrooms 5 and 8 have terrific loch and mountain views. Dine in the brasserie or the formal restaurant.

11 rooms (dinner included) - £ 215/340 £ 275/460

On A 861 ✉ PH36 4HY - ✆ 01967 402257 - www.kilcamblodge.co.uk - Closed January, 1-14 December and restricted opening in winter

STRUAN - Highland ➜ See Skye (Isle of)

TAIN

Highland - Pop. 3 655 - Regional map n° **17**-D2

at Nigg Southeast: 7 mi by A9, B9175 and Pitcalnie Rd

Wemyss House

FAMILY • PERSONALISED Remotely set guesthouse run by charming owners; sit in the conservatory extension or on the terrace to enjoy views across the Cromarty Firth to the mountains. The bright Scandic-style interior features bespoke furniture from Stuart's on-site workshop and Christine often plays the grand piano in the cosy lounge.

3 rooms - £ 115/120 £ 115/120

Bayfield ✉ IV19 1QW - South : 1 mi past church - ✆ 01862 851212 - www.wemysshouse.com - Closed October-Easter

at Cadboll Southeast: 8.5 mi by A9 and B9165 (Portmahomack rd) off Hilton rd✉ Tain

Glenmorangie House

TRADITIONAL • CLASSIC Charming 17C house owned by the famous distillery. Antiques, hand-crafted local furnishings and open peat fires feature; there's even a small whisky tasting room. Luxuriously appointed bedrooms show good attention to detail; those in the courtyard cottages are suites. Communal dining from a classical Scottish menu.

9 rooms (dinner included) - £ 240/300 £ 335/455

Fearn ✉ IV20 1XP - ✆ 01862 871671 - www.theglenmorangiehouse.com - Closed January

TARLAND

Aberdeenshire - Pop. 698 - Regional map n° **16**-D1

Douneside House

COUNTRY HOUSE • CLASSIC A castellated baronial mansion set in 7,000 acres and boasting delightful views. Elegant bedrooms feature antiques, Hypnos beds and underfloor-heated bathrooms. It also serves as a holiday home for servicemen and ex-servicemen. The intimate restaurant offers concise, modern menus.

22 rooms - £ 120/170 £ 145/170 - £ 17 - 8 suites

✉ AB34 4UL - North : 1.25 mi by B 9119 (Aberdeen Rd) - ✆ 01339 881230 - www.dounesidehouse.co.uk

TEANGUE - Highland ➜ See Skye (Isle of)

THORNHILL

Dumfries and Galloway - Pop. 1 674 - Regional map n° **15**-B2

Buccleuch & Queensberry Arms

TOWNHOUSE • CONTEMPORARY Smartly refurbished coaching inn, designed by the owner, who also runs an interiors shop. Boldly coloured bedrooms are named after various estates owned by the Duke of Buccleuch and come with eclectic artwork and superb bathrooms. Informal dining options range from bar snacks to a more adventurous à la carte

13 rooms - £ 70/150 £ 85/175 - 1 suite

112 Drumlanrig St ✉ DG3 5LU - ✆ 01848 323101 - www.bqahotel.com

Gillbank House

TOWNHOUSE • PERSONALISED Red stone house built in 1895; originally the holiday home of the Jenner family of department store fame. A lovely stained glass front door leads to a spacious light-filled interior. The breakfast room has distant hill views and two of the large, simply furnished bedrooms have feature beds; all have wet rooms.

6 rooms - £ 85/95 £ 85/95

8 East Morton St ✉ DG3 5LZ - ✆ 01848 330597 - www.gillbank.co.uk

Holmhill Country House

COUNTRY HOUSE • PERSONALISED An 18C country house given to Charles Douglas by the Duke of Buccleuch; peacefully set beside the river, in 8 acres of woodland. Spacious bedrooms have great country views; west-facing 'Nith' sees some superb sunsets.

3 rooms - £ 90/120 £ 90/120

Holmhill ✉ DG3 4AB - West 0.5mi. by A702 on B 731 - ✆ 01848 332239 - www.holmhill.co.uk - Closed Christmas-February

TIRORAN - Argyll and Bute ➜ See Mull (Isle of)

TOBERMORY - Argyll and Bute ➜ See Mull (Isle of)

TORRIDON

Highland - ✉ Achnasheen - Regional map n° **17**-B2

Torridon Inn

TRADITIONAL CUISINE • INN Tranquil inn geared towards those who enjoy outdoor pursuits. The timbered bar features stags' antlers and an ice axe; the restaurant overlooks the gardens and loch. Satisfying walkers' favourites mix with more elaborate dishes. Simply furnished, modern bedrooms; the larger ones are ideal for families.

Carte £ 20/47 **s**

12 rooms - £ 70 £ 140

✉ IV22 2EY - South : 1.5 mi on A 896 - ✆ 01445 791242 - www.thetorridon.com - Closed mid-December-January and Monday-Thursday November, February and March

Torridon

TRADITIONAL • CLASSIC A former hunting lodge built in 1887 by Lord Lovelace; set in 40 acres and offering superb loch and mountain views. The delightful interior features wood-panelling, ornate ceilings and a peat fire. Bedrooms are spacious and luxurious, with top quality furnishings and feature baths. The whisky bar has over 350 malts and the smart dining room offers a modern daily menu.

18 rooms - £ 165/270 £ 165/270 - 2 suites

✉ IV22 2EY - South : 1.5 mi on A 896 - ✆ 01445 791242 - www.thetorridon.com - Closed January and Monday-Tuesday November-March

TROON

South Ayrshire - Pop. 14 752 - Regional map n° **15**-A2

Lochgreen House

COUNTRY HOUSE • CONTEMPORARY Edwardian country house in a pleasant coastal spot, with sumptuous lounges and a Whisky Room stocked with an extensive range of malts. Bedrooms in the main house are cosy and traditional; those in the extension are more luxurious.

32 rooms - £ 165/205 £ 185/225 - 1 suite

Monktonhill Rd, Southwood ✉ KA10 7EN - Southeast : 2 mi on B 749 - ✆ 01292 313343 - www.costley-hotels.co.uk

TURNBERRY

South Ayrshire - ✉ Girvan - Regional map n° **15**-A2

Trump Turnberry

GRAND LUXURY • ELEGANT An iconic Edwardian hotel built around Ailsa golf course. Elegant guest areas have been taken back to their former glory and many of the luxurious bedrooms boast enviable sea views; for something different, stay in the lighthouse. 1906 offers Italian dishes, while Duel in the Sun serves bistro classics.

204 rooms - £ 129/999 £ 129/999 - 4 suites

✉ KA26 9LT - On A 719 - ✆ 01655 331000 - www.trumpturnberry.com

UDNY GREEN

Aberdeenshire - Regional map n° **16**-D1

Eat on the Green

MODERN BRITISH • ELEGANT XX An attractive former inn overlooking the village green, with a cosy lounge and two traditionally furnished dining rooms. Well-presented modern dishes change with the seasons and feature vegetables and herbs from their smallholding.

Menu £ 25 (weekday lunch)/59

✉ AB41 7RS - ✆ 01651 842337 (booking essential) - www.eatonthegreen.co.uk - Closed Monday and Tuesday

ULLAPOOL

Highland - Pop. 1 541 - Regional map n° **17**-C2

Westlea House

FAMILY • CONTEMPORARY It might look like an ordinary house but inside Westlea has been transformed into a stylish, boutique-style B&B. Individually decorated bedrooms feature bold modern artwork and have a funky feel; two have roll-top baths in the room.

5 rooms - £ 45/55 £ 75/109

2 Market St ✉ IV26 2XE - ✆ 01854 612594 - www.westlea-ullapool.co.uk

WALKERBURN

The Scottish Borders - Pop. 700 - Regional map n° **15**-C2

Windlestraw

LUXURY • ELEGANT An attractive Arts and Crafts property built in 1906 as a wedding gift for the wife of the mill owner John King Ballantyne. It boasts original fireplaces, old plaster ceilings and great valley views; the bedrooms have been stylishly modernised and guest areas include a plush lounge and a comfy bar. The attractive, wood-panelled dining room offers a daily changing menu.

6 rooms - £ 175 £ 220/280

✉ EH43 6AA - On A 72 - ✆ 01896 870636 - www.windlestraw.co.uk - Closed 18 December-13 February

WALES

It may only be 170 miles from north to south, but Wales contains great swathes of beauty, such as the dark and craggy heights of Snowdonia's ninety mountain peaks, the rolling sandstone bluffs of the Brecon Beacons, and Pembrokeshire's tantalising golden beaches. Bottle-nosed dolphins love it here too, arriving each summer at New Quay in Cardigan Bay. Highlights abound: formidable Harlech Castle dominates its coast, Bala Lake has a railway that steams along its gentle shores, and a metropolitan vibe can be found in the capital, Cardiff, home to the Principality Stadium and the National Assembly.

Wales is a country which teems with great raw ingredients and modern-day chefs are employing these to their utmost potential; from succulent slices of Spring lamb farmed on the lush mountains and valleys, through to the humblest of cockles; from satisfying native Welsh Black cattle through to abundant Anglesey oysters, delicious Welsh cheeses and the edible seaweed found on the shores of the Gower and known as laverbread.

- Michelin Road maps n° 503 and 713
- Michelin Green Guide: Great Britain

M. Cristofori/Lithium/age fotostock

Wales

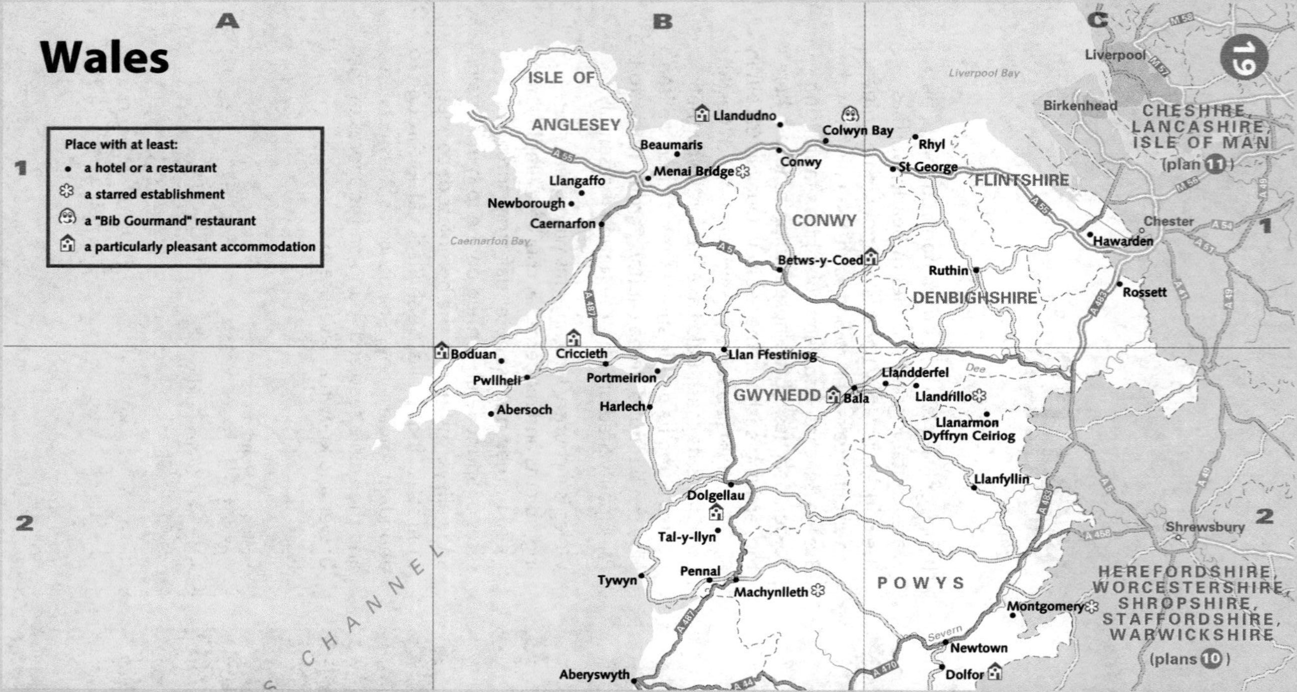
A
B
C
1
2
Place with at least:
• a hotel or a restaurant
a starred establishment
a "Bib Gourmand" restaurant
a particularly pleasant accommodation
ISLE OF ANGLESEY
Llandudno
Colwyn Bay
Rhyl
St George
Beaumaris
Menai Bridge
Conwy
Llangaffo
Newborough
Caernarfon
Caernarfon Bay
Liverpool Bay
Liverpool
Birkenhead
CHESHIRE, LANCASHIRE, ISLE OF MAN
(plan 11)
19
FLINTSHIRE
CONWY
Chester
Hawarden
Betws-y-Coed
Ruthin
DENBIGHSHIRE
Rossett
Boduan
Criccieth
Llan Ffestiniog
Pwllheli
Portmeirion
Llandderfel
Dee
Abersoch
Harlech
GWYNEDD
Bala
Llandrillo
Llanarmon Dyffryn Ceiriog
Llanfyllin
Dolgellau
Tal-y-llyn
Shrewsbury
Tywyn
Pennal
Machynlleth
POWYS
Montgomery
HEREFORDSHIRE, WORCESTERSHIRE, SHROPSHIRE, STAFFORDSHIRE, WARWICKSHIRE
(plans 10)
CHANNEL
Severn
Newtown
Dolfor
Aberyswyth
A 55
A 5
A 487
A 483
A 458
A 470
A 44
A 41
A 49
A 51
A 54
M 56
M 53
M 57

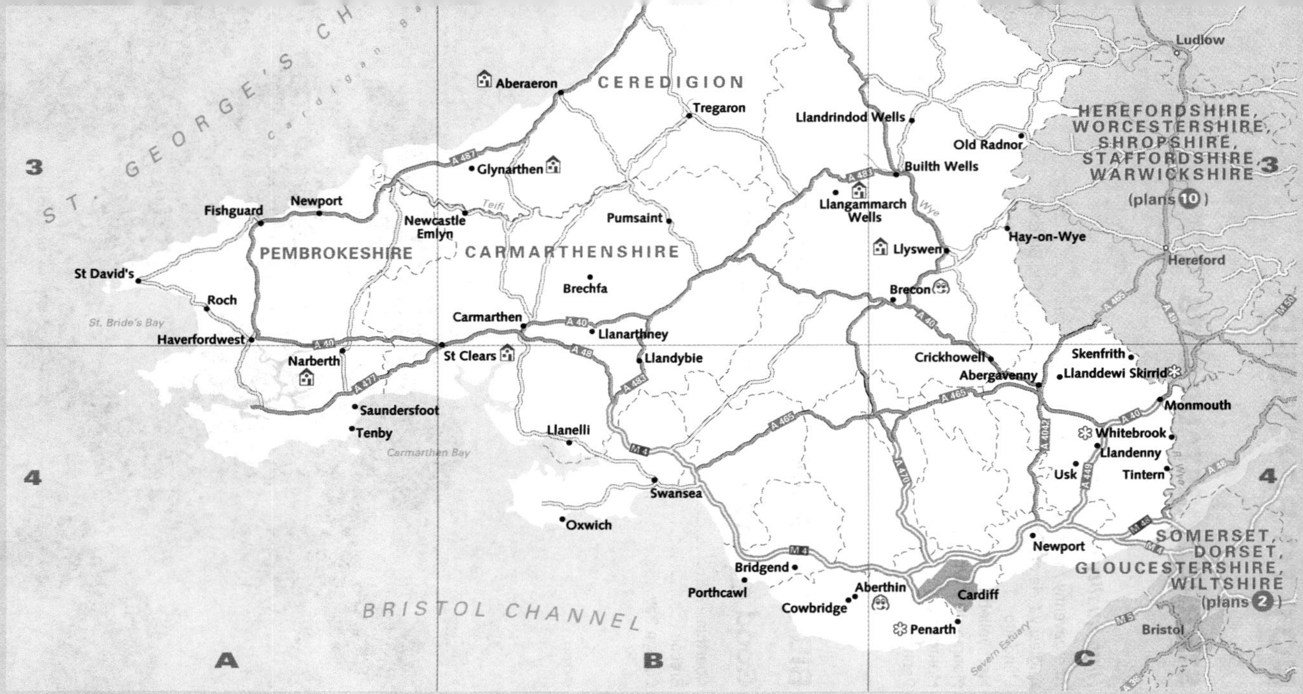
ST. GEORGE'S CH
Cardigan Ba
CEREDIGION
PEMBROKESHIRE
CARMARTHENSHIRE
HEREFORDSHIRE, WORCESTERSHIRE, SHROPSHIRE, STAFFORDSHIRE, WARWICKSHIRE
(plans 10)
SOMERSET, DORSET, GLOUCESTERSHIRE, WILTSHIRE
(plans 2)
BRISTOL CHANNEL
St. Bride's Bay
Carmarthen Bay
Severn Estuary
Aberaeron
Tregaron
Llandrindod Wells
Old Radnor
Ludlow
Glynarthen
Builth Wells
Llangammarch Wells
Fishguard
Newport
Newcastle Emlyn
Teifi
Pumsaint
Wye
Hay-on-Wye
Hereford
Llyswen
St David's
Roch
Brechfa
Brecon
Carmarthen
Llanarthney
Haverfordwest
St Clears
Llandybie
Narberth
Crickhowell
Abergavenny
Skenfrith
Llanddewi Skirrid
Monmouth
Saundersfoot
Tenby
Llanelli
Swansea
Oxwich
Whitebrook
Llandenny
Usk
Tintern
R. Wye
Newport
Bridgend
Porthcawl
Aberthin
Cowbridge
Cardiff
Penarth
Bristol
A 487
A 483
A 40
A 48
A 477
A 465
A 470
A 4042
A 449
A 49
A 38
M 4
M 48
M 5
M 50
3
4
A
B
C

NOT TO BE MISSED

STARRED RESTAURANTS

✿

High quality cooking, worth a stop!

BIB GOURMAND RESTAURANTS

Good quality, good value cooking

Michelin

OUR TOP PICKS

HOTELS WITH SPAS

IT'S ALL ABOUT THE FOOD

MADE THEIR MARK

MORE THAN JUST THE VILLAGE PUB

GLORIOUSLY REMOTE

GOOD VALUE HOME FROM HOME

QUINTESSENTIAL COUNTRY HOUSES

SPECIAL OCCASION

1891
CARDIFF MARKET
LARGE OYSTERS 90p EACH

ABERAERON ABER AERON

Ceredigion - Pop. 1 422 - Regional map n° **19**-B3

Harbourmaster

TRADITIONAL BRITISH • INN A vibrant blue inn with a New England style bar lounge, a modern dining room and lovely harbour views. Choose between an ex tensive bar menu and a more ambitious evening set price menu. Smart bec rooms, split between the house and a nearby cottage, are brightly decorate and well-equipped; some have terraces.

Menu £ 35 (dinner) - Carte £ 24/39

13 rooms - £ 75/155 £ 120/265

Quay Par SA46 0BA - 01545 570755 - www.harbour-master.com - Closed dinner 24-26 December

3 Pen Cei

TOWNHOUSE • PERSONALISED Vibrant blue house on the harbourfront; for merly the Packet Steam Company HQ. Stylish modern bedrooms are name after local rivers: those to the front overlook the water and Aeron has a free standing bath. Great breakfasts range from fruit salad to smoked salmon an scrambled eggs.

5 rooms - £ 80/130 £ 90/140

3 Quay Par SA46 0BT - 01545 571147 - www.pencei.co.uk - Closed 25-26 December

ABERGAVENNY Y-FENNI

Monmouthshire - Pop. 13 423 - Regional map n° **19**-C4

The Court

MODERN BRITISH • CLASSIC DÉCOR XX A country house dining room hun with photos of local scenes. Classic British dishes are given a modern twis and fruit, veg and herbs are from the walled garden. All wines are offered b the glass.

Menu £ 20/38

Llansantffraed Court Hotel, Llanvihangel Gobion NP7 9BA - Southeast : 6.5 m by A 40 and B 4598 off old Raglan rd - 01873 840678 (booking essential) - www.thecourtdiningroom.co.uk - Closed Sunday dinner, Monday and lunch Tuesday

Angel

HISTORIC • PERSONALISED A family-run, Georgian coaching inn and outbuild ings; characterful guest areas have a modern, shabby-chic feel and bedroom are a mix of the traditional and the more contemporary. Have afternoon te in the Wedgewood Room or dine from an all-encompassing menu in th brasserie.

33 rooms - £ 109/159 £ 109/159 - 2 suites

15 Cross St NP7 5EN - 01873 857121 - www.angelabergavenny.com - Close 25 December

Llansantffraed Court

HISTORIC • CLASSIC An attractive Grade II listed William and Mary styl house with an ornamental lake and a 16C church in its 20 acre grounds Bedrooms have a restful feel - the corner rooms have both mountain an valley views.

20 rooms - £ 95/135 £ 125/185

Llanvihangel Gobion NP7 9BA - Southeast : 6.5 mi by A 40 and B 4598 off ol Raglan rd - 01873 840678 - www.llch.co.uk

The Court - See restaurant listing

at Llanddewi Skirrid Northeast: 3.25 mi on B4521 ✉ Abergavenny

Walnut Tree (Shaun Hill)

MODERN BRITISH • COSY A long-standing Welsh institution, set in a wooded valley and always bustling with regulars; start with drinks in the flag-floored lounge-bar. Classic, seasonal dishes are well-priced and refreshingly simple, eschewing adornment and letting the natural flavours of the ingredients speak for themselves.

→ Veal sweetbreads with sauerkraut and mustard dressing. Halibut with spiced mussel broth. Salted caramel apple millefeuille.

Menu £ 30 (lunch) – Carte £ 41/60

✉ NP7 8AW – ✆ 01873 852797 (booking essential) – www.thewalnuttreeinn.com – Closed 1 week Christmas, Sunday and Monday

at Cross Ash Northeast: 8.25 mi on B4521

1861

TRADITIONAL BRITISH • COSY A part-timbered former pub; now a cosy, contemporary restaurant named after the year it was built. Classically based cooking has modern twists – much of the fruit and veg is grown by the owner's father.

Menu £ 25/40 – Carte £ 38/52

✉ NP7 8PB – West : 0.5 mi on B 4521 – ✆ 01873 821297 – www.18-61.co.uk – Closed first 2 weeks January, Sunday dinner and Monday

ABERSOCH

Gwynedd – ✉ Pwllheli – Pop. 783 – Regional map n° **19**-B2

Venetia

ITALIAN • BRASSERIE A double-fronted house once owned by a sea captain, with a cosy bar-lounge and a boldly decorated dining room. Cicchetti is followed by classic Italian dishes presented in a distinctly modern style. Chic bedrooms are well-equipped – one has a jacuzzi with a waterproof TV.

Carte £ 21/40

5 rooms – †£ 65/133 ††£ 80/148

Lon Sarn Bach ✉ LL53 7EB – ✆ 01758 713354 – www.venetiawales.com – dinner only – Restricted opening in winter

at Bwlchtocyn South: 2 mi ✉ Pwllheli

Porth Tocyn

FAMILY • PERSONALISED High on the headland overlooking Cardigan Bay, a traditional hotel that's been in the family for three generations. Relax in the cosy lounges or explore the many leisure and children's facilities. Homely, modernised bedrooms; some with balconies or sea views. Menus offer interesting, soundly executed dishes.

17 rooms – †£ 85/200 ††£ 120/200

✉ LL53 7BU – ✆ 01758 713303 – www.porthtocynhotel.co.uk – Closed early November-mid-March

ABERTHIN

The Vale of Glamorgan – Regional map n° **19**-B4

Hare & Hounds

TRADITIONAL CUISINE • FRIENDLY The chef's passionate desire to make this 300 year old pub the most seasonal in Wales is laudable. Menus change twice daily and produce is from his 3 acre allotment and family farms; he also hunts and forages, so expect plenty of game, mushrooms and hedgerow berries. Cooking is unfussy yet bursts with flavour.

Menu £ 20 (weekday lunch) – Carte £ 18/40

✉ CF71 7LG – ✆ 01446 774892 – www.hareandhoundsaberthin.com – Closed Sunday dinner-Tuesday

ABERYSTWYTH ABERESTUUTH

Ceredigion – Pop. 18 093 – Regional map n° **19**-B2

Gwesty Cymru

TOWNHOUSE • MODERN Grade II listed Georgian townhouse on the seafront with a brightly painted exterior and a terrace overlooking the bay. Thoughtfully designed modern bedrooms vary in size and décor – all are colour themed, with smart bathrooms. Small, stylish basement bar and dining room; ambitious, adventurous dishes.

8 rooms – £ 70/80 £ 90/165

19 Marine Terr ✉ SY23 2AZ
– ✆ 01970 612252 – www.gwestycymru.com
– Closed 23 December-3 January

ANGLESEY (Isle of) SIR YNYS MÔN

Isle of Anglesey – Pop. 68 900 – Regional map n° **19**-B1

Beaumaris

Loft

MODERN BRITISH • ELEGANT XX Formal restaurant under the eaves of an old coaching inn, with a plush, open-fired lounge and an elegant candlelit dining room with exposed beams and immaculately laid tables. Creative modern cooking champions top Anglesey produce.

Menu £ 55

The Bull Hotel, Castle St ✉ LL58 8AP
– ✆ 01248 810329 – www.bullsheadinn.co.uk – dinner only
– Closed 25-26 December, 1 January and Sunday-Tuesday

Brasserie

TRADITIONAL CUISINE • BRASSERIE X Set overlooking a courtyard, a large brasserie in the old stables of a 17C coaching inn, with a Welsh slate floor, oak tables, a fireplace built from local stone and a relaxed feel. Wide-ranging modern menus feature lots of specials.

Carte £ 20/40

The Bull Hotel, Castle St ✉ LL58 8AP
– ✆ 01248 810329 – www.bullsheadinn.co.uk
– Closed 25-26 December and 1 January

The Bull

INN • PERSONALISED Characterful 1670s coaching inn – look out for the old water clock and ducking stool in the bar. Bedrooms in the main house are named after Dickens characters and are traditional; those in the townhouse are more modern and colourful.

25 rooms – £ 85/110 £ 115/195

Castle St ✉ LL58 8AP
– ✆ 01248 810329 – www.bullsheadinn.co.uk
– Closed 25-26 December and 1 January

Brasserie • **Loft** – See restaurant listing

Churchbank

TOWNHOUSE • PERSONALISED Georgian guesthouse with a homely, antique-furnished interior and modern day comforts. Cosy bedrooms look out over the large walled garden and the church opposite; one has a private bathroom. Helpful, amiable owner and hearty breakfasts.

3 rooms – £ 85/95 £ 90/110

28 Church St ✉ LL58 8AB
– ✆ 01248 810353 – www.bedandbreakfastanglesey.co.uk

Llangaffo

Outbuildings

TRADITIONAL · PERSONALISED A tastefully converted former barn set close to a prehistoric burial ground and offering fantastic views over Snowdonia. Stylish modern bedrooms come with local artwork and smart bathrooms; for a romantic hideaway, choose the 'Pink Hut' in the garden. Afternoon tea is served in the cosy open-fired lounge and a concise, seasonally led menu in the spacious dining room.

5 rooms – †£ 65/85 ††£ 75/100

Bodowyr Farmhouse ✉ LL60 6NH – Southeast : 1.5 mi by B 4419 turning left at crossroads and left again by post box – ✆ 01248 430132 – www.theoutbuildings.co.uk

Menai Bridge

Sosban & The Old Butchers (Stephen Stevens)

MODERN CUISINE · INTIMATE A brightly painted restaurant displaying Welsh slate and hand-painted tiles from its butcher's shop days. A well-balanced 6-7 course surprise menu offers boldly flavoured modern dishes with original, personal touches, which demonstrate an innate understanding of cooking techniques and flavour combinations.

→ Cod with yeast, crispy potato purée, pickled onion and ox heart. Salt-aged lamb rump, wild garlic, sheep yoghurt and leek. Rhubarb and custard.

Menu £ 80 – surprise menu only

Trinity House, 1a High St ✉ LL59 5EE – ✆ 01248 208131 (booking essential) – www.sosbanandtheoldbutchers.com – dinner only and Saturday lunch – Closed January-mid-February, Easter, Christmas-New Year and Sunday-Wednesday

Dylan's

MODERN CUISINE · FAMILY An old boat yard timber store; now a smart, busy, two-storey eatery by the water's edge, overlooking Bangor. Extensive menus offer everything from homemade cakes and weekend brunch to sourdough pizzas. Find a spot on the terrace if you can.

Carte £ 18/44

St George's Rd ✉ LL59 5DE – ✆ 01248 716714 – www.dylansrestaurant.co.uk – Closed 25-26 December

Newborough

Marram Grass N

MODERN · RUSTIC The flavour-packed dishes at this homely restaurant reflect the area perfectly. They utilise the best of local produce – including laver and Menai mussels – along with home-grown herbs and salad and home-bred chickens and pigs. One brother is in the kitchen and the other looks after the service.

Menu £ 36 – Carte £ 32/51

White Lodge ✉ LL61 6RS – on A 4080 – ✆ 01248 440077 (booking essential at dinner) – www.themarramgrass.com – Closed first 2 weeks January and Monday-Wednesday

Prices quoted after the symbol † refer to the lowest rate for a single room in low season, followed by the highest rate in high season. The same principle applies to the symbol †† for a double room.

BALA

Gwynedd – ✉ Gwynedd – Pop. 1 974 – Regional map n° **19**-B2

Bryniau Golau

COUNTRY HOUSE • PERSONALISED Original Victorian tiling, plasterwork an fireplaces are proudly shown-off in this elegant house. Bedrooms overlook th lake and mountains: one has a four-poster bed; another, a bath which afford lake views. Their homemade honey features alongside local produce at breakfas

3 rooms – £ 90/110 £ 110/130

Llangower ✉ LL23 7BT – South : 2 mi by A 494 and B 4931 off B 4403 – ✆ 01678 521782 – www.bryniau-golau.co.uk – Closed December-February

BEAUMARIS

→ See Anglesey (Isle of)

BETWS-Y-COED

Conwy – Pop. 255 – Regional map n° **19**-B1

Tan-y-Foel Country House

FAMILY • PERSONALISED Personally run, part-16C country house in 4 acres c grounds, which affords stunning views over the Vale of Conwy and Snowdonia The snug lounge and breakfast room display traditional features. Modern, individ ually styled bedrooms have smart bathrooms; the spacious loft room has vaulted ceiling.

6 rooms – £ 85/165 £ 100/165

✉ LL26 0RE – East : 2.5 mi by A 5, A 470 and Capel Garmon rd on Llanwrst rd – ✆ 01690 710507 – www.tanyfoelcountryhouse.co.uk – Closed November-February

Pengwern

TRADITIONAL • PERSONALISED Cosy Victorian house with stunning mountai and valley views. Warm, well-proportioned bedrooms retain charming origina features like the old fireplaces and are named after famous artists who stayed a the house during the 1800s.

3 rooms – £ 62/67 £ 77/92

Allt Dinas ✉ LL24 0HF – Southeast : 1.5 mi on A 5 – ✆ 01690 710480 – www.snowdoniaaccommodation.co.uk – Closed 22 December-3 January

at Penmachno Southwest: 4.75 mi by A5 on B4406 ✉ Betws-Y-Coed

Penmachno Hall

TRADITIONAL • PERSONALISED A former rectory in a pleasant valley locatior with delightful views. Cosy lounge, eclectic art collection and lovely mature gar dens. Boldly coloured bedrooms contain a host of thoughtful extras. Light suppe by arrangement.

3 rooms – £ 85/95 £ 85/95

✉ LL24 0PU – On Ty Mawr rd – ✆ 01690 760410 – www.penmachnohall.co.uk – Closed Christmas-New Year

BODUAN – Gwynedd

→ See Pwllheli

BRECHFA

Carmarthenshire – Regional map n° **19**-B3

Ty Mawr

TRADITIONAL • TRADITIONAL 16C stone farmhouse in the centre of the village next to the river. It's personally run and boasts plenty of charm and character with exposed bricks, wooden beams, open fires and pine-furnished bedrooms The modern menu has Welsh twists and produce is homemade or from the valley

6 rooms – £ 80 £ 115/130

✉ SA32 7RA – ✆ 01267 202332 – www.wales-country-hotel.co.uk

BRECON

Powys – Pop. 8 250 – Regional map n° **19**-C3

Felin Fach Griffin

MODERN BRITISH • INN Located in picturesque countryside, a rather unique pub with bright paintwork, colourful artwork and an extremely laid-back atmosphere. The young team are friendly and have a good knowledge of what they're serving. Following the motto 'simple things, done well', dishes are straightforward, tasty and refined. Pleasant bedrooms come with comfy beds but no TVs.

Menu £ 24/29 – Carte £ 32/36

7 rooms – £ 110 £ 135

Felin Fach ✉ LD3 0UB – Northeast : 4.75 mi by B 4602 off A 470 – ✆ 01874 620111 – www.felinfachgriffin.co.uk – Closed 25 December and 4 days early January

Felin Glais

TRADITIONAL • COSY 17C stone barn and mill, set in a tranquil hamlet and run with pride. Spacious interior has a pleasant 'lived in' feel; cosy, homely bedrooms have toiletries and linen from Harrods. Large beamed lounge; dine here, at the communal table, or in the conservatory in summer. Lengthy menu – order two days ahead.

4 rooms – £ 95/110 £ 95/110

Aberyscir ✉ LD3 9NP – West : 4 mi by Cradoc rd turning right immediately after bridge – ✆ 01874 623107 – www.felinglais.co.uk – Closed December and January

BRIDGEND PEN-Y-BONT

Bridgend – Pop. 46 757 – Regional map n° **19**-B4

Restaurant Tommy Heaney @ The Great House

MODERN CUISINE • INTIMATE XX A friendly team welcome you to this smart hotel restaurant, where striking sculptures are dotted about the room. Seasonal menus have an emphasis on organic Welsh produce. Dinner sees the most interesting combinations, which arrive with eye-catching presentation.

Menu £ 18 (weekday lunch) – Carte £ 31/43

Great House Hotel, 8 High St, Laleston ✉ CF32 0HP – West : 2 mi on A473 – ✆ 01656 657644 – www.great-house-laleston.co.uk – Closed 26 December, Sunday dinner and bank holidays

Great House

HISTORIC • CLASSIC A welcoming 15C listed property; reputedly a gift from Elizabeth I to the Earl of Leicester and once home to the Lord of the Manor. The guest areas have character and bedrooms are comfy – those in the coach house are the most modern.

13 rooms – £ 80/95 £ 95/135

8 High St, Laleston ✉ CF32 0HP – West : 2 mi on A 473 – ✆ 01656 657644 – www.great-house-laleston.co.uk – Closed 26 December

Restaurant Tommy Heaney @ The Great House – See restaurant listing

BUILTH WELLS LLANFAIR-YM-MUALLT

Powys – Pop. 2 829 – Regional map n° **19**-C3

Rhedyn

FAMILY • PERSONALISED Former forester's cottage with a small garden and pleasant country views, run by very welcoming owners. Tiny lounge with a bookcase full of local info and DVDs; cosy communal dining room where home-cooked, local market produce is served. Good-sized, modern bedrooms feature heavy wood furnishings, good facilities and quirky touches. Tea and cake are served on arrival.

3 rooms – £ 90/100 £ 90/100

Cilmery ✉ LD2 3LH – West : 4 mi on A 483 – ✆ 01982 551944 – www.rhedynguesthouse.co.uk

BWLCHTOCYN - Gwynedd ➜ See Abersoch

CAERNARFON
Gwynedd - Pop. 9 493 - Regional map n° **19**-B1

Plas Dinas
TRADITIONAL • CLASSIC The former home of Lord Snowdon, set in large gardens and filled with family portraits and antiques. The comfy drawing room has an open fire, a piano and an honesty bar. Smart bedrooms come with good extras and immaculate bathrooms. Traditional dinners are served 5 nights a week.

10 rooms - †£ 109/249 ††£ 109/249

LL54 7YF - South : 2.5 mi on A 487 - 01286 830214 - www.plasdinas.co.uk - Closed Christmas

at Seion Northeast: 5.5 mi by A4086 and B4366 on Seion rd Gwynedd

Ty'n Rhos Country House
FAMILY • PERSONALISED Personally run former farmhouse with a large conservatory and a cosy lounge with an inglenook fireplace. Comfortable, modern bedrooms; some have balconies or terraces and others, their own garden. The formal restaurant offers pleasant views over Anglesey; classically based dishes are presented in modern ways.

19 rooms - †£ 90/105 ††£ 105/199

LL55 3AE - Southwest : 0.75 mi - 01248 670489 - www.tynrhos.co.uk

GOOD TIPS!

Wales' capital combines a rich history with top sports venues, big name shops and a lively cultural scene. This is reflected in our selection, with restaurants like the traditional **Park House** – set in a 19C property built by the founder of modern Cardiff – and the ultra-modern glass-fronted **St David's Hotel**. From French and Spanish to Italian and Indian... Cardiff has it all.

CARDIFF

Cardiff – Pop. 346 090 – Regional map n° **19**-C4

Restaurants

Park House

MODERN CUISINE • ELEGANT XXX A striking building overlooking Gorsedd Gardens and designed by William Burgess in the late 1800s; the oak-panelled dining room has a formal air. Ambitious cooking has a strong French base and is flamboyant in its execution. Each dish is matched with a wine from an impressive global list.

Menu £ 25 (lunch) – Carte £ 44/60

Town plan: C1-p – *20 Park Pl. ✉ CF10 3DQ – ✆ 029 2022 4343 – www.parkhouserestaurant.co.uk – Closed 26-27 December, 1-8 January, 28 July-12 August, Sunday and Monday*

Asador 44

SPANISH • ELEGANT XX A dark, moody restaurant divided into lots of different areas; sit overlooking the Asador, the cheese room or the glass-fronted wine cave. The menu focuses on charcoal-cooked meats and much of the produce is imported from Spain.

Menu £ 15 (lunch and early dinner) – Carte £ 25/53

Town plan: C1-a – *14-15 Quay St ✉ CF10 1EA – ✆ 029 2002 0039 – www.asador44.co.uk – Closed 25-26 December, Sunday and Monday*

Purple Poppadom

INDIAN • DESIGN XX Enter via the glass door between the shop fronts and head up to the smart room with bold purple décor. Classic combinations are cooked in a refined modern style and given a personal twist; the seafood dishes are popular.

Menu £ 15 (lunch and early dinner) – Carte £ 20/40

Town plan: B1-n – *185a Cowbridge Rd East ✉ CF11 9AJ – 1st Floor – ✆ 029 2022 0026 – www.purplepoppadom.com – Closed 25-26 December, 1 January and Monday*

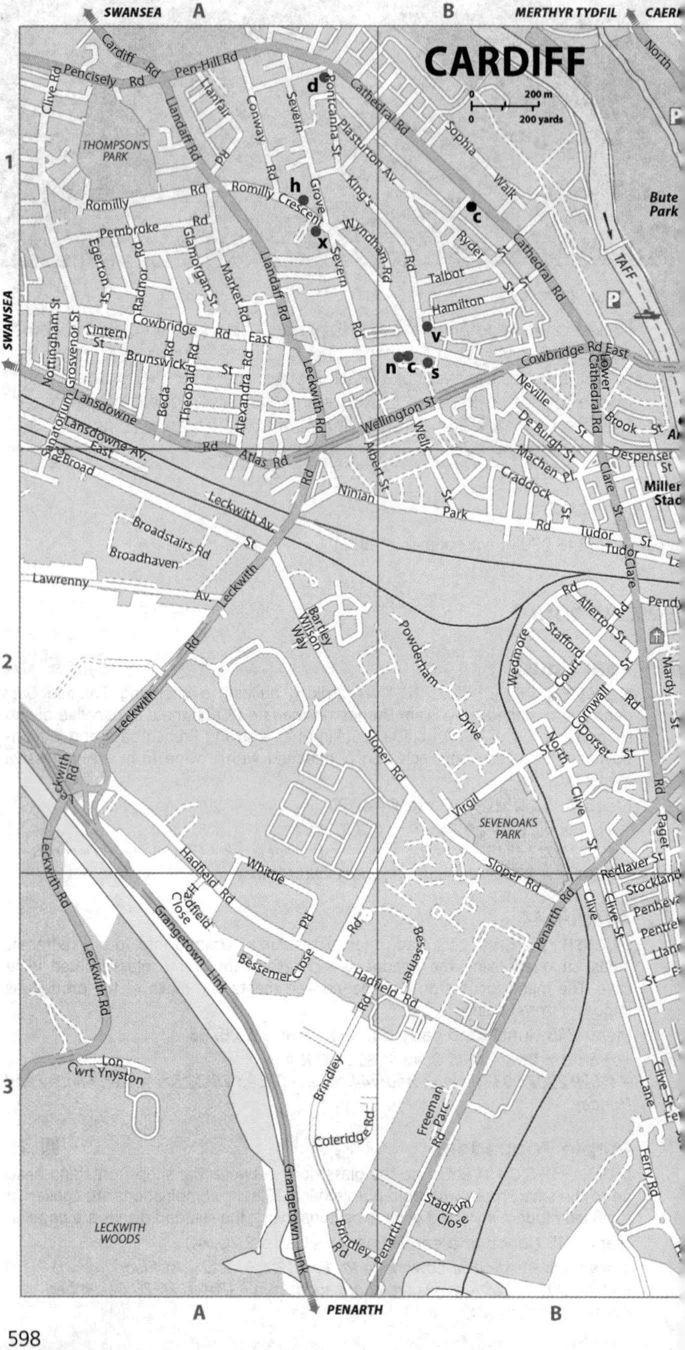
CARDIFF
0 200 m
0 200 yards
SWANSEA
MERTHYR TYDFIL
CAERI
A
B
1
2
3
PENARTH
THOMPSON'S PARK
Bute Park
TAFF
Millen Stad
SEVENOAKS PARK
LECKWITH WOODS
Cardiff Rd
Pen-Hill Rd
Pencisely Rd
Clive Rd
Llandaff Rd
Llanfair Rd
Conway Rd
Severn Grove
Pontcanna St
Cathedral Rd
Plasturton Av.
King's Rd
Sophia Walk
North
Romilly Rd
Romilly Crescent
Wyndham Rd
Severn Rd
Pembroke Rd
Glamorgan St
Market Rd
Egerton St
Radnor Rd
Ryder St
Talbot St
Hamilton St
Cowbridge Rd East
Tintern St
Brunswick St
Nottingham St
Grosvenor St
Sanatorium Rd
Beda Rd
Theobald Rd
Alexandra Rd
Leckwith Rd
Lansdowne Rd
Lansdowne Av. East
Atlas Rd
Wellington St
Lower Cathedral Rd
Neville St
De Burgh St
Brook St
Machen Pl.
Despenser St
Craddock St
Clare St
Albert St
Wells St
Ninian Park Rd
Broad St
Leckwith Av.
Broadstairs Rd
Broadhaven
Lawrenny Av.
Tudor Rd
Tudor St
Tudor Lane
Bartley Wilson Way
Powderham Drive
Wedmore Rd
Allerton St
Stafford Rd
Court Rd
Cornwall St
Dorset St
Pendyris St
Mardy St
Sloper Rd
North Clive St
Virgil St
Paget St
Redlaver St
Stockland St
Penhevad St
Pentre St
Llanmaes St
Clive St
Clive Lane
Penarth Rd
Hadfield Rd
Hadfield Close
Whittle Rd
Bessemer Close
Bessemer Rd
Grangetown Link
Lon Cwrt Ynyston
Brindley Rd
Coleridge Rd
Freeman Parc Rd
Stadium Close
Ferry Rd
d
h
x
c
v
n
s

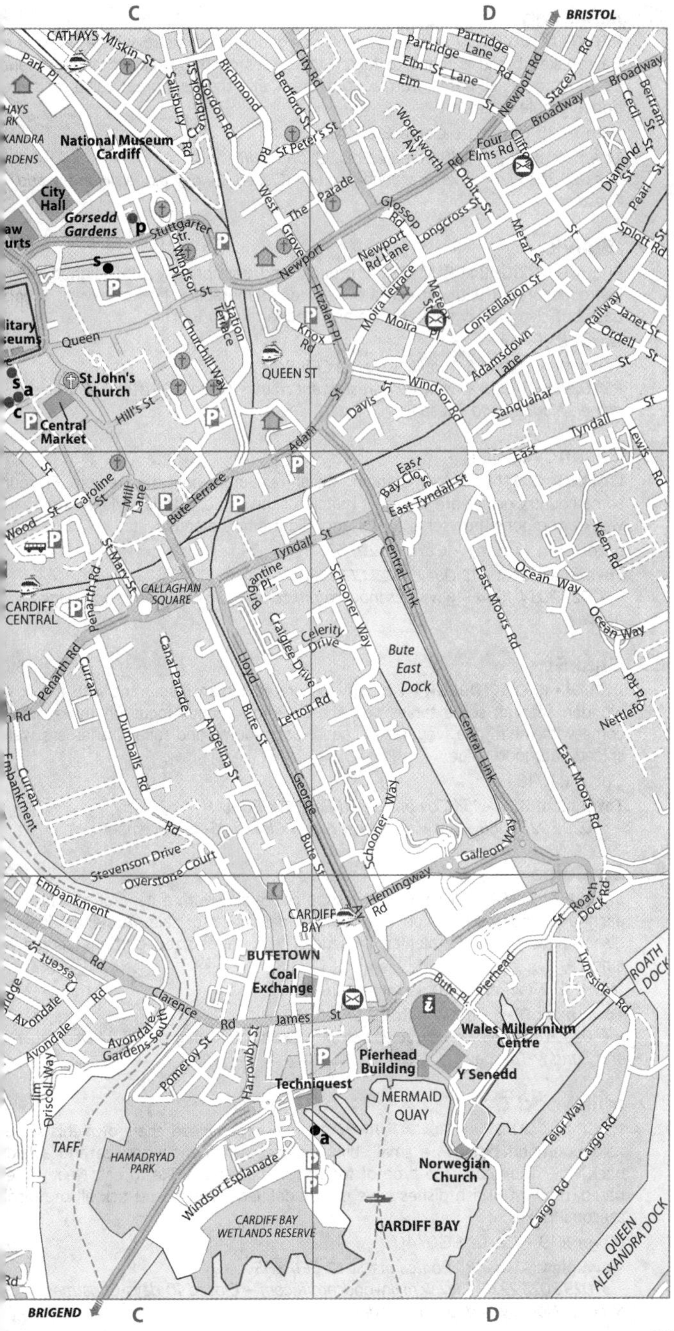
C
D
BRISTOL
CATHAYS
National Museum Cardiff
City Hall
Gorsedd Gardens
St John's Church
Central Market
CARDIFF CENTRAL
CALLAGHAN SQUARE
QUEEN ST
Bute East Dock
CARDIFF BAY
BUTETOWN
Coal Exchange
Wales Millennium Centre
Pierhead Building
Y Senedd
Techniquest
MERMAID QUAY
Norwegian Church
CARDIFF BAY
HAMADRYAD PARK
CARDIFF BAY WETLANDS RESERVE
TAFF
ROATH DOCK
QUEEN ALEXANDRA DOCK
BRIGEND
1
2
3

Arbennig

REGIONAL CUISINE • SIMPLE Homely neighbourhood bistro with a buzzy fee Daily baked bread is made to match the dishes on the weekly changing menu Cooking covers all bases, from soup to steak, and there's a great value set selec tion available at lunch.

Menu £ 15 (lunch) – Carte £ 22/42

Town plan: A1-h – *6-10 Romilly Cres. ✉ CF11 9NR – ✆ 029 2034 1264 – www.arbennig.co.uk – Closed Sunday dinner, Monday and Tuesday*

'Bully's

FRENCH • NEIGHBOURHOOD A proudly and passionately run neighbourhoo bistro decorated with an eclectic array of memorabilia. Menus have a Frenc base but also display some British and Mediterranean touches.

Carte £ 29/47

Town plan: A1-x – *5 Romilly Cres. ✉ CF11 9NP – ✆ 029 2022 1905 – www.bullysrestaurant.co.uk – Closed Christmas, Sunday dinner, Monday and Tuesday*

Casanova

ITALIAN • SIMPLE A long-standing Italian restaurant near the stadium. Flavour some country dishes are a perfect match for the rustic, osteria-style interior; mid week afternoons they serve an Assaggi (light bites) menu.

Menu £ 14 (lunch) – Carte £ 29/39

Town plan: C1-c – *13 Quay St ✉ CF10 1EA – ✆ 029 2034 4044 – www.casanovacardiff.co.uk – Closed Sunday and bank holidays*

Chai St

INDIAN • EXOTIC DÉCOR Vibrantly decorated Indian restaurant with a mix o wooden seating; some tables you share. Simple menus focus on thalis, which come with meat, rice, vegetables, naan, poppadoms and raita. Dishes are well spiced and good value.

Carte £ 11/18

Town plan: B1-s – *153 Cowbridge Rd East ✉ CF11 9AH – ✆ 029 2022 8888 – www.chaistreet.com – Closed 25-26 December*

La Cuina

SPANISH • BISTRO A small, rustic shop conversion with a handful of tables o each level and walls packed with regional delicacies for sale. Authentic Spanis dishes have strong Catalonian influences, with tapas-sized portions served a lunch.

Menu £ 12 (weekdays) – Carte £ 28/50

Town plan: B1-v – *11 Kings Rd ✉ CF11 9BZ – ✆ 029 2019 0265 – www.lacuina.co.uk – Closed 3-24 August, 23-27 December and Sunday-Tuesday*

milkwood (N)

MODERN BRITISH • NEIGHBOURHOOD Two experienced chefs own this swee neighbourhood bistro – a small, bijoux place with friendly service and a laid back vibe. They cook the type of food they themselves like to eat. Neatly pre pared, modern British dishes have clearly defined flavours and tick all the local seasonal boxes.

Menu £ 19 – Carte £ 30/40

Town plan: A1-d – *83 Pontcanna St ✉ CF11 9HS – ✆ 029 2023 2226 – www.milkwoodcardiff.com – Closed 10 days Christmas, Sunday, Monday and lunch Tuesday*

Potted Pig

TRADITIONAL BRITISH • RUSTIC Atmospheric restaurant in a stripped back former bank vault, with brick walls, barrel ceilings and a utilitarian feel. Lesser-known products and cuts of meat are used in robust, tasty dishes. The gin cocktails are a speciality.

Menu £13 (weekday lunch) – Carte £24/55

Town plan: C1-s – *27 High St ✉ CF10 1PU – ✆ 029 2022 4817 – www.thepottedpig.com – Closed 24-28 December, 1-3 January and Sunday dinner*

Hotels

St David's

BUSINESS • MINIMALIST Modern, purpose-built hotel on the waterfront, affording lovely 360° views. Good-sized, minimalist bedrooms have a slightly funky feel; all boast balconies and bay outlooks. Smart spa features seawater pools and a dry floatation tank. Stylish restaurant with superb terrace views serves modern British dishes.

142 rooms – †£ 90/170 ††£ 90/200 – 12 suites

Town plan: D3-a – *Havannah St, Cardiff Bay ✉ CF10 5SD – ✆ 029 2060 7445 – www.phcompany.com*

Park Plaza

BUSINESS • MINIMALIST A light, airy hotel with a stylish lounge, extensive conference facilities and a vast leisure centre boasting a smart stainless steel pool and 8 treatment rooms. Stark modern bedrooms come with slate bathrooms. The informal brasserie and bar serve both international dishes and afternoon teas.

129 rooms – †£ 89/499 ††£ 89/499 – £ 13

Town plan: C1-s – *Greyfriars Rd ✉ CF10 3AL – ✆ 029 2011 1111 – www.parkplazacardiff.com – Closed 25-26 December*

Cathedral 73

TOWNHOUSE • CONTEMPORARY Delightful Victorian terraced house on the edge of the city, with boutique furnishings, designer bedrooms and a chauffeur-driven Rolls Royce. Afternoon tea is served in the spacious sitting room and breakfast, in the orangery.

10 rooms – †£ 89/350 ††£ 89/350 – £ 10

Town plan: B1-c – *73 Cathedral Rd ✉ CF11 9HE – ✆ 029 2023 5005 – www.cathedral73.com – Closed 25 December*

CARMARTHEN

Carmarthenshire – Pop. 15 854 – Regional map n° **19**-B3

at Llanllawddog Northeast: 8 mi by A485

Glangwili Mansion

FAMILY • MODERN Part-17C mansion rebuilt in a Georgian style, set in a great location on the edge of the forest. The spacious interior features sleek tiled floors, contemporary artwork and bright, bold bedrooms with modern oak furnishings.

3 rooms – †£ 94/105 ††£ 105/140

✉ SA32 7JE – ✆ 01267 253735 – www.glangwilimansion.co.uk – Closed 24-26 December

at Nantgaredig East: 5 mi by A4300 on A4310 ✉ Carmarthen

Y Polyn

TRADITIONAL BRITISH • PUB Small, rustic pub on a busy country road, se close to a stream and boasting pleasant views. Cooking is stout, filling and Britis at heart, offering satisfying soups, fresh salads, slow-cooked meats and classic puddings.

Menu £ 40 (dinner) – Carte lunch £ 33/48

✉ SA32 7LH – South : 1 mi on B 4310 – ✆ 01267 290000 – www.ypolyn.co.uk – Closed Sunday dinner and Monday

COLWYN BAY BAE COLWYN

Conwy – Pop. 29 405 – Regional map n° **19**-B1

Bryn Williams at Porth Eirias

MODERN BRITISH • DESIGN If you're looking for a relaxed, friendly enviror ment, this striking beachside brasserie with faux industrial styling and blue leath banquettes is the place to come. The owner is proud of his Welsh roots and shows on the menu. Cooking is pleasingly unfussy and local seafood is to the for

Menu £ 21 (lunch and early dinner) – Carte £ 24/39

The Promenade ✉ LL29 8HH – ✆ 01492 577525 – www.portheirias.com – Closed 25 December

at Rhos-on-Sea Northwest: 1 mi ✉ Colwyn Bay

Plas Rhos House

TRADITIONAL • PERSONALISED Smartly refurbished 19C house with a pleasar terrace, on a small street overlooking the sea. Cosy lounge and bright, chee breakfast room. Bedrooms have modern bathrooms and thoughtful extras suc as chocolates and a decanter of sherry.

5 rooms – †£ 65/110 ††£ 85/110

53 Cayley Promenade ✉ LL28 4EP – ✆ 01492 543698 – www.plasrhos.co.uk – Closed November-April

CONWY

Conwy – Pop. 3 873 – Regional map n° **19**-B1

Signatures

MODERN CUISINE • DESIGN Stylish restaurant with elegantly laid tables and well-versed team – set in a holiday park close to the sea. Brasserie classics an snacks at lunch; more inventive, modern choices at dinner including the chef 'Signature' dishes.

Menu £ 37 (dinner) – Carte lunch £ 26/30

Aberconwy Resort and Spa ✉ LL32 8GA – Northwest 1.5 mi by A 547 – ✆ 01492 583513 – www.signaturesrestaurant.co.uk – Closed Monday and Tuesday

at Rowen South: 3.5 mi by B5106

Tir Y Coed

COUNTRY HOUSE • PERSONALISED 'Tir Y Coed' means 'Place in the Trees' an that sums up the lovely location perfectly; ask for a bedroom overlooking th garden if you like wildlife spotting. It has a contemporary country house loc and offers good comforts throughout. Seasonal dishes feature produce from th local area.

7 rooms – †£ 120/180 ††£ 135/195

✉ LL32 8TP – ✆ 01492 650219 – www.tirycoed.com

COWBRIDGE Y BONT FAEN

The Vale of Glamorgan – Pop. 3 616 – Regional map n° **19**-B4

Arboreal

MEDITERRANEAN CUISINE • RUSTIC There's a lively Antipodean vibe at this all-day bar and café, where the chef uses local produce in dishes with a Mediterranean, Asian and North African edge. Bespoke, wood-fired pizzas are a feature and folk music accompanies.

Carte £ 23/40

68 Eastgate ✉ CF71 7AB - ✆ 01446 775093 - www.arboreal.uk.com - Closed Sunday dinner and Monday

CRICCIETH

Gwynedd - Pop. 1 753 - Regional map n° **19**-B2

Dylan's

MODERN BRITISH • BRASSERIE A striking art deco inspired seafront building designed by Sir Clough Williams-Ellis in the 1950s. Extensive all-day menus offer everything from coffee and cake to seafood specials. Sit in one of two wings or out on the terrace.

Carte £ 17/45

Esplanade ✉ LL52 0HU - ✆ 01766 522773 - www.dylansrestaurant.co.uk - Closed 25-26 December

Bron Eifion

COUNTRY HOUSE • CONTEMPORARY Characterful country house built in 1883 for a slate merchant; the impressive staircase is constructed from pitch pine he brought back from the USA. Some of the spacious, modern bedrooms have carved Middle Eastern beds. Enjoy bistro dishes to a lovely garden backdrop.

17 rooms - †£ 95/135 ††£ 145/175

✉ LL52 0SA - West : 1 mi on A 497 - ✆ 01766 522385 - www.broneifion.co.uk

CRICKHOWELL CRUCYWEL

Powys - Pop. 2 063 - Regional map n° **19**-C4

Bear

TRADITIONAL • COSY A well-known family-run coaching inn which dates from 1432 and is adorned with hanging baskets. Bedrooms in the main house are the most characterful and feature exposed oak beams; those in the old stables across the cobbled courtyard are more modern. Dine from gutsy, traditional dishes in the atmospheric lounge-bar or one of the more formal dining rooms.

36 rooms - †£ 90/145 ††£ 112/182 - 1 suite

High St ✉ NP8 1BW - ✆ 01873 810408 - www.bearhotel.co.uk - Closed 25 December

CROSS ASH - Monmouthshire ➜ See Abergavenny

CROSSGATES - Powys ➜ See Llandrindod Wells

DOLFOR

Powys - Regional map n° **19**-C2

Old Vicarage

TRADITIONAL • PERSONALISED A 19C red-brick vicarage with a classical, country house style lounge and dining room, and large gardens where they grow the produce used in their home-cooked meals. Cosy bedrooms are named after local rivers and mix period furnishings with bright modern colours. Chutney, preserves and soaps are for sale and afternoon tea is served on arrival.

4 rooms - †£ 70/90 ††£ 95/120

✉ SY16 4BN - North : 1.5 mi by A 483 - ✆ 01686 629051 - www.theoldvicaragedolfor.co.uk - Closed Christmas-New Year

DOLGELLAU

Gwynedd – Pop. 2 688 – Regional map n° **19**-B2

Penmaenuchaf Hall

COUNTRY HOUSE • PERSONALISED Personally run Victorian house with woo panelling, ornate ceilings and stained glass windows. Bedrooms blend the trad tional and the modern; some have balconies overlooking the lovely ground mountains and estuary. Classic dishes are accompanied by a well-chosen wine lis

14 rooms – £ 125/205 £ 185/310

Penmaenpool ✉ LL40 1YB – West : 1.75 mi on A 493 (Tywyn Rd) – ✆ 01341 42212 – www.penhall.co.uk – Closed 17-21 December and 2-18 January

Ffynnon

TOWNHOUSE • PERSONALISED A spacious Victorian house which once oper ated as a cottage hospital. Original features and period furnishings abound, offse by stylish modern designs which pay great attention to detail. Keep your win and snacks in the pantry and enjoy homemade crumpets or pancakes for break fast. Outdoor hot tub.

6 rooms – £ 110/180 £ 160/220

Love Ln, off Cader Rd ✉ LL40 1RR – ✆ 01341 421774 – www.ffynnontownhouse.com – Closed Christmas

at Llanelltyd Northwest: 2.25 mi by A470 on A496

Mawddach

MEDITERRANEAN CUISINE • RUSTIC XX Stylish barn conversion run by tw brothers and set on the family farm. The terrace and dining room offer super views of the mountains and estuary. Unfussy Italian-influenced cooking feature lamb from the farm and veg from the garden.

Carte £ 26/39

✉ LL40 2TA – ✆ 01341 421752 – www.mawddach.com – Closed 2 weeks November, 1 week January, 1 week spring and Sunday dinner-Wednesday

FISHGUARD

Pembrokeshire – Pop. 3 419 – Regional map n° **19**-A3

Manor Town House

TOWNHOUSE • PERSONALISED Well-run, listed Georgian townhouse, boastin fabulous harbour views. Stylish, elegant lounges and individually designed, ar tique-furnished bedrooms; some in art deco and some in Victorian styles. Tast breakfasts; charming owners.

6 rooms – £ 80/95 £ 105/135

11 Main St ✉ SA65 9HG – ✆ 01348 873260 – www.manortownhouse.com – Closed 24-27 December

GLYNARTHEN

Ceredigion – Regional map n° **19**-B3

Penbontbren

COUNTRY HOUSE • CONTEMPORARY A collection of enthusiastically run cor verted farm buildings, surrounded by an attractive landscaped garden and 3 acres of rolling countryside. Bedrooms are spacious, stylish and well-equippe and most have a sitting room and patio. The boldly decorated stone-walle breakfast room offers an extensive menu.

6 rooms – £ 79/110 £ 99/140

Glynarthen ✉ SA44 6PE – North : 1 mi taking first left at crossroads then next le onto unmarked lane – ✆ 01239 810248 – www.penbontbren.com – Closed Christmas

HARLECH

Gwynedd – Pop. 1 762 – Regional map n° **19**-B2

Castle Cottage

CLASSIC CUISINE • COSY XX Sweet little cottage behind Harlech Castle, with a cosy yet surprisingly contemporary interior. Start with canapés and an aperitif in the lounge; the table is yours for the evening. Classical menus feature local produce and modern touches. Spacious bedrooms have smart bathrooms and stunning mountain views.

Menu £ 45

7 rooms - £ 85/125 £ 130/175

Pen Llech LL46 2YL - 01766 780479 (booking essential) - www.castlecottageharlech.co.uk - dinner only - Closed 3 weeks November and Sunday-Tuesday

HAVERFORDWEST HWLFFORDD

Pembrokeshire - Pop. 14 596 - Regional map n° **19**-A3

Lower Haythog Farm

TRADITIONAL • COSY Welcoming guesthouse with mature gardens, part-dating from the 14C and set on a working dairy farm. Cosy bedrooms feature bespoke cherry wood furniture and organic toiletries. Pleasant lounge and conservatory. Aga-cooked breakfasts.

4 rooms - £ 45/55 £ 75/85

Spittal SA62 5QL - Northeast : 5 mi on B 4329 - 01437 731279 - www.lowerhaythogfarm.co.uk

Paddock

FAMILY • MODERN Contemporary guesthouse on a working dairy farm. Comfy lounge with books, board games and a wood-burning stove. Modern bedrooms feature chunky wood furniture and sleigh beds made up with Egyptian cotton linen. Home-cooked meals rely on local and market produce; eggs are from their own hens.

3 rooms - £ 65/75 £ 80/90

Lower Haythog, Spittal SA62 5QL - Northeast : 5 mi on B 4329 - 01437 731531 - www.thepaddockwales.co.uk

HAWARDEN PENARLÂG

Flintshire - Pop. 1 858 - Regional map n° **19**-C1

Glynne Arms

TRADITIONAL BRITISH • PUB A 200 year old coaching inn opposite Hawarden Castle; owned by the descendants of PM William Gladstone. Choose from bar snacks, estate steaks and plenty of pub classics. Regular events include quiz nights and gin tastings.

Menu £ 17 (weekday lunch) - Carte £ 24/38

3 Glynne Way CH5 3NS - 01244 569988 - www.theglynnearms.co.uk - Closed 25 December

HAY-ON-WYE Y GELLI

Powys - Pop. 1 846 - Regional map n° **19**-C3

The Swan at Hay

HISTORIC BUILDING • COSY A welcoming 19C coaching inn set in the heart of a pretty town. Relax in the rustic bar or by a wood-burning stove in one of the restful lounges. Bedrooms are cosy with neutral colour schemes and some overlook the hills. Dine on a mix of classic and modern dishes to garden views.

19 rooms - £ 95/105 £ 125/175

Church St HR3 5DQ - 01497 821188 - www.swanathay.co.uk - Closed 2 weeks January

HOWEY - Powys ➔ See Llandrindod Wells

LLANARMON DYFFRYN CEIRIOG

Wrexham - Regional map n° **19**-C2

Hand at Llanarmon

TRADITIONAL CUISINE • INN Nestled at the head of the Ceiriog Valley, t Hand is ideally located for those who like to get away from it all. Choose 'Hand Classic' such as mushrooms on toast or pick from 'Today's Choices' li Welsh lamb cutlets with tomato ragout. Bedrooms are modern and there's ev a small treatment facility.

Carte £ 22/42

13 rooms - £ 79/110 £ 99/140

LL20 7LD - 01691 600666 - www.thehandhotel.co.uk

LLANARTHNEY

Carmarthenshire - Regional map n° **19**-B3

Llwyn Helyg

FAMILY • PERSONALISED A striking modern house with marble floors and styli furnishings. A grand oak staircase leads to luxurious bedrooms with jacuzzi bat and rain showers. Music lovers will appreciate the comfy, well-equipped 'Liste ing Room'.

3 rooms - £ 104/119 £ 135/155

SA32 8HJ - South : 0.25 mi by the side road across from Wright's - 01558 668778 - www.llwynhelygcountryhouse.co.uk - Closed Christmas and 31 December

LLANDDERFEL

Gwynedd - Pop. 4 500 - Regional map n° **19**-C2

Palé Hall

MODERN BRITISH • ELEGANT Sit in the main room of this hotel restaurant take in lovely garden views. Dishes are modern with a creative element; the s priced lunch features some lesser-known ingredients, while the main menu h an element of luxury.

Menu £ 32/65

Palé Hall Hotel, Palé Estate LL23 7PS - 01678 530285 (bookings essential f non-residents) - www.palehall.co.uk

Palé Hall

COUNTRY HOUSE • PERSONALISED An impressive Victorian house built for i dustrialist Henry Robertson; its 1920s hydroelectric generator still heats the w ter. Spacious, elegant rooms boast beautiful marquetry, antique furnishings a ornate design features.

18 rooms - £ 205/790 £ 275/860 - 5 suites

Palé Estate LL23 7PS - 01678 530285 - www.palehall.co.uk

Palé Hall - See restaurant listing

LLANDDEWI SKIRRID - Monmouthshire ➔ See Abergavenny

LLANDENNY

Monmouthshire - Regional map n° **19**-C4

Raglan Arms

MODERN CUISINE • PUB Dine by the open fire in the bar or in the bright co servatory which overlooks the spacious terrace. Menus feature a few pub favou ites but cooking is very much in the modern vein; dishes take on an extra degr of refinement in the evening.

Carte £ 26/44

NP15 1DL - 01291 690800 - www.raglanarms.co.uk - Closed Sunday dinner and Monday

LLANDRILLO

Denbighshire – ✉ Corwen – Pop. 1 048 – Regional map n° **19**-C2

✿ Tyddyn Llan (Bryan Webb)

CLASSIC CUISINE • ELEGANT XXX Attractive former shooting lodge in a pleasant valley location, surrounded by lovely gardens and run by a husband and wife team. Spacious country house lounges and a blue-hued, two-roomed restaurant. Hearty, satisfying cooking is based around the classics; tasting menus show the kitchen's talent to the full. Smart, elegant bedrooms offer a good level of facilities.

→ Dressed langoustine with avocado salsa, fennel and radish salad. Roast local pork 4 ways with black pudding. St Émilion au chocolat with honeycomb and rum & raisin ice cream.

Menu £ 38/70

13 rooms – †£ 130/150 ††£ 130/250

✉ LL21 0ST – ✆ 01490 440264 (booking essential) – www.tyddynllan.co.uk – dinner only and lunch Friday-Sunday – Closed last 2 weeks January, Monday and Tuesday

LLANDRINDOD WELLS

Powys – Pop. 5 309 – Regional map n° **19**-C3

at Crossgates Northeast: 3.5 mi on A483 ✉ Llandrindod Wells

Guidfa House

TRADITIONAL • COSY A Georgian gentleman's residence with a pleasant garden, a smart breakfast room and a period lounge featuring an original cast iron ceiling rose. Bright, airy bedrooms; the best is in the coach house. Friendly owners serve tea on arrival.

6 rooms – †£ 90/125 ††£ 110/145

Crossgates ✉ LD1 6RF – ✆ 01597 851241 – www.guidfahouse.co.uk

at Howey South: 1.5 mi by A483 ✉ Llandrindod Wells

Acorn Court

FAMILY • PERSONALISED Chalet-style house set in 40 acres, with views over rolling countryside towards a river and lake. Welcoming owner and a real family feel. Spacious, well-kept bedrooms come with good extras. Try the Welsh whisky porridge for breakfast.

3 rooms – †£ 65/90 ††£ 80/98

Chapel Rd ✉ LD1 5PB – Northeast : 0.5 mi – ✆ 01597 823543 – www.acorncourt.co.uk – Closed 23-31 December

LLANDUDNO

Conwy – Pop. 15 371 – Regional map n° **19**-B1

Bodysgallen Hall

COUNTRY HOUSE • HISTORIC A stunning National Trust owned country house in 200 acres of delightful parkland, with a 13C tower and a superb outlook to the mountains beyond. It has a welcoming open-fired hall, a characterful wood-panelled lounge and antique-furnished bedrooms - some in cottages and some affording splendid Snowdon views. The grand dining room serves modern versions of classic dishes.

31 rooms – †£ 170/410 ††£ 190/470 – 21 suites

Royal Welsh Way ✉ LL30 1RS – Southeast : 2 mi on A 470 – ✆ 01492 584466 – www.bodysgallen.com

Osborne House

TOWNHOUSE • PERSONALISED Victoriana reigns in this smart townhouse overlooking the bay. Bedrooms are spacious, open-plan suites with canopied bed and lounges; chandeliers cast a romantic glow and marble bathrooms come wit double-ended roll-top baths. Breakfast is served in your room. The opulent restaurant offers a wide-ranging menu.

6 rooms – £ 155/185 £ 155/185

17 North Par ✉ LL30 2LP – ✆ 01492 860330 – www.osbornehouse.co.uk
– Closed 16-31 December

Escape Boutique B&B

TOWNHOUSE • DESIGN Attractive Arts and Crafts house with stained glass windows, parquet floors and a chic, modern interior that sets it apart. Stylish lounge and spacious, contemporary bedrooms; those on the top floor have a stunnin view of the bay.

9 rooms – £ 84/134 £ 99/149

48 Church Walks ✉ LL30 2HL – ✆ 01492 877776 – www.escapebandb.co.uk
– Closed 18-26 December

LLANDYBIE

Carmarthenshire – Pop. 2 813 – Regional map n° **19**-B4

Valans

INTERNATIONAL • FRIENDLY XX Run by a local and his wife, a simple little restaurant with a bright red, white and black colour scheme. Fresh, unfussy dishe rely on local produce and offer classical flavours. The 'Lite Lunch' offers som good value options.

Menu £ 14/25

Primrose House, 29 High St ✉ SA18 3HX – ✆ 01269 851288 – www.valans.co.uk
– Closed 25 December-14 January, Sunday dinner and Monday

LLANELLI

Carmarthenshire – Pop. 43 878 – Regional map n° **19**-B4

Sosban

MODERN CUISINE • ROMANTIC XX This impressive stone building was constructed in 1872 to house the pumping engine for the neighbouring docks; th copper-topped bar is made from the old water tank. Dishes are modern, creativ and often playful, and blend different textures, temperatures and flavours. Service is relaxed and attentive.

Menu £ 19 (weekday lunch) – Carte £ 32/51

The Pump House, North Dock ✉ SA15 2LF – West : 1 mi by Queen Victoria Rd and B 4304. – ✆ 01554 270020 – www.sosban.wales
– Closed 25 December, 1 January, lunch Monday-Tuesday and Sunday dinner

LLANELLTYD - Gwynedd ➜ See Dolgellau

LLAN FFESTINIOG

Gwynedd – Regional map n° **19**-B2

Cae'r Blaidd Country House

TRADITIONAL • PERSONALISED It's all about mountain pursuits at this alpine themed guesthouse: the welcoming owners are mountain guides; ice axes, crampons and skis fill the walls; and there's a climbing wall, a drying room and eve equipment for hire in the basement. Dine on local produce while taking in th stunning panoramic view.

5 rooms – £ 55/90 £ 55/90

✉ LL41 4PH – North : 0.75 mi by A 470 on Blaenau Rd
– ✆ 01766 762765 – www.caerblaidd.com
– Closed January

LANFYLLIN

Powys - Pop. 1 105 - Regional map n° **19**-C2

Seeds

REGIONAL CUISINE • RUSTIC Converted 16C red-brick cottages in a sleepy village; run with pride by a friendly husband and wife team. Cosy, pine-furnished room with an old range and a country kitchen feel. Unfussy, classical dishes and comforting homemade desserts.

Menu £ 29 (dinner) - Carte lunch £ 24/37

5 Penybryn Cottages, High St ✉ SY22 5AP - ✆ 01691 648604 - Closed Thursday in winter and Sunday-Wednesday

LANGAFFO → See Anglesey (Isle of)

LANGAMMARCH WELLS

Powys - Regional map n° **19**-B3

Lake Country House and Spa

TRADITIONAL • PERSONALISED Extended, part-timbered 19C country house in 50 acres of mature gardens and parkland, with a pond, a lake and a river. Comfortable lounges and well-appointed bedrooms with antiques and extras; some are set in a lodge. The impressive spa overlooks the river. Breakfast is in the orangery; the elegant restaurant is perfect for a classical, candlelit dinner.

32 rooms - †£ 147/180 ††£ 205/244 - 8 suites

✉ LD4 4BS - East : 0.75 mi - ✆ 01591 620202 - www.lakecountryhouse.co.uk

LANLLAWDDOG - Carmarthenshire → See Carmarthen

LYSWEN

Powys - ✉ Brecon - Regional map n° **19**-C3

Llangoed Hall

HISTORIC • PERSONALISED A fine country house beside the River Wye, redesigned by Sir Clough Williams-Ellis in 1910 and restored by the late Sir Bernard Ashley. Delightful sitting rooms and sumptuous bedrooms feature rich fabrics, mullioned windows and antiques; the impressive art collection includes pieces by Whistler. Ambitious modern cooking is led by what's fresh in the kitchen garden.

23 rooms - †£ 135/450 ††£ 150/600

✉ LD3 0YP - Northwest : 1.25 mi on A 470 - ✆ 01874 754525 - www.llangoedhall.com

MACHYNLLETH

Powys - Pop. 2 235 - Regional map n° **19**-B2

Ynyshir (Gareth Ward)

CREATIVE • INTIMATE Intimate, Scandic-style restaurant with an open kitchen; set within a beautiful part-Georgian building. The talented chef uses superb local and foraged ingredients to create original dishes with wonderfully balanced flavours; some are finished at the table and for the final course you're invited into the kitchen. Bedrooms have a chic, contemporary country house style.

→ 'Not French onion soup'. Salted Welsh Wagyu rib with shiitake and seaweed. Tiramisu.

Menu £ 75/140 - tasting menu only

10 rooms - †£ 130/400 ††£ 150/420 - 3 suites

Eglwysfach ✉ SY20 8TA - Southwest: 6 mi on A 487 - ✆ 01654 781209 (booking essential) - www.ynyshir.co.uk - Closed 2 weeks Christmas-New Year, 2 weeks summer, 1 week April, 1 week late October-early November and Sunday-Tuesday

MENAI BRIDGE → See Anglesey (Isle of)

MONMOUTH TREFYNWY

Monmouthshire - Pop. 10 110 - Regional map n° **19**-C4

#7 Church Street

MODERN BRITISH • FRIENDLY X A small, family-run restaurant on a pedestri nised lane in the Old Town. The hard-working chef takes pride in his cooki and even does his own butchery. Dishes are fresh, tasty and very filling - a the homemade cakes in the cabinet are hard to resist. Upstairs, 8 simply fur ished bedrooms await.

Carte £ 24/49

8 rooms - £ 65/85 £ 75/95

7 Church St NP25 3BX - 01600 712600 - www.numbersevenchurchstreet.co.uk - Closed dinner 24-26 December, Sunda and Monday

Stonemill

REGIONAL CUISINE • RUSTIC X An attractive 16C cider mill with exposed timbe and an old millstone at the centre of the characterful, rustic restaurant. Go value set menus offer hearty, classically based cooking, with dishes such as ste and lobster offered at a supplement.

Menu £ 23/30

Rockfield NP25 5SW - Northwest : 3.5 mi on B 4233 - 01600 716273 - www.thestonemill.co.uk - Closed 2 weeks January, 25-27 December, Sunday dinner and Monday

at Whitebrook South: 8.25 mi by A466 Monmouth

The Whitebrook (Chris Harrod)

MODERN BRITISH • INTIMATE XX You'll find this relaxed, intimate, whitewash property off the beaten track, in a wooded valley. Cooking is modern and unde stated and menus showcase top quality local and foraged ingredients; descri tions are concise and the elegantly presented dishes are more complex th they first appear. Bedrooms come in muted tones and follow the theme of brin ing nature inside.

→ Wye Valley asparagus with hedgerow pickings, pine and Tintern mead. Hur sham Farm suckling pig with caramelised celeriac and sheep's sorrel. Poach pear, buttermilk ice cream and yoghurt crumble.

Menu £ 39/82

8 rooms - £ 105/210 £ 130/235

NP25 4TX - 01600 860254 (booking essential) - www.thewhitebrook.co.u - Closed first 2 weeks January, Monday and Tuesday

MONTGOMERY TREFALDWYN

Powys - Pop. 986 - Regional map n° **19**-C2

The Checkers (Stéphane Borie)

FRENCH • FRIENDLY XX A charming 18C coaching inn set in a hilltop town a run by an enthusiastic Frenchman and his family. Guests are invited to arrive 7.15pm for aperitifs in the beamed lounge, followed by a tasting menu in the st ish restaurant. Skilfully prepared, classic French dishes are beautifully crafted a flavours pack a punch. Elegant bedrooms are furnished with antiques.

→ Roasted scallop with steamed courgette flower. Gressingham duck with pa d'épices, cherries and liquorice jus. Raspberry soufflé with vanilla ice cream.

Menu £ 65 - tasting menu only

5 rooms - £ 165/230 £ 165/230

Broad St SY15 6PN - 01686 669822 - www.checkerswales.co.uk - dinner or - Closed 3 weeks January, 1 week late summer, 25-26 December, Sunday and Monday

NANTGAREDIG - Carmarthenshire ➜ See Carmarthen

NARBERTH

Pembrokeshire - Pop. 2 265 - Regional map n° **19**-A4

Fernery

MODERN CUISINE • ELEGANT XX A meal in this intimate hotel restaurant is thought of as an event: start with a drink in the bar or in one of the lounges. Modern cooking carefully balances ingredients from the Welsh larder to create some interesting combinations with original touches.

Menu £ 69/94 **s**

Grove Hotel, Molleston ✉ SA67 8BX
- South : 2 mi by A 478 on Herons Brook rd - ✆ 01834 860915
- www.grovenarberth.co.uk
- dinner only

Grove

HISTORIC • PERSONALISED Set in 35 acres, in a charming rural location, the Grove comprises a 15C longhouse and a whitewashed property with Stuart and Victorian additions. Bedrooms blend bold walls and bright fabrics with classical furnishings, and bathrooms boast underfloor heating and deep cast iron baths. Dine on modern dishes in the Fernery or traditional dishes in the cosy Artisan Rooms.

26 rooms - †£ 240/650 ††£ 240/650 - 8 suites

Molleston ✉ SA67 8BX - South : 2 mi by A 478 on Herons Brook rd
- ✆ 01834 860915 - www.thegrovenarberth.co.uk

Fernery - See restaurant listing

NEWBOROUGH ➜ See ANGLESEY (Isle of)

NEWCASTLE EMLYN

Carmarthenshire - Pop. 1 883 - Regional map n° **19**-B3

Gwesty'r Emlyn

INN • CONTEMPORARY This 300 year old coaching inn conceals a surprisingly modern interior. Guest areas include a stylish lounge, a snug bar, a small fitness room and a sauna. Bedrooms are contemporary and well-equipped; one features a glass-covered well. The characterful bistro offers a menu centred around local produce.

29 rooms - †£ 80/95 ††£ 100/120 - 4 suites

Bridge St ✉ SA38 9DU
- ✆ 01239 710317 - www.gwestyremlynhotel.co.uk

NEWPORT

Newport - Pop. 128 060 - Regional map n° **19**-C4

Celtic Manor Resort

RESORT • PERSONALISED A vast resort hotel set in 1,400 acres, boasting two floors of function rooms, a shopping arcade, 3 golf courses and an impressive swimming pool and spa. Bedrooms range from Standards to Presidential Suites and from classical to modern in style. The many restaurants offer everything from grills, buffets and carveries to Asian fusion dishes and modern fine dining menus.

332 rooms - †£ 127/343 ††£ 150/380 - 14 suites

Coldra Woods ✉ NP18 1HQ - East : 3 mi on A 48
- ✆ 01633 410262 - www.celtic-manor.com

NEWPORT TREFDRAETH

Pembrokeshire – Pop. 1 162 – Regional map n° **19**-A3

Llys Meddyg

MODERN CUISINE • RUSTIC XX Centrally located restaurant with a kitchen gard[en] and a slightly bohemian style. Eat in the formal dining room or the characterf[ul] laid-back cellar bar; the owner's father's art is displayed throughout. Cooki[ng] showcases local produce in ambitious, complex dishes. Modern bedrooms ha[ve] a Scandinavian style.

Carte £ 27/42

8 rooms – £ 70/140 £ 90/160

East St ✉ SA42 0SY – ✆ 01239 820008 – www.llysmeddyg.com – dinner only – Restricted opening in winter

Cnapan

TOWNHOUSE • PERSONALISED Part-Georgian house in a busy coastal villag[e] – keenly run by the 3rd generation of the family. The bar and lounge have homely feel. Bright bedrooms are compact but well-maintained; ask for one the back overlooking the garden.

5 rooms – £ 60/75 £ 85/98

East St ✉ SA42 0SY – on A 487 – ✆ 01239 820575 – www.cnapan.co.uk – Close[d] February and Christmas

NEWTOWN

Powys – ✉ Blaenau Gwent – Pop. 11 357 – Regional map n° **19**-C2

The Granary (N)

MODERN CUISINE • RUSTIC XX This was originally a baker's back in the 1900s it's apt that they grind grains in-house to make their sourdough. Dining takes pla[ce] over several levels and there's a Scandic feel both to the décor and the cookin[g]. Creative, highly seasonal dishes feature foraged and fermented ingredients.

Menu £ 50 – Carte £ 25/38

17 Parkers Ln ✉ SY16 2LT – ✆ 01686 621120 – www.thegranaryrestaurant.co.uk – Closed 2 weeks Christmas, Saturday lunch and Sunday-Tuesday

OLD RADNOR PENCRAIG

Powys – Pop. 400 – Regional map n° **19**-C3

Harp Inn

TRADITIONAL CUISINE • INN This 15C stone inn welcomes drinkers and dine[rs] alike. The charming flag-floored rooms boast open fires and beams hung wi[th] hop bines and the terrace offers glorious views. 'Seasonality' and 'sustainabili[ty]' are key, and menus are concise but original. Simple bedrooms come with wo[n]derful views.

Carte £ 22/36

5 rooms – £ 70/80 £ 100/110

✉ LD8 2RH – ✆ 01544 350655 – www.harpinnradnor.co.uk – Closed Monday except bank holidays, Tuesday and lunch Wednesday-Thursday

OXWICH

Swansea – Regional map n° **19**-B4

Beach House

MODERN CUISINE • DESIGN XX The former coal store of the Penrice Estate is charming stone building beside the beach, with a lovely terrace looking out ov[er] the bay. Menus range from a good value set lunch to an 8 course tasting men[u] and showcase interesting dishes which are full of flavour. The room has a nau[ti]cal, New England feel.

Menu £ 28 (lunch) – Carte £ 40/60

Oxwich Beach ✉ SA3 1LS – ✆ 01792 390965 – www.beachhouseoxwich.co.uk – Closed 2 weeks January and Monday-Tuesday

ENARTH

e Vale of Glamorgan - Pop. 27 226 - Regional map n° **19**-C4

James Sommerin

MODERN CUISINE • CONTEMPORARY DÉCOR XX A smart yet laid-back restaurant on the esplanade, which affords panoramic views over the Severn Estuary; five of the spacious bedrooms share the wonderful view. On Friday and Saturday the à la carte is supplemented by two surprise tasting menus. Skilfully-crafted modern dishes exhibit a well-judged blend of complementary textures and flavours; sauces are a highlight.

→ Butter-poached lobster with seed granola, lobster and sweetcorn bisque. Welsh lamb, butternut squash and coconut. Passion fruit soufflé with dark chocolate sorbet.

Menu £ 65/85
- Carte £ 36/54

9 rooms - £ 130/150 £ 150/170

The Esplanade ✉ CF64 3AU - ✆ 029 2070 6559
- www.jamessommerinrestaurant.co.uk - Closed 1 January, 26 December and Monday

Pier 64

MODERN CUISINE • FASHIONABLE XX A bright, airy wood-clad restaurant with a smart bar; set on stilts in an enviable harbourside location - its oversized windows give every table a view. The accessible menu features plenty of seafood and 28 day dry-aged steaks.

Carte £ 24/55

Penarth Marina ✉ CF64 1TT - ✆ 029 2000 0064 - www.pier64.co.uk
- Closed 24-25 December and Sunday dinner

Holm House

MODERN BRITISH • DESIGN X This bright, modern room is a complete contrast to the hotel's 1920s façade. Floor to ceiling windows offer sea views and there's an attractive garden terrace. Daily changing dishes are prepared with restraint and accuracy.

Menu £ 20 (weekday lunch)
- Carte £ 28/49

Holm House Hotel, Marine Par ✉ CF64 3BG - ✆ 029 2070 6029
- www.holmhousehotel.com

Mint and Mustard

INDIAN • NEIGHBOURHOOD X Fashionable high street restaurant with bare brick walls and exposed ducting. The menu features an extensive selection of vibrantly flavoured curries, tandoor dishes and Keralan-inspired recipes. Ingredients are locally sourced.

Menu £ 10 (lunch)
- Carte £ 17/32

33-34 Windsor Terr ✉ CF64 1AB - ✆ 029 2070 0500 - www.mintandmustard.com
- Closed 25 December

Holm House

BOUTIQUE HOTEL • PERSONALISED This characterful Arts and Crafts house sits on the clifftop in a smart residential neighbourhood and looks over the Bristol Channel to the tiny island after which it is named; some of its bedrooms have baths by the window.

13 rooms - £ 115/450 £ 115/450

Marine Par ✉ CF64 3BG - ✆ 029 2070 6029 - www.holmhousehotel.com

Holm House - See restaurant listing

PENMACHNO - Conwy ➔ See Betws-y-Coed

PENNAL

Gwynedd - Regional map n° **19**-B2

Riverside

TRADITIONAL CUISINE • PUB Enter under the 'Glan Yr Afron' (Riverside) si then make for the 'Cwtch' with its wood-burning stove. Despite its Grade II li ing, it has a bright modern feel. Hearty, no-nonsense pub classics are full of f vour and keenly priced.

Carte £ 19/35

SY20 9DW - 01654 791285 - www.riversidehotel-pennal.co.uk - Closed 2 weeks January and Monday October-May

PORTHCAWL

Bridgend - Pop. 15 672 - Regional map n° **19**-B4

Foam Edge

TOWNHOUSE • PERSONALISED A smart, modern, semi-detached house - a fa ily home - set next to the promenade, with great views over the Bristol Chanr Spacious, stylish bedrooms offer good facilities. Comfortable lounge and comn nal breakfasts.

3 rooms - †£ 80/100 ††£ 100/130

9 West Dr CF36 3LS - 01656 782866 - www.foam-edge.co.uk - Closed 25 December

PORTMEIRION

Gwynedd - Regional map n° **19**-B2

Portmeirion

HISTORIC • ART DÉCO A unique, Italianate village built on a private penins and boasting wonderful estuary views - the life work of Sir Clough Williams- lis. Stay in the appealing 1930s hotel or snug, well-appointed bedrooms spre about the village. The art deco style dining room offers a modern internatio menu.

47 rooms - †£ 124/199 ††£ 124/234 - 22 suites

LL48 6ER - 01766 772440 - www.portmerion-village.com - Closed 1-11 September

PUMSAINT

Carmarthenshire - Regional map n° **19**-B3

Dolaucothi Arms

TRADITIONAL BRITISH • RUSTIC A 500 year old drovers' inn set in the pict esque Cothi Valley, close to the Roman gold mines. It's a rustic place with a g den looking out over a river where they have 4 miles of fishing rights. Menus pub classics, which are supplemented by more adventurous specials. Bedroo are comfy and cosy.

Carte £ 20/33

3 rooms - †£ 60/70 ††£ 75/90

SA19 8UW - 01558 650237 - www.thedolaucothiarms.co.uk - Closed 25 December, Tuesday lunch, Monday except bank holidays and mid-week lunch November-February

Prices quoted after the symbol † refer to the lowest rate for a single room in low season, followed by the highest rate in high season. The same principle applies to the symbol †† for a double room.

PWLLHELI

Gwynedd – Pop. 4 076 – Regional map n° **19**-B2

Plas Bodegroes

MODERN CUISINE • INTIMATE XX A charming, Grade II listed Georgian house set in peaceful grounds; inside it's beautifully decorated and features an eclectic collection of modern Welsh art. There's a well-chosen wine list and the kitchen uses the best of the local larder to create classic dishes with a contemporary edge. Understated bedrooms are named after trees and have sleek, modern bathrooms.

Menu £ 45

10 rooms – £ 90/130 £ 120/160

LL53 5TH – Northwest : 1.75 ml on A 497
– 01758 612363 (bookings essential for non-residents) – www.bodegroes.co.uk
– dinner only – Closed January, Sunday and Monday except bank holidays

at Boduan Northwest: 3.75 mi on A497 Pwllheli

Old Rectory

TRADITIONAL • PERSONALISED Lovely part-Georgian family home with well-tended gardens and a paddock. Comfy lounge features a carved wood fireplace; communal breakfasts at a large table include plenty of fresh fruits. Tastefully decorated, homely bedrooms overlook the garden and come with complimentary chocolates and sherry or sloe gin.

3 rooms – £ 85/95 £ 95/125

LL53 6DT – 01758 721519 – www.theoldrectory.net
– Closed Christmas

RHOS-ON-SEA – Conwy → See Colwyn Bay

RHYL

Denbighshire – Pop. 25 149 – Regional map n° **19**-C1

Barratt's at Ty'n Rhyl

TRADITIONAL CUISINE • COSY XX Built in 1672 and retaining many original features, including a carved wooden fireplace reputed to have been the top of a bed owned by Catherine of Aragon! The characterful drawing rooms have a cosy, lived-in feel; the dining room, by contrast, is light and airy. Classically based menu. Traditional bedrooms.

Menu £ 40

3 rooms – £ 80 £ 98

167 Vale Rd. LL18 2PH – South : 0.5 mi on A 525
– 01745 344138 (booking essential) – www.barrattsattynrhyl.co.uk
– dinner only and Sunday lunch – Closed 12-20 July and Sunday-Monday

ROCH

Pembrokeshire – Pop. 463 – Regional map n° **19**-A3

Roch Castle

HISTORIC • DESIGN An intimate 12C castle set over 7 storeys, which has been fully refurbished by its architect owner. It's modern and stylish throughout, from the bedrooms with their quality linens to the fantastic 'Sun Room' with its far-reaching views.

6 rooms – £ 240/270 £ 240/270

SA62 6AQ
– 01437 725566 – www.rochcastle.com

ROSSETT

Wrexham – ✉ Wrexham – Pop. 2 007 – Regional map n° **19**-C1

Machine House

MODERN BRITISH · RUSTIC X This stone-walled barn was once an agricultu machine repair shop and it has retained a characterful, rustic feel. In contra with the surroundings, dishes are modern, with clearly defined flavours and a cr ative element.

Menu £ 23 (lunch and early dinner) – Carte dinner £ 35/42

Chester Rd ✉ LL12 0HW
– ✆ 01244 571678 – www.machinehouse.co.uk – Closed last 2 weeks August, firs 2 weeks January, Sunday and Monday

ROWEN – Conwy → See Conwy

RUTHIN RHUTHUN

Denbighshire – Pop. 5 461 – Regional map n° **19**-C1

On the Hill

TRADITIONAL CUISINE · RUSTIC X Immensely charming 16C house in a busy ma ket town; a real family-run business. It has characterful sloping floors, expos beams and a buzzy, bistro atmosphere. The accessible menu offers keenly price internationally-influenced classics.

Menu £ 14 (lunch) – Carte dinner £ 26/40

1 Upper Clwyd St ✉ LL15 1HY – ✆ 01824 707736 (booking essential)
– www.onthehillrestaurant.co.uk – Closed 25-26 December, 1 January and Sund

Manorhaus Ruthin

TOWNHOUSE · DESIGN A lovely Georgian manor house which retains plenty period character despite its contemporary first impression. The stylish lounge furnished with glass and chrome while the bar has a subtle retro feel; there even a cinema in the basement. The bright conservatory restaurant serves class fare.

8 rooms – †£ 55/95 ††£ 80/120

10 Well St ✉ LL15 1AH – ✆ 01824 704830 – www.manorhaus.com

Firgrove

FAMILY · COSY Attractive stone-built cottage set in stunning gardens. Sit in t snug by the cosy inglenook fireplace in winter or in the delightful plant-fill glasshouse in summer. Two comfortable four-poster bedrooms and a self-co tained cottage offer pleasant valley views. The owners join guests for hear home-cooked dinners which showcase locally sourced farm produce.

3 rooms – †£ 80/120 ††£ 100/120

Llanfwrog ✉ LL15 2LL – West : 1.25 mi by A 494 on B 5105
– ✆ 01824 702677 – www.firgrovecountryhouse.co.uk
– Closed November-February

ST CLEARS

Carmarthenshire – Pop. 1 989 – Regional map n° **19**-B3

Coedllys Country House

TRADITIONAL · PERSONALISED Lovely country house in a peaceful hillside loc tion, complete with a sanctuary where they keep rescued animals – the hens pr vide the eggs at breakfast. Guest areas are comfy and traditional and the char ing antique-furnished bedrooms have good mod cons and binoculars for bi watchers.

4 rooms – †£ 85/90 ††£ 95/110

Llangynin ✉ SA33 4JY – Northwest : 3.5 mi by A 40 turning first left after 30 mph sign on entering village – ✆ 01994 231455
– www.coedllyscountryhouse.co.uk – Closed 18 December-17 January

T DAVIDS TYDDEWI

ımbrokeshire – ✉ Haverfordwest – Pop. 1 959 – Regional map n° **19**-A3

ꟾO cwtch*

TRADITIONAL BRITISH • **RUSTIC** X Popular, laid-back restaurant; its name meaning 'hug'. The three rustic dining rooms boast stone walls, crammed bookshelves and log-filled alcoves. Classic British dishes arrive in generous portions and service is polite and friendly.

Menu £ 34

22 High St ✉ SA62 6SD
– ✆ 01437 720491 – www.cwtchrestaurant.co.uk – dinner only and Sunday lunch October-Easter – Closed January-early February and Monday-Tuesday November-Easter

Twr y Felin

HISTORIC BUILDING • DESIGN Strikingly restored 19C windmill with a cool, modern interior and over 100 pieces of contemporary art on display. The beautiful watchtower is now part of a 3-storey suite and many of the bedrooms have terraces and bay views. Dine in the dark, sultry restaurant or have snacks in the Gallery.

21 rooms – †£ 180/230 ††£ 180/230 – 2 suites

Caerfai Road ✉ SA62 6QT
– ✆ 01437 725555 – www.twryfelinhotel.com

Penrhiw Priory

COUNTRY HOUSE • ELEGANT Built from local red stone and set in 12 acres of gardens offering great country views – a real retreat. Original features have been sympathetically fused with modern designs; the original stained glass door is delightful.

8 rooms – †£ 190/240 ††£ 190/240

✉ SA62 6PG – Northwest : 0.5 mi by A 487 and Quickwell Hill Rd
– ✆ 01437 725588 – www.penrhiwhotel.com

Ramsey House

TRADITIONAL • PERSONALISED An unassuming-looking house on the edge of the UK's smallest city. Smart bedrooms have bold feature walls and either coast or country views. The Italian-tiled shower rooms come with bathrobes and L'Occitane toiletries.

6 rooms – †£ 70/135 ††£ 100/135

Lower Moor ✉ SA62 6RP – Southwest : 0.5 mi on Porth Clais rd
– ✆ 01437 720321 – www.ramseyhouse.co.uk – Closed December-January and restricted opening November and February

T GEORGE LLAN SAIN SIÔR

ɔnwy – Regional map n° **19**-C1

ꟾO Kinmel Arms

MODERN BRITISH • INN An early 17C stone inn hidden away in a hamlet by the entrance to Kinmel Hall. The open-fired bar is delightful and there's and a lovely pantry selling homemade produce. Menus offer modern British dishes and afternoon tea is a feature. Stylish, contemporary bedrooms have their own kitchenettes for breakfast.

Carte £ 27/33

4 rooms – †£ 115/175 ††£ 135/175

The Village ✉ LL22 9BP
– ✆ 01745 832207 – www.thekinmelarms.co.uk – Closed 25 December, 1 January and Monday

SAUNDERSFOOT

Pembrokeshire - Pop. 2 767 - Regional map n° **19**-A4

Coast

MODERN CUISINE • MINIMALIST XX A striking beachfront restaurant with a lovel terrace - every table affords stunning views courtesy of floor to ceiling window Modern menus have a local seafood bias; start with some snacks and move on to assured, carefully crafted dishes with a classical base. Service is friendly and relaxed.

Menu £ 28 (weekday lunch) - Carte £ 40/57

Coppet Hall Beach ✉ SA69 9AJ - ✆ 01834 810800
- www.coastsaundersfoot.co.uk - Closed 2 weeks January,
25-26 December, Monday and Tuesday

St Brides Spa

LUXURY • PERSONALISED Located on the clifftop, overlooking the harbour an the bay, is this nautically styled hotel featuring white wood panelling and contemporary Welsh art. The outdoor infinity pool has a great outlook, as do the restaurant and decked terraces. Smart, well-appointed bedrooms come in white an blue hues.

46 rooms - £ 145/230 £ 190/350 - 6 suites

St Brides Hill ✉ SA69 9NH
- ✆ 01834 812304 - www.stbridesspahotel.com

SEION - Gwynedd ➔ See Caernarfon

SKENFRITH

Monmouthshire - Regional map n° **19**-C4

Bell at Skenfrith

CLASSIC CUISINE • PUB Well-run pub in a verdant valley, offering hearty, classical cooking with the occasional ambitious twist and using ingredients from th organic kitchen garden. There's an excellent choice of champagnes and cognac and service is warm and unobtrusive. Super-comfy bedrooms have an unde stated elegance.

Menu £ 17 (weekday lunch) - Carte £ 31/49

11 rooms - £ 90 £ 150/230

✉ NP7 8UH
- ✆ 01600 750235 (booking essential) - www.skenfrith.co.uk

SWANSEA

Swansea - Pop. 179 485 - Regional map n° **19**-B4

Slice

MODERN BRITISH • INTIMATE X Sweet former haberdashery in a residential are the name reflecting its tapered shape. It's run by two friends who alterna weekly between cooking and serving. Precisely prepared, appealing mode dishes are packed with flavour.

Menu £ 32/55

73-75 Eversley Rd, Sketty ✉ SA2 9DE - West : 2 mi by A 4118
- ✆ 01792 290929 (booking essential) - www.sliceswansea.co.uk - dinner only and lunch Friday-Sunday - Closed 1 week autumn, 1 week Christmas and Monday-Wednesday

Morgans

BUSINESS • PERSONALISED An impressive Edwardian building by the dock with a beautiful façade and a charming interior displaying original plasterwo stained glass windows and a soaring cupola. Bedrooms in the main house are t most spacious. The restaurant boasts a hand-painted mural and a modern men

42 rooms - £ 100/275 £ 100/275

Somerset Pl ✉ SA1 1RR
- ✆ 01792 484848 - www.morganshotel.co.uk

AL-Y-LLYN

ʌynedd - ✉ Tywyn - Regional map n° **19**-B2

Dolffanog Fawr

FAMILY • PERSONALISED This homely 18C farmhouse stands in the shadow of Cadair Idris, just up from a lake; kick-back in the hot tub to make the most of the terrific valley views. Modern bedrooms are furnished in solid oak. Breakfast could include Welsh cakes and dinner might feature local lamb or sea trout caught by the owner.

4 rooms - £ 90/118 £ 110/120

✉ LL36 9AJ - On B 4405
- ✆ 01654 761247 - www.dolffanogfawr.co.uk
- Closed November-March

ENBY

ɘmbrokeshire - Pop. 4 934 - Regional map n° **19**-A4

Salt Cellar

MODERN CUISINE • FRIENDLY XX Four friends own and run this restaurant. It may be in a hotel basement but it's bright and fresh and its pretty terrace over the road offers glorious coastal views. Refined, well-crafted dishes champion local produce.

Carte £ 32/45

The Esplanade ✉ SA70 7DU
- ✆ 01834 844005 - www.thesaltcellartenby.co.uk - Closed 24-26 December

INTERN TYNDYRN

ɔnmouthshire - ✉ Chepstow - Regional map n° **19**-C4

Parva Farmhouse N

MODERN BRITISH • FRIENDLY X A 17C stone farmhouse on the bank of the River Wye, run by a friendly couple. Its simple, rustic interior comprises a spacious lounge and a small 6 table restaurant with an inglenook fireplace. Gutsy modern British cooking has a classic French backbone and the odd Italian or Asian touch. Bedrooms are modest.

Menu £ 42

8 rooms - £ 70 £ 85/90

Riverside ✉ NP16 6SQ - On A 466 - ✆ 01291 689411 (booking essential)
- www.parvafarmhouse.co.uk - dinner only - Closed 24-26 December and Sunday-Tuesday

REDUNNOCK - Newport

➜ See Usk

REGARON

ɘredigion - Regional map n° **19**-B3

Y Talbot

TRADITIONAL CUISINE • CLASSIC DÉCOR Originally a drover's inn dating back to the 17C; the bar rooms are where the action is, and the best place to sit. Seasonal menus offer full-flavoured traditional dishes made with Welsh produce. Bedrooms are bright and modern: ask for one of the newest. Oh, and there's an elephant buried in the garden!

Carte £ 25/43

13 rooms - £ 65/105 £ 90/145

✉ SY25 6JL - ✆ 01974 298208 - www.ytalbot.com - Closed 25-26 December

TYWYN

Gwynedd – Regional map n° **19**-B2

Salt Marsh Kitchen

TRADITIONAL BRITISH • SIMPLE A sweet little bistro run by a proud, hardworki owner. Cooking is honest and generous – the owner is a keen fisherman and will advi you of what's best. He is planning to move to larger premises just down the street.

Menu £ 20 (early dinner) – Carte £ 24/34

6 College Grn ✉ LL36 9BS – ✆ 01654 711949 – www.saltmarshkitchen.co.uk – dinner only – Closed January and Monday-Wednesday November-March

USK

Monmouthshire – Pop. 2 834 – Regional map n° **19**-C4

at Tredunnock South: 4.75 mi by Llangybi rd ✉ Newport

Newbridge on Usk

TRADITIONAL BRITISH • BISTRO 200 year old inn by a bridge over the Riv Usk; choose from several dining areas set over two levels or sit on the terra to have the snack menu. Classic British cooking has a modern twist; sharir plates are popular and include a crumble dessert. The smart, comfortable be rooms are in a separate block.

Menu £ 16 (weekday lunch) – Carte £ 30/53

6 rooms – †£ 70/150 ††£ 80/180

✉ NP15 1LY – East : 0.5 mi – ✆ 01633 451000 – www.celtic-manor.com

WHITEBROOK – Monmouthshire ➜ See Monmouth

Jacek Kadaj/iStock

IRELAND

NORTHERN IRELAND

Think of Northern Ireland and you think of buzzing Belfast, with its impressive City Hall and Queen's University. But the rest of the Six Counties demand attention too. Forty thousand stone columns of the Giants Causeway step out into the Irish Sea, while inland, Antrim boasts nine scenic glens. County Down's rolling hills culminate in the alluring slopes of Slieve Donard in the magical Mourne Mountains, while Armagh's Orchard County is a riot of pink in springtime. Fermanagh's glassy, silent lakelands are a tranquil attraction, rivalled for their serenity by the heather-clad Sperrin Mountains, towering over Tyrone and Derry.

Rich, fertile land, vast waterways and a pride in traditional crafts like butchery and baking mean that Northern Ireland yields a wealth of high quality produce: tender, full-flavoured beef and lamb, and fish and shellfish from the lakes, rivers and sea, including salmon, oysters, mussels and crabs. You can't beat an eel from Lough Neagh – and the seaweed called Dulse is a local delicacy not to be missed.

- Michelin Road maps n° 712, 713 and 501
- Michelin Green Guide: Ireland

20 Northern Ireland

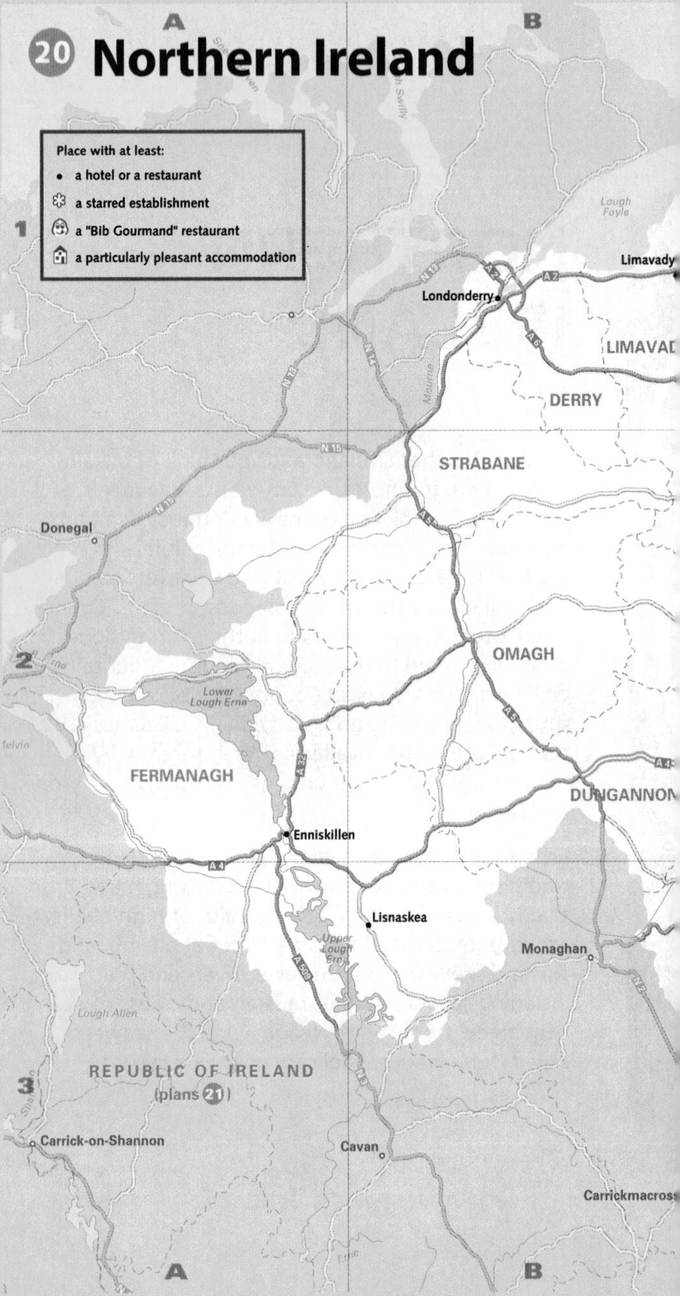

A
B
Place with at least:
• a hotel or a restaurant
a starred establishment
a "Bib Gourmand" restaurant
a particularly pleasant accommodation
1
2
3
Lough Foyle
Limavady
Londonderry
LIMAVADY
DERRY
STRABANE
Donegal
OMAGH
Lower Lough Erne
FERMANAGH
DUNGANNON
Enniskillen
Lisnaskea
Upper Lough Erne
Monaghan
Lough Allen
REPUBLIC OF IRELAND
(plans 21)
Carrick-on-Shannon
Cavan
Carrickmacross
N 13
N 14
N 15
A 2
A 6
A 5
A 32
A 4
A 509
N 2
N 3

C
D
CENTRAL
SCOTLAND
(plans 16)
NORTH CHANNEL
1
2
3
Ballintoy
Portstewart
Portrush
Bushmills
MOYLE
A 37
A 26
BALLYMONEY
Bann
Maghera
Ballymena
MAGHERAFELT
Magherafelt
A 26
A 8
Mounthill
M 22
COOKSTOWN
M 2
Newtownabbey
ANTRIM
Belfast Lough
Bangor
Crumlin
Lough
Neagh
A 2
Holywood
Donaghadee
Belfast
Newtownards
Dungannon
Aghalee
M 1
M 1
Moira
Magheralin
CRAIGAVON
Lisbane
Hillsborough
Killinchy
Strangford
Lough
A 24
A 3
A 1
Ballynahinch
DOWN
BANBRIDGE
Bann
Dundrum
Newcastle
Dundrum Bay
NEWRY
AND MOURNE
A 1
N 1
Carlingford
Lough
Dundalk
Dundalk bay
M 1
C
D

NOT TO BE MISSED

STARRED RESTAURANTS

✿

High quality cooking, worth a stop!

BIB GOURMAND RESTAURANTS

Good quality, good value cooking

Michelin

OUR TOP PICKS

CITY HOTSPOTS

rowns In Town	(Londonderry)	642
dō	(Belfast)	635
uddlers Club	(Belfast)	636
aphyre	(Belfast)	634

IKEABLE LOCALS

hurch Street	(Magherafelt)	643
eanes Deli	(Belfast)	635
Pirata	(Belfast)	636
olly's Yard	(Belfast)	636
leepy Hollow	(Newtownabbey)	644

WARM WELCOME AWAITS

airn Bay Lodge	(Bangor)	631
aldhame Lodge	(Crumlin)	638
auseway Lodge	(Bushmills)	638
denvale House	(Newtownards)	644
ewforge House	(Magheralin)	643
hola Coach House	(Portrush)	644
hitepark House	(Ballintoy)	630

PA RETREATS

ulloden	(Holywood)	641
algorm Resort and Spa	(Galgorm)	630
ough Erne Resort	(Enniskillen)	639

AGHALEE ACHADH LÍ

Lisburn and Castlereagh - Regional map n° **20**-C2

Clenaghans

CLASSIC CUISINE • COSY X This charming former pub dates back over 200 yea and is a hugely characterful place; follow the cobbled path through the garde where hens wander freely, and receive a warm welcome from the friendly tear The experienced chefs skilfully prepare appealingly unfussy, rustic dishes packe with flavour.

Carte £ 24/38

48 Soldierstown Rd ✉ BT67 0ES - Southeast : 1.75 mi on Soldierstown Rd - ☎ 028 9265 2952 - www.clenaghansrestaurant.com - Closed 25-26 December, 1 January, 12 July, Sunday dinner and Monday

ANNAHILT EANACH EILTE - Lisburn ➜ See Hillsborough

BALLINTOY

Moyle - Regional map n° **20**-C1

Whitepark House

TRADITIONAL • CLASSIC Charming 18C house near the Giant's Causeway, dec rated with lovely wall hangings, framed silks and other artefacts from the perso able owner's travels. Large, open-fired lounge where cakes are served on arriv Bright, antique-furnished bedrooms have four-posters or half-testers, and sma modern bathrooms.

3 rooms - †£ 90 ††£ 130

150 Whitepark Rd ✉ BT54 6NH - West : 1.5 mi on A 2 - ☎ 028 2073 1482 - www.whiteparkhouse.com - Closed December and January

BALLYMENA AN BAILE MEÁNACH

Ballymena - Pop. 29 782 - Regional map n° **20**-C2

at Galgorm West: 3 mi on A42

River Room

MODERN BRITISH • INTIMATE XXX Formal, warmly decorated dining room set the ground floor of a stylishly furnished, whitewashed Victorian manor hous with good views across the River Maine. Refined, classically based cooking ar attentive service.

Carte £ 44/49

Galgorm Resort and Spa Hotel, 136 Fenaghy Rd ✉ BT42 1EA - West : 1.5 mi on Cullybacky rd - ☎ 028 2588 1001 - www.galgorm.com - dinner only and Sunday lunch - Closed Monday and Tuesday

Galgorm Resort and Spa

LUXURY • CONTEMPORARY Victorian manor house with newer extensions, set large grounds. Stylish interior with plenty of lounge space, a huge function c pacity and an excellent leisure club with a superb outdoor spa pool. Modern be rooms boast state-of-the-art facilities; some have balconies. Extensive all-d menus served in characterful Gillies; informal Fratelli offers Italian fare.

134 rooms - †£ 105/285 ††£ 130/310 - 1 suite

136 Fenaghy Rd ✉ BT42 1EA - West : 1.5 mi on Cullybacky rd - ☎ 028 2588 1001 - www.galgorm.com

River Room - See restaurant listing

Take note of the classification: you should not expect the same level of service in a X or as in a XXXXX or .

BALLYNAHINCH BAILE NA HINSE

Down – Pop. 5 633 – Regional map n° **20**-D3

Bull & Ram

MEATS AND GRILLS • RUSTIC Stunning Grade I listed former butcher's shop. Sit beneath a herringbone oak ceiling and an old meat-hanging rail, surrounded by original tiling. Meat is the way to go, with beef and lamb dry-aged locally in a Himalayan salt chamber.

Carte £ 20/37

1 Dromore St ✉ BT24 8AG – ☎ 028 9756 0908 – www.bullandram.com – Closed Christmas, 12 July and Monday

BANGOR BEANNCHAR

North Down – Pop. 60 260 – Regional map n° **20**-D2

Wheathill

MODERN CUISINE • NEIGHBOURHOOD Gray's Hill was once known as Wheathill, as it was the route used to transport wheat to the harbour. Choose from hearty, wholesome classics and dishes with an Italian twist. Service is bubbly and the wine list is keenly priced.

Menu £ 18 (early dinner) – Carte £ 24/42

7 Grays Hill ✉ BT20 3BB – ☎ 028 9147 7405 – www.thewheathill.com – Closed 1 week January, 1 week July, Sunday dinner, Monday and Tuesday

Cairn Bay Lodge

FAMILY • COSY Set overlooking the bay, a whitewashed Edwardian house decorated with unusual objets d'art. Bedrooms come with plenty of extras and there's also a small beauty facility. The daytime café offers cakes and brunch-type dishes.

8 rooms – †£ 50/60 ††£ 90/110

278 Seacliffe Rd ✉ BT20 5HS – East : 1.25 mi by Quay St – ☎ 028 9146 7636 – www.cairnbaylodge.com

GOOD TIPS!

Optimism abounds in this city, with industry, commerce, arts and tourism all playing a role. With it has come a vibrant and ever-expanding restaurant scene that offers something for everyone, from delis and fish bars to bistros and brasseries. The Cathedral Quarter is the new dining hub attracting the foodies, while **Eipic** and **OX** have brought Michelin Stars.

BELFAST BÉAL FEIRSTE

Belfast - Pop. 267 742 - Regional map n° **20**-D2

Restaurants

✿ Eipic

MODERN CUISINE • ELEGANT XxX An elegant, intimate restaurant featuring glass-fronted wine room and a smart champagne bar. Top quality local and fc aged ingredients feature on modern seasonal menus and combinations are orig nal and creative. Clearly defined flavours are enhanced by original wine pairin by the glass or shot.

→ Shorthorn beef, leek, mouli, ponzu and cured yolk. BBQ lamb, artichoke, lo age gnocchi with cheese. Chocolate, malt and Guinness.

Menu £ 45/70 - tasting menu only

Town plan: B2-n - *28-40 Howard St ✉ BT1 6PF - ✆ 028 9033 1134 (booking essential) - www.deaneseipic.com - dinner only and Friday lunch - Closed 2-5 January, 17-20 April, 10-24 July, 25-31 December and Sunday-Tuesday*

✿ OX (Stephen Toman)

MODERN BRITISH • BISTRO X Top quality seasonal produce guides the menus this Scandic-style restaurant, where dinner is a daily changing 5 course 'surpris based on around 30 or so ingredients. Ask for a seat in the old minstrels' galle to take in views of the river - and arrive early for an aperitif in the Wine Cave.

→ Scallop with bisque, salsify and squid ink. Wild Wicklow venison with red ca bage, Jerusalem artichoke and chestnut. Caramelised apple, treacle, oats with f leaf ice cream.

Menu £ 22/55

Town plan: B1-m - *1 Oxford St ✉ BT1 3LA - ✆ 028 9031 4121 - www.oxbelfast.com - Closed 10-24 July, 24 December-2 January, 3-10 April, Sunday and Monday*

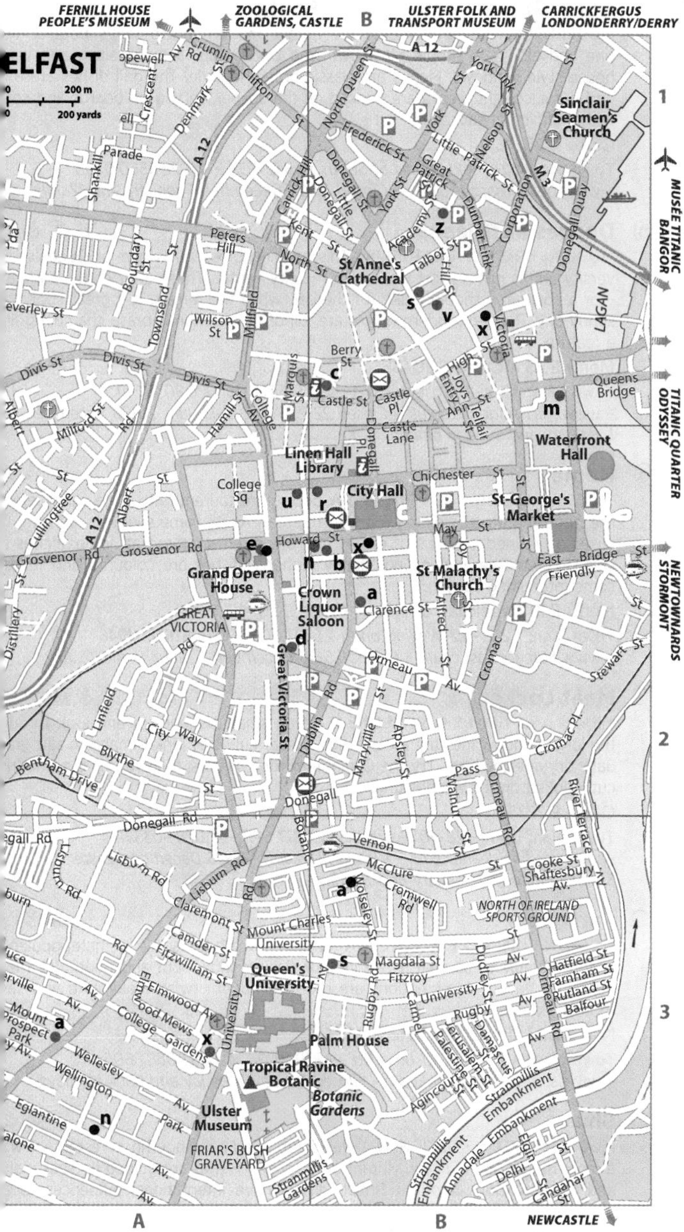
ELFAST
200 m
200 yards
FERNILL HOUSE PEOPLE'S MUSEUM
ZOOLOGICAL GARDENS, CASTLE
ULSTER FOLK AND TRANSPORT MUSEUM
CARRICKFERGUS LONDONDERRY/DERRY
MUSÉE TITANIC BANGOR
TITANIC QUARTER ODYSSEY
NEWTOWNARDS STORMONT
NEWCASTLE
A
B
1
2
3
Sinclair Seamen's Church
St Anne's Cathedral
Linen Hall Library
City Hall
Waterfront Hall
St-George's Market
Grand Opera House
Crown Liquor Saloon
St Malachy's Church
GREAT VICTORIA
Queen's University
Palm House
Tropical Ravine
Botanic
Botanic Gardens
Ulster Museum
FRIAR'S BUSH GRAVEYARD
NORTH OF IRELAND SPORTS GROUND
LAGAN
A 12
M 3
Crumlin Rd
Clifton St
North Queen St
York Link
Frederick St
Little Patrick St
Great Patrick St
Donegall St
Little Donegall St
York St
Carrick Hill
Kent St
North St
Academy St
Talbot St
Hill St
Dunbar Link
Corporation St
Donegall Quay
Victoria St
Peters Hill
Boundary St
Townsend St
Millfield
Wilson St
Shankill Parade
Denmark St
Crescent
Divis St
Berry St
Castle St
Castle Pl.
Castle Lane
High St
Joys Entry
Ann St
Telfair St
Queens Bridge
Marquis St
College Av.
Hamill St
Donegall Pl.
Chichester St
College Sq
Howard St
May St
Joy St
East Bridge St
Friendly St
Clarence St
Alfred St
Cromac St
Stewart St
Grosvenor Rd
Great Victoria St
Ormeau Av.
Dublin Rd
Maryville St
Apsley St
Walnut St
Pass
Ormeau Rd
Cromac Pl.
River Terrace
Linfield Rd
City Way
Blythe St
Bentham Drive
Donegall Pass
Donegall Rd
Botanic Av.
Vernon St
McClure St
Cooke St
Shaftesbury Av.
Lisburn Rd
Wolseley St
Cromwell Rd
Claremont St
Mount Charles
Camden St
Fitzwilliam St
University Rd
University St
Magdala St
Fitzroy Av.
Rugby Rd
Carmel St
Dudley St
Hatfield St
Farnham St
Rutland St
Balfour Av.
Elmwood Av.
Elmwood Mews
College Gardens
Wellesley Av.
Wellington Park
Eglantine Av.
Mount Prospect Park
Jerusalem St
Palestine St
Damascus St
Agincourt St
Stranmillis Embankment
Stranmillis Gardens
Annadale Embankment
Elgin St
Delhi St
Candahar St
Albert St
Milford St
Cullingtree Rd
Distillery St
Beverley St

Bar + Grill at James Street South

MODERN BRITISH • BRASSERIE X A vibrant modern bistro that's popular wi
one and all. It's a simple place with red brick walls, a high ceiling and war
house-style windows. Menus are classic brasserie style. The grill dishes are a h
and the succulent steaks are cooked on the Josper, served on boards and con
with a choice of sauces.

Carte £ 25/33

Town plan: B2-b – *21 James St South ✉ BT2 7GA – ✆ 028 9560 0700 – www.belfastbargrill.co.uk – Closed 25-26 December, 1 January and 12 July*

Deanes at Queens

MODERN BRITISH • BRASSERIE X This bustling brasserie is part of Queen's Ur
versity and is just a short walk from the city centre. Those after coffee and ca
– or a cocktail – should make for the bar, while the terrace is a great spot on
sunny day. Refined modern dishes are full of flavour; the Mibrasa charcoal grill
a feature.

Menu £ 23 – Carte £ 20/35

Town plan: A3-x – *1 College Gdns ✉ BT9 6BQ – ✆ 028 9038 2111 – www.michaeldeane.co.uk – Closed 22-23 April, 12-13 July, 25-26 December, 1 January and Sunday dinner*

Home

TRADITIONAL BRITISH • RUSTIC X A popular restaurant with a deli and café
the front and a rustic dining room to the rear. As its name suggests, cooking f
cuses on refined versions of dishes that are often prepared at home. Menus i
clude gluten free, vegan and 'skinny' options; dishes are colourful and featu
some interesting spicing.

Menu £ 18 (weekday dinner) – Carte £ 26/42

Town plan: B2-r – *22 Wellington Pl ✉ BT1 6GE – ✆ 028 9023 4946 – www.homebelfast.co.uk – Closed 25-26 December, 1 January and 12 July*

Meat Locker

MEATS AND GRILLS • BRASSERIE XX Sit on smart banquettes and look throu
the large window into the meat fridge, where cubes of pink Himalayan salt gra
ually dry age the beef. Try the Carlingford rock oysters, followed by a prime Iri
cut, cooked on the Asador grill.

Carte £ 28/55

Town plan: B2-n – *28-40 Howard St ✉ BT1 6PF – ✆ 028 9033 1134 – www.michaeldeane.co.uk – Closed 12-13 July, 25-26 December, Easter Sunday-Monday, 1 January and Sunday*

Saphyre

MODERN CUISINE • ELEGANT XX A former church houses this intimate, opulent
styled restaurant, as well as an interior design showroom and boutique. Tim
honoured flavour combinations are given a modern twist; make sure you sa
room for dessert.

Menu £ 23 (lunch) – Carte £ 46/54

Town plan: A3-a – *135 Lisburn Rd ✉ BT9 7AG – ✆ 028 9068 8606 – www.saphyrerestaurant.com – Closed Sunday-Tuesday and bank holidays*

Shu

MODERN BRITISH • DESIGN XX A well-established neighbourhood restaurant wi
a modern look and a lively, vibrant atmosphere. Menus are guided by seasonali
and the ambitious, modern British dishes have international influences. Go
value set price menu.

Menu £ 17/31 – Carte £ 21/42

253 Lisburn Rd ✉ BT9 7EN – Southwest : 1.75 mi on A1 – ✆ 028 9038 1655 – www.shu-restaurant.com – Closed 1 January, 11-13 July, 24-26 December and Sunday

Coppi

MEDITERRANEAN CUISINE • BISTRO Set on the ground floor of a purpose built property in the Cathedral Quarter. It's big and buzzy, with rustic furnishings and leather booths, and staff are bright and friendly. Good value Italian dishes; start with a selection of cicchetti.

Menu £ 16 (weekday lunch) - Carte £ 20/46

Town plan: B1-z - *St Annes Sq ✉ BT1 2LD - ✆ 028 9031 1959 - www.coppi.co.uk - Closed 25-26 December*

Cyprus Avenue

TRADITIONAL CUISINE • NEIGHBOURHOOD You'll find something to please everyone at this all-day suburban bistro. Head past the cabinet bursting with home-baked goodies, to one of the intimate booths at the back. Dishes are appealing and full of flavour.

Carte £ 21/44

228 Upper Newtownards Rd ✉ BT4 3ET - East : 2.5 mi by A 2 on A 20 - ✆ 028 9065 6755 - www.cyprusavenue.co.uk - Closed 25 December

Deanes Deli

MODERN BRITISH • BISTRO Glass-fronted city centre eatery. One side is a smart restaurant offering an appealing menu of classical dishes with some Asian and Mediterranean influences; the other side acts as a coffee shop by day and a buzzy tapas bar by night.

Menu £ 19 (early dinner) - Carte £ 21/32

Town plan: B2-a - *42-44 Bedford St ✉ BT2 7FF - ✆ 028 9024 8800 - www.michaeldeane.co.uk - Closed 25-26 December, 12-13 July, 1 January, Sunday dinner and Easter Monday*

Deanes Love Fish

SEAFOOD • ELEGANT If it comes from the sea, they'll serve it here! A glass ceiling makes it light and airy and the décor has a maritime feel. The à la carte offers three sizes of platter and everything from cod croquettes to lobster. Lunch is good value.

Carte £ 22/32

Town plan: B2-n - *28-40 Howard St ✉ BT1 6PF - ✆ 028 9033 1134 - www.michaeldeane.co.uk - Closed Easter Sunday-Monday, dinner 24 December, 12-13 July, 1 January and Sunday*

Edō N

MODERN BRITISH • TRENDY 'I eat' is a smart, modish brasserie in the heart of the city, with rustic-meets-faux-industrial styling and seats at the long kitchen counter for those who want to get in on the action. The international menu allows for sharing and many dishes are cooked over apple or pear wood in the Bertha oven.

Carte £ 30/40

Town plan: A2-u - *3 Capital House, Unit 2, Upper Queen St ✉ BT1 6FB - ✆ 028 9031 3054 - www.edorestaurant.co.uk - Closed 2 weeks July, 1 week January, Christmas, Easter, Sunday and Monday*

Ginger Bistro

TRADITIONAL CUISINE • BISTRO Rustic neighbourhood bistro close to the Grand Opera House. The two rooms feature bright modern artwork and bespoke fish-themed paintings. Good-sized menus feature simply cooked Irish ingredients and display some Asian influences.

Carte £ 24/43

Town plan: A2-d - *68-72 Great Victoria St ✉ BT2 7AF - ✆ 028 9024 4421 - www.gingerbistro.com - Closed Christmas, New Year, Easter, 1 week mid-July, Sunday and lunch Monday-Wednesday*

Hadskis

MEATS AND GRILLS • BISTRO X Hadskis stands in an old building in the up-an coming Cathedral Quarter. It was once part of the area's Iron Foundry and named after the owner. The long, narrow room has a modern feel and you ca watch the chefs in the open kitchen. Cooking showcases market produce and f cuses on the chargrill.

Menu £ 20 (early dinner) – Carte £ 25/42

Town plan: B1-s – *33 Donegall St ✉ BT1 2NB – ✆ 028 9032 5444 – www.hadskis.co.uk – Closed 25-26 December, 1 January and 12 July*

Il Pirata

MEDITERRANEAN CUISINE • RUSTIC X Rustic restaurant with scrubbed wood floors and an open kitchen. Mediterranean-influenced menus offer an extensi range of mainly Italian small plates; 3 or 4 dishes per person (plus desse should suffice. Bright, friendly service.

Carte £ 20/30

279-281 Upper Newtownards Rd ✉ BT4 3JF – East : 3 mi by A 2 on A 20 – ✆ 028 9067 3421 – www.ilpiratabelfast.com

Molly's Yard

TRADITIONAL BRITISH • BISTRO X Split-level bistro in a former coach house a stables, with exposed brickwork and a pleasant courtyard. Simple lunches a more ambitious dinners with classical combinations given a personal twist. Fi selection of ales and stouts.

Menu £ 20 (weekdays) – Carte £ 20/44

Town plan: B3-s – *1 College Green Mews, Botanic Ave ✉ BT7 1LW – ✆ 028 9032 2600 (booking essential) – www.mollysyard.co.uk – Closed 24-26 December, 12 July, 1 January and Sunday*

Mourne Seafood Bar

SEAFOOD • BISTRO X This popular seafood restaurant comes complete with small shop and a cookery school. Blackboard menus offer a huge array of fresh prepared dishes; go for the classics, such as the Carlingford oysters, accompanie by a pint of stout.

Carte £ 24/45

Town plan: B1-c – *34-36 Bank St ✉ BT1 1HL – ✆ 028 9024 8544 (booking essential at dinner) – www.mourneseafood.com – Closed 24-26 December, 1 January, Easter Sunday and 12 July*

Muddlers Club

MODERN CUISINE • DESIGN X Tucked away in a labyrinth of passageways is th modern, industrial-style restaurant named after a 200 year old secret societ Cooking shows off local ingredients: starters and mains are rustic, while desse are more refined.

Menu £ 50 – Carte £ 31/48

Town plan: B1-v – *1 Warehouse Ln ✉ BT1 2DX – (off Waring St) – ✆ 028 9031 3199 – www.themuddlersclubbelfast.com – Closed 2 weeks July, 1 week Easter, 1-8 January, 24-27 December, Sunday and Monday*

Hotels

Merchant

LUXURY • ELEGANT Former Ulster Bank HQ with an impressive Victorian façad Plush, intimately styled bedrooms; those in the annexe have an art deco them Rooftop gym with an outdoor hot tub and a skyline view; relax afterwards the swish cocktail bar. British dishes with a Mediterranean edge in the opule former banking hall. Classic French brasserie dishes and live jazz in Berts.

62 rooms – †£ 170/230 ††£ 180/349 – 2 suites

Town plan: B1-x – *16 Skipper St ✉ BT1 2DZ – ✆ 028 9023 4888 – www.themerchanthotel.com*

Fitzwilliam

LUXURY • CONTEMPORARY Stylish hotel by the Grand Opera House. Smart modern bedrooms have striking colour schemes, contemporary furnishings and good facilities. Have afternoon tea in the lobby, eat informally in the bar or dine on modern Irish dishes in the first floor restaurant. The small function room has great rooftop views.

145 rooms – £ 300/450 £ 310/460 – 1 suite

Town plan: A2-e – *Great Victoria St ✉ BT2 7BQ – ✆ 028 9044 2080 – www.fitzwilliamhotelbelfast.com*

Ten Square

BUSINESS • MODERN Hidden behind the historic City Hall is this Grade I listed Victorian hotel. Bedrooms offer a good level of facilities; the newer ones – in a converted office building – are state-of-the-art. The vibrant bar and terrace is a popular spot, as is Jospers restaurant, which serves steaks and grills.

60 rooms – £ 75/115 £ 115/225

Town plan: B2-x – *10 Donegall Sq South ✉ BT1 5JD – ✆ 028 9024 1001 – www.tensquare.co.uk – Closed 24-25 December*

Malone Lodge

BUSINESS • MODERN Well-run, privately owned townhouse, in a peaceful Victorian terrace. Smart, spacious bedrooms are spread over various annexes and range from corporate rooms to presidential suites and apartments. State-of-the-art function rooms include a large ballroom. Characterful bar and next door grill restaurant.

102 rooms – £ 89/149 £ 89/179 – £ 15 – 3 suites

Town plan: A3-n – *60 Eglantine Ave ✉ BT9 6DY – ✆ 028 9038 8000 – www.malonelodgehotelbelfast.com*

Tara Lodge

TOWNHOUSE • CONTEMPORARY Small hotel close to the Botanic Gardens, not far from town. Smart contemporary bedrooms are split between two buildings; go for a 'Signature' room, which comes with bluetooth speakers, hair straighteners and a coffee machine.

34 rooms – £ 75/105 £ 85/115

Town plan: B3-a – *36 Cromwell Rd ✉ BT7 1JW – ✆ 028 9059 9099 – www.taralodge.com – Closed 24-27 December*

Ravenhill House

TRADITIONAL • CLASSIC Red-brick Victorian house set in the city suburbs. Bright, homely lounge and wood-furnished breakfast room; colourful bedrooms boast good facilities. Organic breakfasts feature homemade muesli and the wheat for the bread is home-milled.

4 rooms – £ 80/105 £ 90/120

690 Ravenhill Rd ✉ BT6 0BZ – Southeast : 1.75 mi on B 506 – ✆ 028 9020 7444 – www.ravenhillhouse.com – Closed 20 December-January and 5-14 July

RYANSFORD – Down ➜ See Newcastle

USHMILLS MUILEANN NA BUAISE

oyle – ✉ Bushmills – Pop. 1 343 – Regional map n° **20**-C1

Bushmills Inn

TRADITIONAL • CLASSIC Proudly run, part-17C whitewashed inn that successfully blends the old with the new. The conference room features a state-of-the-art cinema. Up-to-date bedrooms are split between the original house and an extension. Have a drink beside the peat fire in the old whiskey bar before dining on classic dishes.

41 rooms – £ 120/210 £ 130/440

9 Dunluce Rd ✉ BT57 8QG – ✆ 028 2073 3000 – www.bushmillsinn.com – Closed 24-25 December

Causeway Lodge

FAMILY • CONTEMPORARY Set inland from the Giant's Causeway, in a peace location. Guest areas come with polished wood floors, leather furnishings and a work of local scenes. Spacious, boutique bedrooms have bold feature walls and high level of facilities.

5 rooms – £ 90/150 £ 100/160

52 Moycraig Rd, Dunseverick BT57 8TB – East : 5 mi by A 2 and Drumnagee – 028 2073 0333 – www.causewaylodge.com

CRUMLIN CROMGHLINN

Antrim – Pop. 5 117 – Regional map n° **20**-C2

Caldhame Lodge

FAMILY • PERSONALISED Purpose-built guesthouse near the airport, with pleasant mix of lawns and paved terracing. Comfy guest areas include a conservatory breakfast room and a lounge filled with family photos. Good-sized, individually decorated bedrooms are immaculately kept and feature warm fabrics a iPod docking stations.

8 rooms – £ 45/60 £ 70/80

102 Moira Rd, Nutts Corner BT29 4HG – Southeast : 2 mi on A 26 – 028 9442 3099 – www.caldhamelodge.co.uk

DERRY/LONDONDERRY → See Londonderry

DONAGHADEE DOMHNACH DAOI

Ards – Pop. 6 856 – Regional map n° **20**-D2

Pier 36

TRADITIONAL CUISINE • PUB This vast, family-run pub sits on the quayside a picturesque harbour town. There's a smart bar downstairs and, above it, 'Ha bour and Company', which has two huge windows overlooking the bay. Choo from pub classics, chargrilled seafood and fantastic wood-fired steaks. Brig bedrooms have a seaside feel.

Carte £ 23/46

6 rooms – £ 55/85 £ 79/119

36 The Parade BT21 0HE – 028 9188 4466 – www.pier36.co.uk – Closed 25 December

DUNDRUM DÚN DROMA

Down – Pop. 1 522 – Regional map n° **20**-D3

Buck's Head Inn

SEAFOOD • NEIGHBOURHOOD Have drinks in the lounge of this converted v lage pub, then sit overlooking the garden or in a cosy booth by the fire. Unfus lunches are followed by more ambitious dinners; seafood is a strength, partic larly mussels.

Menu £ 30 (lunch) – Carte £ 22/43

77-79 Main St BT33 0LU – 028 4375 1868 – Closed 24-25 December and Monday October-March

Mourne Seafood Bar

SEAFOOD • RUSTIC Friendly, rustic restaurant on the main street of a bu coastal town. Simple, wood-furnished dining room with nautically themed a work. Classic menus centre around seafood, with oysters and mussels from t owners' beds the specialities.

Carte £ 16/36

10 Main St BT33 0LU – 028 4375 1377 (booking essential) – www.mourneseafood.com – Closed 25-26 December and Monday-Wednesday winter

Carriage House

TRADITIONAL · CLASSIC Sweet, lilac-washed terraced house with colourful window boxes. Homely lounge with books and local info. Simple, antique-furnished bedrooms; some affording pleasant bay views. Breakfast in the conservatory, overlooking the pretty garden.

3 rooms - £ 80/90 £ 110/125

71 Main St ✉ BT33 0LU - ☎ 028 4375 1635 - www.carriagehousedundrum.com

DUNGANNON DÚN GEANAINN

Dungannon - Pop. 14 380 - Regional map n° **20**-C2

Grange Lodge

TRADITIONAL · CLASSIC An attractive Georgian country house with well-kept gardens (an ideal spot for afternoon tea!) Antique-furnished guest areas display fine sketches and lithographs. Snug, well-appointed bedrooms are immaculately kept with good extras.

5 rooms - £ 79/99 £ 99/109

7 Grange Rd, Moy ✉ BT71 7EJ - Southeast : 3.5 mi by A 29 - ☎ 028 8778 4212 - www.grangelodgecountryhouse.com - Closed 20 December-1 February

ENNISKILLEN INIS CEITHLEANN

Fermanagh - Pop. 13 757 - Regional map n° **20**-A2

Lough Erne Resort

LUXURY · MODERN Vast, luxurious golf and leisure resort on a peninsula between two loughs. Bedrooms have a classical style and are extremely well-appointed; the suites and lodges are dotted about the grounds. Relax in the beautiful Thai spa or the huge pool with its stunning mosaic wall. Ambitious, contemporary dining and lough views in Catalina; steaks and grills in the clubhouse.

120 rooms - £ 99/219 £ 99/319 - 6 suites

Belleek Rd ✉ BT93 7ED - Northwest : 4 mi by A 4 on A 46 - ☎ 028 6632 3230 - www.lougherneresort.com

Manor House

TRADITIONAL · MODERN An impressive yellow-washed manor house overlooking Lough Erne and surrounded by mature grounds. Comfy, stylish guest areas mix the traditional and the contemporary. Bedrooms range from characterful in the main house to smart and modern in the extensions. The formal dining room offers classical cooking and there's a more casual all-day menu served in the old vaults.

79 rooms - £ 85/140 £ 90/188 - 2 suites

Killadeas ✉ BT94 1NY - North : 7.5 mi by A 32 on A 47 - ☎ 028 6862 2200 - www.manorhousecountryhotel.com

GALGORM → See Ballymena

HILLSBOROUGH CROMGHLINN

Lisburn - Pop. 3 738 - Regional map n° **20**-C2

Parson's Nose

TRADITIONAL CUISINE · PUB This characterful Georgian property really is a sizeable place. You can eat anywhere: in the charming bar, the contemporary bistro-style Sunroom or the first floor Attic restaurant. Accessible menus are good value and the bespoke sourdough pizzas cooked in the wood-fired oven are a hit.

Carte £ 21/40

48 Lisburn St ✉ BT26 6AB - ☎ 028 9268 3009 - www.theparsonsnose.co.uk - Closed 25 December

Plough Inn

TRADITIONAL CUISINE • PUB A family-run, 18C coaching inn that's two estab lishments in one: a café-cum-bistro and a bar with an adjoining dining room which opens on Friday and Saturday. All-encompassing menus range from ligh snacks and pub classics to more modern, international offerings.

Carte £ 23/43

3 The Square ✉ BT26 6AG – ✆ 028 9268 2985 – www.ploughgroup.com/ploughinn – Closed 25-26 December

Lisnacurran Country House

FAMILY • PERSONALISED Homely Edwardian house, where spacious rooms are furn ished with antiques. Choose a bedroom in the main house, the former milking parlour o the old barn. Breakfasts are hearty – the homemade soda and potato bread is a must

8 rooms – †£ 58/65 ††£ 73/93

6 Listullycurran Rd, Dromore ✉ BT25 1RB – Southwest : 3 mi on A 1 – ✆ 028 9269 8710 – www.lisnacurrancountryhouse.co.uk

at Annahilt Southeast: 4 mi on B177✉ Hillsborough

Pheasant

TRADITIONAL CUISINE • PUB Dark wood and stained glass give this pub Gothic look and the Guinness-themed art, warm welcome and laid-back atmo sphere add a typically Irish feel. Portions are hearty, lunch is good value and th fishcakes are delicious.

Menu £ 13 (lunch and early dinner) – Carte £ 19/33

410 Upper Ballynahinch Rd ✉ BT26 6NR – North : 1 mi on Lisburn rd – ✆ 028 9263 8056 – www.thepheasantrestaurant.co.uk – Closed 25-26 Decembe and 12 July

Fortwilliam

TRADITIONAL • CLASSIC Attractive bay-windowed farmhouse with neat gar dens, surrounded by 80 acres of land. Homely lounge and a country kitche with an Aga. Traditional bedrooms have flowery fabrics, antiques and countr views; two have private bathrooms.

3 rooms – †£ 50/75 ††£ 50/75

210 Ballynahinch Rd ✉ BT26 6BH – Northwest : 0.25 mi on B 177 – ✆ 028 9268 2255 – www.fortwilliamcountryhouse.com – Closed 24-27 Decembe

HOLYWOOD ARD MHIC NASCA

North Down – Pop. 12 131 – Regional map n° **20**-D2

Fontana

MODERN CUISINE • NEIGHBOURHOOD XX This smart, modern, first floor restau rant is a favourite amongst the locals; it's accessed down a narrow town centr passageway and decorated with contemporary art. Menus offer British, Medite ranean and some Asian dishes, with local seafood a speciality. A good value se menu is available at dinner.

Menu £ 27 (weekday dinner) – Carte £ 25/43

61A High St ✉ BT18 9AE – ✆ 028 9080 9908 – www.restaurantfontana.com – Closed 25-26 December, 1-2 January, Saturday lunch, Sunday dinner and Monday

Noble

MODERN CUISINE • NEIGHBOURHOOD X Housed in the centre of a busy tow above a health food shop, is this compact little restaurant where the service i warm and genuine and the room has a happy buzz. The good value weekl menu showcases carefully handled local ingredients; for dessert be sure to tr the chocolate delice.

Menu £ 15 (early dinner) – Carte £ 26/36

27a Church Rd ✉ BT18 9BU – ✆ 028 9042 5655 – www.nobleholywood.com – Closed 24 December-1 January, 1-9 April, 8-23 July, 14-22 October, Monday-Tuesday and lunch Wednesday

Culloden

BUSINESS • CLASSIC An extended Gothic mansion overlooking Belfast Lough, with well-maintained gardens full of modern sculptures, and a smart spa. Charming, traditional, antique-furnished guest areas have open fires and fine ceiling frescoes. Characterful bedrooms offer good facilities. Classical menus and good views in formal Mitre; wide range of traditional dishes in Cultra Inn.

98 rooms - £185/300 £216/350 - 3 suites

142 Bangor Rd ✉ BT18 0EX - East : 1.5 mi on A 2 - ✆ 028 9042 1066 - www.hastingshotels.com

Rayanne House

TRADITIONAL • CLASSIC Keenly run, part-Victorian house in a residential area. Homely, antique-filled guest areas. Smart, country house bedrooms with a modern edge; those to the front offer the best views. Ambitious, seasonal dishes in formal dining room; try the Titanic tasting menu - a version of the last meal served on the ship.

10 rooms - £100/120 £140/160

60 Demesne Rd ✉ BT18 9EX - by My Lady's Mile Rd - ✆ 028 9042 5859 - www.rayannehouse.com

KILLINCHY

ards - Regional map n° **20**-D2

Balloo House

CLASSIC CUISINE • PUB Characterful former farmhouse with a smart dining pub feel. Lengthy menus mix hearty pub classics and dishes with international leanings. Pies are popular, as is High Tea, which is served every day except Saturday.

Menu £20 (weekdays) - Carte £23/41

1 Comber Rd ✉ BT23 6PA - West : 0.75 mi on A 22 - ✆ 028 9754 1210 - www.balloohouse.com - Closed 25 December

LIMAVADY LÉIM AN MHADAIDH

imavady - Pop. 12 669 - Regional map n° **20**-B1

Lime Tree

TRADITIONAL CUISINE • NEIGHBOURHOOD XX Keenly run neighbourhood restaurant; its traditional exterior concealing a modern room with purple velvet banquettes and colourful artwork. Unfussy, classical cooking features meats and veg from the village; try the homemade wheaten bread.

Menu £28 - Carte £28/37

60 Catherine St ✉ BT49 9DB - ✆ 028 7776 4300 - www.limetreerest.com - dinner only and lunch Thursday-Friday - Closed 25-26 December, Sunday and Monday

LISBANE AN LIOS BÁN

rds - ✉ Comber - Regional map n° **20**-D2

Poacher's Pocket

TRADITIONAL BRITISH • PUB Modern-looking building in the centre of a small village; the best seats are in the two-tiered extension overlooking the internal courtyard. Wide-ranging menus offer rustic, hearty dishes; come at the weekend for a laid-back brunch.

Menu £15 (weekdays) - Carte £24/41

181 Killinchy Rd ✉ BT23 5NE - ✆ 028 9754 1589 - www.poacherspocketlisbane.com - Closed 25 December

LISNASKEA

Fermanagh – Pop. 2 880 – Regional map n° **20**-B3

Watermill Lodge

INN • TRADITIONAL A charming red-brick cottage with a thatched roof concea a rustic restaurant with a 25,000 litre aquarium and a delightful terrace. Fro there, superb water gardens lead down to Lough Erne, where airy bedroon with stone floors and heavy wood furnishings boast terraces looking out ov the water.

7 rooms – £ 59/79 £ 89/99

Kilmore Quay BT92 0DT – Southwest: 3 mi by B 127 – 028 6772 4369 – www.watermillrestaurantfermanagh.com

LONDONDERRY/DERRY

Derry – Pop. 85 016 – Regional map n° **20**-B1

Browns

MODERN BRITISH • NEIGHBOURHOOD XX The original Browns sits across fro the railway station and comes with a plush lounge and an intimate, understate dining room. Dishes are eye-catching and showcase top Northern Irish produce some interesting combinations.

Menu £ 25 (weekdays) – Carte £ 35/45

1 Bonds Hill, Waterside BT47 6DW – East : 1 mi by A 2 – 028 7134 5180 – www.brownsrestaurant.com – Closed 24-26 December, Sunday dinner and Monday

Browns In Town

MODERN BRITISH • BRASSERIE X Across the river from the first Browns, is i laid-back bigger sister. A bewildering array of menus offer everything you coul want, from light snacks to hearty Irish meats and veg. Cooking is modern an comprises many elements.

Menu £ 15/25

Strand Rd BT48 7DJ – 028 7136 2889 – www.brownsrestaurant.com – Close 25 December and Sunday lunch

Beech Hill Country House

TRADITIONAL • CLASSIC Once a US Marine HQ, this 18C house is now a we coming hotel and wedding venue. Characterful guest areas feature ornate cov ing and antiques, and most of the bedrooms have a country house style. Dir overlooking the lake and water wheel – traditional menus use produce fro the walled garden.

31 rooms – £ 80/120 £ 120/150 – 2 suites

32 Ardmore Rd BT47 3QP – Southeast : 3.5 mi by A 6 – 028 7134 9279 – www.beech-hill.com – Closed 24-25 December

Da Vinci's

BUSINESS • MODERN The hub of this welcoming hotel is its characterful ba which was once a pub owned by a local artist and now offers informal all da dining. Bedrooms are spacious and modern – and the events rooms are equal stylish. Photos of stars who have stayed here fill the walls.

64 rooms – £ 65/145 £ 65/145 – £ 10

15 Culmore Rd BT48 8JB – North : 1 mi on A 2 (Foyle Bridge rd) – 028 7127 9111 – www.davincishotel.com – Closed 24-25 December

MAGHERA MACHAIRE RÁTHA

Magherafelt – Pop. 3 886 – Regional map n° **20**-C2

Ardtara Country House

COUNTRY HOUSE • CLASSIC Spacious, elegant 19C country house, originally built for a local linen manufacturer. It's set in 8 acres of mature grounds and has a calming, restful air; many period features remain. The intimate wood-panelled restaurant offers a menu of modern classics which feature ingredients foraged for by the chef.

9 rooms – £ 89/238 £ 99/248

8 Gorteade Rd, Upperlands BT46 5SA – 028 7964 4490 – www.ardtara.com – Closed Monday and Tuesday in winter

MAGHERAFELT

Magherafelt – Pop. 8 881 – Regional map n° **20**-C2

Church Street

TRADITIONAL BRITISH • NEIGHBOURHOOD XX Bustling eatery on the main street of a busy country town. The long, narrow room has a mix of bistro, pew and high-backed seating, and there's a second smart room above. Unfussy, classical dishes rely on good quality local produce.

Menu £ 16 (early dinner) – Carte £ 22/42

23 Church St BT45 6AP – 028 7932 8083 – www.churchstreetrestaurant.co.uk – dinner only and Sunday lunch – Closed 8-16 July, Monday and Tuesday

MAGHERALIN

Craigavon – Pop. 1 403 – Regional map n° **20**-C2

Newforge House

COUNTRY HOUSE • PERSONALISED A traditional Georgian building with an old linen mill behind and colourful gardens and a meadow in front. Bedrooms are named after former inhabitants of the house and are tastefully furnished with period pieces. Three course dinners are replaced by simpler suppers on Sundays and Mondays.

6 rooms – £ 95/140 £ 135/199

58 Newforge Rd BT67 0QL – 028 9261 1255 – www.newforgehouse.com – Closed 20 December-1 February

MOIRA MAIGH RATH

Lisburn – Pop. 4 221 – Regional map n° **20**-C2

Wine & Brine

MODERN CUISINE • BISTRO X Local chef Chris McGowan has transformed this fine Georgian house into a bright modern restaurant displaying local art. Top regional ingredients feature in appealing dishes with a comforting feel. As its name suggests, some of the meats and fish are gently brined, using whey from the nearby cheese factory.

Carte £ 19/46

59 Main St BT67 0LQ – 028 9261 0500 – www.wineandbrine.co.uk – Closed 2 weeks January, 2 weeks July, Sunday dinner, Monday and Tuesday

MOUNTHILL

Antrim – Pop. 69 – Regional map n° **20**-D2

Billy Andy's

TRADITIONAL BRITISH • RUSTIC It used to be the village store as well as a pub, and although the groceries are gone, this place still seems to be all things to all people. Cooking is filling, with a strong Irish accent. They offer a fine selection of whiskies, there are four modern bedrooms and Saturday music sessions pack the place out.

Carte £ 23/38

4 rooms – £ 40/65 £ 70/90

66 Browndod Rd BT40 3DX – 028 2827 0648 – www.billyandys.com – Closed 25-26 December

NORTHERN IRELAND

NEWCASTLE AN CAISLEÁN NUA

Down - Pop. 7 723 - Regional map n° **20**-D3

Vanilla

INTERNATIONAL • NEIGHBOURHOOD XX Contemporary restaurant; its black ca opy standing out amongst the town centre shops. The long, narrow room flanked by brushed velvet banquettes and polished tables. Attractively presente internationally influenced modern dishes.

Menu £ 24 (lunch and early dinner) - Carte £ 30/41

67 Main St ✉ BT33 0AE
- ✆ 028 4372 2268 - www.vanillarestaurant.co.uk
- Closed 25-26 December and lunch 1 January

at Bryansford Northwest: 2.75 mi on B180

Tollyrose Country House

FAMILY • PERSONALISED Purpose-built guesthouse beside the Tollymore Fore Park, at the foot of the Mourne Mountains. Simple, modern bedrooms come neutral hues; those on the top floor have the best views. Lots of local info in th lounge. Friendly owners.

6 rooms - £ 60 £ 90

15 Hilltown Rd ✉ BT33 0PX - Southwest : 0.5 mi on B 180
- ✆ 028 4372 6077 - www.tollyrose.com

NEWTOWNABBEY BAILE NUA NA MAINISTREACH

Newtownabbey - Pop. 61 713 - Regional map n° **20**-D2

Sleepy Hollow

MODERN CUISINE • RURAL X This remote, passionately run restaurant is a re find, with its rustic rooms, large terrace and cosy hayloft bar! Cooking is co trastingly modern, and the chef prides himself on using seasonal ingredien with a story.

Menu £ 23 (lunch) - Carte £ 23/33

15 Klin Rd ✉ BT36 4SU - Northwest : 1 mi by Ballyclare Rd and Ballycraig Rd
- ✆ 028 9083 8672 - www.sleepyhollowrestaurant.com
- Closed 25-26 December

NEWTOWNARDS BAILE NUA NA HARDA

Ards - Pop. 28 437 - Regional map n° **20**-D2

Edenvale House

TRADITIONAL • CLASSIC Attractive Georgian farmhouse with a charming own and pleasant lough and mountain views. It's traditionally decorated, with a com drawing room and a wicker-furnished sun room. Spacious, homely bedroom boast good facilities.

3 rooms - £ 65/110 £ 65/110

130 Portaferry Rd ✉ BT22 2AH - Southeast : 2.75 mi on A 20
- ✆ 028 9181 4881 - www.edenvalehouse.com
- Closed Christmas-New Year

PORTRUSH PORT ROIS

Coleraine - Pop. 6 640 - Regional map n° **20**-C1

Shola Coach House

TOWNHOUSE • CONTEMPORARY This attractive stone coach house once be longed to the Victorian manor house next door. Inside it's light and airy, with tasteful contemporary style and modern facilities. Bedrooms are spacious; one in the colourful garden.

4 rooms - £ 90/140 £ 110/140

110A Gateside Rd ✉ BT56 8NP - East : 1.5 mi by Ballywillan Road
- ✆ 028 7082 5925 - www.sholabandb.com - Closed November-January

PORTSTEWART PORT STIÓBHAIRD

Coleraine – Pop. 7 368 – Regional map n° **20**-C1

Harry's Shack

TRADITIONAL CUISINE • **RUSTIC** The location is superb: on a sandy National Trust beach, with views across to Inishowen. It's an appealingly simple place with wooden tables and classroom-style chairs. Concise menus wisely let local ingredients speak for themselves.

Carte £ 27/45

118 Strand Rd BT55 7PG – West : 1 mi by Strand Rd – 028 7083 1783 – Closed Monday November-April

Saltwater House

FAMILY • CONTEMPORARY A great place to escape everyday life: the rooms are light and airy, the atmosphere is serene and the open-plan lounge takes in beach and mountain views. Organic breakfasts feature smoothies, chai porridge and bircher muesli.

5 rooms – †£ 110/130 ††£ 110/130

63 Strand Rd BT55 7LU – 028 7083 3872 – www.saltwaterhouse.co.uk

REPUBLIC OF IRELAND

They say that Ireland offers forty luminous shades of green, but it's not all wondrous hills and down-home pubs: witness the limestone-layered Burren, cut-through by meandering streams, lakes and labyrinthine caves; or the fabulous Cliffs of Moher, looming for mile after mile over the wild Atlantic waves. The cities burst with life: Dublin is one of Europe's coolest capitals, and free-spirited Cork enjoys a rich cultural heritage. Kilkenny mixes a medieval flavour with a strong artistic tradition, while the 'festival' city of Galway is enhanced by an easy, international vibe.

This is a country known for the quality and freshness of its produce, and farmers' markets and food halls yield an array of artisanal cheeses and freshly baked breads. Being an agricultural country, Ireland produces excellent home-reared meat and dairy products and a new breed of chefs are giving traditional dishes a clever modern twist. Seafood, particularly shellfish, is popular – nothing beats sitting on the quayside with a bowl of steaming mussels and the distinctive taste of a micro-brewery beer.

- Michelin Road maps n° 712 and 713
- Michelin Green Guide: Ireland

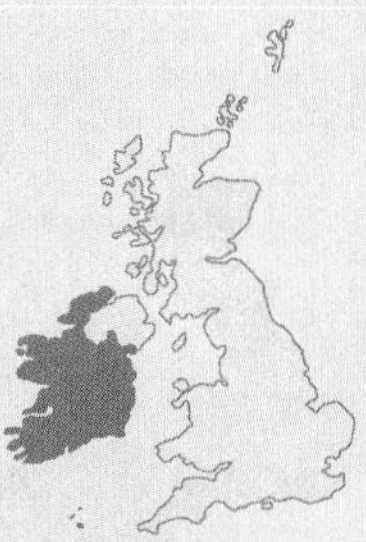

FoodCollection/Photononstop

21 Republic of Ireland

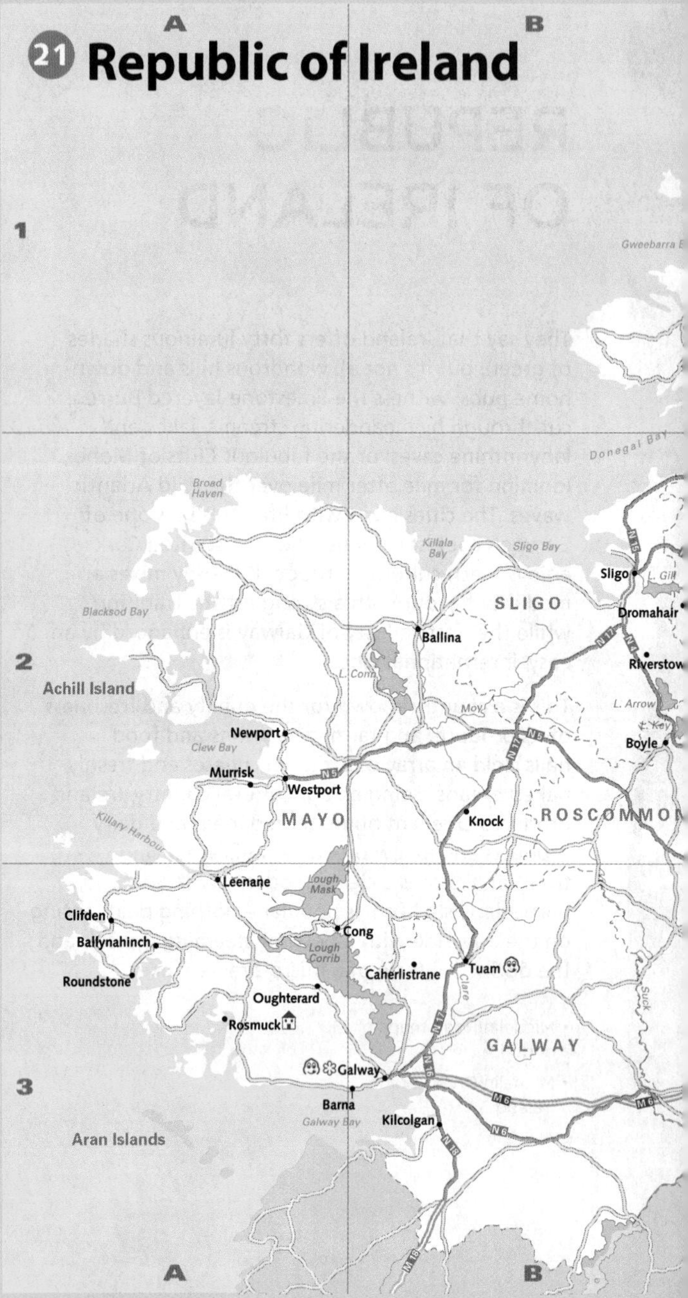

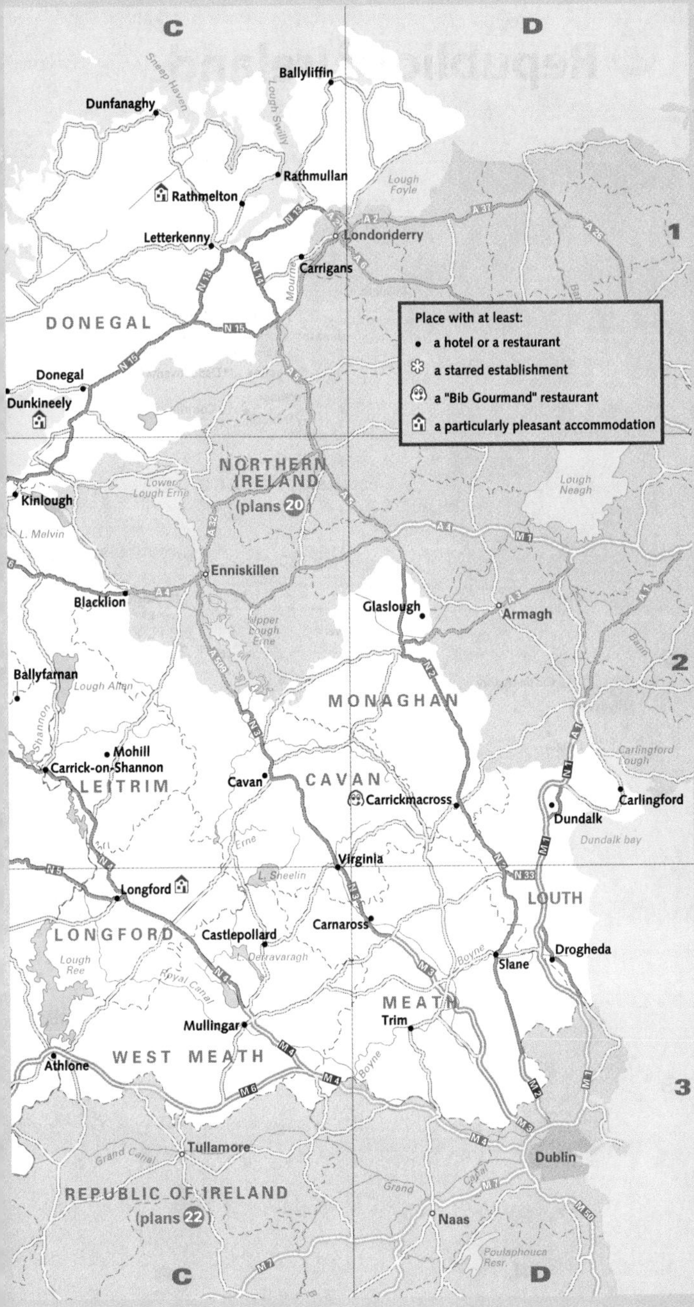

C
D
Sneep Haven
Ballyliffin
Lough Swilly
Dunfanaghy
Rathmullan
Lough Foyle
Rathmelton
Letterkenny
Londonderry
Carrigans
Mourne
1
Place with at least:
a hotel or a restaurant
a starred establishment
a "Bib Gourmand" restaurant
a particularly pleasant accommodation
DONEGAL
Donegal
Dunkineely
NORTHERN IRELAND
(plans 20)
Lower Lough Erne
Lough Neagh
Kinlough
L. Melvin
Enniskillen
Blacklion
Glaslough
Armagh
Upper Lough Erne
2
Ballyfarnan
Lough Allen
MONAGHAN
Shannon
Mohill
Carrick-on-Shannon
LEITRIM
Cavan
CAVAN
Carrickmacross
Carlingford Lough
Carlingford
Dundalk
Dundalk bay
Erne
Virginia
L. Sheelin
Longford
LOUTH
Carnaross
LONGFORD
Castlepollard
L. Derravaragh
Lough Ree
Royal Canal
Boyne
Slane
Drogheda
MEATH
Trim
Mullingar
WEST MEATH
Athlone
Boyne
3
Tullamore
Grand Canal
Dublin
REPUBLIC OF IRELAND
(plans 22)
Grand Canal
Naas
Poulaphouca Resr.
C
D

22 Republic of Ireland

C
D
Dundalk
Dundalk bay
Longford
REPUBLIC OF IRELAND
(plans 21)
Drogheda
FINGAL
1
Malahide
Celbridge
Straffan
Dublin
Clontarf
Ranelagh
Terenure
Blackrock
Dún Laoghaire
Monkstown
KILDARE
Sallins
Naas
Kildare
Kilcullen
Ballymore Eustace
Enniskerry
Greystones
Newtown Mount Kennedy
Delgany
Tullamore
OFFALY
LAOIS
Ballyfin
Portlaoise
Garrykennedy
Athy
Rathnew
WICKLOW
NORTH TIPPERARY
Aughrim
CARLOW
KILKENNY
Kilkenny
Bagenalstown
Clonegall
Gorey
Cashel
Borris
Thomastown
WEXFORD
Ballygarrett
2
Enniscorthy
SOUTH TIPPERARY
Ballymacarbry
Wexford
Rosslare
Arthurstown
Waterford
Duncannon
WATERFORD
Fennor
Carne
Dungarvan
Dungarvan Harbour
Youghal
Castlemartyr
Ardmore
Youghal Bay
Shanagarry
Ballycotton
Midleton
3
Place with at least:
a hotel or a restaurant
a starred establishment
a "Bib Gourmand" restaurant
a particularly pleasant accommodation
C
D

NOT TO BE MISSED

STARRED RESTAURANTS

✿✿

Excellent cooking, worth a detour!

✿

High quality cooking, worth a stop!

BIB GOURMAND RESTAURANTS ☺

Good quality, good value cooking

OUR TOP PICKS

HOTELS WITH SPAS Spa

Michelin

NOTABLY NEIGHBOURHOOD

A TREAT FOR FOODIES

FOR GOLFERS

LITTLE GEMS

Michelin

A SENSE OF GRANDEUR

THE CLASSICS

ADARE ÁTH DARA

Limerick - Pop. 1 106 - Regional map n° **22**-B2

1826

MODERN CUISINE • RUSTIC XX This pretty little thatched cottage was built i 1826 and is cosy and characterful, with a wood burning stove and a rustic feel. In teresting, attractively presented dishes use well-sourced ingredients and have sub tle modern touches. It's owned by an experienced couple: he cooks and she serves

Menu € 25 (early dinner)/29 - Carte € 27/47

Main St - 061 396 004 (booking essential) - www.1826adare.ie - dinner only - Closed last 3 weeks January and Monday-Tuesday

The Oak Room

MODERN CUISINE • INTIMATE XXX Named after the wood panelled walls commis sioned by architect Augustus Pugin, this hotel dining room eschews all the com fort and grandeur one would expect. Confident cooking showcases ingredient from artisan Irish producers and flavours are honest. For garden views sit in th small glassed terrace area.

Menu € 110

Adare Manor Hotel, - 061 605 200 (booking essential) - www.adaremanor.com - dinner only - Closed 24-26 December

Carriage House

MODERN CUISINE • BRASSERIE XX You'd never guess that the smart clubhous was once the stables of this estate. It has a plush bar and an informal conserva tory-like dining room with mosaic tiling and putting green views. Dishes are sim pler than in The Oak Room restaurant but are still fresh and carefully prepared.

Carte € 32/57

Adare Manor Hotel - 061 605 200 - www.adaremanor.com - Closed 24-26 December

Maigue

TRADITIONAL CUISINE • CLASSIC DÉCOR XX There's a formal feel to this tradi tional hotel dining room, which is spread across several adjoining rooms and named after a nearby river. Menus focus on Irish produce and are firmly rooted in tradition; the trolley offering prime roast rib of beef is a feature.

Carte € 27/57 - bar lunch Monday-Saturday

Dunraven Arms Hotel, Main St - 061 605 900 - www.dunravenhotel.com

Adare Manor

GRAND LUXURY • ELEGANT Once the family seat of the Earl of Dunraven, this im pressive 1830s Gothic-style mansion has been extensively restored. It sits in 840 acres and offers a host of outdoor activities. Ornate ceilings and superb wood pa nelling feature throughout and bedrooms have an understated elegance. The Tack Room bar is a fun spot before dinner in the clubhouse or intimate Oak Room.

104 rooms - € 325/595 € 375/700 - 9 suites

- 061 605 200 - www.adaremanor.com - Closed 24-26 December

The Oak Room • **Carriage House** - See restaurant listing

The Dunraven

TRADITIONAL • CLASSIC This charming coaching inn dates from 1792 and is named after Lord Dunraven who once lived opposite at Adare Manor. It's person ally run by the Murphy family and comes with classical lounges and a wood-pa nelled bar. Bedrooms are spacious: those at the front are more modern, those to the back, more peaceful.

87 rooms - € 99/195 € 99/195

Main St - 061 605 900 - www.dunravenhotel.com

Maigue - See restaurant listing

ARAN ISLANDS OILEÁIN ÁRANN

Galway - Pop. 1 280 - Regional map n° **22**-B1

nishmore

Aran Islands

TRADITIONAL • CLASSIC This comfy, cosy hotel is run by a friendly family team and its view across the harbour makes it popular for weddings. Some of the spacious, brightly decorated bedrooms have balconies with bay views. The bustling bar hosts live music in high season and the restaurant focuses on local seafood and steaks.

22 rooms - € 80/140 € 80/140

Kilronan - 099 61104 - www.aranislandshotel.com - Closed November-February

Ard Einne Guesthouse

TRADITIONAL • COSY Close to the airport, an attractive chalet-style guesthouse set back on a hill and boasting superb views of Killeany Bay; take it all in from the comfy lounge. Uniformly decorated bedrooms have pine furnishings and great outlooks.

6 rooms - € 80/90 € 80/100

Killeany - 099 61126 - www.ardeinne.com - Closed November-February

nishmaan

Inis Meáin Restaurant & Suites

REGIONAL CUISINE • FRIENDLY XX Set on a beautiful island, this futuristic stone building is inspired by the surrounding landscapes and features limed walls, sage banquettes and panoramic views. Cooking is modern, tasty and satisfyingly straightforward, showcasing island ingredients including seafood caught in currachs and hand-gathered urchins. Minimalist bedrooms feature natural furnishings.

Menu € 75 - tasting menu only

5 rooms - € 300/600 € 300/600

- 086 826 6026 (booking essential) - www.inismeain.com - dinner only
- Closed mid-October-mid-March, Sunday and Monday, 2 night minimum stay

nisheer

South Aran House

FAMILY • FUNCTIONAL Simple guesthouse on the smallest of the Aran Islands, where traditional living still reigns. With its whitewashed walls and tiled floors, it has a slight Mediterranean feel; bedrooms are homely, with wrought iron beds and modern amenities. Their next door restaurant serves breakfast, snacks and hearty meals.

4 rooms - € 58/65 € 82/86

- 087 340 5687 - www.southaran.com - Restricted opening in winter

RDMORE AIRD MHÓR

Vaterford - Pop. 435 - Regional map n° **22**-C3

House

MODERN CUISINE • DESIGN XXX Full length windows give every table an impressive coastal view at this smart hotel restaurant. Concise menus showcase local and garden produce and cooking is complex - a host of ingredients are used for each course. Creative dishes combine a good range of flavours and textures and presentation is unique.

→ Rose veal with sweetbread crisp, tartare and kombucha. Grilled and pickled halibut with Wagyu lardo, turnips and fish jus. Strawberries with vanilla cream, basil, cucumber and Black Water gin.

Menu € 85/95

Cliff House Hotel, Middle Rd - 024 87800 (booking essential)
- www.cliffhousehotel.ie - dinner only - Closed 24-26 December, Tuesday November-February and Sunday-Monday

Cliff House

LUXURY · MODERN Stylish cliffside hotel with a superb bay outlook and lovely spa. Slate walls, Irish fabrics and bold colours feature throughout. Mod-ern bedrooms have backlit glass artwork and smart bathrooms; some hav balconies and all share the wonderful view. Choose from an extensive men in the delightful bar and on the terrace; the restaurant serves more creativ dishes.

39 rooms – € 180/245 € 225/550 – 3 suites

Middle Rd – 024 87800 – www.cliffhousehotel.ie – Closed 24-26 December

House – See restaurant listing

ARTHURSTOWN COLMÁN

Wexford – Pop. 135 – Regional map n° **22**-D2

Harvest Room

MODERN CUISINE · ELEGANT A light, spacious restaurant in keeping wit the classic Georgian country house in which it sits; bright rugs and chair add a modern touch. Classic dishes feature top Irish and kitchen garde produce.

Menu € 65

Dunbrody Country House Hotel, – 051 389 600 (booking essential) – www.dunbrodyhouse.com – dinner only and Sunday lunch – Closed 9 January-12 February,16-26 December and Monday-Tuesday October-June

Dunbrody Country House

COUNTRY HOUSE · ELEGANT A part-Georgian hunting lodge with a charmin period feel and welcoming open peat fires. It was once owned by the Marqui of Donegal and now celebrity chef Kevin Dundon runs his cookery schoc here.

16 rooms – € 125/190 € 190/320 – 6 suites

– 051 389 600 – www.dunbrodyhouse.com – Closed 9 January-12 February, 16-26 December and Monday-Tuesday October-June

Harvest Room – See restaurant listing

ATHLONE BAILE ÁTHA LUAIN

Westmeath – Pop. 15 558 – Regional map n° **21**-C3

Kin Khao

THAI · FRIENDLY Vivid yellow building with red window frames, hidden down side street near the castle. The upstairs restaurant is decorated with tapestrie and there's a good selection of authentic Thai dishes – try the owner's recom-mendations.

Menu € 10 (weekday lunch)/35 – Carte € 20/47

Abbey Ln. – 090 649 8805 – www.kinkhaothai.ie – dinner only and lunch Wednesday-Friday and Sunday – Closed 25 and 31 December

Left Bank Bistro

INTERNATIONAL · FRIENDLY Keenly run, airy bistro with rough floorboard brick walls and an open-plan kitchen. Extensive menus offer an eclectic mix o dishes, from light lunches and local fish specials to tasty Irish beef and eve Asian-inspired fare.

Menu € 20 (dinner) – Carte € 35/46

Fry Pl – 090 649 4446 – www.leftbankbistro.com – Closed 1 week Christmas, Sunday and Monday

Thyme

REGIONAL CUISINE • FRIENDLY X Welcoming corner restaurant with candles in the windows; set next to the river and run by a chatty, personable team. Hearty, flavoursome dishes are a mix of the traditional and the modern. Local suppliers are listed on the menu.

Menu € 30 - Carte € 31/49

Custume Pl., Strand St
- 090 647 8850 - www.thymerestaurant.ie
- dinner only and Sunday lunch - Closed 27 January-7 February, 24-26 December, 1 January and Good Friday

at Glasson Northeast: 8 km on N55 Athlone

Wineport Lodge

LUXURY • DESIGN A superbly located hotel where the bedroom wing follows the line of the lough shore and each luxurious room boasts a balcony or a waterside terrace (it's worth paying the extra for the Champagne Suite). The outdoor hot tubs make a great place to take in the view. Extensive menus utilise seasonal produce.

30 rooms - € 130 € 160/400

Southwest : 1.5 km
- 090 643 9010 - www.wineport.ie
- Closed 23-26 December

Glasson Stone Lodge

FAMILY • PERSONALISED Smart guesthouse built from local Irish limestone. Pine features strongly throughout; bedrooms boast thoughtful extras and locally made furniture - Room 4 is the best. Breakfast includes homemade bread and fruit from the garden.

6 rooms - € 50/72 € 50/72

- 090 648 5004 - www.glassonstonelodge.com
- Closed November-April

ATHY BAILE ÁTHA Í

Kildare - Pop. 8 218 - Regional map n° **22**-D2

Green Barn

ORGANIC • DESIGN X A charming, shabby-chic shop and café with a laid-back vibe, set in the grounds of an early Georgian villa. It has an admirable organic ethos and overlooks the kitchen garden which informs the unfussy, rustic menu.

Carte € 22/56

Burtown House & Gardens - Northeast : 8 km off N 78
- 059 862 3865 - www.burtownhouse.ie - lunch only and Saturday dinner
- Closed January, Monday and Tuesday except bank holiday Mondays

AUGHRIM EACHROIM

Wicklow - Pop. 1 364 - Regional map n° **22**-D2

Strawberry Tree

ORGANIC • ELEGANT XXX The Strawberry Tree was Ireland's first certified organic restaurant. It's a formal place with an intimate, atmospheric feel, and is set on a village-style hotel estate. Menus feature wild and organic ingredients sourced from local artisan suppliers.

Menu € 65

Brooklodge Hotel, Macreddin Village - North : 3.25 km
- 0402 36444 - www.brooklodge.com - dinner only
- Closed 24-25 December and Monday October-April

Armento

ITALIAN • BISTRO X Informal Italian restaurant set in a smart hotel on a secluded 180 acre estate. Southern Italian menus feature artisan produce imported from Armento and pizzas cooked in the wood-fired oven.

Menu € 35

Brooklodge Hotel, Macreddin Village - North : 3.25 km
- ☎ 0402 36444 - www.brooklodge.com - dinner only
- Closed 24-25 December and Tuesday-Wednesday October-April

Brooklodge H & Wells Spa

SPA AND WELLNESS • CLASSIC Sprawling hotel in 180 peaceful acres in the Wicklow Valley. Flag-floored reception, comfy lounge, informal café and pub. Smart, modern bedrooms with large bathrooms; some in an annexe, along with the conference rooms. State-of-the-art spa.

86 rooms - € 100/140 € 130/200 - 18 suites

Macreddin Village - North : 3.25 km
- ☎ 0402 36444 - www.brooklodge.com
- Closed 24-25 December

Strawberry Tree • **Armento** - See restaurant listing

BAGENALSTOWN MUINE BHEAG

Carlow - Pop. 2 775 - Regional map n° **22**-D2

Kilgraney Country House

COUNTRY HOUSE • PERSONALISED Georgian country house which adopts a truly holistic approach. Period features blend with modern, minimalist furnishings and the mood is calm and peaceful. It boasts a small tea room, a craft gallery and a spa with a relaxation room, along with pleasant herb, vegetable, zodiac and monastic gardens.

7 rooms - € 170/200 € 170/240

South : 6.5 km by R 705 (Borris Rd)
- ☎ 059 977 5283 - www.kilgraneyhouse.com
- Closed November-February and Monday-Wednesday

Lorum Old Rectory

COUNTRY HOUSE • TRADITIONAL A welcoming, double-gabled stone rectory built in 1863, set in a lovely spot at the foot of the Blackstairs Mountains. The traditional interior is decorated with antiques; ask for Room 3 with its 4-poster bed and double-aspect views. Enjoy homemade bread and preserves at breakfast and garden produce at dinner.

4 rooms - € 110/130 € 170/190

Kilgraney - South : 7 km by R 705 (Borris Rd)
- ☎ 059 977 5282 - www.lorum.com
- Closed December-January

BALLINA BÉAL AN ÁTHA

Mayo - Pop. 10 490 - Regional map n° **21**-B2

Library

MODERN CUISINE • ELEGANT XX Start with a drink in the bar, which is fitted out with original pieces from a 16C Spanish galleon, then head for the dramatic candlelit dining room. Seasonal modern dishes include fillet of beef flambéed on a sword at the table!

Menu € 35 (weekdays) - Carte € 49/61

Belleek Castle Hotel, Northeast : 2.5 km by Castle Rd
- ☎ 096 22400 - www.belleekcastle.com - dinner only
- Closed January

Mount Falcon

HISTORIC • ELEGANT Classic former shooting lodge built in 1876, with golf, cycling, fishing and archery available in its 100 acre grounds. Choose between characterful bedrooms in the main house and spacious, contemporary rooms in the extension. The restaurant is located in the old kitchens and serves elaborate modern dishes.

32 rooms - € 150/210 € 160/250 - 2 suites

Foxford Rd - South : 6.25 km on N 26 - ✆ 096 74472 - www.mountfalcon.com - Closed 25 December

Belleek Castle

HISTORIC • ELEGANT An imposing castellated property built on the site of an old medieval abbey and surrounded by 1,000 acres of parkland. An amazing array of characterful rooms come complete with open fires, ornate panelling, antiques and armour.

10 rooms - € 90/150 € 220/270

Northeast : 2.5 km by Castle Rd - ✆ 096 22400 - www.belleekcastle.com - Closed January

Library - See restaurant listing

BALLINGARRY BAILE AN GHARRAÍ

Limerick - Pop. 527 - Regional map n° **22**-B2

Mustard Seed at Echo Lodge

TRADITIONAL • CLASSIC This cosy former convent is surrounded by well-kept gardens and filled with antique furniture, paintings, books and fresh flowers. Bedrooms in the main house have period styling, while those in the former school house are brighter and more modern. Dinner is an occasion - the two grand rooms are candlelit and have gilt mirrors; cooking is elaborate and boldly flavoured.

16 rooms - € 80/165 € 138/360

- ✆ 069 68508 - www.mustardseed.ie - Closed mid-January-early February and 24-26 December

BALLSBRIDGE DROICHEAD NA DOTHRA - Dublin → See Dublin

BALLYBUNION BAILE AN BHUINNEÁNAIGH

Kerry - Pop. 1 354 - Regional map n° **22**-A2

Teach de Broc Country House

FAMILY • MODERN A purpose-built house by the Ballybunion golf course, with a spacious open-plan lounge and bar and eye-catching modern Irish art. Good-sized bedrooms have smart bathrooms; those at the front looks towards the links. The simple bistro-style dining room serves a wide-ranging menu.

16 rooms - € 100/130 € 120/160

Link Rd - South : 2.5 km by Golf Club rd - ✆ 068 27581 - www.ballybuniongolf.com - Closed November-April

Tides

FAMILY • PERSONALISED Generously sized bedrooms, superb views and welcoming hosts are the draw at this purpose-built guesthouse. Quiz David about the local area in the comfy lounge and, at breakfast, enjoy Doreen's pancakes.

7 rooms - € 120 € 120/180

East : 1.75 km. by R 551 on R 553 - ✆ 086 600 0665 - www.ballybunionhotels.com - Closed December-January

BALLYCOTTON BAILE CHOITÍN

Cork - Pop. 476 - Regional map n° **22**-C3

Bayview

FAMILY • PERSONALISED This superbly located hotel sits in an elevated spc overlooking the bay and the island opposite. Many of the spacious, understate bedrooms have Juliet balconies and you can sit in the garden and watch the fish ing boats come in. Menus are modern and ambitious; ask for a seat by the window

34 rooms - € 97/217 € 97/217 - €15

- 021 464 6746 - www.thebayviewhotel.com - Closed November-Easter

BALLYDAVID BAILE NA NGALL

Kerry - Dingle - Regional map n° **22**-A2

Gorman's Clifftop House

FAMILY • CLASSIC Purpose-built house in a wonderfully rural location, offering su perb views out across Ballydavid Head and the Three Sisters. It's family run an has a lovely homely feel. Bright, spacious bedrooms have good facilities; those t the front share the view. The concise menu features home-cooked local produce.

8 rooms - € 95/125 € 110/140

Slea Head Dr, Glashabeg - North : 2 km on Feomanagh rd. - 066 915 5162 - www.gormans-clifftophouse.com - Closed mid-October-mid-March

BALLYDEHOB BÉAL AN DÁ CHAB

Cork - Pop. 271 - Regional map n° **22**-A3

Chestnut (Rob Krawczyk)

MODERN CUISINE • ROMANTIC Locally-born Rob and his partner Elaine hav transformed this old pub into a sweet, intimate restaurant with an elegant styl and a relaxed feel. He has a great understanding of textures and flavours an dishes are understated with a focus on pure, natural flavours and regional produce

→ Scallops with cauliflower, ink and nasturtium. Brill, mussels and lovage. Straw berries with lemon verbena.

Menu € 50/65

Staball Hill - 028 25766 (booking essential) - www.restaurantchestnutwestcork.ie - dinner only and Sunday lunch - Closed 24-26 December, January, February and Monday-Tuesday

BALLYFARNAN BÉAL ÁTHA FEARNÁIN

Roscommon - Pop. 205 - Regional map n° **21**-C2

Kilronan Castle

HISTORIC BUILDING • CLASSIC Impressively restored castle with characterful sit ting rooms, a library and a palm court; wood panelling, antiques and oil painting feature throughout. Smart leisure club and hydrotherapy centre. Opulent red an gold bedrooms offer a high level of comfort. The formal dining room serves classical menu.

85 rooms - € 99/179 € 129/209

Southeast : 3.5 km on Keadew rd - 071 961 8000 - www.kilronancastle.ie

BALLYFIN AN BAILE FIONN

Laois - Pop. 633 - Regional map n° **22**-C1

Ballyfin

GRAND LUXURY • HISTORIC An immaculate Regency mansion built in 1820 an set in 600 acres. The interior is stunning, with its cantilevered staircase, breath taking ceilings and restored antiques. The library features 4,000 books, the draw ing room is decorated in gold leaf and the bedrooms are luxurious. Produce grown in the kitchen garden informs the dishes served in the dining room.

21 rooms - € 440/700 € 670/1415 - 4 suites

- 057 875 5866 - www.ballyfin.com - Closed January

BALLYGARRETT BAILE GHEARÓID

Regional map n° **22**-D2

Clonganny House

COUNTRY HOUSE • ELEGANT Close to the coast you'll find this Georgian manor house, which has been stylishly and comfortably refurbished. Bedrooms are located in the old coach house and have a wonderfully classical style: all feature handmade and antique furnishings and open onto private terraces overlooking the garden. The formal linen-laid dining room offers a traditional set priced menu.

4 rooms – € 165/195 € 195/225

Southwest : 4.5 km. by R 472 – 053 948 2111 – www.clonganny.com

BALLYLICKEY BÉAL ÁTHA LEICE

Cork – Bantry – Regional map n° **22**-A3

Seaview House

TRADITIONAL • CLASSIC Well-run Victorian house that upholds tradition both in its décor and service. It has a pleasant drawing room, a cosy bar and antique-furnished bedrooms – some with sea views. Classic dishes are served at polished tables laid with silver tableware. The attractive gardens lead down to the shore.

26 rooms – € 90/120 € 140/200

– 027 50073 – www.seaviewhousehotel.com – Closed late November-late March

BALLYLIFFIN BAILE LIFÍN

Donegal – Pop. 461 – Regional map n° **21**-C1

Ballyliffin Lodge

TRADITIONAL • MODERN Remote hotel with well-kept gardens, affording a superb outlook over the countryside to the beach. Bedrooms offer good facilities; ask for one facing the front. Relax in the lovely spa and pool, or enjoy afternoon tea with a view in the lounge. Informal, bistro-style dining, with international menus.

40 rooms – € 83/124 € 114/196

Shore Rd – 074 937 8200 – www.ballyliffinlodge.com – Closed 24-26 December

BALLYMACARBRY BAILE MHAC CAIRBRE

Waterford – Clonmel – Pop. 132 – Regional map n° **22**-C2

Glasha Farmhouse

TRADITIONAL • CLASSIC A large farmhouse between the Knockmealdown and Comeragh Mountains. Guest areas include a comfy lounge, airy conservatory and pleasant patio. Bedrooms are immaculately kept and some have jacuzzis. The welcoming owner has good local knowledge. Meals are home-cooked, with picnic lunches available.

6 rooms – € 80/120 € 80/120

Northwest : 4 km by R 671 – 052 613 6108 – www.glashafarmhouse.com – Closed December

BALLYMORE EUSTACE AN BAILE MÓR

Kildare – Pop. 872 – Regional map n° **22**-D1

Ballymore Inn

TRADITIONAL CUISINE • PUB Remote village pub with a deli selling home-made breads, pickles, oils and the like. The owner promotes small, artisan producers, so expect organic veg, meat from quality assured farms and farmhouse cheeses. Portions are generous.

Carte € 31/61

– 045 864 585 – www.ballymoreinn.com

BALLYNAHINCH BAILE NA HINSE

Galway – ✉ Recess – Regional map n° **21**-A3

Owenmore

MODERN CUISINE • INTIMATE XX Within a 17C country house you'll find th bright, elegant restaurant which looks out over the river and the estate. Moder dishes are delicate and subtly flavoured. In winter, end the evening with a drir beside the marble fireplace.

Menu €70 **s**

Ballynahinch Castle Hotel, – ✆ 095 31006 (booking essential) – www.ballynahinchcastle.com – dinner only

Ballynahinch Castle

TRADITIONAL • CLASSIC Dramatically located on the Wild Atlantic Wa amongst 450 acres of woodland, with a salmon fishing river in front and th mountains behind. Relax by a peat fire in one of the cosy sitting rooms. Bec rooms have a country house style.

45 rooms – €180/390 €200/500 – 3 suites

– ✆ 095 31006 – www.ballynahinchcastle.com

Owenmore – See restaurant listing

BALLYVAUGHAN BAILE UÍ BHEACHÁIN

Clare – Pop. 258 – Regional map n° **22**-B1

Gregans Castle

MODERN CUISINE • ELEGANT XX Have an aperitif in the drawing room of th country house hotel before heading through to the restaurant (ask for a tab close to the window, to take in views stretching as far as Galway Bay). Interest ing modern dishes have clean, clear flavours and showcase the latest local pro duce. Service is attentive.

Menu €75 **s**

Gregans Castle Hotel, Southwest : 6 km on N 67 – ✆ 065 707 7005 – www.gregans.ie – dinner only – Closed 2 December-14 February

Gregans Castle

FAMILY • PERSONALISED Well-run, part-18C country house with superb views c The Burren and Galway Bay. The open-fired hall leads to a cosy, rustic bar-loung and an elegant sitting room. Bedrooms are furnished with antiques: two ope onto the garden; one is in the old kitchen and features a panelled ceiling and four-poster bed.

21 rooms – €175/215 €250/290 – 4 suites

Southwest : 6 km on N 67 – ✆ 065 707 7005 – www.gregans.ie – Closed 2 December-14 February

Gregans Castle – See restaurant listing

Ballyvaughan Lodge

TRADITIONAL • PERSONALISED Welcoming guesthouse with a colourful flowe display and a decked terrace. The vaulted, light-filled lounge features a locall made flower chandelier; bedrooms boast co-ordinating fabrics. Breakfast use quality, farmers' market produce.

11 rooms – €60/70 €90/110

– ✆ 065 707 7292 – www.ballyvaughanlodge.com – Closed 23-28 December

BALTIMORE DÚN NA SÉAD

Cork – Pop. 347 – Regional map n° **22**-A3

✿ Mews

MODERN CUISINE • INTIMATE XX Two friends own this cosy, intimate restaurant. County Cork boasts a wealth of top quality produce and the chef uses it to full effect. Fish is from the adjacent harbour and meat from the surrounding area. The appealing modern tasting menu is well-balanced and local herbs and seaweeds are a feature.

→ Cape Clear asparagus. Cod, shore greens, seaweeds and mussel sauce. Wild sorrel, elderflower, elderberry and Alexanders.

Menu € 39/69 – tasting menu only

– ✆ 028 20572 (booking essential) – www.mewsrestaurant.ie – dinner only – Closed November-March, Sunday except bank holidays, Monday-Tuesday except July and August and Wednesday except June-September

BANDON DROICHEAD NA BANDAN

Cork – Pop. 1 917 – Regional map n° **22**-B3

Poachers

TRADITIONAL CUISINE • PUB Sit in the cosy bar, the small snug or the dining room under the eaves. Dishes are boldly flavoured and local seafood is the star of the show – you'll always find fish landed at Union Hall and crabs from Courtmacsherry.

Carte € 25/42

Clonakilty Rd – Southwest : 1.5 km on N 71 – ✆ 023 884 1159 – www.poachers.ie – Closed 25 December

BANTRY BEANNTRAÍ

Cork – Regional map n° **22**-A3

O'Connors

SEAFOOD • BISTRO X Well-run harbourside restaurant, with a compact, bistro-style interior featuring model ships in the windows and modern art on the walls. The menu focuses on local seafood, mostly from the small fishing boats in the harbour.

Menu € 25 (early dinner) – Carte € 25/44

Wolf Tone Sq – ✆ 027 55664 (booking essential) – www.oconnorsbantry.com – dinner only – Closed Tuesday-Wednesday November-April

BARNA BEARNA

Galway – Pop. 1 878 – Regional map n° **21**-B3

Upstairs @ West

MODERN CUISINE • INTIMATE XX Stylish first floor restaurant in a smart boutique hotel, with a chic champagne bar, booth seating and a moody, intimate feel. Seasonal menus offer ambitious, innovative dishes, showcasing meats and seafood from the 'West' of Ireland.

Menu € 38 (weekdays) **s** – Carte € 39/60 **s**

Twelve Hotel, Barna Crossroads – ✆ 091 597 000 – www.westrestaurant.ie – dinner only and Sunday lunch – Closed Monday and Tuesday

O'Grady's on the Pier

SEAFOOD • RUSTIC X In winter, sit in the cosy, rustic downstairs room; in summer, head out onto the terrace or up to the bright first floor with its superb views across the harbour and Galway Bay. Classical dishes showcase fresh local seafood.

Carte € 29/53

– ✆ 091 592 223 – www.ogradysonthepier.com – Closed 24-26 December

Twelve

BUSINESS • MODERN An unassuming exterior hides a keenly run boutique hotel complete with a bakery, a pizza kitchen and a deli. Stylish, modern bedrooms have large g mirrors, mood lighting and designer 'seaweed' toiletries; some even boast cocktail bar Innovative menus in Upstairs @ West; modern European dishes in The Pins.

48 rooms - € 90/140 € 100/160 - 10 suites

Barna Crossroads - 091 597 000 - www.thetwelvehotel.ie

Upstairs @ West - See restaurant listing

BARRELLS CROSS - Cork → See Kinsale

BLACKLION AN BLAIC

Cavan - Pop. 229 - Regional map n° **21**-C2

MacNean House

CREATIVE • ELEGANT XXX A stylish restaurant in a smart townhouse, with a ch lounge, a plush dining room and a cookery school. The 8 course tasting menu offers at tractively presented, ambitious dishes which use complex techniques and feature man different flavours and textures. Bedrooms are a mix of modern and country styles.

Menu € 85 - tasting menu only

19 rooms - € 96 € 134/192

Main St - 071 985 3022 (booking essential) - www.macneanrestaurant.com - dinner only and Sunday lunch - Closed January, Monday and Tuesday

BLACKROCK Dublin → See Dublin

BLARNEY AN BHLARNA

Cork - ✉ Cork - Pop. 2 437 - Regional map n° **22**-B3

Square Table

FRENCH • COSY XX Sweet restaurant with a warm, welcoming, neighbourhoo feel. Menus offer French-influenced dishes crafted from Irish produce; the earl evening menu is good value. It's proudly and enthusiastically run by twins Trici and Martina.

Menu € 27/30 - Carte € 31/48

5 The Square - 021 438 2825 (booking essential) - www.thesquaretable.ie - dinner only and Sunday lunch - Closed January, February, Sunday dinner, Monday and Tuesday

BORRIS AN BHUIRÍOS

Carlow - Pop. 646 - Regional map n° **22**-D2

Clashganny House

CLASSIC CUISINE • INTIMATE XX Hidden away in a lovely valley, this early Victorian house is the setting for the realisation of one couple's dream. The moder restaurant is split over three rooms; appealing menus balance light options wit more gutsy dishes.

Menu € 38

Clashganny - South : 5 km by R 702 and R 729 - 059 977 1003 - www.clashgannyhouse.com - dinner only and Sunday lunch - Closed 24-26 December, Sunday dinner and Monday-Tuesday

1808

MODERN CUISINE • BISTRO X The Step House hotel's restaurant is an appealin bistro deluxe with lots of mahogany, red leather banquettes and French door opening onto the garden. Modern menus use the best of Irish produce. Servic is relaxed and friendly.

Carte € 30/48

Step House Hotel, Main St - 059 977 3209 - www.stephousehotel.ie - Closed 15 January-10 February and Monday-Tuesday

Step House

TOWNHOUSE • PERSONALISED A small heritage village is home to this family-run Georgian townhouse. Sizeable modern bedrooms – many with mountain outlooks – are set at the top of a striking staircase; the suite has a huge terrace and a panoramic view.

20 rooms – € 85/135 € 110/180 – 1 suite

Main St – 059 977 3209 – www.stephousehotel.ie – Closed 15 January-10 February

1808 – See restaurant listing

BOYLE MAINISTIR NA BÚILLE

Roscommon – Pop. 1 459 – Regional map n° **21**-B2

Lough Key House

HISTORIC • CLASSIC Welcoming Georgian house with a neat garden and mature grounds, located next to Lough Key Forest Park. Homely guest areas are filled with antiques and ornaments; bedrooms in the original house are the best, with their antique four-posters and warm fabrics. You're guaranteed a warm Irish welcome.

5 rooms – € 59/69 € 98

Southeast : 3.75 km by R 294 on N 4 – 087 678 7257 – www.loughkeyhouse.com – Closed 4 November-3 May

Rosdarrig House

FAMILY • PERSONALISED Neat house on the edge of town, close to the abbey; the friendly owners offer genuine Irish hospitality. Guest areas include two homely lounges and a linen-laid breakfast room. Simply furnished bedrooms overlook the colourful garden.

5 rooms – € 45/50 € 75/80

Carrick Rd – East : 1.5 km on R 294 – 071 966 2040 – www.rosdarrig.com – Closed November-March

CAHERLISTRANE CATHAIR LOISTREÁIN

Galway – Regional map n° **21**-B3

Lisdonagh House

COUNTRY HOUSE • CLASSIC Ivy-clad Georgian house with lough views. The traditional country house interior boasts eye-catching murals and open-fired lounges. Antique-furnished bedrooms have marble bathrooms; the first floor rooms are brighter. The grand dining room offers 5 course dinners and simpler suppers.

9 rooms – € 120 € 140/240

Northwest : 4 km by R 333 off Shrule rd – 093 31163 – www.lisdonagh.com – Closed December-April

CAHERSIVEEN CATHAIR SAIDHBHÍN

Kerry – Pop. 1 168 – Regional map n° **22**-A2

Quinlan & Cooke

SEAFOOD • BRASSERIE 'QC's, as the locals call it, is an atmospheric restaurant with a nautical theme. Seafood-orientated menus offer unfussy classics and more unusual daily specials; the family also own a local fish wholesalers. Stylish, well-equipped bedrooms are in a townhouse and mews; breakfast is brought to your room.

Carte € 29/53

11 rooms – € 85/120 € 119/179

3 Main St – 066 947 2244 – www.qc.ie – Closed January, February and November and Sunday-Thursday in winter

CARAGH LAKE LOCH CÁRTHAÍ

Kerry - Regional map n° **22**-A2

Ard-Na-Sidhe

COUNTRY HOUSE • CLASSIC 1913 Arts and Crafts house on the shores of Loug Caragh, surrounded by mountains. A subtle modernisation has emphasised orig nal features such as oak-panelled walls and leaded windows; bedrooms are sma and contemporary. The restaurant offers classic dishes with modern twists.

18 rooms - € 200/350 € 220/370

- 066 976 9105 - www.ardnasidhe.com - Closed 7 October-18 April

Carrig Country House

TRADITIONAL • CLASSIC A wooded drive leads down to this Victorian forme hunting lodge on the lough shore. The cosy, country house interior comprises tra ditionally furnished guest areas and individually decorated bedrooms with an tique furnishings. Take in beautiful mountain views from the dining room.

17 rooms - € 150/210 € 150/270

- 066 976 9100 - www.carrighouse.com - Closed November-February and Monday-Tuesday in low season

CARLINGFORD CAIRLINN

Louth - Pop. 1 045 - Regional map n° **21**-D2

Bay Tree

MODERN CUISINE • FRIENDLY XX Keenly run neighbourhood restaurant fronte by bay trees and decorated with branches and hessian. Attractively presentec well-balanced modern dishes feature herbs and salad from the garden and sea food from nearby Carlingford Lough. Service is polite and organised, and th bedrooms are warm and cosy.

Menu € 28/35 - Carte € 32/45

7 rooms - € 65/70 € 89/99

Newry St - 042 938 3848 (booking essential) - www.belvederehouse.ie - dinne only and Sunday lunch - Closed 24-26 December and Monday-Tuesday October-May

Carlingford House

TRADITIONAL • PERSONALISED Early Victorian house close to the old ruine abbey; the owner has lived here all her life. Smart, understated bedrooms hav good mod cons and are immaculately kept. Pleasant breakfast room; tasty locall smoked salmon and bacon.

5 rooms - € 80/110 € 100/120

- 042 937 3118 - www.carlingfordhouse.com - Closed 3 January-1 February

CARNAROSS CARN NA ROS

Meath - Kells - Regional map n° **21**-D3

Forge

TRADITIONAL CUISINE • RUSTIC XX Stone-built former forge in rural Meath; it atmospheric interior features flagged floors and warm red décor. Two fairl priced menus offer hearty dishes made from local produce, with some of the veg and herbs taken from the garden.

Menu € 25 (early dinner)/40 - Carte € 36/53

Pottlereagh - Northwest : 7 km by R 147 and N 3 on L 7112 - 046 924 5003 - www.theforgerestaurant.ie - dinner only and Sunday lunch - Closed 1 week February, 1 week July, 24-26 December, 1 January, Sunday dinner, Monday and Tuesday

CARNE

Wexford - Regional map n° **22**-D3

Lobster Pot

SEAFOOD • PUB Popular pub filled with a characterful array of memorabilia. Large menus feature tasty, home-style cooking. Fresh seafood dishes are a must-try, with oysters and lobster cooked to order being the specialities. No children after 7pm.

Carte € 25/58

Ballyfane
- ✆ 053 913 1110 - www.lobsterpotwexford.ie
- Closed 1 January-10 February, 24-26 December, Tuesday in low season and Monday except bank holidays

CARRICKMACROSS CARRAIG MHACHAIRE ROIS

Monaghan - Pop. 1 978 - Regional map n° **21**-D2

Courthouse

REGIONAL CUISINE • RUSTIC Relaxed, rustic restaurant featuring wooden floors, exposed ceiling rafters and bare brick; ask for table 20, by the window. Great value menus offer carefully prepared, flavourful dishes which are a lesson in self-restraint - their simplicity being a key part of their appeal. Friendly, efficient service.

Menu € 27 (weekdays)
- Carte € 29/46 **s**

1 Monaghan St
- ✆ 042 969 2848 (booking essential) - www.courthouserestaurant.ie - dinner only and Sunday lunch
- Closed 1 week January, 1 week June, 25-26 December, Monday except bank holidays and Tuesday

Nuremore

MODERN CUISINE • ELEGANT Traditional split-level dining room within a well-established Victorian hotel. Formally set, linen-laid tables are well-spaced and service is attentive. Menus showcase luxurious seasonal ingredients and dishes are stylishly presented.

Menu € 37

Nuremore Hotel, South : 2.25 km by R 178 on old N 2
- ✆ 042 966 1438 - www.nuremore.com
- dinner only and Sunday lunch - Restricted opening in winter

Nuremore

COUNTRY HOUSE • PERSONALISED Long-standing Victorian house with extensive gardens and a golf course. Classical interior with a formal bar and a comfy lounge serving three-tiered afternoon tea. Good leisure facilities. Peaceful bedrooms; many have rural views.

72 rooms - € 80/120 € 98/170

South : 2.25 km by R 178 on old N 2 - ✆ 042 966 1438
- www.nuremore.com

Nuremore - See restaurant listing

Shirley Arms

INN • MODERN An early 19C coaching inn, which forms part of the Shirley Estate and sits beside the Courthouse Square. Bedrooms are surprisingly modern; those in the original house are slightly more characterful. There's a welcoming bar, an informal bistro and, for private parties, a stylish bar-cum-nightclub.

25 rooms - € 95/125 € 130/190

Main St. - ✆ 042 967 3100
- www.shirleyarmshotel.ie - Closed 25-26 December

CARRICK-ON-SHANNON CORA DROMA RÚISC

Leitrim – Pop. 3 980 – Regional map n° **21**-C2

St.George's Terrace

MODERN CUISINE • ELEGANT Start with drinks in the plush bar of this impos ing Victorian building before moving into the boldly decorated main dining room with its high ceiling and chandelier. Well-balanced cooking has seasonal Irish pro duce at its heart.

Carte € 36/51

St George's Terr. – 071 961 6546 – www.stgeorgesterrace.com – dinner only an Sunday lunch – Closed 7-21 January, 24-27 December, Monday and Tuesday

Oarsman

TRADITIONAL CUISINE • PUB A traditional family-run pub set close to th river and filled with pottery, bygone artefacts and fishing tackle – it's a real h with the locals. Flavoursome cooking uses local produce and all the bread home-baked; they even have a lager brewed for them. The upstairs restaurar opens later in the week.

Carte € 30/49

Bridge St – 071 962 1733 – www.theoarsman.com – Closed 25-27 December, Good Friday and Sunday-Monday except bank holidays

CARRIGANS AN CARRAIGAIN

Donegal – Pop. 336 – Regional map n° **21**-C1

Mount Royd

TRADITIONAL • PERSONALISED Traditional, creeper-clad house in a quiet vi lage. It's immaculately kept throughout, from the snug lounge and pleasar breakfast room to the four cosy bedrooms – one of which opens onto a terrac overlooking the well-tended gardens and fountain. Tasty, locally smoked salmo features at breakfast.

3 rooms – € 45 € 75/80

– 074 914 0163 – www.mountroyd.com – Closed 1 week Christmas and restricte opening in winter

CASHEL CAISEAL

South Tipperary – Pop. 2 275 – Regional map n° **22**-C2

Chez Hans

TRADITIONAL CUISINE • TRADITIONAL DÉCOR A long-standing family owned restaurant in an imposing former Synod Hall built in 1861. There's a goo value set price menu midweek and a more interesting à la carte of classic dishe at the weekend.

Menu € 33 (weekdays) – Carte € 42/63

Rockside, Moor Ln. – 062 61177 (booking essential) – www.chezhans.net – dinner only – Closed 2 weeks Easter, 1 week autumn, 24-26 December, Sunday and Monday

Cafe Hans

TRADITIONAL CUISINE • FRIENDLY Located just down the road from the Roc of Cashel; a vibrant, popular eatery set next to big sister 'Chez Hans' and run b the same family. Sit at closely set tables amongst an interesting collection of ar Tasty, unfussy lunchtime dishes are crafted from local ingredients. Arrive early a you can't book.

Menu € 16 – Carte € 22/41

Rockside, Moore Lane St – 062 63660 (bookings not accepted) – lunch only – Closed 2 weeks late January, 1 week October, 25 December, Sunday and Monday

Baileys of Cashel

TOWNHOUSE • MODERN Used as a grain store during the Irish famine, this Georgian house conceals a cosy lounge with a library and contrastingly spacious, contemporary bedrooms. The penthouse has superb views of the famous rock. Enjoy live music and classic dishes in the cellar bar or modern European cooking in the restaurant.

20 rooms - € 80/130 € 130/150

42 Main St - 062 61937 - www.baileyshotelcashel.com - Closed 23-28 December

Aulber House

FAMILY • PERSONALISED Within walking distance of the Rock of Cashel and the 13C Cistercian abbey ruins. A bespoke mahogany staircase leads to a galleried landing and many rooms have king-sized beds. Unwind in the gazebo in the beautiful gardens.

11 rooms - € 60/90 € 90/100

Deerpark, Golden Rd - West : 0.75 km on N 74 - 062 63713 - www.aulberhouse.com - Closed November-February

CASTLEGREGORY CAISLEÁN GHRIAIRE

Kerry - Pop. 243 - Regional map n° **22**-A2

Shores Country House

LUXURY • ELEGANT This modern guesthouse is set in a beautiful elevated position between the mountain and the beach and is run by a gregarious owner. Some of the stylish bedrooms have antique beds and all have good attention to detail. There's a great choice at breakfast, including wonderful fruit cocktails and homemade cakes.

6 rooms - € 75/150 € 100/160

Conor Pass Rd, Cappateige - Southwest : 6 km on R 560 - 066 713 9196 - www.theshorescountryhouse.com - Closed 2 November-15 March

CASTLELYONS CAISLEÁN Ó LIATHÁIN

Cork - Pop. 292 - Regional map n° **22**-B2

Ballyvolane House

FAMILY • PERSONALISED Stately 18C Italianate mansion surrounded by lovely gardens, lakes and woodland; children can help feed the hens, collect the eggs, pet the donkeys or go on a tractor tour. Comfy guest areas and bedrooms match the period style of the house, and family antiques and memorabilia feature throughout. The walled garden and latest farm produce guide what's on the menu.

6 rooms - € 200/240 € 210/240

Southeast : 5.5 km by Midleton rd on Britway rd - 025 36349 - www.ballyvolanehouse.ie - Closed 24 December-4 January and restricted opening in winter

CASTLEMARTYR BAILE NA MARTRA

Cork - Pop. 1 277 - Regional map n° **22**-C3

Bell Tower

ITALIAN • LUXURY XXX A bright, formally laid restaurant set on the ground floor of a 17C manor house, with traditional décor and plenty of windows overlooking the attractive gardens. Classic dishes with a modern twist from an experienced team.

Carte € 40/52 **s** - bar lunch Monday-Saturday

- 021 421 9000 - www.castlemartyrresort.ie - Closed Monday and Tuesday October-March

Castlemartyr

COUNTRY HOUSE • MODERN Impressive 17C manor house in 220 acres o grounds, complete with castle ruins, lakes, a golf course and a stunning spa. Lux urious bedrooms have superb marble bathrooms. Look out for the wonderfu original ceiling in the Knight's Bar. Franchini's offers an extensive Italian menu the Bell Tower is more formal.

103 rooms - € 164/274 € 179/289 - 28 suites

- 021 421 9000 - www.castlemartyrresort.ie

Bell Tower - See restaurant listing

CASTLEPOLLARD BAILE NA GCROS

Westmeath - Pop. 1 042 - Regional map n° **21**-C3

Lough Bishop House

TRADITIONAL • PERSONALISED Charming 18C farmhouse on a tranquil, south facing hillside. The hospitable owners and their dogs greet you, and tea an cake are served on arrival in the cosy lounge. Simple bedrooms have neat showe rooms and no TVs. Communal dining - home-cooked dishes include meats an eggs from their own farm.

3 rooms - € 65/130 € 130/195

Derrynagarra, Collinstown - South : 6 km by R 394 taking L 5738 opposite churc and school after 4 km - 044 966 1313 - www.loughbishophouse.com - Closed Christmas-New Year

CAVAN AN CABHÁN

Cavan - Pop. 3 649 - Regional map n° **21**-C2

Radisson Blu Farnham Estate

LUXURY • DESIGN Set in extensive parkland and boasting every conceivable outdoor activity and an impressive spa. Original Georgian feature are combined with contemporary furnishings and the luxurious bedrooms offe superb views. Traditional menus feature local, seasonal ingredients and afternoo teas are a speciality.

158 rooms - € 129/279 € 129/279 - 4 suites

Farnham Estate - Northwest : 3.75 km on R 198 - 049 437 7700 - www.farnhamestate.com

Cavan Crystal

BUSINESS • MODERN Modern hotel next to the Cavan Crystal factory, with ar impressive atrium, a stylish lounge-bar and red and black bedrooms in a uniforr design. It comes with good meeting and leisure facilities and is popular for spa breaks. The contemporary first floor restaurant serves attractively presente modern dishes.

85 rooms - € 85/175 € 110/175

Dublin Rd - 049 436 0600 - www.cavancrystalhotel.com

at Cloverhill North: 12 km by N3 on N54 ✉ Belturbet

Olde Post Inn

TRADITIONAL CUISINE • RUSTIC XX Enjoy a fireside aperitif in the flag-floore bar or the wood-framed conservatory of this red-brick former post office. The well-established restaurant serves traditional dishes made with Irish produce, wherein classic flavour combinations are given a modern twist. Bedrooms are contemporary.

Menu € 45 (early dinner)/63

6 rooms - € 65/85 € 130

- 047 55555 - www.theoldepostinn.com - dinner only and Sunday lunch - Closed 2-16 January, 24-27 December, Monday and Tuesday

CELBRIDGE

Kildare - Pop. 17 262 - Regional map n° **22**-D1

Canteen Celbridge

MODERN CUISINE • FRIENDLY A local chef and his endearing French wife have created this relaxed, understated restaurant, where abstract art stands out against grey walls. Well-crafted dishes are boldly flavoured and Irish produce takes centre stage.

Menu € 29 (weekdays) - Carte € 46/59

4 Main St - ✆ 01 627 4967 - www.canteencelbridge.com - dinner only and Saturday lunch - Closed first week January, last week August, first week September, 25-26 December, Sunday and Monday

CLIFDEN AN CLOCHÁN

Galway - Pop. 2 056 - Regional map n° **21**-A3

Mitchells

SEAFOOD • BISTRO A long-standing, family-run restaurant. It's set over two floors and decorated with regional prints and seascapes. They offer a huge array of traditional seafood dishes; local prawns, mussels and oysters all feature.

Menu € 27 (weekdays) - Carte € 30/48

Market St - ✆ 095 21867 - www.mitchellsrestaurantclifden.com - Closed 5 November-15 March

Quay House

TOWNHOUSE • QUIRKY A former harbourmaster's house and monastery on the quayside, overlooking the river. The quirky, bohemian-style interior is crammed with memorabilia, paintings and pictures. Breakfast takes place in the leafy conservatory.

16 rooms - € 90/120 € 155/175

Beach Rd - ✆ 095 21369 - www.thequayhouse.com - Closed November-April

Sea Mist House

TRADITIONAL • COSY Step back in time at this creeper-clad house, which was built in 1820 and is the owner's family home. Original features are enhanced by interesting paintings; the only TV is in the lounge. Enjoy honey from their bees at breakfast.

4 rooms - € 50/90 € 80/110

- ✆ 095 21441 - www.seamisthouse.com - Closed November-March

CLONAKILTY CLOICH NA COILLTE

Cork - Pop. 4 000 - Regional map n° **22**-B3

Gulfstream

MODERN CUISINE • CHIC Contemporary New England style restaurant set on the first floor of a vast hotel and offering superb views over the beach. Modern menus highlight produce from West Cork and feature plenty of fresh local seafood.

Carte € 52/64

Inchydoney Island Lodge and Spa Hotel, South : 5.25 km by N 71 following signs for Inchydoney Beach - ✆ 023 883 3143 - www.inchydoneyisland.com - dinner only and Sunday lunch - Closed 24-25 December

Deasy's

TRADITIONAL CUISINE • COSY An appealing pub in a picturesque hamlet, offering lovely views out across the bay. Its gloriously dated interior is decorated with maritime memorabilia. Menus are dictated by the seasons and the latest catch from the local boats.

Menu € 34 (early dinner) - Carte € 32/49

Ring - Southeast : 3 km - ✆ 023 883 5741 - Closed 24-26 December, Sunday dinner, Monday, Tuesday and restricted opening in winter

REPUBLIC OF IRELAND

Inchydoney Island Lodge and Spa

SPA AND WELLNESS • MODERN Superbly located on a remote headland and boasting stunning views over the beach and out to sea; all of the cor temporary bedrooms have a balcony or terrace. The impressive spa boasts a sea water pool and 27 treatment rooms. Dine in the modern restaurant or nautical styled bistro-bar.

67 rooms - € 220/260 € 220/260 - 4 suites

South : 5.25 km by N 71 following signs for Inchydoney Beach - ✆ 023 883 3143 - www.inchydoneyisland.com - Closed 24-25 December

Gulfstream - See restaurant listing

CLONEGALL CLUAIN NA NGALL

Carlow - Pop. 245 - Regional map n° **22**-D2

Sha-Roe Bistro

TRADITIONAL CUISINE • FRIENDLY A welcoming 17C former coaching inn se in a picturesque village; it's a simple place with a relaxed, intimate feel and car dlelit tables in the evenings. Menus offer carefully presented, unfussy dishes wit clear flavours and a classical base. Sourcing of local and farmers' market ingred ents is paramount.

Carte € 34/46

Main St - ✆ 053 937 5636 (booking essential) - www.sha-roebistro.ie - dinner only and Sunday lunch - Closed January, 1 week April, 1 week October, Sunday dinner and Monday-Wednesday

CLONTARF CLUAIN TARBH - Dublin → See Dublin

CLOVERHILL DROIM CAISIDE - Cavan → See Cavan

CONG CONGA

Mayo - Pop. 178 - Regional map n° **21**-A3

George V

MODERN CUISINE • ELEGANT A visit to the stunning wine cellars is a must a this grand, sophisticated hotel restaurant, where wood-panelling and Waterfor Crystal chandeliers set the tone. Classic French flavours are delivered using subtl modern techniques.

Carte € 70/85

Ashford Castle Hotel - ✆ 094 954 6003 - www.ashfordcastle.com - dinner only

Cullen's at the Cottage

TRADITIONAL CUISINE • BISTRO Set within the grounds of Ashford Castle i this pretty little thatched cottage with an attractive landscaped terrace an lovely views. It has a stylish, subtly rustic look and a relaxed feel. Menus list ap pealing classics.

Carte € 38/74

Ashford Castle Hotel, - ✆ 094 954 5332 - www.ashfordcastle.com - Closed November-March

Ashford Castle

HISTORIC BUILDING • ELEGANT Hugely impressive lochside castle surrounded b extensive grounds; try archery, falconry, clay pigeon shooting or zip-lining; take to the water; or relax with loch views in the spa. Handsome guest areas displa plenty of historic splendour and bedrooms are sumptuously appointed. Dine i the stone cellars in Dungeon, casually in Cullen's or formally in elegant George V.

83 rooms - € 295/575 € 315/595 - 5 suites

- ✆ 094 954 6003 - www.ashfordcastle.com

George V • **Cullen's at the Cottage** - See restaurant listing

The Lodge at Ashford Castle

BOUTIQUE HOTEL • CONTEMPORARY The attractive Georgian sister to Ashford Castle sits within its grounds and offers lovely views of Lough Corrib. Some of its stylish bedrooms are duplex; the sumptuous Lake View Suites come with bespoke furnishings and great outlooks. Wildes offers a creative fixed price menu; the Quay bar serves simpler fare.

64 rooms – € 130/210 € 150/320 – 20 suites

The Quay – Southeast : 2.25 km by R 345 off R 346 – 094 954 5400 – www.thelodgeac.com – Closed 24-25 December and mid-week in winter

CORK CORCAIGH

Cork – Pop. 119 230 – Regional map n° **22**-B3

Ichigo Ichie (N) (Takashi Miyazaki)

JAPANESE • FASHIONABLE XX This authentic restaurant has dark, moody décor and something of an industrial feel. The interesting monthly omakase menu cleverly mixes long-standing Japanese techniques with local ingredients and modern touches. A lucky few get seats at the counter to watch the Sushi Master's deft preparation.

→ Ox tongue with egg white, wild garlic and onion sauce. Chicken thigh, fish, broad bean, egg and dashi. Soy milk, chocolate, rice cake, mocha and whiskey.

Menu € 95 – tasting menu only

5 Fenns Quay, Sheares St – 021 427 9997 (booking essential) – www.ichigoichie.ie – dinner only – Closed 25-26 December, 1 January, 2 weeks February, Sunday and Monday

Orchids

MODERN CUISINE • ELEGANT XXX Sophisticated formal dining room in a well-appointed country house. Pillars dominate the room, which is laid with crisp white tablecloths. Menus offer refined dishes with some modern twists.

Menu € 69

Hayfield Manor Hotel, Perrott Ave, College Rd – Southwest : 2 km by R 608 – 021 484 5900 (booking essential) – www.hayfieldmanor.ie – dinner only – Closed Tuesday-Thursday in winter and Sunday-Monday

Les Gourmandises

CLASSIC FRENCH • ELEGANT XX Smart, contemporary restaurant which is proudly run by experienced owners – he cooks and she looks after the service. Accomplished dishes have a classic French heart and original Irish twists. The set menus represent good value.

Menu € 33 – Carte € 38/58

17 Cook St – 021 425 1959 (booking essential) – www.lesgourmandises.ie – dinner only – Closed 10 days July, Sunday and Monday

Greenes

MODERN CUISINE • FRIENDLY XX Head down the alleyway at the side of the Isaacs Hotel, towards the waterfall, to access this formal yet friendly restaurant. The chef is a local and uses his cooking to showcase ingredients from West Cork producers.

Menu € 28/35 – Carte € 41/61

48 McCurtain St – 021 455 2279 – www.greenesrestaurant.com – Closed 23 December- 2 January

Perrotts

MODERN CUISINE • BRASSERIE XX A conservatory restaurant overlooking the gardens of a luxurious country house. It's smart but comfortably furnished, with an adjoining wood-panelled bar. The menu offers a modern take on brasserie classics.

Carte € 45/57

Hayfield Manor Hotel, Perrott Ave, College Rd – Southwest : 2 km by R 608 – 021 484 5900 – www.hayfieldmanor.ie – Closed 25 December

Rachel's

TRADITIONAL CUISINE • FRIENDLY XX The service is friendly and energetic at this rustic, industrial-style restaurant and sultry piano bar. Flavoursome, generously proportioned dishes use garden and farm ingredients – go for a dish cooked in the wood-fired oven.

Menu € 35 (early dinner) – Carte € 25/52

28 Washington St – ☎ 021 427 4189 – www.rachels.ie – Closed Sunday

Farmgate Café

REGIONAL CUISINE • BISTRO X Popular, long-standing eatery above a bustling 200 year old market; turn right for self-service or left for the bistro. Daily menus use produce from the stalls below and are supplemented by the latest catch. Dishes are hearty and homemade.

Carte € 22/40

English Market (1st floor), Princes St – ☎ 021 427 8134 – www.farmgate.ie – lunch only – Closed 25-27 December, Sunday and bank holidays

Paradiso

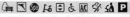

VEGETARIAN • INTIMATE X They've been serving creative, satisfying vegetarian dishes at this stylish restaurant since 1993. The atmosphere is intimate yet lively and the service is bright and friendly. For those dining, they offer a dinner, bed and breakfast deal; spacious bedrooms come in bright, bold colours.

Menu € 25 (early dinner)/45

2 rooms – € 180 € 240

16 Lancaster Quay, Western Rd – ☎ 021 427 7939 (booking essential) – www.paradiso.restaurant – dinner only – Closed 24-27 December, Sunday and bank holidays

Hayfield Manor

HISTORIC • CLASSIC Luxurious country house with wood-panelled hall, impressive staircase and antique-furnished drawing rooms; the perfect spot for afternoon tea. Plush bedrooms have plenty of extras, including putting machines. Well-equipped residents' spa.

88 rooms – € 229/455 € 229/455 – 4 suites

Perrott Ave, College Rd – Southwest : 2 km by R 608 – ☎ 021 484 5900 – www.hayfieldmanor.ie

Orchids • **Perrotts** – See restaurant listing

Lancaster Lodge

BUSINESS • MODERN Purpose-built hotel next to the River Lee and within easy walking distance of the town centre. Spacious, bright bedrooms with bold fabrics and modern artwork; the executive suites have whirlpool baths. A good choice for the business traveller.

48 rooms – € 89/199 € 89/209 – €14

Lancaster Quay, Western Rd – ☎ 021 425 1125 – www.lancasterlodge.com – Closed 23-26 December

CORROFIN CORA FINNE

Clare – Pop. 689 – Regional map n° **22**-B1

Fergus View

FAMILY • PERSONALISED This charming house takes its name from the nearby river and offers pleasant country views from its front rooms. Bedrooms are immaculately kept and the welcome is warm – it's been in the family for four generations.

5 rooms – € 55/58 € 80/84

Kilnaboy – North : 3.25 km on R 476 – ☎ 065 683 7606 – www.fergusview.com – Closed November-February

CROSSHAVEN BUN AN TÁBHAIRNE

Cork – Pop. 2 093 – Regional map n° **22**-B3

Cronin's

SEAFOOD • PUB A classic Irish pub filled with interesting artefacts. It's been in the family since 1970 and is now run by the 3rd generation. Unfussy seafood dishes feature local produce. The limited opening restaurant offers more ambitious fare.

Carte € 25/47

1 Point Rd - ✆ 021 483 1829 - www.croninspub.com - Closed 25 December

DELGANY DEILGNE

Wicklow - ✉ Bray - Pop. 6 682 - Regional map n° **22**-D2

Pigeon House

MODERN BRITISH • BISTRO ✗ This former pub now houses a bakery, a deli and a large restaurant complete with a counter of homemade cakes. Breakfast morphs into coffee, then into lunch and dinner; you can have anything from a bacon sarnie to duck liver parfait.

Carte € 28/45

The Delgany Inn - ✆ 01 287 7103 - www.pigeonhouse.ie - Closed 25-26 December, Monday except bank holidays, dinner Tuesday and Wednesday

DINGLE AN DAINGEAN

Kerry - Pop. 1 965 - Regional map n° **22**-A2

Chart House

REGIONAL CUISINE • RUSTIC ✗ This characterful former boathouse sits in a pleasant quayside spot. The charming open-plan interior features exposed stone and stained glass, and the room has a cosy, intimate feel. Seasonal local ingredients feature in rustic, flavoursome dishes and service is friendly and efficient.

Menu € 35 - Carte € 35/51

The Mall - ✆ 066 915 2255 (booking essential) - www.thecharthousedingle.com - dinner only - Closed 2 January-12 February, 22-27 December and Monday October-May

Global Village

TRADITIONAL CUISINE • BISTRO ✗✗ A homely restaurant with a laid-back feel. Despite having visited 42 countries, the chef likes to keep things local, with meat and vegetables from the peninsula. The local fish dishes are fantastic.

Menu € 35 (early dinner) **s** - Carte € 36/58 **s**

Upper Main St - ✆ 066 915 2325 - www.globalvillagedingle.com - dinner only - Closed January-February and restricted opening in winter

Out of the Blue

SEAFOOD • RUSTIC ✗ Its name is perfectly apt: not only is it painted bright blue, but this simple harbourside restaurant keeps its focus firmly on ingredients that come from the sea. Menus are decided each morning, based on the latest local catch.

Carte € 38/59

Waterside - ✆ 066 915 0811 (booking essential) - www.outoftheblue.ie - dinner only and Sunday lunch - Closed mid-November-February

Castlewood House

COUNTRY HOUSE • PERSONALISED Spacious house overlooking the bay. Modern bedrooms come with whirlpool baths and extras like robes and chocolates. The hot and cold breakfast options are extensive; don't miss the bread and butter pudding.

12 rooms - € 80/130 € 96/170

The Wood - Northwest : 1 km on R 559 - ✆ 066 915 2788 - www.castlewooddingle.com - Closed 6-27 December and 6 January-13 February

Greenmount House

FAMILY • PERSONALISED Well-run hotel in an elevated position above the town with views of the hills and harbour; take it all in over a delicious breakfast. Lounges are comfy and bedrooms are modern; some have balconies or small terraces.

14 rooms – € 70/155 € 102/165

Upper John St, Gortonora - by John St. - 066 915 1414 - www.greenmounthouse.ie - Closed 22-31 December

Heatons

FAMILY • PERSONALISED Large, family-run house close to town, where a warm welcome is guaranteed. Most bedrooms have sea views and some have whirlpool baths. Comprehensive breakfasts include homemade pancakes, omelettes and Drambuie porridge.

16 rooms – € 69/97 € 92/134

The Wood - Northwest : 1 km. on R 559 - 066 915 2288 - www.heatonsdingle.com - Closed 2 January-1 February

DONEGAL DÚN NA NGALL

Donegal – Pop. 2 607 – Regional map n° **21**-C1

Harvey's Point

MODERN CUISINE • CHIC XXX A formal, traditional restaurant set within a family owned country house hotel; its semi-circular windows afford delightful views of the lough. Classic dishes make use of local Donegal produce and are presented in a modern manner.

Menu € 55 – Carte € 48/71

Harvey's Point Hotel, Lough Eske - Northeast : 7.25 km. by N 15 - 074 972 220[illegible] - www.harveyspoint.com - dinner only - Closed Wednesday July-October

Cedars

TRADITIONAL CUISINE • INTIMATE XX Stylish, modern restaurant in a 17C castle close to the lough, with romantic booths to the rear and a slate terrace boasting views over the lawns and woodland. Small menu with international influences but Donegal produce to the fore.

Menu € 55 – Carte € 44/70

Solis Lough Eske Castle Hotel, Northeast : 6.5 km by N 15 - 074 972 5100 - www.lougheskecastlehotel.com - dinner only and Sunday lunch

Harvey's Point

FAMILY • CLASSIC A sprawling, family-run hotel in a peaceful loughside setting with traditional guest areas and huge, very comfortable, country house style bedrooms – all offer a high level of facilities and most have lovely countryside outlooks.

77 rooms – € 190/360 € 250/640

Lough Eske - Northeast : 7.25 km. by N 15 - 074 972 2208 - www.harveyspoint.com

Harvey's Point – See restaurant listing

Solis Lough Eske Castle

LUXURY • CLASSIC Beautifully restored 17C castle, surrounded by 43 acres of sculpture-filled grounds. There's a fantastic spa and a swimming pool overlooking an enclosed garden. Bedrooms are a mix of contemporary and antique furnished; go for a Garden Suite.

96 rooms – € 230/275 € 230/275 – 1 suite

Northeast : 6.5 km by N 15 - 074 972 5100 - www.lougheskecastlehotel.com

Cedars – See restaurant listing

Ardeevin

FAMILY • COSY Friendly, brightly painted house set in peaceful gardens and boasting beautiful views over Lough Eske; personally run by the friendly owner. Warm, pleasantly cluttered guest areas are filled with ornaments and curios. Individually designed bedrooms display quality furnishings and thoughtful extras.

4 rooms – € 85 € 85

Lough Eske, Barnesmore – Northeast : 9 km by N 15 following signs for Lough Eske Drive – 074 972 1790 – www.ardeevinguesthouse.co.uk – Closed November-19 March

DONNYBROOK DOMHNACH BROC – Dublin → See Dublin

DOOLIN DÚLAINM

Clare – Regional map n° **22**-B1

Cullinan's

TOWNHOUSE • COSY A keen husband and wife team run this brightly painted orange property, which stands out in this quaint village in the heart of The Burren. Cosy, contemporary bedrooms are split between the main house and an annexe; the latter look out over the River Aille.

10 rooms – € 60/90 € 80/125

– 065 707 4183 – www.cullinansdoolin.com – Closed November- March

DOONBEG AN DÚN BEAG

Clare – Pop. 272 – Regional map n° **22**-B2

Morrissey's

SEAFOOD • PUB Smartly refurbished pub in a small coastal village; its terrace overlooks the river and the castle ruins. The menu may be simple but cooking is careful and shows respect for ingredients; locally caught fish and shellfish feature heavily and the crabs in particular are worth a try. Bedrooms are modern – two overlook the river – and they have bikes and a kayak for hire.

Carte € 26/46

5 rooms – € 50 € 90/100

– 065 905 5304 (bookings not accepted) – www.morrisseysdoonbeg.com – dinner only and Sunday lunch – Closed January, February, November and Monday-Tuesday March-May

Trump International Golf Links and H. Doonbeg

LUXURY • DESIGN Smart resort complex owned by Donald Trump. Stylish, sumptuous bedrooms and suites are spread about the grounds: some are duplex and feature fully fitted kitchens; all have spacious marble bathrooms and are extremely comfortable. Ocean View offers fine dining with a pleasant outlook over the sea, while Trump's, in the golf clubhouse, serves a traditional menu.

75 rooms – € 180/280 € 180/280

Northeast : 6 km on N 67 – 065 905 5600 – www.trumpirelandhotel.com – Closed Sunday-Thursday November-February

DROGHEDA DROICHEAD ÁTHA

Louth – Pop. 30 393 – Regional map n° **21**-D3

Eastern Seaboard

INTERNATIONAL • BISTRO A lively industrial style bistro; its name a reference to its location within Ireland and also a nod to the USA, which influences the menus. Share several small plates or customise a hearty main course with your choice of sides.

Carte € 20/62

1 Bryanstown Centre, Dublin Rd – Southeast : 2.5 km by N 1 taking first right after railway bridge – 041 980 2570 – www.glasgow-diaz.com – Closed 25-26 December and Wednesday

The Kitchen

WORLD CUISINE • BISTRO Glass-fronted riverside eatery. By day, a café serving homemade cakes, pastries, salads and sandwiches; by night, a more interesting, mainly Eastern Mediterranean menu is served, with influences from North Africa and the Middle East.

Carte € 32/46

2 South Quay – 041 983 4630 – Closed 25-27 December and Monday-Tuesday

Scholars Townhouse

TOWNHOUSE • CLASSIC 19C former priest's house: now a well-run, privately owned hotel with smart wood panelling and ornate coving featuring throughout. Appealing bar and cosy lounge; comfortable, well-kept bedrooms. Dine on classically based dishes under an impressive mural of the Battle of Boyne.

16 rooms – € 75/95 € 89/170

King St – by West St and Lawrence St turning left at Lawrence's Gate – 041 983 5410 – www.scholarshotel.com – Closed 25-26 December

DROMAHAIR

Leitrim – Pop. 748 – Regional map n° **21**-B2

Luna

INTERNATIONAL • FRIENDLY A delightful little cottage on the main road of a sleepy village; the loughside drive over from Sligo is beautiful. It might have a neighbourhood feel but the food has global overtones, from the South of France and Tuscany to Asia.

Carte € 28/47

Main St – 071 913 4332 – dinner only and Sunday lunch – Closed January, dinner Sunday, Monday and Tuesday

GOOD TIPS!

The Celtic Tiger is back, with a purr if not yet a roar, and the capital's food scene continues to show signs of hotting up. A resurgence in informal dining has seen good value neighbourhood restaurants like **Craft**, **Richmond** and **Bastible** become popular – and these sit happily alongside the city's collection of Michelin Stars.

DUBLIN BAILE ÁTHA CLIATH

Dublin – Pop. 527 612 – Regional map n° **22**-D1

Restaurants

✿✿ Patrick Guilbaud (Guillaume Lebrun)

MODERN FRENCH • ELEGANT XXXX Patrick Guilbaud is one of the most celebrated chefs in the country and his highly regarded restaurant is high on the list of any serious foodie living in or visiting Dublin. They have run a tight ship here since 1981 and you cannot deny that they have earned their place in Irish culinary history. The large lounge is decorated in bold, eye-catching colours, while the sumptuous restaurant is decorated in pastel shades which help to soften the space.

The owners are ever-present and they work their way around the room making sure that every diner is warmly welcomed and made to feel special. Accomplished, original cooking is rooted in the traditional French school but introduces some modern techniques. Bold flavours are superbly balanced and the presentation is stunning; luxurious Irish ingredients are always to the fore.

→ Blue lobster ravioli with coconut scented lobster cream, toasted almonds and curry dressing. Caramelised veal sweetbread, with parsnip, Mimolette and coffee. Lime Soufflé with lime leaf ice cream.

Menu € 60/120

Town plan: G3-e – *21 Upper Merrion St* ✉ *D2*
– *✆ 01 676 4192 (booking essential)*
– *www.restaurantpatrickguilbaud.ie*
– *Closed 17 March, 25-31 December, Sunday, Monday and bank holidays*

Don't expect guesthouses to provide the same level of service as a hotel. They are often characterised by a warm welcome and décor which reflects the owner's personality. Those shown in red are particularly charming.

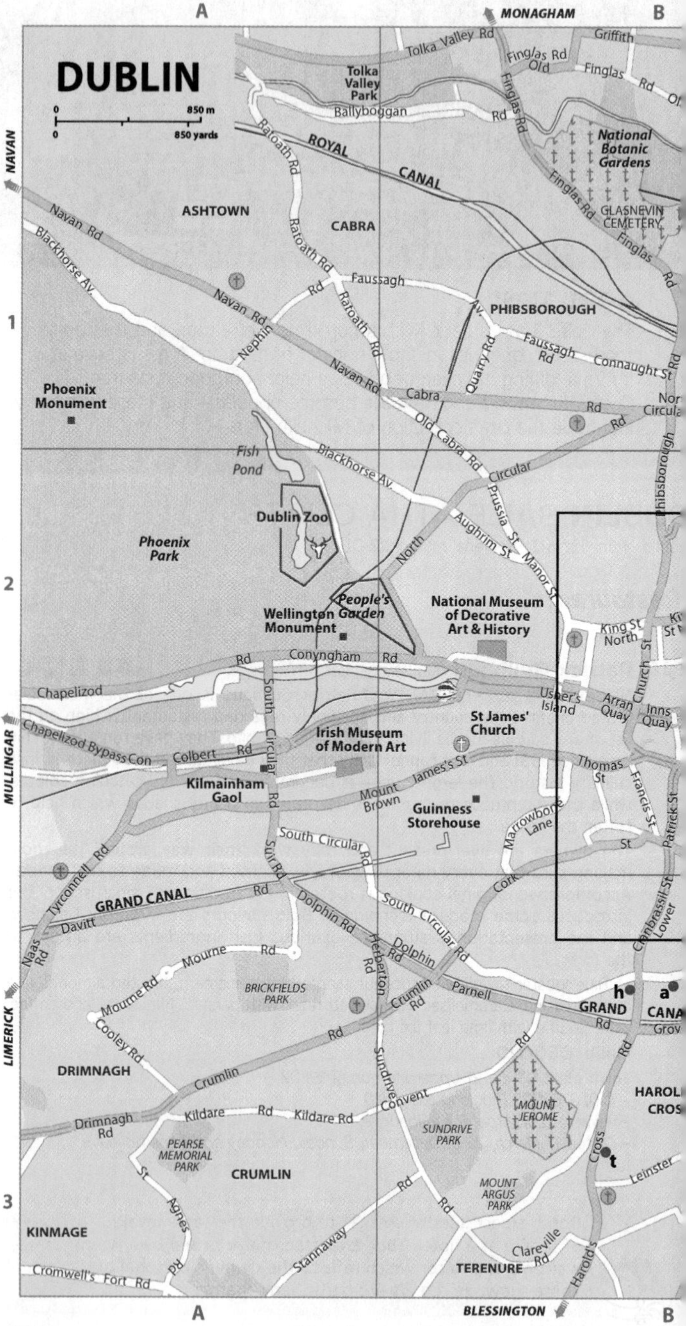

DUBLIN
A
B
MONAGHAM
NAVAN
MULLINGAR
LIMERICK
BLESSINGTON
0
850 m
850 yards
1
2
3
Tolka Valley Park
Tolka Valley Rd
Finglas Rd
Old Finglas Rd
Ballyboggan Rd
Griffith
National Botanic Gardens
GLASNEVIN CEMETERY
ROYAL CANAL
ASHTOWN
CABRA
PHIBSBOROUGH
Navan Rd
Blackhorse Av.
Ratoath Rd
Faussagh Rd
Faussagh Av.
Nephin Rd
Quarry Rd
Connaught St
North Circular Rd
Cabra Rd
Old Cabra Rd
Phibsborough
Phoenix Monument
Fish Pond
Dublin Zoo
Phoenix Park
Prussia St
Aughrim St
Manor St
People's Garden
Wellington Monument
National Museum of Decorative Art & History
King St North
Church St
Conyngham Rd
Chapelizod
Chapelizod Bypass Con
Usher's Island
Arran Quay
Inns Quay
St James' Church
Irish Museum of Modern Art
Colbert Rd
South Circular Rd
Kilmainham Gaol
Mount Brown
James's St
Thomas St
Francis St
Patrick St
Guinness Storehouse
Marrowbone Lane
Cork St
Tyrconnell Rd
GRAND CANAL
Davitt Rd
Naas Rd
Suir Rd
Dolphin Rd
Herberton Rd
Clanbrassil St Lower
Mourne Rd
BRICKFIELDS PARK
Cooley Rd
Crumlin Rd
Parnell Rd
GRAND CANAL
Grove
DRIMNAGH
Drimnagh Rd
Kildare Rd
Sundrive Rd
Convent Rd
MOUNT JEROME
HAROLD'S CROSS
Harold's Cross Rd
Leinster
PEARSE MEMORIAL PARK
SUNDRIVE PARK
CRUMLIN
MOUNT ARGUS PARK
St Agnes Rd
KINMAGE
Stannaway Rd
Clareville Rd
TERENURE
Cromwell's Fort Rd
h
a
t

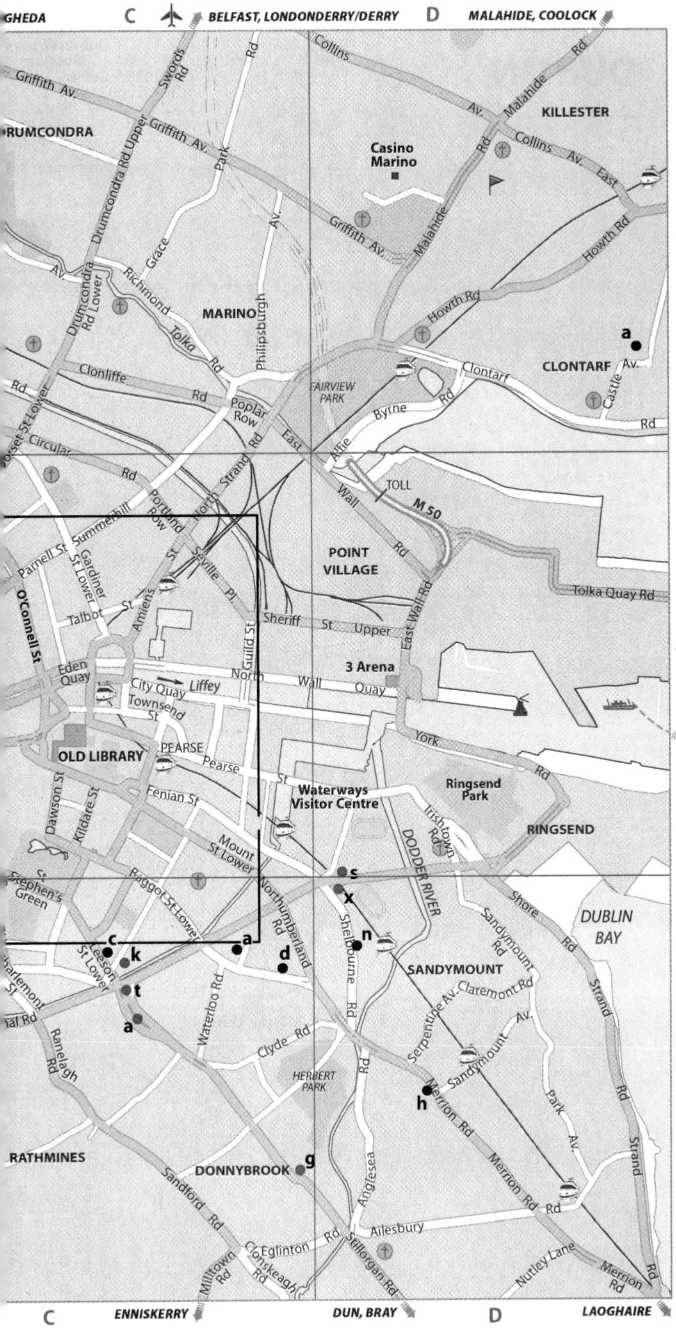
GHEDA
C
BELFAST, LONDONDERRY/DERRY
D
MALAHIDE, COOLOCK
DRUMCONDRA
KILLESTER
Casino Marino
MARINO
FAIRVIEW PARK
CLONTARF
POINT VILLAGE
TOLL
M 50
Tolka Quay Rd
3 Arena
Liffey
OLD LIBRARY
PEARSE
Waterways Visitor Centre
Ringsend Park
RINGSEND
DODDER RIVER
DUBLIN BAY
SANDYMOUNT
HERBERT PARK
RATHMINES
DONNYBROOK
DOUGLAS, HOLYHEAD
LIVERPOOL, MOSTYN
1
2
3
C
ENNISKERRY
DUN, BRAY
D
LAOGHAIRE

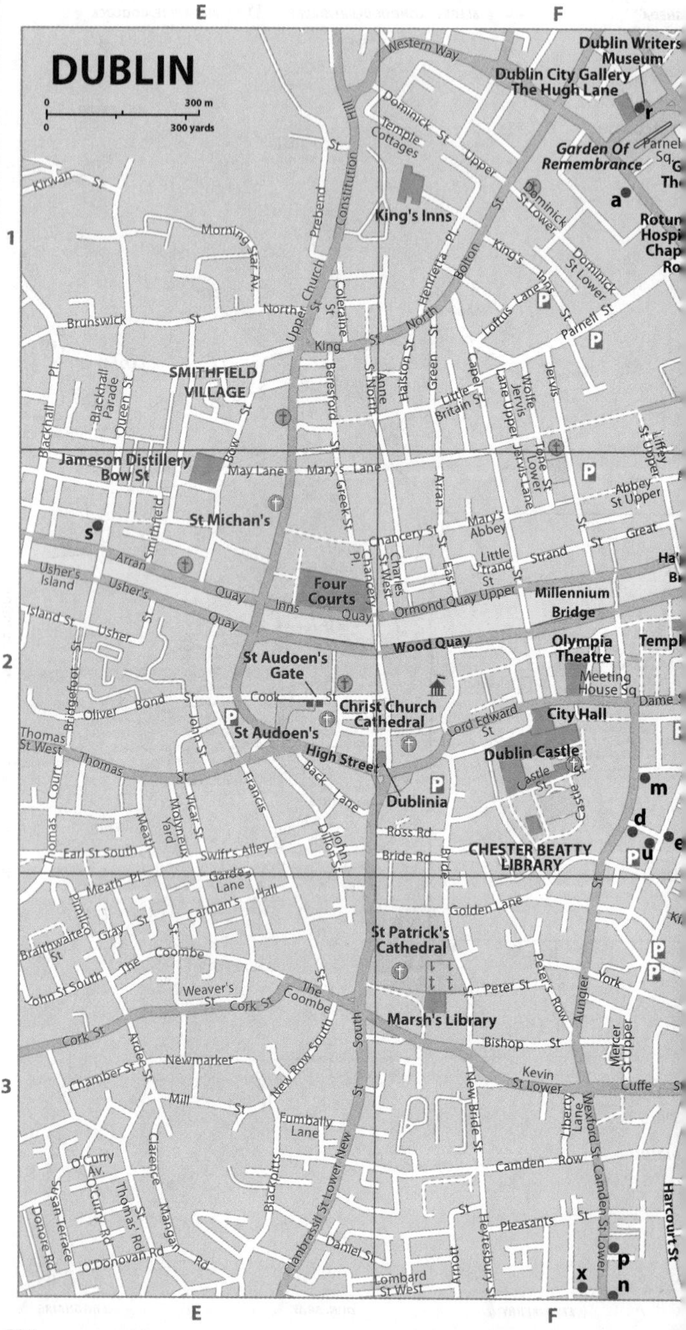
DUBLIN
0
300 m
0
300 yards
E
F
1
2
3
Dublin Writers Museum
Dublin City Gallery The Hugh Lane
Garden Of Remembrance
Parnell Sq
King's Inns
Rotun
Hospi
Chap
Ro
Western Way
Dominick St
Temple Cottages
Upper
Dominick St Lower
King's Inns St
Dominick St Lower
Bolton St
Henrietta Pl.
Loftus Lane
Parnell St
Kirwan St
Morning Star Av.
Prebend St
Constitution Hill
Upper Church St
Coleraine St
North King St
Brunswick St North
SMITHFIELD VILLAGE
Blackhall Pl.
Blackhall Parade
Queen St
Bow St
Beresford St
Anne St North
Halston St
Green St
Capel St
Little Britain St
Lane Upper
Jervis
Wolfe Tone St
Jervis St
Jervis Lane Lower
Liffey St Upper
Jameson Distillery Bow St
May Lane
Mary's Lane
Greek St
Arran St
Abbey St Upper
St Michan's
Smithfield
Chancery St
Mary's Abbey
Little Strand St
Strand St
Great
Chancery Pl.
Charles St West
East
Arran Quay
Usher's Island
Usher's Quay
Inns Quay
Four Courts
Chancery Quay
Ormond Quay Upper
Millennium Bridge
Island St
Usher St
Wood Quay
Olympia Theatre
Templ
St Audoen's Gate
Meeting House Sq
Dame St
Cook St
Christ Church Cathedral
City Hall
Oliver Bond St
Lord Edward St
St Audoen's
Bridgefoot St
Thomas St West
Thomas St
High Street
Dublin Castle
Castle St
Back Lane
Dublinia
John St
Francis St
Vicar St
Molyneux Yard
Meath St
Court
Thomas
John Dillon St
Ross Rd
Bride Rd
Bride St
Earl St South
Swift's Alley
CHESTER BEATTY LIBRARY
Garden Lane
Meath Pl.
Carman's Hall
Golden Lane
Pimlico
Gray St
Braithwaite St
The Coombe
St Patrick's Cathedral
Peter's Row
Aungier St
York St
John St South
Weaver's St
Cork St
The Coombe
Peter St
South St
Marsh's Library
Cork St
Bishop St
Mercer St Upper
Ardee St
Newmarket
Chamber St
New Row South
Kevin St Lower
Cuffe St
Mill St
New Bride St
Liberty Lane
Wexford St
Fumbally Lane
O'Curry Av.
O'Curry Rd
Clarence Mangan Rd
Thomas' Rd
Blackpitts
Clanbrassil St Lower
New St
Camden Row
Camden St Lower
Harcourt St
Susan Terrace
Donore Rd
O'Donovan Rd
Daniel St
Heytesbury St
Arnott St
Pleasants St
Lombard St West
a
r
s
m
d
u
e
p
n
x

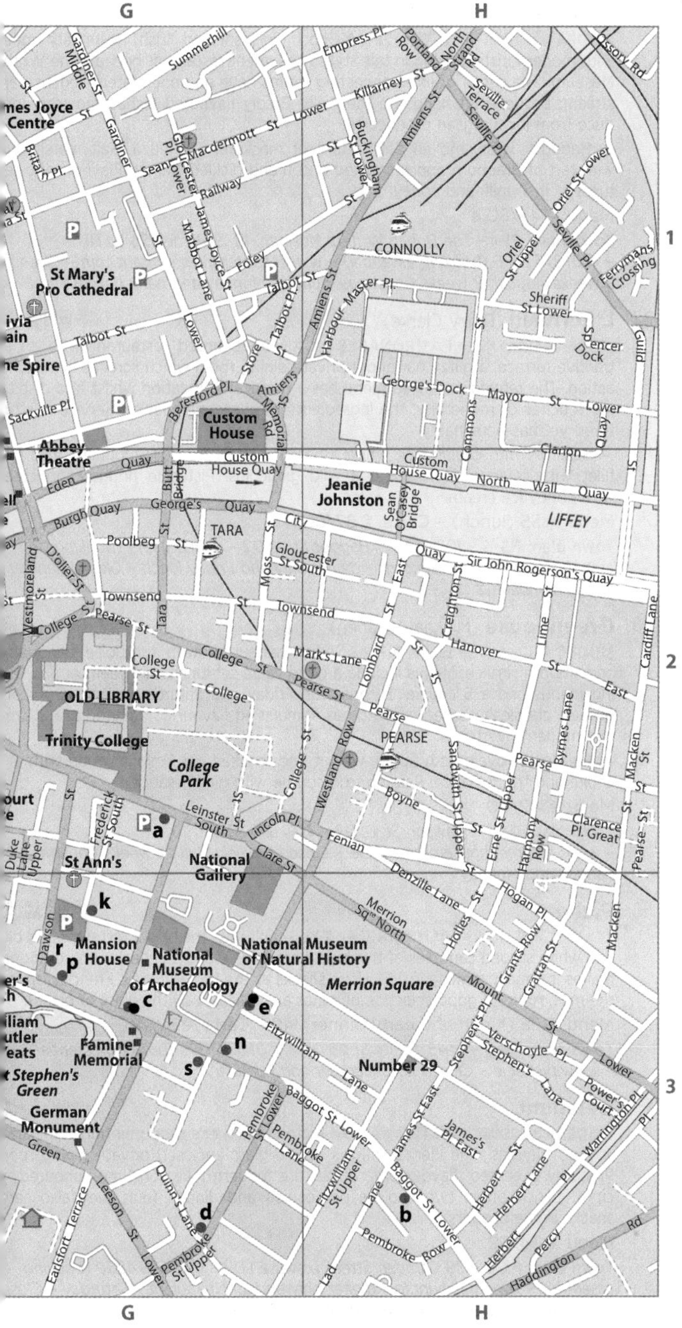
G
H
1
2
3
Summerhill
Gardiner St Middle
Empress Pl.
Portland Row
North Strand Rd
Ossory Rd
James Joyce Centre
Killarney St
Seville Terrace
Seville Pl.
Amiens St
Gardiner St
Sean Macdermott St Lower
Buckingham St Lower
Gloucester Pl. Lower
Railway St
Britain Pl.
Orient St Lower
Oriel St Upper
Seville Pl.
Ferrymans Crossing
CONNOLLY
Mabbot Lane
James Joyce St
Foley St
St Mary's Pro Cathedral
Talbot St
Talbot Pl.
Harbour Master Pl.
Sheriff St Lower
Spencer Dock
Guild St
The Spire
Store St
Amiens St
Beresford Pl.
Memorial Rd
George's Dock
Mayor St Lower
Commons St
Sackville Pl.
Custom House
Abbey Theatre
Custom House Quay
Clarion Quay
Eden Quay
Butt Bridge
Jeanie Johnston
Sean O'Casey Bridge
North Wall Quay
Burgh Quay
George's Quay
City Quay
LIFFEY
TARA
Poolbeg St
Moss St
Gloucester St South
Sir John Rogerson's Quay
D'olier St
Westmoreland St
Townsend St
East St
Creighton St
Lime St
Cardiff Lane
College St
Pearse St
Tara St
Hanover St East
Mark's Lane
Lombard St
College St
OLD LIBRARY
College
Pearse St
PEARSE
Byrnes Lane
Macken St
Trinity College
College Park
Westland Row
Sandwith St Upper
Erne St Upper
Pearse St
Boyne St
Leinster St South
Lincoln Pl.
Clarence Pl. Great
Frederick St South
Fenian St
Harmony Row
Pearse St
Duke Lane Upper
St Ann's
National Gallery
Clare St
Denzille Lane
Hogan Pl.
Merrion Sq North
Holles St
Grants Row
Grattan St
Macken St
Dawson St
Mansion House
National Museum of Archaeology
National Museum of Natural History
Merrion Square
Mount St Lower
Stephen's Pl.
Verschoyle Pl.
Stephen's Lane
Famine Memorial
Fitzwilliam Lane
Number 29
Power's Court
Warrington Pl.
St Stephen's Green
German Monument
Pembroke St Lower
Baggot St Lower
James St East
James's Pl. East
Herbert St
Herbert Lane
Pembroke Lane
Fitzwilliam St Upper
Quinn's Lane
Leeson St Lower
Earlsfort Terrace
Pembroke St Upper
Lad Lane
Pembroke Row
Herbert Pl.
Percy Pl.
Haddington Rd
a
b
c
d
e
k
n
p
r
s

Chapter One (Ross Lewis)

MODERN CUISINE • INTIMATE XXX Good old-fashioned Irish hospitality mee with modern Irish cooking in this stylish basement restaurant beneath the Write Museum. The series of interconnecting rooms have an understated elegance ar striking bespoke art hangs on the walls. Boldly flavoured dishes showcase pr duce from local artisan producers.

→ Haddock with smoked eel, tartare of mackerel and yuzu. Salt marsh du with tart of Braeburn apple, smoked bacon and pickled walnut. Flavours and te tures of Irish milk and honey.

Menu € 42/80 **s**

Town plan: F1-r - *The Dublin Writers Museum, 18-19 Parnell Sq ✉ D1 - ✆ 01 873 2266 (booking essential) - www.chapteronerestaurant.com - Closed 2 weeks August, 2 weeks Christmas, Sunday, Monday and bank holidays*

L'Ecrivain (Derry Clarke)

MODERN CUISINE • FASHIONABLE XXX A well-regarded restaurant with an a tractive terrace, a glitzy bar and a private dining room which screens live kitch action. The refined, balanced menu has a classical foundation whilst also displa ing touches of modernity; the ingredients used are superlative. Service is stru tured yet has personality.

→ Scallops with cauliflower, white asparagus and Lardo di Colonnata. Irish be fillet with celeriac, morels and a wild garlic jus. Pistachio nougat and crea with honey ice cream.

Menu € 35 (lunch) - Carte € 67/88

Town plan: H3-b - *109a Lower Baggot St ✉ D2 - ✆ 01 661 1919 (booking essential) - www.lecrivain.com - dinner only and Friday lunch - Closed Sunday and bank holidays*

Greenhouse (Mickael Viljanen)

MODERN CUISINE • ELEGANT XXX Stylish restaurant with turquoise banquett and smooth service. Menus include a good value set lunch, midweek set and tas ing menus and a 5 course 'Surprise' on Friday and Saturday evenings. Accor plished, classically based cooking has stimulating flavour combinations and cre tive modern overtones.

→ Foie gras royale with apple, walnut and smoked eel. Anjou pigeon with ar choke and truffle sauce. Passion fruit soufflé with ginger sauce.

Menu € 42/90

Town plan: G3-r - *Dawson St ✉ D2 - ✆ 01 676 7015 - www.thegreenhouserestaurant.ie - Closed 2 weeks July, 2 weeks Christmas, Sunday and Monday*

Pichet

CLASSIC FRENCH • FASHIONABLE XX You can't miss the bright red signs and bl and white striped canopies of this buzzy brasserie - and its checkerboard floori makes it equally striking inside. Have snacks at the bar or classic French dishes the main room. A good selection of wines are available by the glass or pichet.

Menu € 28 (lunch and early dinner)/49 - Carte € 32/46

Town plan: F2-g - *14-15 Trinity St ✉ D2 - ✆ 01 677 1060 (booking essential) - www.pichet.ie - Closed 25 December and 1 January*

Delahunt

MODERN CUISINE • BISTRO X An old Victorian grocer's shop mentioned in Jam Joyce's 'Ulysses'; the clerk's snug is now a glass-enclosed private dining roo Precisely executed, flavoursome dishes are modern takes on time-honoured r cipes. Lunch offers two choices per course and dinner, four; they also ser snacks in the upstairs bar.

Menu € 34/39

Town plan: F3-p - *39 Camden Street Lower ✉ D2 - ✆ 01 598 4880 (booking essential) - www.delahunt.ie - dinner only and lunch Thursday-Saturday - Close 15 August-1 September, Sunday and Monday*

Bastible

MODERN CUISINE • SIMPLE X The name refers to the cast iron pot which once sat on the hearth of every family home; they still use it here to make the bread. Modern cooking showcases one main ingredient with minimal accompaniments; menus offer 3 choices per course.

Menu €26/48

Town plan: B3-a – *111 South Circular Rd ✉ D8 – ✆ 01 473 7409 (booking essential) – www.bastible.com – dinner only and lunch Friday-Sunday – Closed Sunday dinner, Monday and Tuesday*

Clanbrassil House Ⓝ

MODERN CUISINE • RUSTIC X Bastible's younger sister is a small place seating just 25. The concise menu focuses on the charcoal grill, with everything from home-made sausages to prime cuts. The hash brown chips are a favourite; the early evening menu is a steal; and if you're in a group you can share dishes 'family-style'.

Menu €25 (early dinner) – Carte €30/47

Town plan: B3-h – *6 Clanbrassil St Upper ✉ D8 – ✆ 01 453 9786 (booking essential) – www.clanbrassilhouse.com – dinner only and Saturday lunch – Closed Sunday and Monday*

Etto

MEDITERRANEAN CUISINE • RUSTIC X The name of this rustic restaurant means 'little' and it is totally apt! Blackboards announce the daily wines and the Worker's Lunch special. Flavoursome dishes rely on good ingredients and have Italian influences; the chef understands natural flavours and follows the 'less is more' approach.

Menu €25 (weekday lunch)/28 – Carte €29/45

Town plan: G3-s – *18 Merrion Row ✉ D2 – ✆ 01 678 8872 (booking essential) – www.etto.ie – Closed last 2 weeks August, 25 December-7 January, 15-23 April, Sunday-Tuesday and lunch Wednesday*

Pig's Ear

MODERN CUISINE • BISTRO X Look out for the bright pink door of this three storey Georgian townhouse overlooking Trinity College Gardens. The first and second floors have a homely retro feel while the third floor is a private dining room its own kitchen and library. Irish produce features in refined yet comforting dishes.

Menu €24 (lunch and early dinner) – Carte €31/49

Town plan: G2-a – *4 Nassau St ✉ D2 – ✆ 01 670 3865 (booking essential) – www.thepigsear.ie – Closed first week January, Sunday and bank holidays*

Richmond

MODERN CUISINE • NEIGHBOURHOOD X A real gem of a neighbourhood restaurant with a rustic look and a lively feel; sit upstairs for a more sedate experience. The vibrant, gutsy dishes change regularly – apart from the Dexter burger and rib-eye which are mainstays; on Tuesdays they serve a good value tasting menu where they try out new ideas.

Menu €24 (early dinner) – Carte €33/44

Town plan: B3-r – *43 Richmond Street South ✉ D2 – ✆ 01 478 8783 – www.richmondrestaurant.ie – dinner only and brunch Saturday-Sunday – Closed Monday*

Glovers Alley Ⓝ

MODERN CUISINE • DESIGN XXX This second floor hotel restaurant looks out over St Stephen's Green and is named in honour of the city's glove-makers who once occupied the neighbouring alleyway. Pinks, greens and floral arrangements give the room a soft touch while dishes display contrastingly bold flavours and textures.

Menu €45 (lunch and early dinner)/80

Town plan: F3-d – *Fitzwilliam Hotel, 127-128 St Stephen's Grn ✉ D2 – ✆ 01 244 0733 (booking essential) – www.gloversalley.com – Closed 25 December-8 January, Sunday, Monday and lunch Tuesday-Wednesday*

One Pico

MODERN CUISINE • ELEGANT XXX This stylishly refurbished restaurant tucke away on a side street is a well-regarded place that's a regular haunt for MPs. S on comfy banquettes or velour chairs, surrounded by muted colours. Modern Iris cooking has plenty of flavour.

Menu € 29 (weekday lunch)/68

Town plan: G3-k - *5-6 Molesworth Pl ✉ D2 - ☏ 01 676 0300 - www.onepico.co - Closed bank holidays*

Amuse

MODERN CUISINE • FRIENDLY XX Modern, understated décor provides the perfe backdrop for the intricate, innovative cooking. Dishes showcase Asian ingredients - inclu ing kombu and yuzu; which are artfully arranged according to their flavours and texture

Menu € 35 (weekday lunch)/55

Town plan: G3-r - *22 Dawson St ✉ D2 - ☏ 01 639 4889 - www.amuse.ie - Close 2 weeks Christmas-New Year, Sunday and Monday*

Bang

MODERN CUISINE • BISTRO XX Stylish restaurant with an intimate powder blu basement, a bright mezzanine level and a small, elegant room above. There a good value pre-theatre menus, a more elaborate à la carte and tasting men showcasing top Irish produce.

Menu € 25/33 - Carte € 38/61

Town plan: G3-a - *11 Merrion Row ✉ D2 - ☏ 01 400 4229 - www.bangrestaurant.com - Closed Christmas and bank holidays*

Dax

FRENCH • BISTRO XX Clubby restaurant in the cellar of a Georgian townhouse ne Fitzwilliam Square. Tried-and-tested French dishes use top Irish produce and flavou are clearly defined. The Surprise Menu best showcases the kitchen's talent.

Menu € 35 (weekday lunch)/39 - Carte € 53/69

Town plan: G3-d - *23 Pembroke St Upper ✉ D2 - ☏ 01 676 1494 (booking essential) - www.dax.ie - Closed 25 December-4 January, 1 week Easter, 1 week mid August, Saturday lunch, Sunday and Monday*

Fade St. Social - Restaurant

MODERN CUISINE • BRASSERIE XX Have cocktails on the terrace then head f the big, modern brasserie. Dishes use Irish ingredients but have a Mediterranea feel; they specialise in sharing and wood-fired dishes, and use large cuts of me such as chateaubriand.

Menu € 35 (lunch and early dinner) - Carte € 36/73

Town plan: F2-u - *4-6 Fade St ✉ D2 - ☏ 01 604 0066 - www.fadestreetsocial.com - dinner only and lunch Thursday-Friday - Closed 25-26 December*

Mr Fox

MODERN CUISINE • INTIMATE XX In the basement of a striking Georgian hous you'll find this light-hearted restaurant with a lovely tiled floor and a small te race. The charming team present tasty international dishes, some of which ha a playful touch.

Menu € 22 (lunch and early dinner) - Carte € 34/48

Town plan: F1-a - *38 Parnell Sq. West ✉ D1 - ☏ 01 874 7778 - www.mrfox.ie - Closed Sunday, Monday and bank holidays*

Pearl Brasserie

CLASSIC FRENCH • BRASSERIE XX Formal basement restaurant with a small ba lounge and two surprisingly airy dining rooms; sit in a stylish booth in one of th old coal bunkers. Intriguing modern dishes have a classical base and Mediterr nean and Asian influences.

Menu € 35/39 - Carte € 47/70

Town plan: G3-n - *20 Merrion St Upper ✉ D2 - ☏ 01 661 3572 - www.pearl-brasserie.com - Closed 25 December and Sunday*

Peploe's

MEDITERRANEAN CUISINE • COSY XX Atmospheric cellar restaurant – formerly a bank vault – named after the artist. The comfy room has a warm, clubby feel and a large mural depicts the owner. The well-drilled team present Mediterranean dishes and an Old World wine list.

Menu € 38 (lunch) – Carte € 46/70

Town plan: G3-p – *16 St Stephen's Grn.* ✉ *D2* – ✆ *01 676 3144 (booking essential) – www.peploes.com – Closed 25-26 December, Good Friday and lunch bank holidays*

Saddle Room

MEATS AND GRILLS • ELEGANT XX Renowned restaurant with a history as long as that of the hotel in which it stands. The warm, inviting room features intimate gold booths and a crustacea counter. The menu offers classic dishes and grills.

Menu € 28 (weekday lunch)/47

Town plan: G3-c – *Shelbourne Hotel, 27 St Stephen's Grn.* ✉ *D2* – ✆ *01 663 4500 – www.shelbournedining.ie*

Suesey Street

MODERN CUISINE • INTIMATE XX An intimate restaurant with sumptuous, eye-catching décor, set in the basement of a Georgian townhouse; sit on the superb courtyard terrace. Refined, modern cooking brings out the best in home-grown Irish ingredients.

Menu € 30 (weekday dinner) – Carte € 38/59

Town plan: C3-k – *26 Fitzwilliam Pl* ✉ *D2* – ✆ *01 669 4600 – www.sueseystreet.ie – Closed 25-30 December, Sunday and Monday*

Camden Kitchen

CLASSIC CUISINE • BISTRO X A simple, modern, neighbourhood bistro set over two floors; watch the owner cooking in the open kitchen. Tasty dishes use good quality Irish ingredients prepared in classic combinations. Service is relaxed and friendly.

Menu € 24/29 – Carte € 31/50

Town plan: F3-x – *3a Camden Mkt, Grantham St* ✉ *D8* – ✆ *01 476 0125 – www.camdenkitchen.ie – Closed 24-26 December, Sunday and Monday*

Drury Buildings

ITALIAN • TRENDY X A hip, laid-back 'New York loft': its impressive terrace has a retractable roof and reclaimed furniture features in the stylish cocktail bar, which offers cicchetti and sharing boards. The airy restaurant serves rustic Italian dishes.

Menu € 24/42 – Carte € 31/59

Town plan: F2-e – *52-55 Drury St* ✉ *D2* – ✆ *01 960 2095 – www.drurybuildings.com – Closed 25-26 December*

Fade St. Social - Gastro Bar

INTERNATIONAL • FASHIONABLE X Buzzy restaurant with an almost frenzied feel. It's all about a diverse range of original, interesting small plates, from a bacon and cabbage burger to a lobster hotdog. Eat at the kitchen counter or on leather-cushioned 'saddle' benches.

Menu € 40 (early dinner) – Carte € 25/57

Town plan: F2-u – *4-6 Fade St* ✉ *D2* – ✆ *01 604 0066 (booking essential) – www.fadestreetsocial.com – dinner only and lunch Saturday-Sunday – Closed 25-26 December and 1 January*

Fish Shop

SEAFOOD • RUSTIC X A very informal little restaurant where they serve a daily changing seafood menu which is written up on the tiled wall. Great tasting, supremely fresh, unfussy dishes could be prepared raw or roasted on the wood-fired oven.

Menu € 29/45 – tasting menu only

Town plan: E2-s – *6 Queen St* ✉ *D7* – ✆ *01 430 8594 – www.fish-shop.ie – dinner only and lunch Friday-Saturday – Closed Sunday-Tuesday*

l'Gueuleton

CLASSIC FRENCH • BISTRO Friendly staff run this long-standing restaura which has a shabby-chic bistro feel and a large pavement terrace. The esta lished kitchen team have a good understanding of French country classics; coc ing is good value, flavoursome and relies on local seasonal produce. The cockt bar is open 'til late.

Menu €29 (early dinner) – Carte €26/52

Town plan: F2-d – *1 Fade St* ✉ *D2* – *☎ 01 675 3708* – *www.lgueuleton.com* – *Closed 25-26 December*

Locks

MODERN CUISINE • BISTRO Locals love this restaurant overlooking the car – downstairs it's buzzy, while upstairs is more intimate, and the personable tea add to the feel. Natural flavours are to the fore and dishes are given subtle mo ern touches; for the best value menus come early in the week or before 7pm.

Menu €25 (early dinner) – Carte €35/55

Town plan: B3-s – *1 Windsor Terr* ✉ *D8* – *☎ 01 416 3655 (booking essential)* – *www.locksrestaurant.ie* – *dinner only and lunch Friday-Sunday* – *Closed Sund dinner and Monday*

Pickle

INDIAN • FASHIONABLE It might not look much from the outside but inside t place really comes alive. Spices are lined up on the kitchen counter and dish are fresh and vibrant; the lamb curry with bone marrow is divine. Try a Tif Box for lunch.

Menu €22 (early dinner) – Carte €32/57

Town plan: F3-n – *43 Lower Camden St* ✉ *D2* – *☎ 01 555 7755* – *www.picklerestaurant.com* – *dinner only and lunch Wednesday-Friday* – *Close 25-27 December*

Saba

THAI • FASHIONABLE Trendy, buzzy restaurant and cocktail bar. Simple, styli rooms have refectory tables, banquettes and amusing photos. Fresh, visual, a thentic cooking is from an all-Thai team, with a few Vietnamese dishes a some fusion cooking too.

Menu €15 (weekday lunch)/35 – Carte €32/48

Town plan: F2-k – *26-28 Clarendon St* ✉ *D2* – *☎ 01 679 2000* – *www.sabadublin.com* – *Closed 25-26 December*

Taste at Rustic by Dylan McGrath

ASIAN • RUSTIC Dylan McGrath's love of Japanese cuisine inspires dishes whi explore the five tastes; sweet, salt, bitter, umami and sour. Ingredients are to notch and flavours, bold and masculine. Personable staff are happy to recor mend dishes.

Carte €34/74

Town plan: F2-m – *17 South Great George's St* ✉ *D2* – *(2nd Floor)* – *☎ 01 526 7701* – *www.tasteatrustic.com* – *dinner only* – *Closed 25-26 Decembe 1 January and Sunday-Tuesday*

Hotels

Shelbourne

GRAND LUXURY • CLASSIC A famed hotel dating from 1824, overlooking St St phen's Green; this is where the 1922 Irish Constitution was signed. It has classic architecture, elegant guest areas, luxurious bedrooms and even a tiny museur The lounge and bars are the places to go for afternoon tea and drinks.

265 rooms – †€350/750 ††€350/750 – 19 suites

Town plan: G3-c – *27 St Stephen's Grn.* ✉ *D2* – *☎ 01 663 4500* – *www.theshelbourne.ie*

Saddle Room – See restaurant listing

Merrion

TOWNHOUSE • CLASSIC A Georgian façade conceals a luxury hotel with a compact spa and impressive pool. Opulent drawing rooms are filled with antiques and fine artwork; enjoy 'Art Afternoon Tea' with a view of the parterre garden. Stylish bedrooms have a classic, understated feel and marble bathrooms. Dine from an all-day menu in the brasserie, whose windows fold back to create a terrace.

143 rooms – € 270/420 € 270/420 – €29 – 9 suites

Town plan: G3-e – *Upper Merrion St ✉ D2 – ✆ 01 603 0600 – www.merrionhotel.com*

Fitzwilliam

BUSINESS • MODERN This stylish hotel is set around an impressive roof garden. Contemporary bedrooms come in striking colours with good facilities – some overlook the courtyard garden and others St Stephen's Green. Dine on original Mediterranean dishes in the brasserie or boldly flavoured dishes in Glovers Alley.

139 rooms – € 189/499 € 189/499 – €22 – 3 suites

Town plan: F3-d – *127-128 St Stephen's Grn ✉ D2 – ✆ 01 478 7000 – www.fitzwilliamhoteldublin.com*

Glovers Alley – See restaurant listing

Number 31

TOWNHOUSE • DESIGN A very quirky, individual property: it's classically styled around the 1960s and features a striking sunken lounge. Most of the stylish bedrooms are found in the Georgian house across the terraced garden.

21 rooms – € 149/450 € 149/450

Town plan: C3-c – *31 Leeson Cl. ✉ D2 – ✆ 01 676 5011 – www.number31.ie*

at Ballsbridge

Chop House

MEATS AND GRILLS • PUB An imposing pub not far from the stadium. For warmer days there's a small terrace; in colder weather head up the steps, through the bar and into the bright conservatory. The relaxed lunchtime menu is followed by more ambitious dishes in the evening when the kitchen really comes into its own.

Carte € 28/57

Town plan: D3-x – *2 Shelbourne Rd ✉ D4 – ✆ 01 660 2390 – www.thechophouse.ie – Closed Saturday lunch*

Old Spot

TRADITIONAL CUISINE • PUB The appealing bar has a stencilled maple-wood floor and a great selection of snacks and bottled craft beers, while the relaxed, characterful restaurant filled with vintage posters serves pub classics with a modern edge.

Menu € 27 – Carte € 27/51

Town plan: D2-s – *14 Bath Ave ✉ D4 – ✆ 01 660 5599 – www.theoldspot.ie – Closed 25-26 December and Good Friday*

InterContinental Dublin

LUXURY • CLASSIC Imposing hotel bordering the RDS Arena. Elegant guest areas, state-of-the-art meeting rooms and impressive ballrooms boast ornate décor, antique furnishings and Irish artwork. Spacious, classical bedrooms have marble bathrooms and plenty of extras. A wide-ranging menu is served in the bright, airy restaurant.

197 rooms – € 270/375 € 270/375 – €28 – 58 suites

Town plan: D3-h – *Simmonscourt Rd. ✉ D4 – ✆ 01 665 4000 – www.intercontinental.com/dublin*

Dylan

TOWNHOUSE • DESIGN An old Victorian nurses' home with a sympathetical styled extension and a funky, boutique interior. Tasteful, individually decorate bedrooms offer a host of extras; those in the original building are the most sp cious. The stylish restaurant offers a menu of modern Mediterranean dishes ar comes complete with a zinc-topped bar and a smartly furnished terrace.

72 rooms – € 169/440 € 169/440 – €25

Town plan: C3-a – *Eastmoreland Pl ✉ D4 – ✆ 01 660 3000 – www.dylan.ie*

Ariel House

TOWNHOUSE • CLASSIC Close to the Aviva Stadium and a DART station; a pe sonally run Victorian townhouse with comfy guest areas and antique furnishing Warmly decorated bedrooms have modern facilities and smart bathroon – some feature four-posters.

37 rooms – € 120/350 € 140/370

Town plan: D3-n – *50-54 Lansdowne Rd ✉ D4 – ✆ 01 668 5512 – www.ariel-house.net – Closed 22 December-4 January*

Pembroke Townhouse

TOWNHOUSE • CLASSIC Friendly, traditionally styled hotel set in 3 Georgia houses. Small lounge with honesty bar and pantry. Sunny breakfast room offerir homemade bread, cakes and biscuits. Variously sized, neutrally hued bedroom go for a duplex room.

48 rooms – € 90/250 € 90/250 – €15

Town plan: C3-d – *88 Pembroke Rd ✉ D4 – ✆ 01 660 0277 – www.pembroketownhouse.ie – Closed 2 weeks Christmas-New Year*

at Donnybrook

Mulberry Garden

MODERN CUISINE • COSY XX Delightful restaurant hidden away in the city su urbs; its interesting L-shaped dining room set around a small courtyard terrac Choice of two dishes per course on the weekly menu; original modern cookir relies on tasty local produce.

Menu € 49

Town plan: C3-g – *Mulberry Ln ✉ D4 – off Donnybrook Rd – ✆ 01 269 3300 (booking essential) – www.mulberrygarden.ie – dinner only – Closed first week January and Sunday-Wednesday*

at Ranelagh

Forest & Marcy

MODERN CUISINE • FASHIONABLE X There's a lively buzz to this lovely little wi kitchen with high-level seating. Precisely prepared, original dishes burst with fl vour; many are prepared at the counter and the chefs themselves often prese and explain what's on the plate. They offer a tasting menu only Friday-Sunday.

Menu € 49 – Carte € 33/42

Town plan: C3-a – *126 Leeson St Upper ✉ D4 – ✆ 01 660 2480 (booking essential) – www.forestandmarcy.ie – dinner only – Closed 25 December-7 January, 20-28 April, last two weeks August and Monday-Tuesd*

Forest Avenue

MODERN CUISINE • NEIGHBOURHOOD X This rustic neighbourhood restaurant named after a street in Queens and has a fitting 'NY' vibe. Elaborately pr sented tasting plates are full of originality and each dish combines many diffe ent flavours.

Menu € 35 (weekday lunch)/68

Town plan: C3-t – *8 Sussex Terr. ✉ D4 – ✆ 01 667 8337 (booking essential) – www.forestavenuerestaurant.ie – Closed last 2 weeks August, 25 December-7 January, 15-23 April, Sunday-Tuesday and lunch Wednesday*

t Terenure

Craft

MODERN CUISINE • **NEIGHBOURHOOD** A busy southern suburb plays host to this neighbourhood bistro. Concise menus evolve with seasonal availability and the lunch and early evening menus really are a steal. Dishes are modern and creative with vibrant colours and fresh, natural flavours. Sweet service from a local team completes the experience.

Menu €29 (early dinner) – Carte €37/50

Town plan: B3-t – *208 Harold's Cross Rd ✉ D6W – ✆ 01 497 8632 – www.craftrestaurant.ie – dinner only and lunch Friday-Sunday – Closed 1 week Christmas-New Year, 1 week July-August, Sunday dinner, Monday and Tuesday*

t Clontarf Northeast: 5.5 km by R 105 ✉ Dublin

Pigeon House

MODERN CUISINE • **NEIGHBOURHOOD** Slickly run neighbourhood bistro that's open for breakfast, lunch and dinner. It's just off the coast road in an up-and-coming area and has a lovely front terrace and a lively feel. Cooking is modern and assured. The bar counter is laden with freshly baked goodies and dishes are full of flavour.

Menu €29 (dinner) – Carte €30/46

11b Vernon Ave ✉ D3 – East : 1km by Clontarf Rd on Vernon Ave (R808) – ✆ 01 805 7567 – www.pigeonhouse.ie – Closed 25-26 December

Fishbone

SEAFOOD • **NEIGHBOURHOOD** A friendly little restaurant opposite the Bull Bridge, with a cocktail bar at its centre and a glass-enclosed kitchen to the rear. Prime seafood from the plancha and charcoal grill is accompanied by tasty house sauces.

Menu €18/22 – Carte €30/48

324 Clontarf Rd ✉ D3 – East : 1.5 km on Clontarf Rd – ✆ 01 536 9066 – www.fishbone.ie – Closed 25-26 December

Clontarf Castle

BUSINESS • **HISTORIC** A historic castle dating back to 1172, with sympathetic Victorian extensions; well-located in a quiet residential area close to the city. Contemporary bedrooms are decorated with bold, warm colours and many have four-poster beds. The restaurant offers local meats and seafood in a medieval ambience.

111 rooms – €200/500 €230/530

Town plan: D1-a – *Castle Ave. ✉ D3 – ✆ 01 833 2321 – www.clontarfcastle.ie*

t Blackrock Southeast : 7.5 km by R 118

Heron & Grey (Damien Grey)

MODERN CUISINE • **FRIENDLY** A homely, candlelit restaurant in a bohemian suburban market; it's personally run by Heron – who leads the service – and Grey, who heads the kitchen. Irish ingredients feature in intensely flavoured dishes which are full of contrasting textures and tastes. The set multi-course dinner menu changes every 2 weeks.

→ Pigeon, beetroot and shiitake. Suckling pig, lovage and juniper. Grapefruit, fermented milk and olive oil.

Menu €74 – tasting menu only

Blackrock Market, 19a Main St – ✆ 01 212 3676 (booking essential) – www.heronandgrey.com – dinner only – Closed 2 weeks Christmas-New Year, 2 weeks late August and Sunday-Tuesday and every alternate Wednesday

at Foxrock Southeast : 13 km by N 11 ✉ Dublin

Bistro One

TRADITIONAL CUISINE • NEIGHBOURHOOD XX Long-standing neighbourhoc bistro above a parade of shops; run by a father-daughter team and a real h with the locals. Good value daily menus list a range of Irish and Italian dishe They produce their own Tuscan olive oil.

Menu € 29 (lunch) – Carte dinner € 29/52

3 Brighton Rd ✉ D18 – ✆ 01 289 7711 (booking essential) – www.bistro-one.ie – Closed 25 December-3 January, 3 April, Sunday dinner, Monday and lunch Tuesday-Thursday

at Dundrum South : 7.5 km by R 117 ✉ Dublin

Ananda

INDIAN • EXOTIC DÉCOR XX Its name means 'bliss' and it's a welcome escap from the bustle of the shopping centre. The stylish interior encompasses a sma cocktail bar, attractive fretwork and vibrant art. Accomplished Indian cooking modern and original.

Menu € 21 (lunch) – Carte € 35/56

Sandyford Rd, Dundrum Town Centre ✉ D14 – ✆ 01 296 0099 – www.anandarestaurant.ie – dinner only and lunch Friday-Sunday – Closed 25-26 December

at Sandyford South : 10 km by R 117 off R 825✉ Dublin

China Sichuan

CHINESE • FASHIONABLE XX A smart interior is well-matched by creative m nus, where Irish produce features in tasty Cantonese classics and some Sichua specialities. It was established in 1979 and is now run by the third generation the family.

Menu € 16 (weekday lunch) – Carte € 29/57

The Forum, Ballymoss Rd. ✉ D18 – ✆ 01 293 5100 – www.china-sichuan.ie – Closed 25-27 December, Good Friday, lunch Saturday and bank holidays

DUNCANNON DÚN CANANN

Wexford – Pop. 328 – Regional map n° **22**-D2

Aldridge Lodge

COUNTRY • FRIENDLY XX This attractive house is set in a great rural location ar run by cheery owners. The constantly evolving menu offers tasty homema bread and veg from the kitchen garden. The focus is on good value fish and she fish (the owner's father is a local fisherman), with some Asian and fusion infl ences. Homely bedrooms come with hot water bottles and home-baked cookie

Menu € 35/40 **s**

3 rooms – € 55/60 € 90/100

South : 2 km on Hook Head rd – ✆ 051 389 116 (booking essential) – www.aldridgelodge.com – dinner only – Closed 2 weeks January, 1 week May, 24-28 December and Monday-Wednesday

DUNDALK DÚN DEALGAN

Louth – Pop. 31 149 – Regional map n° **21**-D2

Rosemount

FAMILY • COSY An attractive dormer bungalow fronted by a delightful flowe filled garden. The welcoming owners serve tea and cake on arrival and a fresh cooked breakfast the next morning. The lounge is warmly decorated and the inc vidually styled, spotlessly kept bedrooms feature fine fabrics and modern facilitie

12 rooms – € 60/70 € 80/100

Dublin Rd – South : 2.5 km on R 132 – ✆ 042 933 5878 – www.rosemountireland.com – Closed 22-27 December

t Jenkinstown Northeast: 9 km by N52 on R173

Fitzpatricks

TRADITIONAL CUISINE • PUB A hugely characterful pub on the coast road, at the foot of the mountains, featuring beautiful flower displays, a wealth of memorabilia and even a petting farm. Extensive menus list hearty, flavoursome dishes; specialities include local steaks and seafood. Don't forget to buy a cake to take home too!

Menu € 35 - Carte € 30/45

Rockmarshall - Southeast : 1 km - ☎ 042 937 6193 - www.fitzpatricks-restaurant.com - Closed 25 December

UNDRUM DÚN DROMA - Dún Laoghaire-Rathdown ➔ See Dublin

UNFANAGHY DÚN FIONNACHAIDH

onegal - ✉ Letterkenny - Pop. 312 - Regional map n° **21**-C1

Mill

TRADITIONAL CUISINE • FRIENDLY XX Converted flax mill on the waterside, with lovely garden edged by reeds and great view of Mount Muckish. Homely inner with conservatory lounge and knick-knacks on display throughout. Antique-furnished dining room has a classical Georgian feel. Traditional menus showcase seasonal ingredients and fish features highly. Cosy, welcoming bedrooms come in individual designs.

Menu € 45

7 rooms - € 75/150 € 120/300

Southwest : 0.75 km on N 56 - ☎ 074 913 6985 - www.themillrestaurant.com - dinner only - Closed November-mid-March

UNGARVAN DÚN GARBHÁN

aterford - Pop. 7 991 - Regional map n° **22**-C3

Tannery

MODERN CUISINE • FRIENDLY XX Characterful 19C stone tannery, close to the harbour; they also run the cookery school here. Have small plates at the counter or head upstairs to the bright restaurant. Attractively presented, classically based dishes use good seasonal ingredients. Stylish bedrooms are in a nearby townhouse.

Menu € 33 (weekdays) - Carte € 22/52

14 rooms - € 70/80 € 105/140

10 Quay St - via Parnell St - ☎ 058 45420 - www.tannery.ie - dinner only and lunch Friday and Sunday - Closed last 2 weeks January, 25-26 December, Sunday dinner except July-August and bank holiday weekends, Good Friday and Monday

UNKINEELY DÚN CIONNAOLA

onegal - Pop. 375 - Regional map n° **21**-C1

Castle Murray House

TRADITIONAL • COSY This extended former farmhouse is perched on a hillside and affords lovely bay and mountain views. The small knick-knack filled bar and flag-floored lounge have a traditional feel. Bedrooms are contrastingly modern and stylish - those to the front share the view; go for the one with the huge roof terrace.

10 rooms - € 130/160 € 130/160

St John's Point - Southwest : 1.5 km by N 56 on St John's Point rd - ☎ 074 973 7022 - www.castlemurray.com - Closed November-March

DUN LAOGHAIRE DÚN LAOGHAIRE

Dún Laoghaire-Rathdown - Pop. 23 857 - Regional map n° **22**-D1

Rasam

INDIAN • EXOTIC DÉCOR XX The scent of roses greets you as you head up to t surprisingly plush lounge and contemporary restaurant. Fresh, authentic dish come in original combinations - they dry roast and blend their own spices.

Menu €25 (early dinner) - Carte €33/56

18-19 Glasthule Rd, 1st Floor (above Eagle House pub) - ✆ 01 230 0600 - www.rasam.ie - dinner only - Closed 25-26 December

Cavistons

SEAFOOD • BISTRO X A landmark restaurant in town, where guests come f fresh, carefully cooked fish and shellfish brought in by the local boats; go for t scallops or lobster when they're in season. Dishes are simple and unadulterat - but why do anything more when the ingredients are so good?

Menu €21 - Carte €28/52

58-59 Glasthule Rd - ✆ 01 280 9245 (booking essential) - www.cavistons.com - lunch only and dinner Thursday-Saturday - Closed Sunday and Monday

Feast N

MODERN BRITISH • NEIGHBOURHOOD X Hidden away on the edge of town this neighbourhood restaurant which has plenty of personality and a good lo following. Dark walls are hung with pictures of people feasting and tables a tightly packed. Colourful modern dishes are full of flavour and keep local fi and meat to the fore.

Menu €28 - Carte €31/46

1a George's St Lower - ✆ 01 444 6546 - www.thefeast.ie - dinner only and lunc Saturday-Sunday - Closed Christmas, bank holidays, Monday and Tuesday

DURRUS DÚRAS

Cork - Pop. 334 - Regional map n° **22**-A3

Blairscove House

MODERN CUISINE • ELEGANT XX Charming 18C barn and hayloft, just a stone throw from the sea, with fantastic panoramic views, pretty gardens, a courtya and a lily pond. Stylish bar and stone-walled, candlelit dining room. Starters a desserts are in buffet format, while the seasonal main courses are cooked on wood-fired chargrill. Luxurious, modern bedrooms are dotted about the place.

Menu €60 **s**

4 rooms ☕ - 🚹 €125/160 🚹🚹 €190/260

Southwest : 1.5 km on R 591 - ✆ 027 61127 (booking essential) - www.blairscove. - dinner only - Closed 3 November-14 March, Sunday and Monday

Gallán Mór

COUNTRY HOUSE • PERSONALISED Proudly run guesthouse named after t 3,500 year old standing stone in its garden; set in a lovely rural location ove looking Dunmanus Bay and Mizen Head. Bedrooms have warm fabrics, good f cilities and handmade wooden beds. The delightful owners welcome you wi homemade cake beside the wood-burning stove.

4 rooms ☕ - 🚹 €90/100 🚹🚹 €130/150

Kealties - West : 5.5 km. on Ahakista rd - ✆ 027 62732 - www.gallanmor.com - Closed October-March. Minimum 2 nights stay.

ENNISCORTHY INIS CÓRTHAIDH

Wexford - Pop. 2 842 - Regional map n° **22**-D2

Monart

SPA AND WELLNESS • GRAND LUXURY Comprehensively equipped destination spa in 100 acres of beautifully landscaped grounds; a haven of peace and tranquility. The Georgian house with its contemporary glass extension houses spacious, stylish bedrooms with a terrace or balcony. The Restaurant serves light, modern dishes; the minimalistic Garden Lounge offers global dishes in a more informal environment.

70 rooms - € 179/599 € 250/599 - 2 suites

The Still - 053 923 8999 - www.monart.ie - Closed 20-27 December

NNISKERRY ÁTH AN SCEIRE

icklow - Pop. 1 811 - Regional map n° **22**-D1

Powerscourt

GRAND LUXURY • CLASSIC Impressive curved building overlooking Sugar Loaf Mountain, featuring stylish guest areas, luxurious bedrooms, state-of-the-art conference facilities and a superb spa; outdoor activities include archery and falconry. Sika offers modern, formal dining, while the plush lounge-bar serves a concise menu of classics. McGills is a traditional Irish pub with a menu to match.

194 rooms - € 150/500 € 185/575 - €28 - 92 suites

Powerscourt Estate - West : 1.5 km by Powerscourt rd - 01 274 8888 - www.powerscourthotel.com

ANORE

are - Regional map n° **22**-B1

Vasco

MODERN CUISINE • SIMPLE Remotely set restaurant opposite the seashore, with a minimalist interior and a glass-screened terrace. The keen owners collect the latest produce on their drive in; the daily menu ranges from sandwiches and cake to soup and light dishes.

Carte € 26/46

Craggagh - West : 1 km on R 477 - 065 707 6020 - www.vasco.ie - Closed October-mid-March, Sunday-Monday and dinner Tuesday-Wednesday

ENNOR FIONNÚIR

aterford - Regional map n° **22**-C2

Copper Hen

TRADITIONAL CUISINE • RUSTIC A likeable little restaurant located above a pub, with rustic décor and a brightly coloured fireplace; set on the coast road from Tramore to Dungarvan. Keenly priced menus offer fresh, hearty, unfussy classics and service is enthusiastic and efficient. The owners raise their own pigs.

Menu € 29

Mother McHugh's Pub - 051 330 300 - www.thecopperhen.ie - Closed 2 weeks September, 1 week January, 25-26 December, Sunday dinner, Monday-Tuesday and lunch Wednesday-Thursday

OTA ISLAND OILEÁN FHÓTA

ork - Regional map n° **22**-B3

Fota Island

LUXURY • DESIGN A resort hotel set within Ireland's only wildlife park. Extensive business and leisure facilities include a golf course and a state-of-the-art spa. Bedrooms are spacious and well-appointed, and most have island views. The stylish restaurant offers modern takes on classical dishes.

131 rooms - € 120/295 € 135/310 - 8 suites

- 021 488 3700 - www.fotaisland.ie - Closed 25 December

OXROCK CARRAIG AN TSIONNAIGH - Dún Laoghaire-athdown

→ See Dublin

GOOD TIPS!

When you think Galway, you think music. An effervescent spirit and a non-conformist attitude helped to put music at the heart of the city. A need to do their own thing is also adopted by the city's restaurants which are an eclectic bunch, from the ground-breaking **Loam** to rustic tapas bar, **Cava Bodega**.

GALWAY GAILLIMH

Galway – Pop. 75 529 – Regional map n° **21**-B3

Restaurants

✿ Loam (Enda McEvoy)

CREATIVE • MINIMALIST XX A large basement with industrial styling; the focus here on the quality of the ingredients, which grow in the fertile local loam. The talented ch understands his craft and produces modern, understated dishes with pure flavour Choose from the 2-3 course fixed price menu or the 7 course tasting menu.

→ Sweetbreads, egg and oyster mushroom. Cod with cauliflower and lardo. Rhu barb with sheep's milk.

Menu € 50/90

Geata na Cathrach, Fairgreen Rd – Northeast : 2 km by R 336 – ✆ 091 569 727 – www.loamgalway.com – dinner only – Closed 17 February-5 March, 25 December, Sunday and Monday

✿ Aniar (JP McMahon)

CREATIVE • SIMPLE X Both the room and the cooking have a back-to-nature etho Aniar means 'From the West' and this is where most of the produce comes from: th 3 set menus are only confirmed once all of the day's ingredients have arrived. Contras in texture and temperature play their part in delicate, Scandic-style dishes.

→ Cod and dulse. Lamb and cherry. Apple and celeriac.

Menu € 65/98 – tasting menu only

Town plan: A2-a – *53 Lower Dominick St – ✆ 091 535 947 (booking essential) – www.aniarrestaurant.ie – dinner only – Closed 25-26 December, Sunday and Monday*

Kai

MEDITERRANEAN CUISINE • NEIGHBOURHOOD X A laid-back eatery with a gl riously cluttered interior and a bohemian feel; the owners run it with real pa sion. Brunch and cakes morph into fresh, simple lunches and are followed by a ternoon tea and tasty dinners. Concise menus list fresh, vibrant dishes ar produce is organic, free range and traceable.

Carte € 40/51

Town plan: A2-x – *22 Sea Rd – ✆ 091 526 003 (booking essential) – www.kaicaferestaurant.com – Closed dinner Sunday-Monday in winter and ba holidays*

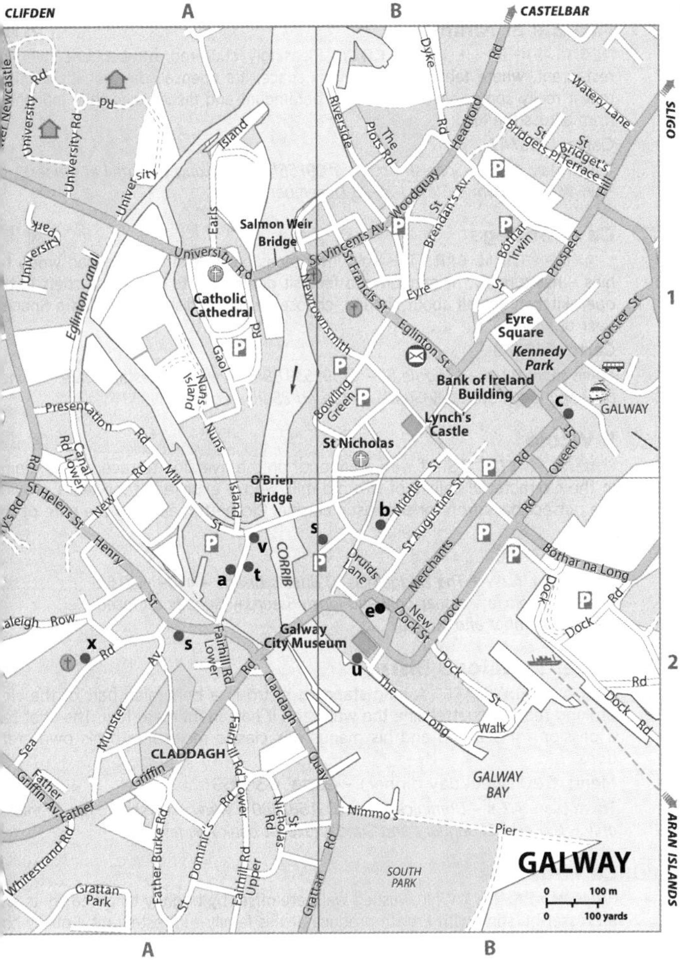

Tartare

MODERN BRITISH • SIMPLE Snug, intimate and endearing, with a rustic feel; this sweet neighbourhood café is a hit with one and all. Sit at multi-level wood-topped tables beneath bright oil paintings and dine on delicious small plates. Simplicity is the key: top seasonal ingredients are well-sourced and carefully prepared.

Carte €18/36

Town plan: A2-t – *56 Lower Dominick St – ✆ 091 567 803 – www.tartaregalway.ie – lunch only and dinner Thursday-Saturday – Closed 25-26 December*

Seafood Bar @ Kirwan's

SEAFOOD • BRASSERIE Well-regarded, long-standing restaurant with a large terrace, in an old medieval lane. Lively brasserie atmosphere, with dining on two levels. Modern menus have a classical base; most dishes consist of tasty seafood – go for the specials.

Carte € 32/48

Town plan: B2-s – *Kirwan's Ln – ✆ 091 568 266 – www.kirwanslane.com – Closed 25-26 December and lunch Sunday and bank holidays*

Ard Bia at Nimmos

MEDITERRANEAN CUISINE • COSY Pleasingly cluttered, atmospheric riversi restaurant, where tables occupy every space; it's open all day but it's at nig that it really comes alive. Sourcing is paramount and dishes take their influenc from across the Med.

Carte € 33/47

Town plan: B2-u - *Spanish Arch - 091 561 114 (booking essential at dinner) - www.ardbia.com - Closed 25-28 December*

Cava Bodega

SPANISH • TAPAS BAR This split-level tapas bar - with its reclaimed wood t bles - has a rustic, neighbourhood feel; sit downstairs to watch the chefs in t open kitchen. It's all about sharing: choose around 3 dishes each and a Spanis beer or wine.

Carte € 16/38

Town plan: B2-b - *1 Middle St - 091 539 884 - www.cavarestaurant.ie - dinne only and lunch Saturday-Sunday - Closed 25-26 December*

Il Vicolo

ITALIAN • BISTRO Start with an aperitif on the riverside terrace before dinir in the characterful cellars of this old mill, whose exposed stone walls provic the perfect backdrop for the rustic cuisine. Cicchetti makes up the core of t menu.

Carte € 31/56

Town plan: A2-v - *The Bridgemills, O'Brien's Bridge - 091 530 515 - www.ilvicolo.ie - dinner only and lunch Saturday-Sunday - Closed 25-26 December and Monday*

Oscar's Seafood Bistro

SEAFOOD • INTIMATE A long-standing bistro in a bohemian part of the cit Striking red banquettes line the walls and it has an intimate feel. The chef h a passion for seafood and his menus mix classic recipes with his own cre tions.

Menu € 20 (weekday dinner) - Carte € 30/59

Town plan: A2-s - *Dominick St - 091 582 180 - www.oscarsbistro.ie - dinner only - Closed 1-21 January and Sunday except bank holidays*

Le Petit Pois

FRENCH • FAMILY Whitewashed walls are offset by brightly coloured lights an a dresser bursting with French produce at this family-run restaurant. Equally co ourful Gallic dishes showcase Irish ingredients and are packed with flavour; t the tasting menu with matching wines.

Menu € 40/60 - Carte € 36/50

Town plan: B1-c - *Victoria Pl - 091 330 880 - www.lepetitpois.ie - dinner onl - Closed 1 week January, Sunday and Monday*

Hotels

Galmont Hotel & Spa

BUSINESS • MODERN A corporate hotel set overlooking a lough and boas ing a striking atrium, vast meeting facilities and a spa with a thermal sui and a salt cave. Bedrooms are spacious and modern - the 5th floor room have balconies and share a business lounge. The brasserie offers interna tional dishes.

262 rooms - € 149/469 € 149/469 - 4 suites

Lough Atalia Rd - Northeast : 2 km by R 336 - 091 538 300 - www.thegalmont.com

G

LUXURY • DESIGN A smart design hotel on a small retail park, with distant views of the bay and mountains from the striking atrium's oversized window. Vibrantly coloured guest areas include blue and pink lounges and a seductive purple restaurant. Spacious bedrooms are more calming, as is the impressive thermal spa.

101 rooms – € 130/380 € 150/420 – 2 suites

Wellpark, Dublin Rd – Northeast : 3 km by R 336 and R 338 – 091 865 200 – www.theghotel.ie – Closed 23-26 December

The House

TOWNHOUSE • DESIGN This unassuming hotel sits in a great central spot, close to the Spanish Arch and the Latin Quarter. Both the guest areas and the bedrooms are decorated in stylish, eye-catching colour schemes; for a quieter stay ask for a room on a higher floor. The laid-back restaurant offers a small menu of classics.

40 rooms – € 130/195 € 145/295 – 1 suite

Town plan: B2-e – *Lower Merchants Rd – 091 538 900 – www.thehousehotel.ie – Closed 25-26 December*

Ardawn House

TRADITIONAL • COSY Set by the stadium, with the city just a stroll away. A small lounge leads to a breakfast room laid with silver-plated cutlery and bedrooms are clean and fresh with modern fabrics. The owners are friendly and helpful.

8 rooms – € 80/200 € 110/220

College Rd. – Northeast : 2.25 km. by R 336 on R 339 – 091 568 833 – www.ardawnhouse.com – Closed 15-27 December

ARRYKENNEDY

orth Tipperary – Regional map n° **22**-C2

Larkins

TRADITIONAL CUISINE • PUB Thatched pub in a charming loughside location. The traditional interior boasts original fireplaces and old flag and timber floors – and plays host to folk music and Irish dancers. Unfussy dishes feature plenty of fresh seafood.

Carte € 26/42

– 067 23232 – www.larkins.ie – Closed 25 December, Good Friday and Monday-Tuesday November-March

LASLOUGH GLASLOCH

onaghan – Monaghan – Regional map n° **21**-D2

Castle Leslie

HISTORIC BUILDING • HISTORIC An impressive castle set in 1,000 acres of peaceful parkland: home to the 4th generation of the Leslie family. Various lounges and drawing rooms are filled with heirlooms and antiques. Bedrooms are individually designed and have a traditional country house style.

20 rooms – € 180/360 € 200/380

Castle Leslie Estate – 047 88100 – www.castleleslie.com – Closed 24-27 December

Lodge at Castle Leslie Estate

HISTORIC • CONTEMPORARY An extended hunting lodge to the main castle, with contrastingly stylish bedrooms. Unwind in the Victorian Treatments Rooms or the charming open-fired bar – or hire an estate horse and explore the 1,000 acre grounds. The restaurant offers modern Mediterranean fare.

29 rooms – € 160/220 € 180/240 – 1 suite

– 047 88100 – www.castleleslie.com

GLASSON - Westmeath ➔ See Athlone

GOLEEN AN GÓILÍN
Cork - Regional map n° **22**-A3

Heron's Cove
TRADITIONAL • PERSONALISED Long-standing guesthouse hidden away in a pret location, with views over a tiny harbour. Bedrooms are tidy and pleasantly furnished: overlook the waterfront and most have a balcony - if you're lucky you might see he ons at the water's edge. The busy restaurant offers seasonal menus of local produce.

4 rooms - € 70/90 € 90/100

The Harbour - 028 35225 - www.heronscove.com
- Closed mid-November-mid-February and restricted opening in winter

GOREY GUAIRE
Wexford - Pop. 3 463 - Regional map n° **22**-D2

The Duck
REGIONAL CUISINE • FRIENDLY X The Duck is a smart, rustic bistro which si within the grounds of a grand country house, next to a superb kitchen garde which informs its menu. Sit on the wonderful terrace with a glass of wine an dine on unfussy, global cuisine.

Carte € 32/63

Marlfield House Hotel, Courtown Rd - Southeast : 1.5 km on R 742
- 053 942 1124 - www.marlfiledhouse.com/dining/the-duck/
- Closed 6-23 January and Monday-Tuesday October-Easter

Marlfield House
COUNTRY HOUSE • ELEGANT Well-appointed, period-style bedrooms look o over the large grounds of this attractive Regency house. Various sitting and draw ing rooms have a homely, classical feel and all are packed with antiques, oil pain ings and curios. Have afternoon tea in the garden while watching the peacoc wander by, then dine in the conservatory restaurant or the terrace café and bar

19 rooms - € 105/135 € 230/670

Courtown Rd - Southeast : 1.5 km on R 742 - 053 942 1124
- www.marlfieldhouse.com - Closed 6-23 January and Monday-Tuesday October-East

The Duck - See restaurant listing

GREYSTONES NA CLOCHA LIATHA
Wicklow - Pop. 10 173 - Regional map n° **22**-D1

Chakra by Jaipur
INDIAN • EXOTIC DÉCOR XX An elegant, intimate restaurant with bold décor, un usually set within a shopping centre. Interesting dishes represent the count from north to south. Spicing is delicate, flavours are refined and desserts are highlight.

Menu € 24 (early dinner) - Carte € 32/55

Meridian Point Centre (1st floor), Church Rd - 01 201 7222 - www.chakra.ie
- dinner only and Sunday lunch - Closed 25 December

HAROLD'S CROSS ➔ See Dublin

INISHEER ➔ See Aran Islands

INISHMAAN INIS MEÁIN - Galway ➔ See Aran Islands

INISHMORE ÁRAINN - Galway ➔ See Aran Islands

JENKINSTOWN BAILE SHEINICÍN - Louth ➔ See Dundalk

KANTURK CEANN TOIRC
Cork - Pop. 2 263 - Regional map n° **22**-B2

Glenlohane

HISTORIC • CLASSIC A Georgian country house set in 260 acres – it has been in the family for over 250 years. Traditional interior hung with portraits and paintings. Colour-themed bedrooms; 'Blue' has an antique four-poster and bathtub. Cosy library and drawing room. Open-fired dining room for home-cooked communal dinners.

3 rooms – € 135/150 € 235/250

– ✆ 029 50014 – www.glenlohane.com

ENMARE NEIDÍN

erry – Pop. 2 175 – Regional map n° **22**-A3

Park

CLASSIC CUISINE • ELEGANT XXX Start with canapés in the lounge then move on to the elegant dining room of this luxurious hotel. Silver candelabras, cloches and gueridon trolleys all feature and service is top-notch. Classically based dishes have a modern touch and local ingredients are kept to the fore.

Menu € 70

Park Hotel, – ✆ 064 664 1200 – www.parkkenmare.com – dinner only – Closed 2 January-16 February, 10-22 December and Sunday in low season

Lime Tree

CLASSIC CUISINE • RUSTIC XX A 19C property that's taken on many guises over the years. The characterful interior has exposed stone walls, an open fire and even its own art gallery. Flavoursome, classical dishes utilise quality local ingredients.

Menu € 48

Shelbourne St. – ✆ 064 664 1225 – www.limetreerestaurant.com – dinner only – Closed January-February and Sunday-Thursday November-May

Mulcahys

MODERN CUISINE • INTIMATE XX Come for cocktails and snacks in the bar or settle in for the evening in the intimate restaurant. Unfussy dishes utilise Irish ingredients, including local fish, which is used in the sushi. For dessert, try the tarte Tatin for two.

Carte € 29/49

Main St – ✆ 064 664 2383 – www.mulcahyskenmare.ie – dinner only – Closed 24-26 December, Tuesday and Monday and Wednesday October-April

Boathouse Bistro

SEAFOOD • BRASSERIE X Converted boathouse in the grounds of Dromquinna Manor; set on the waterside, overlooking the peninsula and mountains. It has a nautical, New England style and a laid-back vibe. Simple, appealing menus focus on seafood.

Carte € 29/53

Dromquinna – West : 4.75 km by N 71 on N 70 – ✆ 064 664 2889 – www.dromquinnamanor.com – Closed December-mid-February, mid-week February, March & November and Monday-Wednesday in October

Mews

MODERN CUISINE • BISTRO X Owners Gary and Maria provide a warm welcome at this cosy, intimate, three-roomed restaurant. Many different ingredients combine to create colourful dishes with rich flavours. There's plenty of choice, including daily specials.

Menu € 32 (early dinner) – Carte € 29/53

Henry Ct, Henry St – ✆ 064 664 2829 (booking essential) – www.themewskenmare.com – dinner only – Closed January-mid-February and Sunday-Thursday November, December and March

Packie's

TRADITIONAL CUISINE • RUSTIC Popular little restaurant in the town centre with two rustic, bistro-style rooms, exposed stone walls, tiled floors and an interesting collection of modern Irish art. Cooking is honest, fresh and seasonal; the seafood specials are a hit.

Carte € 24/50

Henry St – 064 664 1508 (booking essential) – dinner only – Closed 7 January-7 February, Monday in winter and Sunday

Park

GRAND LUXURY • CLASSIC One of Ireland's most iconic country houses sits in the town centre and looks out over wonderful gardens to the bay and the hills. It's elegantly furnished, with a charming drawing room, a cosy cocktail lounge and tastefully styled bedrooms. The stylish spa adds a modern touch.

46 rooms – € 195/475 € 195/475

– 064 664 1200 – www.parkkenmare.com – Closed 2 January-16 February and 10-22 December

Park – See restaurant listing

Sheen Falls Lodge

LUXURY • PERSONALISED Modern hotel in an idyllic spot, where the waterfalls drop away into the bay. It has a welcoming wood-fired lobby, a lovely indoor swimming pool and well-appointed bedrooms overlooking the falls. Unusually, the restaurant serves a brasserie menu on the upper level and more refined dishes on the lower level.

68 rooms – € 195/550 € 195/550 – 14 suites

Southeast : 2 km. by N 71 – 064 664 1600 – www.sheenfallslodge.ie – Closed 2 January-13 February and mid-week in December

Brook Lane

BUSINESS • MODERN Personally run hotel close to the town centre. Bedrooms range from 'Deluxe' to 'Luxury'; the latter have impressive fabric headboards and specially commissioned handmade furniture. The informal bar-bistro offers classic Irish and seafood dishes and hosts regular live music events.

21 rooms – € 75/180 € 99/190

Gortamullen – North : 1.5 km. by N 71 on N 70 – 064 664 2077 – www.brooklanehotel.com – Closed 23-27 December

Sallyport House

FAMILY • CLASSIC Unassuming 1930s house; its charming interior packed with antiques and Irish art. Pleasant lounge with local information. Breakfast is served from the characterful sideboard and features pancakes, stewed fruits and smoked salmon. Traditionally furnished bedrooms are immaculately kept and boast water views.

5 rooms – € 110/140 € 140/150

South : 0.5 km. on N 71 – 064 664 2066 – www.sallyporthouse.com – Closed November-March

KILCOLGAN CILL CHOLGÁIN

Galway – Oranmore – Regional map n° **21**-B3

Moran's Oyster Cottage

SEAFOOD • COSY An attractive thatched pub hidden away in a tiny hamlet – a very popular place come summer. It's all about straightforward cooking and good hospitality. Dishes are largely seafood based and oysters are the speciality.

Carte € 27/52

The Weir – Northwest : 2 km. by N 18 – 091 796 113 – www.moransoystercottage.com – Closed 24-26 December and Good Friday

KILCULLEN

Kildare – Pop. 3 473 – Regional map n° **22**-D1

Fallon's

TRADITIONAL CUISINE • **FASHIONABLE** You'll find plenty of happy locals in the snug, the modern dining room, the conservatory and, in the evening, the rustic, pastel-coloured bistro. Flavoursome dishes are generously proportioned; save room for a homemade dessert.

Carte € 33/52

Main St - 045 481 260 - www.fallonb.ie
- Closed 25 December and Monday

KILDARE CILL DARA

Kildare - Pop. 8 142 - Regional map n° **22**-D1

Harte's

CLASSIC CUISINE • **RUSTIC** Have a local artisan beer in the snug open-fired bar or kick things off with a gin tasting board; then move on to tasty, well-prepared dishes with modern twists in the small restaurant with its large mirrors and exposed brick walls.

Menu € 27 (weekdays) - Carte € 28/42

Market Sq - 045 533 557 - www.harteskildare.ie
- Closed Monday except bank holidays

KILKENNY CILL CHAINNIGH

Kilkenny - Pop. 24 423 - Regional map n° **22**-C2

Campagne (Garrett Byrne)

MODERN BRITISH • **FASHIONABLE** XX A chic, relaxed restaurant with smart booths and contemporary local art, hidden close to the railway arches away from the city centre. Modern cooking has a classic base, and familiar combinations are delivered with an assured touch. The early bird menu is a steal and service is friendly and efficient.

→ Terrine of foie gras with greengage purée, caramelised walnuts and pear chutney. Crisp pork jowl with white cabbage, turnip, quince vinegar and apple. Rhubarb crumble soufflé and ginger ice cream.

Menu € 35 (lunch and early dinner) **s** - Carte € 51/59 **s**

5 The Arches, Gashouse Ln - 056 777 2858 - www.campagne.ie - dinner only and lunch Friday-Sunday
- Closed 2 weeks January, 1 week July, Sunday dinner, Monday and Tuesday

Ristorante Rinuccini

ITALIAN • **CLASSIC DÉCOR** XXX Set in the basement of a townhouse and named after the 17C papal nuncio, this family-owned restaurant is well-known locally. Classic Italian cuisine with homemade ravioli a speciality. Some tables have views through to the wine cellar.

Menu € 29 (lunch and early dinner) - Carte € 30/50

1 The Parade - 056 776 1575 - www.rinuccini.com
- Closed 25-26 December

Anocht

MODERN CUISINE • **DESIGN** XX Set above the Design Centre in an old 1760s grain store is this daytime café, which morphs into an intimate candlelit restaurant at night. Colourful, creative dishes are full of flavour; influences range from the Med to Asia.

Menu € 25 (early dinner) - Carte € 34/46

1st floor, Kilkenny Design Centre, Castle Yard - 056 772 2118
- www.anochtrestaurant.ie - dinner only
- Closed Monday-Wednesday and Sunday except bank holidays

Zuni

MODERN BRITISH • BRASSERIE XX To the front is a small café and a continenta style bar; behind is a sleek, light-filled restaurant with leather panels dividing th tables. Eclectic modern menus rely on local ingredients and desserts are a high light. Comfortable bedrooms are decorated in black and white.

Menu € 30 (early dinner) - Carte € 30/46

13 rooms - € 60/120 € 80/170

26 Patrick St - 056 772 3999 - www.zuni.ie - Closed 24-26 December

Foodworks

TRADITIONAL CUISINE • FRIENDLY X A former bank in the town centre: it bright, fresh look is a perfect match for the style of cooking. Unfussy dishes us top local produce, including fruit and veg from the experienced chef-owner's farm

Menu € 25/35 - Carte € 27/42

7 Parliament St - 056 777 7696 - www.foodworks.ie - Closed 25-26 Decembe and Sunday

Butler House

TOWNHOUSE • ELEGANT A welcoming Georgian townhouse in the city centre with great views over the rear garden towards the impressive castle. Sizeable, sim ply furnished bedrooms have modern oak furnishings and a Scandic feel; ask fo one with a view. The restaurant serves lunch, afternoon tea and evening snacks.

14 rooms - € 135/170 € 135/170

15-16 Patrick St. - 056 776 5707 - www.butler.ie - Closed 24-26 December

Rosquil House

FAMILY • PERSONALISED Modern, purpose-built guesthouse on the main roa out of the city. Leather-furnished lounge filled with books and local informatio spacious, comfortable bedrooms and a smart, linen-laid breakfast room. Exten sive buffet breakfasts with a cooked daily special; omelettes feature. Experi enced, welcoming owners.

7 rooms - € 80/110 € 80/110

Castlecomer Rd - Northwest : 1 km - 056 772 1419 - www.rosquilhouse.com - Closed 3-27 January and 24-27 December

KILLALOE CILL DALUA

Clare - Pop. 1 292 - Regional map n° **22**-B2

Wood & Bell (N)

MODERN BRITISH • ELEGANT XX Above a high street café is this large, elegan country house style restaurant. Deep blue walls are hung with fine oil painting and antique dressers and polished wooden tables add a Georgian feel. Appealin dishes are full of flavour and colour and use good quality local and home-grow ingredients.

Carte € 38/52

Main St (1st Floor) - 061 517 480 - www.woodandbell.com - dinner only - Closed 2 weeks in October, 24-25 December and Sunday-Tuesday,

KILLARNEY CILL AIRNE

Kerry - Pop. 12 740 - Regional map n° **22**-A2

Panorama

MODERN CUISINE • FASHIONABLE XXX Large, formal restaurant set within a lux urious hotel. Panoramic windows afford superb views across the lough to th mountains. Creative modern menus follow the seasons and use the very best Ir ish produce.

Carte € 34/62

Europe Hotel, Fossa - West : 5.75 km. by Port Rd on N 72 - 064 667 1300 - www.theeurope.com - dinner only - Closed 8 December-7 February and Sunda dinner

Park

TRADITIONAL CUISINE • ELEGANT XXX Elegant hotel restaurant with chandeliers, ornate cornicing and a pianist in summer. Classically based menus use some modern combinations; Irish meats are a feature and the tasting menu is a highlight.

Carte € 53/65 – bar lunch

Killarney Park Hotel, – 064 663 5555 – www.killarneyparkhotel.ie – Closed 24-27 December

Brasserie

INTERNATIONAL • BRASSERIE XX Set in a sumptuous lakeside hotel; a modern take on a classical brasserie, with water and mountain views – head for the terrace in warmer weather. The accessible all-day menu ranges from salads to steaks.

Carte € 32/61 **s**

Europe Hotel, Fossa – West : 5.75 km. by Port Rd on N 72 – 064 667 1300 (bookings not accepted) – www.theeurope.com – Closed 8 December-7 February

Europe

GRAND LUXURY • MODERN A superbly located resort boasting stunning views over the lough and mountains. It has impressive events facilities and a sublime three-level spa. Bedrooms are lavishly appointed; some overlook the water.

187 rooms – € 200/350 € 220/370 – 6 suites

Fossa – West : 5.75 km. by Port Rd on N 72 – 064 667 1300 – www.theeurope.com – Closed 8 December-7 February

Panorama • **Brasserie** – See restaurant listing

Aghadoe Heights H. and Spa

LUXURY • DESIGN An unassuming hotel with stunning views over the lakes, mountains and countryside. It boasts an impressive spa and a stylish cocktail bar which comes complete with an evening pianist. Bedrooms are spacious and many have balconies or terraces. The split-level restaurant makes the most of the views.

74 rooms – € 190/290 € 199/299

Northwest : 4.5 km. by N 22 off L 2109 – 064 663 1766 – www.aghadoeheights.com – Closed 21-26 December and weekdays November-April

Killarney Park

LUXURY • CLASSIC A well-versed team run this smart hotel, with its plush library and lavish drawing room. Bedrooms mix modern furnishings with original features. Lunch and afternoon tea are served in the clubby, wood-panelled bar.

67 rooms – € 210/370 € 225/485 – 6 suites

– 064 663 5555 – www.killarneyparkhotel.ie – Closed 24-27 December

Park – See restaurant listing

Fairview

TOWNHOUSE • PERSONALISED Stylish house in the centre of town, with a leather-furnished lounge and modern bedrooms with marble-tiled bathrooms. The Penthouse has a 4-poster, a whirlpool bath for two and mountain views from the balcony.

29 rooms – € 69/249 € 79/299

College St. – 064 663 4164 – www.killarneyfairview.com – Closed 24-25 December

Earls Court House

FAMILY • PERSONALISED A well-run hotel on a quiet residential street close to the town centre. Spacious bedrooms boast good facilities: some feature half-tester or four-poster beds and some have balconies with mountain views.

30 rooms – € 80/140 € 100/160

Woodlawn Rd. – 064 663 4009 – www.killarney-earlscourt.ie – Closed 10 November-1 February

Kathleens Country House

TRADITIONAL • CLASSIC Personally run by a charming hostess: this is Irish h pitality at its best! Comfortable, well-kept and good value hotel, with spacio pine-furnished bedrooms, an open-fired lounge and a cosy first floor library.

17 rooms - € 110/150 € 125/155

Madams Height, Tralee Rd. - North : 3.75 km on N 22 - 064 663 2810 - www.kathleens.net - Closed 24 September-22 April

Killarney Lodge

FAMILY • PERSONALISED Well-located guesthouse on the edge of town. Be rooms are spacious and immaculately kept; No. 12 boasts lovely mountain view Homemade bread and scones feature at breakfast, which is served in a brig airy room.

16 rooms - € 90/120 € 110/160

Countess Rd. - 064 663 6499 - www.killarneylodge.ie - Closed November-10 March

KILLORGLIN CILL ORGLAN

Kerry - Pop. 2 082 - Regional map n° **22**-A2

Giovannelli

ITALIAN • RUSTIC A sweet little restaurant, hidden away in the town centre, w a traditional osteria-style interior and an on-view kitchen. The concise, da changing blackboard menu offers authentic Italian dishes which are unfussy, fre and full of flavour. The pasta is homemade and herbs are from the owners' garde

Carte € 32/56

Lower Bridge St - 087 123 1353 (booking essential) - www.giovannellirestaurant.com - dinner only - Closed Sunday except bank holidays and Monday except July-August

Sol y Sombra

SPANISH • TAPAS BAR Its name means 'Sun and Shade' and the huge tower this former church provides the latter! The cavernous interior still has its pew and stained glass windows. Cooking is fresh and vibrant: go for the raciones.

Menu € 28 - Carte € 26/41

Old Church of Ireland, Lower Bridge St - 066 976 2347 - www.solysombra.ie - dinner only and Sunday lunch - Closed 7 January-2 February and Monday-Tuesday in winter

KINLOUGH CIONN LOCHA

Leitrim - Pop. 1 018 - Regional map n° **21**-C2

Courthouse

ITALIAN • BISTRO Boldly painted former courthouse with a pretty stained gla entrance. The Sardinian chef-owner creates extensive seasonal menus of hone authentic Italian dishes; local seafood and some imported produce feature. T atmosphere is informal and the service, friendly. Simply styled bedrooms off good value.

Menu € 30 (early dinner) - Carte € 31/53

4 rooms - € 55 € 85/95

Main St - 071 984 2391 (booking essential) - www.thecourthouserest.com - dinner only - Closed Wednesday in winter and Monday-Tuesday

KINSALE CIONNE TSÁILE

Cork - Pop. 2 198 - Regional map n° **22**-B3

Bastion

MODERN CUISINE • FRIENDLY A small wine-bar-cum-bistro run by a keen young couple. Modern cooking relies on Irish produce but has Mediterranean influences. Dishes are tasty, carefully prepared and often have an innovative, playful element. The bar serves prosecco on tap, as well as prosecco cocktails.

Menu € 45 - Carte € 38/60

Market St - 021 470 9696 - www.bastionkinsale.com - dinner only and Sunday lunch - Closed last 2 weeks January, first 3 weeks February, Monday and Tuesday

Finns' Table

REGIONAL CUISINE • FRIENDLY Behind the bright orange woodwork lie two attractive rooms - one with colourful banquettes, the other in powder blue with wine box panelling. Meat is from the chef's family farm and everything from bread to ice cream is homemade.

Menu € 36 (early dinner) - Carte € 36/64

6 Main St - 021 470 9636 - www.finnstable.com - dinner only - Closed November, Christmas, Sunday-Thursday January-mid-March and Tuesday-Wednesday

Max's

SEAFOOD • COSY An efficiently run, two-roomed restaurant on a quaint main street, with a simple yet smart rustic style - a spot well-known by the locals! The unfussy, classical seafood menu offers plenty of choice; try the tasty 'Fresh Catches'.

Menu € 26 (early dinner) - Carte € 35/42

Main St - 021 477 2443 - www.maxs.ie - dinner only - Closed mid-December-March, Sunday-Monday, Thursday September-May and bank holidays

Fishy Fishy

SEAFOOD • DESIGN Dine alfresco on the small terrace, amongst 'fishy' memorabilia in the main restaurant or on the quieter first floor; the photos are of the fishermen who supply them. Concise, all-day menus feature some interesting specials.

Carte € 30/50 **s**

Pier Rd - 021 470 0415 - www.fishyfishy.ie - Closed 24-26 December

The Bulman

SEAFOOD • PUB You'll receive a proper Irish welcome from the owner of this cosy pub. Keep an eye out for the Moby Dick mural and the carved Bulman Buoy, which sit alongside some eye-catching Irish art. Dishes have global leanings - go for one of the blackboard specials, which could include locally cured wild smoked salmon.

Carte € 29/51

Summercove - East : 2 km by R 600 and Charles Fort rd. - 021 477 2131 - www.thebulman.ie - Closed 25 December, Good Friday and dinner Sunday-Monday

Perryville House

TOWNHOUSE • CLASSIC A luxuriously appointed house in the heart of town, named after the family that built it in 1820. It boasts three antique-furnished drawing rooms and a small courtyard garden. Bedrooms are tastefully styled - the top rooms have feature beds, chic bathrooms and harbour views.

23 rooms - € 190/390 € 190/390

Long Quay - 021 477 2731 - www.perryvillehouse.com - Closed November-15 April

REPUBLIC OF IRELAND

Old Presbytery

TOWNHOUSE • CLASSIC 18C building which once housed priests from th nearby church – a few ecclesiastical pieces remain. Bedrooms feature Irish pi furniture and either brass or cast iron beds; Room 6 has a roof terrace. Breakfas are comprehensive.

9 rooms – € 95/150 € 100/200

43 Cork St. – 021 477 2027 – www.oldpres.com – Closed mid-November-Marc

at Barrells Cross Southwest: 5.75 km on R600 ✉ Kinsale

Rivermount House

FAMILY • PERSONALISED Spacious, purpose-built dormer bungalow overlookir the countryside and the river, yet not far from town. It has a distinctive mode style throughout, with attractive embossed wallpapers and quality furnishinc Bold, well-appointed bedrooms display high attention to detail and have imma ulate bathrooms.

6 rooms – € 70/100 € 95/140

North : 0.75 km on L 7302 – 021 477 8033 – www.rivermount.com – Closed November-mid-March

KNOCK AN CNOC

Mayo – Pop. 811 – Regional map n° **21**-B2

*Hotels see : **Cong** SW : 58 km by N 17, R 331 R 334 and R 345*

LAHINCH AN LEACHT

Clare – Pop. 642 – Regional map n° **22**-B1

Moy House

COUNTRY HOUSE • ELEGANT An 18C Italianate clifftop villa, overlooking the bay ar run by a friendly, attentive team. Homely guest areas include a small library and a open-fired drawing room with an honesty bar; antiques, oil paintings and heavy fabri feature throughout. Individually designed, classical bedrooms boast good extras ar most have views. Formal dining is from a 6 course set menu.

9 rooms – € 145/165 € 200/395

– 065 708 2800 – www.moyhouse.com – Closed November-April

LEENANE AN LÍONÁN

Galway – ✉ Clifden – Regional map n° **21**-A3

Delphi Lodge

COUNTRY HOUSE • PERSONALISED A former shooting lodge of the Marquis o Sligo, in a lovely loughside spot on a 1,000 acre estate. Bright, simple bedroor with smart bathrooms. 'Special Experience' days, free bike hire and a large wal ers' drying room. Communal dining from a set menu; guests are encouraged t mingle in the drawing room.

13 rooms – € 140/195 € 190/320

Northwest : 13.25 km by N 59 on Louisburgh rd – 095 42222 – www.delphilodge.ie – Closed November-February

LETTERKENNY LEITIR CEANAINN

Donegal – Pop. 15 387 – Regional map n° **21**-C1

Browns on the Green

MODERN CUISINE • FRIENDLY XX Situated on the first floor of a golf club b with views of the mountains rather than the course. A cosy lounge leads in the intimate modern dining room. Refined dishes are modern interpretations o tried-and-tested classics.

Menu € 20/30

Letterkenny Golf Club, Barnhill – Northeast : 5.75 km by R 245 – 074 912 4771 – www.brownsonthegreen.com – Closed 25-26 December, Good Friday, Monday-Wednesday

Lemon Tree

REGIONAL CUISINE • FAMILY XX This established family-run restaurant sees brother, sisters and cousins all working together to deliver surprisingly modern dishes which draw from Donegal's natural larder. The early evening set dinner menu is good value.

Menu € 20 (early dinner) - Carte € 28/43

32 Courtyard Shopping Centre, Lower Main St - 074 912 5788 - www.thelemontreerestaurant.com - dinner only - Closed 24-26 December

LIMERICK LUIMNEACH

Limerick - Pop. 57 106 - Regional map n° **22**-B2

Sash

TRADITIONAL CUISINE • BRASSERIE XX A relaxed, modern bistro with a feature wall of pictures and mirrors, set on the first floor of a boutique hotel - it's named after the type of window found in houses of this era. Menus are wide-ranging.

Menu € 35 (weekday dinner) - Carte € 28/55

No.1 Pery Square Hotel, Pery Sq - 061 402 402 - www.oneperysquare.com - dinner only and lunch Saturday-Sunday - Closed 24-26 December and Monday-Wednesday

No 1. Pery Square

TOWNHOUSE • CONTEMPORARY A charming boutique townhouse in the Georgian Quarter, with a superb spa and a spacious drawing room overlooking the gardens. Choose a luxurious 'Period' bedroom or more contemporary 'Club' room.

20 rooms - € 135/165 € 165/225 - 1 suite

Pery Sq - 061 402 402 - www.oneperysquare.com - Closed 24-26 December

Sash - See restaurant listing

LISCANNOR LIOS CEANNÚIR

Clare - Pop. 129 - Regional map n° **22**-B1

Vaughan's Anchor Inn

SEAFOOD • PUB A characterful family-run pub in a small fishing village. Nautical memorabilia lines the walls and along with the impressive fish tank, gives a clue as to the focus of the menu, where locally sourced seafood underpins the cooking. Bright, stylish bedrooms are hung with photos of local sights.

Carte € 33/56

7 rooms - € 80/120 € 80/120

Main St - 065 708 1548 - www.vaughans.ie - Closed 24-25 December

LISDOONVARNA LIOS DÚIN BHEARNA

Clare - Pop. 739 - Regional map n° **22**-B1

Wild Honey Inn (Aidan McGrath)

CLASSIC CUISINE • INN This personally run inn started life as an 1860s hotel, so it may not look much like a pub, but once inside it's warm, cosy and full of pubby character. Two weekly changing fixed price menus have a classical French base and showcase the county's produce in neat, confidently prepared dishes which are packed with flavour. Comfy bedrooms have a fittingly traditional feel.

→ Black pudding and foie gras with apple purée, celery and olive oil. Lamb rump and neck with tomato and sardine dressing. Poached pineapple with set vanilla cream, hazelnuts, pistachios and pineapple sorbet.

Menu € 50/60

14 rooms - € 120/130 € 140/155

Kincora Rd. - South : 0.5 km on Ennistimon rd - 065 707 4300 - www.wildhoneyinn.com - dinner only - Closed November-February, Tuesday-March, April and October and Sunday-Monday

Sheedy's Country House

FAMILY • CLASSIC Set in the centre of the village and run by the 3rd generatic of the family. Relax in the comfy library, the Lloyd Loom furnished sun lounge the traditional bar. Spacious, well-kept bedrooms have floral fabrics and good fa cilities. A classic menu is offered in the dining room, where service is exacting.

11 rooms – € 90/120 € 135/180

– 065 707 4026 – www.sheedys.com – Closed October-Easter

LISTOWEL LIOS TUATHAIL

Kerry – Pop. 4 205 – Regional map n° **22**-B2

Allo's Bistro

TRADITIONAL CUISINE • COSY Former pub dating back to 1873; now a simpl well-run and characterful restaurant. Series of homely rooms and friendly, eff cient service. Wide-ranging menus rely on regional produce, with theme nigh on Thursdays and an adventurous gourmet menu Fri and Sat evenings. Individu antique-furnished bedrooms.

Carte € 31/46

3 rooms – € 70/100 € 70/100

41-43 Church St – 068 22880 (booking essential)
– www.allosbarbistro-townhouse.com – Closed Sunday-Tuesday and Wednesday dinner

LONGFORD AN LONGFORT

Longford – Pop. 8 002 – Regional map n° **21**-C3

VM

MODERN CUISINE • TRADITIONAL DÉCOR Formal hotel restaurant in the o stables of a Georgian house. The smart, rustic dining room has stone-faced wal and overlooks a Japanese garden. Cooking is interesting, modern and origina and orchard and garden produce features.

Menu € 65

Viewmount House Hotel, Dublin Rd – Southeast : 1.5 km by R 393
– 043 334 1919 – www.viewmounthouse.com – dinner only and Sunday lunch
– Closed 29 October-7 November, Sunday dinner, Monday and Tuesday

Viewmount House

COUNTRY HOUSE • CLASSIC Set in 4 acres of mature grounds, a welcomin Georgian house with a charming period feel – original features include an ornat vaulted ceiling in the breakfast room. Bedrooms are traditionally styled, furnishe with antiques and have good modern facilities; opt for a duplex room. The break fasts are delicious.

12 rooms – € 80/120 € 160/180

Dublin Rd – Southeast : 1.5 km by R 393 – 043 334 1919
– www.viewmounthouse.com – Closed 29 October-7 November

VM – See restaurant listing

MALAHIDE MULLACH ÍDE

Fingal – Pop. 15 846 – Regional map n° **22**-D1

Bon Appetit

MODERN CUISINE • BRASSERIE Smart Georgian terraced house near the har bour. The intimate, dimly lit bar offers cocktails and tapas; below is a moder brasserie with a lively atmosphere. Modern dishes have a classical French base the steaks are a highlight.

Menu € 17 (weekdays) – Carte dinner € 35/60

9 St James's Terr. – 01 845 0314 – www.bonappetit.ie – dinner only and lunch Friday-Sunday – Closed 25 December and Monday

Jaipur

INDIAN • ELEGANT XX A friendly basement restaurant in a Georgian terrace. The origins of the tasty, contemporary Indian dishes are noted on the menu. The monkfish with lime, ginger, coriander root & fried okra is a speciality.

Menu € 24 (early dinner) – Carte € 26/52

5 St James's Terr – 01 845 5455 – www.jaipur.ie – dinner only and Sunday lunch – Closed 25 December

Old Street

MODERN CUISINE • CHIC X A pair of converted cottages house this lively split-level restaurant which boasts designer touches and a stylish cocktail bar with a lovely panelled ceiling. The experienced team carefully craft appealing modern dishes that are made up of numerous different flavours and textures.

Menu € 21 – Carte € 34/53

Old St – 01 845 5614 – www.oldstreet.ie – dinner only and lunch Friday-Saturday – Closed 1-7 January , 25-26 December and Monday

MALLOW MALA

ork – Pop. 8 578 – Regional map n° **22**-B2

Longueville House

HISTORIC • CLASSIC A part-Georgian manor house overlooking Dromaneen Castle and built in William and Mary style. It boasts a lovely stone-tiled hall, a superb flying staircase, a stunning drawing room and well-appointed bedrooms furnished with antiques. Traditional menus use produce from the garden and estate.

20 rooms – € 95/245 € 185/245

West : 5.5 km by N 72 – 022 47156 – www.longuevillehouse.ie – Closed 1-19 January and Monday-Tuesday

MIDLETON MAINISTIR NA CORANN

ork – Pop. 3 733 – Regional map n° **22**-C3

Farmgate Restaurant & Country Store

REGIONAL CUISINE • SIMPLE X A friendly food store with a bakery, a rustic two-roomed restaurant and a courtyard terrace. Lunch might mean soup, a sandwich or a tart; dinner features regional fish and meats – the chargrilled steaks are popular. Cakes served all day.

Carte € 34/54

Broderick St, Coolbawn – 021 463 2771 – www.farmgate.ie – Closed 24 December-2 January, Sunday and Monday

Sage

REGIONAL CUISINE • BISTRO X A passionately run restaurant with a rustic feel. Hearty, classical cooking is full of flavour – ingredients are sourced from within a 12 mile radius and their homemade black pudding is a must. To accompany, try a biodynamic wine or artisan beer. The next door Greenroom café serves lighter dishes.

Menu € 30 (lunch and early dinner) – Carte € 30/48

The Courtyard, 8 Main St – 021 463 9682 – www.sagerestaurant.ie – Closed 25-27 December and Monday

MOHILL MAOTHAIL

eitrim – Pop. 928 – Regional map n° **21**-C2

Lough Rynn Castle

LUXURY • HISTORIC 18C country house with superb gardens and peaceful grounds; popular for weddings. Numerous lounges and a baronial hall with original parquet flooring and an impressive fireplace. Large, well-appointed bedrooms – those in the main house are the most characterful. Formal dining room; ambitious French cuisine.

44 rooms – € 99/175 € 120/250

Southeast : 4 km by R 201 off Drumlish rd – 071 963 2700 – www.loughrynn.ie

Lough Rynn Country House

FAMILY • PERSONALISED Purpose-built stone house in a peaceful country se ting, boasting lovely views over Lough Rynn – three of the homely bedroor share the view and one has a small balcony. There's a comfy lounge and a cc tagey breakfast room, and the delightful owner welcomes guests with hom baked scones or muffins.

4 rooms – € 100 € 100

Southeast : 3.5 km. by R 201 off Drumlish rd – 087 922 8236 – www.loughrynnbandb.ie

MONKSTOWN BAILE NA MANACH

Dublin – Regional map n° **22**-D1

Bresson

MODERN CUISINE • BRASSERIE XX Enter via a small courtyard into this sma characterful neighbourhood brasserie. It's named after a French photograph who pictured subjects in their natural state rather than studio settings – a refle tion of their cooking being honest and natural. Rich, hearty dishes use class French techniques.

Menu € 30/35 – Carte € 41/66

4A The Crescent – 01 284 4286 – www.bresson.ie – Closed 25-26 December, 1 January, Monday and lunch Tuesday-Wednesday

MULLINGAR AN MUILEANN GCEARR

Westmeath – Pop. 9 414 – Regional map n° **21**-C3

Marlinstown Court

TRADITIONAL • COSY Clean, tidy guesthouse close to the N4; a very home personal option for staying away. The light, airy lounge opens into a pleasa pine-furnished breakfast room overlooking the garden. Bedrooms are simply ar brightly decorated.

5 rooms – € 45/50 € 80/90

Old Dublin Rd – East : 2.5 km off N 4 (junction 15) – 044 934 0053 – www.marlinstowncourt.com – Closed 23-27 December

MURRISK MURAISC

Mayo – Pop. 235 – Regional map n° **21**-A2

Tavern

TRADITIONAL CUISINE • PUB A vibrant pink pub where the friendly tea make you feel at home; the collection of rolling pins and vintage signs gives it quirky edge. Fresh ingredients feature in generous, classic dishes; shellfish is fro the nearby bay.

Carte € 19/53

– 098 64060 – www.tavernmurrisk.com – Closed 25 December

NAAS AN NÁS

Kildare – Pop. 20 713 – Regional map n° **22**-D1

Vie de Châteaux

CLASSIC FRENCH • BISTRO X A smart modern bistro with a great terrace ove looking the old harbour. The keenly priced menu of carefully cooked, fully fl voured Gallic dishes will evoke memories of holidays in France; save room fc 'Les Mini Desserts'.

Menu € 22 (lunch) – Carte € 35/51

The Harbour – 045 888 478 (booking essential) – www.viedechateaux.ie – Closed 25-26 December, 1-8 January, lunch Monday, Tuesday, Saturday and bank holidays

at Two Mile House Southwest: 6.5 km by R448 on L 2032

Brown Bear

MODERN BRITISH • BRASSERIE XX Set in a sleepy village, the Brown Bear comprises a locals' bar and a clubby bistro with tan leather booths and candlelit tables. Ambitious dishes are creatively presented and full of flavour. Service is smooth and assured.

Menu € 34 (early dinner) – Carte € 33/53

– ✆ 045 883 561 – www.thebrownbear.ie – dinner only and lunch Saturday-Sunday – Closed 24-27 December, Monday and Tuesday

NEW QUAY BEALACLUGGA

Clare – Regional map n° **22**-B1

Linnane's Lobster Bar

SEAFOOD • PUB A simple but likeable place, with peat fires and full-length windows which open onto a terrace. They specialise in fresh seafood; watch the local boats unload their catch, some of which is brought straight to the kitchen.

Carte € 23/57

New Quay Pier – ✆ 065 707 8120 – www.linnanesbar.com – Closed 25 December, Good Friday and Monday-Thursday November-17 March

Mount Vernon

COUNTRY HOUSE • PERSONALISED Charming whitewashed house with a pretty walled garden, set close to the beach and affording lovely views. Antiques and eclectic curios fill the guest areas; spacious bedrooms have their own personalities – two open onto a terrace. Simply cooked dinners rely on fresh, local produce. Warm, welcoming owners.

5 rooms – € 90/145 € 190/230

Flaggy Shore – North : 0.75 km on coast rd – ✆ 065 707 8126 – www.mountvernon.ie – Closed November-March

NEWPORT BAILE UÍ FHIACHÁIN

Mayo – Pop. 616 – Regional map n° **21**-A2

Newport House

HISTORIC • CLASSIC A delightful 1720s creeper-clad mansion with lovely gardens and river views – they also own neighbouring Lough Beltra, so many guests come to fish. The stunning staircase, topped by a domed cupola, leads up to traditional, antique-filled bedrooms. Dine beneath family portraits and an elegant chandelier.

14 rooms – € 115/135 € 220/260

– ✆ 098 41222 – www.newporthouse.ie – Closed November-mid-March

NEWTOWNMOUNTKENNEDY BAILE AN CHINNÉIDIEH

Wicklow – Pop. 2 548 – Regional map n° **22**-D2

Druids Glen H. & Golf Resort

RESORT • CLASSIC Hidden away in the countryside but just 30mins from Dublin, you'll find this smart resort hotel and its two championship golf courses – along with a great spa and a vast array of other leisure facilities. The delightful bar overlooks the 13th hole and the appealing restaurant has a lovely terrace too.

145 rooms – € 140/275 € 165/375 – 11 suites

– ✆ 01 287 0800 – www.druidsglenresort.com

OUGHTERARD UACHTAR ARD

Galway - Pop. 1 333 - Regional map n° **21**-A3

Currarevagh House

TRADITIONAL • CLASSIC Classically furnished Victorian manor house set in 18 loughside acres and run by the same family for over 100 years. It has a pleas-ingly 'lived-in' feel and offers a real country house experience. Have afternoo tea by the fire or take a picnic out on their boat; set dinners offer unfussy, fla-voursome dishes.

11 rooms - € 85/110 € 160/190

Northwest : 6.5 km on Glann rd - 091 552 312 - www.currarevagh.com - Close November-February

Railway Lodge

COUNTRY HOUSE • RURAL An elegantly furnished house in a remote settin with lovely views across the countryside. Bedrooms come with stripped pine fu nishings and a keen eye for detail. The charming owner offers great local recom mendations.

4 rooms - € 65/110 € 65/110

West : 0.75 km by Shannapheasteen rd taking first right onto unmarked road - 091 552 945 - www.railwaylodge.net

PORTLAOISE PORT LAOISE

Laois - Pop. 20 145 - Regional map n° **22**-C2

Ivyleigh House

TOWNHOUSE • CLASSIC Traditional listed Georgian property in the city centr run by a welcoming owner. Comfy lounge and communal dining area, with ar tiques and ornaments displayed throughout. Good-sized bedrooms are decorate in a period style. Homemade breads, preserves, muesli and a Cashel blue chees cake special at breakfast.

6 rooms - € 70/90 € 120/170

Bank Pl, Church St - 057 862 2081 - www.ivyleigh.com - Closed 12 November-1 April except Christmas and New Year

RAMELTON RÁTH MEALTAIN

Donegal - Pop. 1 212 - Regional map n° **21**-C1

Ardeen

TRADITIONAL • CLASSIC A Victorian house on the edge of the village, wit peaceful gardens and a river nearby. Welcoming owner and homely, personall styled interior. Open-fired lounge with local info; communal breakfasts. Simpl well-kept bedrooms without TVs.

5 rooms - € 45/55 € 45/90

bear left at the fork in the village centre and left at T-junction - 074 915 1243 - www.ardeenhouse.com - Closed October-May

RANELAGH - Dublin → See Dublin

RATHMINES RÁTH MAONAIS - Dublin → See Dublin

RATHMULLAN RÁTH MAOLÁIN

Donegal - Letterkenny - Pop. 518 - Regional map n° **21**-C1

Cook & Gardener

CLASSIC CUISINE • FAMILY XX Formal hotel restaurant comprising several inter connecting rooms. Daily menus list the best of what's in season, including pro duce from the house's original walled kitchen garden. Classic cooking is pre sented in a modern manner.

Carte € 34/63

Rathmullan House Hotel, North : 0.5 mi on R 247 - 074 915 8188 - www.rathmullanhouse.com - Restricted opening in winter

Rathmullan House

TRADITIONAL • CLASSIC Family-run, part-19C house set next to Lough Swilly. Bedrooms in the original house have a fitting country house style; those in the extension are more modern and come with balconies or private terraces overlooking the gardens.

34 rooms - € 90/125 € 180/290

North : 0.5 mi on R 247 - 074 915 8188 - www.rathmullanhouse.com - Restricted opening in winter

Cook & Gardener - See restaurant listing

RATHNEW RÁTH NAOI

Wicklow - Wicklow - Pop. 2 964 - Regional map n° **22**-D2

Brunel

IRISH • ELEGANT XX Spacious, elegant restaurant in a hotel extension, overlooking the gardens: named after the builder of the Great Eastern ship on which Captain Halpin sailed. Flavoursome, traditional dishes use the best Wicklow ingredients.

Menu € 40 - Carte € 40/55

Tinakilly House Hotel, On R 750 - 0404 69274 - www.tinakilly.ie - dinner only and Sunday lunch - Closed 24-26 December

Tinakilly House

HISTORIC • CLASSIC A substantial Victorian house in extensive grounds which stretch to the seashore: built for Captain Robert Halpin. Original features include an impressive staircase. Spacious, classically furnished bedrooms; some have four-posters.

52 rooms - € 100 € 110/190 - 1 suite

On R 750 - 0404 69274 - www.tinakilly.ie - Closed 24-26 December

Brunel - See restaurant listing

RIVERSTOWN BAILE IDIR DHÁ ABHAINN

Sligo - Pop. 374 - Regional map n° **21**-B2

Coopershill

TRADITIONAL • CLASSIC Magnificent Georgian house run by the 7th generation of the same family; set on a working farm within a 500 acre estate. Spacious guest areas showcase original furnishings - now antiques - and family portraits adorn the walls. Warm, country house style bedrooms. Formal dining amongst polished silverware.

8 rooms - € 151/175 € 202/250

- 071 916 5108 - www.coopershill.com - Closed November-March

ROSMUCK

Regional map n° **21**-A3

Screebe House

COUNTRY HOUSE • CLASSIC An old Victorian fishing lodge in a stunning spot on Camus Bay; it has the look of a country house and a friendly, laid-back atmosphere. Enjoy tea by the fire in the sitting room or a beer beneath an enormous stag's head in the bar. Understated bedrooms feature good quality furnishings and character beds.

10 rooms - € 120/200 € 160/260

Northeast : 9 km by R 1204 on R 340 - 091 574 110 - www.screebe.com - Closed 1 December-15 February, Monday, Tuesday and weekdays in winter

ROSSCARBERY ROS Ó GCAIRBRE

Pop. 534 - Regional map n° **22**-B3

Pilgrim's

MODERN CUISINE • RUSTIC It's been a guesthouse and the village booksho among other things, but this cosy, proudly run restaurant has always kept i name. The concise daily menu lists generously proportioned dishes prepar from local and foraged ingredients. The depth of flavours and the warm hospita ity really stand out.

Carte € 34/43

6 South Sq - 023 883 1796 - www.pilgrims.ie - dinner only and Sunday lunch - Closed 16 December-13 March, Sunday dinner, Monday and Tuesday

ROSSLARE ROS LÁIR

Wexford - Pop. 1 547 - Regional map n° **22**-D2

Kelly's Resort

FAMILY • PERSONALISED It started life in 1895 as a beachfront 'refreshme house'; now it's a sprawling leisure-orientated hotel run by the 4th generatic of the Kelly family. An impressive collection of contemporary art is displaye throughout the guest areas and well-appointed bedrooms. Formal 'Beache has an appealing menu and an exceptional wine list; La Marine serves brasser classics.

120 rooms - € 94/132 € 188/394 - 4 suites

- 053 913 2114 - www.kellys.ie - Closed 9 December-15 February

ROUNDSTONE CLOCH NA RÓN

Galway - Pop. 245 - Regional map n° **21**-A3

O'Dowds

SEAFOOD • COSY The blue exterior and proximity to the harbour give a clu as to this pub's speciality: simply prepared, super fresh seafood - much of landed just outside the door. It's been run by the same family for over 100 year

Menu € 20 (early dinner) - Carte € 22/41

- 095 35809 - www.odowdsseafoodbar.com - Closed 25 December

SALLINS NA SOLLÁIN

Pop. 5 283 - Regional map n° **22**-D1

Two Cooks

IRISH • NEIGHBOURHOOD This delightful restaurant on the first floor of a res dential parade is run by - you've guessed it - two chefs; he cooks while sh keeps things running smoothly out front. Cooking is honest and well-judged ar skilled techniques transform even the lesser cuts into dishes packed with flavou

Carte € 38/47

Canal View - 045 853 768 - www.twocooks.ie - dinner only - Closed 15-31 January, 5-16 August, 25-27 December, Sunday and Monday

SANDYFORD ÁTH AN GHAINIMH → See Dublin

SHANAGARRY AN SEANGHARRAÍ

Cork - Midleton - Pop. 414 - Regional map n° **22**-C3

Ballymaloe House

FAMILY • CLASSIC With its pre-18C origins, this is the very essence of a countr manor house. Family-run for 3 generations, it boasts numerous traditional styled guest areas, comfortable, classical bedrooms and a famed cookery schoc The daily changing fixed price menu offers local, seasonal produce.

29 rooms - € 175/215 € 225/270

Northwest : 3 km on R 629 - 021 465 2531 - www.ballymaloe.ie - Closed 7 January-4 February and 24-28 December

SKIBBEREEN AN SCIOBAIRÍN

Cork - Pop. 2 568 - Regional map n° **22**-B3

Liss Ard

HISTORIC • PERSONALISED With 150 acres of grounds - including a lake - this 200 year old manor house, stables and lodge create an idyllic rural retreat. Inside they're surprisingly modern with sleek furnishings and a minimalist Swiss/German style. Staff are friendly and daily menus are led by the availability of local produce.

25 rooms - € 79/99 € 99/189

Liss Ard Estate, Castletownsend Rd - Southeast : 2.5 km on R 596 - 028 40000 - www.lissardestate.com - Closed November-March

SLANE BAILE SHÁINE

Meath - Pop. 1 349 - Regional map n° **21**-D3

Brabazon

MODERN CUISINE • RUSTIC XX Relaxed, rustic restaurant in the former piggery of a delightful manor house. Sit at a painted wooden table by the fire or out on the terrace overlooking the landscaped courtyard. Contemporary cooking uses top quality ingredients.

Menu € 25/30 - Carte € 35/50

Tankardstown Hotel, Northwest : 6 km by N 51 off R 163 - 041 982 4621 - www.tankardstown.ie/dining/brabazon - Closed 24-27 December and Monday-Tuesday

Tankardstown

COUNTRY HOUSE • CONTEMPORARY A fine Georgian manor house with a lavish interior, set up a sweeping tree-lined drive. Bedrooms in the main house are furnished with antiques; those in the courtyard are more modern and come with kitchens. Have afternoon tea in the cottage, wood-fired pizzas in Cellar or contemporary dishes in Brabazon.

25 rooms - € 105/360 € 210/360 - 6 suites

Northwest : 6 km by N 51 off R 163 - 041 982 4621 - www.tankardstown.ie - Closed 24-27 December

Brabazon - See restaurant listing

Conyngham Arms

FAMILY • PERSONALISED 17C coaching inn on the main street of a small but busy town. It has a laid-back feel, an appealing shabby-chic style and a lovely hidden garden. Some of the bedrooms have feature beds and all come with coffee machines and freshly baked biscuits from their nearby bakery. Dine in the bar, with its open kitchen.

15 rooms - € 65/99 € 89/139

- 041 988 4444 - www.conynghamarms.ie - Closed 25-26 December

SLIGO SLIGEACH

Sligo - Pop. 17 568 - Regional map n° **21**-B2

Montmartre

CLASSIC FRENCH • BISTRO XX Smart, modern restaurant in the shadow of the cathedral, with a tiled exterior and wooden blinds. The French chefs prepare classic Gallic menus which follow the seasons. The all-French wine list features interesting, lesser-known wines.

Menu € 27 (early dinner)/37 - Carte € 27/54

Market Yard - 071 916 9901 - www.montmartrerestaurant.ie - dinner only - Closed 7-30 January, Sunday except before a bank holiday and Monday

Hargadons Bros

TRADITIONAL CUISINE • RUSTIC Hugely characterful pub with sloping floor narrow passageways, dimly lit anterooms and a lovely "Ladies' Room" complet with its own serving hatch. Cooking is warming and satisfying, offering the like of Irish stew or bacon and cabbage.

Carte € 21/47

4-5 O'Connell St - ✆ 071 915 3709 (bookings not accepted) - www.hargadons.co - Closed Sunday

Tree Tops

TRADITIONAL • PERSONALISED An unassuming whitewashed house in a res dential area, with immaculately kept bedrooms, a cosy lounge and a smart buff breakfast room overlooking the garden. The chatty, welcoming owners have a interesting Irish art collection.

3 rooms - € 75 € 75

Cleveragh Rd - South : 1.25 km by Dublin rd - ✆ 071 916 2301 - www.sligobandb.com - Closed mid-December-8 January

STRAFFAN TEACH SRAFÁIN

Kildare - Pop. 635 - Regional map n° **22**-D1

K Club

GRAND LUXURY • CLASSIC A golf resort with two championship courses, an ex tensive spa and beautiful formal gardens stretching down to the Liffey. The fin 19C house has elegant antique-filled guestrooms and luxurious bedrooms. Elegar Byerley Turk serves a 6 course tasting menu; grand River Room offers refine classics; Legends has a brasserie menu; and K Thai serves Thai and Malaysian far

134 rooms - € 222/463 € 222/463 - 16 suites

- ✆ 01 601 7200 - www.kclub.ie

Barberstown Castle

COUNTRY HOUSE • HISTORIC This 13C castle with Georgian and Victorian exten sions is set within 20 acres of grounds and makes a popular wedding venue Large, luxurious country house bedrooms feature good facilities; many hav four-poster beds and garden outlooks. Dine from French menus in the Georgia house and stone keep.

55 rooms - € 145/200 € 230/270

North : 0.75 km - ✆ 01 628 8157 - www.barberstowncastle.ie - Closed January-February and 24-26 December

TERENURE ➜ See Dublin

THOMASTOWN BAILE MHIC ANDÁIN

Kilkenny - Pop. 2 273 - Regional map n° **22**-C2

Lady Helen

MODERN CUISINE • ROMANTIC XXX Sited within an impressive Georgian house i this grand, luxurious restaurant which looks out over the estate and the Rive Nore. Ambitious, visually impressive modern dishes are precisely prepared an ingredients come from the estate, the county and the coast; for the full experi ence go for the tasting menu.

➜ Cromesquis of pig and foie gras with Pedro Ximénez and sauce gribiche Squab with cabbage, almond milk and Hen-of-the-wood. Banana and tonk bean with almond sponge and kalamansi.

Menu € 75/110

Manor House Hotel, Mount Juliet Estate - West : 5.5 km by R 448 on L 4206 - ✆ 056 777 3000 (booking essential) - www.mountjuliet.ie - dinner only - Close Sunday-Monday

The Hound

MODERN CUISINE • BRASSERIE XX This eye-catching restaurant is named after the Kilkenny Hounds, who were kept on the estate for many years. Irish ingredients feature in refined dishes with robust flavours. Ask for a table in the conservatory overlooking the greens of the golf course; start with a drink in the Saddle Bar.

Carte €28/47

Hunter's Yard Hotel, Mount Juliet Estate - Southwest : 5.5 km by R 448 on L 4206 - ✆ 056 777 3000 - www.mountjuliet.ie

Manor House

HISTORIC • CLASSIC Within this Irish Estate's 1,500 acres you can enjoy fishing, falconry, horse riding and golf. The house was built in the 1700s and is a fine example of Georgian architecture, with original stuccowork and hand-carved fireplaces. Well-appointed bedrooms have a period style; ask for a River Nore view.

32 rooms - € 179/229 € 239/329 - €23 - 2 suites

Mount Juliet Estate - West : 5.5 km by R 448 on L 4206 - ✆ 056 777 3000 - www.mountjuliet.ie

Lady Helen - See restaurant listing

Hunter's Yard

COUNTRY HOUSE • PERSONALISED The former stable block of the Mount Juliet Estate provides a pleasing contrast to the original Manor House, with bright modern bedrooms and up-to-date amenities. Rooms by the walled garden are quieter and more secluded and come with Juliet balconies. Facilities are shared with the Manor House.

93 rooms - € 150/320 € 170/340 - €22

Mount Juliet Estate - Southwest : 5.5 km by R 448 on L 4206 - ✆ 056 777 3000 - www.mountjuliet.ie

The Hound - See restaurant listing

Abbey House

TRADITIONAL • COSY Attractive whitewashed Victorian house with a neat, lawned garden and a friendly, hospitable owner; set opposite the ruins of Jerpoint Abbey. Traditionally styled lounge with plenty of local info. Simple bedrooms with antique furniture.

6 rooms - € 60/70 € 90/100

Jerpoint Abbey - Southwest : 2 km on R 448 - ✆ 056 772 4166 - www.abbeyhousejerpoint.com - Closed December-February

TIMOLEAGUE TIGH MOLAIGE

Cork - Pop. 323 - Regional map n° **22**-B3

Dillon's

MODERN CUISINE • BISTRO X A former pub-cum-grocer's named after its first owner. The original bar counter and shelves remain and the room has a homely feel. Flavoursome dishes are eye-catchingly presented and make good use of local ingredients, some of which they grow in the garden - the purple sprouting broccoli is wonderful.

Carte €32/50

Mill St - ✆ 023 886 9609 (booking essential) - www.dillonsrestaurant.ie - dinner only and Sunday lunch - Closed Sunday dinner, Wednesday and Thursday

TOORMORE AN TUAR MÓR

Cork - ✉ Goleen - Pop. 207 - Regional map n° **22**-A3

Fortview House

FAMILY • PERSONALISED Well-kept guesthouse on a 120 acre dairy farm, run by a very bubbly owner. It has a rustic, country feel courtesy of its stone walls, timbered ceilings, coir carpets and aged pine furniture. Breakfast is an event, with home-baked scones and bread, eggs from their hens and other local products all featuring.

3 rooms - € 50/100 € 50/100

Gurtyowen - Northeast : 2.5 km on R 591 (Durrus rd) - ✆ 028 35324 - www.fortviewhousegoleen.com - Closed October-April

TRALEE TRÁ LÍ

Kerry - Pop. 20 814 - Regional map n° **22**-A2

Grand

TOWNHOUSE • TRADITIONAL Opened in 1928 and located in the heart of thi bustling town. It has a small first floor lounge and modern bedrooms. The trad tional bar - once the post office - is a popular spot and offers hearty all-day dishe The classical dining room serves a mix of Irish specialities and more global fare.

48 rooms - € 60/130 € 90/200

Denny St - 066 712 1499 - www.grandhoteltralee.com - Closed 25 December

Brook Manor Lodge

TOWNHOUSE • PERSONALISED Spacious detached house with a bright conserva tory breakfast room and views to the Slieve Mish Mountains; perfect if you lik golf, hiking or fishing. Bedrooms are immaculate - those at the back have the view

7 rooms - € 75/120 € 100/175

Fenit Rd, Spa - Northwest : 3.5 km by R 551 on R 558 - 066 712 0406 - www.brookmanorlodge.com - Closed November-March

TRIM BAILE ÁTHA TROIM

Meath - Pop. 1 441 - Regional map n° **21**-D3

Trim Castle

BUSINESS • MODERN Modern family-run hotel opposite the castle, complet with a café, a homeware shop and a delightful roof terrace with a great outloo Good-sized bedrooms come in contemporary hues - those to the front share th view. Dine in the bar or opt for classic European dishes in the stylish first floc restaurant.

68 rooms - € 75/155 € 75/185

Castle St. - 046 948 3000 - www.trimcastlehotel.com

Highfield House

TOWNHOUSE • PERSONALISED Substantial 18C stone house close to the rive and the oldest Norman castle in Europe. Well-appointed lounge and breakfas room, boldly coloured bedrooms and a delightful terraced courtyard. Compre hensive breakfasts; scones on arrival.

10 rooms - € 65/95 € 65/95

Castle St - 046 857 7115 - www.highfieldguesthouse.com - Closed 21 December-2 January

TUAM TUAIM

Galway - Regional map n° **21**-B3

Brownes N

MODERN BRITISH • COSY X A husband and wife own this sweet former pub which previously belonged to the chef's grandfather. The snug front bar has welcoming open coal fire and a collection of family photos - and the dinin room has a homely feel. The availability of ingredients writes the great valu modern daily menu.

Carte € 26/38

The Square - 093 60700 - www.brownestuam.ie - Closed 1-10 January, 25 December, Easter, Monday and Tuesday

TULLAMORE TULACH MHÓR

Offaly - Pop. 11 346 - Regional map n° **22**-C1

Blue Apron

CLASSIC CUISINE • BISTRO Friendly, engaging service sets the tone at this intimate restaurant, which is run by an enthusiastic husband and wife team. All-encompassing menus offer generous, flavoursome dishes that are prepared with care and understanding.

Menu € 28 (weekdays) - Carte € 27/57

Harbour St - 057 936 0106 - www.theblueapronrestaurant.ie - dinner only - Closed 2 weeks August, 24 January-7 February, 24-27 December, Monday and Tuesday

'WO MILE HOUSE → See Naas

'IRGINIA ACHADH AN IÚIR

avan - Pop. 2 282 - Regional map n° **21**-C3

St Kyrans

CLASSIC CUISINE • DESIGN This rurally set restaurant may look plain from the outside but it's a different story on the inside. The smart linen-laid restaurant offers breathtaking views over Lough Ramor and the menu lists classic dishes with an Irish heart and hints of modernity. Five of the modern bedrooms have water views.

Carte € 28/44

8 rooms - € 70/120 € 120/160

Dublin Rd - South : 2.25 km. on N 3 - 049 854 7087 - www.stkyrans.com - Closed January, Christmas, Good Friday, Sunday dinner in Winter, Monday dinner, Wednesday dinner and Tuesday

'VATERFORD PORT LÁIRGE

Vaterford - Pop. 46 732 - Regional map n° **22**-C2

Bay Tree Bistro

MODERN CUISINE • BISTRO You'll find this bistro on the first floor of an old quayside grain store. The chef's enthusiasm for using ingredients from the local larder is palpable and he employs a modern approach and time-honoured techniques to capture natural flavours. The bread selection is a feature and desserts are eye-catching.

Menu € 28 (early dinner) - Carte € 38/51

16 Merchants Quay - 051 858 517 - www.thebaytreebistro.com - dinner only - Closed 24-26 December, 1 January, 2nd week January, Sunday and Monday

La Bohème

FRENCH • INTIMATE Characterful candlelit restaurant in the vaulted cellar of a Georgian house. The French chefs offer an array of Gallic dishes and daily market specials - the simpler dishes are the ones to choose. Service is friendly.

Menu € 26 (early dinner)/37 - Carte € 35/59

2 George's St - 051 875 645 (booking essential) - www.labohemerestaurant.ie - dinner only - Closed 25-27 December, Sunday except bank holidays and Monday

Waterford Castle H. and Golf Resort

HISTORIC BUILDING • CLASSIC An attractive part-15C castle set on a charming 320 acre private island in the river. The carved stone and wood-panelled hall displays old tapestries and antiques, and the beautiful dining room boasts a delightful hand-carved fireplace. Elegant, classical bedrooms have characterful period bathrooms.

19 rooms - € 79/149 € 159/365 - 5 suites

The Island, Ballinakill - East : 4 km by R 683 and private ferry - 051 878 203 - www.waterfordcastleresort.com - Closed 3 weeks January and Christmas

WESTPORT CATHAIR NA MART

Mayo - Pop. 5 543 - Regional map n° **21**-A2

La Fougère

CLASSIC CUISINE • ROMANTIC XXX Spacious hotel restaurant with a large ba several different seating areas and huge windows offering views to Croagh P. trick Mountain. The three menus feature fresh, local produce, including langou tines from the bay below. Formal service.

Carte € 41/70

Knockranny House Hotel & Spa, Castlebar Rd, Knockranny - East : 1.25 km on N - ✆ 098 28600 - www.knockrannyhousehotel.ie - dinner only - Closed 24-26 December

An Port Mór

CLASSIC CUISINE • COSY X Tucked away down a small alleyway and named aft the chef's home village. The compact interior has a shabby-chic, Mediterranea style. Local produce is showcased in elaborate dishes and seafood specials a chalked on the blackboard.

Menu € 24 (early dinner) - Carte € 26/47

Brewery Pl, Bridge St - ✆ 098 26730 - www.anportmor.com - dinner only - Closed 24-26 December

Cíans on Bridge Street

MODERN BRITISH • NEIGHBOURHOOD X A cheery team run this town centre bi tro where you'll find white wooden slatted walls, vintage lighting and modern a The straightforward menu sees modern dishes sitting alongside those of a mo traditional bent. Seafood is always a good bet and local scallops, oysters an mussels feature highly.

Menu € 28 - Carte € 28/44

1 Bridge St - ✆ 098 25914 (booking essential) - www.ciansonbridgestreet.com - dinner only - Closed 25-26 December, 1 January and Monday,

Sheebeen

TRADITIONAL CUISINE • PUB Pretty pub with lovely bay and Croagh Patric views. Hearty, unfussy dishes feature shellfish and lobsters from the bay, an lamb and beef from the fields nearby. Sit outside, in the rustic bar or in the fir floor dining room.

Carte € 23/44

Rosbeg - West : 3 km on R 335 - ✆ 098 26528 - www.croninssheebeen.com - Closed 25 December, Good Friday and weekday lunches September-June

Knockranny House H. & Spa

FAMILY • PERSONALISED Modern hotel in an elevated position overlooking th town, mountains and bay, and furnished in a contemporary yet classical styl Large, smart bedrooms offer excellent comforts; some have marble bathroor or four-poster beds. Superb spa.

97 rooms - € 90/134 € 120/198 - 10 suites

Castlebar Rd, Knockranny - East : 1.25 km on N 5 - ✆ 098 28600 - www.knockrannyhousehotel.ie - Closed 24-26 December

La Fougère - See restaurant listing

WEXFORD LOCH GARMAN

Wexford - Pop. 19 913 - Regional map n° **22**-D2

La Côte

SEAFOOD • NEIGHBOURHOOD X On the main promenade of a historic towr you'll find this welcoming, personally run restaurant. It comprises two home rooms with grey oak flooring and Cape Cod inspired blues. Local seafood is a the heart of the good value menu.

Menu € 36 (early dinner) - Carte € 38/57

Custom House Quay - ✆ 053 912 2122 - www.lacote.ie - dinner only - Closed 2 weeks January, Sunday and Monday

Greenacres

TRADITIONAL BRITISH • BISTRO X Set over 3 floors, with a bistro, deli, wine store, bakery and art gallery. Wide-ranging menu of classic dishes, with daily fish specials. Amazing choice of wine from around the world, with some sensational vintages in the private salon.

Menu € 27 (dinner) - Carte € 35/52

Selskar - ✆ 053 912 2975 - www.greenacres.ie - Closed 25-27 December and Sunday except October-December

Killiane Castle

COUNTRY HOUSE • ELEGANT A 17C house and 14C castle on a family-owned dairy farm. Individually decorated, antique-furnished bedrooms look out over the surrounding farmland; wood-panelled Room 2 is the best. Breakfast includes homemade bread and yoghurt, while the 3 course dinners showcase their own beef, pork and vegetables.

8 rooms - € 85/95 € 120/155

Drinagh - South : 5.5 km by R 730 off N 25 - ✆ 053 915 8885 - www.killianecastle.com - Closed mid-December-mid-February

YOUGHAL EOCHAILL

Cork - Pop. 6 990 - Regional map n° **22**-C3

Aherne's

SEAFOOD • FRIENDLY XX A traditional place dating from 1923, keenly run by the 2nd and 3rd generations of the same family. Have lunch in one of the bars or dinner in the restaurant. Seafood is from the local boats and hot buttered lobster is a speciality. Some of the antique-furnished bedrooms have balconies.

Menu € 35 - Carte € 36/65 - bar lunch

13 rooms - € 95/150 € 120/240

163 North Main St - ✆ 024 92424 - www.ahernes.com - Closed 23-27 December

Walter Raleigh

FAMILY • PERSONALISED It might not look it but this immaculately kept hotel is over 300 years old. It's named after the one-time mayor of Youghal, who would have approved of the charming way it is run. Enjoy breakfast on the balcony overlooking Blackwater and dinner in the traditional bar or restaurant.

39 rooms - € 110 € 120/200

- ✆ 024 92011 - www.walterraleighhotel.com - Closed 25-26 December

INDEX OF TOWNS

C — Page

D Page

E Page

F Page

I — Page

J — Page

K — Page

Y — Page

Z — Page

INDEX OF MAPS

TOWN PLAN KEY

Sights

- Hotels
- Restaurants

	Place of interest
	Interesting place of worship

Road

	Motorway, dual carriageway
0 0	Junctions: complete, limited
	Main traffic artery
	Unsuitable for traffic; street subject to restrictions
	Pedestrian street
Piccadilly P	Shopping street • Car park
	Gateway • Street passing under arch
	Tunnel
	Station and railway
	Funicular
	Cable car, cable way

London

BRENT WEMBLEY	Borough • Area
	Borough boundary
	Congestion Zone • Charge applies Monday-Friday 07.00-18.00
	Nearest Underground station to the hotel or restaurant

Various signs

	Tourist Information Centre
	Place of worship
	Tower or mast • Ruins • Windmill
	Garden, park, wood • Cemetery
	Stadium • Golf course • Racecourse
	Outdoor or indoor swimming pool
	View • Panorama
	Monument • Fountain
	Pleasure boat harbour
	Lighthouse
	Airport
	Underground station
	Coach station
	Tramway
	Ferry services:
	passengers and cars, passengers only
	Main post office with poste restante
	Town Hall • University, College

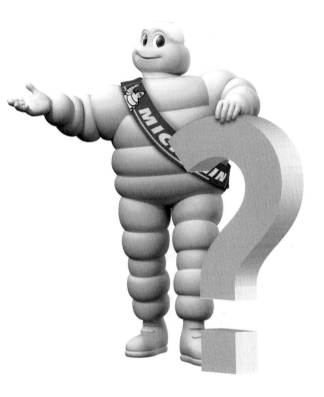

POPULATION - Source:
ONS/Office for National Statistics (www.statistics.gov.uk) [census 2011]
CSO/Central Statistics Office (www.cso.ie) [census 2011]

Michelin Travel Partner

Société par actions simplifiées au capital de 15 044 940 €
27 cours de l'Ile Seguin - 92100 Boulogne-Billancourt (France)
R.C.S. Nanterre 433 677 721

Dépôt légal September 2019
Printed in Italy - August 2019
Printed on paper from sustainably managed forests

Typesetting: JOUVE, Ormes (France)
Printing - Binding: Lego Print (Lavis)